Why Do You Need This New Edition?

1. Enhanced SQ3R Program. The SQ3R learning method continues to be the pedagogical foundation of *Mastering the World of Psychology.* In this edition, we have made the instructions for SQ3R clearer and more concise. We have also created an online SQ3R walk-through on MyPsychLab to guide you through the process to becoming a more efficient student as you read, study, and prepare for exams.

2. New *Map It* Feature and Online Concept Mapping Tool. New to this edition, *Map It* boxes appear in each chapter just after the Summary to encourage you to create a unique note-taking map of the contents of each chapter. You can log onto *www.mypsychlab.com* and click on "Map It" to use preloaded content from each chapter to create a digital version of a chapter map that can be saved, e-mailed to your instructors, and even printed out to use as a study tool. Creating a personalized note-taking map of each chapter is an essential step in SQ3R and will help you better prepare for exams.

3. Streamlined Sections and Numbered Learning Objectives. We have revised, streamlined, and reorganized many sections in this edition to create a better flow of information. In addition, a majority of the numbered learning objectives that appeared in the previous edition have been revised to enhance their pedagogical effectiveness and create a clearer, more focused text.

4. New Chapter Opening *Think About It* Activities. Each chapter now opens with a new *Think About It* feature that gives you the opportunity to become actively involved with the text content right from the beginning of the chapter. The openers invite you to complete an activity (i.e., a quiz, an experiment) that introduces the chapter content in a fun and an interesting way, and gives a brief description of what you will learn about in the pages that follow.

5. In-Text References to MyPsychLab Resources. Icons integrated throughout the text lead to Web-based expansions on topics, giving you access to extra information, videos, and simulations. Many more resources are available in addition to those highlighted in the text, but the icons draw attention to some of the most high-interest materials available at *www.mypsychlab.com*.

6. Improved Art Program. A number of new figures and tables have been added to this edition, while other figures and tables have been revised and updated. Revisions include a number of anatomical figures that now feature color-coded labels and definitions, as well as a number of new *Summarize It* tables (formerly titled *Review and Reflect*).

7. New and Expanded Coverage. There is a wide range of new and expanded topics (including several hundred new research citations) covered in this edition, including, but not limited to: the scientific method (Chapter 1); synesthesia and psychological approaches to pain relief (Chapter 3); the myths and realities of hypnosis (Chapter 4); research on multitasking, electronic games, television, and the Internet (Chapter 5); autobiographical and source memory (Chapter 6); anchoring (Chapter 7); an updated review of research on the universality of Kohlberg's stages (Chapter 8); the effects of stress on the immune system (Chapter 10); Allport's Trait Theory (Chapter 11); and impression formation and impression management (Chapter 14). Please see the Preface for a more detailed list of changes made to this edition.

PEARSON

Mastering the World of Psychology

TB
91

Samuel E. Wood

Ellen Green Wood

Denise Boyd
Houston Community College System

Allyn & Bacon
Boston Columbus Indianapolis
New York San Francisco Upper Saddle River
Amsterdam Cape Town Dubai London
Madrid Milan Munich Paris Montréal Toronto
Delhi Mexico City São Paulo Sydney
Hong Kong Seoul Singapore Taipei Tokyo

VP/Editorial Director: Craig Campanella
Executive Editor: Stephen Frail
Director of Development: Sharon Geary
Development Editor: Deb Hanlon
Editorial Assistant: Kerri Hart-Morris
Director of Marketing: Brandy Dawson
Marketing Manager: Jeannette Koskinas
Marketing Assistant: Shauna Fishweicher
Managing Editor: Maureen Richardson
Project Manager: Annemarie Franklin
Media Editor: Paul DeLuca
Operations Specialist: Sherry Lewis
Art Editor: Maria Piper
Art Director: Anne Nieglos
Text Designer: Wanda España
Cover Designer: Joel Gendron

Manager, Visual Research: Beth Brenzel
Photo Researcher: Sheila Norman
Manager, Rights and Permissions: Zina Arabia
Manager, Cover Visual Research & Permissions: Karen Sanatar
Cover Image Permission Coordinator: Cathy Mazzucca
Cover Art: © Niladri Nath/Getty Images
Text Permissions: Lisa Black
Project Management: Rebecca Dunn/ Prepare, Inc.
Composition: Preparé, Inc.
Printer/Binder: Courier/Kendallville
Cover Printer: Lehigh-Phoenix Color/Hagerstown

This book was set in Sabon 9.75/12.

Credits and acknowledgments borrowed from other sources and reproduced, with permission, in this textbook appear on appropriate page within text (or on page C1).

Library of Congress Cataloging-in-Publication Data
Available upon request from the Library of Congress

10 9 8 7 6 5 4 3 2

Student edition:
ISBN 10: 0-205-00331-1
ISBN 13: 978-0-205-00331-0
Exam Copy:
ISBN 10: 0-205-00520-9
ISBN 13: 978-0-205-00520-8
á la Carte edition:
ISBN 10: 0-205-00505-5
ISBN 13: 978-0-205-00505-5

Allyn & Bacon
is an imprint of

PEARSON

Brief Contents

Contents

1 Introduction to Psychology *1*

2 Biology and Behavior *35*

3   Sensation and Perception   *70*

4   Consciousness   *108*

5 Learning   136

6 Memory   167

9 Motivation and Emotion *282*

10 Health and Stress *317*

11 Personality Theory and Assessment *351*

12 Psychological Disorders 379

13 Therapies 409

14 Social Psychology *438*

APPENDIX: *Statistical Methods* *AP1*

Preface

As psychology instructors, your backgrounds, experiences, and resources are as varied as those of your students. Each of you approaches the course with a unique set of challenges but with common goals: to provide students with a solid introduction to the diverse field of psychology; to show them how psychology applies to their lives; and to teach them how to think critically. We have designed the fourth edition of *Mastering the World of Psychology* to help you meet these goals.

Changes to the Fourth Edition

As with each edition, we have closely examined and thoroughly updated all aspects of the text's content, organization, and pedagogy. Among the improvements made to the fourth edition are the following:

- SQ3R continues to be the pedagogical foundation of *Mastering the World of Psychology*. In the fourth edition, we have made the instructions for SQ3R clearer and more concise. We have also incorporated a new feature into the study system. At the end of each chapter a new *Map It* box tells students how to create a note-taking map for the chapter. The goal of *Map It* is to help students organize their notes around the learning questions and key terms in the chapter and, in so doing, develop a structured summary of it that they can use to study for exams. If they wish, students can use preloaded chapter content in the new Concept Mapping Tool in MyPsychLab (*www.mypsychlab.com*) to create their note-taking maps. The tool allows them to save, share, or print the maps as well. Students can also use the Concept Mapping Tool to create other types of graphic study aids, ranging from simple outlines to complex concept maps that cover multiple chapters. For example, students can use it to outline the principles of classical conditioning to better understand the distinctions among conditioned and unconditioned stimuli and responses. Alternatively, they can use it to create a comprehensive map of psychoanalytic concepts that includes information about the historical significance of Freud's theory from Chapter 1, dream analysis from Chapter 4, repressed memory from Chapter 6, psychosexual development from Chapter 8, and psychodynamic therapy from Chapter 13.

- We have revised and streamlined many of the learning objectives to enhance their pedagogical effectiveness. In addition, the Instructor's Manual and Test Bank now correspond to these same learning objectives, allowing you to design lectures, classroom activities, tests, and quizzes that test specific knowledge or skills.

- Each chapter in *Mastering* now opens with an engaging *Think About It* activity. For example, the activity at the beginning of Chapter 9 (Motivation and Emotion) provides students with a demonstration of the facial feedback hypothesis that they can try for themselves.

- *Explain It* boxes have been made more concise.

- *Review & Reflect* tables from the previous edition have been renamed *Summarize It* tables to more accurately reflect their purpose. Several new *Summarize It* tables appear in the fourth edition.

- In the Instructor's Manual and on the Instructors Resource Center (at *www.pearsonhighered.com*), we have posted a helpful document titled *Goals, Outcomes, and Objectives: How the Fourth Edition of* Mastering the World of Psychology *Can*

Help Instructors Develop an Assessment Strategy for the Introductory Psychology Course. The document explains how to use the text and ancillaries to develop an assessment strategy for the introductory course that satisfies the requirements of most accrediting organizations and state higher education agencies. *Goals, Outcomes, and Objectives* provides instructors with model outcomes and correlates all of the learning objectives in the text with them. In addition, the document includes sample modifications of the outcomes and objectives that can serve as core curricula in introductory psychology for all instructors in a department for the purpose of program-level assessment.

Organizational Changes and Updated Research

We have made a number of text and organizational changes to improve the clarity of the discussions and overall flow of material. We remain dedicated to citing current research and writing the most up-to-date text possible, while promoting an understanding of the foundation of psychology. Several hundred new research citations appear in the fourth edition to ensure that all presentations reflect current thinking about the science of psychology. Here is a chapter-by-chapter list of the major changes we have made in the fourth edition:

Chapter 1: Introduction to Psychology

- New *Think About It*: How Much Do You Know about Psychology?
- Simplified SQ3R instructions
- New figure for the scientific method
- Consolidated material on early theorists, schools of thought, contemporary perspectives, and specialty areas in the field into one section
- Added forensic psychology and school psychology to specialty areas
- New *Summarize It* tables for goals of psychology, research methods

Chapter 2: Biology and Behavior

- New *Think About It*: Hemispheric Specialization and Interpretation of Facial Expressions
- Chapter now opens with methods of studying the brain and nervous system
- Methods section includes discovery of the neuron and electrochemical nature of neuronal transmission
- Added terms with definitions to important anatomical figures
- Reorganized sections on the cerebrum

Chapter 3: Sensation and Perception

- New *Think About It*: The Role of Vision in Balance
- Combined sections on hearing and balance
- New topics: synesthesia, psychological approaches to pain relief
- Added terms with definitions to important anatomical figures

Chapter 4: Consciousness

- New *Think About It*: Lucid Dreaming
- Reorganized discussion of sleep cycles and types of sleep

- New *Summarize It* tables for sleep disorders, theories of hypnosis
- New table contrasts the myths and realities of hypnosis
- Updated the discussion of long-term marijuana use

Chapter 5: Learning

- New *Think About It*: The Power of Variable Reinforcement
- New table for positive/negative reinforcement, positive/negative punishment
- New section, "Learning from Media," that includes multitasking, electronic games, television, other entertainment media, the Internet
- New *Summarize It* table for cognitive theories of learning

Chapter 6: Memory

- New *Think About It*: Creating False Memories
- Significantly reorganized chapter
- New topics: autobiographical memory, source memory, Baddeley's concept of working memory
- New *Summarize It* table for theories of forgetting
- Streamlined *Apply It*: Improving Memory, which includes mnemonic devices, memory strategies, study techniques

Chapter 7: Cognition, Language, and Intelligence

- New *Think About It*: How Anchoring Influences Decision Making
- New topics: anchoring, the difference between human language and animal communication
- New *Summarize It* table for approaches to decision making
- Moved culture-fair testing to the section on reliability and validity
- New *Try It*: Find Your EQ

Chapter 8: Human Development

- New *Think About It*: Kohlberg's Heinz Dilemma
- Improved discussion of schemes, assimilation, accommodation
- Additions: explanation of the distinctions among the physical, cognitive, and social domains of development, a brief discussion of birth
- Updated review of research on the universality of Kohberg's stages

Chapter 9: Motivation and Emotion

- New *Think About It*: What Makes You Jealous?
- New *Summarize It* table for goal orientations
- New discussion of methodological problems associated with determining prevalence of homosexuality
- New topics: affective neuroscience, cognition, and emotion
- New *Apply It*: The Quest for Happiness
- New *Try It*: What Is Your *n* Ach?

Chapter 10: Health and Stress

- New *Think About It*: What Stresses You Out?
- New discussion of the life events approach to stress consolidates topics of Social Readjustment Rating Scale and catastrophic events into a single section
- New section, "The Stress-Health Connection," improves and expands coverage of effects of stress on the immune system
- New topics: risk and resilience model of stress, acculturative stress, distinction between perceived and received social support
- New *Summarize It* table for factors that promote resilience

Chapter 11: Personality Theory and Assessment

- New *Think About It*: Your Locus of Control
- Five-factor model contrasted with five-factor theory of personality
- New *Summarize It* tables for theories of personality, methods of personality assessment
- New *Try It*: Allport's Trait Theory

Chapter 12: Psychological Disorders

- New *Think About It*: Symptoms of Anxiety Disorders
- New topics: negative reinforcement and the development of avoidance and escape behaviors among people with panic disorder; microorganisms as a possible cause of schizophrenia
- Reorganized the section on anxiety disorders
- New *Summarize It* tables for anxiety, somatoform, and dissociative disorders
- New *Try It*: Phobia Names

Chapter 13: Therapies

- New *Think About It*: Identifying Cognitive Triggers for Anxiety and Depression
- Updated discussion of cognitive-behavior therapy with current terminology
- New figure illustrates cognitive-behavior therapy homework
- New table lists cognitive errors addressed by Beck's cognitive therapy
- SNRIs added to discussion of psychiatric drugs

Chapter 14: Social Psychology

- New *Think About It*: Situational and Dispositional Attributions
- New topics: social cognition, impression formation, impression management, viral marketing strategies
- Improved explanations of self-serving bias, actor-observer effect, fundamental attribution error

The SQ3R method will help your students maximize their learning in five steps:
- Survey
- Question
- Read
- Recite
- Review

Sticky notes in Chapter 1 will help your students master this learning system so that they can use it on their own in the remaining chapters.

Our Commitment to Learning: SQ3R

The text's commitment to learning begins with the learning method called SQ3R. Made up of five steps—Survey, Question, Read, Recite, and Review—this method serves as the foundation for your students' success. Introduced in Chapter 1, the SQ3R method is integrated throughout the text to help students make the connection between psychology and life, while promoting a more efficient way to approach reading, studying, and test taking.

Among the key learning features that promote use of the SQ3R method are the following:

Learning Objectives Each chapter in this text is structured around specific learning objectives, which have been streamlined and improved for the fourth edition. These numbered learning objectives are stated as questions, because research shows that open-ended questions help readers locate critical information, process it deeply, and commit it to memory. The learning objectives appear in each chapter opener, in the margins of their corresponding sections, and again in the end-of-chapter Summary, to help focus students' attention on key information.

humans and animals. Today, scientists continue to use both case studies and microscopic tissue studies to answer questions about the nervous system. But since the early 20th century, researchers have also been able to observe the living brain in action.

2.1 What does the electroencephalogram (EEG) reveal about the brain?

The EEG and the Microelectrode

In 1924, Austrian psychiatrist Hans Berger invented the electroencephalograph, a machine that records the electrical activity occurring in the brain. This electrical activity, detected by electrodes placed at various points on the scalp and amplified greatly,

Key Terms Boldfaced key terms are highlighted in the text and defined in the margin on the page on which they first appear. A complete list of key terms, with page references, is supplied at the end of the chapter, and a complete Glossary can be found at the end of the text.

microelectrode A small wire used to monitor the electrical activity of or stimulate activity within a single neuron.

cal problems.

Although the EEG is able to detect electrical activity in different areas of the brain, it cannot reveal what is happening in individual neurons. However, the microelectrode can. A microelectrode is a wire so small that it can be inserted near or into a single neuron without damaging it. Microelectrodes can be used to monitor the electrical activity of a single neuron or to stimulate activity within it.

SUMMARIZE IT

Major Perspectives in Psychology		
PERSPECTIVE	EMPHASIS	EXPLANATION OF A STUDENT'S POOR PERFORMANCE ON EXAMS
Behavioral	The role of environment in shaping and controlling behavior	The student has not been reinforced for getting good grades in the past.
Psychoanalytic	The role of unconscious motivation and early childhood experiences in determining behavior and thought	An unresolved early childhood emotional trauma is distracting the student from his academic work.
Humanistic	The importance of an individual's subjective experience as a key to understanding his or her behavior	Studying for exams does not fit into this student's definition of a meaningful life.
Cognitive	The role of mental processes—perception, thinking, and memory—that underlie behavior	The student does not use effective learning strategies such as the SQ3R method.
Evolutionary	The roles of inherited tendencies that have proven adaptive in humans	The student believes that studying is unimportant because potential mates are more interested in his physical appearance and capacity for social dominance than they are in his grades.
Biological	The role of biological processes and structures, as well as heredity, in explaining behavior	An inappropriate level of emotional arousal (i.e., test anxiety) is preventing this student from performing at an optimal level.
Sociocultural	The roles of social and cultural influences on behavior	The student doesn't want to be perceived as a "nerd," so he studies just enough to avoid failing.

Summarize It These comprehensive summary tables help consolidate major concepts, their components, and their relationships to one another, providing students with a unique visual study tool.

CHAPTER 2 SUMMARY

DISCOVERING THE MYSTERIES OF THE NERVOUS SYSTEM (pp. 36–37)
How researchers study the nervous system

2.1 What do electroencephalograms (EEG) reveal about the nervous system? (p. 36)

An electroencephalogram (EEG) is a record of brain-wave activity. It can reveal an epileptic seizure and can show patterns of neural activity associated with learning disabilities, schizophrenia, Alzheimer's disease, sleep disorders, and other problems.

Key Terms
electroencephalogram (EEG), p. 36
beta wave, p. 36
alpha wave, p. 36
delta wave, p. 36
microelectrode, p. 36

2.2 How do researchers use imaging techniques to study the nervous system? (p. 37)

Both the CT scan and MRI provide detailed images of brain structures. The PET scan reveals patterns of blood flow, oxygen use, and glucose metabolism in the brain. It can also show the action of drugs in the brain and other organs. PET scan studies show that different brain areas are used to perform different tasks. Functional MRI (fMRI) can provide information about brain function and structure more precisely and more rapidly than a PET scan. Two more recently developed technologies, SQUID and MEG, measure magnetic changes to reveal neural activity within the brain as it occurs.

Key Terms
CT scan (computerized axial tomography), p. 37
MRI (magnetic resonance imagery), p. 37
PET scan (positron-emission tomography), p. 37
functional MRI (fMRI), p. 37

Chapter Summary Organized around the learning objectives, each end-of-chapter Summary provides a comprehensive study tool as well as a quick reference to the chapter's key terms, which are listed alphabetically by section.

Map It New to this edition, *Map It* boxes appear in each chapter just after the Summary and encourage students to create their own unique note-taking map of the contents of each chapter. Students can log onto *www.mypsychlab.com* and click on "Map It" to use our new interactive Concept Mapping Tool with preloaded content from each chapter to create a digital version of their chapter map that can be saved, e-mailed to you, and even printed out to use as a study tool. Creating a personalized note-taking map of each chapter is an essential step in SQ3R and will help your students better prepare for exams.

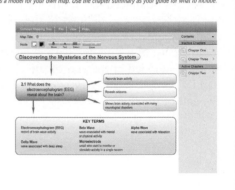

MAP IT

Log on to MyPsychLab and click on "Map It" to prepare a unique digital map of the chapter that you can save for later use, email to your instructor, or print out to use as a study tool. Or, create your own map by drawing one on paper. Use the starter map below as a model for your own map. Use the chapter summary as your guide for what to include. For each item in your map, be sure to include the page number.

Here's one way to *Map It*:
1. Draw a box at the top of the page for the section title.
2. Underneath the section title box, working horizontally across the page, draw a box for each learning question in the section. Write the learning questions in the boxes and draw a line from the section title to each questions box. After you read each subsection, jot an answer for the learning question in the subsection's box.
3. Below each learning question box, insert another box for all of the key terms that are related to the question, along with a very brief reminder of each term's definition. Draw a line from the question box to the key terms box.
4. Below each key terms box, create another box and list all of the helpful figures, tables, and other elements of the text, such as *Try It* and *Apply It* boxes. Draw a line from the key terms box to the helpful elements box.

Map the Chapter on mypsychlab.com

Chapter 2 Study Guide

Answers to all the Study Guide questions are provided at the end of the book.

SECTION ONE: Chapter Review

Discovering the Mysteries of The Nervous System (pp. 36–37)

1. Match the brain-wave pattern with the state associated with it.
   _____ (1) slow-wave (deep) sleep
   _____ (2) deep relaxation while awake
   _____ (3) physical or mental activity

   a. beta wave   c. alpha wave
   b. delta wave

2. The CT scan and MRI are used to
   a. show the amount of activity in various parts of the brain.
   b. produce images of the brain's structures.
   c. measure electrical activity in the brain.
   d. observe neural communication at synapses.

3. Which of the following reveals the electrical activity of the brain by producing a record of brain waves?
   a. electroencephalogram   c. PET scan
   b. CT scan   d. MRI

4. Which of the following does not reveal brain activity?
   a. CT scan   c. PET scan
   b. EEG   d. fMRI

5. Which of the following reveals both brain structure and brain activity?
   a. MRI   c. fMRI
   b. PET scan   d. CT scan

The Neurons and the Neurotransmitters (pp. 37–43)

6. The branchlike extensions of neurons that act as receivers of signals from other neurons are the
   a. dendrites.   c. neurotransmitters.
   b. axons.   d. cell bodies.

7. _____ support neurons, supplying them with nutrients and carrying away their waste products.

8. The junction where the axon of a sending neuron communicates with a receiving neuron is called the
   a. reuptake site.   c. synapse.
   b. receptor site.   d. axon terminal.

Built-in Study Guide In addition to all of the SQ3R features in the text, each chapter concludes with a Study Guide, featuring multiple-choice, true/false, fill-in-the-blank, matching, and critical thinking questions. Answers to the Study Guide questions are located at the end of the text.

Practice Tests At the end of the text, additional Practice Tests for each chapter include multiple-choice, true/false, and essay questions. The solutions are available in the separate Student Solutions Manual and in the Instructor's Resources section of MyPsychLab.

SECTION FOUR: Comprehensive Practice Test

1. Phineas Gage changed from a polite, dependable, well-liked railroad fore-man to a rude and impulsive person who could no longer plan realistically for the future after he suffered serious damage to his

   a. occipital lobe.   **c.** medulla.
   b. frontal lobe.   **d.** cerebellum.

2. A researcher interested in getting information about the brain's activity based on the amount of oxygen and glucose consumed should use a(n)

   a. MRI.   **c.** PET scan.
   b. EEG.   **d.** CT scan.

Learning through Application

To gain a full understanding of psychology, it is vital that students apply the principles they learn about in this course to their own life and the lives of others. We, the authors, have designed five features to help students accomplish this goal.

Think About It Each chapter opens with a *Think About It* feature that encourages students to become actively involved with the content right from the beginning of the chapter. These openers will invite students to complete an activity (i.e., a quiz, an experiment) that introduces the chapter content in a fun and an interesting way.

Think About It

Interpreting others' facial expressions is such a commonplace task that we usually do it without thinking about it. But your eyes can sometimes fool you. See if you can figure out which of the faces below is the happier of the two (Jaynes, 1976).

Which face did you say was the happier one? Your answer probably depended on whether you are right- or left-handed. You see, the brain tends to assign some tasks to the right side of the brain and others to the left. These assignments are correlated to some degree with handedness. For instance, if you are right-handed, you tend to use the right side of the brain to interpret emotions. Since the right side of the brain controls the left side of the body, you would use the left side of people's faces to make inferences about their emotional states (McGee & Skinner, 1987).

Consequently, even though the faces in the drawing are mirror images, right-handed people tend to see the face on the left as the happier one. Left-handers display the opposite pattern. They rely on the left side of the brain to interpret emotions, and because the left side of the brain controls the right side of the body, they usually judge the face on the right to be the happier one.

How the brain divides functions between its left and right halves is just one of many interesting things about the biological foundations of behavior and mental processes that you will read about in this chapter. We will tell you much more about the brain and nervous system, and we will introduce you to the endocrine system. You will also read about genetics. Pay close attention to the information in this chapter because we will refer back to its major concepts in all the chapters that follow.

 APPLY IT   **Should You Consult a Genetic Counselor?**

The purpose of genetic counseling is to estimate individuals' risk of having a child with a genetic disorder or of developing an inherited disorder themselves. If you have relatives who have such disorders, you may have wondered whether you should seek genetic counseling. Such counseling can be helpful to just about anyone, but there are a few situations in which professionals advise that genetic counseling is especially important.

Birth Defects and Inherited Diseases of Childhood
As you may know, prenatal testing can identify many birth defects and genetic disorders before a child is born. However, experts say that screening for such risks should be done prior to conception if any of the following applies to you or your partner (Brundage, 2002):

- You or your partner has previously had a child with a birth defect (e.g., spina bifida) or an inherited disorder (e.g., phenylketonuria).
- There is someone in your or your partner's family who displayed an unexplained developmental delay or disability (i.e., visual or hearing impairment, mental retardation) early in life.
- You or your partner belongs to an ethnic group in which there is a particularly high incidence of a specific inherited disorder (e.g., African Americans: sickle cell disease; European Jews: Tay-Sachs disease; Caucasians: cystic fibrosis; people of Greek, Middle Eastern, or North African descent: thalassemia.)

Adult-Onset Genetic Disorders
Genetic counselors suggest that you seriously consider genetic counseling if anyone in your family has ever been diagnosed with one of these adult-onset genetic disorders:

- Huntington disease
- Myotonic muscular dystrophy
- Amyotrophic lateral sclerosis (ALS, Lou Gehrig disease)
- Schizophrenia

Hereditary Cancers
If someone in your family has been diagnosed with cancer, then genetic counseling can be helpful in determining your own risk of developing the disease. According to the Massey Cancer Center at Virginia Commonwealth University (2006), the following types of family histories are especially indicative of a need for genetic counseling:

- A family history of multiple cases of the same or related types of cancers
- One or more relatives with rare cancers
- Cancers occurring at an earlier age of onset than usual (for instance, under the age of 50 years) in at least one member

- Bilateral cancers (two cancers that develop independently in a paired organ, i.e., both kidneys or both breasts)
- One or more family members with two primary cancers (two original tumors that develop in different sites)
- Eastern European Jewish background

Multifactorial Disorders
Many chronic health conditions are attributable to a combination of genetic and lifestyle factors. While there are no genetic tests for these disorders, a genetic counselor can analyze your family history and help you determine your risk of developing one or more of them. A genetic counselor can also advise you as to the degree to which lifestyle changes might enable you to avoid some of the effects of a disorder that you have seen diminish the quality of life of one of your family members. Thus, you may want to seek genetic counseling if anyone in your family has been diagnosed with one or more of these multifactorial disorders:

- Adult-onset diabetes
- Hypertension
- Glaucoma
- Heart disease
- Rheumatoid arthritis
- Disorders of the endocrine system (e.g., hypothyroidism, pancreatitis)
- Autoimmune disorders (e.g., lupus, multiple sclerosis)
- Liver or kidney disease
- Depression
- Parkinson disease
- Alzheimer's disease

Making the Decision
Even if these checklists have led you to the conclusion that you should consult a genetic counselor, you may find it difficult to confront the possibility that you or your child may have to deal with a serious health problem. Such feelings are common among individuals whose family members have one of the conditions described above. However, researchers have found that people who are uninformed about their personal genetic vulnerability actually tend to overestimate their chances of developing an inherited disorder (Quaid et al., 2001; Tercyak et al., 2001). Thus, genetic counseling will help you formulate a realistic assessment of your own personal risks and will also enable you to develop a plan for coping with them if a genetic disorder is likely to be in your future.

Apply It This feature combines scientific research with practical advice to teach students how to improve their study habits or handle challenging situations that may arise in their personal, academic, or professional lives.

TRY IT　　A Balancing Act

Get a meter stick or yardstick. Try balancing it vertically on the end of your left index finger, as shown in the drawing. Then try balancing it on your right index finger. Most people are better with their dominant hand—the right hand for right-handers, for example. Is this true for you?

　　Now try this: Begin reciting the ABCs out loud as fast as you can while balancing the stick with your left hand. Do you have less trouble this time? Why should that be? The right hemisphere controls the act of balancing with the left hand. However, your left hemisphere, though poor at controlling the left hand, still tries to coordinate your balancing efforts. When you distract the left hemisphere with a steady stream of talk, the right hemisphere can orchestrate more efficient balancing with your left hand without interference.

▶ Watch on mypsychlab.com

Try It This popular feature provides brief applied experiments, self-assessments, and hands-on activities, which help personalize psychology, making it simple for students to actively relate psychological principles to everyday life. For instance, students can find their blind spot (Chapter 3) or take a quiz to find their life stress score (Chapter 10).

Explain It This feature provides psychological explanations for some common everyday occurrences. For instance, "What does your credit score mean, and how is it used by lenders?" (Chapter 1) and "Why are some individuals drawn to dangerous hobbies like skydiving?" (Chapter 9).

EXPLAIN IT　　Why Are Most People Right-Handed?

Scientists have searched for an answer to this question for more than a century and have yet to find a definitive answer. In your own thinking about the matter, you have probably concluded that there are three possibilities:

- Handedness is completely determined by genes.
- Handedness is completely determined by learning.
- Handedness is determined by both genes and learning.

If you are drawn to the first hypothesis, consider the finding that only 82% of identical twins, whose genotypes are identical, have the same hand preference (Klar, 2003). If handedness were completely determined by genes, then identical twins' phenotypes would always be the same for handedness. Therefore, handedness cannot be entirely explained as a function of our genes. Does this mean that handedness is determined by learning? Not necessarily.

The learning hypothesis cannot explain why handedness appears very early in infancy, long before children are exposed to formal instruction that requires them to use one hand or the other (Rönnqvist & Domellöf, 2006). Moreover, the proportions of left-handers and right-handers in the human population have been about the same for thousands of years (Hopkins & Cantalupo, 2004; Wilson, 1998). In fact, these proportions are evident even in the skeletons of humans who died long before writing was invented (Steele & Mays, 1995).

The key to understanding the evidence on handedness is to adopt the view that both genes and learning are at work in the development of hand preferences, but not in the way that you might expect. In most of us, right-handedness is completely determined by our genes, but in a few of us handedness, whether left or right, is influenced by learning. Sound confusing? To clarify, here is the most current thinking on the genetics of handedness.

Researchers suspect that right-handedness is determined by a single dominant gene, *R* (Francks et al., 2003). If an individual receives a copy of *R* from one or both parents, then she will be right-handed. The frequency of *R* in the human population is extremely high, scientists believe, because it is tied to the genes that support left-lateralization of language function in the brain. (Remember, the left side of the brain controls the right side of the body.) It makes sense that

motor functions are linked to language, experts claim, because producing language requires activity in both the language centers and motor cortex of the brain. Putting both on the same side of the brain facilitates the rapid development of neural connections between the two without having to go through the slowly developing membrane between the two hemispheres (corpus callosum). But what happens to the relatively small proportion of humans who do not receive a copy of *R* from either parent?

The dominant gene for right-handedness, *R*, is complemented by a recessive gene, *r* (Francks et al., 2007). You might think that the phenotype of an individual who receives a copy of *r* from both parents would include left-handedness, but, in reality, the phenotype that is associated with *rr* is *non-handedness*. In individuals with the *rr* genotype, learning shapes handedness. Because most people are right-handed, and the tools that humans have developed for use in fine motor activities (e.g., scissors) favor righties, there is a considerable amount of cultural pressure on those who lack innate handedness, those with the genotype *rr*, to become right-handed. Nevertheless, some of them do develop left-handedness. Why?

Researchers believe that other genes come into play as well. Specifically, if a person possesses genes that cause language functions to lateralize to her right rather than her left cerebral hemisphere, then she is also likely to be left-handed. Here again, the lateralization of handedness follows the lateralization of language function. To make matters more complicated, in 2007, scientists discovered a gene that pushes us in the direction of left-handedness when we receive it from our fathers. When we get the gene from our mothers, it seems to have no influence on hand dominance (Francks et al., 2007).

Finally, although genetics appears to play a complex, but important, role in the development of hand preferences, the capacity of individuals to adapt to severe injuries to or the loss of the dominant hand demonstrates the adaptability of the brain with regard to motor functions. Thus, as the trait of hand preference illustrates, nature and nurture are often linked in complex ways. Remember this the next time you are involved in a debate with someone about whether a given trait is *either* genetic or learned.

👁 Watch the **Video** on **mypsychlab.com**

🔊 Listen to the **Podcast** on **mypsychlab.com**

✳ Explore the **Concept** on **mypsychlab.com**

⊙ Simulate the **Experiment** on **mypsychlab.com**

✺ Map the **Chapter** on **mypsychlab.com**

MyPsychLab Icons MyPsychLab icons—Watch, Listen, Explore, Simulate, and Map—are integrated throughout the text in the margins—these icons highlight specific MyPsychLab assets that can be found online.

　　To access MyPsychLab, simply go to *www.mypsychlab.com* and enter your login name and password. First-time users of MyPsychLab can buy access here as well.

Supplements

We have designed a collection of instructor resources for the fourth edition that will help you prepare for class, enhance your course presentations, and assess your students' understanding of the material.

Instructor's Resource DVD (ISBN: 0205005195): Bringing all of the fourth edition's instructor resources together in one place, the Instructor's Resource DVD contains the following resources:

- **Hyperlinked Instructor's Manual:** The Instructor's Manual gives you unparalleled access to a huge selection of classroom-proven assets. First-time instructors will appreciate the detailed introduction to teaching the introductory psychology course, with suggestions for preparing for the course, sample syllabi, and current trends and strategies for successful teaching. Each chapter offers activities, exercises, assignments, handouts, and demos for in-class use, as well as guidelines for integrating media resources into the classroom and syllabus. The material is organized in an easy-to-use Chapter Lecture Outline. A unique hyperlinking system allows for easy reviewing of relevant sections and resources. The Instructor's Manual is also available for download from the Instructor's Resource Center at **http://www.pearsonhighered.com/irc**.

- **Test Bank:** The Fourth Edition Test Bank, authored by Paulina Multhaupt of Macomb Community College, contains over 2,000 multiple-choice, fill-in-the-blank, short-answer, and essay questions, each referencing the relevant page in the text. New to this edition, rationales for the correct answer and closest distracter in the conceptual and applied multiple-choice questions allow you to see the logic of the questions when reviewing them, making it easier to generate an answer key for your students if desired. Feedback from customers indicates that this unique feature is useful for ensuring quality and quick response to student queries. A two-page Total Assessment Guide chapter overview makes creating tests easier by listing all of the test items in an easy-to-reference grid. The Total Assessment Guide organizes all test items by text section and question type/level of difficulty. All multiple-choice questions are categorized as factual, conceptual, or applied. The Test Bank is also available for download from the Instructor's Resource Center at **http://www.pearsonhighered.com/irc**.

- **NEW Interactive PowerPoint Slides:** Available on the Instructor's Resource DVD, these slides bring the design of *Mastering* right into the classroom, drawing students into the lecture and providing wonderful interactive activities and visuals. A video walk-through is available and provides clear guidelines on using and customizing the slides. The slides are built around the text's learning objectives and offer many links across content areas. Icons integrated throughout the slides indicate interactive exercises, simulations, and activities that can be accessed directly from the slides if instructors want to use these resources in the classroom.

- **Standard Lecture PowerPoint Slides:** These slides, presented in a more traditional format with excerpts of the text material, and art work, are also available for download at **http://www.pearsonhighered.com/irc**.

Pearson MyTest Computerized Test Bank mypearsontest ☑ **(www.pearson mytest.com):** The Fourth Edition Test Bank comes with Pearson MyTest, a powerful assessment-generation program that helps instructors easily create and print quizzes and exams. You can do this online, allowing flexibility and the ability to efficiently manage assessments at any time. You can easily access existing questions and edit, create, and store questions using the simple drag-and-drop and Word-like controls. Each question comes with information on its level of difficulty and related page number in the text, mapped to the appropriate learning objective. For more information, go to www.PearsonMyTest.com.

Classroom Response System (CRS) slides: Classroom Response questions ("clicker" questions) created for *Mastering the World of Psychology,* are intended to be the basis of class discussions as well as lectures. Each student uses a personal remote or "clicker" to send immediate communication to the instructor. The system will gather the individual responses and show the compiled feedback for the class as a whole. Based on these results, you can then tailor the pace of each lecture, further explain difficult concepts if needed, and conduct in-class surveys, polls, and quizzes. Pearson offers exclusive, money-saving rebates with several CRS leading systems.

New! Pearson Introductory Psychology Video Series (18 half-hour episodes) (ISBN: 0205035817): Two years in the making, this new video series features exclusive footage from around the United States. Guided by the Design, Development & Review team, a diverse group of introductory psychology instructors, the new series features 18 half-hour episodes organized around the major topics of the introductory psychology course syllabus. The videos take the viewer into the research laboratory, inside the body and brain through breathtaking animations, and out into the street for real-world applications. Each episode features several brief segments that bring psychology to life:

- *The Big Picture* introduces the topic of the episode and provides the hook to draw students in.
- *The Basics* uses the power of video to present foundational topics, especially those that typically trip up students.
- *Special Topics* dives deeper into high-interest and often cutting-edge topics, and often features research in action.
- *In the Real World* focuses on applications of psychological research.
- *What's In It For Me?* These narrated segments emphasize why students should care about the research and how it may have a real impact on their lives.

The Pearson Introductory Psychology Video Series is only available to adopters of Pearson psychology textbooks. An Instructor's Guide to the video series is also available to adopters.

Student Solutions Manual (ISBN: 0205005225): For students who want additional test questions, *Mastering the World of Psychology* offers Practice Tests at the end of the text. The answers to these tests can be found in the Student Solutions Manual, along with corresponding page references where the answers can be found. In addition, sample answers for the essay questions are given. This item can be packaged with the text. Contact your Pearson Higher Education representative for more details.

MyPsychLab mypsychlab **(www.mypsychlab.com)**. MyPsychLab provides instructors with a full suite of tools to assess students' mastery of course material and hold students accountable for the amount of time they spend with the material out of class. Proven in classrooms big and small across the country, and loved by hundreds of thousands of students, MyPsychLab includes the following:

- **An Interactive eBook** with highlighting and note-taking features and powerful embedded media including over 100 simulations, more than 3,000 video clips (available in closed caption), dozens of podcasts, and an interactive timeline that presents the history of psychology.

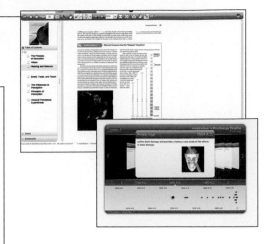

- **Customized Study Plans and Assessments** allow students to take a Pre-Test to self-assess how much they already know about the topics in a section of the chapter they're working on. These Pre-Tests pair together with Post-Tests on the website to generate customized study plans and eBook self-assessments.

- **New! Concept Mapping Tool** Students can use the new Concept Mapping Tool to create a variety of personalized graphic study aids using preloaded content from each chapter. Students can use this flexible and customizable tool to create their own unique organizational aids, to produce aids that conform to instructors' guidelines, or to prepare note-taking maps using the *Map It* instructions in the text. The organizers that the Concept Mapping Tool produces can be saved, e-mailed to you, or printed out to be used as a study tool.

- **New! APA Learning Goals and Outcome Assessments:** For instructors interested in assessing their students progress against the APA Psychology Learning Goals and Outcomes, we have provided a separate bank of assessment items keyed specifically to those goals in MyPsychLab.

- **Pearson Psychology Experiments Tool** presents a suite of data-generating experiment demonstrations, inventories, and surveys that allow students to experience first hand some of the main concepts covered in the text. Each item in the Experiments Tool generates anonymous class data that instructors can download and use in class lectures or for homework assignments. With over 50 assignable demonstrations, such as the Implicit Association Test, Roediger Effect, Inter-hemispheric Transfer Time, IPIP-Neo Personality Inventory, Buss Mate Preference Survey, and general surveys, the Experiments tool holds students accountable for *doing* psychology.

- **New! peerScholar Peer-Graded Writing Assignments** allows instructors to assign online writing assignments, even for large general psychology sections. PeerScholar allows students to read and write about articles relating to course material, evaluate the writing of other students, and receive feedback on their writing. Used successfully for five years in a test market and grounded in ongoing research, this tool provides a fair and pedagogically powerful tool for including open-ended writing assignments in any class context.

- **A Gradebook for Instructors** as well as full course management capabilities for instructors teaching online or hybrid courses are included in the instructor version of MyPsychLab.

- **Audio Files of Each Chapter** benefit students who are blind and others who prefer sound-based materials, and conform to ADA guidelines.

- **New! Podcasting Tool** with preloaded podcasts permits you to easily record and upload podcasts of your own lectures for students to access.

- **Interactive Mobile-Ready Flash Cards** of the key terms from the text can be used by students to build their own stacks, print the cards, or export their flashcards to their cell phones.

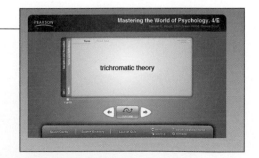

You decide the extent of integration, from independent self-assessment for students to total course management. Students benefit from an easy-to-use site at which they can test themselves on key content, track their progress, and create individually tailored study plans. By transferring faculty members' most time-consuming tasks—content delivery, student assessment, and grading—to automated tools, MyPsychLab allows you to spend more quality time with students.

Additional Course Management Resources:

- **Online Resource MyPsychLab for BlackBoard/MyPsychLab for WebCT**
  The customized BlackBoard cartridge and WebCT epack include the complete Test
  Bank, each chapter's Learning Objectives, Glossary Flashcards, Chapter Summaries,
  a link to MyPsychLab, and Chapter Exams.

- Ask your Pearson representative about custom offerings for other learning management systems or visit **www.mypsychlab.com** for more information.

Acknowledgments

We are thankful for the support of several people at Pearson Education who helped bring our plans for the fourth edition of *Mastering the World of Psychology* to fruition. On the editorial side, Stephen Frail monitored the progress of the text and ensured that the final product is an introductory text that achieves the goal of being thorough while also being timely and accessible. We are grateful for the assistance of our developmental editor, Deb Hanlon, whose suggestions and encouragement helped immeasurably in the pursuit of this goal.

Our Reviewers Numerous reviewers were invaluable to the development of this text. Their help provided a solid foundation for creating *Mastering the World of Psychology*, Fourth Edition:

Carol Anderson, Bellevue College
Bakhtawar Bhadha, Pasadena City College
Dr. Ken Callis, Southeast Missouri State University
Evelyn N. Doody, College of Southern Nevada
Mary Christina Evans, Pierce College
Cecilia Erlund, University of Mary Hardin-Baylor
Hallie Feil, Western Nebraska Community College
Jamie S. Hughes, New Mexico State University
Yasmine Kalkstein, North Hennepin Community College
Eric Kim, Lane Community College
Steve Kittrell, North Metro Technical College
Holly Schofield, Central Carolina Community College
David Shepard, South Texas College
Staci Simmelink-Johnson, Walla Walla Community College
Debra M. Yoder, Mountain View College

In addition, we would also like to thank the reviewers who took part in our Supplements survey for this edition:

Gayle Abbott, New Mexico Junior College
Christan Amundsen, North Lake College
Julie Hanauer, Suffolk County Community College
Annette Jankiewicz, Iowa Western Community College
Warren Lambert, Somerset Community College
Amy Overman, Elon University
Sandra Todaro, Bossier Parish Community College

We would also like to thank reviewers of the first three editions of *Mastering the World of Psychology* for their encouragement and insights:

Elaine P. Adams, Houston Community College
David W. Alfano, Community College of Rhode Island
Jill Barton, Keiser College
Kenneth Benson, Hinds Community College
John Brennecke, Mount San Antonio College
Robin Campbell, Brevard Community College
Cari Cannon, Santiago Canyon College
Dennis Cogan, Texas Tech University

Berry J. Daughenbaugh, Wor-Wic Community College
Wayne Dixon, Southeastern Oklahoma State University
Wendy Domjan, University of Texas
Jim Dorman, St. Charles Community College
Laura Duvall, Heartland Community College
Darlene Earley-Hereford, Southern Union State Community College
Hallie Feil, Western Nebraska Community College
Joseph Feldman, Phoenix College
Colleen L. Gift, Highland Community College
Paula Goolkasian, UNC Charlotte
Chuck Hallock, University of Arizona
Julie Hanauer, Suffolk Community College
Brett Heintz, Delgado Community College
Carmon Weaver Hicks, Ivy Tech Community College
Alan Hughes, Nazareth College (New York)
Carolyn Kaufman, Columbus State Community College
Norman E. Kinney, Southeast Missouri State University
Leslee Koritzke, Los Angeles Trade Technical College
Leslie Minor-Evans, Central Oregon Community College
Paulina Multhaupt, Macomb Community College
Enrique Otero, North Lake College
Debra Parish, North Harris Montgomery Community College
Jeffrey Pedroza, Santa Anna College
Ralph Pifer, Sauk Valley College
Michelle Pilati, Rio Hondo College
Cynthia Reed, Tarrant County College Northeast
Vicki Ritts, St. Louis Community College, Meramec
Amy Shapiro, University of Massachusetts, Amherst
David Shepard, South Texas College
Jason Spiegelman, Community College of Baltimore County
Robert B. Stennett, Gainesville State College
Robert Stickgold, Harvard University
Lisa Valentino, Seminole Community College
Edie Woods, Macomb County Community College

And, last, to all the instructors and students who have taken time out of their busy lives to send along feedback about their experiences teaching and studying from *Mastering the World of Psychology,* we are grateful to you. Please feel free to write *drdeniseboyd@sbcglobal.net* with your comments about the text.

List of Features

APPLY IT

TRY IT

EXPLAIN IT

SUMMARIZE IT

About the Authors

Samuel E. Wood (deceased) received his doctorate from the University of Florida. He taught at West Virginia University and the University of Missouri–St. Louis and was a member of the doctoral faculty at both universities. From 1984 to 1996, he served as president of the Higher Education Center, a consortium of 14 colleges and universities in the St. Louis area. He was a cofounder of the Higher Education Cable TV channel (HEC-TV) in St. Louis and served as its president and CEO from its founding in 1987 until 1996.

Ellen Green Wood received her doctorate in educational psychology from St. Louis University and was an adjunct professor of psychology at St. Louis Community College at Meramec. She has also taught in the clinical experiences program in education at Washington University and at the University of Missouri–St. Louis. In addition to her teaching, Dr. Wood has developed and taught seminars on critical thinking. She received the Telecourse Pioneer Award from 1982 through 1988 for her contributions to the field of distance learning.

Denise Boyd received her Ed.D. in educational psychology from the University of Houston and has been a psychology instructor in the Houston Community College System since 1988. From 1995 until 1998, she chaired the psychology, sociology, and anthropology department at Houston Community College–Central. She has coauthored five other Pearson Allyn and Bacon texts: With Samuel Wood and Ellen Green Wood, *The World of Psychology* (Seventh Edition); with Helen Bee, *Lifespan Development* (Fifth Edition), *The Developing Child* (Twelfth Edition), and *The Growing Child* (First Edition); and with Genevieve Stevens, *Current Readings in Lifespan Development*. A licensed psychologist, she has presented a number of papers at professional meetings, reporting research in child, adolescent, and adult development. She has also presented workshops for teachers whose students range from preschool to college.

Together, Sam, Evie, and Denise have several decades of experience teaching introductory psychology to thousands of students of all ages, backgrounds, and abilities. *Mastering the World of Psychology,* Fourth Edition, is the direct result of their teaching experience.

Introduction to **Psychology**

1 CHAPTER

The SQ3R method will help you maximize your learning in five steps:
- Survey
- Question
- Read
- Recite
- Review

The sticky notes in Chapter 1 will help you master this learning system so that you can use it on your own in the remaining chapters.

Think About It

Here you are taking your first psychology course and wondering what it's all about. When you focus on the word *psychology*, what ideas spring to mind as you concentrate? Do terms such as *therapy, brain, psychological disorder, emotion,* and *hypnosis* come to mind? Your introductory psychology course will touch on all of these concepts, but it will also help you learn how to deal with pressing practical issues in your everyday life. How can you study more effectively? (You can start answering this one by reading the *Apply it* section on page 4.) How can you know which career is right for you? How can you stop feeling so stressed out all the time? These are the kinds of practical questions that a good understanding of psychology can help you answer?

Let's begin your exploration of psychology with an assessment of how much you already know, or think you know, about the topic:

Indicate whether each statement is true (T) or false (F).

1. Once damaged, brain cells never work again.
2. All people dream during a night of normal sleep.
3. As the number of bystanders at an emergency increases, the time it takes for the victim to get help decreases.
4. Humans do not have a maternal instinct.
5. It's impossible for human beings to hear a watch ticking 20 feet away.
6. Eyewitness testimony is often unreliable.
7. Chimpanzees have been taught to speak.
8. Creativity and high intelligence do not necessarily go together.
9. When it comes to close personal relationships, opposites attract.
10. The majority of teenagers have good relationships with their parents.

You may be surprised to learn that all the odd-numbered items are false, and all the even-numbered items are true. Learning all you can from this text is a good first step toward a better understanding of behavior and mental processes. The text's features will help you learn because they are part of a systematic—that is, a goal-oriented, planned, and effortful—way of studying. Similarly, the procedures that scientists use yield reliable answers to questions about behavior and mental processes because they are part of a systematic approach to what some philosophers deem to be the primary goal of science: to search for truth (Popper, 1972).

An Introduction to *Mastering the World of Psychology*

A Ugandan expression says, "The hunter in pursuit of an elephant does not stop to throw stones at birds." In other words, to achieve any goal, including succeeding in a psychology course, one must remain focused on it. The study strategies we have incorporated into *Mastering the World of Psychology* can help you stay focused on your goal of successfully completing your course in introductory psychology. Here is how the features of the text can help you.

SQ3R method A study method involving the following five steps: (1) survey, (2) question, (3) read, (4) recite, and (5) review.

1.1 How will the SQ3R method help you master psychology?

Studying Psychology: Some Tricks of the Trade

To help you maximize your learning, *Mastering the World of Psychology* includes a set of tried and true study strategies—*Survey, Question, Read, Recite,* and *Review*—that are collectively known as the SQ3R method (Robinson, 1970). Here's how to make the most of the SQ3R features that we have included in *Mastering the World of Psychology*:

STEP 1: **Survey.** The goal of the survey step is to get the chapter's "big picture," a mental map of what it's all about. That's the purpose of the outline at the beginning of each chapter. The outline gives you a blueprint to use as you navigate through the chapter and tells you what you will learn in each section. Read it thoroughly. Next, look over the major elements of the chapter. These elements include the chapter-opening activity called *Think About It*, the section headings, *Summarize It* tables, *Try It* activities, *Explain It* boxes, and *Apply It* boxes. You should also survey the learning questions in the margins by each subheading (the same questions that are in the outline) and the boldfaced terms that are also in the margins. Next, skim over the *Chapter Summary*. It includes answers for all the learning questions. At the end of the *Chapter Summary*, you'll find instructions for *Map It*, a study tool that will help you organize the learning questions, answers for the questions, key terms, and important figures and tables in each major section of the chapter. The instructions provide you with a starter map for the first section of the chapter. You can sketch out your own chapter map on paper or log on to **MyPsychLab** (www.mypsychlab.com) and click on "Map It" to create your own digital map, save it, print it, and email it to your instructor if needed. Next, do the *Think About It* activity at the beginning of the chapter, keeping in mind the mental

Step 1: Survey
- Read over the learning objectives in the outline at the beginning of the chapter.
- Look over the other major elements of the chapter. They include:
  - Think About It chapter opener
  - Key terms
  - Summarize It tables
  - Try It activities
  - Explain It boxes
  - Apply It boxes
- Skim the Chapter Summary.
- Follow the Map It instructions on page 31 to create a note-taking map you'll use as you read the chapter. Your map will include these elements:
  - The titles and main ideas of the chapter's sections
  - The learning questions each section answers
- Do the Think About It activity at the beginning of the chapter.

overview of the chapter that you constructed with the help of the outline and *Map It*. Now you're ready to start working your way through the chapter.

STEP 2:　Question. Do the Question step as you come to each subheading in the chapter. This step has two parts: First, read the learning question in the margin. For instance, the learning question for this subsection is "How will the SQ3R method help you master psychology?" Next, think of additional questions you have about the topic and add them to your the *Map It* diagram you created online (www.mypsychlab.com) or on paper in the Survey step.

STEP 3:　Read. Read the text under each subheading and be sure you understand it before you move to the next one. As you read, keep the learning question and your own questions in mind. Use the *Apply It* boxes, *Try It* activities, *Explain It* boxes, and *Summarize It* tables, if any are present, to help you understand the section.

STEP 4:　Recite. When you finish reading each subsection, answer its learning question and your own questions aloud in your own words. Jot your answers in your *Map It* diagram along with brief definitions for the section's key terms. When you're finished, look back at the section to see if you've missed anything and modify your *Map It* notes if necessary. Repeat this process for each subsection and you'll end up with a well organized set of notes on the entire chapter.

STEP 5a: Review I. To be sure you've understood each major section before you move on to the next one, look over the entries in your *Map It* diagram for each of the section's subheadings. Next, log on to MyPsychLab and take the section quiz. You should find many of the answers in your *Map It* diagram. If you don't, you should probably go back and revise it.

STEP 5b: Review II. After you have worked your way through the all the major sections, you need to review the entire chapter to be sure that you're ready to be tested on it. Begin by reading the *Chapter Summary* and comparing it to your *Map It* notes. Revise your notes if necessary. Next, complete the Study Guide and check your answers against the key in the back of the book. Revisit your *Map It* notes and restudy the part of the chapter and study the parts of the chapter you scored the lowest on in the Study Guide. Finally, take the chapter Practice Tests in the back of the book or log on to MyPsychLab to take the online Chapter Exam. Reread the parts of the chapter that relate to any questions that you miss, and be sure that you understand where you went wrong. At this point, you should be feeling confident about your mastery of the chapter.

Now that you know how to study this text effectively, let's consider in more detail what impact the work of psychologists has on our everyday lives. Before we begin, think about all of the ways in which psychology—and the language of psychology—plays an integral role in our lives.

Is Psychology a Science? ▶

Psychology is defined as the scientific study of behavior and mental processes. If you are like most people, you have made many observations about both and perhaps have developed a few of your own theories to explain them. From television, radio, or the Internet, you probably also have had some exposure to "expert" opinions on behavior and mental processes. In fact, those may be the very sources that led you astray on the quiz at the beginning of the chapter.

Many people believe that a field is a science because of the nature of its body of knowledge. Few people question whether physics, for example, is a true science. But a science isn't a science because of its subject matter. A field of study qualifies as a science if it uses the scientific method to acquire knowledge. The scientific method consists of the orderly, systematic procedures that researchers follow as they identify a research problem, design a study to investigate the problem, collect and analyze data, draw conclusions, and communicate their findings. The knowledge gained is dependable because of the method used to obtain it. The scientific method includes these steps (see Figure 1.1 on page 4).

Step 2: Question
Use the question step for each subheading in the chapter. It has two parts:
- Read the learning question in the margin.
- Think of additional questions you have about the topic.

Step 3: Read
Read the text under each subheading and be sure you understand it before you go on to the next one. As you read:
- Keep the learning question in mind.
- Keep your own questions in mind.
- Use the Apply It boxes, Try It activities, Explain It boxes, and Summarize It tables, if any are present, to help you understand the subsection.

Step 4: Recite
When you finish reading each section:
- Answer the learning question and your own questions aloud in your own words.
- Add the answers to your Map It diagram.
- Look back at the section to see if you've missed anything.
- Modify your Map It notes if necessary.
Repeat this process for each subsection and you will end up with a well organized set of notes on the entire chapter.

1.2　Why do psychologists use the scientific method?

psychology The scientific study of behavior and mental processes.

scientific method The orderly, systematic procedures that researchers follow as they identify a research problem, design a study to investigate the problem, collect and analyze data, draw conclusions, and communicate their findings.

APPLY IT   **More Tips for Effective Studying**

Decades of research on learning and memory have uncovered a number of strategies that you can use, in addition to the SQ3R method, to make your study time more efficient and effective.

■ Establish a quiet place, free of distractions, where you do nothing else but study. You can condition yourself to associate this environment with studying, so that entering the room or area will be your cue to begin work.

■ Schedule your study time. Research on memory has proven that spaced learning is more effective than massed practice (cramming). Instead of studying for five hours straight, try five study sessions of one hour each.

■ To be prepared for each class meeting, set specific goals for yourself each week and for individual study sessions. Your goals should be challenging but not overwhelming. If the task for an individual study session is manageable, it will be easier to sit down and face it. Completing the task you have set for yourself will give you a sense of accomplishment.

■ The more active a role you play in the learning process, the more you will remember. Spend some of your study time reciting rather than rereading the material. One effective method is to use index cards as flash cards. Write a key term or study question on the front of each card. On the back, list pertinent information from the text and class lectures. Use these cards to help you prepare for tests.

■ *Overlearning* means studying beyond the point at which you can just barely recite the information you are trying to memorize. Review the information again and again until it is firmly locked in memory. If you are subject to test anxiety, overlearning will help.

■ Forgetting takes place most rapidly within the first 24 hours after you study. No matter how much you have studied for a test, always review shortly before you take it. Refreshing your memory will raise your grade.

■ Sleeping immediately after you study will help you retain more of what you have learned. If you can't study before you go to sleep, at least review what you studied earlier in the day. This is also a good time to go through your index cards.

Once you've mastered these study strategies, use them to improve your comprehension and success in all of your courses.

⊙ Watch on mypsychlab.com

Observe and Theorize. The first step in the scientific method is an interactive one in which a researcher observes some phenomenon and *theorizes*, or develops a hunch, about what might have led to it. For instance, suppose a psychologist observes students playing video games on a big-screen TV in a student lounge and notices that the men tend to get higher scores than the women do. She might speculate that this gender difference results from differences in the amount of time that men and women spend playing video games. In other words, her hunch is that, in general, men get higher scores on video games because they practice more than women do. Such hunches are often derived from a psychological theory, a general principle or set of principles proposed to explain how a number of separate facts are related. In our example, the researcher's hunch seems to be based on a theory that emphasizes the role of experience in shaping behavior; that is, her theory proposes that the more experience people have doing something, the better they are at it.

theory A general principle or set of principles proposed to explain how a number of separate facts are related.

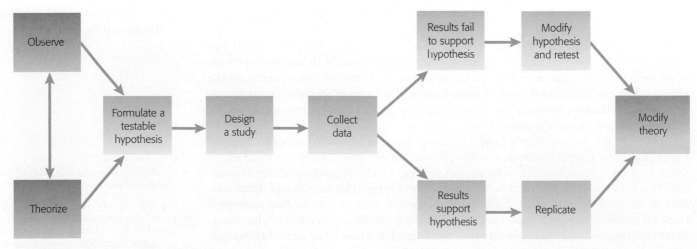

FIGURE 1.1 The Scientific Method
These are the steps involved in the scientific method.

Formulate a Hypothesis. Based on her hunch about the cause of gender differences in video game scores, the researcher next comes up with a hypothesis, a specific prediction that can be tested *empirically*—that is, with data. Although the researchers' theory suggests many possible hypotheses, one, in particular, is key to understanding the contribution of practice to video game scores: *If males and females spend equal amounts of time practicing a game, their scores will be equal.*

Design a Study. Next, to test the hypothesis about equal practice, the researcher could design a study in which she uses the same procedures to teach male and female students how to play a new video game. Then she allows them 30 minutes to practice it on their own. At the end of the practice session, she tells participants to play the game one more time but to try for the highest score possible.

Collect Data. Once the researcher conducts her study, she collects data that are relevant to her hypothesis. First, she calculates an average score for male and female participants. Then she calculates the amount of time that participants actually spent practicing the game. This information could be critical in interpreting the study's results because, even though each participant is allowed 30 minutes to practice, the researcher cannot assume that they will all practice an equal amount of time.

Apply Results to the Hypothesis. If the scores for males and females are equivalent, the researcher can conclude that the data support her hypothesis; given the same amount of practice time, males and females will score equally well. However, she cannot stop there. The researcher must repeat the study using the same procedures to determine whether her findings are a one-time phenomenon or are the result of a true, underlying psychological principle. This process is called replication.

On the other hand, if the researcher finds that males still get higher scores than females, she must concede that the results do not support her hypothesis and she must modify it. However, this is where the researcher's data on actual practice time may come in handy: If the data show that males spent more time engaged in actual practice than the females did, the researcher can assert that the study's outcome supports her hypothesis after all. Still, she must modify her hypothesis to include a testable assertion about why the men in her study chose to practice more than the women did. If she hypothesizes that the practice difference was caused by the type of game used in the study, for example, in a subsequent study, the researcher would go on to examine how different types of games affect practice time.

The Goals of Psychology ▶

1.3 What are the goals of psychology?

What goals do psychological researchers pursue when they plan and conduct their studies? Briefly put, psychologists pursue four broad goals:

- *Description:* Identifying and classifying behaviors and mental processes as accurately as possible
- *Explanation:* Proposing reasons for behaviors and mental processes
- *Prediction:* Offering predictions (or hypotheses) about how a given condition or set of conditions will affect behaviors and mental processes
- *Influence:* Using the results of research to solve practical problems that involve behavior and mental processes

Two types of research help psychologists accomplish the four goals just described: basic research and applied research. The purpose of basic research is to seek new knowledge and to explore and advance general scientific understanding. Basic research explores such topics as the nature of memory, brain function, motivation, and emotional expression. Applied research is conducted specifically for the purpose of solving practical problems and improving the quality of life. Applied research focuses

---

hypothesis A testable prediction about the conditions under which a particular behavior or mental process may occur.

replication The process of repeating a study to verify research findings.

basic research Research conducted to seek new knowledge and to explore and advance general scientific understanding.

applied research Research conducted specifically to solve practical problems and improve the quality of life.

Step 5a: Review I
To be sure you've understood each major section before you move on to the next one:
- Look over your Map It notes for each of the section's subheadings.
- Log on to MyPsychLab and take the section quiz.

on finding methods to improve memory or increase motivation, therapies to treat psychological disorders, ways to decrease stress, and so on. This type of research is primarily concerned with the fourth goal of psychology—influence—because it specifies ways and means of changing behavior.

The scientific method has enabled psychologists to accumulate a vast knowledge base about behavior and mental processes. However, information alone doesn't necessarily advance our understanding of psychological phenomena. As we noted earlier, using knowledge acquired through the scientific method to develop cohesive theories can help us in the quest for understanding. With that point in mind, we'll turn our attention to some early attempts at psychological theory building and the schools of thought and psychological perspectives that arose from the debate stimulated by them.

The *Summarize It* below summarizes the goals of psychology and applies them to the video game hypothesis we discussed earlier.

Psychology Then and Now

If you were to trace the development of psychology from the beginning, you would need to start before the earliest pages of recorded history, beyond even the early Greek philosophers, such as Aristotle and Plato. Psychology became distinct from philosophy when researchers began to use the scientific method to study behavior and mental processes. By the 1920s, the field's earliest researchers had laid the foundations of the major schools of thought and psychological perspectives that exist in psychology today. As the field grew and research findings accumulated, specialty areas within the field began to follow distinctive pathways.

1.4 What did the early psychologists contribute to the field?

Exploring Psychology's Roots

Psychology became a science and an academic discipline in the 19th century when people who wanted to learn more about behavior and mental processes began to use the scientific method. Conventional thought at the time held that such endeavors were the exclusive province of white males. Nevertheless, several researchers overcame gender and ethnic prejudice in the late 19th and early 20th centuries to make notable contributions to the field of psychology.

Structuralism and Functionalism. Who were the "founders" of psychology? Historians acknowledge that three German scientists—Ernst Weber, Gustav Fechner, and Hermann von Helmholtz—were the first to systematically study behavior and mental

SUMMARIZE IT

The Goals of Psychology

GOAL	DEFINITION	EXAMPLE
Description	Describe behavior or mental process as accurately as possible.	Calculate average video game scores for males and females.
Explanation	Suggest causes for behavior or mental processes of interest.	Propose that males score higher on video games because they practice more than females do.
Prediction	Specify conditions under which behavior or mental process is likely to occur.	Hypothesize that males and females will obtain equivalent video game scores if they practice the same amount of time.
Influence	Apply the results of a study to change a condition in order to bring about a desired real-world outcome or prevent an undesired real-world outcome.	Use the results of video game practice studies to develop games that can enhance females' achievement in math and science.

processes. But it is Wilhelm Wundt (1832–1920) who is generally thought of as the "father" of psychology. Wundt's vision for the new discipline included studies of social and cultural influences on human thought (Benjafield, 1996).

Wundt established a psychological laboratory at the University of Leipzig in Germany in 1879, an event considered to mark the birth of psychology as a formal academic discipline. Using a method called *introspection,* Wundt and his associates studied the perception of a variety of visual, tactile, and auditory stimuli, including the rhythm patterns produced by metronomes set at different speeds. Introspection as a research method involves looking inward to examine one's own conscious experience and then reporting that experience.

Wundt's most famous student, Englishman Edward Bradford Titchener (1867– 1927), took the new field to the United States, where he set up a psychological laboratory at Cornell University. He gave the name structuralism to this first formal school of thought in psychology, which aimed at analyzing the basic elements, or the structure, of conscious mental experience. Like Wundt before him, Titchener thought that consciousness could be reduced to its basic elements, just as water (H_2O) can be broken down into its constituent elements—hydrogen (H) and oxygen (O). For Wundt, pure sensations—such as sweetness, coldness, or redness—were the basic elements of consciousness. And these pure sensations, he believed, combined to form perceptions.

▲ Even though these skydivers share the same sensations—the feeling of falling, the rush of air on their faces as they fall, and the sudden lurch of their parachutes opening—their reported introspections of the experience would probably differ.

structuralism The first formal school of thought in psychology, aimed at analyzing the basic elements, or structure, of conscious mental experience.

The work of both Wundt and Titchener was criticized for its primary method, introspection. Introspection is not objective, even though it involves observation, measurement, and experimentation. When different introspectionists were exposed to the same stimulus, such as the click of a metronome, they frequently reported different experiences. Therefore, structuralism was not in favor for long. Later schools of thought in psychology were established, partly as a reaction against structuralism, which did not survive after the death of its most ardent spokesperson, Titchener. Nevertheless, the structuralists were responsible for establishing psychology as a science through their insistence that psychological processes could be measured and studied using methods similar to those employed by scientists in other fields.

As structuralism began losing its influence in the United States in the early 20th century, a new school of psychology called functionalism was taking shape. Functionalism was concerned not with the structure of consciousness but with how mental processes function—that is, how humans and animals use mental processes in adapting to their environment. The influential work of Charles Darwin (1809–1882), especially his ideas about evolution and the continuity of species, was largely responsible for an increasing use of animals in psychological experiments. Even though Darwin, who was British, contributed important seeds of thought that helped give birth to the new school of psychology, functionalism was primarily American in character and spirit.

functionalism An early school of psychology that was concerned with how humans and animals use mental processes in adapting to their environment.

The famous American psychologist William James (1842–1910) was an advocate of functionalism, even though he did much of his writing before this school of psychology emerged. James's best-known work is his highly regarded and frequently quoted textbook *Principles of Psychology,* published more than a century ago (1890). James taught that mental processes are fluid and have continuity, rather than the rigid, or fixed, structure that the structuralists suggested. James spoke of the "stream of consciousness," which, he said, functions to help humans adapt to their environment.

How did functionalism change psychology? Functionalism broadened the scope of psychology to include the study of behavior as well as mental processes. It also allowed the study of children, animals, and the mentally impaired, groups that could not be

▲ During the 1880s, Christine Ladd-Franklin became one of the first women to complete a doctoral degree in psychology, although Johns Hopkins University refused to officially grant her the degree until the mid 1920s.
Archives of the History of American Psychology—The University of Akron.

▲ Kenneth (1914–2005) and Mamie (1917–1983) Clark's research examining self-esteem in African American children was cited in the 1954 U.S. Supreme Court decision *Brown v. Board of Education* that led to the desegregation of public schools in the United States.

1.5 What are the major schools of thought in psychology?

studied by the structuralists because they could not be trained to use introspection. Functionalism also focused on an applied, more practical use of psychology by encouraging the study of educational practices, individual differences, and adaptation in the workplace (industrial psychology).

The Changing Face of Psychology. As we noted earlier, during the early days of psychology, most people believed that academic and scientific pursuits were the exclusive province of white males. However, there were a number of women and minority group members who refused to allow convention to stand in the way of their quest for a better understanding of behavior and mental processes. They broke barriers that paved the way for later scholars and, at the same time, made important contributions to the field. Here are a few examples:

- *Christine Ladd-Franklin (1847–1930):* completed Ph.D. requirements at Johns Hopkins University in the mid-1880s but had to wait 40 years to receive her degree; formulated evolutionary theory of color vision.
- *Mary Whiton Calkins (1863–1930):* completed Ph.D. requirements at Harvard in 1895, but the university refused to grant doctorate to a woman (Dewsbury, 2000); established psychology laboratory at Wellesley College; developed methods for studying memory; first female president of the American Psychological Association in 1905.
- *Margaret Floy Washburn (1871–1939):* received a Ph.D. in psychology from Cornell University; taught at Vassar College (Dewsbury, 2000); wrote influential books on animal behavior and mental imagery.
- *Francis Cecil Sumner (1895–1954):* first African American to earn a Ph.D. in psychology; translated more than 3,000 research articles from German, French, and Spanish; chaired psychology department at Howard University; known as the "father" of African American psychology.
- *Albert Sidney Beckham (1897–1964):* established the first psychological laboratory at an African American institution of higher education (Howard University); studied relationship of intelligence to occupational success.
- *Kenneth Clark (1914–2005) and Mamie Phipps Clark (1917–1983):* conducted studies of detrimental effects of racial segregation on African American children's self-esteem that were cited in Supreme Court ruling that declared racial segregation in U.S. schools unconstitutional (Benjamin & Crouse, 2002; Lal, 2002).
- *George Sánchez (1906–1972):* studied cultural and linguistic bias in intelligence testing during the 1930s (Sánchez, 1932, 1934).

Today, more women than men obtain degrees in psychology, and minority group representation is growing (NCES, 2006, 2008). However, there continues to be a gap between the proportion of minorities in the U.S. population and their representation among professional psychologists (APA, 2008). Consequently, the APA and other organizations have established programs to encourage minority enrollment in graduate programs in psychology.

Schools of Thought in Psychology

Why don't we hear about structuralism and functionalism today? In the early 20th century, the debate between the two points of view sparked a veritable explosion of theoretical discussion and research examining psychological processes. The foundations of the major schools of thought in the field were established during that period and continue to be influential today.

Behaviorism. Psychologist John B. Watson (1878–1958) looked at the study of psychology as defined by the structuralists and functionalists and disliked virtually everything he saw. In his article "Psychology as the Behaviorist Views It" (1913), Watson proposed a radically new approach to psychology, one that rejected the subjectivity of both structuralism and functionalism. This new school redefined psychology as the "science of behavior." Termed behaviorism by Watson, this school of psychology confines itself to the study of behavior because behavior is observable and measurable and, therefore, objective and scientific. Behaviorism also emphasizes that behavior is determined primarily by factors in the environment.

behaviorism The school of psychology that views observable, measurable behavior as the appropriate subject matter for psychology and emphasizes the key role of environment as a determinant of behavior.

Behaviorism was the most influential school of thought in American psychology until the 1960s. It remains a major force in modern psychology, in large part because of the profound influence of B. F. Skinner (1904–1990). Skinner agreed with Watson that concepts such as mind, consciousness, and feelings are neither objective nor measurable and, therefore, not appropriate subject matter for psychology. Furthermore, Skinner argued that these concepts are not needed to explain behavior. One can explain behavior, he claimed, by analyzing the conditions that are present before a behavior occurs and then analyzing the consequences that follow the behavior.

Skinner's research on operant conditioning emphasized the importance of reinforcement in learning and in shaping and maintaining behavior. He maintained that any behavior that is reinforced (followed by pleasant or rewarding consequences) is more likely to be performed again. Skinner's work has had a powerful influence on modern psychology. You will read more about operant conditioning in Chapter 5.

Psychoanalysis. Sigmund Freud (1856–1939), whose work you will study in Chapter 11, developed a theory of human behavior based largely on case studies of his patients. Freud's theory, psychoanalysis, maintains that human mental life is like an iceberg. The smallest, visible part of the iceberg represents the conscious mental experience of the individual. But underwater, hidden from view, floats a vast store of unconscious impulses, wishes, and desires. Freud insisted that individuals do not consciously control their thoughts, feelings, and behavior; these are instead determined by unconscious forces.

psychoanalysis (SY-ko-ah-NAL-ih-sis) The term Freud used for both his theory of personality and his therapy for the treatment of psychological disorders; the unconscious is the primary focus of psychoanalytic theory.

The overriding importance that Freud placed on sexual and aggressive impulses caused much controversy both inside and outside the field of psychology. The most notable of Freud's famous students—Carl Jung, Alfred Adler, and Karen Horney—broke away from their mentor and developed their own theories of personality. These three and their followers are often collectively referred to as *neo-Freudians*. Thus, the psychoanalytic approach continues to be influential, albeit in a form that has been modified considerably over the past several decades by the neo-Freudians.

Humanistic Psychology. Humanistic psychologists reject with equal vigor (1) the behaviorist view that behavior is determined by factors in the environment and (2) the view of the psychoanalytic approach stating that human behavior is determined primarily by unconscious forces. Humanistic psychology focuses on the uniqueness of human beings and their capacity for choice, growth, and psychological health.

humanistic psychology The school of psychology that focuses on the uniqueness of human beings and their capacity for choice, growth, and psychological health.

Abraham Maslow and other early humanists, such as Carl Rogers (1902–1987), pointed out that Freud based his theory primarily on data from his disturbed patients. By contrast, the humanists emphasize a much more positive view of human nature. They maintain that people are innately good and that they possess free will. The humanists believe that people are capable of making conscious, rational choices, which can lead to personal growth and psychological health. As you will learn in Chapter 9, Maslow proposed a theory of motivation that consists of a hierarchy of needs. He considered the need for self-actualization (developing to one's fullest potential) to be the highest need on the hierarchy. Rogers developed what he called *client-centered therapy*, an approach in which the client, or patient, directs a discussion focused on his or her own view of a problem rather than on the therapist's analysis. Rogers and other humanists also popularized group therapy. Thus, the humanistic perspective continues to be important in research examining human motivation and in the practice of psychotherapy.

cognitive psychology The school of psychology that sees humans as active participants in their environment; studies mental processes such as memory, problem solving, reasoning, decision making, perception, language, and other forms of cognition.

Gestalt psychology The school of psychology that emphasizes that individuals perceive objects and patterns as whole units and that the perceived whole is more than the sum of its parts.

information-processing theory An approach to the study of mental structures and processes that uses the computer as a model for human thinking.

evolutionary psychology The school of psychology that studies how human behaviors required for survival have adapted in the face of environmental pressures over the long course of evolution.

▲ Is this person having a bad day? The perceptual processes described by the Gestalt psychologists are observable in everyday life. We often put frustrating events—such as getting up late and then having a flat tire—together to form a "whole" concept, such as "I'm having a bad day."

Cognitive Psychology. Cognitive psychology grew and developed partly in response to strict behaviorism, especially in the United States (Robins, Gosling, & Craik, 1999). Cognitive psychology sees humans not as passive recipients who are pushed and pulled by environmental forces but as active participants who seek out experiences, who alter and shape those experiences, and who use mental processes to transform information in the course of their own cognitive development. It studies mental processes such as memory, problem solving, reasoning, decision making, perception, language, and other forms of cognition. Historically, modern cognitive psychology is derived from two streams of thought: one that began with a small group of German scientists studying human perception in the early 20th century and another that grew up alongside the emerging field of computer science in the second half of the century.

Gestalt psychology made its appearance in Germany in 1912. The Gestalt psychologists, notably Max Wertheimer, Kurt Koffka, and Wolfgang Köhler, emphasized that individuals perceive objects and patterns as whole units and that the perceived whole is more than the sum of its parts. The German word *Gestalt* roughly means "whole, form, or pattern."

To support the Gestalt theory, Wertheimer, the leader of the Gestalt psychologists, performed his famous experiment demonstrating the *phi phenomenon*. In this experiment, two lightbulbs are placed a short distance apart in a dark room. The first light is flashed on and then turned off just as the second light is flashed on. As this pattern of flashing the lights on and off continues, an observer sees what appears to be a single light moving back and forth from one position to another. Here, said the Gestaltists, is proof that people perceive wholes or patterns rather than collections of separate sensations.

When the Nazis came to power in Germany in the 1930s, the Gestalt school disbanded, and its most prominent members emigrated to the United States. Today, the fundamental concept underlying Gestalt psychology—that the mind *interprets* experiences in predictable ways rather than simply reacts to them—is central to cognitive psychologists' ideas about learning, memory, problem solving, and even psychotherapy.

The advent of the computer provided cognitive psychologists with a new way to conceptualize mental structures and processes, known as information-processing theory. According to this view, the brain processes information in sequential steps, in much the same way as a computer does serial processing—that is, one step at a time. But as modern technology has changed computers and computer programs, cognitive psychologists have changed their models. For example, many contemporary researchers are examining the human memory system's capacity for *parallel processing,* the management of multiple bits of information at once, a type of information processing that is commonly used in today's computers (Bajic & Rickard, 2009; Sung, 2008).

Over the past 100 years or so, cognitive psychologists have carried out studies that have greatly increased our knowledge of the human memory system and the mental processes involved in problem solving. Moreover, the principles discovered in these experiments have been used to explain and study all kinds of psychological variables—from gender role development to individual differences in intelligence. As a result, cognitive psychology is currently thought by many psychologists to be the most prominent school of psychological thought (Robins et al., 1999).

Evolutionary Psychology. Why do you think all healthy babies form attachments to their primary caregivers? Why do you think most men prefer mates who are younger than they are? These are the kinds of questions that interest *evolutionary psychologists*. Evolutionary psychology focuses on how the human behaviors required for survival have adapted in the face of environmental pressures over the long course of evolution (Archer, 1996). As such, evolutionary psychology draws heavily on Charles

Darwin's theory of natural selection. Darwin's theory asserts that individual members of a given species who possess characteristics that help them survive are the most likely to pass on the genes underlying those characteristics to subsequent generations. As a result, traits that support individual survival become universal in the species; that is, every individual member of the species has them. For example, every human being possesses the capacity to acquire language. Natural selection would explain this universality as the result of the survival advantage conferred on humans by having an efficient means of communicating information from one person to another.

Evolutionary psychology has been called, simply, a combination of evolutionary biology and cognitive psychology (Barker, 2006; Evans & Zarate, 2000). Two widely recognized proponents of evolutionary psychology, Leda Cosmides and John Tooby, hold that this perspective combines the forces of evolutionary biology, anthropology, cognitive psychology, and neuroscience. They explain that an evolutionary perspective can be applied to any topic within the field of psychology (Tooby & Cosmides, 2005). For example, one of the most influential evolutionary psychologists, David Buss, and his colleagues have conducted a number of fascinating studies examining men's and women's patterns of behavior in romantic relationships (Buss, 1999, 2000a, 2000b, 2001, 2008). You'll read more about Buss's work and that of his critics in Chapter 9.

▲ According to evolutionary psychology, natural selection has provided infants and caregivers with a built-in genetic predisposition to form an emotional attachment to one another because such bonds help infants survive.

Biological (Physiological) Psychology. Sometimes students are confused about the difference between evolutionary psychology and biological psychology (also referred to as *physiological psychology*). After all, many think, isn't evolution "biological" in nature? Yes, it is, but evolutionary psychology provides explanations of how certain biologically based behaviors came to be common in an entire species. Consequently, it focuses on *universals,* traits that exist in every member of a species. For instance, language is a human universal.

biological psychology The school of psychology that looks for links between specific behaviors and equally specific biological processes that often help explain individual differences.

By contrast, biological psychologists look for links between specific behaviors and particular biological factors that often help explain *individual differences.* They study the structures of the brain and central nervous system, the functioning of neurons, the delicate balance of neurotransmitters and hormones, and the effects of heredity to look for links between these biological factors and behavior. For example, the number of ear infections children have in the first year of life (a *biological* individual difference) is correlated with learning disabilities in the elementary school years (a *behavioral* individual difference) (Golz et al., 2005).

Many biological psychologists work under the umbrella of an interdisciplinary field known as neuroscience. Neuroscience combines the work of psychologists, biologists, biochemists, medical researchers, and others in the study of the structure and function of the nervous system. Important findings in psychology have resulted from this work. For example, researchers have learned that defects in nerve cell membranes interfere with the cells' ability to make use of brain chemicals that help us control body movement (Kurup & Kurup, 2002). These findings shed light on the physiological processes underlying serious neurological disorders such as Parkinson's disease and help pharmacological researchers in their efforts to create more effective medications for these disorders.

neuroscience An interdisciplinary field that combines the work of psychologists, biologists, biochemists, medical researchers, and others in the study of the structure and function of the nervous system.

The Sociocultural Approach. How do your background and cultural experiences affect your behavior and mental processing? The sociocultural approach emphasizes social and cultural influences on human behavior and stresses the importance of understanding those influences when interpreting the behavior of others. For example, several psychologists (e.g., Tweed & Lehman, 2002) have researched philosophical differences between Asian and Western cultures that may help explain cross-national achievement differences. Similarly, researcher Lesley Lambright (2003) explored the cultural characteristics that have helped the Vietnamese survive centuries of warfare. In in-depth interviews with Vietnamese men and women ranging in age from 24 to 68, she learned that Vietnam's multicultural background and the tolerance derived from it, the Vietnamese people's strong family system, and their tendencies toward

sociocultural approach The view that social and cultural factors may be just as powerful as evolutionary and physiological factors in affecting behavior and mental processing and that these factors must be understood when interpreting the behavior of others.

optimism, patience, and flexibility were instrumental to the resilience of this group. Another factor that emerged from Lambright's study was the tendency of Vietnamese to endorse forgiveness and practicality over vengeful responses to their enemies. A follow-up study that presented Lambright's interview questions in survey form to Vietnamese college students suggested that younger individuals perceive some of these aspects of traditional culture, such as strong family ties, to be changing. Thus, a sociocultural approach to understanding psychological variables such as resilience can shed light both on how culture and cultural changes shape the individual's experiences.

Social and cultural influences on behavior are often studied within the broader context of a *systems perspective*. The primary idea behind the systems approach is that multiple factors work together holistically; that is, their combined, interactive influences on behavior are greater than the sum of the individual factors that make up the system. A good example of the systems approach may be found in a theory proposed by psychologist Gerald Patterson and his colleagues that explains how variables interact to predispose some teenagers to antisocial behavior (Granic & Patterson, 2006). This systems approach argues that poverty (a sociocultural factor), for example, is predictive of juvenile delinquency, but in and of itself, it is insufficient to produce the behavior. As a result, most teens from poor families do not engage in antisocial behavior. However, poverty may function as part of a system of influential variables that includes disengagement from school, association with peers who encourage antisocial behavior, lack of parental supervision, and a host of other variables to increase the risk of antisocial behavior for individual teenagers. At the same time, these variables interact to maintain themselves and, in some cases, to create a multigenerational cycle. For instance, disengagement from school increases the likelihood that teenagers will live in poverty when they reach adulthood. Poverty, in turn, increases the chances that they will have to work long hours, rendering them less able to supervise their own children's behavior, thus putting another generation at risk for antisocial behavior.

1.6 What are the seven contemporary psychological perspectives?

psychological perspectives General points of view used for explaining people's behavior and thinking, whether normal or abnormal.

Contemporary Psychological Perspectives

The views of modern psychologists are frequently difficult to categorize into traditional schools of thought. Thus, rather than discussing schools of thought, it is often more useful to refer to psychological perspectives—general points of view used for explaining people's behavior and thinking, whether normal or abnormal. For example, a psychologist may adopt a behavioral perspective without necessarily agreeing with all of Watson's or Skinner's ideas. What is important is that the psychologist taking such a view will explain behavior in terms of environmental forces.

▲ A sociocultural approach helps psychologists explain cross-cultural differences in behavior.

The major perspectives in psychology today and the kinds of variables each emphasizes in explaining behavior are as follows:

- *Behavioral perspective:* Environmental factors
- *Psychoanalytic perspective:* Emotions, unconscious motivations, early childhood experiences
- *Humanistic perspective:* Subjective experiences, intrinsic motivation to achieve self-actualization
- *Cognitive perspective:* Mental processes
- *Evolutionary perspective:* Inherited traits that enhance adaptability
- *Biological perspective:* Biological structures, processes, heredity
- *Sociocultural perspective:* Social and cultural variables

The *Summarize It* lists these perspectives and illustrates how each might explain a student's poor performance on exams.

Psychologists need not limit themselves to just one perspective or approach. Many take an *eclectic position,* choosing a combination of approaches to explain a particular behavior. For example, a psychologist may explain a behavior in terms of both environmental factors and mental processes. A child's unruly behavior in school may be seen as maintained by teacher attention (a behavioral explanation) but as initially caused by an emotional reaction to a family event such as divorce (a psychoanalytic explanation). By adopting multiple perspectives, psychologists are able to devise more complex theories and research studies, resulting in improved treatment strategies. In this way, their theories and studies can more closely mirror the behavior of real people in real situations.

Contemporary Perspectives in Psychology

PERSPECTIVE	EMPHASIS	EXPLANATION OF A STUDENT'S POOR PERFORMANCE ON EXAMS
Behavioral	The role of environment in shaping and controlling behavior	The student has not been reinforced for getting good grades in the past.
Psychoanalytic	The role of unconscious motivation and early childhood experiences in determining behavior and thought	An unresolved early childhood emotional trauma is distracting the student from his academic work.
Humanistic	The importance of an individual's subjective experience as a key to understanding his or her behavior	Studying for exams does not fit into this student's definition of a meaningful life.
Cognitive	The role of mental processes—perception, thinking, and memory—that underlie behavior	The student does not use effective learning strategies such as the SQ3R method.
Evolutionary	The roles of inherited tendencies that have proven adaptive in humans	The student believes that studying is unimportant because potential mates are more interested in his physical appearance and capacity for social dominance than they are in his grades.
Biological	The role of biological processes and structures, as well as heredity, in explaining behavior	An inappropriate level of emotional arousal (i.e., test anxiety) is preventing this student from performing at an optimal level.
Sociocultural	The roles of social and cultural influences on behavior	The student doesn't want to be perceived as a "nerd," so he studies just enough to avoid failing.

SUMMARIZE IT

1.7 What specialty areas exist in psychology?

Specialties in Psychology

Stop for a minute and reflect on the definition of psychology: *the study of behavior and mental processes.* Clearly, this definition covers a lot of territory. Thus, it's not surprising that, over the years, psychology has become a highly specialized field. For instance, some psychologists work exclusively with issues related to mental illnesses, such as schizophrenia, that affect a small number of people, while others address questions that concern just about everyone, such as how stress affects health. Likewise, some psychologists focus on research, while others apply the principles of psychology to practical problems. Regardless of specialty area, all psychologists have advanced degrees, typically a Ph.D., in the field. Here is an overview of the major specialty areas in the field today:

- *Clinical psychologists* specialize in the diagnosis and treatment of mental and behavioral disorders, such as anxiety, phobias, and schizophrenia. Some also conduct research in these areas.
- *School psychologists* are clinical psychologists who specialize in the diagnosis and treatment of learning and behavioral problems that interfere with learning.
- *Forensic psychologists* apply their training in clinical psychology to issues involving psychology and law.
- *Counseling psychologists* help people who have adjustment problems (marital, social, or behavioral) that are generally less severe than those handled by clinical psychologists.
- *Physiological psychologists,* also called *biological psychologists* or *neuropsychologists,* study the relationship between physiological processes and behavior.
- *Experimental psychologists* conduct experiments in most areas of psychology—learning, memory, sensation, perception, motivation, emotion, and others.
- *Developmental psychologists* study how people grow, develop, and change throughout the life span.
- *Educational psychologists* specialize in the study of teaching and learning. (*Note:* Do not confuse educational psychology with school psychology. Recall that school psychology is the subfield of clinical psychology that deals with the diagnosis and treatment of learning problems. Educational psychologists study learning in typically developing people. As such, they are trained in theory and research methods but not in the diagnosis and treatment of learning problems.)
- *Social psychologists* investigate how the individual feels, thinks, and behaves in a social setting—in the presence of others.
- *Industrial/organizational (I/O) psychologists* study the relationships between people and their work environments.

At this point, you may be wondering how the psychological perspectives relate to the various specialty areas. Think of it this way. Each perspective is a theoretical point of view that a psychologist in any of the specialty areas can use to explain a behavior or mental process that is relevant to her field of study. For instance, the behavior explained in the *Summarize It* table on page 13, a student's poor performance on exams, falls within the domain of educational psychology. By contrast, a clinical psychologist might use the various perspectives to explain the symptoms of a psychological disorder such as depression. A counseling psychologist might use them to explain how people cope with major life changes such as divorce. An industrial/organizational psychologist would use them to explain individual differences in job satisfaction. In other words, it's possible to apply any of the perspectives within the boundaries of any of the specialty areas. Moreover, regardless of which perspective they adopt or their area of specialization, all psychologists approach questions about behavior and mental processes with a set of intellectual tools that you can acquire with a little practice.

Thinking about Theories and Research

Now that you have read about the various theoretical perspectives in psychology, you probably want to know which of them are "true" and which are "false." However, psychologists don't think about theories in this way. Instead, they evaluate theories in terms of their usefulness.

Likewise, you may wonder whether learning about research methods is of any practical value to people who do not intend to become professional researchers. As you'll see, knowledge about research methods can prove extremely useful in everyday life.

Evaluating Theories

[**1.8** How do psychologists evaluate theories?

As you learned earlier in this chapter, useful theories help psychologists achieve the prediction goal by generating testable hypotheses. When assessed against this criterion, the theories of behaviorists and cognitive psychologists appear more useful than those of psychoanalysts and humanists. B. F. Skinner's prediction that reinforcement increases behavior, for example, is far more testable than Maslow's claim that self-actualization is the highest of all human needs.

Useful theories also lead to the development of solutions to real-world problems. For instance, research based on the information-processing model has resulted in the development of practical strategies for improving memory. Similarly, even though psychoanalytic and humanistic theories have been criticized for lacking testability, they have produced a number of beneficial psychotherapies.

Hypotheses and practical applications are important, but a theory that possesses *heuristic value* is useful even if it falls short in these two areas. A theory that has heuristic value stimulates debate among psychologists and motivates both proponents and opponents of the theory to pursue research related to it. In other words, a theory that possesses heuristic value makes people think and spurs their curiosity and creativity.

All of the theories discussed so far earn high marks for their heuristic value. In fact, even if a theory has limited empirical support, professors who teach introductory psychology are justified in including it in the course if it has been of heuristic importance in the field. This is why we still teach about the structuralists and functionalists and why we continue to rate Freud's theory as one of the most important in the field. Moreover, such theories usually affect students in the same way that they affect psychologists—that is, learning about them stimulates students' thinking about behavior and mental processes. Thus, introducing these theories helps professors achieve one of their most important instructional goals, that of motivating students to think critically.

Evaluating Research

[**1.9** How will critical thinking help you evaluate research?

Another important goal of most professors who teach introductory psychology is to equip students with the intellectual tools needed to evaluate claims based on psychological research. Living in the Information Age, we are bombarded with statistics and claims of all types every day. For instance, a few years ago the news media carried a number of reports warning parents of young children that watching too much television in the early years of life might lead to attention deficit/hyperactivity disorder (ADHD) later in childhood (Clayton, 2004). These warnings were based, reporters said, on a scientific study that was published in the prestigious journal *Pediatrics*. How can a person who is not an expert on the subject in question evaluate claims such as these? ✳—Explore on mypsychlab.com

The thinking strategies used by psychologists and other scientists can help us sift through this kind of information. Critical thinking, the foundation of the scientific method, is the process of objectively evaluating claims, propositions, and conclusions to determine whether they follow logically from the evidence presented. When we engage in critical thinking, we exhibit these characteristics:

✳—Explore the Concept *How to Be a Critical Thinker* on **mypsychlab.com**

critical thinking The process of objectively evaluating claims, propositions, and conclusions to determine whether they follow logically from the evidence presented.

- *Independent thinking:* When thinking critically, we do not automatically accept and believe what we read or hear.
- *Suspension of judgment:* Critical thinking requires gathering relevant and up-to-date information on all sides of an issue before taking a position.
- *Willingness to modify or abandon prior judgments:* Critical thinking involves evaluating new evidence, even when it contradicts preexisting beliefs.

Applying the first of these three characteristics to the television–ADHD study requires recognizing that the validity of any study is not determined by the authority of its source. Prestigious journals—or psychology textbooks for that matter—shouldn't be regarded as sources of fixed, immutable truths. In fact, learning to question accepted "truths" is important to the scientific method itself.

The second and third characteristics of critical thinking, suspension of judgment and willingness to change, may require abandoning some old habits. If you are like most people, you respond to media reports about research on the basis of your own personal experiences, a type of evidence scientists call *anecdotal evidence*. For instance, in response to the media report about television and ADHD, a person might say, "I don't agree with that study because I watched a lot of television when I was a kid, and I don't have ADHD."

Suspension of judgment requires that you postpone either accepting or rejecting the study's findings until you have accumulated more evidence. It might involve determining what, if any, findings other researchers have reported regarding a possible link between television viewing and ADHD. Analysis of other relevant studies can help to create a comprehensive picture of what the entire body of research says about the issue. Ultimately, when enough evidence has been gathered, a critical thinker must be willing to abandon preconceived notions and prior beliefs that conflict with it.

The quality of the evidence is just as important as the quantity. Thus, a critical thinker would evaluate the findings of the television–ADHD study by considering the methods used to obtain them. Did the researchers randomly assign young children to experimental and control groups who watched different amounts of television and then assess whether experimental and control children differed in ADHD symptoms several years later? If so, then the study was an experiment, and media claims that television viewing in early childhood leads to ADHD might be justified. Conversely, if the researchers simply measured television viewing in early childhood and then correlated this variable with a measure of ADHD later on, then claims of a causal relationship between the two variables would not be justified. Instead, the appropriate response would be to look for underlying variables, such as parental involvement, that might explain the connection. In fact, the research cited in these reports was correlational in nature, so the strong causal claims implied by many media accounts of the study (Christakis et al., 2004) were inappropriate.

Descriptive Research Methods

descriptive research methods Research methods that yield descriptions of behavior.

The goals of psychological research are often accomplished in stages. In the early stages of research, descriptive research methods are usually the most appropriate. Descriptive research methods yield descriptions of behavior and include naturalistic and laboratory observation, the case study, and the survey.

1.10 What are the pros and cons of observational and case studies?

Observational and Case Studies

naturalistic observation A descriptive research method in which researchers observe and record behavior in its natural setting, without attempting to influence or control it.

Have you ever sat in an airport or shopping mall and simply watched what people were doing? Such an activity is quite similar to naturalistic observation, a descriptive research method in which researchers observe and record behavior in its natural setting, without attempting to influence or control it. The major advantage of naturalistic observation is the opportunity to study behavior in normal settings, where it occurs more naturally and spontaneously than it does under artificial and contrived laboratory conditions. Sometimes, naturalistic observation is the only feasible way to study behavior—for example, there is no other way to study how people typically react during disasters such as earthquakes and fires.

Naturalistic observation has its limitations, however. Researchers must wait for events to occur; they cannot speed up or slow down the process. And because they have no control over the situation, researchers cannot reach conclusions about cause–effect relationships. Another potential problem with naturalistic observation is *observer bias,* which is a distortion in researchers' observations. Observer bias can result when researchers' expectations about a situation cause them to see what they expect to see or to make incorrect inferences about what they observe. Suppose, for example, that you're a psychologist studying aggression in preschool classrooms. You have decided to count every time a child hits or pushes another child as an aggressive act. Your decision to label this type of physical contact between children as "aggressive" may cause you to notice more such acts and label them as "aggressive" than you would if you were casually watching a group of children play. The effects of observer bias can be reduced substantially when two or more independent observers view the same behavior. If you and another observer independently count, say, 23 aggressive acts in an hour of free play, the findings are considered unbiased. If you see 30 such acts and the other observer records only 15, some kind of bias is at work. In such situations, observers usually clarify the criteria for classifying behavior and repeat the observations. Using video can also help eliminate observer bias because behavior can be reviewed several times prior to making classification decisions.

▲ Naturalistic observation plays an important role in studies of animal behavior.

Another method of studying behavior involves observation that takes place not in its natural setting but in a laboratory. Researchers using laboratory observation can exert more control and use more precise equipment to measure responses. Much of what is known about sleep or the human sexual response, for example, has been learned through laboratory observation. However, like other research methods, laboratory observation has limitations. For one, laboratory behavior may not accurately reflect real-world behavior. For example, in sleep studies, some of the behavior people display while asleep in the laboratory may not occur in their homes. As a result, conclusions based on laboratory findings may not generalize beyond the walls of the laboratory itself. Another disadvantage is that building, staffing, equipping, and maintaining research laboratories can be expensive.

laboratory observation A descriptive research method in which behavior is studied in a laboratory setting.

In a case study, a single individual or a small number of persons are studied in great depth, usually over an extended period of time. A case study involves the use of observations, interviews, and sometimes psychological testing. Like observational studies, case studies are exploratory in nature. Their purpose is to provide a detailed description of some behavior or disorder. This method is particularly appropriate for studying people who have uncommon psychological or physiological disorders or brain injuries. Many case studies are written about patients being treated for such problems. In some instances, the results of detailed case studies have provided the foundation for psychological theories. In particular, the theory of Sigmund Freud was based primarily on case studies of his patients.

case study A descriptive research method in which a single individual or a small number of persons are studied in great depth.

Although the case study has proven useful in advancing knowledge in several areas of psychology, it has certain limitations. Researchers cannot establish the cause of behavior observed in a case study, and observer bias is a potential problem. Moreover, because so few individuals are studied, researchers do not know how applicable, or generalizable, their findings may be to larger groups or to different cultures.

Survey Research ▶

1.11 How do researchers design useful surveys?

Have you ever been questioned about your voting behavior or about the kind of toothpaste you prefer? If you have, chances are that you were a participant in another kind of research study. The survey is a descriptive research method in which researchers use interviews and/or questionnaires to gather information about the attitudes, beliefs, experiences, or behaviors of a group of people. The results of carefully conducted

survey A descriptive research method in which researchers use interviews and/or questionnaires to gather information about the attitudes, beliefs, experiences, or behaviors of a group of people.

population The entire group of interest to researchers, to which they wish to generalize their findings; the group from which a sample is selected.

sample A part of a population that is studied to reach conclusions about the entire population.

representative sample A sample that mirrors the population of interest; it includes important subgroups in the same proportions as they are found in that population.

surveys have provided valuable information about drug use, sexual behavior, and the incidence of various mental disorders.

Researchers in psychology rarely conduct studies using all members of a group. For example, researchers interested in studying the sexual behavior of American women do not survey every woman in the United States. (Imagine trying to interview about 140 million people!) Instead of studying the whole population (the entire group of interest to researchers, to which they wish to apply their findings), researchers select a sample for study. A sample is a part of a population that is studied to reach conclusions about the entire population.

Perhaps you have seen a carton of ice cream that contains three separate flavors—chocolate, strawberry, and vanilla—packed side by side. To properly sample the carton, you would need a small amount of ice cream containing all three flavors in the same proportions as in the whole carton—a representative sample. A representative sample mirrors the population of interest—that is, it includes important subgroups in the same proportions as they are found in that population. A *biased sample,* on the other hand, does not adequately reflect the larger population. Do the *Try It* to find out whether a sample must be large in order to be representative.

The best method for obtaining a representative sample is to select a *random sample* from a list of all members of the population of interest. Individuals are selected in such a way that every member of the larger population has an equal chance of being included in the sample. Using random samples, polling organizations can accurately represent the views of the American public with responses from as few as 1,000 people (O'Brien, 1996).

It might seem that simply interviewing people with a standard set of questions would be the best way to gather survey data. In reality, the truthfulness of participants' responses can be affected by characteristics of the interviewers, such as their gender, age, race, ethnicity, religion, and social class. Thus, to use interviews effectively, survey researchers must select interviewers who have personal characteristics that are appropriate for the intended respondents.

Questionnaires can be completed more quickly and less expensively than interviews, especially when respondents can fill them out in their homes or online. The Internet offers psychologists a fast and inexpensive way of soliciting participants and collecting questionnaire data, and Internet surveys often generate large numbers of responses (Azar, 2000). For example, an Internet survey posted by researchers who wanted to collect data about suicidal feelings attracted more than 38,000 respondents from all over the world (Mathy, 2002). However, researchers who use Web-based surveys must be cautious about generalizing the results of their studies because respondents represent only the population of Internet users who choose to participate, not the general population or even the entire population of Internet users. Moreover, they must take steps to ensure that a respondent can participate in the study only once (Gosling et al., 2004).

If conducted properly, surveys can provide highly accurate information. They can also track changes in attitudes or behavior over time. For example, Johnston and others (Johnston, O'Malley, Bachman, & Schulenberg, 2010) have tracked drug use among high school students since 1975. However, large-scale surveys can be costly and time consuming.

▲ Internet surveys allow psychologists to gather lots of data from large numbers of respondents in a very short period of time. But how representative of the general population are people who respond to Internet surveys? How representative are they of Internet users in general? Questions such as these remain to be answered.

Another important limitation of survey research is that respondents may provide inaccurate information. False information can result from a faulty memory or a desire to please the interviewer. Respondents may try to present themselves in a good light (a phenomenon called the *social desirability response*), or they may even deliberately mislead the interviewer. Finally, when respondents answer questions about sensitive subjects, such as sexual behavior, they are often less candid in face-to-face interviews than in self-administered or computerized questionnaires (Tourangeau, Smith, & Rasinski, 1997).

TRY IT   Can Small Samples Really be Representative?

Sometimes students have a hard time believing that 1,000 people or so can represent the entire population of the United States. This activity will help you see that small samples can be representative. You probably know that when you flip a coin the chance of getting a head or a tail is 50%. This probability is based on an infinite number of coin tosses. But how well does tossing the coin twice represent that whole population of tosses—that is, an infinite number of tosses? If a sample of two tosses (or $n = 2$, as a statistician would express it) doesn't represent the whole population, what about a sample of 5 or 10 or 15 or 20? To answer such a question, you have to take repeated samples of the same size. Toss a coin twice ($n = 2$), and then write the number of heads and tails in the column labeled Sample 1. Repeat the process four more times, recording your results under Sample 2 the second time, under Sample 3 the

third time, and so on, until you have a total of five samples, each of which consists of two coin tosses. When the $n = 2$ row is completely filled in, calculate the overall percentages of heads and tails. Next, use the same process to collect data on samples of $n = 5$, $n = 10$, $n = 15$, and $n = 20$, until you have filled the table with data.

You can see that, as n gets larger, the overall percentages of heads and tails become more balanced (closer to 50/50). However, notice also that $n = 20$ isn't much better than $n = 15$, and it took a lot longer to collect five samples of 20 coin tosses each. In other words, there wasn't much gain in representativeness for the extra cost in time and energy. So, small samples can be representative, and increasing the size of a sample doesn't always pay off when costs are balanced against benefits.

SAMPLE SIZE	SAMPLE 1		SAMPLE 2		SAMPLE 3		SAMPLE 4		SAMPLE 5		OVERALL PERCENTAGES	
	H	T	H	T	H	T	H	T	H	T	H	T
$n = 2$												
$n = 5$												
$n = 10$												
$n = 15$												
$n = 20$												

The Correlational Method

Perhaps the most powerful descriptive method available to psychologists is the correlational method, a method used to establish the degree of relationship (correlation) between two characteristics, events, or behaviors. A group is selected for study, and the variables of interest are measured for each participant. For example, one researcher studied the relationship between attainment of a college degree and subsequent income. Another might look for a correlation between the amount of time students devote to studying and their grade point averages.

Correlations are not just important to scientists, they are also common in our everyday thinking. For example, what is the relationship between the price of a new car and the social status you gain from owning it? Isn't it true that as price goes up, status goes up as well? And isn't status one of the variables that many people take into account when buying a new car? As this example illustrates, correlations are part of our everyday lives, and we often use them in decision making.

When scientists study correlations, they apply a statistical formula to data representing two or more variables to obtain a correlation coefficient. A correlation coefficient is a numerical value that indicates the strength and direction of the relationship between two variables. A correlation coefficient ranges from +1.00 (a perfect positive correlation) to .00 (no relationship) to −1.00 (a perfect negative correlation). The number in a correlation coefficient indicates the relative strength of the relationship between two variables—the higher the number, the stronger the relationship. Therefore, a correlation of −.85 is stronger than a correlation of +.64.

1.12 What are the strengths and weaknesses of the correlational method?

correlational method A research method used to establish the degree of relationship (correlation) between two characteristics, events, or behaviors.

correlation coefficient A numerical value that indicates the strength and direction of the relationship between two variables; ranges from +1.00 (a perfect positive correlation) to −1.00 (a perfect negative correlation).

FIGURE 1.2 Positive and Negative Correlations
Here are two graphs showing positive and negative correlations. (a) When positively correlated scores on two variables are graphed, the points fall along a line that rises from left to right. This graph might represent two variables such as amount of time spent studying and grades on an exam. As study time goes up, exam grades go up as well. (b) When negatively correlated scores on two variables are graphed, the points follow a line that declines from left to right. This graph might represent two variables such as amount of time spent watching television and grades on an exam. As TV time goes up, grades go down.

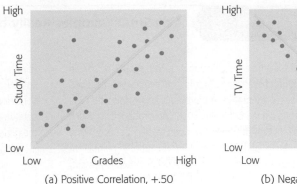

(a) Positive Correlation, +.50

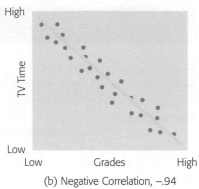

(b) Negative Correlation, –.94

▲ Temperature is correlated with snow-cone sales. As temperature increases, so does the number of snow cones sold. Is this a positive or a negative correlation? What about the corresponding correlation between temperature and coffee sales? Is it positive or negative?

The sign of a correlation coefficient (+ or −) indicates whether the two variables vary in the same or opposite directions. A positive correlation indicates that two variables vary in the same direction, like the price of a car and its associated social status. As another example, there is a positive though weak correlation between stress and illness. When stress increases, illness is likely to increase; when stress decreases, illness tends to decrease (see Figure 1.2).

A negative correlation means that an increase in the value of one variable is associated with a decrease in the value of the other variable. For example, as mileage accumulates on a car's odometer, the less reliable the car becomes. And there is a negative correlation between the number of cigarettes people smoke and the number of years they can expect to live. (For more information about correlation coefficients, see the Appendix.)

Does the fact that there is a correlation between two variables indicate that one variable causes the other? No. For instance, when two variables such as stress and illness are correlated, we cannot conclude that stress makes people sick. It might be that illness causes stress, or that a third factor such as poverty or poor general health causes people to be more susceptible to both illness and stress, as shown in Figure 1.3.

So, you might be thinking, if a researcher can't draw cause–effect conclusions, why do correlational studies? There are four reasons. First, correlations are quite useful for making predictions. One prediction of this type with which you may be familiar involves the use of a college applicant's high school class rank as a factor in admissions decisions. In general, the positive correlation between high school class rank and success in college means that the higher an applicant's rank in high school, the more likely he or she is to succeed in college. Likewise, as you will learn from the *Explain It* on page 21, several correlations determine whether a particular individual gets a credit card or loan.

Correlational studies are also useful when it is impossible, for ethical reasons, to study variables of interest using more direct methods. Scientists can't ethically ask pregnant women to drink alcohol just so they can find out whether it causes birth defects. The only option available in such cases is the correlational method. Researchers have to ask mothers about their drinking habits and note any association with birth defects in their babies. Knowing the correlation between prenatal alcohol consumption and the incidence of birth defects helps scientists make predictions about what may happen when pregnant women consume alcohol.

Another reason for using the correlational method is that many variables of interest to psychologists cannot be manipulated. Everyone wants to know whether biological sex (whether one is male or female) causes the differences we observe in men's and women's behavior. But we can't assign individuals to become male or female as we might ask them to take a drug or a placebo. Again, the only option is to study the correlations between biological sex and particular variables of interest, such as cognitive functioning and personality.

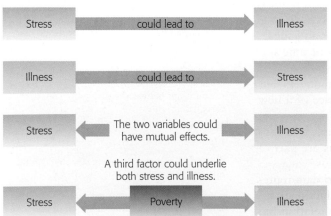

FIGURE 1.3 Correlation Does Not Prove Causation
A correlation between two variables does not prove that a cause–effect relationship exists between them. There is a correlation between stress and illness, but that does not mean that stress necessarily causes illness. Both stress and illness may result from another factor, such as poverty or poor general health.

EXPLAIN IT

What Is a Credit Score?

Have you seen television commercials or pop-up ads that ask, "What's your credit score?" If so, you probably inferred from the ad itself that credit scores are connected in some way to your financial well-being. That's true, but do you really know what a credit score is? You can use what you've just learned about correlations to get a better understanding of what credit scores are and how they are determined.

A credit score is a numerical summary of an individual's financial history that predicts the likelihood that he or she will have a delinquency in the future. A delinquency is failure to pay back a loan, declaration of bankruptcy, or any instance in which a person makes a payment on a loan or credit card more than 90 days after the original due date. The higher a person's credit score, the lower the likelihood of a future delinquency (Equifax, 2006). Thus, the connection between credit scores and delinquencies is a correlation, one that allows financial institutions to make predictions about the likelihood that an applicant will fulfill her financial obligations. Can you determine the nature (positive or negative) of the correlation between credit scores and delinquency risk? The graph in Figure 1.4 may help you visualize it.

If you compare this graph to the scatterplots in Figure 1.2 on p. 20, you will see that the correlation between credit scores and delinquencies is negative. In other words, the higher your score, the lower your chances of a delinquency. Consequently, using credit scores helps lenders minimize the chances that consumers will fail to pay them back.

The credit score itself is based on several correlations. Some of these correlations are positive, and some are negative. See if you can determine which of the three credit score factors below is based on positive correlations and which is derived from negative correlations (see answers following):

- The longer your credit history, the higher your score.
- The more credit cards you have, the lower your score.
- The more reports of late payments there are on your credit report, the lower your score.

If you guessed that a positive correlation is the basis of the first item on the list, and the others are based on negative correlations, you are correct.

Thanks to the association between length of credit history and credit scores, the scores of young adults tend to go up somewhat automatically during the first few years after they get their first loan or credit card. Of course, young consumers don't benefit from this factor unless they also make payments on time, refrain from running up large credit card balances, and resist the temptation to borrow money excessively as they work to build their credit histories. Once young consumers grasp the nature of the correlations that are embodied in credit scores, they can manipulate those correlations in their favor to increase the scores.

👁 Watch on **mypsychlab.com**

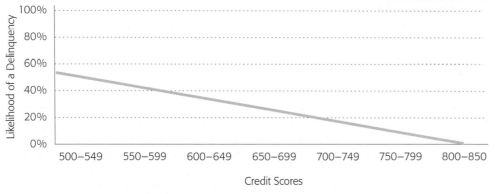

FIGURE 1.4 Predicting Credit Delinquencies.

Finally, correlational studies can often be done fairly quickly. By contrast, as you will learn in the section that follows, *experiments* can be time consuming and complex.

The Experimental Method

What comes to mind when you hear the word *experiment*? Many people use the word to refer to any kind of study. Among psychologists, though, the term *experiment* refers only to one kind of study, the kind in which researchers seek to determine the causes of behavior.

Experiments and Hypothesis Testing ▶

The experimental method, or the experiment, is the *only* research method that can be used to identify cause–effect relationships. An experiment is designed to test a causal hypothesis, a prediction about a cause–effect relationship between two or more variables. A variable is any condition or factor that can be manipulated, controlled, or

experimental method The only research method that can be used to identify cause–effect relationships between two or more conditions or variables.

causal hypothesis A prediction about a cause–effect relationship between two or more variables.

variable Any condition or factor that can be manipulated, controlled, or measured.

1.13 How do researchers use experiments to test causal hypotheses?

measured. One variable of interest to you is the grade you will receive in this psychology course. Another variable that probably interests you is the amount of time you will spend studying for this course. Do you suppose that a cause–effect relationship exists between the amount of time students spend studying and the grades they receive? Consider two other variables, alcohol consumption and aggression. Alcohol consumption and aggressive behavior are often observed occurring at the same time. But can we assume that alcohol consumption causes aggressive behavior?

An Example of an Experimental Study. Alan Lang and his colleagues (1975) conducted a classic experiment to determine whether alcohol consumption itself increases aggression or whether the beliefs or expectations about the effects of alcohol cause the aggressive behavior. The participants in the experiment were 96 male college students. Half of the students were given plain tonic to drink; the other half were given a vodka-and-tonic drink in amounts sufficient to raise their blood alcohol level to .10, which is higher than the .08 level that is the legal limit for intoxication in most states. Participants were assigned to four groups:

> *Group 1:* Expected alcohol, received only tonic
> *Group 2:* Expected alcohol, received alcohol mixed with tonic
> *Group 3:* Expected tonic, received alcohol mixed with tonic
> *Group 4:* Expected tonic, received only tonic

After the students had consumed the designated amount, the researchers had an accomplice, who posed as a participant, purposely provoke half the students by belittling their performance on a difficult task. All the students then participated in a learning experiment, in which the same accomplice posed as the learner. The subjects were told to administer an electric shock to the accomplice each time he made a mistake on a decoding task. Each participant was allowed to determine the intensity and duration of the "shock." (Although the students thought they were shocking the accomplice, no shocks were actually delivered.) The researchers measured the aggressiveness of the students in terms of the duration and the intensity of the shocks they chose to deliver.

What were the results of the experiment? As you might imagine, the students who had been provoked gave the accomplice stronger shocks than those who had not been provoked. But the students who drank the alcohol were not necessarily the most aggressive. Regardless of the actual content of their drinks, the participants who thought they were drinking alcohol gave significantly stronger shocks, whether provoked or not, than those who assumed they were drinking only tonic (see Figure 1.5).

FIGURE 1.5 The Mean Shock Intensity Chosen by Provoked and Unprovoked Participants
In the Lang experiment, participants who thought they were drinking alcohol chose to give significantly stronger shocks, whether provoked or not, than those who believed they were drinking only tonic.
Source: Data from Lang et al. (1995).

> Why would expecting to drink alcohol affect a person's behavior almost as much as actually drinking it?

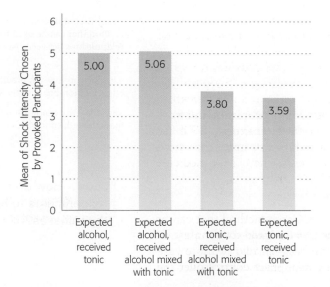

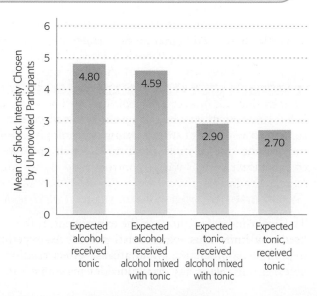

The researchers concluded that it was the *expectation* of drinking alcohol, not the alcohol itself, that caused the students to be more aggressive.

Independent and Dependent Variables. Recall that experiments test hypotheses about cause and effect. Examples of such hypotheses include "Studying causes good grades" and "Taking aspirin causes headaches to go away." Note that each hypothesis involves two variables: One is thought to be the cause (studying, taking aspirin), and the other is thought to be affected by the cause. These two kinds of variables are found in all experiments. An experiment has at least one independent variable—a variable that the researcher believes causes a change in some other variable. The researcher deliberately manipulates the independent variable (hypothesized cause) to determine whether it causes any change in another behavior or condition. Sometimes the independent variable is referred to as the *treatment*. The Lang experiment had two independent variables, the alcoholic content of the drink and the expectation of drinking alcohol.

The second type of variable found in all experiments, the one that the hypothesis states is affected by the independent variable, is the dependent variable. It is measured at the end of the experiment and is presumed to vary (increase or decrease) as a result of the manipulations of the independent variable(s). Researchers must provide operational definitions of all variables in an experiment—that is, they must specify precisely how the variables will be observed and measured. In the Lang study, the dependent variable—aggression—was operationally defined as the intensity and duration of the "shocks" the participants chose to deliver to the accomplice. ◉▸ Simulate on **mypsychlab.com**

independent variable In an experiment, a factor or condition that is deliberately manipulated to determine whether it causes any change in another behavior or condition.

dependent variable The factor or condition that is measured at the end of an experiment and is presumed to vary as a result of the manipulations of the independent variable(s).

◉▸ Simulate the **Experiment**
Distinguishing Independent and Dependent Variables on **mypsychlab.com**

Experimental and Control Groups. Most experiments are conducted using two or more groups of participants. There must always be at least one experimental group—a group of participants who are exposed to the independent variable, or the treatment. The Lang experiment, as noted earlier, used three experimental groups:

Group 1: Expected alcohol, received only tonic
Group 2: Expected alcohol, received alcohol mixed with tonic
Group 3: Expected tonic, received alcohol mixed with tonic

experimental group In an experiment, the group that is exposed to an independent variable.

Most experiments also have a control group—a group that is similar to the experimental group and is also measured on the dependent variable at the end of the experiment, for purposes of comparison. The control group is exposed to the same experimental environment as the experimental group but is not given the treatment. The fourth group in the Lang study was exposed to neither of the two independent variables; that is, this group did not expect alcohol and did not receive alcohol. Because this group was similar to the experimental groups and was exposed to the same experimental environment, it served as a control group.

You may be wondering why a control group is necessary. Couldn't an experimenter just expose one group to the independent variable and see if a change occurs? While this approach is sometimes used, it is usually preferable to have a control group because people and their behaviors often change without intervention. Having a control group reveals what kinds of changes happen "naturally" and provides a way of separating the effect of the independent variable from such changes. Suppose you want to find out if a certain medication relieves headaches. You could just find some people with headaches, give them the medication, and then count how many still have headaches an hour later. But some headaches go away without treatment. So if the medication appears to work, it may be only because a number of headaches went away on their own. Having a control group allows you to know whether the medicine relieves headaches in addition to those that disappear without treatment.

control group In an experiment, a group similar to the experimental group that is exposed to the same experimental environment but is not given the treatment; used for purposes of comparison.

Limitations of the Experimental Method ▸

[**1.14** What are the limitations of the experimental method?

You now know that experiments provide information about cause–effect relationships. But what are their limitations? For one thing, one of the advantages of the experimental method is that it enables researchers to exercise strict control over the setting. However, the more control they exercise, the more unnatural and contrived the research setting becomes. And the more unnatural the setting becomes, the less applicable findings may be to the real world. Another important limitation of the experimental method is that its use is either unethical or impossible for research in many areas of interest to psychologists. Some treatments cannot be given to human participants because their physical or psychological health would be endangered or their constitutional rights violated. However, the most important limitation of the experimental method is that, even when a researcher follows the method's steps scrupulously, confounding variables, factors other than the independent variable(s) that are unequal across groups, can prevent her from concluding that the independent variable caused a change in the dependent variable. Three sources of bias are frequently responsible for the presence of confounding variables in an experiment: selection, the placebo effect, and experimenter bias.

confounding variables Factors other than the independent variable(s) that are unequal across groups.

Selection bias occurs when participants are assigned to experimental or control groups in such a way that systematic differences among the groups are present at the beginning of the experiment. If selection bias occurs, then differences at the end of the experiment may not reflect the change in the independent variable but may be due to preexisting differences in the groups. To control for selection bias, researchers must use random assignment. This process consists of selecting participants by using a chance procedure (such as drawing the names of participants out of a hat) to guarantee that each participant has an equal probability of being assigned to any of the groups. Random assignment maximizes the likelihood that the groups will be as similar as possible at the beginning of the experiment. If there were preexisting differences in students' levels of aggressiveness in the Lang experiment, random assignment would have spread those differences across all the groups.

selection bias The assignment of participants to experimental or control groups in such a way that systematic differences among the groups are present at the beginning of the experiment.

random assignment The process of selecting participants for experimental and control groups by using a chance procedure to guarantee that each participant has an equal probability of being assigned to any of the groups; a control for selection bias.

Can participants' expectations influence an experiment's results? Yes. The placebo effect occurs when a participant's response to a treatment is due to his or her expectations about the treatment rather than to the treatment itself. Suppose a drug is prescribed for a patient and the patient reports improvement. The improvement could be a direct result of the drug, or it could be a result of the patient's expectation that the drug will work. Studies have shown that sometimes patients' remarkable improvement can be attributed solely to the power of suggestion—the placebo effect.

placebo effect The phenomenon that occurs in an experiment when a participant's response to a treatment is due to his or her expectations about the treatment rather than to the treatment itself.

In drug experiments, the control group is usually given a placebo—an inert or harmless substance such as a sugar pill or an injection of saline solution. To control for the placebo effect, researchers do not let participants know whether they are in the experimental group (receiving the treatment) or in the control group (receiving the placebo). If participants getting the real drug or treatment show a significantly greater improvement than those receiving the placebo, then the improvement can be attributed to the drug rather than to the participants' expectations about the drug's effects. In the Lang experiment, some students who expected alcohol mixed with tonic were given only tonic. The tonic without alcohol functioned as a placebo, allowing researchers to measure the effect of the expectations alone in producing aggression.

placebo (pluh-SEE-bo) An inert or harmless substance given to the control group in an experiment as a control for the placebo effect.

Experimenter bias occurs when researchers' preconceived notions or expectations become a self-fulfilling prophecy and cause the researchers to find what they expect to find. A researcher's expectations can be communicated to participants, perhaps unintentionally, through tone of voice, gestures, or facial expressions. These communications can influence the participants' behavior. Expectations can also influence a researcher's interpretation of the experimental results, even if no influence occurred during the experiment. To control for experimenter bias, researchers must not know which participants are assigned to the experimental and control groups until after the research data are collected and recorded. (Obviously, someone assisting the researcher does know.) When neither the participants nor the researchers know which participants are getting the treatment and which are in the control group, the experiment is using the double-blind technique.

experimenter bias A phenomenon that occurs when a researcher's preconceived notions or expectations in some way influence participants' behavior and/or the researcher's interpretation of experimental results.

The *Summarize It* summarizes the different types of research we have discussed in this chapter.

double-blind technique A procedure in which neither the participants nor the experimenters know who is in the experimental and control groups until after the data have been gathered; a control for experimenter bias.

Research Methods in Psychology

METHOD	DESCRIPTION	ADVANTAGES	LIMITATIONS
Naturalistic and laboratory observation	Observation and recording of behavior in its natural setting or in a laboratory.	Behavior studied in everyday setting is more natural. A laboratory setting allows for precise measurement of variables. Can provide basis for hypotheses to be tested later.	Researcher's expectations can distort observations (observer bias). In a natural setting the researcher has little or no control over conditions. Laboratory observations may not generalize to real-world settings, and they can be expensive.
Case study	In-depth study of one or a few individuals using observation, interview, and/or psychological testing.	Source of information for rare or unusual conditions or events. Can provide basis for hypotheses to be tested later.	May not be generalizable. Does not establish cause of behavior. Subject to misinterpretation by the researcher.
Survey	Interviews and/or questionnaires used to gather information about attitudes, beliefs, experiences, or behaviors of a group of people.	Can provide accurate information about large numbers of people. Can track changes in attitudes and behavior over time.	Responses may be inaccurate. Sample may not be representative. Characteristics of the interviewer may influence responses. Can be costly and time consuming.
Correlational method	Method used to determine the relationship (correlation) between two events, characteristics, or behaviors.	Can assess strength of the relationship between variables and can often be done quickly. Provides basis for prediction.	Does not demonstrate cause and effect.
Experimental method	Random assignment of participants to groups. Manipulation of the independent variable(s) and measurement of the effect on the dependent variable.	Enables identification of cause–effect relationships.	Laboratory setting may inhibit natural behavior of participants. Findings may not be generalizable to the real world. In some cases, experiment is unethical or impossible.

SUMMARIZE IT

Research Participants

You have learned about observer and experimenter bias in research, but were you aware that the findings of a study can be biased by the participants themselves? Furthermore, researchers are bound by ethical guidelines that specify how human participants and animal subjects are to be treated.

Participant-Related Bias in Psychological Research

1.15 How can participants' characteristics influence a study's usefulness?

Participant-Related Bias in Psychological Research. Do you remember reading earlier about the importance of representative samples in survey research? With other methods, representativeness becomes an issue when psychologists want to generalize the findings of studies to individuals other than the studies' participants. During the 1990s, several psychologists offered critiques of the lack of representativeness of participants in psychological research. These critiques raised awareness of the failure of psychologists to consider the effects of their sample selection procedures on the results of their studies. As a result, the American Psychological Association and other professional organizations began to require that researchers make every effort to ensure that participants are representative of the population to which the study's results will be generalized. These organizations also require that researchers include detailed information about participants' characteristics (i.e., age, ethnicity) in all published research. Here are a few of the areas of concern.

Researcher Sandra Graham (1992) put forward two important criticisms regarding study participants. She pointed out that whites are often overrepresented in psychological studies because the majority of studies with human participants have drawn from the college student population (Graham, 1992), which has a lower proportion of minorities than the population in general. Moreover, college students, including those of minority ethnicity, are a relatively select group in terms of age, socioeconomic class, and educational level. Thus, they are not representative of the general population. This lack of representativeness in a research sample is called **participant-related bias**. Graham (1992) also reported finding a methodological flaw—failure to include socioeconomic status—in much of the research literature comparing white Americans and African Americans. Graham pointed out that African Americans are overrepresented among the economically disadvantaged. She maintained that socioeconomic status should be incorporated into research designs "to disentangle race and social class effects" in studies that compare white and African Americans (p. 634).

Gender bias is another type of participant-related bias. For example, Ader and Johnson (1994) found that, when conducting research in which all of the participants are of one sex, researchers typically specify the gender of the sample clearly when it is female but not when the sample is exclusively male. Such a practice, according to Ader and Johnson, reveals a "tendency to consider male participants 'normative,' and results obtained from them generally applicable, whereas female participants are somehow 'different,' and results obtained from them are specific to female participants" (pp. 217–218). On a positive note, however, these researchers report that over the decades, gender bias in the sampling and selection of research subjects has been decreasing.

Ageism is another continuing source of participant-related bias and is especially apparent in the language used in psychological research (Schaie, 1993). For example, the titles of research studies on aging often include words such as *loss, deterioration, decline,* and *dependency.* Moreover, researchers are likely to understate the great diversity among the older adults they study. According to Schaie, "most research on adulthood shows that differences between those in their 60s and those in their 80s are far greater than those between 20- and 60-year-olds" (p. 50). Researchers should guard against using descriptions or reaching conclusions that imply that all members of a given age group are defined by negative characteristics.

participant-related bias A type of bias in which a study's participants are not representative of the population to which results will be generalized.

1.16 How do researchers protect human participants' and animals' rights?

Protecting Human Participants' and Animals' Rights

In 2002, the American Psychological Association (APA) adopted its most recent set of ethical standards governing research with human participants so as to safeguard their rights while supporting the goals of scientific inquiry. Following are some of the main provisions of the code:

- *Legality:* All research must conform to applicable federal, state, and local laws and regulations.
- *Institutional approval:* Researchers must obtain approval from all institutions involved in a study. For example, a researcher cannot conduct a study in a school without the school's approval.
- *Informed consent:* Participants must be informed of the purpose of the study and its potential for harming them.
- *Deception:* Deception of participants is ethical when it is necessary. However, the code of ethics cautions researchers against using deception if another means can be found to test the study's hypothesis.
- *Debriefing:* Whenever a researcher deceives participants, including through the use of placebo treatments, he or she must tell participants about the deception as soon as the study is complete.

- *Clients, patients, students, and subordinates:* When participants are under another's authority (for example, a therapist's client, a patient in a hospital, a student in a psychology class, or an employee), researchers must take steps to ensure that participation in a study, and the information obtained during participation, will not damage the participants in any way. Professors, for example, cannot reduce students' grades if the students refuse to participate in a research study.
- *Payment for participation:* Participants can be paid, but the code of ethics requires that they be fully informed about what is expected in return for payment.
- *Publication:* Psychological researchers must report their findings in an appropriate forum, such as a scientific journal, and they must make their data available to others who want to verify their findings.

The APA code of ethics also includes guidelines for using animals in psychological research. Here are a few of the important guidelines:

- *Legality:* Like research with human participants, animal research must follow all relevant federal, state, and local laws.
- *Supervision by experienced personnel:* The use of animals must be supervised by people who are trained in their care. These experienced personnel must teach all subordinates, such as research assistants, how to properly handle and feed the animals and to recognize signs of illness or distress.
- *Minimization of discomfort:* Researchers are ethically bound to minimize any discomfort to research animals. For example, it is unethical to perform surgery on research animals without appropriate anesthesia. And when researchers must terminate the lives of research animals, they must do so in a humane manner.

Even with these safeguards in place, the use of animals in research is controversial. Many animal rights advocates want all animal research stopped immediately. Thus, it is important to address the question of whether animal research is really necessary.

The fact that virtually all of the marvels of modern medicine are at least partially the result of experimentation using animals supports the view that animal research is indeed necessary (Aaltola, 2005). Such research has also increased knowledge in the areas of learning, motivation, stress, memory, and the effects on the unborn of various drugs ingested during pregnancy. Similarly, animal research has helped psychopharmacologists better understand the side effects of drugs that are used to relieve the symptoms of serial mental illnesses such as schizophrenia (Thaaker & Himabindhu, 2009). Thus, animal research is critically important to experiments that involve variables that cannot be ethically manipulated in human beings.

However, the material benefits derived from an action cannot stand alone as an ethical justification for it. For this reason, decisions about the use of animals in research must balance the potential benefits of a given study against the pain and suffering that might be inflicted upon its animal subjects. For example, studying potential cures for cancer might justify intentionally making an animal fatally ill. By contrast, a study that goes to this extreme in search of a cure for male pattern baldness might not. Emphasis on achieving this kind of ethical balance in animal research has led to a search for alternative research methods that is reportedly resulting in a decrease in the numbers of animals needed (Mukerjee, 1997, p. 86).

Looking Back

In this chapter, you have learned a great deal about psychologists, the methods they use, and a tried-and-true approach to studying textbook chapters, the SQ3R method. To be most effective, a general study method such as SQ3R must be adapted to each individual's learning preferences and study skill level. To implement this goal, think about how personally helpful each of the SQ3R features was as you worked your way through

Chapter 1. Use the table on the next page to rate each feature according to this scale: 2 = very useful, 1 = somewhat useful, and 0 = not useful. As you read each chapter, make a conscious effort to follow the SQ3R steps, devoting the most emphasis to those features to which you gave a rating of 1 or 2. Such an approach will enable you to use your study time efficiently and effectively and, we hope, avoid those preexam "all-nighters."

LEARNING TOOLS	USEFULNESS		
Think About It	0	1	2
Learning questions	0	1	2
Key terms	0	1	2
Explain It	0	1	2
Apply It	0	1	2
Try It	0	1	2
Summarize It	0	1	2
Chapter Summary	0	1	2
Map It	0	1	2
Study Guide	0	1	2

Step 5b: Review II

Now you need to review the entire chapter to be sure that you're ready to be tested. Follow these steps:
- Read the Chapter Summary. Your Map It notes should be fairly similar to the learning question answers in the summary.
- Modify your notes if necessary.
- Complete the Study Guide and check your answers against the key in the back of the book. You should be able to find many of the answers in your Map It notes.
- Take the chapter Practice Tests in the back of the book or log on to MyPsychLab to take an online version.

CHAPTER 1 SUMMARY

AN INTRODUCTION TO *MASTERING THE WORLD OF PSYCHOLOGY* (pp. 2-6)

1.1 How will the SQ3R method help you master psychology? (pp. 2-3)

The SQ3R method—survey, question, read, recite, and review—provides you with a systematic approach to studying the material. Using this approach to studying will help you manage your time more efficiently and give you a sense of control over your learning and academic performance.

Key Term
SQ3R method, p. 2

1.2 Why do psychologists use the scientific method? (pp. 3-5)

The scientific method consists of the orderly, systematic procedures researchers follow as they identify a research problem, design a study to investigate the problem, collect and analyze data, draw conclusions, and communicate their findings. Psychologists use it because it is the most objective method known for obtaining dependable knowledge.

Key Terms
psychology, p. 3
scientific method, p. 3
theory, p. 4
hypothesis, p. 5
replication, p. 5

1.3 What are the goals of psychology? (pp. 5-6)

The four goals of psychology are to describe, explain, predict, and influence behavior and mental processes. The purpose of basic research is to seek new knowledge and to expand general scientific understanding. Applied research explores the application of psychological principles to practical problems and everyday life.

Key Terms
basic research, p. 5
applied research, p. 5

PSYCHOLOGY THEN AND NOW (pp. 6-14)

1.4 What did the early psychologists contribute to the field? (pp. 6-8)

Wundt launched the study of psychology as a formal academic discipline. One of his students, Titchener, founded the school of thought called structuralism. Functionalism was the first American school of psychology and broadened the scope of the field to include examination of behavior as well as conscious mental processes. Early female and minority psychologists had to overcome significant educational and professional barriers to work in the field. Still, many of these individuals made noteworthy contributions. Today minority group representation is growing, and more women than men obtain degrees in psychology.

Key Terms
structuralism, p. 7
functionalism, p. 7

1.5 What are the major schools of thought in psychology? (pp. 8-12)

Behaviorists emphasize the environment as the key determinant of behavior. Psychoanalytic theorists claim that an individual's thoughts, feelings, and behavior are determined primarily by the unconscious—the part of the mind that one cannot see and cannot control. Humanistic theorists focus on the uniqueness of human beings and their capacity for choice, personal growth, and psychological health. Cognitive psychology focuses on mental processes such as memory, problem solving, reasoning, decision making, language, perception, and other forms of cognition. Evolutionary psychology focuses on how human behaviors necessary for survival have adapted in the face of environmental pressures over the course of evolution. Biological psychologists look for connections between specific behaviors (such as aggression) and particular biological factors (such as hormone levels) to help explain individual differences. Sociocultural psychology emphasizes social and cultural influences on human behavior and stresses the importance of understanding those influences when interpreting the behavior of others.

Key Terms

behaviorism, p. 9
psychoanalysis, p. 9
humanistic psychology, p. 9
cognitive psychology, p. 10
Gestalt psychology, p. 10
information-processing theory, p. 10
evolutionary psychology, p. 10
biological psychology, p. 11
neuroscience, p. 11
sociocultural approach, p. 11

1.6 What are the seven contemporary psychological perspectives? (pp. 12-13)

Psychological perspectives are general points of view used for explaining people's behavior and thinking that have arisen from the major schools of thought. The seven contemporary perspectives include behavioral, psychoanalytic, humanistic, cognitive, evolutionary, biological, and sociocultural. In taking an eclectic position, psychologists use a combination of two or more perspectives to explain a particular behavior.

Key Term

psychological perspectives, p. 12

1.7 What specialty areas exist in psychology? (p. 14)

Psychology today is highly specialized. Clinical psychologists are members of one specialty group, a subfield that also includes school and forensic psychologists. Other important specialists in the field are counseling psychologists, physiological psychologists, experimental psychologists, developmental psychologists, educational psychologists, social psychologists, and industrial/organizational (I/O) psychologists.

THINKING ABOUT THEORIES AND RESEARCH (pp. 15-16)

1.8 How do psychologists evaluate theories? (p. 15)

Psychologists evaluate theories in terms of their usefulness rather than whether they are true or false. Useful theories generate testable hypotheses and practical solutions to problems. Theories possessing heuristic value are useful for stimulating debate and research.

1.9 How will critical thinking help you evaluate research? (pp. 15-16)

Critical thinkers are independent, able to suspend judgment, and willing to change prior beliefs. These skills help them evaluate claims about research. Critical thinkers also use knowledge of research methods to evaluate research findings.

Key Term

critical thinking, p. 15

DESCRIPTIVE RESEARCH METHODS (PP. 16-21)

1.10 What are the pros and cons of observational and case studies? (pp. 16-17)

In naturalistic observation, researchers observe and record the behavior of human participants or animal subjects in a natural setting without attempting to influence or control it. In laboratory observation, researchers exert more control and use more precise equipment to measure responses. The case study is appropriate for studying people with rare psychological or physiological disorders or brain injuries. Disadvantages of this method include possible observer bias, an inability to establish the cause of behavior, and lack of generalizability.

Key Terms

descriptive research methods, p. 16
naturalistic observation, p. 16

laboratory observation, p. 17
case study, p. 17

1.11 How do researchers design useful surveys? (pp. 17-19)

To be useful, surveys must involve a sample that is representative of the population to which the results will be applied. Useful surveys also avoid wording questions and in ways that influence respondents' answers and employ interviewers whose characteristics are similar to those of respondents.

Key Terms

survey, p. 17
population, p. 18
sample, p. 18
representative sample, p. 18

1.12 What are the strengths and weaknesses of the correlational method? (pp. 19-21)

When the correlation between two variables is known, information about one variable can be used to predict the other. However, a correlation cannot be used to support the conclusion that either variable causes the other.

Key Terms
correlational method, p. 19
correlation coefficient, p. 19

THE EXPERIMENTAL METHOD (pp. 21-25)

1.13 How do researchers use experiments to test causal hypotheses? (pp. 21-23)

The experimental method is the only research method that can identify cause–effect relationships. In an experiment, an independent variable is a condition or factor manipulated by the researcher to determine its effect on the dependent variable. By comparing experimental and control groups, researchers can judge the effects of the independent variable(s) compared to outcomes that occur naturally or in the presence of a placebo.

Key Terms
experimental method, p. 21
causal hypothesis, p. 21
variable, p. 21
independent variable, p. 23
dependent variable, p. 23
experimental group, p. 23
control group, p. 23

1.14 What are the limitations of the experimental method? (pp. 23-25)

Several types of bias introduce confounding variables that make it difficult to conclude that changes in the independent variable caused changes in the dependent variable. Selection bias occurs when there are systematic differences among the groups before the experiment begins. The placebo effect occurs when a person's expectations influence the outcome of a treatment or an experiment. Experimenter bias occurs when the researcher's expectations affect the outcome of the experiment. In addition, experiments are often conducted in unnatural settings, a factor that limits the applicability of results beyond the experimental setting. Also, this method may be unethical or impossible to use for some research.

Key Terms
confounding variables, p. 24
selection bias, p. 24
random assignment, p. 24
placebo effect, p. 24
placebo, p. 24
experimenter bias, p. 24
double-blind technique, p. 24

RESEARCH PARTICIPANTS (pp. 25-27)

1.15 How can participants' characteristics influence a study's usefulness? (pp. 25-26)

Participant-related bias happens when researchers fail to include underrepresented groups in their samples. Historically, psychological researchers have relied heavily on studies in which the primary participants were college students, a group that includes fewer minorities and people of limited means than the general population does. Similarly, many studies have failed to include women. Ageism is another participant-related issue.

Key Term
participant-related bias, p. 00

1.16 How do researchers protect human participants' and animals' rights? (pp. 25-27)

All research must conform to applicable laws and regulations. Researchers must obtain approval from all institutions involved in the study. Participants must give informed consent, may not be deceived unless necessary, and, if deceived, must be debriefed as soon as possible after they participate. Subordinates' participation in a study may not negatively affect them in any way. Participants may be paid after being fully informed about what is expected in return for payment. Researchers must report their findings in an appropriate forum, and results must be made available to participants.

MAP IT

Log on to MyPsychLab and click on "Map It" to prepare a unique digital map of the chapter that you can save for later use, email to your instructor, or print out to use as a study tool. Or, create your own map by drawing one on paper. Use the starter map below as a model for your own map. Use the chapter summary as your guide for what to include. For each item in your map, be sure to include the page number.

Here's one way to *Map It*:

1. Draw a box at the top of the page for the section title.

2. Underneath the section title box, working horizontally across the page, draw a box for each learning question in the section. Write the learning questions in the boxes and draw a line from the section title to each questions box. After you read each subsection, jot an answer for the learning question in the subsection's box.

3. Below each learning question box, insert another box for all of the key terms that are related to the question, along with a very brief reminder of each term's definition. Draw a line from the question box to the key terms box.

4. Below each key terms box, create another box and list all of the helpful figures, tables, and other elements of the text, such as *Try It* and *Apply It* boxes. Draw a line from the key terms box to the helpful elements box.

●─[Map the Chapter on mypsychlab.com

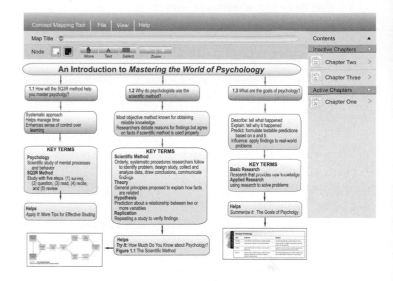

Chapter 1 Study Guide

Answers to all the Study Guide questions are provided at the end of the book.

SECTION ONE: Chapter Review

An Introduction to *Mastering the World of Psychology* (pp. 2-6)

1. The orderly, systematic procedures scientists follow in acquiring a body of knowledge is the _____ _____ .

2. The four goals of psychology are _____, _____, _____, and _____.

3. The purpose of basic research is to seek new knowledge and advance scientific understanding. (true/false)

Psychology Then and Now (pp. 6-14)

4. Classify each of the following people and concepts as being associated with (a) structuralism or (b) functionalism.
   _____ (1) James
   _____ (2) based on Darwin's theory of evolution
   _____ (3) stream of consciousness
   _____ (4) elements of experience
   _____ (5) Titchener
   _____ (6) introspection
   _____ (7) became known in the 19th century

5. Match each of the following individuals with his or her contribution to psychology.
   _____ (1) Francis Cecil Sumner
   _____ (2) Mary Whiton Calkins
   _____ (3) Kenneth Clark
   _____ (4) Christine Ladd-Franklin
   _____ (5) Jorge Sanchez
   a. first female president of APA
   b. published studies on cultural bias in intelligence testing
   c. first African American to receive a PhD in psychology
   d. studied African American children's self-esteem
   e. had to wait 40 years to receive a PhD in psychology after completing the degree requirements

6. Match the major figure with the appropriate school of psychology. Answer(s) may be used more than once.
   _____ (1) Freud
   _____ (2) Skinner
   _____ (3) Maslow
   _____ (4) Wertheimer
   _____ (5) Watson
   _____ (6) Rogers

   a. Gestalt psychology   c. behaviorism
   b. humanistic psychology   d. psychoanalysis

7. Match the school of psychology with its major emphasis.
   _____ (1) the scientific study of behavior
   _____ (2) the perception of whole units or patterns
   _____ (3) the unconscious
   _____ (4) the computer as a model for human cognition
   _____ (5) the uniqueness of human beings and their capacity for growth
   _____ (6) the study of mental processes

   a. Gestalt psychology   d. behaviorism
   b. humanistic psychology e. information-processing theory
   c. cognitive psychology   f. psychoanalysis

8. Match each of the following variables with the psychological approach that is most likely to be interested in it: (a) evolutionary psychology, (b) biological psychology, or (c) sociocultural psychology.
   _____ (1) the effects of drugs and alcohol on reaction time
   _____ (2) the relationship between minority status and self-esteem
   _____ (3) universal behaviors such as infants' attachment to caregivers
   _____ (4) links between hormones and aggression
   _____ (5) gender role beliefs that are consistent across cultures
   _____ (6) gender role beliefs that vary across cultures

9. Match the psychological perspective with its major emphasis.
   _____ (1) the role of biological processes and heredity
   _____ (2) the role of environmental factors
   _____ (3) the role of mental processes
   _____ (4) the role of the unconscious and early childhood experience
   _____ (5) the importance of the individual's own subjective experience
   _____ (6) the role of social and cultural influences
   _____ (7) the role of inherited tendencies that have proved adaptive in humans

   a. psychoanalytic   e. humanistic
   b. biological   f. evolutionary
   c. behavioral   g. sociocultural
   d. cognitive

10. Write "Yes" by the statements below that represent eclecticism in psychology.
    _____ (1) Individual differences in aggression are genetic, but parents and teachers can teach highly aggressive children to be less so.
    _____ (2) Children who are highly aggressive have not received enough punishment for their inappropriate behavior.
    _____ (3) Aggressive children are probably using aggression to release pent-up feelings of frustration.
    _____ (4) Going through a trauma like parental divorce may lead to increased aggression in children because they are experiencing strong emotions, and their parents are likely to be too distracted by their own problems to discipline children effectively.

11. Adjustment problems are the concern of specialists in (clinical/counseling) psychology.

Thinking about Theories and Research (pp. 14-16)

12. Useful theories
    a. lead to practical solutions to problems.
    b. provide researchers with many testable hypotheses.
    c. stimulate debate and research.
    d. all of the above

13. The three characteristics of critical thinkers are _____, _____, and _____.

14. A television reporter claimed that people should stop eating cabbage because scientists have found that it causes cancer. The first response of a critical thinker to this report would be to
    a. find out if the research was published in a prestigious journal.
    b. determine whether the research was correlational or experimental in nature.
    c. find out how many people participated in the study.
    d. stop eating cabbage.

Descriptive Research Methods (pp. 16-21)

15. Which descriptive research method would be best for studying each topic?
    _____ (1) attitudes toward exercise
    _____ (2) gender differences in how people position themselves and their belongings in a library
    _____ (3) physiological changes that occur during sleep
    _____ (4) the physical and emotional effects of a rare brain injury

    a. naturalistic observation   c. case study
    b. laboratory observation   d. survey

16. One problem with _____ _____ is that they often do not generalize to cases other than the one that is the subject of the study.

17. When conducting a survey, a researcher can compensate for a sample that is not representative by using a sample that is very large. (true/false)

18. The correlational method is used to demonstrate cause–effect relationships. (true/false)

19. The _____ is a number describing the strength and direction of a relationship between two variables.

20. Which of the following correlation coefficients indicates the strongest relationship?
    a. +.65   b. −.78   c. .00   d. +.25

21. There is a (positive/negative) correlation between the amount of fat people eat and their body weight.

22. A (positive/negative) correlation exists between the temperature and the number of layers of clothing people wear.

23. The main strength of the correlational method is that it can be used to establish cause–effect relationships. (true/false)

The Experimental Method (pp. 21-25)

24. The experimental method is the *only* research method that can be used to identify cause–effect relationships between variables. (true/false)

25. In an experiment, the _____ _____ is manipulated by the researcher, and its effects on the _____ _____ are measured at the end of the study.

26. A researcher investigates the effectiveness of a new antidepressant drug. She randomly assigns depressed patients to two groups. Group 1 is given the drug, and Group 2 is given a placebo. At the end of the experiment, the level of depression of all participants is measured as a score on a test called a depression inventory. Match the elements of this experiment with the appropriate term.
    _____ (1) score on depression inventory
    _____ (2) the antidepressant drug
    _____ (3) Group 1
    _____ (4) Group 2

    a. experimental group   c. independent variable
    b. control group   d. dependent variable

27. Random assignment is used to control for
    a. experimenter bias.
    b. the placebo effect.
    c. selection bias.
    d. participant bias.

28. The placebo effect occurs when a participant responds according to
    a. the hypothesis.
    b. the actual treatment.
    c. how other participants behave.
    d. his or her expectations.

Research Participants (pp. 25-27)

29. Which of the following groups has *not* been overrepresented as participants in psychological research?
    a. whites
    b. males
    c. females
    d. college students

30. Psychologists are required to debrief participants thoroughly after a research study when the study
    a. violates participants' rights to privacy.
    b. deceives participants about the true purpose of the research.
    c. exposes participants to unreasonable risk or harm.
    d. wastes taxpayers' money on trivial questions.

31. Investigators use animals in psychological research to learn more about humans. (true/false)

SECTION TWO: Who Said This?

Read each statement below and then, in the blank that follows, identify the person mentioned in Chapter 1 who would be most likely to make the statement.

1. I thought that behavior could be explained by analyzing the conditions that were present before it occurs and the consequences it produces. _____

2. I established the first psychological laboratory in Leipzig, Germany. _____

3. I wrote *Principles of Psychology* and advocated functionalism. _____

4. I introduced the term *behaviorism*. _____
5. I proposed a theory of motivation that consists of a hierarchy of needs. _____

6. I was the first African American to earn a PhD in psychology. _____

7. I became the first female president of the American Psychological Association. _____

8. I invented a popular form of psychotherapy called *client-centered therapy*. _____

9. I demonstrated the phi phenomenon. _____

SECTION THREE: Fill in the Blank

1. A _____ is a general principle or set of principles proposed to explain how a number of separate facts are related.

2. Dr. Smith is interested in using _____ _____ to study cooperative versus competitive play in children in nursery school. To accomplish this, she is going to observe and record children's play behaviors at nursery school without attempting to influence or control their behaviors.

3. Dr. Jones is interested in learning about college students in the United States who begin their education after the age of 30. He knows that there are many such students and that he will not be able to study them all, so he decides to carefully define this _____ (the group to which he hopes to generalize his findings) and then study a _____ _____ of these students. He hopes this approach will allow him to make accurate generalizations.

4. A psychologist believes there is an important relationship between test anxiety and test performance. Her _____ predicts that higher levels of anxiety will interfere with test performance.

5. To test her prediction, the psychologist in question 4 randomly assigns psychology students to two different groups. One group is told that the test they are about to take will determine over half of their semester grade. The other group is told that the test will have no bearing on their grade but will help the psychologist prepare better lectures. The psychologist believes the two groups will have different levels of anxiety and that the first group will perform less well than the second group on a standardized psychology test. In this experiment, the _____ variable is the pretest instructions, and the _____ variable is the test scores.

6. Psychologists who use the _____ approach are interested in how social and cultural variables influence individual behavior.

7. Correlations can be useful in allowing you to make _____ but should not be used to draw conclusions about _____ and _____.

8. The first formal school of psychology was known as _____, and members of this school were interested in analyzing the basic elements, or structure, of conscious mental experience.

9. Another early school of psychology was _____. Psychologists who used this approach were interested in how mental processes help humans and animals adapt to their environments.

10. The school of psychology that emphasizes the role of unconscious mental forces and conflicts in determining behavior is known as _____.

11. The _____ perspective in psychology studies the role of mental processes—perception, thinking, and memory—in behavior.

12. Sigmund Freud is associated with the _____ perspective in psychology.

13. _____ psychologists study how people change throughout the life span.

SECTION FOUR: Comprehensive Practice Test

1. Which of the following psychological perspectives likened human mental life to an iceberg?
   a. behaviorism
   b. psychoanalysis
   c. humanistic psychology
   d. structuralism

2. _____ is the approach to psychology that arose from the belief that the study of the mind and consciousness was not scientific.
   a. structuralism
   b. behaviorism
   c. humanistic psychology
   d. psychoanalysis

3. The _____ perspective in psychology would explain behavior by referring to the operation of the brain and the central nervous system.
   a. evolutionary
   b. structuralist
   c. behavioral
   d. biological

4. A _____ psychologist specializes in the diagnosis and treatment of mental and behavioral disorders.

   a. social
   b. developmental
   c. clinical
   d. cognitive

5. "The whole is perceived as greater than the sum of its parts" is a statement you would be most likely to hear from a _____ psychologist.

   a. behavioral
   b. clinical
   c. Gestalt
   d. developmental

6. Description, explanation, prediction, and influence of behavior and mental processes are the _____ of psychology.

   a. reasons
   b. goals
   c. perspectives
   d. methods

7. In an experiment, a researcher would use the double-blind approach to control for _____.

   a. experimenter bias
   b. independent bias
   c. selection bias
   d. random bias

8. The disadvantages of survey research include that

   a. respondents may provide inaccurate information.
   b. they can be costly and time consuming.
   c. the "social desirability effect" may cause respondents to give misleading answers.
   d. all of the above

9. A researcher who wants to establish evidence for a cause–effect relationship between variables should use _____.

   a. naturalistic observation
   b. correlation
   c. the experimental method
   d. the survey method

10. Which of the following psychologists is associated with the humanistic perspective?

    a. Maslow
    b. Darwin
    c. Watson
    d. Freud

11. Researchers who are interested in the adaptive significance of behavior are known as _____ psychologists.

    a. cognitive
    b. humanistic
    c. evolutionary
    d. psychoanalytic

12. A social psychologist would be most interested in how individuals behave in isolated settings, such as when they are alone at home. (true/false)

13. Basic research is aimed at solving practical problems and improving the quality of life. (true/false)

14. Watson would suggest that Freud's psychological approach is invalid because of Freud's emphasis on unconscious motivation and other mental events. (true/false)

15. In an experiment, the experimental group is exposed to all aspects of the treatment except the independent variable. (true/false)

16. Structuralism used introspection to study the basic elements of conscious mental experience. (true/false)

17. Most psychologists believe that animal research is of little value in the study of human mental processes and behavior. (true/false)

18. The best way to establish a cause–effect relationship between variables is to use the case study method because that method gives a researcher an in-depth knowledge of the subject matter from spending so much time with just a few participants. (true/false)

19. A researcher is studying the relationship between styles of computer keyboards and typing accuracy. In this case, the dependent variable is the different types of computer keyboards included in the study. (true/false)

20. You would probably expect to find a negative correlation between the number of alcoholic drinks consumed and the number of accidents a participant has while being tested on an experimental driving simulator. (true/false)

SECTION FIVE: Critical Thinking

1. Consider three of the major forces in psychology: behaviorism, psychoanalysis, and humanistic psychology. Which appeals to you most and which least, and why?

2. Suppose you hear on the news that a researcher claims to have "proven" that day care is harmful to infants. How could you use what you've learned in this chapter about research methods to evaluate this statement?

3. If you became a psychologist, in which area (developmental, educational, clinical, counseling, social, and so on) would you specialize? Why?

Biology and Behavior

2

CHAPTER

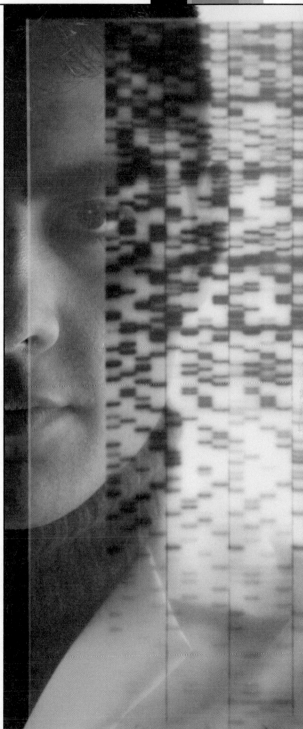

Think About It

Interpreting others' facial expressions is such a commonplace task that we usually do it without thinking about it. But your eyes can sometimes fool you. See if you can figure out which of the faces below is the happier of the two (Jaynes, 1976).

Which face did you say was the happier one? Your answer probably depended on whether you are right- or left-handed. You see, the brain tends to assign some tasks to the right side of the brain and others to the left. These assignments are correlated to some degree with handedness. For instance, if you are right-handed, you tend to use the right side of the brain to interpret emotions. Since the right side of the brain controls the left side of the body, you would use the left side of people's faces to make inferences about their emotional states (McGee & Skinner, 1987).

Consequently, even though the faces in the drawing are mirror images, right-handed people tend to see the face on the left as the happier one. Left-handers display the opposite pattern. They rely on the left side of the brain to interpret emotions, and because the left side of the brain controls the right side of the body, they usually judge the face on the right to be the happier one.

How the brain divides functions between its left and right halves is just one of many interesting things about the biological foundations of behavior and mental processes that you will read about in this chapter. We will tell you much more about the brain and nervous system, and we will introduce you to the endocrine system. You will also read about genetics. Pay close attention to the information in this chapter because we will refer back to its major concepts in all the chapters that follow.

Discovering the Mysteries of the Nervous System

How do we know what we know about the nervous system? Until quite recently, researchers had few techniques for directly studying it. Scientists relied on case studies of people in whom an injury to a specific part of the system, a *lesion*, had led to specific changes in behavior to identify the functions associated with the various parts of the system. For instance, because severe injuries to the back of the head were observed to result in visual problems, researchers were able to infer that the back of the brain was involved in vision. By the mid-19th century, researchers began making great strides in understanding the nervous system thanks to the availability of more powerful microscopes that enabled them to directly examine the nervous system tissues of deceased humans and animals. Today, scientists continue to use both case studies and microscopic tissue studies to answer questions about the nervous system. But since the early 20th century, researchers have also been able to observe the living brain in action.

2.1 What does the electroencephalogram (EEG) reveal about the brain?

The EEG and the Microelectrode

In 1924, Austrian psychiatrist Hans Berger invented the electroencephalograph, a machine that records the electrical activity occurring in the brain. This electrical activity, detected by electrodes placed at various points on the scalp and amplified greatly, provides the power to drive a pen across paper, producing a record of brain-wave activity called an electroencephalogram (EEG). The beta wave is the brain-wave pattern associated with mental or physical activity. The alpha wave is associated with deep relaxation and the delta wave with slow-wave (deep) sleep. (You will learn more about these brain-wave patterns in Chapter 4.)

A computerized EEG imaging technique shows the different levels of electrical activity occurring every millisecond on the surface of the brain (Gevins et al., 1995). It can show an epileptic seizure in progress and can be used to study neural activity in people with schizophrenia, Alzheimer's disease, sleep disorders, and other neurological problems.

Although the EEG is able to detect electrical activity in different areas of the brain, it cannot reveal what is happening in individual neurons. However, the microelectrode can. A microelectrode is a wire so small that it can be inserted near or into a single neuron without damaging it. Microelectrodes can be used to monitor the electrical activity of a single neuron or to stimulate activity within it.

electroencephalogram (EEG) (ee-lek-tro-en-SEFF-uh-lo-gram) A record of brain-wave activity made by a machine called the electroencephalograph.

beta wave (BAY-tuh) The brain-wave pattern associated with mental or physical activity.

alpha wave The brain-wave pattern associated with deep relaxation.

delta wave The brain-wave pattern associated with slow-wave (deep) sleep.

microelectrode A small wire used to monitor the electrical activity of or stimulate activity within a single neuron.

Imaging Techniques ▶

Since the early 1970s, a number of techniques that provide scientists and physicians with images of the brain's structures have become available. For example, a person undergoing a CT scan (computerized axial tomography) of the brain is placed inside a large, doughnut-shaped structure where an X-ray tube encircles the entire head. The tube rotates in a complete circle, shooting X-rays through the brain as it does so. A series of computerized, cross-sectional images reveal the structures within the brain as well as abnormalities and injuries, including tumors and evidence of old or more recent strokes.

MRI (magnetic resonance imaging), which became widely available in the 1980s, produces clearer and more detailed images without exposing people to potentially dangerous X-rays (Potts, Davidson, & Krishman, 1993). MRI can be used to find abnormalities in the central nervous system and in other systems of the body. Although the CT scan and MRI do a remarkable job of showing what the brain looks like both inside and out, they cannot reveal what the brain is doing. But other technological marvels can.

Several techniques capture images of both brain structures and their functions. The oldest of these techniques, the PET scan (positron-emission tomography) has been used since the mid-1970s to identify malfunctions that cause physical and psychological disorders. It has also been used to study normal brain activity. A PET scan maps the patterns of blood flow, oxygen use, and glucose consumption (glucose is the food of the brain). It can also show the action of drugs and other biochemical substances in the brain and other bodily organs (Farde, 1996).

A technique that became available in the 1990s, functional MRI (fMRI), has several important advantages over PET: (1) It can provide images of both brain structure and brain activity; (2) it requires no injections (of radioactive or other material); (3) it can identify locations of activity more precisely than PET can; and (4) it can detect changes that take place in less than a second, compared with about a minute for PET ("Brain Imaging," 1997).

Still other imaging devices are now available. SQUID (superconducting quantum interference device) shows brain activity by measuring the magnetic changes produced by the electric current that neurons discharge when they fire. Another imaging marvel, MEG (magnetoencephalography), also measures such magnetic changes and shows neural activity within the brain as rapidly as it occurs, much faster than PET or fMRI. A new kind of MRI, diffusion tensor imaging (DTI), enables researchers to examine individual neuron bundles.

Brain-imaging techniques have helped neuroscientists accumulate an impressive store of knowledge about brain functions such as memory (Logothetis, 2008). Studies using these imaging techniques have also shown that, to varying degrees, the structures and functions of the brain differ in people who have serious psychological disorders from those who do not. In addition, imaging techniques have revealed where and how drugs affect the brain (Gorman, 2007). And some neuroscientists have experimented with combining virtual reality with fMRI to study how the brain responds to situations and environments that would be impossible to observe using conventional imaging techniques (Wiederhold & Wiederhold, 2008). ◉⬛Watch on **mypsychlab.com**

2.2 How do researchers use imaging techniques to study the nervous system?

CT scan (computerized axial tomography) A brain-scanning technique that uses a rotating, computerized X-ray tube to produce cross-sectional images of the structures of the brain.

MRI (magnetic resonance imaging) A diagnostic scanning technique that produces high-resolution images of the structures of the brain.

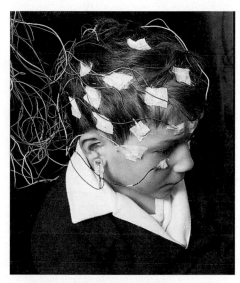

▲ The electroencephalograph, or EEG, uses electrodes placed on the scalp to amplify and record electrical activity in the brain.

PET scan (positron-emission tomography) A brain-imaging technique that reveals activity in various parts of the brain, based on patterns of blood flow, oxygen use, and glucose consumption.

functional MRI (fMRI) A brain-imaging technique that reveals both brain structure and brain activity more precisely and rapidly than PET.

◉⬛Watch the **Video** *Brain Building* on **mypsychlab.com**

The Neurons and the Neurotransmitters

Earlier we mentioned that 19th-century researchers used microscopes to study the nervous system tissues of deceased humans and animals. These studies led to the discovery of the specialized cells that conduct impulses through the nervous system, the neurons. In the early 20th century, the invention of the microelectrode allowed researchers to study the connections between neurons. These studies revealed the existence of chemicals that are essential to nervous system functioning. These chemicals,

neuron (NEW-ron) A specialized cell that conducts impulses through the nervous system.

neurotransmitters Specialized chemicals that facilitate or inhibit the transmission of impulses from one neuron to the next.

2.3 What does each part of the neuron do?

✳⃞ Explore the Concept *The Nerve Impulse and Afferent and Efferent Neurons* on **mypsychlab.com**

cell body The part of a neuron that contains the nucleus and carries out the metabolic functions of the neuron.

dendrites (DEN-drytes) In a neuron, the branch-like extensions of the cell body that receive signals from other neurons.

axon (AK-sahn) The slender, tail-like extension of the neuron that transmits signals to the dendrites or cell body of other neurons and to muscles, glands, and other parts of the body.

axon terminal Bulbous end of the axon where signals move from the axon of one neuron to the dendrites or cell body of another.

glial cells (GLEE-ul) Specialized cells in the brain and spinal cord that support neurons, remove waste products such as dead neurons, and perform other manufacturing, nourishing, and cleanup tasks.

2.4 How do neurons transmit messages through the nervous system?

synapse (SIN-aps) The junction where the axon terminal of a sending neuron communicates with a receiving neuron across the synaptic cleft.

✳⃞ Explore the Concept *The Synapse* on **mypsychlab.com**

the neurotransmitters, can facilitate or inhibit the transmission of impulses from one neuron to the next. Working together, neurons and neurotransmitters convey messages within the nervous system and from the nervous system to other parts of the body.

The Structure of the Neuron

All of our thoughts, feelings, and behavior can ultimately be traced to the activity of neurons. Afferent (sensory) neurons relay messages from the sense organs and receptors—eyes, ears, nose, mouth, and skin—to the brain or spinal cord. Efferent (motor) neurons convey signals from the central nervous system to the glands and the muscles, enabling the body to move. Interneurons, thousands of times more numerous than motor or sensory neurons, carry information between neurons in the brain and between neurons in the spinal cord. ✳⃞ Explore on **mypsychlab.com**

Although no two neurons are exactly alike, nearly all are made up of three important parts: the cell body, the dendrites, and the axon. The cell body, or *soma*, contains the nucleus and carries out the metabolic, or life-sustaining, functions of a neuron. Branching out from the cell body are the dendrites, which look much like the leafless branches of a tree (*dendrite* comes from the Greek word for "tree"). The dendrites are the primary receivers of signals from other neurons, but the cell body can also receive signals directly.

The axon is the slender, tail-like extension of the neuron that sprouts into many branches, each ending in a bulbous axon terminal. Signals move from the axon terminals to the dendrites or cell bodies of other neurons and to muscles, glands, and other parts of the body. In humans, some axons are short—only thousandths of an inch long. Others can be as long as a meter (39.37 inches)—long enough to reach from the brain to the tip of the spinal cord, or from the spinal cord to remote parts of the body. Figure 2.1 shows the structure of a neuron.

Glial cells are specialized cells in the brain and spinal cord that support the neurons. They are smaller than neurons and make up more than one-half the volume of the human brain. Glial cells remove waste products, such as dead neurons, from the brain by engulfing and digesting them, and they handle other manufacturing, nourishing, and cleanup tasks. Glial cells in the spinal cord are also involved in the transmission of pain sensations from the various parts of the body to the brain (Hald, Nedergard, Hansen, Ding, & Heegaard, 2009).

Communication between Neurons

Remarkably, the billions of neurons that send and receive signals are not physically connected. The axon terminals are separated from the receiving neurons by tiny, fluid-filled gaps called *synaptic clefts*. The synapse is the junction where the axon terminal of a sending (presynaptic) neuron communicates with a receiving (postsynaptic) neuron across the synaptic cleft. There may be as many as 100 trillion synapses in the human nervous system (Swanson, 1995). A single neuron may also form synapses with thousands of other neurons (Kelner, 1997). If neurons aren't connected, how do they communicate with one another? ✳⃞ Explore on **mypsychlab.com**

A small but measurable electrical impulse is present every time you move or have a thought. Even though the impulse that travels down the axon is electrical, the axon does not transmit it the way a wire conducts an electrical current. What actually changes is the permeability of the cell membrane (its capability of being penetrated or passed through). In other words, the membrane changes in a way that makes it easier for molecules to move through it and into the cell. This process allows ions (electrically charged atoms or molecules) to move into and out of the axon through ion channels in the membrane.

Body fluids contain ions, some with positive electrical charges and others with negative charges. Inside the axon, there are normally more negative than positive ions. When at rest (not firing), the axon membrane carries a negative electrical potential of

FIGURE 2.1 The Structure of a Typical Neuron
A typical neuron has three important parts: (1) a cell body, which carries out the metabolic functions of the neuron; (2) branched fibers called dendrites, which are the primary receivers of the impulses from other neurons; and (3) a slender, tail-like extension called an axon, the transmitting end of the neuron, which sprouts into many branches, each ending in an axon terminal. The photograph shows human neurons greatly magnified.

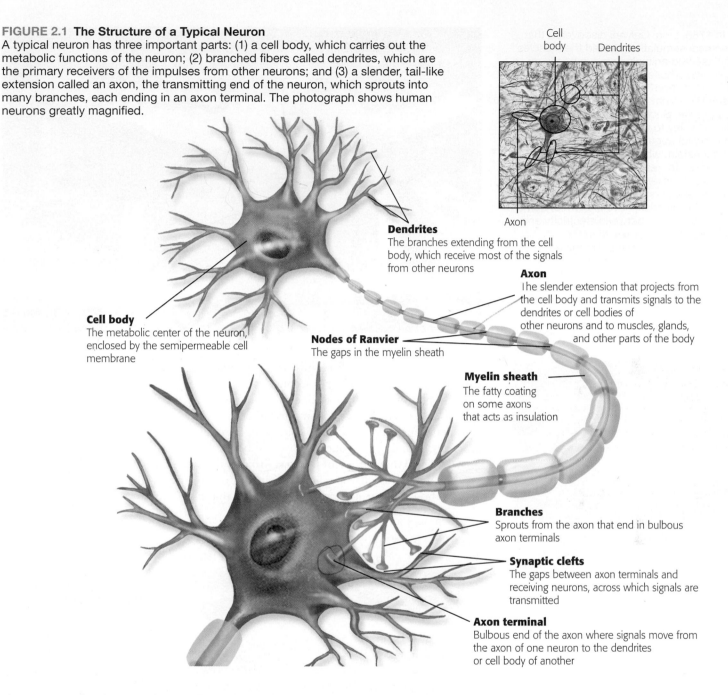

Dendrites
The branches extending from the cell body, which receive most of the signals from other neurons

Axon
The slender extension that projects from the cell body and transmits signals to the dendrites or cell bodies of other neurons and to muscles, glands, and other parts of the body

Cell body
The metabolic center of the neuron, enclosed by the semipermeable cell membrane

Nodes of Ranvier
The gaps in the myelin sheath

Myelin sheath
The fatty coating on some axons that acts as insulation

Branches
Sprouts from the axon that end in bulbous axon terminals

Synaptic clefts
The gaps between axon terminals and receiving neurons, across which signals are transmitted

Axon terminal
Bulbous end of the axon where signals move from the axon of one neuron to the dendrites or cell body of another

about −70 millivolts (−70 thousandths of a volt) relative to the fluid outside the cell. This slight negative charge is referred to as the neuron's resting potential.

When the excitatory effects on a neuron reach a certain threshold, ion channels begin to open in the cell membrane of the axon at the point closest to the cell body, allowing positive ions to flow into the axon (see Figure 2.2 on p. 40). This inflow of positive ions causes the membrane potential to change abruptly, to a positive value of about +50 millivolts (Pinel, 2000). This sudden reversal of the resting potential, which lasts for about 1 millisecond (1 thousandth of a second), is the action potential. Then, the ion channels admitting positive ions close, and other ion channels open, forcing some positive ions out of the axon. As a result, the original negative charge, or resting potential, is restored. The opening and closing of ion channels continues, segment by segment, down the length of the axon, causing the action potential to move along the axon (Cardoso de Mello & Sabbatini, 2000). The action potential operates according to the "all-or-none" law—a neuron either fires completely or does not fire at all. Immediately after a neuron fires, it enters a *refractory period*, during which it cannot

resting potential The slight negative electrical potential of the axon membrane of a neuron at rest, about −70 millivolts.

action potential The sudden reversal of the resting potential, which initiates the firing of a neuron.

▶ In 1786, Luigi Galvani discovered that electrical stimulation caused the muscles of dissected animals to move briefly on their own. These findings led proponents of "reanimation" to speculate that a jolt of electricity might bring dead organisms back to life. Such speculations inspired Mary Shelley to write a shocking (at the time) novel about a scientist, Victor Frankenstein, who developed a procedure for reanimating human corpses, *Frankenstein: The Modern Prometheus*, first published in 1818. Although scientists have known for some time that the link between electricity and life is far more complex than the advocates of reanimation imagined, Shelley's powerful message about the moral dilemmas that arise when science enables humankind to grant and withhold the "spark of life" lives on.

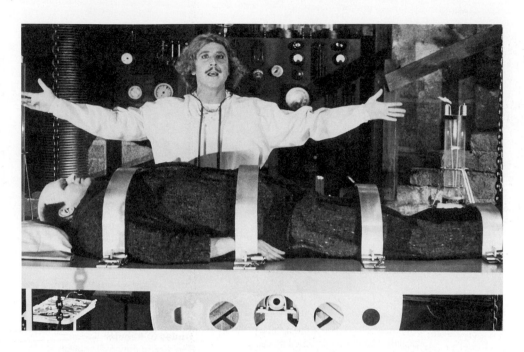

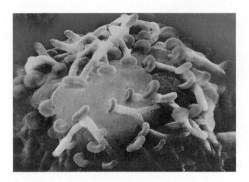

▲ This scanning electron micrograph shows numerous axon terminals (the orange, button-shaped structures) that could synapse with the cell body of the neuron (shown in green).

fire again for 1 to 2 milliseconds. But even with these short resting periods, neurons can fire hundreds of times per second.

If a neuron only fires or does not fire, how can we tell the difference between a very strong and a very weak stimulus? In other words, what is the neurological distinction between feeling anxious about being disciplined by your boss for being late to work and running for your life to avoid being the victim of a criminal attacker? The answer lies in the number of neurons firing at the same time and their rate of firing. A weak stimulus may cause relatively few neurons to fire, while a strong stimulus may trigger thousands of neurons to fire at the same time. Also, a weak stimulus may be

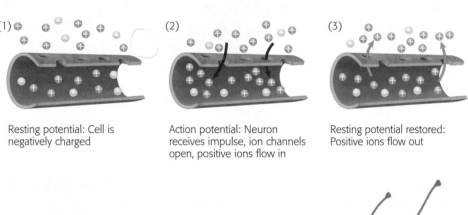

(1) Resting potential: Cell is negatively charged

(2) Action potential: Neuron receives impulse, ion channels open, positive ions flow in

(3) Resting potential restored: Positive ions flow out

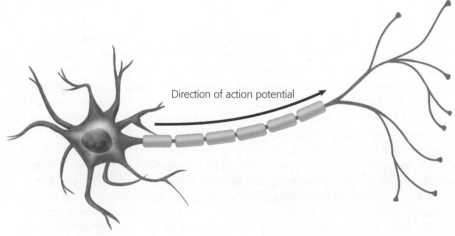

Direction of action potential

FIGURE 2.2 The Action Potential
The action potential moves down the axon to the axon terminals.
Source: Adapted from Lilienfeld, Lynn, Namy, & Wolf (2009).

signaled by neurons firing very slowly; a stronger stimulus may incite neurons to fire hundreds of times per second.

Impulses travel at speeds from about 1 meter per second to approximately 100 meters per second (about 224 miles per hour). The most important factor in speeding the impulse on its way is the myelin sheath—a white, fatty coating wrapped around most axons that acts as insulation. If you look again at Figure 2.1 (p. 39), you will see that the coating has numerous gaps, called *nodes of Ranvier*. The electrical impulse is retriggered or regenerated at each node (or naked gap) on the axon. This regeneration makes the impulse up to 100 times faster than impulses in axons without myelin sheaths. Damage to the myelin sheath causes interruptions in the transmission of neural messages. In fact, the disease multiple sclerosis (MS) involves deterioration of the myelin sheath, resulting in loss of coordination, jerky movements, muscular weakness, and disturbances in speech.

Neurotransmitters ▷

Once a neuron fires, how does it get its message across the synaptic cleft and on to another neuron? Inside the axon terminal are many small, sphere-shaped containers with thin membranes called *synaptic vesicles,* which hold the neurotransmitters. (*Vesicle* comes from a Latin word meaning "little bladder.") When an action potential arrives at the axon terminal, synaptic vesicles move toward the cell membrane, fuse with it, and release their neurotransmitter molecules. This process is shown in Figure 2.3.

Once released, neurotransmitters do not simply flow into the synaptic cleft and stimulate all the adjacent neurons. Each neurotransmitter has a distinctive molecular

myelin sheath (MY-uh-lin) The white, fatty coating wrapped around some axons that acts as insulation and enables impulses to travel much faster.

⌈ **2.5** How do neurotransmitters
⌊ work?

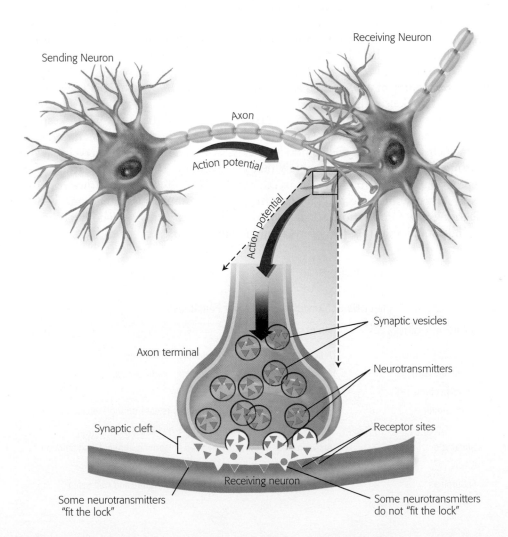

FIGURE 2.3 Synaptic Transmission
Sending neurons transmit their messages to receiving neurons by electrochemical action. When a neuron fires, the action potential arrives at the axon terminal and triggers the release of neurotransmitters from the synaptic vesicles. Neurotransmitters flow into the synaptic cleft and move toward the receiving neuron, which has numerous receptors. The receptors will bind only with neurotransmitters whose molecular shapes match their enclosed volumes. Neurotransmitters influence the receiving neuron to fire or not to fire.

receptors Protein molecules on the surfaces of dendrites and cell bodies that have distinctive shapes and will interact only with specific neurotransmitters.

reuptake The process by which neurotransmitters are taken from the synaptic cleft back into the axon terminal for later use, thus terminating their excitatory or inhibitory effect on the receiving neuron.

shape, as do receptors, which are protein molecules on the surfaces of dendrites and cell bodies. In other words, each receptor is somewhat like a lock that only certain neurotransmitter keys can unlock (Cardoso et al., 2000; Restak, 1993). However, the binding of neurotransmitters with receptors is not as fixed and rigid a process as keys fitting locks or jigsaw puzzle pieces interlocking. Receptors on neurons are somewhat flexible; they can expand and contract their enclosed volumes. And neurotransmitters of different types can have similar shapes. Thus, two different neurotransmitters may compete for the same receptor. The receptor will admit only one of the competing neurotransmitters—the one that fits it best. A receptor may receive a certain neurotransmitter sometimes but not receive it in the presence of a better-fitting neurotransmitter.

When neurotransmitters bind with receptors on the dendrites or cell bodies of receiving neurons, their action is either excitatory (influencing the neurons to fire) or inhibitory (influencing them not to fire). Because a single receiving neuron may have synapses with thousands of other neurons at the same time, it will always be subject to both excitatory and inhibitory influences from incoming neurotransmitters. For the neuron to fire, the excitatory influences must exceed the inhibitory influences by a sufficient amount (the threshold).

You may wonder how the synaptic vesicles can continue to pour out neurotransmitters, yet maintain a ready supply so that the neuron can respond to continuing stimulation. First, the cell body of the neuron is always working to manufacture more of the neurotransmitter. Second, unused neurotransmitters in the synaptic cleft may be broken down into components and reclaimed by the axon terminal to be recycled and used again. Third, by an important process called reuptake, the neurotransmitter is taken back into the axon terminal, intact and ready for immediate use. This terminates the neurotransmitter's excitatory or inhibitory effect on the receiving neuron.

Researchers have identified 75 or more chemical substances that are manufactured in the brain, spinal cord, glands, and other parts of the body and may act as neurotransmitters (Greden, 1994). Table 2.1 lists the major neurotransmitters. As you look over the table, keep in mind that neurotransmitters can serve different functions in different parts of the body. For example, *acetylcholine* (Ach) exerts excitatory effects on the skeletal muscle fibers, causing them to contract so that the body can move. But it has an inhibitory effect on the muscle fibers in the heart, which keeps the heart from beating too rapidly. Thus, when you run to make it to class on time, acetylcholine helps your leg muscles contract quickly, while simultaneously preventing your heart muscle from pumping so rapidly that you pass out. The differing natures of the receptors on the receiving neurons in the two kinds of muscles cause these opposite effects. Acetylcholine also plays an excitatory role in stimulating the neurons involved in learning new information. So, as you are reading this text, acetylcholine is helping you understand and store the information in your memory.

TABLE 2.1 Major Neurotransmitters and Their Functions

NEUROTRANSMITTER	FUNCTIONS
Acetylcholine (Ach)	Affects movement, learning, memory, REM sleep
Dopamine (DA)	Affects movement, attention, learning, reinforcement, pleasure
Norepinephrine (NE)	Affects eating, alertness, wakefulness
Epinephrine	Affects metabolism of glucose, energy release during exercise
Serotonin	Affects mood, sleep, appetite, impulsivity, aggression
Glutamate	Active in areas of the brain involved in learning, thought, and emotion
GABA	Facilitates neural inhibition in the central nervous system
Endorphins	Provide relief from pain and feelings of pleasure and well-being

As you will learn in Chapter 4, drugs influence the nervous system through their action on neurotransmitters. For instance, responses to cocaine involve the neurotransmitters *dopamine* and *glutamate* (Fasano et al., 2009). Moreover, in Chapter 11 you will learn that researchers have discovered links between neurotransmitter functioning and several psychological disorders. For example, researchers suspect that the neurotransmitter *dopamine* plays a role in attention-deficit/hyperactivity disorder (ADHD) (Volkow et al., 2009).

The Human Nervous System

Now that you understand how the cells of the nervous system function, you're ready to learn more about how the system is organized. As you can see in Figure 2.4, there are two major divisions in the system. You'll be happy to learn that it's easy to remember the difference between the two. The peripheral nervous system (PNS) includes all of the nerves (i.e., bundles of neurons) that are not encased in bone, that is, all of the neural tissue that lies outside your skull and backbone. The function of these tissues is to transmit messages to and from the body and brain. The central nervous system (CNS) includes all of the neural tissues inside the skull and backbone. In other words, the CNS is made up of the spinal cord and brain.

The Peripheral Nervous System ▷

What makes your heart pound and palms sweat when you watch a scary movie? Such reactions are the result of signals from the brain's limbic system and other structures that regulate emotions to the peripheral nervous system. The peripheral nervous system (PNS) is made up of all the nerves that connect the central nervous system to the rest of the body. It has two subdivisions: the somatic nervous system and the autonomic nervous system.

▲ The neurotransmitter acetylcholine helps you process new information by facilitating neural transmissions involved in learning.

⌈ 2.6 What are the structures and functions of the peripheral **⌊** nervous system?

peripheral nervous system (PNS) (peh-RIF-er-ul) The nerves connecting the central nervous system to the rest of the body.

central nervous system (CNS) The part of the nervous system comprising the brain and the spinal cord.

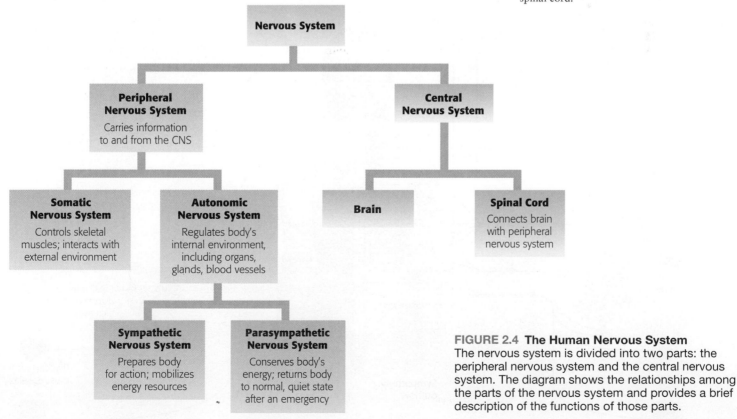

FIGURE 2.4 The Human Nervous System
The nervous system is divided into two parts: the peripheral nervous system and the central nervous system. The diagram shows the relationships among the parts of the nervous system and provides a brief description of the functions of those parts.

sympathetic nervous system The division of the autonomic nervous system that mobilizes the body's resources during stress and emergencies, preparing the body for action.

parasympathetic nervous system The division of the autonomic nervous system that brings the heightened bodily responses back to normal following an emergency.

✳ Explore the Concept *The Autonomic Nervous System* on **mypsychlab.com**

FIGURE 2.5 The Autonomic Nervous System
The autonomic nervous system consists of (1) the sympathetic nervous system, which mobilizes the body's resources during emergencies or stress, and (2) the parasympathetic nervous system, which brings the heightened bodily responses back to normal afterward. This diagram shows the opposite effects of the sympathetic and parasympathetic nervous systems on various parts of the human body.
Source: Lilienfeld, Lynn, Namy, & Woolf (2009).

The *somatic nervous system* consists of (1) all the sensory nerves, which transmit information from the sense receptors—eyes, ears, nose, tongue, and skin—to the central nervous system, and (2) all the motor nerves, which relay messages from the central nervous system to all the skeletal muscles of the body. In short, the nerves of the somatic nervous system make it possible for you to sense your environment and to move, and they are primarily under conscious control.

The *autonomic nervous system* operates without any conscious control or awareness on your part. It transmits messages between the central nervous system and the glands, the cardiac (heart) muscle, and the smooth muscles (such as those in the large arteries and the gastrointestinal system), which are not normally under voluntary control. This system is further divided into two parts—the sympathetic and the parasympathetic nervous systems. ✳ Explore on **mypsychlab.com**

Any time you are under stress or faced with an emergency, the sympathetic nervous system automatically mobilizes the body's resources, preparing you for action. This physiological arousal produced by the sympathetic nervous system was named the *fight-or-flight response* by Walter Cannon (1929, 1935). If an ominous-looking stranger started following you down a dark, deserted street, your sympathetic nervous system would automatically go to work. Your heart would begin to pound, your pulse rate would increase rapidly, your breathing would quicken, and your digestive system would nearly shut down. The blood flow to your skeletal muscles would be enhanced, and all of your bodily resources would be made ready to handle the emergency.

Once the emergency is over, the parasympathetic nervous system brings these heightened bodily functions back to normal. As a result of its action, your heart stops pounding and slows to normal, your pulse rate and breathing slow down, and your digestive system resumes its normal functioning. As shown in Figure 2.5 the

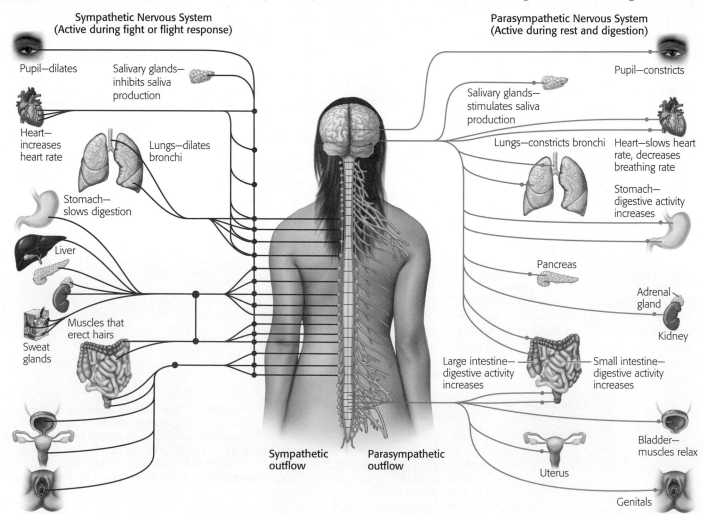

sympathetic and parasympathetic branches act as opposing but complementary forces in the autonomic nervous system. Their balanced functioning is essential for health and survival.

The Central Nervous System ▷

As we noted earlier, the central nervous system includes the spinal cord and the brain. The spinal cord is the link between the peripheral nervous system and the brain. As you will see, the brain itself includes several different components, each of which has distinctive functions.

The Spinal Cord. The spinal cord can best be thought of as an extension of the brain. A cylinder of neural tissue about the diameter of your little finger, the spinal cord reaches from the base of the brain, through the neck, and down the hollow center of the spinal column. It is protected by bone and also by spinal fluid, which serves as a shock absorber. The spinal cord literally links the body with the brain. It transmits messages between the brain and nerves in other parts of the body. Thus, sensory information can reach the brain, and messages from the brain can be sent to the muscles, the glands, and other parts of the body.

Although the spinal cord and the brain usually function together, the spinal cord can act without help from the brain to protect the body from injury. A simple withdrawal reflex triggered by a painful stimulus—touching a hot iron, for example—involves three types of neurons (see Figure 2.6). Sensory neurons in your fingers detect the painful stimulus and relay this information to interneurons in the spinal cord. These interneurons activate motor neurons that control the muscles in your arm and cause you to jerk your hand away. All this happens within a fraction of a second, without any involvement of your brain. However, the brain quickly becomes aware and involved when the pain signal reaches it. At that point, you might plunge your hand into cold water to relieve the pain.

The Hindbrain. Brain structures are often grouped into the *hindbrain*, the *midbrain*, and the *forebrain*, as shown in Figure 2.7 (p. 46). The structures of the hindbrain control heart rate, respiration, blood pressure, and many other vital functions. The part of the hindbrain known as the brainstem begins at the site where the spinal cord enlarges as it enters the skull. The brainstem handles functions that are so critical to physical survival that damage to it is life threatening. The medulla is the part of the brainstem that controls heartbeat, breathing, blood pressure, coughing, and swallowing. Fortunately, the medulla handles these functions automatically, so you do not have to decide consciously to breathe or remember to keep your heart beating.

Extending through the central core of the brainstem into the pons is another important structure, the reticular formation, sometimes called the *reticular activating system* (RAS) (refer to Figure 2.7). The reticular formation plays a crucial role in arousal and attention (Gadea et al., 2004; Kinomura et al., 1996; Steriade, 1996). For example, a driver may be listening intently to a radio program when, suddenly, a car cuts in front of her. In response, the reticular formation blocks the sensory information coming from the radio and fixes the driver's attention on the potential danger posed by the other driver's action. Once the traffic pattern returns to normal, the reticular formation allows her to attend to the radio again, while continuing to monitor the traffic situation.

2.7 **What are the structures and functions of the central nervous system?**

spinal cord An extension of the brain, from the base of the brain through the neck and spinal column, that transmits messages between the brain and the peripheral nervous system.

hindbrain A link between the spinal cord and the brain that contains structures that regulate physiological functions, including heart rate, respiration, and blood pressure.

brainstem The structure that begins at the point where the spinal cord enlarges as it enters the brain and handles functions critical to physical survival. It includes the medulla, the reticular formation, and the pons.

medulla (muh-DUL-uh) The part of the brainstem that controls heartbeat, blood pressure, breathing, coughing, and swallowing.

reticular formation A structure in the brainstem that plays a crucial role in arousal and attention and that screens sensory messages entering the brain.

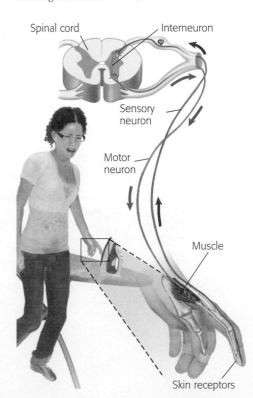

FIGURE 2.6 The Spinal Reflex
The sequence that begins with a sensory stimulus (such as touching something hot) and ends with a behavioral response (withdrawing the hand) involves sensory neurons, interneurons, and motor neurons.
Source: Adapted from Lilienfeld et al. (2009).

The reticular formation also determines how alert we are. When it slows down, we doze off or go to sleep. But thanks to the reticular formation, important messages get through even when we are asleep. This is why parents may be able to sleep through a thunderstorm but will awaken to the slightest cry of their baby.

Above the medulla and at the top of the brainstem is a bridgelike structure called the pons that extends across the top front of the brainstem and connects to both halves of the cerebellum. The pons plays a role in body movement and even exerts an influence on sleep and dreaming.

The cerebellum is critically important to the body's ability to execute smooth, skilled movements (Spencer et al., 2003). It also regulates muscle tone and posture. Furthermore, it has been found to play a role in motor learning (Orban et al., 2009).

pons The bridgelike structure that connects the medulla and the cerebellum.

cerebellum (sehr-uh-BELL-um) The brain structure that helps the body execute smooth, skilled movements and regulates muscle tone and posture.

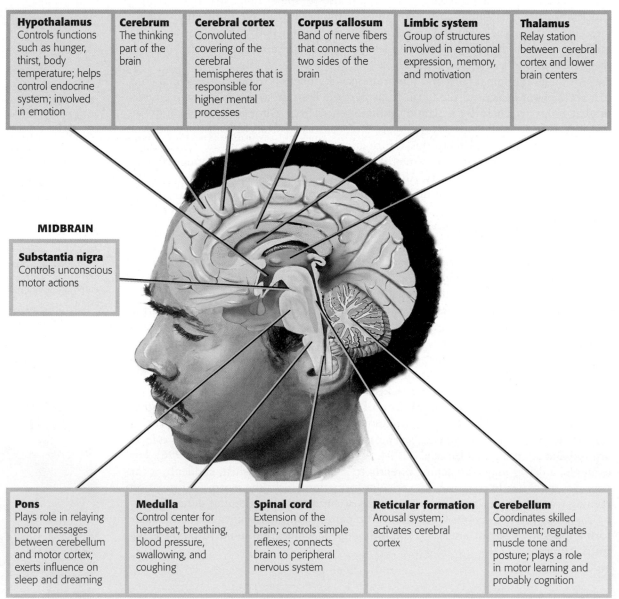

FOREBRAIN

Hypothalamus
Controls functions such as hunger, thirst, body temperature; helps control endocrine system; involved in emotion

Cerebrum
The thinking part of the brain

Cerebral cortex
Convoluted covering of the cerebral hemispheres that is responsible for higher mental processes

Corpus callosum
Band of nerve fibers that connects the two sides of the brain

Limbic system
Group of structures involved in emotional expression, memory, and motivation

Thalamus
Relay station between cerebral cortex and lower brain centers

MIDBRAIN

Substantia nigra
Controls unconscious motor actions

Pons
Plays role in relaying motor messages between cerebellum and motor cortex; exerts influence on sleep and dreaming

Medulla
Control center for heartbeat, breathing, blood pressure, swallowing, and coughing

Spinal cord
Extension of the brain; controls simple reflexes; connects brain to peripheral nervous system

Reticular formation
Arousal system; activates cerebral cortex

Cerebellum
Coordinates skilled movement; regulates muscle tone and posture; plays a role in motor learning and probably cognition

HINDBRAIN

FIGURE 2.7 Major Structures of the Human Brain
This drawing shows some of the major structures of the brain with a brief description of the function of each. The brainstem contains the medulla, the reticular formation, and the pons.

It coordinates the series of movements necessary to perform many simple activities—such as walking in a straight line or touching your finger to the tip of your nose—without conscious effort. For people who have damage to their cerebellum or who are temporarily impaired by too much alcohol, such simple acts may be difficult or impossible to perform.

The Midbrain. As shown in Figure 2.7, the midbrain lies between the hindbrain and the forebrain. The structures of this brain region act primarily as relay stations through which the basic physiological functions of the hindbrain are linked to the cognitive functions of the forebrain. For example, when you burn your finger, the physical feeling travels through the nerves of your hand and arm, eventually reaching the spinal cord, resulting in the reflexive action of dropping a pot, for example. From there, nerve impulses are sent through the midbrain to the forebrain, where they are interpreted ("Next time, I'll remember to use a potholder!").

midbrain Area that contains structures linking the physiological functions of the hindbrain to the cognitive functions of the forebrain.

The substantia nigra is located in the midbrain. This structure is composed of the darkly colored nuclei of nerve cells that control our unconscious motor actions. When you ride a bicycle or walk up stairs without giving your movements any conscious thought, the nuclei of the cells that allow you to do so are found in the substantia nigra. Research suggests that the defects in dopamine-producing neurons in the substantia nigra may explain the inability of people with Parkinson's disease to control their physical movements (Bergman et al., 2010).

substantia nigra (sub-STAN-sha NI-gra) The structure in the midbrain that controls unconscious motor movements.

The Forebrain. The largest part of the brain is the forebrain. This is the part of the brain where cognitive and motor functions are controlled. Two important forebrain structures lie just above the brainstem (see Figure 2.7). The thalamus, which has two egg-shaped parts, serves as the relay station for virtually all the information that flows into and out of the forebrain, including sensory information from all the senses except smell. (You'll learn more about the sense of smell in Chapter 3.)

forebrain The largest part of the brain where cognitive functions as well as many of the motor functions of the brain are carried out.

thalamus (THAL-uh-mus) The structure, located above the brainstem, that acts as a relay station for information flowing into or out of the forebrain.

The thalamus, or at least one small part of it, affects our ability to learn new verbal information (Soei, Koch Schwarz, & Daum, 2008). Another function of the thalamus is the regulation of sleep cycles, which is thought to be accomplished in cooperation with the pons and the reticular formation (Saper, Scammell, & Lu, 2005). The majority of people who have had acute brain injury and remain in an unresponsive "vegetative" state have suffered significant damage to the thalamus, to the neural tissue connecting it to parts of the forebrain, or to both (Young, 2009).

The hypothalamus lies directly below the thalamus and weighs only about 2 ounces. It regulates hunger, thirst, sexual behavior, and a wide variety of emotional behaviors. The hypothalamus also regulates internal body temperature, starting the process that causes you to perspire when you are too hot and to shiver to conserve body heat when you are too cold. It also houses the biological clock—the mechanism responsible for the timing of the sleep/wakefulness cycle and the daily fluctuation in more than 100 body functions (Wirz-Justice, 2009). Because of the biological clock, once your body gets used to waking up at a certain time, you tend to awaken at that time every day—even if you forget to set your alarm. The physiological changes in the body that accompany strong emotion—sweaty palms, a pounding heart, a hollow feeling in the pit of your stomach—are also initiated by neurons concentrated primarily in the hypothalamus.

hypothalamus (HY-po-THAL-uh-mus) A small but influential brain structure that regulates hunger, thirst, sexual behavior, internal body temperature, other body functions, and a wide variety of emotional behaviors.

The limbic system, shown in Figure 2.8 (p. 48) is a group of structures in the brain, including the amygdala and the hippocampus, that are collectively involved in emotional expression, memory, and motivation. The amygdala plays an important role in emotion, particularly in response to unpleasant or punishing stimuli (Cain & LeDoux, 2008; Tye et al., 2008). Heavily involved in the learning of fear responses, the amygdala helps form vivid memories of emotional events, which enable humans and other animals to avoid dangerous situations (Roozendaal, et al., 2008). Damage to the amygdala can impair a person's ability to recognize facial expressions and tones of voice that are associated with fear and anger (Ariatti, Benuzzi, & Nichelli, 2008).

limbic system A group of structures in the brain, including the amygdala and hippocampus, that are collectively involved in emotional expression, memory, and motivation.

amygdala (ah-MIG-da-la) A structure in the limbic system that plays an important role in emotion, particularly in response to unpleasant or punishing stimuli.

hippocampus (hip-po-CAM-pus) A structure in the limbic system that plays a central role in the storing of new memories, the response to new or unexpected stimuli, and navigational ability.

The hippocampus is an important brain structure of the limbic system located in the interior temporal lobes (see Figure 2.8). If your hippocampal region—the hippocampus and the underlying cortical areas—were destroyed, you would not be able to store any new personal or cognitive information, such as that day's baseball score or the phone number of the person you met at dinner (Wirth et al., 2003). Yet, memories already stored before the hippocampal region was destroyed would remain intact. You will learn more about the central role of the hippocampal region in the formation of memories in Chapter 6.

The hippocampus also plays a role in the brain's internal representation of space in the form of neural "maps" that help us learn our way about in new environments and remember where we have been (Wilson & McNaughton, 1993). A widely cited study of taxi drivers in London revealed that their posterior (rear) hippocampus was significantly larger than that of participants in a control group who did not have extensive experience navigating the city's streets (Maguire et al., 2000). In fact, the more experience a taxi driver had, the larger that part of the hippocampus was. This study shows that the posterior hippocampus is important for navigational ability. Finally, the *cerebral cortex* is the forebrain structure that is responsible for the functions we usually associate with the word *brain*. It is the wrinkled, gray covering of the *cerebrum*, or the thinking part of the brain. In the next section, you will read about the cerebrum in more detail.

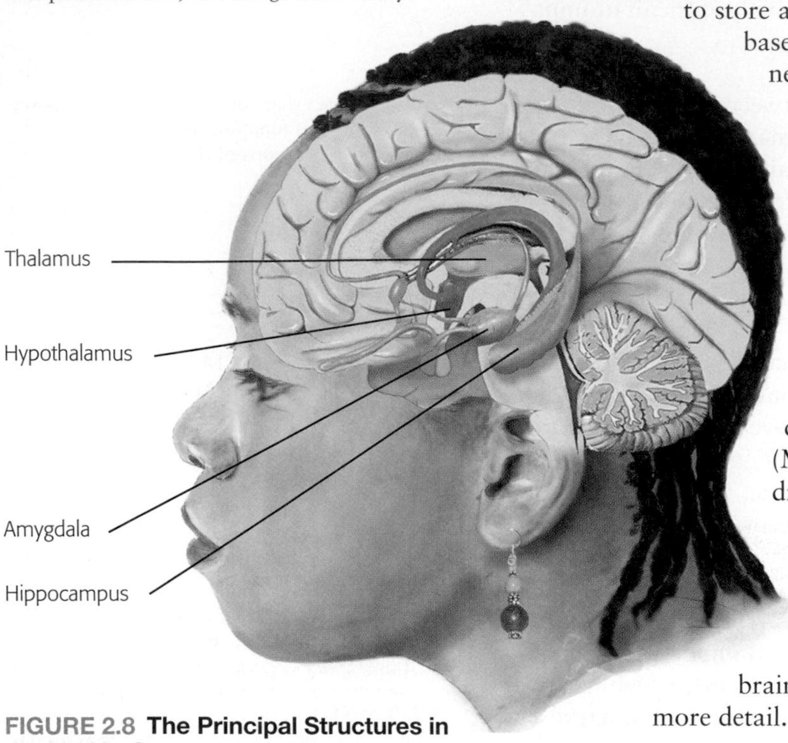

FIGURE 2.8 The Principal Structures in the Limbic System
The amygdala plays an important role in emotion; the hippocampus is essential in the formation of new memories.

Thalamus

Hypothalamus

Amygdala

Hippocampus

A Closer Look at the Thinking Part of the Brain

Researchers have known for more than a century that the majority of the functions that distinguish the human species from others, such as language, reside in the part of the forebrain known as the *cerebrum*. Modern techniques, such as the EEG and the CT and MRI scans, have enabled researchers to localize many important functions, such as planning and logic, to specific parts of the cerebrum. They have also learned a great deal about the communication that goes on between the two sides and four lobes of the cerebrum.

cerebrum (seh-REE-brum) The largest structure of the human brain, consisting of the two cerebral hemispheres connected by the corpus callosum and covered by the cerebral cortex.

2.8 What are the components of the cerebrum?

Components of the Cerebrum

If you could peer into your skull and look down on your brain, what you would see would resemble the inside of a huge walnut. Like a walnut, which has two matched halves connected to each other, the cerebrum is composed of two cerebral hemispheres—a left and a right hemisphere resting side by side (see Figure 2.9). The two hemispheres are physically connected at the bottom by a thick band of nerve fibers called the corpus callosum. This connection makes possible the transfer of information and the coordination of activity between the hemispheres. In general, the right cerebral hemisphere controls movement and feeling on the left side of the body; the left hemisphere controls the right side of the body.

The cerebral hemispheres have a thin outer covering about $1/8$ inch thick called the cerebral cortex, which is primarily responsible for the higher mental processes of language, memory, and thinking. The presence of the cell bodies of billions of neurons in the cerebral cortex gives it a grayish appearance. Thus, the cortex is often referred to as *gray matter*. Immediately beneath the cortex are the white myelinated axons

cerebral hemispheres (seh-REE-brul) The right and left halves of the cerebrum, covered by the cerebral cortex and connected by the corpus callosum; they control movement and feeling on the opposing sides of the body.

corpus callosum (KOR-pus kah-LO-sum) The thick band of nerve fibers that connects the two cerebral hemispheres and makes possible the transfer of information and the synchronization of activity between the hemispheres.

cerebral cortex (seh-REE-brul KOR-tex) The gray, convoluted covering of the cerebral hemispheres that is responsible for the higher mental processes of language, memory, and thinking.

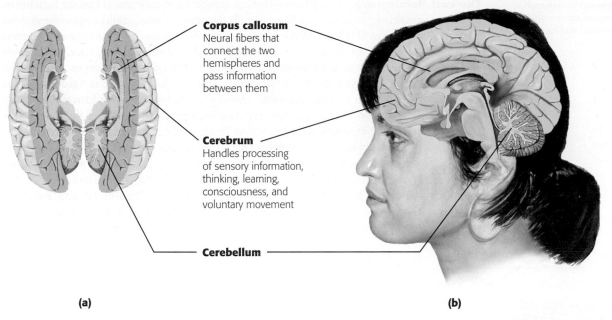

Corpus callosum
Neural fibers that connect the two hemispheres and pass information between them

Cerebrum
Handles processing of sensory information, thinking, learning, consciousness, and voluntary movement

Cerebellum

(a)

(b)

FIGURE 2.9 Two Views of the Cerebral Hemispheres
(a) The two hemispheres rest side by side like two matched halves, physically connected by the corpus callosum. (b) An inside view of the right hemisphere.

(referred to as *white matter*) that connect the neurons of the cortex with those of other brain regions. Research suggests that the amount of gray matter is positively correlated with intelligence in humans (Narr, 2007).

In humans, the cerebral cortex is very large—if it were spread out flat, it would measure about 2 feet by 3 feet. Because the cortex is roughly three times the size of the cerebrum itself, it does not fit smoothly around the cerebrum. Rather, it is arranged in numerous folds or wrinkles, called *convolutions*. About two-thirds of the cortex is hidden from view in these folds. The cortex of less intelligent animals is much smaller in proportion to total brain size and, therefore, is much less convoluted. The cerebral cortex contains three types of areas: (1) sensory input areas, where vision, hearing, touch, pressure, and temperature register; (2) motor areas, which control voluntary movement; and (3) association areas, which house memories and are involved in thought, perception, and language.

Finally, the brain assigns different functions to different regions of the cerebral cortex. The first functional division involves the left and right sides of the cortex. The second involves areas known as the *lobes*—the front (frontal), top (parietal), side (temporal), and back (occipital) of the cortex. As you read about the various neurological divisions of labor in the next two sections, keep in mind that all parts of the brain are in communication with one another at all times. Consequently, everything we do involves the coordination of neural activity in several areas of the brain at once.

association areas Areas of the cerebral cortex that house memories and are involved in thought, perception, and language.

The Cerebral Hemispheres ▷

We all know that some people are right-handed and others are left-handed. As discussed in the *Explain It* (p. 50), handedness is neurologically based. Consequently, discussions in the media about the differences between "right-brained" and "left-brained" people might seem to make sense. However, there is no scientific basis for the notion that hemisphere dominance varies across individuals in the same way that hand preference does. In everyone's brain, the right and left hemispheres are in constant contact with one another, thanks to the corpus callosum (shown in Figure 2.9). But research has shown that some lateralization of the hemispheres exists; that is, each hemisphere is specialized to handle certain functions. Let's look at the specific functions associated with the left and right hemispheres.

2.9 What are the specialized functions of the left and right cerebral hemispheres?

lateralization The specialization of one of the cerebral hemispheres to handle a particular function.

left hemisphere The hemisphere that controls the right side of the body, coordinates complex movements, and, in most people, handles most of the language functions.

The Left Hemisphere. The left hemisphere handles most of the language functions, including speaking, writing, reading, speech comprehension, and comprehension of written information (Hellige, 1990; Long & Baynes, 2002). Many of these functions have specific regions of the left hemisphere devoted to them. For instance, the sounds and meanings associated with spoken language are processed in different areas of the left hemisphere (Poldrack & Wagner, 2004). The left hemisphere is specialized for mathematics and logic as well (Piazza & Dehaene, 2004). Moreover, researchers have learned that information about the self, including one's sense of well-being, is processed in the left hemisphere (Heatherton et al., 2004; Urry et al., 2004).

The left hemisphere coordinates complex movements by directly controlling the right side of the body and by indirectly controlling the movements of the left side of the body. It accomplishes this by sending orders across the corpus callosum to the right hemisphere so that the proper movements will be coordinated and executed smoothly. (Remember that the cerebellum also plays an important role in helping coordinate complex movements.)

EXPLAIN IT ▶ Why Are Most People Right-Handed?

Scientists have searched for an answer to this question for more than a century and have yet to find a definitive answer. In your own thinking about the matter, you have probably concluded that there are three possibilities:

- Handedness is completely determined by genes.
- Handedness is completely determined by learning.
- Handedness is determined by both genes and learning.

If you are drawn to the first hypothesis, consider the finding that only 82% of identical twins, whose genotypes (genetic makeup) are identical, have the same hand preference (Klar, 2003). If handedness were completely determined by genes, then identical twins' phenotypes (actual characteristics) would always be the same for handedness. Therefore, handedness cannot be entirely explained as a function of our genes. Does this mean that handedness is determined by learning? Not necessarily.

The learning hypothesis cannot explain why handedness appears very early in infancy, long before children are exposed to formal instruction that requires them to use one hand or the other (Rönnqvist & Domellöf, 2006). Moreover, the proportions of left-handers and right-handers in the human population have been about the same for thousands of years (Hopkins & Cantalupo, 2004; Wilson, 1998). In fact, these proportions are evident even in the skeletons of humans who died long before writing was invented (Steele & Mays, 1995).

The key to understanding the evidence on handedness is to adopt the view that both genes and learning are at work in the development of hand preferences, but not in the way that you might expect. In most of us, right-handedness is completely determined by our genes, but in a few of us handedness, whether left or right, is influenced by learning. Sound confusing? To clarify, here is the most current thinking on the genetics of handedness.

Researchers suspect that right-handedness is determined by a single dominant gene, R (Francks et al., 2003). If an individual receives a copy of R from one or both parents, then she will be right-handed. The frequency of R in the human population is extremely high, scientists believe, because it is tied to the genes that support left-lateralization of language function in the brain. (Remember, the left side of the brain controls the right side of the body.) It makes sense that motor functions are linked to language, experts claim, because producing language requires activity in both the language centers and motor cortex of the brain. Putting both on the same side of the brain facilitates the rapid development of neural connections between the two without having to go through the slowly developing membrane between the two hemispheres (corpus callosum). But what happens to the relatively small proportion of humans who do not receive a copy of R from either parent?

The dominant gene for right-handedness, R, is complemented by a recessive gene, r (Francks et al., 2007). You might think that the phenotype of an individual who receives a copy of r from both parents would include left-handedness, but, in reality, the phenotype that is associated with rr is *non-handedness*. In individuals with the rr genotype, learning shapes handedness. Because most people are right-handed, and the tools that humans have developed for use in fine motor activities (e.g., scissors) favor righties, there is a considerable amount of cultural pressure on those who lack innate handedness, those with the genotype rr, to become right-handed. Nevertheless, some of them do develop left-handedness. Why?

Researchers believe that other genes come into play as well. Specifically, if a person possesses genes that cause language functions to lateralize to her right rather than her left cerebral hemisphere, then she is also likely to be left-handed. Here again, the lateralization of handedness follows the lateralization of language function. To make matters more complicated, in 2007, scientists discovered a gene that pushes us in the direction of left-handedness when we receive it from our fathers. When we get the gene from our mothers, it seems to have no influence on hand dominance (Francks et al., 2007).

Finally, although genetics appears to play a complex, but important, role in the development of hand preferences, the capacity of individuals to adapt to severe injuries to or the loss of the dominant hand demonstrates the adaptability of the brain with regard to motor functions. Thus, as the trait of hand preference illustrates, nature and nurture are often linked in complex ways. Remember this the next time you are involved in a debate with someone about whether a given trait is *either* genetic *or* learned.

The Right Hemisphere. The right hemisphere is generally considered to be the hemisphere more adept at visual-spatial relations. And the auditory cortex in the right hemisphere appears to be far better able to process music than the left (Zatorre, Belin, & Penhune, 2002). When you arrange your bedroom furniture or notice that your favorite song is being played on the radio, you are relying primarily on your right hemisphere.

The right hemisphere also augments the left hemisphere's language-processing activities. For example, it produces the unusual verbal associations characteristic of creative thought and problem solving (Kounios et al., 2008). As Van Lancker (1987) pointed out, "although the left hemisphere knows best what is being said, the right hemisphere figures out how it is meant and who is saying it" (p. 13). It is the right hemisphere that is able to understand familiar idiomatic expressions, such as "She let the cat out of the bag."

To experience an effect of the specialization of the cerebral hemispheres, try your hand at the *Try It* below.

People with right hemisphere damage may have difficulty understanding metaphors or orienting spatially, as in finding their way around, even in familiar surroundings. They may have attentional deficits and be unaware of objects in the left visual field, a condition called *unilateral neglect* (Saevarsson, Kristiansson, & Hjaltason, 2009). People with this condition may eat only the food on the right side of a plate, read only the words on the right half of a page, groom only the right half of the body, or even deny that the arm on the side opposite the brain damage belongs to them. Researchers have found that a treatment combining visual training with forced movement of limbs on the neglected side helps some people (Brunila et al., 2002).

As you read earlier, the left hemisphere processes the linguistic aspects of speech. However, researchers have found that the processing of natural language involves an interaction between the two halves of the brain in which the right hemisphere carries out a number of critical functions (Berckmoes & Vingerhoets, 2004). One such function is the comprehension of causal links between statements such as "I fell off my bicycle yesterday. My knee is killing me" (Mason & Just, 2004). The right hemisphere also responds to the emotional message conveyed by another's tone of voice (LeDoux, 2000). Reading and interpreting nonverbal behavior, such as gestures and facial expressions, is another right hemisphere task (Hauser, 1993; Kucharska-Pietura & Klimkowski, 2002). For example, the subtle clues that tell us someone is lying (such as excessive blinking or lack of eye contact) are processed in the right hemisphere (Etcoff et al., 2000). Figure 2.10 summarizes the functions associated with the left and right hemispheres.

right hemisphere The hemisphere that controls the left side of the body and, in most people, is specialized for visual-spatial perception.

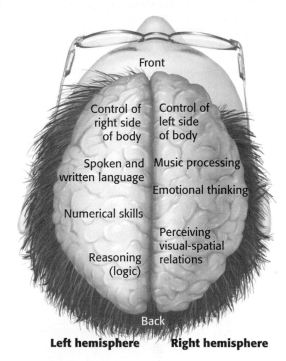

FIGURE 2.10 Lateralized Functions of the Brain
Assigning functions to one hemisphere or the other allows the brain to function more efficiently.
Source: Based on Gazzaniga (1983).

TRY IT ▶ **A Balancing Act**

Get a meter stick or yardstick. Try balancing it vertically on the end of your left index finger, as shown in the drawing. Then try balancing it on your right index finger. Most people are better with their dominant hand—the right hand for right-handers, for example. Is this true for you?

Now try this: Begin reciting the ABCs out loud as fast as you can while balancing the stick with your left hand. Do you have less trouble this time? Why should that be? The right hemisphere controls the act of balancing with the left hand. However, your left hemisphere, though poor at controlling the left hand, still tries to coordinate your balancing efforts. When you distract the left hemisphere with a steady stream of talk, the right hemisphere can orchestrate more efficient balancing with your left hand without interference.

👁 Watch on **mypsychlab.com**

split-brain operation A surgical procedure, performed to treat severe cases of epilepsy, in which the corpus callosum is cut, separating the cerebral hemispheres.

FIGURE 2.11 Testing a Split-Brain Person
Using special equipment, researchers are able to study the independent functioning of the hemispheres in split-brain patients. In this experiment, when a visual image (an orange) is flashed on the right side of the screen, it is transmitted to the left (talking) hemisphere. When asked what he sees, the split-brain patient replies, "I see an orange." When an image (an apple) is flashed on the left side of the screen, it is transmitted only to the right (nonverbal) hemisphere. Because the split-brain patient's left (language) hemisphere did not receive the image, he replies, "I see nothing." But he can pick out the apple by touch if he uses his left hand, proving that the right hemisphere "saw" the apple.
Source: Based on Gazzaniga (1983).

The Split Brain. A great deal of knowledge about lateralization has been gained from studies involving individuals in whom the corpus callosum is absent or has been surgically modified. Many such individuals have had their corpus callosum severed in a drastic surgical procedure called the split-brain operation. Neurosurgeons Joseph Bogen and Philip Vogel (1963) found that people with severe epilepsy, who had frequent and uncontrollable grand mal seizures, could be helped by surgery that severed their corpus callosum, rendering communication between the two hemispheres impossible. The operation decreases the frequency of seizures in two-thirds of such people and causes minimal loss of cognitive functioning or change in personality (Washington University School of Medicine, 2003).

Research with split-brain patients by Roger Sperry (1964) and colleagues Michael Gazzaniga (1970, 1989) and Jerre Levy (1985) expanded knowledge of the unique capabilities of the individual hemispheres. Sperry (1968) found that when the brain was surgically separated, each hemisphere continued to have individual and private experiences, sensations, thoughts, and perceptions. However, most sensory experiences are shared almost simultaneously because each ear and eye has direct sensory connections to both hemispheres.

Sperry's research, for which he won a Nobel Prize in medicine in 1981, revealed some fascinating findings. In Figure 2.11, a split-brain patient sits in front of a screen that separates the right and left fields of vision. If an orange is flashed to the right field of vision, it will register in the left (verbal) hemisphere. If asked what he saw, the patient will readily reply, "I saw an orange." Suppose that, instead, an apple is flashed to the left visual field and is relayed to the right (nonverbal) hemisphere. The patient will reply, "I saw nothing."

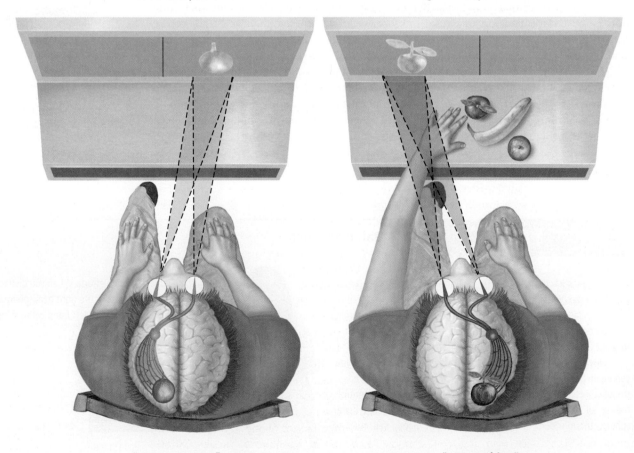

Left Hemisphere   Right Hemisphere

"I see an orange."   "I see nothing."

Why could the patient report that he saw the orange but not the apple? Sperry (1964, 1968) maintains that in split-brain patients, only the verbal left hemisphere can report what it sees. In these experiments, the left hemisphere does not see what is flashed to the right hemisphere, and the right hemisphere is unable to report verbally what it has viewed. But did the right hemisphere actually see the apple that was flashed in the left visual field? Yes, because with his left hand (which is controlled by the right hemisphere), the patient can pick out from behind a screen the apple or any other object shown to the right hemisphere. The right hemisphere knows and remembers what it sees just as well as the left, but unlike the left hemisphere, the right cannot name what it has seen. (In these experiments, images must be flashed for no more than $1/10$ or $2/10$ of a second so that the subjects do not have time to refixate their eyes and send the information to the opposite hemisphere.)

The Four Cerebral Lobes ▶

Each of the cerebral hemispheres has four further divisions. These divisions, or *lobes*, are named for the skull bones to which they are adjacent, the *frontal*, *parietal*, *occipital*, and *temporal* bones (see Figure 2.12 on p. 54). Each lobe is responsible for a different set of functions.

The Frontal Lobes. The largest of the brain's lobes, the frontal lobes, begin at the front of the brain and extend to the top center of the skull. They contain the motor cortex, Broca's area, and the frontal association areas.

The motor cortex is the area that controls voluntary body movement (refer to Figure 2.12). The right motor cortex controls movement on the left side of the body, and the left motor cortex controls movement on the right side of the body. In 1937, Canadian neurosurgeon Wilder Penfield applied electrical stimulation to the motor cortex of conscious human patients undergoing neurosurgery. He then mapped the primary motor cortex in humans. The parts of the body that are capable of the most finely coordinated movements, such as the fingers, lips, and tongue, have a larger share of the motor cortex. Movements in the lower parts of the body are controlled primarily by neurons at the top of the motor cortex, whereas movements in the upper body parts (face, lips, and tongue) are controlled mainly by neurons near the bottom of the motor cortex. For example, when you wiggle your right big toe, the movement is produced mainly by the firing of a cluster of brain cells at the top of the left motor cortex.

How accurately and completely does Penfield's map account for the control of body movement? Although it may be useful in a broad sense, more recent research has shown that there is not a precise one-to-one correspondence between specific points on the motor cortex and movement of particular body parts. Motor neurons that control the fingers, for example, play a role in the movement of more than a single finger. In fact, the control of movement of any single finger is handled by a network of neurons that are widely distributed over the entire hand area of the motor cortex (Sanes & Donoghue, 2000; Sanes et al., 1995; Schieber & Hibbard, 1993).

In 1861, physician Paul Broca performed autopsies on two patients—one who had been totally without speech and another who could say only four words (Jenkins et al., 1975). Broca found that both individuals had damage in the left hemisphere, slightly in front of the part of the motor cortex that controls movements of the jaw, lips, and tongue. He concluded that the site of left hemisphere damage he identified through the autopsies was the part of the brain responsible for speech production, now called Broca's area (refer to Figure 2.12). Broca's area is involved in directing the pattern of muscle movement required to produce speech sounds.

If Broca's area is damaged as a result of head injury or stroke, Broca's aphasia may result. Aphasia is a general term for a loss or impairment of the ability to use or understand language, resulting from damage to the brain (Kirshner & Jacobs, 2008). Characteristically, patients with Broca's aphasia know what they want to say but can

frontal lobes The largest of the brain's lobes, which contain the motor cortex, Broca's area, and the frontal association areas.

motor cortex The strip of tissue at the rear of the frontal lobes that controls voluntary body movement and participates in learning and cognitive events.

Broca's area (BRO-kuz) The area in the frontal lobe, usually in the left hemisphere, that controls the production of speech sounds.

Broca's aphasia (BRO-kuz uh-FAY-zyah) An impairment in the physical ability to produce speech sounds or, in extreme cases, an inability to speak at all; caused by damage to Broca's area.

aphasia (uh-FAY-zyah) A loss or impairment of the ability to use or understand language, resulting from damage to the brain.

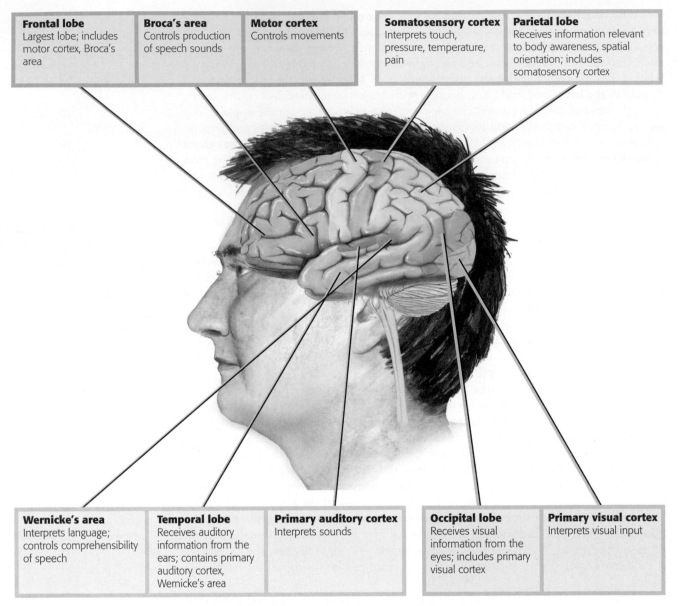

| **Frontal lobe**
Largest lobe; includes motor cortex, Broca's area | **Broca's area**
Controls production of speech sounds | **Motor cortex**
Controls movements | **Somatosensory cortex**
Interprets touch, pressure, temperature, pain | **Parietal lobe**
Receives information relevant to body awareness, spatial orientation; includes somatosensory cortex |

| **Wernicke's area**
Interprets language; controls comprehensibility of speech | **Temporal lobe**
Receives auditory information from the ears; contains primary auditory cortex, Wernicke's area | **Primary auditory cortex**
Interprets sounds | **Occipital lobe**
Receives visual information from the eyes; includes primary visual cortex | **Primary visual cortex**
Interprets visual input |

FIGURE 2.12 The Four Lobes of the Cerebral Cortex
This illustration of the left cerebral hemisphere shows the four lobes: (1) the frontal lobe, including the motor cortex and Broca's area; (2) the parietal lobe, with the somatosensory cortex; (3) the occipital lobe, with the primary visual cortex; and (4) the temporal lobe, with the primary auditory cortex and Wernicke's area.

speak very little or not at all. If they are able to speak, their words are produced very slowly, with great effort, and are poorly articulated.

Much of the frontal lobes consists of association areas involved in thinking, motivation, planning for the future, impulse control, and emotional responses (Stuss et al., 1992). Damage to the frontal association areas produces deficiencies in the ability to plan and anticipate the consequences of actions. One of the best known cases involving this type of damage, that of the unfortunate railroad construction worker Phineas Gage, took place on September 13, 1848. Twenty-five-year-old Gage was using dynamite to blast rocks and dirt out of the pathway of the railroad tracks he was helping to lay that would connect the east and west coasts of the United States by rail. Suddenly, an unplanned explosion sent a 3-foot-long, 13-point metal rod under his left cheekbone and out through the top of his skull. Much of the brain tissue in his frontal lobe was torn away, and he was rendered unconscious for a few minutes. A few weeks later, Gage appeared to be fully recovered. However, prior to the accident, Gage had been an easygoing fellow. Afterward, he was rude and impulsive. His changed personality cost him his job, and he lived out the rest of his life as a circus sideshow exhibit (adapted from Harlow, 1848).

The Parietal Lobes. The parietal lobes lie directly behind the frontal lobes, in the top middle portion of the brain (refer back to Figure 2.12). The parietal lobes are involved in the reception and processing of touch stimuli. The front strip of brain tissue in the parietal lobes is the somatosensory cortex, the site where touch, pressure, temperature, and pain register in the cerebral cortex (Stea & Apkarian, 1992). The somatosensory cortex also makes you aware of movement in your body and the positions of your body parts at any given moment.

The two halves of the somatosensory cortex, in the left and right parietal lobes, are wired to opposite sides of the body. Also, cells at the top of the somatosensory cortex govern feeling in the lower extremities of the body. If you drop a brick on your right foot, the topmost brain cells of the left somatosensory cortex will fire and register the pain sensation. (*Note:* This is *not* a *Try It!*) The large somatosensory areas are connected to sensitive body parts such as the tongue, lips, face, and hand, particularly the thumb and index finger.

Other parts of the parietal lobes are responsible for spatial orientation and sense of direction—for example, helping you to retrace your path when you take a wrong turn. The hippocampus cooperates with these parts of the parietal lobes in performing such functions, as the study of London taxi drivers discussed on page 48 indicates (Maguire et al., 2000). Association areas in the parietal lobes also house memories of how objects feel against the human skin, a fact that explains why we can identify objects by touch. People with damage to these areas could hold a computer mouse, a CD, or a baseball in their hand but not be able to identify the object by touch alone.

The Occipital Lobes. Behind the parietal lobes at the rear of the brain lie the occipital lobes, which are involved in the reception and interpretation of visual information (refer to Figure 2.12). At the very back of the occipital lobes is the primary visual cortex, the site where vision registers in the cortex.

Each eye is connected to the primary visual cortex in both the right and the left occipital lobes. Look straight ahead and draw an imaginary line down the middle of what you see. Everything to the left of the line is referred to as the left visual field and registers in the right visual cortex. Everything to the right of the line is the right visual field and registers in the left visual cortex. A person who sustains damage to one half of the primary visual cortex will still have partial vision in both eyes because each eye sends information to both the right and the left occipital lobes.

The association areas in the occipital lobes are involved in the interpretation of visual stimuli. They hold memories of past visual experiences and enable us to recognize what is familiar among the things we see. That's why the face of a friend stands out in a crowd of unfamiliar people. When these areas are damaged, people can lose the ability to identify objects visually, although they will still be able to identify the same objects by touch or through some other sense.

The Temporal Lobes. The temporal lobes, located slightly above the ears, are involved in the reception and interpretation of auditory stimuli. The site in the cortex where hearing registers is known as the primary auditory cortex. The primary auditory cortex in each temporal lobe receives sound inputs from both ears. Injury to one of these areas results in reduced hearing in both ears, and the destruction of both areas causes total deafness.

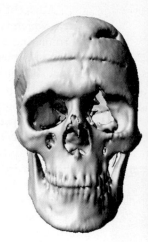

▲ The skull of Phineas Gage is on display at the Warren Anatomical Museum at Harvard University. As you can see, the tamping rod tore through his frontal lobes leaving him with an altered personality.

parietal lobes (puh-RY-uh-tul) The lobes that contain the somatosensory cortex (where touch, pressure, temperature, and pain register) and other areas that are responsible for body awareness and spatial orientation.

somatosensory cortex (so-MAT-oh-SENS-or-ee) The strip of tissue at the front of the parietal lobes where touch, pressure, temperature, and pain register in the cerebral cortex.

occipital lobes (ahk-SIP-uh-tul) The lobes that are involved in the reception and interpretation of visual information; they contain the primary visual cortex.

primary visual cortex The area at the rear of the occipital lobes where vision registers in the cerebral cortex.

temporal lobes The lobes that are involved in the reception and interpretation of auditory information; they contain the primary auditory cortex, Wernicke's area, and the temporal association areas.

primary auditory cortex The part of each temporal lobe where hearing registers in the cerebral cortex.

Wernicke's area (VUR-nih-keys) The language area in the left temporal lobe involved in comprehending the spoken word and in formulating coherent speech and written language.

Wernicke's aphasia Aphasia that results from damage to Wernicke's area and in which the person's speech is fluent and clearly articulated but does not make sense to listeners.

Adjacent to the primary auditory cortex in the left temporal lobe is Wernicke's area, which is the language area involved in comprehending the spoken word and in formulating coherent written and spoken language (refer to Figure 2.12). When you listen to someone speak, the sound registers first in the primary auditory cortex. The sound is then sent to Wernicke's area, where the speech sounds are unscrambled into meaningful patterns of words.

Wernicke's aphasia is a type of aphasia resulting from damage to Wernicke's area. Although speech is fluent and words are clearly articulated, the actual message does not make sense to listeners (Kirshner & Jacobs, 2008). The content may be vague or bizarre and may contain inappropriate words, parts of words, or a gibberish of non-existent words. One Wernicke's patient, when asked how he was feeling, replied, "I think that there's an awful lot of mung, but I think I've a lot of net and tunged in a little wheat duhvayden" (Buckingham & Kertesz, 1974). People with Wernicke's aphasia are not aware that anything is wrong with their speech. Thus, this disorder is difficult to treat.

The remainder of the temporal lobes consists of the association areas that house memories and are involved in the interpretation of auditory stimuli. For example, the association area where your memories of various sounds are stored enables you to recognize the sounds of your favorite band, a computer booting up, your roommate snoring, and so on. There is also a special association area where familiar melodies are stored.

▲ Because the left hand of a professional string player like Boyd Tinsley of the Dave Matthews Band must rapidly and accurately execute fine movements and slight pressure variations, it is not surprising that these musicians have an unusually large area of the somatosensory cortex dedicated to the fingers of that hand.

2.11 How does the brain change across the lifespan?

pruning The process through which the developing brain eliminates unnecessary or redundant synapses.

Age, Gender, and the Brain

How many adults express concern that the moon might be following them? It is likely that you have never heard an adult express such a concern. Nevertheless, it is one of several irrational worries that are frequently expressed by preschoolers. Nowadays, most people have heard something about the link between brain development and such differences in children's and adults' thinking. And it is common to hear people attribute the cognitive deficits displayed by some elderly people to deterioration of their brains. Likewise, interest never seems to wane in the idea that men's and women's brains process information differently. What is the evidence regarding these popular notions about age and gender differences in the brain?

The Ever-Changing Brain

When do you think the brain reaches full maturity? The answer to this question might surprise you. In fact, the brain grows in spurts from conception until well into adulthood (Fischer & Rose, 1994). In childhood and adolescence, many of these spurts are correlated with major advances in physical and intellectual skills, such as the acquisition of fluency in language that happens around age 4 for most children. Each growth spurt also seems to involve a different brain area. For example, the spurt that begins around age 17 and continues into the early 20s mainly affects the frontal lobes, where the abilities to plan and to control one's emotions are located. Differences between teens and adults in these abilities may be due to this growth spurt. Changes in brain function are influenced by several development processes.

Synapses develop as a result of the growth of both dendrites and axons. This process, known as *synaptogenesis,* occurs in spurts throughout the life span. Each spurt is followed by a period of pruning, the process through which the developing brain eliminates unnecessary or redundant synapses. The activity of neurotransmitters within the synapses also varies with age. For example, acetylcholine is less plentiful in the brains of children than in the brains of teens and adults. This difference may help explain age differences in memory and other functions influenced by this excitatory neurotransmitter.

The process of *myelination,* or the development of myelin sheaths around axons, begins prior to birth but continues well into adulthood. For example, the brain's association areas are not fully myelinated until age 12 or so (Tanner, 1990). And the reticular formation, which regulates attention, isn't fully myelinated until the mid-20s (Spreen et al., 1995). Thus, differences in myelination may account for differences between children and adults in processing speed, memory, and other functions.

Some degree of hemispheric specialization is present very early in life. Language processing, for example, occurs primarily in the left hemisphere of the fetal and infant brain, just as it does in the adult brain (Chilosi et al., 2001; de Lacoste et al., 1991). Other functions, such as spatial perception, aren't lateralized until age 8 or so. Consequently, children younger than age 8 exhibit much poorer spatial skills than do older children (Roberts & Bell, 2000). For instance, children younger than 8 have difficulty using maps and distinguishing between statements such as *It's on your left* and *It's on my left.*

The brain's plasticity—its capacity to adapt to changes such as brain damage—is maintained throughout life. This plasticity allows synapses to strengthen and reorganize their interconnections when stimulated by experience and practice. Plasticity is greatest in young children within whom the hemispheres are not yet completely lateralized. However, researchers have found that the correction of hearing defects in late-middle-aged adults results in changes in all the areas of the brain that are involved in sound perception (Fallon, Irvine, & Shepherd, 2008). Moreover, the brains of these individuals appear to develop responses to sounds in areas in which the brains of people with normal hearing do not.

Despite the retention of some degree of plasticity, the brain is subject to the physical effects of aging. For example, the brain both gains and loses synapses throughout life. At some point in adulthood, however, losses begin to exceed gains (Huttenlocher, 1994). Brain weight begins to decline around age 30 (Raz et al., 2006). Age-related deficits due to the loss of brain weight are common. For example, elderly people tend to experience problems with balance, they become less steady on their feet, and their gait is affected.

In addition, as you will learn in Chapter 10, the health of the heart and blood vessels often deteriorates as adults get older. With this deterioration comes an increased risk of stroke, an event in the cardiovascular system in which a blood clot or plug of fat blocks an artery and cuts off the blood supply to a particular area of the brain. Strokes cause brain damage that can range from mild to severe. Some survivors have long-term intellectual and physical impairments. However, physical therapy can help most of them recover at least partial motor functions, providing yet another example of the brain's plasticity (Bruno-Petrina, 2009).

plasticity The capacity of the brain to adapt to changes such as brain damage.

stroke An event in the cardiovascular system in which a blood clot or plug of fat blocks an artery and cuts off the blood supply to a particular area of the brain.

Gender Differences in the Brain ▶

[**2.12 How do the brains of men and women differ?**

Throughout development, the brains of males and females differ to some degree. However, these differences and their possible links to behavior have been most thoroughly researched among adults. One such difference is that the brains of men have a higher proportion of white matter than do the brains of women (Gur et al., 1999). Moreover, men have a lower proportion of white matter in the left brain than in the right brain. In contrast, in women's brains, the proportions of gray matter and white matter in the two hemispheres are equivalent. Such findings have led some neuropsychologists to speculate that gender differences in the distribution of gray and white matter across the two hemispheres may explain men's superior performance on right-hemisphere tasks such as mental rotation of geometric figures. Likewise, women's superior abilities in the domain of emotional perception (more on this in Chapter 9) may be attributable to the fact that they have more gray matter than men do in the area of the brain that controls emotions (Gur et al., 2002).

Other research has revealed that some tasks stimulate different parts of the brain in men and women. For example, imaging studies have shown that men process navigational information, such as that needed to find the way out of a maze, in the left hippocampus. By contrast, women who are engaged in the same task use the right parietal cortex and the right frontal cortex (Gron et al., 2000). Similarly, studies show that men and women use different areas of the brain when searching for the location of a sound (Lewald, 2004).

What is the meaning of these gender differences in the brain? The short answer is that scientists won't know for certain until a great deal more research is done. Moreover, studies that look for links between these brain differences and actual behavior are needed before any conclusions can be drawn regarding the possible neurological bases for gender differences in behavior.

Beyond the Nervous System

The body has two additional systems that influence how we function both physically and psychologically. The glands of the *endocrine system* exert their influences by producing, secreting, and regulating *hormones*. By contrast, in some cases, information encoded in our *genes* affects us from the moment of conception; in others, the influences of the genes appear later in life or depend on input from the environment.

2.13 What are the functions of the glands of the endocrine system?

The Endocrine System

Most people think of the reproductive system when they hear the word *hormones*. Or they may associate hormones with particular physical changes, such as those of puberty, pregnancy, or menopause. However, these substances regulate many other physical and psychological functions, and their influence reaches far beyond the reproductive system.

The endocrine system is a series of ductless glands, located in various parts of the body, that manufacture and secrete the chemical substances known as hormones, which are manufactured and released in one part of the body but have an effect on other parts of the body. Hormones are released into the bloodstream and travel throughout the circulatory system, but each hormone performs its assigned job only when it connects with the body cells that have receptors for it. Some of the same chemical substances that are neurotransmitters act as hormones as well—norepinephrine and vasopressin, to name two. Figure 2.13 shows the glands in the endocrine system and their locations in the body.

The pituitary gland rests in the brain just below the hypothalamus and is controlled by it (see Figure 2.13). The pituitary is considered to be the "master gland" of the body because it releases the hormones that activate, or turn on, the other glands in the endocrine system—a big job for a tiny structure about the size of a pea. The pituitary also produces the hormone that is responsible for body growth (Howard et al., 1996). Too little of this powerful substance will make a person a dwarf; too much will produce a giant.

The pineal gland lies deep within the brain. Its function is to produce and regulate the hormone *melatonin*. As you will learn in Chapter 4, this hormone regulates sleep and wakefulness. Deficiencies are associated with jet lag and other disturbances of the sleep/wakefulness cycle.

The thyroid gland rests in the front, lower part of the neck just below the voice box (larynx). The thyroid produces the important hormone thyroxine, which regulates the rate at which food is metabolized, or transformed into energy. The parathyroid glands are attached to the left and right lobes of the thyroid. Parathyroid hormone (PTH) is involved in the absorption of calcium and magnesium from the diet and regulates the levels of these minerals in the bloodstream. Dysfunctions of the parathyroid are also linked to depression and memory loss (Kim & Makdissi, 2009).

endocrine system (EN-duh-krin) A system of ductless glands in various parts of the body that manufacture hormones and secrete them into the bloodstream, thus affecting cells in other parts of the body.

hormone A chemical substance that is manufactured and released in one part of the body and affects other parts of the body.

pituitary gland The endocrine gland located in the brain that releases hormones that activate other endocrine glands as well as growth hormone; often called the "master gland."

pineal gland The endocrine gland that secretes the hormone that controls the sleep/wakefulness cycle.

thyroid gland The endocrine gland that produces thyroxine and regulates metabolism.

parathyroid glands The endocrine glands that produce PTH, a hormone that helps the body absorb minerals from the diet.

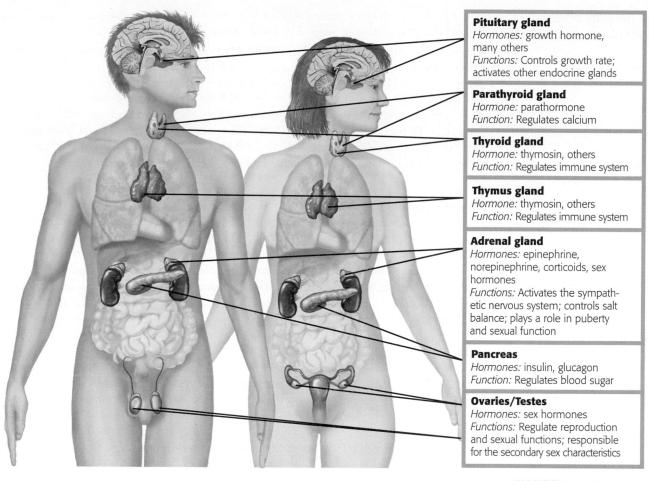

Pituitary gland
Hormones: growth hormone, many others
Functions: Controls growth rate; activates other endocrine glands

Parathyroid gland
Hormone: parathormone
Function: Regulates calcium

Thyroid gland
Hormone: thymosin, others
Function: Regulates immune system

Thymus gland
Hormone: thymosin, others
Function: Regulates immune system

Adrenal gland
Hormones: epinephrine, norepinephrine, corticoids, sex hormones
Functions: Activates the sympathetic nervous system; controls salt balance; plays a role in puberty and sexual function

Pancreas
Hormones: insulin, glucagon
Function: Regulates blood sugar

Ovaries/Testes
Hormones: sex hormones
Functions: Regulate reproduction and sexual functions; responsible for the secondary sex characteristics

FIGURE 2.13 The Endocrine System
The endocrine system is a series of glands that manufacture and secrete hormones. The hormones travel through the circulatory system and have important effects on many bodily functions.

The thymus gland, as you will learn in Chapter 10, produces hormones such as thymosin that are needed for the production of specialized white blood cells that circulate throughout the body and destroy microorganisms that can cause diseases. When the body is threatened by one of these invaders, the thymus gland signals the body to produce more of these cells. The pancreas regulates the body's blood sugar levels by releasing the hormones insulin and glucagon into the bloodstream. In people with diabetes, too little insulin is produced. Without insulin to break down the sugars in food, blood-sugar levels can get dangerously high.

The two adrenal glands, which rest just above the kidneys (as shown in Figure 2.13), produce epinephrine and norepinephrine. By activating the sympathetic nervous system, these two hormones play an important role in the fight-or-flight syndrome. A group of adrenal hormones called the corticoids are also involved in the fight-or-flight syndrome. Animal research suggests that these hormones contribute to both the emotion of rage and aggressive behavior by signaling the brain to maintain the fight-or-flight response long after the threat that initiated the response has passed (Kruk et al., 2004).

The adrenals also produce small amounts of sex hormones. However, the gonads—the ovaries in females and the testes in males—have the primary responsibility for these hormones (refer to Figure 2.13). Activated by the pituitary gland, the gonads release the sex hormones that make reproduction possible and that are responsible for the secondary sex characteristics—pubic and underarm hair in both sexes, breasts in females, and facial hair and a deepened voice in males. Androgens, the male sex hormones, influence sexual motivation. Estrogen and progesterone, the female sex hormones, help regulate the menstrual cycle. Although both males and females have androgens and estrogens, males have considerably more androgens, and females have considerably more estrogens. (The sex hormones and their effects are discussed in more detail in Chapter 9.)

thymus gland The endocrine gland that produces hormones that are essential to immune system functioning.

pancreas The endocrine gland responsible for regulating the amount of sugar in the bloodstream.

adrenal glands (ah-DREE-nal) A pair of endocrine glands that release hormones that prepare the body for emergencies and stressful situations and also release corticoids and small amounts of the sex hormones.

gonads The ovaries in females and the testes in males; endocrine glands that produce sex hormones.

2.14 **How does heredity affect physical and psychological traits?**

Genes and Behavioral Genetics

You may have heard of the Human Genome Project, a 13-year enterprise spearheaded by the U.S. Department of Energy and devoted to mapping the entire human genetic code. Remarkably, in April 2003, only 50 years after scientists James Watson and Francis Crick discovered the structure of DNA (of which genes consist), the international team of scientists involved in the project announced that they had achieved their goal (U.S. Department of Energy, 2009). Of course, you received your own genetic code from your parents. But just how do the chemical messages that make up your genes affect your body and your behavior? ◉⎯|Watch on **mypsychlab.com**

◉⎯|**Watch** the **Video** *How the Human Genome Affects You* on **mypsychlab.com**

genes The segments of DNA that are located on the chromosomes and are the basic units for the transmission of all hereditary traits.

chromosomes Rod-shaped structures in the nuclei of body cells, which contain all the genes and carry all the genetic information necessary to make a human being.

The Mechanisms of Heredity. Genes are segments of DNA located on rod-shaped structures called chromosomes. The nuclei of normal body cells, with two exceptions, have 23 pairs of chromosomes (46 in all). The two exceptions are the sperm and egg cells, each of which has 23 single chromosomes. At conception, the sperm adds its 23 chromosomes to the 23 of the egg. From this union, a single cell called a *zygote* is formed; it has the full complement of 46 chromosomes (23 pairs), which contain about 20,000 to 25,000 genes (U.S. Department of Energy, 2009). These genes carry all the genetic information needed to make a human being. The Human Genome Project is aimed at identifying the functions of all the genes and their locations on the chromosomes.

Twenty-two of the 23 pairs of chromosomes are matching pairs, called *autosomes,* and each member of these pairs carries genes for particular physical and mental traits. The chromosomes in the 23rd pair are called *sex chromosomes* because they carry the genes that determine a person's sex. The sex chromosomes of females consist of two X chromosomes (XX); males have an X chromosome and a Y chromosome (XY). The egg cell always contains an X chromosome. Half of a man's sperm cells carry an X chromosome, and half carry a Y. Thus, the sex of an individual depends on which type of chromosome is carried by the sperm that fertilizes the egg. A single gene found only on the Y chromosome causes a fetus to become a male. This gene, which has been labeled Sry, orchestrates the development of the male sex organs (Capel, 2000).

genotype An individual's genetic makeup.

phenotype An individual's actual characteristics.

Our individual genetic codes include some genes that are expressed and some that are not expressed. For example, some people carry the gene for a disease but do not have the disorder associated with it. To help distinguish genetic traits that are expressed from those that are not expressed, scientists use the term genotype to refer to an individual's genetic makeup and phenotype to refer to his or her actual traits. Thus, if a person carries the gene for a disease but does not have it, the disease is part of her genotype but not part of her phenotype. The *Apply It* feature (p. 62) outlines some situations in which you might consider genetic counseling. Scientists still do not fully understand all of the factors that govern the expression of genes. However, a few of the rules that determine which aspects of an individual's genotype are expressed in her phenotype have been well established by research.

dominant-recessive pattern A set of inheritance rules in which the presence of a single dominant gene causes a trait to be expressed but two genes must be present for the expression of a recessive trait.

Many traits are influenced by complementary gene pairs, one from the sperm and the other from the egg. In most cases, these gene pairs follow a set of inheritance rules known as the dominant-recessive pattern. The gene for curly hair, for example, is dominant over the gene for straight hair. Thus, a person having one gene for curly hair and one for straight hair will have curly hair, and people with straight hair have two recessive genes.

Several neurological and psychological characteristics are associated with dominant or recessive genes. Hand preference appears to follow the dominant recessive pattern, although in a somewhat complex way, as discussed in the *Explain It* on page 50. However, most of the traits of interest to psychologists follow more complex inheritance patterns.

In polygenic inheritance, many genes influence a particular characteristic. For example, skin color is determined by several genes. When one parent has dark skin and the other is fair skinned, the child will have skin that is somewhere between the two. Many polygenic characteristics are subject to multifactorial inheritance; that is, they are influenced by both genes and environmental factors. For instance, a man's genes may allow him to reach a height of 6 feet, but if he suffers from malnutrition while still growing, his height may not reach its genetic potential. As you'll learn in later chapters, both intelligence (Chapter 7) and personality (Chapter 11) are believed to be polygenic and multifactorial in nature. In addition, many psychological disorders are both polygenic and multifactorial (Leonardo & Hen, 2006; McMahon et al., 2010).

Sex-linked inheritance involves the genes on the X and Y chromosomes. In females, the two X chromosomes function pretty much like the autosomes: If one carries a harmful gene, the other usually has a gene that offsets its effects. In males, however, if the single X chromosome carries a harmful gene, there is no offsetting gene on the Y chromosome because it is very small and carries only the genes needed to create the male body type. Consequently, disorders caused by genes on the X chromosome occur far more often in males than in females. For example, one fairly common sex-linked disorder you will read about in Chapter 3 is *red-green color blindness*. About 5% of men have the disorder, but less than 1% of women have it (Mather, 2006). About 1 in every 4,000 males and 1 in every 8,000 females have a far more serious sex-linked disorder called *fragile-X syndrome*, which can cause mental retardation (Jewell, 2009).

Behavioral Genetics. Behavioral genetics is a field of research that investigates the relative effects of heredity and environment—nature and nurture—on behavior (Loehlin, 2009). In twin studies, behavioral geneticists study identical twins (monozygotic twins) and fraternal twins (dizygotic twins) to determine how much they resemble each other on a variety of characteristics (Johnson, Turkheimer, Gorresman, & Bouchard, 2009). Identical twins have exactly the same genes because a single sperm of the father fertilizes a single egg of the mother, forming a cell that then splits and forms two human beings—"carbon copies." In the case of fraternal twins, two separate sperm cells fertilize two separate eggs that happen to be released at the same time during ovulation. Fraternal twins are no more alike genetically than any two siblings born to the same parents.

Twins who are raised together, whether identical or fraternal, have similar environments. If identical twins raised together are found to be more alike on a certain trait than fraternal twins raised together, then that trait is assumed to be more influenced by heredity. But if the identical and fraternal twin pairs do not differ on the trait, then that trait is assumed to be influenced more by environment.

In adoption studies, behavioral geneticists study children adopted shortly after birth. Researchers compare the children's abilities and personality traits to those of their adoptive parents and those of their biological parents. This strategy allows researchers to disentangle the effects of heredity and environment (Plomin, DeFries, & Fulker, 1988).

Because heredity and environment work together to influence so many of the variables of interest to psychologists, you'll be reading a great deal more in later chapters about the debate concerning their relative influence.

▲ This child's *phenotype* includes curly hair. What can you infer about her *genotype*? How likely is it that neither of her parents has curly hair?

polygenic inheritance A pattern of inheritance in which many genes influence a trait.

multifactorial inheritance A pattern of inheritance in which a trait is influenced by both genes and environmental factors.

behavioral genetics A field of research that uses twin studies and adoption studies to investigate the relative effects of heredity and environment on behavior.

Should You Consult a Genetic Counselor?

The purpose of genetic counseling is to estimate individuals' risk of having a child with a genetic disorder or of developing an inherited disorder themselves. If you have relatives who have such disorders, you may have wondered whether you should seek genetic counseling. Such counseling can be helpful to just about anyone, but there are a few situations in which professionals advise that genetic counseling is especially important.

Birth Defects and Inherited Diseases of Childhood

As you may know, prenatal testing can identify many birth defects and genetic disorders before a child is born. However, experts say that screening for such risks should be done prior to conception if any of the following applies to you or your partner (Brundage, 2002):

- You or your partner has previously had a child with a birth defect (e.g., spina bifida) or an inherited disorder (e.g., phenylketonuria).
- There is someone in your or your partner's family who displayed an unexplained developmental delay or disability (i.e., visual or hearing impairment, mental retardation) early in life.
- You or your partner belongs to an ethnic group in which there is a particularly high incidence of a specific inherited disorder (e.g., African Americans: sickle cell disease; European Jews: Tay-Sachs disease; Caucasians: cystic fibrosis; people of Greek, Middle Eastern, or North African descent: thalassemia.)

Adult-Onset Genetic Disorders

Genetic counselors suggest that you seriously consider genetic counseling if anyone in your family has ever been diagnosed with one of these adult-onset genetic disorders:

- Huntington disease
- Myotonic muscular dystrophy
- Amyotrophic lateral sclerosis (ALS, Lou Gehrig disease)
- Schizophrenia

Hereditary Cancers

If someone in your family has been diagnosed with cancer, then genetic counseling can be helpful in determining your own risk of developing the disease. According to the Massey Cancer Center at Virginia Commonwealth University (2006), the following types of family histories are especially indicative of a need for genetic counseling:

- A family history of multiple cases of the same or related types of cancers
- One or more relatives with rare cancers
- Cancers occurring at an earlier age of onset than usual (for instance, under the age of 50 years) in at least one member

- Bilateral cancers (two cancers that develop independently in a paired organ, i.e., both kidneys or both breasts)
- One or more family members with two primary cancers (two original tumors that develop in different sites)
- Eastern European Jewish background

Multifactorial Disorders

Many chronic health conditions are attributable to a combination of genetic and lifestyle factors. While there are no genetic tests for these disorders, a genetic counselor can analyze your family history and help you determine your risk of developing one or more of them. A genetic counselor can also advise you as to the degree to which lifestyle changes might enable you to avoid some of the effects of a disorder that you have seen diminish the quality of life of one of your family members. Thus, you may want to seek genetic counseling if anyone in your family has been diagnosed with one or more of these multifactorial disorders:

- Adult-onset diabetes
- Hypertension
- Glaucoma
- Heart disease
- Rheumatoid arthritis
- Disorders of the endocrine system (e.g., hypothyroidism, pancreatitis)
- Autoimmune disorders (e.g., lupus, multiple sclerosis)
- Liver or kidney disease
- Depression
- Parkinson disease
- Alzheimer's disease

Making the Decision

Even if these checklists have led you to the conclusion that you should consult a genetic counselor, you may find it difficult to confront the possibility that you or your child may have to deal with a serious health problem. Such feelings are common among individuals whose family members have one of the conditions described above. However, researchers have found that people who are uninformed about their personal genetic vulnerability actually tend to overestimate their chances of developing an inherited disorder (Quaid et al., 2001; Tercyak et al., 2001). Thus, genetic counseling will help you formulate a realistic assessment of your own personal risks and will also enable you to develop a plan for coping with them if a genetic disorder is likely to be in your future.

Looking Back

One of the many things you learned about the nervous system in this chapter is that adaptability is one of its important features. For instance, as the case of Phineas Gage illustrates, many areas of the adult brain are irrevocably committed to certain functions, leaving us with a more vulnerable but more efficient brain than we had as children. Nevertheless, even in the face of devastating injury, the brain may continue to function. The complementary functions of excitatory and inhibitory neurotransmitters enable our brains to respond appropriately to different kinds of situations. Individuals who have split-brain surgery function quite well in everyday life; only in certain kinds of tasks do they show any effects from the loss of interhemispheric communication. When we need to react to an emergency, our endocrine and peripheral nervous systems collaborate to produce the temporary burst of energy we need. Finally, although a few characteristics and diseases are fully determined by our genes, most of our psychological traits are shaped by both heredity and environment, a theme that will be emphasized repeatedly in the coming chapters.

CHAPTER 2 SUMMARY

DISCOVERING THE MYSTERIES OF THE NERVOUS SYSTEM (pp. 36–37)

2.1 What does the electroencephalogram (EEG) reveal about the brain? (p. 36)

An electroencephalogram (EEG) is a record of brain-wave activity. It can reveal an epileptic seizure and can show patterns of neural activity associated with learning disabilities, schizophrenia, Alzheimer's disease, sleep disorders, and other problems.

Key Terms

electroencephalogram (EEG), p. 36
beta wave, p. 36
alpha wave, p. 36
delta wave, p. 36
microelectrode, p. 36

2.2 How do researchers use imaging techniques to study the nervous system? (p. 37)

Both the CT scan and MRI provide detailed images of brain structures. The PET scan reveals patterns of blood flow, oxygen use, and glucose metabolism in the brain. It can also show the action of drugs in the brain and other organs. PET scan studies show that different brain areas are used to perform different tasks. Functional MRI (fMRI) can provide information about brain function and structure more precisely and more rapidly than a PET scan. Two more recently developed technologies, SQUID and MEG, measure magnetic changes to reveal neural activity within the brain as it occurs.

Key Terms

CT scan (computerized axial tomography), p. 37
MRI (magnetic resonance imagery), p. 37
PET scan (positron-emission tomography), p. 37
functional MRI (fMRI), p. 37

THE NEURONS AND THE NEUROTRANSMITTERS (pp. 37–43)

2.3 What does each part of the neuron do? (p. 38)

The cell body carries out metabolic functions. The dendrites receive messages from cell bodies and other neurons. The axon transmits messages to the dendrites and cell bodies of other neurons and to the muscles, glands, and other parts of the body. Glial cells support neurons' vital functions.

Key Terms

neuron, p. 37
neurotransmitters, p. 38
cell body, p. 38
dendrites, p. 38
axon, p. 38
axon terminal, p. 38
glial cells, p. 38

2.4 How do neurons transmit messages through the nervous system? (pp. 38–41)

The action potential, the primary means by which the brain and body communicate with one another via the nervous system, is the sudden reversal (from a negative to a positive value) of the resting potential on the cell membrane of a neuron; this reversal initiates the firing of a neuron. A strong stimulus will cause many more neurons to fire and to fire much more rapidly than a weak stimulus will.

Key Terms

synapse, p. 38
resting potential, p. 39
action potential, p. 39
myelin sheath, p. 41

2.5 How do neurotransmitters work? (pp. 41–43)

Neurotransmitters are chemicals released into the synaptic cleft from the axon terminal of the sending neuron. They cross the synaptic cleft and bind to receptors on the receiving neuron, influencing the cell to fire or not to fire. Neurotransmitters work by speeding up, slowing down, or blocking messages between neurons. Drugs affect the nervous system by altering or mimicking neurotransmitters. Some neurotransmitters contribute to psychological disorders.

Key Terms

receptors, p. 42
reuptake, p. 42

THE HUMAN NERVOUS SYSTEM (pp. 43–48)

2.6 What are the structures and functions of the peripheral nervous system? (pp. 43–45)

The peripheral nervous system includes all of the nerves that connect the various parts of the body to the central nervous system. The somatic subdivision governs voluntary control of the body; the autonomic subdivision governs involuntary processes. Within the autonomic subdivision, the sympathetic nervous system mobilizes the body's resources during emergencies or during stress, and the parasympathetic nervous system brings the heightened bodily responses back to normal after an emergency.

Key Terms
peripheral nervous system, p. 43
central nervous system, p. 43
sympathetic nervous system p. 44
parasympathetic nervous system, p. 44

2.7 What are the structures and functions of the central nervous system? (pp. 45–48)

The spinal cord transmits information from the body to the brain and from the brain to the body. The hindbrain contains the cerebellum, which regulates movement, muscle tone, and posture. The brainstem contains the medulla, which controls vital functions; the reticular formation, which controls arousal and attention; and the pons, which connects the two halves of the cerebellum. The substantia nigra, a structure in the midbrain, controls unconscious motor actions, such as riding a bicycle. The structures of the forebrain include (1) the thalamus, the relay station for information flowing into and out of the brain; (2) the hypothalamus, which regulates hunger, thirst, sexual behavior, internal body temperature, and emotional behaviors; (3) the limbic system, including the amygdala and the hippocampus, which is involved in emotional expression, memory, and motivation. The cerebrum is also part of the forebrain.

Key Terms
spinal cord, p. 45
hindbrain, p. 45
brainstem, p. 45
medulla, p. 45
reticular formation, p. 45
pons, p. 46
cerebellum, p. 46
midbrain, p. 47
substantia nigra, p. 47
forebrain, p. 47
thalamus, p. 47
hypothalamus, p. 47
limbic system, p. 47
amygdala, p. 47
hippocampus, p. 48

A CLOSER LOOK AT THE THINKING PART OF THE BRAIN (pp. 48–56)

2.8 What are the components of the cerebrum? (pp. 48–49)

The cerebral hemispheres are connected by the corpus callosum and covered by the cerebral cortex, which is primarily responsible for higher mental processes such as language, memory, and thinking.

Key Terms
cerebrum, p. 48
cerebral hemispheres, p. 48
corpus callosum, p. 48
cerebral cortex, p. 48
association areas, p. 49

2.9 What are the specialized functions of the left and right cerebral hemispheres? (pp. 49–53)

The left hemisphere controls the right side of the body, coordinates complex movements, and handles most of the language functions, including speaking, writing, reading, and understanding the written and the spoken word. The right hemisphere controls the left side of the body. It is specialized for visual-spatial perception, the interpretation of nonverbal behavior, and the recognition and expression of emotion.

Key Terms
lateralization, p. 49
left hemisphere, p. 50
right hemisphere, p. 51
split-brain operation, p. 52

2.10 Which functions are associated with each of the four lobes of the cerebral cortex? (pp. 53–56)

The frontal lobes contain (1) the motor cortex, which controls voluntary motor activity; (2) Broca's area, which functions in speech production; and (3) the frontal association areas, which are involved in thinking, motivation, planning for the future, impulse control, and emotional responses. The somatosensory cortex, where touch, pressure, temperature, and pain register, is in the parietal lobes. The occipital lobes receive and interpret visual information. The temporal lobes contain

(1) the primary auditory cortex, where hearing registers in the cortex; (2) Wernicke's area, which processes the spoken word and formulates coherent speech and written language; and (3) the temporal association areas, which interpret auditory stimuli.

Key Terms
frontal lobes, p. 53
motor cortex, p. 53
Broca's area, p. 53

Broca's aphasia, p. 53
aphasia, p. 53
parietal lobes, p. 55
somatosensory cortex, p. 55
occipal lobes, p. 55
primary visual cortex, p. 55
temporal lobes, p. 55
primary auditory cortex, p. 55
Wernicke's area, p. 56
Wernicke's aphasia, p. 56

AGE, GENDER, AND THE BRAIN (pp. 56–58)

2.11 How does the brain change across the lifespan? (pp. 56–57)

The brain grows in spurts, each of which is followed by a period of pruning of unnecessary synapses. The activity of neurotransmitters within the synapses also varies with age. Few neurons are myelinated at birth, but the process of myelination continues into the adult years. Language appears to be lateralized very early in life, but other functions, such as spatial perception, aren't fully lateralized until age 8 or so. Aging eventually leads to a reduction in the number of synapses.

Key Terms
pruning, p. 56
plasticity, p. 57
stroke, p. 57

2.12 How do the brains of men and women differ? (pp. 57–58)

Men's brains have a lower proportion of white matter in the left than in the right brain; women have equal proportions of gray and white matter in the two hemispheres. Some tasks tap different areas in men's brains than they do in the brains of women.

BEYOND THE NERVOUS SYSTEM (pp. 58–61)

2.13 What are the functions of the glands of the endocrine system? (pp. 58–59)

The pituitary gland releases hormones that control other glands in the endocrine system and also releases a growth hormone. The thyroid gland produces thyroxine, which regulates metabolism. The pancreas produces insulin and glucagon and regulates blood sugar levels. The adrenal glands release epinephrine and norepinephrine, which prepare the body for emergencies and stressful situations; these glands also release corticoids and small amounts of the sex hormones. The gonads are the sex glands, which produce the sex hormones and make reproduction possible.

Key Terms

endocrine system, p. 58
hormone, p. 58
pituitary gland, p. 58
pineal gland, p. 58
thyroid gland, p. 58
parathyroid glands, p. 58
thymus gland, p. 59

pancreas, p. 59
adrenal glands, p. 59
gonads, p. 59

2.14 How does heredity affect physical and psychological traits? (pp. 60–61)

Some genetic traits follow the dominant-recessive pattern in which pairs of genes control their manifestation. Others involve multiple genes (polygenic), and still others depend on the combined effects of genes and environmental factors (multifactorial). Behavioral geneticists use twin studies to examine the relative effects of heredity and environment on behavior as well as adoption and family studies. Such studies suggest that both intelligence and personality are polygenic and multifactorial.

Key Terms
genes, p. 60
chromosomes, p. 60
genotype, p. 60
phenotype, p. 60
dominant-recessive pattern, p. 60
polygenic inheritance, p. 61
multifactorial inheritance, p. 61
behavioral genetics, p. 61

MAP IT

Log on to MyPsychLab and click on "Map It" to prepare a unique digital map of the chapter that you can save for later use, email to your instructor, or print out to use as a study tool. Or, create your own map by drawing one on paper. Use the starter map below as a model for your own map. Use the chapter summary as your guide for what to include. For each item in your map, be sure to include the page number.

Here's one way to *Map It*:

1. Draw a box at the top of the page for the section title.
2. Underneath the section title box, working horizontally across the page, draw a box for each learning question in the section. Write the learning questions in the boxes and draw a line from the section title to each questions box. After you read each subsection, jot an answer for the learning question in the subsection's box.
3. Below each learning question box, insert another box for all of the key terms that are related to the question, along with a very brief reminder of each term's definition. Draw a line from the question box to the key terms box.
4. Below each key terms box, create another box and list all of the helpful figures, tables, and other elements of the text, such as *Try It* and *Apply It* boxes. Draw a line from the key terms box to the helpful elements box.

 Map the **Chapter** on **mypsychlab.com**

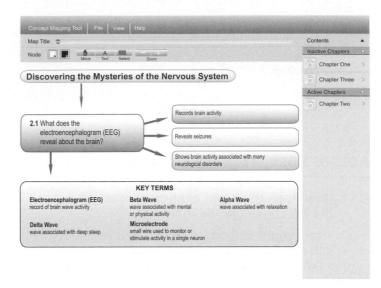

Chapter 2 Study Guide

Answers to all the Study Guide questions are provided at the end of the book.

SECTION ONE: Chapter Review

Discovering the Mysteries of The Nervous System (pp. 36–37)

1. Match the brain-wave pattern with the state associated with it.
_____ **(1)** slow-wave (deep) sleep
_____ **(2)** deep relaxation while awake
_____ **(3)** physical or mental activity

  a. beta wave   **c.** alpha wave
  b. delta wave

2. The CT scan and MRI are used to
  a. show the amount of activity in various parts of the brain.
  b. produce images of the brain's structures.
  c. measure electrical activity in the brain.
  d. observe neural communication at synapses.

3. Which of the following reveals the electrical activity of the brain by producing a record of brain waves?
  a. electroencephalogram   **c.** PET scan
  b. CT scan   **d.** MRI

4. Which of the following does not reveal brain activity?
  a. CT scan   **c.** PET scan
  b. EEG   **d.** fMRI

5. Which of the following reveals both brain structure and brain activity?
  a. MRI   **c.** fMRI
  b. PET scan   **d.** CT scan

The Neurons and the Neurotransmitters (pp. 37–43)

6. The branchlike extensions of neurons that act as receivers of signals from other neurons are the
  a. dendrites.   **c.** neurotransmitters.
  b. axons.   **d.** cell bodies.

7. _____ support neurons, supplying them with nutrients and carrying away their waste products.

8. The junction where the axon of a sending neuron communicates with a receiving neuron is called the
  a. reuptake site.   **c.** synapse.
  b. receptor site.   **d.** axon terminal.

9. When a neuron fires, neurotransmitters are released from the synaptic vesicles in the _____ terminal into the synaptic cleft.

   a. dendrite
   b. cell body's
   c. receptor
   d. axon

10. The (resting, action) potential is the firing of a neuron that results when the charge within the neuron becomes more positive than the charge outside the cell membrane.

11. Receptor sites on the receiving neuron
   a. receive any available neurotransmitter molecules.
   b. receive only neurotransmitter molecules of specific shapes.
   c. can only be influenced by neurotransmitters from a single neuron.
   d. are located only on the dendrites.

12. The neurotransmitter called *acetylcholine* is involved in
   a. memory.
   b. motor function.
   c. rapid eye movement during sleep.
   d. all of the above

13. _____ is a neurotransmitter that may be associated with ADHD.

14. _____ are neurotransmitters that act as natural painkillers.

15. Responses to cocaine involve the neurotransmitters _____ and _____.

16. The _____ nervous system connects the central nervous system to the rest of the body.

   a. central
   b. peripheral
   c. somatic
   d. autonomic

17. The _____ nervous system mobilizes the body's resources during times of stress; the _____ nervous system brings the heightened bodily responses back to normal when the emergency is over.
   a. somatic; autonomic
   b. autonomic; somatic
   c. sympathetic; parasympathetic
   d. parasympathetic; sympathetic

The Human Nervous System (pp. 43–48)

18. Match the brain structure with its description.
   _____ (1) connects the brain with the peripheral nervous system
   _____ (2) controls heart rate, breathing, and blood pressure
   _____ (3) consists of the medulla, the pons, and the reticular formation
   _____ (4) influences attention and arousal
   _____ (5) coordinates complex body movements
   _____ (6) serves as a relay station for sensory information flowing into the brain
   _____ (7) controls unconscious movements

   a. medulla
   b. spinal cord
   c. reticular formation
   d. thalamus
   e. cerebellum
   f. brainstem
   g. substantia nigra

19. The hypothalamus regulates all the following *except*

   a. internal body temperature.
   b. coordinated movement.
   c. hunger and thirst.
   d. sexual behavior.

20. The part of the limbic system primarily involved in the formation of memories is the (amygdala, hippocampus).

21. The _____ is associated with emotions, and the _____ is involved in memory.

A Closer Look at the Thinking Part of the Brain (pp. 48–56)

22. What is the thick band of fibers connecting the two cerebral hemispheres?

   a. cortex
   b. corpus callosum
   c. cerebrum
   d. motor cortex

23. The outer covering of the cerebrum is the

   a. cerebral cortex.
   b. cortex callosum.
   c. myelin sheath.
   d. white matter.

24. Match the lobes with the brain areas they contain.
   _____ (1) primary auditory cortex
   _____ (2) primary visual cortex
   _____ (3) motor cortex
   _____ (4) somatosensory cortex

   a. frontal lobes
   b. parietal lobes
   c. occipital lobes
   d. temporal lobes

25. Match the specialized area with the appropriate description of function.
   _____ (1) hearing registers
   _____ (2) vision registers
   _____ (3) touch, pressure, and temperature register
   _____ (4) voluntary movement
   _____ (5) thinking, motivation, impulse control

   a. primary visual cortex
   b. motor cortex
   c. association areas
   d. auditory cortex
   e. somatosensory cortex

26. Match the hemisphere with the specialized abilities usually associated with it.
   _____ (1) visual-spatial skills
   _____ (2) speech
   _____ (3) recognition and expression of emotion
   _____ (4) musical perception
   _____ (5) mathematics
   a. right hemisphere
   b. left hemisphere

27. Which of these statements is *not* true of the split-brain operation?
   a. It is used on people with severe epilepsy.
   b. It provides a means of studying the functions of the individual hemispheres.
   c. It causes major changes in intelligence, personality, and behavior.
   d. It makes transfer of information between hemispheres impossible.

Age, Gender, and the Brain (pp. 56–58)

28. Synaptic development (synaptogenesis) involves growth of

   a. dendrites.
   b. axons.
   c. both dendrites and axons.

29. One developmental process that contributes to differences in processing speed between children and adults is _____.

30. Men have a lower proportion of _____ _____ in the left hemisphere than in the right.

31. Navigational tasks stimulate (different, the same) areas of the brain in men and women.

32. As adults get older, brain weight (increases, decreases).

33. As adults get older, the risk of brain damage from _____ increases.

Beyond The Nervous System (pp. 58–61)

34. Match the endocrine gland with the appropriate description.
_____ (**1**) keeps body's metabolism in balance
_____ (**2**) acts as a master gland that activates the other glands
_____ (**3**) regulates the blood sugar
_____ (**4**) makes reproduction possible
_____ (**5**) releases hormones that prepare the body for emergencies
_____ (**6**) regulates sleep

a. pituitary gland   **d.** thyroid gland
b. adrenal glands   **e.** pancreas
c. gonads   **f.** pineal gland

35. A _____ gene will not be expressed unless an individual carries two copies of it.

36. Characteristics that are affected by both genes and environment are said to be

a. polygenic.   **c.** recessive.
b. dominant.   **d.** multifactorial.

37. Researchers use _____ and _____ to examine the effects of heredity and environment.

SECTION TWO: Label the Brain

Identify each of the numbered parts in the brain diagram.

1. _____   **5.** _____
2. _____   **6.** _____
3. _____   **7.** _____
4. _____   **8.** _____

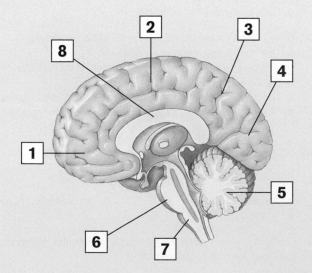

SECTION THREE: Fill in the Blank

1. The _____ is the part of the neuron that receives chemical messages from other neurons.

2. Dopamine, serotonin, and acetylcholine are all examples of _____.

3. The amygdala and the hippocampus are structures in the _____ system.

4. The _____ _____ _____ is at the back of the occipital lobe.

5. The somatosensory cortex is located in the _____ lobe.

6. Phineas Gage suffered damage to his _____ lobe.

7. Broca's area and Wernicke's area are important for language and are located in the _____ hemisphere.

8. The longest part of a neuron is called the _____.

9. The central nervous system is composed of the _____ and the _____ _____ .

10. The fight-or-flight response is related to the activity of the _____ nervous system.

11. The _____ monitors and regulates internal body temperature.

12. The _____ _____ occurs when the neuron ion channels open and allow a sudden influx of positive ions into the axon.

13. _____ aphasia is an impairment in the ability to produce speech sounds or, in extreme cases, an inability to speak at all.

14. The limbic system structure thought to play a central role in the formation of memories is the _____.

15. The primary auditory cortex is located in the _____ lobe.

16. You can write notes in class or execute other smooth, skilled body movements because of the action of the _____.

17. The somatic and the autonomic nervous systems are the two primary divisions of the _____ nervous system.

18. People who have Parkinson's disease may have damage to neurons whose nuclei are in the _____ _____.

19. In carrying out navigational tasks, men rely more on the _____ _____ than women do.

20. _____ _____ is a sex-linked disorder that causes mental retardation.

21. _____ _____ is lateralized to the left hemisphere in the fetal brain, just as it is in children and adults.

SECTION FOUR: Comprehensive Practice Test

1. Phineas Gage changed from a polite, dependable, well-liked railroad foreman to a rude and impulsive person who could no longer plan realistically for the future after he suffered serious damage to his

a. occipital lobe.   **c.** medulla.
b. frontal lobe.   **d.** cerebellum.

2. A researcher interested in getting information about the brain's activity based on the amount of oxygen and glucose consumed should use a(n)

a. MRI.   **c.** PET scan.
b. EEG.   **d.** CT scan.

3. Functional MRI (fMRI) reveals both brain structure and brain activity. (true/false)

4. Afferent is to efferent as

   a. sensory is to sensation.
   b. sensation is to perception.
   c. motor is to sensory.
   d. sensory is to motor.

5. _____ plays an important role in regulating mood, sleep, impulsivity, aggression, and appetite.

   a. Dopamine
   b. Norepinephrine
   c. Acetylcholine
   d. Serotonin

6. Neurons can conduct messages faster if they have

   a. an axon with a myelin sheath.
   b. a positive resting potential.
   c. more than one cell body.
   d. fewer dendrites.

7. The electrical charge inside a neuron is about -70 millivolts and is known as the _____ potential.

   a. action
   b. refractory
   c. resting
   d. impulse

8. The main divisions of the nervous system are the _____ and the _____ systems.

   a. somatic; autonomic
   b. central; peripheral
   c. brain; spinal cord
   d. sympathetic; parasympathetic

9. The structure that is located above the brainstem and serves as a relay station for information flowing into or out of the forebrain is the

   a. pituitary gland.
   b. hypothalamus.
   c. thalamus.
   d. hippocampus.

10. The structure that is located in the brainstem and is important for basic life functions such as heartbeat and breathing is the

   a. pons.
   b. medulla.
   c. hypothalamus.
   d. amygdala.

11. The _____ is sometimes referred to as the body's thermostat because it controls temperature, hunger, thirst, and emotional behaviors.

   a. corpus callosum
   b. pituitary gland
   c. cerebellum
   d. hypothalamus

12. The lobe that contains the primary visual cortex is the

   a. parietal lobe.
   b. occipital lobe.
   c. temporal lobe.
   d. frontal lobe.

13. The primary motor cortex is located in the _____ lobe.

   a. frontal
   b. occipital
   c. temporal
   d. oculovisual

14. The pituitary gland, known as the master gland, is part of the _____ system.

   a. somatic
   b. peripheral nervous
   c. endocrine
   d. central nervous

15. The _____ nervous system controls skeletal muscles and allows the body to interact with the external environment.

   a. autonomic
   b. parasympathetic
   c. sympathetic
   d. somatic

16. Damage to Broca's area will result in a type of aphasia that impairs one's ability to produce speech sounds. (true/false)

17. _____ _____ isn't lateralized to the right hemisphere until age 8 or so.

18. Women are more likely than men to process navigational tasks in the _____ _____ _____ and _____ _____ _____.

19. Red-green color blindness is caused by a defective gene on the _____.

SECTION FIVE: Critical Thinking

1. Much of the brain research you have read about in this chapter was carried out using animals. In many studies, it is necessary to euthanize animals to study their brain tissues directly. Many people object to this practice, but others say it is justified because it advances knowledge about the brain. Prepare arguments to support both of the following positions:

   a. The use of animals in brain research projects is ethical and justifiable because of the possible benefits to humankind.

   b. The use of animals in brain research projects is not ethical or justifiable on the grounds of possible benefits to humankind.

2. How would your life change if you had a massive stroke affecting your left hemisphere? How would it change if the stroke damaged your right hemisphere? Which stroke would be more tragic for you, and why?

CHAPTER

3 Sensation and Perception

Think About It

Try standing on one foot like the woman in the accompanying illustration. You'll probably have no trouble maintaining your balance for at least 30 seconds. But what will happen if you try to maintain this position with your eyes closed? Try it and find out.

No doubt you found it more difficult to keep your balance with your eyes closed. Your body's system for maintaining balance is a complex one that depends on several types of input. As you just learned, visual input is critical. In fact, visual input is so important that doctors use the one-leg/eyes-closed test to assess neurological health (Chaitow & DeLany, 2002). And because performance on the test normally declines as we get older (due to the aging of the cerebellum), it can also be used to determine whether your brain is aging normally. Studies suggest that, if you're between the ages of 20 and 49, and you can't maintain your

balance on one foot with your eyes closed for at least 25 seconds, your brain might be aging more rapidly than those of your peers (Bohannon et al., 1984). But take heart, exercise regimens that emphasize balance, such as the ancient Chinese practice of *Tai Chi*, can help to counteract the effects of aging (Fuzhong, Harmer, Fisher, & McAutey, 2004).

Your body's ability to maintain its position is just one of many topics that we'll address as we explore the interactive processes of *sensation* and *perception*.

First, we'll consider the two dominant senses: vision and hearing. Then we'll turn our attention to the other senses: smell, taste, touch, pain, and balance. You will learn how the senses detect sensory information and how this sensory information is actively organized and interpreted by the brain.

The Process of Sensation

Sensation is the process through which the senses pick up visual, auditory, and other sensory stimuli and transmit them to the brain. **Perception** is the process by which the brain actively organizes and interprets sensory information. Sensation furnishes the raw material of sensory experience, whereas perception provides the finished product. However, sensation and perception are not entirely discrete, independent processes. Instead, they are interactive: Sensation provides the data for perception, but perceptual processes influence sensation. Keep this in mind as you read about sensory and perceptual processes throughout the chapter. Before we consider perception, we will take a look at the process of sensation.

sensation The process through which the senses pick up visual, auditory, and other sensory stimuli and transmit them to the brain.

perception The process by which the brain actively organizes and interprets sensory information.

The Absolute and Difference Thresholds ▶

3.1 What are the absolute and difference thresholds?

What is the softest sound you can hear, the dimmest light you can see, the most diluted substance you can taste? Researchers in sensory psychology have performed many experiments over the years to answer these questions. Their research has established measures for the senses known as absolute thresholds. Just as the threshold of a doorway is the dividing point between being outside a room and inside, the **absolute threshold** of a sense marks the difference between not being able to perceive a stimulus and being just barely able to perceive it. Psychologists have arbitrarily defined this absolute threshold as the minimum amount of sensory stimulation that can be detected 50% of the time. The absolute thresholds for vision, hearing, taste, smell, and touch are illustrated in Figure 3.1 (p. 72).

absolute threshold The minimum amount of sensory stimulation that can be detected 50% of the time.

If you are listening to music, the very fact that you can hear it means that the absolute threshold has been crossed. But how much must the volume be turned up or down for you to notice a difference? Or, if you are carrying some bags of groceries, how much weight must be added or taken away for you to be able to sense that your load is heavier or lighter? The **difference threshold** is a measure of the smallest increase or decrease in a physical stimulus that is required to produce the **just noticeable difference (JND)**. The JND is the smallest change in sensation that a person is able to detect 50% of the time. If you were holding a 5-pound weight and 1 pound were added, you could easily notice the difference. But if you were holding 100 pounds and 1 additional pound were added, you could not sense the difference. Why not?

More than 150 years ago, researcher Ernst Weber (1795–1878) observed that the JND for all the senses depends on a proportion or percentage of change in a stimulus

difference threshold A measure of the smallest increase or decrease in a physical stimulus that is required to produce a difference in sensation that is noticeable 50% of the time.

just noticeable difference (JND) The smallest change in sensation that a person is able to detect 50% of the time.

FIGURE 3.1 Absolute Thresholds
Just as the threshold of a doorway is the dividing point between being outside a room and being inside it, the absolute threshold of a sense marks the difference between not being able to perceive a stimulus and being just barely able to perceive it.

(a)
For vision, a candle flame 30 miles away on a clear night

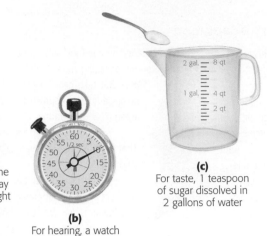

(b)
For hearing, a watch ticking 20 feet away

(c)
For taste, 1 teaspoon of sugar dissolved in 2 gallons of water

(d)
For smell, a single drop of perfume in a three-room house

(e)
For touch, a bee's wing falling a distance of 1 centimeter onto the cheek

▲ What is the dimmest light this lifeguard could perceive in the darkness? Researchers in sensory psychology have performed many experiments over the years to answer such questions. Their research has established measures known as absolute thresholds. Just as the threshold of a doorway is the dividing point between being outside a room and being inside it, the absolute threshold of a sense marks the difference between not being able to perceive a stimulus and being just barely able to perceive it.

rather than on a fixed amount of change. This observation became known as Weber's law. A weight you are holding must increase or decrease by $\frac{1}{50}$, or 2%, for you to notice the difference; in contrast, if you were listening to music, you would notice a difference if a tone became slightly higher or lower in pitch by about only 0.33%. According to Weber's law, the greater the original stimulus, the more it must be increased or decreased for the difference to be noticeable.

As you might suspect, the difference threshold is not the same for all the senses. A very large ($\frac{1}{5}$, or 20%) difference is necessary for some changes in taste to be detected. Moreover, Weber's law best applies to people with average sensitivities and to sensory stimuli that are neither very strong (loud thunder) nor very weak (a faint whisper). For instance, expert wine tasters would know if a particular vintage was a little too sweet, even if its sweetness varied by only a fraction of the 20% necessary for changes in taste. Furthermore, people who have lost one sensory ability often gain greater sensitivity in others. One study found that children with early-onset blindness were more capable of correctly labeling 25 common odors than were sighted children, whereas another found that congenitally deaf students possessed motion-perception abilities superior to those of hearing students (Bavelier et al., 2000). Moreover, students who are deaf appear to be more easily distracted by visual stimuli than are their counterparts who can hear (Dye, Hauser, & Bavelier, 2008).

3.2 How does transduction change sensory information?

Transduction and Adaptation

Would you be surprised to learn that our eyes do not actually see and that our ears do not hear? The sense organs provide only the beginning of sensation, which must be completed by the brain. As you learned in Chapter 2, specific clusters of neurons in specialized parts of the brain must be stimulated for us to see, hear, taste, and so on. Yet the brain itself cannot respond directly to light, sound waves, odors, and tastes. How, then, does it get the message? The answer is through the sensory receptors.

The body's sense organs are equipped with highly specialized cells called **sensory receptors** that detect and respond to one type of sensory stimulus—light, sound waves, odors, and so on.

Weber's law The law stating that the just noticeable difference (JND) for all the senses depends on a proportion or percentage of change in a stimulus rather than on a fixed amount of change.

sensory receptors Highly specialized cells in the sense organs that detect and respond to one type of sensory stimulus—light, sound, or odor, for example—and transduce (convert) the stimuli into neural impulses.

TRY IT   **Sensory Adaptation**

Take three large cereal bowls or small mixing bowls. Fill one with very cold water, another with hot water (*not* boiling or scalding), and the third with luke-warm water. Hold your left hand in the cold water and your right hand in the hot water for at least 1 minute. Then quickly plunge both hands into the lukewarm water at the same time.

Why do you experience the illusion that the lukewarm water feels simultane-ously warmer and colder than its actual temperature? The answer is adaptation. You perceive the lukewarm water as warm on your cold-adapted left hand and as cold on your warm-adapted right hand. This illustrates that our perceptions of sensory stimuli are relative and are affected by differences between stimuli we are already adapted to and new stimuli.

Through a process known as transduction the sensory receptors convert the sensory stimulation into neural impulses, the electrochemical language of the brain. The neural impulses are then transmitted to precise locations in the brain, such as the primary visual cortex for vision or the primary auditory cortex for hearing. We experience a sensation only when the appropriate part of the brain is stimulated. The sense receptors provide the essential link between the physical sensory world and the brain.

After a time, the sensory receptors grow accustomed to constant, unchanging lev-els of stimuli—sights, sounds, or smells—so we notice them less and less, or not at all. For example, smokers become accustomed to the smell of cigarette smoke in their homes and on their clothing. This process is known as sensory adaptation (see the *Try It* above). Even though it reduces our sensory awareness, sensory adaptation enables us to shift our attention to what is most important at any given moment. However, sen-sory adaptation is not likely to occur in the presence of a very strong stimulus, such as the smell of ammonia, an earsplitting sound, or the taste of rancid food.

transduction The process through which sensory receptors convert the sensory stimulation into neural impulses.

sensory adaptation The process in which sensory receptors grow accustomed to constant, unchanging levels of stimuli over time.

Vision

Vision is the most studied of all the senses. One thing vision researchers have known for a long time is that there is a great deal more information in the sensory environ-ment than our eyes can take in. Our eyes can respond only to visible light waves, which form a small subgroup of *electromagnetic waves,* a band called the visible spectrum (see Figure 3.2). These waves are measured in wavelengths, the distance from the peak of one wave to the peak of the next. The shortest light waves we can see appear violet, while the longest visible waves appear red. But sight is much more than just response to light.

visible spectrum The narrow band of electromagnetic waves that are visible to the human eye.

wavelength A measure of the distance from the peak of a light wave to the peak of the next.

Invisible Long Waves	Visible Light Spectrum	Invisible Short Waves
Infrared rays (beyond red)		Ultraviolet rays (beyond violet)

1500 ... 800   700   600   500   400   300

Wavelength (in nanometers)

AC circuits	Broadcast bands	Radar	Microwaves	IR		UV	X-rays	Gamma rays	Cosmic rays

FIGURE 3.2 The Electromagnetic Spectrum
Human eyes can perceive only a very thin band of electromagnetic waves, known as the visible spectrum.

3.3 How does each part of the eye function in vision?

cornea (KOR-nee-uh) The tough, transparent, protective layer that covers the front of the eye and bends light rays inward through the pupil.

lens The transparent disk-shaped structure behind the iris and the pupil that changes shape as it focuses on objects at varying distances.

accommodation The flattening and bulging action of the lens as it focuses images of objects on the retina.

retina The layer of tissue that is located on the inner surface of the eyeball and contains the sensory receptors for vision.

✳─Explore the Concept *Normal Vision, Nearsightedness* on **mypsychlab.com**

The Eye

The globe-shaped human eyeball, shown in Figure 3.3, measures about 1 inch in diameter. Curving outward from the eye's surface is the cornea—the tough, transparent, protective layer covering the front of the eye. The cornea performs the first step in vision by bending the light rays inward. It directs the light rays through the *pupil*, the small, dark opening in the center of the *iris*, or colored part of the eye. The iris dilates and contracts the pupil to regulate the amount of light entering the eye.

Suspended just behind the iris and the pupil, the lens is composed of many thin layers and looks like a transparent disk. The lens performs the task of focusing on viewed objects. It flattens as it focuses on objects at a distance and becomes more spherical, bulging in the center, as it focuses on close objects. This flattening and bulging action of the lens is known as accommodation. With age, the lens loses the ability to change its shape to accommodate for near vision, a condition called *presbyopia* ("old eyes"). This is why many people over age 40 must hold a book or newspaper at arm's length or use reading glasses to magnify the print.

The lens focuses the incoming image onto the retina—a layer of tissue about the size of a small postage stamp and as thin as onion skin, located on the inner surface of the eyeball and containing the sensory receptors for vision. The image that is projected onto the retina is upside down and reversed from left to right, as illustrated in Figure 3.4.

In some people, the distance through the eyeball (from the lens to the retina) is either too short or too long for proper focusing. Nearsightedness (*myopia*) occurs when the lens focuses images of distant objects in front of, rather than on, the retina. A person with this condition will be able to see near objects clearly, but distant images will be blurred. Farsightedness (*hyperopia*) occurs when the lens focuses images of close objects behind, rather than on, the retina. The individual is able to see far objects clearly, but close objects are blurred. Both conditions are correctable with eyeglasses or contact lenses or by surgical procedures. ✳─Explore on **mypsychlab.com**

FIGURE 3.3
The Major Parts of the Human Eye

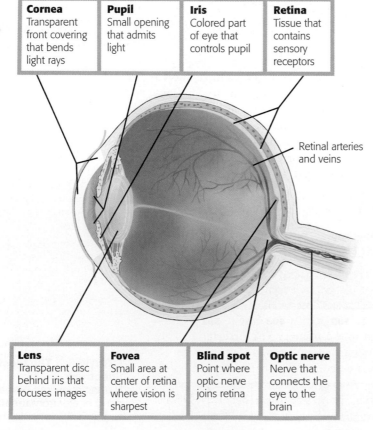

Cornea	**Pupil**	**Iris**	**Retina**
Transparent front covering that bends light rays	Small opening that admits light	Colored part of eye that controls pupil	Tissue that contains sensory receptors

Retinal arteries and veins

Lens	**Fovea**	**Blind spot**	**Optic nerve**
Transparent disc behind iris that focuses images	Small area at center of retina where vision is sharpest	Point where optic nerve joins retina	Nerve that connects the eye to the brain

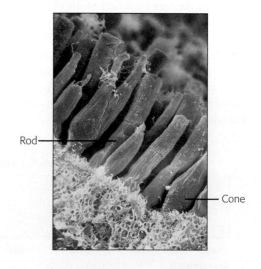

Rod

Cone

At the back of the retina is a layer of light-sensitive receptor cells—the rods and the cones. Named for their shapes, the rods look like slender cylinders, and the cones appear shorter and more rounded. There are about 120 million rods and 6 million cones in each retina. The cones are the receptor cells that enable us to see color and fine detail in adequate light, but they do not function in very dim light. By contrast, the rods in the human eye are extremely sensitive, allowing the eye to respond to as few as five photons of light (Hecht, Shlaer, & Pirenne, 1942).

A substance called *rhodopsin* present in the rods enables us to adapt to variations in light. Rhodopsin has two components, *opsin* and *retinal* (a chemical similar to vitamin A). In bright light, opsin and retinal break apart, as the process of *light adaptation* takes place. During *dark adaptation*, opsin and retinal bond to one another, re-forming rhodopsin. As you've no doubt experienced, when you move from bright light to total darkness, as when you enter a darkened movie theater, you are momentarily blind until the opsin and retinal recombine. Similarly, when you leave the theater again, you become temporarily blind until the two substances break apart once again.

At the center of the retina is the fovea, a small area about the size of the period at the end of this sentence. When you look directly at an object, the image of the object is focused on the center of your fovea. The fovea contains no rods but has about 30,000 cones tightly packed together, providing the clearest and sharpest area of vision in the whole retina. The cones are most densely packed at the center of the fovea; their density decreases sharply just a few degrees beyond the fovea's center and then levels off more gradually to the periphery of the retina.

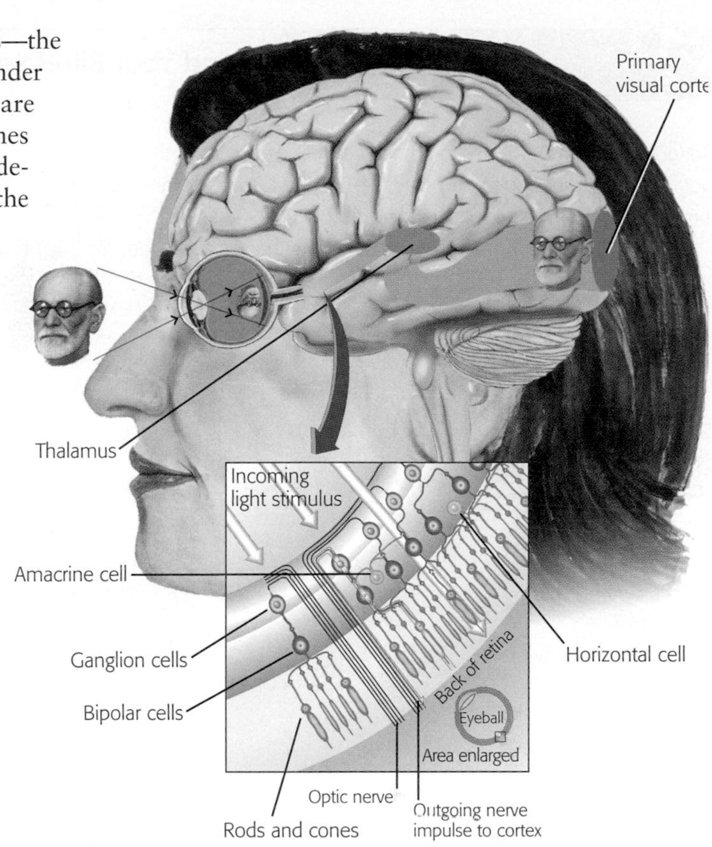

FIGURE 3.4 From Retinal Image to Meaningful Information Because of the way the lens alters light rays in order to produce a clear image, images are upside down on the retina. The brain's visual processing system takes the upside-down retinal image and flips it so it is properly orientated.

Vision and the Brain ▶

As you can see in Figure 3.4, the brain is responsible for converting the upside-down retinal images into meaningful visual information. But the first stages of neural processing actually take place in the retina itself. Before light rays reach the sensory receptors on the rods and cones, they pass through four layers of tissue, each of which contains specialized neurons—*ganglion cells, amacrine cells, bipolar cells,* and *horizontal cells* (see the inset in Figure 3.4). When the light rays reach the sensory receptors (the rods and cones), the receptors tranduce, or change, them to neural impulses. The impulses are then transmitted to the bipolar, amacrine, and horizontal cells, which carry them to the ganglion cells. The approximately 1 million axonlike extensions of the ganglion cells are bundled together in a pencil-sized cable that extends through the wall of the retina, leaving the eye and leading to the brain. There are no rods or cones where the cable runs through the retinal wall, so this point is a blind spot in each eye (see *Try It* on p. 76).

Beyond the retinal wall of each eye, the cable becomes the optic nerve (refer to Figure 3.3). The two optic nerves come together at the *optic chiasm,* a point where some of their nerve fibers cross to the opposite side of the brain. The nerve fibers from the right half of each retina go to the right hemisphere, and those from the left half of each retina go to the left hemisphere. This crossing over is important because it allows visual information from a single eye to be represented in the primary visual cortex of both hemispheres of the brain. Moreover, it plays an important part in depth perception.

From the optic chiasm, the optic nerve fibers extend to the thalamus, where they form synapses with neurons that transmit the impulses to the primary visual cortex, the part of the brain that is devoted to visual processing. Thanks to researchers David Hubel and Torsten Wiesel (1959, 1979; Hubel, 1963, 1995), who won a Nobel Prize for their

[**3.4** How does visual information get from the retina to the primary visual cortex?

rods The light-sensitive receptor cells in the retina that look like slender cylinders and allow the eye to respond to as few as five photons of light.

cones The light-sensitive receptor cells in the retina that enable humans to see color and fine detail in adequate light but do not function in very dim light.

fovea (FO-vee-uh) A small area at the center of the retina that provides the clearest and sharpest vision because it has the largest concentration of cones.

blind spot The point in each retina where there are no rods or cones because the cable of ganglion cells is extending through the retinal wall.

optic nerve The nerve that carries visual information from each retina to both sides of the brain.

primary visual cortex The part of the brain in which visual information is processed.

TRY IT ▶ Find Your Blind Spot

To locate one of your blind spots, hold this book at arm's length. Close your right eye and look directly at the magician's eyes. Now slowly bring the book closer, keeping your eye fixed on the magician.

When the rabbit disappears, you have found the blind spot in your left eye.

👁 Watch on **mypsychlab.com**

feature detectors Neurons in the brain that respond only to specific visual patterns (for example, to lines or angles).

work in 1981, we know a great deal about how specialized the neurons of the primary visual cortex are. By inserting tiny microelectrodes into single cells in the visual cortexes of cats, Hubel and Wiesel (1959) were able to determine what was happening in individual cells when the cats were exposed to different kinds of visual stimuli. They discovered that each neuron responded only to specific patterns. Some neurons responded only to lines and angles, while others fired only when the cat saw a vertical or horizontal line. Still others were responsive to nothing but right angles or lines of specific lengths. Neurons of this type are known as feature detectors, and they are already coded at birth to make their unique responses. Yet we see whole images, not collections of isolated features, because visual perceptions are complete only when the primary visual cortex transmits the millions of pieces of visual information it receives to other areas in the brain, where they are combined and assembled into whole visual images (Self & Zeki, 2005).

The major structures of the visual system are summarized in the *Summarize It*.

SUMMARIZE IT

Major Structures of the Visual System

STRUCTURE	FUNCTION
Cornea	Translucent covering on the front of the eyeball that bends light rays entering the eye inward through the pupil
Iris	Colored part of the eye that adjusts to maintain a constant amount of light entering the eye through the pupil
Pupil	Opening in the center of the iris through which light rays enter the eye
Lens	Transparent disk-shaped structure behind the pupil that adjusts its shape to allow focusing on objects at varying distances
Retina	Layer of tissue on the inner surface of the eye that contains sensory receptors for vision
Rods	Specialized receptor cells in the retina that are sensitive to light changes
Cones	Specialized receptor cells in the retina that enable humans to see fine detail and color in adequate light
Fovea	Small area at the center of the retina, packed with cones, on which objects viewed directly are clearly and sharply focused
Optic nerve	Nerve that carries visual information from the retina to the brain
Blind spot	Area in each eye where the optic nerve joins the retinal wall and no vision is possible

3.5 How does color vision work? ⊐◄   **Color Vision**

Why does the skin of an apple appear to be red, while its flesh is perceived as an off-white color? What we actually see is reflected light. Some light waves striking an object are absorbed by it; others are reflected from it. So, why does an apple's skin look red?

Sensing Color. If you hold a red apple in bright light, light waves of all the different wavelengths strike the apple, but more of the longer red wavelengths of light are reflected from the apple's skin. The shorter wavelengths are absorbed, so you see only the reflected red. Bite into the apple, and it looks off-white. Why? You see the near-white color because, rather than being absorbed, almost all of the wavelengths of the visible spectrum are reflected from the inside part of the apple. The presence of all visible wavelengths gives the sensation of a near-white color. If an object does indeed reflect 100% of visible wavelengths, it appears to be pure white.

Our everyday visual experience goes far beyond the colors in the rainbow. We can detect thousands of subtle color shadings. What produces these fine color distinctions? Researchers have identified three dimensions of light that combine to provide the rich world of color we experience: The chief dimension is hue, which refers to the specific color perceived—red, blue, or yellow, for example. Saturation refers to the purity of a color; a color becomes less saturated, or less pure, as other wavelengths of light are mixed with it. Brightness refers to the intensity of the light energy that is perceived as a color and corresponds to the amplitude (height) of the color's light wave.

hue The dimension of light that refers to the specific color perceived.

saturation The purity of a color, or the degree to which the light waves producing it are of the same wavelength.

brightness The intensity of light energy perceived as a color; based on amplitude of light wave.

Theories of Color Vision. Scientists know that the cones are responsible for color vision, but exactly how do they work to produce color sensations? Two major theories have been offered to explain color vision, and both were formulated before the development of laboratory technology capable of testing them (Stabell & Stabell, 2009). The trichromatic theory, first proposed by Thomas Young in 1802, was modified by Hermann von Helmholtz about 50 years later. This theory states that there are three kinds of cones in the retina and that each kind makes a maximal chemical response to one of three colors—blue, green, or red. Research conducted in the 1950s and the 1960s by Nobel Prize winner George Wald (1964; Wald, Brown, & Smith, 1954) supports the trichromatic theory. Wald discovered that even though all cones have basically the same structure, the retina does indeed contain three kinds of cones. Subsequent research demonstrated that each kind of cone is particularly sensitive to one of three colors—blue, green, or red (Roorda & Williams, 1999).

trichromatic theory The theory of color vision suggesting that three types of cones in the retina each make a maximal chemical response to one of three colors—blue, green, or red.

The other major attempt to explain color vision is the opponent-process theory, which was first proposed by physiologist Ewald Hering in 1878 and revised in 1957 by researchers Leon Hurvich and Dorthea Jamison. According to the opponent-process theory, three kinds of cells respond by increasing or decreasing their rate of firing when different colors are present. The red/green cells increase their firing rate when red is present and decrease it when green is present. The yellow/blue cells have an increased response to yellow and a decreased response to blue. A third kind of cells increase their response rate for white light and decrease it in the absence of light.

opponent-process theory The theory of color vision suggesting that three kinds of cells respond by increasing or decreasing their rate of firing when different colors are present.

If you look long enough at one color in the opponent-process pair and then look at a white surface, your brain will give you the sensation of the opposite color—a negative afterimage, a visual sensation that remains after the stimulus is withdrawn. After you have stared at one color in an opponent-process pair (red/green, yellow/blue, white/black), the cell responding to that color tires and the opponent cell begins to fire, producing the afterimage. Demonstrate this for yourself in the *Try It*.

afterimage A visual sensation that remains after a stimulus is withdrawn.

TRY IT **A Negative Afterimage**

Stare at the dot in the green, black, and yellow flag for approximately 1 minute. Then shift your gaze to the dot in the blank rectangle. You will see the American flag in its true colors—red, white, and blue, which are the opponent-process opposites of green, black, and yellow.

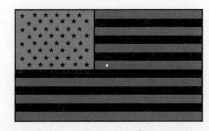

▲ On the left a hot air balloon is shown as it would appear to a person with normal color vision; on the right is the same balloon as it would appear to a person with red-green color blindness.

But which theory of color vision is correct? It turns out that each theory explains a different phase of color processing. It is now generally accepted that the cones perform color processing in a way that is best explained by the trichromatic theory. The cones pass on information about wavelengths of light to the ganglion cells, the site of opponent processes. And color perception appears to involve more than just these two phases. Researchers think that color processing starts at the level of the retina, continues through the bipolar and ganglion cells, and is completed in the color detectors in the visual cortex (Masland, 1996; Sokolov, 2000). However, the trichromatic theory alone does not fully explain color perception because the cones are not distributed evenly across the surface of the retina. New theories that include motoric aspects of vision, such as the nearly invisible movements of the eyes called *saccades,* may turn out to provide researchers with a more comprehensive understanding of color vision (Wittenberg, Bremmer, & Wachter, 2008).

Color Blindness. You may have wondered what it means if someone is "color-blind." Does that person see the world in black and white? No—the term color blindness refers to an inability to distinguish certain colors from one another. About 8% of males experience some kind of difficulty in distinguishing colors, most commonly red from green (Mather, 2006). By contrast, fewer than 1% of females suffer from color blindness. (Recall from Chapter 2 that this sex difference is explained by the fact that genes for color vision are carried on the X chromosome.)

Research has shown that color blindness can have degrees; it isn't simply a matter of either-you-have-it-or-you-don't. Why are some of us better able to make fine distinctions between colors, as we must do when sorting black and navy blue socks, for instance? These differences appear to be related to the number of color vision genes individuals have. Researchers have found that, in people with normal color vision, the X chromosome may contain as few as two or as many as nine genes for color perception (Neitz & Neitz, 1995). Those who have more of such genes appear to be better able to make very fine distinctions between colors. These genetic differences lead to differences in the way that the various kinds of cones are distributed on an individual's retina (Hofer et al., 2005). Moreover, animal studies suggest that gene therapy aimed at increasing the number of cones in the retinas of individuals with color blindness may cure the condition (Simunovic, 2010).

color blindness The inability to distinguish certain colors from one another.

Hearing and Balance

"In space, no one can hear you scream!" Years ago, the frightening science fiction movie *Alien* was advertised this way. Although the movie was fiction, the statement is true. Light can travel through the vast nothingness of space, a vacuum, but sound cannot.

Sound ▶

┌ **3.6** **What are the physical**
└ **characteristics of sound?**

Sound requires a medium, such as air, water, or a solid object, through which to move. This fact was first demonstrated by Robert Boyle in 1660 when he suspended a ringing pocket watch by a thread inside a specially designed jar. When Boyle pumped all the air out of the jar, he could no longer hear the watch ring. But when he pumped the air back into the jar, he could again hear the watch ringing.

Frequency is determined by the number of cycles completed by a sound wave in one second. The unit used to measure a wave's frequency, or cycles per second, is known as the hertz (Hz). The *pitch*—how high or low the sound is—is chiefly determined by frequency—the higher the frequency (the more cycles per second), the higher the sound. The human ear can hear sound frequencies from low bass tones of around 20 Hz up to high-pitched sounds of about 20,000 Hz. However, as discussed in *Explain It* on page 81, adults' ability to hear such high frequencies varies a lot from one individual to another. By contrast, many mammals, such as dogs, cats, bats, and rats, can hear tones much higher in frequency than 20,000 Hz. Amazingly, dolphins can respond to frequencies up to 100,000 Hz. ✳⎡**Explore** on **mypsychlab.com**

frequency The number of cycles completed by a sound wave in one second, determining the pitch of the sound; expressed in the unit called the hertz.

✳⎡**Explore** the **Concept** *Frequency and Amplitude of Sound Waves* on **mypsychlab.com**

The loudness of a sound is determined by a measure called amplitude. The force or pressure with which air molecules move chiefly determines loudness, which is measured using a unit called the *bel*, named for Alexander Graham Bell. Because the bel is a rather large unit, sound levels are expressed in tenths of a bel, or decibels (dB). The threshold of human hearing is set at 0 dB, which does not mean the absence of sound but rather the softest sound that can be heard in a very quiet setting. Each increase of 10 decibels makes a sound 10 times louder. Figure 3.5 shows comparative decibel levels for a variety of sounds.

amplitude The measure of the loudness of a sound; expressed in the unit called the decibel.

decibel (dB) (DES-ih-bel) A unit of measurement for the loudness of sounds.

Another characteristic of sound is timbre, the distinctive quality of a sound that distinguishes it from other sounds of the same pitch and loudness. Have you ever thought about why a given musical note sounds different when played on a piano, a guitar, and a violin, even though all three instruments use vibrating strings to produce sounds? The characteristics of the strings, the technique used to initiate the vibrations, and the way the body of the instrument amplifies the vibrations work together to produce a unique "voice," or timbre, for each instrument. Human voices vary in timbre as well, providing us with a way of recognizing individuals when we can't see their faces. Timbres vary from one instrument to another, and from one voice to another, because most sounds consist of several different frequencies rather than a single pitch. The range of those frequencies gives each musical instrument, and each human voice, its unique sound.

timbre (TAM-burr) The distinctive quality of a sound that distinguishes it from other sounds of the same pitch and loudness.

Psychological Response	Decibel Scale	Example
Threshold of severe pain	140	
Painfully loud		Rock band at 15 feet
Prolonged exposure produces damage to hearing	120	Jet takeoff at 200 feet
		Riveting machine
	100	Subway train at 15 feet
Very loud		Water at foot of Niagara Falls
	80	Automobile interior at 55 mph
		Freeway traffic at 50 feet
	60	Normal conversation at 3 feet
Quiet		Quiet restaurant
	40	Quiet office
		Library
Very quiet	20	Whisper at 3 feet
Just audible		Normal breathing
Threshold of hearing	0	

FIGURE 3.5 Decibel Levels of Various Sounds
The loudness of a sound (its amplitude) is measured in decibels. Each increase of 10 decibels makes a sound 10 times louder. A normal conversation at 3 feet measures about 60 decibels, which is 10,000 times louder than a soft whisper of 20 decibels. Any exposure to sounds of 130 decibels or higher puts a person at immediate risk for hearing damage, but levels as low as 90 decibels can cause hearing loss if one is exposed to them over long periods of time.

3.7 How does each part of the ear function in hearing?

audition The sensation and process of hearing.

outer ear The visible part of the ear, consisting of the pinna and the auditory canal.

middle ear The portion of the ear containing the ossicles, which connect the eardrum to the oval window and amplify sound waves.

inner ear The innermost portion of the ear, containing the cochlea, the vestibular sacs, and the semicircular canals.

cochlea (KOK-lee-uh) The fluid-filled, snail-shaped, bony chamber in the inner ear that contains the basilar membrane and its hair cells (the sound receptors).

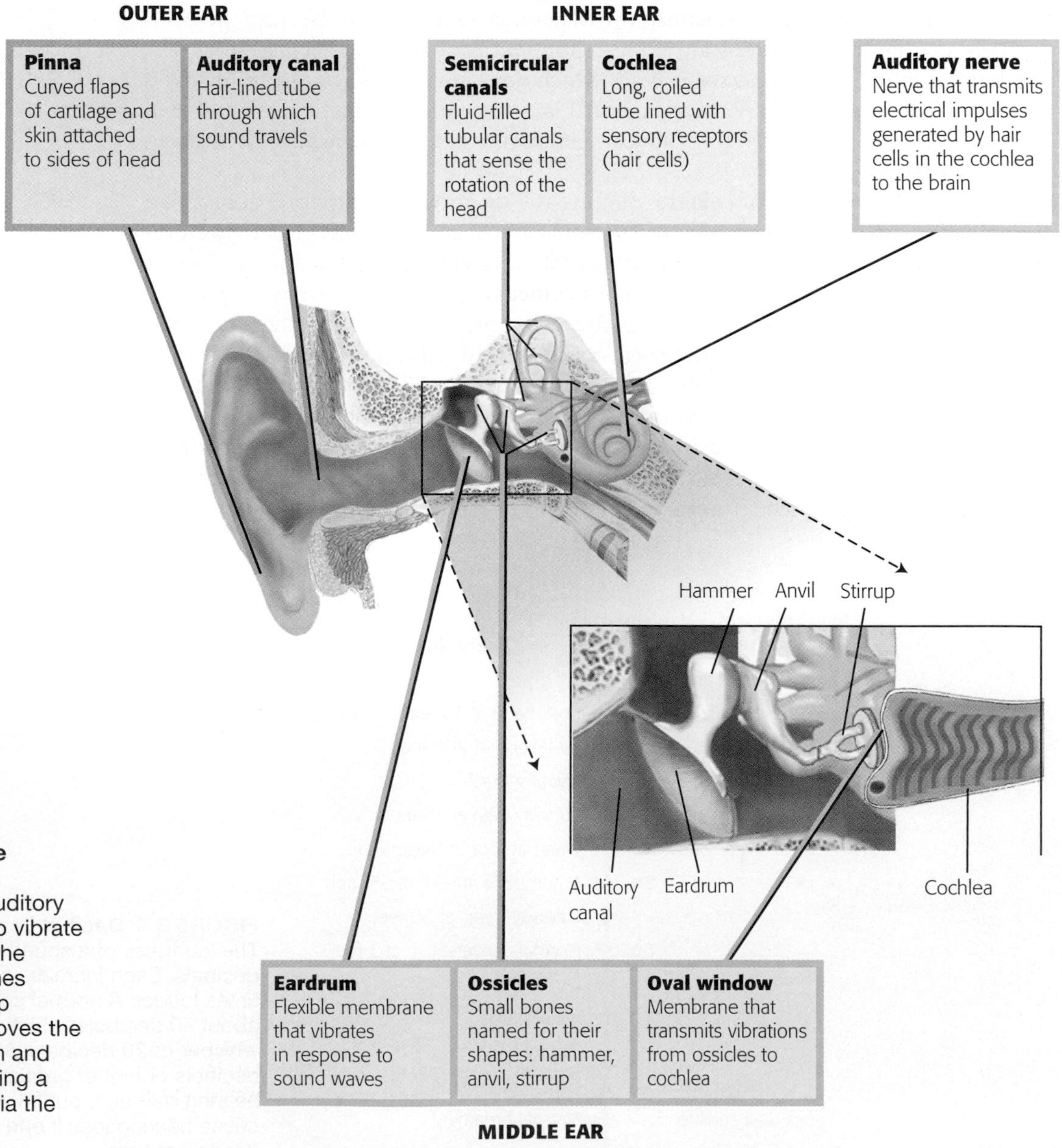

The Ear and Hearing

Audition is the sensation and process of hearing. The oddly shaped, curved flap of cartilage and skin called the *pinna* is the visible part of the outer ear (see Figure 3.6). Inside the ear, the *auditory canal* is about 1 inch long, and its entrance is lined with hairs. At the end of the auditory canal is the *eardrum* (or *tympanic membrane*), a thin, flexible membrane about $1/3$ inch in diameter. The eardrum moves in response to the sound waves that travel through the auditory canal and strike it.

The middle ear is no larger than an aspirin tablet. Inside its chamber are the *ossicles*, the three smallest bones in the human body. Named for their shapes, the ossicles—the hammer, the anvil, and the stirrup—are connected in that order, linking the eardrum to the oval window (see Figure 3.6). The ossicles amplify sound waves some 22 times (Békésy, 1957). The inner ear begins at the inner side of the oval window, at the cochlea—a fluid-filled, snail-shaped, bony chamber. When the stirrup pushes against the oval window, it sets up vibrations that move the fluid in the cochlea back and forth in waves. Inside the cochlea, attached to its thin basilar membrane are about

OUTER EAR

Pinna
Curved flaps of cartilage and skin attached to sides of head

Auditory canal
Hair-lined tube through which sound travels

INNER EAR

Semicircular canals
Fluid-filled tubular canals that sense the rotation of the head

Cochlea
Long, coiled tube lined with sensory receptors (hair cells)

Auditory nerve
Nerve that transmits electrical impulses generated by hair cells in the cochlea to the brain

Hammer   Anvil   Stirrup

Auditory canal   Eardrum   Cochlea

Eardrum
Flexible membrane that vibrates in response to sound waves

Ossicles
Small bones named for their shapes: hammer, anvil, stirrup

Oval window
Membrane that transmits vibrations from ossicles to cochlea

MIDDLE EAR

FIGURE 3.6 The Anatomy of the Human Ear
Sound waves pass through the auditory canal to the eardrum, causing it to vibrate and set in motion the ossicles in the middle ear. When the stirrup pushes against the oval window, it sets up vibrations in the inner ear. This moves the fluid in the cochlea back and forth and sets in motion the hair cells, causing a message to be sent to the brain via the auditory nerve.

15,000 sensory receptors called hair cells, each with a bundle of tiny hairs protruding from it. The tiny hair bundles are pushed and pulled by the motion of the fluid inside the cochlea. If the tip of a hair bundle is moved only as much as the width of an atom, an electrical impulse is generated, which is transmitted to the brain by way of the auditory nerve. As noted in the *Explain It*, damage to the cochlea's hair cells is a major

hair cells Sensory receptors for hearing that are attached to the basilar membrane in the cochlea.

EXPLAIN IT   Why Can't Everyone Hear the "Mosquito" Ring Tone?

Have you ever tested your hearing to find out if you can hear the "Mosquito," a tone with a frequency of about 17,000 Hz? If not, search online for "mosquito ringtone hearing test" and you'll be directed to dozens of websites where you can do so. As the figure to the right suggests, the ability to hear the Mosquito declines with age. However, research suggests that the truth about age differences in sensitivity to the Mosquito is that the ability to hear it is nearly universal in the teens and early 20s but highly variable from the mid-20s on (Lawton, 2001). What accounts for the variability in sensitivity to high-pitched tones among adults?

The ability to hear high-pitched tones declines with age for a variety of reasons. A few conditions that are more common to middle-aged and older adults (e.g., excessive ear wax, chronic fluid in the ear, overgrowth of the bones in the inner ear) than to younger adults explain some of the decline (Mathur & Roland, 2009). However, hearing loss in adulthood often results from lifelong exposure to excessive noise. Noise above 85 decibels or so, if experienced repeatedly for long periods of time, damages the tiny hair cells inside the cochlea (Mathur & Roland, 2009). And the longer the exposure to excessive noise goes on, the more hearing people who are exposed to it lose. For instance, many long-time rock and pop musicians who are now in their middle- and late-adulthood years—Bono, Pete Townshend, Eric Clapton, Ozzy Osbourne, Ted Nugent, Phil Collins, Trent Reznor, to name a few—have much poorer hearing than others their age. Moreover, Townshend has reported that he began to notice his hearing loss

when he was still in his 20s. Classical musicians who regularly play in orchestras show similar losses (Laitinen, 2005).

What can you do to increase your chances of maintaining the ability to hear the Mosquito and other high-pitched sounds, which happen to be critical to the ability to understand speech, for as long as possible? If you're a musician, investigate hearing protectors that shield your inner ear from potentially damaging noise but still allow you to hear the sounds you need to in order to play and perform effectively. Even if you're not a musician, you should be aware that regular use of headphones greatly increases your risk of suffering the kind of hearing loss that is common among professional musicians (Britt, 2006). To protect your hearing, adopt a practice that experts call the "60/60 rule": Use headphones no more than a total of 60 minutes each day with the player set on 60% of its maximum volume (Mayo Clinic, 2006a).

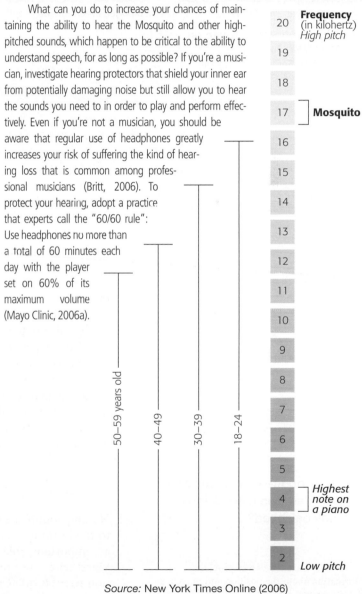

Frequency
(in kilohertz)
High pitch

17   **Mosquito**

50–59 years old   40–49   30–39   18–24

4   *Highest note on a piano*

2   *Low pitch*

Source: New York Times Online (2006)

◀ Trent Reznor is one of many rock musicians who began to experience hearing problems in early adulthood due to exposure to excessive noise.

Normal inner ear "hair" cells

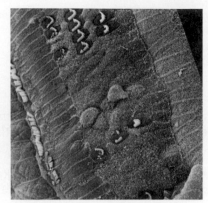

Damaged inner ear "hair" cells

FIGURE 3.7 Effects of Noise on Cochlear Hair Cells
Source: House Ear Institute (2006).

place theory The theory of hearing that holds that each individual pitch a person hears is determined by the particular location along the basilar membrane of the cochlea that vibrates the most.

frequency theory The theory of hearing that holds that hair cell receptors vibrate the same number of times per second as the sounds that reach them.

source of hearing loss. Figure 3.7 dramatically illustrates the effects of excessive noise on these delicate cells.

We can hear some sounds through *bone conduction,* the vibrations of the bones in the face and skull. When you click your teeth or eat crunchy food, you hear these sounds mainly through bone conduction. And if you have heard a recording of your voice, you may have thought it sounded odd. This is because recordings do not reproduce the sounds you hear through bone conduction when you speak, so you are hearing your voice as it sounds to others.

Having two ears, one on each side of the head, enables you to determine the direction from which sounds are coming (Konishi, 1993). Unless a sound is directly above, below, in front of, or behind you, it reaches one ear very shortly before it reaches the other (Spitzer & Semple, 1991). The brain can detect differences as small as 0.0001 second and interpret them, revealing the direction of the sound (Rosenzweig, 1961). The source of a sound may also be determined by the difference in the intensity of the sound reaching each ear, as well as the position of the head when the sound is detected (Kopinska & Harris, 2003; Middlebrooks & Green, 1991).

Scientists have proposed two theories to explain hearing. In the 1860s, Hermann von Helmholtz helped develop place theory. This theory of hearing holds that each individual pitch a person hears is determined by the particular spot or place along the basilar membrane that vibrates the most. Observing the living basilar membrane, researchers verified that different locations do, indeed, vibrate in response to differently pitched sounds (Ruggero, 1992). Even so, place theory seems to apply only to frequencies higher than 150 Hz.

Another attempt to explain hearing is frequency theory. According to this theory, the hair cells vibrate the same number of times per second as the sounds that reach them. Thus, a tone of 500 Hz would stimulate the hair cells to vibrate 500 times per second. However, frequency theory cannot account for frequencies higher than 1,000 Hz because individual neurons linked to the hair cells cannot fire more than about 1,000 times per second. So, even if a receptor vibrated as rapidly as the sound wave associated with a higher tone, the information necessary to perceive the pitch wouldn't be faithfully transmitted to the brain. Consequently, frequency theory seems to be a good explanation of how we hear low-frequency tones (lower than 500 Hz), but place theory better describes the way in which tones with frequencies higher than 1,000 Hz are heard (Matlin & Foley, 1997). Both frequency and location are involved when we hear sounds with frequencies between 500 and 1,000 Hz.

3.8 How do the kinesthetic and vestibular senses help us move and stay balanced?

kinesthetic sense The sense providing information about the position and movement of body parts.

Balance and Movement

No one doubts the importance of the ears and the auditory information they provide to the brain in everyday life, but did you know that structures in the ears also play an important role in your ability to move and to maintain your balance? The kinesthetic sense provides information about (1) the position of body parts in relation to each other and (2) the movement of the entire body or its parts. This information is detected by receptors in the joints, ligaments, and muscles. The other senses provide additional information about body position and movement. For example, as you learned at the beginning of the chapter, the kinesthetic sense functions poorly when the brain is deprived of visual information. Still, it does function fairly well, even without visual input. If you tried the balance activity we described, you probably found that your body maintained its balance by prompting you to periodically lower your raised foot and make contact with the floor. Consequently, although you were unable to continuously maintain your balance on one leg, you didn't fall over completely. That's because the kinesthetic sense is capable of compensating for missing sensory information either by using information from the other senses or by prompting us to move in particular ways. As a result, we are usually able to maintain control of our bodies without visual feedback or a studied, conscious effort.

The visual and kinesthetic systems work with the *vestibular sense* to enable you to execute smooth, coordinated movements. The vestibular sense detects movement and provides information about the body's orientation in space. The vestibular sense organs are located in the semicircular canals and the *vestibular sacs* in the inner ear. The semicircular canals sense the rotation of your head, such as when you are turning your head from side to side or when you are spinning around (see Figure 3.8). Because the canals are filled with fluid, rotating movements of the head in any direction send the fluid coursing through the tubelike semicircular canals. In the canals, the moving fluid bends the hair cells, which act as receptors and send neural impulses to the brain. Because there are three canals, each positioned on a different plane, rotation in a given direction will cause the hair cells in one canal to bend more than the hair cells in the other canals.

The semicircular canals and the vestibular sacs signal only changes in motion or orientation. If you were blindfolded and had no visual or other external cues, you would not be able to sense motion once your speed reached a constant rate. For example, in an airplane, you would feel the takeoff and the landing, as well as any sudden changes in speed. But once the plane leveled off and maintained a fairly constant cruising speed, your vestibular organs would not signal the brain that you are moving, even if you were traveling at a rate of hundreds of miles per hour.

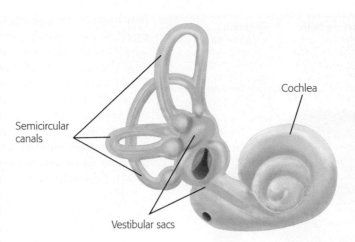

Semicircular canals

Cochlea

Vestibular sacs

FIGURE 3.8 Sensing Balance and Movement
You sense the rotation of your head in any direction because the movement sends fluid coursing through the tubelike semicircular canals in the inner ear. The moving fluid bends the hair cell receptors, which, in turn, send neural impulses to the brain.

vestibular sense (ves-TIB-yu-ler) The sense that provides information about the body's orientation in space.

semicircular canals Three fluid-filled tubular canals in the inner ear that sense the rotation of the head.

Smell, Taste, and Touch

Clearly, our sensory experiences would be extremely limited without vision and hearing, but what about the chemical senses—smell and taste?

Smell ▶

3.9 How do smell sensations get from the nose to the brain?

If you suddenly lost your capacity for olfaction (the sense of smell), you might think, "This isn't so bad. I can't smell flowers or food, but, on the other hand, I no longer have to endure the foul odors of life." But your *olfactory system*—the technical name for the organs and brain structures involved in the sense of smell—aids your survival. You smell smoke and can escape before the flames of a fire envelop you. Your nose broadcasts an odor alarm to the brain when certain poisonous gases or noxious fumes are present. Smell, aided by taste, provides your line of defense against putting spoiled food or drink into your body. Olfactory experiences also influence our emotional states, that is, taking advice such as "stop and smell the roses" literally could actually cheer you up when you're feeling down (Gottfried, 2010). And as you probably know, distinctive odors can serve as memory cues, both pleasant and unpleasant. For instance, the smell of peanut butter may transport you back to your elementary school lunchroom and, in turn, remind you either of the bully who stole your cookies or the best friend who sat next to you every day.

You cannot smell a substance unless some of its molecules vaporize—that is, pass from a solid or liquid into a gaseous state. Heat speeds up the vaporization of molecules, which is why food that is cooking has a stronger and more distinct odor than uncooked food. When odor molecules vaporize, they become airborne and make their way up each nostril to the olfactory epithelium. The olfactory epithelium consists of

olfaction (ol-FAK-shun) The sense of smell.

olfactory epithelium Two 1-square-inch patches of tissue, one at the top of each nasal cavity, which together contain about 10 million olfactory neurons, the receptors for smell.

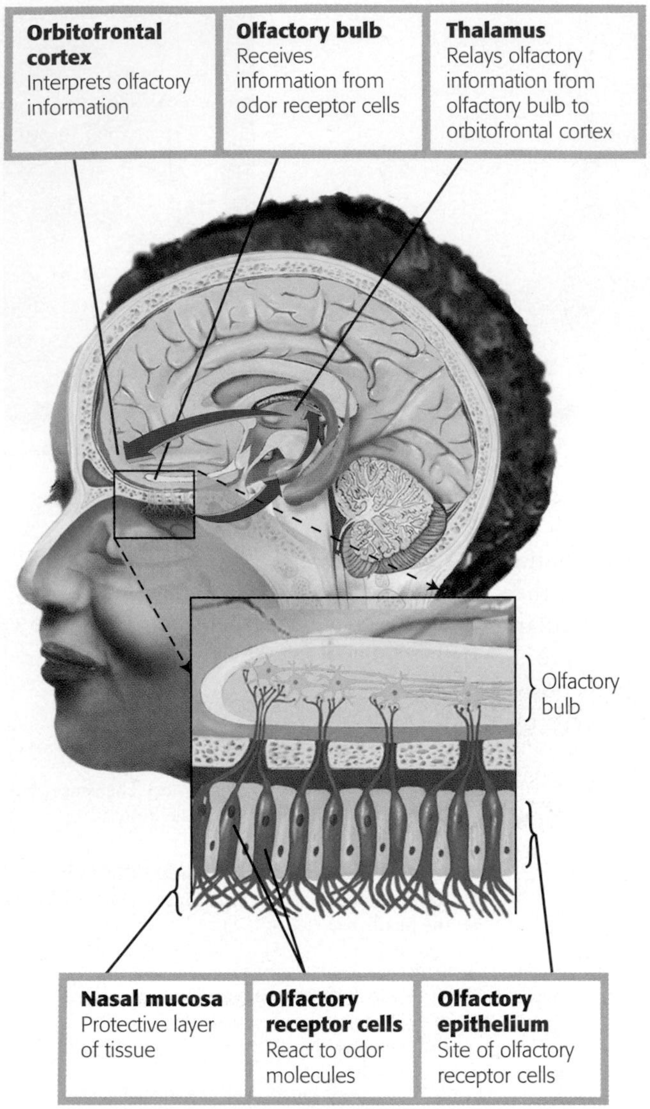

Orbitofrontal cortex	Olfactory bulb	Thalamus
Interprets olfactory information	Receives information from odor receptor cells	Relays olfactory information from olfactory bulb to orbitofrontal cortex

Olfactory bulb

Nasal mucosa	Olfactory receptor cells	Olfactory epithelium
Protective layer of tissue	React to odor molecules	Site of olfactory receptor cells

FIGURE 3.9 The Olfactory System
Odor molecules travel up the nostrils to the olfactory epithelium, which contains the receptor cells for smell. Olfactory receptors are special neurons whose axons form the olfactory nerve. The olfactory nerve relays smell messages to the olfactory bulbs, which pass them on to the amygdala and olfactory cortex. From there, they go to the limbic system, the thalamus, and orbitofrontal cortex.

3.10 How do we detect the primary taste sensations?

olfactory bulbs Two matchstick-sized structures above the nasal cavities, where smell sensations first register in the brain.

gustation The sense of taste.

two 1-square-inch patches of tissue, one at the top of each nasal cavity; together these patches contain about 10 million olfactory neurons, which are the receptor cells for smell. Each of these neurons contains only one of the 1,000 different types of odor receptors (Bargmann, 1996). Because humans are able to detect some 10,000 odors, each of the 1,000 types of odor receptors must be able to respond to more than one kind of odor molecule. Moreover, some odor molecules trigger more than one type of odor receptor (Axel, 1995). The intensity of a smell stimulus—how strong or weak it is—is apparently determined by the number of olfactory neurons firing at the same time (Freeman, 1991). Figure 3.9 shows a diagram of the human olfactory system.

Have you ever wondered why dogs have a keener sense of smell than humans? Not only do many dogs have a long snout, but, in some breeds, the olfactory epithelium can be as large as the area of a handkerchief and can contain 20 times as many olfactory neurons as in humans (Engen, 1982). It is well known that dogs use scent to recognize not only other members of their species but also the humans with whom they live. Humans have this ability, too. The mothers of newborns can recognize their own babies by smell within hours after birth. But can humans recognize the scents of other species—their own pets, for example? Yes, to a remarkable degree. When presented with blankets permeated with the scents of dogs, some 89% of the dog owners easily identified their own dog by smell (Wells & Hepper, 2000).

Olfactory neurons are different from all other sensory receptors: They both come into direct contact with sensory stimuli and reach directly into the brain. These neurons have a short life span; after functioning for only about 60 days, they die and are replaced by new cells (Bensafi et al., 2004).

The axons of the olfactory neurons relay a smell message directly to the olfactory bulbs—two brain structures the size of matchsticks that rest above the nasal cavities (refer to Figure 3.9). Smell sensations then travel to the amygdala, part of the limbic system, and the nearby olfactory cortex. Olfactory messages leave the amygdala and olfactory cortex via two pathways. One of these pathways carries smell sensations to other parts of limbic system for emotional interpretation. The other pathway sends olfactory information to cells in the thalamus that relay it to the orbitofrontal cortex for cognitive interpretation.

The process of sensing odors is the same in every individual, but there are large differences in sensitivity to smells. For example, perfumers and whiskey blenders can distinguish subtle variations in odors that are indistinguishable to the average person. Young people are more sensitive to odors than older people, and nonsmokers are more sensitive than smokers (Boyce & Shone, 2006; Danielides et al., 2009).

Taste

You might be surprised to learn that much of the pleasure you attribute to the sense of taste actually arises from smells, when odor molecules are forced up the nasal cavity by the action of the tongue, cheeks, and throat when you chew and swallow. Even without a sense of taste, your sense of smell would provide you with some taste sensations. Still, life without the ability to fully experience the tastes of the foods we love would, no doubt, be less enjoyable.

Psychology textbooks long maintained that gustation, the sense of taste, produced four distinct kinds of taste sensations: sweet, sour, salty, and bitter. This is true. But researchers now know that there is a fifth taste sensation in humans (Herness, 2000). This fifth taste sensation, called *umami*, is triggered by the substance glutamate, which, in the form of monosodium glutamate (MSG), is widely used as a flavoring in

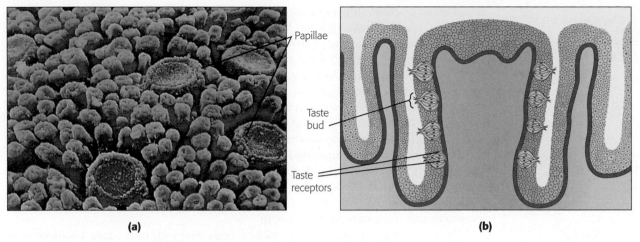

FIGURE 3.10 The Tongue's Papillae and Taste Buds
(a) A photomicrograph of the surface of the tongue shows several papillae. (b) This vertical cross-section through a papilla reveals the location of the taste buds and taste receptors.

Asian foods (Matsunami, Montmayeur, & Buck, 2000). Many protein-rich foods, such as meat, milk, aged cheese, and seafood, also contain glutamate.

All five taste sensations can be detected on all locations of the tongue. Indeed, even a person with no tongue could still taste to some extent, thanks to the taste receptors found in the palate, in the mucous lining of the cheeks and lips, and in parts of the throat, including the tonsils. When tastes are mixed, the specialized receptors for each type of flavor are activated and send separate messages to the brain (Sugita & Shiba, 2005). In other words, your brain perceives the two distinctive flavors present in sweet-and-sour sauce quite separately. This analytical quality of the sense of taste prevents your being fooled into eating spoiled or poisoned food when the characteristic taste of either is combined with some kind of pleasant flavor.

If you look at your tongue in a mirror, you will see many small bumps called *papillae*. Taste buds lie alongside some of these papillae (see Figure 3.10). Each taste bud is composed of 60 to 100 receptor cells. The life span of the taste receptors is very short—only about 10 days—and they are continually being replaced.

Research indicates that individuals vary widely in their capacity for experiencing taste sensations (Yackinous & Guinard, 2002). Nontasters are unable to taste certain sweet and bitter compounds, but they do taste most other substances, albeit with less sensitivity. Supertasters taste these sweet and bitter compounds with far stronger intensity than other people. Researchers are currently investigating links between taste sensitivity, eating behaviors, and health status variables, such as obesity (Tepper, 2008). For example, supertasters who are particularly sensitive to the chemical that gives fruits and vegetables a bitter taste eat less salad than medium tasters and nontasters (Yackinous & Guinard, 2002). Still, supertasters appear no more likely to be overweight than medium tasters or nontasters. In fact, among individuals who report that they never deliberately restrict their diets to try to lose weight, supertasters of the bitter chemical have less body fat than medium tasters or nontasters (Tepper & Ullrich, 2002). So, researchers know that taste sensitivity is linked to food preferences but not how these preferences may be connected to nutritional status.

▲ Cultures vary widely in their taste preferences. Curry, for example, is commonly used in Indian foods. Westerners may find it to be too spicy for their tastes when they first try Indian food, but the process of sensory adaptation will occur if they regularly consume such foods.

taste buds Structures along the sides of many of the tongue's papillae that are composed of 60 to 100 receptor cells for taste.

Touch and Pain ▶

Your natural clothing, the skin, is the largest organ of your body. It performs many important biological functions while also providing much of what is known as sensual pleasure. Tactile information is conveyed to the brain when an object touches and depresses the skin, stimulating one or more of the several distinct types of receptors found in the nerve endings. These sensitive nerve endings in the skin send the

⌐ **3.11** How does the skin provide pleasant and unpleasant ⌐ sensations?

tactile Pertaining to the sense of touch.

touch message through nerve connections to the spinal cord. The message travels up the spinal cord and through the brainstem and the midbrain, finally reaching the somatosensory cortex. (Recall from Chapter 2 that the somatosensory cortex is the strip of tissue at the front of the parietal lobes where touch, pressure, temperature, and pain register.) Once the somatosensory cortex has been activated, you become aware of where and how hard you have been touched. In the 1890s, one of the most prominent researchers of the tactile sense, Max von Frey, discovered the *two-point threshold*—the measure of how far apart two touch points on the skin must be before they are felt as two separate touches.

If you could examine the skin from the outermost to the deepest layer, you would find a variety of nerve endings that differ markedly in appearance. Most or all of these nerve endings appear to respond in some degree to all types of tactile stimulation. The more densely packed with these sensory receptors a part of the body's surface is, the more sensitive it is to tactile stimulation.

How important is the sense of touch? Classic research in the mid-1980s demonstrated that premature infants who were massaged for 15 minutes three times a day gained weight 47% faster than other premature infants who received only regular intensive care treatment (Field et al., 1986). The massaged infants were more responsive and were able to leave the hospital about 6 days earlier on average than those who were not massaged. Thus, the sense of touch is not only one of the more pleasant aspects of life, but is also critical to our survival.

Scientists are not certain how pain works, but one major theory that attempts to answer this question is the *gate-control theory* of Ronald Melzack and Patrick Wall (1965, 1983). These researchers contend that an area in the spinal cord can act like a "gate" and either block pain messages or transmit them to the brain. Only so many messages can go through the gate at any one time. You feel pain when pain messages carried by small, slow-conducting nerve fibers reach the gate and cause it to open. Large, fast-conducting nerve fibers carry other sensory messages from the body; these can effectively tie up traffic at the gate so that it will close and keep many of the pain messages from getting through. What is the first thing you do when you stub your toe or pound your finger with a hammer? If you rub or apply gentle pressure to the injury, you are stimulating the large, fast-conducting nerve fibers, which get their message to the spinal gate first and block some of the pain messages from the slower-conducting nerve fibers. Applying ice, heat, or electrical stimulation to the painful area also stimulates the large nerve fibers and closes the spinal gate.

The gate-control theory also accounts for the fact that psychological factors, both cognitive and emotional, can influence the perception of pain. Melzack and Wall (1965, 1983) contend that messages from the brain to the spinal cord can inhibit the transmission of pain messages at the spinal gate, thereby affecting the perception of pain. This phenomenon explains why soldiers injured in battle or athletes injured during games can be so distracted that they do not experience pain until some time after the injury. Likewise, distraction can be an effective pain management strategy. In one study, researchers applied a vibrator to one of the children's arms while they were getting an injection in the other. They also instructed the children to watch as the vibrator moved up and down their arms. The study showed that the children who were in the vibrator group experienced little or no pain from the injection.

But what about long-term pain? Not surprisingly, distraction is of little use in managing the ongoing pain of conditions such as *arthritis*, chronic inflammation of the joints. Still, there are psychological techniques that help. Strategies such as relaxation techniques, which you will read about in Chapter 4, provide some relief for the anxiety associated with chronic pain (Dixon et al., 2007). However, they do not seem to actually prevent pain sensations.

Intense types of pain seem to be resistant to psychological management as well. For example, many pregnant women attend prepared childbirth classes in which they learn controlled breathing, focused massage, and other strategies for managing labor pains. However, research indicates that women who use them are no less likely to request pharmacological pain relief than

▼ The skills that women learn in prepared childbirth classes help them cope with the anxieties that accompany the pain of childbirth. However, women who attend such classes are no less likely to request pain-relieving drugs than women who do not.

are those who do not (Bergström, Kieler, & Waldenström, 2009). Nevertheless, these strategies help women manage the anxieties associated with labor and delivery (Kimber et al., 2008).

Although psychological pain management may not be of much help during childbirth, research suggests that the mind gets a lot of help from the body when it comes to managing the pain of labor and delivery. During the last few weeks of pregnancy, a woman's body is flooded with higher levels of estrogen than she experiences at any other time of life. Estrogen levels determine how sensitive a woman's neurons are to the effects of endorphins, the pain-blocking neurotransmitters you learned about in Chapter 2 (Smith et al., 2006). The higher estrogen levels are, the better the neurons are at using endorphins. Moreover, the quantity of endorphins in a woman's system increases dramatically in the last few weeks of pregnancy and rises again when she goes into labor (Abboud et al., 1983; Hughes, Levinson, Rosen, & Shnider, 2002). Even after administration of pain-relieving drugs, the laboring woman's level of endorphins remains much higher than is typical in the nonpregnant state.

Similarly, endorphins are released when you are injured, when you experience stress or extreme pain, and when you laugh, cry, or exercise. Recent findings suggest that the release of endorphins that occurs during acupuncture treatments may be one of the factors involved in individuals who respond favorably to such treatments for conditions such as chronic back pain (Cabýoglu, Ergene, & Tan, 2006).

Some people release endorphins even when they merely *think* they are receiving pain medication but are being given, instead, a placebo in the form of a sugar pill or an injection of saline solution (Zubieta et al., 2005). Imaging studies confirm that placebo administration causes a reduction of activity in the regions of the brain that are associated with pain perception (Price, Finniss, & Benedetti, 2008). Why? Apparently, when patients believe that they have received a drug for pain, that belief stimulates the release of their own natural pain relievers, the endorphins.

Finally, the proportion of people who suffer from chronic pain, or pain that lasts for three months or longer, varies across cultures. Why? Researchers don't have a definitive answer. However, they do know that the experience of pain has both physical and emotional components, both of which vary from person to person. Animal studies showing that biochemical changes take place in the cells of the amygdala when chronic pain is experienced support the notion that pain and emotion are linked (Narita et al., 2006). Thus, pain experts distinguish between pain and suffering—suffering being the affective, or emotional, response to pain. Sullivan and others (1995) found that people suffered most from pain when they harbored negative thoughts about it, feared its potential threat to their well-being, and expressed feelings of helplessness. Thus, cross-cultural variations in chronic pain may be linked to differences in people's emotional states.

endorphins (en-DOR-fins) The body's own natural painkillers, which block pain and produce a feeling of well-being.

Influences on Perception

So far, you have been reading about *sensation*, the process of taking in information from the outside world through the senses. We've discussed vision, hearing, smell, taste, touch, and the spatial orientation senses. However, we have yet to discuss *perception*, the process through which the brain assigns meaning to sensations. For instance, your senses provide you with information about the color, taste, and smell of an apple, as well as the sound that happens when you bite into one. Sensation even provides you with the kinesthetic sense needed to toss an apple to your roommate. By contrast, perception enables you to link these sensations to the knowledge that apples are food, that you either like or dislike them, and that they have a variety of symbolic associations (e.g., "an apple for the teacher").

Perception is influenced by a number of factors. Before we discuss some of the principles that govern perception in all human beings, we will consider three factors that contribute to perceptual processes: attention, prior knowledge, and cross-modal perception.

3.12 What do we gain and lose when we attend to a stimulus?

Attention

In some cases, linking sensations to meanings—the essence of the process of perception—requires very little mental effort. For instance, when reading familiar words, the sensation of seeing the word and the perception of its meaning occur almost simultaneously (Heil Rolke, & Pecchineda, 2004). Likewise, while we are driving, perceiving that the other objects on the road with us are cars takes very little mental effort because we are so familiar with them. In other words, connecting the sensation of seeing a car with the perception that the object is a car is an *automatic* (noneffortful) mental process. However, more mental effort is required to determine which cars we should watch most closely. When we engage in this kind of mental effort, the process of *attention* is at work. Attention is defined as the process of sorting through sensations and selecting some of them for further processing. Without attention, perception of all but the most familiar sensations would be impossible.

attention The process of sorting through sensations and selecting some of them for further processing.

inattentional blindness The phenomenon in which we shift our focus from one object to another and, in the process, fail to notice changes in objects to which we are not directly paying attention.

Of course, we cannot pay attention to everything at once. Thus, in a complex perceptual task, such as the everyday experience of driving in traffic, it's important to realize that attention carries certain perceptual costs. Research examining the phenomenon of inattentional blindness has helped to illustrate these costs (Bressan & Pizzighello, 2008; Simons & Rensink, 2005). Inattentional blindness occurs when we shift our attention from one object to another and, in the process, fail to notice changes in objects to which we are not directly paying attention (Woodman & Luck, 2003). In many studies of inattentional blindness, experimenters have presented participants with a scene and asked them to attend to a particular element in it. For example, in a classic study, Daniel Simons and colleagues (e.g., Simons & Chabris, 1999) showed participants a videotape of a basketball game in which one team wore white uniforms and the other team wore black uniforms. Participants were instructed to count how many times the ball was passed from one player to another, either on the white team or on the black team. Under such conditions, about one-third of participants typically failed to later recall the appearance on the screen of even extremely incongruent stimuli (for example, a man dressed in a gorilla costume). The inattentional blindness happens even when the incongruous stimulus is present on the screen for a long period of time. Interestingly, too, expertise does not influence inattentional blindness; that is, a person is just as likely to exhibit the phenomenon when observing scenes that depict activities in which she has a great deal of knowledge and experience as she is when observing other types of scenes (Memmert, Simons, & Grimme, 2009). Simons's research helps us understand why we sometimes exclaim, "Where did that car come from?" when a car we had been ignoring suddenly swerves into our path. Read the *Apply It* feature to learn about the possible dangers of using a cell phone while driving.

▲ When you look at this photograph, you can easily notice the gorilla-costumed figure. However, this photo is actually a frame from a video used in Simons's inattentional blindness studies. Participants are shown the video after being told to keep track of how many times a basketball is passed from one person to another. Under these conditions, participants typically fail to notice when the gorilla-costumed figure enters the scene.

Similar costs arise when we attend to auditory sensations. Suppose you are standing in a crowded room in which a large number of conversations are going on simultaneously. What would happen if someone mentioned your name? Research shows that you would zero in on the conversation that included your name and ignore others. This *cocktail party phenomenon* was documented in classic research by E. C. Cherry (1953). Remember, perception is the process of attaching meaning to sensations—and what is more meaningful to a person than his or her own name? Thus, when you hear your name, you assume that whatever is to follow will be personally meaningful to you. The process of attending to the conversation that included your name, however, would prevent you from adequately perceiving other conversations. Thus, you might fail to pick up on other conversations that might have more meaning for you but are free from obvious attentional cues such as your name.

Although attending to a stimulus is associated with deficits in the ability to attend to other stimuli, attention is clearly not an all-or-nothing process. We can, and often do, process more than one stimulus at a time. Indeed, research shows that we are

APPLY IT How Dangerous Is It to Talk on a Cell Phone or Text while Driving?

When you read about the research demonstrating inattentional blindness, did it raise your level of concern about the possible dangers of driving while talking or texting on a cell phone? Interestingly, surveys suggest that we are more concerned about other drivers' cell phone use than our own. In one study, researchers found that just 6% of drivers reported that their cell phone use had caused them to get into a potentially dangerous situation on the road. Remarkably, when participants were asked whether another driver's cell phone use had ever put them at risk, 66% said yes (Troglauer, Hels, & Christens, 2006). As much as we would like to believe that cell phones affect other drivers' behavior but not our own, research clearly shows that talking or texting on a cell phone, or engaging in other kinds of attention-demanding tasks, results in potentially dangerous changes in our behind-the-wheel behavior.

Behavioral Effects of Cell Phone Use

Most experiments examining cell phone use while driving take place in laboratories in which participants use driving simulators. Experimental group participants talk or text on the cell phone while driving, but those in the control groups do not. Studies of this type show that cell phone use affects drivers' behavior in the following ways (Beede & Kass, 2006; Harrold et al., 2009; Liu & Lee, 2006):

- Drivers slow down when using the phone.
- Drivers have slower reaction times when engaged in phone conversations or texting.
- Drivers who talk on a cell phone often fail to stay within the boundaries of the lane in which they are driving.
- Cell-phone-using drivers sometimes stop at green lights but drive through red lights and stop signs.

These effects have been observed just as often in studies using hands-free phones as conventional handheld models (Strayer & Drews, 2004). However, one study suggested that hands-free phone use gave drivers a false sense of safety (Langer, Holzner, Magnet, & Kopp, 2005). Thus, experimental studies show definitively that, on average, cell phone use impairs driving ability.

Compensating for the Effects of Cell Phone Use

Despite the clear findings of these studies, other research suggests that several factors help drivers compensate for the distractions associated with cell phone use (Hunton & Rose, 2005; Pöysti, Rajalin, & Summala, 2005; Shinar, Tractinsky, & Compton, 2005). Here are a few of them:

- Experience with multitasking improves drivers' ability to juggle the demands of cell phone use and driving.

- Reducing other distractions, such as turning off the radio, helps drivers keep their minds on driving while also talking on the phone.
- Some drivers end a cell phone call with "I'll call you back later when I'm not driving," when they realize that the attentional demands of a specific conversation are incompatible with those of driving.

These findings show that drivers are well aware of the potentially risk-enhancing effects of behavior changes caused by distractions. As a result, they actively work to manage the number of demands on their attention while driving.

It's about Attention, Not Cell Phones

You may know from personal experience that several attention-demanding tasks impair driving behaviors just as much as cell phone use does. For example, talking to a passenger or searching for a radio station while driving produces the same kinds of detrimental effects on drivers' behavior as cell phone use (Amado & Ulupinar, 2005; Horberry et al., 2006). Therefore, for drivers, the takeaway message from this chapter's discussion of inattentional blindness is clear. When drivers pay attention to anything that is not relevant to the task of operating a vehicle—be it a cell phone, a radio, or a conversation with a passenger—they limit their ability to focus on driving. Consequently, the goal of anyone who is operating a vehicle ought to be to minimize distractions to as great a degree as possible:

- Texting is more dangerous than talking on a cell phone because you must divert your eyes from the road (Harrold et al., 2009). Therefore, experts recommend that drivers NEVER text while driving.
- If possible, drivers should pull off the road to talk on their cell phones.
- Radio station adjustments should be postponed until drivers are stopped at a red light or stop sign.
- Whenever passengers are distracting them, drivers should politely request that they refrain from talking.

By taking these measures, drivers will reduce their risk of missing important cues such as traffic lights and decrease the likelihood that they will, at best, get a traffic ticket, or, at worst, cause an accident.

Watch on **mypsychlab.com**

capable of accurately perceiving some sensations to which we do not pay direct attention. For example, in the same series of classic studies that led to the discovery of the cocktail party phenomenon, E. C. Cherry (1953) discovered that listeners who were presented with different verbal messages in either ear could remember the content of only the message to which the experimenter directed their attention (e.g., "Pay attention to the message in your left ear"). Nevertheless, they were able to remember many things about the unattended message, such as whether it had been delivered by a male or a female.

But what happens when we get conflicting information from two or more senses? How do we know which one to pay attention to? Experiments in which participants are exposed to conflicting visual and auditory information have shown that cross-modal perception, a process through which the brain integrates information from more than one sense, depends on the comparative accuracy of the conflicting sensations. For example, you have participated in a cross-modal perception "experiment" if you have ever seen a movie in which the actors' lip movements didn't match their spoken language. Research shows that it is very difficult to understand speech under such conditions (Thomas & Jordan, 2004). In effect, we must block out the visual information to understand what the speakers are saying. The opposite happens when facial expressions and vocal characteristics seem to be conveying different emotional messages. When a person looks angry but speaks in a happy voice, the visual information is typically judged to be more reliable than the auditory input (Vroomen, Driver, & Degelder, 2001).

cross-modal perception A process whereby the brain integrates information from more than one sense.

3.13 How does prior knowledge influence perception?

Prior Knowledge

Think back to the example of attending to cars on the road while driving. How do we make judgments about which cars require most of our attention? To a great extent, our past driving experiences, or prior knowledge, help us make such decisions. Prior knowledge is helpful when interpreting the meanings of sensations, but it can lead to perceptual errors as well.

Suppose you were presented with this array of letters and numbers. How would you go about trying to use your prior knowledge to make sense of it?

DP
6-4-3

If you don't immediately recognize the array, you might begin trying to decipher it by guessing what the letters *DP* stand for, a classic example of bottom-up processing or *data-driven* processing. This strategy involves looking for patterns in individual bits of information that can be interpreted using prior knowledge. For example, bottom-up processing might lead you to call up compound nouns (nouns made up of two words) from your memory, such as "Detroit Police" or "data projector," that the letters might stand for. Perhaps you would try to decide which of these two possible meanings of "DP" was more feasible based on the information given in "6–4–3." Ultimately, you would probably give up and declare the array either meaningless or indecipherable.

bottom-up processing Information processing in which individual components or bits of data are combined until a complete perception is formed.

Suppose we told you that the array has something to do with baseball. Now, if you have some knowledge of the game, you might try to think of baseball terms that could be represented by the letters *DP*. In so doing, you would be using top-down processing or *concept-driven* processing. In top-down processing, prior knowledge limits the range of one's guesses by providing a "whole" that can serve as a context for individual bits of information. Thus, given that baseball is the context for the array, neither "Detroit Police" nor "data projector" will fit. Of course, if you know how to score a baseball game, you probably instantly moved into top-down processing mode when you saw the array. No doubt, you recognized the array as representing a double play (DP) in which the short-stop (6) threw the ball to the second baseman (4) who, in turn, threw it to the first baseman (3) to get two runners out. ☀ Explore on mypsychlab.com

top-down processing Information processing in which previous experience and conceptual knowledge are applied to recognize the whole of a perception and thus easily identify the simpler elements of that whole.

☀ Explore the Concept *Top Down Processing* on mypsychlab.com

This example might lead you to think that bottom-up processing seldom leads to accurate perceptions. However, there are some situations in which only bottom-up processing will work. A "find the differences" activity, such as the one in Figure 3.11, provides a good example of a task that can only be accomplished through bottom-up processing. Why? Top-down processing causes you to perceive the scene as a whole and, as a result, to overlook details. To find the differences, you have to look at the items individually, without allowing the picture to contextualize them.

> If you created titles for these two scenes, would you be using bottom-up or top-down processing?

FIGURE 3.11 A Bottom-Up Processing Task
A bottom-up processing strategy is the best approach to some kind of tasks because top-down processing prevents you from processing the details in the two scences pictured.
Source: Highlights for Children (May, 1995).

However, as you'll learn from doing the *Try It*, bottom-up and top-down processes are interactive. Technically speaking, decoding tasks like the one in the *Try It* call for bottom-up processing. Thus, you'll probably start out using the key to decode the first couple of letters in each word (bottom-up processing). But after you decode one or two letters in each work, you're likely to develop a hunch about what the word might be. Subsequently, when you look at the key, your hunch will guide your search (top-down processing).

Prior knowledge also contributes to perception by leading us to expect certain perceptions. For example, if you ordered raspberry sherbet and it was colored green, would it still taste like raspberry, or might it taste more like lime? The perceptual set—what we expect to perceive—determines, to a large extent, what we actually see, hear, feel, taste, and smell. Such expectations are, of course, based on prior knowledge (that lime sherbert is usually green). Such expectations do seem to influence perception. So, green raspberry sherbert might, indeed, taste a bit like lime.

In a classic study of perceptual set, psychologist David Rosenhan (1973) and some of his colleagues were admitted as patients to various mental hospitals with "diagnoses" of schizophrenia. Once admitted, they acted normal in every way. The purpose? They wondered how long it would take the doctors and the hospital staff to realize that they were not mentally ill. But the doctors and the staff members saw what they expected to see and not what actually occurred. They perceived everything the pseudo-patients said and did, such as note taking, to be symptoms of their illness. But the real patients were not fooled; they were the first to realize that the psychologists were not really mentally ill.

perceptual set An expectation of what will be perceived, which can affect what actually is perceived.

TRY IT ▶ Bottom-Up and Top-Down Processing

Decode these words:

1. GIVV

2. DRMWLD

3. ELOFMGVVI

4. NZTRX

5. YILMGLHZFIFH

KEY

A = Z	H = S	O = L	V = E
B = Y	I = R	P = K	W = D
C = X	J = Q	Q = J	X = C
D = W	K = P	R = I	Y = B
E = V	L = O	S = H	Z = A
F = U	M = N	T = G	
G = T	N = M	U = F	

ANSWERS: 1. TREE; 2. WINDOW; 3. VOLUNTEER; 4. MAGIC; 5. BRONTOSAURUS

Principles of Perception

Some influences on perception—particularly the application of prior knowledge to perceptual tasks—can lead to wide variations in how a stimulus is perceived. However, researchers have found a few principles that appear to govern perceptions in all human beings.

3.14 What are the Gestalt principles of perceptual organization?

Gestalt (geh-SHTALT) A German word that roughly refers to the whole form, pattern, or configuration that a person perceives.

Perceptual Organization and Constancy

The Gestalt psychologists maintained that people cannot understand the perceptual world by breaking down experiences into tiny parts and analyzing them separately. When sensory elements are brought together, something new is formed. That is, the whole is more than just the sum of its parts. The German word Gestalt has no exact English equivalent, but it roughly refers to the whole form, pattern, or configuration that a person perceives. The Gestalt psychologists claimed that sensory experience is organized according to certain basic principles of perceptual organization:

- *Figure–ground.* As we view the world, some object (the figure) often seems to stand out from the background (the ground) (see Figure 3.12).
- *Similarity.* Objects that have similar characteristics are perceived as a unit. In Figure 3.12, dots of a similar color are perceived as belonging together to form horizontal rows on the left and vertical columns on the right.
- *Proximity.* Objects that are close together in space or time are usually perceived as belonging together. Because of their spacing, the lines in Figure 3.12 are perceived as four pairs of lines rather than as eight separate lines.
- *Continuity.* We tend to perceive figures or objects as belonging together if they appear to form a continuous pattern such as a line or wave, as in Figure 3.12.
- *Closure.* We perceive figures with gaps in them to be complete. Even though parts of the figure in Figure 3.12 are missing, we use closure and perceive it as a triangle.

When you say good-bye to friends and watch them walk away, the image they cast on your retina grows smaller and smaller until they finally disappear in the distance. So how does your brain know that they are still the same size? Scientists call this phenomenon perceptual constancy. Thanks to perceptual constancy, when you watch someone walk away, the information that the retina sends to the brain (the sensation that that person is shrinking in size) does not fool the perceptual system. As objects or people move farther away, you continue to perceive them as being about the same size. This perceptual phenomenon is known as *size constancy.* You do not make a literal

perceptual constancy The phenomenon that allows us to perceive objects as maintaining stable properties, such as size, shape, and brightness, despite differences in distance, viewing angle, and lighting.

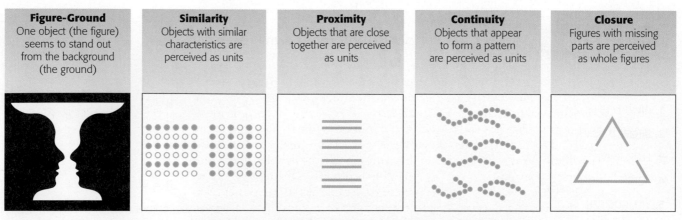

Figure-Ground	Similarity	Proximity	Continuity	Closure
One object (the figure) seems to stand out from the background (the ground)	Objects with similar characteristics are perceived as units	Objects that are close together are perceived as units	Objects that appear to form a pattern are perceived as units	Figures with missing parts are perceived as whole figures

FIGURE 3.12 Gestalt Principles of Perceptual Organization
Gestalt psychologists proposed several principles of perceptual organization, including figure–ground, similarity, proximity, continuity, and closure.

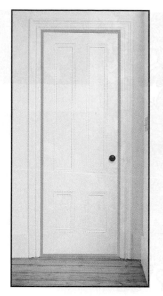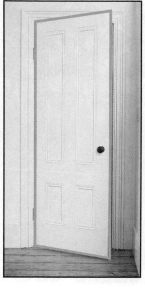

interpretation about the size of an object from its retinal image—the image of the object projected onto the retina. If you did, you would believe that objects become larger as they approach and smaller as they move away. ⊙►─Simulate on **mypsychlab.com**

The shape or image of an object projected onto the retina changes according to the angle from which it is viewed. But your perceptual ability includes *shape constancy*—the tendency to perceive objects as having a stable or unchanging shape, regardless of changes in the retinal image resulting from differences in viewing angle. In other words, you perceive a door as rectangular and a plate as round from whatever angle you view them (see Figure 3.13).

We normally see objects as maintaining a constant level of brightness, regardless of differences in lighting conditions—a perceptual phenomenon known as *brightness constancy*. Nearly all objects reflect some part of the light that falls on them, and white objects reflect more light than black objects. However, a black asphalt driveway at noon in bright sunlight actually reflects more light than a white shirt does indoors at night in dim lighting. Nevertheless, the driveway still looks black, and the shirt still looks white. Why? We learn to infer the brightness of an object by comparing it with the brightness of all other objects viewed at the same time.

Depth Perception ▶

Depth perception is the ability to perceive the visual world in three dimensions and to judge distances accurately. We judge how far away objects and other people are. We climb and descend stairs without stumbling and perform numerous other actions requiring depth perception. Depth perception is three dimensional. Yet each eye is able to provide only a two-dimensional view. The images cast on the retina do not contain depth; they are flat, just like a photograph. How, then, do we perceive depth so vividly?

Some cues to depth perception depend on both eyes working together. These binocular depth cues include convergence and binocular disparity. *Convergence* occurs when the eyes turn inward to focus on nearby objects—the closer the object, the more the two objects appear to come together. Hold the tip of your finger about 12 inches in front of your nose and focus on it. Now, slowly begin moving your finger toward your nose. Your eyes will turn inward so much that they virtually cross when the tip of your finger meets the tip of your nose. Many psychologists believe that the tension of the eye muscles as they converge conveys to the brain information that serves as a cue for depth perception. Fortunately, the eyes are just far enough apart, about $2\frac{1}{2}$ inches or so, to give each eye a slightly different view of the objects being focused on and, consequently, a slightly different retinal image. The difference between the two retinal images, known as *binocular disparity* (or *retinal disparity*), provides an important cue

⊙►─**Simulate** the **Experiment**
Distinguising Figure–Ground Relationships on **mypsychlab.com**

3.15 What do monocular and binocular cues contribute to perception?

depth perception The ability to perceive the visual world in three dimensions and to judge distances accurately.

binocular depth cues Depth cues that depend on both eyes working together.

that your eyes, not the lights, are moving. Because of the darkness of the room, the brain has no stable visual reference point to use in deciding whether the lights are actually moving (Gibson, 1994). But when the room is lit up, the brain immediately "fixes" the error because it has a stable visible background for the lights.

In one kind of study of false-motion perceptions, several stationary lights in a dark room are flashed on and off in sequence, causing participants to perceive a single light moving from one spot to the next. This type of illusion, called the *phi phenomenon* (sometimes called *stroboscopic motion*), was first discussed by Max Wertheimer (1912), one of the founders of Gestalt psychology. You encounter one of the most common examples of the phi phenomenon whenever you go to the movies. As you probably know, movies are simply a series of still photographs shown in rapid succession.

Unusual Perceptual Experiences

Having read about the senses and the factors that influence and govern perception, you are probably convinced by now that sensation and perception enable us to make sense of the world we live in. But what happens when these vital processes are fooled, that is, when they lead us to believe that we see or hear something that really isn't there? Further, is it possible to perceive without sensing?

3.17 What are three puzzling perceptions?

Puzzling Perceptions

Not only can we perceive motion that doesn't exist, but we can also perceive objects that aren't present in a stimulus and misinterpret those that are.

When you are faced for the first time with an *ambiguous figure*, you have no experience to call on. Your perceptual system is puzzled and tries to resolve the uncertainty by seeing the ambiguous figure first one way and then another, but not both ways at once. You never get a lasting impression of ambiguous figures because they seem to jump back and forth beyond your control. In some ambiguous figures, two different objects or figures are seen alternately. The best known of these, "Old Woman/Young Woman," by E. G. Boring, is shown in Figure 3.16(a). If you direct your gaze to the left of the drawing, you are likely to see an attractive young woman, her face turned away. But the young woman disappears when you suddenly perceive the image of the old woman. Such examples of object ambiguity offer striking evidence that perceptions are more than the mere sum of sensory parts. It is hard to believe that the same drawing (the same sum of sensory parts) can convey such dramatically different perceptions. ✳─⌐Explore on **mypsychlab.com**

✳─⌐Explore the **Concept** *Five Well-Known Illusions* on **mypsychlab.com**

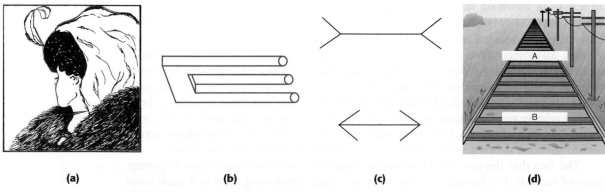

(a)   (b)   (c)   (d)

FIGURE 3.16 Some Puzzling Perceptions
(a) Do you see an old woman or a young woman? (b) Why couldn't you build a replica of this three-pronged device? (c) Which horizontal line appears to be longer? (d) Which bar, A or B, is longer?
Source: "A New Ambiguous Figure" by E. G. Boring (1930).

At first glance, many impossible figures do not seem particularly unusual—at least not until you examine them more closely. Would you invest your money in a company that manufactured the three-pronged device shown in Figure 3.16(b)? Such an object could not be made as pictured because the middle prong appears to be in two different places at the same time. However, this type of impossible figure is more likely to confuse people from Western cultures. Classic research in the 1970s showed that people in some African cultures do not represent three-dimensional visual space in their art, and they do not perceive depth in drawings that contain pictorial depth cues. These people see no ambiguity in drawings similar to the three-pronged trident, and they can draw the figure accurately from memory much more easily than people from Western cultures can (Bloomer, 1976).

An *illusion* is a false perception or a misperception of an actual stimulus in the environment. We can misperceive size, shape, or the relationship of one element to another. We need not pay to see illusions performed by magicians. Illusions occur naturally, and we see them all the time. An oar in the water appears to be bent where it meets the water. The moon looks much larger at the horizon than it does overhead. Why? One explanation of the *moon illusion* involves relative size. This idea suggests that the moon looks very large on the horizon because it is viewed in comparison to trees, buildings, and other objects. When viewed overhead, the moon cannot be directly compared with other objects, and it appears smaller.

In Figure 3.16(c), the two lines are the same length, but the diagonals extending outward from both ends of the upper line make it look longer than the lower line, which has diagonals pointing inward, a phenomenon known as the *Müller-Lyer illusion*. The *Ponzo illusion* also plays an interesting trick on our estimation of size. Look at Figure 3.16(d). Contrary to your perceptions, bars A and B are the same length. Again, perceptions of size and distance, which we trust and which are normally accurate in informing us about the real world, can be wrong. If you saw two obstructions like the ones in the illusion on real railroad tracks, the one that looks larger would indeed be larger. So the Ponzo illusion is not a natural illusion but a contrived one. In fact, all these illusions are really misapplications of principles that nearly always work properly in normal everyday experience.

Because responses to a number of illusions are universal, many psychologists believe they are inborn. However, British psychologist R. L. Gregory believed that susceptibility to the Müller-Lyer and other such illusions is not innate. Rather, the culture in which people live is responsible to some extent for the illusions they perceive. To test whether susceptibility to the Müller-Lyer and similar illusions is due to experience, Segall and others (1966) tested 1,848 adults and children from 15 different cultures in Africa, the Philippines, and the United States. Included were a group of Zulus from South Africa and a group of Illinois residents. The study revealed that "there were marked differences in illusion susceptibility across the cultural groups included in this study" (Segall, 1994, p. 137). People from all the cultures showed some tendency to perceive the Müller-Lyer illusion, indicating a biological component, but experience was clearly a factor. Zulus, who have round houses and see few corners of any kind, are not fooled by this illusion. Illinois residents saw the illusion readily, while the Zulu tribespeople tended not to see it.

In another classic cross-cultural study of illusions, Pedersen and Wheeler (1983) studied perceptions of the Müller-Lyer illusion among two groups of Navajos. The group who lived in rectangular houses and had experienced corners, angles, and edges tended to see the illusion. The members of the other group, like the Zulus, tended not to see it because their cultural experience consisted of round houses.

illusion A false perception or a misperception of an actual stimulus in the environment.

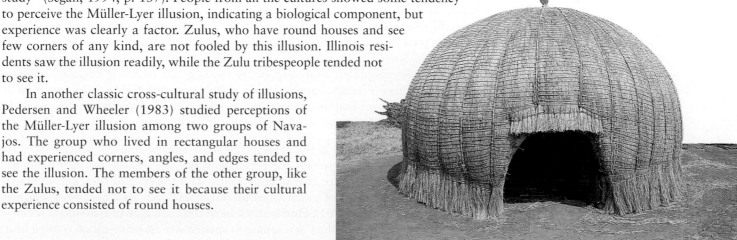

▼ Some visual illusions seem to be culture dependent. For example, Zulus and people from other cultures in which the houses lack straight sides and corners do not perceive the Müller-Lyer illusion.

3.18 What do studies of subliminal perception, ESP, and synesthesia show?

◁ ## Subliminal Perception, Extrasensory Perception, and Synesthesia

Illusions result from misperceptions of sensory input. By contrast, the phenomena you will read about in this section involve perceptions that are entirely independent of sensory input. Thus, they represent perception without sensation, or at least an awareness of sensation.

Subliminal Perception. Synesthesia involves perception without sensation. For decades, psychologists have studied a similar phenomenon known as subliminal perception, the capacity to perceive and respond to stimuli that are presented below the threshold of awareness. Neuroimaging studies show that the brain does, indeed, respond physiologically to subliminally presented stimuli (Kouider et al., 2009). Moreover, subliminal information can influence behavior to some degree. For example, when people are subliminally exposed to a picture of one person hitting another, they are more likely to judge a consciously perceived neutral scene, such as two people talking in a restaurant, as involving some kind of aggression (Todorov & Bargh, 2002).

But how strongly does subliminal perception affect behavior? The use of messages presented below the threshold of awareness in advertising, often called *subliminal persuasion,* has been around for decades. However, most research on subliminal perception suggests that, although the phenomenon does exist, it probably cannot produce the kinds of behavior changes claimed by the proponents of its use for advertising purposes (Greenwald, 1992).

Similarly, people who want to lose weight sometimes download commercially available MP3s containing subliminal messages, such as "I will eat less," embedded in recordings of music or ocean waves in the hopes that listening to them will help them control their appetite. Recordings of this kind are also marketed to people who want to quit smoking. However, experimental, placebo-controlled studies have found that such subliminal messages have no effect on behavior (Greenwald, 1992; Greenwald et al., 1991; Russell, Rowe, & Smouse, 1991).

Extrasensory Perception. Extrasensory perception (ESP) is defined as gaining information about objects, events, or another person's thoughts through some means other than the known sensory channels. Several different kinds of ESP have been proposed to exist. *Telepathy* means gaining awareness of the thoughts, feelings, or activities of another person without the use of the senses—in other words, reading a person's mind. *Clairvoyance* means gaining information about objects or events without use of the senses, such as knowing the contents of a letter before opening it. *Precognition* refers to an awareness of an event before it occurs. Most of the reported cases of precognition in everyday life have occurred while people were dreaming.

Many studies of ESP employ the *Ganzfeld procedure,* a study design in which two individuals, a "sender" and a "receiver," are placed in separate rooms. The rooms are specially designed to minimize distractions and to facilitate deep concentration. Experimenters provide senders with messages that they are supposed to attempt to transmit to receivers. Some studies using the Ganzfeld technique have suggested that ESP exists and that some people are more capable of sending and receiving extrasensory messages than others (Pérez-Navarro, Lawrence, & Hume, 2009). However, in almost all cases, attempts at replication of these studies have failed (Milton & Wiseman, 2001). Thus, most psychologists remain skeptical about the existence of ESP.

Synesthesia. Synesthesia is the capacity for experiencing unusual sensations along with ordinary ones. For instance, one person with synesthesia who has been examined by researchers sees the color blue simultaneously with the taste of beef, and an orange blob appears in his field of vision when he consumes foods that have been seasoned with ginger (Carpenter, 2001). However, the most common type of synesthesia is one in which individuals sense colors in response to spoken words, or so-called colored hearing (Carpenter, 2001). Neuroimaging studies suggest that colored hearing is not the

subliminal perception The capacity to perceive and respond to stimuli that are presented below the threshold of awareness.

extrasensory perception (ESP) Gaining information about objects, events, or another person's thoughts through some means other than the known sensory channels.

synesthesia The capacity for experiencing unusual sensations along with ordinary ones.

result of learned associations. These studies show that different brain areas are active in people with synesthesia who associate words with colors than in research participants who have been trained to consciously engage in such associations (Nunn et al., 2002).

Some psychologists speculate that all newborn brains are synesthetic and that the capacity for synesthesia is lost in most people as the various brain areas become more specialized over the years of childhood and adolescence (Spector & Maurer, 2009). However, some drugs produce temporary synesthesia, leading a few scientists to hypothesize that the neural connections that underlie synesthetic experiences are present in everyone (Grossenbacher & Lovelace, 2001). Nevertheless, the jury is still out with regard to both the origin and neurological basis of synesthesia (Carpenter, 2001). A great deal more research needs to be done.

Looking Back

We began the chapter by demonstrating to you how our senses work together to enable our bodies to do the tasks we require them to do. We ended this chapter with an examination of some unusual kinds of perceptual experiences. In synesthesia, one kind of perception (e.g., visual) occurs in response to stimuli that normally elicit another kind of perception (e.g., auditory). Subliminal perception occurs in response to stimuli that we are unaware of having sensed. ESP, if it exists, involves perception in the absence of any sensory stimulus. While such phenomena are intriguing, navigating through our everyday sensory environments would be much more difficult without reliable connections among sensory stimuli, the process of sensation, and the process of perception that mark our more typical sensory and perceptual experiences.

CHAPTER 3 SUMMARY

THE PROCESS OF SENSATION (pp. 71–73)

3.1 What are the absolute and difference thresholds? (pp. 71–72)

The absolute threshold is the minimum amount of sensory stimulation that can be detected 50% of the time. The difference threshold is a measure of the smallest increase or decrease in a physical stimulus that can be detected 50% of the time.

Key Terms
sensation, p. 71
perception, p. 71
absolute threshold, p. 71
difference threshold, p. 71
just noticeable difference (JND) p. 71
Weber's law, p. 72

3.2 How does transduction change sensory information? (pp. 72–73)

For each of the senses, the body has sensory receptors that detect and respond to sensory stimuli. Through the process of transduction, the receptors change the sensory stimuli into neural impulses, which are then transmitted to precise locations in the brain.

Key Terms
sensory receptors, p. 72
transduction, p. 72
sensory adaptation, p. 73

VISION (pp. 73–78)

3.3 How does each part of the eye function in vision? (pp. 74–75)

The cornea bends light rays inward through the pupil—the small, dark opening in the eye. The iris dilates and contracts the pupil to regulate the amount of light entering the eye. The lens changes its shape as it focuses images of objects at varying distances on the retina, a thin layer of tissue that contains the sensory receptors for vision. The cones detect color and fine detail; they function best in adequate light. The rods are extremely sensitive and enable vision in dim light.

Key Terms
visible spectrum, p. 73
wavelength, p. 73
cornea, p. 74

lens, p. 74
accommodation, p. 74
retina, p. 74
rods, p. 75
cones, p. 75
fovea, p. 75

3.4 How does visual information get from the retina to the primary visual cortex? (pp. 75–76)

The rods and the cones transduce light waves into neural impulses that pass from the bipolar, amacrine, and horizontal cells to the ganglion cells, whose axons form the optic nerve beyond the retinal wall of each eye. At the optic chiasm, the two optic nerves come together, and some of the nerve fibers from each eye cross to the opposite side of the brain. They synapse with neurons in the thalamus, which transmit the neural impulses to the primary visual cortex.

Key Terms
blind spot, p. 75
optic nerve, p. 75
primary visual cortex, p. 75
feature detectors, p. 75

3.5 How does color vision work? (pp. 76–78)

The perception of color results from the reflection of particular wavelengths of the visual spectrum from the surfaces of objects. For example, an object that appears to be red reflects light of longer wavelengths than one that appears to be blue. Color blindness is the inability to distinguish certain colors from one another, rather than the total absence of color vision. Two major theories that attempt to explain color vision are the trichromatic theory and the opponent-process theory.

Key Terms
hue, p. 77
saturation, p. 77
brightness, p. 77
trichromatic theory, p. 77
opponent-process theory, p. 77
afterimage, p. 77
color blindness, p. 78

HEARING AND BALANCE (pp. 78–83)

3.6 What are the physical characteristics of sound? (p. 79)

The pitch of a sound is determined by the frequency of the sound waves, which is measured in hertz. The loudness of a sound is determined largely by the amplitude of the sound waves, which is measured in decibels.

Key Terms
frequency, p. 79
amplitude, p. 79
decibel (dB), p. 79
timbre, p. 79

3.7 How does each part of the ear function in hearing? (pp. 80–82)

Sound waves enter the pinna, the visible part of the outer ear, and travel to the end of the auditory canal, causing the eardrum to vibrate. This sets in motion the ossicles in the middle ear, which amplify the sound waves. The vibration of the oval window causes activity in the inner ear, setting in motion the fluid in the cochlea. The moving fluid pushes and pulls the hair cells attached to the thin basilar membrane, which transduce the vibrations into neural impulses. The auditory nerve then carries the neural impulses to the brain.

Key Terms
audition, p. 80
outer ear, p. 80
middle ear, p. 80
inner ear, p. 80
cochlea, p. 80
hair cells, p. 81
place theory, p. 82
frequency theory, p. 82

3.8 How do the kinesthetic and vestibular senses help us move and stay balanced? (pp. 82–83)

The kinesthetic sense provides information about the position of body parts in relation to one another and movement of the entire body or its parts. This information is detected by sensory receptors in the joints, ligaments, and muscles. The vestibular sense detects movement and provides information about the body's orientation in space. Sensory receptors in the semicircular canals and the vestibular sacs sense changes in motion and the orientation of the head.

Key Terms
kinesthetic sense, p. 82
vestibular sense, p.82
semicircular canals, p. 83

Think About It

Have you ever awakened in the midst of a dream that was so good that you wished you could continue it? If so, then you might be interested to learn the steps involved in a technique that researchers have devised to study the controllability of dreams. Here are the steps:

1. Relax.

2. Close your eyes and focus on an imaginary spot in your field of vision.

3. Focus on your intention to control your dream.

4. Tell yourself that you're going to dream about whatever you want.

5. Imagine yourself having the dream that you are trying to create.

6. Repeat the steps until you fall asleep.

As you will learn later in the chapter, dreams may indeed be, at least to some degree, under conscious control. But what do we mean when we say "conscious" control? It stands to reason that psychologists need a working definition of *consciousness* before they can understand the processes, such as dreaming, that modify it. Thus, we begin our exploration of phenomena such as biological rhythms, sleep, meditation, and the brain's response to mind-altering substances with a discussion of states of awareness.

What Is Consciousness?

What if, in a middle-of-the-night phone call, your mother told you that your grand-mother had had a stroke and had been in a coma for a short while, but then had regained consciousness? You would most likely understand your mother to mean that your grandmother was in a state of unawareness of her own and others' activities but then returned to a state of awareness, or wakefulness. One way of understanding the meaning of consciousness is to think of it in contrast to its opposite, unconsciousness. But is that all there is to consciousness—simply being awake? What about when you arrive home from shopping but have no recollection of the drive from the mall to your home? Certainly, you were awake, so the reason you don't remember is *not* that you were unconscious. Thus, consciousness is defined as everything of which we are aware at any given time—our thoughts, feelings, sensations, and perceptions of the external environment.

consciousness Everything of which we are aware at any given time—our thoughts, feelings, sensations, and perceptions of the external environment.

Changing Views of Consciousness ▶

4.1 How do psychologists view consciousness?

The early psychologists held widely varying views of the nature of consciousness. William James likened consciousness to a flowing stream (the stream of consciousness) that sometimes is influenced by the will and sometimes is not. Sigmund Freud emphasized the notion that unconscious wishes, thoughts, and feelings are hidden from consciousness because they evoke too much anxiety. In contrast to both James and Freud, behaviorist John Watson urged psychologists to abandon the study of consciousness, claiming that it could not be studied scientifically. Because of the strong influence of behaviorism, especially in the United States, psychologists did not study consciousness for several decades (Nelson, 1996).

In recent decades, though, psychological researchers have returned to the study of consciousness, in examining physiological rhythms, sleep, and altered states of consciousness (changes in awareness produced by sleep, meditation, hypnosis, or drugs). Modern brain-imaging techniques have allowed psychologists to accumulate a large body of evidence leading to a better understanding of the neurological basis of consciousness. Consequently, today's psychologists think about consciousness largely in neurobiological terms. In other words, psychologists tend to equate the subjective experience of consciousness with objective observations of what's actually happening in the brain during states such as sleep and hypnosis (Morsella, Krieger, & Bargh, 2010).

altered state of consciousness Change in awareness produced by sleep, meditation, hypnosis, or drugs.

4.2 What is the connection between altered states of consciousness and culture?

Culture and Altered States of Consciousness

Religious and cultural traditions the world over have proposed supernatural explanations for naturally occurring altered states of consciousness. For example, the ancient Greeks believed that a special group of gods and goddesses, the *muses,* were responsible for inducing the trance-like state that artists and musicians often experience in association with their creative activities. In today's world, many people continue to express such culturally based views of altered states. For instance, beliefs about the spirit world strongly influence the ways in which Puerto Ricans interpret nightmares and other emotion-provoking dreams (Jacobson, 2009).

The belief that an altered state can be a pathway to the supernatural world has led people in many cultures to develop rituals that enable them to intentionally induce altered states of consciousness. For example, in the United States, the use of an illegal drug called *peyote* by members of the Native American Church, sometimes called *peyotism,* is controversial (Feeney, 2007). Some mental health professionals have argued that the religious use of peyote may lead to the development of substance abuse problems among church members. In response to these critics, advocates for the use of peyote in the Native American Church argue that church officials take care to regulate the dosages of the drug that are available for consumption during their rituals. In support of this claim, advocates cite the fact that there has never been a reported case of peyote overdose resulting from a church ceremony (Jones, 2005). The church's official doctrines also condemn substance dependence as a moral failing. As a result, advocates say, dependence is unlikely to develop.

The fact that so many different means of altering consciousness are practiced by members of so many cultures around the world has led some experts to wonder whether "there may be a universal human need to produce and maintain varieties of conscious experiences" (Ward, 1994, p. 60). This may be why some people use drugs to deliberately induce altered states of consciousness.

Circadian Rhythms

circadian rhythm (sur-KAY-dee-un) Within each 24-hour period, the regular fluctuation from high to low points of certain bodily functions and behaviors.

Do you notice changes in the way you feel throughout the day—fluctuations in your energy level, moods, or efficiency? More than 100 bodily functions and behaviors follow circadian rhythms—that is, they fluctuate regularly from a high to a low point over a 24-hour period (Dement, 1974).

4.3 How do circadian rhythms affect physiological and psychological functions?

The Influence of Circadian Rhythms

Physiological functions such as blood pressure, heart rate, appetite, secretion of hormones and digestive enzymes, sensory acuity, elimination, and even the body's response to medication all follow circadian rhythms (Hrushesky, 1994; Morofushi et al., 2001). Many psychological functions—including learning efficiency, the ability to perform a wide range of tasks, and even moods—ebb and flow according to these daily rhythms (Boivin et al., 1997; Johnson et al., 1992; Manly et al., 2002). Indeed, the circadian timing system is involved in the 24-hour variation of virtually every physiological and psychological variable researchers have studied (Kunz & Herrmann, 2000).

suprachiasmatic nucleus (SCN) A pair of tiny structures in the brain's hypothalamus that control the timing of circadian rhythms; the biological clock.

The biological clock that controls circadian rhythms along with other kinds of timekeeping mechanisms in the brain (see the *Explain It*) is the suprachiasmatic nucleus (SCN), located in the brain's hypothalamus (Ruby et al., 2002). However, the ebb and flow of circadian rhythms is not strictly biological. Environmental cues also play a part. The most significant environmental cue is bright light, particularly sunlight. Specialized cells (photoreceptors) in the retina at the back of each eye respond to the amount of light reaching the eye and relay this information via the optic nerve

> ## EXPLAIN IT   How Does the Brain Keep Track of Time?
>
> Have you ever been in this situation? You stop at a red light and wait patiently for it to change to green. As time goes on, you start to think that the light has been red for an unusually long period of time. You look around at other drivers, wondering if they have the same impression. Finally, you decide that the light is malfunctioning and cautiously proceed through the intersection even though the light is still red. What happened?
>
> An interval timer in your brain functions similarly to the device in your kitchen that you use to remind yourself to take a pizza out of the oven before it burns. The brain's interval timer consists of a network of neurons in the cerebral cortex that fire randomly and independently until something gets their attention (Wright, 2002). When an attention-getting stimulus that has time characteristics (e.g., a traffic light) occurs, the substantia nigra sends out a pulse of dopamine that signals these neurons to fire simultaneously. This simultaneous firing becomes a neurological marker for the beginning of the event. When the event ends, the substantia nigra does the same thing, creating a marker for the end of the event. The brain's timer compares its measurements to time-stamped memories of similar events. This is what happens when you are sitting at a traffic light and have the impression that the light has been red too long.
>
> How accurate is the brain's interval timer? Here's a prime illustration. Your alarm goes off, but you decide to allow yourself to sleep 10 more minutes. Sometimes, you wake up again, look at the clock, and note that you have slept for about 10 minutes, just as you planned. But on other occasions, you wake up to
>
> find that you have slept for two hours rather than 10 minutes. What accounts for such variations in accuracy?
>
> In such cases, the interval timer is superseded by another of the brain's clocks, the one that governs sleep cycles. When you go back to sleep after a brief period of awakening, your brain begins a new sleep cycle. If your target waking-up time happens to fall within the brief initial phase of the new sleep cycle when you are merely drowsy, you will probably not sleep past it. But if you slip into a deeper sleep phase before the interval timer wakes you up, you are likely to sleep for 90 minutes or so. This happens because, when you enter a deeper phase of sleep, your brain automatically switches off its interval timer. Thus, when you want to get a few extra minutes of shut-eye, turn to your alarm clock, one of the many devices humans have invented to compensate for the inaccuracies of our built-in neurological timers.

to the SCN (Foster, Hankins, & Peirson, 2007). From dusk until just before dawn, the message from the retina to the SCN is relayed to the pineal gland, causing it to secrete the hormone *melatonin*. During the daylight hours, the pineal gland does not produce melatonin (Kripke et al., 2005). Melatonin induces sleep, perhaps through its ability to keep all of the body's tissues aware of both the time of day and the time of year (Benarroch, 2008).

Two circadian rhythms of particular importance are the sleep/wakefulness cycle and the daily fluctuation in body temperature. Normal human body temperature ranges from a low of about 97 to 97.5°F between 3:00 and 4:00 a.m. to a high of about 98.6°F between 6:00 and 8:00 p.m. People sleep best when their body temperature is at its lowest, and they are most alert when their body temperature is at its daily high point. Alertness also follows a circadian rhythm, one that is quite separate from the sleep/wakefulness cycle (Monk, 1989). For most people, alertness decreases between 2:00 and 5:00 p.m. and between 2:00 and 7:00 a.m. (Webb, 1995).

Disruptions in Circadian Rhythms ▶

Suppose you fly from Chicago to London, and the plane lands at 12:00 a.m. Chicago time, about the time you usually go to sleep. At the same time that it is midnight in Chicago, it is 6:00 a.m. in London, almost time to get up. The clocks, the sun, and everything else in London tell you it is early morning, but you still feel as though it is midnight. You are experiencing jet lag. ◉ Watch on mypsychlab.com

Chronic jet lag, such as that experienced by many airline pilots and flight attendants, produces memory deficits that may be permanent (Cho, 2001; Cho et al., 2000). You might think that airline employees who regularly fly across time zones would adjust to their schedules. However, research indicates that experienced airline workers are just as likely to suffer from jet lag as passengers on their first intercontinental flight (Ariznavaretta et al., 2002). Melatonin supplements have been found to

[**4.4** How do disruptions in circadian rhythms affect the body and mind?

◉ Watch the **Video** *The Effects of Sleep and Stress on Memory: Jessica Payne* on **mypsychlab.com**

▲ Research indicates that frequent flyers, such as this airline employee, are just as likely to suffer from jet lag when crossing several time zones as travelers who are on their first intercontinental journey.

subjective night The time during a 24-hour period when the biological clock is telling a person to go to sleep.

be helpful for alleviating jet lag in some long-distance travelers (Doghramji, Brainard, & Balaicuis, 2010). However, melatonin is most effective when taken during the day, when natural melatonin levels are low. People who take it at night, just before bedtime, are likely to see little effect because natural melatonin levels are near their peak at that time. Thus, for some people with jet lag, other remedies are preferable. For instance, some travelers benefit from exposure to bright sunlight during the early morning hours, and avoidance of bright lights during the evening may be more effective than melatonin for restoring circadian rhythms (Arendt, 2009).

Similarly, alertness and performance deteriorate if people work during subjective night, when their biological clock is telling them to go to sleep (Sack et al., 2007a). During subjective night, energy and efficiency are at their lowest points, reaction time is slowest, productivity is diminished, and industrial accidents are significantly higher. In one study, researchers found that pilots who were flying between midnight and 6:00 a.m. were 50% more likely to make errors (de Mello et al., 2008). Furthermore, shift workers get less sleep overall than nonshift workers (Bonnefond et al., 2006). Some studies show that the deleterious effects of shift work persist for months or even years after shift work ends (Rouch, Wild, Ansiau, & Marquie, 2005).

Moving work schedules forward from days to evenings to nights makes adjustment easier because people find it easier to go to bed later and wake up later than the reverse. And rotating shifts every three weeks instead of every week lessens the effect on sleep even more (Karlson, Eck, Ørbœk, & Österberg, 2009). Some researchers are investigating the use of a new wakefulness drug called *modafinil* that helps people remain alert without the side effects of stimulants such as caffeine (Morgenthaler et al., 2007). Others have used a device called a "light mask" to reset shift workers' biological clocks. This mask allows researchers to control the amount of light to which the closed eyelids of research participants are exposed. The findings of light mask studies suggest that exposing participants to bright light during the last 4 hours of sleep is an effective treatment for the kinds of sleep-phase delays experienced by shift workers (Cole et al., 2002). Thus, this device may become important in the treatment of sleep disorders associated with shift work.

Sleep

As noted earlier, the sleep/wakefulness cycle is a circadian rhythm. But what actually happens during our periods of sleep? Before the 1950s, there was little understanding of what goes on during the state of consciousness known as sleep. Then, in the 1950s, several universities set up sleep laboratories where people's brain waves, eye movements, chin-muscle tension, heart rate, and respiration rate were monitored through a night of sleep. From analyses of sleep recordings, known as *polysomnograms*, researchers discovered the characteristics of two major types of sleep.

4.5 How do the restorative and circadian theories explain sleep?

Why We Sleep

Are you one of those people who regards sleep as a waste of time—especially when you have a term paper due the next day? (Of course, you wouldn't be facing a sleepless night if you hadn't procrastinated about the paper in the first place!) In fact, consistent sleep habits are probably important to getting good grades. Why?

restorative theory of sleep The theory that the function of sleep is to restore body and mind.

Two complementary theories have been advanced to explain why we need to sleep. Taken together, they provide us with a useful explanation. One, the restorative theory of sleep, holds that being awake produces wear and tear on the body and the brain, while sleep serves the function of restoring body and mind (Gökcebay et al., 1994). There is now convincing evidence for this theory: The functions of sleep do include the restoration of energy and the consolidation of memory (Kunz & Herrmann, 2000). The second explanation, the circadian theory of sleep, sometimes called the *evolutionary or adaptive theory,* is based on the premise that sleep evolved to keep humans out of harm's way during the dark of night, possibly from becoming prey for some nocturnal predator (Siegel, 2009).

Alexander Borbely (1984; Borbely et al., 1989) explains how a synthesis of the circadian and restorative theories can be used to explain the function of sleep. That people feel sleepy at certain times of day is consistent with the circadian theory. And that sleepiness increases the longer a person is awake is consistent with the restorative theory. In other words, the urge to sleep is partly a function of how long a person has been awake and partly a function of the time of day (Sack et al., 2007a).

How We Sleep ▶

Sleep follows a fairly predictable pattern each night. Each sleep cycle lasts about 90 minutes and consists of the stages shown in Figure 4.1. The type of sleep we experience in all four stages is known as NREM (non-REM) sleep. It is a type of sleep in which our heart and respiration rates are slow and steady, our movements are minimal, and our blood pressure and brain activity are at their lowest points of the 24-hour period.

As you can see in Figure 4.1, when we are fully awake, beta waves predominate. As we become drowsy, alpha waves begin to appear. When alpha waves outnumber beta waves, we enter the first of the four NREM sleep stages:

- *Stage 1:* Transition from waking to sleeping; irregular waves with occasional alpha waves
- *Stage 2:* Transition from light to deeper sleep; sleep spindles (waves with alternating periods of calm and flashes of intense activity) appear
- *Stage 3:* Deeper sleep; slow-wave sleep begins when EEG shows 20% of brain waves are delta waves
- *Stage 4:* Deepest sleep; Stage 4 sleep begins when 50% of waves are delta waves

About 40 minutes after we enter Stage 4 sleep, delta waves begin to disappear. When that happens, we transition back through Stage 3 and Stage 2 until we reach Stage 1 sleep again. As we reenter Stage 1, our pathway through the night takes a brief side trip into REM (rapid eye movement) sleep. During the REM period, our brains are highly active. Epinephrine is released into the system, causing blood pressure to

4.6 What types of sleep occur during a typical night of sleep?

circadian theory of sleep The theory that sleep evolved to keep humans out of harm's way during the night; also known as the evolutionary or adaptive theory.

sleep cycle A period of sleep lasting about 90 minutes and including one or more stages of NREM sleep, followed by REM sleep.

NREM (non-REM) sleep Four sleep stages characterized by slow, regular respiration and heart rate, little body movement, and blood pressure and brain activity that are at their 24-hour low points.

sleep spindles Sleep Stage 2 brain waves that feature short periods of calm interrupted by brief flashes of intense activity.

slow-wave sleep Deep sleep; associated with Stage 3 and Stage 4 sleep.

Stage 4 sleep The deepest stage of NREM sleep, characterized by an EEG pattern of more than 50% delta waves.

REM (rapid eye movement) sleep A type of sleep characterized by rapid eye movements, paralysis, fast and irregular heart and respiration rates, increased brain-wave activity, and vivid dreams.

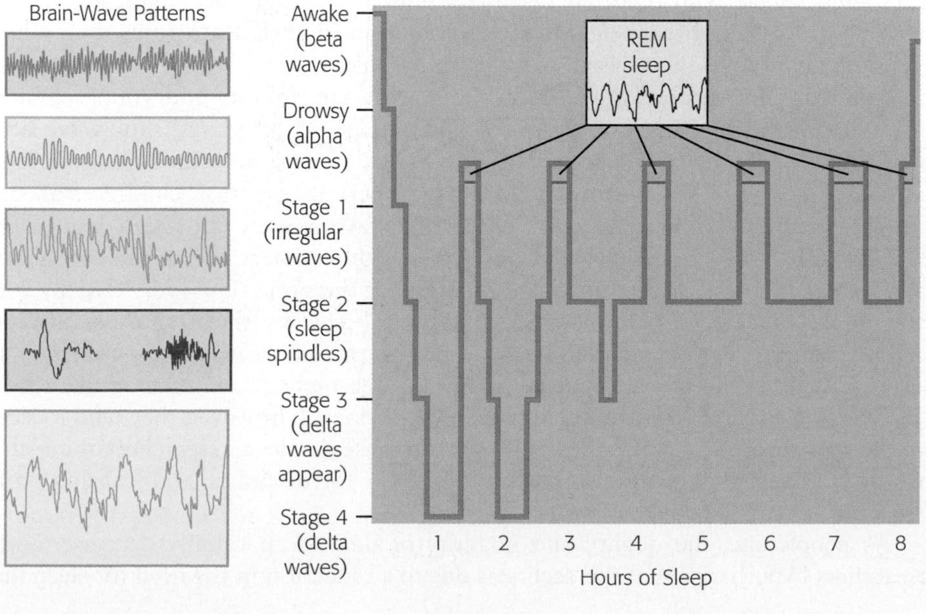

FIGURE 4.1 Brain-Wave Patterns Associated with Different Stages of Sleep
By monitoring brain-wave activity on an EEG throughout a night's sleep, researchers have identified the brain-wave patterns associated with different stages of sleep. As sleepers progress through the four NREM stages, the brain-wave pattern changes from faster, smaller waves in Stages 1 and 2 to the slower, larger delta waves in Stages 3 and 4.

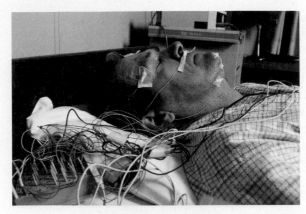

▲ In a sleep laboratory or sleep clinic, researchers attach electrodes to a person's head to monitor brain-wave activity, eye movements, and muscle tension.

REM rebound The increased amount of REM sleep that occurs after REM deprivation.

rise and heart rate and respiration to become faster and less regular. In contrast to this storm of internal activity, there is an external calm during REM sleep. The large muscles of the body—arms, legs, trunk—become paralyzed.

Observe a sleeper during the REM state and you will see her or his eyes darting around under the eyelids. Eugene Azerinsky first discovered these bursts of rapid eye movements in 1952, and William Dement and Nathaniel Kleitman (1957) made the connection between rapid eye movements and dreaming. It is during REM sleep that the most vivid dreams occur. When awakened from REM sleep, most people report that they were dreaming.

Researchers have also found that REM sleep may be critical to the consolidation of memories after learning (Nishida, Pearsall, Buckner, & Walker, 2008; Valeo, 2008). Several experiments have shown that participants' performance on previously acquired motor and verbal tasks improves after a period of normal sleep (Walker & Stickgold, 2006). In one classic study, Karni and others (1994) found that research participants who were learning a new perceptual skill showed an improvement in performance, with no additional practice, 8 to 10 hours later if they had a normal night's sleep or if the researchers disturbed only their NREM sleep. Performance did not improve, however, in those who were deprived of REM sleep. This may be why, when people are deprived of REM sleep, they make up for it by getting an increased amount of REM sleep afterward, a phenomenon called REM rebound.

After the first REM period of the night ends, a new sleep cycle begins. However, the remaining sleep cycles differ from the first one (refer again to Figure 4.1). Typically, the second cycle includes only Stages 2, 3, and 4, followed by a REM period. The third cycle usually includes Stages 2, 3, and a REM period. Later cycles include only Stage 2 and REM sleep. In addition, with each cycle, the REM period increases in duration, from a few minutes at the end of the first cycle to a half-hour or longer at the end of the fifth cycle. Overall, sleepers average five cycles in a 7- to 8-hour night of sleep, which provides them with a total of 1 to 2 hours of slow-wave sleep and 1 to 2 hours of REM sleep.

4.7 How does age influence sleep patterns?

Variations in Sleep

The amount of sleep people get varies a lot from one person to another. But how much sleep do we need? Many of us have heard that eight hours of sleep are required for optimal health. Research suggests that this is not true. In a longitudinal study begun in 1982, more than a million Americans were asked about their sleep habits. Twenty years later, people who reported sleeping six or fewer hours per night, along with those who slept more than eight, showed somewhat higher death rates than adults who slept about seven hours each night (Kripke et al., 2002).

As Figure 4.2 demonstrates, sleep varies with age. Infants and young children have the longest sleep time and the highest percentages of REM and slow-wave sleep (Siegel, 2005). However, infants and children also have more erratic sleep patterns than individuals in other age groups (Millman, 2005). By contrast, children from age 6 to puberty are the most consistent sleepers and wakers. They fall asleep easily, sleep soundly for 10 to 11 hours at night, and feel awake and alert during the day. Moreover, they tend to fall asleep and wake up at about the same time every day. By contrast, adolescents' sleep patterns are strongly influenced by their schedules. Factors such as part-time employment and early school start times cause many teenagers to sleep little more than seven hours on a typical week night (Carskadon et al., 1998). When adolescents are free from such scheduling pressures, however, they tend to sleep even longer than elementary-aged children. Thus, some sleep researchers think that insufficient sleep may be at least partly responsible for discipline and learning problems in secondary schools.

As people age, the quality and quantity of their sleep usually decrease. Some researchers hypothesize that the decline is due to a reduction in the need for sleep that

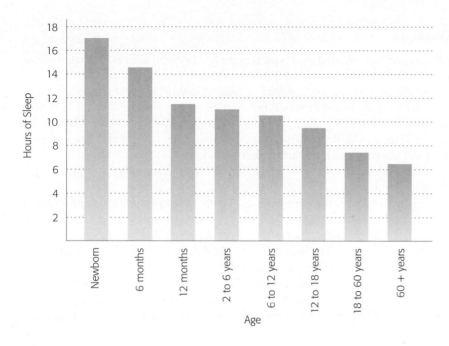

Maturational explanations for age differences in sleep might seem to make sense, but in what ways might social factors also contribute to these variations?

FIGURE 4.2 Average Hours of Daily Sleep across the Life Span
The number of hours devoted to sleep in each 24-hour period decreases dramatically across the life span.

Sources: Foley, Ancoli-Israel, Britz, & Walsh, 2004; Iglowstein, Jenni, Molinari, & Largo, 2003; Hansen, Janssen, Schiff, & Zee, 2005; Millman, 2005; Mindell, 1999; Ohayan, Carskadon, Guilleminault, & Vitiello, 2004.

is a part of the natural aging process (Klerman & Dijk, 2008). Nevertheless, many older adults view the decline as a threat to their quality of life. Large-scale surveys of older adults in North America, Europe, and Japan suggest that up to two-thirds of them experience daytime sleepiness, nighttime awakenings, and insomnia on a regular basis (Diaper & Hindmarch, 2005).

Sleep Deprivation ▷

4.8 What are the effects of sleep deprivation?

What is the longest you have ever stayed awake? Most people have missed no more than a few consecutive nights of sleep, perhaps studying for final exams. If you have ever missed two or three nights of sleep, you may remember having had difficulty concentrating, lapses in attention, and general irritability. Research indicates that even the rather small amount of sleep deprivation associated with delaying your bedtime on weekends leads to decreases in cognitive performance (Chee et al., 2008).

How does a lack of sleep affect the brain? The effects of sleep deprivation go beyond simply feeling tired. In fact, research has shown that failing to get enough sleep affects your ability to learn. So, if you stay up all night to study for a test, you may actually be engaging in a somewhat self-defeating behavior. In a ground-breaking study Drummond and others (2000) used brain-imaging techniques to map the patterns of brain activity during a verbal learning task in two groups of participants—those in an experimental group who were deprived of sleep for about 35 hours, and those in a control group who slept normally. In the control group, the prefrontal cortex was highly active, as were the temporal lobes. As expected, on average, these rested participants scored significantly higher on the learning task than did their sleep-deprived counterparts. Surprisingly, however, areas of the prefrontal cortex were even more active in the sleep-deprived participants than in those who slept normally. Moreover, the temporal lobes that were so active in the rested group were almost totally inactive in the sleep-deprived group. The parietal lobes of the latter group became highly active, however, as if to compensate for their sleep-deprived condition. And, the more active the parietal lobes, the higher a sleep-deprived participant scored on the learning task.

This study, the first to use brain-imaging techniques to examine the effects of sleep deprivation on verbal learning, indicates that the cognitive functions used in such learning are significantly impaired by sleep deprivation. It also shows that there are compensatory mechanisms in the parietal lobes that can reduce this impairment to some degree (Drummond et al., 2000, 2004).

▲ Health care professionals who work in hospitals often work long hours including, in some cases, two or more consecutive 24-hour shifts. How do you think these working conditions affect their on-the-job performance?

4.9 What are the various sleep disorders?

⊣| **Sleep Disorders**

So far, our discussion has centered on a typical night for a typical sleeper. But what about the one-third of people who report sleep problems (Lubit, Bonds, & Lucia, 2009)?

Do you walk or talk in your sleep? If you do, you suffer from one of the parasomnias, sleep disturbances in which behaviors and physiological states that normally occur only in the waking state take place during sleep (Schenck & Mahowald, 2000). Sleepwalking, or *somnambulism*, occurs during a partial arousal from Stage 4 sleep in which the sleeper does not come to full consciousness. *Somniloquy*, the technical term for sleeptalking, can occur in any stage. Typically, sleeptalkers mumble nonsensical words and phrases.

Frightening dreams are also parasomnias. *Sleep terrors* happen during Stage 4 sleep and often begin with a piercing scream. The sleeper springs up in a state of panic—eyes open, heart pounding, perspiring, breathing rapidly, and so on. Typically, such sleep terrors resolve quickly, and the individual falls back to sleep. *Nightmares* are more frightening than sleep terrors because they occur during REM sleep and, as a result, are far more vivid. Moreover, sleepers often awaken to full consciousness during a nightmare and remember it in detail. Whereas sleep terrors occur early in the night, nightmares more often occur in the early-morning hours, when REM periods are the longest.

Physicians often begin the process of treating a parasomnia by investigating hidden illnesses and/or psychological factors in the patient's life that may be causing her sleep disturbances (Sharma, 2006). If such an underlying condition is discovered, then the physician treats it directly and assumes that curing it will also relieve the patient's parasomnia symptoms. Sleep-inducing medications, whether over-the-counter or prescription drugs, are regarded as a last resort in the treatment of parasomnias. The reason for medication avoidance is that the potential side effects of sleep medications and the possibility that a patient will become dependent on them outweigh the temporary benefits. Instead, physicians recommend that patients practice the principles of *sleep hygiene* that are outlined in the *Apply It* feature.

In contrast to parasomnias, dyssomnias are disorders that involve the timing, quantity, or quality of sleep. For instance, narcolepsy is an incurable sleep disorder characterized by excessive daytime sleepiness and uncontrollable attacks of REM sleep, usually lasting 10 to 20 minutes (Bozorg & Benbadis, 2009). People with narcolepsy, who number from 250,000 to 350,000 in the United States alone, tend to be involved in accidents virtually everywhere—while driving, at work, and at home. Narcolepsy is caused by an abnormality in the part of the brain that regulates sleep, and it appears to have a strong genetic component. Some dogs are subject to narcolepsy, and much has been learned about the genetics of this disorder from research on canine subjects (Lamberg, 1996). Although there is no cure for narcolepsy, stimulant medications improve daytime alertness in most patients. ⊙⊣Watch on **mypsychlab.com**

More than 1 million Americans—mostly obese men—suffer from another sleep disorder, sleep apnea. Sleep apnea consists of periods during sleep when breathing stops, and the individual must awaken briefly to breathe (Becker & Wallace, 2010). The major symptoms of sleep apnea are excessive daytime sleepiness and extremely loud snoring, often accompanied by snorts, gasps, and choking noises. A person with sleep apnea will drop off to sleep, stop breathing altogether, and then awaken struggling

parasomnias Sleep disturbances in which behaviors and physiological states that normally take place only in the waking state occur while a person is sleeping.

dyssomnias Sleep disorders in which the timing, quantity, or quality of sleep is impaired.

narcolepsy An incurable sleep disorder characterized by excessive daytime sleepiness and uncontrollable attacks of REM sleep.

⊙⊣**Watch** the **Video** *Living with a Sleep Disorder-Narcolepsy* on **mypsychlab.com**

sleep apnea A sleep disorder characterized by periods during sleep when breathing stops and the individual must awaken briefly in order to breathe.

▶ This dog is experiencing a narcoleptic sleep attack. Much has been learned about narcolepsy through research with dogs.

APPLY IT   How to Get a Good Night's Sleep

Hand washing may come to mind when you hear the term *hygiene,* but health care professionals use it as a catch-all term for all kinds of preventive health measures. Thus, *sleep hygiene* refers to practices that reduce your risk of developing sleep problems. The Mayo Clinic (2006b) has compiled a list of tips for practicing sleep hygiene that you will find at *http://mayoclinic.com/health/sleep/HQ01387.* Here are a few highlights:

- Keep a regular schedule that includes fairly consistent going-to-bed and getting-up times.

- Avoid eating or drinking to excess just before going to bed.

- Limit your intake of nicotine and caffeine throughout the day.

- Get regular exercise.

- Maintain a comfortable temperature and light level in the place where you sleep.

- Do not nap during the day.

- Make your bed as comfortable as possible.

- Establish a going-to-bed routine that relaxes you.

- Do not lie in bed awake for more than 30 minutes. Get up and do something until you feel sleepy enough to go back to bed.

- Don't push yourself to stay awake beyond the point at which you begin to feel sleepy.

- Avoid resorting to sleep medications unless absolutely necessary.

⊙ Watch on **mypsychlab.com**

---

for breath. After gasping several breaths in a semiawakened state, the person falls back to sleep and stops breathing again. People with severe sleep apnea may partially awaken as often as 1 to 2 times per minute to gasp for air. Alcohol and sedatives aggravate the condition (Valipour et al., 2007).

Severe sleep apnea can lead to chronic high blood pressure and other types of cardiovascular disease (Somers et al., 2008). Neuroscientists have also found that sleep apnea may cause mild brain damage (Macey et al., 2002). Physicians sometimes treat sleep apnea by surgically modifying the upper airway. When the surgery is effective, sleep apnea sufferers not only sleep better but also exhibit higher levels of performance on tests of verbal learning and memory (Dahloef et al., 2002). These findings suggest that the interrupted sleep experienced by individuals with this disorder affects cognitive as well as physiological functioning.

Many adults in the United States suffer from insomnia, a sleep disorder characterized by difficulty falling or staying asleep, by waking too early, or by sleep that is light, restless, or of poor quality (Passaro, 2009). Any of these symptoms can lead to distress and impairment in daytime functioning (Sateia et al., 2000). Transient (temporary) insomnia, lasting three weeks or less, can result from jet lag, emotional highs (as when preparing for an upcoming wedding) or lows (losing a loved one or a job), or a brief illness or injury that interferes with sleep (Passaro, 2009). Much more serious is chronic insomnia, which lasts for months or even years and plagues about 10% of the adult population (Passaro, 2009). The percentages are even higher for women, the elderly, and people suffering from psychiatric and medical disorders. Chronic insomnia may begin as a reaction to a psychological or medical problem but persist long after the problem is resolved.

Earlier you read that physicians avoid using sleep medicines to treat parasomnias. The same is true for the dyssomnias, but the life-threatening nature of some of these conditions means that individuals who suffer from them are more likely to be prescribed medications than those who have parasomnias. Narcolepsy sufferers, for example, may be given stimulant drugs to keep them awake during times when it would be dangerous for them to fall asleep, such as when they are driving (Bozorg & Benbadis, 2009). Sleep apnea may also be treated with medications. Electronic devices that awaken sleepers who stop breathing may also be used, and there are surgical treatments for sleep apnea as well (Dahloef et al., 2002). Finally, insomnia may be treated with drugs, but, in most cases, physicians encourage patients to adopt sleep hygiene practices to obtain long-term relief (Passaro, 2009).

The *Summarize It* on page 118 lists the various sleep disorders.

insomnia A sleep disorder characterized by difficulty falling or staying asleep, by waking too early, or by sleep that is light, restless, or of poor quality.

Sleep Disorders

DISORDER	DESCRIPTION
PARASOMNIAS	
Somnambulism	Sleepwalking; occurs during partial arousal from Stage 4 sleep
Sleep terrors	Frightening dreams that occur during partial arousal from Stage 4 sleep; sleeper springs up in a state of panic, usually shortly after falling asleep
Nightmares	Frightening dreams that occur during REM sleep; likely to be remembered in vivid detail
Somniloquy	Sleeptalking; can occur during any sleep stage
DYSSOMNIAS	
Narcolepsy	Excessive daytime sleepiness; uncontrollable attacks of REM sleep; incurable
Sleep apnea	Periods during sleep when breathing stops; individual must awaken briefly in order to breathe
Insomnia	Difficulty falling or staying asleep, waking too early, and/or sleep that is light, restless, or of poor quality

Dreams

What does a young woman mean when she says, "I met the guy of my dreams last night?" Or how about a telemarketer who promises you a "dream vacation" in exchange for listening to a sales pitch? Most of the time, we think of dreaming as a pleasant, imaginative experience. But when a fellow student exclaims, "That exam was a nightmare!" he or she means, of course, that the exam was somewhat less than pleasant, like a frightening dream. Good or bad, just exactly what is a dream?

4.10 What have researchers learned about dreams?

REM dream A type of dream occurring almost continuously during each REM period and having a storylike quality; typically more vivid, visual, and emotional than NREM dreams.

NREM dream A type of dream occurring during NREM sleep that is typically less frequent and less memorable than REM dreams are.

The Content of Our Dreams

The vivid dreams people remember and talk about are usually REM dreams, the type that occur almost continuously during each REM period. But people also have NREM dreams, which occur during NREM sleep, although these are typically less frequent and less memorable than REM dreams (McNamara McLaren & Durso, 2007). REM dreams have a storylike or dreamlike quality and are more visual, vivid, and emotional than NREM dreams (Hobson, 1989). Blind people who lose their sight before age 5 usually do not have visual dreams, although they do have vivid dreams involving the other senses.

Brain-imaging studies suggest that the general perception that events in REM dreams are stranger and more emotion provoking than waking experiences is probably true. The areas of the brain responsible for emotions, as well as the primary visual cortex, are active during REM dreams (Dang-Vu et al., 2007). Similarly, vivid REM dreams are associated with distributions of activity in the forebrain that are very similar to those exhibited by individuals with delusional disorders while they are awake (Schwartz & Maquet, 2002). By contrast, the prefrontal cortex, the more rational part of the brain, is suppressed during REM sleep, suggesting that the bizarre events that happen in REM dreams result from the inability of the brain to structure perceptions logically during that type of sleep. Areas associated with memory are also suppressed during REM sleep, which may explain why REM dreams are difficult to remember.

What is it about REM sleep that predisposes people to bizarre dreams? One hypothesis is based on the finding that different neurotransmitters are dominant in the cortex during wakefulness and during REM sleep (Gottesmann, 2000). When we are awake, powerful inhibiting influences exert control over the functioning of the cortex, keeping us anchored to reality, less subject to impulsive thoughts and acts, and more or less "sane." These inhibiting influences are maintained principally by cortical neurons that are responding to serotonin and norepinephrine. These neurotransmitters are far less plentiful during REM dreaming, when a higher level of dopamine causes other cortical neurons to show intense activity. This uninhibited, dopamine-stimulated activity of the dreaming brain has been likened to a psychotic mental state (Gottesmann, 2000).

Finally, as you learned at the beginning of the chapter, researchers have devised procedures designed to control dreams, so you won't be surprised to learn that some people have been taught to deliberately control dream content in order to stop unwanted, recurrent dreams. In lucid dreams, people attempt to exert control over a dream while it is in progress. Research suggests that individuals who are good at controlling their thoughts when awake are also successful at lucid dreaming (Blagrove & Hartnell, 2000). Moreover, lucid dreams about exercising appear to actually improve heart function (Erlacher & Schredl, 2008). Lucid dreaming has even been advocated as an intervention for depression, although its effects appear to be inconsistent among depressed individuals (Newell & Cartwright, 2000), perhaps because the ability to control thoughts is impaired in many of these people. ◉ Watch on **mypsychlab.com**

lucid dream A dream that an individual is aware of dreaming and whose content the individual is often able to influence while the dream is in progress.

◉ Watch the **Video** *Lucid Dreaming* on **mypsychlab.com**

Interpreting Dreams ▶

4.11 How do the various theorists explain dreams?

Most people believe that dreams, especially those that frighten us or that recur, have hidden meanings (Morewedge & Norton, 2009). Sigmund Freud believed that dreams function to satisfy unconscious sexual and aggressive desires. Because such wishes are unacceptable to the dreamer, they have to be disguised and therefore appear in dreams in symbolic forms. Freud (1900/1953a) claimed that objects such as sticks, umbrellas, tree trunks, and guns symbolize the male sex organ; objects such as chests, cupboards, and boxes represent the female sex organ. Freud differentiated between the manifest content of a dream—the content of the dream as recalled by the dreamer—and the latent content—or the underlying meaning of the dream—which he considered more significant.

▲ If you dream that you are an Omaticayan warrior who lives in a world known as Pandora, the cognitive theory of dreaming would predict that you had recently watched a movie that included such content. The evolutionary theory would say that the adaptive function of the dream is to help you be ready to defend yourself against your enemies.

Beginning in the 1950s, psychologists began to move away from the Freudian interpretation of dreams. For example, Hall (1953) proposed a cognitive theory of dreaming in which he suggested that dreaming is simply thinking while asleep. Advocates of Hall's approach argued for a greater focus on the manifest content—the actual dream itself—which is seen as an expression of a broad range of the dreamer's concerns rather than as an expression of sexual impulses (Glucksman & Kramer, 2004).

Well-known sleep researcher J. Allan Hobson (1988) rejects the notion that nature would equip humans with the capability of having dreams that would require a specialist to interpret. Hobson and McCarley (1977) advanced the activation-synthesis hypothesis of dreaming. This hypothesis suggests that dreams are simply the brain's attempt to make sense of the random firing of brain cells during REM sleep. Just as people try to make sense of input from the environment during their waking hours, they try to find meaning in the conglomeration of sensations and memories that are generated internally by this random firing of brain cells. Hobson (1989) believes that dreams also have psychological significance, because the meaning a person imposes on the random mental activity reflects that person's experiences, remote memories, associations, drives, and fears.

Finally, advocates of the evolutionary theory of dreaming suggest that vivid, emotionally charged REM dreams serve a protective function (Barrett, 2007). Such dreams often involve threatening situations in which we may actually find ourselves. For example, an individual may dream that he is driving at 70 miles per hour on a highway when his car's brakes suddenly go out. According to the evolutionary view, such a dream would provide the dreamer with an opportunity to rehearse strategies that may help him manage a similar threat in real life.

manifest content Freud's term for the content of a dream as recalled by the dreamer.

latent content Freud's term for the underlying meaning of a dream.

cognitive theory of dreaming The view that dreaming is thinking while asleep.

activation-synthesis hypothesis of dreaming The hypothesis that dreams are the brain's attempt to make sense of the random firing of brain cells during REM sleep.

evolutionary theory of dreaming The view that vivid REM dreams enable people to rehearse the skills needed to fend off threats and predators.

Meditation and Hypnosis

We all have to sleep. Even if you fight it, your body will eventually force you to sleep. But there are other forms of altered consciousness that we may experience only if we choose to do so. Meditation and hypnosis are two of these.

4.12 What are the benefits of meditation?

meditation A group of techniques that involve focusing attention on an object, a word, one's breathing, or one's body movements in an effort to block out all distractions, to enhance well-being, and to achieve an altered state of consciousness.

Meditation

Do you know that a mental and physical relaxation technique can actually induce an altered state of consciousness? Meditation is a group of techniques that involve focusing attention on an object, a word, one's breathing, or one's body movements in an effort to block out all distractions, to enhance well-being, and to achieve an altered state of consciousness. Some forms of meditation, such as yoga, Zen, and transcendental meditation (TM), have their roots in Eastern religions and are practiced by followers of those religions to attain a higher spiritual state. In the United States, these approaches are often used to increase relaxation, reduce arousal, or expand consciousness (Wolsko et al., 2004). Brain-imaging studies support the conclusion that meditation, in addition to being relaxing, induces an altered state of consciousness (Cahn & Polich, 2006; Newberg et al., 2001).

Studies suggest that meditation can be helpful for a variety of physical and psychological problems. Researchers have found that regular meditation helps individuals, even those who are severely depressed, learn to control their emotions (Butler et al., 2008). In addition, meditation may prove helpful in lowering blood pressure, cholesterol levels, and other measures of cardiovascular health (Seeman, Dubin, & Seeman, 2003). Keep in mind, though, that meditation is not a "quick fix" for either mental or physical health problems. Deriving benefits from meditation requires self-discipline and commitment (Murray, 2002). Use the steps in the *Try It* to learn how to induce a relaxation state that is very similar to that experienced by those who meditate; practice the technique until you become proficient in it. You will then be ready to incorporate it into your daily routine.

hypnosis A procedure through which one person, the hypnotist, uses the power of suggestion to induce changes in thoughts, feelings, sensations, perceptions, or behavior in another person, the subject.

sociocognitive theory of hypnosis A theory suggesting that the behavior of a hypnotized person is a function of that person's expectations about how subjects behave under hypnosis.

Neuroimaging studies have suggested that several areas of the brain may be permanently changed by the long-term practice of meditation (Lutz et al., 2008; Newberg, 2010). However, these findings are preliminary. Much research remains to be done before neuroscientists will have a complete understanding of how such neurological changes affect meditators' cognitive or emotional functioning.

TRY IT   The Relaxation Response

Find a quiet place and sit in a comfortable position.

1. Close your eyes.

2. Relax all your muscles deeply. Beginning with your feet and moving slowly upward, relax the muscles in your legs, buttocks, abdomen, chest, shoulders, neck, and finally your face. Allow your whole body to remain in this deeply relaxed state.

3. Now concentrate on your breathing, and breathe in and out through your nose. Each time you breathe out, silently say the word *one* to yourself.

4. Repeat this process for 20 minutes. (You can open your eyes to look at your watch periodically, but don't use an alarm.) When you are finished, remain seated for a few minutes— first with your eyes closed, then with them open.

⊙ Watch on **mypsychlab.com**

Hypnosis ▶

Hypnosis may be formally defined as a procedure through which one person, the hypnotist, uses the power of suggestion to induce changes in thoughts, feelings, sensations, perceptions, or behavior in another person, the subject. Interestingly, research shows that some people cannot be hypnotized (Milling et al., 2010). Individual differences in the degree to which people are open to suggestions when they are fully conscious is linked to hypnotizability. Moreover, there are many misconceptions about hypnosis. Have you ever heard of the myths listed in Table 4.1?

Hypnosis has come a long way from the days when it was used mainly by entertainers. It is now recognized as a viable technique to be used in medicine, dentistry, and psychotherapy (Weisberg, 2008). Hypnosis is accepted by the American Medical Association, the American Psychological Association, and the American Psychiatric Association. It has been particularly helpful in the control of pain (Uman, Chambers, McGrath, & Kisely, 2008). Experimental studies have shown that patients who are hypnotized and exposed to suggestions designed to induce relaxation prior to surgery experience less postsurgery pain than do nonhypnotized patients (Montgomery et al., 2002).

According to the sociocognitive theory of hypnosis, the behavior of a hypnotized person is a function of that person's expectations about how subjects behave under hypnosis. People are motivated to be good subjects, to follow the suggestions of the hypnotist, and to fulfill the social role of the hypnotized person as they perceive it (Spanos, 1986, 1991, 1994). The *Summarize It* on page 122 lists the theories that explain hypnosis. Does this mean that hypnotized people are merely acting or faking it? No, "most hypnotized persons are neither faking nor merely complying with suggestions" (Kirsch & Lynn, 1995, p. 847). In fact, using the single most effective and reliable indicator of deception in the laboratory—skin conductance, which indicates emotional response by measuring perspiration—Kinnunen and others (1994) found that 89% of supposedly hypnotized people had been truly hypnotized.

Ernest Hilgard (1986, 1992) has proposed a theory to explain why hypnotized individuals can accomplish very difficult acts, even undergoing surgery without anesthesia. According to his neodissociation theory of hypnosis, hypnosis induces a split, or dissociation, between two aspects of the control of consciousness: the planning function and the monitoring function. During hypnosis, it is the planning function that

4.13 How and why does hypnosis influence the body and mind?

▲ A hypnotized person is in a state of heightened suggestibility. This hypnotherapist may therefore be able to help the woman control chronic or postsurgery pain.

neodissociation theory of hypnosis A theory proposing that hypnosis induces a split, or dissociation, between two aspects of the control of consciousness: the planning function and the monitoring function.

TABLE 4.1 What Do You Know about Hypnosis?

IF YOU THINK ...	THE REALITY IS ...
It's all a matter of having a good imagination.	Ability to imagine vividly is unrelated to hypnotizability.
Relaxation is an important feature of hypnosis.	It's not. Hypnosis has been induced during vigorous exercise.
It's mostly just compliance.	Many highly motivated subjects fail to experience hypnosis.
It's a matter of willful faking.	Physiological responses indicate that subjects are not lying.
It is dangerous.	Standard procedures are no more distressing than lectures.
It has something to do with a sleeplike state.	It does not. Hypnotized subjects are fully awake.
Certain personality types are likely to be hypnotizable.	There are no substantial correlates with personality measures.
People who are hypnotized lose control of themselves.	Subjects are capable of saying no or terminating hypnosis.
Hypnosis can enable people to "relive" the past.	Age-regressed adults behave like adults playacting as children.
A person's responsiveness to hypnosis depends on the technique used and who administers it.	Neither is important under laboratory conditions. It is the subject's capacity that is important.
When hypnotized, people can remember more accurately.	Hypnosis may actually muddle the distinction between memory and fantasy and may artificially inflate confidence.
Hypnotized people can be led to do acts that conflict with their values.	Hypnotized subjects fully adhere to their usual moral standards.
People do not remember what happens during hypnosis.	Posthypnotic amnesia does not occur spontaneously.
Hypnosis can enable people to perform otherwise impossible feats of strength, endurance, learning and sensory acuity.	Performance following hypnotic suggestions for increased muscle strength, learning and sensory acuity does not exceed what can be accomplished by motivated subjects outside hypnosis.

carries out the suggestions of the hypnotist and remains a part of the subject's conscious awareness. The monitoring function monitors or observes everything that happens to the subject, but without his or her conscious awareness. Hilgard called the monitoring function, when separated from conscious awareness, "the hidden observer."

Bowers and his colleagues (Bowers, 1992; Woody & Bowers, 1994) have proposed a view of hypnosis as an authentic altered state of consciousness. Their theory of dissociated control maintains that hypnosis does not induce a splitting of different aspects of consciousness, as Hilgard's model suggests. Rather, they believe that hypnosis weakens the control of the executive function over other parts (subsystems) of consciousness, allowing the hypnotist's suggestions to contact and influence those subsystems directly. Bowers further believes that the hypnotized person's responses are automatic and involuntary, like reflexes, and are not controlled by normal cognitive functions (Kirsch & Lynn, 1995). Indeed, some research supports this viewpoint (Bowers & Woody, 1996; Hargadon, Bowers, & Woody, 1995).

Although the majority of hypnosis researchers seem to support the sociocognitive theory, most clinicians, and some influential researchers in the field, apparently believe that hypnosis is a unique altered state of consciousness (Kallio & Revonsuo, 2003). Kihlstrom (2007) has suggested that a more complete picture of hypnosis could emerge from some combination of the sociocognitive and neodissociation theories. But even though researchers still have theoretical differences, hypnosis is being increasingly used in clinical practice and in selected areas of medicine and dentistry.

theory of dissociated control The theory that hypnosis weakens the control that the executive function exerts over other subsystems of consciousness.

SUMMARIZE IT

Theories of Hypnosis

THEORY	EXPLANATION OF HYPNOSIS
Sociocognitive	Expectations and a desire to be a "good subject" motivate people to respond to the suggestions of a hypnotist.
Neodissociation	The mind's planning function consciously responds to a hypnotist's suggestions while its monitoring function observes these responses unconsciously.
Dissociated control	Subjects respond to a hypnotist's suggestions because hypnosis weakens the influence of the executive control system over other aspects of consciousness.

Psychoactive Drugs

The last time you took a pain reliever or an antibiotic, you probably didn't think of yourself as engaging in a mind-altering experience. However, all chemical substances, even the aspirin you take for a headache, affect the brain because they alter the functioning of neurotransmitters (Munzar et al., 2002). As you can probably guess, most such substances have no noticeable effect on your state of consciousness. Some drugs, however, have especially powerful effects on the brain and induce dramatically altered states of consciousness.

A psychoactive drug is any substance that alters mood, perception, or thought. When psychoactive drugs, such as antidepressants, are approved for medical use, they are called *controlled substances*. The term *illicit* denotes psychoactive drugs that are illegal. Many *over-the-counter drugs,* such as antihistamines and decongestants, as well as many herbal preparations, are psychoactive. Certain foods, such as chocolate, may also alter our moods (Macht & Mueller, 2007). Note to restaurant servers: Giving customers a piece of chocolate along with their checks increases tips (Strohmetz et al., 2002).

psychoactive drug Any substance that alters mood, perception, or thought; called a controlled substance if approved for medical use.

4.14 How do drugs affect the brain's neurotransmitter system?

How Drugs Affect the Brain

You may recall from Chapter 2 that drugs affect our brains and behavior through their influence on neurotransmitters, the chemicals that regulate communication between neurons. For instance, did you know that all kinds of physical pleasure have the same neurological basis? Whether derived from sex, a psychoactive chemical, or any other source, a subjective sense of physical pleasure is brought about by an increase in the availability of the neurotransmitter dopamine in a part of the brain's limbic system known as the *nucleus accumbens* (Koob & Le Moal, 2008; Panksepp, 2010). Thus, it isn't surprising that researchers have found that a surge of dopamine is involved in the rewarding and motivational effects produced by most psychoactive drugs (Carlson, 1998), including marijuana, heroin (Tanda, Pontieri, & DiChiara, 1997), and nicotine (Pich et al., 1997; Pontieri et al., 1996). Why, then, does the altered state associated with alcohol feel different from that associated with nicotine or marijuana? Because the effect drugs have on the dopamine system is just the beginning of a cascade of effects that involve the brain's entire neurotransmitter system. Each drug influences the whole system differently and is associated with a distinctive altered state of consciousness. Consider a few examples of how different drugs act on neurotransmitters and the associated beneficial effects:

- Opiates such as morphine and heroin mimic the effects of the brain's own endorphins, chemicals that have pain-relieving properties and produce a feeling of well-being. For this reason, opiates are useful in pain management.

- Depressants such as alcohol, barbiturates, and benzodiazepines (Valium and Librium, for example) act on GABA receptors to produce a calming, sedating effect (Harris, Brodie, & Dunwiddie, 1992). Thus, depressants can play a role in reducing a patient's nervousness prior to undergoing a medical procedure.

- Stimulants such as amphetamines and cocaine mimic the effects of epinephrine, the neurotransmitter that triggers the sympathetic nervous system. The effects of the sympathetic nervous system include suppressed hunger and digestion; this is why "diet pills" typically contain some kind of stimulant, such as caffeine.

As we all know, drugs don't always have solely beneficial effects. Why? Because too much of a good thing, or the wrong combination of good things, can lead to disaster. For example, opiates, when taken regularly, will eventually completely suppress the production of endorphins. As a result, natural pain management systems break down, and the brain becomes dependent on the presence of opiates to function normally. Similarly, if ingestion of too much alcohol, or of a combination of alcohol and other depressants, floods the brain with GABA, consciousness will be lost, and death may follow. Excessive amounts of a stimulant can send heart rates and blood pressure levels zooming; death can even result from the ingestion of a single, large dose.

Substance Abuse and Addiction ▶

When people intentionally use drugs to induce an altered state of consciousness, they risk developing a *substance abuse* problem. Psychologists usually define substance abuse as continued use of a substance after several episodes in which use of the substance has negatively affected an individual's work, education, and social relationships (American Psychiatric Association, 2000a). For example, a person who has missed work several times because of alcohol intoxication, but who continues to drink, has a substance abuse problem. 👁 Watch on **mypsychlab.com**

What causes people to progress from substance use to substance abuse? The physical pleasure associated with drug-induced altered states of consciousness is one reason. Genetically based differences in the way people respond physiologically to drugs also contribute to substance abuse (Ehlers et al., 2010). For example, some people feel intoxicated after drinking very small amounts of alcohol; others require a much larger "dose" to feel the same effects. People who have to drink more to experience intoxication are more likely to become alcoholics. Genetic researchers are currently searching for the gene or genes that contribute to low response to alcohol (Schuckit et al., 2001). Of course, personality and social factors contribute to substance abuse as well. Impulsivity, for instance, is associated with experimentation with drugs (Simons & Carey, 2002). Stress-related variables, such as a history of having been a victim of child abuse or domestic violence, are also associated with substance abuse (Goeders, 2004;

4.15 How do physical and psychological drug dependence differ?

substance abuse Continued use of a substance that affects an individual's work, education, and social relationships.

👁 Watch the Video *Kathy: Substance Abuse* on **mypsychlab.com**

▲ Seeing the paraphernalia that are associated with the drug an addict uses can trigger a craving for the drug's psychological effects. Thus, learning to avoid such cues is important in the process of recovery from addiction.

physical drug dependence A compulsive pattern of drug use in which the user develops a drug tolerance coupled with unpleasant withdrawal symptoms when the drug use is discontinued.

drug tolerance A condition in which the user becomes progressively less affected by the drug and must take increasingly larger doses to maintain the same effect or high.

withdrawal symptoms The physical and psychological symptoms that occur when a regularly used drug is discontinued and that terminate when the drug is taken again.

psychological drug dependence A craving or irresistible urge for a drug's pleasurable effects.

Gordon, 2002; Sussman & Dent, 2000). Social and cultural factors play important roles in the development of substance abuse problems, too. For instance, associating with peers who use drugs may influence teenagers to begin doing so or may help to maintain substance abuse behavior once it begins (Curran, Stice, & Chassin, 1997).

Some people progress from substance abuse to full-blown substance dependence, commonly called *addiction*. Physical drug dependence results from the body's natural ability to protect itself against harmful substances by developing a drug tolerance. That is, the user becomes progressively less affected by the drug and must take increasingly larger doses to achieve the same effect or high (Koob, 2008). Tolerance occurs because the brain adapts to the presence of the drug by responding less intensely to it. In addition, the liver produces more enzymes to break down the drug. The various bodily processes adjust so that they can continue to function with the drug in the system.

Once drug tolerance is established, a person cannot function normally without the drug. If the drug is taken away, the user begins to suffer withdrawal symptoms. These withdrawal symptoms, which are both physical and psychological, are usually the exact opposite of the effects produced by the drug. For example, withdrawal from stimulants leaves a person exhausted and depressed; withdrawal from tranquilizers leaves a person nervous and agitated. Because taking the drug is the only way to escape these unpleasant symptoms, withdrawal supports continued addiction. Moreover, the lasting behavioral and cognitive effects of abused substances on the brain often interfere with attempts to stop using them. Among other effects, researchers have learned that addiction is associated with attention and memory deficits, loss of the ability to accurately sense the passage of time, and declines in the capacity to plan and control behavior (Bates, Laboovie, & Voelbel, 2002; Buhusi & Meck, 2002). Abusers need all of these skills to overcome addiction and rebuild their lives, but regaining them once drug abuse is stopped—if they can be recovered at all—takes time.

Psychological drug dependence is a craving or irresistible urge for the drug's pleasurable effects; it is even more difficult to combat than physical dependence (O'Brien, 1996). Continued use of drugs to which an individual is physically addicted is influenced by the psychological component of the habit. Some drugs that are probably not physically addictive (e.g., marijuana) may nevertheless create psychological dependence.

Learning processes are important in the development and maintenance of psychological dependence. For example, drug-taking cues—the people, places, and things associated with using the drug—can trigger a strong craving for the substance of abuse (Koob, 2008). PET scans of cocaine addicts' brains indicate that such cues arouse a cue-specific neural network, which may explain why it is difficult for addicts to divert their attention from them (Bonson et al., 2002). Furthermore, research with animals indicates that drug-related cues elicit the same responses in the brain as the drugs themselves (Kiyatkin & Wise, 2002). These findings underscore the need for further research aimed at revealing the relationships among the physiological effects of drugs and the social contexts in which drug use occurs (Crombag & Robinson, 2004).

4.16 How do stimulants affect behavior?

stimulants A category of drugs that speed up activity in the central nervous system, suppress appetite, and can cause a person to feel more awake, alert, and energetic; also called "uppers."

Stimulants

Have you ever advised a friend to "switch to decaf"? This advice comes from a bit of drug knowledge we all share: Caffeine can make us jumpy. Stimulants (also called "uppers") speed up activity in the central nervous system, suppress appetite, and can make a person feel more awake, alert, and energetic. Stimulants increase pulse rate, blood pressure, and respiration rate, and they reduce cerebral blood flow (Mathew & Wilson, 1991). In higher doses, stimulants make people feel nervous, jittery, and restless, and they can cause shaking or trembling and interfere with sleep.

Caffeine. Coffee, tea, cola drinks, chocolate, energy drinks such as Red Bull, and more than 100 prescription and over-the-counter drugs contain caffeine. Caffeine makes people more mentally alert and can help them stay awake (Wesensten et al., 2002). Caffeine may even improve visual acuity by making the retina more sensitive to light (Arushanyan & Shikina, 2004). However, contrary to popular opinion, mixing alcohol with caffeine does not enable a person to party for a longer period of time than she would without the caffeine (Gulick & Gould, 2009). In fact, combining alcohol and caffeine can lead to severe dehydration which, it so happens, is the underlying cause of the constellation of symptoms popularly known as a "hangover." Thus, anyone who wants to avoid a hangover should also avoid mixing caffeine with alcohol. Moreover, caffeine appears to impair drinkers' ability to assess the degree to which they are intoxicated, an effect that leads to poor decision making about driving under the influence of alcohol and other risky behaviors (Ferreira et al., 2006).

When moderate to heavy caffeine users abstain, they suffer withdrawal symptoms such as nervousness, instability, headaches, drowsiness, and decreased alertness. Using EEGs and sonograms, researchers looked at the effects of caffeine withdrawal symptoms on the brain and were able to correlate the symptoms with significant increases in blood pressure and in the velocity of blood flow in all four of the cerebral arteries. The EEGs also showed an increase in slower brain waves, which correlates with decreased alertness and drowsiness (Jones et al., 2000).

Nicotine. Like caffeine, nicotine increases alertness, but few people who have tried to quit smoking doubt its addictive power. (The many serious health problems associated with smoking are discussed in Chapter 10.) Many treatment methods advertised as being helpful to smokers who are trying to quit appear to have limited value. For example, Green and Lynn (2000) reviewed the results of 59 studies of hypnosis and smoking and concluded that hypnosis cannot be considered effective in helping smokers break the habit. However, experiments have shown that over-the-counter nicotine patches help about one in five smokers quit and enable many others to cut down on the number of cigarettes they smoke (Jolicoeur et al., 2003).

Amphetamines. Amphetamines increase arousal, relieve fatigue, improve alertness, suppress the appetite, and give a rush of energy. Research suggests that in high doses (100 milligrams or more) amphetamines can cause confused and disorganized behavior, extreme fear and suspiciousness, delusions and hallucinations, aggressiveness and antisocial behavior, even manic behavior and paranoia (Thirthalli & Benegal, 2006). The powerful amphetamine methamphetamine (known as "crank" or "speed") comes in a smokable form ("ice"), which is highly addictive and can be fatal.

Withdrawal from amphetamines leaves a person physically exhausted; he or she will sleep for 10 to 15 hours or more, only to awaken in a stupor, extremely depressed and intensely hungry. Stimulants constrict the tiny capillaries and the small arteries. Over time, high doses can stop blood flow, causing hemorrhaging and leaving parts of the brain deprived of oxygen. In fact, victims of fatal overdoses of stimulants usually have multiple hemorrhages in the brain.

Cocaine. Cocaine, a stimulant derived from coca leaves, can be sniffed as a white powder, injected intravenously, or smoked in the form of crack. The effects of snorting cocaine are felt within 2 to 3 minutes, and the high lasts 30 to 45 minutes. The euphoria from cocaine is followed by an equally intense crash, marked by depression, anxiety, agitation, and a powerful craving for more of the drug.

Cocaine stimulates the reward, or "pleasure," pathways in the brain, which use the neurotransmitter dopamine (Landry, 1997). With continued use, these reward systems fail to function normally, and the user becomes incapable of feeling any pleasure except from the drug. The main withdrawal symptoms are psychological—the inability to feel pleasure and the craving for more cocaine.

Cocaine constricts the blood vessels, raises blood pressure, speeds up the heart, quickens respiration, and can even cause epileptic seizures in people who have no history of epilepsy (Pascual-Leone et al., 1990). Over time, or even quickly in high doses, cocaine can cause heart palpitations, an irregular heartbeat, and heart attacks, and high doses can cause strokes in healthy young individuals. Chronic cocaine use can

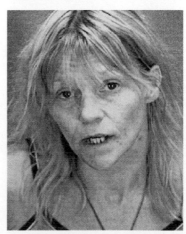

▲ Methamphetamine abuse leads to dramatic changes in appearance, because the drug interferes with the body's ability to maintain and repair the skin, hair, and teeth (Wells, 2007).

also result in holes in the nasal septum (the ridge of cartilage running down the middle of the nose) and in the palate (the roof of the mouth) (Greenfield & Hennessy, 2008).

Animals become addicted more readily to cocaine than to any other drug, and those who are addicted to multiple substances prefer cocaine when offered a choice of drugs (Manzardo, Stein, & Belluzi, 2002). Given unlimited access to cocaine, animals will lose interest in everything else, including food, water, and sex, and will rapidly and continually self-administer cocaine. They tend to die within 14 days, usually from cardiopulmonary collapse (Gawin, 1991). Cocaine-addicted monkeys will press a lever as many as 12,800 times to get one cocaine injection (Yanagita, 1973).

Crack, or "rock," the most dangerous form of cocaine, can produce a powerful dependency in several weeks. Users who begin with cocaine in powder form are likely to progress to crack, while users who start on crack are more likely to continue using it exclusively. When both powder and crack are used interchangeably, a mutual reinforcement seems to occur, and the user develops a dependence on both forms of cocaine (Shaw et al., 1999).

4.17 How do depressants affect behavior?

depressants A category of drugs that decrease activity in the central nervous system, slow down bodily functions, and reduce sensitivity to outside stimulation; also called "downers."

Depressants

Another class of drugs, the depressants, decrease activity in the central nervous system, slow down bodily functions, and reduce sensitivity to outside stimulation. Within this category are the sedative-hypnotics (alcohol, barbiturates, and minor tranquilizers) and the narcotics (opiates). When different depressants are taken together, their sedative effects are additive and, thus, potentially dangerous.

Alcohol. The more alcohol a person consumes, the more the central nervous system is depressed (Knapp, Ciraulo, & Kramzler, 2008). As drinking increases, the symptoms of drunkenness mount—slurred speech, poor coordination, staggering. Impaired depth perception—one good reason to avoid driving after you have been drinking—is another feature of alcohol intoxication (Nawrot et al., 2004). (We will discuss the health consequences of alcohol abuse in detail in Chapter 10.) Alcohol also decreases the ability to form new memories (Kirchner & Sayette, 2003; Ray & Bates, 2006). That's why an episode of heavy drinking is often followed by a "morning after," during which the drinker is unable to remember the events that occurred while he or she was under the influence of alcohol. Interestingly, alcohol placebos have similar effects on memory function, so a drinker's expectations contribute to alcohol's effects to some extent (Assefi & Garry, 2003). ✳—Explore on mypsychlab.com

✳—Explore the Concept *Behavioral Effects Associated with Various Blood Alcohol Levels* on mypsychlab.com

Barbiturates. Barbiturates, such as *phenobarbital* and *propofol*, depress the central nervous system (Lafferty, 2008). Depending on the dose, a barbiturate can act as an anesthetic, sedative, or a sleeping pill. People who abuse barbiturates become drowsy and confused, their thinking and judgment suffer, and their coordination and reflexes are affected. Barbiturates can kill if taken in overdose. Alcohol and barbiturates, when taken together, are a potentially fatal combination.

Minor Tranquilizers. The popular minor tranquilizers, the *benzodiazepines,* came on the scene in the early 1960s and are sold under the brand names Valium, Librium, Dalmane, and, more recently, Xanax (also used as an antidepressant). Benzodiazepines are prescribed for several medical and psychological disorders (Mantooth, 2010). Abuse of these drugs is associated with both temporary and permanent impairment of memory and other cognitive functions. (A more detailed discussion of tranquilizers can be found in Chapter 13.)

narcotics A class of depressant drugs derived from the opium poppy that produce both pain-relieving and calming effects.

Narcotics. Narcotics are derived from the opium poppy and produce both pain-relieving and calming effects. Opium affects mainly the brain, but it also paralyzes the intestinal muscles, which is why it is used medically to treat diarrhea. If you have ever taken paregoric, you have had a tincture (extract) of opium. Because opium suppresses the cough center, it is used in some cough medicines. Morphine and codeine, natural constituents of opium, may be found in some drugs prescribed for pain relief. Such drugs, including Oxycontin and Vicodin, are addictive and are sold illegally to millions of people in the United States every year (Meehan & Adelman, 2010).

A highly addictive narcotic derived from morphine is heroin. Heroin addicts describe a sudden "rush" of euphoria, followed by drowsiness, inactivity, and impaired concentration. Withdrawal symptoms begin about 6 to 24 hours after use, and the addict becomes physically sick. Nausea, diarrhea, depression, stomach cramps, insomnia, and pain grow worse and worse until they become intolerable—unless the person gets another "fix."

Hallucinogens ▶

[**4.18** How do hallucinogens affect behavior?

The hallucinogens, or *psychedelics,* are drugs that can alter and distort perceptions of time and space, alter mood, and produce feelings of unreality. As the name implies, hallucinogens also cause hallucinations, sensations that have no basis in external reality (Malik & Disouza, 2006; Thirthalli & Benegal, 2006). Rather than producing a relatively predictable effect like most other drugs, hallucinogens usually magnify the mood of the user at the time the drug is taken. Contrary to the belief of some, hallucinogens hamper rather than enhance creative thinking (Bourassa & Vaugeois, 2001).

Marijuana. *THC* (tetrahydrocannabinol), the ingredient in marijuana that produces the high, remains in the body "for days or even weeks" (Julien, 1995). Marijuana impairs attention and coordination and slows reaction time, and these effects make operating complex machinery such as an automobile dangerous, even after the feeling of intoxication has passed. Marijuana can interfere with concentration, logical thinking, formation of new memories, and retrieval of stored memories (Niyuhire et al., 2007; Verdejo-Garcia et al., 2005). Many of the receptors for THC are in the hippocampus, which explains why the drug affects memory (Rubino et al., 2009).

Studies comparing marijuana users who began taking the drug before age 17 with those who started later show that early marijuana use is associated with a somewhat smaller brain volume and a lower percentage of the all-important gray matter in the brain's cortex. Marijuana users who started younger were also shorter and weighed less than users who started when older (Wilson et al., 2000). Longitudinal studies also suggest that marijuana causes the cerebral cortices of users who begin smoking it in adolescence to age more rapidly than those of nonusers (Mata et al., 2010). At the same time, marijuana appears to permanently stunt the development of neurons in the hippocampal regions of the brains of young users, an effect that may lead to memory impairment that persists into adulthood (Rubino et al., 2009). Further, early marijuana use affects the capacity of the prefrontal cortex to respond to danger alerts from the amygdala, a factor that may explain correlations between marijuana use and other risky behaviors among adolescents and young adults (Lin et al., 2008). Taken together, these results suggest that marijuana's effects on the developing brain are complex.

However, an advisory panel of the National Institute on Drug Abuse, after reviewing the scientific evidence, concluded that marijuana shows promise as a treatment for certain medical conditions. It has been found effective for treating the eye disease glaucoma, for controlling nausea and vomiting in cancer patients receiving chemotherapy, and for improving appetite and curtailing weight loss in some AIDS patients (Fackelmann, 1997). It may also be helpful in the treatment of spinal cord injuries and other

▲ Many Americans believe that the use of marijuana for medical purposes ought to be legal. However, the U.S. Food and Drug Administration insists that there are no legitimate medical uses for smoked marijuana (FDA, 2006). They point out that the active ingredient in marijuana, THC, is available in pill form and can be legally prescribed to patients by any licensed physician in the United States.

hallucinogens (hal-LU-sin-o-jenz) A category of drugs that can alter and distort perceptions of time and space, alter mood, produce feelings of unreality, and cause hallucinations; also called *psychedelics.*

kinds of nerve damage (Wade et al., 2003). However, because pills containing the active ingredients in marijuana are already legally available by prescription, many experts contend that it is not necessary to legalize the use of marijuana cigarettes for medical purposes. These experts point out that marijuana smoke contains many of the same irritants and carcinogens as cigarette smoke and, as a result, increases users' risk of pulmonary diseases and lung cancer (Vawter & Fisher, 2007). Moreover, the U.S. Food and Drug Administration has stated unequivocally that smoked marijuana has no known medical benefits and should continue to be regarded as a dangerous drug (U.S. Food and Drug Administration, 2006).

LSD (Lysergic Acid Diethylamide). LSD is lysergic acid diethylamide, sometimes referred to simply as "acid." The average LSD "trip" lasts for 10 to 12 hours and usually produces extreme perceptual and emotional changes, including visual hallucinations and feelings of panic (Weaver & Schnoll, 2008). On occasion, bad LSD trips have ended tragically in accidents, death, or suicide. Former LSD users sometimes experience *flashbacks,* brief recurrences of previous trips that occur suddenly and without warning. Some develop a syndrome called *hallucinogen persisting perception disorder (HPPD),* in which the visual cortex becomes highly stimulated whenever the individuals shut their eyes, causing them to experience chronic visual hallucinations whenever they try to sleep (Abraham & Duffy, 2001).

Designer Drugs. Designer drugs are so called because they are specially formulated to mimic the pleasurable effects of other drugs without, supposedly, their negative side effects. STP (for Serenity, Tranquility, and Peace) and Ecstasy are two common designer drugs. All designer drugs are derived from amphetamines but have hallucinogenic as well as stimulant effects.

Users of MDMA (methylene-dioxy-methamphetamine, the chemical for Ecstasy) describe a wonderfully pleasant state of consciousness, in which even the most backward, bashful, self-conscious people shed their inhibitions (U.S. Department of Health and Human Services, 2001; Verdejo-García et al., 2005). However, MDMA is known to impair a variety of cognitive functions, including memory, sustained attention, analytical thinking, and self-control (Weaver & Schnoll, 2008). More specifically, the drug is believed to have devastating effects on the critically important neurotransmitter serotonin (Buchert et al., 2004). Serotonin, as you learned in Chapter 2, influences cognitive performance (including memory), as well as moods, sleep cycles, and the ability to control impulses. Overdoses of MDMA can be fatal (Drug Enforcement Administration, 2003). In addition, MDMA causes dehydration, a side effect that can lead to fatal heat exhaustion (Hahn & Yew, 2009).

Moreover, MDMA seems to impair the capacity for judging social cues in frequent users. In one study, Ecstasy users were more likely than nonusers to incorrectly classify the actions of others as having aggressive intent (Hoshi et al., 2006). As you will learn in Chapter 14, poor social judgments of this type are thought to be the cognitive basis of some acts of aggression. Thus, by changing the way Ecstasy users think about social cues, the drug may indirectly increase their proclivity for aggressive behavior.

The *Summarize It* provides a summary of the effects and withdrawal symptoms of the major psychoactive drugs.

The Effects and Withdrawal Symptoms of Some Psychoactive Drugs

PSYCHOACTIVE DRUG	EFFECTS	WITHDRAWAL SYMPTOMS
STIMULANTS		
Caffeine	Produces wakefulness and alertness; increases metabolism but slows reaction time	Headache, depression, fatigue
Nicotine (tobacco)	Effects range from alertness to calmness; lowers appetite for carbohydrates; increases pulse rate and other metabolic processes	Irritability, anxiety, restlessness, increased appetite
Amphetamines	Increase metabolism and alertness; elevate mood, cause wakefulness, suppress appetite	Fatigue, increased appetite, depression, long periods of sleep, irritability, anxiety
Cocaine	Brings on euphoric mood, energy boost, feeling of excitement; suppresses appetite	Depression, fatigue, increased appetite, long periods of sleep, irritability
DEPRESSANTS		
Alcohol	First few drinks stimulate and enliven while lowering anxiety and inhibitions; higher doses have a sedative effect, slowing reaction time, impairing motor control and perceptual ability	Tremors, nausea, sweating, depression, weakness, irritability, and in some cases hallucinations
Barbiturates	Promote sleep, have calming and sedative effect, decrease muscular tension, impair coordination and reflexes	Sleeplessness, anxiety; sudden withdrawal can cause seizures, cardiovascular collapse, and death
Tranquilizers (e.g., Valium, Xanax)	Lower anxiety, have calming and sedative effect, decrease muscular tension	Restlessness, anxiety, irritability, muscle tension, difficulty sleeping
Narcotics	Relieve pain; produce paralysis of intestines	Nausea, diarrhea, cramps, insomnia
HALLUCINOGENS		
Marijuana	Generally produces euphoria, relaxation; affects ability to store new memories	Anxiety, difficulty sleeping, decreased appetite, hyperactivity
LSD	Produces excited exhilaration, hallucinations, experiences perceived as insightful and profound	None
MDMA (Ecstasy)	Typically produces euphoria and feelings of understanding others and accepting them; lowers inhibitions; often causes overheating, dehydration, nausea; can cause jaw clenching, eye twitching, and dizziness	Depression, fatigue, and in some cases a "crash," during which the person may be sad, scared, or annoyed

ᏉᎡ Looking Back

This chapter began with a look at dreams. Studies of sleep and dreams have been important to researchers' attempts to understand consciousness. The strong tendency across cultural groups to identify ways of altering consciousness suggests that this domain of experience is important in everyday lives as well. As you learned, however, consciousness itself is regulated by circadian rhythms. Waking and sleeping, too, occur in natural cycles. Still, humans sometimes take control of these natural regulatory mechanisms through meditation, hypnosis, and by using psychoactive drugs. As is always the case, more research is needed to help us more fully understand both involuntary and voluntary alterations of consciousness.

CHAPTER 4 SUMMARY

WHAT IS CONSCIOUSNESS? (pp. 109-110)

4.1 How do psychologists view consciousness? (p. 109)

Early psychologists saw consciousness, or awareness, as psychological in nature. Freud distinguished between conscious and unconscious experiences. James emphasized the continuous flow of thought and feeling in consciousness. Today's pschologists view consciousness as a neurobiological phenomenon rather than an exclusively psychological one.

Key Terms
consciousness, p. 109
altered states of consciousness, p. 109

4.2 What is the connection between altered states of consciousness and culture? (p. 110)

Practices in many cultures allow individuals to deliberately induce altered states, often as part of tribal ceremonies or religious rituals.

CIRCADIAN RHYTHMS (pp. 110-112)

4.3 How do circadian rhythms affect physiological and psychological functions? (pp. 110-111)

The suprachiasmatic nucleus (SCN) is the body's biological clock, which regulates circadian rhythms and signals the pineal gland to secrete or suppress secretion of melatonin, a hormone that acts to induce sleep. The amount of melatonin released by the pineal gland depends on the amount of light perceived by specialized photoreceptor cells on the retina.

Key Terms
circadian rhythm, p. 110
suprachiasmatic nucleus (SCN), p. 110

4.4 How do disruptions in circadian rhythms affect the body and mind? (pp. 111-112)

Jet lag and shift work disrupt circadian rhythms, which can lead to sleep difficulties as well as reduced alertness during periods of wakefulness.

Key Term
subjective night, p. 112

SLEEP (pp. 112-118)

4.5 How do the restorative and circadian theories explain sleep? (pp. 112-113)

The restorative theory of sleep claims that being awake causes stress on the body and the brain; repairs are made during sleep. The circadian (evolutionary) theory maintains that circadian rhythms, which evolved to protect humans from predators during the night, dictate periods of sleep and alertness.

Key Terms
restorative theory of sleep, p. 112
circadian theory of sleep, p. 113

4.6 What types of sleep occur during a typical night of sleep? (pp. 113-114)

During a typical night of sleep, a person goes through about five sleep cycles, each lasting about 90 minutes. During NREM sleep, heart rate and respiration are slow and regular, and blood pressure and brain activity are at a 24-hour low point; there is little body movement and no rapid eye movements. During REM sleep, the large muscles of the body are paralyzed, respiration and heart rate are fast and irregular, brain activity increases, and rapid eye movements and vivid dreams occur. REM sleep appears to be essential to the consolidation of memories. The first sleep cycle contains Stages 1, 2, 3, and 4 of NREM sleep as well as a period of REM sleep; the second contains Stages 2, 3, and 4 of NREM sleep and a period of REM sleep. In the third cycle, only Stages 2 and 3 are present, along with a period of REM sleep. In the remaining sleep cycles, the sleeper alternates mainly between Stage 2 and REM sleep, with each sleep cycle having progressively longer periods of REM.

Key Terms
sleep cycle, p. 113
NREM sleep, p. 113
sleep spindles, p. 113
slow-wave sleep, p. 113
Stage 4 sleep, p. 113
REM sleep, p. 113
REM rebound, p. 114

4.7 How does age influence sleep patterns? (pp. 114-115)

Infants and young children have the longest sleep time and largest percentages of REM and slow-wave sleep. Children from age 6 to puberty sleep best. Older adults typically have shorter total sleep time, more awakenings, and substantially less slow-wave sleep.

4.8 What are the effects of sleep deprivation? (p. 115)

Sleep deprivation can lead to lapses in concentration and emotional irritability. Research examining the effects of sleep deprivation on verbal learning have shown that sleep deprivation may lead to suppression of neurological activity in the temporal lobes.

4.9 What are the various sleep disorders? (pp. 116-118)

Parasomnias occur during partial arousal from Stage 4 sleep. In a sleep terror, the sleeper awakens in a panicked state with a racing heart. Episodes last 5 to 15 minutes, and then the person falls back to sleep. Nightmares occur during REM sleep and are usually remembered in vivid detail. Somniloquy (sleeptalking) can occur during any sleep stage and is more common in children than adults. The symptoms of narcolepsy include excessive daytime sleepiness and sudden attacks of REM sleep. Sleep apnea is a sleep disorder in which a sleeper's breathing stops and the person must awaken briefly to breathe. Its symptoms are excessive daytime sleepiness and loud snoring. Insomnia is a sleep disorder characterized by difficulty falling or staying asleep, waking too early, or sleep that is light, restless, or of poor quality.

Key Terms
parasomnias, p. 116
dyssomnia, p. 116
narcolepsy, p. 116
sleep apnea, p. 116
insomnia, p. 117

DREAMS (pp. 118-119)

4.10 What have researchers learned about dreams? (pp. 118-119)

REM dreams have a storylike or dreamlike quality and are more visual, vivid, and emotional than NREM dreams. Common dream themes include falling or being attacked or chased. During REM dreams, areas of the brain responsible for emotions and the primary visual cortex are active, but the neurotransmitters serotonin and norepinephrine are less plentiful. Lucid dreaming is a set of techniques that enables dreamers to exert cognitive control over the content of their dreams.

Key Terms
REM dream, p. 118
NREM dream, p. 118
lucid dream, p. 119

4.11 How do the various theorists explain dreams? (p. 119)

Freud claimed that dreams carry hidden meanings and function to satisfy unconscious sexual and aggressive desires. He claimed that the manifest content of dreams differs from their latent content. Today, some psychologists support the cognitive theory of dreaming, which claims that dreaming is thinking while asleep; others support the activation-synthesis hypothesis, which claims that dreams are the brain's attempt to make sense of the random firing of brain cells during REM sleep and others support the evolutionary theory of dreaming, which says that vivid REM dreams enable people to rehearse the skills they need to fend off predators.

Key Terms
manifest content, p. 119
latent content, p. 119
cognitive theory of dreaming, p. 119
activation-synthesis hypothesis of dreaming, p. 119
evolutionary theory of dreaming, p. 119

MEDITATION AND HYPNOSIS (pp. 120-122)

4.12 What are the benefits of meditation? (p. 120)

Meditation promotes relaxation, reduces arousal, or expands consciousness. It may also help prevent and treat cardiovascular disease.

Key Terms
meditation, p. 120

4.13 How and why does hypnosis influence the body and mind? (pp. 121-122)

Hypnosis is a procedure through which a hypnotist uses the power of suggestion to induce changes in the thoughts, feelings, sensations, perceptions, or behavior of a subject. It has been used most successfully for the control of pain. The three main theories proposed to explain hypnosis are the sociocognitive theory, the neodissociation theory, and the theory of dissociated control.

Key Terms
hypnosis, p. 120
sociocognitive theory of hypnosis, p. 120
neodissociation theory of hypnosis, p. 121
theory of dissociated control, p. 122

PSYCHOACTIVE DRUGS (pp. 122-129)

4.14 How do drugs affect the brain's neurotransmitter system? (pp. 122-123)

Psychoactive drugs increase the availability of dopamine in the nucleus accumbens. Beyond that, each drug has a unique influence on a specific neurotransmitter or group of neurotransmitters.

Key Terms
psychoactive drug, p. 122

4.15 How do physical and psychological drug dependence differ? (pp. 123-124)

With physical drug dependence, the user develops a drug tolerance, and so larger and larger doses of the drug are needed to get the same effect or high. Withdrawal symptoms appear when the drug is discontinued and disappear when the drug is taken again. Psychological drug dependence involves an intense craving for the drug's pleasurable effects.

Key Terms
substance abuse, p. 123
physical drug dependence, p. 124
drug tolerance, p. 124
withdrawal symptoms, p. 124
psychological drug dependence, p. 124

4.16 How do stimulants affect behavior? (pp. 124-126)

Stimulants (amphetamines, cocaine, caffeine, and nicotine) speed up activity in the central nervous system, suppress appetite, and make a person feel more awake, alert, and energetic.

Key Terms
stimulants, p. 124

4.17 How do depressants affect behavior? (pp. 126-127)

Depressants decrease activity in the central nervous system, slow down bodily functions, and reduce sensitivity to outside stimulation. Depressants include sedative-hypnotics (alcohol, barbiturates, and minor tranquilizers) and narcotics (opiates such as opium, codeine, morphine, and heroin), which have both pain-relieving and calming effects.

Key Terms
depressants, p. 126
narcotics, p. 126

4.18 How do hallucinogens affect behavior? (pp. 127-129)

Hallucinogens—including marijuana, LSD, and MDMA—can alter and distort perceptions of time and space, alter mood, produce feelings of unreality, and cause hallucinations.

Key Terms
hallucinogens, p. 127

MAP IT

Log on to MyPsychLab and click on "Map It" to prepare a unique digital map of the chapter that you can save for later use, email to your instructor, or print out to use as a study tool. Or, create your own map by drawing one on paper. Use the starter map below as a model for your own map. Use the chapter summary as your guide for what to include. For each item in your map, be sure to include the page number.

Here's one way to *Map It*:

1. Draw a box at the top of the page for the section title.
2. Underneath the section title box, working horizontally across the page, draw a box for each learning question in the section. Write the learning questions in the boxes and draw a line from the section title to each questions box. After you read each subsection, jot an answer for the learning question in the subsection's box.
3. Below each learning question box, insert another box for all of the key terms that are related to the question, along with a very brief reminder of each term's definition. Draw a line from the question box to the key terms box.
4. Below each key terms box, create another box and list all of the helpful figures, tables, and other elements of the text, such as *Try It* and *Apply It* boxes. Draw a line from the key terms box to the helpful elements box.

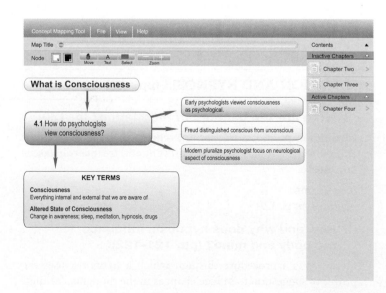

Map the **Chapter** on **mypsychlab.com**

Chapter **4** Study Guide

Answers to all the Study Guide questions are provided at the end of the book.

SECTION ONE: Chapter Review

What Is Consciousness? (pp. 109–110)

1. Which of the following best defines consciousness?

a. awareness

b. wakefulness

c. receptiveness

d. rationality

Circadian Rhythms (pp. 110–112)

2. The structure that regulates the body's internal clock is the _____ _____.

3. People who are suffering from jet lag or the effects of working rotating shifts or night shifts are experiencing

a. a deficiency in melatonin production.

b. an excess of melatonin production.

c. a defect in their suprachiasmatic nucleus.

d. a disturbance in their circadian rhythms.

4. The performance of shift workers is enhanced during their subjective night. (true/false)

Sleep (pp. 112–118)

5. The circadian theory of sleep is also known as the _____ or _____ theory of sleep.

6. State the type of sleep—NREM or REM—that corresponds to each characteristic.

_____ **(1)** paralysis of large muscles

_____ **(2)** slow, regular respiration and heart rate

_____ **(3)** rapid eye movements

_____ **(4)** intense brain activity

_____ **(5)** vivid dreams

a. REM   b. NREM

7. The average length of a sleep cycle in adults is

a. 30 minutes.

b. 60 minutes.

c. 90 minutes.

d. 120 minutes.

8. After the first two sleep cycles, most people get equal amounts of deep sleep and REM sleep. (true/false)

9. Which type of sleep seems to aid learning and memory?

a. Stage 1

b. Stage 2

c. Stages 3 and 4

d. REM sleep

10. Following REM deprivation, there is usually

a. an absence of REM sleep.

b. an increase in REM sleep.

c. a decrease in REM sleep.

d. no change in the amount of REM sleep.

11. Match the age group with the appropriate description of sleep.

_____ **(1)** have most difficulty sleeping

_____ **(2)** sleep 10 to 11 hours

_____ **(3)** have highest percentage of REM and deep sleep

a. infants and young children

b. children aged 6 to puberty

c. elderly adults

12. Sleepwalking and sleep terrors occur during a partial arousal from

a. Stage 1 sleep.

b. Stage 2 sleep.

c. Stage 4 sleep.

d. REM sleep.

13. Sleep terrors typically occur in Stage 2 sleep. (true/false)

14. Match each sleep problem with the description or associated symptom.

_____ **(1)** uncontrollable sleep attacks during the day

_____ **(2)** cessation of breathing during sleep

_____ **(3)** difficulty falling or staying asleep

_____ **(4)** very frightening REM dream

a. sleep apnea

b. nightmare

c. insomnia

d. narcolepsy

Dreams (pp. 118–119)

15. Compared to REM dreams, NREM dreams are

a. more emotional.

b. more visual.

c. less storylike.

d. more vivid.

16. Dreams are difficult to remember because most of them occur during Stage 4 sleep. (true/false)

17. According to researchers,

a. most dreams are bizarre in nature.

b. dreams involving bizarre content are more likely to be remembered than other kinds of dreams.

c. people who have delusional disorders rarely have bizarre dreams.

d. only children have bizarre dreams.

18. Experts tend to agree on how dreams should be interpreted. (true/false)

Meditation and Hypnosis (pp. 120–122)

19. Which is not a proposed use of meditation?

a. to promote relaxation

b. to substitute for anesthesia during surgery

c. to bring a person to a higher level of spirituality

d. to alter consciousness

20. Many people who meditate are motivated by a desire to attain a higher spiritual state of consciousness. (true/false)

21. Meditation can help people control their emotions. (true/false)

22. Which of the following statements is true of people under hypnosis?

a. They will often violate their moral code.

b. They are much stronger than they are in the normal waking state.

c. They can be made to experience distortions in their perceptions.

d. Their memory is more accurate than it is during the normal waking state.

23. For a fairly hypnotizable person, which use of hypnosis would probably be most successful?
    a. for relief from pain
    b. instead of a general anesthetic during surgery
    c. for treating drug addiction
    d. for improving memory

24. The three main theories proposed to explain hypnosis are the _____, _____, and _____ theories.

Psychoactive Drugs (pp. 122–129)

25. Psychoactive drugs create pleasurable sensations in the brain by stimulating the _____ _____ .

26. Which of the following does not necessarily occur with drug tolerance?
    a. The body adjusts to functioning with the drug in the system.
    b. The user needs increasingly larger doses of the drug to achieve the desired effect.
    c. The user becomes progressively less affected by the drug.
    d. The user develops a craving for the pleasurable effects of the drug.

27. During withdrawal from a drug, the user experiences symptoms that are the opposite of the effects produced by the drug. (true/false)

28. Psychological dependence on a drug is more difficult to combat than physical dependence. (true/false)

29. Match the stimulant with the appropriate description.
    _____ (1) used to increase arousal, relieve fatigue, and suppress appetite
    _____ (2) found in coffee
    _____ (3) snorted or injected
    _____ (4) smokable form of cocaine
    a. caffeine   c. crack
    b. amphetamines   d. cocaine

30. Decreased activity in the central nervous system is the chief effect of
    a. stimulants.   c. hallucinogens.
    b. depressants.   d. narcotics.

31. Which of the following is a narcotic?
    a. cocaine   c. LSD
    b. heroin   d. Valium

32. Narcotics have
    a. pain-relieving effects.
    b. stimulating effects.
    c. energizing effects.
    d. perception-altering effects.

33. Which category of drugs alters perception and mood and can cause feelings of unreality?
    a. stimulants   c. hallucinogens
    b. depressants   d. narcotics

34. People who stop smoking marijuana usually experience no withdrawal symptoms. (true/false)

35. Some addictive drugs increase the effect of the neurotransmitter _____ in the nucleus accumbens.
    a. acetylcholine   c. dopamine
    b. GABA   d. serotonin

SECTION TWO: Identify the Drug

Match the description of drug effects with the drug.
    _____ (1) Produces excited exhilaration and hallucinations
    _____ (2) Produces wakefulness and alertness with increased metabolism but slowed reaction time
    _____ (3) Increases metabolism and alertness, elevates mood and wakefulness, and decrease appetite
    _____ (4) Produces euphoria and relaxation but also affects ability to store new memories
    _____ (5) Produces an energy boost and feeling of excitement while suppressing appetite
    _____ (6) Initial doses stimulate and enliven while lowering anxiety, but higher doses have a sedative effect
    _____ (7) Produces euphoria and feelings of social acceptance; stimulates appetite; leads to depression and fatigue
    a. alcohol   e. cocaine
    b. hallucinogens   f. amphetamines
    c. marijuana   g. MDMA (Ecstasy)
    d. caffeine

SECTION THREE: Fill in the Blank

1. The text defined _____ as an awareness of one's own perceptions, thoughts, feelings, sensations, and external environment.

2. The _____ wave is the slowest brain wave and occurs during Stages 3 and 4 sleep.

3. After a person loses REM sleep, he or she might experience _____.

4. Luis awoke in the middle of a strange dream in which he flew across a river. This dream probably occurred during _____ sleep.

5. A person who experiences sleepwalking or sleeptalking is suffering from one of a class of sleep disturbances collectively known as _____.

6. Sleep _____ is a condition in which breathing stops during sleep.

7. _____ is characterized by daytime sleepiness and sudden REM sleep.

8. Psychoactive drugs are a group of substances that alter _____, _____, or _____.

9. _____ is a group of techniques designed to block out all distractions so as to achieve an altered state of consciousness.

10. A compulsive pattern of drug use in which the user develops a tolerance coupled with unpleasant withdrawal symptoms when drug use is discontinued is referred to as physical drug _____.

11. The euphoric high from cocaine lasts only a short time and is followed by an equally intense _____, which is marked by depression, anxiety, agitation, and a powerful craving for more cocaine.

12. Cocaine's action in the human brain includes influencing the neurotransmitter _____, thereby leading to the continual excitatory stimulation of the reward pathways in the brain.

13. The most highly addictive drug is _____.

SECTION FOUR: Comprehensive Practice Test

1. The suprachiasmatic nucleus signals the pineal gland to secrete _____ from dusk until dawn.

2. People who work during their _____, when their biological clock is telling them it is time to sleep, can suffer lowered efficiency and productivity.
   - **a.** REM rebound
   - **b.** subjective night
   - **c.** circadian rebound
   - **d.** episodes of narcolepsy

3. Which theory proposes that the purpose of sleep is to allow the body to rest and recover?
   - **a.** restorative theory of sleep
   - **b.** evolutionary theory of sleep
   - **c.** adaptive theory of sleep
   - **d.** circadian theory of sleep

4. REM sleep is the _____ stage of sleep in a typical sleep cycle.
   - **a.** first
   - **b.** second
   - **c.** last
   - **d.** middle

5. Delta waves appear primarily in Stages _____ sleep.
   - **a.** 1 and 2
   - **b.** 2 and 3
   - **c.** 3 and 4
   - **d.** 1 and 4

6. Researchers have found that REM sleep
   - **a.** is increased in the elderly.
   - **b.** is associated with memory consolidation.
   - **c.** occurs only in some sleep cycles.
   - **d.** is rarely associated with dreaming.

7. As we grow older we sleep more than when we were younger; we also sleep more deeply, with more REM sleep. (true/false)

8. Freud believed dreams functioned to satisfy unconscious _____ and _____ urges.
   - **a.** parental; childhood
   - **b.** sexual; superego
   - **c.** aggressive; violent
   - **d.** sexual; aggressive

9. J. Allan Hobson believes dreams are merely the brain's attempt to make sense of the random firing of brain cells. This view is known as the
   - **a.** Hobson dream hypothesis.
   - **b.** somniloquy hypothesis.
   - **c.** activation-synthesis hypothesis.
   - **d.** physiological activation hypothesis.

10. The technical term for sleepwalking is
    - **a.** somniloquy.
    - **b.** mobile insomnia.
    - **c.** narcolepsy.
    - **d.** somnambulism.

11. People who talk in their sleep often mumble nonsensical words and phrases. (true/false)

12. Some people suffer from a sleep disorder known as _____, which causes them to stop breathing and then to wake for a brief time so as to start breathing again.
    - **a.** narcolepsy
    - **b.** sleep apnea
    - **c.** somniloquy
    - **d.** somnambulism

13. The sleep disorder characterized by either difficulty falling asleep or frequently waking is known as
    - **a.** sleep apnea.
    - **b.** insomnia.
    - **c.** somnambulism.
    - **d.** REM rebound.

14. Jack pleaded not guilty to his public indecency charges. He claimed he would never do such a thing if he were in his right mind and that he was the victim of the effects of hypnosis. A psychologist would probably support this claim. (true/false)

15. Personality has little impact on substance abuse. (true/false)

16. LSD, MDMA, and marijuana are classified as
    - **a.** narcotics.
    - **b.** stimulants.
    - **c.** hallucinogens.
    - **d.** depressants.

17. Animals addicted to several drugs prefer _____ when offered a choice of drugs.
    - **a.** marijuana
    - **b.** heroin
    - **c.** cocaine
    - **d.** alcohol

18. Caffeine is a depressant. (true/false)

SECTION FIVE: Critical Thinking

1. Suppose you have been hired by a sleep clinic to formulate a questionnaire for evaluating patients' sleep habits. List 10 questions you would include in your questionnaire.

2. Luanne is a full-time student who wants to find a way to keep up her class schedule while working full-time. She decides to work the 11:00 p.m. to 7:00 a.m. shift at a hospital and then attend morning classes. After her classes end at noon, she intends to sleep from 1:00 p.m. until 7:00 p.m., at which time she will get up and study until it is time to leave for work. Based on what you have learned about circadian rhythms in this chapter, what kinds of problems do you think Luanne will encounter in trying to carry out her plan?

3. You have been asked to make a presentation to 7th and 8th graders about the dangers of drugs. What are the most persuasive general arguments you can give to convince them not to start using drugs? What are some convincing, specific arguments against using each of these drugs: alcohol, marijuana, cocaine, and MDMA (Ecstasy)?

5 Learning

Think About It

On an episode of a popular cable television comedy program, the hosts offered $100 to any studio audience member who would eat an entire stick of butter. As you would probably predict, they had no trouble finding a volunteer; we all know that the expectation of some kind of a payoff influences our behavior. But do all rewards influence behavior in the same way? Would the hosts have been successful if they had offered $1 instead of $100? Not likely—the reward would have to be worth completing the task. In addition, what if there was only a 75% chance that the audience member would actually receive the $100 after eating the stick of butter—would this affect his or her willingness to participate?

The predictability of an expected reward does matter, but not in the way that you might think. To find out what we mean, estimate the likelihood that each behavior in the accompanying chart will actually yield its associated payoff. Use a scale of 0 to 10, with 0 = no chance at all and 10 = absolute certainty that the behavior, if executed correctly, will lead to the payoff. For example, how likely is it that you will find a TV program you want to watch when you channel-surf? Is there no chance (0)? Some chance (5)? Will you definitely find a program (10)? Make your estimations for this and the other items listed in the chart.

Chances are good that your ratings for some behaviors were higher than for others; for example, the likelihood that you would get money from an ATM was probably rated higher than the likelihood that you would win the lottery. But now take a moment to think about which of these behaviors you could get so involved in that you continue them for much longer than you originally intended. The chances are good that you don't see yourself repetitively punching in your PIN at an ATM or baking cookies for hours on end, even if these have a high probability of paying off. On the other hand, who hasn't wasted time channel-surfing or playing video games? And how many people regularly buy lottery tickets despite having never won any money? In this way, everyday experience confirms an important principle that you will read about in this chapter: Unpredictable rewards usually influence behavioral changes (what psychologists call *learning*) more strongly than predictable rewards do.

Behavior	Potential Payoff	Probability of Payoff
Channel-surfing	Find a program you want to watch	0 ←——→ 10
Using an ATM	Get cash	0 ←——→ 10
Playing a video game	Beat opponent or your own past performance	0 ←——→ 10
Baking cookies according to a recipe	Cookies turn out as expected	0 ←——→ 10
Buying lottery tickets	Win money	0 ←——→ 10

Psychologists define learning as a relatively permanent change in behavior, knowledge, capability, or attitude that is acquired through experience and cannot be attributed to illness, injury, or maturation. Several parts of this definition warrant further explanation. First, defining learning as a "relatively permanent change" excludes temporary changes that could result from illness, fatigue, or fluctuations in mood. Second, limiting learning to changes that are "acquired through experience" excludes some readily observable changes in behavior that occur as a result of brain injuries or certain diseases. Also, certain observable changes that occur as individuals grow and mature have nothing to do with learning. For example, technically speaking, infants do not *learn* to crawl or walk. Basic motor skills and the maturational plan that governs their development are a part of the genetically programmed behavioral repertoire of every species. The first kind of learning we'll consider is classical conditioning.

learning A relatively permanent change in behavior, knowledge, capability, or attitude that is acquired through experience and cannot be attributed to illness, injury, or maturation.

Classical Conditioning

Why do sodas that contain artificial sweeteners (so-called diet drinks) make some people hungry? The answer can be found in the principles of classical conditioning, a type of learning through which an organism learns to associate one stimulus with another. This kind of learning is sometimes referred to as *Pavlovian conditioning* or *respondent conditioning*. A stimulus (the plural is *stimuli*) is any event or object in the environment to which an organism responds. Be patient; at the end of this section, we'll explain why drinking diet sodas might actually cause you to gain weight. As you read about classical conditioning, see if you can figure it out on your own.

classical conditioning A type of learning through which an organism learns to associate one stimulus with another.

stimulus (STIM-yu-lus) Any event or object in the environment to which an organism responds; plural is *stimuli*.

Pavlov and the Process of Classical Conditioning ▶

5.1 How does the kind of learning Pavlov discovered happen?

Ivan Pavlov (1849–1936) organized and directed research in physiology at the Institute of Experimental Medicine in St. Petersburg, Russia, from 1891 until his death 45 years later. There, he conducted his classic experiments on the physiology of digestion, which won him a Nobel Prize in 1904—the first time a Russian received this honor.

Pavlov's contribution to psychology came about quite by accident. Pavlov, a physician by training and profession, was engaged in research aimed at clarifying the

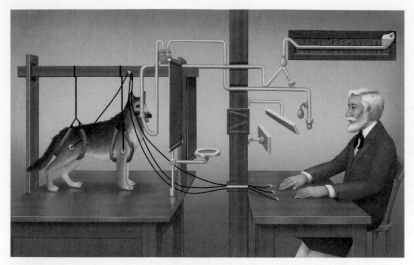

FIGURE 5.1 The Experimental Apparatus Used in Pavlov's Classical Conditioning Studies
In Pavlov's classical conditioning studies, the dog was restrained in a harness in the cubicle and isolated from all distractions. An experimenter observed the dog through a one-way mirror and, by remote control, presented the dog with food and other conditioning stimuli. A tube carried the saliva from the dog's mouth to a container where it was measured.

role of saliva in the process of digestion. In pursuit of this goal, he developed a procedure for collecting and measuring the amount of saliva in a dog's mouth (Figure 5.1). Pavlov's purpose was to collect the saliva that the dogs would secrete naturally in response to food placed inside the mouth. But he noticed that, in many cases, the dogs would begin to salivate even before the food was presented. Pavlov observed drops of saliva collecting in the containers when the dogs heard the footsteps of the laboratory assistants coming to feed them. He observed saliva collecting when the dogs heard their food dishes rattling, saw the attendant who fed them, or spotted their food. How could an involuntary response such as salivation come to be associated with the sights and sounds involved in feeding? Pavlov spent the rest of his life studying this question. The type of learning he studied is known today as classical conditioning.

Pavlov (1927/1960) used tones, bells, buzzers, lights, geometric shapes, electric shocks, and metronomes in his conditioning experiments. In a typical experiment, food powder was placed in the dog's mouth, causing salivation. Because dogs do not need to be conditioned to salivate to food, salivation to food is an unlearned response, or unconditioned response (UR). Any stimulus, such as food, that without prior learning will automatically elicit, or bring forth, an unconditioned response is called an unconditioned stimulus (US).

Following is a list of some common unconditioned reflexes, showing their two components: the unconditioned stimulus and the unconditioned response.

UNCONDITIONED REFLEXES

Unconditioned Stimulus (US)	*Unconditioned Response (UR)*
food	salivation
loud noise	startle
light in eye	contraction of pupil
puff of air in eye	eyeblink response

unconditioned response (UR) A response that is elicited by an unconditioned stimulus without prior learning.

unconditioned stimulus (US) A stimulus that elicits a specific unconditioned response without prior learning.

conditioned stimulus (CS) A neutral stimulus that, after repeated pairing with an unconditioned stimulus, becomes associated with it and elicits a conditioned response.

conditioned response (CR) The learned response that comes to be elicited by a conditioned stimulus as a result of its repeated pairing with an unconditioned stimulus.

higher-order conditioning Conditioning that occurs when conditioned stimuli are linked together to form a series of signals.

Pavlov demonstrated that dogs could be conditioned to salivate to a variety of stimuli never before associated with food, as shown in Figure 5.2. During the conditioning process, the researcher would present a neutral stimulus such as a musical tone shortly before placing food powder in the dog's mouth. The food powder would cause the dog to salivate. Pavlov found that after the tone and the food were paired many times, usually 20 or more, the tone alone would elicit salivation (Pavlov, 1927/1960). Pavlov called the tone the learned stimulus, or conditioned stimulus (CS), and salivation to the tone the learned response, or conditioned response (CR).

Pavlov also discovered that a neutral stimulus could become a conditioned stimulus simply by pairing it with a previously acquired conditioned stimulus, a process called higher-order conditioning. Higher-order conditioning is quite common. Think about what happens when you must have some kind of blood test. Typically, you sit in a chair next to a table on which are arranged materials such as needles, syringes, and such. Next, some kind of constricting device is tied around your arm, and the nurse or technician pats on the surface of your skin until a vein becomes visible. Each step in the sequence tells you that the unavoidable "stick" of the needle and the pain, which is largely the result of reflexive muscle tension, is coming. The stick itself is the unconditioned stimulus, to which you reflexively respond. But all the steps that precede it are conditioned stimuli that cause you to anticipate the pain of the stick itself. And with each successive step, a conditioned response occurs, as your muscles respond to your anxiety by contracting a bit more in anticipation of the stick. Chains of cues such as this are the result of higher-order conditioning.

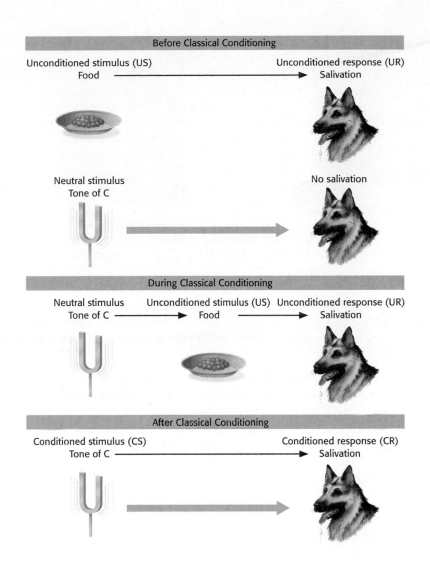

FIGURE 5.2 Classically Conditioning a Salivation Response
A neutral stimulus (a tone) elicits no salivation until it is repeatedly paired with the unconditioned stimulus (food). After many pairings, the neutral stimulus (now called the conditioned stimulus) alone produces salivation. Classical conditioning has occurred.

Changing Conditioned Responses ▷

5.2 What causes classically conditioned responses to change?

After conditioning an animal to salivate to a tone, what would happen if you continued to sound the tone but no longer paired it with food? Pavlov found that without the food, salivation to the tone became weaker and weaker and then finally disappeared altogether—a process known as extinction. After the response had been extinguished, Pavlov allowed the dog to rest for 20 minutes and then brought it back to the laboratory. He found that the dog would again salivate to the tone. Pavlov called this recurrence spontaneous recovery. But the spontaneously recovered response was weaker and shorter in duration than the original conditioned response. Figure 5.3 (p. 140) shows the processes of extinction and spontaneous recovery.

Assume that you have conditioned a dog to salivate when it hears the tone middle C played on the piano. Would it also salivate if you played B or D? Pavlov found that a tone similar to the original conditioned stimulus would produce the conditioned response (salivation), a phenomenon called generalization. But the salivation decreased the farther the tone was from the original conditioned stimulus, until the tone became so different that the dog would not salivate at all (Figure 5.4, p. 140).

It is easy to see the value of generalization in daily life. For instance, if you get a new clock, you will not have to relearn what to do when the alarm goes off, even if you have never heard it before. Even if the sound of the alarm varies considerably from that of your old clock, you will still recognize it as a sound that is telling you that it's time to wake up and get ready for your early-morning class.

extinction In classical conditioning, the weakening and eventual disappearance of the conditioned response as a result of repeated presentation of the conditioned stimulus without the unconditioned stimulus.

spontaneous recovery The reappearance of an extinguished response (in a weaker form) when an organism is exposed to the original conditioned stimulus following a rest period.

generalization In classical conditioning, the tendency to make a conditioned response to a stimulus that is similar to the original conditioned stimulus.

FIGURE 5.3 Extinction of a Classically Conditioned Response
When a classically conditioned stimulus (a tone) was presented in a series of trials without the unconditioned stimulus (food), Pavlov's dogs salivated less and less until there was virtually no salivation. But after a 20-minute rest, one sound of the tone caused the conditioned response to reappear in a weakened form (producing only a small amount of salivation), a phenomenon Pavlov called *spontaneous recovery*.
Source: Data from Pavlov (1927/1960), p. 58.

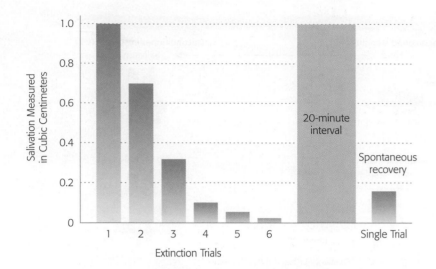

discrimination The learned ability to distinguish between similar stimuli so that the conditioned response occurs only to the original conditioned stimulus but not to similar stimuli.

Let's return to the example of a dog being conditioned to a musical tone to trace the process of discrimination, the learned ability to distinguish between similar stimuli so that the conditioned response occurs only to the original conditioned stimulus but not to similar stimuli:

Step 1. The dog is conditioned to salivate in response to the tone C.

Step 2. Generalization occurs, and the dog salivates to a range of musical tones above and below C. The dog salivates less and less as the tone moves farther away from C.

Step 3. The original tone C is repeatedly paired with food. Neighboring tones are also sounded, but they are not followed by food. The dog is being conditioned to discriminate. Gradually, the salivation response to the neighboring tones (A, B, D, and E) is extinguished, while salivation to the original tone C is strengthened.

Like generalization, discrimination has survival value. Discriminating between the odors of fresh and spoiled milk will spare you an upset stomach. Discriminating between a rattlesnake and a garter snake could save your life.

5.3 What did Watson's "Little Albert" experiment show?

John Watson and Emotional Conditioning

You may recall from Chapter 1 that John B. Watson (1878–1958) claimed that the influence of environmental factors could explain nearly all variations in human behavior. Recall, too, that Watson coined the term *behaviorism* to refer to the school of thought that proposed limiting psychology to the study of overtly observable behavior. In 1919, Watson and his assistant, Rosalie Rayner, conducted a now-famous study to prove that fear could be classically conditioned. The subject of the

FIGURE 5.4 Generalization of a Conditioned Response
Pavlov attached small vibrators to different parts of a dog's body. After conditioning salivation to stimulation of the dog's thigh, he stimulated other parts of the dog's body. Due to generalization, the salivation also occurred when other body parts were stimulated. But the farther away from the thigh the stimulus was applied, the weaker the salivation response.
Source: From Pavlov (1927/1960).

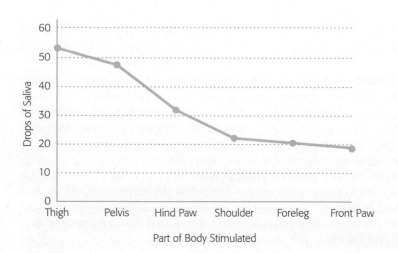

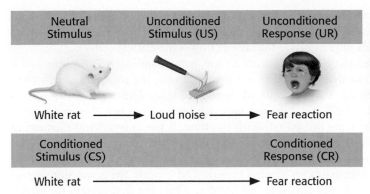

Neutral Stimulus	Unconditioned Stimulus (US)	Unconditioned Response (UR)
White rat ——→	Loud noise ——→	Fear reaction

Conditioned Stimulus (CS)		Conditioned Response (CR)
White rat ——————————————→		Fear reaction

FIGURE 5.5 The Conditioned Fear Response
Little Albert's fear of a white rat was a conditioned response that was generalized to other stimuli, including a rabbit and, to a lesser extent, a Santa Claus mask.
Archives of the History of American Psychology—The University of Akron.

study, known as Little Albert, was a healthy and emotionally stable 11-month-old infant. When tested, he showed no fear except of the loud noise Watson made by striking a hammer against a steel bar near his head.

In the laboratory, Rayner presented Little Albert with a white rat. As Albert reached for the rat, Watson struck the steel bar with a hammer just behind Albert's head. This procedure was repeated, and Albert "jumped violently, fell forward and began to whimper" (Watson & Rayner, 1920, p. 4). A week later, Watson continued the experiment, pairing the rat with the loud noise five more times. Then, at the sight of the white rat alone, Albert began to cry.

When Albert returned to the laboratory five days later, the fear had generalized to a rabbit and, somewhat less, to a dog, a seal coat, Watson's hair, and a Santa Claus mask (see Figure 5.5). After 30 days, Albert made his final visit to the laboratory. His fears were still evident, although they were somewhat less intense. Watson concluded that conditioned fears "persist and modify personality throughout life" (Watson & Rayner, 1920, p. 12).

Although Watson had formulated techniques for removing conditioned fears, Albert moved out of the city before they could be tried on him. Because Watson apparently knew that Albert would be moving away before these fear-removal techniques could be applied, he clearly showed a disregard for the child's welfare. The American Psychological Association now has strict ethical standards for the use of human and animal participants in research experiments and would not sanction an experiment such as Watson's. ◉—Watch on mypsychlab.com

Some of Watson's ideas for removing fears laid the groundwork for certain behavior therapies used today. Three years after his experiment with Little Albert, Watson and a colleague, Mary Cover Jones (1924), worked with 3-year-old Peter, who was afraid of white rabbits. Peter was brought into the laboratory, seated in a high chair, and given candy to eat. A white rabbit in a wire cage was brought into the room but kept far enough away from Peter that it would not upset him. Over the course of 38 therapy sessions, the rabbit was brought closer and closer to Peter, who continued to enjoy his candy. Occasionally, some of Peter's friends were brought in to play with the rabbit at a safe distance from Peter so that he could see firsthand that the rabbit did no harm. Toward the end of Peter's therapy, the rabbit was taken out of the cage and eventually put in Peter's lap. By the final session, Peter had grown fond of the rabbit.

◉—Watch the **Video** *Little Albert* on **mypsychlab.com**

The Cognitive Perspective ▶

5.4 What did Rescorla demonstrate about classical conditioning?

Which aspect of the classical conditioning process is most important? Both Pavlov and Watson believed that the critical element in classical conditioning was the repeated pairing of the conditioned stimulus and the unconditioned stimulus, with only a brief interval between the two. Beginning in the late 1960s, though, researchers began to discover exceptions to some of the general principles Pavlov had identified.

Robert Rescorla (1967, 1968, 1988; Rescorla & Wagner, 1972) is largely responsible for changing how psychologists view classical conditioning. Rescorla was able to demonstrate that the critical element in classical conditioning is not the repeated pairing of the conditioned stimulus and the unconditioned stimulus (Rescorla, 2008).

Rather, the important factor is whether the conditioned stimulus provides information that enables the organism to reliably *predict* the occurrence of the unconditioned stimulus. How was Rescorla able to prove that prediction is the critical element?

Using rats as his subjects, Rescorla used a tone as the conditioned stimulus and a shock as the unconditioned stimulus. For one group of rats, the tone and shock were paired 20 times—the shock always occurred during the tone. The other group of rats also received a shock 20 times while the tone was sounding, but this group also received 20 shocks that were not paired with the tone. If the only critical element in classical conditioning were the number of pairings of the conditioned stimulus and the unconditioned stimulus, both groups of rats should have developed a conditioned fear response to the tone, because both groups experienced exactly the same number of pairings of tone and shock. But this was not the case. Only the first group, for which the tone was a reliable predictor of the shock, developed the conditioned fear response to the tone. The second group showed little evidence of conditioning because the shock was just as likely to occur without the tone as with it. In other words, for this group, the tone provided no additional information about the shock.

5.5 How do biological predispositions affect classical conditioning?

biological predispositions Genetically programmed tendencies to acquire classically conditioned fear responses to potentially life-threatening stimuli.

taste aversion The intense dislike and/or avoidance of a particular food that has been associated with nausea or discomfort.

Biological Predispositions

Remember that Watson conditioned Little Albert to fear the white rat by pairing the presence of the rat with the loud noise of a hammer striking against a steel bar. Do you think Watson could just as easily have conditioned a fear response to a flower or a piece of ribbon? Probably not. Research has shown that humans are more easily conditioned to fear stimuli, such as snakes, that can have very real negative effects on their well-being (Mineka & Oehlberg, 2008). Moreover, fear of snakes and other potentially threatening animals is just as common in apes and monkeys as in humans, suggesting a biological predisposition to develop these fearful responses.

According to Martin Seligman (1972), most common fears "are related to the survival of the human species through the long course of evolution" (p. 455). Seligman (1970) has suggested that humans and other animals are prepared to associate only certain stimuli with particular consequences. One example of this preparedness is the tendency to develop taste aversion—the intense dislike and/or avoidance of particular foods that have been associated with nausea or discomfort.

Experiencing nausea and vomiting after eating a certain food is often enough to condition a long-lasting taste aversion. You may have had some personal experience with this phenomenon if you have ever thrown up after eating spaghetti, chili, or some other food with a very distinctive taste and smell. If so, you know that, for weeks afterward, just the smell of the offending food was sufficient to prompt a wave of nausea. ✳ Explore on **mypsychlab.com**

✳ Explore the Concept *Taste Aversion* on **mypsychlab.com**

▲ Chemotherapy treatments can result in a conditioned taste aversion, but providing patients with a "scapegoat" target for the taste aversion can help them maintain a proper diet.

In a classic study on taste aversion, Garcia and Koelling (1966) exposed rats to a three-way conditioned stimulus: a bright light, a clicking noise, and flavored water. For one group of rats, the unconditioned stimulus was being exposed to either X-rays or lithium chloride, either of which produces nausea and vomiting several hours after exposure; for the other group, the unconditioned stimulus was an electric shock to the feet. The rats that were made ill associated the flavored water with the nausea and avoided it at all times, but they would still drink unflavored water when the bright light and the clicking sound were present. The rats receiving the electric shock continued to prefer the flavored water over unflavored water, but they would not drink at all in the presence of the bright light or the clicking sound. The rats in one group associated nausea only with the flavored water; those in the other group associated electric shock only with the light and the sound.

Garcia and Koelling's research established two exceptions to traditional ideas of classical conditioning. First, the finding that rats formed an association between nausea and flavored water ingested several hours earlier contradicted the principle that the conditioned stimulus must be presented shortly before the unconditioned stimulus.

Second, the finding that rats associated electric shock only with noise and light and nausea only with flavored water revealed that animals are apparently biologically predisposed to make certain associations and that associations cannot be readily conditioned between just any two stimuli.

Knowledge about conditioned taste aversion is useful in solving other problems as well. Bernstein and others (1982; Bernstein, 1985) devised a technique to help cancer patients avoid developing aversions to desirable foods. A group of cancer patients were given a novel-tasting, maple-flavored ice cream before chemotherapy. The nausea caused by the treatment resulted in a taste aversion to the ice cream. The researchers found that when an unusual or unfamiliar food becomes the "scapegoat," or target for a taste aversion, other foods in the patient's diet may be protected, and the patient will continue to eat them regularly. So, cancer patients should refrain from eating preferred or nutritious foods prior to chemotherapy. Instead, they should be given an unusual-tasting food shortly before treatment. As a result, they are less likely to develop aversions to foods they normally eat and, in turn, are more likely to maintain their body weight during treatment.

Classical Conditioning in Everyday Life ▶

5.6 What are some examples of classical conditioning in everyday life?

Do you suddenly experience hunger pangs when you smell fresh-baked chocolate chip cookies? Do you cringe in response to the sound of a dental drill? In either case, classical conditioning is the most likely explanation for your behavior. Your stomach rumbles when you smell fresh-baked cookies because smell and taste are so closely linked that food odors, functioning as conditioned stimuli, can actually make you think you are hungry even if you have just finished a large meal. Recall that we began our discussion of classical conditioning by saying that its principles can explain why diet sodas make some people hungry. This can happen because the distinctive flavors of foods can become conditioned stimuli for the digestive processes that typically follow them.

For instance, researchers have found that the pancreas quickly adapts to food cues through the process of classical conditioning (e.g., Stockhorst et al., 2004). Most of the time, the presence of a sweet taste on the tongue (a CS) is a reliable cue indicating that a rise in blood sugar (a UR) will soon occur. As a result, the pancreas "learns" to pump out insulin, the hormone that lowers blood sugar levels, whenever you eat or drink something sweet. A likely consequence of this adaptation is that the pancreas will respond to an artificial sweetener in the same way. Without the presence of real sugar to bring up the blood sugar level, however, the insulin will cause the blood sugar level to drop below normal. Whenever the blood sugar level drops below normal, the body signals the brain to motivate you to eat; in other words, you begin to feel hungry (more on this mechanism in Chapter 10). Over time, of course, the pancreas will probably learn to discriminate between the taste of artificially sweetened beverages and drinks that contain real sugar. The insulin response to artificial sweeteners will then become extinguished, while the link between the taste of sugared beverages and the insulin response will be maintained.

Through classical conditioning, environmental cues associated with drug use become conditioned stimuli and later produce the conditioned responses of drug craving (Epstein, Willner-Reid, & Preston, 2010). The conditioned stimuli associated with drugs become powerful, often irresistible forces that lead individuals to seek out and use those substances (Porrino & Lyons, 2000). Consequently, drug counselors strongly urge recovering addicts to avoid any cues (people, places, and things) associated with their past drug use.

The prevalence of classical conditioning in our everyday lives raises questions about the degree to which laboratory studies may or may not faithfully represent the process of classical conditioning. As noted earlier, laboratory learning typically requires a large number of trial pairings of conditioned and unconditioned stimuli, but many kinds of everyday conditioning (e.g., taste aversion) can happen after just one experience.

▲ Classical conditioning has proved to be a highly effective tool for advertisers. Here, a neutral product (milk) is paired with an image of an attractive celebrity. Can you identify the UCS, UCR, CS, and CR at work here?

This and other differences have led experts in the field to hypothesize that a stimulus that has *ecological relevance* is more likely to function as a conditioned stimulus (Domjan, 2005). In other words, to serve as a conditioned stimulus, a neutral stimulus must have some authentic connection to the unconditioned stimulus. For example, real links exist among smells, tastes, and digestive processes. Likewise, a dental drill really can cause pain, and drugs do create altered states of consciousness. Compare these everyday conditioned stimuli to the arbitrary ones that Pavlov used—musical tones, buzzers, and the like. Research indicates that ecologically valid conditioned stimuli are acquired much more quickly than arbitrary stimuli and are also more resistant to extinction (Domjan, 2005).

Operant Conditioning

Understanding the principles of classical conditioning can provide a great deal of insight into human behavior. But is there more to human learning than simply responding reflexively to stimuli? Think about a ringing telephone, for example. Do you respond to this stimulus because it has been paired with a natural stimulus of some kind or because of a consequence you anticipate when you hear it? The work of two psychologists, Edward L. Thorndike and B. F. Skinner, helps answer this question.

5.7 What did Thorndike and Skinner discover about the consequences of behavior?

Thorndike, Skinner, and the Consequences of Behavior

Have you ever watched a dog learn how to turn over a trash can, or a cat learn how to open a door? If so, you probably observed the animal fail several times before finding just the right physical technique for accomplishing the goal. Based on his observations of animal behavior, Edward Thorndike (1874–1949) formulated several laws of learning, the most important being the law of effect (Thorndike, 1911/1970). The law of effect states that the consequence, or effect, of a response will determine whether the tendency to respond in the same way in the future will be strengthened or weakened. Responses closely followed by satisfying consequences are more likely to be repeated. Thorndike (1898) insisted that it was "unnecessary to invoke reasoning" to explain how the learning took place.

law of effect One of Thorndike's laws of learning, which states that the consequence, or effect, of a response will determine whether the tendency to respond in the same way in the future will be strengthened or weakened.

In Thorndike's best-known experiments, a hungry cat was placed in a wooden box with slats, which was called a *puzzle box*. The box was designed so that the animal had to manipulate a simple mechanism—pressing a pedal or pulling down a loop—to escape and claim a food reward that lay just outside the box. The cat would first try to squeeze through the slats; when these attempts failed, it would scratch, bite, and claw the inside of the box. In time, the cat would accidentally trip the mechanism, which would open the door. Each time, after winning freedom and claiming the food reward, the cat was returned to the box. After many trials, the cat learned to open the door almost immediately after being placed in the box.

operant conditioning A type of learning in which the consequences of behavior are manipulated so as to increase or decrease the frequency of an existing response or to shape an entirely new response.

operant A voluntary behavior that accidentally brings about a consequence.

reinforcer Anything that follows a response and strengthens it or increases the probability that it will occur.

shaping An operant conditioning technique that consists of gradually molding a desired behavior (response) by reinforcing any movement in the direction of the desired response, thereby gradually guiding the responses toward the ultimate goal.

Thorndike's law of effect was the conceptual starting point for B. F. Skinner's work in operant conditioning, the process through which consequences increase or decrease the frequency of a behavior. Skinner's research revealed that the process begins with an operant, or voluntary behavior, that accidentally brings about some kind of consequence. A consequence that increases the frequency of an operant is known as a reinforcer, while one that decreases an operant's frequency is called a *punisher*. We will examine both these processes later in the chapter.

5.8 How do shaping, generalization, and discriminative stimuli influence operant conditioning?

The Process of Operant Conditioning

Have you ever attended a show that featured trained animals? Trainers use an operant conditioning technique called shaping in which animals learn their tricks in small steps rather than all at once. Moreover, like learning based on classical conditioning, behaviors acquired through operant conditioning can be altered in a variety of ways.

B. F. Skinner first demonstrated that shaping was particularly effective in training animals to exhibit complex behaviors. With shaping, rather than waiting for the desired response to occur and then reinforcing it, a researcher reinforces any movement in the direction of the desired response, thereby gradually guiding the responses toward the ultimate goal.

Skinner designed a soundproof apparatus, commonly called a Skinner box, with which he conducted his experiments in operant conditioning. One type of box is equipped with a lever, or bar, that a rat presses to gain a reward of food pellets or water from a dispenser. A record of the animal's bar pressing is registered on a device called a *cumulative recorder,* also invented by Skinner. Through the use of shaping, a rat in a Skinner box is conditioned to press a bar for rewards. It may be rewarded first for simply turning toward the bar. The next reward comes only when the rat moves closer to the bar. Each step closer to the bar is rewarded. Next, the rat must touch the bar to receive a reward; finally, it is rewarded only when it presses the bar.

Shaping—rewarding successive approximations of the desired response—has been used effectively to condition complex behaviors in people as well as other animals. Parents may use shaping to help their children develop good table manners, praising them each time they show an improvement. Teachers often use shaping with disruptive children, reinforcing them at first for very short periods of good behavior and then gradually expecting them to work productively for longer and longer periods. Through shaping, circus animals have earned to perform a wide range of amazing feats, and pigeons have learned to bowl and play Ping-Pong.

Of course, the motive of the shaper is very different from that of the person or animal whose behavior is being shaped. The shaper seeks to change another's behavior by controlling its consequences. The motive of the person or animal whose behavior is being shaped is to gain rewards or avoid unwanted consequences.

What happens when reinforcement is no longer available? In operant conditioning, extinction occurs when reinforcers are withheld. A rat in a Skinner box will eventually stop pressing a bar when it is no longer rewarded with food pellets.

In humans and other animals, the withholding of reinforcement can lead to frustration or even rage. Consider a child having a temper tantrum. If whining and loud demands do not bring the reinforcer, the child may progress to kicking and screaming. If a vending machine takes your coins but fails to deliver candy or soda, you might shake the machine or even kick it before giving up. When we don't get something we expect, it makes us angry.

The process of *spontaneous recovery,* which we discussed in relation to classical conditioning, also occurs in operant conditioning. A rat whose bar pressing has been extinguished may again press the bar a few times when it is returned to the Skinner box after a period of rest.

Skinner conducted many of his experiments with pigeons placed in a specially designed Skinner box. The box contained small illuminated disks that the pigeons could peck to receive bits of grain from a food tray. Skinner found that generalization occurs in operant conditioning, just as in classical conditioning. A pigeon reinforced for pecking at a yellow disk is likely to peck at another disk similar in color. The less similar a disk is to the original color, the lower the rate of pecking will be.

Discrimination in operant conditioning involves learning to distinguish between a stimulus that has been reinforced and other stimuli that may be very similar. Discrimination develops when the response to the original stimulus is reinforced but responses to similar stimuli are not reinforced. For example, to encourage discrimination, a researcher would reinforce the pigeon for pecking at the yellow disk but not for pecking at the orange or red disk. Pigeons have even been conditioned to discriminate between a cubist-style Picasso painting and a Monet with 90% accuracy ("Psychologists' pigeons . . . ," 1995).

Certain cues come to be associated with reinforcement or punishment. For example, children are more likely to ask their parents for a treat when the parents are smiling than when they are frowning. A stimulus that signals whether a certain response or behavior

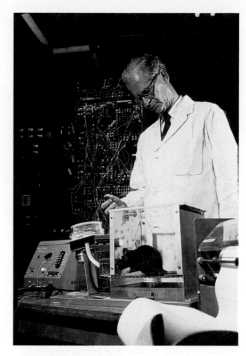

▲ B. F. Skinner shapes a rat's bar-pressing behavior in a Skinner box.

Skinner box A soundproof chamber with a device for delivering food to an animal subject; used in operant conditioning experiments.

successive approximations A series of gradual steps, each of which is more similar to the final desired response.

extinction In operant conditioning, the weakening and eventual disappearance of the conditioned response as a result of the withholding of reinforcement.

generalization In operant conditioning, the tendency to make the learned response to a stimulus similar to that for which the response was originally reinforced.

discriminative stimulus A stimulus that signals whether a certain response or behavior is likely to be rewarded, ignored, or punished.

is likely to be rewarded, ignored, or punished is called a discriminative stimulus. If a pigeon's peck at a lighted disk results in a reward but a peck at an unlighted disk does not, the pigeon will soon be pecking exclusively at the lighted disk. The presence or absence of the discriminative stimulus—in this case, the lighted disk—will control whether the pecking takes place.

Why do children sometimes misbehave with a grandparent but not with a parent, or make one teacher's life miserable yet be model students for another? The children may have learned that in the presence of some people (the discriminative stimuli), their misbehavior will almost certainly lead to punishment, but in the presence of certain other people, it may even be rewarded.

5.9 How do positive and negative reinforcement affect behavior?

Reinforcement

How did you learn the correct sequence of behaviors involved in using an ATM machine? Simple—a single mistake in the sequence will prevent you from getting your money, so you learn to do it correctly. What about paying bills on time? Doesn't prompt payment allow you to avoid those steep late-payment penalties? In each case, your behavior is reinforced, but in a different way.

reinforcement Any event that follows a response and strengthens or increases the probability that the response will be repeated.

Positive and Negative Reinforcement. Reinforcement is a key concept in operant conditioning and may be defined as an increase in behavior that occurs as a result of a consequence. Another way to say this is that reinforcement involves learning or increasing the frequency of a behavior in order to make something happen. Reinforcement can be either positive or negative. These terms are used in their mathematical sense in operant conditioning. Thus, *positive* is equivalent to *added,* and *negative* is equivalent to *subtracted* or *removed*.

positive reinforcement Any pleasant or desirable consequence that follows a response and increases the probability that the response will be repeated.

Combining two of the concepts you have just learned yields the definition of positive reinforcement: an increase in behavior that results from an added consequence. For instance, performing the correct sequence of behaviors at the ATM machine is the only way to obtain money. Thus, you are careful to get the sequence right (increased behavior) because doing so will cause the machine to dispense the money (added consequence) that you need. Here are a few more examples of positive reinforcement:

- Rat learns to press a lever (increased behavior) to obtain a food pellet (added consequence)
- College student studies more often (increased behavior) after getting an *A* on an exam for which she studied more than usual (added consequence)
- Person buys more lottery tickets (increased behavior) after hitting a $100 jackpot (added consequence)

negative reinforcement The termination of an unpleasant condition after a response, which increases the probability that the response will be repeated.

You may have already predicted the definition of negative reinforcement because it follows logically from the definitions of its constituent terms (negative + reinforcement). It simply means an increase in behavior (reinforcement) that is brought about by the subtraction of something that is typically unpleasant. Stated differently, negative reinforcement involves learning or increasing a behavior in order to make something unpleasant go away. For instance, you take cough medicine (learned behavior) to make your coughing go away (removed consequence). Here are a few more examples:

- Rat learns to press a lever (increased behavior) to turn off an annoying stimulus such as a loud buzzer (removed consequence)
- College student studies more often (increased behavior) in order to avoid getting another *F* on an exam (removed consequence)
- Individual calls his mother more often (increased behavior) in order to keep the mother from nagging him (removed consequence)

primary reinforcer A reinforcer that fulfills a basic physical need for survival and does not depend on learning.

Primary and Secondary Reinforcers. Are all reinforcers created equal? Not necessarily. A primary reinforcer is one that fulfills a basic physical need for survival and does not depend on learning. Food, water, sleep, and termination of pain are examples of primary reinforcers. And sex is a powerful reinforcer that fulfills a basic physical need for survival of the species. Fortunately, learning does not depend solely on primary reinforcers. If that were the case, people would need to be hungry, thirsty, or sex starved before they would respond at all. Much observed human behavior occurs in response to secondary reinforcers. A secondary reinforcer is acquired or learned through association with other reinforcers. Some secondary reinforcers (money, for example) can be exchanged at a later time for other reinforcers. Praise, good grades, awards, applause, attention, and signals of approval, such as a smile or a kind word, are all examples of secondary reinforcers.

Schedules of Reinforcement ▶

Think about the difference between an ATM and a slot machine. Under the right conditions, you can get money from either of them. But the ATM gives you a reinforcer every time you use the right procedure (*continuous reinforcement*), while the slot machine does so only intermittently (*partial reinforcement*). These two familiar machines use different schedules of reinforcement, or systematic processes for administering reinforcement.

The two basic types of schedules of reinforcement are ratio and interval schedules. Both the ATM and the slot machine use ratio schedules—that is, behavior brings about reinforcement. With interval schedules, a given amount of time must pass before a reinforcer is administered. Workers who get weekly paychecks are reinforced on an interval schedule. Ratio and interval schedules are further subdivided into fixed and variable categories (see Figure 5.6). Each kind of schedule has a different effect on behavior.

On a fixed-ratio (FR) schedule, a reinforcer is given after a fixed number of correct, nonreinforced responses. For example, if your favorite coffee bar offers a frequent buyer program in which you get a free cup of coffee for every 10 cups you buy, it is reinforcing you on a fixed ratio schedule. This schedule is a very effective way to maintain a high response rate because the number of reinforcers received depends directly on the response rate. The faster people or animals respond, the more reinforcers they earn and the sooner they earn them. When large ratios are used, people and animals tend to pause after each reinforcement but then return to the high rate of responding.

Intermittent reinforcement is characteristic of a variable-ratio (VR) schedule in which a reinforcer is provided after a varying number of nonreinforced responses. For instance,

▲ Recall that negative reinforcement involves learning a behavior in order to make something unpleasant go away. For many students, studying with classmates (learned behavior) reduces test anxiety (removed consequence). Thus, for these students, test anxiety is an important source of negative reinforcement, one that encourages them to engage in effective study behaviors.

secondary reinforcer A reinforcer that is acquired or learned through association with other reinforcers.

schedule of reinforcement A systematic process for administering reinforcement.

fixed-ratio (FR) schedule A schedule in which a reinforcer is given after a fixed number of correct, nonreinforced responses.

[**5.10** **What are the four types of schedules of reinforcement?**

variable-ratio (VR) schedule A schedule in which a reinforcer is given after a varying number of non-reinforced responses, based on an average ratio.

FIGURE 5.6 Four Types of Reinforcement Schedules
Skinner's research revealed distinctive response patterns for four reinforcement schedules (the reinforcers are indicated by the diagonal marks). The ratio schedules, based on the number of responses, yielded a higher response rate than the interval schedules, which are based on the amount of time elapsed between reinforcers.

Fixed ratio   Variable ratio

Reinforcers

Rapid responding near time for reinforcement

Fixed interval

Variable interval

Steady responding

Number of Responses

1250
1000
750
500
250
0

0   10   20   30   40   50   60   70   80
Time (minutes)

▲ Two examples of variable-ratio schedules of reinforcement: Gamblers can't predict when the payoff (reinforcement) will come, so they are highly motivated to keep playing. Likewise, many computer users find themselves in the predicament of knowing they should stop playing solitaire and get to work, but they just can't seem to tear themselves away from the game. Why? The power of variable-ratio reinforcement motivates them to stick with the game until the next win, and the next, and the next. . . .

partial reinforcement effect The typical outcome of a variable ratio of reinforcement in which a slow rate of initial learning is coupled with resistance to extinction.

fixed-interval (FI) schedule A schedule in which a reinforcer is given following the first correct response after a specific period of time has elapsed.

variable-interval (VI) schedule A schedule in which a reinforcer is given after the first correct response that follows a varying time of nonreinforcement, based on an average time.

suppose your favorite coffee bar offers you a chance to participate in a drawing each time you purchase a drink. You draw a card out of a jar that contains dozens of cards, 1 in 10 of which says "Get a free coffee next time you visit" and 9 in 10 of which say "Sorry. Try again next time." The coffee bar is using a variable-ratio schedule of reinforcement. This kind of schedule takes longer to produce learning than a fixed-ratio schedule does. However, once learned, behaviors that are acquired through variable reinforcement are highly resistant to extinction. This is known as the partial reinforcement effect. For instance, how many times have you sat down at your computer to work on a research paper and found yourself still playing solitaire or some other PC game hours later? Many other enjoyable leisure pursuits—hunting, fishing, channel surfing, and even shopping for bargains—involve variable schedules of reinforcement and are often difficult to break away from. In fact, when you set your MP3 player to "shuffle," you are creating a variable ratio schedule in which the songs you like most are serving as unpredictable reinforcers that maintain the behavior of listening to music. Likewise, video games involve the partial reinforcement effect because players don't succeed every time they play. Finally, slot machines and other forms of gambling employ a variable-ratio reinforcement schedule. For some gamblers, the partial reinforcement produces a self-destructive behavior pattern (i.e., *compulsive gambling*) that requires professional help to overcome.

On a fixed-interval (FI) schedule, a specific period of time must pass before a response is reinforced. For example, a teacher who gives weekly exams is reinforcing the behavior of studying on a fixed-interval schedule. Characteristic of the fixed-interval schedule is a pause or a sharp decline in responding immediately after each reinforcement and a rapid acceleration in responding just before the next reinforcer is due (the "scalloping" effect). In other words, with weekly exams, students are likely to slack off for a few days after each exam and study intensely the day before the next test.

Variable-interval schedules eliminate the pause after reinforcement typical of the fixed-interval schedule. On a variable-interval (VI) schedule, a reinforcer is given after the first correct response following a varying time of nonreinforced responses. For instance, a teacher who gives pop quizzes at unpredictable intervals is reinforcing studying on a variable-interval schedule. This schedule maintains remarkably stable and uniform rates of responding, but the response rate is typically lower than that for ratio schedules because reinforcement is not tied directly to the number of responses made. Thus, pop quizzes are more likely to influence students to study continuously than weekly exams are.

The *Summarize It* will help you review the characteristics of the four schedules of reinforcement.

SUMMARIZE IT

Reinforcement Schedules Compared

SCHEDULE OF REINFORCEMENT	RESPONSE RATE	PATTERN OF RESPONSES	RESISTANCE TO EXTINCTION
RATIO			
Fixed-ratio (FR) schedule	Very high	Steady response with low ratio. Brief pause after each reinforcement with very high ratio.	The higher the ratio, the more resistance to extinction.
Variable-ratio (VR) schedule	Highest response rate	Constant response pattern, no pauses.	Most resistance to extinction.
INTERVAL			
Fixed-interval (FI) schedule	Lowest response rate	Long pause after reinforcement, followed by gradual acceleration.	The longer the interval, the more resistance to extinction.
Variable-interval (VI) schedule	Moderate	Stable, uniform response.	More resistance to extinction than fixed-interval schedule with same average interval.

Punishment ▸

┌ **5.11 How does punishment**
└ **affect behavior?**

You may be wondering about one of the most common types of consequences, punishment. Punishment is the opposite of reinforcement. Thus, it is a decrease in the frequency of a behavior that follows some kind of consequence.

Positive and Negative Punishment. Like reinforcement, punishment can involve either positive (added) or negative (removed) consequences. In positive punishment behavior decreases after the addition of a consequence, usually an unpleasant one. For example, a driver avoids taking a particular route (decreased behavior) because it has caused him to become bogged down in traffic jams in the past (added consequence). Here are a few more examples:

- Rat stops pressing a lever (decreased behavior) when doing so causes a loud, annoying buzzing sound (added consequence)
- Student stops staying up late (decreased behavior) after sleeping through an important exam (added consequence)

Students sometimes confuse negative reinforcement and positive punishment because both involve unpleasant stimuli. However, negative reinforcement increases behavior, whereas positive punishment decreases the behavior that it follows. The simplest examples are those that happen in the context of laboratory experiments. In a negative reinforcement experiment, a rat might be put into a cage with an electrical current running through its metal floor, causing an unpleasant sensation on the rat's feet. By pressing a lever, the rat can turn off the current. After some trial and error, the rat stands on his hind legs and uses his front paws to keep the lever in the depressed position, thus eliminating the electric shocks. His lever-pressing behavior has increased (reinforcement) as a result of the removal of the unpleasant shock sensation.

In a positive punishment experiment, the lever would turn on the electricity instead of turning it off. As a result, the rat would learn to not press the lever (a decrease in behavior) because he gets a shock when he does so.

Negative punishment happens when a behavior decreases after the removal of a consequence. The consequence usually involves the loss of something desirable. For example, a driver who speeds less often (decreased behavior) after suffering through a six-month suspension of his license (removed consequence) has experienced negative punishment. Here are a few more examples:

- Rat stops pressing a lever (decreased behavior) when doing so causes a dish of food to disappear from his cage (removed consequence)
- Teenager stops coming home late (decreased behavior) after parents take away her going-out privileges for two weeks (removed consequence)

Table 5.1 includes definitions and examples for positive reinforcement, negative reinforcement, positive punishment, and negative punishment.

punishment The removal of a pleasant stimulus or the application of an unpleasant stimulus, thereby lowering the probability of a response.

positive punishment A decrease in behavior that results from an added consequence.

negative punishment A decrease in behavior that results from a removed consequence.

TABLE 5.1 **The Effects of Reinforcement and Punishment**

REINFORCEMENT (INCREASES OR STRENGTHENS A BEHAVIOR)	PUNISHMENT (DECREASES OR SUPRESSES A BEHAVIOR)
Adding a pleasant stimulus (positive reinforcement)	**Adding an aversive stimulus (positive punishment)**
Presenting food, money, praise, attention, or other rewards.	Delivering a pain-producing or otherwise aversive stimulus, such as a spanking or an electric shock.
Subtracting an aversive stimulus (negative reinforcement)	**Subtracting a pleasant stimulus (negative punishment)**
Removing or terminating some pain-producing or otherwise aversive stimulus, such as an electric shock.	Removing some pleasant stimulus or taking away privileges, such as TV watching, use of automobile.

The Disadvantages of Punishment. If punishment can suppress behavior, why do so many people oppose its use? A number of potential problems are associated with the use of punishment:

1. According to Skinner, punishment does not extinguish an undesirable behavior; rather, it suppresses that behavior when the punishing agent is present. But the behavior is apt to continue when the threat of punishment is removed or in settings where punishment is unlikely. If punishment (imprisonment, fines, and so on) reliably extinguished unlawful behavior, there would be fewer repeat offenders in the criminal justice system.

2. Punishment indicates that a behavior is unacceptable but does not help people develop more appropriate behaviors. If punishment is used, it should be administered in conjunction with reinforcement or rewards for appropriate behavior.

3. The person who is severely punished often becomes fearful and feels angry and hostile toward the punisher. These reactions may be accompanied by a desire to retaliate or to avoid or escape from the punisher and the punishing situation. Many runaway teenagers leave home to escape physical abuse. Punishment that involves a loss of privileges is more effective than physical punishment and engenders less fear and hostility (Fasotti, 2003).

4. Punishment frequently leads to aggression. Those who administer physical punishment, such as spanking, may become models of aggressive behavior, by demonstrating aggression as a way of solving problems and discharging anger. Children of abusive, punishing parents are at greater risk than other children of becoming aggressive and abusive themselves (Huesmann & Podolski, 2003).

If punishment can cause these problems, what can be done to discourage undesirable behavior?

Alternatives to Punishment. Are there other ways to suppress behavior? Many psychologists believe that removing the rewarding consequences of undesirable behavior is the best way to extinguish a problem behavior. According to this view, parents should extinguish a child's temper tantrums not by punishment but by never giving in to the child's demands during a tantrum. A parent might best extinguish problem behavior that is performed merely to get attention by ignoring it and giving attention to more appropriate behavior. Sometimes, simply explaining why a certain behavior is not appropriate is all that is required to extinguish the behavior.

Using positive reinforcement such as praise will make good behavior more rewarding for children. This approach brings with it the attention that children want and need—attention that often comes only when they misbehave.

It is probably unrealistic to believe that punishment will ever become unnecessary. If a young child runs into the street, puts a finger near an electrical outlet, or reaches for a hot pan on the stove, a swift punishment may save the child from a potentially disastrous situation.

Making Punishment More Effective. When punishment is necessary (e.g., to stop destructive behavior), how can we be sure that it will be effective? Research has revealed several factors that influence the effectiveness of punishment: its timing, its intensity, and the consistency of its application (Parke, 1977):

1. Punishment is most effective when it is applied during the misbehavior or as soon afterward as possible. Interrupting the problem behavior is most effective because doing so abruptly halts its rewarding aspects. The longer the delay between the response and the punishment, the less effective the punishment is in suppressing the response (Camp, Raymond, & Church, 1967). When there is a delay, most animals do not make the connection between the misbehavior and the punishment. For example, anyone who has tried to housebreak a puppy knows that it is necessary to catch the animal in the act of soiling the carpet for the punishment to be effective. With

humans, however, if the punishment must be delayed, the punisher should remind the perpetrator of the incident and explain why the behavior was inappropriate.

2. Ideally, punishment should be of the minimum severity necessary to suppress the problem behavior. Animal studies reveal that the more intense the punishment, the greater the suppression of the undesirable behavior (Church, 1963). But the intensity of the punishment should match the seriousness of the misdeed. Unnecessarily severe punishment is likely to produce the negative side effects mentioned earlier. The purpose of punishment is not to vent anger but, rather, to modify behavior. Punishment meted out in anger is likely to be more intense than necessary to bring about the desired result. Yet, if the punishment is too mild, it will have no effect. Similarly, gradually increasing the intensity of the punishment is not effective because the perpetrator will gradually adapt, and the unwanted behavior will persist (Azrin & Holz, 1966). At a minimum, if a behavior is to be suppressed, the punishment must be more punishing than the misbehavior is rewarding. In human terms, a $200 ticket is more likely to suppress the urge to speed than a $2 ticket.

3. To be effective, punishment must be applied consistently. A parent cannot ignore misbehavior one day and punish the same act the next. And both parents should react to the same misbehavior in the same way. An undesired response will be suppressed more effectively when the probability of punishment is high. Would you be tempted to speed if you saw a police car in your rearview mirror?

Culture and Punishment. Do you think stoning is an appropriate punishment for adultery? Probably not, unless you come from a culture in which such punishments are acceptable. Punishment is used in every culture to control and suppress people's behavior. It is administered when important values, rules, regulations, and laws are violated. But not all cultures share the same values or have the same laws regulating behavior. U.S. citizens traveling in other countries need to be aware of how different cultures view and administer punishment. For example, selling drugs is a serious crime just about everywhere. In the United States, it carries mandatory prison time; in some other countries, it is a death penalty offense.

Escape and Avoidance Learning ▶

Do you pay bills on time to avoid late fees? Learning to perform a behavior because it prevents or terminates an aversive event is called *escape learning,* and it reflects the power of negative reinforcement. Running away from a punishing situation and taking aspirin to relieve a pounding headache are examples of escape behavior. In these situations, the aversive event has begun, and an attempt is being made to escape it.

Avoidance learning, in contrast, depends on two types of conditioning. Through classical conditioning, an event or condition comes to signal an aversive state. Drinking and driving may be associated with automobile accidents and death. Because of such associations, people may engage in behaviors to avoid the anticipated aversive consequences. Making it a practice to avoid riding in a car with a driver who has been drinking is sensible avoidance behavior.

Much avoidance learning is maladaptive, however, and occurs in response to phobias. Students who have had a bad experience speaking in front of a class may begin to fear any situation that involves speaking before a group. Such students may avoid taking courses that require class presentations or taking leadership roles that necessitate public speaking. Avoiding such situations prevents them from suffering the perceived dreaded consequences. But the avoidance behavior is negatively reinforced and thus strengthened through operant conditioning.

Likewise, procrastination is a maladaptive avoidance behavior that plagues many students. The behavior patterns that contribute to procrastination are negatively reinforced because they enable students to avoid the confusion, anxiety, and boredom they experience while studying. While maladaptive behavior patterns of this

▲ What strategies other than punishment might a parent use to get this child to behave more appropriately?

5.12 How do escape and avoidance learning occur?

avoidance learning Learning to avoid events or conditions associated with aversive consequences or phobias.

APPLY IT   How to Win the Battle against Procrastination

Have you often thought that you could get better grades if only you had more time? Do you often find yourself studying for an exam or completing a term paper at the last minute? If so, it makes sense for you to learn how to overcome the greatest time waster of all—procrastination. Research indicates that academic procrastination arises partly out of a lack of confidence in one's ability to meet expectations (Wolters, 2003). Other studies suggest that a preference for short-term over long-term gratification is sometimes to blame (Knipe, 2010). In other words, when students procrastinate, they may be choosing the immediate pleasures of activities such as watching television or chatting with friends over the sense of satisfaction that they will experience in the future by meeting academic goals. Once procrastination has become established as a behavior pattern, it often persists for years (Lee, Kelly, & Edwards, 2006). Nevertheless, anyone can overcome procrastination, and gain self-confidence in the process, by using behavior modification techniques. Systematically apply the following suggestions to keep procrastination from interfering with your studying:

■ *Identify the environmental cues that habitually interfere with your studying*. Television, computer or video games, and even food can be powerful distractors that consume hours of valuable study time. However, these distractors can be useful positive reinforcers to enjoy after you've finished studying.

■ *Schedule your study time and reinforce yourself for adhering to your schedule*. Once you've scheduled it, be just as faithful to your schedule as you would be to a work schedule set by an employer. And be sure to schedule something you enjoy to immediately follow the study time.

■ *Get started*. The most difficult part is getting started. Give yourself an extra reward for starting on time and, perhaps, a penalty for starting late.

■ *Use visualization*. Much procrastination results from the failure to consider its negative consequences. Visualizing the consequences of not studying, such as trying to get through an exam you haven't adequately prepared for, can be an effective tool for combating procrastination.

■ *Beware of jumping to another task when you reach a difficult part of an assignment*. This procrastination tactic gives you the feeling that you are busy and accomplishing something, but it is, nevertheless, an avoidance mechanism.

■ *Beware of preparation overkill*. Procrastinators may actually spend hours preparing for a task rather than working on the task itself. For example, they may gather enough library materials to write a book rather than a five-page term paper. This enables them to postpone writing the paper.

■ *Keep a record of the reasons you give yourself for postponing studying or completing important assignments*. If a favorite rationalization is "I'll wait until I'm in the mood to do this," count the number of times in a week you are seized with the desire to study. The mood to study typically arrives after you begin, not before.

Don't procrastinate! Begin now! Apply the steps outlined here to gain more control over your behavior and win the battle against procrastination.

---

learned helplessness A passive resignation to aversive conditions that is learned through repeated exposure to inescapable or unavoidable aversive events.

sort are difficult to extinguish, they can be overcome. The *Apply It* feature contains a number of useful tips for overcoming procrastination.

There is an important exception to the ability of humans and other animals to learn to escape and avoid aversive situations: Learned helplessness is a passive resignation to aversive conditions, learned by repeated exposure to aversive events that are inescapable or unavoidable. The initial experiment on learned helplessness was conducted by Overmeier and Seligman (1967). Dogs in the experimental group were strapped into harnesses from which they could not escape and were exposed to electric shocks. Later, these same dogs were placed in a box with two compartments separated by a low barrier. The dogs then experienced a series of trials in which a warning signal was followed by an electric shock administered through the box's floor. However, the floor was electrified only on one side, and the dogs could have escaped the electric shocks simply by jumping the barrier. Surprisingly, the dogs did not do so. Dogs in the control group had not previously experienced the inescapable shock and behaved in an entirely different manner and quickly learned to jump the barrier when the warning signal sounded and thus escaped the shock. Seligman (1975) later reasoned that humans who have suffered painful experiences they could neither avoid nor escape may also experience learned helplessness. For example, children who fail repeatedly in school may stop doing their school work because they believe that it is impossible for them to succeed. Similarly, people who are abused by their intimate partners may adopt the view that they deserve such treatment and submit to their partners' aggressive behavior. As a result, says Seligman, such people become inactive, withdrawn, and depressed (Seligman, 1991).

5.13 What are some applications of operant conditioning?

Applications of Operant Conditioning

You have probably realized that operant conditioning is an important learning process that we experience almost every day. Operant conditioning can also be used intentionally by one person to change another person's behavior.

Can you train yourself to control your body's responses to stress? For years, scientists believed that internal responses such as heart rate, brain-wave patterns, and blood flow were not subject to operant conditioning. It is now known that when people are given very precise feedback about these internal processes, they can learn, with practice, to exercise control over them. Biofeedback is a way of getting information about internal biological states. Biofeedback devices have sensors that monitor slight changes in these internal responses and then amplify and convert them into visual or auditory signals. Thus, people can see or hear evidence of internal physiological processes, and by trying out various strategies (thoughts, feelings, or images), they can learn which ones routinely increase, decrease, or maintain a particular level of activity.

Biofeedback has been used to regulate heart rate and to control migraine and tension headaches, gastrointestinal disorders, asthma, anxiety tension states, epilepsy, sexual dysfunctions, and neuromuscular disorders such as cerebral palsy, spinal cord injuries, and stroke (Field, 2009).

Can operant conditioning help you get better grades? Perhaps, if you apply its principles to your study behavior. Behavior modification is a method of changing behavior through a systematic program based on the learning principles of classical conditioning, operant conditioning, or observational learning (which we will discuss soon). The majority of behavior modification programs use the principles of operant conditioning. The *Try It* below challenges you to create your own behavior modification plan.

Behavior modification programs have been used to change self-injurious behavior in autistic children and adults. Such programs are highly individualized and are frequently studied in a "one-subject" design, meaning that the study includes only one participant. One such study was designed to address a common problem among adults with autism and their caretakers (Beare et al., 2004). Adults with autism frequently reside in group homes and are employed in modified work settings. However, self-injurious behaviors can disturb these individuals' co-workers and supervisors, interfere with the performance of their duties, and cause them to lose their jobs. In the study, researchers successfully used behavior modification to stop a 41-year-old man with autism from exhibiting such behavior in his workplace, thereby enabling him to keep his job.

Some institutions, such as schools, mental hospitals, and prisons, use a token economy—a program that motivates socially desirable behavior by reinforcing it with tokens. The tokens (poker chips or coupons) may later be exchanged for desired items such as candy and privileges such as free time or participation in desired activities.

▼ With biofeedback devices, people can see or hear evidence of internal physiological states and learn how to control them through various mental strategies.

biofeedback The use of sensitive equipment to give people precise feedback about internal physiological processes so that they can learn, with practice, to exercise control over them.

behavior modification A method of changing behavior through a systematic program based on the learning principles of classical conditioning, operant conditioning, or observational learning.

token economy A program that motivates socially desirable behavior by reinforcing it with tokens that can be exchanged for desired items or privileges.

 TRY IT ▷ **Using Behavior Modification**

Use conditioning to modify your own behavior.

1. *Identify the target behavior.* It must be both observable and measurable. You might choose, for example, to increase the amount of time you spend studying.
2. *Gather and record baseline data.* Keep a daily record of how much time you spend on the target behavior for about a week. Also note where the behavior takes place and what cues (or temptations) in the environment precede any slacking off from the target behavior.
3. *Plan your behavior modification program.* Formulate a plan and set goals to either decrease or increase the target behavior.
4. *Choose your reinforcers.* Any activity you enjoy more can be used to reinforce any activity you enjoy less. For example, you could reward yourself with a movie after a specified period of studying.
5. *Set the reinforcement conditions and begin recording and reinforcing your progress.* Be careful not to set your reinforcement goals so high that it becomes nearly impossible to earn a reward. Keep in mind Skinner's concept of shaping through rewarding small steps toward the desired outcome. Be perfectly honest with yourself and claim a reward only when you meet the goals. Chart your progress as you work toward gaining more control over the target behavior.

◉ Watch on **mypsychlab.com**

People in the program know in advance exactly what behaviors will be reinforced and how they will be reinforced. Token economies have been used effectively in mental hospitals to encourage patients to attend to grooming, to interact with other patients, and to carry out housekeeping tasks (Kazdin, 2000). Prisons also sometimes use token economies to encourage prosocial behavior among inmates (Seegert, 2004). Even schoolchildren's behavior can be modified with a well-designed token economy that is based on age-appropriate statements of desired behavior (Reitman et al., 2004). Although the positive behaviors generally stop when the tokens are discontinued, this does not mean that the programs are not worthwhile. After all, most people who are employed would probably quit their jobs if they were no longer paid.

Many classroom teachers and parents use *time out*—a behavior modification technique in which a child who is misbehaving is removed for a short time from sources of positive reinforcement. (Remember, according to operant conditioning, a behavior that is no longer reinforced will extinguish.)

Behavior modification is also used successfully in business and industry to increase profits and to modify employee behavior related to health, safety, and job performance (Hickman & Geller, 2003). To keep their premiums low, some companies give annual rebates to employees who do not use up the deductibles in their health insurance plan. To reduce costs associated with automobile accidents and auto theft, insurance companies offer incentives in the form of reduced premiums for installing airbags and burglar alarm systems. To encourage employees to take company-approved college courses, some companies offer tuition reimbursement to employees who complete such courses with acceptable grades. Many companies promote sales by giving salespeople bonuses, trips, and other prizes for increasing sales. One of the most successful applications of behavior modification has been in the treatment of psychological problems ranging from phobias to addictive behaviors. In this context, behavior modification is called behavior therapy (discussed in Chapter 13).

The *Summarize It* table lists the principles of classical and operant conditioning.

SUMMARIZE IT

Classical and Operant Conditioning Compared

CHARACTERISTICS	CLASSICAL CONDITIONING	OPERANT CONDITIONING
Type of association	Between two stimuli	Between a response and its consequence
State of subject	Passive	Active
Focus of attention	On what precedes response	On what follows response
Type of response typically involved	Involuntary or reflexive response	Voluntary response
Bodily response typically involved	Internal responses; emotional and glandular reactions	External responses; muscular and skeletal movement and verbal responses
Range of responses	Relatively simple	Simple to highly complex
Responses learned	Emotional reactions; fears, likes, dislikes	Goal-oriented responses

Cognitive Learning

By now, you are probably convinced of the effectiveness of both classical and operant conditioning. But can either type of conditioning explain how you learned a complex mental function like reading? Behaviorists such as Skinner and Watson believed that any kind of learning could be explained without reference to internal mental processes. Today, however, a growing number of psychologists stress the role of mental processes. They choose to broaden the study of learning to include such cognitive processes as thinking, knowing, problem solving, remembering, and forming mental representations. According to cognitive theorists, understanding these processes is critically

cognitive processes (COG-nih-tiv) Mental processes such as thinking, knowing, problem solving, remembering, and forming mental representations.

important to a more complete, more comprehensive view of learning. We will consider the work of three important researchers in the field of cognitive learning: Wolfgang Köhler, Edward Tolman, and Albert Bandura.

Learning by Insight ▷

Have you ever been worried about a problem, only to have a crystal clear solution suddenly pop into your mind? If so, you experienced an important kind of cognitive learning first described by Wolfgang Köhler (1887–1967). In his book *The Mentality of Apes* (1925), Köhler described experiments he conducted on chimpanzees confined in caged areas. In one experiment, Köhler hung a bunch of bananas inside the caged area but overhead, out of reach of the chimps; boxes and sticks were left around the cage. Köhler observed the chimps' unsuccessful attempts to reach the bananas by jumping up or swinging sticks at them. Eventually, the chimps solved the problem by piling the boxes on top of one another and climbing on the boxes until they could reach the bananas.

Köhler observed that the chimps sometimes appeared to give up in their attempts to get the bananas. However, after an interval, they returned with the solution to the problem, as if it had come to them in a flash of insight. They seemed to have suddenly realized the relationship between the sticks or boxes and the bananas. Köhler insisted that insight, rather than trial-and-error learning, accounted for the chimps' successes, because they could easily repeat the solution and transfer this learning to similar problems. In human terms, a solution gained through insight is more easily learned, less likely to be forgotten, and more readily transferred to new problems than a solution learned through rote memorization (Rock & Palmer, 1990). Brain-imaging studies indicate that insight learning is associated with a unique pattern of interaction involving several different brain areas (Jing, 2004).

Latent Learning and Cognitive Maps ▷

Like Köhler, Edward Tolman (1886–1959) held views that differed from the prevailing ideas on learning. First, Tolman (1932) believed that learning could take place without reinforcement. Second, he differentiated between learning and performance. He maintained that latent learning could occur; that is, learning could occur without apparent reinforcement and not be demonstrated until the organism was motivated to do so. A classic experimental study by Tolman and Honzik (1930) supports this position. ◉▷ Simulate on mypsychlab.com

Three groups of rats were placed in a maze daily for 17 days. The first group always received a food reward at the end of the maze. The second group never received a reward, and the third group did not receive a food reward until the 11th day. The first group showed a steady improvement in performance over the 17-day period. The second group showed slight, gradual improvement. The third group, after being rewarded on the 11th day, showed a marked improvement the next day and, from then on, outperformed the rats that had been rewarded daily (see Figure 5.7, p. 156). The rapid improvement of the third group indicated to Tolman that latent learning had occurred—that the rats had actually learned the maze during the first 11 days but were not motivated to display this learning until they were rewarded for it. Tolman concluded that the rats had learned to form a cognitive map, a mental representation or picture, of the maze but had not demonstrated their learning until they were reinforced. In later studies, Tolman showed how rats quickly learn to rearrange their established cognitive maps and readily find their way through increasingly complex mazes.

Observational Learning ▷

Have you ever wondered why you slow down when you see another driver getting a speeding ticket? In all likelihood, no one has ever reinforced you for slowing down under these conditions, so why do you do it? Psychologist Albert Bandura (1986) contends that many behaviors or responses are acquired through observational learning,

---

5.14 **How does insight affect learning?**

insight The sudden realization of the relationship between elements in a problem situation, which makes the solution apparent.

5.15 **What did Tolman discover about the necessity of reinforcement?**

◉▷ Simulate the Experiment *Latent Learning* on **mypsychlab.com**

latent learning Learning that occurs without apparent reinforcement and is not demonstrated until the organism is motivated to do so.

cognitive map A mental representation of a spatial arrangement such as a maze.

5.16 **How do we learn by observing others?**

FIGURE 5.7 Latent Learning
Rats in Group 1 were rewarded every day for running the maze correctly, while rats in Group 2 were never rewarded. Group 3 rats were rewarded only on the 11th day and thereafter outperformed the rats in Group 1. The rats had "learned" the maze but were not motivated to perform until rewarded, demonstrating that latent learning had occurred.
Source: From Tolman & Honzik (1930).

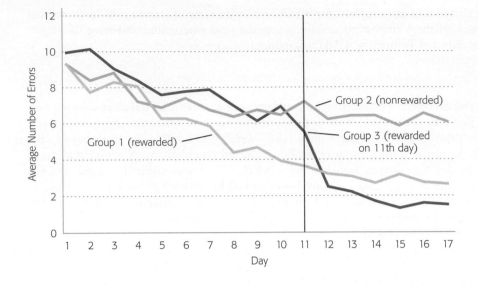

observational learning (social-cognitive learning) Learning by observing the behavior of others and the consequences of that behavior; learning by imitation.

model The individual who demonstrates a behavior or whose behavior is imitated.

✳—⸢**Explore** the **Concept** *Bandura's Study on Observational Learning* on **mypsychlab.com**

or *social-cognitive learning.* Observational learning results when people observe the behavior of others and note the consequences of that behavior. Thus, you slow down when you see another driver getting a ticket because you assume that person's consequence will also be your consequence. The same process is involved when we see another person get a free soft drink by hitting the side of a vending machine. We assume that if we hit the machine, we will also get a free drink.

A person who demonstrates a behavior or whose behavior is imitated is called a model. Parents, movie stars, and sports personalities are often powerful models for children. The effectiveness of a model is related to his or her status, competence, and power. Other important factors are the age, sex, attractiveness, and ethnicity of the model. Moreover, observers' own characteristics influence the degree to which they learn from models. For instance, women who are dissatisfied with their appearance pay more attention to and are more likely to try to emulate physically attractive models than women who are satisfied with the way they look.

✳—⸢**Explore** on **mypsychlab.com**

Whether learned behavior is actually performed depends largely on whether the observed models are rewarded or punished for their behavior and whether the observer expects to be rewarded for the behavior (Bandura, 1969, 1977). Note, too, that a model doesn't have to be a person. For instance, Bandura would agree that the instructions in Chapter 1 that show you how to use the SQ3R method to study this textbook constitute an important kind of model, as do the diagrams that accompany "ready-to-assemble" furniture.

As you may have learned in math, chemistry, and physics classes, or in other subjects in which teachers use modeling to teach students how to solve problems, simply watching a model does not necessarily result in learning. Bandura proposed that four processes determine whether observational learning will occur:

- *Attention:* The observer must attend to the model.
- *Retention:* The observer must store information about the model's behavior in memory.
- *Reproduction:* The observer must be physically and cognitively capable of performing the behavior to learn it. In other words, no matter how much time you devote to watching Serena Williams play tennis or listening to Beyoncé sing, you won't be able to acquire skills like theirs unless you possess talents that are equal to theirs. Likewise, it is doubtful that a kindergartener will learn geometry from watching her high-school-aged sister do her homework.
- *Reinforcement:* Ultimately, to exhibit a behavior learned through observation, an observer must be motivated to practice and perform the behavior on his own.

Just as there are factors that determine whether an observer will learn from a model, there are varying types of learning that involve models and observers. These different types of learning are called *effects* because they represent the different ways in which models affect the behavior of observers. See whether you can determine which of these effects is involved in the examples of observational learning we have given so far:

- *Modeling:* The modeling effect involves learning a new behavior.
- *Facilitation:* In the facilitation effect, an observer learns a behavior that is similar to that of a model in an unfamiliar situation.
- *Inhibition:* The tendency of observers to suppress socially unacceptable behaviors for which they see models punished is the inhibitory effect.
- *Disinhibition:* When observers see models get away with or be rewarded for exhibiting socially unacceptable behavior, the disinhibitory effect can occur.

Here is how our examples would be classified. The modeling effect is in evidence when you successfully learn how to solve a math problem from a teacher's demonstration. When you watch gifted athletes and artists perform and try to imitate them, you are demonstrating the facilitation effect. Slowing down when you see a fellow motorist getting a speeding ticket is an example of the inhibitory effect. Spending your time at work surfing the Internet because you have seen your co-workers do so without getting caught represents the disinhibitory effect.

The *Summarize It* table below reviews the principles of cognitive learning that we have discussed in this section. Now that you have learned about various principles of learning, read the *Explain It* feature (p. 158) to see how they explain the behavior of smoking cigarettes.

modeling effect Learning a new behavior from a model through the acquisition of new responses.

facilitation effect Exhibiting a behavior similar to that shown by a model in an unfamiliar situation.

inhibitory effect Suppressing a behavior because a model is punished for displaying the behavior.

disinhibitory effect Displaying a previously suppressed behavior because a model does so without receiving punishment.

Learning from Media ▷

5.17 What has research shown regarding learning from media?

How much of your day is spent in the presence of information that is flowing from some kind of electronic source? Many people nowadays are exposed to such information almost every waking minute. There is even a 24/7 cable television channel just for babies these days ("Round-the-clock baby TV ...," 2006).

Effects of the Multitasking Environment. The various kinds of electronic information media that are common in today's world comprise what some researchers call an *electronic multitasking environment* in which we attempt to manage several different sources of information at once (Rideout, Roberts, & Foehr, 2005). In one observational study of college computer labs, researchers found that many college students worked on papers and other assignments in a split-screen format, with one part of the screen devoted to their work and another to a game (Jones, 2003). And many of these students were listening to music on their MP3 players at the same time.

Cognitive Learning

TYPE OF LEARNING	DESCRIPTIONS	MAJOR CONTRIBUTORS	CLASSIC RESEARCH
Insight	Sudden realization of how to solve a problem	Wolfgang Köhler	Observations of chimpanzees' attempts to retrieve bananas suspended from the tops of their cages
Latent learning	Learning that is hidden until it is reinforced	Edward Tolman	Comparisons of rats that were rewarded for learning to run a maze with others that were allowed to explore it freely but were not rewarded
Observational learning	Learning from watching others	Albert Bandura	Comparisons of children who observed an adult model behaving aggressively with those who did not observe such an aggressive model

SUMMARIZE IT

EXPLAIN IT

How Do the Principles of Learning Explain the Behavior of Smoking Cigarettes?

Now that you have studied all of the major principles of learning, you may be able to use them to develop a comprehensive explanation for the health-threatening behavior of smoking cigarettes. It may help to break the behavior of smoking, and that of quitting smoking, into several components: the learning phase, the maintenance phase, and the quitting phase. Before going on, think for a few minutes about how the principles of classical conditioning, operant conditioning, and observational learning contribute to each of these phases. Your analysis may be different from ours, but here's how we see it.

The Learning Phase

Observational learning is critical to the initiation of cigarette smoking. Non-smokers see models whom they believe to be competent and successful—popular peers, movie characters, models in magazine advertisements—smoking cigarettes and think that this behavior helps people make friends or makes them look sophisticated and sexy. Operant conditioning comes into play when the mild brain-stimulating effects of nicotine are experienced by the new smoker as rewarding. At the same time, the aversive antismoking reactions of the lungs gradually subside with increased exposure to cigarette smoke. As a result, a behavior that began in response to social influences is now maintained by physiological factors.

The Maintenance Phase

Once the smoking habit is established, several different learning principles work together to keep it going. For instance, many smokers light up immediately after a meal. As a result of classical conditioning, the physiological feeling of being full becomes associated with the effects of nicotine, and the feeling of fullness becomes a stimulus that triggers a desire for a cigarette. Social settings in which most people are smoking bring observational principles to the fore as smokers feel freer to engage in the habit when others are doing so. In addition, negative reinforcement, an operant learning principle, is at work in the maintenance of smoking behavior. Specifically, smoking a cigarette makes a smoker's craving for nicotine go away.

The Quitting Phase

In the quitting phase, success depends on taking control of the principles of learning. First, those who hope to quit must learn to suppress classically conditioned triggers such as the feeling of fullness after a meal. Likewise, smokers can harness the power of observational learning by avoiding social situations in which many people are likely to be smoking and spending more time in settings in which smoking is prohibited or strongly discouraged. Finally, smokers who want to quit can exploit the fact that the negative reinforcement that occurs as a result of smoking a cigarette (i.e., alleviating craving) operates on a continuous schedule of reinforcement. Recall that behaviors that involve a continuous schedule are more easily learned than those that involve a variable schedule, but they are also more easily extinguished. Thus, smokers who want to quit should be aware that while the first three days or so of denying one's cravings can be quite miserable, the cravings diminish considerably thereafter.

▲ In Bandura's observational learning research, children learned to copy aggression by observing adult models act aggressively toward a Bobo doll.

Research examining the effects on learning of the multitasking environment is still too preliminary to support definitive conclusions, but the questions being examined are likely to be of great interest to people who spend their days juggling multiple information sources. One such question concerns the degree to which the brain adapts to multiple sources of information by changing its attentional strategies (e.g., Zhang et al., 2005). Another has led researchers to examine the possibility that simultaneous exposure to multiple information sources degrades learning from any one of those sources (e.g., Law, Logie, & Pearson, 2006). Other hypotheses currently being investigated include the possibility that keeping track of multiple streams of information induces anxiety (e.g., Bailey & Konstan, 2006).

Researchers are also interested in how multitasking influences our cognitive abilities beyond the multitasking environment. Surprisingly, these studies show that the more time people spend multitasking, the less capable they are of managing their thought processes when they are not multitasking (Ophir, Nass, & Wagner, 2009). Psychologists say that these results suggest that multitasking reduces our ability to differentiate between relevant and irrelevant information. In other words, multitasking causes us to develop the habit of attending to everything in the environment rather than filtering out information that is unimportant.

Television and Other Entertainment Media. More than four decades ago, Albert Bandura raised concerns regarding the impact of televised violence on children's behavior with a classic series of studies. Bandura suspected that aggression and violence on television programs, including cartoons, tend to increase aggressive behavior in children. His pioneering work has greatly influenced current thinking on these issues. In several classic experiments, Bandura demonstrated how children are influenced by exposure to aggressive models. One study involved three groups of preschoolers. Children in one group individually observed an adult model punching, kicking, and hitting a 5-foot, inflated plastic "Bobo Doll" with a mallet, while uttering aggressive phrases (Bandura et al., 1961, p. 576). Children in the second group observed a nonaggressive model who ignored the Bobo Doll and sat quietly assembling Tinker Toys. The children in the control group were placed in the same setting with no adult present. Later, each child was observed through a one-way mirror. Those children exposed to the aggressive model imitated much of the aggression and also engaged in significantly more nonimitative aggression than did children in either of the other groups. The group that observed the nonaggressive model showed less aggressive behavior than the control group. ⊙ Watch on mypsychlab.com

A further study compared the degree of aggression in children following exposure to (1) an aggressive model in a live situation, (2) a filmed version of the same situation, or (3) a film depicting an aggressive cartoon character using the same aggressive behaviors in a fantasylike setting (Bandura et al., 1963). A control group was not exposed to any of the three situations of aggression. The groups exposed to aggressive models used significantly more aggression than the control group. The researchers concluded that "of the three experimental conditions, exposure to humans on film portraying aggression was the most influential in eliciting and shaping aggressive behavior" (p. 7).

Bandura's research sparked interest in studying the effects of violence and aggression portrayed in other entertainment media. For example, researchers have also shown in a variety of ways—including carefully controlled laboratory experiments with children, adolescents, and young adults—that violent video games increase aggressive behavior (Anderson & Carnagey, 2009). Moreover, the effects of media violence are evident whether the violence is presented in music, music videos, advertising, or on the Internet (Villani, 2001). Such research has spawned a confusing array of rating systems that parents may refer to when choosing media for their children. However, researchers have found that the various rating systems do a poor job of communicating the frequency and intensity of violent acts in programs (Linder & Gentile, 2009). Moreover, researchers have found that labeling media as "violent" may enhance children's desire to experience it, especially in boys over age 11 (Bushman & Cantor, 2003).

But, you might argue, if televised violence is followed by appropriate consequences, such as an arrest, it may actually teach children not to engage in aggression. However, experimental research has demonstrated that children do not process information about consequences in the same ways as adults do (Krcmar & Cooke, 2001). Observing consequences for aggressive acts does seem to help preschoolers learn that violence is morally unacceptable. By contrast, school-aged children appear to judge the rightness or wrongness of an act of violence on the basis of provocation; that is, they believe that violence demonstrated in the context of retaliation is morally acceptable even if it is punished by an authority figure.

Remarkably, too, recently published longitudinal evidence shows that the effects of childhood exposure to violence persist well into the adult years. Psychologist L. Rowell Huesmann and his colleagues (2003) found that individuals who had watched the greatest number of violent television programs in childhood were the most likely to have engaged in actual acts of violence as young adults. This study was the first to show that observations of media violence during childhood are linked to real acts of violence in adulthood. Brain-imaging studies suggest that these long-term effects may be the result of patterns of neural activation that underlie emotionally laden behavioral scripts that children learn while watching violent programming (Murray et al., 2006).

But just as children imitate the aggressive behavior they observe on television, they also imitate the prosocial, or helping, behavior they see there. Programs such as *Mister Rogers' Neighborhood* and *Sesame Street* have been found to have a positive influence on children. And, hopefully, the findings of Huesmann and his colleagues also apply to the positive effects of television.

Electronic Games. In recent years, concerns about media violence have shifted away from television and toward an emphasis on electronic games. This shift has occurred because children and teenagers now spend as much time playing these games as they do watching television (Cummings & Vandewater, 2007). Adults also

⊙ **Watch** the **Video** *Bandura's Bobo Doll Experiment* on **mypsychlab.com**

▲ Aggressive behaviors aren't the only kinds of behaviors people can learn from watching television. Rachael Ray became famous by showing millions of viewers how to add creativity to everyday activities such as preparing family meals.

devote a considerable amount of time to gaming (see Figure 5.8). A number of studies have shown that playing violent games increases feelings of hostility and decreases sensitivity to violent images (Carnagey, Anderson, & Bushman, 2007).

Despite these findings, some psychologists argue that violent electronic games allow individuals, especially adolescent and young adult males, to express socially unacceptable feelings in a socially acceptable and safe manner (Jansz, 2005). They point out that these games are most often played in groups and are a central shared activity in many young males' peer relationships (Jansz & Martens, 2005). Consequently, learning to channel aggressive impulses into competitive play among friends, even when such play involves simulated violence, may be an essential part of the social development of adolescent males.

Like television, video games can be used to teach positive messages and skills (Greitmeyer & Osswald, 2010). For example, researchers at the University of Michigan have found that video games are an effective medium through which to teach teenagers how to drive more safely (University of Michigan Transportation Research Institute [UMTRI], 2003). Furthermore, playing video games appears to enhance women's spatial cognitive skills, a domain in which females typically perform more poorly than males (Achtman, Green, & Bavelier, 2008; Terlecki & Newcombe, 2005).

The Internet. Educators agree that the Internet holds great promise as a teaching tool (Schofield, 2006). Still, researchers note that teachers ought not to assume that media-rich, Internet-based instruction is, by default, more effective than conventional approaches (Mayer, 2010). For instance, when text is presented online, embedded video and audio help to maintain students' attention, but such links don't necessarily contribute to learning (Liu, Liao, & Pratt, 2009). Moreover, physical manipulations of the computer itself, such as typing and moving the mouse, distract online readers and hinder their ability to comprehend and remember what they are reading (Mangen, 2008). Several well-designed studies have also shown that conventional classroom lectures and textbooks are just as useful for learning complex material as multimedia presentations are (Mayer, Hegarty, Mayer, & Campbell, 2005).

Research suggests that educators must be especially cautious when using Internet-based instruction with children. For one thing, until they are about 10 years old, children have difficulty recognizing online advertising even though they recognize television advertisements as early as age 5 (Ali, Blades, Oates, & Blumberg, 2009). As a result, younger children who are using Web-based materials are more likely to be distracted by ads than older children are. Moreover, researcher Teena Willoughby and her colleagues have found that, even among college students, differences in background knowledge contribute significantly to individual differences in learning from online references such as Wikipedia (Willoughby, Anderson, Wood, Mueller, & Ross, 2009). Thus, it is likely such sources would be even less useful for children whose background

FIGURE 5.8 "Gamers" in Four Age Groups Researchers at the Pew Internet & American Life Project track all kinds of media use among children and adults in the United States. One of their findings is that younger adults are more likely to play video games at least occasionally than those who are older. However, older adults who play are more likely to do so every day than younger adults are.
Source: Lenhart, Jones, & Macgill, 2008.

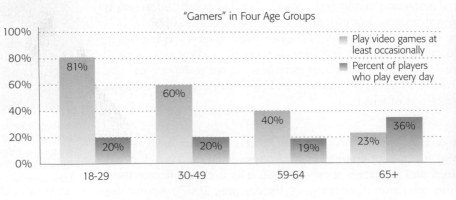

How would you explain these findings? Could both age trends be caused by the same underlying variable?

"Gamers" in Four Age Groups

- Play video games at least occasionally
- Percent of players who play every day

Age group	Play occasionally	Play every day
18-29	81%	20%
30-49	60%	20%
59-64	40%	19%
65+	23%	36%

knowledge is, generally, much less developed than that of adults. Thus, educators who study the phenomenon of online reading suggest that children be allowed time to develop both background knowledge and reading skill from conventional materials before they are introduced to online text (Ali et al., 2009; Mangen, 2008).

Looking Back

At the beginning of this chapter, you learned that the principles of learning can be used to explain why some activities are more engaging than others. As you read through the chapter, you encountered examples of other kinds of everyday experiences that involve classical conditioning, operant conditioning, and cognitive learning. At this point, you may be wondering how the various topics covered in this chapter relate to the mental processes that we commonly associate with academic learning, such as memory and problem solving. The answer is that the principles explained in this chapter represent only a few of the many different kinds of learning that we experience in our daily lives. Other aspects of learning, including memory and problem solving, will be considered in the next two chapters.

CHAPTER 5 SUMMARY

CLASSICAL CONDITIONING (pp. 137-144)

5.1 How does the kind of learning Pavlov discovered happen? (pp. 137-138)

Pavlov's study of a conditioned reflex in dogs led him to discover a model of learning called classical conditioning. In classical conditioning, a neutral stimulus (a tone in Pavlov's experiments) is presented shortly before an unconditioned stimulus (food in Pavlov's experiments), which naturally elicits, or brings forth, an unconditioned response (salivation for Pavlov's dogs). After repeated pairings, the conditioned stimulus alone (the tone) comes to elicit the conditioned response (salivation).

Key Terms
learning, p. 137
classical conditioning, p. 137
stimulus, p. 137
unconditioned response (UR), p. 138
unconditioned stimulus (US), p. 138
conditioned stimulus (CS), p. 138
conditioned response (CR), p. 138
higher-order conditioning, p. 138

5.2 What causes classically conditioned responses to change? (pp. 139-140)

If the conditioned stimulus (tone) is presented repeatedly without the unconditioned stimulus (food), the conditioned response (salivation) eventually disappears, a process called extinction. That response can reappear in a weaker form if the organism is exposed to the conditioned stimulus again after a period of rest, which is a process called spontaneous recovery. Generalization occurs when an organism makes a conditioned response to a stimulus that is similar to the original conditioned stimulus. Discrimination is the ability to distinguish between similar stimuli.

Key Terms
extinction, p. 139
spontaneous recovery, p. 139
generalization, p. 139
discrimination, p. 140

5.3 What did Watson's "Little Albert" experiment show? (pp. 140-141)

Watson showed that fear could be classically conditioned by presenting a white rat to Little Albert along with a loud, frightening noise, thereby conditioning the child to fear the white rat.

5.4 What did Rescorla demonstrate about classical conditioning? (pp. 141–142)

Rescorla found that the critical element in classical conditioning is whether the conditioned stimulus provides information that enables the organism to reliably predict the occurrence of the unconditioned stimulus.

5.5 How do biological predispositions affect classical conditioning? (pp. 142-143)

Garcia and Koelling conducted a study in which rats formed an association between nausea and flavored water ingested several hours earlier. This represented an exception to the principle that the conditioned stimulus must be presented shortly before the unconditioned stimulus. It also revealed that animals appear to be biologically predisposed to make certain associations, meaning associations cannot be conditioned between just any two stimuli.

Key Terms
biological predispositions, p. 142   taste aversion, p. 142

5.6   What are some examples of classical conditioning in everyday life? (pp. 143-144)

Types of responses acquired through classical conditioning include positive and negative emotional responses (including likes, dislikes, fears, and phobias), responses to environmental cues associated with drug use, responses to advertisements, and conditioned immune system responses. Studies of classical conditioning in everyday life indicate that neutral stimuli cannot serve as conditioned stimuli unless they have authentic connections to unconditioned stimuli (ecological relevance).

OPERANT CONDITIONING (pp. 144-154)

5.7   What did Thorndike and Skinner discover about the consequences of behavior? (p. 144)

Thorndike concluded that most learning occurs through trial and error. He claimed that the consequences of a response determine whether the tendency to respond in the same way in the future will be strengthened or weakened (the law of effect). In Skinner's operant conditioning, behaviors change as a result of the consequences they produce. Reinforcement occurs when consequences cause behaviors to increase. Punishment occurs when consequences cause behaviors to decrease.

Key Terms

law of effect, p. 144
operant conditioning, p. 144
operant, p. 144
reinforcer, p. 144

5.8   How do shaping, generalization, and discriminative stimuli influence operant conditioning? (pp. 144–146)

In one kind of operant conditioning, shaping, complex behaviors are learned in small steps. In extinction, behaviors disappear when the consequences they formerly produced are no longer available. A discriminative stimulus is one that through its association with reinforcement signals learners about behaviors that are likely to be reinforced.

Key Terms

shaping, p. 144
Skinner box, p. 145
successive approximations, p. 145
extinction, p. 145
generalization, p. 145
discriminative stimulus, p. 146

5.9   How do positive and negative reinforcement affect behavior? (pp. 146-147)

Both positive (added) and negative (subtracted, removed) reinforcement increase behavior. In positive reinforcement, a behavior occurs more frequently because it produces a desired consequence. In negative reinforcement, a behavior is learned because it makes an undesirable condition or stimulus go away. Primary reinforcers are consequences that satisfy basic needs. Secondary reinforcers are those that have some kind of association with a primary reinforcer.

Key Terms

reinforcement, p. 146
positive reinforcement, p. 146
negative reinforcement, p. 146
primary reinforcer, p. 146
secondary reinforcer, p. 147

5.10   What are the four types of schedules of reinforcement? (pp. 147-148)

The four types of schedules of reinforcement are the fixed-ratio, variable-ratio, fixed-interval, and variable-interval schedules. The variable-ratio schedule provides the highest response rate and the most resistance to extinction. The partial-reinforcement effect is the greater resistance to extinction that occurs when responses are maintained under partial reinforcement, rather than under continuous reinforcement.

Key Terms

schedule of reinforcement, p. 147
fixed-ratio (FR) schedule, p. 147
variable-ratio (VR) schedule, p. 147
partial reinforcement effect, p. 148
fixed-interval (FI) schedule, p. 148
variable-interval (VI) schedule, p. 148

5.11   How does punishment affect behavior? (pp. 149-151)

Punishment happens when either an added (positive) or a removed (negative) consequence leads to a reduction in the frequency of a behavior. Generally, punishment does not help people develop more appropriate behaviors, and it can cause fear, anger, hostility, and aggression in the punished person. Punishment is most effective when it is given immediately after undesirable behavior, when it is consistently applied, and when it is just intense enough to suppress the behavior.

Key Terms

punishment, p. 149
positive punishment, p. 149
negative punishment, p. 149

5.12   How do escape and avoidance learning occur? (pp. 151-152)

Avoidance learning is desirable when it leads to a beneficial response, such as buckling a seat belt to stop the annoying sound of a buzzer. It is maladaptive when it occurs in response to fear. For example, fear of speaking to a group may lead you to skip class on the day your oral report is scheduled.

Key Terms

avoidance learning, p. 151
learned helplessness, p. 152

27. You are most likely to learn a modeled behavior if you
   a. repeat the behavior in different settings.
   b. are physically capable of performing the behavior.
   c. have never seen the behavior before.
   d. are personally acquainted with the model.

28. Match each of the effects of modeling with its definition:

   _____ **(1)** modeling   _____ **(3)** inhibitory

   _____ **(2)** facilitation   _____ **(4)** disinhibitory

   a. exhibiting a behavior similar to that of a model
   b. exhibiting a previously learned unacceptable behavior after seeing a model do so
   c. learning a new behavior from a model
   d. suppressing a previously learned unacceptable behavior after seeing a model be punished for it

29. Match the researcher with the subject(s) researched.

   _____ **(1)** Edward Tolman

   _____ **(2)** Albert Bandura

   _____ **(3)** Wolfgang Köhler

   a. observational learning
   b. learning by insight
   c. latent learning

30. _____ was a pioneer in the study of the ways in which observing aggressive behavior on television and in films influences children's behavior.

SECTION TWO: Identify the Concept

In the blank following each statement below, list the learning principle(s) illustrated by the statement.

1. Ben continues to play a slot machine even though he never knows when it will pay off. _____

2. Tamake watched a movie about tornadoes and is now afraid of bad storms. _____

3. Joey is crying and asking for a candy bar. His mother gives in because doing so will make him stop crying for now—but Joey will most likely behave this way again. _____

4. Hans got sick eating lasagna and now never eats food containing tomato sauce. _____

5. Helen washed the dinner dishes, and her mother allowed her to watch television for 30 extra minutes that evening. From then on, Helen dutifully washed the dishes after every family meal. _____

6. Natasha's parents are advised to stop paying attention to her crying when it is time for bed and instead ignore it. _____

7. Jorge is paid for his factory job once every two weeks. _____

8. Maria is scolded for running into the road and never does it again. _____

9. Ellen watches her lab partner mix the chemicals and set up the experiment. She then repeats the same procedure and completes her assignment. _____

10. Through associations with such things as food and shelter, pieces of green paper with pictures of past U.S. presidents on them become very powerful reinforcers. _____

11. Although he studied the problem, Jack did not seem to be able to figure out the correct way to reconnect the pipes under the sink. He took a break before he became too frustrated. Later he returned and immediately saw how to do it. _____

12. Morgan often listens to her iPod while chatting with friends online and watching television. _____

SECTION THREE: Fill in the Blank

1. Classical conditioning is based on the association between _____, and operant conditioning is based on the association between a _____ and its _____.

2. _____ is a relatively permanent change in behavior, knowledge, capability, or attitude that is acquired through experience and cannot be attributed to illness, injury, or maturation.

3. Ed feeds the horses on his ranch every day at the same time. He notices that the horses now run to their feed troughs and whinny as if they know dinner is on its way as soon as they hear his truck coming up the drive. In this example, the conditioned stimulus is _____.

4. In question 3, the unconditioned stimulus is _____.

5. The unconditioned response of Pavlov's dogs was _____.

6. In Pavlov's classic experiment, the bell was originally a(n) _____ stimulus.

7. To get coyotes to stop eating sheep, ranchers poison sheep carcasses in the hope that coyotes that eat the carcasses will get sick enough to avoid eating sheep from that point on. The ranchers hope that the coyotes will avoid all types and sizes of sheep—which is an example of _____ in classical conditioning.

8. The ranchers in question 7 also hope that the coyotes will be able to distinguish between sheep and other more appropriate sources of food. This is an example of _____ in classical conditioning.

9. Eduardo loved eating at a certain fast-food restaurant. After a while even the giant logo sign in front of the restaurant would make him hungry every time he saw it. The restaurant ran a TV ad showing a clown standing by the logo sign. Pretty soon, every time Eduardo saw a clown, he became hungry. Eduardo's responses are examples of _____ conditioning.

10. If Watson had wanted to extinguish Little Albert's conditioned fear of white furry things, he would have presented the _____ stimulus without presenting the _____ stimulus.

11. The law of _____, developed by _____, states that a response that is followed by a satisfying consequence will tend to be repeated, while a response followed by discomfort will tend to be weakened.

12. Since researchers cannot tell rats to press the bar in a Skinner box for food or have them read "The Skinner Box Owner's Manual," they must initiate the bar-pressing response by rewarding _____ _____, an approach known as *shaping*.

13. Reinforcement is any event that follows a response and increases the probability of the response. _____ reinforcement involves the removal of a stimulus and _____ reinforcement involves the presentation of a stimulus.

14. You're driving on an interstate highway and suddenly notice that you've been going 80 miles per hour without realizing it. Immediately after you slow down, you see the flashing light of a state police car, and you know you're about to be pulled over. In this case the flashing light is a _____ stimulus.

15. Food is considered a _____ reinforcer; money is considered a _____ reinforcer.

16. If you were going to train a rat to press a bar for food, you would probably use _____ reinforcement for the initial training period and a _____-reinforcement schedule to strengthen the learned bar-pressing behavior.

17. Bandura's research demonstrated that children may learn _____ behaviors from watching models perform them on television.

18. Research shows that children learn to identify advertising on _____ several years before they can do the same for ads on _____.

SECTION FOUR: Comprehensive Practice Test

1. Pavlov is associated with _____ conditioning.
   a. classical
   b. operant
   c. cognitive
   d. Watsonian

2. This theorist believed that the causes of behavior are in the environment and that inner mental events are themselves shaped by environmental forces.
   a. Bandura
   b. Pavlov
   c. Skinner
   d. Tolman

3. Which of the following theorists developed the concepts of latent learning and cognitive mapping?
   a. Pavlov
   b. Köhler
   c. Tolman
   d. Skinner

4. This theorist researched observational learning and the effects of modeling on behavior.
   a. Köhler
   b. Thorndike
   c. Skinner
   d. Bandura

5. Which of the following theorists is associated with research on reinforcement theory?
   a. Pavlov
   b. Skinner
   c. Tolman
   d. Bandura

6. The concept that is associated with cognitive learning is
   a. negative reinforcement.
   b. positive reinforcement.
   c. latent learning.
   d. the discriminative stimulus.

7. Jim has been sober since he completed a treatment program for alcoholics. He was told to stay away from his old drinking places. The danger is that he may start drinking again as a result of the conditioned stimuli in those environments. If he did, it would be a practical example of _____ in classical conditioning.
   a. extinction
   b. spontaneous recovery
   c. stimulus generalization
   d. observational response sets

8. The seductive nature of a slot machine in a gambling casino is based on its _____ schedule of reinforcement.
   a. continuous
   b. fixed-interval
   c. variable-ratio
   d. variable-interval

9. For Little Albert, the conditioned stimulus was _____.
   a. the white rat
   b. a loud noise
   c. Watson
   d. based on negative reinforcement

10. Positive reinforcement increases behavior; negative reinforcement _____ behavior.
   a. decreases
   b. has no effect on
   c. removes a
   d. also increases

11. A good example of a fixed-interval schedule of reinforcement is _____.
   a. factory piecework.
   b. a child's weekly allowance.
   c. a slot machine.
   d. turning on a light switch.

12. The nice thing about continuous reinforcement is that it creates a behavior that is very resistant to extinction. (true/false)

13. Taste aversion is a real-world example of
   a. operant conditioning.
   b. classical conditioning.
   c. observational learning.
   d. cognitive mapping.

14. In _____ learning, a person or animal learns a response that _____ a negative reinforcer.
   a. escape; prevents the occurrence of
   b. escape; terminates
   c. avoidance; terminates
   d. avoidance; initiates

15. Ms. Doe, a new teacher, is having a difficult time with her misbehaving second graders. When the principal enters the room, the children behave like perfect angels. In this case, the principal may be thought of as a(n) _____.
   a. positive reinforcer.
   b. unconditioned stimulus.
   c. shaping reinforcer.
   d. discriminative stimulus.

16. According to Tolman, _____ is defined as learning that occurs without apparent reinforcement but is not demonstrated until the organism is sufficiently reinforced to do so.
   a. classical conditioning
   b. modeling behavior
   c. latent learning
   d. cognitive mapping

17. Which statement best sums up research on learning from video games?
   a. Video games can have both positive and negative effects.
   b. Videos games influence learning in males but not in females.
   c. Only violent games influence learning.
   d. Video games influence learning in children and teens, but not in adults.

SECTION FIVE: Critical Thinking

1. Outline the strengths and limitations of classical conditioning, operant conditioning, and observational learning in explaining how behaviors are acquired and maintained.

2. The use of behavior modification has been a source of controversy among psychologists and others. Prepare arguments supporting each of these positions:
   a. Behavior modification should be used in society to shape the behavior of others.
   b. Behavior modification should not be used in society to shape the behavior of others.

3. Think of a behavior of a friend, family member, or professor that you would like to change. Using what you know about classical conditioning, operant conditioning, and observational learning, formulate a detailed plan for changing the targeted behavior.

Memory

Think About It

Perhaps you have heard that people sometimes suddenly "remember" an event that happened long ago only to find out that the event never actually happened. Such "false" memories make us wonder about the accuracy of human memory—just how easy is it to create such a memory? Read all these words aloud at a rate of about one word per second. Then close your book and write down all the words you can remember.

bed	dream	nap	rest
wake	yawn	awake	snooze
snore	tired	doze	slumber

Now check your list. Did you "remember" the word *sleep*? Many people do, even though it is not one of the words on the list (Deese, 1959). As you can see, creating a false memory really isn't all that difficult, and it is something that can happen to anyone.

As you will learn later in the chapter, the memory process is subject to distortion for a variety of reasons. Clearly, the human memory system does not function like a camera. Instead, the system combines new input with previously stored information to create a representation of an event rather than a copy of it. In this chapter, you will read about the fascinating processes that, together, make up human memory.

The Structure of Human Memory

How do our minds create memories? Psychologists have been studying memory for more than a century. However, the need to break down the memory process into its constituent parts that was necessitated by the invention of modern computers and computer programming has opened the doors to psychologists' understanding of how the human memory system works.

6.1 How does information-processing theory describe memory?

information-processing theory A framework for studying memory that uses the computer as a model of human cognitive processes.

encoding The process of transforming information into a form that can be stored in memory.

storage The process of keeping or maintaining information in memory.

retrieval The process of bringing to mind information that has been stored in memory.

What Is Memory?

Most current studies aimed at understanding human memory are conducted within a framework known as information-processing theory (Klatzky, 1984). This approach makes use of modern computer science and related fields to provide models that help psychologists understand the processes involved in memory (Bishop, 2005). In keeping with the computer analogy, information-processing theorists sometimes apply such terms as *hardware* (e.g., brain structures that are involved in memory) and *software* (e.g., learned memory strategies) to various aspects of the human memory system.

Note that information-processing theory is a perspective, or general framework, that yields *microtheories* that explain specific memory processes or outcomes using the general principles of the information-processing approach. One such microtheory might explain how study participants remember lists of words in laboratory experiments, whereas another might focus on how our memories keep track of everyday tasks such as, "I have to remember to go to the library after class."

The general principles of the information processing approach to memory include the notion that memory involves three distinct processes. The first process, encoding, is the transformation of information into a form that can be stored in memory. For example, if you witness a car crash, you might try to form a mental picture of it to enable yourself to remember it. The second memory process, storage, involves keeping or maintaining information in memory. In order for encoded information to be stored, some physiological change must take place in the brain—a process called *consolidation*. The final process, retrieval, occurs when information stored in memory is brought to mind. To remember something, you must perform all three processes—

FIGURE 6.1 The Processes Required for Remembering
The act of remembering requires successful completion of all three of these processes: encoding, storage, and retrieval.

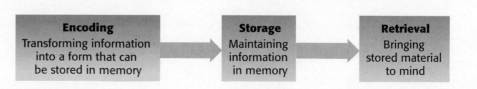

Encoding	**Storage**	**Retrieval**
Transforming information into a form that can be stored in memory	Maintaining information in memory	Bringing stored material to mind

encode the information, store it, and then retrieve it. Thus, memory is a cognitive process that includes encoding, storage, and retrieval of information (see Figure 6.1).

✳ Explore on mypsychlab.com

Information-processing theory is not associated with any one theorist. However, several theorists have been especially influential, two of these influential theorists are Richard Atkinson and Richard Shiffrin. They proposed the model of memory that almost all researchers employ (Atkinson & Shiffrin, 1968; Shiffrin, 1999). Their model characterizes memory as three different, interacting memory systems: sensory memory, short-term memory, and long-term memory. We will examine each of these three memory systems, which are shown in Figure 6.2, in detail.

Sensory Memory ▶

Virtually everything we see, hear, or otherwise sense is held in sensory memory, where each piece of information is stored only for the briefest period of time. As shown in Figure 6.2, sensory memory normally holds visual images for a fraction of a second and sounds for about 2 seconds (Crowder, 1992; Klatzky, 1980).

Exactly how long does visual sensory memory last? Glance at the three rows of letters shown below for a fraction of a second and then close your eyes. How many of the letters can you recall?

```
X   B   D   F
M   P   Z   G
L   C   N   H
```

Most people can correctly recall only four or five of the letters when they are briefly presented. Does this indicate that visual sensory memory can hold only four or five letters at a time? To find out, researcher George Sperling (1960) briefly flashed 12 letters, as shown above, to participants. Immediately upon turning off the display, he sounded a high, medium, or low tone that signaled the participants to report only the top, middle, or bottom row of letters. Before they heard the tone, the participants had no way of knowing which row they would have to report. Yet Sperling found that when the participants could view the rows of letters for $^{15}/_{1000}$ to $^{1}/_{2}$ second, they could report correctly all the items in any one row nearly 100% of the time. But the items faded from sensory memory so quickly that during the time it took to report three or four of them, the other eight or nine had already disappeared. Thus, sensory memory can take in an enormous amount of information, but it can only hold on to it for a very brief period of time.

A very small proportion of individuals, most of them children, have an exceptional ability to extend the amount of time that an image is present in sensory memory

✳ Explore the Concept *Encoding, Storage, and Retrieval in Memory* on **mypsychlab.com**

memory The process of encoding, storage, and retrieval of information.

⌐ **6.2** What are the characteristics
∟ of sensory memory?

sensory memory The memory system that holds information from the senses for a period of time ranging from only a fraction of a second to about 2 seconds.

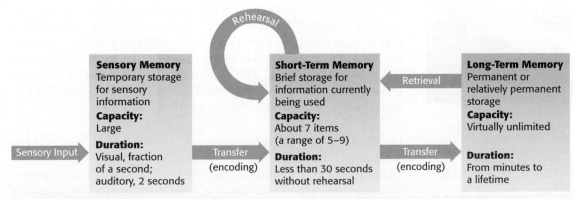

FIGURE 6.2 Characteristics of and Processes Involved in the Three Memory Systems Proposed by Atkinson and Shiffrin
The three memory systems differ in what and how much they hold and for how long they store it.
Source: Peterson & Peterson (1959).

eidetic imagery (eye-DET-ik) The ability to retain the image of a visual stimulus for several minutes after it has been removed from view and to use this retained image to answer questions about the visual stimulus.

(Haber, 1980). This ability is called eidetic imagery, and it is the memory phenomenon that comes closest to the popular notion of a "photographic memory" (Solso, MacLin, & MacLin, 2008). People with eidetic imagery abilities can retain the image of a visual stimulus, such as a picture, for several minutes after it has been removed from view and use this retained image to answer questions about the visual stimulus. However, they generally have no better long-term memory than others, and virtually all children with eidetic imagery lose it before adulthood.

6.3 What happens to information in short-term memory?

Short-Term Memory

So, you might be thinking, if almost everything flows out of sensory memory, how do we ever remember anything? Fortunately, our ability to attend allows us to grab on to some sensory information and send it to the next stage of processing, short-term memory (STM). Whatever you are thinking about right now is in your STM (see Figure 6.2). Short-term memory usually codes information according to sound. For example, the letter *T* is coded as the sound "tee," not as the shape T. ◉ Watch on **mypsychlab.com**

◉ Watch the **Video** *Short-Term Memory* on **mypsychlab.com**

short-term memory (STM) The component of the memory system that holds about seven (from five to nine) items for less than 30 seconds without rehearsal; also called working memory.

displacement The event that occurs when short-term memory is filled to capacity and each new, incoming item pushes out an existing item, which is then forgotten.

chunking A memory strategy that involves grouping or organizing bits of information into larger units, which are easier to remember.

rehearsal The act of purposely repeating information to maintain it in short-term memory.

Capacity. Short-term memory has a very limited capacity—about seven (plus or minus two) different items or bits of information at one time. This is just enough for phone numbers and ordinary ZIP codes. (Nine-digit ZIP codes strain the capacity of most people's STM.) When short-term memory is filled to capacity, displacement can occur. In displacement, each new incoming item pushes out an existing item, which is then forgotten. Think of what happens when the top of your desk gets too crowded. Things start to "disappear" under other things; some items even fall off the desk. So, you can remember that short-term memory is the limited component of the memory system by associating it with the top of your desk: The desk is limited in size, causing you to lose things when it gets crowded, and the same is true of short-term memory. (See the *Explain It.*)

One way to overcome the limitation of seven or so bits of information is to use a strategy that George A. Miller (1956), a pioneer in memory research, calls chunking—organizing or grouping separate bits of information into larger units, or chunks. A *chunk* is an easily identifiable unit, such as a syllable, a word, an acronym, or a number (Cowan, 1988). For example, nine digits, such as 5 2 9 7 3 1 3 2 5, can be divided into three more easily memorized chunks, 529 73 1325. (Notice that this is the form of Social Security numbers in the United States.)

Any time you chunk information on the basis of knowledge stored in long-term memory—that is, by associating it with some kind of meaning—you increase the effective capacity of short-term memory (Baddeley, 2009). As a result, chunking is just as useful in remembering large amounts of information as it is in remembering short bits of data such as telephone numbers. For instance, the headings, subheadings, and margin questions in this textbook help you sort information into manageable chunks. Thus, you will remember more of a chapter if you use them as organizers for your notes and as cues to recall information when you are reviewing for an exam.

▲ Suppose the person with whom this driver is talking is giving her directions. As you can see, the driver has no way to write down the directions, and her short-term memory is trying to juggle the tasks of driving and talking on the phone while also trying to understand and remember the directions. If you have ever been in this situation, you probably learned the hard way that your performance on at least one of the tasks suffered because of the limitation of short-term memory.

Duration. As you might have guessed, chunking alone won't do the trick. In fact, items in short-term memory are lost in less than 30 seconds unless you repeat them over and over to yourself. This process is known as rehearsal. But rehearsal is easily disrupted. It is so fragile, in fact, that an interruption can cause information to be lost in just a few seconds. In a series of early studies, participants were briefly

EXPLAIN IT   Why Is Cramming an Ineffective Study Method?

Have you ever found yourself in a situation like this one? It's the night before your psychology exam, and you have not read the three chapters that will be covered on the exam. Seeing no other option, you stay awake all night cramming for the test. Despite your best efforts, when you are faced with the exam the next day, you find yourself able to recall only fragments of information from the three chapters you studied so diligently the night before. Do you think that the characteristics of short-term memory might have something to do with your inability to remember what you were sure you had learned the night before? Think for a moment about how these characteristics come into play when you cram for an exam.

Did the limited capacity of short-term memory come to mind? It should have because cramming, by its nature, overloads the short-term memory. Although cramming strains the memory system in many other ways as well, the primary cause of its ineffectiveness is this tendency to exceed the capacity of STM.

For clarity, let's consider an example. Suppose you are cramming for an exam over this chapter, and you need to learn the characteristics of the STM. You skim the text and predict that what you need to know for the exam boils down to these units of information:

- Capacity limited to 7 ± 2 bits of information
- Information lost through decay, displacement, and interference
- Information lost in 30 seconds if not rehearsed
- Also known as working memory
- Strategies executed in STM
- Chunking can increase its capacity

You might be thinking that, since there are only six items on this list, they easily fit within the seven-unit capacity of the STM. This observation might be valid if rote memorization were sufficient for the purposes of a college-level exam. But, as you probably know by now, most college exams require more than simple memorization.

Let's look at just how complex this six-item list really is from the perspective of your STM. The first item is fairly straightforward, but take a look at the second one. It is essentially a summary statement that requires you to know what the terms *decay, displacement,* and *interference* mean to process it. The definitions of these terms also include multiple bits of information that must be understood in order to be stored in memory before you can use them to understand the summary statement. Thus, this single item includes numerous bits of information. The entire list encompasses several dozen bits of information, all of which must be understood and stored in meaningful networks in your long-term memory in order to be accessible when you take the exam.

Given the limitations of STM, the only way to learn complex material of this kind is to employ a chunking strategy. Building up the underlying knowledge that you must have before you can even begin to chunk the information takes time and effort. Thus, it could take an hour or more just to learn the characteristics of STM. And, remember, your task for the purposes of this example is to learn the entire chapter, not just the characteristics of STM.

Clearly, then, an all-night cram session during which you are tired and anxious as well as engaged in a task that taxes your information-processing system beyond its limits is a poor approach to learning even a single chapter in a college textbook. And how often do you have an exam that covers only one chapter? In most cases, college exams are based on several textbook chapters and, often, extra reading material and lecture notes to boot. That's why sound advice about studying usually begins with an admonition to forestall the need to cram by developing a disciplined and realistic approach to time management.

---

shown three consonants (such as H, G, and L) and then asked to count backward by threes from a given number (738, 735, 732, and so on) (Peterson & Peterson, 1959). After intervals lasting from 3 to 18 seconds, participants were instructed to stop counting backward and recall the three letters. Following a delay of 9 seconds, the participants could recall an average of only one of the three letters. After 18 seconds, there was practically no recall whatsoever. An 18-second distraction had completely erased the three letters from short-term memory.

Short-Term Memory and Working Memory. Allan Baddeley (2009) has suggested that short-term memory is one component of a broader system of temporary storage structures and processes known as working memory. Simply put, working memory is the memory subsystem with which you work on information to understand it, remember it, or use it to solve a problem or to communicate with someone. Baddeley argues that STM is largely speech-based. Consequently, other kinds of information (e.g., visual) that we need to carry out an information-processing task are sent to other components of the working memory system for temporary storage while the STM is engaged in processing verbal information. Research shows that the

working memory The memory subsystem that we use when we try to understand information, remember it, or use it to solve a problem or communicate with someone.

prefrontal cortex is the site that is activated when we are using our working memories (Schreppel et al., 2008).

So, just what kind of "work" goes on in working memory? One of the most important working memory processes is the application of *memory strategies*, such as chunking. Using a memory strategy involves manipulating information in ways that make it easier to remember. We use some memory strategies almost automatically, but others require more effort. For example, sometimes we repeat information over and over again until we can recall it easily. (Remember learning those multiplication tables in elementary school?) This strategy, called maintenance rehearsal, works well for remembering telephone numbers and license plate numbers, particularly when the information is needed for only a short time. However, it isn't the best way to remember more complex information, such as the kind you find in a textbook. For this kind of information, the best strategy is elaborative rehearsal, which involves relating new information to something you already know. For example, suppose you are taking a French class and have to learn the word *escaliers*, which is equivalent to *stairs* in English. You might remember the meaning of *escaliers* by associating it with the English word *escalator*.

maintenance rehearsal Repeating information over and over again until it is no longer needed; may eventually lead to storage of information in long-term memory.

elaborative rehearsal A memory strategy that involves relating new information to something that is already known.

Levels of Processing in Working Memory. Maintenance and elaborative rehearsal were first described by memory researchers Fergus Craik and Robert Lockhart (1972) in the context of their levels-of-processing model of memory (Baddeley, 1998). This model proposed that maintenance rehearsal involves "shallow" processing (encoding based on superficial features of information, such as the sound of a word), whereas elaborative rehearsal involves "deep" processing (encoding based on the meaning of information). Craik and Lockhart hypothesized that deep processing is more likely to lead to long-term retention than is shallow processing. Their hypothesis was tested in classic research by Craik and Tulving (1975). They had participants answer "yes" or "no" to questions asked about words just before the words were flashed to them for $^1/_5$ of a second. The participants had to process the words in three ways: (1) visually (Is the word in capital letters?); (2) acoustically (Does the word rhyme with another particular word?); and (3) semantically (Does the word make sense when used in a particular sentence?). Thus, this test required shallow processing for the first question, deeper processing for the second question, and still deeper processing for the third question. Later retention tests showed that the deeper the level of processing, the higher the accuracy of memory.

levels-of-processing model The memory model that describes maintenance rehearsal as "shallow" processing and elaborative rehearsal as "deep" processing.

Automaticity. The combined effects of memory strategies and repeated retrieval can lead to the development of automaticity for some information. For instance, when you first learned to tell time on an analogical clock, the process of translating the positions of the short and long hands into time-of-day information required a great deal of mental effort. But with practice, you became capable of instantly knowing the time by simply glancing at the clock. When information can be retrieved automatically, working memory space is freed up for other tasks. So, thanks to automaticity, you can look at your clock, realize that you're going to be late for class, and, within microseconds, formulate a plan to get there as quickly as possible.

automaticity The ability to recall information from long-term memory without effort.

Do Some People Have "Super-Memories"? You may have heard stories about people who are capable of seemingly impossible feats of memory, such as memorizing the value of *pi* to thousands of digits. In all such cases research has shown that the people involved used the kinds of strategies you have just read about and those you will see in the *Try It* and the *Apply It* on page 173 (Guenther, 2002). Moreover, many people who display exceptional memory abilities have neurological conditions that have both positive and negative effects on memory functioning. For example,

TRY IT   Organizing for Memory Improvement

Have a pencil and a sheet of paper handy. Read the following list of items out loud and then write down as many as you can remember.

peas	shaving cream	cookies
toilet paper	fish	grapes
carrots	apples	bananas
ice cream	pie	ham
onions	perfume	chicken

If you organize this list, the items are much easier to remember. Now read each category heading and the items listed beneath it. Write down as many items as you can remember.

Desserts	Fruits	Vegetables	Meat	Toilet Articles
pie	bananas	carrots	chicken	perfume
ice cream	apples	onions	fish	shaving cream
cookies	grapes	peas	ham	toilet paper

APPLY IT   Improving Memory

Writing notes, making lists, writing on a calendar, or keeping an appointment book is often more reliable and accurate than trusting to memory (Intons-Peterson & Fournier, 1986). But what if you need information at some unpredictable time, when you do not have external aids handy? Several *mnemonics,* or memory devices, and study strategies have been developed over the years to aid memory.

Mnemonics

Rhymes are a common aid to remembering material that otherwise might be difficult to recall. Perhaps as a child you learned to recite "*i* before *e* except after *c*" when you were trying to spell a word containing that vowel combination.

The *method of loci* is a mnemonic device that can be used when you want to remember a list of items such as a grocery list or when you give a speech or a class report and need to make your points in order without using notes. The word *loci* (pronounced "LOH-sye") is the plural form of *locus,* which means "location" or "place." Select any familiar place—your home, for example—and simply associate the items to be remembered with locations there. Progress in an orderly fashion. For example, visualize the first item or idea you want to remember in its place on the driveway, the second in the garage, the third at the front door, and so on, until you have associated each item you want to remember with a specific location. When you want to recall the items, take an imaginary walk starting at the first place—the first item will pop into your mind. When you think of the second place, the second item will come to mind, and so on.

Another useful mnemonic is to take the first letter of each item to be remembered and form a word, a phrase, or a sentence with those letters. For example, suppose you had to memorize the seven colors of the visible spectrum in their proper order:

Red

Orange

Yellow

Green

Blue

Indigo

Violet

You could make your task easier by using the first letter of each color to form the name Roy G. Biv. Three chunks are easier to remember than seven different items.

Study Strategies

Mnemonics are helpful for some kinds of information, but much of what you need to learn from textbooks calls for more comprehensive strategies. For example, *organization* is a powerful study strategy. Try to organize items you want to remember in alphabetical order, or according to categories, historical sequence, important people, or in any other way that will make retrieval easier for you.

Overlearning is practicing or studying material beyond the point where it can be repeated once without error. It makes material more resistant to forgetting. So, the next time you study for a test, don't stop studying as soon as you think you know the material. Spend another hour or so going over it, using features of your textbook such as margin questions. You will be surprised at how much more you will remember.

Most students have tried cramming for examinations, a strategy that psychologists call *massed practice*. But *spaced practice*, a strategy that breaks studying into several brief sessions with rest periods in between, is generally more effective. Long periods of memorizing make material particularly subject to forgetting and often result in fatigue and poor concentration.

Research shows that you will recall more if you increase the amount of *recitation* in your study. For example, it is better to read a page or a few paragraphs and then recite what you remember of what you have read. Then, continue reading, stop and practice reciting again, and so on.

Finally, memory researcher Henry Roediger and his colleagues have demonstrated in countless studies that there is no better strategy for studying textbook material than *repeated testing* (e.g., Karpicke, Butler, & Roediger, 2009). Roediger's research shows that repeatedly taking quizzes and looking back at the book to figure out why you missed items is a highly effective approach to creating long-term, accessible memories of the kinds of detailed information that students must master to succeed on exams. That's why we keep reminding you to complete the Study Guide, take the practice quizzes in the back of the book, and take the additional quizzes on MyPsychLab. It's a lot of work, but Roediger's studies show that it pays off in better performance on exams.

Watch on **mypsychlab.com**

Kim Peek, the man who was portrayed by Dustin Hoffman in the movie *Rainman*, was capable of rapidly carrying out complex mental calculations and could memorize hundreds of pages of text. Yet, his developmental disability, *autism*, prevented him from forming long-term memories of the types of interpretive information that people who do not have such disabilities use to understand the world. Thus, Peek could memorize a novel but lacked the knowledge he needed to understand it. Research suggests that having a good memory isn't some kind of mysterious gift that some have and others lack. It results from using effective strategies, a practice that anyone can adopt.

6.4 What are the subsystems of long-term memory?

long-term memory (LTM) The memory system with a virtually unlimited capacity that contains vast stores of a person's permanent or relatively permanent memories.

declarative memory The subsystem within long-term memory that stores facts, information, and personal life events that can be brought to mind verbally or in the form of images and then declared or stated; also called explicit memory.

episodic memory (ep-ih-SOD-ik) The type of declarative memory that records events as they have been subjectively experienced.

semantic memory The type of declarative memory that stores general knowledge, or objective facts and information.

nondeclarative memory The subsystem within long-term memory that stores motor skills, habits, and simple classically conditioned responses; also called implicit memory.

Long-Term Memory

If information is processed effectively in short-term memory, it makes its way to long-term memory. Long-term memory (LTM) is a person's vast storehouse of permanent or relatively permanent memories (refer to Figure 6.2). There are no known limits to the storage capacity of this memory system, and long-term memories can persist for years, some of them for a lifetime. Information in long-term memory is usually stored in semantic form, although visual images, sounds, and odors can be stored there as well.

Declarative Memory. Some experts believe that there are two main subsystems within long-term memory. The first, declarative memory (also called *explicit memory*), stores facts, information, and personal life events that can be brought to mind verbally or in the form of images and then declared or stated. It holds information that we intentionally and consciously recollect. There are two types of declarative memory, episodic memory and semantic memory. Episodic memory is the type of declarative memory that records events as they have been subjectively experienced (Wheeler, Stuss, & Tulving, 1997). It is somewhat like a mental diary, a record of the episodes of your life—the people you have known, the places you have seen, and the personal experiences you have had. Using episodic memory, a person might make this statement: "I remember being in Florida on my vacation last spring, lying on the sand, soaking up some rays, and listening to the sound of the waves rushing to the shore." Semantic memory, the other type of declarative memory, is memory for general knowledge, or objective facts and information. Semantic memory is involved when a person recalls that Florida is bounded by the Atlantic Ocean on the east and the Gulf of Mexico on the west. It is not necessary to have ever visited Florida to know these facts. Consequently, semantic memory is more like an encyclopedia or a dictionary than a personal diary.

Memory researcher Endel Tulving (1995) points out that the two types of declarative memory do not function independently. For instance, your memory of lying on a beach in Florida (episodic) relies on your understanding of what a beach is (semantic). Likewise, the experience of actually being there (episodic) undoubtedly enhanced your general knowledge of the state (semantic).

Nondeclarative Memory. The second kind of memory, called nondeclarative memory (also called *implicit memory*), is the subsystem within long-term memory that stores procedures, motor skills, habits, and simple classically conditioned responses (Squire et al., 1993). Motor skills are acquired through repetitive practice and include such things as eating with a fork, riding a bicycle, or driving a car. Although acquired slowly, once learned, these skills become habit, are quite reliable, and can be carried out with little or no conscious effort. For example, you probably use the keyboard on a computer without consciously being able to name the keys in each row from left to right. Figure 6.3 shows the two subsystems of long-term memory.

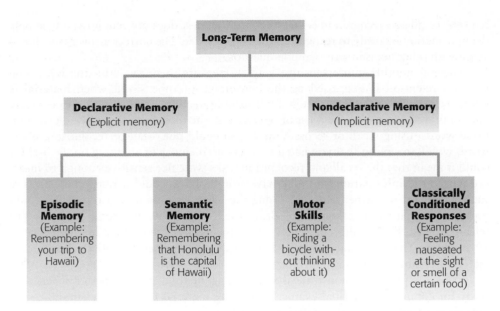

Long-Term Memory

Declarative Memory
(Explicit memory)

Nondeclarative Memory
(Implicit memory)

Episodic Memory
(Example: Remembering your trip to Hawaii)

Semantic Memory
(Example: Remembering that Honolulu is the capital of Hawaii)

Motor Skills
(Example: Riding a bicycle without thinking about it)

Classically Conditioned Responses
(Example: Feeling nauseated at the sight or smell of a certain food)

FIGURE 6.3 Subsystems of Long-Term Memory
Declarative memory can be divided into two subsystems: episodic memory, which stores memories of personally experienced events, and semantic memory, which stores facts and information. Nondeclarative memory consists of motor skills acquired through repetitive practice and simple classically conditioned responses.

A Closer Look at Retrieval

Now that you have an idea of how information flows through the information-processing system, we will turn to a closer examination of the process of extracting information from long-term memory. Wilder Penfield (1969), a Canadian neurosurgeon, proposed an interesting metaphor when he likened memory to a recording, implying that retrieval involves pushing the play button on a mental memory recorder. As you will see, the process is a bit more complex than Penfield's metaphor suggests.

Measuring Retrieval ▷

As we noted earlier, *retrieval* is the process of bringing information that has been encoded and stored to mind. In general, memory researchers use three types of tasks to measure retrieval. In recall, a person must produce required information simply by searching memory. Trying to remember someone's name, the items on a shopping list, or the words of a speech or a poem is a recall task. Which of the following test questions do you think is easier?

What are the three basic memory processes?

Which of the following is *not* one of the three basic memory processes?

a. retrieval   **b.** encoding   **c.** relearning   **d.** storage

Most people think that the second question is easier because it requires only recognition, whereas the first requires recall.

A recall task may be made a little easier if cues are provided to jog memory. A retrieval cue is any stimulus or bit of information that aids in retrieving a particular memory. Think about how you might respond to these two test questions:

What are the four basic memory processes?

The four processes involved in memory are e_____, s_____, c_____, and r_____.

Both questions require you to recall information. However, most students would find the second question easier to answer because it includes four retrieval cues.

Recognition is exactly what the name implies. A person simply recognizes something as familiar—a face, a name, a taste, a melody. Multiple-choice, matching, and true/false questions are examples of test items based on recognition. The main difference

recall A memory task in which a person must produce required information by searching memory.

retrieval cue Any stimulus or bit of information that aids in retrieving particular information from long-term memory.

recognition A memory task in which a person must simply identify material as familiar or as having been encountered before.

6.5 What are the differences among the recall, recognition, and relearning methods of measuring retrieval?

▲ Are you better at remembering faces than names? Have you ever wondered why? It's because the task involves recognition rather than recall. You must recall the name but merely recognize the face.

relearning method A measure of memory in which retention is expressed as the percentage of time saved when material is relearned compared with the time required to learn the material originally.

between recall and recognition is that a recognition task does not require you to supply the information but only to recognize it when you see it. The correct answer is included along with other items in a recognition question.

There is another, more sensitive way to measure memory. With the relearning method, retention is expressed as the percentage of time saved when material is relearned relative to the time required to learn the material originally. Suppose it took you 40 minutes to memorize a list of words, and one month later you were tested on those words, using recall or recognition. If you could not recall or recognize a single word, would this mean that you had absolutely no memory of anything on the list? Or could it mean that the recall and recognition tasks were not sensitive enough to measure what little information you may have stored? How could a researcher measure such a remnant of former learning? Using the relearning method, a researcher could time how long it would take you to relearn the list of words. If it took 20 minutes to relearn the list, this would represent a 50% savings over the original learning time of 40 minutes. The percentage of time saved—the *savings score*—reflects how much material remains in long-term memory.

College students demonstrate the relearning method each semester when they study for comprehensive final exams. Relearning material for a final exam takes less time than it took to learn the material originally.

6.6 How do the serial position, context, and state-dependent memory effects influence retrieval?

Influences on Retrieval

As you have probably learned from everyday experience, retrieval sometimes happens effectively and efficiently. But there are also times when retrieval is more elusive. Studies show that a number of factors influence the process.

The Serial Position Effect. What would happen if you were introduced to a dozen people at a party? You would most likely recall the names of the first few people you met and the last one or two, but forget many of the names in the middle. The reason is the serial position effect—the finding that, for information learned in a sequence, recall is better for items at the beginning and the end than for items in the middle of the sequence.

serial position effect The finding that, for information learned in a sequence, recall is better for the beginning and ending items than for the middle items in the sequence.

primacy effect The tendency to recall the first items in a sequence more readily than the middle items.

recency effect The tendency to recall the last items in a sequence more readily than those in the middle.

Information at the beginning of a sequence is subject to the primacy effect—the tendency to recall the first items in a sequence more readily than the middle items. Such information is likely to be recalled because it already has been placed in long-term memory. Information at the end of a sequence is subject to the recency effect—the tendency to recall the last items in a sequence more readily than those in the middle. This information has an even higher probability of being recalled because it is still in short-term memory. The poorer recall of information in the middle of a sequence occurs because that information is no longer in short-term memory and has not yet been placed in long-term memory. The serial position effect lends strong support to the notion of separate systems for short-term and long-term memory (Postman & Phillips, 1965). ✲—Explore on mypsychlab.com

✲—Explore the Concept *Retrieval of Long-Term Memories* on mypsychlab.com

context effect The tendency to encode elements of the physical setting in which information is learned along with memory of the information itself.

The Context Effect. Have you ever stood in your living room and thought of something you needed from your bedroom, only to forget what it was when you got there? Did the item come to mind again when you returned to the living room? Tulving and Thompson (1973) suggest that many elements of the physical setting in which a person learns information are encoded along with the information and become part of the memory, a process called the context effect. If part or all of the original context is reinstated, it may serve as a retrieval cue. That is why returning to the living room elicits the memory of the object you intended to get from the bedroom. In fact, just visualizing yourself in the living room might do the trick (Smith, Glenberg, & Bjork, 1978). (*Hint:* Next time you're taking a test and having difficulty recalling something, try visualizing yourself in the room where you studied.)

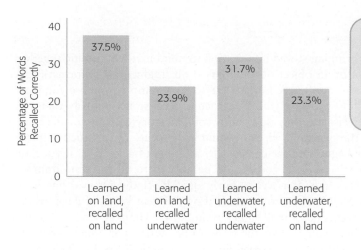

According to research on context and memory, is it a good idea to review your notes while you're waiting for an exam to begin? Why or why not?

FIGURE 6.4 **The Context Effect**

Godden and Baddeley (1975) conducted one of the early studies of context and memory with members of a university diving club. Participants memorized a list of words when they were either 10 feet underwater or on land. They were later tested for recall of the words in the same or a different environment. Words learned underwater were best recalled underwater, and words learned on land were best recalled on land. In fact, when the divers learned and recalled the words in the same context, their scores were 47% higher than when the two contexts were different (see Figure 6.4).

Odors can also supply powerful and enduring retrieval cues for memory. In one study, researchers introduced vanilla scent into a room in which participants were learning a memory-for-location task (Schwab & Wolf, 2009). When the experimenters tested participants on the task the next day, those who were tested in a vanilla-scented room outperformed those who were tested in an unscented setting.

The State-Dependent Memory Effect. The emotional state that a person was in when she formed a memory affects her ability to recall it. Psychologists call this the state-dependent memory effect. The effect appears to be greater for episodic than for semantic memories (Eysenck & Keane, 2010). It is also stronger when positive emotions are involved. However, animal studies suggest that anxiety is one negative emotion for which state-dependent memory effects are pronounced (Packard, 2009).

Research with human participants has also revealed an association between anxiety and the state-dependent memory effect. For example, when researchers exposed college students to spiders and/or snakes while they were learning lists of words (presumably an anxiety-inducing experience!), the students recalled more words when the creatures were also present during tests of recall (Lang et al., 2001).

state-dependent memory effect The tendency to recall information better if one is in the same pharmacological or psychological state as when the information was encoded.

Remembering as Reconstruction

Memory researcher Henry Roediger (1980) has pointed out that the Atkinson-Shiffrin model and others like it seem to suggest that getting information out of memory requires little more than opening the door to a mental closet and pulling out a needed item. However, quite often, the process of remembering more closely resembles creating a multicolored, multitextured work of art than searching a mental closet (Loftus & Loftus, 1980). Thus, in addition to retrieval, the act of remembering often includes a creative element.

6.7 What does "Memory is reconstructive" mean?

reconstruction An account of an event that has been pieced together from a few highlights.

schemas Frameworks of knowledge and assumptions that we have about people, objects, and events.

The Process of Reconstruction

In some cases, the act of bringing stored information to mind involves piecing together a plausible representation of an object or event based on fragmentary information, a process called reconstruction (Loftus & Loftus, 1980). For example, suppose you were asked to recall the last time you saw your best friend. Because it's unlikely that you encoded the date of your last meeting along with your memory of it, you can't truly "retrieve" an answer to the question. So, you would have to use reconstructive memory. You would probably begin with the current day and think backwards. If you saw your friend within the last few days, you should be able to recall the time frame—yesterday, a couple of days ago, last week—fairly quickly. If the interval has been longer, your backward search is likely to be marked by different kinds of days (weekdays, weekends), special events (a football game), or holidays (Thanksgiving) that serve as reference points that help you narrow the time frame. When you finally arrive at your best judgment, you are likely to say something like "a couple of weeks ago," a time frame that may be very close to or very far from the actual date of your last meeting.

Pioneering memory researcher Sir Frederick Bartlett (1886–1969) suggested that reconstructive memory processes of this kind employ schemas, frameworks of knowledge and assumptions that we have about people, objects, and events. Schemas are helpful to memory because they provide us with meaningful ways of chunking individual bits of information, thereby increasing the efficiency of working memory. The *Think About It* activity at the beginning of the chapter shows how schemas work. All of the words in the activity are related to the "sleep" schema; that is, they represent the typical objects, behaviors, and experiences that we associate with sleep (e.g., bed, yawn, dream). As a result, our memory systems use the sleep schema to encode and store the list of words. The upside of schema-based processing in this case is that it makes the words easier to remember. The downside is that it causes most of us to falsely recall that the word "sleep" appeared on the list. Thus, there are both advantages and disadvantages to reconstructive memory processes.

Schema-based processing is even more evident when we process more complex types of information. For instance, suppose you read the headline, "Dog Saves Boy from Drowning." What facts would you expect to be included in the story? You might expect to read about where the incident took place; perhaps it happened at a beach or in a neighborhood swimming pool. But you would be unlikely to expect to read about a canine rescue that occurred in a bathtub. Why?—because schemas are based on situational averages. Drownings occur most often in bodies of water in which people swim. Thus, the schema evoked by the headline would cause you to picture the incident taking place in the setting that would be most likely.

Once invoked, schemas focus our attention on the essential elements in new information and increase the chances that we will store them in long-term memory. At the same time, schema-based processing causes us to ignore unimportant details. Thus, in the "Dog Saves Boy ..." story, the fact that the incident happened in a lake rather than a swimming pool would be an essential element, but the name of the lake would not be. Consequently, you would probably remember that the episode took place in a lake but fail to remember its name. If, while recounting the story at a later time, you were asked about the name of the lake, you would reconstruct your memory of it by considering plausible alternatives, a process that is somewhat like entering terms in an Internet search engine such as Google. The possible names that you generated would be based on your knowledge of lakes or on some feature of the name that you recall from the story, such as that it started with W. The name you finally settle on, if any, as a result of using these reconstructive strategies may or may not be accurate, but it will be plausible. You won't mistakenly use the name of a river or an ocean.

As you can see, using schemas to reconstruct memories can lead to inaccuracies. Bartlett (1932) studied the distorting effects of reconstruction by giving participants stories to read and asking them to reproduce the stories after varying amounts of time. Accurate reports were rare. Participants made the stories shorter and substituted familiar objects for the unusual ones that the stories described. These errors increased over time, and participants were unable to distinguish between the parts of their reproduced stories that they actually remembered from those that they had created.

Source, Flashbulb, and Autobiographical Memories

6.8 What have researchers learned about source, flashbulb, and autobiographical memories?

You might be thinking that reconstructive memory processes should be avoided because of their potential for distorting our recollections. Perhaps we should make an effort to commit every detail of our experiences to memory. Following this practice might enable us to reduce the chances of generating inaccurate memories, but we would lose a great deal of efficiency in the process. Thus, reconstructive memory processes are common in everyday life. Moreover, there are some types of memories that are best understood as a function of reconstructive processes.

Source Memory. A source memory is a recollection of the circumstances in which you formed a memory. Most of our memories do not include source information. For example, you know that Paris is the capital of France, but you probably have no idea exactly when or how you acquired the information. Thus, when we need to know the source of a memory, we usually must reconstruct it (Johnson, Hashtroudi, & Lindsay, 1993). For instance, suppose you see a new brand of shampoo on a store shelf, recognize it as one you have heard of, but are unable to remember how you learned about it. If you are really curious about the source, you could use your "ways-of-learning-about-products" schemas to search your memory for the most plausible source. You would probably consider television commercials, pop-up ads, and so on. And, as is true of all schema-based processing, the source you come up with might not be accurate.

In order to encode source information along with a memory, you must engage in source monitoring, the practice of intentionally keeping track of the sources of incoming information. Source monitoring is particularly important when you are working on a research paper. This is so because the memory system tends to focus on the meaning of information rather than its source, especially when forming semantic memories. Thus, when you read a passage of text in an article or other reference and store it in your semantic memory for future use, reconstructive memory processes may lead you to mistakenly believe that you thought of it yourself when you are writing your paper (a phenomenon called *cryptomnesia*). As a result, you may, at best, omit a needed citation, or, at worst, unknowingly commit plagiarism (Carroll & Perfect, 2002). Fortunately, research shows that, when we consciously practice source monitoring, we can protect our memories from distortions of this kind.

Flashbulb Memories. Do you remember how you learned about the terrorist attacks of September 11, 2001? Memories for shocking, emotion-provoking events that include information about the source from which the information was acquired are called flashbulb memories. This term reflects early researchers' hypothesis (e.g., Brown & Kulik, 1977) that the shocking nature of such events works somewhat like a camera flash that freezes a moment in time. They believed that flashbulb memories were photographic, highly detailed, and resistant to change. However, since the early 1990s, psychologists have thought of flashbulb memory as a subcategory of source memory. Studies showing that the inclusion of source information is the primary characteristic that distinguishes flashbulb from other types of memories were responsible for this shift (Brewer, 1992).

Research has also shown that flashbulb memories are reconstructive in nature (Curci, 2009). That is, we don't pull up a mental snapshot when we recall them. Instead, we rebuild flashbulb memories piece by piece. As a result, like other kinds of reconstructed recollections, flashbulb memories change over time. Results such as those of researcher William Hirst and his colleagues illustrate this pattern of findings (Hirst et al., 2009). Hirst and his team questioned participants about their memories of September 11 a few days after the event, one year later, and three years later. At all

source memory A recollection of the circumstances in which you formed a memory.

source monitoring Intentionally keeping track of the sources of incoming information.

flashbulb memories Memories for shocking, emotion-provoking events that include information about the source from which the information was acquired.

▲ Eyewitnesses to the aftermath of the terrorist attacks on the World Trade Center almost certainly formed flashbulb memories of the horrific events they witnessed. Do you remember where you were and what you were doing when you heard the news on September 11, 2001?

three points, the researchers asked flashbulb/source memory questions, such as "How did you hear about the attacks?" along with event memory questions, such as "How many planes were involved?" They found that over the three-year period, participants forgot source and event details at about the same rate. Nevertheless, participants expressed far more confidence in their flashbulb memories than they did in their event memories. Research findings on the unshakable faith that participants have in the accuracy of their flashbulb memories are so consistent that most researchers now agree that a high degree of confidence (justified or not) in their accuracy is a defining feature of flashbulb memories (Talarico & Rubin, 2009).

Autobiographical Memories. Autobiographical memories are recollections that a person includes in an account of his or her own life (Markowitsch, Welzer, & Emmans, 2010). They are reconstructive in nature and include factual, emotional, and interpretive information. For example, an autobiographical memory of your first day at college would include facts such as which classes you attended, images such as the classroom where you heard your psychology professor's first lecture of the term, and emotions such as the anxiety you felt about finding your way around campus. Your interpretation of the day might be reflected in the content of an e-mail you sent to your best friend that evening in which you summarized the events of the day and your feelings of relief that your first day was over. As a result, the text of the e-mail is likely to be linked to your other memories of the day in your long-term memory and become the outline for the "first-day-of-college-story" that you retell every time the topic comes up in conversation. Years later, you might pass on the same story to your children when they go to college. (Failure to engage in source monitoring would probably cause you to forget that the story began as an e-mail to a friend, by the way.)

Interestingly, research has shown that autobiographical memories are particularly subject to positive bias, the tendency for pleasant autobiographical memories to be more easily recalled than unpleasant ones and memories of unpleasant events to become more emotionally positive over time (Rubin, Boals, & Klein, 2010; Wood & Conway, 2006). In one study of positive bias that examined college students' memories of their high school grades, nearly all of the participants remembered their As accurately, but only 29% remembered their Ds (Bahrick, Hall, & Berger, 1996). Researchers speculate that positive bias results when our current need for emotional well-being serves as a schema that we use to reconstruct unpleasant memories (Kennedy, Mather, & Carstensen, 2004).

Influences on Reconstructive Memory

You learned earlier that some features of information, such as the headlines of news stories, influence reconstructive memory processes by invoking schemas. Like other information we acquire through experience, schemas are stored in long-term memory. Thus, research on schema-based processing shows that prior knowledge contributes to reconstructive memory processes. Two important sources of prior knowledge are *expertise* and *culture*.

Expertise. If you possess an extensive amount of relevant background knowledge, or expertise, for a reconstructive memory task, your performance on the task will exceed that of others who are less knowledgeable. In classic research, Chase and Simon (1973) presented chess champions and volunteers who had little or no experience with the game with several arrays of pieces on chess boards. Some of the arrays were plausible within the rules of the game, but others were random. After participants viewed each array for a few seconds, the researchers removed the pieces from the board and asked the participants to reproduce the configuration they had just seen. Chase and Simon found that the champions were much better than the non-champions at reproducing the plausible configurations both immediately and after a brief delay. That is, the experts introduced fewer reconstructive distortions into the

---

autobiographical memories Recollections that a person includes in an account of the events of his or her own life.

positive bias The tendency for pleasant autobiographical memories to be more easily recalled than unpleasant ones and memories of unpleasant events to become more emotionally positive over time.

6.9 How do expertise and culture influence reconstructive memory?

expertise An extensive amount of background knowledge that is relevant to a reconstructive memory task.

reproduction task than the nonexperts did. By contrast, there were no group differences with regard to the random arrangements. Chase and Simon concluded that the expertise the chess champions had acquired over many years of playing the game enabled them to integrate the individual pieces into meaningful chunks, rendering their reconstructive memories for the arrays more efficient and more accurate than those of the nonchampions.

Researchers have examined the impact of expertise on reconstructive memory in knowledge domains ranging from baseball to waiting tables. The results of all of these studies are consistent with the classic findings of Chase and Simon. That is, people who know a lot about baseball can reconstruct the events of a baseball game more accurately than nonexperts can (Ricks & Wiley, 2009). Similarly, professional restaurant servers can faithfully reconstruct complicated food orders from memory, while nonservers perform poorly on the task (Bekinschtein, Cardozo, & Manes, 2008). Researchers attribute the effects of expertise on reconstructive memory to increased efficiency in working memory (Ricks & Wiley, 2009). Thus, having a lot of relevant knowledge for a reconstructive memory task enables you to take in more information, encode it more efficiently, and apply it more accurately than you can to tasks for which you do not possess much relevant knowledge.

Culture. The effects of expertise are evident in research examining cultural influences on reconstructive memory as well. In one classic study, Sir Frederick Bartlett (1932) described the amazing ability of the Swazi people of Africa to remember the slight differences in individual characteristics of their cows. One Swazi herdsman, Bartlett claimed, could remember details of every cow he had tended the year before. Such a feat is less surprising when you consider that the key component of traditional Swazi culture is the herds of cattle the people tend and depend on for their living. Do the Swazi people have super memory powers? Bartlett asked young Swazi men and young European men to recall a message consisting of 25 words. In this case, the Swazi had no better recall ability than the Europeans.

The effects of cultural schemas on reconstructive memory are also evident in studies showing that people more easily remember stories set in their own cultures than those set in others, just as they more easily recognize photographs of people of their own ethnic group than they do those of others (Corenblum & Meissner, 2006). In one of the first of these studies, researchers told women in the United States and Aboriginal women in Australia a story about a sick child (Steffensen & Calker, 1982). Participants were randomly assigned to groups for which story outcomes were varied. In one version, the girl got well after being treated by a physician. In the other, a traditional native healer was called in to help the girl. Aboriginal participants better recalled the story with the native healer, while the American women were more accurate in their recall of the story in which a physician treated the girl. Most likely, these results reflect the influence of culturally based schemas. Aboriginal participants' schemas led them to expect a story about a sick child to include a native healer, and the story that fit with these expectations was easier for them to understand and remember. Just the opposite was true for the Western participants.

In addition, cultural values prompt oral historians to engage in source monitoring as they recount important information, thereby protecting information that must be passed on verbatim (i.e., word-for-word) from the potentially distorting effects of reconstructive memory. Source monitoring provides such protection by enabling oral historians to distinguish the original material they learned from older group members from their own interpretive thoughts about the material and from ideas proposed by others.

For example, among many tribal peoples in Africa, the history of the tribe is preserved orally by specialists, who

▲ In many traditional cultures, elders are oral historians, remembering and passing on the details of tribal traditions and myths as well as genealogical data.

must be able to encode, store, and retrieve huge volumes of historical data (D'Azevedo, 1982). Elders of the Iatmul people of New Guinea are also said to have committed to memory the lines of descent for the various clans of their people, stretching back for many generations (Bateson, 1982). The unerring memory of the elders for the kinship patterns of their people is used to resolve disputed property claims (Mistry & Rogoff, 1994).

Barbara Rogoff, an expert in cultural psychology, maintains that such phenomenal memory feats are best explained and understood in their cultural context (Rogoff & Mistry, 1985). The tribal elders perform their impressive memory feats because the information is an integral and critically important part of the culture in which they live. Most likely, their ability to remember nonmeaningful information would be no better than your own.

Forgetting

forgetting The inability to bring to mind information that was previously remembered.

As you have seen, both retrieval and reconstruction are associated with memory failure to some degree. Forgetting, the inability to bring to mind information that was previously remembered, represents another kind of memory failure. Pioneering researcher Hermann Ebbinghaus (1850–1909) studied forgetting extensively. Since Ebbinghaus's time, memory researchers have proposed a number of different explanations of forgetting.

6.10 What did Ebbinghaus discover about forgetting?

Ebbinghaus and the Curve of Forgetting

Hermann Ebbinghaus (1850–1909) conducted the first experimental studies on learning and memory. He performed his studies on memory using 2,300 nonsense syllables as his material and himself as the only participant (1885/1964). He carried out all his experiments at about the same time of day in the same surroundings, eliminating all possible distractions. Ebbinghaus memorized lists of nonsense syllables (strings of letters such as LEJ and XIZ) by repeating them over and over at a constant rate of 2.5 syllables per second, marking time with a metronome or a ticking watch. He repeated a list until he could recall it twice without error, a measure he called *mastery*.

Ebbinghaus recorded the amount of time or the number of trials it took to memorize his lists to mastery. Then, after different periods of time had passed and forgetting had occurred, he recorded the amount of time or number of trials needed to relearn the same list to mastery. Ebbinghaus compared the time or number of trials required for relearning with that for original learning and then computed the percentage of time saved. This savings score represented the percentage of the original learning that remained in memory.

curve of forgetting The pattern of forgetting discovered by Ebbinghaus, which shows that forgetting tapers off after a period of rapid information loss that immediately follows learning.

Ebbinghaus learned and relearned more than 1,200 lists of nonsense syllables to discover how rapidly forgetting occurs. Figure 6.5 shows his famous curve of forgetting, which consists of savings scores at various time intervals after the original learning. The curve of forgetting shows that the largest amount of forgetting occurs very quickly, after which forgetting tapers off. Of the information Ebbinghaus retained after a day or two, very little more would be forgotten even a month later. But, remember, this curve of forgetting applies to nonsense syllables. Meaningful material is usually forgotten more slowly, as is material that has been carefully encoded, deeply processed, and frequently rehearsed.

What Ebbinghaus learned about the rate of forgetting is relevant for everyone. Do you, like most students, cram before a big exam? If so, don't assume that everything you memorize on Monday can be held intact until Tuesday. So much forgetting occurs within the first 24 hours that it is wise to spend at least some time reviewing the material on the day of the test. The less meaningful the material is to you, the more you will forget and the more necessary a review is. Recall from Chapter 4 that the quantity and quality of sleep you get between studying and taking the test also influences how much you will remember.

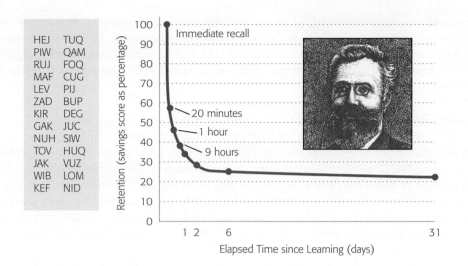

FIGURE 6.5 Ebbinghaus's Curve of Forgetting
After memorizing lists of nonsense syllables similar to those at left, Ebbinghaus measured his retention after varying intervals of time using the relearning method. Forgetting was most rapid at first, as shown by his retention of only 58% after 20 minutes and 44% after 1 hour. Then, the rate of forgetting tapered off, with a retention of 34% after 1 day, 25% after 6 days, and 21% after 31 days.
Source: Data from Ebbinghaus (1885/1964, 1913).

Why Do We Forget?   ▶

6.11 Why do we forget?

Why do we fail to remember, even when we put forth a lot of effort aimed at remembering? Psychologists have proposed several explanations. Studies examining these proposals have led researchers to conclude that there are several different causes for forgetting.

Encoding Failure. The inability to remember is sometimes a result of encoding failure—the information was never put into long-term memory in the first place. Of the many things we encounter every day, it is surprising how little we actually encode. Can you recall accurately, or even recognize, something you have seen thousands of times before? Read the *Try It* below to find out.

In your lifetime, you have seen thousands of pennies, but unless you are a coin collector, you probably have not encoded the details of a penny's appearance. If you did poorly on the *Try It*, you have plenty of company. After studying a large group of participants, Nickerson and Adams (1979) reported that few people could reproduce a penny from recall. In fact, only a handful of participants could even recognize an accurate drawing of a penny when it was presented along with incorrect drawings. (The correct penny is the one labeled A in the *Try It*.)

encoding failure A cause of forgetting that occurs when information was never put into long-term memory.

Decay. Decay theory, which is probably the oldest theory of forgetting, assumes that memories, if not used, fade with time and ultimately disappear entirely. The word *decay* implies a physiological change in the neurons that recorded the experience. According to this theory, the neuronal record may decay or fade within seconds, days, or even much longer periods of time. While decay, or the fading of memories, is

decay theory The oldest theory of forgetting, which holds that memories, if not used, fade with time and ultimately disappear altogether.

TRY IT   A Penny for your Thoughts

On a sheet of paper, draw a sketch of a U.S. penny from memory using recall. In your drawing, show the direction in which President Lincoln's image is facing and the location of the date and include all the words on the heads side of the penny. Or try the easier recognition task and see if you can recognize the real penny in the drawings. (From Nickerson & Adams, 1979.)

Tip: The next time someone you know claims to have "photographic" memory, use this *Try It* to put him or her to the test.

probably a cause of forgetting in sensory and short-term memory, there does not appear to be a gradual, inevitable decay of long-term memories. In one study, Harry Bahrick and others (1975) found that after 35 years, participants could recognize 90% of their high school classmates' names and photographs, the same percentage as for recent graduates.

interference A cause of forgetting that occurs because information or associations stored either before or after a given memory hinder the ability to remember it.

Interference. A major cause of forgetting that affects people every day is interference, when information stored either before or after a given memory can hinder the ability to remember it. For example, a well-known experiment in psychology called the *Stroop test* requires research participants to memorize color words that are shown in colored type (see Figure 6.6). As you might guess, remembering the word *red* is much easier when it is written in red than when it is written in yellow. The colors of the words interfere with retrieval of their meanings because the colors prime, or prompt, participants to retrieve the names of the colors rather than the meanings of the words. ⊙→⌐Simulate on **mypsychlab.com**

⊙→⌐**Simulate** the **Experiment** *The Stroop Effect* on **mypsychlab.com**

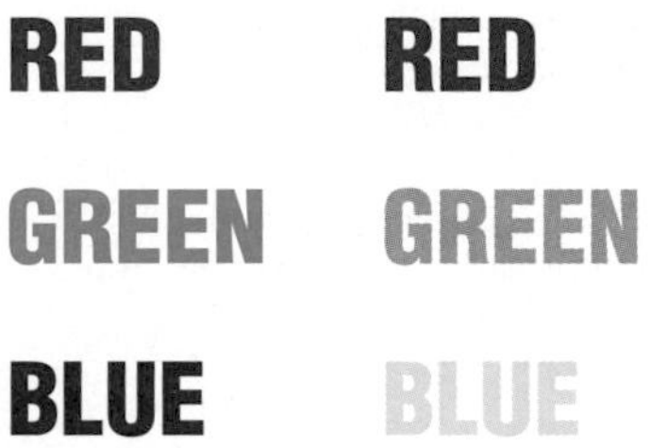

Whenever you try to recall any given memory, two types of interference can hinder the effort. Information or associations stored either *before* or *after* a given memory can interfere with the ability to remember it (see Figure 6.7). Also, the more similar the interfering associations are to the information a person is trying to recall, the more difficult it is to recall the information (Underwood, 1964).

Proactive interference occurs when information or experiences already stored in long-term memory hinder the ability to remember newer information (Underwood, 1957). For example, Laura's romance with her new boyfriend, Todd, got off to a bad start when she accidentally called him "Dave," her former boyfriend's name. One explanation for proactive interference is the competition between old and new responses (Bower, Thompson-Schill, & Tulving, 1994).

Retroactive interference happens when new learning interferes with the ability to remember previously learned information. The more similar the new material is to that learned earlier, the more interference there is. For example, when you take a psychology class, it may interfere with your ability to remember what you learned in your sociology class, especially with regard to theories (e.g., psychoanalysis) that are shared by the two disciplines but applied and interpreted differently. However, research shows that the effects of retroactive interference are often temporary (Lustig, Konkel, & Jacoby, 2004). In fact, after some time has passed, the old information may be better remembered than the information that was learned more recently. As a consequence, what a student learned in a previous sociology course may appear to fade

RED　**RED**

GREEN　**GREEN**

BLUE　**BLUE**

FIGURE 6.6 The Stroop Test
Which list of words do you think would be easier to remember?

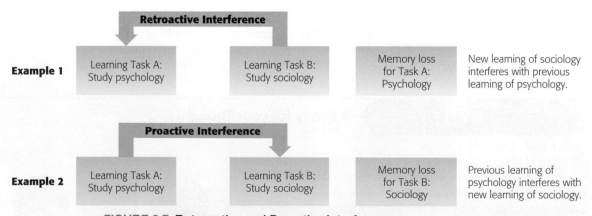

FIGURE 6.7 Retroactive and Proactive Interference
As shown in Example 1, retroactive interference occurs when new learning hinders the ability to recall information learned previously. As shown in Example 2, proactive interference occurs when prior learning hinders new learning.

when she encounters similar information presented in a somewhat different light in a psychology course. In the long run, however, her sociology knowledge may outlast what she learned in psychology.

Consolidation Failure. *Consolidation* is the physiological process by which encoded information is stored in memory. Consolidation failure can result from anything that disrupts the consolidation process, typically an event that causes a person to lose consciousness—a car accident, a blow to the head, an epileptic seizure, or an electroconvulsive shock treatment given for severe depression. Moreover, as you learned in Chapter 4, REM sleep is critical to memory consolidation (Walker & Stickgold, 2006). As a result, when you don't get enough REM sleep, the information you acquired during the day may be lost due to consolidation failure (Fogel, Smith, & Beninger, 2010).

consolidation failure Any disruption in the consolidation process that prevents a long-term memory from forming.

Motivated Forgetting. We have discussed ways to avoid forgetting, but there are occasions when people may want to avoid remembering—times when they want to forget. Victims of rape or physical abuse, war veterans, and survivors of airplane crashes or earthquakes all have had terrifying experiences that may haunt them for years. These victims are certainly motivated to forget their traumatic experiences, but even people who have not experienced any trauma use motivated forgetting to protect themselves from experiences that are painful, frightening, or otherwise unpleasant. With one form of motivated forgetting, *suppression,* a person makes a conscious, active attempt to put a painful, disturbing, anxiety- or guilt-provoking memory out of mind, but the person is still aware that the painful event occurred. With another type of motivated forgetting, *repression,* unpleasant memories are literally removed from consciousness, and the person is no longer aware that the unpleasant event ever occurred (Freud, 1922).

motivated forgetting Forgetting through suppression or repression in an effort to protect oneself from material that is painful, frightening, or otherwise unpleasant.

Prospective Forgetting. Prospective forgetting is not remembering to carry out some intended action (e.g., forgetting to go to your dentist appointment). People are most likely to forget to do the things they view as unimportant, unpleasant, or burdensome. They are less likely to forget things that are pleasurable or important to them (Winograd, 1988). However, as you probably know, prospective forgetting isn't always motivated by a desire to avoid something. Have you ever arrived home and suddenly remembered that you had intended to go to the bank to deposit your paycheck? If so, then you have personally experienced prospective forgetting.

prospective forgetting Not remembering to carry out some intended action.

Retrieval Failure. How many times have you had this experience? While taking a test, you can't remember the answer to a question that you are sure you know. Often, people are certain they know something but are not able to retrieve the information when they need it. This type of forgetting is called retrieval failure. A common experience with retrieval failure is known as the tip-of-the-tongue (TOT) phenomenon (Brown & McNeil, 1966). You have surely experienced trying to recall a name, a word, or some other bit of information, knowing that you knew it but are not able to come up with it. You were on the verge of recalling the word or name, perhaps aware of the number of syllables and the beginning or ending letter. It was on the tip of your tongue, but it just wouldn't quite come out.

retrieval failure Not remembering something one is certain of knowing.

tip-of-the-tongue (TOT) phenomenon The experience of knowing that a particular piece of information has been learned but being unable to retrieve it.

The tip-of-the-tongue phenomenon is one of the most thoroughly researched of all of our everyday memory experiences (Gollan & Brown, 2006). A similar experience, *tip-of-the-fingers phenomenon (TOF),* occurs in individuals who use sign language to communicate. In both speakers and signers, proper names are the subject of this kind of retrieval failure more often than other kinds of words (Thompson, Emmorey, & Gollan, 2005). Regardless of the object of a TOT event, research suggests that the best strategy for overcoming this kind of retrieval failure is to divert

Forgetting

TYPE OF FORGETTING	DESCRIPTION	EXAMPLE
Encoding failure	Information was never stored in memory	Failing to remember details of everyday objective such as coins
Decay	Unused information fades over time	Information in sensory memory disappears if not moved on to short-term memory
Interference	One piece of information displaces another	A person recalls her old phone number when she intends to recall her new one
Consolidation failure	Disruption of consolidation prevents information from being stored in long-term memory	A blow to the head causes a person to forget everything that happened in the minutes immediately preceding the blow
Motivated forgetting	Loss of information that is emotionally unpleasant	A soldier forgets about witnessing the combat-related death of his best friend
Prospective forgetting	Forgetting to carry out an intended action	A student forgets to transfer his laundry from the washer to the dryer until he discovers the washer full of wet clothes the next day
Retrieval failure	Forgetting something you are sure that you know	Remembering the answer to a test question after you turn in the exam

your attention from it for a brief period and return to your retrieval efforts at a later time (Choi & Smith, 2005). This finding provides support for one frequently heard test-taking tip: Skip items for which answers do not immediately come to mind and return to them after you have answered all of the questions that you are sure you know the answers to.

Biology and Memory

Obviously, a person's vast store of memories must exist physically somewhere in the brain. Neuronal processes are also involved in the storage of information in the brain. Trauma and disorders that affect brain structures, neuronal health, or both can seriously impair memory function.

6.12 What brain structures are associated with memory?

The Hippocampus and Hippocampal Region

Researchers continue to identify specific locations in the brain that mediate functions and processes in memory. One important source of information comes from people who have experienced memory loss resulting from damage to specific brain areas. One especially significant case is that of H. M., a man who suffered from such severe epilepsy that, out of desperation, he agreed to a radical surgical procedure. The surgeon removed the part of the brain believed to be causing H. M.'s seizures—the medial portions of both temporal lobes, containing the amygdala and the hippocampal region, which includes the hippocampus itself and the underlying cortical areas. It was 1953, and H. M. was 27 years old.

After his surgery, H. M. remained intelligent and psychologically stable, and his seizures were drastically reduced. But unfortunately, the tissue cut from H. M.'s brain housed more than the site of his seizures. It also contained his ability to use working memory to store new information in long-term memory. Although the capacity of his short-term memory remained the same and he remembered life events that were stored before the operation, H. M. was unable to remember a single event that occurred after the surgery. And when H. M. passed away in 2008 at the age of 82, as far as his conscious long-term memory was concerned, it was still 1953 and he was still 27 years old.

hippocampal region A part of the limbic system, which includes the hippocampus itself and the underlying cortical areas, involved in the formation of semantic memories.

Surgery affected only H. M.'s declarative, long-term memory—his ability to store facts, personal experiences, names, faces, telephone numbers, and the like. But researchers were surprised to discover that he could still form nondeclarative memories; that is, he could still acquire skills through repetitive practice, although he could not remember having done so. For example, after the surgery, H. M. learned to play tennis and improve his game, but he had no memory of ever having played (Milner, 1966, 1970; Milner et al., 1968).

Most research supports the hypothesis that the hippocampus is especially important in forming episodic memories (Eichenbaum & Fortin, 2003). Semantic memory, however, depends not only on the hippocampus but also on the other parts of the hippocampal region (Hoenig & Sheef, 2005). Once stored, memories can be retrieved without the involvement of the hippocampus (Gluck & Myers, 1997; McClelland, McNaughton, & O'Reilly, 1995). Consequently, many researchers argue that the neurological underpinnings of episodic and semantic memories are entirely separate (e.g., Tulving, 2002). But the degree to which the brain processes associated with episodic and semantic memories can be clearly distinguished is being questioned by some neuroscientists. Research involving older adults who suffer from semantic dementia due to frontal lobe damage shows that many of them suffer from deficiencies in episodic memory (Nestor et al., 2002). Moreover, other studies show that damage to the temporal and occipital lobes can affect episodic memory (Wheeler & McMillan, 2001).

An interesting series of studies (Maguire, Nannery, & Spiers, 2006; Maguire et al., 2000), which were described briefly in Chapter 2, suggest that the hippocampus may serve special functions in addition to those already known. A part of the hippocampus evidently specializes in navigational skills by helping to create intricate neural spatial maps. Using magnetic resonance imaging (MRI) scans, researchers found that the rear (posterior) region of the hippocampus of London taxi drivers was significantly larger than that of participants in a matched control group whose living did not depend on navigational skills (see Figure 6.8). In addition, the more time spent as a taxi driver, the greater the size of this part of the hippocampus.

Neuronal Changes and Memory ▶

6.13 Why is long-term potentiation important?

Some researchers are exploring memory at deeper levels than the structures of the brain. Some look at the actions of single neurons; others study collections of neurons and their synapses and the neurotransmitters whose chemical action begins the

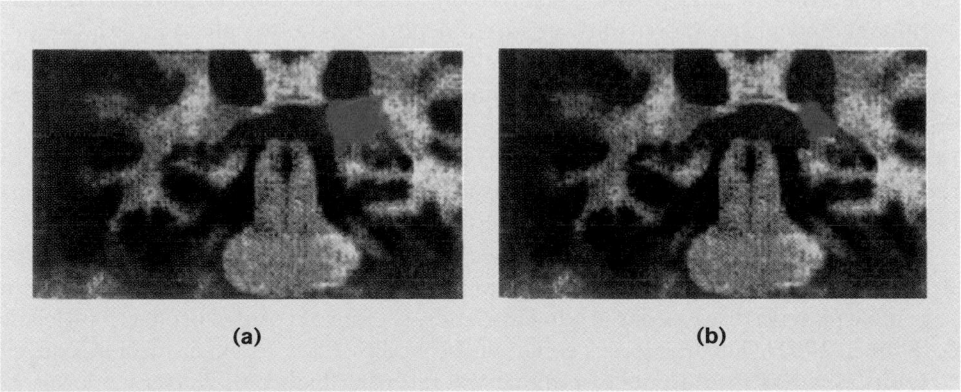

(a)   (b)

FIGURE 6.8 MRI Scans Showing the Larger Size of the Posterior Hippocampus in the Brain of an Experienced Taxi Driver
The posterior (rear) hippocampus of an experienced London taxi driver, shown in red in the MRI scan on the left, is significantly larger than the posterior hippocampus of a research participant who was not a taxi driver, shown in red in the scan on the right.
Source: Adapted from Maguire et al. (2000).

process of recording and storing a memory (Kesner, 2009). The first close look at how memory works in single neurons was provided by Eric Kandel and his colleagues, who traced the effects of learning and memory in the sea snail *Aplysia* (Dale & Kandel, 1990). Using tiny electrodes implanted in several single neurons in this snail, the researchers mapped the neural circuits that are formed and maintained as the animal learns and remembers. They also discovered the different types of protein synthesis that facilitate short-term and long-term memory (Sweatt & Kandel, 1989). Kandel won a Nobel Prize in 2000 for his work.

The studies of learning and memory in *Aplysia* reflect only simple classical conditioning, which is a type of nondeclarative memory. Other researchers studying mammals report that physical changes occur in the neurons and synapses in brain regions involved in declarative memory (Lee & Kesner, 2002).

As far back as the 1940s, Canadian psychologist Donald O. Hebb (1949) argued that learning and memory must involve the enhancement of transmission at the synapses between neurons. The most widely studied model for learning and memory at the level of the neurons meets the requirements of the mechanism Hebb described (Fischbach, 1992). Long-term potentiation (LTP) is an increase in the efficiency of neural transmission at the synapses that lasts for hours or longer (De Roo et al., 2008). (*Potentiate* means "to make potent, or to strengthen.") Long-term potentiation does not take place unless both the sending neurons and the receiving neurons are activated at the same time by intense stimulation. Also, the receiving neuron must be depolarized (ready to fire) when the stimulation occurs, or LTP will not happen. LTP is common in the hippocampal region, which, as you have learned, is essential in the formation of declarative memories (Eichenbaum & Otto, 1993). When a disruption in this process occurs, a long-term memory usually does not form.

If the changes in synapses produced by LTP are the same changes that take place during learning, then blocking or preventing LTP should interfere with learning. And it does. When Davis and others (1992) gave rats a drug that blocks certain receptors in doses large enough to interfere with a maze-running task, they discovered that LTP in the rats' hippocampi was also disrupted. In contrast, Riedel (1996) found that LTP was enhanced and the rats' memory improved when a drug that excites those same receptors was administered shortly after maze training.

long-term potentiation (LTP) An increase in the efficiency of neural transmission at the synapses that lasts for hours or longer.

6.14 How do hormones influence memory?

Hormones and Memory

The strongest and most lasting memories are usually those fueled by emotion. Research by McGaugh and Cahill (2009) suggests that there may be two pathways for forming memories—one for ordinary information and another for memories that are fired by emotion. When a person is emotionally aroused, the adrenal glands release the hormones epinephrine (adrenalin) and norepinephrine (noradrenaline) into the bloodstream. Long known to be involved in the "fight-or-flight response," these hormones enable humans to survive, and they also imprint powerful and enduring memories of the circumstances surrounding threatening situations. Such emotionally laden memories activate the amygdala (known to play a central role in emotion) and other parts of the memory system. This widespread activation in the brain may be the most important factor in explaining the intensity of flashbulb memories.

Other hormones may have important effects on memory. Excessive levels of the stress hormone *cortisol*, for example, have been shown to interfere with memory in patients who have diseases of the adrenal glands, the site of cortisol production (Jelicic & Bonke, 2001). Furthermore, people whose bodies react to experimenter-induced stressors, such as forced public speaking, by releasing higher than average levels of cortisol perform less well on memory tests than those whose bodies release lower than average levels in the same situations (Al'absi et al., 2002).

Estrogen, the female sex hormone, appears to improve working memory efficiency (Dohanich, 2003). This hormone, along with others produced by the ovaries, also plays some role in the development and maintenance of synapses in areas of the brain known to be associated with memory (e.g, the hippocampus). This finding caused researchers to hypothesize that hormone replacement therapy might prevent or reverse the effects of Alzheimer's disease (Dohanich, 2003). However, research shows that postmenopausal women who take a combination of synthetic estrogen and progesterone, the two hormones that regulate the menstrual cycle, may actually increase their risk of developing the disease (Espeland et al., 2009). Some researchers have explained these seemingly contradictory findings by claiming that the timing of estrogen replacement is the most critical factor in its effect on memory function (Marriott & Wenk, 2004). Most researchers agree, however, that much more research is needed to ascertain the definitive role of hormone treatment in the prevention and treatment of age-related memory loss.

Memory Loss ▶

[**6.15** What kinds of memory loss occur in amnesia and dementia?

Everyone has lapses of memory at one time or another, but for individuals such as H. M., whose story you read at the beginning of this section, memory loss is an enduring feature of their everyday lives. Such cases result from some kind of physical or psychological trauma or disease process in the brain. There are two broad categories that involve this kind of memory loss, *amnesia* and *dementia*.

Amnesia. Amnesia is a general term that can signify either a partial or total loss of memory. Unlike the memory disorders that are experienced by some older adults that you will read about in a moment, amnesia can be experienced at any age. In some cases, such as that of H. M., amnesia takes the form of an inability to store new information. This kind of amnesia is known as anterograde amnesia.

Some individuals with amnesia can form new memories, but they cannot remember the past, a disorder known as retrograde amnesia. Retrograde amnesia typically involves episodic rather than semantic memories, however, so people who have it usually have a clear understanding of the world around them. What they often lack is knowledge of themselves and/or the events surrounding the development of their memory loss. The character who is known by the name "Jason Bourne" in the popular books and films *The Bourne Identity*, *The Bourne Supremacy*, *The Bourne Ultimatum*, and the rest, has this kind of amnesia.

Most cases of amnesia are far less dramatic than those that are common in novels and movies. For example, it is not unusual for a person to have both retrograde and anterograde amnesia with regard to the events that immediately preceded and followed a serious car crash or other traumatic event. In such cases, researchers believe that the fear and panic induced by the trauma interfered with the process of long-term potentiation such that the victim actually did not store any memories of the "forgotten" events. Paradoxically, the biochemical processes associated with these memory deficits also enhance the victims' memories of other aspects of the event such as visual images in which the size of a train or bus that hit their car is far out of proportion to other objects in the environment (Strange, Hurlemann, & Dolan, 2003). Thus, emotion may be better thought of as a source of memory distortion rather than of true amnesia.

In some cases, debilitating anterograde and retrograde amnesia occur in the same individual. H. M. had retrograde amnesia with respect to the two years or so immediately prior to his surgery. However, this aspect of his condition, though it was distressing to him at times, proved to be far less consequential to his daily life than his anterograde amnesia. By contrast, in another well-known case of memory loss, that of British musician Clive Wearing, a combination of anterograde and retrograde amnesia has left him psychologically suspended entirely in the present. Because of a severe infection that destroyed the hippocampal regions in both sides of his brain many years ago, Wearing is able neither to form new memories nor to retrieve information that was stored in his long-term memory prior to his illness. Well-practiced skills such as self-care, language, and the ability to read and play music have been preserved in Wearing's brain. However, he is often at a loss to recall

amnesia A partial or complete loss of memory due to loss of consciousness, brain damage, or some psychological cause.

anterograde amnesia The inability to form long-term memories of events occurring after a brain injury or brain surgery, although memories formed before the trauma are usually intact and short-term memory is unaffected.

retrograde amnesia (RET-ro-grade) A loss of memory for experiences that occurred shortly before a loss of consciousness.

▲ British musician Clive Wearing suffers from a combination of anterograde and retrograde amnesia that prevents him from forming new memories and from retrieving old ones.

his family members' names and has no awareness of the fact that he was once a professional musician. If asked, he will adamantly insist that he has never played a single note of music in his life though he continues to play on a regular basis.

Dementia. The lost sense of connection to one's own past that has been so dramatically demonstrated in the life of Clive Wearing is a prominent feature of the dementias, a collection of neurological disorders in which degenerative processes in the brain diminish people's ability to remember and process information. Dementia can result from such conditions as cerebral arteriosclerosis (hardening of the arteries in the brain), chronic alcoholism, and irreversible damage by a series of small strokes. Dementia is most common among older adults—it occurs in about 5 to 8% of those over age 65, 15 to 20% of those over 75, and 25 to 50% of those over 85 (American Psychiatric Association, 1997). However, diseases such as HIV/AIDS can cause dementia to develop in a younger person as well.

Individuals with dementia lose touch with both their episodic and semantic memories. Most have difficulty forming new memories as well. Repeatedly asking the same questions or expressing confusion about location and time are behaviors that are exhibited by many individuals with amnesia. Many become completely incapable of carrying out daily activities such as cooking, financial transactions, and self-care routines such as dressing themselves.

About 50 to 60% of all cases of dementia result from Alzheimer's disease. In Alzheimer's disease, there is a progressive deterioration of intellect and personality that results from widespread degeneration of brain cells. At first, victims show a gradual impairment in memory and reasoning and in efficiency in carrying out everyday tasks (Salmon & Bondi, 2009). Many have difficulty finding their way around in familiar locations. As the disorder progresses, people with Alzheimer's disease become confused and irritable, tend to wander away from home, and become increasingly unable to take care of themselves. Eventually, their speech becomes unintelligible, and they become unable to control bladder and bowel functions. If they live long enough, they reach a stage where they do not respond when spoken to and no longer recognize even spouse or children.

Age and a family history of Alzheimer's disease are two risk factors that have been consistently associated with the disorder (Farrer & Cupples, 1994; Payami et al., 1994; Williams, 2003). Can Alzheimer's disease be delayed? According to brain reserve theory, a high IQ coupled with lifelong intellectual activity may delay or lessen Alzheimer's symptoms in those who are at risk for the disease (Fratiglioni & Wang, 2007). Unfortunately, though, research aimed at finding ways to prevent or cure the disease have yielded little in the way of positive findings. Vitamins, anti-inflammatory drugs, and the female hormone estrogen have all been ruled out as potential cures or preventives for Alzheimer's disease. However, scientists say that a new drug, *bapineuzumab*, that prevents the development of neurofibrillary tangles shows promise (Jeffrey, 2009). A similar vaccine was used in trials with humans a few years ago, but studies were terminated because the vaccine caused swelling in the brains of participants. Investigators now believe that they have solved the swelling problem and will soon reinitiate clinical trials with human beings (Okura et al., 2006).

Memory in Legal and Therapeutic Settings

In most cases, memory failure is an annoyance. But there are times when it has profound consequences. For example, you have probably heard news reports about people being convicted of crimes on the basis of eyewitness testimony who are later exonerated by DNA evidence. Likewise, the news media from time to time carry reports of cases in which adults "recover" decades-old memories of childhood abuse. As you'll see, research on remembering, forgetting, and the biology of memory can help us understand both eyewitness testimony and the controversy surrounding "recovered" memories.

dementia A state of mental deterioration characterized by impaired memory and intellect and by altered personality and behavior.

Alzheimer's disease (ALZ-hye-mer's) An incurable form of dementia characterized by progressive deterioration of intellect and personality, resulting from widespread degeneration of brain cells.

Eyewitness Testimony ▶

The U.S. Department of Justice issued the first set of national guidelines for the collection of eyewitness evidence in the United States in 1999 (Wells et al., 2000). Research attesting to the inaccuracy of such testimony and the number of wrongful convictions that occur because of its poor reliability rendered these guidelines necessary (Laney & Loftus, 2009). According to one of the leading researchers in this area, Elizabeth Loftus, studies on the reconstructive nature of human memory suggest that eyewitness testimony is highly subject to error and that it should always be viewed with caution (Loftus, 1979).

Why is the reliability of eyewitness testimony in question? One reason is biological. Witnessing a crime causes physiological stress, and, as you learned earlier, stress hormones disrupt memory functioning (Wolf, 2009). Yet, it is also true that fear can enhance memory. The combined effects of stress and fear on eyewitnesses causes them to remember the central, most frightening details of the event, but to fail to encode less emotion-provoking details (Burke, Heuer, & Reisberg, 1992; Christianson, 1992). As a result, eyewitnesses typically experience memory gaps (Yovell, Bannett, & Shalev, 2003). These gaps may involve just the sort of information investigators need, such as license plate numbers, addresses, the clothing worn by the perpetrator, and so on.

As you might suspect, when eyewitnesses experience memory gaps, reconstructive processes come to the fore to fill in the missing information. Consequently, distortions and even false memories sometimes replace such gaps. Moreover, misleading information that is inadvertently supplied to an eyewitness during the process of an investigator's interview can result in erroneous recollections of the actual event, a phenomenon known as the misinformation effect (Laney & Loftus, 2009). Interestingly, the misinformation effect appears to be stronger for emotionally negative events, such as witnessing a crime, than it is for emotionally positive events, such as being a guest at a party (Porter et al., 2010).

An example will help you see how the misinformation effect works. Suppose you are walking across campus one day, thinking about an upcoming exam, and a man suddenly accosts you and steals your backpack. Because of the stress involved in being a crime victim, your hippocampus records only a vague recollection of what the man looked like. Your memory includes his height, weight, and ethnicity, but lacks a definitive image of his face. When you talk to a campus police officer, she shows you a photo of a man who is suspected of committing several such crimes and says, "Is this the man who stole your backpack?" The photo and question set into motion the process of retroactive interference (new information displaces old information) in which the photo and its verbal label "man who stole your backpack" fill in the gaps in your own incomplete memory of the man's appearance (Chan, Thomas, & Bulevich, 2009). Remember, too, that source monitoring isn't something we normally do, so you are likely to forget that you have replaced your own memory with information suggested by the photo and the officer's question. As a result, you may mentally superimpose the photo over your own incomplete memory of the perpetrator's face and believe that it is what you actually saw during the event. Furthermore, over the course of the investigation and in chatting with friends, you are likely to repeat your story several times. Your story may include a verbal description of the perpetrator based on the misinformation that is now part of your memory of the event. Research shows that, after eyewitnesses have repeatedly recalled information, whether accurate or inaccurate, they become more confident of the information's accuracy (Shaw, 1996). That is, by "practicing" your distorted memory through repetition, you will become even more convinced of its accuracy and resistant to the suggestion that you may have identified the wrong person.

Furthermore, the confidence eyewitnesses have in their testimony is not necessarily an indication of its accuracy (Laney & Loftus, 2009). In fact, eyewitnesses who perceive themselves to be more objective have more confidence in their testimony,

6.16 What factors influence the reliability of eyewitness testimony?

misinformation effect Erroneous recollections of witnessed events that result from information learned after the fact.

▲ When people recall an event, such as a car accident, they are actually reconstructing it from memory by piecing together bits of information that may or may not be totally accurate.

regardless of its accuracy, and are more likely to include incorrect information in their verbal descriptions (Geiselman et al., 2000). When witnesses make incorrect identifications with great certainty, they can be highly persuasive to judges and jurors alike.

Fortunately, eyewitness mistakes can be minimized. For instance, training interviewers to use questioning strategies that minimize the effects of reconstructed memory can prevent the misinformation effect (U.S. Department of Justice, 1999). Such interviewing strategies usually involve asking open-ended questions that prompt the eyewitness to tell his or her own story of the event prior to being asked specific questions. Moreover, investigators typically separate witnesses so that their stories are as free from the distorting effects of others' recollections as possible.

Similarly, if eyewitnesses view photographs of a suspect before viewing the lineup, eyewitnesses may mistakenly identify that suspect in the lineup because the person looks familiar. Research suggests that it is better to have an eyewitness first describe the perpetrator and then search for photos matching that description than to have the eyewitness start by looking through photos and making judgments as to their similarity to the perpetrator (Pryke, Lindsay, & Pozzulo, 2000).

The composition of the lineup is also important. Other subjects in a lineup must resemble the suspect in age, body build, and certainly race. Even then, if the lineup does not contain the guilty party, eyewitnesses may identify the person who most closely resembles the perpetrator (Gonzalez, Ellsworth, & Pembroke, 1993). Eyewitnesses are less likely to make errors if a sequential lineup is used—that is, if the members of the lineup are viewed one after the other, rather than simultaneously (Loftus, 1993). Some police officers and researchers prefer a "showup," in which the witness sees only one suspect at a time and indicates whether or not that person is the perpetrator. There are fewer misidentifications with a showup but also more failures to make a positive identification (Wells, 1993).

6.17 What is the "repressed memory controversy"?

repression A psychological process in which traumatic memories are buried in the unconscious.

The Repressed Memory Controversy

Memory distortions, as well as "memories" that turn out to be entirely false, have been the subject of debate in regard to the claims made by some therapists about their clients' recoveries of memories of child abuse (Haaken & Reavey, 2010). These therapists, like Freud and other psychoanalysts before them, believe that a process called repression, a form of motivated forgetting, can cause traumatic memories to be so deeply buried in an individual's unconscious mind that he or she has lost all awareness of them. In 1988, Ellen Bass and Laura Davis published a best-selling book called *The Courage to Heal*. It became the "bible" for sex abuse victims and the leading "textbook" for some therapists who specialized in treating them. Bass and Davis not only sought to help survivors who remember having suffered sexual abuse but also reached out to other people who had no memory of any sexual abuse and tried to help them determine whether they might have been abused. They suggested that "if you are unable to remember any specific instances ... but still have a feeling that something abusive happened to you, it probably did" (p. 21). They offered a definite conclusion: "If you think you were abused and your life shows the symptoms, then you were" (p. 22). And they freed potential victims of sexual abuse from the responsibility of establishing any proof: "You are not responsible for proving that you were abused" (p. 37).

However, many psychologists are skeptical about such "recovered" memories, claiming that they are actually false memories created by the suggestions of therapists. Critics charge that recovered memories of sexual abuse are suspect because of the techniques therapists usually use to uncover them—namely, hypnosis and guided imagery. As you have learned (in Chapter 4), hypnosis does not improve the accuracy of memory, only the confidence that what one remembers is accurate. And a therapist using guided imagery might tell a patient something similar to what Wendy Maltz (1991) advocates in her book:

Spend time imagining that you were sexually abused, without worrying about accuracy, proving anything, or having your ideas make sense. ... Ask yourself ... these questions: What time of day is it? Where are you? Indoors or outdoors? What kind of things are happening? (p. 50)

Can merely imagining experiences in this way lead people to believe that those experiences had actually happened to them? Yes, according to some studies. The research of eyewitness testimony expert Elizabeth Loftus on the misinformation effect has been instrumental in helping psychologists and the public understand how these techniques lead to both false and distorted memories. Many research participants who are instructed to imagine that a fictitious event happened do, in fact, develop a false memory of that imagined event (Laney & Loftus, 2009; Mazzoni & Memon, 2003).

False childhood memories can also be experimentally induced. Garry and Loftus (1994) were able to implant a false memory of being lost in a shopping mall at 5 years of age in 25% of participants aged 18 to 53, after verification of the fictitious experience by a relative. Repeated exposure to suggestions of false memories can create those memories (Zaragoza & Mitchell, 1996). Further, researchers have found that adults who claim to have recovered memories of childhood abuse or of abduction by extraterrestrials are more vulnerable to experimentally induced false memories than are adults who do not report such recovered memories (McNally, 2003). So, individual differences in suggestibility may play a role in the recovery of memories.

Critics are especially skeptical of recovered memories of events that occurred in the first few years of life, in part because the hippocampus, vital in the formation of episodic memories, is not fully developed then. And neither are the areas of the cortex where memories are stored (Squire, Knowlton, & Musen, 1993). Furthermore, young children, who are still limited in language ability, do not store semantic memories in categories that are accessible to them later in life. The relative inability of older children and adults to recall events from the first few years of life is referred to as infantile amnesia.

In light of these developmental limitations, is it possible that some individuals cannot recall incidents of childhood sexual abuse? Widom and Morris (1997) found that 64% of a group of women who had been sexually abused as children reported no memory of the abuse in a two-hour interview 20 years later. Following up on women who had documented histories of sexual victimization, Williams (1994) found that 38% of them did not report remembering the sexual abuse some 17 years later. Memories of abuse were better when the victimization took place between the ages of 7 and 17 than when it occurred in the first six years of life. Keep in mind, however, that it is possible that some of these women may have remembered the abuse but, for whatever reason, chose not to admit it. There is also some indication that individuals who are traumatized develop an attentional style that involves distracting themselves from potentially unpleasant stimuli (DePrince & Freyd, 2004; Goodman, Quas, & Ogle, 2010). It is this attentional style, some researchers argue, that prevents such individuals from forming memories of abuse that can be easily recalled.

The American Psychological Association (1994), the American Psychiatric Association (1993a), and the American Medical Association (1994) have issued status reports on memories of childhood abuse. The position of all three groups is that current evidence supports both the possibility that repressed memories exist and the likelihood that false memories can be constructed in response to suggestions of abuse. Moreover, individuals who hold false memories are often thoroughly convinced that they are accurate because of the details such memories contain and the strong emotions associated with them (Dodson, Koutstaal, & Schacter, 2000; Gonsalves et al., 2004; Henkel et al., 2000; Loftus, 2004; Loftus & Bernstein, 2005; McNally et al., 2004). Neuroimaging studies suggest that engaging in visually vivid mental replays of false memories may serve to strengthen them even further (Lindsay et al., 2004). For these reasons, many experts recommend that recovered memories of abuse should be verified independently before they are accepted as facts.

infantile amnesia The relative inability of older children and adults to recall events from the first few years of life.

ᚖᛃ Looking Back

Sometimes psychologists learn more about a mental process from situations in which it goes wrong than they do from those in which it functions as expected. This is especially true of human memory. For instance, by breaking down the inaccurate memories of eyewitnesses and people who claim to have recovered long-lost memories, psychologists have developed a good understanding of how reconstruction, despite its drawbacks, contributes to the efficiency of memory. Moreover, cases in which a physical trauma or condition has caused massive memory failure, such as those of H. M. and Clive Wearing, have helped neuroscientists better understand the biology of memory. And the scientist who initiated the scientific study of memory, Hermann Ebbinghaus, learned a lot about remembering by studying forgetting. You can take a cue from the history of the study of memory the next time you experience a memory failure of your own. Use what you have learned in this chapter to figure out exactly where your effort to remember went awry. Your analysis should equip you with the knowledge you need to avoid similar failures in the future.

CHAPTER 6 SUMMARY

THE STRUCTURE OF HUMAN MEMORY (pp. 168-175)

6.1 How does information-processing theory describe memory? (pp. 168-169)

The information-processing approach uses the computer as an analogy to describe human cognition. It conceptualizes memory as involving the processes of encoding, storage, and retrieval. The model proposes that information flows through a three-part system—sensory memory, short-term memory, and long-term memory.

Key Terms
information-processing theory, p. 168
encoding, p. 168
storage, p. 168
retrieval, p. 168
memory, p. 169

6.2 What are the characteristics of sensory memory? (pp. 169-170)

Sensory memory holds information coming in through the senses for up to 2 seconds, just long enough for the nervous system to begin to process it.

Key Terms
sensory memory, p. 169
eidetic imagery, p. 170

6.3 What happens to information in short-term memory? (pp. 170-174)

Short-term (working) memory holds about seven (plus or minus two) unrelated items of information for less than 30 seconds without rehearsal. Short-term memory also acts as a mental workspace for carrying out any mental activity.

Key Terms
short-term memory, p. 170
displacement, p. 170
chunking, p. 170
rehearsal, p. 170
working memory, p. 171
maintenance rehearsal, p. 172
elaborative rehearsal, p. 172
levels-of-processing model, p. 172
automaticity, p. 172

6.4 What are the subsystems of long-term memory? (pp. 174-175)

The subsystems of long-term memory are (1) declarative memory, which holds facts and information (semantic memory) along with personal life experiences (episodic memory); and (2) nondeclarative memory, which consists of motor skills, conditioned behaviors, and other types of memories that are difficult or impossible to put into verbal form.

Key Terms
long-term memory, p. 174
declarative memory, p. 174
episodic memory, p. 174
semantic memory, p. 174
nondeclarative memory, p. 174

A CLOSER LOOK AT RETRIEVAL (pp. 175-177)

6.5 What are the differences among the recall, recognition, and relearning methods of measuring retrieval? (pp. 175-176)

Three methods of measuring retention of information in memory are (1) recall, where information must be supplied with few or no retrieval cues; (2) recognition, where information must simply be recognized as having been encountered before; and (3) the relearning method, which measures retention in terms of time saved when relearning material compared with the time required to learn it originally.

Key Terms
recall, p. 175
retrieval cue, p. 175
recognition, p. 175
relearning method, p. 176

6.6 How do the serial position, context, and state-dependent memory effects influence retrieval? (pp. 176-177)

The serial position effect is the tendency, when recalling a list of items, to remember the items at the beginning of the list (primacy effect) and the items at the end of the list (recency effect) better than items in the middle. People tend to recall material more easily if they are in the same physical location during recall as during the original learning. The state-dependent memory effect is the tendency to recall information better if one is in the same pharmacological or psychological state as when the information was learned.

Key terms
serial position effect, p. 176
primacy effect, p. 176
recency effect, p. 176
context effect, p. 176
state-dependent memory effect, p. 177

REMEMBERING AS RECONSTRUCTION (pp. 177-182)

6.7 What does "Memory is reconstructive" mean? (pp. 178-179)

People reconstruct memories, piecing them together using schemas to organize fragments of information, a process that has both advantages and disadvantages. Information that fits with preexisting schemas can be efficiently remembered, but schemas can also introduce distortions into memory. Sir Frederick Bartlett's research demonstrated how reconstructive processing changes memory over time.

Key Terms
reconstruction, p. 178
schemas, p. 178

6.8 What have researchers learned about source, flashbulb, and autobiographical memories? (pp. 179-180)

Most memories do not include source information, so memories for sources must be reconstructed. Source monitoring results in encoding of source memories. Flashbulb memories are different from others in that they always include source information, although the source information is subject to reconstruction changes over time. Auto-biographical memories are reconstructed memories that include factual, emotional, and interpretive elements. They are subject to positive bias.

Key Terms
source memory, p. 179
source monitoring, p. 179
flashbulb memories, p. 179
autobiographical memories, p. 180
positive bias, p. 180

6.9 How do expertise and culture influence reconstructive memory? (pp. 180-182)

People with extensive background knowledge (expertise) introduce fewer distortions into reconstructive memory tasks than nonexperts do. Culturally based schemas influence reconstructive memory in the same way that expertise does. In addition, cultural schemas that emphasize the valued status of information such as oral histories encourage source monitoring that protects the information from the distorting effects of reconstruction.

Key Term
expertise, p. 180

FORGETTING (pp. 182-186)

6.10 What did Ebbinghaus discover about forgetting? (pp. 182-183)

In conducting the first experimental studies of learning and memory, Ebbinghaus invented the nonsense syllable, used the relearning method as a test of memory, and plotted the curve of forgetting. He discovered that the largest amount of forgetting occurs very quickly and then tapers off.

Key Terms
forgetting, p. 182
curve of forgetting, p. 182

6.11 Why do we forget? (pp. 183-186)

Encoding failure happens when an item is perceived as having been forgotten but, in fact, was never stored in memory. Decay theory, the oldest theory of forgetting, assumes that information that has not been retrieved from memory for a long time may fade and ultimately disappear entirely. Interference occurs when information or associations stored either before or after a given memory hinder the ability to remember it. Consolidation failure results from a loss of consciousness as new memories are being encoded. Sometimes, we forget because we don't want to remember something, a process called motivated forgetting. Other times, an item is stored in memory, but we are unable to retrieve it (retrieval failure).

Key Terms
encoding failure, p. 183
decay theory, p. 183
interference, p. 184
consolidation failure, p. 185
motivated forgetting, p. 185
prospective forgetting, p. 185
retrieval failure, p. 185
tip-of-the-tongue (TOT) phenomenon, p. 185

BIOLOGY AND MEMORY (pp. 186-190)

6.12 What brain structures are associated with memory? (pp. 186-187)

The hippocampus itself is involved primarily in the formation of episodic memories; the rest of the hippocampal region is involved in forming semantic memories.

Key Term
hippocampal region, p. 186

6.13 Why is long-term potentiation important? (pp. 187-188)

Long-term potentiation (LTP) is a long-lasting increase in the efficiency of neural transmission at the synapses. LTP is important because it may be the basis for learning and memory at the level of the neurons.

Key Term
long-term potentiation (LTP), p. 188

6.14 How do hormones influence memory? (pp. 188-189)

Memories of threatening situations tend to be more powerful and enduring than ordinary memories because of the hormones associated with the strong emotions aroused in such situations.

6.15 What kinds of memory loss occur in amnesia and dementia? (pp. 189-190)

Trauma and disease in the brain can cause anterograde amnesia (inability to learn new information) and/or retrograde amnesia (inability to remember a specific period of time in the past). Patients with Alzheimer's disease and other types of dementia forget the names of people and objects they have known all their lives as well as how to do everyday tasks such as managing money.

Key Terms
amnesia, p. 189
anterograde amnesia, p. 189
retrograde amnesia, p. 189
dementia, p. 190
Alzheimer's disease, p. 190

MEMORY IN LEGAL AND THERAPEUTIC SETTINGS (pp. 190-193)

6.15 What factors influence the reliability of eyewitness testimony? (pp. 191-192)

Stress hormones may disrupt witnesses' memories, leading to gaps that eventually are filled in through reconstructive memory processes. Interviewers' questions can introduce information that witnesses believe is a part of their own memory of the event. The reliability of eyewitness testimony is reduced when witnesses view a photograph of the suspect before viewing the lineup, when members of a lineup don't sufficiently resemble each other; when members of a lineup are viewed at the same time rather than one by one, and when the perpetrator's race is different from that of the eyewitness.

Key Term

misinformation effect, p. 191

6.17 What is the "repressed memory controversy"? (pp. 192-193)

Critics argue that therapists using hypnosis and guided imagery to help their patients recover repressed memories of childhood sexual abuse are actually implanting false memories in those patients. They are especially critical of claims of recovered memories in the first three years of life, because the hippocampus isn't well developed enough to store long-term memories. Therapists who use these techniques believe that a number of psychological problems can be treated successfully by helping patients recover repressed memories of sexual abuse.

Key Terms

repression, p. 192
infantile amnesia, p. 193

MAP IT

Log on to MyPsychLab and click on "Map It" to prepare a unique digital map of the chapter that you can save for later use, email to your instructor, or print out to use as a study tool. Or, create your own map by drawing one on paper. Use the starter map below as a model for your own map. Use the chapter summary as your guide for what to include. For each item in your map, be sure to include the page number.

Here's one way to *Map It*:

1. Draw a box at the top of the page for the section title.
2. Underneath the section title box, working horizontally across the page, draw a box for each learning question in the section. Write the learning questions in the boxes and draw a line from the section title to each questions box. After you read each subsection, jot an answer for the learning question in the subsection's box.
3. Below each learning question box, insert another box for all of the key terms that are related to the question, along with a very brief reminder of each term's definition. Draw a line from the question box to the key terms box.
4. Below each key terms box, create another box and list all of the helpful figures, tables, and other elements of the text, such as *Try It* and *Apply It* boxes. Draw a line from the key terms box to the helpful elements box.

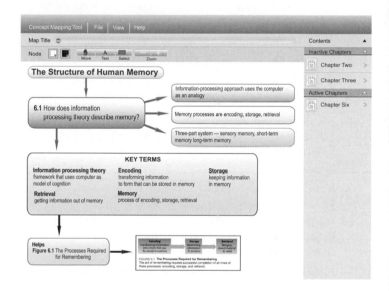

Map the Chapter on mypsychlab.com

Chapter 6 Study Guide

Answers to all the Study Guide questions are provided at the end of the book.

SECTION ONE: Chapter Review

The Structure of Human Memory (pp. 168–175)

1. Transforming information into a form that can be stored in memory is called _____; bringing to mind the material that has been stored is called _____.
   - **a.** encoding; decoding
   - **b.** consolidation; retrieval
   - **c.** consolidation; decoding
   - **d.** encoding; retrieval

2. Match the memory system with the best description of its capacity and the duration of time it holds information.
   - _____ **(1)** sensory memory
   - _____ **(2)** short-term memory
   - _____ **(3)** long-term memory
   - **a.** virtually unlimited capacity; long duration
   - **b.** large capacity; short duration
   - **c.** very limited capacity; short duration

3. Match each example with the appropriate memory system:
   - _____ **(1)** semantic memory
   - _____ **(2)** episodic memory
   - _____ **(3)** nondeclarative memory

a. movements involved in playing tennis
b. names of the presidents of the United States
c. what you did during spring break last year

4. In which subsystem of long-term memory are responses that make up motor skills stored?
   a. episodic memory
   b. semantic memory
   c. nondeclarative memory
   d. declarative memory

A Closer Look at Retrieval (pp. 175–177)

5. Which of the following methods can detect learning when other methods cannot?
   a. recall
   b. recognition
   c. relearning
   d. retrieval

6. Match the example with the corresponding method of measuring retention:
   _____ (1) identifying a suspect in a lineup
   _____ (2) answering a fill-in-the-blank question on a test
   _____ (3) having to study less for a comprehensive final exam than for all of the previous exams put together
   _____ (4) answering multiple-choice questions in this Study Guide
   _____ (5) reciting one's lines in a play
   a. recognition
   b. relearning
   c. recall

7. When children learn the alphabet, they often learn "A, B, C, D" and "W, X, Y, Z" before learning the letters in between. This is due to the
   a. primacy effect.
   b. recency effect.
   c. serial position effect.
   d. state-dependent memory effect.

8. Recall is best when it takes place in the same context in which information was learned. (true/false)

9. Scores on recognition tests (either multiple-choice or true/false) will be higher if testing and learning take place in the same physical environment. (true/false)

10. Which best explains why information learned when one is feeling anxious is best recalled when experiencing feelings of anxiety?
    a. consistency effect
    b. state-dependent memory effect
    c. context-dependent effect
    d. consolidation failure

Remembering as Reconstruction (pp. 177–182)

11. Which of the following is *not* true of schemas?
    a. Schemas are the integrated frameworks of knowledge and assumptions a person has about people, objects, and events.
    b. Schemas affect the way a person encodes information.
    c. Schemas affect the way a person retrieves information.
    d. When a person uses schemas, memories are always accurate.

12. In order to prevent plagiarism, it is important to practice _____ _____ while you are doing research for a research paper.

13. When you remember where you were and what you were doing when you received a shocking piece of news, you are experiencing
    a. flashbulb memory.
    b. sensory memory.
    c. semantic imagery.
    d. interference.

14. Expertise influences reconstructive memory by making _____ function more efficiently.

a. sensory memory
b. working memory
c. semantic memory
d. source memory

15. Cultural values protect some information from the distorting effects of reconstructive memory. (true/false)

16. In general, reconstructed memories of unpleasant events become more (positive/negative) over time.

Forgetting (pp. 182–186)

17. Who plotted the curve of forgetting?
    a. George Sperling
    b. E. Burtt
    c. Frederick Bartlett
    d. Hermann Ebbinghaus

18. The curve of forgetting shows that memory loss
    a. occurs most rapidly at first and then levels off to a slow decline.
    b. begins to occur about 3 to 4 hours after learning.
    c. occurs at a fairly steady rate over a month's time.
    d. occurs slowly at first and increases steadily over a month's time.

19. Match the example with the appropriate cause of forgetting.
    _____ (1) encoding failure
    _____ (2) consolidation failure
    _____ (3) retrieval failure
    _____ (4) repression
    _____ (5) interference
    a. failing to remember the answer on a test until after you turn in the test
    b. forgetting a humiliating childhood experience
    c. not being able to describe the back of a dollar bill
    d. calling a friend by someone else's name
    e. waking up in the hospital and not remembering you had an automobile accident

20. Retroactive interference is most likely to occur when prior knowledge and new information are
    a. very different
    b. recently learned
    c. learned from the same source
    d. similar

21. Most psychologists accept decay theory as a good explanation for the loss of information from long-term memory. (true/false)

22. According to the text, a major cause of forgetting is interference. (true/false)

Biology and Memory (pp. 186–190)

23. H. M. retained his ability to add to his nondeclarative memory. (true/false)

24. The hippocampus itself is involved primarily in the formation of _____ memories; the entire hippocampal region is involved primarily in the formation of _____ memories.

25. What is the term for the long-lasting increase in the efficiency of neural transmission at the synapses that may be the basis for learning and memory at the level of the neurons?
    a. long-term potentiation
    b. synaptic facilitation
    c. synaptic potentiation
    d. presynaptic potentiation

26. Memories of circumstances surrounding threatening situations that elicit the "fight-or-flight response" tend to be more powerful and enduring than ordinary memories. (true/false)

27. When eyewitnesses incorporate details from an interviewer's questions into their memories of an event, they are demonstrating
    a. source monitoring.
    b. the content effect.
    c. the misinformation effect.
    d. event monitoring.

28. There are fewer errors in eyewitness testimony if
  a. eyewitnesses are identifying a person of their own race.
  b. eyewitnesses view suspects' photos prior to a lineup.

c. a weapon has been used in the crime.
d. questions are phrased to provide retrieval cues for the eyewitness.

29. Experts agree that there is no such thing as a recovered memory. (true/false)

SECTION TWO: Complete the Diagrams

Fill in the blanks in each diagram with the missing words.

Sensory Input → **Sensory Memory** — Temporary storage for sensory information — Capacity: (1) _____ — Duration: (2) _____

Rehearsal

Transfer → **Short-Term Memory** — Brief storage for information currently being used — Capacity: (3) _____ — Duration: (4) _____

Retrieval / **Transfer** → **Long-Term Memory** — Permanent or relatively permanent storage — Capacity: (5) _____ — Duration: (6) _____

Long-Term Memory

(7) _____ **Memory** (Explicit memory)

Nondeclarative Memory (Implicit memory)

(8) _____ memory

Semantic memory

(9) _____ skills

(10) _____ conditioned responses

SECTION THREE: Fill in the Blank

1. The first step in the memory process is _____.

2. Short-term memory seems to have a limited life span—less than 30 seconds. If you want to keep a phone number in short-term memory, you will need to use some form of _____, such as repeating the number several times.

3. Another name for short-term memory is _____ memory.

4. The capacity of short-term memory can be expanded through the use of _____.

5. When you take a test in your psychology class, you may be asked to list the names of famous psychologists and their major contributions to psychology. For this task you would use _____ memory.

6. A fill-in-the-blank question requires you to _____ the correct answers.

7. In a list of items, those in the _____ position are the items least easily remembered.

8. The _____ _____ memory effect is the tendency to remember best when in the same physical or psychological state as when the information was encoded.

9. _____ memories are a special type of source memory.

10. When Raquel moved to a new town, she had trouble remembering her new ZIP code. Every time she tried to think of her new ZIP code, her old ZIP code seemed to interfere with her recall. This is probably an example of _____ interference.

11. Serge found himself in trouble during his physics test—he could not remember the formulas from class. He realized that he should have been paying more attention during the lectures. His current memory problem is probably due to _____ failure.

12. The _____ _____ of the brain appears to be very important in the formation of long-term memory.

13. One theory of memory suggests that neural transmission becomes more efficient at certain synapses along neural paths. This increase in transmission efficiency is known as long-term _____.

14. A patient survived delicate brain surgery and displayed no signs of personality change or loss of intelligence. Days after the surgery, the doctor realized that the patient was unable to form long-term memories. He was, however, able to remember everything from before the surgery. The patient was diagnosed as having _____ _____.

15. The misinformation effect is associated with _____ interference and a lack of _____ _____ .

16. Freud suggested that traumatic memories are forgotten as a result of _____, a form of motivated forgetting.

SECTION FOUR: Comprehensive Practice Test

1. The first step in the memory process is known as _____, when information is transformed into a form that can be stored in short-term memory.
   a. retrieval
   b. storage
   c. encoding
   d. rehearsal

2. The process in which information is stored in permanent memory involves a change in the brain's physiology. This change is known as
   a. consolidation.
   b. transformation.
   c. hippocampal transformation.
   d. recalcitration.

3. You are at a party and meet someone you are really interested in. You get that person's phone number but have no way to write it down, so you use the process of _____ to get it into memory.
   a. encoding
   b. latent retrieval
   c. rehearsal
   d. recalcitration

4. The kind of memory that has a large capacity but a very short duration is _____ memory.
   a. short-term
   b. sensory
   c. long-term
   d. temporary

5. Alice's ability to remember all the actions required to ride her motorcycle is due to her repetitive practice, to the point where riding it is almost reflexive. Any set of skills acquired this way is part of _____ memory.

6. Implicit memory is to explicit memory as _____ are to _____.
   a. motor skills; facts and information
   b. episodic memories; semantic memories
   c. semantic memories; episodic memories
   d. facts and information; motor skills

7. Cristina and her friends were talking about some great times they had in high school. Recounting those stories as if they had happened yesterday, the friends were relying on _____ memory.
   a. semantic
   b. implicit
   c. personal
   d. episodic

8. You use _____ memory when you answer questions such as "What is the capital of California?"
   a. episodic
   b. semantic
   c. geographic
   d. flashbulb

9. An example of good recall is doing well on an essay test. (true/false)

10. An example of good recognition ability is doing well on a fill-in-the-blank test. (true/false)

11. Freud did extensive research on memory. He used nonsense syllables to determine forgetting curves. (true/false)

12. When she was 16 years old, Sarah was severely injured in a car accident and was unconscious for 14 days. She can remember nothing immediately preceding the accident. This is known as _____ amnesia.
    a. trauma
    b. retroactive
    c. proactive
    d. retrograde

13. With retroactive interference, _____ information interferes with _____ information.
    a. new; old
    b. old; new
    c. unpleasant; pleasant
    d. factual; emotional

14. Using _____, a person removes an unpleasant memory from consciousness.
    a. regression
    b. traumatic amnesia
    c. repression
    d. degeneration

15. Psychologists doubt the validity of people's recovered memories of having been abused in infancy because the hippocampal region of the infant brain is not sufficiently developed to form such memories. (true/false)

16. It appears that the _____ is important in the formation of episodic memory.
    a. hippocampus
    b. cerebellum
    c. amygdala
    d. temporal lobe

17. Pablo's vivid memory of the day Princess Diana was killed is known as a _____ memory.
    a. histrionic
    b. flashbulb
    c. semantic
    d. retroactive

18. Eyewitnesses are more likely to identify the wrong person if the person is of a different race. (true/false)

19. Autobiographical memories are highly resistant to reconstructive distortions. (true/false)

20. Flashbulb memories are a subcategory of _____ memory.
    a. nondeclarative
    b. sensory
    c. photographic
    d. source

SECTION FIVE: Critical Thinking

1. Some studies cited in this chapter involved only one or a few participants.
   a. Select two of these studies and discuss the possible problems in drawing conclusions based on results from so few participants.
   b. Suggest several possible explanations for the findings other than those proposed by the researchers.

2. Drawing on your knowledge, formulate a plan that you can put into operation to help improve your memory and avoid the pitfalls that cause forgetting.

Cognition, Language, and Intelligence

Think About It

On a scale of 1 to 100, with 1 = not very important and 100 = very important, how vital is each of the following to your long-term happiness?

Being involved in a stable romantic relationship
Having enough money to live comfortably
Achieving professional goals

Now look at these three issues from a different perspective. Imagine your life 10 years from now and assume that you are 100% happy, or perfectly, totally happy at that point. How much would each of these three factors contribute to your sense that you were totally happy? Make a proportional estimate of the contribution of each factor such that they add up to 100%:

_____ % Romance +

_____ % Money +

_____ % Professional goals =

__100__ % Happiness

Did you notice that the emphasis you placed on each factor changed when you thought about balancing them rather than when you thought about them individually? That's because our thinking is distorted by a process called *anchoring,* or the *focusing effect,* when we think about one factor in isolation from others that affect a decision (Tversky & Kahneman, 1974). As a result, we often overestimate the importance of the factor we happen to be thinking about at the moment. In fact, focusing on a single factor, such as a desire for money, can actually make us quite miserable because it causes us to emphasize what we lack rather than what we have (Kahneman et al., 2006).

We address distortions such as anchoring, and how the information-processing system manages and compensates for them, in the opening section of this chapter. In it, we introduce you to the universal intellectual tools that we use to make sense of the world—reasoning, imagery, and concepts—and discuss how we put these tools to work to make decisions, solve problems, and develop technological devices that mirror our own thought processes. Next, we turn to another vital cognitive tool: language. Finally, we end with a discussion of intelligence, creativity, and other aspects of cognitive functioning that vary from one person to another.

cognition The mental processes that are involved in acquiring, storing, retrieving, and using information and that include sensation, perception, imagery, concept formation, reasoning, decision making, problem solving, and language.

imagery The representation in the mind of a sensory experience—visual, auditory, gustatory, motor, olfactory, or tactile.

7.1 How do imagery and concepts help us think?

Cognition

All of us have an idea of what thinking is. We say, "I think it's going to rain" (a prediction) and "I think this is the right answer" (a decision). But our everyday use of the word *think* obscures the fact that thinking actually involves a number of coordinated sub-processes. Psychologists use the term cognition to refer collectively to these processes, which include acquiring, storing, retrieving, and using information (Matlin, 1989). You have already learned about some of them (sensation, perception, and memory) in earlier chapters. Now we turn our attention to some of the other cognitive processes.

Imagery and Concepts

Can you imagine hearing a recording of your favorite song or someone calling your name? In doing such a thing, you take advantage of your own ability to use mental imagery—that is, to represent or picture a sensory experience.

According to psychologist Stephen Kosslyn (1988), we mentally construct our images of objects one part at a time. Stored memories of how the parts of an object look are retrieved and assembled in working memory to form a complete image. Such images can be directly analogous to the real world or they can be creative. In the *Apply It* box in Chapter 6, you read about several mnemonic devices that rely on imagery. Such images can be extremely helpful to memory. For example, to remember that the independent variable is the one in an experiment that is manipulated by the experimenter, you might imagine a puppeteer with a large "I" on his forehead manipulating a marionette.

Images can also be helpful in learning or maintaining motor skills. Brain-imaging studies show that, in general, the same brain areas are activated whether a person is performing a given task or mentally rehearsing the same

▲ Many professional athletes use visualization to improve performance.

task using imagery (Fourkas, Bonavolonta, Avenanti & Aglioti, 2008). Thus, it isn't surprising that professionals whose work involves repetitive physical actions, such as musicians and athletes, use imaging effectively. One remarkable demonstration of the power of imagery may be found in the case of professional pianist Liu Chi Kung, who was imprisoned for 7 years during China's cultural revolution. He mentally rehearsed all the pieces he knew every day and was able to play them all immediately following his release (Garfield, 1986).

The ability to form concepts is another important aid to thinking. A concept is a mental category used to represent a class or group of objects, people, organizations, events, situations, or relations that share common characteristics or attributes. *Furniture, tree, student, college,* and *wedding* are all examples of concepts. As fundamental units of thought, concepts are useful tools that help us to organize our peceptions of the world and to think and communicate with speed and efficiency.

Thanks to our ability to use concepts, we are not forced to consider and describe everything in great detail before we make an identification. If you see a hairy, brown-and-white, four-legged animal with its mouth open, tongue hanging out, and tail wagging, you recognize it immediately as a representative of the concept *dog. Dog* is a concept that stands for a class of animals that share similar characteristics or attributes, even though they may differ in significant ways. Great Danes, dachshunds, collies, Chihuahuas, and other breeds—you recognize all these varied creatures as fitting into the concept *dog.* Moreover, the concepts we form do not exist in isolation, but rather in hierarchies. For example, dogs represent one subset of the concept animal; at a higher level, animals are a subset of the concept *living things.* Thus, concept formation has a certain logic to it.

Psychologists identify two basic types of concepts: formal concepts and natural concepts. A formal concept is one that is clearly defined by a set of rules, a formal definition, or a classification system. Most of the concepts we form and use are natural concepts, acquired not from definitions but through everyday perceptions and experiences. A leading cognition researcher, Eleanor Rosch, and her colleagues studied concept formation in its natural setting and concluded that in real life, natural concepts (such as *fruit, vegetable,* and *bird*) are not clear-cut and systematic (Rosch, 1973, 1978).

Many formal concepts are acquired in school. For example, we learn that an equilateral triangle is one in which all three sides are the same size. We acquire many natural concepts through experiences with examples, or positive instances of the concept. When children are young, parents may point out examples of a car—the family car, the neighbor's car, cars on the street, and pictures of cars in books. But if a child points to some other type of moving vehicle and says "car," the parent will say, "No, that's a truck," or "This is a bus." *Truck* and *bus* are negative instances, or nonexamples, of the concept *car.* After experience with positive and negative instances of the concept, a child begins to grasp some of the properties of a car that distinguish it from other wheeled vehicles.

How do we use concepts in our everyday thinking? One view suggests that, in using natural concepts, we are likely to picture a prototype of the concept—an example that embodies its most common and typical features. Your *bird* prototype is more likely to be a robin or a sparrow than either a penguin or a turkey: Those birds can fly, while penguins and turkeys can't. Nevertheless, both penguins and turkeys are birds. So not all examples of a natural concept fit it equally well. This is why natural concepts often seem less clear-cut than formal ones. Nevertheless, the prototype most closely fits a given natural concept, and other examples of the concept most often share more attributes with that prototype than with the prototype of any other concept.

A more recent theory of concept formation suggests that concepts are represented by their exemplars—individual instances, or examples, of a concept that are stored in memory from personal experience (Estes, 1994). So, if you work with penguins or turkeys every day, your exemplar of *bird* might indeed be a penguin or a turkey. By contrast, most people encounter robins or sparrows far more often than penguins or turkeys (except the roasted variety!). Thus, for the majority of people, robins or sparrows are exemplars of the *bird* concept.

concept A mental category used to represent a class or group of objects, people, organizations, events, situations, or relations that share common characteristics or attributes.

formal concept A concept that is clearly defined by a set of rules, a formal definition, or a classification system.

natural concept A concept acquired not from a definition but through everyday perceptions and experiences.

prototype An example that embodies the most common and typical features of a concept.

exemplars The individual instances, or examples, of a concept that are stored in memory from personal experience.

▶ A prototype is an example that embodies the most typical features of a concept. Which of the animals shown here best fits your prototype for the concept of *bird*?

As noted earlier, the concepts we form do not exist in isolation, but rather in hierarchies, or nested categories. Thus, concept formation has a certain orderliness about it, just as the process of *decision making* does—or, at least, sometimes does.

7.2 How do we make decisions? ┤◀ **Decision Making**

decision making The process of considering alternatives and choosing among them.

Do you recall the last time you made an important decision? Would you describe the process you used to make the decision as a logical one? Psychologists define decision making as the process of considering alternatives and choosing among them. Some psychologists and other scientists with an interest in decision making—particularly economists—maintain that humans make decisions by systematically examining all possible alternatives and then choosing the one that will be most beneficial to them (Loewenstein, Rick, & Cohen, 2008).

The belief that decision making always proceeds in this fashion was challenged by psychologist Herbert Simon in 1956, when he introduced the notion of *bounded rationality* into the discussion. Bounded rationality simply means that boundaries, or limitations, around the decision-making process prevent it from being entirely logical. One important limitation is the size of working memory. We can think about only so much at any given time. Another limitation is our inability to predict the future. For example, if you are considering marrying someone, how do you know that you will still feel the same way about him or her 20 years from now? Obviously, you can't know, so you have to make an educated guess. For the past several decades, research on decision making has focused on how we form such educated guesses.

Elimination by Aspects. In one of the most important early studies of decision making along these lines, psychologist Amos Tversky (1972) suggested that we deal with the limitations on decision making by using a strategy he called elimination by aspects. With this approach, the factors on which the alternatives are to be evaluated are ordered from most important to least important. Any alternative that does not satisfy the most important factor is automatically eliminated. The process of elimination continues as each factor is considered in order. The alternative that survives is the one chosen. For example, if the most important factor for your apartment search was that you could afford a maximum rent of $800 per month, then you would automatically eliminate all the apartments that rented for more than that. If the second most important factor was availability of parking, you would then look at the list of apartments that cost $800 or less per month and weed out those without appropriate parking. You would then continue with your third most important factor and so on, until you had trimmed the list down.

elimination by aspects A decision-making approach in which alternatives are evaluated against criteria that have been ranked according to importance.

Heuristics. Of course, decision making is often less systematic than Tversky's model suggests. For instance, have you ever decided to leave home a bit earlier than necessary so as to allow time for a possible traffic jam? Such decisions are often based on a *heuristic*—a rule of thumb that is derived from experience. Several kinds of heuristics exist. One that has been studied a great deal is the availability heuristic, a rule stating that the perceived probability of an event corresponds to the ease with which the event comes to mind. Thus, a decision to leave home early to avoid a possible traffic jam may result from having been stuck in one recently. The availability heuristic can cause us to overestimate probabilities in our daily lives as well (see the *Explain It*). Another type of heuristic is the representativeness heuristic, a decision strategy based on how closely a new situation resembles a familiar one. For instance, a decision about whether to go out with someone you have just met may be based on how much the person resembles someone else you know.

The recognition heuristic, a strategy in which the decision-making process terminates as soon as a factor that moves one toward a decision has been recognized, has also been the subject of much research. Suppose you are voting and the only information you have is the list of names vying for a particular office on the ballot. If you recognize one of the candidates' names as being that of a woman, and you have a predisposition toward seeing more women elected to public office, the recognition heuristic may cause you to decide to vote for the female candidate. Be aware, however,

heuristic (yur-RIS-tik) A rule of thumb that is derived from experience and used in decision making and problem solving, even though there is no guarantee of its accuracy or usefulness.

availability heuristic A cognitive rule of thumb that says that the perceived probability of an event or the importance assigned to it is based on its availability in memory.

representativeness heuristic A thinking strategy based on how closely a new object or situation is judged to resemble or match an existing prototype of that object or situation.

recognition heuristic A strategy in which decision making stops as soon as a factor that moves one toward a decision has been recognized.

EXPLAIN IT   Why Do People Overestimate the Likelihood of Rare Events?

When was the last time you read a news story about someone who bought a lottery ticket and didn't win? By its nature, the news focuses on the unusual, so the good fortune of lottery winners is trumpeted by the news media, while the more typical outcome of buying a lottery ticket is ignored. How does such news affect our ability to estimate probabilities in our everyday lives? Think about how heuristics may be involved in such effects before reading on.

If you are like most people who have favorable attitudes toward playing the lottery, you probably don't think about the results of your personal experiences with gambling when you are deciding whether to buy a lottery ticket. Instead, you think about the story you read on the Internet about a college student who won $30 million on a $1 Powerball ticket. You should recognize this thought process as an instance of the availability heuristic.

Research suggests that focusing on the possible benefits associated with buying a lottery ticket can lead you to overestimate your chances of winning (Griffiths, 2003). Such irrationality isn't limited to just buying the ticket; this kind of thinking extends to people's number-picking strategies as well. For example, surveys show that 21% of regular ticket buyers believe their chances of winning the lottery are better if they choose the same numbers every time they play (BBC World Service, 2007). Faulty thinking of this kind may reflect our inability to grasp very large numbers (Griffiths, 2003). Moreover, brain-imaging studies suggest that we tend to rely on our emotions when our minds have difficulty interpreting and integrating all of the facts that are relevant to a decision (De Martino et al., 2006). The fact that most people don't think of wasting a single dollar as all that important, especially as compared to the possibility of winning millions in return, contributes to the decision as well (Camerer, 2005). Thus, with the

thought "Wouldn't it be great if I win the lottery?" firmly ensconced in our minds, we plunk down a dollar for a lottery ticket.

Wasting money on a lottery ticket is hardly a life-and-death matter. By contrast, the availability heuristic sometimes leads to tragic outcomes. For example, immediately after the terrorist attacks of September 11, 2001, researchers hypothesized that the number of deaths due to traffic accidents in the United States would increase dramatically in the ensuing weeks (Gigerenzer, 2004). They believed that memories of the attacks would serve as availability heuristics that would cause people to choose to travel by car rather than by plane. These decisions, hypothesized researchers, would reflect people's tendency to rely on the availability heuristic rather than on knowledge that their chances of being the target of a terrorist attack were far less than those of getting into an automobile accident. To test the hypothesis, researchers compared police records of fatal car crashes during September, October, and November of 2001 to the same months in 1996 through 2000. They found that there were substantially more such accidents in the months immediately after September 11, 2001 than during the same period in the five previous years.

To avoid making poor decisions, we need to be aware of the availability heuristic and be on guard against it. Sometimes this requires a conscious effort to shift our attention from the most cognitively available outcome of a decision to its actual statistical likelihood. So, if you would like to avoid spending your hard-earned money on lottery tickets, use imagery to develop a mental picture of yourself tossing yet another losing ticket into the trash and get into the habit of substituting it for the media images of winners that spring to mind when you think about buying a ticket.

👁 Watch on **mypsychlab.com**

▲ How do you decide which fast-food restaurant to patronize when you want a quick bite to eat? Chances are you use a representativeness heuristic, a prototype that guides your expectations about how long it will take to get your food and what it will taste like. Fast-food chains use the same ingredients and food preparation methods at every location in order to maintain patrons' representativeness heuristics as guides for their future fast-food buying decisions.

framing The way information is presented so as to emphasize either a potential gain or a potential loss as the outcome.

intuition Rapidly formed judgments based on "gut feelings" or "instincts."

that researchers have found that decision-makers rely on recognition heuristics only when they lack relevant information (Newell, Lagnado & Shanks, 2007). Thus, with regard to voting, the more information people gather before an election, the less likely they are to vote for someone simply because the candidate's name is associated with one gender or the other or is suggestive of a particular ethnic group.

Framing. Whether we use heuristics or more time-consuming strategies, we should be aware that the manner in which information is presented can affect the decision-making process. For example, framing refers to the way information is presented so as to emphasize either a potential gain or a potential loss as the outcome. To study the effects of framing on decision making, Kahneman and Tversky (1984) presented the following options to a group of participants. Which program would you choose?

The United States is preparing for the outbreak of a dangerous disease, which is expected to kill 600 people. There have been designed two alternative programs to combat the disease. If program A is adopted, 200 people will be saved. If program B is adopted, there is a one-third probability that all 600 will be saved and a two-thirds probability that no people will be saved.

The researchers found that 72% of the participants selected the "sure thing" of program A over the "risky gamble" of program B. Now consider the options as they were reframed:

If program C is adopted, 400 people will die. If program D is adopted, there is a one-third probability that nobody will die and a two-thirds probability that all 600 people will die.

Which program did you choose? Of research participants given this version of the problem, 78% chose program D. A careful reading will reveal that program D has exactly the same consequences as program B in the earlier version. How can this result be explained? The first version of the problem was framed to focus attention on the number of lives that could be saved. And when people are primarily motivated to achieve gains (save lives), they are more likely to choose a safe option over a risky one, as 72% of the participants did. The second version was framed to focus attention on the 400 lives that would be lost. When trying to avoid losses, people appear much more willing to choose a risky option, as 78% of the participants were.

Intuition. How often have you heard someone advise another to "go with your gut feelings"? Psychologists use the term intuition to refer to rapidly formed judgments based on "gut feeling" or "instincts." Despite our faith in intuition, it's important to understand that it is strongly influenced by emotion. Thus, at times, intuition can interfere with logical reasoning. Researchers have found this to be the case even when people are asked to make judgments about emotionally neutral issues, such as whether a given string of words constitutes a grammatically correct statement (Topolinski & Strack, 2009). Including emotion-provoking words in such strings (e.g., fight, death) influences study participants' accuracy in judging their grammaticality.

Intuition can also lead us to base important decisions on the degree to which one of the available options offers us some kind of gain. For example, what if you had to make an on-the-spot decision about whether you would rather purchase an $18,000 car and receive a $1,000 rebate or buy a $17,000 car? Information-processing researchers argue that, in the face of such decisions, intuitive judgments are generated by a mental representation of the gist of a body of information rather than by its factual details (Reyna, 2004). The gist of a car dealer's advertisement for a $1,000 rebate on an $18,000 automobile is "you'll save money if you buy it here," not "$18,000 − $1,000 = $17,000; therefore, it doesn't matter where you buy the car." Furthermore, researchers have found that intuition can lead to errors in reasoning about decisions that carry far greater risks than those associated with buying a car. One study found that intuitive thought processes caused physicians to overestimate the degree to which condoms reduce the risk of sexually transmitted diseases (Adam & Reyna, 2005). Study participants' assessments of the comparative risks of sexual behavior with and without condoms tended to ignore infections that have modes of transmission other than sexual intercourse (e.g., chlamydia).

Anchoring. At the beginning of the chapter, we introduced you to the concept of anchoring, the notion that focusing on a single factor magnifies the importance of that factor relative to others that are relevant to a decision. In one series of studies, British psychologist Neil Stewart examined how anchoring on the minimum payment required on a credit card bill influences decisions about repayment (Stewart, 2009). First, researchers conducted a survey in which participants answered questions about their most recent credit card bill. Respondents reported their balances, minimum payments required on their accounts, and actual payments. The researchers found that the smaller the required minimum payments were, the smaller participants' actual payments were. Moreover, there was no correlation between account balances and actual payments. In other words, survey participants anchored their payment decisions on the size of the minimum payment rather than on the size of the balance.

> anchoring Overestimation of the importance of a factor by focusing on it to the exclusion of other relevant factors.

In a follow-up laboratory experiment, Stewart presented participants with credit card bills on which the full balance was about $900. Half of the bills included a minimum payment, while half did not. Participants were asked to think about how big a payment they would be able to afford if the bill were theirs and then to tell the researchers how much they would probably pay on the bill. On average, participants who were given bills without minimum payments reported that they would pay nearly twice as much as those whose bills included minimum payments. Extrapolating from these results, Stewart predicted that banks and other financial institutions double the amount of interest they make off the average credit card balance (about $4,000) by requiring small minimum payments without warning consumers of the effects of such payments on interest charges. Stewart suggests that the effects of anchoring might be lessened if credit card bills included tables showing the effects of various payment amounts on interest charges.

The *Summarize It* (p. 208) recaps the various approaches to decision making.

Problem Solving

> **7.3** How do the basic approaches and obstacles to problem solving differ?

The process of decision making shares many features with problem solving, the thoughts and actions required to achieve a desired goal. Notably, heuristics are just as important in problem solving as they are in decision making.

> problem solving Thoughts and actions required to achieve a desired goal that is not readily attainable.

Heuristics and Algorithms in Problem Solving. The analogy heuristic involves comparing a problem to others you have encountered in the past. The idea is that if a particular strategy worked with similar problems in the past, it will be effective for solving a new one.

> analogy heuristic A rule of thumb that applies a solution that solved a problem in the past to a current problem that shares many features with the past problem.

Another heuristic that is effective for solving some problems is working backward, sometimes called the *backward search*. This approach starts with the solution, a known condition, and works back through the problem. Once the backward search has revealed the steps to be taken and their order, the problem can be solved. Try working backward to solve the water lily problem in the *Try It* (p. 208).

> working backward A heuristic strategy in which a person discovers the steps needed to solve a problem by defining the desired goal and working backward to the current condition; also called *backward search*.

SUMMARIZE IT

Approaches to Decision Making

APPROACH	DESCRIPTION
Elimination by aspects	Factors on which alternatives are to be evaluated are ordered from most to least important; any alternatives that do not satisfy the most important factor are eliminated; elimination of alternatives then continues factor by factor until one choice remains.
Availability heuristic	Information that comes easily to mind determines the decision that is made, often because of a recent experience.
Representativeness heuristic	The decision is based on how closely an object or situation resembles or matches an existing prototype.
Recognition heuristic	A rapid decision based on recognition of one of the alternatives.
Framing	Potential gains and losses associated with alternatives are emphasized and influence the decision.
Intuition	Decisions are motivated by "gut feelings" that may be influenced by perceptions of gains.
Anchoring	Decisions are influenced by focusing on a single factor, thereby overestimating its importance.

TRY IT — Water Lily Problem

Water lilies double the area they cover every 24 hours. At the beginning of the summer there is one water lily on a pond. It takes 60 days for the pond to become covered with water lilies. On what day is the pond half covered? (From Fixx, 1978.)

Answer: The most important fact is that the lilies double in number every 24 hours. If the pond is to be completely covered on the 60th day, it has to be half covered on the 59th day.

Source: Fixx (1978).

Watch on **mypsychlab.com**

means–end analysis A heuristic strategy in which the current position is compared with the desired goal and a series of steps are formulated and taken to close the gap between them.

algorithm A systematic, step-by-step procedure, such as a mathematical formula, that guarantees a solution to a problem of a certain type if applied appropriately and executed properly.

functional fixedness The failure to use familiar objects in novel ways to solve problems because of a tendency to view objects only in terms of their customary functions.

mental set The tendency to apply a familiar strategy to the solution of a problem without carefully considering the special requirements of that problem.

Another popular heuristic strategy is means–end analysis, in which the current position is compared with a desired goal, and a series of steps are formulated and then taken to close the gap between the two (Sweller & Levine, 1982). Many problems are large and complex and must be broken down into smaller steps or subproblems before a solution can be reached. If your professor assigns a term paper, for example, you probably do not simply sit down and write it. You must first determine how you will approach the topic, research the topic, make an outline, and then write the sections over a period of time. At last, you will be ready to assemble the complete term paper, write several drafts, and put the finished product in final form before handing it in and receiving your *A*.

When you adopt a heuristic strategy, it may or may not lead to a correct solution. By contrast, an algorithm is a problem-solving strategy that always leads to a correct solution if it is applied appropriately. For example, the formula you learned in school for finding the area of a rectangle (width × length) is an algorithm.

Obstacles to Problem Solving. In some cases, we are hampered in our efforts to solve problems in daily life because of functional fixedness—the failure to use familiar objects in novel ways to solve problems. We tend to see objects only in terms of their customary functions. Just think of all the items you use daily—tools, utensils, and other equipment—that help you perform certain functions. Often, the normal functions of such objects become fixed in your thinking so that you do not consider using them in new and creative ways (German & Barrett, 2005).

Suppose you wanted a cup of coffee, but the glass pot for your coffeemaker was broken. If you suffered from functional fixedness, you might come to the conclusion that there was nothing you could do to solve your problem at that moment. But, rather than thinking about the object or utensil that you don't have, think about the function that it needs to perform. What you need is something to catch the coffee, not necessarily the specific type of glass pot that came with the coffeemaker. Could you catch the coffee in a bowl or cooking utensil, or even in coffee mugs?

Another impediment to problem solving is mental set, the tendency to continue to use the same old method even though another approach might be better. Perhaps you hit on a way to solve a problem once in the past and continue to use the same technique in similar situations, even though it is not highly effective or efficient. People are much more susceptible to mental set when they fail to consider the special requirements of a problem. Not surprisingly, the same people who are subject to mental set are also more likely to have trouble with functional fixedness when they attempt to solve problems (McKelvie, 1984).

Why do people tend to hang on to ineffective problem-solving strategies? The cognitive process that underlies both functional fixedness and mental set is confirmation bias, the tendency to selectively pay attention to information that confirms preexisting beliefs and ignore data that contradict them. For example, when faced with an operating system "crash," most computer users know that the first line of defense is to reboot. Every time rebooting solves the problem, confirmation bias in favor of rebooting as a solution for computer problems becomes stronger. As a result, when a problem arises that proves resistant to rebooting, most of us try rebooting a few more times before we confront the reality that rebooting isn't going to solve the problem. Confirmation bias (i.e., "it worked last time") is responsible for the fact that multiple reboots are required before the belief that rebooting will solve any computer problem gives way and we look for a different approach.

Artificial Intelligence

In the previous section you read that mathematical formulas are algorithms, or problem-solving strategies that always lead to a correct solution. Another kind of algorithm tests all possible solutions and then executes the one that works best. In most situations, the limits of human working memory render this kind of algorithm difficult, if not impossible, to employ. By contrast, computers are capable of completing such an algorithm and doing so in a matter of seconds. This particular feature of computer "thinking" has been well illustrated by artificial intelligence programs that have been designed to match the skills of human experts in games such as chess. You may have heard of the series of chess matches that pitted renowned player Garry Kasparov against IBM computers named "Deep Blue" and "Deep Junior." The best Kasparov has been able to do is to play the computers to a draw.

If a computer can beat a human at chess, does it mean that computers process information in exactly the same way as the human brain does? Not necessarily. However, computer scientists hope to design artificial intelligence that accomplishes that goal. Programs designed to mimic human brain functioning are called artificial neural networks (ANNs). Such networks have proved very useful in computer programs designed to carry out highly specific functions within a limited domain, known as expert systems. One of the first expert systems was MYCIN, a program used by physicians to diagnose blood diseases and meningitis. For the most part,

▲ Many of us are hampered in our efforts to solve problems in daily life because of functional fixedness—the failure to use familiar objects in novel ways to solve problems.

confirmation bias Selective attention to information that confirms preexisting beliefs about the best way to solve a problem.

artificial intelligence The programming of computer systems to simulate human thinking in solving problems and in making judgments and decisions.

artificial neural networks (ANNs) Computer systems that are intended to mimic human cognitive functioning.

expert systems Computer programs designed to carry out highly specific functions within a limited domain.

[**7.4** How have computer scientists applied research on artificial intelligence?

▲ World champion Garry Kasparov contemplates a move against Deep Blue, an IBM computer that exhibited artificial intelligence in the area of top-level chess play.

expert systems offer the greatest benefits when acting as assistants to humans. For example, medical diagnosis programs are most often used to confirm doctors' hypotheses or to generate possible diagnoses that have not occurred to them (Brunetti et al., 2002). Remember, too, that any expert system relies on the accumulated knowledge of human experts. Thus, it is impossible for computers to totally replace human professionals.

Moreover, many cognitive tasks that humans find relatively easy to perform are actually quite difficult to teach a computer to do. Many aspects of language processing, for instance, are extremely difficult for computers to manage (Athanasselis et al., 2005). For example, what kind of scene comes to mind when you hear the word *majestic?* Perhaps you see a range of snow-capped mountains. Computer scientists are currently working to develop programs that can enable computers to retrieve images on the basis of such vague, abstract cues (Araujo, 2009). As you will see in the next section, human language, although we use it effortlessly most of the time, is an extremely complex phenomenon.

Language

language A means of communicating thoughts and feelings using a system of socially shared but arbitrary symbols (sounds, signs, or written symbols) arranged according to rules of grammar.

Language is a means of communicating thoughts and feelings using a system of socially shared but arbitrary symbols (sounds, signs, or written symbols) arranged according to rules of grammar. Language expands our ability to think because it allows us to consider abstract concepts—such as justice—that are not represented by physical objects. Further, thanks to language, we can share our knowledge and thoughts with one another in an extremely efficient way. Thus, whether spoken, written, or signed, language is our most important cognitive tool. In Chapter 8, we will discuss how language is acquired by infants. Here, we explore the components and the structure of this amazing form of human communication.

7.5 What are the components language?

psycholinguistics The study of how language is acquired, produced, and used and how the sounds and symbols of language are translated into meaning.

phonemes The smallest units of sound in a spoken language.

morphemes The smallest units of meaning in a language.

syntax The aspect of grammar that specifies the rules for arranging and combining words to form phrases and sentences.

The Structure of Language

Psycholinguistics is the study of how language is acquired, produced, and used and how the sounds and symbols of language are translated into meaning. Psycholinguists use specific terms for each of the five basic components of language.

The smallest units of sound in a spoken language—such as *b* or *s* in English—are known as **phonemes**. Three phonemes together form the sound of the word *cat: c* (which sounds like *k*), *a,* and *t.* Combinations of letters that form particular sounds are also phonemes, such as the *th* in *the* and the *ch* in *child.* The same phoneme may be represented by different letters in different words; this occurs with the *a* in *stay* and the *ei* in *sleigh.* And the same letter can serve as different phonemes. The letter *a,* for example, is sounded as four different phonemes in *day, cap, watch,* and *law.*

Morphemes are the smallest units of meaning in a language. A few single phonemes serve as morphemes, such as the article *a* and the personal pronoun *I.* The ending *-s* gives a plural meaning to a word and is thus a morpheme in English. Many words in English are single morphemes—*book, word, learn, reason,* and so on. In addition to root words, morphemes may be prefixes (such as *re-* in *relearn*) or suffixes (such as *-ed* to show past tense, as in *learned*). The single morpheme *reason* becomes a dual morpheme in *reasonable.* The morpheme *book* (singular) becomes two morphemes in *books* (plural).

Syntax is the aspect of grammar that specifies the rules for arranging and combining words to form phrases and sentences. The rules of word order, or syntax, differ from one language to another. For example, an important rule of syntax in English is that adjectives usually come before nouns. So English speakers refer to the residence of the U.S. president as "the White House." In Spanish, in contrast, the noun usually comes before the adjective, and Spanish speakers say "*la Casa Blanca*," or "the House White."

Semantics refers to the meaning derived from morphemes, words, and sentences. The same word can have different meanings depending on how it is used in sentences: "I don't mind." "Mind your manners." "He has lost his mind." Or consider another example: "Loving to read, the young girl read three books last week." Here, the word *read* is pronounced two different ways and, in one case, is the past tense.

Finally, pragmatics is the term psycholinguists use to refer to aspects of language such as *intonation*, the rising and falling patterns that are used to express meaning. For example, think about how you would say the single word *cookie* to express each of the following meanings: "Do you want a cookie?" or "What a delicious looking cookie!" or "That's a cookie." The subtle differences reflect your knowledge of the pragmatic rules of English; for example, questions end with a rising intonation, while statements end with a falling intonation. Pragmatic rules also come into play when you speak in one way to your friend and another to your professor. That is, the social rules associated with language use are also included in pragmatics. Likewise, the differences between expressions such as "break a leg" (i.e., "good luck" for people in a theatrical production) and "when pigs fly" (i.e., referring to an outcome that is extremely unlikely) and their literal counterparts lie within the domain of pragmatics.

▲ Gestural languages, such as American Sign Language, include all of the same elements of spoken language. The "phonemes" of sign language are (1) hand shape, (2) location, (3) palm orientation, (4) movements, and (5) holds. Thus, any sign can be analyzed in terms of these elements just as spoken words can be broken down into their constituent sounds. For example, the sign for "cat" shown above includes more phonemes than its spoken equivalent, which, has only three (k/a/t).

Animal Language ▶

[**7.6 What is the evidence concerning animal communication?**

Ask people what capability most reliably sets humans apart from all other animal species, and most will answer "language." And for good reason. As far as scientists know, humans are the only species to have developed this rich, varied, and complex system of communication. Moreover, linguists assert that human language includes several key elements and that all known animal communication systems lack one or more of them (Hockett, 1959). Linguists differ to some degree as to just what the unique features of human language are (Anderson & Patrick, 2006). However, here are a few key elements that most agree on:

- *Duality of patterning:* Phonemes are combined in rule-governed patterns to create words; words are combined in rule-governed patterns to create sentences.
- *Productivity:* A finite number of sounds is used to produce an infinite number of unique utterances.
- *Arbitrariness:* There is no meaningful link between an object, event, or thought and the way it is expressed phonologically.
- *Interchangeability:* Any sound that can be heard can be reproduced.
- *Specialization:* Language sounds are used only for communication.
- *Displacement:* Utterances can be about objects and events that are not present.
- *Cultural transmission:* A social environment is required for language learning; it does not develop on its own.
- *Prevarication:* Language can express ideas that are untrue.
- *Reflexiveness:* Language can describe itself.

Despite their limitations, however, it is clear that animals communicate with one another. Moreover, researchers have taught several different kinds of animals to communicate with humans.

semantics The meaning or the study of meaning derived from morphemes, words, and sentences.

pragmatics The patterns of intonation and social roles associated with a language.

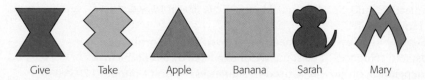

Give   Take   Apple   Banana   Sarah   Mary

FIGURE 7.1 Sarah's Symbols
A chimpanzee named Sarah learned to communicate using plastic chips of various shapes, sizes, and colors to represent words in an artificial language developed by her trainer, David Premack.
Source: Premack (1971).

As early as 1933 and 1951, researchers attempted to teach chimpanzees to speak by raising the chimps in their homes. These experiments failed because the vocal tract in chimpanzees and the other apes is not adapted to human speech, so researchers turned to sign language. Psychologists Allen and Beatrix Gardner (1969) took in a 1-year-old chimp named Washoe and taught her sign language. Washoe learned signs for objects and certain commands, such as *flower, give me, come, open,* and *more.* By the end of her fifth year, she had mastered about 160 signs (Fleming, 1974).

Psychologist David Premack (1971) taught another chimp, Sarah, to use an artificial language he developed. Its symbols consisted of magnetized chips of various shapes, sizes, and colors, as shown in Figure 7.1. Premack used operant conditioning techniques to teach Sarah to select the magnetic chip representing a fruit and place it on a magnetic language board. The trainer would then reward Sarah with the fruit she had requested. Sarah mastered the concepts of similarities and differences, and eventually she could signal whether two objects were the same or different with nearly perfect accuracy (Premack & Premack, 1983).

At the Yerkes Primate Research Center at Emory University, a chimp named Lana participated in a computer-controlled language training program. She learned to press keys imprinted with geometric symbols that represented words in an artificial language called Yerkish. Researcher Sue Savage-Rumbaugh and a colleague (1986; Rumbaugh, 1977) varied the location, color, and brightness of the keys, so Lana had to learn which symbols to use no matter where they were located. One day, her trainer Tim had an orange that she wanted. Lana had available symbols for many fruits—apple, banana, and so on—but none for an orange. Yet there was a symbol for the color orange. So Lana improvised and signaled, "Tim give apple which is orange."

Researcher Herbert Terrace (1979, 1981) and his co-workers taught sign language to a chimp they called Nim Chimpsky (after the famed linguist Noam Chomsky) and reported Nim's progress from the age of 2 weeks to 4 years. Nim learned 125 symbols, which is respectable, but does not amount to language, according to Terrace (1985, 1986). Terrace believed that chimps like Nim and Washoe were simply imitating their trainers and making responses to get reinforcers, according to the laws of operant conditioning, not the laws of language. Finally, Terrace suggested that the studies with primates were probably influenced by experimenter bias; trainers might unconsciously tend to interpret the behavior of the chimps as more indicative of progress toward developing language than it really was. However, Terrace had not heard of Kanzi when he expressed his skepticism.

As impressive as the feats of Washoe, Sarah, and the rest of these talented primates were, the linguistic skills that were acquired by a bonobo chimp named Kanzi eclipsed them all. During the mid-1980s, researchers had taught Kanzi's mother to press symbols representing words. Her progress was not remarkable; but her infant son Kanzi, who stood by and observed her during training, was learning rapidly (thanks to observational learning, discussed in Chapter 5). When

▲ From their studies of communication among chimps and other animals, researchers have gained useful insights into the nature of language. The bonobo chimp Kanzi became skilled at using a special symbol board to communicate.

Kanzi had a chance at the symbol board, his performance quickly surpassed that of his mother and of every other chimp the researchers had tested.

Kanzi demonstrated an advanced understanding (for chimps) of spoken English and could respond correctly even to new commands, such as "Throw your ball to the river," or "Go to the refrigerator and get out a tomato" (Savage-Rumbaugh, 1990; Savage-Rumbaugh et al., 1992). By the time Kanzi was 6 years old, a team of researchers who worked with him had recorded more than 13,000 "utterances" and reported that Kanzi could communicate using some 200 different geometric symbols (Gibbons, 1991). Kanzi could press symbols to ask someone to play chase with him and even ask two others to play chase while he watched. And if Kanzi signaled someone to "chase" and "hide," he was insistent that his first command, "chase," be done first (Gibbons, 1991). Kanzi was not merely responding to nearby trainers whose actions or gestures he might have copied. He responded just as well when requests were made over earphones so that no one else in the room could signal to him purposely or inadvertently.

Most animal species studied by language researchers are limited to motor responses, such as sign language, gestures, using magnetic symbols, or pressing keys on symbol boards. But these limitations do not extend to some bird species such as parrots, which are capable of making humanlike speech sounds. One remarkable case is Alex, an African gray parrot that not only mimics human speech but also seems to do so intelligently. Able to recognize and name various colors, objects, and shapes, Alex answers questions about them in English. Asked "Which object is green?" Alex easily names the green object (Pepperberg, 1991, 1994b). And he can count as well. When asked such questions as "How many red blocks?" Alex answers correctly about 80% of the time (Pepperberg, 1994a). Studies even suggest that Alex may be able to add (Pepperberg, 2006).

Research with sea mammals such as whales and dolphins has established that they apparently use complicated systems of grunts, whistles, clicks, and other sounds to communicate within their species (Quick & Janik, 2008; Schulz, Whitehead, Gero, & Rendell, 2008). Researchers at the University of Hawaii have trained dolphins to respond to fairly complex commands requiring an understanding of directional and relational concepts. Dolphins can learn to pick out an object and put it on the right or left of a basket, for example, and comprehend such commands as "in the basket" and "under the basket" (Chollar, 1989).

Language and Thinking ▶

7.7 **How does language influence thinking?**

If language is unique to humans, then does it drive human thinking? Does the fact that you speak English mean that you reason, think, and perceive your world differently than does someone who speaks Spanish, or Chinese, or Swahili? According to one hypothesis presented about 50 years ago, it does. Benjamin Whorf (1956) put forth his linguistic relativity hypothesis, suggesting that the language a person speaks largely determines the nature of that person's thoughts (Tohidian, 2009). According to this hypothesis, people's worldview is constructed primarily by the words in their language. As proof, Whorf offered his classic example. The languages used by the Inuit people have a number of different words for snow—"*apikak,* first snow falling; *aniv,* snow spread out; *pukak,* snow for drinking water"—while the English-speaking world has but one word, *snow* (Restak, 1988, p. 222). Whorf claimed that such a rich and varied selection of words for various snow types and conditions enabled the Inuit to think differently about snow than do people whose languages lack such a range of words.

Eleanor Rosch (1973) tested whether people whose language contains many names for colors would be better at thinking about and discriminating among colors than people whose language has only a few color names. Her participants were English-speaking Americans and the Dani, members of a remote tribe in New Guinea whose language has only two names for colors—*mili* for dark, cool colors and *mola* for bright, warm colors. Rosch showed members of both groups single-color chips of

linguistic relativity hypothesis The notion that the language a person speaks largely determines the nature of that person's thoughts.

11 colors—black, white, red, yellow, green, blue, brown, purple, pink, orange, and gray—for 5 seconds each. Then, after 30 seconds, she had the participants select the 11 colors they had viewed from an assortment of 40 color chips. Did the Americans outperform the Dani participants, for whom brown, black, purple, and blue are all *mili*, or dark? No. Rosch found no significant differences between the Dani and the Americans in discriminating, remembering, or thinking about those 11 basic colors. Rosch's study did not support the linguistic relativity hypothesis.

Clearly, however, it would be a mistake to go too far in the opposite direction and assume that language has no influence on how people think. Thought both influences and is influenced by language, and language appears to reflect cultural differences more than it determines them (Pinker, 1994; Rosch, 1987).

7.8 How does bilingualism affect thinking and language development?

Learning a Second Language

Do you speak more than one language? Most native-born Americans speak only English. But in many other countries around the world, the majority of citizens speak two or even more languages (Snow, 1993). In European countries, most students learn English in addition to the languages of the countries bordering their own. Dutch is the native language of the Netherlands, but all Dutch schoolchildren learn German, French, and English. College-bound German students also typically study three languages (Haag & Stern, 2003). What about the effect of learning two languages on the process of language development itself? (You'll learn more about this process in Chapter 8).

Research suggests that there are both advantages and disadvantages to learning two languages early in life. One of the pluses is that, among preschool and school-age children, bilingualism, fluency in at least two languages, is associated with better *executive control* skills on language tasks (Luo, Luk, & Bialystok, 2010). Executive control skills enable bilingual children to suppress impulsive responses to verbal tasks and, as a result, think more carefully about them. Thus, executive control skills are important in learning to read and write. On the downside, even in adulthood, bilingualism is sometimes associated with decreased efficiency in memory tasks involving words (Craik & Bialystok, 2010). However, bilinguals appear to develop compensatory strategies that allow them to make up these inefficiencies. Consequently, they often perform such tasks as accurately as monolinguals, though they may respond more slowly. Many people would argue, however, that the advantages associated with fluency in two languages are worth giving up a bit of cognitive efficiency. ◉—Watch on **mypsychlab.com**

bilingualism Fluency in at least two languages.

◉—Watch the **Video** *Bilingual Education* on **mypsychlab.com**

So, you may ask, what about people who did not have the good fortune to grow up bilingual? Is it still possible to become fluent in a second language after reaching adulthood? Researchers have found that there is no age at which it is impossible to acquire a new language. While it is true that those who begin earlier reach higher levels of proficiency, age is not the only determining factor. Kenji Hakuta and his colleagues (2003) used census data to examine relationships among English proficiency, age at entry into the United States, and educational attainment for Chinese- and Spanish-speaking immigrants. The results of their study are shown in Figure 7.2. As you can see, even when immigrants entered the United States in middle and late adulthood, their ability to learn English was predicted by their educational backgrounds. And other studies have shown that the more you know about your first language—its spelling rules, grammatical structure, and vocabulary—the easier it will be for you to learn another language (Meschyan & Hernandez, 2002).

It may be that children attain second-language fluency more easily than adults simply because they practice more. Older individuals may rely more on passive strategies such as listening to others' conversations or watching television to pick up a new language. Research has shown that passive listening can help us learn new vocabulary, but it is of no help in learning grammar (Van Lommel,

▲ Growing up in a bilingual home provides distinct advantages in adolescence and adulthood. Spanish and English are the languages spoken by the majority of bilinguals in the United States.

Why do you think immigrants with college educations who arrive in the United States in late adulthood achieve higher levels of English fluency that those with fewer than five years of schooling who arrive in early childhood? What do these findings mean to the popular notion that it is easier to learn a second language in childhood than in adulthood?

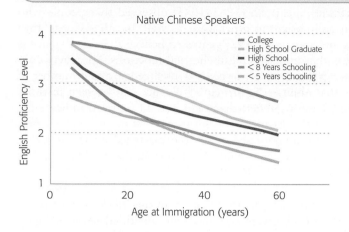

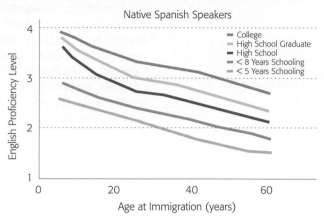

FIGURE 7.2 English Proficiency in Chinese- and Spanish-Speaking Immigrants to the United States These research results, based on census data involving more than 2 million individuals, suggest that it is never too late to learn a second language. *Source:* Hakuta et al. (2003).

Laenen, & d'Ydewalle, 2006). In fact, listening to others speak actually appears to cause us to forget the grammatical knowledge that we already have. This may happen because natural conversation includes fragmentary expressions rather than complete sentences. For example, a friend might say to you, "How long did you study for the psychology exam?" In reply, you would probably say "about three hours" rather than "I studied about three hours for the psychology exam." Thus, when you take a foreign language class, some of the required exercises may seem silly. (How often does anyone say something like "Here is my aunt's big yellow pencil" or "There is Lucy's beautiful blue hat" in real life?) Yet, they are essential to your acquisition of the language's grammar.

There is one clear advantage to learning two languages earlier in life, however. People who are younger when they learn a new language are far more likely to be able to speak it with an appropriate accent (McDonald, 1997). One reason for this difference between early and late language learners may have to do with slight variations in neural processing in Broca's area, the area of the brain that controls speech production. Research by Kim and others (1997) suggests that bilinguals who learned a second language early (younger than age 10 or 11) rely on the same patch of tissue in Broca's area for both of the languages they speak. In those who learned a second language at an older age, two different sections of Broca's area are active while they are performing language tasks—one section for the first language and another for the second language. Yet, the two sections are very close, only 1/3 inch apart.

Intelligence

Have you ever stopped to think what you really mean when you say someone is "intelligent"? Do you mean that the person learns quickly or that he or she can solve problems that appear to mystify others? Spending a few minutes thinking about intelligence in this way will help you realize that defining intelligence in ways that can be measured is quite a challenge.

The Nature of Intelligence ▸

A task force of experts from the American Psychological Association (APA) defined intelligence as possessing several basic facets: an individual's "ability to understand complex ideas, ... to adapt effectively to the environment, ... to learn from experience, to engage in various forms of reasoning, and to overcome obstacles by taking thought" (Neisser et al., 1996, p. 77). As you will see, however, there's more to intelligence than this simple definition suggests.

7.9 How do the theories of Spearman, Thurstone, Gardner, and Sternberg differ?

intelligence An individual's ability to understand complex ideas, to adapt effectively to the environment, to learn from experience, to engage in various forms of reasoning, and to overcome obstacles through mental effort.

The APA's definition of intelligence includes several factors, such as the ability to understand complex ideas and the capacity for adapting to the environment. But are these manifestations of a single entity or truly separate abilities? This question has fascinated psychologists for more than a century.

English psychologist Charles Spearman (1863–1945) observed that people who are bright in one area are usually bright in other areas as well. In other words, they tend to be generally intelligent. Spearman (1927) came to believe that intelligence is composed of a general ability that underlies all intellectual functions. Spearman concluded that intelligence tests tap this *g* factor, or general intelligence, and a number of *s* factors, or specific intellectual abilities. Spearman's influence can be seen in those intelligence tests, such as the Stanford–Binet, that yield one IQ score to indicate the level of general intelligence. Over the decades since Spearman first published his work, many studies have supported his hypotheses about the existence of the *g* factor and that it strongly influences how we acquire information from the world around us (e.g., Neisser et al., 1996; Meyer et al., 2010).

Another early researcher in testing, Louis L. Thurstone (1938), rejected Spearman's notion of general intellectual ability, or *g* factor. After analyzing the scores of many participants on some 56 separate ability tests, Thurstone identified seven primary mental abilities: verbal comprehension, numerical ability, spatial relations, perceptual speed, word fluency, memory, and reasoning. He maintained that all intellectual activities involve one or more of these primary mental abilities. Thurstone and his wife, Thelma G. Thurstone, developed their Primary Mental Abilities Tests to measure these seven abilities. Thurstone believed that a single IQ score obscured more than it revealed. He suggested that a profile showing relative strengths and weaknesses on the seven primary mental abilities would provide a more accurate picture of a person's intelligence.

Harvard psychologist Howard Gardner (Gardner & Hatch, 1989) also denies the existence of a *g* factor. Instead, he proposes a theory of multiple intelligences that includes eight independent forms of intelligence, or *frames of mind,* as illustrated in Figure 7.3. The eight frames of mind are linguistic, logical-mathematical, spatial, bodily-kinesthetic, musical, interpersonal, intrapersonal, and naturalistic. Furthermore, Gardner continues to

g factor Spearman's term for a general intellectual ability that underlies all mental operations to some degree.

primary mental abilities According to Thurstone, seven relatively distinct capabilities that singly or in combination are involved in all intellectual activities.

theory of multiple intelligences Howard Gardner's proposal that there are several independent forms of intelligence.

FIGURE 7.3 Gardner's Eight Frames of Mind

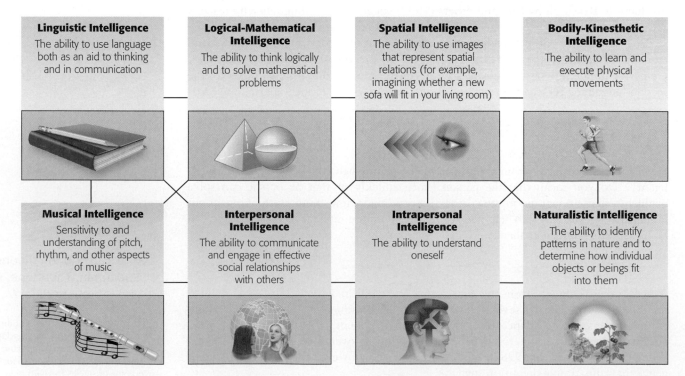

Linguistic Intelligence
The ability to use language both as an aid to thinking and in communication

Logical-Mathematical Intelligence
The ability to think logically and to solve mathematical problems

Spatial Intelligence
The ability to use images that represent spatial relations (for example, imagining whether a new sofa will fit in your living room)

Bodily-Kinesthetic Intelligence
The ability to learn and execute physical movements

Musical Intelligence
Sensitivity to and understanding of pitch, rhythm, and other aspects of music

Interpersonal Intelligence
The ability to communicate and engage in effective social relationships with others

Intrapersonal Intelligence
The ability to understand oneself

Naturalistic Intelligence
The ability to identify patterns in nature and to determine how individual objects or beings fit into them

refine his model. In recent years, he has proposed that a ninth type of intelligence, one that he calls *existential intelligence,* deals with the spiritual realm and enables us to contemplate the meaning of life (Halama & Strízenec, 2004). ✳┤Explore on mypsychlab.com

Gardner (1983) first developed his theory by studying patients with different types of brain damage that affect some forms of intelligence but leave others intact. He also studied reports of people with *savant syndrome,* who show a combination of mental retardation and unusual talent or ability. (You'll read more about this phenomenon later in this chapter.) Finally, Gardner considered how various abilities and skills have been valued differently in other cultures and periods of history.

Perhaps the most controversial aspect of Gardner's theory is his view that all forms of intelligence are of equal importance. In fact, different cultures asign varying degrees of importance to the types of intelligence. For example, linguistic and logical mathematical intelligences are valued most in the United States and other Western cultures; bodily-kinesthetic intelligence is more highly prized in cultures that depend on hunting for survival.

Psychologist Robert Sternberg (2000) is also critical of heavy reliance on Spearman's *g* factor for measuring intelligence. But Sternberg is not merely a critic; he has developed his own theory of intelligence. Sternberg (1985a; 1986a) has formulated a triarchic theory of intelligence, which proposes that there are three types of intelligence (see Figure 7.4). The first type, *componential intelligence,* refers to the mental abilities most closely related to success on conventional IQ and achievement tests. He claims that traditional IQ tests measure only componential, or analytical, intelligence. ✳┤Explore on mypsychlab.com

The second type, *experiential intelligence,* is reflected in creative thinking and problem solving. People with high experiential intelligence are able to solve novel problems and deal with unusual and unexpected challenges. Another aspect of experiential intelligence is finding creative ways to perform common daily tasks more efficiently and effectively.

The third type, *contextual intelligence,* or practical intelligence, might be equated with common sense or "street smarts." People with high contextual intelligence are survivors, who capitalize on their strengths and compensate for their weaknesses. They either adapt well to their environment, change the environment so that they can succeed, or, if necessary, find a new environment.

Sternberg and others (1995) argue that IQ-test performance and real-world success are based on two different types of knowledge: *formal academic knowledge,* or the knowledge we acquire in school, and *tacit knowledge.* Unlike formal academic knowledge, tacit knowledge is action oriented and is acquired without direct help from others. According to Sternberg, tacit knowledge is more important to successful

✳┤Explore the **Concept**
Gardner's Multiple Intelligences on
mypsychlab.com

triarchic theory of intelligence Sternberg's theory that there are three types of intelligence: componential (analytical), experiential (creative), and contextual (practical).

✳┤Explore the **Concept** *Sternberg's Triarchic Theory of Intelligence* on* **mypsychlab.com**

FIGURE 7.4 Sternberg's Triarchic Theory of Intelligence
According to Sternberg, there are three types of intelligence: componential, experiential, and contextual.

Componential Intelligence
Mental abilities most closely related to success on traditional IQ and achievement tests

Experiential Intelligence
Creative thinking and problem solving

Contextual Intelligence
Practical intelligence or "street smarts"

real-world performance. Research supports Sternberg's contention that the two forms of knowledge are different (Grigorenko et al., 2004; Taub et al., 2001). However, investigators have found that measures of formal academic knowledge, such as traditional IQ tests, better predict real-world success than do Sternberg's tests of practical intelligence. Sternberg and those who agree with him contend that imperfections in the tests themselves are responsible for such results. Thus, in recent years, Sternberg and his colleagues have focused on developing a reliable and valid intelligence test that measures each of the three hypothesized types of intelligence (Chart, Grigorenko & Sternberg, 2008).

Sternberg's ideas have become popular among educators. Several studies have shown that teaching methods designed to tap into all three types of intelligence can be effective with students who are low achievers (Jarvin et al., 2008). In such instruction, teachers emphasize the practical relevance of formal academic knowledge and help students apply it to real-world problems.

The *Summarize It* recaps the various theories of intelligence.

SUMMARIZE IT

Theories of Intelligence

THEORY	DESCRIPTION
Spearman's *g* factor	Intelligence consists of a single factor known as *g*, which represents a general intellectual ability.
Thurstone's primary mental abilities	Intelligence has seven separate components: verbal comprehension, numerical ability, spatial relations, perceptual speed, word fluency, memory, and reasoning.
Gardner's frames of mind	There are eight independent forms of intelligence: linguistic, logical-mathematical, spatial, bodily-kinesthetic, musical, interpersonal, intrapersonal, and naturalistic.
Sternberg's triarchic theory	There are three types of intelligence: componential, experiential, and contextual.

7.10 What are the characteristics of good cognitive ability tests?

Measuring Cognitive Abilities

To better understand how psychologists measure intelligence, it may be helpful to you to gain some insight into the various kinds of tests of cognitive ability. Scores on these tests, as you might suspect, tend to overlap somewhat. That is, if an individual does well on one kind, he or she usually gets good scores on the others as well. However, research has also demonstrated that the three kinds of tests you will read about measure distinctive aspects of cognition.

achievement test A measure of what a person has learned up to a certain point in his or her life.

When you were in elementary school, you probably took an achievement test every year or two. These tests tap knowledge and skills that a person has acquired through experiences such as formal education up to the point at which the test is taken. *Norm-referenced* achievement tests compare individual students' scores to the average score of all students at their grade level. *Criterion-referenced* achievement tests compare the performance of an individual or group against a predetermined standard. For example, a goal that states "all children in the fourth grade will be able to multiply two-digit numbers with 70% accuracy" is such a standard.

aptitude test A test that predicts future performance in a particular setting or on a specific task.

Aptitude tests are norm-referenced tests that are designed to predict a person's probable achievement or performance in a particular setting or in reference to a specific task at some future time. For example, many colleges include scores on aptitude tests such as the SAT and the American College Testing Program (ACT) in the criteria they use to make admissions decisions. These tests are useful because they predict variations in indicators of college success, such as freshman GPAs and degree attainment (Schmitt et al., 2009). Another familiar aptitude test is the Armed Services Vocational Aptitude Battery (ASVAB) that is given to individuals who have applied to serve in the armed forces of the United States. Test scores on the ASVAB help military officials place inductees into the educational programs in which they are most likely to be successful. Similarly, when a company administers tests of mechanical ability to applicants who are seeking positions in which such ability is important, they use aptitude tests specifically designed for that purpose.

An intelligence test is a measure of general intellectual ability. An individual's score is determined by how his responses compare to others of his or her age. Thus, intelligence tests are norm-referenced. They attempt to measure all of the aspects of intelligence that are included in the definition of intelligence that you learned a few pages back. Let's look at what distinguishes a good test from a not-so-good test.

All psychological tests, including all the various types of tests that measure cognitive ability, are judged according to the same criteria. First, they must provide consistent results. What if your watch gains 6 minutes one day and loses 3 or 4 minutes the next day? It would not be reliable. You want a watch you can rely on to give the correct time day after day. Like a watch, an intelligence test must have reliability; the test must consistently yield nearly the same score when the same person is tested and then retested on the same test or an alternative form of the test. The higher the correlation between the two scores, the more reliable the test.

Tests can be highly reliable but worthless if they are not valid. Validity is the ability or power of a test to measure what it is intended to measure. For example, a thermometer is a valid instrument for measuring temperature; a bathroom scale is valid for measuring weight. But no matter how reliable your bathroom scale is, it will not take your temperature. It is valid only for weighing.

Once a test is proven to be valid and reliable, the next requirement is norm-referenced standardization. There must be standard procedures for administering and scoring the test. Exactly the same directions must be given, whether written or oral, and the same amount of time must be allowed for every test taker. But even more important, standardization means establishing norms, age-based averages, by which all scores are interpreted. A test is standardized by administering it to a large sample of people who are representative of those who will be taking the test in the future. The group's scores are analyzed, and then the average score, standard deviation, percentile rankings, and other measures are computed. These comparative scores become the norms used as the standard against which all other scores on that test are measured.

Reliability, validity, and standardization are especially important with regard to intelligence tests because the kinds of decisions that are sometimes based on intelligence test scores can have grave consequences. For instance, a few years ago the U.S. Supreme Court ruled that it is unconstitutional to execute individuals who have *mental retardation,* an intellectual disability that will be explained in greater detail shortly. Thus, a psychologist who is charged with the responsibility of administering an intelligence test to a person who will or will not be subject to the death penalty at least partly on the basis of his or her intelligence test score must ensure that the test given is reliable and valid and has been properly standardized. Likewise, children's scores on these tests are often used to place them in special school programs that, in a very real sense, change the course of their lives for years to come. In fact, such a goal was the impetus for the development of the first standardized intelligence test.

One criticism that continues to plague advocates of IQ testing is the suggestion that minority children and those for whom English is a second language are at a disadvantage when they are assessed on conventional tests because their cultural backgrounds differ from that assumed by the tests' authors. In response, attempts have been made to develop a culture-fair intelligence test designed to minimize cultural bias. The questions do not penalize individuals whose cultural experience or language differs from that of the mainstream or dominant culture. See Figure 7.5 (p. 220) for an example of the type of test item found on a culture-fair test. Research shows that such tests are moderately correlated with other measures of intellectual ability, such as the SAT (Frey & Detterman, 2004). Likewise, high-IQ minority children are more likely to

intelligence test A test of individual differences in general intellectual ability.

reliability The ability of a test to yield nearly the same score when the same people are tested and then retested on the same test or an alternative form of the test.

validity The ability of a test to measure what it is intended to measure.

standardization Establishing norms for comparing the scores of people who will take a test in the future; administering tests using a prescribed procedure.

norms Age-based averages.

culture-fair intelligence test An intelligence test that uses questions that will not penalize those whose culture differs from the mainstream or dominant culture.

FIGURE 7.5 An Example of an Item on a Culture-Fair Test
This culture-fair test item does not penalize test takers whose language or cultural experiences differ from those of the urban middle or upper classes. Test takers select, from the six samples on the right, the patch that completes the pattern. Patch number 3 is the correct answer.
Source: Adapted from the Raven Standard Progressive Matrices Test.

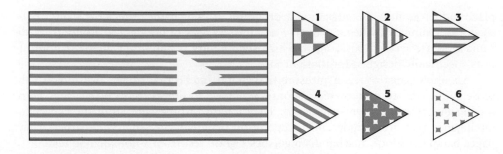

7.11 What did Binet, Terman, and Weschler contribute to the study of intelligence?

be identified as gifted when culture-fair tests are used than when school officials use conventional IQ tests to screen students for inclusion in programs for the gifted (Shaunessy, Karnes, & Cobb, 2004).

Intelligence Testing: Past and Present

The first successful effort to measure intelligence resulted not from a theoretical approach but as a practical means of solving a problem. In 1903, the French government formed a special commission to look for a way of assessing the intellectual potential of individual schoolchildren. The commission's goal was to find a way to identify children who might need additional instructional support. One of the commission members, Alfred Binet (1857–1911), with the help of his colleague, psychiatrist Theodore Simon, developed a variety of tests that eventually became the first intelligence test, the *Binet–Simon Intelligence Scale,* first published in 1905.

The Binet–Simon Scale used a type of score called *mental age.* A child's mental age was based on the number of items she or he got right as compared with the average number right for children of various ages. In other words, if a child's score equaled the average for 8-year-olds, the child was assigned a mental age of 8, regardless of her or his chronological age (age in years). To determine whether children were bright, average, or had mental retardation, Binet compared the children's mental and chronological ages. A child who was mentally 2 years ahead of his or her chronological age was considered bright; one who was 2 years behind was classified as having mental retardation. But there was a flaw in Binet's scoring system. A 4-year-old with a mental age of 2 is farther behind her peers than a 12-year-old with a mental age of 10. How could a similar degree of retardation at different ages be expressed?

German psychologist William Stern (1914) provided an answer. In 1912, he devised a simple formula for calculating an index of intelligence—*the intelligence quotient.* But it was American psychologist Lewis M. Terman, a professor at Stanford University, who perfected this new way of scoring intelligence tests. In 1916, Terman published a thorough revision of the Binet–Simon scale, consisting of items adapted for use with American children. Terman also established new norms, based on the scores of large numbers of children. Within 3 years, 4 million American children had taken Terman's revision, known as the *Stanford–Binet Intelligence Scale.* It was the first test to make use of Stern's concept of the intelligence quotient (IQ). (Terman also introduced the abbreviation *IQ.*) Terman's formula for calculating an IQ score was

$$\frac{\text{Mental age}}{\text{Chronological age}} \times 100 = \text{IQ}$$

For example,

$$\frac{14}{10} \times 100 = 140 \text{ (superior IQ)}$$

The highly regarded Stanford–Binet is an individually administered IQ test for those aged 2 to 23. It contains four subscales: verbal reasoning, quantitative reasoning, abstract visual reasoning, and short-term memory. An overall IQ score is derived from scores on the four subscales, and the test scores correlate well with achievement

intelligence quotient (IQ) An index of intelligence, originally derived by dividing mental age by chronological age and then multiplying by 100, but now derived by comparing an individual's score with the scores of others of the same age.

test scores (Laurent, Swerdik, & Ryburn, 1992). Intelligence testing became increasingly popular in the United States in the 1920s and 1930s, but it quickly became obvious that the Stanford–Binet was not useful for testing adults. The original IQ formula could not be applied to adults because at a certain age people achieve maturity in intelligence. According to the original IQ formula, a 40-year-old with the same IQ test score as the average 20-year-old would be considered mentally retarded, with an IQ of only 50. Obviously, something was wrong with the formula when applied to populations of all ages.

To address this problem, psychologist David Wechsler developed the first individual intelligence test for individuals over the age of 16 (Wechsler, 1939). Rather than being based on mental and chronological ages, scores on the *Wechsler Adult Intelligence Scale (WAIS)* were based on how much an individual deviated from the average score for adults. Wechsler's new IQ score was so well received that he subsequently published similarly scored tests for children *(Wechsler Intelligence Scale for Children, WISC)* and preschoolers *(Wechsler Preschool and Primary Scale of Intelligence, WPPSI)*.

Both Terman's and Wechsler's tests continue to be among the most frequently used of all psychological tests. Psychologists have revised each of them several times. The Stanford–Binet is now known as the SB-V, meaning the fifth revision of the original scale. The current editions of Wechsler's scales are the WAIS-III, WISC-IV, and the WPPSI-III. These scales have changed somewhat since their introduction and now yield several types of scores, a feature of modern intelligence tests that is perhaps best exemplified by the WISC-IV.

When psychologists who work in schools need to find out why a particular child is exhibiting learning problems, they most often turn to the WISC-IV for guidance in determining the child's intellectual strengths and weaknesses. The scale consists of 15 separate subtests. Five of these tests, those that make up the *verbal comprehension index*, measure verbal skills such as vocabulary. The remaining 10 tests demand nonverbal types of thinking, such as arranging pictures to tell a story and repeating digits back to an examiner. The nonverbal tests are divided among the *perceptual reasoning index, processing speed index*, and *working memory index*. Each of these indexes measures a different kind of nonverbal intelligence and generates its own IQ score. The WISC-IV also provides a comprehensive *full-scale IQ* score that takes all four types of tests into account. Many psychologists find comparisons of the different kinds of IQ scores generated by the WISC-IV to be helpful in gaining insight into a child's learning difficulties.

Individual intelligence tests such as the Stanford–Binet and the Wechsler scales must be given to one person at a time by a psychologist or educational diagnostician. For testing large numbers of people in a short period of time (often necessary due to budget limitations), group intelligence tests are the answer. Group intelligence tests, such as the *California Test of Mental Maturity*, the *Cognitive Abilities Test*, and the *Otis–Lennon Mental Ability Test*, are widely used.

▲ Working with psychiatrist Theodore Simon to develop a test for evaluating children's intelligence, Alfred Binet (shown here) began testing Parisian students in 1904.

The Range of Intelligence ▷

> **7.12** How do people at both ends of the IQ score continuum differ from those in the middle?

You may have heard the term *bell curve* and wondered just exactly what it is. When large populations are measured on intelligence or physical characteristics such as height and weight, the frequencies of the various scores or measurements usually conform to a *bell-shaped* distribution known as the *normal curve*—hence the term *bell curve*. The majority of the scores cluster around the mean (average). The more scores deviate from the mean (that is, the farther away from it they fall), either above or below, the fewer there are. And the normal curve is perfectly symmetrical; that is, there are just as many cases above as below the mean. The average IQ test score for all people in the same age group is arbitrarily assigned an IQ score of 100. On the Wechsler intelligence tests, approximately 50% of the scores are in the average range, between 90 and 110. About 68% of the scores fall between 85 and 115, and about 95% fall between 70 and 130. Some 2% of the scores are above 130,

FIGURE 7.6 **The Normal Curve**
When a large number of test scores are compiled, they are typically distributed in a normal (bell-shaped) curve. On the Wechsler scales, the average, or mean, IQ score is set at 100. As the figure shows, about 68% of the scores fall between 15 IQ points (1 standard deviation) above and below 100 (from 85 to 115), and about 95.5% of the scores fall between 30 points (2 standard deviations) above and below 100 (from 70 to 130).

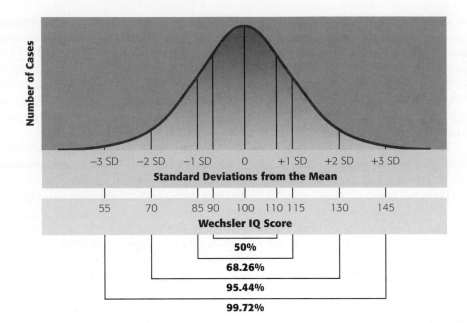

⊙→ Simulate the Experiment *The Normal Curve* on **mypsychlab.com**

mental retardation Subnormal intelligence reflected by an IQ below 70 and by adaptive functioning severely deficient for one's age.

which is considered superior, and about 2% fall below 70, in the range of mental retardation (see Figure 7.6). ⊙→ Simulate on **mypsychlab.com**

But what does it mean to have a "superior" IQ? In 1921, to try to answer this question, Lewis Terman (1925) launched a longitudinal study, now a classic, in which 1,528 gifted students were selected and measured at different ages throughout their lives. Tested on the Stanford–Binet, the participants—857 males and 671 females—had unusually high IQs, ranging from 135 to 200, with an average of 151. Terman's early findings put an end to the myth that mentally superior people are more likely to be physically inferior. In fact, Terman's gifted participants excelled in almost all the abilities he studied—intellectual, physical, emotional, moral, and social. Terman also exploded many other myths about the mentally gifted (Terman & Oden, 1947). For example, you may have heard the saying that there is a thin line between genius and madness. Actually, Terman's gifted group enjoyed better mental health than the general population. Terman's participants also earned more academic degrees, achieved higher occupational status and higher salaries, were better adjusted both personally and socially, and were healthier than their less mentally gifted peers. However, most women at that time did not pursue careers outside of the home, so the findings related to occupational success applied primarily to the men. Terman (1925) concluded that "there is no law of compensation whereby the intellectual superiority of the gifted is offset by inferiorities along nonintellectual lines" (p. 16). The Terman study continues today, with the surviving participants in their 80s or 90s. In a report on Terman's study, Shneidman (1989) states its basic findings—that "an unusual mind, a vigorous body, and a relatively well-adjusted personality are not at all incompatible" (p. 687).

At the opposite end of the continuum from Terman's sample are the 2% of the U.S. population whose IQ scores are in the range of mental retardation. These individuals have IQ scores below 70 and have problems carrying out the everyday activities that are easily managed by others of the same age (Sattler, 2008). There are many causes of mental retardation, including brain injuries, chromosomal abnormalities such as Down syndrome, chemical deficiencies, and hazards present during fetal development. And studies continue to document the enduring mental deficits produced by early exposure to lead (CDC, 2008). The degrees of retardation range from mild to profound (American Psychiatric Association, 2000a). Individuals with IQs ranging from 55 to 70 have mild mental retardation. Those whose scores fall between 40 and 54 have moderate retardation, and those whose IQs are between 25 and 39 have severe mental retardation. An IQ score lower than 25 is required for an individual to be diagnosed with profound mental retardation. Individuals with mild mental retardation are able to acquire academic skills such as reading up to about a sixth-grade level and may be able to become economically self-supporting. The academic skills of those with moderate retardation are usually limited to the first- or second-grade level; these individuals can learn self-care skills and often function well in sheltered work environments. People with severe levels of retardation typically are unable to acquire academic skills but can communicate verbally and learn self-care skills such as brushing their teeth. At the profound level of retardation, individuals usually learn only rudimentary motor skills and limited self-help skills such as feeding themselves.

Before the late 1960s, children with mental retardation in the United States were educated almost exclusively in special schools. Since then, there has been a movement toward inclusion—or educating such students in classes with other students. Inclusion, also called *mainstreaming,* may involve placing these students in classes with nonhandicapped students for part or all of the day. Resources spent on educational programs for students with mental retardation are proving to be sound investments. Such programs rely heavily on behavior modification techniques and are making it possible for some individuals with mental retardation to become employed. Everyone benefits—the individual, his or her family, and society as a whole. 👁—|Watch on **mypsychlab.com**

inclusion Educating students with mental retardation by placing them in classes with nonhandicapped students for part or all of the day; also called *mainstreaming.*

👁—|Watch the **Video** *Mainstreaming Children with Special Needs* on **mypsychlab.com**

Explaining Differences in Intelligence

We use several words to refer to people we believe to be intellectually superior—bright, clever, intelligent, smart, and so on. Likewise, we have just as many to describe our peers who seem to possess less intelligence than others. In fact, the presence of these terms in our vocabularies demonstrates that a wide range of differences in intellectual functioning are readily apparent in our everyday interactions with other people. What accounts for these differences?

Nature, Nurture, and IQ ▶

In many cases, biological factors, such as the presence of an extra chromosome, are to blame for mental retardation. But what about normal variations in intelligence? To what degree do they result from biological, or genetic, influences? This question arises out of perhaps the most vocal area of disagreement concerning intelligence, the nature–nurture debate, the debate over whether intelligence is primarily the result of heredity or environment. Englishman Sir Francis Galton (1874) initiated this debate, which has raged for more than 100 years, and coined the term. After studying a number of prominent families in England, Galton concluded that intelligence was inherited. Hereditarians agree with Galton, claiming that intelligence is largely inherited—the result of nature. Environmentalists, in contrast, insist that it is influenced primarily by one's environment—the result of nurture. Most psychologists now agree that both nature and nurture contribute to intelligence, but they continue to debate the proportions contributed by each.

7.13 What is the evidence for each side of the nature–nurture debate?

nature–nurture debate The debate over whether intelligence and other traits are primarily the result of heredity or environment.

Heritability. As you learned in Chapter 2, *behavioral genetics* is the study of the relative influence of genetics and environment on human behavior and mental processes. Behavioral geneticists sometimes express the results of their studies in terms of heritability, an index of the degree to which a characteristic is estimated to be influenced by heredity. Figure 7.7 (p. 224) shows estimates of the proportional contributions of genetic and environmental factors to intelligence. Some research using the adoption study method, comparing children to both their adoptive and biological parents, also supports the assertion that genes strongly influence IQ scores.

Minnesota is the site of the most extensive U.S. study of identical and fraternal twins. Since the early 1980s, the Minnesota Center for Twin and Adoption Research has been recruiting fraternal and identical twins to participate in research projects examining genetic and environmental influences on a variety of psychological

heritability An index of the degree to which a characteristic is estimated to be influenced by heredity.

FIGURE 7.7 Correlations between the IQ Scores of Persons with Various Relationships
The more closely related two individuals are, the more similar their IQ scores tend to be. Thus, there is a strong genetic contribution to intelligence.
Source: Based on data from Bouchard & McGue (1981); Erlenmeyer-Kimling & Jarvik (1963).

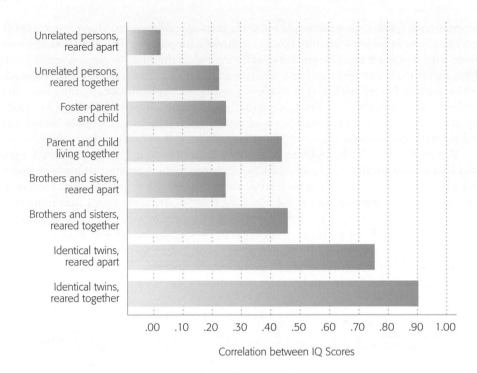

variables, including intelligence. In 1997, the center's first director, Thomas Bouchard, summarized all of the studies of intelligence that had been done at the center up to that point. Bouchard reported that, taken together, the studies yielded heritability estimates of .60 to .70. (A heritability of 1.00 would mean that all of the variation in intelligence is due to genes.) The center's more recent studies have produced similar estimates (e.g., Johnson et al., 2007).

Other twin studies suggest that the Minnesota researchers may have overestimated the heritability of intelligence. For example, British researchers associated with another large-scale study of twins, the Twins Early Development Study, found estimates of heritability ranging from .34 to .42 in a group of twins they tested at 7, 9, and 10 years of age (Kovas, Haworth, Dale, & Plomin, 2007). Similar heritability estimates were found by researchers in another longitudinal twin study, the Western Reserve Reading Project in Ohio, in which twins were tested at 6, 7, and 8 years of age (Hart, Petrill, Thompson, & Plomin, 2009).

Adoption and Early Intervention. Several studies indicate that IQ test scores are not fixed but can be modified with an enriched environment. Several decades ago, Sandra Scarr and Richard Weinberg (1976) studied 140 African American and interracial children who had been adopted by highly educated, upper-middle-class white American families; 99 of the children had been adopted in the first year of life. The adoptees were fully exposed to middle-class cultural experiences and vocabulary, the "culture of the tests and the school" (p. 737). How did the children perform on IQ and achievement tests? The average IQ score of the 130 adoptees was 106.3. Their achievement test scores were slightly above the national average, not below. On the average, the earlier the children were adopted, the higher their IQs. The mean IQ score of the 99 early adoptees was 110.4, about 10 IQ points above the average for white Americans. Similarly, studies in France show that IQ scores and achievement are substantially higher when children from lower-class environments are adopted by middle- and upper-middle-class families (Duyme, 1988; Schiff & Lewontin, 1986).

In addition to these encouraging adoption studies, research examining the effects of early childhood interventions on the IQ scores of children from poor families clearly indicates that early educational experiences can affect intellectual development (Ramey, Ramey, & Lanzi, 2007; Reynolds & Temple, 2008). Some of the best known of these interventions have been carried out by developmental psychologist Craig Ramey. And unlike many studies of early interventions, Ramey's research involves true experiments—so it is clear that the outcomes are caused by the interventions.

In one of Ramey's programs (Campbell & Ramey, 1994), 6- to 12-month-old infants of low-IQ, low-income mothers were randomly assigned to either an intensive 40-hour-per-week day-care program that continued throughout the preschool years or a control group that received only medical care and nutritional supplements. When the children reached school age, half in each group (again based on random assignment) were enrolled in a special after-school program that helped their families learn how to support school learning with educational activities at home. Ramey followed the progress of children in all four groups through age 12, giving them IQ tests at various ages. Figure 7.8 shows that those who participated in the infant and preschool program scored higher on IQ tests than peers who received either no intervention or only the school-aged intervention. Perhaps more important, during the elementary school years, about 40% of the control group participants had IQ scores classified as borderline or retarded (scores below 85), compared with only 12.8% of those who were in the infant program. More recent research shows that the cognitive advantage enjoyed by the infant intervention groups has persisted into adulthood (Campbell et al., 2008). Ramey's work clearly shows that the environment has great potential to influence IQ scores. Does education have similar effects on adults' IQ scores? The *Apply It* discussion (p. 226) addresses this question.

Historical evidence also suggests that environmental factors have a strong influence on IQ scores. Americans and similarly advantaged populations all over the world have gained about 3 IQ points per decade since 1940. James Flynn (1987, 1999; Dickens & Flynn, 2001; Must, te Njienhuis, Must, & van Vianen, 2009) analyzed 73 studies involving some 7,500 participants ranging in age from 12 to 48 and found that "every Binet and Wechsler [standardization group] from 1932 to 1978 has performed better than its predecessor" (Flynn, 1987, p. 225). Studies in developing countries, such as Kenya and the Sudan, have shown that IQ gains can happen over much shorter periods of time when the standard of living improves drastically (Daley et al., 2003; Khaleefa, Abdelwahid, Abdulradi, & Lynn, 2008). This consistent improvement in IQ scores over time is known as the *Flynn effect*.

It should not be surprising that enriched environments alter traits that are highly heritable. Consider the fact that American and British adolescents are 6 inches taller on average than their counterparts a century and a half ago (Tanner, 1990). Height has the same heritability (.90) today as it did in the mid-19th century. So this tremendous average gain in height of 6 inches is entirely attributable to environmental influences: better health, better nutrition, and so on. The highest heritability estimates for intelligence are

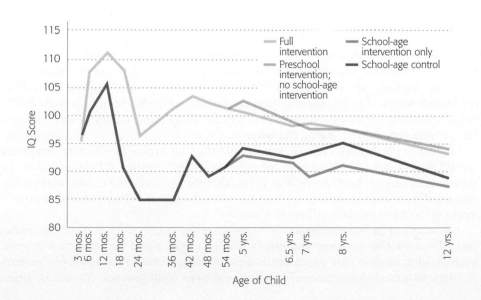

FIGURE 7.8 Ramey's Infant Intervention
In the Ramey study, children were randomly assigned in infancy to an experimental group with special day care (the "full intervention" group) or to a control group. From kindergarten through third grade, half of each group received supplementary family support, and the other half did not. The difference in IQ between the intervention and control groups remained statistically significant even at age 12.

Source: Campbell & Ramey, (1994).

APPLY IT **How to Build a Powerful Vocabulary**

Researchers have often found that vocabulary tests are strongly correlated with IQ scores (Sattler & Dumont, 2004). These correlations provide one of the best arguments in favor of the view that learning is at least as important to the development of intelligence as any ability with which we are born. Clearly, too, of all the cognitive skills we possess, none is more important for clarity of thinking and academic success than vocabulary. Thus, you may be able to make yourself smarter, in a practical sense, by improving your vocabulary. How can you accomplish this goal? The best way is to realize that almost all words belong to larger networks of meaning and to understand that your mind is already geared toward organizing information in terms of meaning. Thus, with a little effort, you can greatly increase your vocabulary by supporting the kind of learning your brain is already inclined to do. Here are a few techniques for following this advice.

Learn to Think Analytically about Words You Already Know and Relate New Words to Them.
What do the words *antiseptic* and *septic tank* have in common? You use an *antiseptic* to prevent bacterial infection of a wound; a *septic tank* is used for removing harmful bacteria from water containing human waste. A logical conclusion would be that *septic* has something to do with bacteria. Knowing this, what do you think a doctor means when she says that a patient is suffering from *sepsis*? By linking *sepsis* to *septic tank* and *antiseptic,* you can guess that she is referring to some kind of bacterial infection.

Be Aware of Word Connections That May Be Hidden by Spelling Differences.
You may know that both *Caesar* and *Czar* refer to some kind of ruler or leader. But you may not know that they are exactly the same word spoken and spelled somewhat differently in Ancient Rome *(Caesar)* and in Russia *(Czar)*. Now, if you learn in a history class about *Kaiser Wilhelm* who led Germany during World War I, thinking analytically about his title may help you realize that it is exactly the same word as *Caesar* and *Czar* but with a German spelling. Here's another example: Can you guess something about the location and climate of the nation of *Ecuador* by relating its name to a word that differs only slightly in spelling?

Use Your Knowledge of Word Parts to Actively Seek Out New Words.
Don't learn new words one at a time. Instead, be on the lookout for "word families"—root words and prefixes and suffixes. Here is one important root word, *spect*. You've seen it in many words. *Spect* means "look," "look at," "watch," "see." And *spect* appears in dozens of different words, such as *inspect*. What do you do when you *inspect* something? You *look* closely at it. Once you are equipped with this knowledge, other *spect* words may start to come to mind along with an entirely new way of thinking about their meanings: *spectacular, spectator, spectacle, spectacles, perspective, prospect, respect, disrespect, retrospect, suspect,* and so on. The word *circumspect* may be new to you. Look it up in a dictionary and think about how the literal meaning of the word ("look around") relates to the way this word is frequently used. And, when you read Chapter 1, might it have been easier to understand and remember the meaning of Wundt's research method, *introspection,* if you had thought about the *spect* part of the word? Probably so.

A strong vocabulary based on root words, prefixes, and suffixes will yield the word power that will profit you in many ways.

far lower than those for height. It seems clear, then, that environmental influences have the power to affect intelligence and achievement. For example, poverty affects nutrition, and research clearly shows that malnutrition, especially early in life, can harm intellectual development (Grigorenko, 2003).

7.14 How do theorists explain ethnic group differences in IQ scores?

Race and IQ

The nature–nurture debate has also been important in the discussion of race differences in intelligence test scores. Historically, most studies have shown that blacks score, on average, about 15 points lower than whites on standardized IQ tests in the United States (e.g., Loehlin, Lindzey, & Spuhler, 1975; Rushton & Jensen, 2005). Other studies have shown similar differences for blacks and whites in other nations (e.g., Rushton & Jensen, 2003). But why?

In 1969, psychologist Arthur Jensen published an article in which he attributed the IQ gap to genetic differences between the races. Further, he claimed that the genetic influence on intelligence is so strong that the environment cannot make a significant difference. Jensen even went so far as to claim that blacks and whites possess qualitatively different kinds of intelligence.

Beliefs such as those expressed by Jensen run counter to the results of the studies carried out by Craig Ramey and others that you read about earlier in this chapter. Such studies suggest that racial differences are more likely to result from poverty and lack of access to educational opportunities than from genetics. Moreover, a new testing technique called *dynamic assessment* supports the environmental explanation. In dynamic assessment, examinees are taught the goal and format of each IQ subtest before they are actually tested. The rationale behind the technique is the assumption that children from middle-class backgrounds have more experience with testing procedures and better understand that the goal of testing is to demonstrate competency (Haywood & Lidz, 2007). However, some experts argue that dynamic assessment has more potential as a tool for identifying effective teaching strategies for individual students than as a replacement for intelligence tests (Elliott, 2003; Jeltova et al., 2007). Thus, more research is needed before psychologists will be able to make definitive statements about the validity of dynamic assessment for intelligence testing.

In recent years, psychologists have begun to investigate another variable called *stereotype threat* that may help explain racial differences in IQ scores. The stereotype threat theory was first proposed by psychologist Claude Steele (Steele & Aronson, 1995). According to Steele, when minority individuals hear discussions of group differences in IQ scores, they may assume that their own intellectual ability is inferior to that of individuals in the majority group. Therefore, when faced with an IQ test, they "disengage," to avoid the threat of being stereotyped as having limited intellectual ability. This disengagement becomes a self-fulfilling prophecy: It causes individuals to obtain low scores, thereby appearing to validate the stereotype. Research has shown that programs designed to help people talk about and overcome the degree to which they sense stereotype threat when they take cognitive ability tests helps them achieve higher scores (Abrams et al., 2008; Alter et al., 2010). Other psychologists have pointed out that, although studies have shown that stereotype threat does exist, it explains only a fraction of the total average score differences among racial groups (Sackett, Hardison, & Cullen, 2004).

Before leaving the topic of race and IQ, stop and consider why the debates spawned by findings showing that one group has a higher average IQ than another group have stirred so much emotional intensity. One reason might be that in Western societies such as the United States intellectual ability is highly valued. Studies show that Asians place little value on intellectual ability even though they tend to get higher scores on cognitive ability tests than whites or other groups (Li, 2003; Lynn, 2006). Instead, Asians emphasize hard work and perseverance as the routes to academic and other kinds of life success (Stevenson, 1992). By contrast, by the time Americans reach the age of 11 or 12, a large majority believe that achievement results more from ability than from effort (Altermatt & Pomerantz, 2003; Heyman, Gee, & Giles, 2003). Psychologists suggest that this belief leads American students to fail to appreciate the importance of effort to academic achievement, even for people who are high in ability. It may also help explain research such as that of two researchers who compared the achievement test scores of Australian school children of Asian descent to those of English/Irish ancestry (Dandy & Nettelbeck, 2002). Their findings showed that Asian Australian students scored higher than their English/Irish peers on achievement tests even when they were matched on IQ (Dandy & Nettelbeck, 2002). These results suggest that, on a practical level, teachers and parents should probably be more concerned about helping each student work to achieve his or her full intellectual potential than about the student's IQ score.

Gender Differences in Cognitive Abilities

7.15 How do the cognitive abilities of males and females differ?

Psychologist Janet Shibley Hyde has studied gender differences for more than three decades. She points out that although there are a few physical characteristics on which males and females differ to a large degree (e.g., arm strength), the few gender gaps that exist for cognitive variables are quite small (Hyde, 2005). Thus, it is important not to exaggerate these differences to such a degree that they cause us to develop gender stereotypes. As you read through the discussion of gender differences, keep your antistereotyping guard up.

Figure 7.9 (p. 228) shows some types of problems on which each gender tends to excel. But you need to keep two important points in mind: First, in general, the differences

FIGURE 7.9 Problem-Solving Tasks Favoring Women and Men
(a) A series of problem-solving tasks on which women generally do better than men. (b) Problem-solving tasks on which men do better.
Source: Kimura (1992).

Women tend to perform better than men on tests of perceptual speed, in which subjects must rapidly identify matching items—for example, pairing the house on the far left with its twin:

In addition, women remember whether an object, or a series of objects, has been displaced:

On some tests of ideational fluency—for example, those in which subjects must list objects that are the same color—and on tests of verbal fluency—in which participants must list words that begin with the same letter—women outperform men:

L _ _ _	Limp, Livery, Love, Laser, Liquid, Low, Like, Lag, Live, Lug, Light, Lift, Liver, Lime, Leg, Load, Lap, Lucid…

Women do better on precision manual tasks—that is, those involving fine motor coordination—such as placing the pegs in holes on a board:

And women do better than men on mathematical calculation tests:

77	$14 \times 3 - 17 + 52$
43	$2(15 + 3) + 12 - \frac{15}{3}$

(a)

Men tend to perform better than women on certain spatial tasks. They do well on tests that involve mentally rotating an object or manipulating it in some fashion, such as imagining turning this three-dimensional object:

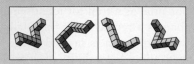

or determining where the holes punched in a folded piece of paper will fall when the paper is unfolded:

Men also are more accurate than women in target-directed motor skills, such as guiding or intercepting projectiles:

They do better on disembedding tests, in which they have to find a simple shape, such as the one on the left, once it is hidden within a more complex figure:

And men tend to do better than women on tests of mathematical reasoning:

1,100	If only 60 percent of seedlings will survive, how many must be planted to obtain 660 trees

(b)

within each gender are greater than the differences between the genders. Second, even though gender differences in cognitive abilities have been generally small on average, there tends to be more variation in such abilities among males than among females (that is, the range of test scores is typically greater for males).

Girls as young as 18 months of age have been found to have, on average, larger vocabularies than boys of the same age, a difference that persists throughout childhood (Wallentin, 2009). In one frequently cited large-scale study, Hedges and Nowell (1995) analyzed the results of the National Assessment of Educational Progress (NAEP), which has tested a nationally representative sample of 70,000 to 100,000 9-, 13-, and 17-year-olds annually in reading comprehension, writing, math, and science. The researchers compared the achievements of the 17-year-olds from 1971 through 1992 and reported that females outperformed males in reading and writing, while males did better in science and math.

Interestingly, however, girls get higher grades than boys do in all subjects (Duckworth & Seligman, 2006; Kenney-Benson et al., 2006). Researchers often attribute this finding to girls' approach to schoolwork. They have discovered that girls are more likely to take an effortful approach to their work and, as a result, they develop more effective learning strategies than boys do (Kenney-Benson et al., 2006). Studies have also shown that girls, on average, also tend to be more self-disciplined than boys (Duckworth & Seligman, 2006; Else-Quest et al., 2006).

As noted above, analyses of NAEP data show that boys display higher levels of achievement in mathematics than girls. More recent studies show the same pattern (Liu & Wilson, 2009). Some data suggest that hormonal factors explain this difference (Josephs et al., 2003). Other findings indicate that differences in brain structure and function are responsible. For example, some researchers attribute the finding that gender differences favoring males first appear or greatly increase during adolescence to the fact that males' brains develop more slowly than those of females do (Ellison & Nelson, 2009). However, most researchers agree that social influences are probably more important.

One possible social factor influencing the difference in math achievement is that parents often expect boys to do better than girls in math (Tiedemann, 2000). Could parental expectations become a self-fulfilling prophecy, leading girls to lack confidence in their math ability and to decide not to pursue advanced math courses? Yes, says sex difference researcher Jacqueline Eccles. Eccles's longitudinal research has shown that parents' beliefs about their children's talents at age 6 predict those children's beliefs about their own abilities at age 17 (Fredricks & Eccles, 2002). However, Eccles's research has also revealed that the gender gap in beliefs about math ability is somewhat smaller among today's high school students than it was in the past, suggesting that educators' efforts to increase girls' interest and success in mathematics have been effective.

Another way in which parents influence boys' and girls' ideas about math competence is their tendency to see academically successful girls as "hard workers" and academically successful boys as "talented" (Ratty et al., 2002). Thus, parents' beliefs may help explain why teenage girls who obtain top scores on standardized mathematics tests typically explain their scores as resulting from effort, while their male peers believe that their scores are due to superior natural mathematical talent (Rebs & Park, 2001). Thus, even girls with extraordinary levels of mathematical achievement may see themselves as lacking in ability. Perhaps it isn't surprising that mathematically gifted girls are far less likely than similarly gifted boys to choose math-oriented careers (Webb, Lubinski, & Benbow, 2002).

Researchers have found that, in general, males tend to perform somewhat better than females on some, but not all, spatial tasks (Geary, 1996; Kimura, 1992, 2000). Some research has shown that spatial abilities appear to be enhanced by prenatal exposure to high levels of androgens (Berenbaum, Korman, & Leveroni, 1995). Further, high blood levels of testosterone in men are associated with good performance on spatial tasks such as route learning (Choi & Silverman, 2002). However, these findings do not minimize the role of social experiences and expectations in shaping children's abilities and interests. Women also outperform men on some kinds of spatial tasks.

Beyond Intelligence

Perhaps the most important contribution of Gardner, Sternberg, and others who have suggested multicomponent models of intelligence is their emphasis on the notion that there are many aspects of cognitive functioning that are not captured by standardized tests of intelligence. Such tests cannot measure how well we relate to others, for example. Nor can they assess our ability to use our imaginations to escape the limitations of present reality.

7.16 What are the components of emotional intelligence?

Emotional intelligence The ability to apply knowledge about emotions to everyday life.

Emotional Intelligence

Whether one is male or female, the understanding we possess about our own and others' emotions influences how we think about ourselves and manage our interactions with others. Emotional intelligence is the ability to apply knowledge about emotions to everyday life (Salovey & Pizarro, 2003). Two leading researchers in the field, Peter Salovey and David Pizarro, argue that emotional intelligence is just as important to many important outcome variables, including how we fare in our chosen careers, as the kind of intelligence that is measured by IQ tests. Research supports this view, showing that emotional intelligence is unrelated to IQ scores (Lam & Kirby, 2002; van der Zee, Thijs, & Schakel, 2002). At the same time, emotional intelligence is correlated with both academic and social success (DiFabio & Palazzeschi, 2009).

Emotional intelligence includes two sets of components. The first, known as the *personal* aspects of emotional intelligence, includes awareness and management of our own emotions. People who are able to monitor their feelings as they arise are less likely to be ruled by them. However, managing emotions does not mean suppressing them; nor does it mean giving free rein to every feeling. Instead, effective management of emotions involves expressing them appropriately. Emotion management also involves engaging in activities that cheer us up, soothe our hurts, or reassure us when we feel anxious.

The *interpersonal* aspects of emotional intelligence make up the second set of components. *Empathy*, or sensitivity to others' feelings, is one such component. One key indicator of empathy is the ability to read others' nonverbal behavior—the gestures, vocal inflections, tones of voice, and facial expressions of others. Another of the interpersonal components is the capacity to manage relationships. However, it is related to both the personal aspects of emotional intelligence and to empathy. In other words, to effectively manage the emotional give-and-take involved in social relationships, we have to be able to manage our own feelings and be sensitive to those of others.

In a recent study, men were found to process emotions, especially positive ones, predominantly in the left hemisphere of the brain, whereas women were found to use both cerebral hemispheres more equally for processing emotions (Coney & Fitzgerald, 2000). This finding could account for some of the emotional difference between the genders. You can find your own *emotional quotient*, or *EQ*, by completing the *Try It*.

TRY IT   Find Your EQ

Emotional intelligence may be just as important to success in your chosen career as your actual job skills. Take this short test to assess your EQ by checking one response for each item.

1. I'm always aware of even subtle feelings as I have them.

_____ Always _____ Usually _____ Sometimes
_____ Rarely _____ Never

2. I can delay gratification in pursuit of my goals instead of getting carried away by impulse.

_____ Always _____ Usually _____ Sometimes
_____ Rarely _____ Never

3. Instead of giving up in the face of setbacks or disappointments, I stay hopeful and optimistic.

_____ Always _____ Usually _____ Sometimes
_____ Rarely _____ Never

4. My keen sense of others' feelings makes me compassionate about their plight.

_____ Always _____ Usually _____ Sometimes
_____ Rarely _____ Never

5. I can sense the pulse of a group or relationship and state unspoken feelings.

_____ Always _____ Usually _____ Sometimes
_____ Rarely _____ Never

6. I can soothe or contain distressing feelings, so that they don't keep me from doing things I need to do.

_____ Always _____ Usually _____ Sometimes
_____ Rarely _____ Never

Score your responses as follows: Always = 4 points; Usually = 3 points; Sometimes = 2 points; Rarely = 1 point; Never = 0 points. The closer your total number of points is to 24, the higher your EQ probably is.

Creativity ▶

┌ **7.17** How does creativity differ
└ from other forms of cognition?

Have you ever known a person who was intellectually bright but lacked creativity? Creativity can be thought of as the ability to produce original, appropriate, and valuable ideas and/or solutions to problems. Research indicates that there is only a weak to moderate correlation between creativity and IQ (Lubart, 2003). Remember the mentally gifted individuals studied by Lewis Terman? Not one of them has produced a highly creative work (Terman & Oden, 1959). No Nobel laureates, no Pulitzer prizes. Geniuses, yes; creative geniuses, no. Thus, high intelligence does not necessarily mean high creativity.

creativity The ability to produce original, appropriate, and valuable ideas and/or solutions to problems.

Cartoonists often illustrate creative thinking as a flash of insight, a lightbulb that suddenly turns on in the mind. But research studies indicate that useful and genuine creativity rarely appears in the form of sudden flashes (Haberlandt, 1997). For the most part, creative ideas that come to conscious awareness have been incubating for some time. Most experts agree that genuine creativity "is an accomplishment born of intensive study, long reflection, persistence and interest" (Snow, 1993, p. 1033).

There are basically four stages in the creative problem-solving process (Goleman, Kaufman, & Ray, 1992):

1. **Preparation**—searching for information that may help solve the problem
2. **Incubation**—letting the problem "sit" while the relevant information is digested
3. **Illumination**—being suddenly struck by the right solution
4. **Translation**—transforming the insight into useful action

The incubation stage, perhaps the most important part of the process, takes place below the level of awareness.

What is unique about creative thought? According to psychologist J. P. Guilford (1967), who studied creativity for several decades, creative thinkers are highly proficient at divergent thinking. Divergent thinking is the ability to produce multiple ideas, answers, or solutions to a problem for which there is no agreed-on solution (Guilford, 1967). More broadly, divergent thinking is novel, or original, and involves the synthesis of an unusual association of ideas; it is flexible, switching quickly and smoothly from one stream of thought or set of ideas to another; and it requires fluency, or the ability to formulate an abundance of ideas (Csikszentmihalyi, 1996). For example, divergent thinking would help policymakers come up with new answers to questions such as "What is the most efficient way of distributing surplus agricultural products grown in developed nations to hungry people in the developing world?" In contrast to divergent thinking, Guilford defined *convergent thinking* as the type of mental activity measured by IQ and achievement tests; it consists of solving precisely defined, logical problems for which there is a known correct answer. For instance, convergent thinking would be required to answer a question such as "How much surplus food is grown in each of the world's developed nations?"

divergent thinking The ability to produce multiple ideas, answers, or solutions to a problem for which there is no agreed-on solution.

However, divergent and convergent thinking are not always separate phenomena. Both are required for most cognitive tasks. For example, to be creative, a person must develop divergent thinking, but convergent thinking is required to discriminate between good and bad ideas (Csikszentmihalyi, 1996). Similarly, solving precisely defined problems can involve divergent thinking, as one tries to think of possible solutions.

Researchers are identifying the different brain areas involved in convergent and divergent thinking. In general, convergent thinking is characterized by greater activity in the left frontal cortex, while divergent thinking is marked by higher levels of activity in the right frontal cortex (Razoumnikova, 2000). Other studies show that processes involved in convergent thinking, such as searching for patterns in events, are carried out in the left hemisphere (Wolford, Miller, & Gazzaniga, 2000). Studies by Carlsson and others (2000) that measured regional cerebral blood flow (rCBF) revealed striking differences in frontal lobe activity between participants who were

FIGURE 7.10 Maps of Regional Cerebral Blood Flow (rCBF)
(a) Highly creative thinking is associated with activity in both hemispheres, but with significantly higher levels in the right hemisphere (red indicates activity).
(b) During thinking that is not creative, activity is largely restricted to the left hemisphere.
Source: Adapted from Carlsson et al. (2000).

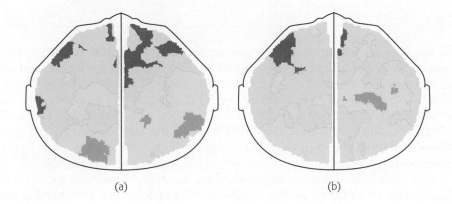

(a)   (b)

engaged in highly creative thinking and those who were not. Figure 7.10(a) shows the frontal lobe activity during highly creative thinking. There is activity in both hemispheres but a significantly greater amount in the right frontal cortex. In contrast, Figure 7.10(b) shows that during periods when no creative thinking is occurring, the left frontal lobe is highly active, and there is very little activity in the right hemisphere.

How might individual differences in creativity be measured? Tests designed to measure creativity emphasize original approaches to arriving at solutions for open-ended problems or to producing artistic works (Gregory, 1996). One creativity test, the Unusual Uses Test, asks respondents to name as many uses as possible for an ordinary object (such as a brick). Another measure of creativity is the Consequences Test, which asks test takers to list as many consequences as they can that would be likely to follow some basic change in the world (such as the force of gravity being reduced by 50%). And researchers Mednick and Mednick (1967), who reasoned that the essence of creativity consists of the creative thinker's ability to fit together ideas that to the noncreative thinker might appear remote or unrelated, created the Remote Associates Test (RAT).

Psychologists studying exceptionally creative individuals (e.g., Bloom, 1985) have learned that they share a number of characteristics that distinguish them from less creative individuals. For one, they have a great deal of expertise in a specific area that has been built up over years of disciplined study and practice. Creative individuals are also open to new experiences and ideas, even those that may seem quite odd to others; moreover, they seem to be inherently curious and inquisitive (Sternberg, 1985a). Creative people also tend to be independent thinkers who are less influenced by the opinions of others than their less creative counterparts are. Perhaps because of their independence, creative individuals are more likely to be motivated by the anticipation, excitement, and enjoyment of their work than by a desire to please others. Finally, creative endeavor requires hard work and persistence in the face of failure. For instance, Albert Einstein published 248 papers on his theory of relativity before it was finished, and Mozart, when he died at age 35, had created 609 musical compositions (Haberlandt, 1997).

ᦁᦞ Looking Back

We began this chapter by introducing you to anchoring, after which you learned about the cognitive strategies we use to think, make decisions, and solve problems. Next, we discussed human language and animal communication. Thinking about cognition and language, a vast body of knowledge and skills, highlights the narrowness of some of the ways in which intelligence has been measured in the past. That is, all humans possess a remarkable set of cognitive and linguistic tools, yet intelligence testing emphasizes our differences. Thus, it's important to remember that intelligence tests measure only one aspect of human functioning.

CHAPTER 7 SUMMARY

COGNITION (pp. 202-210)

7.1 How do imagery and concepts help us think? (pp. 202-204)

Imagery is helpful for learning new skills and for practicing those we already know. It can also help us store and retrieve information. Concepts are categories that allow us to quickly comprehend information. Rules and definitions determine formal concepts, whereas natural concepts arise out of everyday experiences. We also match information with prototypes, or examples, that include most or all of the features associated with the concepts they represent. Exemplars are examples of concepts with which we have the most familiarity.

Key Terms

cognition, p. 202
imagery, p. 202
concept, p. 203
formal concept, p. 203
natural concept, p. 203
prototype, p. 203
exemplars, p. 203

7.2 How do we make decisions? (pp. 204-207)

Systematic processes involve considering all possible options prior to making a decision. Sometimes we use priorities to eliminate some of these options to speed up the decision-making process. By contrast, heuristics, or "rules of thumb," allow us to make decisions quickly, with little effort. Framing causes us to weigh a decision's gains and losses, and intuition relies on "gut feelings." Anchoring on one piece of information rather than considering all of the factors that are relevant to a decision may cause distortions in thinking.

Key Terms

decision making, p. 204
elimination by aspects, p. 204
heuristic, p. 205
availability heuristic, p. 205
representativeness heuristic, p. 205
recognition heuristic, p. 205
framing, p. 206

intuition, p. 206
anchoring, p. 207

7.3 How do the basic approaches and obstacles to problem solving differ? (pp. 207-209)

Analogy, working backward, and means–end analysis are problem solving heuristics that may or may not lead to a correct solution. Analogy heuristics apply proven solutions to new problems. Working backward discovers the steps to solving a problem by first defining the solution. In means-end analysis, the current state is compared to the desired state, and a series of steps are proposed to close the gap between the two. An algorithm is a strategy that always yields a correct solution. Obstacles to problem solving include functional fixedness, the inability to see new uses for familiar objects, and mental set, using a previously successful problem-solving strategy without determining whether it is appropriate for a new problem.

Key Terms

problem solving, p. 207
analogy heuristic, p. 207
working backward, p. 207
means–end analysis, p. 208
algorithm, p. 208
functional fixedness, p. 208
mental set, p. 208
confirmation bias, p. 209

7.4 How have computer scientists applied research on artificial intelligence? (pp. 209-210)

Artificial neural networks (ANNs) are used to simulate human thinking. They process information like human experts and learn from experience. ANNs are the basis for expert systems, computer programs that do the work of human decision makers.

Key Terms

artificial intelligence, p. 209
artificial neural networks (ANNs), p. 209
expert systems, p. 209

LANGUAGE (pp. 210-215)

7.5 What are the components of language? (pp. 210-211)

The components of language are (1) phonemes, (2) morphemes, (3) syntax, (4) semantics, and (5) pragmatics. Phonemes are the basic units of sound, and morphemes are the basic units of meaning. Syntax includes all of a language's rules for combining words into phrases and sentences. Semantics includes the rules for combining units of meaning such as morphemes, words, and sentences. Pragmatics includes the social and nonverbal aspects of language.

Key Terms

language, p. 210
psycholinguistics, p. 210
phonemes, p. 210
morphemes, p. 210

syntax, p. 210
semantics, p. 211
pragmatics, p. 211

7.6 What is the evidence concerning animal communication? (pp. 211-213)

Chimpanzees can learn to use sign language to communicate. Birds that can vocalize have been taught to use words to communicate. For the most part, research indicates that animals string symbols together rather than create true sentences.

7.7 How does language influence thinking? (pp. 213-214)

In general, thinking has a greater influence on language than language has on thinking. Whorf's linguistic relativity hypothesis has not been supported by research.

Key Term
linguistic relativity hypothesis, p. 213

7.8 How does bilingualism affect thinking and language development? (pp. 214-215)

People who learn a second language when they are younger than age 10 or 11 usually speak it without an accent. However, adolescents and adults know more about their own languages, and they can use this knowledge when they are learning a second one.

Key Term
bilingualism, p. 214

INTELLIGENCE (pp. 215-223)

7.9 How do the theories of Spearman, Thurstone, Gardner, and Sternberg differ? (pp. 215-218)

Spearman believed that intelligence is composed of a general ability factor (*g*) and a number of specific abilities (*s*). Thurstone proposed seven primary mental abilities. Gardner claims that there are eight kinds of intelligence, and Sternberg's triarchic theory proposed that three types exist.

Key Terms
intelligence, p. 215
g factor, p. 216
primary mental abilities, p. 216
theory of multiple intelligences, p. 216
triarchic theory of intelligence, p. 217

7.10 What are the characteristics of good cognitive ability tests? (pp. 218-220)

Achievement tests measure learning, while an aptitude test predicts future performance on a specific task. Intelligence tests measure general intellectual ability. Reliable tests yield consistent results. Tests are valid if they predict appropriate outcome variables. Standardization is necessary so that individuals' scores can be compared. Cultural bias threatens the validity of a test, so test makers must reduce it as much as possible.

Key Terms
achievement test, p. 218
aptitude test, p. 218
intelligence test, p. 219
reliability, p. 219
validity, p. 219

standardization, p. 219
norms, p. 219
culture-fair intelligence test, p. 219

7.11 What did Binet, Terman, and Wechsler contribute to the study of intelligence? (pp. 220-221)

Binet developed the first standardized intelligence test. Terman adapted Binet's test for use in the United States and adopted Stern's "intelligence quotient" or "IQ" as the scoring system for the new test. Wechsler developed tests for children and adults. Scores in Wechsler's tests are based on deviation from age-based averages.

Key Term
intelligence quotient (IQ), p. 220

7.12 How do people at both ends of the IQ score continuum differ from those in the middle? (pp. 221-223)

Graphing the frequencies of a large number of IQ scores produces a symmetrical curve (the normal curve) shaped like a bell. Half of scores fall above and half below the mean. Terman's longitudinal study revealed that, in general, gifted individuals enjoy better physical and mental health and are more successful than members of the general population. To be classified as having mental retardation, an individual must have an IQ score below 70 and show a severe deficiency in everyday adaptive functioning.

Key Terms
mental retardation, p. 222
inclusion, p. 223

EXPLAINING DIFFERENCES IN INTELLIGENCE (pp. 223-229)

7.13 What is the evidence for each side of the nature–nurture debate? (pp. 223-226)

The nature-nurture debate concerns the relative contributions of heredity and environment to variations in IQ test scores.

Studies involving identical twins are important to this debate because twins have exactly the same genes. If identical twins raised together are found to be more alike on a certain trait than are fraternal twins raised together, then that trait is

Human Development

Think About It

Do you consider yourself a moral person? Most people do, but we sometimes face questions for which there are no simple yes-no, right-wrong answers. A "dilemma" is a situation in which all of the options are viewed as undesirable or mutually exclusive. By asking people to reflect on various kinds of dilemmas, psychologists have learned a lot about how social reasoning changes with age. For instance, consider the following dilemma and the exercise that follows it.

> In Europe a woman was near death from a special kind of cancer. There was one drug the doctors thought might save her. It was a form of radium that a druggist in the same town had recently discovered. The drug was expensive to make, and the druggist was charging ten times what it cost him. He paid $200 for the radium and charged $2,000 for a small dose of the drug. The sick woman's husband, Heinz, went to everyone he knew to borrow the money, but he could only get together $1,000, which was half of what the drug cost. He told the druggist that his wife was dying and asked him to sell it cheaper or let him pay later. But the druggist said, "No, I discovered the drug, and I am going to make money from it." So Heinz got desperate and broke into the man's store to steal the drug for his wife. (Colby et al., 1983, p. 77)

If Heinz had asked for your advice before he broke into the store, how important would each of the following factors have been to you? Rank them in their order of importance based on your own personal values.

_____ Heinz may go to jail if he steals the drug.

_____ Heinz promised to "love and honor" his wife when he got married.

_____ In general, people ought to obey the law and respect others' rights; otherwise society will break down.

_____ Heinz's wife's right to life is more important than the druggist's right to profit from his discovery.

Do you detect any general themes or principles in these statements? The first item is about Heinz and how stealing the drug might affect him. The second is about Heinz's relationship with his wife. The third is about the implications of Heinz's actions for society as a whole, and the fourth is about competing individual rights. As you can imagine, the ranking that you assign to each item might reveal something about how you think about moral issues. As you will learn later in the chapter, researchers have used similar procedures to show how people's thinking about moral issues evolves from childhood, through adolescence, and across early, middle, and late adulthood.

Historically, psychologists considered childhood and adolescence to be periods of change culminating in physical, social, and intellectual maturity. Next, most believed, came several decades of behavioral and psychological stability in adulthood. Finally, the conventional wisdom said, old age ushered in an era of rapid decline that resulted in death. Today, psychologists' approach to all of these periods is strongly influenced by the belief that change happens throughout the human life span.

developmental psychology The study of how humans grow, develop, and change throughout the life span.

We begin this chapter with a discussion of several theories that have strongly influenced the field of developmental psychology, the scientific study of how humans grow, develop, and change throughout the life span. Then, we will consider the challenges and milestones associated with each of the major phases of development. Note that when we discuss changes in the *physical domain*, we are referring to changes that take place in the body. The *cognitive domain* includes changes in thinking, memory, and so on. The *psychosocial domain* includes changes in how we relate to others and understand the social world.

Theories of Development

You may not realize it, but you have already learned about several theories of development. The learning theories you studied in Chapter 5, for instance, can explain many age-related changes as resulting from conditioned stimuli, reinforcement, punishment, observational learning, and the like. Learning theories favor the nurture side of the nature–nurture debate you read about in earlier chapters.

All developmental theories take a position in the nature–nurture debate. Most also address the question of whether development is continuous or occurs in stages. The learning theories assume that development happens in a continuous fashion as the result of environmental influences. Stage theories, by contrast, assert that development occurs in phases—or "leaps" to put it metaphorically—that are distinct from one another. We will begin our discussion of developmental theories with perhaps the most influential of all stage theories, that of Swiss developmentalist Jean Piaget.

Piaget's Theory of Cognitive Development ▶

Thanks to the work of Swiss psychologist Jean Piaget (PEE-ah-ZHAY) (1896–1980), psychologists have gained insights into the cognitive processes of children.

How Development Happens. According to Piaget, cognitive development begins with a few basic schemes—plans of action to be used in similar circumstances. For instance, once you've experienced the series of actions involved in using a fast-food restaurant's drive-through service, you can construct a drive-through scheme and apply it to any such restaurant. Each time you use this scheme at a different restaurant, there will be a few differences from your experience at other places, but the basic plan of action you follow will be the same. The point is that you don't have to start from scratch every time you go to a new fast-food restaurant; experience has provided you with a general plan of action—a scheme—to follow.

schemes Plans of action, based on previous experiences, to be used in similar circumstances.

The essence of cognitive development, for Piaget, is the refinement of schemes. For example, an infant who has had experience playing with rubber balls has constructed a scheme that she uses whenever she encounters a ball-like object. The scheme leads her to expect anything resembling a ball to bounce. Consequently, when she is presented with a plum, her ball scheme (her mental plan of action to be applied to ball-like objects) leads her to throw the plum to the floor, expecting it to bounce. Piaget used the term assimilation to refer to the mental process by which we incorporate new objects, events, experiences, and information into existing schemes.

assimilation The process by which new objects, events, experiences, or information is incorporated into existing schemes.

When the infant sees that the plum doesn't bounce, her ball scheme changes (although she may try bouncing plums a few more times just to be sure!). This change of scheme will result in a better intellectual adaptation to the real world because the revised scheme includes the knowledge that some ball-like objects bounce but others do not. Piaget used the term accommodation for the mental process of modifying existing schemes and creating new ones to incorporate new objects, events, experiences, and information.

accommodation The process by which existing schemes are modified and new schemes are created to incorporate new objects, events, experiences, or information.

According to Piaget (1963, 1964; Piaget & Inhelder, 1969), changes in schemes underlie four stages of cognitive development, each of which reflects a qualitatively different way of reasoning and understanding the world. The stages occur in a fixed sequence in which the accomplishments of one stage provide the foundation for the next stage. Although children throughout the world seem to progress through the stages in the same order, they show individual differences in the rate at which they pass through them. And each child's rate is influenced by her or his level of maturation and experiences, such as going to school. The transition from one stage to another is gradual, not abrupt, and children often show aspects of two stages while going through these transitions.

The Sensorimotor Stage. In Piaget's first stage, the *sensorimotor stage* (age birth to 2 years), infants gain an understanding of the world through their senses and their motor activities (actions or body movements). An infant's behavior, which is mostly reflexive at birth, becomes increasingly complex and gradually evolves into intelligent behavior. At this stage, thought is confined to objects that are present and events that are directly perceived. The child learns to respond to and manipulate objects and to use them in goal-directed activity.

The major achievement of the sensorimotor period is the development of object permanence—the realization that objects (including people) continue to exist, even when they are out of sight. This concept develops gradually and is complete when the child is able to represent objects mentally in their absence. The attainment of this ability marks the end of the sensorimotor period.

object permanence The realization that objects continue to exist, even when they can no longer be perceived.

The Preoperational Stage. According to Piaget, children move into the *preoperational stage* of cognitive development when they begin to exhibit signs of the symbolic function—the understanding that one thing can stand for another. Children act on the

symbolic function The understanding that one thing—an object, a word, a drawing—can stand for another.

world in ways that help them develop symbolic schemes throughout this stage, which is typical of children between the ages of 2 and 7 years. Two ways in which children display the symbolic function are through the use of words to represent objects and through *pretend play,* such as imagining that a block is a car or a doll is a real baby. As children practice using symbols, they become increasingly able to represent objects and events mentally with words and images.

During the preoperational stage, children exhibit a tendency Piaget called *egocentrism:* They believe that everyone sees what they see, thinks as they think, and feels as they feel. As a result, their thinking is often illogical. In addition, their thinking about objects is dominated by appearances. For example, a 3-year-old may believe that a cookie is ruined when it breaks. Adults' attempts to convince her otherwise usually fail because adult thinking is based on the assumption that the identity of an object does not change when its appearance changes, a concept that is not yet understood by children in this stage.

The Concrete Operations Stage. In the third stage, the *concrete operations stage* (age 7 to 11 or 12 years), new schemes allow children to understand that a given quantity of matter remains the same despite rearrangement or change in its appearance, as long as nothing is added or taken away—a concept Piaget called conservation. Conservation develops because new schemes enable children in this stage to understand the concept of reversibility—the understanding that any change in the shape, position, or order of matter can be reversed mentally. As a result, they can think about a broken cookie before and after it broke, realizing that the change in appearance did not change the substance that makes up the cookie. You can see how younger and older children differ in their reasoning about such problems by doing the *Try It.*

The concepts of conservation of number, substance (liquid or mass), length, area, weight, and volume are not all acquired at once. They come in a certain sequence and usually at specific ages (see Figure 8.1, on page 244). Moreover, children in the concrete operations stage are unable to apply logic to hypothetical situations. For instance, they find it difficult to think logically about careers they might pursue as adults. They also have difficulty with problems that involve systematically coordinating several variables. For example, they usually cannot solve reasoning problems like these: If Mary is taller than Bill, and Bill is taller than Harry, is Harry shorter than Mary? or, How many different two-letter, three-letter, and four-letter combinations of the letters *A, B, C,* and *D* are possible? This kind of reasoning isn't possible until children enter the next stage.

The Formal Operations Stage. The *formal operations stage* (age 11 or 12 years and beyond) is Piaget's fourth and final stage of cognitive development. At this stage, preadolescents and adolescents can apply logical thought to abstract, verbal, and hypothetical situations and to problems in the past, present, or future—a capacity Piaget called hypothetico-deductive thinking. Teenagers can comprehend abstract subjects, such as philosophy and politics, and they become interested in the world of ideas as they begin to formulate their own theories. However, not all people attain full formal operational thinking (Kuhn, 1984; Neimark, 1981). High school math and science experience seems to facilitate it (Sharp, Cole, & Lave, 1979).

Formal operational thinking enables adolescents to think of what might be. Thus, they begin to conceive of "perfect" solutions to the world's and their own problems. For example, a teen whose parents are divorced may idealize her noncustodial parent and believe that her life would be wonderful if only she could live with that parent. Piaget used the term naive idealism to refer to this kind of thinking.

Psychologist David Elkind (1967, 1974) claims that the early teenage years are marked by another kind of unrealistic thought, *adolescent egocentrism,* which takes two forms, the imaginary audience and the personal fable. The imaginary audience consists of admirers and critics that adolescents conjure up and that exist only in their imagination. In their minds, they are always on stage. Teens may spend hours in front of the mirror trying to please this audience. Teenagers also have an exaggerated sense of personal

conservation The concept that a given quantity of matter remains the same despite being rearranged or changed in appearance, as long as nothing is added or taken away.

reversibility The realization that any change in the shape, position, or order of matter can be reversed mentally.

hypothetico-deductive thinking The ability to base logical reasoning on a hypothetical premise.

naive idealism A type of thought in which adolescents construct ideal solutions for problems.

imaginary audience A belief of adolescents that they are or will be the focus of attention in social situations and that others will be as critical or approving as they are of themselves.

TRY IT ▸ Conservation of Volume*

Show a preschooler two glasses of the same size and then fill them with the same amount of juice. After the child agrees they are the same, pour the juice from one glass into a taller, narrower glass and place that glass beside the other original one. Now ask the child if the two glasses have the same amount of juice or if one glass has more than the other. Children at this stage will insist that the taller, narrower glass has more juice, although they will quickly agree that you neither added juice nor took any away.

Now, repeat the procedure with a school-aged child. The older child will be able to explain that even though there appears to be more liquid in the taller glass, pouring liquid into a different container doesn't change its quantity.

*Be sure to get permission from the child's parents before you do this *Try It*.

◉ Watch on **mypsychlab.com**

uniqueness and indestructibility that Elkind calls the personal fable. Many believe they are somehow indestructible and protected from the misfortunes that befall others, such as unwanted pregnancies or drug overdoses (Alberts, Elkind, Ginsberg, 2007).

personal fable An exaggerated sense of personal uniqueness and indestructibility, which may be the basis for adolescent risk taking.

Cross-Cultural Research. The *Summarize It* (on p. 245) provides a recap of Piaget's four stages. Cross-cultural studies have affirmed the universality of the types of reasoning and the sequence of stages formulated by Piaget. But cross-cultural research has also revealed differences in the rates of cognitive development in various domains. Whereas the children Piaget observed began to acquire the concept of conservation between ages 5 and 7, Australian Aboriginal children show this change between the ages of 10 and 13 (Dasen, 1994). Yet the Aboriginal children function at the concrete operations level earlier on spatial tasks than on quantification (counting) tasks, while the reverse is true for Western children. This difference makes sense in light of the high value Aborigines place on spatial skills and the low premium they place on quantification. In the Australian desert, moving from place to place, hunting, gathering, and searching for water, Aborigines have few possessions and rarely count things. Their language has words for numbers up to five, and their word for "many" applies to anything above five.

Conservation task	Typical age of acquisition (years)	Original presentation	Transformation

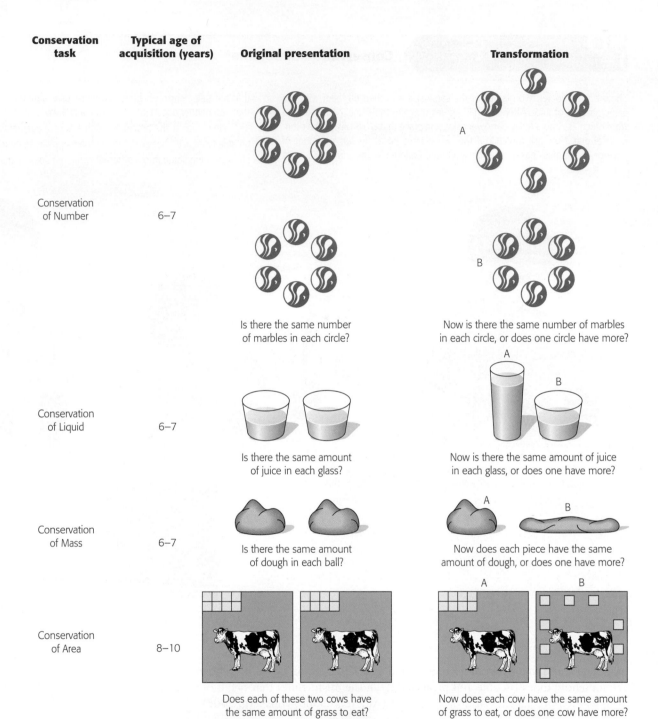

FIGURE 8.1 Piaget's Conservation Tasks
Piaget's research involved several kinds of conservation tasks. He classified children's thinking as concrete operational with respect to a particular task if they could correctly solve the problem and provide a concrete operational reason for their answer. For example, if a child said, "The two circles of marbles are the same because you didn't add any or take any away when you moved them," the response was judged to be concrete operational. Conversely, if a child said, "The two circles are the same, but I don't know why," the response was not classified as concrete operational.
Source: Bee & Boyd, *The Developing Child,* 11e.

Piaget's Stages of Cognitive Development

STAGE		DESCRIPTION
Sensorimotor (0 to 2 years)		Infants experience the world through their senses, actions, and body movements. At the end of this stage, toddlers develop the concept of object permanence and can mentally represent objects in their absence.
Preoperational (2 to 7 years)		Children are able to represent objects and events mentally with words and images. They can engage in imaginary play (pretend), using one object to represent another. Their thinking is egocentric; that is, they fail to consider the perspective of others.
Concrete operational (7 to 11 or 12 years)		Children at this stage become able to think logically in concrete situations. They acquire the concepts of conservation and reversibility, can order objects in a series, and can classify them according to multiple dimensions.
Formal operational (11 or 12 years and beyond)		At this stage, adolescents learn to think logically in abstract situations, learn to test hypotheses systematically, and become interested in the world of ideas. Not all people attain full formal operational thinking.

Another important cultural variable that contributes to cognitive development is formal education. Developmental psychologists know that children who live in cultures in which they have access to formal education progress more rapidly through Piaget's stages than peers whose societies do not require them to attend school or do not provide them with educational opportunities (Mishra, 1997). Moreover, formal operational thinking is so strongly correlated with formal education that some psychologists have suggested that it may be more a product of specific learning experiences than of a universal developmental process, as Piaget hypothesized.

8.2 How do the neo-Piagetians and Vygotsky explain cognitive development?

Alternatives to Piaget's theory

Although Piaget's genius and his monumental contribution to scientists' knowledge of mental development are rarely disputed, his methods and some of his findings and conclusions have been criticized (Halford, 1989). It now seems clear that children are more advanced cognitively and adults are less competent cognitively than Piaget concluded (Flavell, 1985, 1992; Mandler, 1990; Siegler, 1991). Nevertheless, decades of research, much of which was aimed at challenging Piaget's original findings, strongly suggest that cognitive development follows the sequence that Piaget's stages describe (Morra, Gobbo, Marini, & Sheese, 2008). However, a number of important questions about the process of age-related cognitive change remain, and other theories have proposed answers to them.

The Neo-Piagetian Approach. Some developmentalists, called neo-Piagetians, explain age-based differences in performance on the problems Piaget used in his studies as a function of changes in children's use of their working memories (Morra et al., 2008). Research has shown, for instance, that the younger children are, the more slowly they process information (Kail, 2000). Because they process information more slowly, they are more likely to fail to store information in long-term memory before new information comes along and pushes the old information out of working memory. (Recall the interference explanation of forgetting from Chapter 6.) Think about how this might affect children's responses to the conservation of number task shown in Figure 8.1 (refer back to p. 244). If the neo-Piagetians are correct, then children younger than age 6 or 7 will likely forget what the original presentation of marbles looked like when they are shown the transformation. As a result, they cannot mentally compare the original and transformed arrays. By contrast, older children, with their faster rates of information processing and more efficient working memories, can keep both presentations in mind as well as the process that was used to make the transformation. Thus, the older children can come up with a correct solution because they are better able to integrate all of the relevant information in working memory.

Vygotsky's Sociocultural Approach. The Russian developmentalist Lev Vygotsky (1896–1934) claimed that Piaget's theory of cognitive development placed too much emphasis on forces within the child. Vygotsky hypothesized that much of cognitive development results from the child's internalization of information that is acquired socially, primarily through the medium of language.

For instance, have you ever noticed children talking to themselves as they assemble a puzzle or paint a picture? Vygotsky believed that this and other spontaneous language behaviors exhibited by children are important to the process of cognitive development. Vygotsky maintained that human infants come equipped with basic skills such as perception, the ability to pay attention, and certain capacities of memory not unlike those of many other animal species (Vygotsky, 1934/1986). During the first two years of life, these skills grow and develop naturally through direct experiences and interactions with the child's sociocultural world. As children develop the ability to represent ideas, activities, and so on through speech, they are often observed "talking to themselves." Vygotsky believed that talking to oneself—*private speech*—is a key component in cognitive development. Through private speech, children can specify the components of a problem and verbalize steps in a process to help them work through a puzzling activity or situation. As young children develop greater competence, private speech fades into barely audible mumbling and muttering, and finally becomes simply thinking.

Vygotsky saw a strong connection among social experience, speech, and cognitive development. He also maintained that a child's readiness to learn resides within a zone of proximal development (*proximal* means "potential"). This zone, according to Vygotsky, is a range of cognitive tasks that the child cannot yet perform alone but can learn to perform with the instruction and guidance of a parent, teacher, or more advanced peer. This kind of help, in which a teacher or parent adjusts the quality and

zone of proximal development A range of cognitive tasks that a child cannot yet do but can learn to do through the guidance of an older child or adult.

▼ This father teaching his daughter to ride a bike is using Vygotsky's technique called *scaffolding*. A parent or teacher provides direct and continuous instruction at the beginning of the learning process and then gradually withdraws from active teaching as the child becomes more proficient at the new task or skill. How might scaffolding help a child acquire cognitive skills such as reading?

degree of instruction and guidance to fit the child's present level of ability or perform-ance, is often referred to as scaffolding. In scaffolding, direct instruction is given, at first, for unfamiliar tasks (Maccoby, 1992). But as the child shows increasing compe-tence, the teacher or parent gradually withdraws from direct and active teaching, and the child may continue toward independent mastery of the task. Vygotsky hypothe-sized that such scaffolding episodes occur frequently within the context of parent–child relationships and are essential to children's cognitive development.

Kohlberg's Theory of Moral Development ▶

Lawrence Kohlberg (1927–1987) proposed a stage theory of moral reasoning that has been extremely influential in the study of moral development. Long before Kohlberg's work began, both Vygotsky and Piaget applied their theories to moral development. Vygotsky (1926/1992) asserted that culture, by means of language and religious instruction, molds individuals to conform to its standards of acceptable behavior. Piaget did not deny the role that culture plays in moral development. However, he hypothesized that children's levels of cognitive development interact with society's efforts to instill moral values in them such that moral reasoning develops in stages that parallel those of cognitive development (Piaget, 1927/1965).

Measuring Moral Reasoning. Kohlberg studied changes in moral reasoning across the life span by presenting study participants with moral dilemmas like the story about Heinz you read at the beginning of the chapter. However, instead of asking partici-pants to rank different kinds of responses, Kohlberg asked open-ended questions such as "What do you think Heinz should do?" After participants offered their opinions, Kohlberg would ask for their reasons. By analyzing participants' responses to such questions, Kohlberg found that he could classify moral reasoning into three levels, each of which has two stages.

Levels and Stages. At Kohlberg's first level of moral development, the preconventional level, moral reasoning is governed by the physical consequences of behavior rather than one's own internalized standards of right and wrong. An act is judged good or bad based on its physical consequences. In Stage 1, "right" is whatever avoids punishment; in Stage 2, "right" is whatever is rewarded, benefits the individual, or results in a favor being returned. "You scratch my back and I'll scratch yours" is the type of thinking common at this stage. Children usually function at the preconventional level through age 10.

At Kohlberg's second level of moral development, the conventional level, the indi-vidual has internalized the standards of others and judges right and wrong in terms of those standards. At Stage 3, sometimes called the *good boy–nice girl orientation,* "good behavior is that which pleases or helps others and is approved by them" (Kohlberg, 1968, p. 26). At Stage 4, the orientation is toward "authority, fixed rules, and the maintenance of the social order. Right behavior consists of doing one's duty, showing respect for authority, and maintaining the given social order for its own sake" (p. 26). Kohlberg believed that a person must function at Piaget's concrete operations stage to reason morally at the conventional level.

Kohlberg's highest level of moral development is the postconventional level, which requires the ability to think at Piaget's stage of formal operations. At this level, people do not simply internalize the standards of others. Instead, they weigh moral alternatives, realizing that the law may sometimes conflict with basic human rights. At Stage 5, the person believes that laws are formulated to protect both soci-ety and the individual and should be changed if they fail to do so. At Stage 6, ethical decisions are based on universal ethical principles, which emphasize respect for human life, justice, equality, and dignity for all people. People who reason morally at Stage 6 believe that they must follow their conscience even if it results in a viola-tion of the law.

scaffolding A type of instruction in which an adult adjusts the amount of guidance provided to match a child's present level of ability.

[**8.3** How does Kohlberg's theory explain moral reasoning?

preconventional level Kohlberg's lowest level of moral development, in which moral reasoning is based on the physical consequences of an act; "right" is whatever avoids punishment or gains a reward.

conventional level Kohlberg's second level of moral development, in which right and wrong are based on the internalized standards of others; "right" is whatever helps or is approved of by others, or whatever is consistent with the laws of society.

postconventional level Kohlberg's highest level of moral development, in which moral reasoning involves weighing moral alternatives; "right" is whatever furthers basic human rights.

Ages, Stages, and Culture. The *Summarize It* describes Kohlberg's six stages of moral development. Kohlberg claimed that people progress through these stages one at a time in a fixed order, without skipping any stage. If movement occurs, it is to the next higher stage. Moreover, each level is associated with a prerequisite stage of cognitive development. Conventional moral reasoning is based on concrete operational thought, and postconventional reasoning is impossible until an individual has attained Piaget's formal operational stage.

Nevertheless, cognitive development alone is insufficient to produce advances in moral reasoning. In addition to the prerequisite level of cognitive development, individuals' environments must provide them with ample opportunities to apply their reasoning skills to moral issues. Direct teaching of moral principles also supports movement from one stage to the next, especially when parents and teachers explicitly explain such principles to children and teenagers and help them relate the principles to issues in their own lives (Narvaez, 2002; Weinstock, Assor, & Broide, 2009). Consequently, moral development tends to lag behind cognitive development, as suggested by Figure 8.2. Notice that conventional moral reasoning does not predominate until after age 12, even though most children attain the required

SUMMARIZE IT

Kohlberg's Stages of Moral Development

LEVEL	STAGE
Level I: Preconventional Level Moral reasoning is governed by the physical consequences of behavior; an act is good or bad depending on its physical consequences—whether it is punished or rewarded.	**Stage 1** The stage in which behavior that avoids punishment is right. Children obey out of fear of punishment. **Stage 2** The stage of self-interest. What is right is what benefits the individual or gains a favor in return. "You scratch my back and I'll scratch yours."
Level II: Conventional Level The child internalizes the standards of others and judges right and wrong according to those standards.	**Stage 3** The morality of mutual relationships. The "good boy–nice girl" orientation. Child acts to please and help others. **Stage 4** The morality of the social system and conscience. Orientation toward authority. Morality is doing one's duty, respecting authority, and maintaining the social order.
Level III: Postconventional Level Moral conduct is under internal control; this is the highest level and the mark of true morality.	**Stage 5** The morality of contract; respect for individual rights and laws that are democratically agreed on. Rational valuing of the wishes of the majority and the general welfare. Belief that society is best served if citizens obey the law. **Stage 6** The highest stage of the highest social level. The morality of universal ethical principles. The person acts according to internal standards independent of legal restrictions or opinions of others.

level of cognitive development (i.e., concrete operations) at age 6 or 7. Similarly, postconventional thought does not appear until adulthood, many years after most individuals have shown the first signs of formal operational thinking. Notice, too, that postconventional reasoning is the exception rather than the rule even among adults in their 30s. These findings suggest that moral development is a lifelong process.

There is a great deal of evidence that Kohlberg's stages of moral reasoning occur in all cultures. In a classic review of 45 studies of Kohlberg's theory conducted in 27 countries, Snarey (1985) found support for the universality of Stages 1 through 4 and for the invariant sequence of these stages in all groups studied. Although extremely rare, Stage 5 was found in almost all samples from urban or middle-class populations and was absent in all of the tribal or village folk societies studied. A more recent review by Snarey and others of a large number of studies across more than 20 countries supports the conclusions of Snarey's earlier work (Gibbs, Basinger, Grime, & Snarey, 2007).

Challenges to Kohlberg's View. One controversy concerning Kohlberg's theory involves the possibility of gender bias. Kohlberg indicated that the majority of women remain at Stage 3, while most men attain Stage 4. Do men typically attain a higher level of moral reasoning than women? Carol Gilligan (1982) asserts that Kohlberg's theory is sex biased. Not only did Kohlberg fail to include females in his original research, Gilligan points out, but he also limited morality to abstract reasoning about moral dilemmas. And, at his highest level, Stage 6, Kohlberg emphasized justice and equality but not mercy, compassion, love, or concern for others. Gilligan suggests that females, more than males, tend to view moral behavior in terms of compassion, caring, and concern for others. Thus, she agrees that the content of moral reasoning differs between the sexes, but she contends that males and females do not differ in the complexity of their moral reasoning.

More recent evidence suggests that females do tend to emphasize care and compassion in resolving moral dilemmas, while males tend to stress justice or at least to give it equal standing with caring (Garmon et al., 1996; Wark & Krebs, 1996). Although Kohlberg's theory does emphasize rights and justice over concern for others, researchers, nevertheless, have found that females score as high as males in moral reasoning (Walker, 1989). For this reason, Gilligan and others who have carried out research inspired by her approach have come to think of the caring and justice ethics as different dimensions of moral reasoning that contribute to both males' and females' thinking about issues of right and wrong (Jorgensen, 2006).

Finally, some critics point out that moral reasoning and moral behavior are not one and the same. Kohlberg readily acknowledged that people can be capable of making mature moral judgments yet fail to live morally (Kohlberg, 1968). Yet, researchers have found group differences in moral reasoning when groups that are extremely different in moral behavior are compared. For example, researchers have found that teenagers who are less able than their peers to look at situations from others' perspectives are more likely to engage in criminal behavior (Marshall, Marshall, & Serran, 2009). However, critics justifiably point out that such findings tell us little about how variations in moral development contribute to everyday decisions about moral behavior, such as office workers' decisions about whether to break their employers' rules about surfing the Internet on the job. Learning theorists suggest that decisions of this kind are influenced by the rewards associated with rule violation, the likelihood and consequences of getting caught, and the behavior of others (i.e., "everybody does it") rather than by abstract moral reasoning (Bandura 1977, 1989).

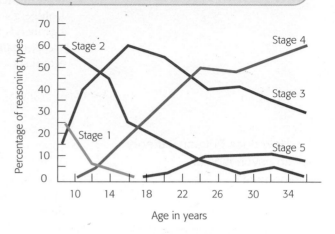

Why do you think Stage 2 reasoning persists into adulthood in some people?

FIGURE 8.2 Longitudinal Study of Moral Development
These findings are from Colby and Kohlberg's long-term longitudinal study of a group of boys who were asked about Kohlberg's moral dilemmas every few years from age 10 through early adulthood. Note that postconventional, or principled, reasoning was quite uncommon, even in adulthood.
Source: Colby et al. (1983).

In support of this view, psychologists Dennis Krebs and Kathy Denton have found that people exhibit lower levels of reasoning in response to real-life dilemmas than they do when formulating judgments about the hypothetical scenarios used in Kohlberg's research (Krebs & Denton, 2005). Regardless of whether we agree with Kohlberg's theory, most of us would agree that moral reasoning and moral behavior are critically important aspects of human development. Moral individuals make moral societies.

8.4 How does Erikson's theory explain psychosocial development?

Erikson's Theory of Psychosocial Development

Piaget's, Vygotsky's, and Kohlberg's theories deal with the intellectual aspects of development. Moral reasoning, of course, involves reasoning about the social world, but it doesn't address the process through which individuals come to feel a part of the families, neighborhoods, and cultures in which they live. By contrast, the theories of the psychoanalysts, first mentioned in Chapter 1, focus on precisely this domain of development. We will discuss the developmental theory of the founder of psychoanalysis, Sigmund Freud, in Chapter 11. But the theory of one of Freud's most important revisionists, Erik Erikson (1902–1994), is best discussed in the context of life-span development, because Erikson (1980) proposed the only major theory of development to include the entire life span. According to Erikson, individuals progress through eight psychosocial stages, each of which is defined by a conflict involving the individual's relationship with the social environment, which must be resolved satisfactorily for healthy development to occur (Erikson, 1980).

According to Erikson's view, the foundations of adult personality are laid in four childhood stages. During the first stage, *basic trust versus basic mistrust,* infants (birth to 1 year) develop a sense of trust or mistrust depending on the degree and regularity of care, love, and affection they receive from the mother or primary caregiver. Erikson (1980) considered "basic trust as the cornerstone of a healthy personality" (p. 58). During the second stage, *autonomy versus shame and doubt,* children aged 1 to 3 begin to express their independence (often by saying "No!") and develop their physical and mental abilities. In the third stage, *initiative versus guilt,* 3- to 6-year-old children go beyond merely expressing their autonomy and begin to develop initiative. During the fourth stage, *industry versus inferiority,* school-aged children (age 6 years to puberty) begin to enjoy and take pride in making things and doing things.

Erikson's later stages begin with puberty, but they are not as strongly tied to chronological age as those that occur during childhood. Instead, the adolescent and adult stages represent important themes of adult life. These themes occur in a fixed sequence, Erikson claimed, because the resolution of each depends on how well prior stages were resolved.

The first of these stages is *identity versus role confusion,* during which adolescents experience a phenomenon Erikson called the *identity crisis.* During the identity crisis, teens must develop an idea of how they will fit into the adult world. A healthy identity, Erikson claimed, is essential to the next stage, *intimacy versus isolation,* which begins around age 18. During this stage, young adults must find a life partner or come to a healthy acceptance of living in a single state. The next major theme of adult life, *generativity versus stagnation,* is at its peak during the years of middle age. Generativity, according to Erikson, is the desire to guide the next generation, through parenting, teaching, or mentoring. Finally, in later years, adults experience *ego integrity versus despair.* The goal of this stage is an acceptance of one's life in preparation for facing death. The *Summarize It* outlines Erikson's psychosocial stages.

psychosocial stages Erikson's eight developmental stages for the entire life span; each is defined by a conflict that must be resolved satisfactorily for healthy personality development to occur.

Most research on Erikson's theory has focused on trust in infants, identity formation in adolescents, and generativity in middle-aged adults. Specific predictions derived from Erikson's descriptions of these three stages have received mixed research support. On the positive side, there is a great deal of evidence that a relationship with a trusted caregiver in infancy is critical to later development.

In contrast, most research examining the development of identity has shown that the process does begin in adolescence, but it is not complete until well into the early adult years (Marcia, 2002; Waterman, 1985). Many college students, for example, have not yet settled on a major or future career when they begin taking classes, and they use experiences in their first few semesters to make these important decisions. One reason for the apparent delay may be that advances in logical reasoning, such as those associated with Piaget's formal operational stage, are strongly related to identity formation (Klaczynski, Fauth, & Swanger, 1998). Formal operational thinking evolves slowly across the adolescent years. Consequently, people may not have the cognitive ability to engage in the kind of thinking necessary for the development of identity until the early adult years.

With regard to generativity, in studies of young, midlife, and older women, researchers have found that generativity increases in middle age as Erikson's theory predicts (Warburton, McLaughlin, & Pinsker, 2006; Zucker, Ostrove, & Stewart, 2002). However, it does not decline in old age. So, generativity may be more a characteristic of middle than of early adulthood, as Erikson predicted, but it appears to continue to be important in old age.

Erikson's Psychosocial Stages of Development

STAGE	AGES	DESCRIPTION
Trust vs. mistrust	Birth to 1 year	Infants learn to trust or mistrust depending on the degree and regularity of care, love, and affection provided by parents or caregivers.
Autonomy vs. shame and doubt	1 to 3 years	Children learn to express their will and independence, to exercise some control, and to make choices. If not, they experience shame and doubt.
Initiative vs. guilt	3 to 6 years	Children begin to initiate activities, to plan and undertake tasks, and to enjoy developing motor and other abilities. If not allowed to initiate or if made to feel stupid and considered a nuisance, they may develop a sense of guilt.
Industry vs. inferiority	6 years to puberty	Children develop industriousness and feel pride in accomplishing tasks, making things, and doing things. If not encouraged or if rebuffed by parents and teachers, they may develop a sense of inferiority.
Identity vs. role confusion	Adolescence	Adolescents must make the transition from childhood to adulthood, establish an identity, develop a sense of self, and consider a future occupational identity. Otherwise, role confusion can result.
Intimacy vs. isolation	Young adulthood	Young adults must develop intimacy—the ability to share with, care for, and commit themselves to another person. Avoiding intimacy brings a sense of isolation and loneliness.
Generativity vs. stagnation	Middle adulthood	Middle-aged people must find some way of contributing to the development of the next generation. Failing this, they may become self-absorbed and emotionally impoverished and reach a point of stagnation.
Ego integrity vs. despair	Late adulthood	Individuals review their lives, and if they are satisfied and feel a sense of accomplishment, they will experience ego integrity. If dissatisfied, they may sink into despair.

SUMMARIZE IT

Now that you have had an introduction to developmental theories, we will turn our attention to the major milestones of each phase of development. *Prenatal development* refers to the period prior to birth. The first 2 years constitute the period of *infancy*. The period from 2 to 6 years of age is *early childhood*, and *middle childhood* is the period from age 6 to puberty. *Adolescence* begins at puberty and ends when an individual is considered to be an adult in his or her culture. Finally, the adult years are typically divided into phases of *early adulthood* (18 to 40 or 45), *middle adulthood* (40 or 45 to 65), and *late adulthood* (65 and older).

Prenatal Development and Infancy

What is the phase of life during which change takes place at the most rapid rate? You might be surprised to learn that it is during the first eight weeks after the first of life's developmental milestones, *conception*, the joining of a sperm and an egg. But the changes that occur in the first two years after birth also happen very quickly, as you will soon learn.

8.5 What happens in each stage of prenatal development?

From Conception to Birth

Many people divide the 9 months of pregnancy into *trimesters*, three periods of 3 months' duration. However, the division of pregnancy into trimesters is arbitrary and has nothing to do with prenatal development. In fact, the final stage of prenatal development, or development from conception to birth, begins before the first trimester ends.

prenatal development Development from conception to birth.

The Stages of Prenatal Development. Conception, of course, marks the beginning of prenatal development and typically takes place in one of the fallopian tubes. Over the next 2 weeks, the zygote, the cell that results from the union of a sperm and an ovum, travels to the uterus and attaches itself to the uterine wall. This stage is known as the *period of the zygote* or the *germinal stage*. At the end of this stage, the zygote is only the size of the period at the end of this sentence. The second stage is the *period of the embryo*, when the major systems, organs, and structures of the body develop. Lasting from week 3 through week 8, this period ends when the first bone cells form. Only 1 inch long and weighing 1/7 of an ounce, the embryo already resembles a human being, with limbs, fingers, toes, and many internal organs that have begun to function. The final stage of prenatal development, called the *period of the fetus,* lasts from the end of the second month until birth. The fetus undergoes rapid growth and further development of the structures, organs, and systems of the body. Table 8.1 describes the characteristics of each stage of prenatal development.

zygote Cell that results from the union of a sperm and an ovum.

embryo The developing human organism during the period (week 3 through week 8) when the major systems, organs, and structures of the body develop.

fetus The developing human organism during the period (week 9 until birth) when rapid growth and further development of the structures, organs, and systems of the body occur.

During the last several weeks of prenatal development, the fetus is capable of responding to stimuli from the outside world, particularly sounds. Further, newborns

TABLE 8.1 Stages of Prenatal Development

STAGE	TIME AFTER CONCEPTION	MAJOR ACTIVITIES OF THE STAGE
Period of the zygote	1 to 2 weeks	Zygote attaches to the uterine lining. At 2 weeks, zygote is the size of the period at the end of this sentence.
Period of the embryo	3 to 8 weeks	Major systems, organs, and structures of the body develop. Period ends when first bone cells appear. At 8 weeks, embryo is about 1 inch long and weighs 1/7 of an ounce.
Period of the fetus	9 weeks to birth (38 weeks)	Rapid growth and further development of the body structures, organs, and systems.

remember the stimuli to which they were exposed prior to birth (Kisilevsky et al., 2003). In a classic study of prenatal learning, DeCasper and Spence (1986) had 16 pregnant women read *The Cat in the Hat* to their developing fetuses twice a day during the final 6 weeks of pregnancy. A few days after birth, the infants could adjust their sucking on specially designed, pressure-sensitive nipples to hear their mother reading either *The Cat in the Hat* or *The King, the Mice, and the Cheese,* a story they had never heard before. By their sucking behavior, the infants showed a definite preference for the familiar story.

Negative Influences on Prenatal Development. As wondrous as the process of prenatal development is, ample evidence indicates that the developing embryo and the fetus are vulnerable to a number of potentially harmful factors. One is lack of prenatal care, and another is maternal health. The babies of women who have chronic conditions such as diabetes may experience retardation or acceleration of fetal growth (Murray, 2009). And when the mother has a viral disease such as *rubella, chicken pox,* or *HIV,* she may deliver an infant with physical and behavioral abnormalities (Amato, 1998; Kliegman, 1998).

Teratogens are substances that can have a negative impact on prenatal development, causing birth defects and other problems. A teratogen's impact depends on both its intensity and the time during prenatal development when it is present. Teratogens generally have their most devastating consequences during the period of the embryo. During this time, there are critical periods when certain body structures develop. If drugs or other harmful substances interfere with development during a critical period, the body structure will not form properly, nor will it develop later (Kopp & Kaler, 1989). (Note that there are critical periods throughout development. You'll read about another one in the section on language development.)

teratogens Harmful agents in the prenatal environment, which can have a negative impact on prenatal development or even cause birth defects.

critical period A period so important to development that a harmful environmental influence at that time can keep a bodily structure from developing normally or can impair later intellectual or social development.

The use of heroin, cocaine, and crack during pregnancy has been linked to miscarriage, prematurity, low birth weight, breathing difficulties, physical defects, and fetal death. Alcohol also crosses the placental barrier, and alcohol levels in the fetus almost match the levels in the mother's blood (Little et al., 1989). Women who drink heavily during pregnancy risk having babies with fetal alcohol syndrome. Babies with this syndrome have mental retardation and abnormally small heads with wide-set eyes and a short nose. They also have behavioral problems such as hyperactivity (Julicn, 1995). Some children prenatally exposed to alcohol have *fetal alcohol effects*—they show some of the characteristics of fetal alcohol syndrome but in less severe form. The Surgeon General warns women to abstain from drinking alcohol altogether during pregnancy (Rosenblatt, 2008). However, a review of survey data from 1991 to 2005 found that the percentage of pregnant women who reported using alcohol, approximately 13%, did not change significantly during the period despite nationwide campaigns aimed at informing pregnant women about the dangers associated with drinking during pregnancy (Denny, Tsai, Floyd, & Green, 2009).

fetal alcohol syndrome A condition, caused by maternal alcohol intake during pregnancy, in which the baby is born with mental retardation, with a small head and facial, organ, and behavioral abnormalities.

Smoking decreases the amount of oxygen and increases the amount of carbon monoxide crossing the placental barrier. The embryo or fetus is exposed to nicotine and several thousand other chemicals as well. Smoking while pregnant increases the

▼ These photos show the fertilization of an egg by a sperm (left), an embryo at 7 weeks (center), and a fetus at 22 weeks (right).

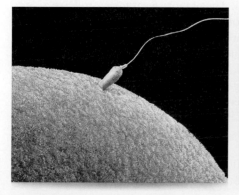

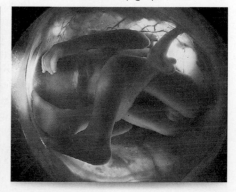

⊙─|Watch the **Video** *Effects of Prenatal Smoking on Children's Development* on **mypsychlab.com**

neonate A newborn infant up to 1 month old.

low-birth-weight baby A baby weighing less than 5.5 pounds.

preterm infant An infant born before the 37th week and weighing less than 5.5 pounds; a premature infant.

8.6 How do infants' abilities change over the first 18 months of life?

reflexes Built-in responses to certain stimuli that neonates need to ensure survival in their new world.

probability that the baby will be premature or of low birth weight (Nigg & Breslau, 2007). Further, because researchers disagree as to whether heavy caffeine consumption has an adverse effect on the fetus, the wisest course of action is to restrict caffeine consumption to less than 300 milligrams (3 cups) daily. ⊙─|Watch on **mypsychlab.com**

Birth. In Chapter 3 you learned that, near the end of pregnancy, the woman's body begins to prepare for the physical discomfort of birth by increasing the levels of *endorphins*, the body's natural painkillers, in her system. At the same time, her levels of *oxytocin*, the hormone that stimulates the uterus to contract during labor, rise as the uterine tissues become more sensitive to its effects (Smith & Brennan, 2009). Interestingly, too, oxytocin seems to influence the woman's emotions in ways that help to prepare her psychologically for both the anxieties of labor and the process of bonding with the infant after birth (Neumann, 2008).

At some point, physiological factors within the woman's body along with biochemical signals from the fetus and placenta, trigger the beginning of labor, a three-stage process. In Stage 1, the uterus contracts, and the cervix flattens out and gradually increases in diameter to about 10 centimeters. The fetus makes its way through the vagina and into the world in Stage 2. Finally, in Stage 3, the woman's uterus expels the placenta.

Immediately after birth, health care professionals assess the health of the neonate (newborn baby). Her weight and *gestational age*, the length of the mother's pregnancy, are key factors. Low-birth-weight babies are those weighing less than 5.5 pounds. Infants of this weight born at or before the 37th week are considered preterm infants. The smaller and more premature the baby, the greater the risk of problems that range from subtle learning and behavior problems in babies closer to normal birth weight to "severe retardation, blindness, hearing loss, and even death" in the smallest newborns (Apgar & Beck, 1982, p. 69).

Perceptual and Motor Development

Neonates come equipped with an impressive range of reflexes—built-in responses to certain stimuli that are needed to ensure survival in their new world. Sucking, swallowing, coughing, and blinking are some necessary behaviors that newborns can perform right away. Newborns will move an arm, a leg, or other body part away from a painful stimulus and will try to remove a blanket or cloth placed over the face. Stroke a baby on the cheek and you will trigger the rooting reflex—the baby opens his or her mouth and actively searches for a nipple. Moreover, all five senses are working at birth, although a number of refinements are still to come.

The newborn already has preferences for certain odors, tastes, sounds, and visual configurations. Hearing is much better developed than vision in the neonate (Busnel, Granier-Deferre, & Lecanuet, 1992). A newborn is able to turn his or her head in the direction of a sound and shows a general preference for female voices. Newborns are able to discriminate among and show preferences for certain odors and tastes (Bartoshuk & Beauchamp, 1994; Leon, 1992). They favor sweet tastes and are able to differentiate between salty, bitter, and sour solutions. Newborns are also sensitive to pain (Porter, Porges, & Marshall, 1988) and are particularly responsive to touch, reacting positively to stroking and fondling (Field, 2002).

Robert Fantz (1961) made a major breakthrough when he realized that a baby's interest in an object can be gauged by the length of time it fixates on it. Fantz demonstrated that infants prefer the image of a human face to other images, such as a black-and-white abstract pattern (see Figure 8.3). Fantz's study and others have shown that newborns have clear preferences and powers of discrimination—and even memory recognition and learning ability.

At birth, an infant's vision is about 20/600, and it typically does not reach 20/20 until the child is about 2 years old (Courage & Adams, 1990; Held, 1993). Newborns

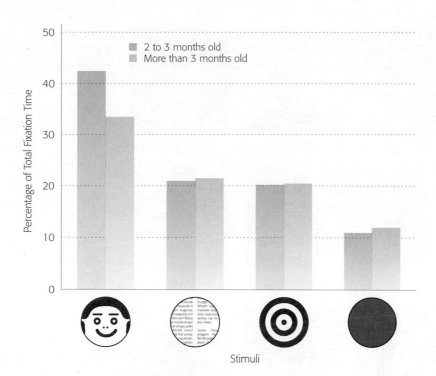

FIGURE 8.3 Results of Fantz's Study
Using a device called a *viewing box* to observe and record infants' eye movements, Fantz (1961) found that infants preferred faces to black-and-white abstract patterns.

focus best on objects about 9 inches away, and they can follow a slowly moving object. Infants from 22 to 93 hours old already indicate a preference for their own mother's face over that of an unfamiliar female (Field et al., 1984). Although newborns prefer colored stimuli to gray ones, they can't distinguish all of the colors adults normally can until they are about 4 months old (Franklin, Pilling, & Davies, 2005).

One famous experiment was devised to study depth perception in infants. Gibson and Walk (1960) designed an apparatus called the visual cliff, which is "a board laid across a sheet of heavy glass, with a patterned material directly beneath the glass on one side and several feet below it on the other" (p. 65). This arrangement made it appear that there was a sudden drop-off, or "visual cliff," on one side. Most babies aged 6 to 14 months could be coaxed by their mothers to crawl to the shallow side, but only three would crawl onto the deep side. Gibson and Walk concluded that most babies "can discriminate depth as soon as they can crawl" (p. 64).

Simulate on **mypsychlab.com**

Like perceptual skills, an infant's motor skills become increasingly sophisticated over the first 18 months. The rapid changes in motor skills babies undergo arise primarily because of maturation. Maturation occurs naturally according to the infant's own genetically determined biological timetable of development. Many motor milestones, such as sitting, standing, and walking (shown in Figure 8.4), depend on the growth and development of the central nervous system.

Still, experience does have some influence on the development of motor skills. For instance, the rate at which milestones are achieved is slowed when an infant is subjected to extremely unfavorable environmental conditions, such as severe malnutrition or maternal or sensory deprivation. Further, cross-cultural research reveals that in some African cultures in Uganda and Kenya, mothers use special motor-training techniques that enable their infants to attain some of the major motor milestones earlier than most infants in the United States (Kilbride & Kilbride, 1975; Super, 1981). But speeding up the attainment of motor skills has no lasting impact on development. Babies will walk, talk, and be toilet trained according to their own developmental schedules.

visual cliff An apparatus used to test depth perception in infants.

maturation Changes that occur according to one's genetically determined biological timetable of development.

Simulate the **Experiment** *The Visual Cliff* on **mypsychlab.com**

▲ When placed on the visual cliff, most infants older than 6 months will not crawl out over the deep side, indicating that they can perceive depth.

FIGURE 8.4 The Progression of Motor Development
Most infants develop motor skills in the sequence shown in the figure. The ages indicated are only averages, so normal, healthy infants may develop any of these milestones a few months earlier or several months later than the average.
Source: Based on Frankenburg et al. (1992).

Lifts head up
2 months

Rolls over
3 months

Sits propped up
3 months

Sits without support
6 months

Stands holding on
7 months

Walks holding on
9 months

Stands momentarily
10 months

Stands alone
11 months

Walks alone
12 months

Walks backwards
14 months

Walks up steps
17 months

Kicks ball forward
18 months

8.7 How does temperament affect infants' behavior?

temperament A person's behavioral style or characteristic way of responding to the environment.

Temperament

Is each baby born with an individual behavior style or characteristic way of responding to the environment—a particular temperament? The New York Longitudinal Study was undertaken in 1956 to investigate temperament and its effect on development. Thomas, Chess, and Birch (1970) studied 2- to 3-month-old infants and followed them into adolescence and adulthood using observation, interviews with parents and teachers, and psychological tests. Three general types of temperament emerged from the study.

"Easy" children—40% of the group studied—had generally pleasant moods, were adaptable, approached new situations and people positively, and established regular sleeping, eating, and elimination patterns. "Difficult" children—10% of the group—had generally unpleasant moods, reacted negatively to new situations and people, were intense in their emotional reactions, and showed irregularity of bodily functions. "Slow-to-warm-up" children—15% of the group—tended to withdraw, were slow to adapt, and were "somewhat negative in mood." The remaining 35% of the children studied were too inconsistent to categorize. ◉ Watch on mypsychlab.com

◉ Watch the Video *Temperament* on mypsychlab.com

Research suggests that variations in infant temperament are strongly influenced by heredity and are somewhat predictive of personality differences later in life (e.g., Caspi, 2000; Crockenberg & Leerkes, 2005; Saudino, 2005). Thus, most developmentalists who study temperament believe that personality is molded by the continuous interaction of temperament and environment, although the environment can intensify, diminish, or modify these inborn behavioral tendencies. Adjustment in children seems to rest in part on the fit between individual temperament and the accommodation of family and environment to behavioral style. A difficult child may stimulate hostility and resentment in parents and others, which, in turn, may perpetuate the child's negative behavior. On the other hand, an easy child usually elicits a positive response from parents and others, which reinforces the child's behavior and increases the likelihood that the behavioral style will continue.

Attachment ▶

Almost all infants form a strong attachment to their mothers or primary caregivers. But what precisely is the glue that binds caregiver (usually the mother) and infant?

A series of classic studies conducted by Harry Harlow on attachment in rhesus monkeys was critical to developmentalists' understanding of infant–caregiver attachment. Harlow constructed two surrogate (artificial) monkey "mothers." One was a plain wire-mesh cylinder with a blocky wooden head; the other was a wire-mesh cylinder that was padded, covered with soft terry cloth, and fitted with a somewhat more monkeylike head. A baby bottle could be attached to either surrogate mother for feeding. Newborn monkeys were placed in individual cages where they had equal access to a cloth surrogate and a wire surrogate. The source of their nourishment (cloth or wire surrogate) was unimportant. "The infants developed a strong attachment to the cloth mothers and little or none to the wire mothers" (Harlow & Harlow, 1962, p. 141). Harlow found that it was *contact comfort*—the comfort supplied by bodily contact—rather than nourishment that formed the basis of the infant monkey's attachment to its mother. If the cloth mother was not present when unfamiliar objects were placed in the cage, the monkey would huddle in the corner, clutching its head, rocking, sucking its thumb or toes, and crying in distress. But when the cloth mother was present, it would first cling to her and then explore and play with the unfamiliar objects.

Numerous studies have shown that the attachment process is similar in human infants (Posada et al., 2002). The mother holds, strokes, and talks to the baby and responds to the baby's needs, and the baby gazes at and listens to the mother and even moves in synchrony with her voice (Condon & Sander, 1974; Lester, Hoffman, & Brazelton, 1985). Once the attachment has formed, infants show separation anxiety— fear and distress when the parent leaves them. Occurring from about 8 months to 24 months, separation anxiety peaks between 12 and 18 months of age (Fox & Bell, 1990). At about 6 or 7 months of age, infants develop a fear of strangers called stranger anxiety, which increases in intensity until the first birthday and then declines in the second year (Marks, 1987). Stranger anxiety is greater in an unfamiliar setting, when the parent is not close at hand, and when a stranger abruptly approaches or touches the child.

There are important differences in the quality of attachment. In a classic study of mother–child attachment, Mary Ainsworth (1973, 1979) observed mother–child interactions in the home during the infants' first year and then again at age 12 months in a laboratory. Based on infants' reactions to their mothers after brief periods of separation, Ainsworth and others (1978; Main & Solomon, 1990) identified four patterns of attachment.

The first pattern is *secure attachment* (observed in about 65% of American infants). Although usually distressed when separated from their mother, securely attached infants eagerly seek to reestablish the connection and then show an interest in play. They use the mother as a safe base of operation from which to explore and are typically more responsive, obedient, cooperative, and content than other infants. In addition, secure attachment seems to protect infants from the potentially adverse effects of risk factors such as poverty (Belsky & Fearon, 2002). Further, preschoolers who were securely attached as infants display more advanced social skills, such as the ability to maintain friendships, than peers who were not securely attached to their caregivers (McElwain & Volling, 2004).

8.8 What are the causes, characteristics, and consequences of infant–caregiver attachment?

attachment The strong affectionate bond a child forms with the mother or primary caregiver.

separation anxiety The fear and distress shown by a toddler when the parent leaves, occurring from 8 to 24 months and reaching a peak between 12 and 18 months.

stranger anxiety A fear of strangers common in infants at about 6 months and increasing in intensity until about 12 months, and then declining in the second year.

▲ Harlow found that infant monkeys developed a strong attachment to a cloth-covered surrogate mother and little or no attachment to a wire surrogate mother— even when the wire mother provided nourishment.

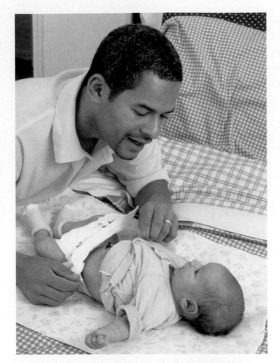

▲ Fathers tend to engage in more physical play with their children than mothers. However, many fathers today share basic child-care responsibilities, such as feeding and diaper changing, with mothers.

Infants with a pattern called *avoidant attachment* (approximately 20% of American infants) are usually not responsive to their mother when she is present and not troubled when she leaves. When the parent returns, the infant may actively avoid contact with her or, at least, not be quick to greet her. In short, these infants do not act much more attached to the parent than to a stranger. Mothers of avoidant infants tend to show little affection and to be generally unresponsive to their infants' needs and cries.

Prior to a period of separation, infants who show *resistant attachment* (10 to 15% of American infants) seek and prefer close contact with their mother. Yet, in contrast to securely attached infants, they do not tend to branch out and explore. And when the mother returns to the room after a period of separation, the resistant infant displays anger and may push the mother away or hit her. When picked up, the infant is hard to comfort and may continue crying.

The pattern of *disorganized/disoriented attachment* (seen in 5 to 10% of American infants) is the most puzzling and apparently the least secure pattern. When reunited with the mother, the infant with this pattern of attachment exhibits contradictory and disoriented responses. Rather than looking at the mother while being held, the child may purposely look away or approach the mother with an expressionless or depressed demeanor. Also characteristic are a dazed and vacant facial expression and a peculiar, frozen posture after being calmed by the mother.

Although mother–child, rather than father–child, attachment relationships have been the traditional focus of research, fathers can be as responsive and competent as mothers (Roberts & Moseley, 1996), and their attachments can be just as strong. Indeed, father–child interactions have many enduring positive influences on children (Bronte-Tinkew, Moore, & Carrano, 2006; Stein, Milburn, Zane, & Rotheram-Borus, 2009). Children who experience regular interaction with their fathers tend to have higher IQs and to do better in social situations and at coping with frustration than children lacking such interaction. They also persist longer in solving problems and are less impulsive and less likely to become violent. Positive father–son relationships are also associated with higher-quality parenting behavior by sons when they have children of their own (Shears, Robinson, & Emde, 2002).

Interactions with fathers may be important for development because mothers and fathers interact differently with infants and children. Fathers engage in more exciting and arousing physical play with children (Paquette, 2004). Mothers are more likely to protect their children from overstimulation and potential injury. By contrast, fathers allow infants to crawl farther away, up to twice as far as mothers usually allow. And fathers remain farther away as the infant explores novel stimuli and situations. Ideally, of course, children need both kinds of influences.

Early and Middle Childhood

Think about how remarkable it is that, at birth, an infant's only means of communication is crying, but by age 11 or so, the average child has a vocabulary of more than 60,000 words (Anglin, 1995). Mastery of language, both spoken and written, is just one of several important developmental processes that happen in early and middle childhood.

8.9 What are the phases of language development, and how do various theorists explain them?

Language Development

During their first few months, infants communicate distress or displeasure through crying. But then they begin rapidly to acquire language. Language development depends on both physical maturation, especially of the brain, and linguistic input from the environment. If children do not have access to human language during the first two years of life, their ability to acquire language is permanently impaired (Baird, 2010). Thus, these years are a critical period for language development.

Phases of Language Development. During the second or third month, infants begin *cooing*—repeatedly uttering vowel sounds such as "ah" and "oo." At about 4 to 6 months, infants begin babbling. They utter *phonemes*—the basic speech sounds of any language, which form words when combined. During the first part of the babbling stage, infants babble all the basic speech sounds that occur in all the languages of the world. Language up to this point seems to be biologically determined, because all babies throughout the world, even deaf children, vocalize this same range of speech sounds.

At about 8 months, babies begin to focus attention on those speech sounds (phonemes) common to the language spoken around them and on the rhythm and intonation of that language. And by 1 year, the babbling stage gives way to the one-word stage. The first words usually represent objects that move or those that infants can act on or interact with. From 13 to 18 months of age, children markedly increase their vocabulary (Woodward, Markham, & Fitzsimmons, 1994), and 2-year-olds know about 270 words (Brown, 1973).

Initially a child's understanding of words differs from that of an adult. When they lack the correct word, children may act on the basis of shared features and apply a word to a broader range of objects than is appropriate. This is known as overextension. For example, any man may be called "dada" and any four-legged animal, "doggie." Underextension occurs, too; this is when children fail to apply a word to other members of the class. The family's poodle is a "doggie," but the German shepherd next door is not.

Between 18 and 20 months of age, when their vocabulary is about 50 words, children begin to put nouns, verbs, and adjectives together in two-word phrases and sentences. At this stage, children depend to a great extent on gesture, tone, and context to convey their meaning (Slobin, 1972). Depending on intonation, their sentences may indicate questions, statements, or possession. Children adhere to a rigid word order. You might hear "mama drink," "drink milk," or "mama milk," but not "drink mama," "milk drink," or "milk mama."

Between 2 and 3 years of age, children begin to use short sentences, which may contain three or more words. Labeled telegraphic speech by Roger Brown (1973), these short sentences follow a rigid word order and contain only essential content words, leaving out all plurals, possessives, conjunctions, articles, and prepositions. Telegraphic speech reflects the child's understanding of *syntax*—the rules governing how words are ordered in a sentence. When a third word is added to a sentence, it usually fills in the word missing from the two-word sentence (for example, "mama drink milk"). After using telegraphic speech for a time, children gradually begin to add modifiers to make their sentences more precise.

Children pick up grammatical rules intuitively and apply them rigidly. Overregularization is the kind of error that results when a grammatical rule is misapplied to a word that has an irregular plural or past tense (Marcus, 1996). Thus, children who have correctly used the words "went," "came," and "did" incorrectly apply the rule for past tenses and begin to say "goed," "comed," and "doed." What the parents see as a regression in speech actually means that the child has acquired a grammatical rule. ⊙—[Watch on **mypsychlab.com**

Theories of Language Development. *Learning theorists* have long maintained that language is acquired in the same way as other behaviors—as a result of learning through reinforcement and imitation. B. F. Skinner (1957) asserted that parents selectively criticize incorrect speech and reinforce correct speech through praise, approval, and attention. Thus, the child's utterances are progressively shaped in the direction of grammatically correct speech. Others believe that children acquire vocabulary and sentence construction mainly through imitation (Bandura, 1977). However, imitation cannot account for patterns of speech such as telegraphic speech or for systematic errors such as overregularization. And parents seem to reinforce children more for the content of the utterance than for the correctness of the grammar (Brown, Cazden, & Bellugi, 1968).

---

babbling Vocalization of the basic speech sounds (phonemes), which begins between 4 and 6 months.

overextension The act of using a word, on the basis of some shared feature, to apply to a broader range of objects than is appropriate.

underextension Restricting the use of a word to only a few, rather than to all, members of a class of objects.

telegraphic speech Short sentences that follow a strict word order and contain only essential content words.

overregularization The act of inappropriately applying the grammatical rules for forming plurals and past tenses to irregular nouns and verbs.

⊙—[Watch the **Video** *Learning Language* on **mypsychlab.com**

▲ Mothers who are deaf use sign language to communicate with their young children, but they do so in *motherese,* signing slowly and with frequent repetitions.

Noam Chomsky (1957) believes that language ability is largely innate, and he has proposed a very different theory. Chomsky (1968) maintains that the brain contains a *language acquisition device (LAD),* which enables children to acquire language and discover the rules of grammar easily and naturally. Language develops in stages that occur in a fixed order and appear at about the same times in most normal children. Thus, it appears that biological maturation underlies language development in much the same way as it underlies physical and motor development. These claims are known as the *nativist position.*

The nativist position is better able than learning theory to account for the fact that children throughout the world go through the same basic stages in language development. It also accounts for the similar errors all children make when they are first learning to form plurals, past tenses, and negatives—errors not acquired through imitation or reinforcement.

Nevertheless, some environmental factors do contribute to language development. For example, babies whose parents are responsive to their babbling vocalize more than infants whose parents are not responsive to them (Whitehurst et al., 1989). Moreover, parents can facilitate language acquisition by adjusting their speech to their infant's level of development. Parents often use *motherese*—highly simplified speech with shorter phrases and sentences and simpler vocabulary, which is uttered slowly, at a high pitch, and with exaggerated intonation and much repetition (Fernald, 1993; R. Jones, 2003). Mothers who are deaf communicate with their infants in a similar way, signing more slowly and with exaggerated hand and arm movements and frequent repetition (Masataka, 1996). Thus, most researchers endorse an *interactionist* approach to explaining language development that acknowledges the crucial role of infants' apparently inborn capacity for acquiring language but also recognizes that environmental influences contribute to language development as well (MacWhinney, 2005).

Literacy. Throughout the industrialized world, children must master written as well as spoken language. As you might expect, many aspects of the development of spoken language are critical to the process of learning to read. *Phonological awareness,* or sensitivity to the sound patterns of a language and how they are represented as letters, is particularly important. Children who can correctly answer questions such as "What would bat be if you took away the [b]?" by the age of 4 or so learn to read more rapidly than their peers who cannot (de Jong & van der Leij, 2002). Moreover, children who have good phonological awareness skills in their first language learn to read more easily even when reading instruction is conducted in a second language (Mumtaz & Humphreys, 2002; Quiroga et al., 2002).

Children seem to learn phonological awareness skills through word play. Among English-speaking children, learning nursery rhymes facilitates the development of these skills (Layton et al., 1996). Japanese parents foster phonological awareness in their children by playing a game with them called *shiritori,* in which one person says a word and another must supply a word that begins with its ending sound (Serpell & Hatano, 1997). Activities in which parents and children work together to read or write a story also foster the development of phonological awareness (Aram & Levitt, 2002).

8.10 What do parenting styles and peer relationships contribute to socialization?

socialization The process of learning socially acceptable behaviors, attitudes, and values.

Socialization `

The process of learning socially acceptable behaviors, attitudes, and values is called socialization. Although parents have the major role in their children's socialization, peers affect the process as well.

Parenting Styles. The methods parents use to control children's behavior also contribute to socialization. Diane Baumrind (1971, 1980, 1991) studied the continuum of parental control and identified three parenting styles: authoritarian, authoritative, and permissive. Each style appears to have distinctive effects on children's behavior.

Authoritarian parents make the rules, expect unquestioned obedience from their children, punish misbehavior (often physically), and value obedience to authority. Rather than giving a rationale for a rule, authoritarian parents consider "because I said so" a sufficient reason for obedience. Parents using this parenting style tend to be uncommunicative, unresponsive, and somewhat distant, and Baumrind (1967) found preschool children disciplined in this manner to be withdrawn, anxious, and unhappy. The authoritarian style has been associated with low intellectual performance and lack of social skills, especially in boys (Maccoby & Martin, 1983). However, research suggests that there are some circumstances in which authoritarian parenting is beneficial to children's development. For instance, children of authoritarian parents who live in impoverished neighborhoods display more favorable developmental outcomes than their peers whose parents are more permissive (Steinberg, Blatt-Eisengart, & Cauffman, 2006).

authoritarian parents Parents who make arbitrary rules, expect unquestioned obedience from their children, punish transgressions, and value obedience to authority.

Authoritative parents set high but realistic and reasonable standards, enforce limits, and at the same time encourage open communication and independence. They are willing to discuss rules and supply rationales for them. Knowing why the rules are necessary makes it easier for children to internalize them and to follow them, whether in the presence of their parents or not. Authoritative parents are generally warm, nurturant, supportive, and responsive, and they show respect for their children and their opinions. Their children are more mature, happy, self-reliant, self-controlled, assertive, socially competent, and responsible than their peers. The authoritative parenting style is associated with higher academic performance, independence, higher self-esteem, and internalized moral standards in middle childhood and adolescence (Lamborn et al., 1991; Steinberg, Elman, & Mounts, 1989).

authoritative parents Parents who set high but realistic standards, reason with the child, enforce limits, and encourage open communication and independence.

Although they are rather warm and supportive, **permissive parents** make few rules or demands and usually do not enforce those that are made. They allow children to make their own decisions and control their own behavior. Children raised in this manner are the most immature, impulsive, and dependent, and they seem to be the least self-controlled and self-reliant (Steinberg et al., 2006).

permissive parents Parents who make few rules or demands and allow children to make their own decisions and control their own behavior.

Permissive parents also come in the indifferent, unconcerned, uninvolved variety (Maccoby & Martin, 1983). This parenting style is associated with drinking problems, promiscuous sex, delinquent behavior, and poor academic performance in adolescents.

The positive effects of authoritative parenting have been found across all ethnic groups in the United States (Querido, Warner, & Eyberg, 2002; Steinberg & Dornbusch, 1991). The one exception is among first-generation Asian immigrants, where the authoritarian style is more strongly associated with academic achievement (Chao, 2001). Developmental psychologist Ruth Chao suggests that this finding may be explained by the traditional idea in Asian culture that making a child obey is an act of affection (Chao & Aque, 2009). Moreover, strict parenting tends to be tempered by emotional warmth in Asian families, so children probably get the idea that their parents expect unquestioning obedience because they love them. However, research also shows that the longer first-generation immigrants have lived in the United States, the more the pattern of association between authoritative parenting and social competence resembles that found in other groups (Kim & Chung, 2003).

Peer Relationships. Friendships begin to develop by the age of 3 or 4, and relationships with peers become increasingly important. These early relationships are usually based on shared activities; two children think of themselves as friends while they are playing together. During the elementary school years, friendships tend to be based on mutual trust (Dunn, Cutting, & Fisher, 2002). By middle childhood, membership in a peer group is central to a child's happiness. Peer groups are usually composed of children of the same race, sex, and social class (Schofield & Francis, 1982). The peer group serves a socializing function by providing models of behavior, dress, and language. Peer groups provide objective measures against which children can evaluate their own traits. They are also a continuing source of both reinforcement for appropriate behavior and punishment for deviant behavior. In fact, peer rejection often results in excessive aggression (Wood, Cowan, & Baker, 2002).

8.11 How do theorists explain gender role development?

⊢⊣ Gender Role Development

gender roles Cultural expectations about the behavior appropriate for each gender.

Traditionally, males have been expected to be independent and competitive; females have been expected to be warm and nurturant. Psychologists use the term gender roles to refer to such expectations. Children display play behavior that is consistent with gender roles fairly early in life, by age 2 or so. Psychologists differ in how they explain gender role development.

According to the biological view, genes and prenatal sex hormones have an important influence on gender role development. In a review of studies on the effects of prenatal androgens (male sex hormones), Collaer and Hines (1995) found that these hormones have a reasonably strong influence on children's play behavior. Girls exposed to prenatal androgens are more likely than girls not exposed to these hormones to prefer to play with toys favored by boys, such as trucks, cars, and fire engines (Berenbaum & Snyder, 1995). Prenatal androgens are also known to affect brain development and functioning in humans and many other animal species (Beyenburg et al., 2000).

Of course, biological influences on gender role development don't operate in an environmental vacuum. For example, from infancy on, most of the presents children receive are gender consistent: Girls are given dolls and tea sets, while boys get trucks and sports equipment. And while a girl may feel complimented if someone calls her a "tomboy," almost every boy considers it an insult to be called a "sissy" (Doyle & Paludi, 1995).

As you might expect, for *social learning theorists* environmental influences are considered more important than biological forces in explaining gender role development (Mischel, 1966). These theorists point out that children are usually reinforced for imitating behaviors considered appropriate for their gender. When behaviors are not appropriate (a boy puts on lipstick, or a girl pretends to shave her face), children are quickly informed, often in a reprimanding tone, that boys or girls do not do that. However, there is little evidence that parents reinforce gender role–appropriate behavior in girls and boys often enough to account for the early age at which children begin to show gender-typed behavior (Fagot, 1995). Thus, imitation and reinforcement probably play some part in gender role development, but they do not provide a full explanation of this phenomenon.

Cognitive developmental theory, proposed by Lawrence Kohlberg (1966; Kohlberg & Ullian, 1974), suggests that an understanding of gender is a prerequisite to gender role development. According to Kohlberg, children go through a series of stages in acquiring the concept of gender. Between ages 2 and 3, children acquire *gender identity*—their sense of being a male or a female. Between ages 4 and 5, children acquire the concept of *gender stability*—awareness that boys are boys and girls are girls for a lifetime. Finally, between ages 6 and 8, children understand *gender constancy*—that gender does not change regardless of the activities people engage in or the clothes they wear. Moreover, according to Kohlberg, when children realize their gender is permanent, they are motivated to seek out same-sex models and learn to act in ways considered appropriate for their gender.

Cross-cultural studies reveal that Kohlberg's stages of gender identity, gender stability, and gender constancy occur in the same order in cultures as different as those in Samoa, Kenya, Nepal, and Belize (Munroe, Shimmin, & Munroe, 1984). Moreover, research shows that children's knowledge of gender stereotypes and the value that they attach to being male or female increase as they progress through the gender stability and constancy stages (Ruble et al., 2007). However, this theory fails to explain why many gender-appropriate behaviors and preferences are observed in children as young as age 2 or 3, long before gender constancy is acquired (Bussey & Bandura, 1999; Jacklin, 1989; Martin & Little, 1990).

Gender-schema theory, proposed by Sandra Bem (1981), provides a more complete explanation of gender role development. Like social learning theory, gender-schema theory

▲ Theorists differ in their explanations for gender differences in play preferences. Learning theorists emphasize the effects of models. Cognitive developmental theorists propose that gender role development is a consequence of general cognitive development. Gender-schema theories use the information-processing approach to explain these differences. What do you think?

suggests that young children are motivated to pay attention to and behave in a way consistent with gender-based standards and stereotypes of the culture. Like cognitive developmental theory, gender-schema theory stresses that children begin to use gender as a way to organize and process information (Bussey & Bandura, 1999; Martin & Ruble, 2004). But gender-schema theory holds that this process occurs earlier, when gender identity rather than gender constancy is attained, and children exhibit strong preferences for sex-appropriate toys and clothing and favor same-sex peers over those of the other sex (Powlishta, 1995). To a large extent, children's self-concepts and self-esteem depend on the match between their abilities and behaviors and the cultural definition of what is desirable for their gender. Consequently, the desire to maintain self-esteem, according to gender-schema theory, motivates children to align their behavior with culturally defined gender roles.

Adolescence

The concept of adolescence—a period of transition from childhood to adulthood—did not exist until psychologist G. Stanley Hall first wrote about it in his book by that name in 1904. He portrayed this stage in life as one of "storm and stress," the inevitable result of biological changes occurring during the period.

adolescence The developmental stage that begins at puberty and encompasses the period from the end of childhood to the beginning of adulthood.

Puberty and Sexual Behavior ▶

8.12 How does puberty influence adolescents' bodies, self-concepts, and behavior?

Adolescence begins with the onset of puberty—a period of rapid physical growth and change that culminates in sexual maturity. Although the average onset of puberty is age 10 for girls and age 12 for boys, the normal range extends from age 7 to age 14 for girls and from 9 to 16 for boys (Tanner, 1990). Puberty begins with a surge in hormone production followed by a marked acceleration in growth known as the *adolescent growth spurt*. On average, the growth spurt occurs from age 10 to 13 in girls and about 2 years later in boys, from age 12 to 15 (Tanner, 1990). Girls attain their full height between ages 16 and 17 and boys between ages 18 and 20 (Tanner, 1990).

puberty A period of rapid physical growth and change that culminates in sexual maturity.

During puberty, the reproductive organs in both sexes mature and secondary sex characteristics appear—those physical characteristics not directly involved in reproduction that distinguish the mature male from the mature female. In girls, the breasts develop, and the hips round; in boys, the voice deepens, and facial and chest hair appears; and in both sexes, there is growth of pubic and underarm (axillary) hair. The major landmark of puberty for males is the first ejaculation, which occurs, on average, at age 13 (Jorgensen & Keiding, 1991). For females, it is menarche—the onset of menstruation—which occurs at an average age of 12, although from 9 to 16 is considered the normal range (Tanner, 1990; Kaplowitz, 2009).

secondary sex characteristics Those physical characteristics that are not directly involved in reproduction but distinguish the mature male from the mature female.

menarche (men-AR-kee) The onset of menstruation.

The timing of puberty can have important psychological consequences, coming as it does at a time when a sense of security is gained from being like other members of the peer group. Many studies show that early-maturing boys, taller and stronger than their classmates, have an advantage in sports and are likely to have a positive body image; to feel confident, secure, independent, and happy; and to be more successful academically (Susman & Dorn, 2009). However, early-maturing boys may also be more hostile and aggressive than later-maturing peers (Arim & Shapka, 2008). In addition, earlier-than-average puberty is correlated with affiliation with deviant peers and substance abuse (Westling, Andrews, Hampton, & Peterson, 2008).

Early-maturing girls, who may tower over their peers, feel more self-conscious about their developing bodies and their size. Consequently, they are more likely than late-maturing girls to develop eating disorders (Kaltiala-Heino et al., 2001). In addition to having earlier sexual experiences and more unwanted pregnancies than late-maturing girls, early-maturing girls are more likely to be exposed to alcohol and drug use (Caspi et al., 1993; Cavanaugh, 2004). Late-maturing girls often experience

FIGURE 8.5 **Incidence of Sexual Activity in U.S. High School Students** This graph shows that the proportions of sexually active boys and girls increase dramatically from grade 9 to 12. *Source:* Data from CDC (2008).

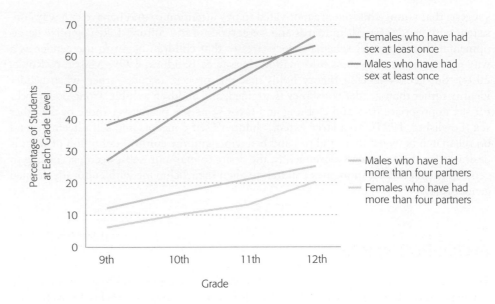

considerable stress when they fail to develop physically along with their peers, but they are likely to be taller and slimmer than their early-maturing age mates.

Puberty brings with it the awakening of sexual desire. As Figure 8.5 indicates, the incidence of sexual activity among teenagers in the United States increases dramatically across grades 9 to 12 (Centers for Disease Control and Prevention [CDC], 2004). One particularly alarming statistic is the proportion of teens who have had multiple sex partners before leaving high school, because the more partners an individual has (whether teen or adult), the more likely he or she is to contract a sexually transmitted disease.

In addition, the rate of teenage pregnancy is higher in the United States than in any other developed country. For example, there are about 41 births per year for every 1,000 teenage girls in the United States, while the rate is less than 7 per 1,000 in Japan, Korea, Switzerland, the Netherlands, and Sweden (National Center for Health Statistics, 2006; Kmietowicz, 2002). It's important to keep in mind, though, that most teen pregnancies occur after the age of 16 and that the incidence of teen pregnancy has actually declined in the United States since the 1960s. What has increased is the number of births to *unmarried* adolescent mothers. In the 1960s, about 80% of teen mothers were married, compared with only 20% today (Martin et al., 2003).

Teens who tend to be less experienced sexually attend religious services frequently and live with both biological parents, who are neither too permissive nor too strict in their discipline and rules (Blinn-Pike et al., 2004; Miller et al., 1998; White & DeBlassie, 1992). Early intercourse is also less prevalent among adolescents whose academic achievement is above average and who are involved in sports (Brooks-Gunn & Furstenberg, 1989; Savage & Holcomb, 1999).

8.13 What do parents and peers contribute to teens' development?

Social Relationships

Most adolescents have good relationships with their parents (Steinberg, 1990). In fact, research shows that good relationships with parents are important to the development of self-esteem in adolescents (Wilkinson, 2004). Moreover, of the three parenting styles discussed earlier in the chapter—authoritative, authoritarian, and permissive—the authoritative style appears to be most effective and the permissive least effective for adolescents (Baumrind, 1991; Steinberg et al., 1994). In a study of about 2,300 adolescents, those with permissive parents were more likely to use alcohol and drugs and to have conduct problems and less likely to be interested in academic success than were those with authoritative or authoritarian parents (Lamborn et al., 1991). The authoritarian style was related to more psychological distress and less self-reliance and self-confidence in adolescents.

EXPLAIN IT   Why Are Peer Groups Important in Adolescence?

Several years ago, residents of an upscale suburb of Houston, Texas, were shocked when they learned that a group of teenaged girls from their community, armed with handguns, had been responsible for a string of convenience store holdups. When arrested, the girls characterized the robberies as "entertainment" and revealed that they had named their group the "Queens of Armed Robbery." Why would teenagers who, at least in a material sense, had everything they could want or need turn to armed robbery for amusement? Think for a moment about how the features of Erikson's identity versus role confusion stage might be used to explain some teenagers' attraction to gangs.

In traditional societies, teenagers are initiated into adult roles through formal rites of passage at around the same time that they go through puberty. Afterward, boys either enter adult occupations or became apprentices. Girls marry or devote themselves to acquiring domestic skills in preparation for marriage. Teenagers who live in such societies rarely experience doubts about what their adult roles will be and how to transition into them. By contrast, there are no longer any formal rites of passage in the industrialized world, and teenagers are expected to develop their own pathways to adulthood. Moreover, society provides them with no formal role of their own; they are too old for some activities but too young for others. As a result, the state that Erikson called "role confusion," together with all of its associated anxieties, is a daily experience for most teenagers.

Erikson thought that peer groups help teenagers cope with the stress of role confusion by providing them with a temporary resolution, a temporary identity, if you will (Erikson, 1968). To facilitate this temporary identity, group members dress similarly, listen to the same bands, go places together, share criticisms of other groups, and develop standards for what constitutes an acceptable plan for the future. Some of these groups have informal names, such as "jocks" or "nerds" or "preps."

For most teens, group membership serves a constructive purpose by providing them with an escape from the anxieties that go along with being in limbo between childhood and adulthood. But for others, the drive to gain an identity through group membership leads to a self-destructive pathway, one that will interfere with their transition into the adult world. Teen groups whose bonds are maintained through substance abuse represent one example of this kind of group. Likewise, when adolescents forge their bonds with others through criminal activities, they risk not only their present status and comfort but also their future adult roles. This message was driven home to several members of the "Queens of Armed Robbery" who, at age 17, were considered adults under Texas criminal law. The crime spree they referred to as "entertainment" netted them several years in prison. Thus, the temporary reprieve from role confusion that these girls enjoyed ultimately undermined their journey to adulthood.

Of course, the experiences of the "Queens of Armed Robbery" seem somewhat benign when compared to those of teens who, for the same psychosocial reasons, get caught up in violent gangs that endanger not only their pathway to adulthood but their very lives. Erikson suggested that in contrast to other kinds of teenaged groups, society responds to criminally oriented youth gangs by viewing their members collectively rather than as individuals, thereby confirming members' use of the gang as a means of avoiding role confusion (Erikson & Erikson, 1957). To forestall an individual teenager's making a lifelong commitment to a criminal identity, he argued, society should develop policies that allow officials to deal with gang activity at the level of the individual gang member. Thus, Erikson would endorse policies in which school administrators, judges, and other authorities are given a certain degree of latitude in deciding how individual youthful offenders should be dealt with.

👁️—[Watch on **mypsychlab.com**

Even adolescents who have good relationships with their parents usually feel the need to separate from them to some degree. As a result, friends become a vital source of emotional support and approval for most of them. Adolescents usually choose friends of the same sex and race (Clark & Ayers, 1992), who have similar values, interests, and backgrounds (Duck, 1983; Epstein, 1983). Interactions with peers are critical while young people are forming their identities. Adolescents can try out different roles and observe the reactions of their friends to their behavior and their appearance. The peer group provides teenagers with a standard of comparison for evaluating their personal assets, as well as a vehicle for developing social skills (Berndt, 1992). Read the *Explain It* feature to learn more about the importance of peer groups.

Emerging Adulthood ▷

8.14 What are the characteristics of emerging adulthood?

Physically speaking, the body is fully mature by age 18. There are varied legal definitions of adulthood—voting age, drinking age, and the like. But what are the psychological and social criteria that distinguish an adolescent from an adult? In search of an answer to this question, developmental psychologist Jeffrey Arnett has proposed that the educational, social, and economic demands of modern culture have given rise to a new developmental period he calls emerging adulthood, the period from the late teens to the early 20s when individuals experiment with options prior to taking on adult roles (Arnett, 2000). Arnett's studies and those of other researchers indicate that, at least in the United States, young people do not tend to think of themselves as having fully attained adulthood until the age of 25 or so (Galambos, Turner, & Tilton-Weaver, 2005).

Neuroimaging studies have provided some support for the notion that emerging adulthood is a unique period of life. These studies suggest that the parts of the brain that underlie rational decision making, impulse control, and self-regulation mature during these years (Crone et al., 2006; Gogtay et al., 2004). As a result, early on in this phase of life, individuals make poorer decisions about matters such as risky behaviors (e.g., unprotected sex) than they do when these brain areas reach full maturity in the early to mid-20s.

The neurological changes of the emerging adult period combine with cultural demands to shape the psychosocial features of this period of development. Researcher Glenn Roisman and his colleagues have hypothesized that emerging adults must address developmental tasks in five domains: academic, friendship, conduct, work, and romantic (Roisman et al., 2004). Roisman's research suggests that skills within the first three of these domains transfer easily from adolescence to adulthood. By contrast, emerging adults must approach the work and romantic domains differently than they did as adolescents. Certainly, many teenagers have jobs and are involved in romances. However, the cultural expectations associated with emerging adulthood require them to commit to a career path that will enable them to achieve full economic independence from their families. Likewise, emerging adults must make decisions about the place of long-term romantic relationships in their present and future lives as well as participate in such relationships. As predicted by his hypothesis, Roisman's findings and those of other researchers suggest that emerging adults experience more adjustment difficulties related to these two domains than they do in the academic, friendship, and conduct domains (Korobov & Thorne, 2006).

Early and Middle Adulthood

As noted earlier, the long period of 50 or more years known as adulthood is generally divided into three parts: young or early adulthood (ages 20 to 40 or 45), middle adulthood (ages 40 or 45 to 65), and late adulthood (after age 65 or 70). These ages are only approximate because there are no biological or psychological events that neatly define the beginning or ending of a period. Obviously, some things change; but, in many ways, adults remain much the same as they were in their earlier years. The most obvious changes are usually physical ones.

8.15 How do the body and mind change in early and middle adulthood?

Physical and Cognitive Changes

Most people enjoy good general health and vitality in their 20s and 30s, but the first of these decades is the period of top physical condition, when physical strength, reaction time, reproductive capacity, and manual dexterity all peak. After age 30, there is a slight decline in these physical capacities, which is barely perceptible to most people other than professional athletes. Middle-aged people often complain about a loss of physical vigor and endurance. But such losses have to do less with aging than with exercise, diet, and health habits (Boul, 2003). One unavoidable change in the mid- to late 40s, though, is presbyopia, a condition in which the lenses of the eyes no longer accommodate adequately for near vision, and reading glasses or bifocals are required for reading.

The major biological event for women during middle age is menopause—the cessation of menstruation, which usually occurs between ages 45 and 55 and signifies the end of reproductive capacity. The most common symptom associated with menopause and the sharp decrease in the level of estrogen is *hot flashes*—sudden feelings of being uncomfortably hot. Some women also experience symptoms such as anxiety, irritability, and/or mood swings, and about 10% become depressed. However, most women do not experience psychological problems in connection with menopause (Busch, Zonderwan, & Costa, 1994; Matthews, 1992).

Although men do not have a physical event equivalent to menopause, they do experience a gradual decline in testosterone from age 20 until about age 60. During late middle age, many men also experience a reduction in the functioning of the prostate gland that affects the production of semen. Usually coupled with these reductions in testosterone and semen production is a reduction in the sex drive. Still, in contrast to women, men are capable of fathering a child throughout their lives. However, the DNA carried by their sperm show increasing amounts of fragmentation as they get older (Wyrobek, 2006). Scientists have not yet determined if or how damage of this kind is linked to either male fertility or to pregnancy outcomes.

Changes in intellectual functioning also occur across the early and middle adulthood years. However, they're a bit more complicated than you might think. For example, young adults outperform middle-aged and older adults on tests requiring speed or rote memory. But on tests measuring general information, vocabulary, reasoning ability, and social judgment, older participants usually do better than younger ones because of their greater experience and education (Salthouse, 2004). Adults actually continue to gain knowledge and skills over the years, particularly when they lead intellectually challenging lives.

Schaie and his colleagues (Schaie, 2005) analyzed data from the Seattle Longitudinal Study, which assessed the intellectual abilities of some 5,000 participants. Many of the participants were tested six times over the course of 50 years. Schaie found that in five areas—verbal meaning, spatial orientation, inductive reasoning, numerical reasoning, and word fluency—participants showed modest gains from young adulthood to the mid-40s. Decline did not occur, on average, until after age 60, and even then the decline was modest until the 80s. Half of the participants, even at age 81, showed no decline compared to their earlier performance. The study also revealed several gender differences: Females performed better on tests of verbal meaning and inductive reasoning; males tended to do better on tests of numerical reasoning and spatial orientation. The only ability found to show a continuous decline from the mid-20s to the 80s was perceptual speed.

To better understand changes in intellectual functioning in adulthood, researchers often distinguish between two types of intelligence (Horn, 1982): Crystallized intelligence—one's verbal ability and accumulated knowledge—tends to increase over the life span. Fluid intelligence—abstract reasoning and mental flexibility—peaks in the early 20s and declines slowly as people age.

crystallized intelligence Aspects of intelligence involving verbal ability and accumulated knowledge, which tend to increase over the life span.

fluid intelligence Aspects of intelligence involving abstract reasoning and mental flexibility, which peak in the early 20s and decline slowly as people age.

Social Development

8.16 What are the themes of social development in early and middle adulthood?

In days gone by, the primary social tasks of adulthood were marriage and starting a family. While it remains true that the majority of adults marry and have children, there is now a great deal of variability in the ages at which they do so. In 1960, the median age at first marriage was 20 for females and 23 for males; today, the median age is 26 for females and 28 for males (U.S. Census Bureau, 2010).

Living Arrangements. Government surveys indicate that households in the United States are now about evenly divided between those that are headed by a married couple and living arrangements that involve other kinds of relationships (U.S. Census Bureau, 2006). Most non-married-couple households are headed by single adults. Despite stereotypes that they are unhappy or searching for a life partner, most single adults say that they are satisfied with their status and do not seek to change it (Davies, 2003).

One important reason for the increase in age at which adults marry is the popularity of cohabitation. In the United States, nearly 5% of all households are headed by a cohabiting opposite-sex couple (U.S. Census Bureau, 2006). An additional 1%

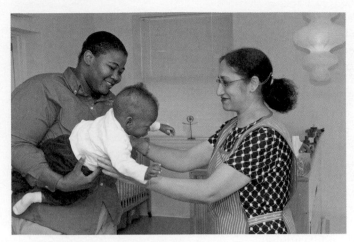

▲ The challenges associated with juggling the demands of family and career are familiar to most working mothers.

of households are headed by a cohabiting same-sex couple. Some studies suggest that if they marry, couples who cohabit are more prone to divorce than those who don't live together prior to marriage. However, these findings may be somewhat misleading in that they often do not take into account the firmness of couples' intention to marry. More careful studies show that couples who undertake a cohabiting relationship with a clear understanding by both partners that the arrangement is a prelude to marriage differ little in relationship satisfaction or stability from those who do not cohabit before marriage (Kline et al., 2004; Teachman, 2003).

As is true for heterosexuals, gay and lesbian committed couples report greater satisfaction with their sex lives than do singles (Home & Biss, 2005). Moreover, same-sex couples argue about the same things as heterosexuals do and report higher levels of satisfaction when partners are equally committed to the relationship (Solomon, Rothblum, & Balsam, 2004). Thus, Erikson's view that the status of one's intimate partnerships is an important facet of adult life appears to hold true regardless of sexual orientation.

Marriage and Divorce. Despite the rising age at first marriage and the diversity of living arrangements among today's adults, it is nevertheless true that the vast majority of adults marry at some time during their lives. Research suggests that more than 80% of adults will marry at least once in their lives (Whitehead & Popenoe, 2005). In addition to its economic benefits, marriage is associated with numerous physical and mental health benefits (e.g., lower rates of depression) for both men and women (Bierman, Fazio, & Milkie, 2006; Umberson et al., 2006).

Some studies suggest that an unhappy, stress-filled marriage may actually be detrimental to the health of one or both spouses (Umberson et al., 2006). Thus, conflict within a marriage sometimes leads to divorce. However, conflict is only one of several factors that are associated with divorce. Overall, the marriages most likely to fail are those between teenagers, nonreligious couples in which the bride was pregnant before marriage, and marriages of people whose parents divorced (Popenoe & Whitehead, 2000).

Divorce often radically alters the course of an adult's life, especially for a woman. For one thing, women who have children often experience a reduced standard of living after divorce. For another, both women and men must often find new networks of friends and often new places to live.

Parenthood. As with the increased age at which people get married, a growing number of couples are delaying parenthood until their 30s. But whenever a person becomes a parent, the adjustment is one of the most challenging—and rewarding—in life. One of the challenges is that both mothers and fathers are more likely to exhibit behaviors that are stereotypically associated with their respective gender roles after becoming parents than they were beforehand (Katz-Wise, Priess, & Hyde, 2010). However, this pattern may reflect gender differences in the availability of leave time from work or other practical factors rather than the preferences of either mothers or fathers. Moreover, research suggests that the quality of a couple's relationship before parenthood predicts how satisfied they are with their relationship after a child is born. For example, low levels of conflict before childbirth predispose couples to maintain high levels of relationship satisfaction during the transition to parenthood (Kluwer & Johnson, 2007).

Careers. Issues involving work and careers constitute an important theme of adult life. As discussed in the *Apply It*, psychologists' studies of career development have focused on both personality variables and the stages involved in pursuing a career. Personality and stages aside, how we feel about our work situations, our level of *job satisfaction*,

Have you ever wondered what type of work you are best suited for? If so, you may want to begin your quest for an answer by looking at two models of career development, the process of choosing and adjusting to a particular career. Recommendations about what you might do to enhance your search for the ideal career can be derived from both. Ultimately, though, the degree to which you are satisfied with your career may depend on how you integrate your work into your life as a whole.

Holland's Personality Types

The work of John Holland has been very influential in shaping psychologists' ideas about personality and career. Holland proposes six basic personality types: realistic, investigative, artistic, social, enterprising, and conventional. His research shows that each of the six types is associated with work preferences. (The types and their associated work preferences are summarized in Table 8.2.) As Holland's theory predicts, people whose personality matches their job are also more likely to be satisfied with their work. Thus, a personality assessment may help you make an appropriate occupational choice and give you confidence about the decision (Francis-Smyth & Smith, 1997).

Super's Career Development Stages

Psychologist Donald Super proposed that career development happens in stages that begin in infancy (Super, 1971, 1986). First comes the growth stage (from birth to 14 years), in which you learn about your abilities and interests. Next is the exploratory stage, roughly between the ages of 15 and 24. According to Super, there's a lot of trial and error in this stage, so job changes happen frequently. Next is the establishment stage (also called the stabilization stage), from 25 to 45. This stage begins with learning how things work in your career, the culture of your organization, and progression through the early steps of the career ladder. Sometimes, additional formal training is required during this stage. Setting goals is also important in this stage. You must decide how far you want to go and how you intend to get there. Mentoring by an experienced co-worker often helps you negotiate this stage successfully. Once an individual has become well established in a career, she or he enters the maintenance phase (age 45 through retirement), in which the goal is to protect and maintain the gains made in earlier years. Of course, in today's rapidly changing economy, people are often required to change careers. Thus, an individual may reenter the exploratory stage at any time. As with most stage theories, the ages associated with Super's stages of career development are less important than the sequence of the stages.

TABLE 8.2 Holland's Personality Types and Work Preferences

TYPE	PERSONALITY TRAITS	WORK PREFERENCES
Realistic	Aggressive, masculine, physically strong, often with low verbal or interpersonal skills	Mechanical activities and tool use; often chooses a job such as mechanic, electrician, or surveyor
Investigative	Oriented toward thinking (particularly abstract thinking), organizing, and planning; low in social skills	Ambiguous, challenging tasks; often a scientist or engineer
Artistic	Asocial	Unstructured, highly individual activity; often an artist
Social	Extraverted; people-oriented, sociable, and needing attention; avoids intellectual activity and dislikes highly ordered activity	Working with people in service jobs like nursing and education
Enterprising	Highly verbal and dominating; enjoys organizing and directing others; persuasive and a strong leader	Often chooses a career in sales
Conventional	Prefers structured activities and subordinate roles; likes clear guidelines; accurate and precise	May choose an occupation such as bookkeeping or filing

Source: Holland (1973, 1992).

Akosua
PRE-PHARMACY

◉ Watch on **mypsychlab.com**

predicts not only how happy and productive we are on the job but also how positively we feel about other aspects of our lives. For example, workers' job satisfaction is strongly related to how satisfied they are with their romantic relationships (Sonnentag, 2003). Thus, these two important themes of adult life are intertwined. The more satisfied a person is with one, the better he or she is likely to feel about the other.

Other aspects of adults' lives are interconnected with their careers as well. For example, child-rearing issues are often central in the lives of working women. In the 1960s, only 18% of mothers with children were employed. Today, 66% of mothers of children younger than age 6 and about 80% of the mothers of school-aged children work outside the home (Parker, 2009). Further, the idea that a career is an important component of a satisfying life is now shared by men and women alike. However, studies show that women are less likely than men to actively seek promotions to upper-level management positions because of potential conflicts between their work and family roles (Sarrio et al., 2002; van Vianen & Fischer, 2002).

The Myths of Middle Age. You may have heard that parents experience an *empty nest syndrome* when their grown children leave home. Contrary to this popular stereotype, parents often appreciate the opportunity to reexamine their identity that is afforded by their children's departure from home (Noriko, 2004). Moreover, analyses show that the presence of an empty nest has little or no relationship to the appearance of mental disorders such as depression at midlife (Schmidt et al., 2004). Thus, the concept of an empty nest syndrome seems to have little basis in reality.

Similarly, the term *midlife crisis* has been used to describe the angst middle-aged people feel over their lost youth. Research refutes the idea that middle-aged people go through such a crisis, however. More often, individuals between the ages of 40 and 60 are more likely to experience what psychologist David Almeida calls *stressor overload* than either younger or older adults (Clay, 2003). This condition arises when middle-aged people must balance the demands of mentoring teenaged and young adult children with those associated with caring for aging parents, managing their own careers, finding time for intimate relationships, and looking ahead to retirement. Surprisingly, though, Almeida has found that successful management of these challenges enhances middle-aged adults' sense of competence (Serido, Almeida, & Wethington, 2004).

Later Adulthood

In the early years of the 20th century, life expectancy in the United States was only 49 years. By the century's end, the expected life span of someone born in the United States was about 76 years. According to the most recent census, people older than age 65 constitute about 15% of the U.S. population; by 2030, that percentage will rise to 20% (FIFARS, 2004; U.S. Census Bureau, 2001). A sizable number of these elders are likely to be older than age 100. What are your perceptions of life after 65? The statistics in the *Try It* might surprise you.

8.17 How do the body and mind change in the later adult years?

Physical and Cognitive Changes

It was long assumed that the number of neurons in the brain declined sharply in later adulthood, but this assumption appears to be false (Gallagher & Rapp, 1997). Research has shown that the shrinking volume of the aging cortex is due more to breakdown of the myelin that covers the axons in the white matter than to loss of the neurons that make up the gray matter, a process that begins in the early 30s (Bartzokis et al., 2004; Peters et al., 1994; Wickelgren, 1996). As you learned in Chapter 2, the myelin sheath facilitates the rapid conduction of neural impulses. The breakdown of myelin thus explains one of the most predictable characteristics of aging—the general slowing of behavior—a process in which the reductions in the speed of neural transmission lead to a slowing of physical and mental functions (Birren & Fisher, 1995).

general slowing A process in which the reductions in the speed of neural transmission lead to a slowing of physical and mental functions.

TRY IT   Stereotypes about Later Adulthood

Estimate the percentages of people older than age 65 in the United States who exhibit these indicators of well-being:

1. Live alone or with a spouse
2. Have incomes above the poverty level
3. Interact with family at least once every two weeks
4. Need no help with daily activities
5. Need no assistive devices (e.g., cane, wheelchair)
6. Go out to eat at least once every two weeks
7. Attend religious services regularly
8. Are sexually active

Sources: FIFARS (2000, 2004); Gingell et al. (2003).

ANSWERS
1. 94% 2. 90% 3. 90% 4. 89% 5. 85% 6. 60% 7. 50% 8. 50%

◉ Watch on **mypsychlab.com**

With degeneration of the myelin, the brain takes longer to process information, and reaction time is slower.

With advancing age, the elderly typically become more farsighted, have increasingly impaired night vision, and experience hearing loss in the higher frequencies (Long & Crambert, 1990; Slawinski, Hartel, & Kline, 1993). Joints become stiffer, and bones lose calcium and become more brittle, increasing the risk of fractures from falls.

About 80% of Americans older than age 65 have one or more chronic conditions. The most common of these ailments is hypertension (high blood pressure), a condition that afflicts 52% of women and 47% of men older than age 65 (FIFARS, 2004). Arthritis, an inflammatory condition that causes stiffness in the joints, is next, with prevalence rates of 39% among females and 31% among males. However, these two conditions can be controlled with medication, and many older adults who have them manage quite well.

Research suggests that physical exercise improves the physical fitness levels of older adults (Small, 2005). In one study, 100 frail nursing-home residents, average age 87, exercised their thigh and hip muscles vigorously on exercise machines for 45 minutes three times a week. At the end of 10 weeks, participants had increased their stair-climbing power by 28.4% and their walking speed by 12%, and four of them were able to exchange their walkers for canes (Fiatarone et al., 1994). For many of us, remaining fit and vigorous as we age lies within our power.

General slowing also helps to explain the finding you read about earlier regarding age differences in performance on cognitive tests that require speed. However, intellectual decline in late adulthood is not inevitable. Older adults who keep mentally and physically active tend to retain their mental skills as long as their health is good (Schaie, 2005). They do well on tests of vocabulary, comprehension, and general information, and their ability to solve practical problems is generally higher than that of young adults. In laboratory memory tasks, older people do as well or almost as well as younger people on recognition tasks (Hultsch & Dixon, 1990) and on recall of information in their areas of expertise (Charness, 1989). And they are just as capable as younger adults at learning new cognitive strategies (Saczynski, Willis, & Schaie, 2002).

Several factors are positively correlated with good cognitive functioning in the elderly: a higher education level, a complex work environment, a long marriage to an intelligent spouse, and a higher income (Schaie, 2005; vander Elst et al., 2006). And gender is a factor as well. Women not only outlive men, but they also generally show less cognitive decline during old age. But intellectual functioning can be hampered by physical problems (Manton, Siegler, & Woodbury, 1986) or by psychological problems such as depression. A study by Shimamura and others (1995) revealed that people who continue to lead intellectually stimulating and mentally active lives are far less likely to suffer mental decline as they age. So, "use it or lose it" is good advice if you want to remain mentally sharp as you age.

8.18 What adjustment challenges do older adults face?

Social Adjustment

As noted earlier, most elderly adults are both physically and cognitively healthy. Yet old age involves many losses. Adjusting to these losses is one of the challenges of getting older. Fortunately, most older adults are able to cope effectively. For instance, in the United States, 60% of 65- to 69-year-olds and 80% of those over 70 have retired from paid employment (Fifars, 2008). Despite stereotypes, most of them are happy to leave work and do not experience a great deal of stress in adjusting to retirement. Generally, the people who are most reluctant to retire are those who are better educated, hold high-status jobs with a good income, and find fulfillment in their work. Bosse and others (1991) found that only 30% of retirees reported finding retirement stressful, and most of those were likely to be in poor health and to have financial problems.

Another common event that may affect life satisfaction for older adults is the loss of a spouse. For most people, losing a spouse is the most stressful event in a lifetime. Disruption of sleep patterns is among the many physical effects associated with this loss (Steeves, 2002). These physical effects take their toll on the bereaved elderly and lead to tiredness and anxiety. In addition, both widows and widowers are at a greater risk for health problems due to suppressed immune function and have a higher mortality rate, particularly within the first 6 months, than their age-mates who are not bereaved (Martikainen & Valkonen, 1996).

Loss of a spouse often brings with it another challenge for the 44% of women and 14% of older men who experience it (FIFARS, 2004): They must decide whether to alter their living arrangements. In the United States, older Americans of all ethnic groups have a strong preference for remaining independent as long as possible (FIFARS, 2004; Martinez, 2002). As a result, only 5% of elderly women and 9% of older men live with their relatives (FIFARS, 2004). The living arrangements of elders in European countries are similar to those in the United States (Hellstrom & Hallberg, 2004; Osborn et al., 2003). Predictably, maintaining the ability to live alone is an important factor in elders' life satisfaction in these societies (Osborn et al., 2003).

▲ Older adults take more time to learn new skills, but, once learned, they apply new skills as accurately as those who are younger.

In other countries, the situation is just the opposite. For instance, in Mexico, 90% of elderly widows live with relatives, usually their adult children (Varley & Blasco, 2003). Multigenerational households are commonplace in other Latin American countries as well (De Vos, 1990). Living with relatives is also more common among the elderly in Asian countries than in the United States or Europe (Sung, 1992). Consequently, the psychological effects of living alone are quite different among elders in Latin American and Asian societies than in the United States and Europe. Elders who live alone in societies in which it is considered normative for older adults to live with their adult children express lower levels of life satisfaction than their peers who live with family (Yeh & Lo, 2004).

8.19 What are the components of successful aging?

Successful Aging

As you have learned, for older adults to maintain a sense of life satisfaction, they must be able to adjust to both physical and social changes. Knowing this, you shouldn't be surprised to learn that a majority of older adults rate their health as good (see Figure 8.6), even though 80% of them suffer from some kind of chronic ailment (FIFARS, 2008). One reason for this seeming contradiction is that the tendency toward having a generally optimistic outlook on life increases as people get older (Charles, Mather, & Carstengen, 2003). Further, most older adults have learned to think of their lives in relative terms. That is, most believe that others are worse off than they are (Heckhausen & Brim, 1997). In other words, older adults grade their health "on a curve," so to speak.

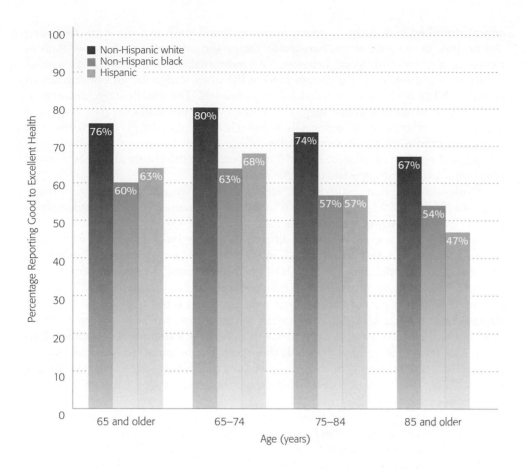

FIGURE 8.6 **Percentage of People Age 65 and Older Who Reported Having Good to Excellent Health, by Age Group and Race and Hispanic Origin, 2004–2006**
Source: FIFARS (2008).

An optimistic outlook is one of the key components of successful aging, the term researchers use to describe maintaining one's physical health, mental abilities, social competence, and overall satisfaction with life as one gets older (Rowe & Kahn, 1997, 1998). Successful aging has been the focus of much aging-related research in recent years. As defined by authors John Rowe and Robert Kahn (1997, 1998), successful aging has three components: good physical health, retention of cognitive abilities, and continuing engagement in social and productive activities.

Much of what happens to us as we age, of course, is somewhat beyond our control. However, successful aging also includes behaviors aimed at warding off age-related declines, such as eating a healthy diet and remaining mentally and socially active, and adaptive responses to the challenges that inevitably accompany aging. For instance, after a stroke, some older adults work diligently to recover lost abilities, while others despair and put little effort into the rehabilitation regimens prescribed for them by doctors and therapists (Ushikubo, 1998). Not surprisingly, individuals who are willing to do the work required for optimal recovery of functioning gain the most from rehabilitation. The kind of attitude that motivates an individual to try to get better after a devastating event such as a stroke represents the spirit of Rowe and Kahn's successful aging concept.

successful aging Maintaining one's physical health, mental abilities, social competence, and overall satisfaction with life as one gets older.

Death and Dying ▶

8.20 How do people respond to approaching death and bereavement?

One of the developmental tasks for every elderly person is to accept the inevitability of death and to prepare for it. At no time, however, does this task become more critical than when an individual—no matter what age—faces a terminal illness. Elisabeth Kübler-Ross (1969) interviewed some 200 terminally ill people and found they shared common reactions to their impending death. In her book *On Death and Dying,* she identifies five stages people go through in coming to terms with death.

In the first stage, *denial,* most patients react to the diagnosis of their terminal illness with shock and disbelief (surely, the doctors must be wrong). The second stage, *anger,* is marked by feelings of anger, resentment, and envy of those who are young and healthy. In the third stage, *bargaining,* the person attempts to postpone death in return for a promise of "good behavior." An individual may offer God some special service or a promise to live a certain kind of life in exchange for an opportunity to attend a child's wedding or a grandchild's graduation. The fourth stage, *depression,* brings a great sense of loss and may take two forms—depression over past losses and depression over impending losses. Given enough time, patients may reach the final stage, *acceptance,* in which they stop struggling against death and contemplate its coming without fear or despair. Kübler-Ross claims that the family also goes through stages similar to those experienced by the patient.

Critics deny the universality of Kübler-Ross's proposed stages and their invariant sequence (Wright, 2003). Each person is unique. The reactions of all the terminally ill cannot be expected to conform to some rigid sequence of stages.

Similarly, there are cross-cultural differences in how individuals deal with death (Westerhof et al., 2001). For individuals in Western societies, maintenance of individual autonomy over the dying process is of great importance. Moreover, people often view death as an enemy that must be battled at all costs. By contrast, Native American cultures see death as part of nature's cycle and, as such, it is not to be feared or fought (DeSpelder & Strickland, 1983). In Mexican culture, people's deaths are seen as reflections of their lives. As a result, their behavior during the dying process is assumed to reveal much about what kind of people they were. Furthermore, in Mexican culture, death is discussed frequently and is even celebrated on the Day of the Dead (DeSpelder & Strickland, 1983). Thus, Kübler-Ross's stages of denial, anger, bargaining, and so on, may not exist in such cultures.

Death comes too soon for most people, but not soon enough for others. Some who are terminally ill and subject to intractable pain would welcome an end to their suffering. Should dying patients be left with no choice but to suffer to the end? Today most medical ethicists distinguish between two forms of euthanasia (also known as "mercy killing"). *Passive euthanasia* occurs when a person (typically, a physican) hastens death by not using life support systems or medication that would prolong a patient's life or by withdrawing life support or other treatment that may be keeping a patient alive. *Active euthanasia* (also called "assisted suicide") occurs when a physician or other individual (at a patient's request) hastens a patient's death by active means, such as by administering a fatal dose of a drug.

Active euthanasia is the focus of an ongoing debate. The state of Oregon legalized physician-assisted suicide in 1997. Most patients who request death cite as their reasons loss of control over bodily functions, loss of autonomy, and inability to take part in activities that make life enjoyable (Sullivan, Hedberg, & Fleming, 2000). However, when Oregon physicians provide such patients with prescriptions for lethal doses of drugs, the patients often do not fill the prescriptions, illustrating that the desire to live is a powerful motivator even among people who wish to escape from pain and suffering (Quill, 2007).

A rapidly growing alternative to hospitals and nursing homes is *hospice care.* Hospices are agencies that care for the needs of the dying more humanely and affordably than hospitals can and that use special facilities or, in some cases, the patient's own home. A hospice follows a set of guidelines that make it more attuned to the patient's personal needs and preferences than a hospital or nursing home typically can be.

Finally, many of us have experienced the *grieving process*—the period of bereavement that follows the death of a loved one and sometimes lingers long after the person has gone. Contrary to what many believe, research (Bonanno et al., 1995) has shown that bereaved individuals who suffer the most intense grief initially, who weep inconsolably and feel the deepest pain, do not get through their bereavement more quickly than others. And other research (Folkman et al., 1996) has found that the grieving process for male caregivers whose partners have died of AIDS is very similar to that experienced by spouses.

Death and dying are not pleasant subjects, but remember that life itself is a terminal condition, and each day of life should be treasured like a precious gift.

ᨀ Looking Back

Our discussion of death and dying has brought us to the end of the human life span. As you have seen, gains and losses occur in every phase of development. The accumulated experience available to the elderly is punctuated by losses in physical and psychological speed for most and more serious declines for others. In middle adulthood, many people occupy important social roles at the same time that their reproductive capacity is diminishing. For young adults, the joys of youth are left behind as the responsibilities of adulthood are assumed. In similar fashion, adolescents look back wistfully at the time they spent playing during their childhood years as they use their newly acquired mental and physical abilities to make important decisions about their lives. School-aged children think more logically than when they were younger, but, at the same time, they have forever left behind the pleasures associated with a day spent pretending to be a superhero, for example. The capacity to use one's own behavior as a symbolic representation of something else is the most important ability gained in the preschool years, but it comes with the loss of caregivers' tolerance of dependency. Finally, the infant trades the warm safety of the womb for the opportunity to take in all the sights and sounds of the outside world and to embark on a journey of unknown length but of certain destination.

CHAPTER 8 SUMMARY

THEORIES OF DEVELOPMENT (pp. 240-252)

8.1 How does Piaget's theory explain cognitive development? (pp. 241-245)

Piaget proposed that humans construct schemes, or general action plans, on the basis of experiences. Schemes change through assimilation and accommodation until they work effectively in the real world. During the sensorimotor stage (ages birth to 2 years), infants act on the world through their senses and motor activities and develop object permanence. Children at the preoperational stage (ages 2 to 6 years) are increasingly able to use symbols, but they exhibit egocentrism. When working real-world problems, children at the concrete operations stage (ages 6 to 11 or 12 years) are able to apply logical operations to problems that can be tested in the real world. At the formal operations stage (ages 11 or 12 years and beyond), adolescents can apply logic to abstract problems and hypothetical situations. Piaget may have underestimated the abilities of children and overestimated those of adults, but research supports the sequence of cognitive development that he proposed.

Key Terms

developmental psychology, p. 240
schemes, p. 241
assimilation, p. 241
accommodation, p. 241
object permanence, p. 241
symbolic function, p. 241
conservation, p. 242
reversibility, p. 242
hypothetico-deductive thinking, p. 242
naive idealism, p. 242
imaginary audience, p. 242
personal fable, p. 243

8.2 How do the neo-Piagetians and Vygotsky explain cognitive development? (pp. 246-247)

Neo-Piagetians explain cognitive development as a function of working memory development. Vygotsky argued that private speech helps children verbalize problem-solving steps. In scaffolding, a teacher or parent adjusts the quality and degree of instruction to fit the child's present level of ability. It allows a child to gradually perform a task independently within her zone of proximal development.

Key Terms

zone of proximal development, p. 246
scaffolding, p. 247

8.3 How does Kohlberg's theory explain moral reasoning? (pp. 247-250)

At the preconventional level, moral reasoning is governed by the physical consequences of an act. At the conventional level, judgments of right and wrong are based on the internalized standards of others. Postconventional moral reasoning involves weighing moral alternatives and realizing that laws may conflict with basic human rights.

Key Terms

preconventional level, p. 247
conventional level, p. 247
postconventional level, p. 247

8.4 How does Erikson's theory explain psychosocial development? (pp. 250-251)

Erikson proposed that individuals progress through eight psychosocial stages that span the entire period from birth to death. Each stage is defined by a conflict involving the individual's relationship with the social environment. A positive resolution of each conflict makes it more likely that an individual will be successful in later stages.

Key Term

psychosocial stages, p. 250

PRENATAL DEVELOPMENT AND INFANCY (pp. 252-258)

8.5 What happens in each stage of prenatal development? (p. 252-254)

In the germinal stage, from conception to 2 weeks, the egg is fertilized, and the zygote attaches itself to the uterine wall. During the embryonic stage, from week 3 through week 8, all of the major systems, organs, and structures form. In the fetal stage, from week 9 until birth, the fetus experiences rapid growth and body systems, structures, and organs continue their development. Fetuses can hear and remember sounds that they hear repeatedly. Negative influences on prenatal development include drugs, environmental hazards, poor maternal nutrition, and maternal illness. Exposure is most harmful in the period of the embryo during critical periods of development for the various body structures. Physiological signals from the woman's body, the fetus, and the placenta trigger labor, a three-stage process. Low-birth-weight and preterm infants are at risk for poor developmental outcomes.

Key Terms
prenatal development, p. 252
zygote, p. 252
embryo, p. 252
fetus, p. 252
teratogens, p. 253
critical period, p. 253
fetal alcohol syndrome, p. 253
neonate, p. 254
low-birth-weight baby, p. 254
preterm infant, p. 254

8.6 How do infants' abilities change over the first 18 months of life? (pp. 254-256)

Neonates are born with reflexes that help them survive, and all of their senses are functional at birth. As maturation proceeds, controlled motor skills, such as grasping and walking, develop. Experience can retard or accelerate motor development, but the sequence of motor milestones is universal.

Key Terms
reflexes, p. 254
visual cliff, p. 255
maturation, p. 255

8.7 How does temperament affect infants' behavior? (pp. 256-257)

Temperament refers to an individual's behavioral style or characteristic way of responding to the environment. The three temperament types identified by Thomas, Chess, and Birch are easy, difficult, and slow-to-warm-up. Current research indicates that dimensions of temperament include activity level, sociability, inhibition, negative emotionality, and effortful control.

Key Term
temperament, p. 256

8.8 What are the causes, characteristics, and consequences of infant–caregiver attachment? (pp. 257-258)

Harlow found that the basis of attachment in infant monkeys is contact comfort. According to Bowlby, the infant has usually developed a strong attachment to the mother at age 6 to 8 months. Ainsworth identified four attachment patterns in infants: secure, avoidant, resistant, and disorganized/disoriented. Fathers' patterns of interaction with children differ from those of mothers. Thus, mothers and fathers exert unique influences on children's development, and, ideally, children need both influences. Children who interact regularly with their fathers tend to have higher IQs, do better in social situations, and manage frustration better than children lacking such interaction.

Key Terms
attachment, p. 257
separation anxiety, p. 257
stranger anxiety, p. 257

EARLY AND MIDDLE CHILDHOOD (pp. 258-263)

8.9 What are the phases of language development, and how do various theorists explain them? (pp. 258-260)

Babbling begins at age 6 months, followed by single words sometime during the second year, two-word sentences at ages 18 to 20 months, and telegraphic speech between 2 and 3 years of age, and then the acquisition of grammatical rules. Learning theory suggests that language is acquired through imitation and reinforcement. The nativist position is that language ability is largely innate, because it is acquired in stages that occur in a fixed order at the same ages in most children throughout the world.

Key Terms
babbling, p. 259
overextension, p. 259
underextension, p. 259
telegraphic speech, p. 259
overregularlization, p. 259

8.10 What do parenting styles and peer relationships contribute to socialization? (pp. 260-261)

The three parenting styles identified by Baumrind are authoritarian, authoritative, and permissive. Research suggests that the

TABLE 9.1 Intrinsic and Extrinsic Motivation

	DESCRIPTION	EXAMPLES
Intrinsic motivation	An activity is pursued as an end in itself because it is enjoyable and rewarding.	A person anonymously donates a large sum of money to a university to fund scholarships for deserving students.
		A child reads several books each week because reading is fun.
Extrinsic motivation	An activity is pursued to gain an external reward or to avoid an undesirable consequence.	A person agrees to donate a large sum of money to a university for the construction of a building, provided it will bear the family name.
		A child reads two books each week to avoid losing TV privileges.

that no true instincts motivate human behavior. However, most also agree that biological forces underlie some human behaviors.

One biological approach to motivation, drive-reduction theory, was popularized by Clark Hull (1943). According to Hull, all living organisms have certain biological needs that must be met if they are to survive. A need gives rise to an internal state of tension called a drive, and the person or organism is motivated to reduce it. For example, when you are deprived of food or go too long without water, your biological need causes a state of tension—in this case, the hunger or thirst drive. You become motivated to seek food or water to reduce the drive and satisfy your biological need.

Drive-reduction theory is derived largely from the biological concept of homeostasis—the tendency of the body to maintain a balanced, internal state to ensure physical survival. Body temperature, blood sugar level, water balance, blood oxygen level—in short, everything required for physical existence—must be maintained in a state of equilibrium, or balance. When such a state is disturbed, a drive is created to restore the balance, as shown in Figure 9.1 (p. 286).

Drive-reduction theory assumes that humans are always motivated to reduce tension. Other theorists argue just the opposite, that humans are sometimes motivated to increase tension. These theorists use the term arousal to refer to a person's state of alertness and mental and physical activation. Arousal levels can range from no arousal (when a person is comatose), to moderate arousal (when pursuing normal day-to-day activities), to high arousal (when excited and highly stimulated). Arousal theory states that people are motivated to maintain an optimal level of arousal. If arousal is less than the optimal level, we do something to stimulate it; if arousal exceeds the optimal level, we seek to reduce the stimulation (see the *Explain It*, p. 287).

When arousal is too low, stimulus motives—such as curiosity and the motives to explore, to manipulate objects, and to play—cause humans and other animals to increase stimulation. Think about sitting in an airport or at a bus stop or any other place where people are waiting. How many people do you see playing games on their cellphones or laptops? Waiting is boring; in other words, it provides no sources of arousal. Thus, people turn to electronic games to raise their level of arousal.

There is often a close link between arousal and performance. According to the Yerkes–Dodson law, performance on tasks is best when the person's arousal level is appropriate to the difficulty of the task. Performance on simple tasks is better when

drive-reduction theory A theory of motivation suggesting that biological needs create internal states of tension or arousal—called drives—which organisms are motivated to reduce.

drive An internal state of tension or arousal that is brought about by an underlying need and that an organism is motivated to reduce.

homeostasis The natural tendency of the body to maintain a balanced internal state in order to ensure physical survival.

arousal A state of alertness and mental and physical activation.

arousal theory A theory of motivation suggesting that people are motivated to maintain an optimal level of alertness and physical and mental activation.

stimulus motives Motives that cause humans and other animals to increase stimulation when the level of arousal is too low (examples are curiosity and the motive to explore).

Yerkes–Dodson law The principle that performance on tasks is best when the arousal level is appropriate to the difficulty of the task: higher arousal for simple tasks, moderate arousal for tasks of moderate difficulty, and lower arousal for complex tasks.

▲ Which is the more powerful motivator in a game of poker, the gratification that comes from devising a successful strategy (intrinsic motivation) or the money you get when you win (extrinsic motivation)? As is true of many activities, poker is an engaging hobby (or profession, depending on your skill level) that involves both intrinsic and extrinsic motivators.

FIGURE 9.1 Drive-Reduction Theory
Drive-reduction theory is based on the biological concept of homeostasis—the natural tendency of a living organism to maintain a state of internal balance, or equilibrium. When the equilibrium becomes disturbed (by a biological need such as thirst), a drive (internal state of arousal) emerges. Then the organism is motivated to take action to satisfy the need, thus reducing the drive and restoring equilibrium.

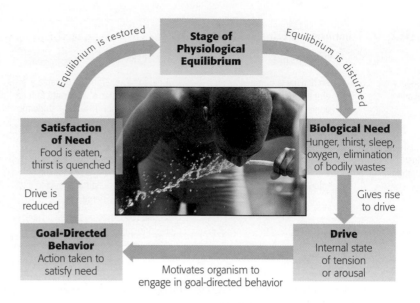

arousal is relatively high. Tasks of moderate difficulty are best accomplished when arousal is moderate; complex or difficult tasks, when arousal is lower (see Figure 9.2, p. 288). But performance suffers when arousal level is either too high or too low for the task. For instance, how often have you heard great athletes who "choke" in critical situations compared to those who "come through" under pressure? Perhaps high-pressure situations push the athletes who choke past the optimal point of arousal but have just the opposite effect on the reliable athletes.

The relationship between arousal and performance is most often explained in terms of attention. Low arousal allows the mind to wander, so performance declines for tasks that require concentration, such as taking a test. By contrast, high arousal interferes with concentration by taking up all the available space in working memory. The ideal level of arousal for test taking, then, is an amount that is sufficient to keep the mind from wandering but not so great as to interfere with the memory demands of taking the test. Critics of this theory have argued that arousal is merely one of many variables that influence attention (Hanoch & Vitouch, 2004; Landers, 2007). Moreover, they point out that the Yerkes-Dodson law is based primarily on animal research (Hancock & Ganey, 2003). For these reasons, they caution against generalizing arousal theory to complex human behaviors such as test performance without taking into account other factors that influence how humans allocate attention.

9.3 How do behavioral and social-cognitive theories explain work and achievement motivation?

Behavioral and Social-Cognitive Approaches to Motivation

The biological approaches that you have read about so far are helpful for understanding motivation on a physiological level, but they don't help us answer questions about the more complex social motives. To better understand motivation in work and school settings, we have to consider behavioral and social-cognitive approaches. You should remember from Chapter 5 that behavioral theories emphasize learning from consequences and social-cognitive theories focus on how people think about models, consequences, and other factors that influence their decisions about behavior.

industrial/organizational (I/O) psychologists
Psychologists who apply their knowledge in the workplace and are especially interested in work motivation and job performance.

goal setting An approach to work motivation that involves establishing specific, difficult goals rather than simply telling people to do their best in the absence of assigned goals.

Work Motivation. What motivates workers to perform well on the job? Psychologists who apply their knowledge in the workplace are known as industrial/organizational (I/O) psychologists. I/O psychologists design behavior modification plans that use reinforcers such as supervisor praise, bonuses, and extra time off to motivate employees to improve job performance. They may also use a strategy called goal setting in which supervisors provide employees with specific, difficult goals, which leads to higher levels of performance than simply telling people to do their best (Latham & Pinder, 2005).

EXPLAIN IT   **Why Are Dangerous Hobbies Appealing to Some People?**

Suppose you had unlimited funds and unlimited time to pursue the hobby of your dreams. Would you choose skydiving, or would you prefer to spend your time developing an organic garden? Think for a minute about how drive-reduction and arousal theory might be used to explain your choice of a hobby.

Recall that drive-reduction theory proposes that we are motivated to reduce tension. But what is more tension inducing than jumping out of an airplane? Yet some people seem to crave such thrills. By the same token, what could be more calming than patiently working a plot of land until you succeed in getting it to produce the fruits and vegetables that you are trying to grow? Devoted gardeners would probably agree with this observation, but those who prefer skydiving would, no doubt, be bored to tears if they were forced to spend their time tending a garden. Consequently, drive-reduction theory cannot explain why people vary in their choices of leisure activities.

By contrast, arousal theorists would argue that hobby choices reflect individuals' standing with regard to *sensation seeking*, a variable that reflects our tendency to seek stimulation when our levels of arousal are low. Psychological researchers have found that differences in sensation seeking are correlated with activity choices. Thus, if you think you would prefer skydiving to gardening, you might be high in sensation seeking. If gardening is more appealing to you, then you are probably low in sensation seeking. If you are unsure as to where you might fall on a measure of sensation seeking, here are a few questions that can help you decide.

Circle the choice A or B that better describes your feelings:

1. A. I am invigorated by a brisk, cold day.
   B. I can't wait to get indoors on a cold day.
2. A. I get bored seeing the same old faces.
   B. I like the comfortable familiarity of everyday friends.
3. A. I sometimes like to do things that are a little frightening.
   B. A sensible person avoids activities that are dangerous.
4. A. The most important goal of life is to live it to the fullest and experience as much as possible.
   B. The most important goal of life is to find peace and happiness.
5. A. I would like to try parachute jumping.
   B. I would never want to try jumping out of a plane, with or without a parachute.
6. A. I enter cold water gradually, giving myself time to get used to it.
   B. I like to dive or jump right into the ocean or a cold pool.

7. A. A good painting should shock or jolt the senses.
   B. A good painting should give one a feeling of peace and security.
8. A. People who ride motorcycles must have some kind of unconscious need to hurt themselves.
   B. I would like to drive or ride a motorcycle.

Count one point for each of the following items that you have circled: 1A, 2A, 3A, 4A, 5A, 6B, 7A, 8B. Add up your total and compare it with the norms: 0–1, Very low; 2–3, Low; 4–5, Average; 6–7, High; 8, Very high.

If your score is low, you may want to start saving now for a set of sturdy gardening tools. Be aware, however, that a low level of sensation seeking may also help you avoid the potentially health-threatening behaviors of substance abuse and even crossing busy streets against "Don't Walk" signals (Brecht, Greenwell, & Anglin, 2007; Rosenbloom, 2006). Thus, it may seem that high sensation-seekers have more fun, but they are also more vulnerable to risks that involve high levels of arousal.

⊙ Watch on **mypsychlab.com**

An organization can enhance employees' commitment to goals by (1) having them participate in the goal setting, (2) making goals specific, attractive, difficult, and attainable, (3) providing feedback on performance, and (4) rewarding the employees for attaining the goals (Katzell & Thompson, 1990).

Several social-cognitive theories have been applied to research on work motivation. According to one of these—expectancy theory—motivation to engage in a given

expectancy theory An approach that explains work motivation in terms of workers' beliefs about the effectiveness and value of the effort they put forth on the job.

FIGURE 9.2 The Yerkes–Dodson Law
The optimal level of arousal varies according to the difficulty of the task. Arousal levels should be relatively high for simple tasks, moderate for moderately difficult tasks, and lower for difficult tasks.

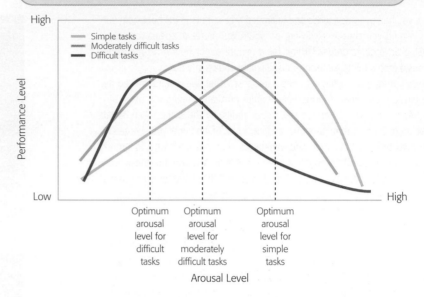

How would the amount of preparation you did for an exam affect the arousal curve that would be activated when you actually take the test?

need for achievement (*n* Ach) The need to accomplish something difficult and to perform at a high standard of excellence.

activity is determined by (1) *expectancy,* a person's belief that more effort will result in improved performance; (2) *instrumentality,* the person's belief that doing a job well will be noticed and rewarded; and (3) *valence,* the degree to which a person values the rewards that are offered. Several studies have supported expectancy theory by showing that employees work harder when they believe that more effort will improve their performance, when they think that a good performance will be acknowledged and rewarded, and when they value the rewards that are offered (Fairbank et al., 2003).

Achievement Motivation. In early research, social-cognitive theorist Henry Murray (1938) developed the *Thematic Apperception Test (TAT),* which consists of a series of pictures of ambiguous situations. The person taking the test is asked to create a story about each picture—to describe what is going on in the picture, what the person or persons pictured are thinking about, what they may be feeling, and what is likely to be the outcome of the situation. The stories are presumed to reveal the test taker's needs and the strength of those needs. One of the motives identified by Murray was the need for achievement (abbreviated *n* Ach), or the motive to accomplish something difficult and to maintain a high standard of performance. The need for achievement, rather than being satisfied with accomplishment, seems to grow as it is fed.

Researchers David McClelland and John Atkinson have conducted many studies of the *n* Ach (McClelland, 1958, 1961, 1985; McClelland et al., 1953). People with a high *n* Ach pursue goals that are challenging yet attainable through hard work, ability, determination, and persistence. Goals that are too easy, those anyone can reach, offer no challenge and hold no interest because success would not be rewarding (McClelland, 1985). Impossibly high goals and high risks are not pursued because they offer little chance of success and are considered a waste of time. The goals of those with high *n* Ach are self-determined and linked to perceived abilities; thus, these goals tend to be realistic (Roberts, Treasure, & Conroy, 2007).

By contrast, people with low *n* Ach, the researchers claim, are not willing to take chances when it comes to testing their own skills and abilities. They are motivated more by their fear of failure than by their hope and expectation of success. This is why they set either ridiculously low goals, which anyone can attain, or impossibly high goals (Geen, 1984). After all, who can fault a person for failing to reach a goal that is impossible for almost anyone? Complete the *Try It,* which describes a game that is said to reveal a high or low need for achievement.

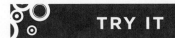

TRY IT   **What is Your *N* ACH?**

Imagine yourself involved in a ring-toss game. You have three rings to toss at any of the six pegs pictured here. You will be paid a few pennies each time you are able to ring a peg.

Which peg would you try to ring with your three tosses—peg 1 or 2 nearest you, peg 3 or 4 at a moderate distance, or peg 5 or 6 at the far end of the row?

Another social-cognitive theory known as goal orientation theory provides a somewhat different view of achievement motivation. According to this perspective, achievement motivation varies according to which of four goal orientations an individual adopts (Wolters, 2004). Here's how each of the orienations might affect a college student. Students with a *mastery/approach* orientation will study and engage in other behaviors (e.g., attend class) so as to increase their knowledge and overcome challenges. Those who have a *mastery/avoidance* orientation will exhibit whatever behaviors are necessary to avoid failing to learn (a different outcome than a failing grade, by the way). Students with a *performance/avoidance* orientation will measure their performance against that of other students and are motivated to work to the point where they are at least equal to their peers. Finally, those who have a *performance/approach* orientation try to surpass the performance of their peers in an attempt to enhance their own sense of self-worth. (Table 9.2 summarizes the four goal orientations. Stop for a minute and think about which orientation best describes your own.) Research indicates that the performance/approach orientation is more strongly associated with high grades than any of the others (Church et al., 2001).

goal orientation theory The view that achievement motivation depends on which of four goal orientations (mastery/approach, mastery/avoidance, performance/avoidance, performance/approach) an individual adopts.

TABLE 9.2 Goal Orientations

Mastery/Approach
Working to attain something of self-determined intrinsic value (e.g., knowledge).

Mastery/Avoidance
Working to avoid an outcome that threatens self-worth (e.g., being unable to learn something new).

Performance/Avoidance
Limiting efforts in order to avoid surpassing the performance of others (e.g., getting mediocre grades to fit in with a peer group).

Performance/Approach
Doing just enough work to ensure that one's performance will be superior to that of others (e.g., working for an A in a difficult class to feel superior to others in a class or being satisfied with a D because most other students are failing).

Note: Mastery involves working toward a personally meaningful goal. *Performance* involves working toward a goal defined by social comparison. *Approach* means that the goal helps the individual move toward something that is desirable. *Avoidance* means that the goal helps the individual move away from something that is undesirable.

9.4 What are Maslow's views on motivation?

self-actualization The pursuit of self-defined goals for personal fulfillment and growth.

✳ Explore the Concept *Maslow's Hierarchy of Needs* on **mypsychlab.com**

Maslow's Hierarchy of Needs

Another view of motivation, associated with the humanistic personality theory of Abraham Maslow, suggests that physiological motivations are the foundation for so-called higher-level motives (Maslow, 1970). He proposed that motivation is the process through which humans seek to meet their needs. Human needs, Maslow claimed, are hierarchical in nature, with our need for food and shelter at the bottom and our need for self-actualization at the top. Self-actualization is the pursuit of self-defined goals for personal fulfillment and growth. Thus, as Figure 9.3 suggests, in Maslow's view, it is impossible for an individual to attain self-actualization without first meeting his or her needs at the lower levels of the hierarchy. ✳ Explore on **mypsychlab.com**

One implication of Maslow's theory is that we must work through our lower needs to experience the fulfillment that comes from pursuing personal growth for its own sake. However, the hierarchy also implies that humans are motivated by their lowest unmet need. If we ask, for example, why a student in school is failing to achieve one of Maslow's esteem needs, it is possible that the student has an unmet lower need. He or she may be hungry (physiological need), feel threatened in the school environment (safety need), or be concerned about peer rejection (belongingness need). Consequently, Maslow's theory has helped educators understand that providing students with adequate nutrition, ensuring their safety while at school, and supporting their social development may be as critical to achievement as curriculum materials and teaching strategies are.

Despite the practical implications of Maslow's theory, critics have often charged that self-actualization is an elusive concept. Maslow agreed to some extent and, in an effort to better illustrate the phenomenon, he studied people he believed were using their talents and abilities to their fullest. He studied some historical figures, such as Abraham Lincoln and Thomas Jefferson, and some individuals who made significant contributions during his own lifetime, including Albert Einstein, Eleanor Roosevelt, and Albert Schweitzer. Maslow found these self-actualizers to be accurate in perceiving reality—able to judge honestly and to spot quickly the fake and the dishonest. Most of them believed that they had a mission to accomplish or need to devote their life to some larger good. Finally, the hallmark of self-actualizers is frequently occurring *peak experiences*—experiences of deep meaning, insight, and harmony within and with the universe.

The *Summarize It* recaps the theoretical approaches to motivation we have discussed in this section.

FIGURE 9.3 Maslow's Hierarchy of Needs
According to humanistic psychologist Abraham Maslow, "higher" motives, such as the need for love, go unheeded when "lower" motives, such as the need for safety, are not met.

Approaches to Motivation

SUMMARIZE IT

APPROACH	DESCRIPTION	EXAMPLE
Drive-reduction theory	Behavior results from the need to reduce an internal state of tension or arousal.	Eating to reduce hunger
Arousal theory	Behavior results from the need to maintain an optimal level of arousal.	Climbing a mountain for excitement; listening to classical music for relaxation
Goal setting	Behavior results from establishing specific, difficult goals.	Reducing employees' absences by inviting them to participate in establishing the criteria for an attendance bonus
Expectancy theory	Behavior results from expectancy, instrumentality, and valence.	Employees working harder because they believe that their efforts will be effective and will be noticed by supervisors, and the employees value supervisors' approval
Need for achievement (*n* Ach)	Behavior results from the need to accomplish something difficult and to perform at a high level of excellence.	A medical school graduate choosing a specialty that requires a 6-year residency because he wants to challenge himself to attain the highest, most difficult goal possible
Goal orientation theory	Behavior depends on which of four goal orientations a person adopts (see Table 9.2 on page 289).	A student adopting the performance/approach orientation feeling satisfied with getting a C on an exam when he learns that all of the other students received Ds and Fs
Maslow's hierarchy of needs	Lower needs must be met before higher needs motivate behavior.	Schoolchildren not being able to focus on achievement if they are hungry or don't feel safe

Hunger

Earlier we told you that primary drives are unlearned motives that serve to satisfy biological needs. For instance, thirst is a basic biological drive. The motivation to drink is largely governed by physiological variables, such as the amount of salt in the body's cells. But what about hunger?

Internal and External Cues

9.5 How do internal and external cues influence eating?

Like thirst, hunger is influenced by physiological processes. For instance, you may recall reading in Chapter 4 that eating stimulates the brain's pleasure system. Thus, one of the reasons that we eat is because it is pleasurable. However, some researchers speculate that, as is true for some drugs, something can go awry in the brain's pleasure system such that food loses its capacity for inducing pleasure and, instead, becomes the object of compulsive behavior (Berridge, 2009). As a result, a person becomes driven to eat or to avoid eating without regard to hunger, the pleasure associated with eating, or the consequences of compulsive consumption or avoidance of food.

Excessive food avoidance or consumption may also be caused by dysfunctions in the brain's feeding/satiety system. As researchers discovered long ago, the lateral hypothalamus (LH) acts as a *feeding center* to excite eating. Stimulating the feeding center causes animals to eat even when they are full (Delgado & Anand, 1953). And when the feeding center is destroyed, animals initially refuse to eat (Anand & Brobeck, 1951). The ventromedial hypothalamus (VMH) apparently acts as a *satiety* (or *fullness*) *center* that inhibits eating (Hernandez & Hoebel, 1989). If the VMH is surgically removed, animals soon eat their way to gross obesity (Hetherington & Ranson, 1940; Parkinson & Weingarten, 1990). Moreover, some of the substances

lateral hypothalamus (LH) The part of the hypothalamus that acts as a feeding center to incite eating.

ventromedial hypothalamus (VMH) The part of the hypothalamus that acts as a satiety (fullness) center to inhibit eating.

TABLE 9.3 Biological and Environmental Factors That Inhibit and Stimulate Eating

	BIOLOGICAL	ENVIRONMENTAL
Factors that inhibit eating	Activity in ventromedial hypothalamus Raised blood glucose levels Distended (full) stomach CCK (hormone that acts as satiety signal) Sensory-specific satiety	Unappetizing smell, taste, or appearance of food Acquired taste aversions Learned eating habits Desire to be thin Reaction to stress, unpleasant emotional state
Factors that stimulate eating	Activity in lateral hypothalamus Low blood levels of glucose Increase in insulin Stomach contractions Empty stomach	Appetizing smell, taste, or appearance of food Acquired food preferences Being around others who are eating Foods high in fat and sugar Learned eating habits Reaction to boredom, stress, unpleasant emotional state

✳ Explore the Concept *The Effects of the Hypothalamus on Eating Behavior* on **mypsychlab.com**

secreted by the gastrointestinal tract during digestion, such as the hormone cholecystokinin (CCK), act as satiety signals (Geary, 2004). ✳ Explore on **mypsychlab.com**

More recent studies have suggested that referring to the LH as the brain's hunger center and the VMH as its satiety center fails to convey the subtle ways in which the neurons in these organs influence eating and body weight (King, 2006; Pinel, 2007). For one thing, animals eventually recover from LH damage and resume eating (Teitelbaum, 1957). Similarly, the effects of VMH damage are not permanent. A rat whose VMH is damaged will eventually stop overeating. In addition, damage to the VMH renders laboratory rats less willing to work (i.e., press a lever) in order to get food and more particular about what kinds of foods they are willing to eat. Thus, on balance, it's difficult to see how damage to the VMH alone might lead to obesity. Therefore, although the hypothalamus clearly plays a role in eating behavior, researchers have yet to determine precisely how its role is shaped by both its own neurons and biochemical signals from other components of the body's hunger management system.

Changes in blood sugar level and the hormones that regulate it also contribute to sensations of hunger. Blood levels of the sugar called *glucose* are monitored by nutrient detectors in the liver that send this information to the brain (Friedman, Tordoff, & Ramirez, 1986). Hunger is stimulated when the brain receives the message that blood levels of glucose are low. Similarly, insulin, a hormone produced by the pancreas, chemically converts glucose into energy that is usable by the cells. Elevations in insulin cause an increase in hunger, in food intake, and in a desire for sweets (Rodin et al., 1985). In fact, chronic oversecretion of insulin stimulates hunger and often leads to obesity.

As you may have learned from everyday experience, hunger can also be stimulated by external cues. What happens when you smell a steak sizzling on the grill or chocolate chip cookies baking in the oven? For many, the hands of the clock alone, signaling mealtime, are enough to prompt a quest for food. Table 9.3 summarizes the factors that stimulate and inhibit eating.

9.6 What factors contribute to individual differences in body weight?

body mass index (BMI) A measure of weight relative to height.

Explaining Variations in Body Weight

Health care professionals classify individuals' body weights using a measure of weight relative to height called the body mass index (BMI). A BMI that is less than 18.5 is considered underweight, while one in excess of 25 is classified as overweight. To calculate your BMI, use this formula or use the BMI calculator at http://www.cdc.gov/nccdphp/dnpa/bmi/index.htm:

$$BMI = [Weight\ in\ pounds \div (height\ in\ inches \times height\ in\ inches)] \times 703$$

Why are there variations in human body weight? Heredity is one reason. A review of studies that included more than 100,000 participants found that 74% of identical twin pairs had similar body weights. Only 32% of fraternal twins, however, had comparable body weights. The researchers reported an estimated heritability for body weight between .50 and .90 (Barsh, Farooqi, & O'Rahilly, 2000). More than 40 genes appear to be related to body weight regulation (Barsh et al., 2000).

But what exactly do people inherit that affects body weight? Researchers Friedman and colleagues identified the hormone *leptin,* which affects the hypothalamus and may be an element in the regulation of body weight (Geary, 2004). Leptin is produced by the body's fat tissues. Decreases in body fat cause lower levels of leptin in the body. Lower levels of leptin stimulate food intake because the body "thinks" that it may be in danger of starvation. When leptin levels increase sufficiently people begin to lose weight due to the appetite-suppressing effects of rising levels of leptin. In one study, obese mice injected with leptin lost 30% of their body weight within 2 weeks (Halaas et al., 1995). However, the bodies of humans who are obese appear to develop a tolerance for the effects of leptin. Consequently, researchers are currently searching for a way to counteract this tolerance in hopes of developing a leptin-based anti-obesity drug (Ozcan et al., 2009).

The rate at which the body burns calories to produce energy is called the metabolic rate, and it is also influenced by genes. Further, *set-point theory* suggests that each person is genetically programmed to carry a certain amount of body weight (Keesey, 1978). Set point—the weight the body maintains when one is trying neither to gain nor to lose weight—is affected by the number of fat cells in the body and by metabolic rate, both of which are influenced by the genes (Gurin, 1989).

Researchers think that fat cells send biochemical messages indicating how much energy is stored in them to the hypothalamus (Hallschmid et al., 2004). Presumably, the genes influence what the hypothalamus "believes" to be the appropriate amount of energy to store. One of the most important current lines of research in this area aims to identify these biochemical messages and influence them in ways that will lower the set points of obese individuals (Hallschmid et al., 2004).

metabolic rate (meh-tuh-BALL-ik) The rate at which the body burns calories to produce energy.

set point The weight the body normally maintains when one is trying neither to gain nor to lose weight.

Obesity and Weight Loss

9.7 What does research suggest about obesity and dieting?

Variations in body weight have emerged as an important public health topic in recent years because of the link between excessive weight and health problems, such as heart disease and arthritis (National Center for Health Statistics, 2004). As you can see in Figure 9.4, the prevalence of both overweight (BMI between 25 and 29.9) and obesity (BMI over 30) has risen dramatically over the past three decades. More than one-third of adults in the United States are obese.

obesity BMI over 30.

Most individuals who are obese require the help of a physician to attain a healthy weight. For one thing, many suffer from other health problems, such as diabetes, that are linked to their weight problems in complex ways. Thus, any weight-loss program they undertake must be managed in such a way that does not aggravate other conditions. Children who are obese also require medical assistance to lose weight because caloric restriction diets can interfere with their growth (Overby, 2002).

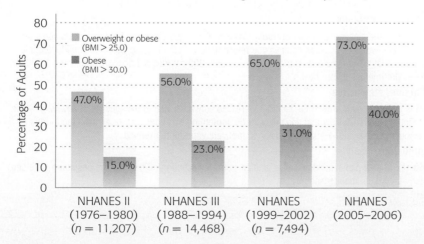

FIGURE 9.4 Age-Adjusted[*] **Prevalence of Overweight and Obese among U.S. Adults, Age 20–74 Years**

*Age-adjusted by the direct method to the year 2000 U.S. Bureau of the Census estimates using the age groups 20–39, 40–59, and 60–74 years.

Source: National Center for Health Statistics (2008).

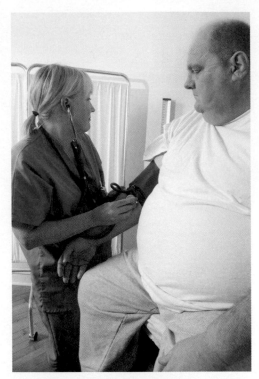

▲ Surgical techniques that limit the amount of food that an individual's digestive system can take in at one time (e.g., gastric bypass) are a last resort for some individuals who are obese. Most patients lose weight after the surgery, but they must adopt a healthy diet and increase their physical activity to maintain a healthy body weight.

For unknown reasons, some people who suffer from obesity appear to be unable to reverse the trend of continual weight gain. For these individuals, *gastric bypass surgery,* a procedure in which the size of the stomach is reduced, may be the only alternative. Candidates for gastric bypass surgery must have a BMI in excess of 40. Individuals with BMIs ranging from 35 to 39 may be considered for the surgery if they have a weight-related health problem, such as diabetes or high blood pressure. Among more than 80% of patients, gastric bypass surgery results in both weight reduction below the obesity threshold and improvements in weight-related health conditions (Schauer et al., 2000). However, physicians stress that any person who undergoes the surgery must be willing to commit to postoperative lifestyle changes, including following a healthy diet and exercise regimen. These changes are needed because, even with reduced stomach capacity, it is quite possible to return to an obese state after a period of postoperative weight loss. Moreover, gastric bypass surgery is associated with risks, such as the possibility of postoperative infection. In general, the heavier the patient is, the greater the risk of postsurgical complications (Livingston et al., 2002).

For individuals who are not obese, the principles of successful dieting are fairly simple. There is no need to spend your hard-earned money on special foods, food supplements, or the latest celebrity or fad diet. In fact, the Mayo Clinic in Rochester, Minnesota, is one of many health care institutions that have posted everything you need to know about weight loss on the Internet (Mayo Clinic, 2005). Table 9.4 summarizes the strategies the clinic recommends for achieving and maintaining a healthy weight. At their Web site, you can enter your own personal information and get a customized weight-loss plan that includes recipes and menus (see https://www.mayoclinic.com/health/weight-loss/HQ01625).

The complexities of the processes involved in appetite regulation and energy metabolism explain why diets often do not work (Campbell & Dhand, 2000). To be effective, any weight-loss program must help people decrease energy intake (eat less), increase energy expenditure (exercise more), or both (Bray & Tartaglia, 2000). Unfortunately, most people who are trying to lose weight focus only on cutting calories.

TABLE 9.4 Six Weight-Loss Strategies from the Mayo Clinic

Make a commitment.

Approach weight loss as an effortful task, one in which you are likely to have some setbacks. Be determined to persist toward your weight-loss goal.

Get emotional support.

Share your goals with people whom you know will support and encourage you. If possible, participate in an informal weight-loss support group, or suggest to a friend who also wants to lose weight that the two of you become "accountability partners."

Set realistic goals.

Do some research to determine your body type and a target weight that is appropriate for you. A realistic time frame is important as well. Permanent weight loss is best achieved over a long, rather than a short, period of time with a reasonable diet and exercise program that you can stick to.

Enjoy healthier foods.

Making permanent changes in your everyday diet is the best way to insure that the pounds you shed during dieting won't reappear as soon as you return to your normal eating patterns. The Mayo Clinic states, too, that extreme calorie restriction—less than 1,200 calories per day for women and 1,400 for men—is detrimental to your health.

Get active, stay active.

There is simply no way around the fact that increased activity is vital to the success of any weight-loss plan. Find a physical activity that you enjoy, or do something that you enjoy (e.g., listening to music) while engaging in a calorie-burning activity, to motivate yourself to exercise.

Change your lifestyle.

Devise your entire plan, eating, exercise, and all, with the idea in mind that you are designing a lifelong strategy for weight maintenance.

Source: Mayo Clinic (2005).

Eating Disorders ▶

Eating disorders are a category of mental disorders in which eating and dieting behaviors go far beyond the everyday extremes of overeating and dieting many people experience. One eating disorder, Anorexia nervosa, is characterized by an overwhelming, irrational fear of gaining weight or becoming fat, compulsive dieting to the point of self-starvation, and excessive weight loss. Some people with anorexia lose as much as 20 to 25% of their original body weight. The disorder typically begins in adolescence, and most of those afflicted are females. About 1 to 4% of females are diagnosed this disorder (American Psychiatric Association, 2006). The greater prevalence of eating disorders among females appears to be a general phenomenon rather than a culturally specific one. In a large sample of Norwegian adults, for example, women were twice as likely as men to have an eating disorder (Augestad, 2000). ◉ Watch on mypsychlab.com

There are important differences between dieting (even obsessive dieting) and anorexia nervosa. For one, among people with anorexia, perceptions of body size are grossly distorted (Kittler, Menard, & Phillips, 2007). No matter how emaciated they become, they continue to perceive themselves as fat. Researchers have learned that such unrealistic perceptions may result from a general tendency toward distorted thinking (Tchanturia et al., 2001). Moreover, most individuals with anorexia—as many as 74% in some studies—suffer from another kind of psychiatric disorder along with their eating disorder (Dyl et al., 2006; Milos et al., 2002). These findings suggest that, for some sufferers anorexia may be only one component of a larger psychiatric problem.

Frequently, people with anorexia not only starve themselves but also exercise relentlessly in an effort to accelerate the weight loss. Further, they don't necessarily avoid food or the ritual of eating. Indeed, most people with anorexia are fascinated with food and the process of preparing it (Faunce, 2002). Many become skilled in giving the appearance of eating while not actually swallowing food. To accomplish this, some of them habitually chew and spit out their food, often with such dexterity that others with whom they eat don't notice (Kovacs, Mahon, & Palmer, 2002).

Among young females with anorexia, progressive and significant weight loss eventually results in amenorrhea (cessation of menstruation). Some may also develop low blood pressure, impaired heart function, dehydration, electrolyte disturbances, and sterility (American Psychiatric Association, 2006a), as well as decreases in the gray matter volume in the brain, which are thought to be irreversible (Lambe et al., 1997). Moreover, prolonged self-starvation induces changes in the lining of the stomach that can make it extremely difficult for people with anorexia to recover normal functioning of the digestive system even after they have begun eating normally (Ogawa et al., 2004). Unfortunately, as many as 20% of those suffering from anorexia nervosa eventually die of starvation or complications from organ damage (Brotman, 1994).

It is difficult to pinpoint the cause of this disorder. Most sufferers are well behaved and academically successful (Vitousek & Manke, 1994). Psychological risk factors for eating disorders include being overly concerned about physical appearance, worrying about perceived attractiveness, and feeling social pressure in favor of thinness (Whisenhunt et al., 2000). Some investigators believe that young women who refuse to eat are attempting to control a portion of their lives, which they may feel unable to control in other respects.

Anorexia is very difficult to treat. Most people with anorexia are steadfast in their refusal to eat, while insisting that nothing is wrong with them. The main thrust of treatment, therefore, is to get the individual to gain weight. The patient may be admitted to a hospital, fed a controlled diet, and given rewards for small weight gains and increases in food intake. The treatment usually includes some type of psychotherapy and/or a self-help group. Some studies show that antidepressant drugs may help in the treatment of anorexia (Barbarich et al., 2004). Others suggest that protein-rich supplements help

9.8 What are the characteristics of eating disorders?

anorexia nervosa An eating disorder characterized by an overwhelming, irrational fear of gaining weight or becoming fat, compulsive dieting to the point of self-starvation, and excessive weight loss.

◉ Watch the Video *Speaking Out: Natasha: Living with Anorexia Nervosa* on **mypsychlab.com**

▲ Victoria Beckham is one of many young women who have struggled with anorexia. Individuals with anorexia usually have a distorted body image that causes them to believe they are overweight when they are actually dangerously underweight.

individuals with anorexia regain their normal appetites (Latner & Wilson, 2004). Multidimensional treatment programs—that is, those that combine medication, nutritional therapy, and psychotherapy—may prove to be the most successful approach (Bean et al., 2004). However, no matter which treatment approach is used, most individuals with anorexia experience relapses (Hogan & McReynolds, 2004).

As many as 50% of those with anorexia also develop bulimia nervosa, a chronic disorder characterized by repeated and uncontrolled (and often secretive) episodes of binge eating (American Psychiatric Association, 2006a). And individuals who do not have anorexia can develop bulimia alone. Many people with bulimia come from families in which family members make frequent negative comments about others' physical appearances (Crowther et al., 2002).

bulimia nervosa An eating disorder characterized by repeated and uncontrolled (and often secretive) episodes of binge eating.

An episode of binge eating has two main features: (1) the consumption of much larger amounts of food than most people would eat during the same period of time, and (2) a feeling that one cannot stop eating or control the amount eaten. Binges—which generally involve foods that are rich in carbohydrates, such as cookies, cake, and candy—are frequently followed by purging. Purging consists of self-induced vomiting and/or the use of large quantities of laxatives and diuretics. People with bulimia may also engage in excessive dieting and exercise. Athletes are especially susceptible to this disorder.

Bulimia nervosa can cause a number of physical problems. The stomach acid in vomit eats away at the teeth and may cause them to rot, and the delicate balance of body chemistry is destroyed by excessive use of laxatives and diuretics. People with bulimia may have a chronic sore throat as well as a variety of other symptoms, including dehydration, swelling of the salivary glands, kidney damage, and hair loss. The disorder also has a strong emotional component; the person with bulimia is aware that the eating pattern is abnormal and feels unable to control it. Depression, guilt, and shame accompany both binging and purging. Some evidence suggests that decreased function of the neurotransmitter serotonin appears to contribute to this disorder (Jimerson et al., 1997).

Bulimia nervosa tends to appear in the late teens and affects about 1 in 25 women (Kendler et al., 1991). Like those with anorexia, people with bulimia have high rates of obsessive-compulsive disorder (Milos et al., 2002). Further, perhaps as many as one-third of them have engaged in other kinds of self-injurious behavior, such as cutting themselves intentionally (Paul et al., 2002).

About 10 to 15% of all people with bulimia are males, and homosexuality or bisexuality seems to increase males' risk for bulimia (Carlat, Camargo, & Herzog, 1997). In addition, researchers are finding more evidence of a cultural component to bulimia. Westernized attitudes in Turkey, for example, are clashing with the country's traditional values and, according to researchers, creating an increase in cases of bulimia (Elal et al., 2000). Apparently, some Turkish citizens are succumbing to Western media pressure to have an ultrathin body.

Bulimia, like anorexia, is difficult to treat. Sometimes treatment is complicated by the fact that a person with an eating disorder is likely to have a personality disorder as well or to be too shy to interact effectively with therapists (Goodwin & Fitzgibbon, 2002; Rosenvinge, Matinussen, & Ostensen, 2000). Some behavior modification programs have helped extinguish bulimic behavior (Traverso et al., 2000), and cognitive-behavioral therapy has been used successfully to help those with bulimia modify their eating habits and their abnormal attitudes about body shape and weight (Wilson & Sysko, 2006). Certain antidepressant drugs have been found to reduce the frequency of binge eating and purging in some individuals with bulimia.

Sexual Motivation

Alfred Kinsey and his coauthors' *Sexual Behavior in the Human Male* (1948) and *Sexual Behavior in the Human Female* (1953) shattered many widely held beliefs about sexuality. Though his work has been called into question by many other researchers on both theoretical and methodological grounds, most admit that the topic of sexuality is discussed more openly now than was true before Kinsey's land-mark research findings became known. We will begin our consideration of this important motivational domain with a discussion of cultural and gender differences in sexual attitudes and behavior.

Sexual Attitudes and Behavior ▶

9.9 How do sexual attitudes and behavior vary across cultures and genders?

You probably won't be surprised to learn that a large majority of adults all over the world are sexually active. As you can see in Table 9.5, the average frequency of sexual intercourse varies considerably from one culture to another (Durex Global Sex Survey, 2005). Surveys suggest that the number of times that men and women 16 and older engage in intercourse in a year range from a low of 45 times in Japan to a high of 138 times in Greece. Of course, individuals vary considerably around these averages. Some people have sex several times each day; while others never have sex at all. Perhaps the reasons behind relatively high rates of sexual activity are simple: People enjoy sex, and attitudes have changed such that they feel free to do so. But what explains the low rate of sexual activity in Japan? Japanese officials, concerned about their country's plummeting birth rate and growing number of elderly, blame long work days, the high cost of raising children, and the increasing number of women who choose to focus on their careers rather than to become mothers (Reuters, 2006). Of course, these trends are found throughout the industrialized world, so they cannot explain why Japanese sexual activity rates are lower than those of other nations.

As you learned in Chapter 8, sexual activity continues throughout the life span. In one very large survey involving people aged 40 to 80 in 13 different countries, researchers found that 83% of men and 66% of women had engaged in intercourse at least once in the last year (Gingell et al., 2003). One reason why intercourse frequency was lower among women was that many of the elderly women in the study were widows who lacked access to a partner. Nevertheless, men and women of all ages differ with regard to sexual attitudes and behavior, even when both have equal access to a partner.

On average, men are more interested in sex and think about it more often than women do (Peplau, 2003). And they are more likely than women to be interested in purely physical sex and to have more permissive attitudes toward sex (Baldwin & Baldwin, 1997; Dantzker & Eisenman, 2003). Nevertheless, the gender gap has narrowed considerably since the mid-20th century. Psychologists Brooke Wells and Jean Twenge analyzed the results of attitude surveys from 1958 to 1987 (Wells & Twenge, 2005). They found that among young women (ages 12 to 27), approval rates for premarital sex rose dramatically, from 30% in the early years of their study to 91% in

TABLE 9.5 Selected Findings from the Durex Global Sex Survey

COUNTRY	FREQUENCY OF INTERCOURSE IN THE PAST YEAR	PERCENTAGE WHO ARE SATISFIED WITH THEIR SEX LIVES
Greece	138	43%
United States	113	52%
Chile	112	50%
South Africa	109	46%
Canada	108	46%
Italy	106	36%
Israel	100	36%
China	96	22%
Sweden	92	45%
Japan	45	24%

Source: Durex Global Sex Survey (2005).

parental investment A term used by evolutionary psychologists to denote the amount of time and effort men or women must devote to parenthood.

1987. Behavior, too, had changed. Twenge's analysis showed that about 13% of teenaged girls admitted to being sexually active during the 1950s. By the 1990s, the proportion had increased to 47%. Thus, even though recent surveys show that there are still gender differences in both sexual attitudes and behavior, the historical perspective helps us see that, over time, this gender gap has narrowed considerably. However, critics of such studies say that what has really changed is people's willingness to talk about their sexual experiences rather than their actual attitudes and behavior (Dobson & Baird, 2006).

Why do these gender differences exist? Evolutionary psychologists often explain these differences as resulting from the influence of evolution on men's and women's mating behaviors. Many use the term parental investment to denote the amount of time and effort men or women must devote to parenthood. According to parental investment theory, women and men have adopted mating strategies that correspond to their respective investments in parenting (Buss, 1999, 2000b). Men are assumed to be interested in making only a short-term biological investment in parenting, so they typically seek women who are young, healthy (physical attractiveness is taken as a sign of good health), and well suited for child bearing. Because parenting requires a greater investment from women (9 months of pregnancy and a long period of dependency), they tend to prefer men who are somewhat older, more stable and with sufficient resources, generous, emotionally attached, and strong enough to provide protection for the family (Buss, 1999). These and related gender differences are apparently not culture specific, since they have been found in 37 different countries (Buss, 1994).

As you learned in Chapter 1, and as the *Think About It* activity at the beginning of this chapter illustrated, Buss's research also shows that men are mostly concerned about sexual fidelity, presumably because they want to be certain that any children conceived are their own. Women, by contrast, are most interested in emotional fidelity, or the idea that they should be able to count on a man to be fully committed to a psychological and social partnership with them. Other researchers have replicated these findings in more recent work (Hughes, Harrison, & Gallup, 2004). Moreover, Buss and his colleagues have replicated them in both elderly (average age = 67) and young adult (average age = 20) samples (Shackelford et al., 2004).

As evolutionary theory would predict, women appear to have the strongest desire for sex around the time of ovulation when they are most likely to conceive a child (Pillsworth, Haselton, & Buss, 2004). Similarly, studies conducted by Viennese researcher Karl Grammar (cited in Holden, 1996) indicate that increases in men's testosterone levels are linked to the *pheromones,* odor-producing hormones, that are found in women's vaginal secretions at the time of ovulation. Thus, it is likely that men are the most rapidly aroused in the presence of female partners who are ovulating. ◉─|Watch on **mypsychlab.com**

◉─|**Watch** the **Video** *Evolution and Sex: Michael Bailey* on **mypsychlab.com**

Other researchers question whether women's reported mate preferences and concerns about emotional fidelity are thoroughly biological in nature. Researchers Wood and Eagly (2007) cite research demonstrating that gender differences in mate preferences are significantly smaller when economic and social conditions for males and females are more equal, as they are becoming in developed countries in the 21st century. In other words, when women are economically dependent on men, the mating "rules" described by evolutionary psychologists may apply; however, gender differences in mate preferences decline as women gain independence. Under conditions of equality, physical attractiveness in a mate would be likely to be just as important to women as to men. And a woman's earning capacity might be more highly valued by men.

Eagly and Wood may be right. Research indicates that, in societies with egalitarian attitudes about gender roles, marital status and income are correlated. Longitudinal, prospective research has shown that the higher a woman's economic status, the more likely she is to get married (Ono, 2003). Moreover, the sexual/emotional fidelity distinction appears to be larger among older women than among college students, so younger cohorts of women may be developing beliefs about fidelity that are more similar to those held by men (Shackelford et al., 2004). Today's men may be looking for more in their mates than just good looks and child-bearing potential, and today's women may be more concerned about sexual fidelity than their mothers and grandmothers were.

Sexual Desire and Arousal ▷

Dr. William Masters and Dr. Virginia Johnson conducted the first laboratory investigations of the human sexual response in 1954. They monitored their volunteer participants, who engaged in sex while connected to electronic sensing devices. Masters and Johnson (1966) concluded that both males and females experience a sexual response cycle with four phases.

The *excitement phase* is the beginning of the sexual response. Visual cues, such as watching a partner undress, are more likely to initiate the excitement phase in men than in women. Tender, loving touches coupled with verbal expressions of love arouse women more readily than visual stimulation. And men can become aroused almost instantly, while arousal for women is often a more gradual, building process. For both partners, muscular tension increases, heart rate quickens, and blood pressure rises. As additional blood is pumped into the genitals, the male's penis becomes erect, and the female feels a swelling of the clitoris. Vaginal lubrication occurs as the inner two-thirds of the vagina expands and the inner lips of the vagina enlarge. In women especially, the nipples harden and stand erect.

After the excitement phase, the individual enters the *plateau phase,* when excitement continues to mount. Blood pressure and muscle tension increase still more, and breathing becomes heavy and more rapid. The man's testes swell, and drops of liquid, which can contain live sperm cells, may drip from the penis. The outer part of the woman's vagina swells as the increased blood further engorges the area. The clitoris withdraws under the clitoral hood (its skin covering), and the breasts become engorged with blood. Excitement builds steadily during the plateau phase.

The *orgasm,* the shortest of the phases, is the highest point of sexual pleasure, marked by a sudden discharge of accumulated sexual tension. Involuntary muscle contractions may seize the entire body during orgasm, and the genitals contract rhythmically. Orgasm is a two-stage experience for the male. First is his awareness that ejaculation is near and that he can do nothing to stop it; second is the ejaculation itself, when semen is released from the penis in forceful spurts. The experience of orgasm in women builds in much the same way as for men. Marked by powerful, rhythmic contractions, the female's orgasm usually lasts longer than that of the male. About 40 to 50% of women regularly experience orgasm during intercourse (Wilcox & Hager, 1980).

The orgasm gives way to the *resolution phase,* a tapering-off period, when the body returns to its unaroused state. Men experience a *refractory period* in the resolution phase, during which they cannot have another orgasm. The refractory period may last from only a few minutes for some men to as long as several hours for others. Women do not have a refractory period and may, if restimulated, experience another orgasm right away.

The sexual response cycle is strongly influenced by hormones. The sex glands manufacture hormones—*estrogen* and *progesterone* in the ovaries and androgens in the testes. The adrenal glands in both sexes also produce small amounts of these hormones. Females have considerably more estrogen and progesterone than males do, so these are known as the female sex hormones. Males have considerably more androgens, the male sex hormones.

Testosterone, the most important androgen, influences the development and maintenance of male sex characteristics, as well as sexual motivation. Males must have a sufficient level of testosterone to maintain sexual interest and have an erection. Females, too, need small amounts of testosterone in the bloodstream to maintain sexual interest and responsiveness (Andersen & Cyranowski, 1995). Deficiencies in sexual interest and activity can sometimes be reversed in both men and women with the use of testosterone patches or ointments (Meyer, 1997). However, researchers point out that many hormones work in concert with testosterone to regulate the sexual response cycle and warn against the assumption that pharmacological manipulation of testosterone alone is adequate to solve problems with sexual functioning (Halaris, 2003). You will learn more about the topic of sexual dysfunctions in Chapter 12.

9.10 What are the phases of the human sexual response cycle?

sexual response cycle The four phases—excitement, plateau, orgasm, and resolution—that make up the human sexual response in both males and females, according to Masters and Johnson.

▲ Psychological factors play an important role in sexual attraction and arousal. Such factors include preferences and attitudes we learn from our culture.

9.11 What does research show regarding sexual orientation?

sexual orientation The direction of one's sexual interest—toward members of the opposite sex (heterosexuality), toward one's own sex (homosexuality), or toward both sexes (bisexuality).

Psychological factors play a large role in sexual arousal. Part of the psychological nature of sexual behavior stems from preferences and practices that people learn from their culture. And cultural norms about sexual behavior vary widely, covering everything from the age at which initiation of sexual behavior is proper to the partners, conditions, settings, positions, and specific sexual acts that are considered acceptable. Moreover, what is perceived as sexually attractive in a male and a female may differ dramatically from culture to culture.

Sexual fantasies also influence sexual arousal. Both men and women are likely to fantasize during intercourse. Most sexual fantasies involve conventional imagery about one's current or past partner or an imaginary lover. There are consistent gender differences in fantasies: "Men more than women imagine doing something sexual to their partner, whereas women more than men imagine something sexual being done to them" (Leitenberg & Henning, 1995, p. 491). Men's fantasies generally involve more specific visual imagery, and women's fantasies have more emotional and romantic content. Although 95% of males and females admit to having sexual fantasies, about 25% experience strong guilt about them (Leitenberg & Henning, 1995). But research seems to suggest an association between a higher incidence of sexual fantasies and a more satisfactory sex life and fewer sexual problems.

Sexual Orientation

Now we turn our attention to sexual orientation—the direction of an individual's sexual preference, erotic feelings, and sexual activity. In heterosexuals, the human sexual response is oriented toward members of the opposite sex; in homosexuals, toward those of the same sex; and in bisexuals, toward members of both sexes.

Prevalence. Estimating the prevalence of homosexuality is difficult. One problem is that, as you learned in Chapter 1, people sometimes give inaccurate information in response to researchers' questions about personal matters. But the biggest obstacle involves the definition of homosexuality itself. Is a person classified as homosexual if he or she has ever been attracted to someone of the same sex? What if they have had only one sexual experience with someone of the same sex? And if researchers limit the definition of homosexuality to those whose current sexual activity is restricted to partners of the same sex, will they underestimate the prevalence of homosexuality? These questions demonstrate two things. First, that sexual orientation is not a matter of strict categories. Sexual expression can be thought of as a continuum of experience, from, for instance, zero interest and participation in same-sex relations to exclusive interest and participation in same-sex relations. Second, when we are trying to make sense of survey data on homosexual behavior, we must find out how the researchers defined homosexuality, what specific questions they asked, and how they analyzed the data.

Because of the complexities involved in defining sexual orientation combined with people's reluctance to share information about the intimate details of their lives, reliable studies of the prevalence of homosexuality are few and far between. That's why researchers continue to look to studies that were done decades ago, and to compare more recent data to them, in order to determine patterns in the prevalence of homosexuality rather than specific percentages. For instance, Kinsey and his associates (1948, 1953) estimated that 4% of the male participants had nothing but homosexual relations throughout life, and 2 to 3% of the female participants had been in mostly or exclusively lesbian relationships. However, he also found that nearly half of men and one-third of women reported having been attracted to someone of the same sex. In one of the most important surveys of sexual orientation, Laumann and others (1994) reported that the percentages of Americans who identified themselves as homosexual or bisexual were 2.8% of men and 1.4% of women. But 5.3% of men and 3.5% of women said that they had had a sexual experience with a person of the same sex at least once since puberty. And even larger percentages of those surveyed—10%

of males and 8 to 9% of females—said that they had felt some same-sex desires. Kinsey's and Laumann's data suggest two patterns. First, homosexuality and bisexuality are more prevalent among men than among women. Second, homosexual attraction and brief experiences with same-sex relations are far more prevalent than exclusive identification with a homosexual orientation.

Patterns of homosexuality prevalence in more recent studies have been both consistent and inconsistent with earlier research. For instance, gender differences in exclusive homosexuality in a national survey of several thousand respondents in the United States were similar to those found by Kinsey and Laumann (Mosher, Chandra, & Jones, 2005). Two percent of male and 1.3% of female respondents described themselves as exclusively homosexual. However, the gender difference for bisexuality in earlier research was reversed. Some 2.8% of women described themselves as bisexual, while only 1.8% of men did. The researchers hypothesized that their study's methodology was responsible for this unexpected finding. By allowing respondents to enter answers to survey questions on laptop computers rather than in face-to-face or telephone interviews, the researchers may have enabled participants to answer more honestly than those in earlier studies did.

Another unexpected finding was that 11% of female respondents reported having had a sexual experience with a woman at some time in their lives, while the figure was just 6% for males. Here again, the use of computerized questionnaires rather than interviews may have played a role. However, the researchers pointed out that this finding probably resulted from variations in the questions they posed to male and female respondents. Men were asked, "Have you ever had anal or oral sex with a man?" By contrast, women were asked, "Have you ever had a sexual experience with a woman?" As a result, female participants responded to their own definition of "sexual experience," while men responded to a yes/no question about two specific behaviors. The specific nature of the men's question may have artificially restricted respondents' answers by not allowing for other forms of sexual contact. Thus, this survey provides us with valuable insight into the current prevalence of homosexual orientation, but it also reminds us that we need to know something about the methodological details of a survey before we can draw conclusions about its results.

Causes. Ample evidence exists to support the hypothesis that some kind of genetic predisposition increases the likelihood of a homosexual orientation in both men and women. Twin studies show that 50 to 60% of the identical twins of gay men are also gay, and slightly less than 50% of the identical twins of lesbian women are also lesbians (Bailey & Pillard, 1991; Bailey et al., 1993; Whitam, Diamond, & Martin, 1993). However, researchers have yet to identify a specific set of genes that accounts for homosexual orientation or the molecular mechanism through which genes may influence sexual orientation (Mustanski, Chivers, & Bailey, 2002).

In the last few years, researchers have examined the relationship between prenatal hormones and sexual orientation (Hershberger & Segal, 2004). Many of these studies have focused on associations between these hormones and inconsistencies between the left and right sides of the body. One such difference involves the ratio of the second and fourth fingers on the left and right hands (Rahman & Wilson, 2003a). It has long been known that fluctuations of androgen levels in the prenatal environment can produce these inconsistencies. Thus, researchers reason that, if prenatal androgens contribute to sexual orientation, then such physical inconsistencies should occur more frequently in homosexuals than in heterosexuals. Studies have shown that this is indeed the case (Rahman, 2005; Rahman & Wilson, 2003a).

Neuroscientist Simon LeVay (1991) reported that an area in the hypothalamus governing sexual behavior is about twice as large in heterosexual men as in homosexual men. Critics were quick to point out that all of the gay men included in LeVay's sample died of AIDS. Many researchers questioned whether the brain differences LeVay observed might have resulted from AIDS rather than being associated with sexual orientation (Byne, 1993). However, recent animal studies have also suggested a link between the hypothalamus and sexual orientation. Among domestic species of sheep, about 10% of males (i.e., rams) exhibit homosexual behavior. Researchers have found that, like LeVay's subjects, male-oriented rams have a smaller hypothalamus than those who prefer exclusively female partners do (Roselli et al., 2004).

Consequently, many psychologists, such as Charlotte Patterson (1995), suggest that sexual orientation should be studied as a complex interaction of nature and nurture, using theoretical models similar to those used by developmental psychologists to explain other phenomena. For instance, developmentalists often study the ways in which family characteristics contribute to the development of children's traits and behavior. In one early study that examined homosexuality from this perspective, Bell, Weinberg, and Hammersmith (1981) conducted extensive face-to-face interviews with 979 homosexual participants (293 women, 686 men) and 477 heterosexual controls. The researchers found no single condition of family life that in and of itself appeared to be a factor in either homosexual or heterosexual development.

homophobia An intense, irrational hostility toward or fear of homosexuals.

9.12 How have attitudes toward homosexuality changed in recent decades?

Social Attitudes toward Gays and Lesbians

No discussion of sexual orientation would be complete without consideration of the social challenges that have been faced by gays and lesbians and society's increasing tolerance of homosexual relationships. For instance, the American Psychiatric Association considered homosexuality a disorder until 1973 but now views it as such only if the individual considers it a problem. Thanks to such changes, more gay men and lesbians are "coming out," preferring to acknowledge and express their sexual orientation. Such individuals appear to be as healthy psychologically as heterosexuals (Strickland, 1995).

Homophobia is an intense, irrational hostility toward or fear of homosexuals that can lead to discrimination against gays and lesbians or even motivate acts of violence against them. Fortunately, most people's views of homosexuality stop short of full-blown homophobia, although negative attitudes toward homosexuality are still common in U.S. society (Herek, 2002). Generally, men are more likely to express such views. For instance, in one survey, 54% of women believed that homosexuality is morally acceptable, while only 45% of men approved of same-sex relationships (Pew Research Center, 2006).

Importantly, though, most people are opposed to discrimination based on sexual orientation. (Moreover, such discrimination is illegal.) Surveys show that more than three-quarters of Americans believe that homosexuality should not be a factor in hiring public school teachers (Herek, 2002). Similarly, an overwhelming majority of Americans, including those who are strongly opposed to homosexual behavior, adamantly support the rights of homosexuals to speak out and to try to influence public policy. Thus, objections to homosexuality appear to be focused on the behavior itself and not on those who exhibit it.

▲ Social attitudes toward homosexuality vary widely around the world. In the United States, court rulings and legislation in several states have paved the way for same-sex couples to marry. Same-sex couples can be legally partnered in civil unions in other states and in domestic partnerships in many cities. In Canada, same-sex marriage is legal throughout the country, as it is in the Netherlands, Spain, and Belgium. By contrast, homosexual behavior is illegal in many nations of Africa and southern Asia, and those who engage in such behavior are subject to the death penalty in Saudi Arabia, Iran, the Sudan, and Mauritania.

Emotion

Much of our motivation to act is fueled by emotional states. In fact, the root of the word *emotion* means "to move," indicating the close relationship between motivation and emotion. Psychologists define emotion as a state involving physiological arousal, a cognitive appraisal of the stimulus that brought about the state, and an outward behavior expressing the state. But what, precisely, are emotions?

emotion A state involving physiological arousal, a cognitive appraisal of the situation that produced the state, and an outward behavior expressing the state.

Theories of Emotion

Typically, psychologists have studied emotion in terms of three components: the physical, the cognitive, and the behavioral (Wilken et al., 2000). The three components appear to be interdependent. For instance, in one study, participants who were better at detecting heartbeat variations (the physical component) rated their subjective experiences of emotion (the cognitive component) as being more intense than did participants who were less able to detect physical changes (Wilken et al., 2000). However, neither the physical nor the cognitive components completely determine how emotion is expressed (the behavioral component). Moreover, there is a long-standing debate among psychologists about which component comes first in the overall experience of emotion.

American psychologist William James (1884) argued that an event causes physiological arousal and a physical response, after which the individual perceives the physical response as an emotion. At about the same time James proposed his theory, a Danish physiologist and psychologist, Carl Lange, independently formulated nearly the same theory. The James–Lange theory of emotion (Lange & James, 1922) suggests that different patterns of arousal in the autonomic nervous system produce the different emotions people feel, and that the physiological arousal appears before the emotion is perceived. (See Figure 9.5.)

Another early theory of emotion that challenged the James-Lange theory was proposed by Walter Cannon (1927), who did pioneering work on the fight-or-flight response and the concept of homeostasis. Cannon claimed that the bodily changes caused by the various emotions are not sufficiently distinct to allow people to distinguish one emotion from another. Cannon's original theory was later expanded by physiologist Philip Bard (1934). The Cannon–Bard theory suggests that the following chain of events occurs when a person feels an emotion: Emotion-provoking stimuli are received by the senses and are then relayed simultaneously to the cerebral cortex, which provides the conscious mental experience of the emotion, and to the sympathetic nervous system, which produces the physiological state of arousal. In other words, the feeling of an emotion (fear, for example) occurs at about the same time as the experience of physiological arousal (a pounding heart). One does not cause the other.

Stanley Schachter believed that the early theories of emotion left out a critical component—the subjective cognitive interpretation of why a state of arousal has occurred. Schachter and Singer (1962) proposed the *two-factor theory*. According

9.13 What theories have been proposed to explain emotion?

James–Lange theory The theory that emotional feelings result when an individual becomes aware of a physiological response to an emotion-provoking stimulus (for example, feeling fear because of trembling).

Cannon–Bard theory The theory that an emotion-provoking stimulus is transmitted simultaneously to the cerebral cortex, providing the conscious mental experience of the emotion, and to the sympathetic nervous system, causing the physiological arousal.

FIGURE 9.5 The James–Lange Theory of Emotion
The James–Lange theory of emotion is the exact opposite of what subjective experience tells us. If a dog growls at you, the James–Lange interpretation is that the dog growls, your heart begins to pound, and only after perceiving that your heart is pounding do you conclude that you must be afraid.

Schachter–Singer theory A two-factor theory stating that for an emotion to occur, there must be (1) physiological arousal and (2) a cognitive interpretation or explanation of the arousal, allowing it to be labeled as a specific emotion.

Lazarus theory The theory that a cognitive appraisal is the first step in an emotional response and all other aspects of an emotion, including physiological arousal, depend on it.

to the Schachter–Singer theory, two things must happen for a person to feel an emotion: (1) The person must first experience physiological arousal; and (2) there must then be a cognitive interpretation, or explanation, of the physiological arousal so that the person can label it as a specific emotion. Thus, Schachter concluded, a true emotion can occur only if a person is physically aroused and can find some reason for it. When people are in a state of physiological arousal but do not know why they are aroused, they tend to label the state as an emotion that is appropriate to their situation at the time.

The theory of emotion that most heavily emphasizes the cognitive aspect has been proposed by Richard Lazarus (1991a, 1991b, 1995). According to the Lazarus theory, a cognitive appraisal is the first step in an emotional response; all other aspects of an emotion, including physiological arousal, depend on the cognitive appraisal. This theory is most compatible with the subjective experience of an emotion's sequence of events—the sequence that William James reversed long ago. Faced with a stimulus—an event—a person first appraises it. This cognitive appraisal determines whether the person will have an emotional response and, if so, what type of response. The physiological arousal and all other aspects of the emotion flow from the appraisal. In short, Lazarus contends that emotions are provoked when cognitive appraisals of events or circumstances are positive or negative—but not neutral.

Critics of the Lazarus theory point out that some emotional reactions are instantaneous—occurring too rapidly to pass through a cognitive appraisal (Zajonc, 1980, 1984). Lazarus (1984, 1991a) responds that some mental processing occurs without conscious awareness. And there must be some form of cognitive realization, however brief, or else a person would not know what he or she is responding to or what emotion to feel—fear, happiness, embarrassment, and so on. Further, researchers have found that reappraisal, or changing one's thinking about an emotional stimulus, is related to a reduction in physiological response (Gross, 2002).

The *Summarize It* below recaps the four major theories of emotion: James–Lange, Cannon–Bard, Schachter–Singer, and Lazarus.

SUMMARIZE IT

Theories of Emotion

THEORY	VIEW	EXAMPLE
James–Lange theory	An event causes physiological arousal. You experience an emotion only *after* you interpret the physical response.	You are walking home late at night and hear footsteps behind you. Your heart pounds and you begin to tremble. You interpret these physical responses as fear.
Cannon–Bard theory	An event causes a physiological *and* an emotional response simultaneously. One does not cause the other.	You are walking home late at night and hear footsteps behind you. Your heart pounds, you begin to tremble, and you feel afraid.
Schachter–Singer theory (two-factor theory)	An event causes physiological arousal. You must then be able to identify a reason for the arousal to label the emotion.	You are walking home late at night and hear footsteps behind you. Your heart pounds and you begin to tremble. You know that walking alone at night can be dangerous, so you feel afraid.
Lazarus theory	An event occurs, a cognitive appraisal is made, and then the emotion and physiological arousal follow.	You are walking home late at night and hear footsteps behind you. You think it could be a mugger. So you feel afraid, your heart starts to pound, and you begin to tremble.

9.14 **What have affective neuroscientists learned about emotion and the brain?**

affective neuroscience The study of the neurological foundations of emotion.

Emotion and the Brain

Researchers have used many of the techniques you learned about in Chapter 2—EEG, MRI, fMRI, PET scans, and so on—to study the neurological foundations of emotion, a field called affective neuroscience (Dalgleish, 2004). One thing that they have learned

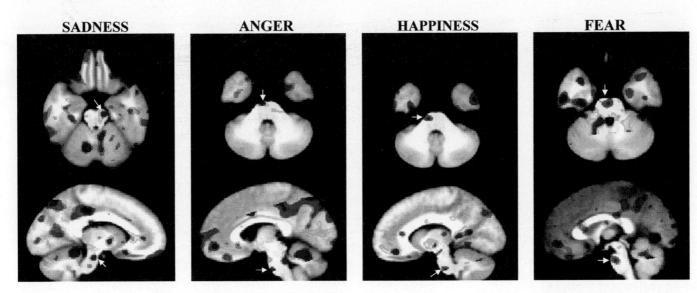

| SADNESS | ANGER | HAPPINESS | FEAR |

FIGURE 9.6 Neuroimaging of Emotions
PET scans show distinct patterns of brain activation for the various emotions. Red areas show areas of activation, and purple areas show areas of deactivation.
Source: Damasio et. al. (2000).

is that each emotion appears to have a distinctive system within the brain, as the PET scan images in Figure 9.6 suggest (Dalgleish, 2004). In addition, researchers have identified several brain structures that play key roles in our emotional experiences.

You should recall from Chapter 2 that the amygdala is part of the limbic system and is closely associated with fear (LeDoux, 2000). Information comes to the amygdala directly from all five of the senses and is acted on immediately, without initial involvement of the primary "thinking" area of the brain, the cortex. But, as with reflex actions, the cortex does become involved as soon as it "catches up" with the amygdala (LeDoux, 2000). Once it does so, the cortex tempers the amygdala's fear response with its interpretation of the fear-provoking situation. The ability of the cortex to control the amygdala's fear response is also vital to our ability to overcome previously learned fears (Sotres-Bayon, Bush, & LeDoux, 2004). Thus, when people manage to conquer, say, the fear associated with taking an important exam, they can thank their cortex's ability to regulate the amygdala.

When the emotion of fear first materializes, much of the brain's processing is non-conscious. The person becomes conscious of it later, because the cortex monitors the physiological signals that accompany emotion, such as changes in heart rate. The cortex uses these signals to relate our current circumstances to emotion-provoking experiences that are stored in memory (Dalgleish, 2004). This monitoring function of the cortex contributes to our ability to use stored information about the meaning of our emotions to make decisions in situations in which logic and information are insufficient (Damasio, 1995). Consequently, people who have sustained damage to the parts of the cortex that perform the monitoring function have difficulty making such decisions. For example, researchers have found that such people have a very limited ability to develop effective strategies for playing games that require *intuition*, which you should remember from Chapter 7 is often described as a "hunch" or "gut feeling" (e.g., Clark et al., 2008). An example will help you see how this works. Suppose you are playing a video game in which you have to make split-second, yes/no decisions about choices that are offered to a character that you are controlling, such as deciding whether the character should turn left or right, go through a door, or jump to a new level. The pace of the game does not allow for a logical analysis of all of the possible consequences that may follow these actions. As a result, you must rely on intuition to make choices for the character (Kuo et al., 2009). The emotion-monitoring system in your cortex guides these decisions based on information stored in your memory about past choices and the emotions they elicited. It does the same when everyday life confronts us with situations in which we must make decisions quickly as well, such as when you notice dark clouds and must make a quick, yes/no decision about taking an umbrella with you to class.

Of course, there are times when decision-making processes must ignore emotion to be effective, as is the case when we must resist the lure of an immediate reward in order to achieve a long-term goal. In such cases, affective neuroscientists say that the *anterior cingulate cortex (ACC)*, the front part of a band that surrounds the corpus callosum, works with the cortex to suppress the emotional cues that are associated with the immediate reward (Dalgleish, 2004). As a result, we are able to focus our attention on the long-term goal and act thoughtfully rather than impulsively. Thus, it isn't surprising that researchers have found links between delayed maturity of the ACC and serious behavior problems among preadolescent boys (De Brito et al., 2009). Similarly, animal studies show that damage to the ACC disrupts animals' social relationships (Rudebeck et al., 2007). This finding makes sense when you consider how important the inhibition of impulses is to social relationships. For instance, most people agree that you will be better off in the long run if you refrain from telling off your boss every time you are angry with her. Thanks to your ACC, you can resist the pull of fantasies about how good you think you will feel in the short run if you tell her off in favor of the long-term goal of keeping your job.

9.15 How do males and females differ with regard to emotion?

Gender Differences in Emotion

Do females and males differ significantly in the way they experience their emotions? According to the evolutionary perspective, your answer to the following question is likely to be gender specific: What emotion would you feel first if you were betrayed or harshly criticized by another person? When asked to respond to this question, male research participants in a classic study were more likely to report that they would feel angry; female participants were more likely to say that they would feel hurt, sad, or disappointed (Brody, 1985). Of course, both males and females express anger, but typically not in the same ways. Women are just as likely as men to express anger in private (at home) but much less likely than men to express it publicly (Cupach & Canary, 1995). The reason that women may fail to show anger in public is that emotion display rules are, at least to some extent, gender specific. Researchers in the United States have found that, in general, women are expected to suppress negative emotions and express positive ones (Simpson & Stroh, 2004). The pattern of expectations is just the opposite for men.

Researchers have also found sex differences in the intensity of emotional response. Grossman and Wood (1993) tested male and female participants for the intensity of emotional responses on five basic emotions—joy, love, fear, sadness, and anger. They found that "women reported more intense and more frequent emotions than men did, with the exception of anger" (p. 1013). More joy, more sadness, more fear, more love! But these were self-reports. How did Grossman and Wood know that the female participants actually felt four of the five emotions more intensely than the males? The researchers also measured physiological arousal. The participants viewed slides depicting the various emotions while they were hooked up to an electromyograph, which measured tension in the facial muscles. The researchers found that "women not only reported more intense emotional experience than men, but they also generated more extreme physiological reactions" (p. 1020). Other researchers agree that, in general, women respond with greater emotional intensity than men and thus can experience both greater joy and greater sorrow (Fujita, Diener, & Sandvik, 1991).

In another interesting study of gender differences in emotional intensity, researchers measured levels of *cortisol*, a stress hormone that increases with emotional arousal, in husbands and wives after discussions of positive and negative events in their relationships

▲ Do you think that gender differences in experiencing emotions affect the ways in which men and women argue? If so, how?

(Kiecolt-Glaser, 2000). The researchers found that women's cortisol levels increased after discussions of negative events, while men's levels remained constant. This finding suggests that women are more physiologically sensitive to negative emotions than men are.

The Expression of Emotion ▶

9.16 How do humans express and influence emotion?

Expressing emotion comes as naturally to humans as breathing. Two leading researchers on emotion, Paul Ekman (1993) and Carroll Izard (1992), insist that there are a limited number of basic emotions. Basic emotions are unlearned and universal; that is, they are found in all cultures, are reflected in the same facial expressions, and emerge in children according to their own biological timetable of development. Fear, anger, disgust, surprise, joy or happiness, and sadness or distress are usually considered basic emotions. Izard (1992, 1993) suggests that there are distinct neural circuits that underlie each of the basic emotions, and Levenson and others (1990) point to specific autonomic nervous system activity associated with the basic emotions.

In studying the range of emotion, Ekman (1993) has suggested considering emotions as comprising families. The anger family would range from annoyed to irritated, angry, livid, and, finally, enraged. Furthermore, the anger family, if it exists, also includes various forms in which the emotion is expressed, according to Ekman (1993). Resentment, for example, is a form of anger "in which there is a sense of grievance" (p. 386). Just as there are many words in the English language to describe the variations in the range of any emotion, Ekman and Friesen claim that subtle distinctions in the facial expression of a single emotion convey its intensity (Ekman, 1993).

Charles Darwin (1872/1965) maintained that most emotions and the facial expressions that convey them are genetically inherited and characteristic of the entire human species. If Darwin was right, then everyone should label the expressions in the *Try It* the same way. Do your labels agree with those of others? To test his belief, Darwin asked missionaries and people of different cultures around the world to record the facial expressions that accompany the basic emotions. Based on those data, he concluded that facial expressions were similar across cultures. Modern researchers agree that Darwin was right.

basic emotions Emotions that are unlearned and universal, that are reflected in the same facial expressions across cultures, and that emerge in children according to their biological timetable of development; fear, anger, disgust, surprise, happiness, and sadness are usually considered basic emotions.

TRY IT   Recognizing Basic Emotions

Look carefully at the six photographs. Which basic emotion is portrayed in each?
Match the number of the photograph with the basic emotion it conveys.

a. happiness   **b.** sadness   **c.** fear   **d.** anger   **e.** surprise   **f.** disgust

         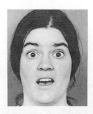      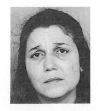

1. _____   **2.** _____   **3.** _____   **4.** _____   **5.** _____   **6.** _____

ANSWERS: 1.d   2.c   3.f   4.e   5.a   6.b

Watch on **mypsychlab.com**

Other researchers have found evidence for universality as well as for cultural variations. Scherer and Wallbott (1994) found very extensive overlap in the patterns of emotional experiences reported across cultures in 37 different countries on five continents. They also found important cultural differences in the ways emotions are elicited and regulated and in how they are shared socially. Recent research suggests that Asians pay more attention to indicators of emotion, such as tone of voice, than Westerners do (Ishii, Reyes, & Kitayama, 2003).

Moreover, each culture appears to have an "accent" for facial expressions (Marsh, Elfenbein, & Ambady, 2007). This accent is a pattern of minute muscle movements that are used by most members of a culture when they exhibit a particular facial expression. In other words, there is a Japanese way to make a happy face, an American way to make a happy face that is somewhat different, and a German way of making a happy face that differs from both. In fact, these differences are enough to influence perceptions of emotion even when individuals come from very similar cultural backgrounds. In one classic study, researchers found that white Americans more quickly identified the facial expressions of other white Americans than did white Europeans (Izard, 1971).

display rules Cultural rules that dictate how emotions should generally be expressed and when and where their expression is appropriate.

Each culture has very different display rules—cultural rules that dictate how emotions should generally be expressed and where and when their expression is appropriate (Ekman, 1993; Ekman & Friesen, 1975; Scherer & Wallbott, 1994). Often a society's display rules require people to give evidence of certain emotions that they may not actually feel or to disguise their true feelings. For example, Americans are expected to look sad at funerals, to hide disappointment at not winning, and to refrain from making facial expressions of disgust when served food that tastes bad. Display rules in Japanese culture dictate that negative emotions must be disguised when other people are present (Ekman, 1972; Triandis, 1994). In East Africa, young males from traditional Masai society are expected to appear stern and stony-faced and to "produce long, unbroken stares" (Keating, 1994).

There are variations in display rules across groups within the same culture as well. For instance, researchers have found that, in most work settings, supervisors expect the workers they manage to express more positive than negative emotions (Diefendorff & Richard, 2004). Similarly, researchers have learned that, in the United States, teens conform to unspoken display rules acquired from peers that discourage public displays of emotion. The resulting subdued emotional expressions can cause them to appear to be aloof, uncaring, and even rude to parents and other adults (Salisch, 2001). Psychologists speculate that conformity to these peer-based display rules may be the basis of much miscommunication between teens and their parents and teachers.

Could controlling one's facial expressions be a means of controlling the emotions themselves? The idea that the muscular movements involved in certain facial expressions

▶ There are many situations in which people must disguise their emotions to comply with the display rules of their culture, which dictate when and how feelings should be expressed. For example, these soccer players—both winners and losers—are expected to be good sports, even if it means hiding their true feelings.

produce the corresponding emotion is called the facial-feedback hypothesis (Strack, Martin, & Stepper, 1988). Some evidence supports this notion. In classic research, Ekman and colleagues (1983) demonstrated that physiological measures of emotion such as heart rate and muscle tension changed in response to changes in research participants' facial expressions. More recently, researchers have found that people's facial expressions are more likely to change the intensity of the emotion they are really feeling than to enable them to change from one state to another (Soussignan, 2002). Thus, if you are angry and you adopt an angry expression, you will feel angrier. However, such findings could be interpreted to mean that neutralizing your facial expression is the first step toward gaining control when your emotions are heading in a direction that you think may be more harmful than helpful.

If we can control our emotions, is it a good idea to do so? You may have heard that "venting" anger can make you feel better. However, there is no evidence to support this view, and, in fact, venting may actually make you feel worse (Lohr et al., 2007). Moreover, it can lead to aggressive behavior. Thus, research suggests that learning to regulate and manage anger is a better option than venting.

One of today's most influential clinical psychologists, Martin Seligman, enthusiastically endorses the idea that people can and should exert control over their emotions to maintain positive emotional states (e.g., happiness) and avoid negative ones (e.g., anger) (Seligman et al., 2005). Moreover, he has argued that the field of psychology can help people do so by devoting as much time and energy to studying human strengths such as *optimism*, a positive outlook on life, as we do to studying weaknesses such as psychological disorders, an approach called positive psychology (Seligman & Csikszentmihalyi, 2000). Positive psychologists such as Barbara Fredrickson (2009) suggest that positive emotions enable us to focus on applying and modifying the coping strategies that have worked well for us in the past to new challenges. By contrast, negative feelings direct our attention to our problems. The *Apply It* provides you with important tips for maintaining a positive outlook.

facial-feedback hypothesis The idea that the muscular movements involved in certain facial expressions produce the corresponding emotions (for example, smiling makes one feel happy).

positive psychology The view that psychologists should study and promote the development of human strengths such as optimism.

APPLY IT   The Quest for Happiness

Happiness is closely related to life satisfaction—people who feel happy also tend to believe that their lives are satisfying. Of course, there are factors in everyone's life that can't be changed, and some of them can result in unhappiness. However, people can use certain strategies to exercise greater control over the way they respond emotionally to their life situations.

Remove Your Rose-Colored Glasses
Having a generally positive outlook on life is an important factor in maintaining a sense of well-being. However, do you know what it means to "see the world through rose-colored glasses"? The expression derives from a French metaphor, *voire la vie en rose* ("to see life in pink"), that means to see things more favorably than they really are. Psychologist Daniel Gilbert has studied the connection between decision making and happiness (Gilbert, 2006). He points out that we are often disappointed when we make decisions based on what we believe will make us happy. For example, the belief that a new house will make us happy motivates us to save money, spend time searching for a house, and go through the stressful experience of moving. But within a very short time, we discover that the new house did not bring us the bliss we expected. Gilbert says that we do the same thing in relationships. In pursuit of happiness, we date, marry, have affairs, divorce, have children, reconcile with estranged relatives, cut off communication with troublesome relatives, join clubs to find new friends, and on and on, only to find that we revert to our original emotional state after all is said and done.

Count Your Blessings
Perhaps we can avoid the hope–disappointment cycle Gilbert describes by learning to be more appreciative of what we already have. Psychologist Martin Seligman and his colleagues (2005) have used a number of exercises geared toward increasing people's sense of well-being by getting them to focus on the positive aspects of their experiences. One such exercise is "Three Good Things." Seligman instructs participants in his studies to keep a journal in which they record three positive things that happen each day. They have found that participants report feeling happier after having kept the "three good things" journal for only a week. Furthermore, those who continue the practice after their participation in the study has ended report enduring effects.

Keep Busy
You will also feel happier if you get so caught up in an activity that you become oblivious to your surroundings. Psychologists refer to this state as *flow*. To be in flow is to be unself-consciously absorbed (Csikszentmihalyi et al., 2005). People who are caught up in some activity that engages their skills—whether it is work, play, or simply driving a car—report more positive feelings.

You may not be able to control every aspect of your life situation, but you do have some control over how you respond to it.

ᜃ Looking Back

Now that you have finished reading about motivation and emotion, you can probably see how individual differences in optimism contribute to the various topics that were discussed in this chapter. With regard to work motivation, for example, a person who is optimistic may be more strongly motivated to take on new challenges and thereby gain access to opportunities than more pessimistic employees are. Likewise, in romantic relationships, it seems that a basic belief in one's ability to bring about good outcomes, another way of thinking optimistically,

would be likely to motivate a person to tolerate the risk of rejection that goes along with approaching a potential romantic party. As a result, optimistic people may have more opportunities to explore relationships than those who are pessimistic. Thus, if you find yourself tending toward the pessimistic side of the optimism–pessimism continuum, it might be worth your while to consult a counselor who is an adherent of positive psychology and who knows how to help you develop a more positive outlook on life.

CHAPTER 9 SUMMARY

EXPLAINING MOTIVATION (pp. 283-291)

9.1 How do psychologists define and classify motivation? (pp. 283-284)

Activation is the component of motivation in which an individual takes the first steps toward a goal. Persistence is the component of motivation that enables a person to continue to work toward the goal even when he or she encounters obstacles. The intensity component of motivation refers to the energy and attention a person must employ to reach a goal. Primary drives are unlearned biological motives, such as thirst and hunger. Social motives are learned from experience and interactions with others. With intrinsic motivation, an act is performed because it is satisfying or pleasurable. With extrinsic motivation, an act is performed to gain a reward or avert an undesirable consequence.

Key Terms
motivation, p. 283
motives, p. 284
primary drives, p. 284
social motives, p. 284
work motivation, p. 284
achievement motivation, p. 284
intrinsic motivation, p. 284
incentive, p. 284
extrinsic motivation, p. 284

9.2 How do drive-reduction and arousal theory explain motivation? (pp. 284-286)

Drive-reduction theory suggests that a biological need creates an unpleasant state of emotional arousal that compels the organism to engage in behavior that will reduce the arousal level. Arousal theory suggests that the aim of motivation is to maintain an optimal level of arousal.

Key Terms
drive-reduction theory, p. 285
drive, p. 285

homeostasis, p. 285
arousal, p. 285
arousal theory, p. 285
stimulus motives, p. 285
Yerkes–Dodson law, p. 285

9.3 How do behavioral and social-cognitive theories explain work and achievement motivation? (pp. 286-289)

Behavioral techniques such as reinforcement and goal setting are used by industrial-organizational psychologists to enhance workers' motivation. Expectancy theory is a social-cognitive theory that focuses on workers' beliefs about the effectiveness and value of their efforts. Two other social-cognitive theories, need for achievement theory and goal orientation theory, help to explain achievement motivation.

Key Terms
industrial/organizational (I/O) psychologists, p. 286
goal setting, p. 286
expectancy theory, p. 287
need for achievement (n Ach), p. 288
goal orientation theory, p. 289

9.4 What are Maslow's views on motivation? (p. 290)

According to Maslow, higher needs cannot be addressed until lower needs are met. Lower needs include both physiological needs (e.g., for food) and the need for safety. Once these are satisfied, behavior can be motivated by higher needs, such as the needs for belonging, esteem, and self-actualization.

Key Term
self-actualization, p. 290

HUNGER (pp. 291-296)

9.5 How do internal and external cues influence eating behavior? (pp. 291-292)

The brain's pleasure system influences eating behavior. The lateral hypothalamus (LH) signals us to eat when we are hungry, and the ventromedial hypothalamus (VMH) motivates us to stop eating when we are full. Other internal hunger signals are low blood glucose levels and high insulin levels. Some satiety signals are high blood glucose levels and the presence in the blood of other satiety substances (such as CCK) that are secreted by the gastrointestinal tract during digestion. External hunger cues, such as the taste, smell, and appearance of food; eating with other people; and the time of day can cause people to eat more food than they actually need.

Key Terms
lateral hypothalamus (LH), p. 291
ventromedial hypothalamus (VMH), p. 291

9.6 What factors contribute to individual differences in body weight? (pp. 292-293)

Variations in body weight are influenced by genes, hormones, metabolic rate, activity level, number of fat cells, and eating habits. Fat-cell theory claims that individuals who are overweight have more fat cells in their bodies. Set-point theory suggests that an internal homeostatic system functions to maintain body weight by adjusting appetite and metabolic rate.

Key Terms
body mass index (BMI), p. 292
metabolic rate, p. 293
set point, p. 293

9.7 What does research suggest about obesity and dieting? (pp. 293-294)

Some people who are obese cannot lose weight and must undergo gastric bypass surgery to attain a healthy body weight. Weight-loss programs for such individuals and those for children must be carefully supervised by health professionals. To be effective, a weight-loss strategy must include calorie reduction and exercise.

Key Term
obesity, p. 293

9.8 What are the characteristics of eating disorders? (pp. 295-296)

The symptoms of anorexia nervosa are an overwhelming, irrational fear of being fat, compulsive dieting to the point of self-starvation, and excessive weight loss. It damages the heart and other organs and can be fatal. The symptoms of bulimia nervosa are repeated and uncontrolled episodes of binge eating, usually followed by purging. Intentional vomiting can cause dental and digestive problems for people who have bulimia nervosa. Both anorexia and nervosa are more common in females than in males, are difficult to treat, and often occur along with other psychiatric disorders.

Key Terms
anorexia nervosa, p. 295
bulimia nervosa, p. 296

SEXUAL MOTIVATION (pp. 296-302)

9.9 How do sexual attitudes and behavior vary across cultures and genders? (pp. 297-298)

Men are more likely than women to think of sex in purely physical terms and to have more permissive attitudes toward sex. The frequency of sexual activity varies across cultures. During ovulation women have the strongest desire for sex, and men are likely to be most rapidly aroused by ovulating female partners. Evolutionary psychologists say that differences in parental investment explain gender differences in attitudes and behavior, but others argue that social factors are responsible.

Key Term
parental investment, p. 298

9.10 What are the phases of the human sexual response cycle? (pp. 299-300)

The sexual response cycle consists of four phases: the excitement phase, the plateau phase, orgasm, and the resolution phase. Hormones influence the cycle in both men and women.

Key Term
sexual response cycle, p. 299

9.11 What does research show regarding sexual orientation? (pp. 300-302)

Two general patterns in the prevalence of homosexuality are that males are more likely to identify with an exclusive homosexual orientation than women are, and same-sex attraction is more common than homosexual behavior. The biological factors suggested as possible causes of a gay or lesbian sexual orientation are (1) androgens; (2) structural differences in an area of the hypothalamus of gay men; and (3) genetic factors.

Key Term
sexual orientation, p. 300

9.12 How have attitudes toward homosexuality changed in recent decades? (p. 302)

Prior to 1973, homosexuality was considered to be a disorder by mental health professionals. Today most people are opposed

to discrimination based on homosexuality. Homosexual relationships are similar to those involving heterosexuals. Gay men are more tolerant of sexual infidelity than heterosexual and lesbian couples. Like heterosexual women, lesbians place more emphasis on mutual emotional support than they do on sexual intimacy.

Key Term
homophobia, p. 302

EMOTION (pp. 302-309)

9.13 What theories have been proposed to explain emotion? (pp. 303-304)

The three components of emotions are the physiological arousal that accompanies the emotion, the cognitive appraisal of the stimulus or situation, and the outward behavioral expression of the emotion. According to the James–Lange theory of emotion, environmental stimuli produce a physiological response, and then awareness of this response causes the emotion to be experienced. The Cannon–Bard theory suggests that emotion-provoking stimuli received by the senses are relayed simultaneously to the cerebral cortex, providing the mental experience of the emotion, and to the sympathetic nervous system, producing physiological arousal. The Schachter–Singer theory states that for an emotion to occur, (1) there must be physiological arousal, and (2) the person must perceive some reason for the arousal in order to label the emotion. According to the Lazarus theory, an emotion-provoking stimulus triggers a cognitive appraisal, which is followed by the emotion and the physiological arousal.

Key Terms
emotion, p. 302
James–Lange theory, p. 303
Cannon–Bard theory, p. 303
Schachter–Singer theory, p. 304
Lazarus theory, p. 304

9.14 What have affective neuroscientists learned about emotion and the brain? (pp. 304-306)

Affective neuroscientists have identified associations between emotions and different areas of the brain, and most believe a distinct neurological system underlies each emotion. The amygdala contributes to fear-based learning. The cortex monitors physiological cues associated with emotion and relates them to past experiences to help us make decisions. The anterior cingulate cortex suppresses emotional cues to help us control impulsivity.

Key Term
affective neuroscience, p. 304

9.15 How do males and females differ with regard to emotion? (pp. 306-307)

Men and women appear to manage emotions differently. Women are more likely to feel hurt or disappointed after a betrayal or harsh criticism from another person, while men are more likely to feel angry. Men and women also differ in their likeliness to express anger publicly.

9.16 How do humans express and influence emotion? (pp. 307-309)

The basic emotions (happiness, sadness, disgust, and so on) are those that are unlearned and universal and that emerge in children according to their biological timetable of development. Studies also show that there is variation across cultures in the ways emotions are elicited and regulated and how they are shared socially. The customs of an individual's culture determine when, where, and under what circumstances various emotions are exhibited. Children learn these rules as they mature so that, as adults, they will be able to suppress and exhibit emotions in accordance with the rules of their cultures. Violating a culture's display rules can cause a person's behavior to be interpreted as rude or offensive. The facial-feedback hypothesis suggests that the muscular movements involved in certain facial expressions trigger corresponding emotions (for example, smiling triggers happiness). Positive psychologists study the impact of positive emotional states on other aspects of functioning.

Key Terms
basic emotions, p. 307
display rules, p. 308
facial-feedback hypothesis, p. 309
positive psychology, p. 309

MAP IT

Log on to MyPsychLab and click on "Map It" to prepare a unique digital map of the chapter that you can save for later use, email to your instructor, or print out to use as a study tool. Or, create your own map by drawing one on paper. Use the starter map below as a model for your own map. Use the chapter summary as your guide for what to include. For each item in your map, be sure to include the page number.

Here's one way to *Map It*:

1. Draw a box at the top of the page for the section title.

2. Underneath the section title box, working horizontally across the page, draw a box for each learning question in the section. Write the learning questions in the boxes and draw a line from the section title to each questions box. After you read each subsection, jot an answer for the learning question in the subsection's box.

3. Below each learning question box, insert another box for all of the key terms that are related to the question, along with a very brief reminder of each term's definition. Draw a line from the question box to the key terms box.

4. Below each key terms box, create another box and list all of the helpful figures, tables, and other elements of the text, such as *Try It* and *Apply It* boxes. Draw a line from the key terms box to the helpful elements box.

 Map the Chapter on mypsychlab.com

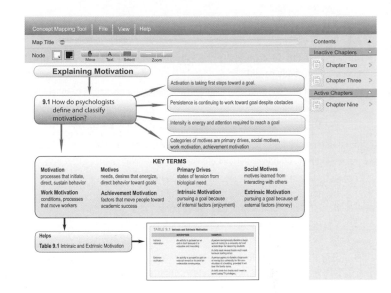

Chapter 9 Study Guide

Answers to all the Study Guide questions are provided at the end of the book.

SECTION ONE: Chapter Review

Explaining Motivation (pp. 283–291)

1. Motives move us toward goals. (true/false)

2. When you engage in an activity to gain a reward or to avoid an unpleasant consequence, your motivation is (intrinsic, extrinsic).

3. Drive-reduction theory states that people are motivated to
   a. reduce tension created by biological drives.
   b. seek emotional highs such as the feelings you have on a roller coaster.
   c. obey genetically programmed instincts.
   d. maintain appropriate levels of arousal.

4. According to arousal theory, people seek _____ arousal.
   a. minimized
   b. increased
   c. decreased
   d. optimal

5. According to Maslow's hierarchy of needs, which needs must be satisfied before a person will try to satisfy the belonging and love needs?
   a. safety and self-actualization needs
   b. self-actualization needs and esteem needs
   c. physiological and safety needs
   d. physiological and esteem needs

6. Murray used the Thematic Apperception Test (TAT) to study the need for achievement. (true/false)

7. Individuals who have a _____ goal orientation are motivated by a desire to outperform others.

8. Industrial/organizational psychologists use reinforcement and goal setting to increase
   a. achievement motivation.
   b. mastery motivation.
   c. performance motivation.
   d. work motivation.

9. According to _____ theory, an employee's belief that increased effort will lead to improved performance is an important element of work motivation.

Hunger (pp. 291–296)

10. The lateral hypothalamus (LH) acts as a (feeding, satiety) center; the ventromedial hypothalamus (VMH) acts as a (feeding, satiety) center.

11. All of the following are hunger signals *except*
    a. activity of the lateral hypothalamus.
    b. low levels of glucose in the blood.
    c. the hormone CCK.
    d. a high insulin level.

12. The smell of food
    a. has little effect on hunger.
    b. can substitute for food itself when you are dieting.
    c. may make you feel hungry even when you are not.
    d. motivates you to eat only when you are very hungry.

13. Which factor is most responsible for how fast your body burns calories to produce energy?
    a. calories consumed
    b. fat cells
    c. eating habits
    d. metabolic rate

14. According to set-point theory, the body works to (increase, decrease, maintain) body weight.

15. Which of the following might indicate a tendency for obesity to be inherited?
    a. metabolic rate
    b. set point
    c. hormones
    d. all of the above

16. Adopted children are more likely to be very thin or obese if their (biological, adoptive) parents are very thin or obese.

17. To be effective, a weight loss program should
    a. focus more on calorie reduction than on exercise
    b. include specially prepared "diet" foods
    c. include both calorie reduction and increased exercise
    d. exclude all high-fat foods

18. Self-starvation is the defining symptom of _____; binge eating followed by purging is the main symptom of _____.

Sexual Motivation (pp. 296–302)

19. Who conducted the first major surveys of sexual attitudes and behaviors of American males and females?
    a. Alfred Kinsey
    b. Masters and Johnson
    c. George Gallup
    d. Laumann and others

20. Which of the following statements about the human sexual response is *false*?
    a. It consists of four phases.
    b. It occurs in sexual intercourse and can occur in other types of sexual activity.
    c. It is very different in males and females.
    d. It was researched by Masters and Johnson.

21. Androgens, estrogen, and progesterone are present in both males and females. (true/false)

22. Testosterone plays a role in maintaining sexual interest in males and females. (true/false)

23. The direction of one's sexual interest—toward members of the opposite sex or members of one's own sex—is termed one's
    a. sexual role.
    b. sexual orientation.
    c. sexual desire.
    d. sexual motive.

24. Statistics suggest that homosexuality is more common in males than in females. (true/false)

25. Which of the following did Bell, Weinberg, and Hammersmith's study reveal about the childhood experiences of their gay and lesbian participants?
    a. Abuse was more common in their families than in those of heterosexuals.
    b. No single characteristic of family life distinguished their families from those of heterosexuals.

c. Most were raised in single-parent homes.
d. Most were from middle-class backgrounds.

26. Evolutionary theory suggests that gender differences in sexual behavior are caused by gender differences in
    a. hormones.
    b. parental investment.
    c. cultural roles.
    d. ideas about the importance of physical attractiveness.

Emotion (pp. 302–310)

27. According to the text, emotions have all of the following *except* a _____ component.
    a. physical
    b. cognitive
    c. sensory
    d. behavioral

28. Which theory of emotion holds that you feel a true emotion only when you become physically aroused and can identify some cause for the arousal?
    a. Schachter–Singer theory
    b. James–Lange theory
    c. Cannon–Bard theory
    d. Lazarus theory

29. Which theory of emotion suggests that you would feel fearful because you were trembling?
    a. Schachter–Singer theory
    b. James–Lange theory
    c. Cannon–Bard theory
    d. Lazarus theory

30. Which theory suggests that the feeling of emotion and the physiological response to an emotional situation occur at about the same time?
    a. Schachter–Singer theory
    b. James–Lange theory
    c. Cannon–Bard theory
    d. Lazarus theory

31. Which theory suggests that the physiological arousal and the emotion flow from a cognitive appraisal of an emotion-provoking event?
    a. Schachter–Singer theory
    b. James–Lange theory
    c. Cannon–Bard theory
    d. Lazarus theory

32. Which of the following is *not* true of the basic emotions?
    a. They are reflected in distinctive facial expressions.
    b. They are found in all cultures.
    c. There are several hundred known to date.
    d. They are unlearned.

33. All of the following are true of display rules *except* that they
    a. are the same in all cultures.
    b. dictate when and where emotions should be expressed.
    c. dictate what emotions should not be expressed.
    d. often cause people to display emotions they do not feel.

34. The idea that making a happy, sad, or angry face can actually trigger the psychological response and feeling associated with the emotion is called the
    a. emotion production theory.
    b. emotion and control theory.
    c. facial-feedback hypothesis.
    d. facial expression theory.

SECTION TWO: Important Concepts and Psychologists

On the line opposite each name, list the major concept or theory discussed in this chapter.

Name	Major Concept or Theory
1. Hull	_____
2. Maslow	_____
3. Murray	_____
4. James and Lange	_____
5. Cannon and Bard	_____
6. Lazarus	_____
7. Salovey and Pizarro	_____

SECTION THREE: Fill in the Blank

1. _____ are needs or desires that energize and direct behavior toward a goal.

2. Anthony mows his parents' lawn and, in the winter, shovels his own and his elderly neighbor's sidewalk. He does this because he enjoys helping others. Anthony is responding to _____ motivation.

3. Cleo will help around the house only if she receives a financial reward or special privilege. Cleo responds to _____ motivation.

4. Jack always wants to ride the wildest rides at the amusement park. He also seems to get bored very easily and then finds a way to create action in his environment. His behavior would probably best be explained by the _____ theory of motivation.

5. Expectancy theory's term for the degree to which an employee values the rewards that her employer offers for improved performance is _____.

6. The _____ hypothalamus acts as the feeding center, and the _____ hypothalamus acts as the satiety center.

7. _____ is an important factor in successful long-term weight loss.

8. _____ nervosa involves rigid restriction of calorie intake; _____ nervosa involves a cycle of binging and purging.

9. The _____ theory of emotion says that we experience emotion as a result of becoming aware of our physical response to a situation.

10. The _____ theory of emotion says that our physical response to a stimulus and our emotional response occur at the same time.

11. The _____ theory of emotion says that we experience a physical response to a stimulus and then give it meaning; from this comes our emotional response.

12. Feelings of fear, anger, disgust, surprise, joy, or happiness have been identified as _____ emotions.

13. The _____ phase is the beginning of the human sexual response cycle.

14. Males must have a sufficient level of _____ to maintain sexual interest and have an erection.

15. The tendency of the body to maintain a balanced internal state with regard to oxygen level, body temperature, blood sugar, water balance, and so forth is called _____.

16. Simon LeVay, a neuroscientist, reported that an area in the hypothalamus governing sexual behavior is about twice as large in _____ men as in _____ men.

SECTION FOUR: Comprehensive Practice Test

1. If James is responding to an incentive, he is responding to an _____ stimulus.
  a. extrinsic
  b. internal
  c. explicit
  d. intrinsic

2. Courtney reads books on research and statistics because these subjects fascinate her; she really enjoys learning about new approaches to research and the results of major research projects. Courtney is being driven by _____ motivation.
  a. intrinsic
  b. intellectual
  c. academic
  d. extrinsic

3. Keisha studies chemistry every night because she wants to excel in this field; she believes she will make a great deal of money as a chemist. Keisha is being driven mainly by _____ motivation.
  a. career
  b. intrinsic
  c. extrinsic
  d. academic

4. A _____ is a state of tension or arousal brought about by an underlying need, which motivates one to engage in behavior that will satisfy the need and reduce the tension.
  a. drive
  b. balance stimulus
  c. tension stimulus
  d. homeostatic condition

5. Angel's behavior sometimes scares his friends. He drives his motorcycle fast, he loves bungee jumping, and he can't wait for his first parachute jump. These interests could be explained by the _____ theory of motivation.
  a. instinct
  b. risky shift
  c. arousal
  d. homeostasis

6. According to Maslow, the need for love and affiliation is satisfied _____ basic biological needs and the need for safety.
  a. instead of
  b. before
  c. at the same time as
  d. after

7. Cody realizes that the goals he has set for himself are going to take too much time and effort, so he decides to compromise and go for what he considers less difficult but more rational goals. Cody has a high *n* Ach.? (true/false)

8. When you are hungry, you experience the effects of the _____ hypothalamus; when you have eaten and feel full, you experience the effects of the _____ hypothalamus.
  a. proximal; distal
  b. distal; proximal
  c. ventromedial; lateral
  d. lateral; ventromedial

9. Murray developed the Thematic Apperception Test as a way to measure
  a. anger.
  b. personal perceptions of success.
  c. social needs.
  d. extrinsic motivation.

10. Which of the following theories asserts that, when presented with an emotion-producing stimulus, we feel the physiological effects and the subjective experience of emotion at about the same time?

    a. James–Lange   c. Cannon–Bard
    b. Lazarus   d. Schachter–Singer

11. Researchers agree that all humans experience basic emotions. (true/false)

12. Trina smiled and thanked her friend for a birthday gift that she really did not like. Trina has learned the _____ of her culture.
    a. social rules
    b. interpersonal rules
    c. display rules
    d. expressive rules

13. The facial-feedback hypothesis states that the muscular movements that cause facial expressions trigger the corresponding emotions. (true/false)

14. The orgasm is the shortest phase in the sexual response cycle. (true/false)

15. Boys who display early effeminate behavior usually are homosexual in adulthood. (true/false)

16. Which of the following is the most accurate description of sexual orientation?
    a. Homosexuality is inherited.
    b. Homosexuality is determined by prenatal hormones.
    c. Homosexuality results from alterations in brain structures.
    d. Homosexuality is associated with both biological and environmental causal factors.

17. Homophobia is
    a. a type of sexual orientation.
    b. an irrational fear of homosexuals.
    c. the belief that homosexuals should not be discriminated against in employment.
    d. found more often in women than in men.

18. The study of the neurological foundations of emotion is called _____ neuroscience.
    a. affective
    b. emotional
    c. motivational
    d. limbic

SECTION FIVE: Critical Thinking

1. In your view, which theory or combination of theories best explains motivation: drive-reduction theory, arousal theory, or Maslow's hierarchy of needs? Which theory do you find least convincing? Support your answers.

2. Which level of Maslow's hierarchy provides the strongest motivation for your behavior in general? Give specific examples to support your answer.

3. In your view, which is the better explanation of gender differences in sexual attitudes and behavior: parental investment theory or the social factors proposed by Wood and Eagly?

Health and Stress

Think About It

What kinds of things make you feel "stressed out"? If you are like most students, one of the things that irritates you is the feeling that you don't have enough time. In fact, having too much to do and not enough time to do it is one of the topics addressed by the "Hassles Scale," a test that measures people's stress levels (Kanner et al., 1981). The questions on the test came from a survey of college students taken in 1981. The researchers presented students with a list of potentially irritating things and asked them to identify the items that were currently causing stress for them. The following table lists the things that the researchers asked about and the percentage of students that identified each one as a current cause of stress. How many of them are sources of stress in your own life?

SOURCES OF STRESS	PERCENTAGE STRESSED	SOURCE OF STRESS FOR YOU?
Troubling thoughts about the future	77	
Not getting enough sleep	73	
Wasting time	71	
Inconsiderate smokers	70	
Too many things to do	69	
Misplacing or losing things	67	
Not enough time to do the things you need to do	66	
Concerns about meeting high standards	64	
Being lonely	61	

Source: Table from "Comparison of Two Modes of Stress Measurement; Daily Hassles and Uplifts versus Major Life Events by A. D. Kanner, J. C. Coyne, C. Shaefer, and R. S. Lazarus. (1981). *Journal of Behavioral Medicine*, 4, pp. 1-39. Copyright © 1981 by Springer Publishing Group. Reprinted by permission of Copyright Clearance Center on behalf of the publisher.

Thinking about the sources of stress listed in the table may make you more aware of just how stressful your own life is at the moment. This chapter will acquaint you with some strategies for managing stress. It will also introduce you to theories and research that will help you understand more about what stresses us, how we respond to stress, and how stress affects our health.

Sources of Stress

stress The physiological and psychological response to a condition that threatens or challenges a person and requires some form of adaptation or adjustment.

stressor Any stimulus or event capable of producing physical or emotional stress.

Psychologists define stress as the physiological and psychological response to a condition that threatens or challenges an individual and requires some form of adaptation or adjustment. A stressor is a stimulus or an event that is capable of producing a stress response. Everyone would probably agree that major events such as changing jobs, breaking up with an intimate partner, and so on, are stressful. But do such events cause us more stress than the everyday stressors that we asked you reflect on in the *Think About It* activity above? As you might guess, there's evidence to support both points of view.

10.1 How does the life events approach describe stress?

The Life Events Approach

life events approach The view that a person's state of well-being can be threatened by major life changes.

Social Readjustment Rating Scale (SRRS) Holmes and Rahe's measure of stress, which ranks 43 life events from most to least stressful and assigns a point value to each.

One way of describing, measuring, and explaining stress is the life events approach, the view that a person's state of well-being can be threatened by major life changes. This approach includes events that most people experience at one time or another, such as beginning and ending romantic relationships. It also includes events that most of us never or rarely experience first-hand, such as combat, sexual assault, and natural disasters.

The Social Readjustment Rating Scale. The classic studies of researchers Thomas Holmes and Richard Rahe are representative of this approach. Holmes and Rahe (1967) developed the Social Readjustment Rating Scale (SRRS) to measure stress by ranking different life events from most to least stressful and assigning a point value to each event. Life events that produce the greatest life changes and require the greatest adaptation are considered the most stressful, regardless of whether the events are positive or negative. The 43 life events on the scale range from death of a spouse (assigned 100 stress points) to minor law violations, such as getting a traffic ticket (11 points). Find your life stress score by completing the *Try It* below.

Holmes and Rahe claim that there is a connection between the degree of life stress and major health problems. People who score 300 or more on the SRRS, the researchers say, run about an 80% risk of suffering a major health problem within the next two years. Those who score between 150 and 300 have a 50% chance of becoming ill within a two-year period (Rahe et al., 1964). More recent research has shown that the weights given to life events by Holmes and Rahe continue to be appropriate for adults in North America and that SRRS scores are correlated with a variety of health indicators (Dohrenwend, 2006; Thorsteinsson & Braun, 2009).

▲ Even positive life events, such as getting married, can cause stress.

 TRY IT   **Finding a Life Stress Score**

To assess your level of life changes, check all of the events that have happened to you in the past year. Add up the points to derive your life stress score. (Based on Holmes & Masuda, 1974.)

Rank	Life Event	Life Change Unit Value	Your Points	Rank	Life Event	Life Change Unit Value	Your Points
1	Death of spouse	100	___	23	Son or daughter leaving home	29	___
2	Divorce	73	___	24	Trouble with in-laws	29	___
3	Marital separation	65	___	25	Outstanding personal achievement	28	___
4	Jail term	63	___	26	Spouse beginning or stopping work	26	___
5	Death of close family member	63	___	27	Beginning or ending school	26	___
6	Personal injury or illness	53	___	28	Change in living conditions	25	___
7	Marriage	50	___	29	Revision of personal habits	24	___
8	Getting fired at work	47	___	30	Trouble with boss	23	___
9	Marital reconciliation	45	___	31	Change in work hours or conditions	20	___
10	Retirement	45	___	32	Change in residence	20	___
11	Change in health of family member	44	___	33	Change in schools	20	___
12	Pregnancy	40	___	34	Change in recreation	19	___
13	Sex difficulties	39	___	35	Change in church activities	19	___
14	Gain of new family member	39	___	36	Change in social activities	18	___
15	Business readjustment	39	___	37	Taking out loan for lesser purchase (e.g., car or TV)	17	___
16	Change in financial state	38	___	38	Change in sleeping habits	16	___
17	Death of close friend	37	___	39	Change in number of family get-togethers	15	___
18	Change to different line of work	36	___	40	Change in eating habits	15	___
19	Change in number of arguments with spouse	35	___	41	Vacation	13	___
20	Taking out loan for major purchase (e.g., home)	31	___	42	Christmas	12	___
21	Foreclosure of mortgage or loan	30	___	43	Minor violation of the law	11	___
22	Change in responsibilities at work	29	___		**Life stress score:**		___

One of the main shortcomings of the SRRS is that it assigns a point value to each life change without taking into account how an individual copes with that stressor. One study found that SRRS scores did reliably predict disease progression in multiple sclerosis patients (Mohr et al., 2002). But the patients who used more effective coping strategies displayed less disease progression than did those who experienced similar stressors but coped poorly with them.

Catastrophic Events. Catastrophic events such as the terrorist attacks of September 11, 2001, the deadly Indian Ocean tsunami of 2004, the devastating hurricanes that hit the Gulf Coast of the United States in 2005, and the earthquake that struck Haiti in 2010 are stressful both for those who experience them directly and for people who learn of them via news media. Most people are able to manage the stress associated with such catastrophes. However, for some, these events lead to posttraumatic stress disorder (PTSD), a prolonged and severe stress reaction to a catastrophic event (such as a plane crash or an earthquake) or to severe, chronic stress (such as that experienced by soldiers engaged in combat or residents of neighborhoods in which violent crime is a daily occurrence) (Kilpatrick et al., 2003).

Studies show that the effects of such traumatic events can linger for years, particularly for those who have some kind of personal connection to them. For example, surveys of New York City residents indicate that some were continuing to suffer from symptoms of PTSD up to six years after the terrorist attacks of 2001 (Brackbill et al., 2009). Moreover, PTSD sometimes does not appear until many years after an event has been experienced, and in some cases, it is triggered by the anniversary of a traumatic event. For example, mental health professionals in the United States reported that the number of World War II veterans seeking treatment from the Veterans Administration for war-related symptoms of PTSD increased substantially in the years that followed the fiftieth anniversary of the war's end in 1945 (Johnston, 2000). Researchers hypothesize that age-related changes in the brain lessened some older veterans' ability to manage the emotions that were associated with traumatic combat experiences, an effect that was particularly marked in veterans who also suffered from dementia. ◉—Watch on **mypsychlab.com**

People with PTSD often have flashbacks, nightmares, or intrusive memories that make them feel as though they are actually reexperiencing the traumatic event. They suffer increased anxiety and startle easily, particularly in response to anything that reminds them of the trauma (Green, Lindy, & Grace, 1985). Many survivors of war or catastrophic events experience *survivor guilt* because they lived while others died; some feel that perhaps they could have done more to save others. Extreme combat-related guilt in Vietnam veterans is a risk factor for suicide or preoccupation with suicide (Hendin & Haas, 1991). One study of women with PTSD revealed that they were twice as likely as women without PTSD to experience first-onset depression and three times as likely to develop alcohol problems (Breslau et al., 1997). PTSD sufferers also experience cognitive difficulties, such as poor concentration (Vasterling et al., 2002).

Everyday Stressors

Which is more stressful—major life events or those little problems and frustrations that seem to crop up every day? Richard Lazarus believes that everyday stressors, which he calls hassles, cause more stress than major life events do (Lazarus & DeLongis, 1983). Daily hassles include irritating, frustrating experiences such as standing in line, being stuck in traffic, being put on hold when you are trying to resolve an issue over the phone, and so on. Relationships are another frequent source of hassles, such as happens when another person misunderstands us or when co-workers or customers are hard to get along with. Likewise, environmental conditions such as traffic noise and pollution are among the daily hassles reported by city dwellers (Moser & Robin, 2006).

To illustrate the usefulness of Lazarus's approach, Kanner and others (1981) developed the Hassles Scale that you learned about in the *Think About It* activity at the beginning of the chapter to assess various categories of hassles. Unlike the Holmes and Rahe scale, the Hassles Scale takes into account the facts that items may or may not represent stressors to individuals and that the amount of stress produced by an

---

posttraumatic stress disorder (PTSD) A prolonged and severe stress reaction to a catastrophic event or to severe, chronic stress.

◉—Watch the **Video** *9/11 Post Traumatic Stress Disorder* on **mypsychlab.com**

10.2 What do hassles, uplifts, and choices contribute to stress?

hassles Irritating demands that occur daily and may cause more stress than major life changes do.

item varies from person to person. People completing the scale indicate the items that have been a hassle for them and rate those items for severity on a 3-point scale.

DeLongis, Folkman, & Lazarus (1988) studied 75 American couples over a 6-month period and found that daily stress (as measured on the Hassles Scale) related significantly to present and future "health problems such as flu, sore throat, headaches, and backaches" (p. 486). Research also indicates that minor hassles that accompany stressful major life events, such as those measured by the SRRS, are better predictors of a person's level of psychological distress than the major events themselves (Pillow, Zautra, & Sandlar, 1996).

According to Lazarus, uplifts, or positive experiences in life, may neutralize the effects of many hassles. Lazarus and his colleagues also constructed an Uplifts Scale. As with the Hassles Scale, people completing this scale make a cognitive appraisal of what they consider to be an uplift. Research has demonstrated links among hassles, uplifts, and a personal sense of well-being. It appears that a hectic daily schedule increases hassles, decreases uplifts, and diminishes their subjective sense of how well they feel (Erlandsson & Eklund, 2003). However, items viewed as uplifts by some people may actually be stressors for others. For middle-aged people, uplifts are often health- or family-related (Pinquart & Sorensen, 2004). For college students uplifts often take the form of having a good time (Kanner et al., 1981).

Hassles and uplifts aren't the only sources of everyday stress that we experience. Making choices is stressful as well. Some decisions cause us stress by forcing us to choose between equally desirable alternatives. Such dilemmas are known as approach-approach conflicts. Some approach-approach conflicts are minor, such as deciding which movie to see. Others can have major consequences, such as the conflict between building a promising career or interrupting that career to raise a child. In an avoidance-avoidance conflict, a person must choose between two undesirable alternatives. For example, you may want to avoid studying for an exam, but at the same time you want to avoid failing the test. An approach-avoidance conflict involves a single choice that has both desirable and undesirable features. The person facing this type of conflict is simultaneously drawn to and repelled by a choice—for example, wanting to take a wonderful vacation but having to empty a savings account to do so.

Stress in the Workplace

Have you ever had a boss who was difficult to work with? If so, then you are well acquainted with the phenomenon of work-related stress, an experience that varies somewhat from both the life events and everyday stressors approaches you read about earlier. Work-related stress is unique in that it has more to do with the characteristics of the setting in which a person is functioning than with specific life events or the cumulative effects of everyday stressors.

Albrecht (1979) suggested that if people are to function effectively and find satisfaction on the job, the following nine variables must fall within their comfort zone (see also Figure 10.1):

- *Workload.* Too much or too little to do can cause people to feel anxious, frustrated, and unrewarded.

- *Clarity of job description and evaluation criteria.* Anxiety arises from confusion about job responsibilities and performance criteria or from a job description that is too rigidly defined to leave room for individual initiative.

- *Physical variables.* Temperature, noise, humidity, pollution, amount of workspace, and the physical positions (standing or sitting) required to carry out job duties should fall within a person's comfort zone.

- *Job status.* People with very low-paying, low-status jobs may feel psychological discomfort; those with celebrity status often cannot handle the stress that fame brings.

- *Accountability.* Accountability overload occurs when people have responsibility for the physical or psychological well-being of others but only a limited degree of

uplifts The positive experiences in life, which may neutralize the effects of many hassles.

approach-approach conflict A conflict arising from having to choose between equally desirable alternatives.

avoidance-avoidance conflict A conflict arising from having to choose between undesirable alternatives.

approach-avoidance conflict A conflict arising when the same choice has both desirable and undesirable features.

10.3 What variables contribute to workers' comfort zone?

FIGURE 10.1 Variables in Work Stress
For a person to function effectively and find satisfaction on the job, these nine variables should fall within the person's comfort zone.
Source: Albrecht (1979).

How would you rank these factors with regard to stress potential? That is, which are likely to cause the most on-the-job stress, and which are likely to cause the least?

Accountability

Job status

Task variety

Physical variables (noise, temperature, space, etc.)

Human contact

Clarity of job description and evaluation criteria

Physical challenge

Workload

Mental challenge

▲ Air-traffic controllers have an extremely high-stress job. The on-the-job stress they experience increases the risk of coronary disease and stroke.

burnout Lack of energy, exhaustion, and pessimism that results from chronic stress.

control (air-traffic controllers, emergency room nurses and doctors); accountability underload occurs when workers perceive their jobs as meaningless.

- *Task variety.* To function well, people need a comfortable amount of variety and stimulation.

- *Human contact.* Some workers have virtually no human contact on the job (forest-fire lookouts); others have almost continuous contact with others (welfare and employment office workers). People vary greatly in how much interaction they enjoy or even tolerate.

- *Physical challenge.* Jobs range from being physically demanding (construction work, professional sports) to requiring little to no physical activity. Some jobs (firefighting, police work) involve physical risk.

- *Mental challenge.* Jobs that tax people beyond their mental capability, as well as those that require too little mental challenge, can be frustrating.

Workplace stress can be especially problematic for women because of sex-specific stressors, including sex discrimination and sexual harassment in the workplace and difficulties in combining work and family roles. These added stressors have been shown to increase the negative effects of occupational stress on the health and well-being of working women (Buchanan & Fitzgerald, 2008).

Job stress can have a variety of consequences. Perhaps the most frequently cited is reduced effectiveness on the job. But job stress can also lead to absenteeism, tardiness, accidents, substance abuse, and lower morale (Wilhelm et al., 2004). Chronic stress can also lead to work-related burnout (Freudenberger & Richelson, 1981). People with burnout lack energy, feel emotionally drained, and are pessimistic about the possibility of changing their situations. People who feel that their work is unappreciated are more subject to burnout than others. For example, one survey suggested that nearly half of the social workers in the United Kingdom suffer from burnout, and the sense of being unappreciated was the best predictor of the condition (Evans et al., 2006).

10.4 What are some social sources of stress?

┤◀ **Social Sources of Stress**

Like work-related stress, social stress is largely a function of the characteristics of the overall context in which a person faces the challenges of life. For example, members of ethnic minority groups are exposed to stressors that rarely affect the lives of those in the so-called dominant group. Likewise, aspects of economic status, such as poverty and unemployment, are also characterized by unique sources of stress.

Racism. Some theorists have proposed that a phenomenon called *historical racism*—experienced by members of groups that have a history of repression, such as Hispanic Americans, Native Americans, and African Americans—is a source of social stress (Alamilla, Kim, & Lam, 2010; Belcourt-Dittloff & Stewart, 2000; Troxel et al., 2003). Researchers interested in the effects of historical racism have focused primarily on African Americans. Many of these researchers claim that the higher incidence of high blood pressure among African Americans is attributable to stress associated with historical racism. Surveys have shown that African Americans experience more race-related stress than members of other minority groups do (Utsey et al., 2002). Those African Americans who express the highest levels of concern about racism display higher levels of cardiovascular reactivity to experimentally induced stressors, such as sudden loud noises, than do peers who express less concern (Bowen-Reid & Harrell, 2002). At least one study has demonstrated a correlation between African Americans' perceptions of racism and hypertension (Din-Dzietham et al., 2004). Researchers found that African Americans who reported the highest levels of race-related stressors in their workplaces were more likely to have high blood pressure than workers who reported fewer such stressors.

▲ A strong sense of ethnic identity helps African Americans cope with the stress that may arise from living with racism.

African Americans are also more likely than members of other minority groups to have a strong sense of ethnic identity, a factor that helps moderate the effects of racial stress (Utsey et al., 2002). But some studies show that personal characteristics, such as hostility, may increase the effects of racial stress (Fang & Myers, 2001; Raeikkoenen, Matthews, & Saloman, 2003). So, the relationship between historical racism and cardiovascular health is probably fairly complex and varies considerably across individuals.

Socioeconomic Status. The term socioeconomic status is often used to refer to differences in income levels, but it includes much more than just financial resources. Occupation and education are also important components of socioeconomic status, as is the more subjective variable of social status. These variables interact to influence the status that is assigned to an individual, and these interactions can vary differently from one setting to another. For example, in some neighborhoods, police officers have low status even though they may have more education and higher incomes than the people who live in the communities they serve. In other neighborhoods, police officers have high status despite having less education and lower incomes than many members of the community. Thus, socioeconomic status is a fairly complex variable.

socioeconomic status A collective term for the economic, occupational, and educational factors that influence an individual's relative position in society.

Despite these complexities, large-scale studies of health and other variables of interest often rely on data such as income and educational level to sort people into socioeconomic status categories. When this technique is used, as you can probably predict, people who are low in socioeconomic status are usually found to more frequently have stress-related health conditions such as colds and the flu. In addition, health risk factors such as high levels of LDL cholesterol are typically more common among them (Goodman et al., 2005).

Closer scrutiny of the variables associated with socioeconomic status reveals other factors that help us interpret links between socioeconomic status and health. For example, one frequent finding is that people of lower socioeconomic status have higher levels of stress hormones than people of higher status (Cohen, Doyle, & Baum, 2006). Looking further into this relationship, researchers have identified several behavioral and social factors among such people that help to explain the relationship between status and stress hormones. These factors included higher rates of smoking, more limited social networks, and less regular patterns of eating as compared to people at higher levels of socioeconomic status. This is not to say that these factors apply to everyone who has a low income, but they are found more frequently among those who are economically disadvantaged. Their presence affects the averages of health variables among low-income groups, thus creating correlations between socioeconomic status and these variables.

Unemployment. Unemployment is another aspect of socioeconomic status that is related to stress and health. People who are forced out of their jobs experience heightened risks of stress-related illnesses in the months that follow (Isaksson et al., 2004). These effects are found among people of low, middle, and high socioeconomic status, by the way. This consistency is the result of the financial strain that accompanies the loss of income and the uncertainty about the future that is part of the experience of looking for a new job. These aspects of unemployment are stressful no matter how much money people made in their former jobs. However, unemployment is also stressful because it diminishes people's sense of control over what happens to them.

Acculturative Stress. You can probably guess that adjusting to life in a new culture can be extremely stressful, a phenomenon that researchers call *acculturative stress* (Berry, Kim, Minde, & Mok, 1987). Some theorists suggest that immigrants who develop an *integration orientation*, the belief that they will be able to fit into the social structure of the new culture while retaining links to their home cultures, are well equipped to manage the stresses that go along with transitioning from one culture to another (Berry, 2003; Schwartz & Zamboanga, 2008). Research shows that immigrants with an integration orientation are more satisfied with their lives than those who adopt a different way of thinking about the immigration experience (Peeters & Oerlemans, 2009). Thus, cultural psychologists suggest that schools and other institutions encourage immigrants to maintain ties to their cultures of origin as they acquire the skills they need to fit in to their new surroundings.

The Health-Stress Connection

There's no doubt that stress affects the quality of our lives, but can it actually threaten our health? The answer to this question depends at least partially on how we define health. It also depends on a careful analysis of the physiological and psychological effects of stress, and the factors that protect us against it, on the body and mind.

10.5 How does the biopyschosocial model approach health and illness?

biomedical model A perspective that explains illness solely in terms of biological factors.

The Biopsychosocial Model of Health and Illness

For centuries researchers focused on an explanatory model that defined health as the absence of disease. This approach, known as the biomedical model, explains illness exclusively in terms of biological factors. Consequently, it focuses on illness more than it does on health. In some cases, the biomedical model works quite well. For example, streptococcus bacteria cause many infections of the respiratory system. Thus, when a person who has one of these ailments takes an antibiotic drug that kills streptococcus, she usually experiences a speedy and complete recovery. But why doesn't everyone who is exposed to streptococcus get sick?

Individual differences in people's responses to *pathogens* (microorganisms that cause illness) such as streptococcus suggest that there's more to health than the biomedical model suggests. Thus, researchers and practitioners have turned to the biopsychosocial model—an approach that includes psychological and social factors in addition to physical causes of disease—in their search for more comprehensive explanations of health than the biomedical model can provide. As you can see in Figure 10.2, these explanations often include psychological factors. Moreover, the biopsychosocial model seeks answers to questions about what keeps us healthy as well as what makes us sick.

biopsychosocial model A perspective that focuses on health as well as illness and holds that both are determined by a combination of biological, psychological, and social factors.

Interest in the contributions of psychological factors to health and illness among psychologists has led to the development of the specialized field of health psychology. Health psychologists use principles of psychology to prevent illness and to help restore people who are ill to health. Furthermore, for health psychologists, the concept of health extends beyond the simple absence of disease. It includes all aspects of well-being in the

health psychology The subfield within psychology that is concerned with the psychological factors that contribute to health, illness, and recovery.

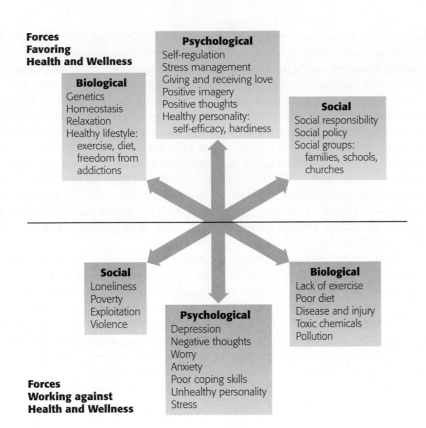

Forces Favoring Health and Wellness

Biological
Genetics
Homeostasis
Relaxation
Healthy lifestyle:
  exercise, diet,
  freedom from
  addictions

Psychological
Self-regulation
Stress management
Giving and receiving love
Positive imagery
Positive thoughts
Healthy personality:
  self-efficacy, hardiness

Social
Social responsibility
Social policy
Social groups:
  families, schools,
  churches

Social
Loneliness
Poverty
Exploitation
Violence

Psychological
Depression
Negative thoughts
Worry
Anxiety
Poor coping skills
Unhealthy personality
Stress

Biological
Lack of exercise
Poor diet
Disease and injury
Toxic chemicals
Pollution

Forces Working against Health and Wellness

FIGURE 10.2 The Biopsychosocial Model of Health and Illness
The biopsychosocial model focuses on health as well as on illness and holds that both are determined by a combination of biological, psychological, and social factors. Most health psychologists endorse the biopsychosocial model.
Source: Green & Shellenberger (1990).

physical, psychological, and social domains (Brannon & Feist, 2010). Consequently, the scope of health psychology is quite broad. One important goal of health psychology is to find ways to improve communication between health care professionals and the people they serve. Another is to identify the psychological, behavioral, and social factors that contribute to conditions such as chronic pain, asthma, heart disease, diabetes, cancer, and so on. Health psychologists also design strategies for helping people make behavioral changes that can enhance people's health.

Health psychologists have found that stress contributes to individual differences in each of these areas. For example, some patients find communicating with health professionals about their condition to be highly stressful (Cruess et al., 2010). Researchers hypothesize that stress distracts such patients from the information that care providers are attempting to convey to them. As a result, these patients are less likely to follow instructions about medication and other aspects of their treatment than those for whom communication with providers is less stressful. Thus, patients' responses to providers' instructions may improve if they learn how to manage their stress responses more effectively.

Another important finding in health psychology is that providing people with training in stress management can improve their health in more direct ways. For example, some people who have chronic pain conditions learn to manage their discomfort more effectively if their treatment includes training in stress management techniques such as meditation (Rosenzweig et al., 2010). Likewise, such training is critical to helping people who have a low tolerance for stress make health-related behavior changes such as giving up smoking (Siahpush et al., 2009). But what is it about stress that influences health?

The Physiology of the Health-Stress Connection

10.6 How does the fight-or-flight response affect health?

You should recall from Chapter 2 that the sympathetic nervous system responds to threats (stressors) by preparing the body to resist or escape. It does so by increasing heart rate, blood pressure, and respiration rate while at the same time shutting down unnecessary functions, such as those of the digestive system. This set of reactions is

fight-or-flight response A response to stress in which the sympathetic nervous system and the endocrine glands prepare the body to fight or flee.

lymphocytes The white blood cells—including B cells and T cells—that are the key components of the immune system.

psychoneuroimmunology (sye-ko-NEW-ro-IM-you-NOLL-oh-gee) A field in which psychologists, biologists, and medical researchers combine their expertise to study the effects of psychological factors on the immune system.

called the fight-or-flight response because it enables us to fight the stressor or flee from it. When the stressor is no longer present, the parasympathetic nervous system reverses the fight-or-flight response, and the body returns to normal. But when stressors are present for long periods of time, and the person's efforts to adjust to them fail, the body's tendency to keep the fight-or-flight response going can threaten our health.

Maintaining the fight-or-flight response over an extended period of time influences health in two ways. First, research suggests that the biochemicals associated with the fight-or-flight response directly affect how the body functions. For example, when we are exposed to stressors, our bodies pump out large amounts of a substance called *neuropeptide Y (NPY)* (Dutton, Lee, & Zukowska, 2006). NPY helps us adapt to stress by reducing anxiety (Sajdyk et al., 2008). However, it also constricts the blood vessels that serve the heart and brain. As a result, the vessels become more vulnerable to blockages, an important cause of heart attacks and strokes (Kuo, Abe, & Zukowska, 2007; Li, Lee, Ji, & Zukowska, 2003).

Second, the fight-or-flight response indirectly affects health by suppressing the body's immune system. Composed of an army of highly specialized cells and organs, the immune system works to identify and search out and destroy bacteria, viruses, fungi, parasites, and any other foreign matter that may enter the body. The key components of the immune system are white blood cells known as lymphocytes, which include B cells and T cells. *B cells* are so named because they are produced in the bone marrow. *T cells* derive their name from the thymus gland, where they are produced. All cells foreign to the body, such as bacteria, viruses, and so on, are known as *antigens*. B cells produce proteins called *antibodies,* which are highly effective in destroying antigens that live in the bloodstream and in the fluid surrounding body tissues (Paul, 1993). For defeating harmful foreign invaders that have taken up residence inside the body's cells, however, T cells are critically important.

Psychoneuroimmunology is a field of study in which psychologists, biologists, and medical researchers combine their expertise to learn the effects of psychological factors—stress, emotions, thinking, and behavior—on the immune system (Fleshner & Laudenslager, 2004. Robles, Glaser, & Kiecolt-Glaser, 2005). Their studies show that periods of high stress are correlated with increased symptoms of many infectious diseases, including oral and genital herpes, mononucleosis, colds, and flu. Stress may also decrease the effectiveness of certain kinds of vaccines (Miller et al., 2004; Moynihan et al., 2004) and decrease levels of the immune system's B and T cells.

Stress has the power to suppress the immune system long after the stressful experience is over. An experimental group of medical students who were enduring the stress of major exams was compared with a control group of medical students who were on vacation from classes and exams. When tested for the presence of disease-fighting antibodies, participants in the exam group, but not those in the control group, had a significant reduction in their antibody count because of the stress. The lowered antibody count was still present 14 days after the exams were over. At that point, the students were not even aware that they were still stressed and reported feeling no stress (Deinzer et al., 2000).

In addition to academic pressures, poor marital relationships and sleep deprivation have been linked to lowered immune response (Kiecolt-Glaser et al., 1987; Maier & Laudenslager, 1985). Likewise, for several months after the death of a spouse, the widow or widower suffers weakened immune system function and is at a higher risk of mortality. Severe bereavement weakens the immune system, increasing a person's chance of suffering from a long list of physical and mental ailments for as long as two years following a partner's death (Prigerson et al., 1997).

10.7 How do theorists explain physiological and psychological responses to stress?

Theories of Stress Response

As you have seen, prolonged stress threatens health. However, the body doesn't simply surrender to the stressors. Instead, it calls upon a variety of resources to defend itself against the stressors' potentially damaging effects. Theories of stress response explain how the body does so. One important theory focuses on the body's physiological response, and another emphasizes psychological responses to stress.

The General Adaptation Syndrome. Hans Selye (1907–1982), the researcher most prominently associated with the effects of stress on health, established the field of stress research. At the heart of Selye's concept of stress is the general adaptation syndrome (GAS), the predictable sequence of reactions that organisms show in response to stressors. It consists of three stages: the alarm stage, the resistance stage, and the exhaustion stage (Selye, 1956; see Figure 10.3).

The first stage of the body's response to a stressor is the alarm stage, in which the adrenal cortex releases hormones called *glucocorticoids* that increase heart rate, blood pressure, and blood sugar levels, supplying a burst of energy that helps the person deal with the stressful situation, that is, the fight-or-flight syndrome (Pennisi, 1997). Next, the organism enters the resistance stage, during which the adrenal cortex continues to release glucocorticoids to help the body resist stressors. The length of the resistance stage depends both on the intensity of the stressor and on the body's power to adapt. If the organism finally fails in its efforts to resist, it reaches the exhaustion stage, at which point all the stores of deep energy are depleted, and disintegration and death follow.

Selye found that the most harmful effects of stress are due to the prolonged secretion of glucocorticoids, which can lead to permanent increases in blood pressure, suppression of the immune system, weakening of muscles, and even damage to the hippocampus (Stein-Behrens et al., 1994). Thanks to Selye, the connection between extreme, prolonged stress and certain diseases is now widely accepted by medical experts.

Lazarus's Cognitive Theory of Stress. Is it the stressor itself that upsets us, or the way we think about it? Richard Lazarus (1966; Lazarus & Folkman, 1984) contends that it is not the stressor that causes stress but rather a person's perception of it. According to Lazarus, when people are confronted with a potentially stressful event, they engage in a cognitive process that involves a primary and a secondary appraisal. A primary appraisal is an evaluation of the meaning and significance of the situation—whether its effect on one's well-being is positive, irrelevant, or negative. An event appraised as stressful could involve (1) harm or loss—that is, damage that has already occurred; (2) threat, or the potential for harm or loss; or (3) challenge—that is, the opportunity to grow or to gain. An appraisal of threat, harm, or loss can occur in relation to anything important to you—a friendship, a part of your body, your property, your finances, your self-esteem. When people appraise a situation as involving threat, harm, or loss, they experience negative emotions, such as anxiety, fear, anger, and resentment (Folkman, 1984). An appraisal that sees a challenge, on the other hand, is usually accompanied by positive emotions such as excitement, hopefulness, and eagerness.

During secondary appraisal, if people judge the situation to be within their control, they make an evaluation of available resources—physical (health, energy, stamina), social (support network), psychological (skills, morale, self-esteem), material (money,

general adaptation syndrome (GAS) The predictable sequence of reactions (alarm, resistance, and exhaustion stages) that organisms show in response to stressors.

alarm stage The first stage of the general adaptation syndrome, in which the person experiences a burst of energy that aids in dealing with the stressful situation.

resistance stage The second stage of the general adaptation syndrome, when there are intense physiological efforts to either resist or adapt to the stressor.

exhaustion stage The third stage of the general adaptation syndrome, which occurs if the organism fails in its efforts to resist the stressor.

primary appraisal A cognitive evaluation of a potentially stressful event to determine whether its effect is positive, irrelevant, or negative.

secondary appraisal A cognitive evaluation of available resources and options prior to deciding how to deal with a stressor.

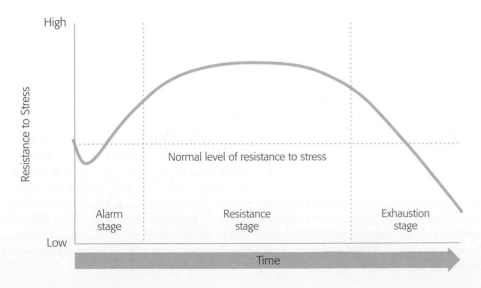

FIGURE 10.3 The General Adaptation Syndrome
The three stages in Selye's general adaptation syndrome are (1) the alarm stage, during which there is emotional arousal and the defensive forces of the body are mobilized for fight or flight; (2) the resistance stage, in which intense physiological efforts are exerted to resist or adapt to the stressor; and (3) the exhaustion stage, when the organism fails in its efforts to resist the stressor.
Source: Selye (1956).

tools, equipment), and time. Then, they consider the options and decide how to deal with the stressor. The level of stress they feel is largely a function of whether their resources are adequate to cope with the threat, and how severely those resources will be taxed in the process. Figure 10.4 summarizes the Lazarus and Folkman psychological model of stress. Research supports their claim that the physiological, emotional, and behavioral reactions to stressors depend partly on whether the stressors are appraised as challenging or threatening. The *Summarize It* below recaps the theories of stress response we have discussed.

FIGURE 10.4 Lazarus and Folkman's Psychological Model of Stress
Lazarus and Folkman emphasize the importance of a person's perceptions and appraisal of stressors. The stress response depends on the outcome of the primary and secondary appraisals, whether the person's coping resources are adequate to cope with the threat, and how severely the resources are taxed in the process.
Source: Folkman (1984).

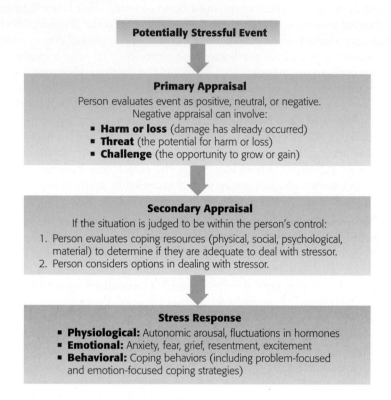

Potentially Stressful Event

Primary Appraisal
Person evaluates event as positive, neutral, or negative.
Negative appraisal can involve:
- **Harm or loss** (damage has already occurred)
- **Threat** (the potential for harm or loss)
- **Challenge** (the opportunity to grow or gain)

Secondary Appraisal
If the situation is judged to be within the person's control:
1. Person evaluates coping resources (physical, social, psychological, material) to determine if they are adequate to deal with stressor.
2. Person considers options in dealing with stressor.

Stress Response
- **Physiological:** Autonomic arousal, fluctuations in hormones
- **Emotional:** Anxiety, fear, grief, resentment, excitement
- **Behavioral:** Coping behaviors (including problem-focused and emotion-focused coping strategies)

SUMMARIZE IT

Theories of Stress Responses

THEORY	DESCRIPTION
Selye's general adaptation syndrome (GAS)	Three stages: alarm, resistance, and exhaustion
Lazarus's cognitive theory	Primary appraisal (evaluation of stressor), followed by secondary appraisal (evaluation of resources and options)

10.8 What factors promote resilience in the face of stress?

Risk and Resilience

risk/resilience model A perspective that proposes that risk and protective factors interact to produce or protect us from illness.

Fortunately, stressors and our responses to them aren't the only factors that determine how our bodies respond to stress. A helpful way to understand how stress and other factors interact to influence our health is to think about stress in terms of a risk/resilience model. This perspective proposes that risk and protective factors interact to produce or protect us from illness. Risk factors such as stress increase the chances of getting sick. Protective factors counteract the effects of risk factors and enable us to "bounce back" from their effects, that is, to exhibit *resilience* (Almeida, 2005). Researchers have identified several factors that promote resilience in the face of stress.

Coping Strategies. If you're like most people, the stresses you have experienced have helped you develop some coping strategies. Coping refers to a person's efforts through action and thought to deal with demands perceived as taxing or overwhelming. Problem-focused coping is direct; it consists of reducing, modifying, or eliminating the source of stress itself. If you are getting a poor grade in history and appraise this as a threat, you may study harder, talk over your problem with your professor, form a study group with other class members, get a tutor, or drop the course (see the *Explain It*).

Emotion-focused coping involves reappraising a stressor to reduce its emotional impact. Research has shown that emotion-focused coping can be a very effective way of managing stress (Austenfeld & Stanton, 2004). If you lose your job, you may decide that it isn't a major tragedy and instead view it as a challenge, an opportunity to find a better job with a higher salary. Despite what you may have heard, ignoring a stressor—one form of emotion-focused coping—can be an effective way of managing stress. Researchers studied 116 people who had experienced heart attacks (Ginzburg, Soloman, & Bleich, 2002). All of the participants reported being worried about suffering another attack. However, those who tried to ignore their worries were less likely to exhibit anxiety-related symptoms such as nightmares and flashbacks. Other emotion-focused strategies, though, such as keeping a journal in which you write about your worries and track how they change over time, may be even more effective (Pennebaker & Seagal, 1999; Solano et al., 2003).

A combination of problem-focused and emotion-focused coping is probably the best stress-management strategy (Folkman & Lazarus, 1980). For example, a heart patient may ignore her anxiety (emotion-focused coping) while conscientiously adopting recommended lifestyle changes such as increasing exercise (problem-focused coping). Moreover, people who respond to stressors with emotion- or problem-focused coping, or a combination of the two, tend to be healthier than those whose behavioral responses to stress include eating more or less, drugs, alcohol, or social withdrawal (Wang et al., 2009). ✳—Explore on mypsychlab.com

coping Efforts through action and thought to deal with demands that are perceived as taxing or overwhelming.

problem-focused coping A direct response aimed at reducing, modifying, or eliminating a source of stress.

emotion-focused coping A response involving reappraisal of a stressor to reduce its emotional impact.

✳—Explore the Concept *Coping Strategies and Their Effects* on **mypsychlab.com**

EXPLAIN IT   **Why Do Pop Quizzes Facilitate Learning?**

What happens when your professor walks into class and announces in a seemingly gleeful tone, "Good morning, class. We're going to start today with a pop quiz"? On hearing these words, you think back to your decision to watch a poker tournament on television instead of reading your assigned chapter, and your heart rate increases dramatically. This is a sure sign that your sympathetic nervous system has triggered the fight-or-flight response, and you are in the throes of a stressful experience. But you suppress the urge you feel to run from the room by resolving never to be caught off guard again in this particular class. The next time you are tempted to while away an evening in front of the television, you force yourself to study instead. How do the various types of coping come into play in this series of events?

As you have learned, emotion-focused coping is the strategy we use when we are faced with a stressor about which we can do little. Being faced with a pop quiz for which you are unprepared is just such a situation. To counter the fight-or-flight response, you modify your thinking about the situation in an effort to indirectly quell the tumultuous emotions you are experiencing. That's why your resolution to be better prepared next time around makes you feel better.

Problem-focused coping addresses the actual stressor and attempts to modify it. Obviously, resolving to be better prepared won't get the job done. You have to actually follow through on your goal. If you do, then you are engaging in

problem-focused coping. In so doing, you are exerting some degree of control over the future appearance of this particular stressor. Recall from our discussion of controllability earlier in the chapter that we cope more effectively with stressors over which we believe we have control.

What do these coping strategies have to do with learning? To find out, we have to examine what might happen the next time your professor announces a pop quiz, assuming that you have kept your resolution to prepare for class. If you have read the assigned material, your emotional response to the quiz announcement is likely to be less intense than it was when you were unprepared. However, it is unlikely that you will perform well on the quiz unless you have actually learned the material. In other words, pop quizzes give prepared students feedback about the effectiveness of their study strategies. Presumably, if you took the time to prepare, but you are disappointed by your quiz grade, you will take steps to not only prepare for class but also to be certain that you are effectively processing what you read. This, of course, is exactly what professors are trying to get you to do when they employ pop quizzes as an instructional strategy. And research suggests that, whether professors count pop quizzes as regular grades or use them for extra credit, they are effective both for motivating students to prepare for class and for helping them learn (Ruscio, 2001; Thorne, 2000).

proactive coping Active measures taken in advance of a potentially stressful situation in order to prevent its occurrence or to minimize its consequences.

Some stressful situations can be anticipated in advance, allowing people to use a strategy called proactive coping, which consists of efforts or actions taken in advance of a potentially stressful situation to prevent its occurrence or to minimize its consequences (Greenglass & Fiksenbaum, 2009). Proactive copers anticipate and then prepare for upcoming stressful events and situations. For example, one certain stressor associated with attending college is that college bookstores are very busy at the beginning of the semester. To cope with this stress proactively, that is, to avoid the stress associated with standing in line with a heavy stack of books, you may order some of your books online or go to the bookstore well in advance of the start of the semester. Parents proactively cope, too, when they take along their children's favorite snacks and toys in anticipation of the children becoming hungry and restless at a relative's home or a doctor's office.

Optimism. People who are generally optimistic tend to cope more effectively with stress, which in turn may reduce their risk of illness (Seligman, 1990). An important characteristic shared by optimists is that they generally expect good outcomes. Such positive expectations help make them more stress-resistant than pessimists, who tend to expect bad outcomes. Similarly, individuals who are optimistic seem to be able to find positives even in the darkest of circumstances (Rini et al., 2004). An especially lethal form of pessimism is hopelessness. A longitudinal study of a large number of Finnish men revealed that participants who reported feeling moderate to high hopelessness died from all causes at two to three times the rates of those reporting low or no hopelessness (Everson et al., 1996).

hardiness A combination of three psychological qualities—commitment, control, and challenge—shared by people who can handle high levels of stress and remain healthy.

Hardiness. Studying male executives with high levels of stress, psychologist Suzanne Kobasa (1979; Kobasa, Maddi, & Kahn, 1982) found three psychological characteristics that distinguished those who remained healthy from those who had a high incidence of illness. The three qualities, which she referred to collectively as hardiness, are *commitment, control,* and *challenge.* Hardy individuals feel a strong sense of commitment to both their work and their personal life. They see themselves not as victims of whatever life brings but as people who have control over consequences and outcomes. They act to solve their own problems, and they welcome challenges in life, viewing them not as threats but as opportunities for growth and improvement. Other researchers have found that the dimensions of hardiness are related to the subjective sense of well-being among the elderly (Smith, Young, & Lee, 2004).

Religious and Social Involvement. Another personal factor that contributes to resilience is religious involvement (Hunter & Lewis, 2010; Prati & Pietrantoni, 2009). For example, a meta-analysis of 42 separate studies combined data on some 126,000 individuals and revealed that religious involvement is positively associated with measures of physical health and lower rates of cancer, heart disease, and stroke (McCullough et al., 2000). Why is religious involvement linked to health? Researchers are currently examining a number of hypotheses (Powell, Shahabi, & Thresen, 2003). One proposal is that attendance at religious services is linked to healthy habits and positive emotions (Koenig & Vaillant, 2009). For example, people who attend church regularly are less likely to smoke and to drink alcohol to excess than other adults. In addition, they are more likely to tell researchers that they are content with their lives than nonattenders are.

Researchers also note that religious involvement may contribute to health because it provides people with a variety of opportunities for social involvement. In support of this conclusion, health psychologists cite research showing that other forms of social involvement, such as serving as a volunteer at a community agency, promote health. In one study, researchers gave volunteers nasal drops containing a cold virus. Within the next few days, symptoms of the viral infection rose sharply in some of the 151 women and 125 men who participated in the study, but less so or not at all in others. Participants with a rich social life in the form of frequent interactions with others—spouses, children, parents, co-workers, friends, and volunteer and religious groups—seemed to enjoy a powerful shield of protection against the virus infection. This pattern of protection held across age and racial groups, for both sexes, at all educational levels, and at every season of the year (Ader, 2000; Cohen et al., 1997).

Social Support. Religious and social involvement may also provide people with a stronger form of social support than is available to others (Seeman et al., 2003). Social support is support provided, usually in time of need, by a spouse, other family members, friends, neighbors, colleagues, support groups, or others. It can involve tangible aid, information, and advice, as well as emotional support. It can also be viewed as the feeling of being loved, valued, and cared for by those toward whom we feel a similar obligation.

▲ A strong social support network can help a person recover faster from an illness.

Social support appears to have positive effects on the body's immune system as well as on the cardiovascular and endocrine systems (Kiecolt-Glaser, Gouin, & Hantsoo, 2010). Social support may help encourage health-promoting behaviors and reduce the impact of stress so that people are less likely to resort to unhealthy methods of coping, such as smoking or drinking. Further, social support has been shown to reduce depression and enhance self-esteem in individuals who suffer from chronic illnesses, such as kidney disease (Symister & Friend, 2003).

It's important to note here that researchers distinguish between *perceived support*, the degree to which a person believes help is available when needed, and *received support*, the actual help a person receives from others. Interestingly, many have found that perceived support is more important than received support (Reinhardt et al., 2006). Other research has shown that high levels of perceived social support are associated with lower levels of depression (Sheets & Mohr, 2009). Such perceived support may be more a function of individual personality than of the actual availability of family and friends who can offer help. One longitudinal study found that college-aged participants who had sociable, outgoing personalities were more likely to report having high levels of perceived social support later in adulthood (Von Dras & Siegler, 1997). These results underscore the importance of psychological variables in health.

social support Tangible and/or emotional support provided in time of need by family members, friends, and others; the feeling of being loved, valued, and cared for by those toward whom we feel a similar obligation.

Perceived Control. Resilience is also influenced by *perceived control*, the degree to which we feel a sense of control over our lives (Rodin & Salovey, 1989). Langer and Rodin (1976) studied the effects of perceived control on nursing-home residents. Residents in one group were given some measure of control over their lives, such as choices in arranging their rooms and in the times they could see movies. They showed improved health and well-being and had a lower death rate than another group who were not given such control. Within 18 months, 30% of the residents given no choices had died, compared with only 15% of those who had been given some control over their lives. Perceived control is important for cancer patients, too. Some researchers suggest that a sense of control over their daily physical symptoms and emotional reactions may be even more important for cancer patients than control over the course of the disease itself (Thompson et al., 1993).

Several studies suggest that we are less subject to stress when we have the power to do something about it, whether we exercise that power or not (John, 2004). Glass and Singer (1972) subjected two groups of participants to the same loud noise. Participants in one group were told that they could, if necessary, terminate the noise by pressing a switch. These participants suffered less stress, even though they never did exercise the control they were given. Friedland and others (1992) suggest that when people experience a loss of control because of a stressor, they are motivated to try to reestablish control in the stressful situation. Failing this, they often attempt to increase their sense of control in other areas of their lives.

Factors That Promote Resilience

FACTOR	DESCRIPTION
Coping	Problem-focused coping, directed toward stress; emotion-focused coping, directed toward the emotional response to the stressor; proactive coping, actions taken to prevent future stress
Optimism	Positive expectations for the future
Hardiness	Commitment to work and personal life; sense of control over outcomes; view stressors as challenges
Religious faith	Healthy habits, positive emotions, social involvement
Social support	Tangible, emotional support provided by family, friends, other; perceived support may be more important than actual support
Perceived control	Belief that one has some degree of control over stressors

Health and Illness

As we noted earlier, health psychologists apply the biopsychosocial model to better understand the prevention and treatment of specific illnesses. For example, they have studied two life-threatening illnesses, heart disease and cancer, extensively. In addition, the biopsychosocial model has helped health psychologists explain gender and ethnic group differences in health and illness.

10.9 How do lifestyle, heredity, and personality influence coronary heart disease?

Coronary Heart Disease

To survive, the heart muscle requires a steady, sufficient supply of oxygen and nutrients carried by the blood. Coronary heart disease is caused by the narrowing or the blockage of the coronary arteries, the arteries that supply blood to the heart muscle. As you learned earlier, stress-related biochemicals play an important role in this process. Although coronary heart disease remains the leading cause of death in the United States, responsible for 25% of all deaths, deaths due to this cause have declined 50% during the past 40 years (Xu, Kochanek & Tejada-Vera, 2009).

A health problem of modern times, coronary heart disease is largely attributable to lifestyle and is therefore an important field of study for health psychologists. A *sedentary lifestyle*—one that includes a job at which one spends most of the time sitting and less than 20 minutes of exercise three times per week—is the primary modifiable risk factor contributing to death from coronary heart disease (Gallo et al., 2003). Other modifiable risk factors are high serum cholesterol level, cigarette smoking, and obesity. ✳ Explore on **mypsychlab.com**

✳ Explore the **Concept** *Heart Disease in America* on **mypsychlab.com**

Though not modifiable, another important risk factor is family history. The association between family history and coronary heart disease is both genetic and behavioral. For instance, individuals whose parents have high blood pressure, but who have not yet developed the disorder themselves, exhibit the same kinds of emotional reactivity and poor coping strategies as their parents (Frazer, Larkin, & Goodie, 2002).

Personality type is also associated with an individual's risk of heart disease. After extensive research, cardiologists Meyer Friedman and Ray Rosenman (1974) concluded that there are two types of personality: Type A, associated with a high rate of coronary heart disease, and Type B, commonly found in persons unlikely to develop heart disease.

Type A behavior pattern A behavior pattern marked by a sense of time urgency, impatience, excessive competitiveness, hostility, and anger; considered a risk factor in coronary heart disease.

Type B behavior pattern A behavior pattern marked by a relaxed, easygoing approach to life, without the time urgency, impatience, and hostility of the Type A pattern.

People with the Type A behavior pattern have a strong sense of time urgency and are impatient, excessively competitive, hostile, and easily angered. They are "involved in a chronic, incessant struggle to achieve more and more in less and less time" (Friedman & Rosenman, 1974, p. 84). In contrast, people with the Type B behavior pattern are relaxed and easygoing and are not driven by a sense of time urgency. They are not impatient or hostile and are able to relax without guilt. They play for fun and relaxation rather than to exhibit superiority over others. Yet, a Type B individual may be as bright and ambitious as a Type A person, and more successful as well.

Research indicates that the lethal core of the Type A personality is not time urgency but anger and hostility, which fuel an aggressive, reactive temperament (Smith & Ruiz, 2002). These associations have been found across cultures and in both men and women (Mohan, 2006; Olson et al., 2005).

However, careful studies have shown that anger and hostility may be part of a larger complex of variables that includes other forms of emotional distress (Kubzansky et al., 2006; Olson et al., 2005). When anger and hostility are considered as single variables, both prove to be predictive of coronary heart disease. However, when other distress variables, such as anxiety and cynicism, are added to them, statistical analyses suggest that it is the whole cluster of negative emotions that best predicts heart disease rather than any one of the variables alone.

The finding that negative emotions collectively predict coronary disease better than any one of the variables alone has led some researchers to propose a new classification, Type D behavior pattern ("D" for distress; Denollet, 1997). People with this profile exhibit a chronic pattern of emotional distress combined with a tendency to suppress negative emotions. In one study of men who were enrolled in a rehabilitative therapy program after having had a heart attack, those with the Type D profile were found to have four times the risk of death as other patients in the program (Sher, 2004). Researchers speculate that the high mortality rate of individuals with Type D personality may come from their body's heightened tendency to produce an inflammatory response to invasive medical procedures such as surgery (Molloy, Perkios-Porras, Strike, & Steptoe, 2008; Pedersen & Denollet, 2003). However, more research is needed before the physiology associated with Type D personality will be fully understood.

Whatever the physiological link between personality and coronary disease, its relationship to both health behaviors and social support may turn out to be equally important. For example, individuals who, like those with Type D personality, tend to have a negative view of life, are less likely to abstain from tobacco after completing a smoking cessation program (Hooten et al., 2005). Furthermore, researchers have found that Type D personality in the partners of patients who have coronary heart disease impairs these partners' ability to be supportive (Pedersen, van Domburg, & Theuns, 2004). As you can see, the ramifications of personality for heart disease may turn out to be quite comprehensive. Hostility not only is highly predictive of coronary heart disease but also is associated with ill health in general (Miller et al., 1996).

▲ Hostility is a key component of the Type A behavior pattern.

Type D behavior pattern People who exhibit chronic emotional distress combined with a tendency to suppress negative emotions.

Cancer ▶

10.10 How do psychological factors influence cancer patients' quality of life?

Cancer is the second leading cause of death in the United States, accounting for 23% of all deaths (Xu, Kochanek, & Tejada-Vera, 2009). Cancer strikes frequently in the adult population, and about 30% of Americans will develop cancer at some time in their lives. The young are not spared the scourge of cancer, for it takes the lives of more children aged 3 to 14 than any other disease.

Cancer, a collection of diseases rather than a single illness, can invade cells in any part of a living organism—humans, other animals, and even plants. Normal cells in all parts of the body divide, but fortunately they have built-in instructions about when to stop dividing. Unlike normal cells, cancer cells do not stop dividing. And, unless caught in time and destroyed, they continue to grow and spread, eventually killing the organism. Health psychologists point out that an unhealthy diet, smoking, excessive alcohol consumption, promiscuous sexual behavior, or becoming sexually active in the early teens (especially for females) are all behaviors that increase the risk of cancer.

▲ This group of cancer patients is involved in art therapy, which is believed to lower the stress level associated with having a serious illness.

Moreover, while there is no solid evidence that stress causes cancer, it does influence how people with the disease respond to and cope with treatment (Garssen, 2004; Pedersen et al., 2009).

The 1.5 million people in the United States who are diagnosed with cancer each year have the difficult task of adjusting to a potentially life-threatening disease and the chronic stressors associated with it (American Cancer Society, 2009). Thus, researchers claim that cancer patients need more than medical treatment. Their therapy should include help with psychological and behavioral factors that can influence their quality of life. Carver and others (1993) found that 3 months and 6 months after surgery, breast cancer patients who maintained an optimistic outlook, accepted the reality of their situation, and maintained a sense of humor experienced less distress. Patients who engaged in denial—refusal to accept the reality of their situation—and had thoughts of giving up experienced much higher levels of distress. Dunkel-Schetter and others (1992) found that the most effective elements of a strategy for coping with cancer were social support (such as through self-help groups), a focus on the positive, and distraction. Avoidant coping strategies, such as fantasizing, denial, and social withdrawal, were associated with more emotional distress.

10.11 How do males and females differ with regard to health?

Gender and Health

Most medical research in the past, primarily funded by the U.S. government, rejected women as participants in favor of men (Matthews et al., 1997). One area where the failure to study women's health care needs has been particularly evident is in research examining mortality risk following open-heart surgery. Women are more likely to die after such surgery than are men. To date, studies have shown that the gender gap in surgical survival narrows with age, but researchers are still investigating why women's postsurgical mortality rate is higher than men's (Vaccarino et al., 2002). One reason for the disparity is that women have higher rates of postsurgical infection and stroke than men do (Rogers et al., 2006). Higher rates of blood transfusion among female patients may be responsible for the gender gap in postoperative infections (Rogers et al., 2007). Both men and women who receive transfusions during or after heart surgery have higher infection rates than nontransfused patients do, but women are about 50% more likely than men to require transfusions during or after surgery.

In general, however, men have higher death rates from all causes than women do, although women tend to be less healthy. These seemingly contradictory findings have puzzled researchers for decades (Rieker & Bird, 2005). The finding that women are more likely than men are to seek medical care explains some of this difference (Addis & Mahalik, 2003). However, differences in care seeking fall short of fully explaining gender differences in illness and death.

In recent years, researchers have begun to examine how the progression of potentially fatal diseases varies across gender (Case & Paxson, 2004). For example, lung diseases that are caused by smoking afflict women and men about equally. However, for unknown reasons, men with these diseases are more seriously ill, as indicated by gender differences in the frequency of hospitalization, and males are more likely to die from them than are women. Researchers are looking at physiological gender differences such as hormone levels in search of explanations for these patterns. Some have also pointed out that interactions among gender differences in the physiological, psychological, and social domains must be examined as well (Rieker & Bird, 2005).

Ethnic Group Differences in Health ▶

10.12 How do researchers explain ethnic group differences in health?

Like gender, racial categories are associated with different patterns of health outcomes. Remember as you read that the methods used to collect health statistics often obscure important variations among subgroups of the five major groups whose health is tracked by government agencies—White Americans, African Americans, Hispanic Americans, Asian Americans and Pacific Islanders, and Native Americans. Here are a few highlights from the many findings in this area.

Group Differences in Health. African Americans have higher rates of many chronic conditions than do White Americans. For example, they have higher rates of diabetes, arthritis, and high blood pressure (National Center for Health Statistics, 2010). African Americans are 40% more likely than White Americans to die of heart disease and 30% more likely to die of cancer. Even when African and White Americans of the same age suffer from similar illnesses, the mortality rate of African Americans is higher (NCHS, 2010). And the rate of AIDS is more than three times higher among African Americans than among White Americans.

Hypertension is more prevalent among Hispanic Americans than among non-Hispanic White Americans. However, heart problems are less prevalent (NCHS, 2010). Rates of diabetes are also dramatically higher among Hispanic Americans than for other groups (NCHS, 2010).

Asian Americans are comparatively healthy. However, there are wide disparities among subgroups. For example, Vietnamese women are five times more likely to suffer from cervical cancer than White women are (CDC, 2005a). Similarly, the overall age-adjusted death rate for Asian American males is 40% lower than that for White American males, but their death rate from stroke is 8% higher.

Among Native Americans, diabetes rates are higher than they are among Whites (NCHS, 2010). Rates of alcohol abuse are higher among Native Americans as well, leading to high rates of liver disease. Deaths from liver disease are far more frequent among Native Americans than in other groups (NCHS, 2010).

Explaining Group Differences. How can such differences be explained? As you learned earlier, historical racism is one possible explanatory factor. Another is socioeconomic status. About one-fifth of African Americans, Native Americans, and Hispanic Americans live in poverty (U.S. Census Bureau, 2010). Thus, we might conclude that variables related to poverty—nutritional status, access to health care, and education, for example—explain racial differences in health.

However, studies that provide us with a closer look at the links among race, income, and health suggest otherwise. For instance, in one study, researchers found that the general health of African American and White children from middle-class families was quite similar; however, the African American children had much higher rates of asthma than did the White children in the study (Weitzman, Byrd, & Auinger, 2005). Large-scale studies of health trends also show that poor White Americans and African Americans have similar rates of health-related activity limitations in old age (NCHS, 2005). However, the rate of such limitations is nearly 50% less among older Hispanic Americans who live in poverty.

As these findings illustrate, group differences in socioeconomic factors do not fully account for group differences in health, so what other variables might contribute to them? Bioethics professor Pilar Ossorio and sociologist Troy Duster suggest that the phenomenon of *racial patterning* underlies such differences (Ossorio & Duster, 2005). Racial patterning is the tendency of groups of people to maintain their collective identities through shared behavior patterns (e.g., diet). Moreover, groups tend to share certain aspects of living conditions that may have health consequences as well (e.g., the concentration of Hispanic Americans in the desert regions of the southwestern United States). As a result of these patterns, risk and protective factors occur at different rates in different groups.

Lifestyle and Health

Thanks to the proliferation of computers all over the world and to the availability of the Internet, people who live in the industrialized nations of the world have something very important in common with those who live in the remotest regions of the developing world: a penchant for turning to the Internet for information about health (see the *Apply It;* Borzekowski, Fobil, & Asante, 2006; Cohen & Stussman, 2010). If you have searched the Net for health information, you know that any health-related search term will turn up dozens of Web sites that remind you of what you probably already know: For most of us, health enemy number one is our own habits—lack of exercise, too little sleep, alcohol or drug abuse, an unhealthy diet, and overeating. What can make someone change an unhealthy lifestyle? Perhaps vanity is the key. Health psychologists have found that people are more likely to adopt healthy behaviors if they believe behavioral change will make them look better or appear more youthful than if they simply receive information about the health benefits of the suggested change (Mahler et al., 2003). Still, there are some health-threatening behaviors that carry such grave risks that everyone ought to take them seriously. The most dangerous unhealthy behavior of all is smoking.

10.13 How does smoking affect health?

Smoking and Health

Smoking remains the foremost cause of preventable diseases and deaths in the United States (U.S. Department of Health and Human Services, 2000). That message appears to be taking root because the prevalence of smoking among American adults has been decreasing and is currently less than 20% (National Center for Health Statistics, 2010). Moreover, smoking is more likely to be viewed as a socially unacceptable behavior now than in the past (Chassin et al., 2003). But there are wide variations in smoking habits according to gender and ethnic group. The highest rates of smoking are found among Native American men (31%) and women (24%), while the lowest rates are reported for Asian American men (17%) and women (5%) (NCHS, 2010).

APPLY IT   **Interpreting Health Information on the Internet**

How reliable is the information available on the Internet? In a large-scale study of health-related Web sites sponsored by the American Medical Association, researchers found that the quality of information varied widely from one site to another (Eysenbach et al., 2002). A study of Internet-based advice for managing children's fever sponsored by the British Medical Association found that most Web sites contained erroneous information. Moreover, in a follow-up study done four years later, the researchers found that about half of the sites were no longer available; those that remained showed little improvement in the quality of information.

Despite these difficulties, physicians' organizations acknowledge the potential value of the Internet in helping patients learn about and manage their own health. And because so many older adults are using the Internet to learn about health issues, the American Association of Retired Persons (2002) has published a list of points to keep in mind when surfing the Web for health information and advice:

- *Remember that there are no rules governing what is published on the Internet.* Unlike scientific journal articles, which are usually written and reviewed by experts in the field, Internet articles can be posted by anyone, without review of any kind. Without expert knowledge, it is extremely difficult to tell whether the information and advice these articles contain are valid.

- *Consider the source.* Generally, Web sites sponsored by medical schools, government agencies, and public health organizations are reliable. Others, especially those promoting a health-related product, should be considered suspect.

- *Get a second opinion.* Ask your health care provider about Internet-based information or read what's available from several different sources on the topic.

- *Examine references.* Sites that refer to credible sources (e.g., books, other Web sites) that you can find on the Internet or in a library or bookstore are probably more reliable than sites that offer no references to support their advice.

- *How current is the information?* Health-related information changes frequently. Be certain that you are reading the most current findings and recommendations.

- *Is it too good to be true?* As in all areas of life, if something sounds too good to be true (e.g., a vitamin that cures cancer), it probably is. Try to find experimental, placebo-controlled studies that support any claims.

Using these guidelines, you can become a better consumer of Internet-based health information.

Megan
ELEMENTARY EDUCATION

 Watch on **mypsychlab.com**

Smoking increases the risk for heart disease, lung cancer, other smoking-related cancers, and emphysema. It is now known that smoking suppresses the action of T cells in the lungs, increasing susceptibility to respiratory tract infections and tumors (McCue et al., 2000). Other negative consequences from smoking include the widespread incidence of chronic bronchitis and other respiratory problems; the deaths and injuries from fires caused by smoking; and the low birth weight and retarded fetal development in babies born to smoking mothers. Furthermore, mothers who smoke during pregnancy tend to have babies who are at greater risk for anxiety and depression and who are five times more likely to become smokers themselves (Cornelius et al., 2000). And millions of nonsmokers engage in *passive smoking* by breathing smoke-filled air—with proven ill effects. Research indicates that nonsmokers who are regularly exposed to *second-hand smoke* have twice the risk of heart attack of those who are not exposed (National Center for Chronic Disease Prevention and Health Promotion, 2006). ◉⊸Watch on **mypsychlab.com**

◉⊸**Watch** the **Video** *Smoking Damage* on **mypsychlab.com**

There are many ways to quit smoking, but overall success rates for these methods, or for smoking cessation in general, can be somewhat misleading. There are many variables that affect success rates other than the desire to quit and the cessation method that a person chooses. Thus, if a study shows that only 20% of smokers using nicotine replacement, such as patches or chewing gum, succeed, reasons other than the purely physical aspects of nicotine addiction may be to blame (Rose, 2006).

The circumstances in smokers' lives may affect the outcome of their attempts to quit smoking. In one study involving more than 600 college students, researchers found that those who perceived that their lives were not very stressful had more success than other participants who felt more stress (Norman et al., 2006). Participants' overall success rate over the 18-month-long study was only 18%, but the low-perceived-stress group achieved a success rate of 52%. By contrast, only 13% of participants who perceived their lives to be highly stressful managed to quit in 18 months. The implication of these findings for others who want to quit smoking is that the often-heard recommendation that they choose a "quit date" is probably good advice. Planning a quit date to coincide with times of reduced stress, such as immediately after final exams, might be better than trying to quit at times of great stress.

Alcohol Abuse ▶

10.14 What are some health risks of alcohol abuse?

Do you use alcohol regularly? Many Americans do. Recall from Chapter 4 that *substance abuse* is defined as continued use of a substance that interferes with a person's major life roles at home, in school, at work, or elsewhere and contributes to legal difficulties or any psychological problems (American Psychiatric Association, 2000a). Alcohol is perhaps the most frequently abused substance of all, and the health costs of alcohol abuse are staggering—in fatalities, medical bills, lost work, and family problems.

When consumed to excess, alcohol can damage virtually every organ in the body, but it is especially harmful to the liver. Moreover, even a person who has never previously had a drink in his or her life can die from ingesting too much alcohol over a short period of time (see Table 10.1, p. 338). One Norwegian longitudinal study involving more than 40,000 male participants found that the rate of death prior to age 60 was significantly higher among alcoholics than nonalcoholics (Rossow & Amundsen, 1997). Alcoholics are about three times as likely to die in automobile accidents or of heart disease as nonalcoholics, and they have twice the rate of deaths from cancer.

Damage to the brains of alcoholics has been found by researchers using MRI scans (Dauringac et al., 2005). CT scans also show brain shrinkage in a high percentage of alcoholics, even in those who are young and in those who show normal cognitive functioning (Lishman, 1990). Moreover, heavy drinking can cause cognitive impairment that continues for several months after the drinking stops (Sullivan et al., 2002). The only good news in recent studies is that some of the effects of alcohol on the brain seem to be partially reversible with prolonged abstinence.

TABLE 10.1 Alcohol Poisoning

How much alcohol does it take to cause alcohol poisoning?
- This varies according to weight and tolerance for alcohol.
- Eight to ten drinks in one hour is sufficient to induce alcohol poisoning in anyone.

Are there any quick ways to sober up?
- No. There is no way to speed up elimination of alcohol from the body.
- Coffee, cold showers, walking it off, and sleeping it off don't work.

What are the signs of alcohol poisoning?
- Confusion, stupor, coma, or person can't be roused
- No response to pinching the skin
- Vomiting while asleep
- Seizures
- Slow breathing (fewer than 8 breaths per minute)
- Irregular breathing (10 seconds or more between breaths)
- Low body temperature, bluish skin, paleness

What should I do if I think someone has alcohol poisoning?
- Call 911.
- Stay with the person.
- Keep the person from choking on vomit.
- Tell paramedics how much and what type of alcohol the person drank.

Source: National Highway and Traffic Safety Administration (2007).

Since the late 1950s, the American Medical Association has maintained that alcoholism is a disease and that once an alcoholic, always an alcoholic. According to this view, even a small amount of alcohol can cause an irresistible craving for more, leading alcoholics to lose control of their drinking (Jellinek, 1960). Thus, total abstinence is seen as the only acceptable and effective method of treatment. Alcoholics Anonymous (AA) also endorses both the disease concept and the total abstinence approach to treatment. And there is a drug that may make abstinence somewhat easier. Researchers report that the drug acamprosate helps prevent relapse in recovering alcoholics (Mason et al., 2006).

Some studies suggest a genetic influence on alcoholism and lend support to the disease model. For example, the late neuroscientist Henri Begleiter (1935–2006) and his colleagues have accumulated a large body of evidence suggesting that the brains of alcoholics respond differently to visual and auditory stimuli than those of nonalcoholics (Hada et al., 2000, 2001; Prabhu et al., 2001). Further, many relatives of alcoholics, even children and adults who have never consumed any alcohol in their lives, display the same types of response patterns (Rangaswamy et al., 2007). The relatives of alcoholics who do display these patterns are more likely to become alcoholics themselves or to suffer from other types of addictions (Anokhin et al., 2000; Beirut et al., 1998). Consequently, Begleiter suggested that the brain-imaging techniques he used in his research may someday be used to determine which relatives of alcoholics are genetically predisposed to addiction (Porjesz et al., 1998).

10.15 What is the difference between bacterial and viral STDs?

Sexually Transmitted Diseases

What is the most common infectious disease in the United States? You might be surprised to learn that it is *chlamydia,* a sexually transmitted disease (CDC, 2005d). Sexually transmitted diseases (STDs) are infections spread primarily through sexual contact. The incidence of many STDs has increased dramatically over the past 30 years or so. This trend can be partly explained by more permissive attitudes toward sex and increased sexual activity among young people, some of whom have had

sexually transmitted diseases (STDs) Infections that are spread primarily through intimate sexual contact.

several sexual partners by the time they graduate from high school (look back at Figure 8.5 on page 264). Another factor is the greater use of nonbarrier methods of contraception, such as the birth control pill, which do not prevent the spread of STDs. Barrier methods, such as condoms and vaginal spermicide, provide some protection against STDs.

Chlamydia is one of many bacterial STDs, diseases that can be cured by antibiotics. It can be transmitted through many kinds of physical contact involving the genitals as well as actual intercourse (CDC, 2009a). Women are about three times as likely as men to suffer from chlamydia. The prevalence of another bacterial STD, *gonorrhea,* has declined considerably in recent years, but the strains that exist today are far more resistant to antibiotics than those that existed decades ago (CDC, 2009a). One of the long-term effects of both chlamydia and gonorrhea is *pelvic inflammatory disease,* an infection of the female reproductive tract that can cause infertility.

Another bacterial STD is *syphilis,* which can lead to serious mental disorders and death if it is not treated in the early stages of infection. At one time, syphilis had been almost completely eradicated. However, in 2008, about 46,000 cases were reported to the Centers for Disease Control and Prevention (CDC, 2009a). Most of these cases involved homosexual males who live in urban areas (CDC, 2009a). Educating such men about the dangers of syphilis and measures that may be taken to prevent its transmission has become a major focus of public health officials in recent years.

Unlike STDs caused by bacteria, viral STDs cannot be treated with antibiotics and are considered to be incurable. One such disease is *genital herpes,* a disease that can be acquired through either intercourse or oral sex. The Centers for Disease Control and Prevention reports that 17% of the adult population in the United States is infected with herpes (CDC, 2009a). Outbreaks of the disease, which include the development of painful blisters on the genitals, occur periodically in most people who carry the virus.

A more serious viral STD is *genital warts* caused by infection with *human papillomavirus (HPV).* The primary symptom of the disease, the presence of growths on the genitals, is not its most serious effect, however. HPV is strongly associated with cervical cancer (CDC, 2009a). Studies indicate that, in the United States, 29% of women in their twenties and 13% of women in their thirties are infected with HPV.

Recently, the Food and Drug Administration approved a vaccine that officials believe will protect young women against four types of HPV (CDC, 2006a). However, the vaccine is licensed for use only in females between the ages of 9 and 26, and researchers do not yet know how long the vaccine's protective effects will last. Moreover, officials point out that there are other forms of HPV against which the vaccine offers no protection. For these reasons, public health officials state that women who get the vaccine should continue to be vigilant about safe sex practices and routine medical screening.

The most feared STD is acquired immune deficiency syndrome (AIDS), caused by infection with the human immunodeficiency virus (HIV). The virus attacks the immune system until it is essentially nonfunctional. Although the first case was diagnosed in this country in 1981, there is still no cure for AIDS. Test your knowledge about AIDS in the *Try It* (p. 340).

The long search for effective treatments for HIV, chronicled in Figure 10.5 (p. 341), has produced two major victories. First, the discovery that drugs such as AZT can prevent the transmission of HIV from a pregnant woman to her fetus has saved thousands of lives. During the 1990s, nearly 2,000 infants were diagnosed with HIV each year. Thanks to widespread prenatal HIV screening and to the availability of these preventive drugs, just under 100 infants were diagnosed with HIV in 2007 (CDC, 2009b).

Second, the advent of *antiretroviral drugs* has probably prevented millions of deaths from AIDS by interfering with HIV's ability to invade healthy cells, the process through which HIV destroys its victims' immune systems. At present, the United Nations, aided by the World Bank, governments throughout the industrialized world, corporations, charitable foundations, and celebrity spokespersons, such as U2 singer Bono, is working

bacterial STDs Sexually transmitted diseases that are caused by bacteria and can be treated with antibiotics.

viral STDs Sexually transmitted diseases that are caused by viruses and are considered to be incurable.

acquired immune deficiency syndrome (AIDS) A devastating and incurable illness that is caused by infection with the human immunodeficiency virus (HIV) and progressively weakens the body's immune system, leaving the person vulnerable to opportunistic infections that usually cause death.

human immunodeficiency virus (HIV) The virus that causes AIDS.

TRY IT   AIDS Quiz

Answer *true* or *false* for each statement.

1. AIDS is a single disease. (true/false)

2. AIDS symptoms vary widely from country to country and even from risk group to risk group. (true/false)

3. Those at greatest risk for getting AIDS are people who have sex without using condoms, drug users who share needles, and infants born to AIDS-infected mothers. (true/false)

4. AIDS is one of the most highly contagious diseases. (true/false)

5. One way to avoid contracting AIDS is to use an oil-based lubricant with a condom. (true/false)

Watch on **mypsychlab.com**

Answers:

1. *False:* AIDS is not a single disease. Rather, a severely impaired immune system leaves a person with AIDS highly susceptible to a whole host of infections and diseases.

2. *True:* In the United States and Europe, AIDS sufferers may develop Kaposi's sarcoma (a rare form of skin cancer), pneumonia, and tuberculosis. In Africa, people with AIDS usually waste away with fever, diarrhea, and symptoms caused by tuberculosis.

3. *True:* Those groups are at greatest risk. Screening of blood donors and testing of donated blood have greatly reduced the risk of contracting AIDS through blood transfusions. Today, women make up the fastest-growing group of infected people worldwide, as AIDS spreads among heterosexuals, especially in Africa.

4. *False:* AIDS is not among the most highly infectious diseases. You cannot get AIDS from kissing, shaking hands, or using objects handled by people who have AIDS.

5. *False:* Do not use oil-based lubricants, which can eat through condoms. Latex condoms with an effective spermicide are safer. Learn the sexual history of any potential partner, including HIV test results. Don't have sex with prostitutes.

to provide the funding needed to supply antiretroviral drugs to developing regions in which HIV-infection rates are particularly high, such as sub-Saharan Africa (Global Fund to Fight AIDS, Tuberculosis, and Malaria, 2005; Merson, 2006). Preliminary results suggest that these efforts have been quite effective. The number of new cases of HIV/AIDS in developing regions has leveled off and may even be declining (United Nations, 2008). These programs have also reduced rates of mother-to-child transmission of the disease as well as HIV-related infant deaths in these parts of the world (Violari et al., 2008).

Researchers believe that HIV is transmitted primarily through the exchange of blood, semen, or vaginal secretions during sexual contact or when IV (intravenous) drug users share contaminated needles or syringes. In the United States, about 11% of those with AIDS are IV drug users, but homosexual men represent the largest number of HIV carriers and AIDS cases (CDC, 2009b). Anal intercourse is more dangerous than coitus because rectal tissue often tears during penetration, allowing HIV ready entry into the bloodstream. However, it is a mistake to view AIDS as a disease confined to gay men; about 30% of those diagnosed with AIDS are women. Figure 10.6 (p. 342) illustrates the rates of infection in the United States in 2007 for four different modes of transmission: (1) male/male sexual relations; (2) male/female sexual relations; (3) intravenous drug use; and (4) male/male sexual relations combined with intravenous drug use (CDC, 2009b). You may be surprised to learn that almost a third of new HIV cases in that year resulted from heterosexual contact.

Researchers have recently discovered that circumcision substantially reduces the risk of HIV transmission (Siegfried et al., 2009). In response, public health officials in many of the developing nations that have large populations of HIV-positive men, such as Uganda, have begun educating the public about the procedure along with other ways of reducing risk of infection (Cassell et al., 2006). Screening and treatment for other STDs are vital to the prevention of HIV (CDC, 2009a) as well. Research has shown that the presence of another STD in an HIV-infected person causes him or her to have higher levels of the communicable form of the virus in his or her bodily fluids. Anyone who has sex with such a person is, therefore, at a greatly increased risk of becoming infected with HIV.

What are the psychological effects on people who struggle to cope with this fearsome disease? The reaction to the news that one is HIV-positive is frequently shock,

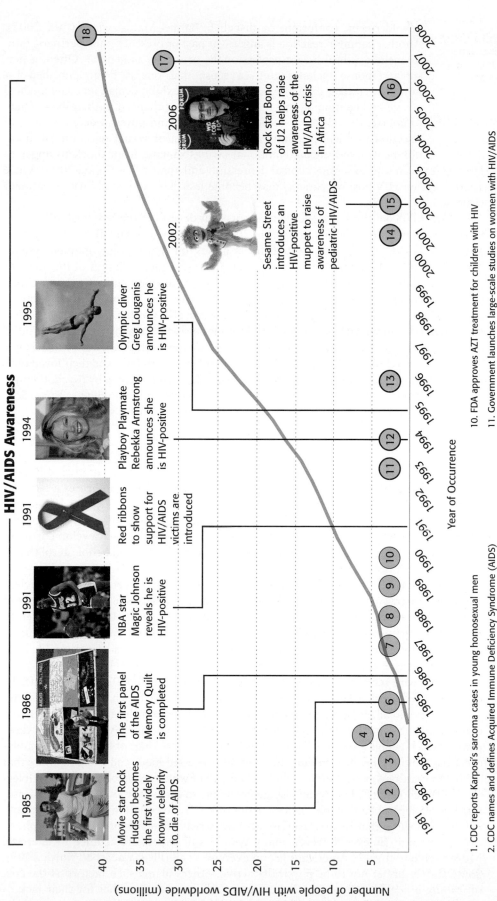

HIV/AIDS Awareness

Number of people with HIV/AIDS worldwide (millions)

Year of Occurrence

1985 — Movie star Rock Hudson becomes the first widely known celebrity to die of AIDS

1986 — The first panel of the AIDS Memory Quilt is completed

1991 — NBA star Magic Johnson reveals he is HIV-positive

1991 — Red ribbons to show support for HIV/AIDS victims are introduced

1994 — Playboy Playmate Rebekka Armstrong announces she is HIV-positive

1995 — Olympic diver Greg Louganis announces he is HIV-positive

2002 — Sesame Street introduces an HIV-positive muppet to raise awareness of pediatric HIV/AIDS

2006 — Rock star Bono of U2 helps raise awareness of the HIV/AIDS crisis in Africa

1. CDC reports Karposi's sarcoma cases in young homosexual men
2. CDC names and defines Acquired Immune Deficiency Syndrome (AIDS)
3. Officials warn public about infection risk associated with blood transfusions
4. Researchers identify HIV as cause of AIDS
5. Officials issue advisories about infection risk associated with IV-drug use
6. Blood banks begin screening supplies for HIV
7. FDA approves experimental drugs for AIDS
8. CDC mails brochure about HIV/AIDS to every home in the United States
9. Government changes policies to speed up drug approval process
10. FDA approves AZT treatment for children with HIV
11. Government launches large-scale studies on women with HIV/AIDS
12. FDA approves AZT for pregnant women with HIV
13. HIV/AIDS cases decline for the first time since 1982 in the U.S.
14. Lower-cost generic drugs for HIV/AIDS become available
15. FDA approves first finger-prick test for HIV
16. FDA approves triple-drug therapy
17. Experts recommend circumcision to reduce risk of HIV transmission
18. Number of HIV-positive adults receiving antiretroviral drugs in poor countries has increased seven-fold since 2004.

FIGURE 10.5 Milestones from the History of HIV/AIDS
Source: Kaiser Family Foundation (2010).

341

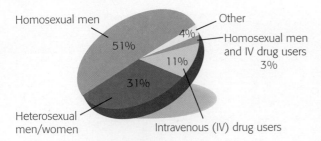

FIGURE 10.6 How HIV Is Transmitted in AIDS Cases in the United States
Source: CDC (2009c).

bewilderment, confusion, or disbelief (Bargiel-Matusiewicz et al., 2005). Another common reaction is anger—at past or present sexual partners, family members, health care professionals, or society in general. Often, a person's response includes guilt, a sense that one is being punished for homosexuality or drug abuse. Other people exhibit denial, ignoring medical advice and continuing to act as if nothing has changed in their lives. Then, of course, there is fear—of death; of mental and physical deterioration; of rejection by friends, family, and co-workers; of sexual rejection; of abandonment. Experiencing emotional swings ranging from shock to anger to guilt to fear can lead to serious clinical depression and apathy (Tate et al., 2003). Once apathy sets in, HIV-positive patients may become less likely to comply with treatment (Dilorio et al., 2009).

Once AIDS develops, a sequence of events that devastates the brains of 40% of its victims is set in motion (Thompson et al., 2005). The cortex of an AIDS victim gradually thins as the disease gains ground in its attack on the person's immune system. Motor and language impairments often result from slow deterioration of the areas of the cortex that are involved in these functions. Cortical thinning causes some AIDS patients to develop *AIDS-related dementia,* a disorder that is similar to Alzheimer's disease. Researchers say that some people who are HIV-positive but who have not developed full-blown AIDS show cortical thinning to some extent as well. Thus, studies are currently underway to determine the best way to approach this effect of the virus.

To cope psychologically, AIDS patients, those infected with HIV, and their loved ones need education and information about the disease. They can be helped by psychotherapy, self-help groups, and medications such as antidepressants and anti-anxiety drugs. Self-help groups and group therapy may serve as an extended family for some patients.

10.16 How do diet and exercise affect health?

Diet and Exercise

In Chapter 9, you learned about obesity as it relates to the primary motive of hunger and read that a BMI in excess of 30 is considered obese. Obesity increases a person's chances of developing several chronic diseases (CDC, 2006e). These conditions include high blood pressure, type 2 diabetes, gallbladder disease, arthritis, and respiratory disorders. In addition, people who are obese are more likely to develop coronary heart disease and to have elevated levels of LDL cholesterol (the bad cholesterol that is associated with heart disease).

Health problems may also develop in people whose diets have insufficient amounts of particular nutrients (CDC, 2006e). For example, a diet that is deficient in iron leads to *anemia,* a condition that impairs the blood's ability to deliver oxygen to the body's organs. Likewise, a diet that lacks sufficient calcium may cause degeneration of the bones. And pregnant women whose diets lack folic acid are more likely to deliver infants with spinal defects.

People who regularly consume fast foods are at risk for both obesity and specific nutritional deficiencies. Thus, nutrition experts recommend that such food be eaten infrequently or not at all. To help consumers achieve this goal, experts have also developed several strategies for improving overall diet quality. One simple approach is the "5-a-day" plan in which people are advised to try to eat at least five servings of fruits and vegetables every day. Another involves reading the labels of processed foods and avoiding those that are high in saturated fats, trans fats, and sodium, all of which are associated with high levels of LDL cholesterol. Labels can also guide people to foods that are high in monosaturated fats, a type of fat that may increase levels of HDL cholesterol (the good cholesterol).

Studies show that regular exercise also pays rich dividends in the form of physical and mental fitness. However, many people still express reluctance to exercise. More than one-third of Americans get no exercise at all (Pleis, Lucas, & Ward, 2009). Some simply prefer not to be physically active; others blame such factors as the cost of joining a health club or even the unpredictability of the weather for their lack of physical activity (Salmon et al., 2003). Such individuals are missing out on one of the simplest and most effective ways of enhancing one's health.

Aerobic exercise (such as running, swimming, brisk walking, bicycling, rowing, and jumping rope) is exercise that uses the large muscle groups in continuous, repetitive action and increases oxygen intake and breathing and heart rates. To improve cardiovascular fitness and endurance and to lessen the risk of heart attack, an individual should perform aerobic exercise regularly—five times a week for 20 to 30 minutes (CDC, 2006b). Less than 20 minutes of aerobic exercise three times a week has "no measurable effect on the heart," and more than 3 hours per week "is not known to reduce cardiovascular risk any further" (Simon, 1988, p. 3). However, individuals who engage in more than 3 hours of aerobic activity each week are more successful at losing excess weight and keeping it off than are those who exercise less (Votruba, Horvitz, & Schoeller, 2000).

In case you are not yet convinced, consider the following benefits of exercise (Mayo Clinic, 2009):

▲ Regular aerobic exercise improves cardiovascular fitness in people of all ages.

- Improves mood
- Combats chronic diseases such as high blood pressure, diabetes, and osteoporosis
- Helps manage weight
- Boosts energy level
- Promotes better sleep
- Improves sexual intimacy
- Enhances enjoyment of life

Exercise also appears to moderate the effects of aging on the body. Strength training, for example, has been found to reduce *sarcopenia,* an age-related process in which the muscles deteriorate (CDC, 2006b). Such training appears to prevent the loss of bone mass, or *osteoporosis,* as well. Moreover, physical exercise helps seniors with balance, coordination, and stamina.

aerobic exercise (ah-RO-bik) Exercise that uses the large muscle groups in continuous, repetitive action and increases oxygen intake and breathing and heart rates.

alternative medicine Any treatment or therapy that has not been scientifically demonstrated to be effective.

Alternative Medicine ▶

Americans spend billions of dollars each year on unconventional treatments—herbs, massage, self-help groups, megavitamins, folk remedies, and homeopathy—for a variety of illnesses and conditions. In one such survey, the National Science Foundation (NSF, 2002) found that 88% of Americans believe that there are valid ways of preventing and curing illnesses that are not recognized by the medical profession. Thus, it isn't surprising that some 40% of adults and children in the United States take at least one vitamin pill each day for the purpose of preventing or treating some kind of health condition (NHANES, 2002). In addition, 38% of adults and 12% of children use some kind of nonmedical therapy to treat a current medical condition (Barnes, Bloom, & Nahin, 2008). Figure 10.7 shows the most popular therapies. The "other" category in the figure includes treatments such as acupuncture, biofeedback, guided imagery, progressive relaxation, hypnosis, Pilates, traditional healers, and a host of other alternative therapies.

The National Science Foundation (2002) defines alternative medicine as any treatment or therapy that has not been scientifically demonstrated to be effective. Even a simple practice such as taking vitamins sometimes falls into this category. For instance, if you take Vitamin C to protect yourself against the common cold, you are using alternative medicine because Vitamin C has not been scientifically proven to prevent colds.

Most people who use alternative treatments do not inform their physicians about them. Health professionals cite this tendency toward secrecy as a major risk factor in the use of alternative medicine (Yale-New Haven Hospital, 2003). They point out that many therapies, especially those that involve food supplements,

10.17 What are the benefits and risks associated with alternative medicine?

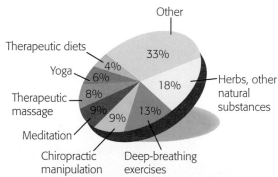

FIGURE 10.7 Alternative Therapies
In the United States, 38% of adults and 12% of children use one or more alternative treatments to treat or prevent disease. The "other" category includes acupuncture, biofeedback, guided imagery, progressive relaxation, hypnosis, Pilates, traditional healers, and a host of other treatments.
Source: Barnes et al. (2007).

▲ Many individuals turn to vitamins and other nutritional supplements to improve their health and fight disease. These substances can interact with prescription medications, so health care professionals strongly recommend that patients inform their doctors if they are taking some kind of supplement.

have pharmacological effects that can interfere with treatments prescribed by physicians. Consequently, individuals who use alternative treatments should tell their physicians about them. While doctors may be skeptical about the utility of the alternative treatments, they need to have this information about their patients to practice conventional medicine effectively. Moreover, faith in an alternative treatment may cause an individual to delay seeking necessary conventional medical treatment.

Although it is true that some alternative therapies may be helpful in both preventing and treating illness, most health professionals agree that lifestyle changes bring greater health benefits than do any methods of alternative medicine. Unfortunately, many people resist making lifestyle changes because they see them as taking too long to be effective or being too difficult to carry out. However, Table 10.2 shows that the benefits of various lifestyle changes, some of which are fairly easy to achieve, can be well worth the effort.

TABLE 10.2 **Benefits of Lifestyle Changes**

LIFESTYLE CHANGE	BENEFITS
If overweight, lose just 10 pounds.	34% reduction in triglyceride levels; 16% decrease in total cholesterol; 18% increase in HDL ("good" cholesterol); significant reduction in blood pressure; decreased risk of diabetes, sleep apnea, and osteoarthritis (Still, 2001).
Add 20 to 30 grams of fiber to your diet each day.	Improved bowel function; reduced risk of colon cancer and other digestive system diseases; decrease in total cholesterol; reduced blood pressure; improved insulin function in both diabetics and nondiabetics (HCF, 2003).
Engage in moderate physical activity every day (e.g., walk up and down stairs for 15 minutes; spend 30 minutes washing a car).	Reduced feelings of anxiety and sadness; increased bone density; reduced risk of diabetes, heart disease, high blood pressure, and many other life-shortening diseases (CDC, 1999).
Stop smoking at any age, after any number of years of smoking.	*Immediate:* improved circulation; reduced blood level of carbon monoxide; stabilization of pulse rate and blood pressure; improved sense of smell and taste; improved lung function and endurance; reduced risk of lung infections such as pneumonia and bronchitis. *Long-term:* reduced risk of lung cancer (declines substantially with each year of abstinence); decreased risk of other smoking-related illnesses such as emphysema and heart disease; decreased risk of cancer recurrence in those who have been treated for some form of cancer (National Cancer Institute, 2000).
Get recommended annual or 5-year screenings beginning at these ages	*Women:* (21) Chlamydia, cervical cancer screenings if sexually active; (35), cholesterol test; (50) mammogram, colorectal exam; (65) vision, hearing tests *Men:* (30) EKG, cholesterol test; (40) PSA test for prostate cancer; (50) colorectal exam; (65) vision, hearing tests

☉⚬ Looking Back

In the section of this chapter that discussed stress, you learned that exerting control over controllable stressors can help you cope. The same is true of health. And, although the list of lifestyle changes in Table 10.2 may be intimidating, you need not make *all* of them to improve your chances of a healthy future. You might consider starting with just one. Even if you never make another change, you are likely to live longer and be healthier than you would have otherwise been.

CHAPTER 10 SUMMARY

SOURCES OF STRESS (pp. 318-324)

10.1 How does the life events approach describe stress? (pp. 318-320)

The life events approach focuses on individuals' responses to the stresses associated with major life changes. The SRRS assesses stress in terms of major life events, positive or negative, that necessitate change and adaptation. Holmes and Rahe found a relationship between degree of life stress (as measured on the scale) and major health problems. Research on responses to catastrophic events shows that people respond differently to such stressors. Some people develop posttraumatic stress disorder (PTSD), a prolonged, severe stress reaction, often characterized by flashbacks, nightmares, or intrusive memories of the traumatic event.

Key Terms
stress, p. 318
stressor, p. 318
life events approach, p. 318
Social Readjustment Rating Scale (SRRS), p. 318
posttraumatic stress disorder (PTSD), p. 320

10.2 What do hassles, uplifts, and choices contribute to stress? (pp. 320–321)

Some theorists argue that everyday stressors are more important than major life events. According to Lazarus, daily hassles typically cause more stress than major life changes. Positive experiences in life—or uplifts—can neutralize the effects of many of the hassles, however. Choices are another important source of stress in everyday life. In an approach-approach conflict, a person must decide between equally desirable alternatives. In an avoidance-avoidance conflict, the choice is between two undesirable alternatives. In an approach-avoidance conflict, a person is both drawn to and repelled by a single choice.

Key Terms
hassles, p. 320
uplifts, p. 321
approach-approach conflict, p. 321
avoidance-avoidance conflict, p. 321
approach-avoidance conflict, p. 321

10.3 What variables contribute to workers' comfort zone? (pp. 321-322)

Nine variables influence a worker's comfort zone. They include workload, clarity of job description and evaluation criteria, physical variables, job status, accountability, task variety, human contact, physical challenge, and mental challenge. Discrimination and harassment contribute to work-related stress. Job stress affects employees' effectiveness, absenteeism, tardiness, accidents, substance abuse, and morale. Chronic work stress can lead to burnout.

Key Term
burnout, p. 322

10.4 What are some social sources of stress? (pp. 322-324)

People of low socioeconomic status have more stress-related health problems than those of higher status. Stressors associated with low SES include lifestyle factors such as smoking as well as higher levels of stress hormones. Perceived status may predict health outcomes better than objective status. Unemployment is another status variable that is related to health. People who lose their jobs suffer more stress-related illnesses in the months following job loss than peers who are still employed.

Key Term
socioeconomic status, p. 323

THE HEALTH-STRESS CONNECTION (pp. 324-332)

10.5 How does the biopsychosocial model approach health and illness? (pp. 324-325)

The biomedical model focuses on illness rather than on health and explains illness in terms of biological factors. The biopsychosocial model focuses on health as well as on illness and holds that both are determined by a combination of biological, psychological, and social factors. Health psychologists use the biopsychosocial model to understand and influence the contributions of psychological factors to communication between health care professionals and patients, pain management, the influence of psychological and behavioral factors on specific diseases, gender and group differences in health, and health-related lifestyle behaviors. They have found that stress plays a role in all of these domains.

Key Terms
biomedical model, p. 324
biopsychosocial model, p. 324
health psychology, p. 324

10.6 How does the fight-or-flight response affect health? (pp. 325-326)

When a stressor occurs, the sympathetic nervous system prepares the body to oppose it or flee from it (the fight-or-flight response). Prolonged stress causes the body to try to maintain the fight-or-flight response over a long period of time. The biochemicals associated with the fight-or-flight response can make the body more vulnerable to illness through their direct actions on tissues. The fight-or-flight response also influences health indirectly because it suppresses the immune system.

Key Terms
fight-or-flight response, p. 326
lymphocytes, p. 326
psychoneuroimmunology, p. 326

10.7 How do theorists explain physiological and psychological responses to stress? (pp. 326-328)

The general adaptation syndrome (GAS) proposed by Selye is the predictable sequence of reactions that organisms show in response to stressors. It consists of the alarm stage, the resistance stage, and the exhaustion stage. Lazarus maintains that when confronted with a potentially stressful event, a person engages in a cognitive appraisal process consisting of (1) a primary appraisal, to evaluate the relevance of the situation to one's well-being (whether it will be positive, irrelevant, or negative), and (2) a secondary appraisal, to evaluate one's resources and determine how to cope with the stressor.

Key Terms
general adaptation syndrome (GAS), p. 327
alarm stage, p. 327
resistance stage, p. 327
exhaustion stage, p. 327
primary appraisal, p. 327
secondary appraisal, p. 327

10.8 What factors promote resilience in the face of stress? (pp. 328-332)

Coping strategies help us overcome stress. Problem-focused coping is a direct response aimed at reducing, modifying, or eliminating the source of stress; emotion-focused coping involves reappraising a stressor in order to reduce its emotional impact. Other factors that promote resilience include optimism, hardiness, social involvement, social support, and perceived control.

Key Terms
risk/resilience model, p. 328
coping, p. 329
problem-focused coping, p. 329
emotion-focused coping, p. 329
proactive coping, p. 330
hardiness, p. 330
social support, p. 331

HEALTH AND ILLNESS (pp. 332-335)

10.9 How do lifestyle, heredity, and personality influence coronary heart disease? (pp. 332-333)

The Type A behavior pattern, often cited as a risk factor for coronary heart disease, is characterized by a sense of time urgency, impatience, excessive competitive drive, hostility, and easily aroused anger. The Type B behavior pattern is characterized by a relaxed, easygoing approach to life, without the time urgency, impatience, and hostility of the Type A pattern. People with the Type D behavior pattern experience high levels of negative emotions that they usually suppress.

Key Terms
Type A behavior pattern, p. 332
Type B behavior pattern, p. 332
Type D behavior pattern, p. 333

10.10 How do psychological factors influence cancer patients' quality of life? (p. 333-334)

Research does not support the idea that stress causes cancer. However, stress associated with cancer treatment affects how the immune system responds to treatment. In addition, variables such as optimism contribute to cancer patients' resistance to stress. Therapy can help patients maintain a positive emotional state and cope more effectively with the pain they experience.

10.11 How do males and females differ with regard to health? (p. 334)

Women are more likely than men to die following heart surgery. Generally, though, men are more likely than women to die from most diseases, but women are generally less healthy. When men and women have the same diseases, men are often more seriously ill. Researchers suspect these patterns may be caused by the unique physiology of each gender.

10.12 How do researchers explain ethnic group differences in health? (p. 335)

Some researchers believe that African Americans have greater levels of high blood pressure than members of other groups because of stress due to historical racism. African Americans who express high levels of concern about racism display larger cardiovascular responses to experimentally induced stressors than do their peers who express lower levels of concern. Racial patterning produces correlations between race and health through its influence on group differences in risk and protective factors.

LIFESTYLE AND HEALTH (pp. 336-344)

10.13 **How does smoking affect health? (pp. 336-337)**

Smoking is considered the most dangerous health-related behavior because it is directly related to over 400,000 deaths each year, including deaths from heart disease, lung cancer, and respiratory diseases.

10.14 **What are some health risks of alcohol abuse? (pp. 337-338)**

Alcohol abuse damages virtually every organ in the body, including the liver, heart, and brain. Alcoholics are three times as likely to die in motor vehicle accidents as nonalcoholics.

10.15 **What is the difference between bacterial and viral STDs? (pp. 338-342)**

The major sexually transmitted diseases caused by bacteria are chlamydia, gonorrhea, and syphilis. All can be cured with antibiotics. However, chlamydia and gonorrhea pose a particular threat to women because, unlike men, women with these infections typically have no symptoms or very mild symptoms, making prompt diagnosis and treatment less likely. If the infection spreads, it may result in infertility. Viral STDs include the human papilloma virus (HPV), genital herpes, and HIV/AIDS. Viral infections presently are not curable, but a vaccine is available to protect women against some strains of HPV. HIV gradually renders the immune system nonfunctional. Psychotherapy, self-help groups, and antidepressant medication can be helpful to those coping with HIV/AIDS.

Key Terms

sexually transmitted diseases (STDs), p. 338

bacterial STDs, p. 339
viral STDs, p. 339
acquired immune deficiency syndrome (AIDS), p. 339
human immunodeficiency virus (HIV), p. 339

10.16 **How do diet and exercise affect health? (pp. 342-343)**

Obesity is related to many chronic health conditions. Nutrient deficiencies also cause problems. Fast-food consumers are at risk for both obesity and dietary deficiencies. Guidelines based on the latest research are available to help people improve the quality of their diets. Regular aerobic exercise reduces the risk of cardiovascular disease, increases muscular strength, makes bones denser and stronger, and helps one maintain a desirable weight.

Key Terms

aerobic exercise, p. 343

10.17 **What are the benefits and risks associated with alternative medicine? (pp. 343-344)**

Alternative medicine, or the use of any treatment that has not been proven scientifically to be effective, may be helpful in both preventing and treating illness in some instances. However, many patients increase their risk of poor outcomes by not telling their physicians about their use of alternative treatments. And some people delay seeking necessary conventional medical treatment because they believe that alternative approaches will work.

Key Term

alternative medicine, p. 343

MAP IT

Log on to MyPsychLab and click on "Map It" to prepare a unique digital map of the chapter that you can save for later use, email to your instructor, or print out to use as a study tool. Or, create your own map by drawing one on paper. Use the starter map below as a model for your own map. Use the chapter summary as your guide for what to include. For each item in your map, be sure to include the page number.

Here's one way to *Map It*:

1. Draw a box at the top of the page for the section title.
2. Underneath the section title box, working horizontally across the page, draw a box for each learning question in the section. Write the learning questions in the boxes and draw a line from the section title to each questions box. After you read each subsection, jot an answer for the learning question in the subsection's box.
3. Below each learning question box, insert another box for all of the key terms that are related to the question, along with a very brief reminder of each term's definition. Draw a line from the question box to the key terms box.
4. Below each key terms box, create another box and list all of the helpful figures, tables, and other elements of the text, such as *Try It* and *Apply It* boxes. Draw a line from the key terms box to the helpful elements box.

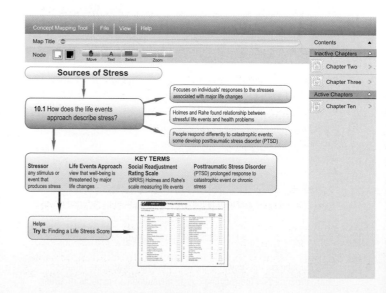

Chapter 10 Study Guide

Answers to all the Study Guide questions are provided at the end of the book.

SECTION ONE: Chapter Review

Sources of Stress (pp. 318–324)

1. On the Social Readjustment Rating Scale, only negative life changes are considered stressful. (true/false)

2. The Social Readjustment Rating Scale takes account of the individual's perceptions of the stressfulness of the life change in assigning stress points. (true/false)

3. Posttraumatic stress disorder is a prolonged and severe stress reaction that results when a number of common sources of stress occur simultaneously. (true/false)

4. According to Lazarus, hassles typically account for more life stress than major life changes. (true/false)

5. Lazarus's approach to measuring hassles and uplifts considers individual perceptions of stressful events. (true/false)

6. Travis cannot decide whether to go out or stay home and study for his test. What kind of conflict does he have?
   - **a.** approach-approach
   - **b.** avoidance-avoidance
   - **c.** approach-avoidance
   - **d.** ambivalence-ambivalence

7. Sources of workplace stress for women include
   - **a.** sexual harassment.
   - **b.** discrimination.
   - **c.** balancing family and work demands.
   - **d.** all of the above.

8. The group that has received the most attention from researchers interested in the association between stress and racism is
   - **a.** Native Americans.
   - **b.** Hispanic Americans.
   - **c.** Asian Americans.
   - **d.** African Americans.

The Stress-Health Connection (pp. 324–332)

9. The biomedical model focuses on _____; the biopsychosocial model focuses on _____.
   - **a.** illness; illness
   - **b.** health and illness; illness
   - **c.** illness; health and illness
   - **d.** health and illness; health and illness

10. Lowered immune response has been associated with
    - **a.** stress.
    - **b.** depression.
    - **c.** stress and depression.
    - **d.** neither stress nor depression.

11. The stage of the general adaptation syndrome marked by intense physiological efforts to adapt to the stressor is the (alarm, resistance) stage.

12. Susceptibility to illness increases during the (alarm, exhaustion) stage of the general adaptation syndrome.

13. Selye focused on the (psychological, physiological) aspects of stress; Lazarus focused on the (psychological, physiological) aspects of stress.

14. During secondary appraisal, a person
    - **a.** evaluates his or her coping resources and considers options for dealing with the stressor.
    - **b.** determines whether an event is positive, neutral, or negative.
    - **c.** determines whether an event involves loss, threat, or challenge.
    - **d.** determines whether an event causes physiological or psychological stress.

15. Coping aimed at reducing, modifying, or eliminating a source of stress is called (emotion-focused, problem-focused) coping; that aimed at reducing an emotional reaction to stress is called (emotion-focused, problem-focused) coping.

16. People typically use a combination of problem-focused and emotion-focused coping when dealing with a stressful situation. (true/false)

17. Some research suggests that optimists are more stress-resistant than pessimists. (true/false)

18. Which of the following is not a dimension of psychological hardiness?
    - **a.** a feeling that adverse circumstances can be controlled and changed
    - **b.** a sense of commitment and deep involvement in personal goals
    - **c.** a tendency to look on change as a challenge rather than a threat
    - **d.** close, supportive relationships with family and friends

19. Social support tends to reduce stress but is unrelated to health outcomes. (true/false)

Health and Illness (pp. 332–335)

20. Most research has pursued the connection between the Type A behavior pattern and
    - **a.** cancer.
    - **b.** coronary heart disease.
    - **c.** stroke.
    - **d.** ulcers.

21. Recent research suggests that the most toxic component of the Type A behavior pattern is
    - **a.** hostility.
    - **b.** impatience.
    - **c.** a sense of time urgency.
    - **d.** perfectionism.

22. Stress causes cancer. (true/false)

23. Which statement about gender differences in health is false?
    - **a.** Women are more likely than men to die within a year of having heart surgery.
    - **b.** Men seek medical care more often than women.
    - **c.** Fatal diseases progress more quickly in men than in women.
    - **d.** Smoking-related diseases afflict male and female smokers about equally.

24. Which ethnic group has the highest rate of death from liver disease?
    - **a.** Whites
    - **b.** African Americans
    - **c.** Hispanic Americans
    - **d.** Native Americans

Lifestyle and Health (pp. 336–344)

25. Which is the most important factor leading to disease and death?
    - **a.** unhealthy lifestyle
    - **b.** a poor health care system
    - **c.** environmental hazards
    - **d.** genetic disorders

26. Which health-compromising behavior is responsible for the most deaths?
    - **a.** overeating
    - **b.** smoking
    - **c.** lack of exercise
    - **d.** excessive alcohol use

27. (Alcohol, Smoking) damages virtually every organ in the body.

28. Viral STDs are those that can be effectively treated with antibiotics. (true/false)

29. HIV eventually causes a breakdown in the _____ system.
   a. circulatory
   b. vascular
   c. immune
   d. respiratory

30. The incidence of AIDS in the United States is highest among
   a. IV drug users.
   b. hemophiliacs.
   c. homosexuals.
   d. heterosexuals.

31. To improve cardiovascular fitness, aerobic exercise should be done
   a. 15 minutes daily.
   b. 1 hour daily.
   c. 20 to 30 minutes five times a week.
   d. 20 to 30 minutes three or four times a week.

32. Alternative health treatments have proven to be just as effective as traditional approaches to illness. (true/false)

SECTION TWO: The Biopsychosocial Model of Health and Illness

List at least two forces for each of the following:

1. Biological forces favoring health and wellness _____ _____

2. Biological forces working against health and wellness _____ _____

3. Psychological forces favoring health and wellness _____ _____

4. Psychological forces working against health and wellness _____ _____

5. Social forces favoring health and wellness _____ _____

6. Social forces working against health and wellness _____ _____

SECTION THREE: Fill in the Blank

1. Medicine has been dominated by the _____ model, which focuses on illness rather than on health, whereas the _____ model asserts that both health and illness are determined by a combination of biological, psychological, and social factors.

2. The field of psychology that is concerned with the psychological factors that contribute to health, illness, and recovery is known as _____ _____.

3. The fight-or-flight response is controlled by the _____ _____ _____ and the endocrine glands.

4. The first stage of the general adaptation syndrome is the _____ stage.

5. The stage of the general adaptation syndrome during which the adrenal glands release hormones to help the body resist stressors is called the _____ stage.

6. Lazarus's theory is considered a _____ theory of stress and coping.

7. Noelle knew that her upcoming job interview would be difficult, so she tried to anticipate the kinds of questions she would be asked and practiced the best possible responses. Noelle was practicing _____ coping.

8. The most feared disease related to the immune system is _____.

9. The primary means of transmission of HIV is through sexual contact between _____ _____ .

10. Daily _____ are the "irritating, frustrating, distressing demands and troubled relationships that plague us day in and day out."

11. Tiffany is a psychologist who works with biologists and medical researchers to determine the effects of psychological factors on the immune system. Tiffany works in the field of _____ _____.

12. People with the Type _____ behavior pattern have a strong sense of time urgency and are impatient, excessively competitive, hostile, and easily angered.

13. The effects of alcohol on _____ may continue for several months after an alcoholic stops drinking.

14. _____ appraisal is an evaluation of the significance of a potentially stressful event according to how it will affect one's well-being—whether it is perceived as irrelevant or as involving harm, loss, threat, or challenge.

15. African Americans may have a greater incidence of _____ _____ _____ than White Americans because of the stress associated with historical racism.

16. A _____ is any event capable of producing physical or emotional stress.

17. Cole wants to get a flu shot, but he is also very afraid of needles. He is faced with an _____ _____ conflict.

18. The Social Readjustment Rating Scale is an example of the _____ _____ approach to identifying stressors.

SECTION FOUR: Comprehensive Practice Test

1. Stress consists of the threats and problems we encounter in life. (true/false)

2. Hans Selye developed the
   a. diathesis stress model.
   b. general adaptation syndrome model.
   c. cognitive stress model.
   d. conversion reaction model.

3. The fight-or-flight response is seen in the _____ stage of the general adaptation syndrome.
   a. alarm
   b. exhaustion
   c. resistance
   d. arousal

4. Lack of exercise, poor diet, and disease and injury are considered to be _____ forces that work against health and wellness.
   a. environmental
   b. psychological
   c. biological
   d. social

5. Charlotte has been looking for new bedroom furniture and has found two styles that she really likes. She is trying to decide which one she will purchase. Charlotte is experiencing an _____ conflict.
   a. approach-approach
   b. approach-avoidance
   c. avoidance-avoidance
   d. avoidance-approach

6. Perceived control over a situation can have an important beneficial influence on how a stressor affects you even if you do not exercise that control. (true/false)

7. Posttraumatic stress disorder leaves some people more vulnerable to future mental health problems. (true/false)

8. Which of the following is not a variable in work stress?

a. workload
b. clarity of job description
c. perceived equity of pay for work
d. task variety

9. Research indicates that African Americans who are highly concerned about _____ are more sensitive to stressors than their peers who are less concerned.

10. Religious faith can help people cope with negative life events. (true/false)

11. Lazarus's term for the positive experiences that can serve to cancel out the effects of day-to-day hassles is
a. stress assets.
b. coping mechanisms.
c. uplifts.
d. appraisals.

12. Type B behavior patterns seem to be more correlated with heart disease than do Type A behavior patterns. (true/false)

13. B cells produce antibodies that are effective in destroying antigens that live _____ the body cells; T cells are important in the destruction of antigens that live _____ the body cells.
a. outside; inside
b. inside; outside

14. AIDS is caused by HIV, often called the AIDS virus. (true/false)

15. HIV weakens the immune system by attacking T cells. (true/false)

SECTION FIVE: Critical Thinking

1. In your view, which is more effective for evaluating stress: the Social Readjustment Rating Scale or the Hassle Scale? Explain the advantages and disadvantages of each.

2. Prepare two arguments: one supporting the position that alcoholism is a genetically inherited disease, and the other supporting the position that alcoholism is not a medical disease but results from learning.

3. Choose several stress-producing incidents from your life and explain what problem-focused and emotion-focused coping strategies you used. From the knowledge you have gained in this chapter, list other coping strategies that might have been more effective.

Personality Theory and Assessment

Think About It

Who or what is in control of your life? We all know that we don't have total control, but what do you believe about your ability to at least influence what happens to you? Give some serious thought to your beliefs about control by responding to the following statements. For each one, indicate whether you agree or disagree.

1. Heredity determines most of a person's personality.
2. Chance has a lot to do with being successful.
3. Whatever plans you make, something will always interfere.
4. Being at the right place at the right time is essential for getting what you want in life.
5. Intelligence is a given, and it cannot be improved.
6. If I successfully accomplish a task, it's because it was an easy one.
7. You cannot change your destiny.
8. School success is mostly a result of one's socioeconomic background.
9. People are lonely because they are not given the chance to meet new people.
10. Setting goals for yourself is of little use because nobody knows what might happen in the future to interfere with them.

Give yourself 1 point for each "agree" and 0 points for each "disagree." Is your score closer to 0 or closer to 10? Scores ranging from 0 to 4 suggest that you believe that you have some degree of control over what happens to you, and scores from 7 to 10 indicate just the opposite. As you learned in Chapter 10, believing you have at least some degree of control over a stressor helps you cope with it effectively. A sense of personal control is an important feature of personality.

personality A person's characteristic patterns of behaving, thinking, and feeling.

psychoanalysis (SY-co-ah-NAL-ih-sis) Freud's theory of personality and his therapy for treating psychological disorders; focuses on unconscious processes.

conscious (KON-shus) The thoughts, feelings, sensations, or memories of which a person is aware at any given moment.

11.1 What concepts did Freud propose to explain personality?

preconscious The thoughts, feelings, and memories that a person is not consciously aware of at the moment but that may be easily brought to consciousness.

unconscious (un-KON-shus) For Freud, the primary motivating force of human behavior, containing repressed memories as well as instincts, wishes, and desires that have never been conscious.

id (ID) The unconscious system of the personality, which contains the life and death instincts and operates on the pleasure principle; source of the libido.

▲ Sigmund Freud (1856–1939), with his daughter Anna.

Psychoanalytic Theories

Personality is a person's characteristic patterns of behaving, thinking, and feeling. You learned about one important theory of personality in Chapter 1. You may recall that the term psychoanalysis refers not only to Freud's approach to therapy but also to the influential personality theory he proposed. The central idea of psychoanalytic theory is that unconscious forces shape human thought and behavior.

Freud's Theory of Personality

Freud proposed that there are three levels of awareness in consciousness: the conscious, the preconscious, and the unconscious. The conscious consists of whatever we are aware of at any given moment—thoughts, feelings, sensations, or memories. The preconscious is somewhat like long-term memory: It contains all the memories, feelings, experiences, and perceptions that we are not consciously thinking about at the moment but that may be easily brought to consciousness.

The most important of the three levels is the unconscious, which Freud believed to be the primary motivating force of human behavior. The unconscious holds memories that once were conscious but were so unpleasant or anxiety provoking that they were repressed (involuntarily removed from consciousness). The unconscious also contains all of the instincts (sexual and aggressive), wishes, and desires that have never been allowed into consciousness. Freud traced the roots of psychological disorders to these impulses and repressed memories and proposed a three-part model of personality to explain how the unconscious, preconscious, and conscious minds interact.

The Id, Ego, and Superego. Freud also proposed three systems of personality. Figure 11.1 shows these three systems and how they relate to his conscious, preconscious, and unconscious levels of awareness. These systems do not exist physically; they are only concepts, or ways of looking at personality.

The id is the only part of the personality that is present at birth, and it is often compared to a newborn infant who never grows up. It is inherited, primitive, inaccessible, and completely unconscious. The id contains (1) the life instincts, which are the sexual instincts and the biological urges, such as hunger and thirst; and (2) the death instinct, which accounts for aggressive and destructive impulses (Freud, 1933/1965). Operating according to the *pleasure principle,* the id tries to seek pleasure, avoid pain, and gain immediate gratification of its wishes. The id is the source of the *libido,* the psychic energy that fuels the entire personality; yet, the id can only fantasize and demand.

The ego is the logical, rational, realistic part of the personality. The ego evolves from the id and draws its energy from the id. One of the ego's functions is to satisfy the id's urges. But the ego, which is mostly conscious, acts according to the *reality principle*. It considers the constraints of the real world in determining appropriate times, places, and

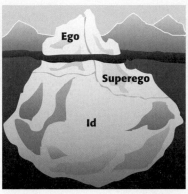

Conscious mind
(current state of awareness)

Preconscious
(outside awareness but accessible)

Unconscious mind
(outside awareness and inaccessible)

FIGURE 11.1 Freud's Conception of Personality
According to Freud, personality, which may be conceptualized as a giant iceberg, is composed of three structures: the id, the ego, and the superego. The id, completely unconscious, is wholly submerged, floating beneath the surface. The ego is largely conscious and visible, but partly unconscious. The superego also operates at both the conscious and unconscious levels.

objects for gratification of the id's wishes. The art of the possible is its guide, and sometimes compromises must be made—such as settling for a fast-food hamburger instead of steak or lobster.

When a child is age 5 or 6, the superego, the moral component of the personality, is formed. The superego has two parts: (1) The *conscience* consists of all the behaviors for which the child has been punished and about which he or she feels guilty; and (2) the *ego ideal* comprises the behaviors for which the child has been praised and rewarded and about which he or she feels pride and satisfaction. At first, the superego reflects only the parents' expectations of what is good and right, but it expands over time to incorporate teachings from the broader social world. In its quest for moral perfection, the superego sets guidelines that define and limit the ego's flexibility. A harsher judge than any external authority, including one's parents, the superego judges not only behavior, but also thoughts, feelings, and wishes. ✳Explore on mypsychlab.com

ego (EE-go) In Freud's theory, the logical, rational, largely conscious system of personality, which operates according to the reality principle.

superego (sue-per-EE-go) The moral system of the personality, which consists of the conscience and the ego ideal.

✳Explore the Concept *The Id, Ego, and Super Ego* on **mypsychlab.com**

Defense Mechanisms. All would be well if the id, the ego, and the superego had compatible aims. But the id's demands for pleasure are often in direct conflict with the superego's desire for moral perfection. At times the ego needs some way to defend itself against the anxiety created by the excessive demands of the id and the harsh judgments of the superego. When it cannot solve problems directly, the ego may use a defense mechanism, a technique used to defend against anxiety and to maintain self-esteem. All people use defense mechanisms to some degree, but research supports Freud's view that the overuse of defense mechanisms can adversely affect mental health (Watson, 2002). Table 11.1 (p. 354) lists and defines the various defense mechanisms along with examples of each one.

According to Freud, *repression* is the most frequently used defense mechanism. It involves removing painful or threatening memories, thoughts, or perceptions from consciousness and keeping them in the unconscious. It may also prevent unconscious sexual and aggressive impulses from breaking into consciousness. Several studies have shown that people do, indeed, try to repress unpleasant thoughts (Koehler, Tiede, & Thoens, 2002). Freud believed that repressed thoughts lurk in the unconscious and can cause psychological disorders in adults. He thought that the way to cure such disorders was to bring the repressed material back to consciousness, and this was the basis for his system of therapy—psychoanalysis.

defense mechanism A means used by the ego to defend against anxiety and to maintain self-esteem.

psychosexual stages A series of stages through which the sexual instinct develops; each stage is defined by an erogenous zone around which conflict arises.

fixation Arrested development at a psychosexual stage occurring because of excessive gratification or frustration at that stage.

The Psychosexual Stages of Development ▶

11.2 What is the role of the psychosexual stages in Freud's theory?

The sex instinct, Freud said, is the most important factor influencing personality. It is present at birth and then develops through a series of psychosexual stages. Each stage centers on a particular part of the body that provides pleasurable sensations (an *erogenous zone*) and around which a conflict arises (Freud, 1905/1953b, 1920/1963b). If the conflict is not readily resolved, the child may develop a fixation.

TABLE 11.1 Freud's Defense Mechanisms

DEFENSE MECHANISM	DESCRIPTION	EXAMPLE
Repression	Involuntarily removing an unpleasant memory, thought, or perception from consciousness or barring disturbing sexual and aggressive impulses from consciousness	Jill forgets a traumatic incident from childhood.
Projection	Attributing one's own undesirable traits, thoughts, behavior, or impulses to another	A very lonely divorced woman accuses all men of having only one thing on their minds.
Denial	Refusing to acknowledge consciously the existence of danger or a threatening situation	Amy fails to take a tornado warning seriously and is severely injured.
Rationalization	Supplying a logical, rational, or socially acceptable reason rather than the real reason for an action or event	Fred tells his friend that he didn't get the job because he didn't have connections.
Regression	Reverting to a behavior that might have reduced anxiety at an earlier stage of development	Susan bursts into tears whenever she is criticized.
Reaction formation	Expressing exaggerated ideas and emotions that are the opposite of disturbing, unconscious impulses and desires	A former purchaser of pornography, Bob is now a tireless crusader against it.
Displacement	Substituting a less threatening object or person for the original object of a sexual or aggressive impulse	After being spanked by his father, Bill hits his baby brother.
Sublimation	Rechanneling sexual and aggressive energy into pursuits or accomplishments that society considers acceptable or even admirable	Tim goes to a gym to work out when he feels hostile and frustrated.

Oedipus or Elektra complex (ED-uh-pus) Occurring in the phallic stage, a conflict in which the child is sexually attracted to the opposite-sex parent and feels hostility toward the same-sex parent (Oedipus for males; Elektra for females).

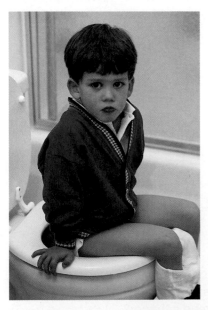

▲ Freud believed that a fixation at the anal stage, resulting from harsh parental pressure, could lead to an anal retentive personality—characterized by excessive stubbornness, rigidity, and neatness.

This means that a portion of the libido (psychic energy) remains invested at that particular stage, leaving less energy to meet the challenges of future stages. Overindulgence at any stage may leave a person psychologically unwilling to move on to the next stage, whereas too little gratification may leave the person trying to make up for unmet needs. Freud believed that certain personality characteristics develop as a result of difficulty at one or another of the stages. The *Summarize It* summarizes Freud's psychosexual stages.

One of the most controversial features of Freud's theory is the central theme of the phallic stage, the Oedipus complex. Freud named the complex after the central character in the ancient Greek tragedy *Oedipus Rex* by Sophocles, in which the ill-fated king discovers that he has unknowingly married his mother. When it is used in reference to females, the complex is called the Elektra complex after a similar play in which a woman is the main character. These two plays were quite popular in Europe during the later years of the 19th century, and Freud thought that their popularity was due to the fact that their theme, love for one's opposite-sex parent, represented a universal conflict that all human beings must resolve early on in their development (Freud, 1900/1953a).

Working from this assumption of universality, Freud claimed that, during the phallic stage, "boys concentrate their sexual wishes upon their mother and develop hostile impulses against their father as being a rival" (1925/1963a, p. 61). The boy usually resolves the Oedipus complex by identifying with his father and repressing his sexual feelings for his mother. With identification, the child takes on his father's behaviors, mannerisms, and superego standards; in this way, the superego develops (Freud, 1930/1962).

Freud proposed an equally controversial developmental process for girls (the Elektra complex) in the phallic stage. When they discover they have no penis, girls in this stage develop "penis envy," and they turn to their father because he has the desired organ (Freud, 1933/1965). They feel sexual desires for him and develop jeal-

Freud's Psychosexual Stages of Development

STAGE		PART OF THE BODY	CONFLICTS/ EXPERIENCES	ADULT TRAITS ASSOCIATED WITH PROBLEMS AT THIS STAGE
Oral (birth to 1 year)		Mouth	Weaning Oral gratification from sucking, eating, biting	Optimism, gullibility, dependency, pessimism, passivity, hostility, sarcasm, aggression
Anal (1 to 3 years)		Anus	Toilet training Gratification from expelling and withholding feces	Excessive cleanliness, orderliness, stinginess, messiness, rebelliousness, destructiveness
Phallic (3 to 5 or 6 years)		Genitals	Oedipal conflict Sexual curiosity Masturbation	Flirtatiousness, vanity, promiscuity, pride, chastity
Latency (5 or 6 years to puberty)		None	Period of sexual calm Interest in school, hobbies, same-sex friends	
Genital (from puberty on)		Genitals	Revival of sexual interests Establishment of mature sexual relationships	

ousy and rivalry toward their mother. But eventually girls, too, experience anxiety as a result of their hostile feelings. They repress their sexual feelings toward the father and identify with the mother, leading to the formation of their superego (Freud, 1930/1962).

According to Freud, failure to resolve these conflicts can have serious consequences for both boys and girls: Tremendous guilt and anxiety may be carried over into adulthood and cause sexual problems, great difficulty relating to members of the opposite sex, or homosexuality. ✳ Explore on mypsychlab.com

✳ Explore the Concept *Freud's Five Psychosexual Stages of Personality Development* on mypsychlab.com

11.3 How do modern psychologists evaluate Freud's ideas?

Evaluating Freud's Contribution

Do you believe that a person can be motivated by impulses of which he or she is unaware? Or that someone's current problems are the result of a long-forgotten childhood trauma or emotional conflict? If so, then you are a living example of the lasting influence of Freud's psychoanalytic theory on Western culture. Psychologists disagree as to whether Freudian ideas have benefited or harmed society. Critics such as E. Fuller Torrey argue that the infusion of psychoanalytic concepts into Western culture has led to an overemphasis on sexual pleasure (Torrey, 1992). Freud's supporters argue that the popularization of his theory has made people more aware of the importance of sexuality in their lives and of the significance of early childhood experiences to later development. Supporters often claim, too, that critics mischaracterize Freud's ideas both in the popular media and in academic circles (Knafo, 2009).

What about the scientific status of Freud's theory? Some have pointed out that Freud's work on defense mechanisms foreshadowed theories such as those of Lazarus in which cognitive appraisals are thought to shape emotional experiences (Knafo, 2009). In addition, some aspects of psychoanalytic theory, such as Freud's emphasis on family dynamics, continue to be important in explanations of psychological disorders (e.g., Clark, 2009). Moreover, today's *psychodynamic* therapies are direct descendants of Freud's techniques (Borden, 2009).

However, in Chapter 4 you learned that neurological approaches to dreaming have overtaken Freud's notions regarding symbolism in dreams. Likewise, in Chapter 6 you learned that, generally, people do not repress traumatic memories as Freud claimed. These challenges to psychoanalytic theory have arisen largely because of psychoanalysts' failure to adequately test the causal hypotheses found in psychoanalytic theory by means other than after-the-fact analyses of clinical case studies (Grünbaum, 2006). Moreover, a few observers claim that the unquestioning acceptance of Freud's theory by many therapists in the early decades of the 20th century went against Freud's own perception of psychoanalysis as a scientific theory that ought to be tested like any other.

When tests of Freud's hypotheses are available, the results show a mixed pattern. For instance, his suggestion that *catharsis,* the release of pent-up emotions, is good for one's psychological health has been refuted by studies showing that expressing negative emotions such as anger actually intensifies such feelings (Farber, Khurgin-Bott, & Feldman, 2009). In contrast, his assertion that childhood trauma leads to the development of psychological disorders in adulthood has received partial support. One study found that more than 70% of women who had been sexually victimized in childhood were diagnosed with some kind of psychological disorder in adulthood (Katerndahl, Burge, & Kellogg, 2005). At the same time, though, studies show that individual differences among victims better predict adult outcomes than the experience of victimization itself (Eisold, 2005). Thus, many victims of sexual abuse display a greater degree of resilience—the capacity to overcome potentially damaging early experiences—than psychoanalytic theory might predict.

11.4 How do the views of the neo-Freudians differ from those of Freud?

The Neo-Freudians

Is it possible to construct a theory of personality that builds on the strengths of Freud's approach and avoids its weaknesses? Several personality theorists, referred to as *neo-Freudians,* have attempted to do so. Most started their careers as followers of Freud but began to disagree on certain basic principles of psychoanalytic theory.

One of the most important neo-Freudians, Carl Jung (1875–1961), did not consider the sexual instinct to be the main factor in personality, nor did he believe that the personality is almost completely formed in early childhood. For Jung (1933), middle age was an even more important period for personality development. Jung conceived

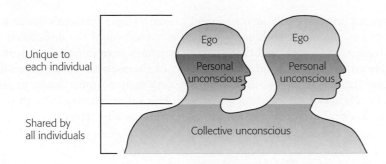

Unique to each individual

Shared by all individuals

Ego

Personal unconscious

Ego

Personal unconscious

Collective unconscious

FIGURE 11.2 Jung's Conception of Personality
Like Freud, Jung saw three components in personality. The ego and the personal unconscious are unique to each individual. The collective unconscious accounts for the similarity of myths and beliefs in diverse cultures.

Structure	Characteristics
Ego	The conscious component of personality; carries out normal daily activities.
Personal unconscious	The component containing all the individual's memories, thoughts, and feelings that are accessible to consciousness, and all repressed memories, wishes, and impulses; similar to a combination of Freud's preconscious and unconscious.
Collective unconscious	The most inaccessible layer of the unconscious, shared by all people; contains the universal experiences of humankind, as well as the archetypes.

of the personality as consisting of three parts: the ego, the personal unconscious, and the collective unconscious, as shown in Figure 11.2. He saw the ego as the conscious component of personality, which carries out normal daily activities. Like Freud, he believed the ego to be secondary in importance to the unconscious.

The **personal unconscious** develops as a result of one's own experience and is therefore unique to each person. It contains all the experiences, thoughts, and perceptions accessible to the conscious, as well as repressed memories, wishes, and impulses. The **collective unconscious**, the most inaccessible layer of the unconscious, contains the universal experiences of humankind. This is how Jung accounted for the similarity of certain myths, dreams, symbols, and religious beliefs in cultures widely separated by distance and time. Moreover, the collective unconscious contains what he called **archetypes**, inherited tendencies to respond to universal human situations in particular ways. Jung would say that the tendencies of people to believe in a god, a devil, evil spirits, and heroes all result from inherited archetypes that reflect the shared experience of humankind.

Another neo-Freudian, Alfred Adler (1870–1937), emphasized the unity of the personality rather than the separate warring components of id, ego, and superego. Adler (1927, 1956) also maintained that the drive to overcome feelings of inferiority acquired in childhood motivates most of our behavior. He claimed that people develop a "style of life" at an early age—a unique way in which the child and later the adult will go about the struggle to achieve superiority (Adler, 1956). Sometimes inferiority feelings are so strong that they prevent personal development, a condition Adler called the *inferiority complex* (Dreikurs, 1953). Because Adler's theory stresses the uniqueness of each individual's struggle to achieve superiority and refers to the "creative self," a conscious, self-aware component of an individual's personality, it is known as *individual psychology*.

The work of neo-Freudian Karen Horney (1885–1952) (pronounced *horn-eye*) centered on two main themes: the neurotic personality (Horney, 1937, 1945, 1950) and feminine psychology (Horney, 1967). Horney did not accept Freud's division of personality into id, ego, and superego, and she flatly rejected his psychosexual stages and the concepts of the Oedipus complex and penis envy. Furthermore, Horney thought Freud overemphasized the role of the sexual instinct and neglected cultural and environmental influences on personality. While she did stress the importance of early childhood experiences, Horney (1939) believed that personality could continue to develop and change throughout life.

personal unconscious In Jung's theory, the layer of the unconscious that contains all of the thoughts, perceptions, and experiences accessible to the conscious, as well as repressed memories, wishes, and impulses.

collective unconscious In Jung's theory, the most inaccessible layer of the unconscious, which contains the universal experiences of humankind.

archetype (AR-ka-type) Existing in the collective unconscious, an inherited tendency to respond to universal human situations in particular ways.

▲ Carl Gustav Jung (1875–1961).

Horney argued forcefully against Freud's notion that a woman's desire to have a child and to have a man is nothing more than a conversion of the unfulfilled wish for a penis. Horney (1945) believed that many of women's psychological difficulties arise from failure to live up to an idealized version of themselves. To be psychologically healthy, she claimed, women—and men, for that matter—must learn to overcome irrational beliefs about the need for perfection. Her influence may be seen in modern cognitive-behavioral therapies, which we will explore in Chapter 13.

Humanistic Theories

In *humanistic psychology*, people are assumed to have a natural tendency toward growth and the realization of their fullest potential. Thus, humanistic personality theories are more optimistic than Freud's psychoanalytic theory. However, like Freud's theory, these perspectives are often criticized as being difficult to test scientifically.

11.5 How do humanistic theorists explain personality?

Two Humanistic Theories

For humanistic psychologist Abraham Maslow (1908–1970), motivational factors are at the root of personality. You may remember from Chapter 9 that Maslow constructed a hierarchy of needs, ranging from physiological needs at the bottom upward to safety needs, belonging and love needs, esteem needs, and finally to the highest need—self-actualization (refer back to Figure 9.3 on page 290). Self-actualization means developing to one's fullest potential. A healthy person is continually striving to become all that he or she can be.

In his research, Maslow found self-actualizers to be accurate in perceiving reality—able to judge honestly and to spot quickly the fake and the dishonest. Most of them believe they have a mission to accomplish or the need to devote their life to some larger good. Self-actualizers tend not to depend on external authority or other people but seem to be inner driven, autonomous, and independent. Finally, the hallmark of self-actualizers is having frequently occurring *peak experiences*—experiences of deep meaning, insight, and harmony within themselves and with the universe. Current researchers have modified Maslow's definition of self-actualization to include effective personal relationships as well as peak experiences (Dy-Liacco et al., 2009; Hanley & Abell, 2002).

According to another humanistic psychologist, Carl Rogers (1902–1987), our parents set up conditions of worth, or conditions on which their positive regard hinges. Conditions of worth force us to live and act according to someone else's values rather than our own. In our efforts to gain positive regard, we deny our true selves by inhibiting some of our behavior, denying or distorting some of our perceptions, and closing off parts of our experience. In so doing, we experience stress and anxiety, and our whole self-structure may be threatened.

For Rogers, a major goal of psychotherapy is to enable people to open themselves up to experiences and begin to live according to their own values rather than living by the values of others in an attempt to gain positive regard. He called his therapy *person-centered therapy,* preferring not to use the term *patient* (Rogers's therapy will be discussed further in Chapter 13). Rogers believed that the therapist must give the client unconditional positive regard—that is, unqualified caring and nonjudgmental acceptance, no matter what the client says, does, has done, or is thinking of doing. Unconditional positive regard is designed to reduce threat, eliminate conditions of worth, and bring the person back in tune with his or her true self. If successful, the therapy helps the client become what Rogers called a *fully functioning person,* one who is functioning at an optimal level and living fully and spontaneously according to his or her own inner value system.

Although humanists have been criticized for being unscientific and for seeing, hearing, and finding no evil within the human psyche, they have inspired the study of

self-actualization Developing to one's fullest potential.

conditions of worth Conditions on which the positive regard of others rests.

unconditional positive regard Unqualified caring and nonjudgmental acceptance of another.

positive personality qualities, including altruism, cooperation, love, acceptance of others, and especially self-esteem. Most of us do not form a global idea about our own self-worth on the basis of a single area of competence. Instead, we view ourselves in terms of strengths and weaknesses.

Self-Esteem ▶

11.6 What have psychologists learned about self-esteem?

No doubt you have heard discussions of the importance of self-esteem, a person's sense of self-worth, to mental health. Although humanists have been criticized for being unscientific and for seeing, hearing, and finding no evil within the human psyche, they have inspired the study of positive personality qualities, including altruism, cooperation, love, acceptance of others, and especially self-esteem. Complete the *Try It* below to estimate your current level of self-esteem.

self-esteem A person's sense of self-worth.

How does self-esteem develop? One source of variations in self-esteem arises from comparisons of actual to desired traits. For example, a tone-deaf person who desires to be an accomplished musician might suffer from low self-esteem. However, most of us do not form a global idea about our own self-worth on the basis of a single area of competence. Instead, we view ourselves in terms of strengths and weaknesses. When our strengths lie in areas that we value and believe to be important, we have high self-esteem. Conversely, even outstanding achievements in areas we consider to be of little value may not affect our self-esteem. So, a person who is a great plumber, but who believes that being a good plumber isn't very important, is likely to have low self-esteem. At the same time, a person who feels incompetent because he has to pay a plumber a handsome sum to fix a leaking faucet might be in awe of the plumber's skill.

Developmental psychologists have found that self-esteem is fairly stable from childhood through the late adult years (Robins & Trzesniewski, 2005). So, the self-worth beliefs we adopt in childhood can affect us for a lifetime. Children and adolescents form ideas about their competencies in various domains—academics, sports, fine arts—that become increasingly stable across the elementary and secondary school years (Harter, 2006). And by age 7, most children have a sense of global self-esteem as well. These judgments come from both actual experiences and information provided by others. Thus, to develop high self-esteem, children need to experience success in domains they view as important and to be encouraged by parents, teachers, and peers to value themselves.

Trait Theories

Traits are personal qualities or characteristics that make it possible for us to face a wide variety of situational demands and deal with unforeseen circumstances (De Raad & Kokkonen, 2000). For example, persistence is a trait that helps us overcome adversity. *Trait theories* are attempts to explain personality and differences among people in terms of personal characteristics that are stable across situations.

trait A personal characteristic that is stable across situations and is used to describe or explain personality.

TRY IT ▶ **Allport's Trait Theory**

Which adjectives in this list best describe you? Which characterize your mother? Your father?

In Allport's terms you are describing your or their central traits, those you might mention in response to the request "Tell me about your mother."

decisive	outgoing	generous	industrious
funny	inhibited	sloppy	deceptive
intelligent	religious	laid-back	cooperative
disorganized	arrogant	rebellious	reckless
shy	loyal	calm	sad
fearful	competitive	good-natured	honest
jealous	liberal	nervous	happy
controlled	friendly	serious	selfish
responsible	compulsive	humble	organized
rigid	quick	lazy	quiet

11.7 What ideas did the early trait theorists propose?

Early Trait Theories

One of the early trait theorists, Gordon Allport (1897–1967), claimed that each person inherits a unique set of raw materials for given traits, which are then shaped by experiences (Allport & Odbert, 1936). A *cardinal trait* is "so pervasive and so outstanding in a life that … almost every act seems traceable to its influence" (Allport, 1961, p. 365). It is so strong a part of a person's personality that he or she may become identified with or known for that trait. For example, what comes to mind when you hear the name *Einstein*? Most likely, you associate this name with intellectual genius; in fact, it is sometimes used as a synonym for genius. Thus, for Albert Einstein, genius is a cardinal trait. *Central traits* are those, said Allport (1961), that we would "mention in writing a careful letter of recommendation" (p. 365). 👁 Watch on **mypsychlab.com**

👁 Watch the **Video** *Gordon Allport Discusses Personality Traits* on **mypsychlab.com**

Raymond Cattell (1950) referred to observable qualities of personality as *surface traits*. Using observations and questionnaires, Cattell studied thousands of people and found certain clusters of surface traits that appeared together time after time. He thought these were evidence of deeper, more general, underlying personality factors, which he called *source traits*. People differ in the degree to which they possess each source trait. For example, Cattell claimed that intelligence is a source trait: Everyone has it, but the amount possessed varies from person to person.

Cattell found 23 source traits in normal individuals, 16 of which he studied in great detail. Cattell's Sixteen Personality Factor Questionnaire, commonly called the *16PF*, yields a personality profile (Cattell, 1950; Cattell, Eber, & Testsuoka, 1977). This test continues to be widely used in research (e.g., Fan et al., 2008) and for personality assessment in career counseling, schools, and employment settings. Results from the 16PF are usually plotted on a graph such as that shown in Figure 11.3.

> How well do yo think the profile of "Eric" (solid line) matches that of business executives (broken line)? What types of conflicts is Eric likely to have with other executives if he chooses this career path?

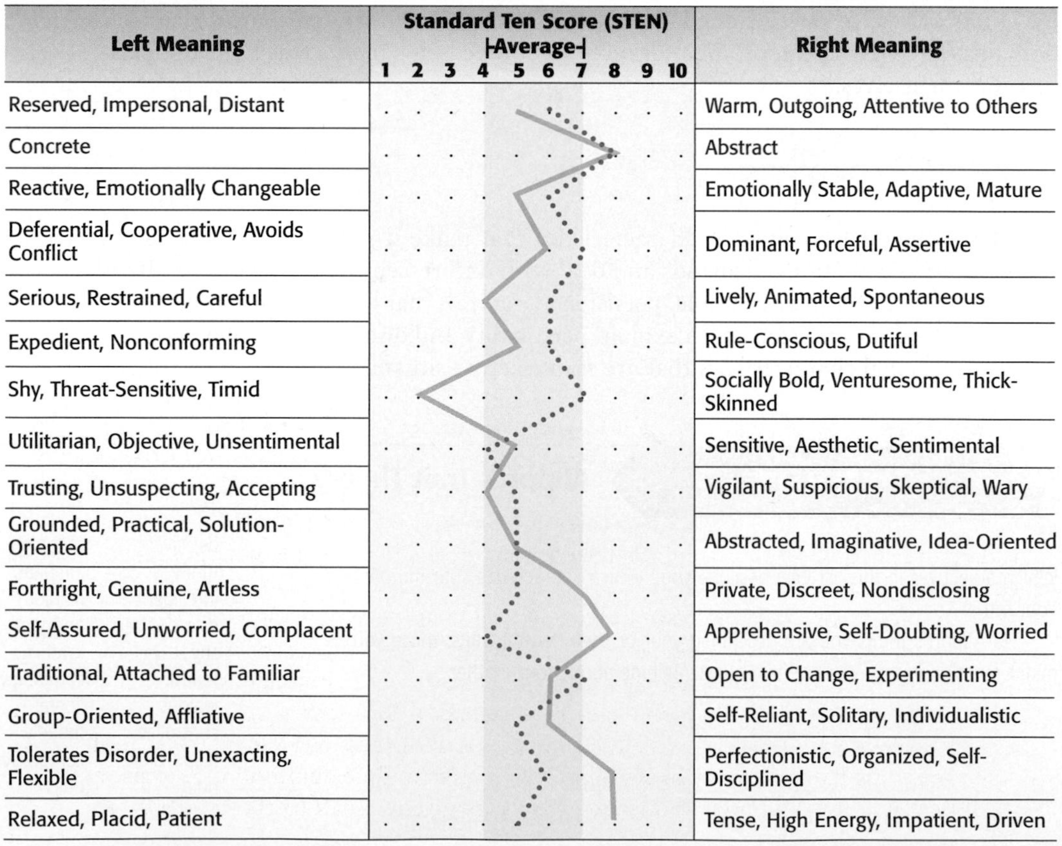

FIGURE 11.3 The 16PF Personality Profile
The solid line represents the 16PF profile for a man named "Eric" (Cattell, Cattell & Cattell, 2003). The broken line is the average 16PF profile for business executives.

Source: Cattell, Cattell & Cattell (2003).

Left Meaning	Standard Ten Score (STEN) |Average| 1 2 3 4 5 6 7 8 9 10	Right Meaning
Reserved, Impersonal, Distant		Warm, Outgoing, Attentive to Others
Concrete		Abstract
Reactive, Emotionally Changeable		Emotionally Stable, Adaptive, Mature
Deferential, Cooperative, Avoids Conflict		Dominant, Forceful, Assertive
Serious, Restrained, Careful		Lively, Animated, Spontaneous
Expedient, Nonconforming		Rule-Conscious, Dutiful
Shy, Threat-Sensitive, Timid		Socially Bold, Venturesome, Thick-Skinned
Utilitarian, Objective, Unsentimental		Sensitive, Aesthetic, Sentimental
Trusting, Unsuspecting, Accepting		Vigilant, Suspicious, Skeptical, Wary
Grounded, Practical, Solution-Oriented		Abstracted, Imaginative, Idea-Oriented
Forthright, Genuine, Artless		Private, Discreet, Nondisclosing
Self-Assured, Unworried, Complacent		Apprehensive, Self-Doubting, Worried
Traditional, Attached to Familiar		Open to Change, Experimenting
Group-Oriented, Affliative		Self-Reliant, Solitary, Individualistic
Tolerates Disorder, Unexacting, Flexible		Perfectionistic, Organized, Self-Disciplined
Relaxed, Placid, Patient		Tense, High Energy, Impatient, Driven

Building on Cattell's notion of personality factors, the late British psychologist Hans Eysenck (1916–1997) proposed a three-factor model that is sometimes called the *PEN* model (Eysenck, 1990). The first of the dimensions, *psychoticism,* is a continuum that represents an individual's link to reality. At one extreme are "psychotics," those who live in a world of hallucinations and delusions. At the other end are people whose thought processes are so rigidly tied to the material world that they lack creativity. The second dimension, *extraversion,* ranges from people who are outgoing to those who are shy. The third, *neuroticism,* describes emotional stability, with highly stable people at one end and anxious, irritable people at the other.

Eysenck proposed that all three of the PEN dimensions are rooted in neurological functioning. As a result, his theory has served as a useful framework for neurological studies of personality. For example, researchers have found a link between dopamine activity in the brain and extraversion (Munafó et al., 2008). Studies using electroencephalography (EEG) have shown that neuroticism is correlated with a distinctive pattern of brain-wave activity (Knyazev, 2009). In addition, Eysenck developed a series of personality tests that are still widely used by researchers and clinicians today (Danielsson et al., 2010).

The Five-Factor Model

[11.8 How does the five-factor model describe personality?

The most talked-about trait approach today is the five-factor model, the view that personality consists of five broad dimensions, each of which is composed of a cluster of personality traits. The assertion that five factors are needed to account for personality, as opposed to Eysenck's three factors, dates back to the early 1960s (e.g., Norman, 1963). However, over the past three decades, the model has become most closely associated with the research of Robert McCrae and Paul Costa (Costa & McCrae, 1985). Another important five-factor model, known as the *Big Five,* proposed by psychologist Lewis Goldberg, varies somewhat from that of McCrae and Costa in its approach to measuring the factors (Goldberg, 1993). However, research based on both models supports the hypothesis that personality can be usefully described in terms of five factors. You will notice that the names of these factors can be easily remembered by using the acronym OCEAN. ✷ Explore on mypsychlab.com

five-factor model A model that describes personality using five broad dimensions, each of which is composed of a constellation of personality traits.

✷ Explore the Concept *The Five-Factor Model* on **mypsychlab.com**

Openness. Are you eager to try new things and consider new ideas? If so, then you might get a high score on a test that measures openness. This dimension contrasts individuals who seek out varied experiences and who are imaginative, intellectually curious, and broad minded with those whose interests are narrower.

Openness may also be an important factor in adapting to new situations. In one 4-year study, researchers found that college students who scored high on this factor as freshmen adjusted to college life more easily than peers who scored lower (Harms, Roberts, & Winter, 2006). Apparently, students who were higher in openness were better able to adapt their own personality characteristics to the demands of the college environment than their low-scoring peers.

Conscientiousness. Do you always fold your laundry before putting it away? Individuals who score high on measures of conscientiousness pay more attention to such details than those who get lower scores. They are often viewed as reliable by others. By contrast, those at the lower end of this dimension may be perceived as lazy and undependable, but they also tend to be more spontaneous than people who get higher scores on this dimension.

Research suggests that the components of conscientiousness include order, self-control, and industriousness (Jackson et al., 2009). Thus, it isn't surprising that conscientiousness is correlated with measures of health. Longitudinal studies, for example, suggest that, compared to peers who obtained low scores on measures of conscientiousness, children who were high in conscientiousness as elementary school students were less likely to be smokers or to be obese in middle adulthood (Hampson et al., 2006). Likewise, conscientiousness shows long-term links to the tendency to maintain health-protective factors, such as avoiding obesity, during middle adulthood (Brummett et al., 2006).

Conscientiousness also predicts both academic and job performance. Among elementary school students, those who are highest in conscientiousness tend to be the highest achievers later in high school (Shiner, 2000). Likewise, across the years of undergraduate and graduate school, assessments of conscientiousness during students' first year predict their standing at the end of their programs of study (Chamorro-Premuzic & Furnham, 2003). Finally, variations in conscientiousness are correlated with measures of job performance among adults no matter what type of job is considered (Barrick, Mount, & Judge, 2001).

Extraversion. If you have a free evening, would you rather go to a party or stay home and read a book or watch a movie? Individuals who are high in extraversion prefer being around people. Chances are that anyone who is known as "the life of the party" is an extravert. Those at the opposite end of the continuum, introverts, may feel most comfortable when they are on their own.

Extraverts may have an easier time getting a job than their more introverted peers (Tay, Ang, & Dyne, 2006). Researchers have found that extraverts receive more job offers after being interviewed than do introverts. However, extraverts also may be more likely than introverts to engage in risky behaviors, such as unprotected sex (Miller et al., 2004).

Agreeableness. Do people describe you as easygoing? Individuals who are high in agreeableness are often characterized in this way. This dimension is composed of a collection of traits that range from compassion to antagonism toward others. A person who is low in agreeableness would not be viewed as easygoing. Instead, this individual would be described as unfriendly, argumentative, cold, and perhaps vindictive.

Like conscientiousness, agreeableness is predictive of job performance (Witt et al., 2002). As you might guess, it is also related to employees' ability to function well in work teams (Stewart, Fulmer, & Barrick, 2005). However, people who are high in agreeableness also seem to be more likely to succumb to peer influence with regard to decisions about risky behavior, such as binge drinking (van Schoor, Bott, & Engels, 2008).

Neuroticism. If you see an 8-ounce glass that contains 4 ounces of water, is it half empty or half full? People who are high in neuroticism tend to be pessimistic and always see the negative aspects of situations—the "half-empty" interpretation of life. At the same time, they are prone to emotional instability because of their tendency to overreact to the kinds of daily annoyances that most people take in stride. For example, an individual who is high in neuroticism might be very demonstrative about his or her frustration while standing in a slow-moving line at the campus bookstore. When such behaviors are exhibited by neurotic characters in television shows (e.g., George Costanza on *Seinfeld*, Larry David on *Curb Your Enthusiasm*), they are often perceived as humorous by audiences and regarded sympathetically by other characters. However, in real life, individuals who are high in neuroticism have difficulty maintaining social relationships and are at higher risk than others for a variety of psychological disorders (Hur, 2009; Kurdek, 2009).

Predictably, individuals who get high scores on measures of neuroticism receive low ratings on cooperativeness from their co-workers (Stewart et al., 2005). There is also evidence that high neuroticism impedes learning (Robinson & Tamir, 2005). It appears that the worrisome thoughts that result from neuroticism distract individuals with this characteristic from information that they are trying to learn, thereby interfering with the transfer of information from short- to long-term memory.

Gender Differences in the Five Factors. As you read through the discussions of the various traits, you may have speculated about whether males and females differ with regard to them. In general, researchers have found that women score higher than men do on measures of conscientiousness, agreeableness, and neuroticism, while men tend to score more highly on the trait of openness to experience (Goodwin & Gotlib,

2004). Both hormonal and social factors have been proposed as explanations for these differences. Importantly, though, gender differences across the five factors are small. Moreover, as is true of most variables that are not directly linked to the anatomical differences between males and females, the range of individual differences within each gender is far greater than the differences across genders (Hyde, 2005).

Nature, Nurture, and Personality Traits ▸

Critics of the five-factor model point out that, while it may describe personality well, it does not explain individual differences. In response, McCrae and Costa (2003) have proposed a behavioral genetic theory known as the *five-factor theory of personality*. The theory asserts that heredity is largely responsible for individual differences in the Big Five, although environmental factors, such as parenting and culture, also influence them. McCrae and Costa cite twin and adoption studies in support of their theory.

In one classic twin study, Rushton and colleagues (1986) found that nurturance, empathy, and assertiveness are substantially influenced by heredity. Even altruism and aggressiveness, traits we might expect to be strongly influenced by parental upbringing, are actually more heavily influenced by heredity. A meta-analysis by Miles and Carey (1997) revealed that the heritability of aggressiveness may be as high as .50. (Recall from Chapter 7 that *heritability* is an estimate of the percentage of variation in a trait that is due to genes. So, a heritability estimate of .50 means that 50% of the variation in aggressiveness is due to heredity.)

A number of longitudinal studies indicate that heredity makes substantial contributions to individual differences in the Big Five personality dimensions, as shown in Figure 11.4 (Bouchard, 1994; Caspi, 2000; Loehlin, 1992; Lonsdorf et al., 2009). These studies suggest that genes exert more influence on extraversion and neuroticism than on the other dimensions of the Big Five (Krueger & Johnson, 2004). Thus, genetically based similarities in personality, rather than modeling, may be responsible for the ways in which our adult lives relate to those of our parents.

Adoption studies have also shown that heredity strongly influences personality. Loehlin and others (1987) assessed the personalities of 17-year-olds who had been adopted at birth. When the adopted children were compared to other children in the family, the researchers found that the shared family environment had virtually no influence on their personalities. In another study, Loehlin and colleagues (1990) measured

11.9 What does research say about the effects of heredity and environment on personality traits?

FIGURE 11.4 Estimated Influence of Heredity and Environment on the Big Five Personality Dimensions
The Minnesota study of twins reared apart yielded an average heritability estimate of .41 (41%) for the Big Five personality factors; the Loehlin twin studies, a heritability estimate of .42 (42%). Both studies found the influence of the shared environment to be only about .07 (7%). The remaining percentage represents a combination of nonshared environmental influences and measurement error.
Source: Adapted from Bouchard (1994).

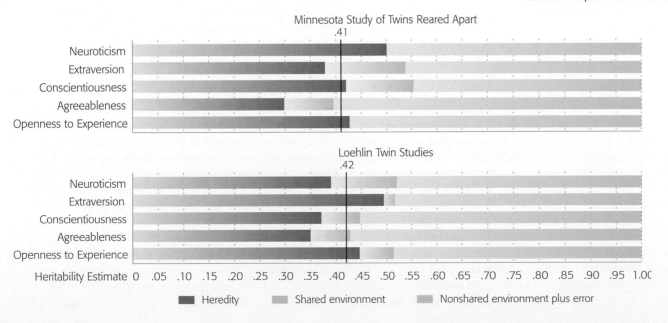

change in personality of adoptees over a 10-year period and found that children tended "to change on the average in the direction of their genetic parents' personalities" (p. 221). The prevailing thinking among behavioral geneticists, then, is that the shared environment plays a negligible role in the formation of personality (Loehlin et al., 1988), although there has been some opposition to this view (Rose et al., 1988).

Clearly, heredity influences personality. However, it is equally clear that personality is not determined by genes in the same way that physical traits such as eye color and blood type are. Instead, according to many psychologists, genes *constrain* the ways in which environments affect personality traits (Kagan, 2003). For example, a child who has a genetic tendency toward shyness may be encouraged by parents to be more sociable. As a result, he will be more outgoing than he would have been without such encouragement but will still be less sociable than a child who is genetically predisposed to be more sociable. Read the *Explain It* feature below to learn how trait theories explain the absence of a conscience.

11.10 How do personality traits vary across cultures?

Personality and Culture

Most advocates of the five-factor theory assert that the factors are universal, but does research support this claim? Evidence for the universality of the five factors comes from research in which psychologists have successfully measured them in Canada, Finland, Poland, Germany, Russia, Hong Kong, Croatia, Italy, South Korea, China, Mexico, Scotland, India, and New Zealand (Gow et al., 2005; Guenole & Chernyshenko, 2005; McCrae et al., 2000; Paunonen et al., 1996; Rodríguez & Church, 2003; Sahoo, Sahoo, & Harichandan, 2005; Zhang, 2002). Similarly, the five factors predict health status and other outcomes with about the same degree of accuracy in all ethnic groups in the United States (Worrell & Cross, 2004).

However, research also suggests that culture influences personality in ways that may not be captured by the five-factor model. In classic research, Hofstede (1980, 1983)

EXPLAIN IT ▸ **Why Do Some People Fail to Develop a Conscience?**

You may recall that Pinocchio's six-legged friend, Jiminy Cricket, advised him when he left home to always let his conscience be his guide. This is sound advice for the vast majority of people, but about 1% of human beings appear to lack a conscience, a condition known as *psychopathy* (Hare, 1998). How do personality theories explain the absence of a conscience? Before reading on, consider for a moment how Freud and the other theorists you have learned about so far in this chapter would answer this question.

Recall that Freud claimed that the superego develops in the context of child–parent relationships. According to his view, then, any disruption of these relationships could potentially disrupt the process of conscience development. A humanistic theorist would counter that a conscience is unlikely to develop in a child whose parents failed to provide him or her with unconditional positive regard, while a social-cognitive perspective would lead to a hypothesis that emphasizes parental discipline and modeling. Surprisingly, though, while all of these theories touch upon important and influential factors in a child's upbringing, none of them can fully explain why some adults appear to be completely without a conscience and, as a result, lack the capacity to feel guilty when they harm others (Aksan & Kochaska, 2005).

In our quest to explain the failure to develop a conscience, the trait approach may turn out to be the most helpful. For many years, researcher Paul Frick of the University of New Orleans and his colleagues have been studying *callous-unemotional (CU) traits* in children (Frick et al., 2003). Children who possess these traits lack empathy and the capacity to feel guilt. Frick and others have identified

CU traits in children as young as 4 years of age (Dadds et al., 2005). Moreover, longitudinal studies have shown that these children are at greater risk of engaging in behaviors that are hurtful to others than their peers who lack CU traits.

As is true for the traits that are associated with the five-factor model of personality, twin studies suggest that CU traits are inherited rather than the product of environmental influence (Larsson, Andershed, & Lichtenstein, 2006; Viding et al., 2005). Furthermore, individuals who lack a conscience are far more likely than others to suffer from psychological disorders (Assadi et al., 2006). Taken together, these findings suggest that the failure to develop a conscience might be best explained by a genetic vulnerability model in which an inherited risk can either be enhanced or mitigated by factors in a child's environment.

Do such findings mean that some human beings are simply destined to grow up without a conscience? Not necessarily, because studies have identified therapies that can help some of these children modify their CU traits. And if therapies can help them, then it might be possible to identify parenting strategies that could prevent these traits from condemning a child to an adult life that is sure to be fraught with social difficulties at best and incarceration at worst. The key is to recognize that, to be effective, both therapeutic approaches and parenting strategies must be adapted in light of the emotional limitations of children with CU traits. Paul Frick and his research team are committed to finding out exactly what those adaptations are. You can learn more about their research at *http://fs.uno.edu/pfrick/*.

analyzed questionnaire responses measuring the work-related values of more than 100,000 IBM employees in 53 countries around the world. Factor analysis revealed four separate dimensions related to culture and personality, of which one, the individualism/collectivism dimension, is of particular interest here. In individualist cultures, more emphasis is placed on individual achievement than on group achievement. High-achieving individuals are accorded honor and prestige in individualist cultures. People in collectivist cultures, on the other hand, tend to be more interdependent and define themselves and their personal interests in terms of their group membership. Asians, for example, have highly collectivist cultures, and collectivism is compatible with Confucianism, an ethical and philosophical system that is found in many Asian cultures. In fact, according to the Confucian values, the individual finds his or her identity in interrelatedness, as a part of the larger group. Moreover, this interrelatedness is an important ingredient of happiness for Asians (Kitayama & Markus, 2000).

Hofstede rank-ordered the 53 countries from the IBM study on each of the four dimensions. The United States ranked as the most individualist culture in the sample, followed by Australia, Great Britain, Canada, and the Netherlands. At the other end of the continuum were the most collectivist cultures: Guatemala, Ecuador, Panama, Venezuela, and Colombia, all Latin American countries.

Although, according to Hofstede, the United States ranks first in individualism, there are many distinct minority cultural groups in the United States, which may be decidedly less individualist. Native Americans number close to 2 million, but even within this relatively small cultural group, there are more than 200 different tribes, and no single language, religion, or culture (Bennett, 1994). Yet, Native Americans have many shared (collectivist) values, such as the importance of family, community, cooperation, and generosity. Native Americans value a generous nature as evidenced by gift giving and helpfulness. Such behaviors bring more honor and prestige than accumulating property and building individual wealth. Hispanic Americans and African Americans also tend to be more collectivist than individualist.

It is important to note that some psychologists warn against overemphasizing cultural differences in personality. For example, Constantine Sedikides and his colleagues have argued that the goal of all individuals, regardless of cultural context, is to enhance self-esteem (Sedikides, Gaertner, & Toguchi, 2003; Gaertner, Sedikides, & Chang, 2008). That is, even in collectivist cultures, the process of conforming to one's culture is motivated by an individualistic concern, the desire for self-esteem. Consequently, at least to some degree, an individualist orientation is universal. Furthermore, while members of different cultures display varying commitments to an individualistic philosophy, autonomy—a sense of personal control over one's life—predicts well-being in all cultures (Ryan, Kim, & Kaplan, 2003).

Social-Cognitive Theories

As useful as the five-factor model is, it still does not provide psychologists with a complete explanation of individual differences in personality. For instance, why are even the most extraverted individuals among us sometimes quiet and withdrawn? How do people who are disorganized—that is, who are low in conscientiousness—manage to complete tasks that require attention to detail, such as college research papers? Researchers who examine the influence of learning on personality have provided psychologists with some clues as to how these questions might be answered. For the most part, their hypotheses come from social-cognitive theory, the view that personality is a collection of learned behaviors that have been acquired through interactions with others.

The Situation–Trait Debate ▶

Social-cognitive theorist Walter Mischel has been among the most vocal critics of the five-factor model and of trait theories in general (Mischel, 1968, 2004). Mischel initiated the situation–trait debate, an ongoing discussion among psychologists about the relative

▲ For these native Alaskans, participating in the traditional blanket toss ceremony is one manifestation of their culture's values related to community and cooperation.

individualism/collectivism dimension A measure of a culture's emphasis on either individual achievement or social relationships.

social-cognitive theory The view that personality can be defined as a collection of learned behaviors acquired through social interactions.

situation–trait debate A discussion among theorists about the relative influence of traits and situations on personality.

⌈ **11.11** How do Mischel and Bandura address the situation–trait debate?

▲ Research on personality suggests that some traits, such as agreeableness, actually increase as we get older.

reciprocal determinism Bandura's concept of a mutual influential relationship among behavior, cognitive factors, and environment.

self-efficacy The perception a person has of his or her ability to perform competently whatever is attempted.

FIGURE 11.5 Bandura's Reciprocal Determinism
Bandura takes a social-cognitive view of personality. He suggests that three components—the external environment, individual behaviors, and cognitive factors, such as beliefs, expectancies, and personal dispositions—are all influenced by each other and play reciprocal roles in determining personality.

11.12 What do self-efficacy and locus of control contribute to personality?

locus of control Rotter's concept of a cognitive factor that explains how people account for what happens in their lives—either seeing themselves as primarily in control of their behavior and its consequences (internal locus of control) or perceiving what happens to them to be in the hands of fate, luck, or chance (external locus of control).

importance of factors within the situation and factors within the person in accounting for behavior (Rowe, 1987). For instance, you probably wouldn't steal money from a store, but what if you see a stranger unknowingly drop a $5 bill? Mischel and those who agree with him say that characteristics of the two situations dictate your behavior, not a trait such as honesty. Stealing from a store might require devising and carrying out a complicated plan, and it would carry a heavy penalty if you were caught, so you opt for honesty. Picking up a $5 bill is easy and may only result in embarrassment if you get caught, so you may do it. Mischel (1973, 1977) later modified his original position and admitted that behavior is influenced by both the person and the situation. Mischel views a trait as a conditional probability that a particular action will occur in response to a particular situation (Wright & Mischel, 1987).

The weight of evidence supports the view that there are internal traits that strongly influence behavior across situations (Costa & McCrae, 2009). Still, situational variables do affect personality traits. Consequently, social-cognitive theorist Albert Bandura, whose research on observational learning you learned about in Chapter 5, has proposed a comprehensive theory of personality that takes both traits and situations into account (1977, 1986). Moreover, Bandura's model incorporates cognitive variables into the mix. Because the model includes so many variables and provides a systematic explanation of how these variables interact, it has generated a great deal of research and has helped psychologists better understand both consistencies and inconsistencies in personality.

Bandura has proposed that internal, environmental, and behavioral variables interact to influence personality. He calls this interaction reciprocal determinism, a term that conveys his view that mutual influences contribute to variations across all three types of variables (see Figure 11.5). Internal variables, or *person* variables as they are usually called, include traits such as the five factors, information-processing variables such as short-term memory strategies, individual differences in intelligence, stages of cognitive and social development, learned expectancies about how the environment will respond to behaviors, and physiological factors such as neurological functioning. Environmental variables include social sources of information, the various kinds of consequences that are elicited by our behaviors, and the characteristics of specific situations. Behavioral variables are our actual behaviors.

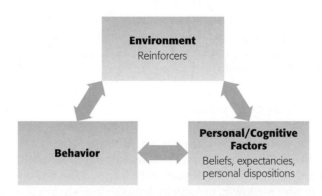

Self-Efficacy and Locus of Control

One of the cognitive factors that Bandura (1997a, 1997b) considers especially important is self-efficacy, the perception people have of their ability to perform competently whatever they attempt. Cross-cultural researchers examining self-efficacy in 25 countries found it to be an important individual difference in all of them (Scholz et al., 2002). According to Bandura, people high in self-efficacy approach new situations confidently, set high goals, and persist in their efforts because they believe success is likely. People low in self-efficacy, on the other hand, expect failure; consequently, they avoid challenges and typically give up on tasks they find difficult. Bandura's research has shown that people with high self-efficacy are less likely to experience depression than those with low self-efficacy (Bandura, 1997b).

Similarly, Julian Rotter proposed that a cognitive factor known as locus of control has effects on personality. Some people see themselves as primarily in control of their behavior and its consequences. This perception Rotter (1966, 1971, 1990) defines as an *internal locus of control*. Other people perceive that whatever happens to them is in the hands of fate, luck, or chance. These individuals exhibit an *external locus of control* and may claim that it does not matter what they do because "whatever will be, will be." Rotter contends that people with an external locus of control are less likely to change their behavior as a result of reinforcement, because they do not see reinforcers as being tied to their own actions. Students who have an external locus of control tend to be procrastinators and, thus, are less likely to be academically successful than those with an internal locus of control (Janssen & Carton, 1999). Similarly, construction workers who have an internal locus of control are more likely than their external-locus co-workers to take the time to implement safety procedures before beginning a dangerous project (Kuo & Tsaur, 2004). External locus of control is also associated with lower levels of life satisfaction (Kirkcaldy, Shephard, & Furnham, 2002). Where is your locus of control? Look back at the *Think About It* activity at the beginning of the chapter. The statements in the activity are similar to those Rotter used to assess locus of control. To translate the scoring instructions in the activity into Rotter's terms: 0–4 = internal locus of control, 7–10 = external locus of control. Scores of 5 and 6 suggest that your views are consistent with the internal view for some outcomes but are more akin to the external end of the continuum for others. The *Summarize It* below recaps the theories of personality.

▲ Individuals who are high in self-efficacy pursue challenging goals and persist until they reach them.

Theories of Personality

SUMMARIZE IT

THEORY	MAIN IDEAS
PSYCHOANALYTIC THEORIES	
Freud's Psychosexual Theory	Unconscious forces shape personality; three components of personality are id, ego, superego; defense mechanisms protect self-esteem; personality stages are characterized by a focus on different areas of the body.
Neo-Freudians	Jung distinguished between personal and collective unconscious; Adler emphasized the inferiority complex and striving for superiority; Horney focused on neurotic personality and feminine psychology.
HUMANISTIC THEORIES	
Maslow's and Rogers's Theories	Maslow emphasized self-actualization; Rogers believed that unconditional positive regard helped individuals attain potential.
Self-Esteem	Humanistic theory promotes research on self-esteem, which is somewhat stable across the life span; there is global and domain-focused self-esteem.
TRAIT THEORIES	
Early Theories	Allport proposed cardinal and central traits; Cattell developed the 16PF personality test to measure source traits; Eysenck's three-factor model includes psychoticism, extraversion, and neuroticism.
Five-Factor Model	The five-factor model (Big Five) includes openness, conscientiousness, extraversion, agreeableness, neuroticism (OCEAN); traits are influenced by heredity and environment; they are generally stable from childhood through adulthood and predict important outcomes.
SOCIAL-COGNITIVE THEORIES	
Situation–Trait Debate	Trait theorists argue that traits influence behavior more than situations; social-cognitive theorists argue that situations matter more than traits.
Reciprocal Determinism	Bandura claims that personal/cognitive factors (traits, thinking), the environment (reinforcement), and behavior interact to shape personality.
Self-Efficacy/Locus of Control	Two cognitive factors that influence personality are self-efficacy (Bandura) and locus of control (Rotter).

Personality Assessment

Have you ever taken a personality test? You may have as part of a job application and screening process. Personality assessment is commonly used in business and industry to aid in hiring decisions. Various ways of measuring personality are used by clinical psychologists, psychiatrists, and counselors in the diagnosis of patients and in the assessment of progress in therapy.

11.13 How do psychologists use observations, interviews, and rating scales?

Observation, Interviews, and Rating Scales

Psychologists use observation in personality assessment in a variety of settings—hospitals, clinics, schools, and workplaces. Behaviorists, in particular, prefer observation to other methods of personality assessment. Using an observational technique known as *behavioral assessment*, psychologists can count and record the frequency of particular behaviors. This method is often used in behavior modification programs in settings such as psychiatric hospitals, where psychologists may chart the progress of people with psychological disorders toward reducing aggressive acts or other undesirable behaviors. However, behavioral assessment is time consuming, and behavior may be misinterpreted. Probably the most serious limitation is that the very presence of the observer can alter the behavior being observed.

Clinical psychologists and psychiatrists use interviews to help in the diagnosis and treatment of people with psychological disorders. Counselors use interviews to screen applicants for admission to college or other special programs, and employers use them to evaluate job applicants and employees for job promotions. Interviewers consider not only a person's answers to questions but the person's tone of voice, speech, mannerisms, gestures, and general appearance also. Interviewers often use a *structured interview,* in which the content of the questions and even the manner in which they are asked are carefully planned ahead of time. The interviewer tries not to deviate in any way from the structured format so that more reliable comparisons can be made between different subjects. As you probably know from experience, interviews are also an integral part of any job search, and the *Apply It* includes numerous tips for using the interview process to your advantage.

Examiners sometimes use *rating scales* to record data from interviews or observations. Such scales are useful because they provide a standardized format, including a list of traits or behaviors to evaluate. A rating scale helps to focus the rater's attention on all the relevant traits to be considered so that none is overlooked or weighed too heavily. The major limitation of these scales is that the ratings are often subjective. A related problem is the *halo effect*—the tendency of raters to be excessively influenced in their overall evaluation of a person by one or a few favorable or unfavorable traits. Often, traits or attributes that are not even on the rating scale, such as physical attractiveness or similarity to the rater, heavily influence a rater's perception of an individual. To overcome these limitations, it is often necessary to have individuals rated by more than one interviewer.

11.14 What do the MMPI-2, the CPI, and the MBTI reveal about personality?

Personality Inventories

As useful as observations, interviews, and rating scales are, another method of measuring personality offers greater objectivity. This method is the inventory, a paper-and-pencil test with select-response questions (i.e., true/false, multiple-choice) about an individual's thoughts, feelings, and behaviors, which measures several dimensions of personality and can be scored according to a standard procedure. Psychologists favoring the trait approach prefer the inventory because it reveals where people fall on various dimensions of personality, and it yields a personality profile.

The most widely used personality inventory is the Minnesota Multiphasic Personality Inventory (MMPI) or its revision, the MMPI-2. Developed in the late 1930s and early 1940s by researchers J. Charnley McKinley and Starke Hathaway, the MMPI was

inventory A paper-and-pencil test with questions about a person's thoughts, feelings, and behaviors, which measures several dimensions of personality and can be scored according to a standard procedure.

Minnesota Multiphasic Personality Inventory (MMPI) The most extensively researched and widely used personality test, which is used to screen for and diagnose psychiatric problems and disorders; revised as MMPI-2.

APPLY IT · Put Your Best Foot Forward

Did you ever think of a job interview as a personality assessment? You should, because that's precisely what it is. The interviewer isn't measuring your personality as a psychologist would. Instead, he or she is assessing whether you fit the organization's needs and whether you can fit in with the others who work there. Here are a few tips for successful interviewing.

Impression Management

Think of the interview as an opportunity to make a particular impression on a potential employer. However, you should refrain from exaggerating your qualifications or experience. Experienced interviewers are skilled at recognizing such exaggerations and tend to look unfavorably upon interviewees who use them (Paulhus et al., 2003).

Educate Yourself

Learn as much as you can about the business or industry you want to work in and about the particular firm to which you are applying. Study the qualifications for the job you are seeking, both required and preferred, if they're available, and get a good idea of how your qualifications match up.

Prepare an Effective Resume

Even if the job you're applying for doesn't require a resume, it's a good idea to prepare one and take it—along with some extra copies—with you to the interview. A good resume is a quick source of information for the interviewer, who needs to know about your entire work history to create questions based on it. Most colleges and universities have career centers that provide advice on résumé preparation and related services.

Practice

Practice answering interview questions with a friend. Many college career centers have lists of frequently asked interview questions, and you should always create your own list of questions that you think the interviewer might ask. Try to avoid saying negative things about yourself. Remember, too, that consistent eye contact will show the interviewer that you have confidence.

Dress Professionally

When you are interviewing for a job, your clothing, visible adornments on your body (e.g., tattoos, jewelry), how well groomed you are, and even the way you smell can be forms of communication. Your appearance should communicate to the interviewer that you understand the environment in which you hope to be working. Keep in mind, too, that your appearance influences your own self-confidence. Researchers have found that the more formal interviewees' clothing is, the more positive are the remarks they make about themselves during the interview (Hannover & Kuehnen, 2002).

Be Punctual

Do you feel frustrated when others keep you waiting? Interviewers respond emotionally to tardiness, just as you do. Consequently, it's best to arrive early. And if you are unavoidably delayed, call and reschedule.

Greet the Interviewer Appropriately

Your greeting plays an important role in the interview process as well. In the United States, it's best to look your interviewer directly in the eyes, shake hands firmly, pronounce her or his name correctly, and have good posture.

Follow Up

After the interview, it's a good idea to send a thank-you note. If you met with more than one interviewer, send a note to each of them, mentioning some specific aspect of the discussion that you found interesting. This will indicate that you were fully engaged in the conversation, listening intently, and interested in the interviewer's knowledge about the open position and the organization. The note should also express your appreciation for the interviewer's time and your interest in the position.

Watch on **mypsychlab.com**

originally intended to identify tendencies toward various types of psychiatric disorders. The researchers administered more than 1,000 questions about attitudes, feelings, and specific symptoms to groups of people at the University of Minnesota hospital who had been clearly diagnosed with various specific disorders and to a control group of individuals who had no diagnosed disorders. They retained the 550 items that differentiated the specific groups of people with psychological disorders from the group of participants without disorders.

The MMPI-2 was published in 1989 (Butcher et al., 1989). Most of the original test items were retained, but new items were added to more adequately cover areas such as alcoholism, drug abuse, suicidal tendencies, eating disorders, and the Type A behavior pattern. New norms were established to reflect national census data and achieve a better geographical, racial, and cultural balance (Ben-Porath & Butcher, 1989).

Table 11.2 shows the 10 clinical scales of the MMPI-2. Following are examples of items on the test, which are to be answered "true" or "false."

I wish I were not bothered by thoughts about sex.

When I get bored, I like to stir up some excitement.

In walking I am very careful to step over sidewalk cracks.

If people had not had it in for me, I would have been much more successful.

TABLE 11.2 The Clinical Scales of the MMPI-2

SCALE NAME	INTERPRETATION
1. Hypochondriasis (Hs)	High scorers exhibit an exaggerated concern about their physical health.
2. Depression (D)	High scorers are usually depressed, despondent, and distressed.
3. Hysteria (Hy)	High scorers complain often about physical symptoms that have no apparent organic cause.
4. Psychopathic deviate (Pd)	High scorers show a disregard for social and moral standards.
5. Masculinity/femininity (Mf)	High scorers show "traditional" masculine or feminine attitudes and values.
6. Paranoia (Pa)	High scorers demonstrate extreme suspiciousness and feelings of persecution.
7. Psychasthenia (Pt)	High scorers tend to be highly anxious, rigid, tense, and worrying.
8. Schizophrenia (Sc)	High scorers tend to be socially withdrawn and to engage in bizarre and unusual thinking.
9. Hypomania (Ma)	High scorers are usually emotional, excitable, energetic, and impulsive.
10. Social introversion (S)	High scorers tend to be modest, self-effacing, and shy.

A high score on any of the scales does not necessarily mean that a person has a problem or a psychiatric symptom. Rather, the psychologist looks at the individual's MMPI profile—the pattern of scores on all the scales—and then compares it to the profiles of normal individuals and those with various psychiatric disorders.

But what if someone lies on the test to appear mentally healthy or to try to "fake" a psychological disorder? The MMPI-2 includes questions that help psychologists assess test takers' truthfulness. Collectively, these questions comprise the *validity scales* of the MMPI-2. One variable that the validity scales measure is *social desirability,* or the degree to which a test taker desires to appear to conform to society's concept of a "good" person. For instance, a test taker who is influenced by social desirability is likely to claim to have never told a lie. In addition, validity scales control for people who are faking a psychiatric illness, as in the case of someone hoping to be judged not guilty of a crime by reason of insanity. They also help psychologists identify individuals who are trying to appear healthier than they actually are, perhaps in order to be released from a psychiatric hospital. Thus, an individual's scores on the clinical scales of the MMPI-2 are always interpreted in light of his or her scores on the validity scales.

The MMPI-2 is reliable, easy to administer and score, and inexpensive to use. It is useful in the screening, diagnosis, and clinical description of abnormal behavior, but it does not reveal normal personality differences very well. A special form of the test, the MMPI-A, was developed for adolescents in 1992. The MMPI-A includes some items that are especially relevant to adolescents, such as those referring to eating disorders, substance abuse, and problems with school and family. There have been more than 115 recognized translations of the MMPI-2, and it is used in more than 65 countries (Butcher & Graham, 1989).

An important limitation of the MMPI-2, though, is that it was designed specifically to assess psychopathology. By contrast, the California Personality Inventory (CPI) is a highly regarded personality test developed especially for typical individuals aged 13 and older. Similar to the MMPI, the CPI even has many of the same questions, but it does not include any questions designed to reveal psychiatric illness (Gough, 1987). The CPI is valuable for predicting behavior, and it has been "praised for its technical competency, careful development, cross-validation and follow-up, use of sizable samples and separate sex norms" (Domino, 1984, p. 156). The CPI is particularly

California Personality Inventory (CPI) A highly regarded personality test developed especially for typical individuals aged 13 and older.

useful in predicting school achievement in high school and beyond, leadership and executive success, and the effectiveness of police, military personnel, and student teachers (Gregory, 1996).

The Myers-Briggs Type Indicator (MBTI) is another personality inventory that is useful for measuring individual differences. This test is based on Jung's personality theory. The MBTI is scored on four separate bipolar dimensions:

Extraversion (E) ⟷ Introversion (I)
Sensing (S)   ⟷ Intuition (N)
Thinking (T)   ⟷ Feeling (F)
Judging (J)   ⟷ Perceptive (P)

A person can score anywhere along a continuum for each of the four bipolar dimensions, and these individual scores are usually summarized according to a system of personality types. Sixteen types of personality profiles can be derived from the possible combinations of the four bipolar dimensions. For example, a person whose scores were more toward the Extraversion, Intuition, Feeling, and Perceptive ends of the four dimensions would be labeled an ENFP personality type, which is described as follows:

> Relates more readily to the outer world of people and things than to the inner world of ideas (E); prefers to search for new possibilities over working with known facts and conventional ways of doing things (N); makes decisions and solves problems on the basis of personal values and feelings rather than relying on logical thinking and analysis (F); and prefers a flexible, spontaneous life to a planned and orderly existence (P). (Gregory, 1996)

The MBTI is growing in popularity, especially in business and educational settings (Sample, 2004). Critics point to the absence of rigorous, controlled validity studies of the inventory (Pittenger, 1993). And it has also been criticized for being interpreted too often by unskilled examiners, who have been accused of making overly simplistic interpretations (Gregory, 1996). However, sufficiently sophisticated methods for interpreting the MBTI do exist, as revealed by almost 500 research studies to date (Allen, 1997). Many of these studies have shown that the MBTI personality types are associated with career choices and job satisfaction. For example, physicians who choose different specialties (e.g., pediatrics, surgery) tend to have different MBTI types (Stilwell et al., 2000). Consequently, the MBTI continues to enjoy popularity among career counselors.

Projective Tests ▶

Responses on interviews and questionnaires are conscious responses and, for this reason, are less useful to therapists who wish to probe the unconscious. Such therapists may choose a completely different technique called a projective test. A projective test is a personality test consisting of inkblots, drawings of ambiguous human situations, or incomplete sentences for which there are no correct or incorrect responses. People respond by projecting their inner thoughts, feelings, fears, or conflicts onto the test materials.

One of the oldest and most popular projective tests is the Rorschach Inkblot Method developed by Swiss psychiatrist Hermann Rorschach (ROR-shok) in 1921. It consists of 10 inkblots, which the test-taker is asked to describe (see Figure 11.6). Rorschach experimented with thousands of inkblots on different

Myers-Briggs Type Indicator (MBTI)
A personality inventory useful for measuring individual differences; based on Jung's theory of personality.

projective test A personality test in which people respond to inkblots, drawings of ambiguous human situations, or incomplete sentences by projecting their inner thoughts, feelings, fears, or conflicts onto the test materials.

Rorschach Inkblot Method (ROR-shok) A projective test composed of 10 inkblots that the test taker is asked to describe; used to assess personality, make differential diagnoses, plan and evaluate treatment, and predict behavior.

⌈ **11.15** How do projective tests
⌊ provide insight into personality?

FIGURE 11.6 An Inkblot Similar to One Used for the Rorschach Inkblot Method

groups of people and found that 10 of the inkblots could be used to discriminate among different diagnostic groups, such as people with bipolar disorder, schizophrenia, and other serious disorders. These 10 inkblots—5 black and white, and 5 with color—were standardized and are still widely used.

The Rorschach can be used to describe personality, make differential diagnoses, plan and evaluate treatment, and predict behavior (Ganellen, 1996; Weiner, 1997, 2004). For the last 20 years, it has been second in popularity to the MMPI for use in research and clinical assessment (Butcher & Rouse, 1996). The test taker is shown the 10 inkblots and asked to tell everything that he or she thinks about what each inkblot looks like or resembles. The examiner writes down the test taker's responses and then goes through the cards again, asking questions to clarify what the test taker has reported. In scoring the Rorschach, the examiner considers whether the test taker has used the whole inkblot in the description or only parts of it. The test taker is asked whether the shape of the inkblot, its color, or something else prompted the response. The examiner also considers whether the test taker sees movement, human figures or parts, animal figures or parts, or other objects in the inkblots.

Until the 1990s, the main problem with the Rorschach was that the results were too dependent on the interpretation and judgment of the examiner. In response to such criticisms, Exner (1993) developed the Comprehensive System, a more reliable procedure for scoring the Rorschach. It provides some normative data so that the responses of a person taking the test can be compared to those of others with known personality characteristics. Using this system, some researchers have found high agreement among different raters interpreting the same responses (interrater agreement) (McDowell & Acklin, 1996). Others believe that more research is necessary before it can be concluded that the Comprehensive System yields reliable and valid results (Wood, Nezworski, & Stejskal, 1996). However, a number of meta-analyses indicate that the Rorschach Inkblot Method has "psychometric soundness and practical utility" (Weiner, 1996).

Another projective test is the Thematic Apperception Test (TAT) developed by Henry Murray and his colleagues in 1935 (Morgan & Murray, 1935; Murray, 1938). You may remember from Chapter 9 that researchers have used the TAT to study the need for achievement, but it is also useful for assessing other aspects of personality. The TAT consists of one blank card and 19 other cards showing vague or ambiguous black-and-white drawings of human figures in various situations. If you were taking the TAT, this is what you would be told:

> This is a test of your creative imagination. I shall show you a picture, and I want you to make up a plot or story for which it might be used as an illustration. What is the relation of the individuals in the picture? What has happened to them? What are their present thoughts and feelings? What will be the outcome? (Morgan & Murray, 1962, p. 532)

The TAT is time consuming and difficult to administer and score. Although it has been used extensively in research, it suffers from the same weaknesses as other projective techniques: (1) It relies heavily on the interpretation skills of the examiner, and (2) it may reflect too strongly a person's temporary motivational and emotional states and not indicate more permanent aspects of personality. The *Summarize It* on page 373 recaps the three approaches to personality assessment discussed in this chapter.

Thematic Apperception Test (TAT)
A projective test consisting of drawings of ambiguous human situations, which the test taker describes; thought to reveal inner feelings, conflicts, and motives, which are projected onto the test materials.

▲ The Thematic Apperception Test requires test takers to make inferences about drawings that can be interpreted in a variety of ways. The drawings typically include human figures in different kinds of settings. To get a feeling for the projective technique, make up a story to explain what the two people in this photo are discussing.

Three Approaches to Personality Assessment

METHOD	EXAMPLES	DESCRIPTION
Observation and rating	Observation	Performance (behavior) is observed in a specific situation, and personality is assessed based on the observation.
	Interviews	In interviews, the responses to questions are taken to reveal personality characteristics.
	Rating scales	Rating scales are used to score or rate test takers on the basis of traits, behaviors, or results of interviews.
		Assessment is subjective, and accuracy depends largely on the ability and experience of the evaluator.
Inventories	Minnesota Multiphasic Personality Inventory-2 (MMPI-2)	Test takers reveal their beliefs, feelings, behavior, and/or opinions on paper-and-pencil tests.
	California Personality Inventory (CPI)	Scoring procedures are standardized, and responses of test takers are compared to group norms.
	Myers-Briggs Type Indicator (MBTI)	Used for measuring individual differences; based on Jung's theory of personality.
Projective tests	Rorschach Inkblot Method	Test takers respond to ambiguous test materials and presumably reveal elements of their own personalities by what they report they see in inkblots and by themes they write about scenes showing possible conflict.
	Thematic Apperception Test (TAT)	

Looking Back

The development of reliable and valid measures of personality has been a boon to psychologists' attempts to define and explain individual differences in this important domain. Comprehensive theories of personality have been useful to these attempts as well. To review, psychoanalytic theories emphasize unconscious forces, while humanistic approaches focus on individuals' attempts to better themselves and find acceptance. Trait theories describe personality in terms of individual differences across a number of universal dimensions. Social-cognitive theories assert that personality traits are influenced by learning and that their manifestation is often dependent on situational factors. Each of these perspectives has been used to explain how and why variations in mental health develop. Keep them in mind as you read the upcoming chapter about psychological disorders.

CHAPTER 11 SUMMARY

PSYCHOANALYTIC THEORIES (pp. 352-358)

11.1 What concepts did Freud propose to explain personality? (pp. 352-353)

The three levels of awareness in consciousness are the conscious, the preconscious, and the unconscious. The conscious mind includes everything we are thinking about at any given moment. The preconscious includes thoughts and feelings we can easily bring to mind. The unconscious contains thoughts and feelings that are difficult to call up because they have been repressed. The id is the primitive, unconscious part of the personality, which contains the instincts and operates on the pleasure principle. The ego is the rational, largely conscious system, which operates according to the reality principle. The superego is the moral system of the personality, consisting of the conscience and the ego ideal. A defense mechanism is a means used by the ego to defend against anxiety and to maintain self-esteem.

Key Terms

personality, p. 352
psychoanalysis, p. 352
conscious, p. 352
preconscious, p. 352
unconscious, p. 352
id, p. 352
ego, p. 353
superego, p. 353
defense mechanism, p. 353

11.2 What is the role of the psychosexual stages in Freud's theory? (pp. 353-355)

Freud asserted that the sexual instinct is present at birth and develops through a series of psychosexual stages, providing the driving force for all feelings and behaviors. The stages are the oral stage, anal stage, phallic stage (followed by the latency period), and genital stage. One of the most controversial features of Freud's stage theory is the Oedipus complex, a conflict that arises during the phallic stage in which the child is sexually attracted to the opposite-sex parent and feels hostility toward the same-sex parent.

Key Terms
psychosexual stages, p. 353
fixation, p. 353
Oedipus or Elektra complex, p. 354

11.3 How do modern psychologists evaluate Freud's ideas? (p. 356)

Freud is credited with calling attention to the unconscious, the importance of early childhood experiences, and the role of defense mechanisms. However, his theory is often criticized because it defies scientific testing.

11.4 How do the views of the neo-Freudians differ from those of Freud? (pp. 356-358)

Jung's model of personality includes three parts: the ego, the personal unconscious, and the collective unconscious. Adler claimed that the predominant force of the personality is not sexual in nature but rather the drive to overcome and compensate for feelings of weakness and inferiority and to strive for superiority or significance. Horney took issue with Freud's sexist view of women and added the feminine dimension to the world of psychology.

Key Terms
personal uncosncious, p. 357
collective unconscious, p. 357
archetype, p. 357

HUMANISTIC THEORIES (pp. 358-359)

11.5 How do humanistic theorists explain personality? (pp. 358-359)

According to Maslow, the goal of personality development is to reach a level where most behavior is motivated by self-actualization, the drive to attain one's fullest potential. According to Rogers, individuals often do not become fully functioning persons because in childhood they did not receive unconditional positive regard from their parents. To gain positive regard, they had to meet their parents' conditions of worth.

Key Terms
self-actualization, p. 358
conditions of worth, p. 358
unconditional positive regard, p. 358

11.6 What have psychologists learned about self-esteem? (p. 359)

The sense of self-esteem is influenced by comparisons of one's real self to one's desired self. Most people's self-esteem is based on what they perceive to be their strengths and weaknesses rather than on a single desired accomplishment or trait. By age 7, most children have a global sense of self-esteem and continue developing beliefs about their competencies in specific domains (e.g., sports) for several years.

Key Term
self-esteem, p. 359

TRAIT THEORIES (pp. 359-365)

11.7 What ideas did the early trait theorists propose? (pp. 360-361)

Allport defined a cardinal trait as a personal quality that pervades a person's personality to the point where he or she may become identified with that trait. A central trait is the type you might mention when writing a letter of recommendation. Cattell used the term surface traits to refer to observable qualities of personality. Source traits, which underlie the surface traits, are possessed in varying amounts by people. Eysenck considered the three most important dimensions of personality to be psychoticism, extraversion, and neuroticism.

Key Term
traits, p. 359

11.8 How does the five-factor model describe personality? (pp. 361-363)

According to the five-factor model, personality is influenced by five dimensions. The Big Five are neuroticism, extraversion, conscientiousness, agreeableness, and openness to experience.

Key Term
five-factor model, p. 361

11.9 What does research say about the effects of heredity and environment on personality traits? (pp. 363-364)

Both twin and adoption studies have shown that heredity strongly influences personality. However, some traits change over time, suggesting that the environment also contributes to personality traits.

11.10 How do personality traits vary across cultures? (pp. 364-365)

The cultural dimension known as individualism/collectivism is associated with personality. Individualist cultures encourage people to view themselves as separate from others and to value independence and assertiveness. Collectivist cultures emphasize social connectedness among people and encourage individuals to define themselves in terms of their social relationships.

Key Terms
individualism/collectivism dimension, p. 365

SOCIAL-COGNITIVE THEORIES (pp. 365-367)

11.11 How do Mischel and Bandura address the situation–trait debate? (pp. 365-366)

Mischel initiated the situation-trait debate to show how situations influence the manifestation of personality traits. He views a trait as a conditional probability that an action will occur in response to a specific situation. Bandura's reciprocal determinism model explains how traits and situations interact. The external environment (situation), behavior (partly due to traits), and cognitive factors (partly due to traits) are the three components of reciprocal determinism, each influencing and being influenced by the others.

Key Terms
social-cognitive theory, p. 365
situation-trait debate, p. 365
reciprocal determinism, p. 366

11.12 What do self-efficacy and locus of control contribute to personality? (pp. 366-367)

Self-efficacy gives people the confidence they need to accomplish goals. An internal locus of control helps them do so as well. An external locus of control may lead to procrastination.

Key Terms
self-efficacy, p. 366
locus of control, p. 366

PERSONALITY ASSESSMENT (pp. 368-372)

11.13 How do psychologists use observations, interviews, and rating scales? (p. 368)

During observations, psychologists count behaviors that may be representative of an individual's personality. They use structured interviews to compare the responses of one interviewee to those of others given under similar circumstances. Rating scales are used to quantify behaviors that occur during observations or interviews.

11.14 What do the MMPI-2, the CPI, and the MBTI reveal about personality? (pp. 368-371)

An inventory is a paper-and-pencil test with questions about a person's thoughts, feelings, and behaviors, which measures several dimensions of personality and can be scored according to a standard procedure. The MMPI-2 is designed to screen and diagnose psychiatric problems, and the CPI is designed to assess the normal personality. The MBTI uses examinees' scores to group them into sixteen categories that represent combinations of four dimensions: extraversion/introversion, sensing/intuition, thinking/feeling, judging/perceptive.

Key Terms
inventory, p. 368
Minnesota Multiphasic Personality Inventory (MMPI), p. 368
California Personality Inventory (CPI), p. 370
Myers-Briggs Type Indicator (MBTI), p. 371

11.15 How do projective tests provide insight into personality? (pp. 371-372)

In a projective test, people respond to inkblots or drawings of ambiguous human situations or by projecting their inner thoughts, feelings, fears, or conflicts onto the test materials. Examples are the Rorschach Inkblot Method and the Thematic Apperception Test (TAT).

Key Terms
projective test, p. 371
Rorschach Inkblot Method, p. 371
Thematic Apperception Test (TAT), p. 372

MAP IT

Log on to MyPsychLab and click on "Map It" to prepare a unique digital map of the chapter that you can save for later use, email to your instructor, or print out to use as a study tool. Or, create your own map by drawing one on paper. Use the starter map below as a model for your own map. Use the chapter summary as your guide for what to include. For each item in your map, be sure to include the page number.

Here's one way to *Map It*:

1. Draw a box at the top of the page for the section title.

2. Underneath the section title box, working horizontally across the page, draw a box for each learning question in the section. Write the learning questions in the boxes and draw a line from the section title to each questions box. After you read each subsection, jot an answer for the learning question in the subsection's box.

3. Below each learning question box, insert another box for all of the key terms that are related to the question, along with a very brief reminder of each term's definition. Draw a line from the question box to the key terms box.

4. Below each key terms box, create another box and list all of the helpful figures, tables, and other elements of the text, such as *Try It* and *Apply It* boxes. Draw a line from the key terms box to the helpful elements box.

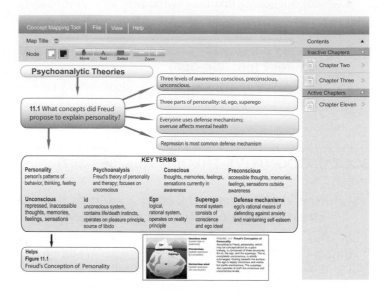

⚫⚙ ⌐Map the Chapter on mypsychlab.com

Chapter 11 Study Guide

Answers to all the Study Guide questions are provided at the end of the book.

SECTION ONE: Chapter Review

Psychoanalytic Theories (pp. 352–358)

1. Psychoanalysis is both a theory of personality and a therapy for the treatment of psychological disorders. (true/false)

2. Freud considered the (conscious, unconscious) to be the primary motivating force of human behavior.

3. The part of the personality that would make you want to eat, drink, and be merry is your
   a. id.   **b.** ego.   **c.** superego.

4. You just found a gold watch in a darkened movie theater. Which part of your personality would urge you to turn it in to the lost and found?
   a. id   **b.** ego   **c.** superego

5. The part of the personality that determines appropriate ways to satisfy biological urges is the
   a. id.
   b. ego.
   c. superego.

6. Defense mechanisms are used only by psychologically unhealthy individuals. (true/false)

7. Repression is used to avoid unpleasant thoughts. (true/false)

8. According to Freud, the sex instinct arises at (birth, puberty).

9. Which of the following lists presents Freud's stages in the order in which they occur?
   a. latency, anal, oral, genital, phallic
   b. genital, anal, latency, oral, phallic
   c. oral, phallic, anal, genital, latency
   d. oral, anal, phallic, latency, genital

10. Rich's excessive concern with cleanliness and order could indicate a fixation at the _____ stage.
    a. oral   **c.** phallic
    b. anal   **d.** genital

11. When a young boy develops sexual feelings toward his mother and hostility toward his father, he is said to have a conflict called the _____ _____.

12. According to Freud, which of the following represents a primary source of influence on personality?
    a. heredity
    b. life experiences after beginning school
    c. the relative strengths of the id, ego, and superego
    d. the problems experienced during adolescence

13. In Jung's theory, the inherited part of the personality that stores the experiences of humankind is the (collective, personal) unconscious.

14. Which personality theorist believed that the basic human drive is to overcome and compensate for inferiority and strive for superiority and significance?
  a. Sigmund Freud
  b. Carl Jung
  c. Alfred Adler
  d. Karen Horney

15. On which of the following did Horney focus?
  a. psychoanalysis
  b. trait theory
  c. feminine psychology
  d. humanistic psychology

Humanistic Theories (pp. 358–359)

16. Humanistic psychologists would *not* say that
  a. human nature is innately good.
  b. human beings have a natural tendency toward self-actualization.
  c. human beings have free will.
  d. researchers should focus primarily on observable behavior.

17. Which psychologist identified characteristics that he believed self-actualized persons share?
  a. Carl Rogers
  b. Gordon Allport
  c. Abraham Maslow
  d. Hans Eysenck

18. Which psychologist believed that individuals often do not become fully functioning persons because, in childhood, they fail to receive unconditional positive regard from their parents?
  a. Carl Rogers
  b. Gordon Allport
  c. Abraham Maslow
  d. Hans Eysenck

19. Self-esteem includes assessments of competence in different domains such as academics and sports. (true/false)

Trait Theories (pp. 359–365)

20. According to Allport, the kind of trait that is a defining characteristic of one's personality is a _____ trait.
  a. common
  b. source
  c. secondary
  d. cardinal

21. According to Cattell, the differences between people are explained by the number of source traits they possess. (true/false)

22. Who claimed that psychologists can best understand personality by assessing people on two major dimensions, Extraversion and Neuroticism?
  a. Hans Eysenck
  b. Gordon Allport
  c. Raymond Cattell
  d. Carl Jung

23. This chapter suggests that, according to a growing consensus among trait theorists, there are _____ major dimensions of personality.
  a. 3
  b. 5
  c. 7
  d. 16

24. Behavioral geneticists have found that the shared family environment has a (strong, negligible) effect on personality development.

25. Children adopted at birth are more similar in personality to their adoptive parents than to their biological parents. (true/false)

Social-Cognitive Theories (pp. 365–367)

26. The situation–trait debate was initiated by
  a. Albert Bandura
  b. Walter Mischel
  c. Robert McCrae
  d. Julian Rotter

27. Bandura's concept of reciprocal determinism refers to the mutual effects of
  a. a person's behavior, personality, and thinking.
  b. a person's feelings, attitudes, and thoughts.
  c. a person's behavior, personal/cognitive factors, and the environment.
  d. classical and operant conditioning and observational learning.

28. Which statement is *not* true of people low in self-efficacy?
  a. They persist in their efforts.
  b. They lack confidence.
  c. They expect failure.
  d. They avoid challenge.

29. Who proposed the concept of locus of control?
  a. B. F. Skinner
  b. Albert Bandura
  c. Hans Eysenck
  d. Julian Rotter

Personality Assessment (pp. 368–372)

30. Match each personality test with its description.
  _____ **(1)** MMPI-2
  _____ **(2)** Rorschach
  _____ **(3)** TAT
  _____ **(4)** CPI
  _____ **(5)** MBTI
  a. inventory used to diagnose psychopathology
  b. inventory used to assess typical personality
  c. projective test using inkblots
  d. projective test using drawings of ambiguous human situations
  e. inventory used to assess personality types

31. Clay has an unconscious resentment toward his father. Which test might best detect this?
  a. MMPI-2
  b. CPI
  c. MBTI
  d. TAT

32. Which of the following items might appear on the MMPI-2?
  a. What is happening in the picture?
  b. Hand is to glove as foot is to _____.
  c. My mother was a good person.
  d. What is your favorite food?

SECTION TWO: Complete the Table

Approach	Key Theorist(s)	Major Assumption about Behavior
1. Psychoanalytic	_____	_____
2. Humanistic	_____	_____
3. Trait	_____	_____
4. Social-cognitive	_____	_____

SECTION THREE: Fill in the Blank

1. According to Freud, the _____ is the personality structure that is completely unconscious and operates on the pleasure principle.

2. According to Freud, the _____ is the logical and rational part of the personality.

3. Freud's _____ is very much like long-term memory.

4. The stages of psychosexual development, in the proper order, are _____, _____, _____, _____, and _____.

5. Mother Teresa would be said to have possessed the _____ trait of altruism.

6. According to Cattell, _____ traits are the observable qualities of personality.

7. Bandura asserted that personal/cognitive factors, one's behavior, and the external environment all influence each other and are influenced by each other. He called this relationship _____ _____.

8. According to Jung, the _____ _____ accounts for the similarity of certain myths, dreams, symbols, and religious beliefs in different cultures.

9. Psychologists who adopt a behavioral perspective on personality usually prefer the _____ method to other methods of personality assessment.

10. The Myers-Briggs Type Indicator is a personality inventory that is based on _____ theory of personality.

11. The Rorschach Inkblot Method is an example of a _____ test.

12. The _____ is the most widely used of the many different personality inventories.

13. _____ refers to a person's belief that he or she can perform competently in what is attempted.

14. Cattell defined _____ traits as those traits that make up the most basic personality structure and cause behavior.

15. In Jung's view, an _____ exists in the collective unconscious and is an inherited tendency to respond in particular ways to universal human situations.

16. Cultures that encourage people to define themselves in terms of social relationships represent the _____ side of the _____/_____ dimension.

17. A person's sense of self-worth is also known as _____.

SECTION FOUR: Comprehensive Practice Test

1. A person's unique pattern of behaving, thinking, and feeling is his or her
   a. motivation.
   b. emotion.
   c. personality.
   d. cognition.

2. Freud's theory of personality and his therapy for the treatment of psychological disorders are both known as
   a. behaviorism.
   b. psychosocialism.
   c. psychoanalysis.
   d. humanism.

3. Of Freud's three conceptual systems of personality, the _____ is mainly in the conscious, the _____ is split between the conscious and the unconscious, and the _____ is completely unconscious.
   a. id; ego; superego
   b. ego; superego; id
   c. superego; ego; id
   d. ego; id; superego

4. The libido is Freud's name for the psychic or sexual energy that comes from the superego and provides the energy for the entire personality. (true/false)

5. Ava is 13 months old, and whatever she can pick up is likely to go into her mouth. Ava is in Freud's _____ stage of psychosexual development.
   a. anal
   b. oral
   c. phallic
   d. genital

6. Clint is 5 years old, and he thinks his mother is as beautiful as a princess; he would rather spend time with her than with his father. Clint is in Freud's _____ stage of psychosexual development.
   a. anal
   b. oral
   c. phallic
   d. genital

7. A central theme in Adler's theory is the individual's quest for feelings of
   a. superiority.
   b. the collective unconscious.
   c. adequacy.
   d. ego integrity.

8. According to Horney, maladjustment is often caused by
   a. guilt related to failing to live up to an ideal self.
   b. observation of maladjusted role models.
   c. inherited traits.
   d. repressed memories.

9. Allport and Cattell were proponents of the _____ theory of personality.
   a. stage
   b. trait
   c. biological
   d. humanistic

10. Which of the following Big Five personality factors has been found to be a requirement for creative accomplishment?
    a. extraversion
    b. conscientiousness
    c. neuroticism
    d. openness to Experience

11. Bandura's theory includes the concept of _____, the belief a person has regarding his or her ability to perform competently whatever is attempted.
    a. reciprocal determinism
    b. self-efficacy
    c. extraversion
    d. conditions of worth

12. Trey believes that what happens to him is based on fate, luck, or chance, and his philosophy of life is "whatever will be, will be." Rotter would say that Trey has a(n) _____ locus of control.
    a. internal
    b. explicit
    c. external
    d. regressed

13. Rogers's theory included the concept of conditions of worth—the idea that our parents teach us important values in life and that we as individuals will be motivated to seek out those values. (true/false)

14. The MMPI-2 is a good example of a projective personality test. (true/false)

15. The California Psychological Inventory was developed to evaluate the personalities of
    a. the mentally ill.
    b. males.
    c. typical people
    d. females.

16. You are shown a black-and-white drawing of people and asked to tell a story about it. You are probably responding to
    a. the Rorschach Inkblot Method.
    b. the CPI.
    c. the Myers-Briggs Type Indicator.
    d. the TAT.

SECTION FIVE: Critical Thinking

1. In your opinion, which of the major personality theories discussed in this chapter is the most accurate, reasonable, and realistic? Which is the least accurate, reasonable, and realistic? Give reasons to support your answers.

2. Most social scientists say that American culture is individualist. What aspects of culture in the United States exemplify individualism? Are there some features of American culture that are collectivist in nature? If so, what are they?

3. How do you think the Big Five dimensions of personality affect your behavior?

Psychological Disorders

12 CHAPTER

Think About It

Have you ever worried about what might happen in the future? Who hasn't? Being concerned about what lies ahead, a state that psychologists call *anxiety*, is an experience shared by all humans. But sometimes anxiety becomes so frequent or so intense that it interferes with or even takes over a person's life. If you are wondering whether you or someone close to you has reached that point, thinking about the following descriptions may help you decide. Read each one and place a check mark beside each description that sounds like you or someone about whom you are concerned.

_____ 1. You are always worried about things, even when there are no signs of trouble. You have frequent aches and pains that can't be traced to physical illness or injury. You tire easily, and yet you have trouble sleeping. Your body is constantly tense.

_____ 2. You have stopped leaving home because that seems to be the only way you can avoid situations in which, out of the blue, your heart starts pounding. You feel dizzy. You can't breathe. You feel like you are about to die.

_____ 3. Every day, you fear you will do something embarrassing. You've stopped going to parties because you're afraid to meet new people. When other people look at you, you break out in a sweat and shake uncontrollably. You stay home from work because you're terrified of being called on in a staff meeting.

_____ 4. You are so afraid of germs that you wash your hands repeatedly until they are raw and sore. You can't leave the house until you check the locks on every window and door over and over again. You are terrified that you will harm someone you care about. You just can't get those thoughts out of your head.

Later in the chapter, you will learn about the conditions that correspond to these descriptions. The first represents *generalized anxiety disorder* and the second describes *panic disorder*. The third description refers to *social phobia*, and the fourth is associated with *obsessive-compulsive disorder*. In recent years, psychologists have learned a great deal about psychological disorders like these, including what causes them and how to help people who have them. This chapter addresses those findings. But first let's ask the obvious question: What is abnormal?

Defining Psychological Disorders

psychological disorders Mental processes and/or behavior patterns that cause emotional distress and/or substantial impairment in functioning.

Psychological disorders are mental processes and/or behavior patterns that cause emotional distress and/or substantial impairment in functioning. We begin our examination of them with a basic question: What is abnormal?

12.1 What criteria do psychologists use to classify behavior as abnormal?

What Is Abnormal Behavior?

Human behavior lies along a continuum, from well adjusted to maladaptive. But where along the continuum does behavior become abnormal? Several questions can help determine when behavior is abnormal:

■ *Is the behavior considered strange within the person's own culture?* What is considered normal or abnormal in one culture is not necessarily considered so in another. In some cultures, it is normal for women to appear in public bare breasted, but it would be abnormal for a female executive in an industrialized culture to go to work that way.

■ *Does the behavior cause personal distress?* When people experience considerable emotional distress without any life experience that warrants it, they may be diagnosed as having a psychological or mental disorder. Some people may be sad and depressed, and some anxious; others may be agitated or excited; and still others may be frightened, or even terrified, by delusions and hallucinations.

■ *Is the behavior maladaptive?* Some experts believe that the best way to differentiate between normal and abnormal behavior is to consider whether it leads to healthy or impaired functioning. Washing your hands before you eat is adaptive; washing them 100 times a day is maladaptive.

■ *Is the person a danger to self or others?* Another consideration is whether people pose any danger to themselves or others. To be committed to a mental hospital, a person must be judged both mentally ill and a danger to self or others.

▲ Abnormal behavior is defined by each culture. For example, homelessness is considered abnormal in some cultures and completely normal in others.

- *Is the person legally responsible for his or her acts?* Often, the term *insanity* is used to label those who behave abnormally, but mental health professionals do not use this term. It is a legal term used by the courts to declare people not legally responsible for their acts. You should remember from Chapter 1 that *forensic psychologists* are clinical psychologists who specialize in the legal aspects of psychology. They sometimes testify in cases in which a defendant claims to have been insane at the time he or she committed a crime. However, the insanity defense is rarely successful. Mass murderer Jeffrey Dahmer was ruled legally responsible for his acts, yet his behavior was clearly abnormal.

Classifying and Tracking Psychological Disorders ▷

12.2 How do clinicians use the *DSM-IV-TR*?

In 1952, the American Psychiatric Association published a manual providing a diagnostic system for describing and classifying psychological disorders. Over the years, the manual has been revised several times. The most recent edition, the *Diagnostic and Statistical Manual of Mental Disorder (DSM-IV-TR)*, Fourth Edition, Text Revision, commonly known as the *DSM-IV-TR* appeared in 2000. Work is now underway on the fifth edition that is scheduled for publication in 2011.

　　The *DSM-IV-TR* contains descriptions of about 300 specific psychological disorders and lists criteria that must be met in order to make a particular diagnosis. Further, the manual organizes these disorders into categories (see Table 12.1, p. 382). The manual is used by researchers, therapists, mental health workers, and most insurance companies. This common language enables professionals to speak the same language when diagnosing, treating, researching, and conversing about a variety of psychological disorders (Clark, Watson, & Reynolds, 1995). Moreover, the *DSM-IV-TR* provides clinicians with a multidimensional diagnostic system. This system is known as the *multiaxial system* and is described in Table 12.2 (p. 383). A complete description of any case includes information for each of the five axes. ✳ Explore on mypsychlab.com

DSM-IV-TR, 2000 The Diagnostic and Statistical Manual of Mental Disorders, 4th Edition, Text Revision; a manual published by the American Psychiatric Association, which describes the criteria used to classify and diagnose mental disorders.

✳ Explore the Concept *The Axes of the DSM* on mypsychlab.com

　　Widespread use of the *DSM-IV-TR* by mental health professionals has enabled public health officials to keep track of the frequency with which the various categories and individual disorders are diagnosed, just as they do for physical ailments. Their

TABLE 12.1 Major *DSM-IV-TR* Categories of Mental Disorders

CATEGORY	SYMPTOMS	EXAMPLES
Schizophrenia and other psychotic disorders	Disorders characterized by the presence of psychotic symptoms, including hallucinations, delusions, disorganized speech, bizarre behavior, and loss of contact with reality	Schizophrenia, paranoid type Schizophrenia, disorganized type Schizophrenia, catatonic type Delusional disorder, jealous type
Mood disorders	Disorders characterized by periods of extreme or prolonged depression or mania or both	Major depressive disorder Bipolar disorder
Anxiety disorders	Disorders characterized by anxiety and avoidance behavior	Panic disorder Social phobia Obsessive-compulsive disorder Posttraumatic stress disorder
Somatoform disorders	Disorders in which physical symptoms are present that are psychological in origin rather than due to a medical condition	Hypochondriasis Conversion disorder
Dissociative disorders	Disorders in which one handles stress or conflict by forgetting important personal information or one's whole identity, or by compartmentalizing the trauma or conflict into a split-off alter personality	Dissociative amnesia Dissociative fugue Dissociative identity disorder
Personality disorders	Disorders characterized by long-standing, inflexible, maladaptive patterns of behavior beginning early in life and causing personal distress or problems in social and occupational functioning	Antisocial personality disorder Histrionic personality disorder Narcissistic personality disorder Borderline personality disorder
Substance-related disorders	Disorders in which undesirable behavioral changes result from substance abuse, dependence, or intoxication	Cocaine abuse Cannabis dependence Alcohol abuse
Disorders usually first diagnosed in infancy, childhood, or adolescence	Disorders that include mental retardation, learning disorders, communication disorders, pervasive developmental disorders, attention-deficit and disruptive behavior disorders, tic disorders, and elimination disorders	Conduct disorder Autistic disorder Tourette's syndrome Stuttering
Eating disorders	Disorders characterized by severe disturbances in eating behavior	Anorexia nervosa Bulimia nervosa

Source: Based on *DSM-IV-TR* (American Psychiatric Association, 2000a).

findings indicate that psychological disorders are more common than many physical ailments. For instance, each year in the United States, less than 1% of adults, about 1.5 million people, are diagnosed with cancer (American Cancer Society, 2009). By contrast, 26%, or more than 44 million adults, are diagnosed with a mental disorder of some kind (Freeman et al., 2010).

Another way of thinking about the frequency of a disorder is to examine how likely an individual is to be diagnosed with it in his or her lifetime. The lifetime prevalence rate of cancer in the United States is about 30%; in other words, about 30% of Americans will be diagnosed with cancer sometime in their lives (National Center for Health Statistics, 2000). Again, mental disorders are more common, with a lifetime prevalence rate of nearly 50% (Freeman et al., 2010). Lifetime rates of a few disorders are shown in Figure 12.1. Clearly, mental disorders represent a significant source of personal misery for individuals and of lost productivity for society. Thus, research aimed at identifying their causes and treatments is just as important as research examining the causes and treatments of physical diseases.

TABLE 12.2 The Multiaxial System

AXIS	DESCRIPTION	EXPLANATION
I	Clinical disorders	Psychological disorders or the main reason for an individual's visit to a clinician is recorded on Axis I. The clinician can enter as many diagnoses or problems as needed but, typically, designates one of them as primary.
II	Personality disorders; Mental retardation	Axis II includes only two types of disorders, personality disorders and mental retardation. These two classes of disorders are separated because they usually call for special treatment strategies.
III	General medical conditions	Any relevant health condition is recorded on Axis III. The clinician also notes any recommendations made to the person regarding the need to look for a medical cause for his or her psychological problems.
IV	Psychosocial, environmental problems	Life issues, such as strained romantic relationships, unemployment, or lack of social support that may be relevant to treatment are recorded on Axis IV.
V	Global assessment of functioning	Axis V usually includes a "global functioning" score ranging from 0 to 100 that describes the degree to which the person's psychological problems have affected his or her life.

Source: American Psychiatric Association (2000a).

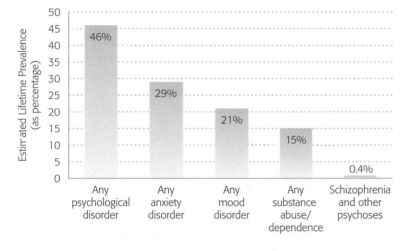

FIGURE 12.1 Lifetime Prevalence of Psychological Disorders
The percentages of people in the United States who suffer from various psychological disorders during their lifetime are based on the findings of the National Comorbidity Survey.
Source: Data from Bhugra (2005) & Freeman et al. (2010).

Explaining Psychological Disorders

> **12.3** What are the five perspectives that psychologists use to explain psychological disorders?

What causes psychological disorders, and how can they be treated? Psychologists employ five theoretical perspectives to answer these questions. Each perspective has its place in the description, analysis, and treatment of psychological disorders.

The *biological perspective* views abnormal behavior as arising from a physical cause, such as genetic inheritance, biochemical abnormalities or imbalances, structural abnormalities within the brain, and/or infection. Thus, its adherents favor biological treatments, such as drug therapy.

The *biopsychosocial perspective* agrees that physical (biological) causes are of central importance but also recognizes the influence of psychological and social factors in the study, identification, and treatment of psychological disorders. Consequently, biopsychosocial psychologists often advocate treatment strategies that include both drugs and psychotherapy.

Originally proposed by Freud, the *psychodynamic perspective* maintains that psychological disorders stem from early childhood experiences and unresolved, unconscious conflicts, usually of a sexual or aggressive nature. The cause assumed by the psychodynamic approach also suggests the cure—psychoanalysis, which Freud developed to uncover and resolve such unconscious conflicts.

SUMMARIZE IT

Five Perspectives on Psychological Disorders

PERSPECTIVE	CAUSES OF PSYCHOLOGICAL DISORDERS	TREATMENT
Biological perspective	A psychological disorder is a symptom of an underlying physical disorder caused by a structural or biochemical abnormality in the brain, by genetic inheritance, or by infection.	Diagnose and treat like any other physical disorder. Drugs, electroconvulsive therapy, or psychosurgery
Biopsychosocial perspective	Psychological disorders result from a combination of biological, psychological, and social causes.	Employ eclectic treatments that include both drugs and psychotherapy
Psychodynamic perspective	Psychological disorders stem from early childhood experiences and unresolved, unconscious sexual or aggressive conflicts.	Bring disturbing repressed material to consciousness and help patient work through unconscious conflicts. Psychoanalysis
Learning perspective	Abnormal thoughts, feelings, and behaviors are learned and sustained like any other behaviors, or there is a failure to learn appropriate behaviors.	Use classical and operant conditioning and modeling to extinguish abnormal behavior and to increase adaptive behavior. Behavior therapy Behavior modification
Cognitive perspective	Faulty thinking or distorted perceptions can cause psychological disorders.	Change faulty, irrational, and/or negative thinking. Beck's cognitive therapy Rational-emotive therapy

According to the *learning perspective*, psychological disorders are thought to be learned and sustained in the same way as any other behavior. According to this view, people who exhibit abnormal behavior either are victims of faulty learning or have failed to learn appropriate patterns of thinking and acting. Behavior therapists use the learning principles of classical and operant conditioning to eliminate distressing behavior and to establish new, more appropriate behavior in its place.

The *cognitive perspective* suggests that faulty thinking or distorted perceptions can contribute to some types of psychological disorders. Treatment based on this perspective is aimed at changing thinking, which presumably will lead to a change in behavior.

The *Summarize It* feature lists the main ideas and treatment approaches for each of the theoretical perspectives. You should remember from Chapter 1 that many psychologists favor an eclectic approach rather than a rigid commitment to a single perspective. Thus, mental health professionals often adopt the perspective and treatment method that they believe will be most helpful in each individual case.

Anxiety Disorders

What would you do if your lifelong dream of being a professional entertainer came true? No doubt you would be overjoyed, but what if a severe case of stage fright robbed you of that joy and prevented you from taking advantage of many of the opportunities to perform that came your way? Surprisingly, this is precisely what has happened to many highly talented and successful performers. For example, stage fright prevented Barbara Streisand from performing before live audiences for 27 years. Similarly, actress Scarlett Johansson made her stage debut as a confident 8-year-old child actress. But by the time she reached her teens, Johansson had developed such a severe case of stage fright that she feared she would never be able to perform before a live audience again. Despite her successful film career, Johansson turned down numerous offers to appear on the stage before finally overcoming her fears in early 2010 to play the leading role in a Broadway play. However it isn't always the prospect of facing a live audience that

▲ Stage fright led actress Scarlett Johansson to refuse several offers to appear on the Broadway stage until early 2010.

leads to paralyzing stage fright. Film star Hugh Grant reports that he often freezes up in front of the cameras, leading to embarrassment and filming delays.

Stage fright is one manifestation of a fearful state of mind that psychologists call *anxiety*. When anxiety is so severe that it interferes with a person's educational or occupational functioning, it can develop into a serious psychological disorder. Anxiety disorders are the most common category of mental disorders and account for more than 4 million visits to doctors' offices each year in the United States (National Center for Health Statistics, 2002b).

anxiety disorders Psychological disorders characterized by frequent fearful thoughts about what might happen in the future.

Panic Attacks, Agoraphobia, and Panic Disorder ▶

Feeling anxious is an extremely common experience. However, anxious feelings, even when they occur for unknown reasons and seem to be irrational, are not psychological disorders (American Psychiatric Association, 2000a). There are, however, two types of anxious feelings for which people often seek professional help, panic attacks and agoraphobia.

[**12.4** What are the characteristics of panic attacks, agoraphobia, and panic disorder?

Panic Attacks. A panic attack is a sudden feeling of fear in which the heart pounds, the body shakes, and the person has a choking sensation. Panicky feelings that have known cues, such as the feeling a person might get while driving through an intersection where she once had a traffic accident, are more often viewed as the result of learning rather than as signs of a disorder. By contrast, uncued attacks are more likely to be symptomatic of a psychological disorder.

panic attack An episode of overwhelming anxiety, fear, or terror.

Uncued attacks appear to be brought about by a dysfunction in the autonomic nervous system's fight-or-flight system in which the brain misperceives a normal change in bodily functioning to be a danger signal (National Alliance for Mental Illness, 2003). For example, a person's heart rate normally increases after consuming a beverage that contains caffeine. For unknown reasons, in panic attack sufferers, this normal change may be perceived as a danger signal by the brain, thereby causing the sympathetic nervous system to put the body's autonomic systems on alert. Next, the person's higher cognitive functions spring into action—"I'm having a heart attack! I'm going to die!"—thus amplifying the sensation of danger. These cognitive interpretations prolong the attack by short-circuiting the parasympathetic system's efforts to counteract the sympathetic system's influence on physiological functions. Thus, clinicians often treat panic attacks by teaching people how to control their cognitive responses to the sensations that accompany these attacks (Teachman, Marker, & Smith-Janik, 2008).

Agoraphobia. A person with agoraphobia has an intense fear of being in a situation from which immediate escape is not possible or in which help would not be available if she or he should become overwhelmed by anxiety or experience. In some cases, a person's entire life is planned around avoiding feared situations such as busy streets, crowded stores, restaurants, and/or public transportation. Many will not leave home unless accompanied by a friend or family members, and, in severe cases, not even then.

agoraphobia (AG-or-uh-FO-bee-ah) An intense fear of being in a situation from which escape is not possible or in which help would not be available if one experienced overwhelming anxiety or a panic attack.

Although agoraphobia can occur without panic attacks, it often begins during the early adult years with repeated panic attacks (American Psychiatric Association, 2000a). The intense fear of having another attack causes the person to avoid any place or situation where previous attacks have occurred. Thus, although agoraphobia itself is not a psychological disorder, when it begins to interfere so dramatically with a person's everyday life, clinicians often find that it is one of many debilitating symptoms that a person is experiencing as a result of having developed an anxiety disorder.

Panic Disorder. People who have recurring panic attacks may be diagnosed with panic disorder. Panic disorder sufferers must cope with both repeated attacks and anxiety about the occurrence and consequences of further attacks. This anxiety can lead people to develop agoraphobia, as noted earlier. The presence of agoraphobia complicates clinicians' efforts to help people who have panic disorder because confronting

panic disorder An anxiety disorder in which a person experiences recurring, unpredictable episodes of overwhelming anxiety, fear, or terror.

situations in which panic attacks are likely to occur is part of the process of learning to live with this persistent disorder. Obviously, clinicians have a much harder time getting people with agoraphobia to take on this challenging aspect of their treatment. For this reason, panic disorder with agoraphobia is among the most debilitating of all psychological disorders. However, most individuals with this disorder respond to a combination of medication and psychotherapy (Lamplugh et al., 2008). ◉─|Watch on **mypsychlab.com**

◉─|**Watch** the **Video** *Panic Disorder* on **mypsychlab.com**

Explaining Panic Disorder. You should remember from Chapter 5 that negative reinforcement increases behaviors that enable us to avoid something unpleasant. Each time a person with panic disorder behaves in a way that prevents or interrupts a panic attack, their behavior is reinforced because it enables them to escape from the unpleasant sensations that are associated with anxiety (e.g., rapidly beating heart, rapid breathing, feelings of doom, and impending death). Over time, the frequency of avoidance behaviors increases to the point that the person leaves home only when absolutely necessary and is prone to suddenly returning home in the midst of even the most essential excursions (e.g., doctor's appointments) if a panic attack happens. As a result, a cycle of anxiety, avoidance, and escape becomes established and gains dominance over the life of the person who has panic disorder.

In order to break this cycle, most therapists encourage people with panic disorder to confront situations in which they may experience a panic attack. When people with panic disorder follow this recommendation, they learn that the anxiety they experience when a panic attack occurs will eventually subside on its own (Lamplugh et al., 2008). Thus, relief from anxiety becomes a reinforcer for confronting anxiety-provoking situations rather than for avoiding them.

12.5 How do generalized anxiety disorder, social phobia and specific phobia differ?

Generalized Anxiety Disorder and Phobias

At the beginning of this section, you read about several entertainers' battles with stage fright. Like them, millions of people struggle with and overcome anxiety disorders.

generalized anxiety disorder (GAD) An anxiety disorder in which people experience chronic, excessive worry for 6 months or more.

Generalized Anxiety Disorder. Generalized anxiety disorder (GAD) is the diagnosis given to people who experience chronic, excessive worry for 6 months or more. These people expect the worst; their worrying is either unfounded or greatly exaggerated and, thus, difficult to control. Their excessive anxiety may cause them to feel tense, tired, and irritable and to have difficulty concentrating and sleeping. Other symptoms may include trembling, palpitations, sweating, dizziness, nausea, diarrhea, or frequent urination. This disorder affects twice as many women as men and leads to considerable distress and impairment (Brawman-Mintzer & Lydiard, 1996, 1997; Kranzler, 1996).

phobia (FO-bee-ah) A persistent, irrational fear of some specific object, situation, or activity that poses little or no real danger.

social phobia An irrational fear and avoidance of any social or performance situation in which one might embarrass or humiliate oneself in front of others by appearing clumsy, foolish, or incompetent.

Social Phobia. A phobia is a persistent, irrational fear of some specific object, situation, or activity that poses no real danger (or whose danger is blown out of proportion). Most people realize that their phobias are irrational, but they nevertheless feel compelled to avoid the feared situations or objects. People who have social phobia are intensely afraid of any social or performance situation in which they might embarrass or humiliate themselves in front of others—by shaking, blushing, sweating, or in some other way appearing clumsy, foolish, or incompetent. Social phobia may take the specific form of *performance anxiety*. About one-third of people with social phobia only fear speaking in public (Kessler, Stein, & Berglund, 1998). If you are one of the millions who are afraid of public speaking, see the *Apply It* for advice on overcoming your fear.

Social phobia can be a disabling disorder (Yates, 2008). In its extreme form, it can seriously affect people's performance at work, preventing them from advancing in their careers or pursuing an education and severely restricting their social lives (Bruch, Fallon, & Heimberg, 2003; Stein & Kean, 2000; Yates, 2008). Those with social phobia sometimes turn to alcohol and tranquilizers to lessen their anxiety in social situations.

APPLY IT ▸ Overcoming the Fear of Public Speaking

Do you break out in a cold sweat and start trembling when you have to speak in public? If so, cheer up; you're in good company: Fear of public speaking is the number one fear reported by American adults in surveys. More people fear public speaking than flying, sickness, or even death (CBS News, July 31, 2002)!

What Causes It?
Fear of public speaking is a form of performance anxiety, a common type of social phobia. Much of the fear of public speaking stems from fear of being embarrassed or of being judged negatively by others. Some people cope with this fear by trying to avoid situations in which they may be required to speak in public. A more practical approach is to examine the incorrect beliefs that can cause the fear of public speaking and then take specific steps to overcome it. Here are some incorrect beliefs associated with public speaking (Orman, 1996):

- To succeed, a speaker has to perform perfectly. (Not true; no audience expects perfection.)
- A good speaker presents as many facts and details about the subject as possible. (Not true; all you need is two or three main points.)
- If some members of the audience aren't paying attention, the speaker needs to do something about it. (Not true; you can't please everyone, and it's a waste of time to try to do so.)

What Can You Do?
Some of the steps you can take to manage fear of public speaking deal with how you present yourself to your audience; others focus on what's going on inside you. Here are some of the many suggestions offered by experts at Toastmasters International (2003), an organization devoted to helping people improve their public speaking skills:

- *Know your material well.* Practice aloud and revise your speech, if necessary.
- *Visualize your speech.* Imagine yourself giving your speech in a confident, clear manner.
- *Relax.* Reduce your tension by doing deep breathing or relaxation exercises.
- *Be familiar with the place where you will speak.* Arrive early and practice using the microphone and any other equipment you plan to use.
- *Connect with the audience.* Greet some members of the audience as they arrive; then, when you give your speech, speak to the audience as though they were a group of your friends.
- *Project confidence through your posture.* Stand or sit in a self-assured manner, smile, and make eye contact with the audience.
- *Focus on your message, not on yourself.* Turn your attention away from your nervousness and focus on the purpose of your speech, which is to transmit information to your audience.
- *Remember that the audience doesn't expect you to be perfect.* Don't apologize for any problems you think you have with your speech. Just be yourself.

By applying these few simple tips, you can overcome nervousness and speak confidently on any topic—even on the spur of the moment.

◉ Watch on **mypsychlab.com**

Specific Phobia. A specific phobia is a marked fear of a specific object or situation. This general label is applied to any phobia other than agoraphobia and social phobia. Faced with the object or situation they fear, people who have a specific phobia experience intense anxiety, even to the point of shaking or screaming. The categories of specific phobias, in order of frequency of occurrence, are (1) situational phobias (fear of elevators, airplanes, enclosed places, heights, tunnels, or bridges); (2) fear of the natural environment (fear of storms or water); (3) animal phobias (fear of dogs, snakes, insects, or mice); and (4) blood-injection-injury phobia (fear of seeing blood or an injury or of receiving an injection) (Fredrikson et al., 1996). Two types of situational phobias—*claustrophobia* (fear of closed spaces) and *acrophobia* (fear of heights)—are the specific phobias treated most often by therapists (see the *Try It*, p. 388).

specific phobia A marked fear of a specific object or situation; a general label for any phobia other than agoraphobia and social phobia.

Explaining Generalized Anxiety Disorder and Phobias. Psychologist Timothy Brown (2007) has argued convincingly that GAD and social phobia are manifestations of the Big Five personality trait of neuroticism. You should remember from Chapter 11 that people who are high in neuroticism have a negative outlook on life and tend to be emotionally unstable. That is, they tend to react to stressors in the same way that other people do, but their reactions are more intense and extreme. For example, everyone gets anxious when they have an important exam coming up. But people who are high

Phobia Names

You may know that the Greek word *phobia* means "fear." Thus, phobias are named by creating a compound word that includes the Greek or Latin word for the feared object with *-phobia*. For example, *agoraphobia* literally means "fear of the marketplace" (*agora* = marketplace) and, by usage, has come to mean a fear of open spaces or of being anywhere other than one's home. Likewise, *claustrophobia* combines the Latin word *claustrum*, which means "prison," with *-phobia* to denote a fear of enclosed places. Think about the following phobias and see whether you can match them with their definitions.

_____ **(1)** ablutobphobia
_____ **(2)** glossophobia
_____ **(3)** gynephobia
_____ **(4)** lactophobia
_____ **(5)** haptephobia
_____ **(6)** hemophobia
_____ **(7)** xenophobia
_____ **(8)** erythrophobia

a. fear of the color red
b. fear of public speaking
c. fear of washing or bathing
d. fear of strangers
e. fear of women
f. fear of blood
g. fear of being touched
h. fear of milk

ANSWERS: (1) c, (2) b, (3) e, (4) h, (5) g, (6) f, (7) d, (8) a

in neuroticism may worry about the exam so much that they can't sleep or eat, and they may irritate those around them by constantly talking about how stressed they are over the exam. Brown's research suggests that these reactions can develop into generalized anxiety disorder and/or social phobia (as well as depression, which you'll read about later in the chapter). Moreover, he has found that people with these disorders who are high in neuroticism benefit less from treatment than those who are low in the trait.

Neuroticism is also a risk factor for the development of specific phobias (Bienvenu et al., 2007). However, classical conditioning, which you will recall involves associations between neutral stimuli and fear-provoking situations or objects, is important as well. To cite a simple example: A dog barks menacingly at 3-year-old Bobby (fear-provoking situation); Bobby associates all dogs (neutral stimulus) with the experience. As a result, he cries and runs away every time he sees a dog. Consequently, principles of learning are often used to treat specific phobias. A therapist may use classical conditioning principles to teach people with phobias to associate pleasant emotions with feared objects or situations. For example, a child who fears dogs might be given ice cream while in a room where a dog is present. Behavior modification, in which people with phobias are reinforced for exposing themselves to fearful stimuli, may also be useful. Observation of models who do not exhibit fear in response to the object or situation of which a person with a phobia is afraid has also been an effective treatment technique.

12.6 What are the symptoms of obsessive-compulsive disorder?

Obsessive-Compulsive Disorder

What would your life be like if every time you left your home you were so fearful of having left your door unlocked that you had to go back and check it again and again? Obsessive-compulsive disorder (OCD) is an anxiety disorder in which a person has recurrent obsessions or compulsions, or both.

obsessive-compulsive disorder (OCD) An anxiety disorder in which a person has recurrent obsessions and/or compulsions.

obsession A persistent, involuntary thought, image, or impulse that invades consciousness and causes great distress.

compulsion A persistent, irresistible, and irrational urge to perform an act or ritual repeatedly.

Obsessions and Compulsions. Obsessions are persistent, involuntary thoughts, images, or impulses that invade consciousness and cause a person great distress. People with obsessions might worry about contamination by germs or about whether they performed a certain act, such as turning off the stove or locking the door (Greenberg, 2009). Other types of obsessions center on aggression, religion, or sex.

A person with a compulsion feels a persistent, irresistible, irrational urge to perform an act or ritual repeatedly. The individual knows such acts are senseless but cannot resist performing them without experiencing an intolerable buildup of anxiety—which can be relieved only by yielding to the compulsion. Many of us have engaged in compulsive behavior like stepping over cracks on the sidewalk, counting stairsteps, or performing little rituals from time to time. The behavior becomes a psychological problem only if the person cannot resist performing it, if it is very time consuming, and if it interferes with the person's normal activities and relationships with others.

Compulsions exhibited by people with obsessive-compulsive disorder often involve cleaning and washing behaviors, counting, checking, touching objects, hoarding, and excessive organizing. These cleaning and checking compulsions affect 75% of OCD patients receiving treatment (Ball, Baer, & Otto, 1996). People with OCD realize that their behavior is not normal, but they simply cannot help themselves, as shown in the following example.

Mike, a 32-year-old patient, performed checking rituals that were preceded by a fear of harming other people. When driving, he had to stop the car often and return to check whether he had run over people, particularly babies. Before flushing the toilet, he had to check to be sure that a live insect had not fallen into the toilet, because he did not want to be responsible for killing a living thing. At home he repeatedly checked to see that the doors, stoves, lights, and windows were shut or turned off. . . . Mike performed these and many other checking rituals for an average of 4 hours a day. (Kozak, Foa, & McCarthy, 1988, p. 88)

Explaining Obsessive-Compulsive Disorder. An important feature of OCD is that individuals with the disorder fear or are disgusted by things that everyone would prefer not to be exposed to. Likewise, their compulsions are typically exaggerated forms of behaviors that most people exhibit from time to time. In other words, most of us would prefer to be clean, and most of us have checked an appliance to be sure that it is turned off from time to time. Thus, the problem in OCD is that normal aversions are taken to extremes (Deacon & Olatunji, 2007). Experimental studies in which people with and without OCD are exposed to the same kinds of potentially disgusting and anxiety-inducing stimuli have demonstrated this to be true (Olatunji et al., 2007).

But where does the tendency of individuals with OCD toward extreme responses come from? Studies have shown that early autoimmune system diseases, early strep infections, and changes in the brain caused by infection may predispose a person to develop OCD (Swedo & Grant, 2004). Several twin and family studies suggest that a genetic factor is involved in the development of OCD as well (Hur, 2009; Kirvan et al., 2006). Genes affecting serotonin functioning are suspected of causing OCD in some people, many of whom are helped by antidepressant drugs that increase serotonin levels in the brain (Ravindran et al., 2009).

▲ Like this woman, many people with obsessive-compulsive disorder take great pains to avoid contamination from germs and dirt.

Mood Disorders

Actor and comedian Jim Carrey is known for his exaggerated humorous facial expressions and slapstick humor, so few people would guess that he has struggled with periods of profound sadness at various points during his successful show business career. A sense of sadness that is severe enough to interfere with a person's work is one of several mood disorders, a group of psychological disorders that are characterized by extreme and unwarranted disturbances in emotion. Of course, everyone experiences ups and downs, but true mood disorders involve changes in mood that are characterized by the criteria for abnormality you read about at the beginning of the chapter. In other words, people with these disorders have symptoms that are severe enough to interfere with their normal functioning.

mood disorders Disorders characterized by extreme and unwarranted disturbances in emotion or mood.

Major Depressive Disorder ▷

> **12.7** What are the characteristics of major depressive disorder?

People with major depressive disorder feel an overwhelming sadness, despair, and hopelessness, and they usually lose their ability to experience pleasure. They may have changes in appetite, weight, or sleep patterns; loss of energy; and difficulty in thinking or concentrating. Key symptoms of major depressive disorder are psychomotor disturbances

major depressive disorder A mood disorder marked by feelings of great sadness, despair, and hopelessness as well as the loss of the ability to experience pleasure.

(Bhalla, Moraille-Bhalla, & Aronson, 2010). For example, body movements, reaction time, and speech may be so slowed that some depressed people seem to be doing everything in slow motion. Others experience the opposite extreme and are constantly moving and fidgeting, wringing their hands, and pacing. Depression can be so severe that people develop delusions or hallucinations, which are symptoms of *psychotic depression*. The more deeply a person descends into depression over an extended period, the more she or he withdraws from social activities (Judd et al., 2000).

According to the American Psychiatric Association (2000a), one year after their initial diagnosis of major depressive disorder, 40% of people diagnosed with depression are without symptoms; 40% are still suffering from the disorder; and 20% are depressed, but not enough to warrant a diagnosis of major depression. Slightly less than one-half of those hospitalized for major depressive disorder are fully recovered after one year (Keitner et al., 1992). For many, recovery is aided by antidepressant drugs. However, some studies show that psychotherapy can be just as effective (Hollon, Thase, & Markowitz, 2002). Some people have only one major depressive episode, but 50 to 60% will have a recurrence. Risk of recurrence is greatest for females (Winokur et al., 1993) and for individuals with an onset of depression before age 15 (Brown, 1996). Recurrences may be frequent or infrequent, and for 20 to 35% of people with depression, the episodes are chronic, lasting two years or longer. Thus, finding a way to prevent recurrences is important in depression research. Most researchers suggest that medication, psychotherapy, social support, and even physical exercise may all play some role in the prevention of recurrent episodes of depression (Sher, 2004a).

12.8 What kinds of mood changes do people with bipolar disorder experience?

bipolar disorder A mood disorder in which manic episodes alternate with periods of depression, usually with relatively normal periods in between.

manic episode (MAN-ik) A period of excessive euphoria, inflated self-esteem, wild optimism, and hyperactivity, often accompanied by delusions of grandeur and by hostility if activity is blocked.

Bipolar Disorder

Bipolar disorder is a condition in which individuals exhibit two radically different moods—the extreme highs of manic episodes (or *mania*) and the extreme lows of major depression—usually with relatively normal periods in between. Manic episodes are marked by excessive euphoria, inflated self-esteem, wild optimism, and hyperactivity. People in a manic state have temporarily lost touch with reality and frequently have delusions of grandeur along with their euphoric highs. They may waste large sums of money on get-rich-quick schemes. If family members or friends try to stop them, they are likely to become irritable, hostile, enraged, or even dangerous. Quite often, individuals must be hospitalized during manic episodes to protect them and others from the disastrous consequences of their poor judgment.

Bipolar disorder is much less common than major depressive disorder, affecting about 1% of the U.S. population in any given year, and the lifetime prevalence rates are about the same for males and females (Soreff & McInnes, 2008). Bipolar disorder tends to appear in late adolescence or early adulthood. About 90% of those with the disorder have recurrences, and about 50% experience another episode within a year of recovering from a previous one. The good news is that 70 to 80% of people with bipolar disorder return to a state of emotional stability (American Psychiatric Association, 2000a), even though mild cognitive deficits, such as difficulty with planning, persist in many of them following a manic episode (Chowdhury, Ferrier, & Compson, 2003). Still, in many cases, individuals with bipolar disorder can manage their symptoms, and thereby live a normal life, with the help of drugs such as lithium and divalproex. Moreover, psychotherapy can help them cope with the stress of facing life with a potentially disabling mental illness (Hollon et al., 2002). ◉─|Watch on **mypsychlab.com**

◉─|**Watch** the **Video** *Bipolar Disorder* on **mypsychlab.com**

12.9 What are some risk factors for mood disorders?

Explaining Mood Disorders

Many factors contribute to the development of mood disorders. Biological factors appear to be central. However, an individual's life circumstances are important as well, along with cultural factors and gender roles.

Neurological Correlates of Mood Disorders. PET scans have revealed abnormal patterns of brain activity in people with mood disorders (Drevets, Price, & Furey, 2008).

Drevets and others (1997) located a brain area that may trigger both the sadness of major depression and the mania of bipolar disorder. A small, thimble-size patch of brain tissue in the lower prefrontal cortex (about 2 to 3 inches behind the bridge of the nose) is a striking 40 to 50% smaller in people with major depression. Earlier research established that this area of the brain plays a key role in the control of emotions. Moreover, the personality trait called *neuroticism* is associated with both depression and abnormalities in the brain's serotonin levels (Fanous et al., 2002; Lesch, 2003). Research has shown that abnormal levels of serotonin are strongly linked to depression and to suicidal thoughts (Oquendo et al., 2003). Thus, individuals who are at the neurotic end of the Big Five personality dimension of neuroticism (discussed in Chapter 11) may be predisposed to develop depression and to have suicidal thoughts.

Researchers have also found that the production, transport, and reuptake patterns for dopamine, GABA, and norepinephrine in people with mood disorders differ from those in other individuals (Kaladindi & McGuffin, 2003). Neurotransmitter abnormalities may reflect genetic variations, thus helping to explain the significant heritability rates for mood disorders.

Heredity. Evidence for a genetic basis for bipolar disorder is also strong. In one twin study, researchers found that 50% of the identical twins of bipolar sufferers had also been diagnosed with a mood disorder, compared to only 7% of fraternal twins (Kalidindi & McGuffin, 2003). Mounting evidence indicates that the genetic and neurological bases of bipolar disorder are more like those of schizophrenia than those of major depressive disorder (Molnar et al., 2003). These findings may explain why biological relatives of people with bipolar disorder are at increased risk of developing a number of mental disorders, while relatives of those with major depressive disorder display an increased risk only for that disorder (Kaladindi & McGuffin, 2003).

Stressors. Life stresses are also associated with depression. The vast majority of first episodes of depression strike after major life stress (Brown, Harris, & Hepworth, 1994; Frank et al., 1994; Tennant, 2002). A longitudinal study of Harvard graduates that continued for over 40 years found that negative life events as well as family history played significant roles in the development of mood disorders (Cui & Vaillant, 1996). This seems particularly true of women, who are more likely to have experienced a severe negative life event just prior to the onset of depression (Welsh, 2009). Yet, recurrences of depression, at least in people who are biologically predisposed, often occur without significant life stress (Brown et al., 1994).

Culture. How is it possible to study depression—or any mental disorder, for that matter—across cultures, since cultural context must be taken into consideration when defining abnormality? Indeed, it is extremely difficult to construct surveys or other instruments for measuring mental disorders that are valid in a variety of cultures (Girolamo & Bassi, 2003). Nevertheless, a few researchers have managed to produce a limited, but informative, body of data about cross-cultural differences in depression (Girolamo & Bassi, 2003). One large study involving participants from 10 countries revealed that the lifetime risk for developing depression varied greatly around the world (see Figure 12.2, p. 392), with Asian countries (Taiwan and Korea) having significantly lower rates of the disorder (Weissman et al., 1996). Researchers explain these differences as the result of cross-cultural differences in ideal emotional states (Tsai, Knutson, & Fung, 2006). The experience of depression in individuals who live in non-Asian cultures appears to be influenced by those cultures' ideas about how people *ought* to feel, a phenomenon that psychologist Daniel Gilbert (2006) claims to be an important factor in individual differences in happiness (see the *Explain It* feature, p. 392).

Gender. In most countries, the rate of depression for females is about twice that for males (World Health Organization, 2010). Before boys reach puberty, they are more

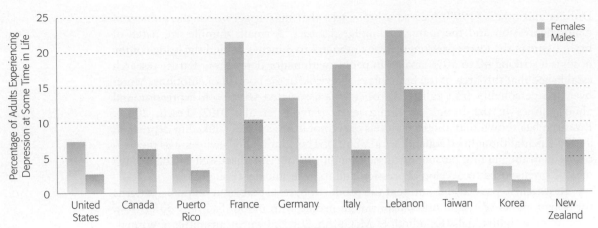

FIGURE 12.2 Lifetime Risk for Developing Depression in 10 Countries
The lifetime prevalence of depression for 38,000 men and women in 10 different countries reveals that women are more susceptible to depression worldwide.
Source: Data from Weissman et al. (1996).

likely than girls to be depressed, but a dramatic reversal of the gender-related depression rates takes place in adolescence (Cyranowski et al., 2000). Not only are women more likely than men to suffer from depression, but they are also more likely to be affected by negative consequences as a result. Early-onset major depressive disorder adversely affects the educational attainment and earning power of women, but not men (Berndt et al., 2000). The National Task Force on Women and Depression suggests that the higher rate of depression in women is largely due to social and cultural factors. In fulfilling her many roles—mother, wife, lover, friend, daughter, neighbor—a woman is likely to put the needs of others ahead of her own (Schmitt, Fuchs, & Kirch, 2008).

EXPLAIN IT   How Do Cultural Beliefs about Ideal Emotional States Lead to Depression?

Cross-cultural researchers' assert that cultural differences in beliefs about how people *ought* to feel might lead to cultural differences in depression rates. Think about how a thought pattern in which people measure their own emotional state against a cultural ideal might contribute to depression. For example, did you notice in Figure 12.2 that depression rates are much lower in Taiwan and Korea than they are in Europe, North America, and New Zealand? Some researchers attribute this finding to the belief of people in Western cultures that they should be happy most of the time (Uchida, Norasakkunkit, & Kitayama, 2004). As a result, people in such cultures have difficulty coping with the unpleasant emotional states that are a part of everyday life and are at increased risk of depression. Moreover, say these researchers, people in Western cultures devote their energies to pursuing achievements that they believe will ensure their future happiness. By contrast, researchers hypothesize that people in East Asian cultures such as Korea and Taiwan focus more on maintaining a balance between positive and negative emotional states (Uchida et al., 2004). This belief leads East Asians to focus more energy on maintaining social connections that provide them with support in times of emotional distress than they do to the pursuit of happiness.

In his book *Stumbling on Happiness* psychologist Daniel Gilbert (2006) offered evidence in support of the view that people in Western cultures often base their life goals on beliefs about how they can attain lasting happiness. He points out that individuals in these societies are often disappointed when they make decisions based on overly optimistic predictions about what will make them happy (Gilbert, 2006). For example, soap operas, movies, and even ads for Valentine's Day cards and treats lead people to believe that their lives will be perfect if they find the right romantic partner. In search of that partner, many people date, marry, have affairs, divorce, date again, marry again, and so on. Why? Because the emotional perfection that they think will come to them as a result of each change in status never materializes. As a result, they perpetually predict that the next relationship will be the perfect one.

The other side of the unrealistic expectation coin is the overestimation of the emotional impact of an imagined loss (Kermer et al., 2006). Just as some people move from partner to partner in search of the perfect one, others stay in unsatisfactory relationships because they fear the emotional trauma that they expect to experience as a result of being alone. This kind of thought pattern leads people to avoid taking risks. As a result, they feel perpetually unhappy both because of the features of the relationships in which they choose to remain and because they are plagued by thoughts about the good outcomes that they might have experienced if they had the courage to take a risk. Here again, people's belief in the necessity of maintaining an ideal emotional state, as defined by Western culture, is the fundamental error in thinking that they are making, in Gilbert's view.

Suicide and Race, Gender, and Age ▷

┌ **12.10** What are some of the risk
└ factors for suicide?

Some people with depression commit the ultimate act of desperation—suicide. Mood disorders and schizophrenia, along with substance abuse, are major risk factors for suicide in all age groups (Mościcki, 1995; Pinikahana, Happell, & Keks, 2003; Shaffer et al., 1996). Suicide risk also increases when people are exposed to particularly troubling life stressors, such as the violent death of a spouse (Ajdacic-Gross et al., 2008). There is also evidence that suicidal behavior runs in families (Brent et al., 1996, 2002). Even among people who have severe mood disturbances, such as bipolar disorder, those with a family history of suicide attempts are far more likely to kill themselves than are those without such history (Tsai et al., 2002).

About 32,000 suicides are reported annually in the United States. Figure 12.3 shows the differences in U.S. suicide rates according to race, gender, and age (Bergen et al., 2008). As you can see, White Americans are more likely than African Americans to commit suicide. Native American suicide rates are similar to those of White Americans; rates for Hispanic Americans are similar to those of African Americans (National Center for Health Statistics, 2006a). Asian Americans have the lowest suicide rates of all ethnic groups in the United States until they reach old age when, for unknown reasons, suicide rates among Asian American males rise dramatically (National Center for Health Statistics, 2006a). Nevertheless, the suicide rate among Asian Americans who are over the age of 65, at 17 per 100,000, is half that of White American males.

You will also note in Figure 12.3 that suicide rates are far lower for both White and African American women than for men. However, studies show that women are four times more likely than men to attempt suicide (Anderson, 2002). The higher rate of completed suicides in males is due to the methods men and women use. Emergency room records show that the rate of firearms use by suicide attempters and completers is 10 times higher in males than in females, while the rates of poisoning and drug overdose are higher in females (Centers for Disease Control and Prevention, 2002). Consequently, a higher proportion of male suicide attempters succeed in killing themselves.

Although suicide rates among teens and young adults have increased in the past few decades, older Americans are at far greater risk for suicide than younger people.

▲ Evidence suggests that suicidal behavior tends to run in families. Les Franklin founded the Shaka Franklin Foundation for Youth, a suicide prevention organization, in memory of his son Shaka, who had killed himself. Ten years later, Franklin's other son, Jamon, also committed suicide.

Students are often surprised to learn that suicide rates are higher in late adulthood than they are in the teen and early adult years. Why do you think that is the case? Do you think society places more emphasis on early-life than on late-life suicides? If so, why?

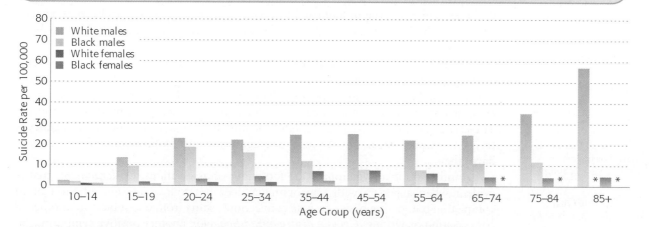

FIGURE 12.3 Differences in Suicide Rates According to Race, Gender, and Age
In every age group, the suicide rate is highest for White American males and second-highest for African American males. The general conclusion is that males are more likely to commit suicide than females and that White Americans are more likely to do so than are African Americans. Suicide rates indicated by asterisks (*) are too low to be statistically reliable.
Source: Data from National Center for Health Statistics (2006a).

▲ Tracy Moore's plans to become a professional singer were cut short by symptoms of schizophrenia when she was a college student. Still, once her doctors found an effective medication for her symptoms, she was able to fulfill her dream of auditioning for *American Idol*.

12.11 What are the positive and negative symptoms of schizophrenia?

psychosis (sy-CO-sis) A condition characterized by loss of contact with reality.

schizophrenia (SKIT-soh-FREE-nee-ah) A severe psychological disorder characterized by loss of contact with reality, hallucinations, delusions, inappropriate or flat affect, some disturbance in thinking, social withdrawal, and/or other bizarre behavior.

hallucination An imaginary sensation.

delusion A false belief, not generally shared by others in the culture.

delusion of grandeur A false belief that one is a famous person or a powerful or important person who has some great knowledge, ability, or authority.

delusion of persecution A false belief that some person or agency is trying in some way to harm one.

White males aged 85 and older have the highest recorded suicide rate, with more than 51 suicides for every 100,000 people in that age group, about five times the average national suicide rate of 11 per 100,000 (National Center for Health Statistics, 2006a). Poor general health, serious illness, loneliness (often due to the death of a spouse), and decline in social and economic status are conditions that may push many older Americans, especially those aged 75 and older, to commit suicide.

About 90% of individuals who commit suicide leave clues (NIMH, 2009). They may communicate verbally: "You won't be seeing me again." They may provide behavioral clues, such as giving away their most valued possessions; withdrawing from friends, family, and associates; taking unnecessary risks; showing personality changes; acting and looking depressed; and losing interest in favorite activities. These warning signs should always be taken seriously. If you suspect you are dealing with a suicidal person, the best thing you can do is to encourage the person to get professional help. There are 24-hour suicide hotlines all over the country. A call might save a life.

Schizophrenia

After high school, Tracy Moore enrolled in Musictech College in Minneapolis to pursue her goal of becoming a professional singer (Roberts, 2006). Soon Moore started hearing voices and became convinced that aliens were trying to take over her body, a condition referred to as psychosis among psychologists. Doctors determined that she was suffering from schizophrenia, a serious psychological disorder in which a person loses contact with reality. Medication relieved Moore's symptoms well enough that she was able to audition for the 2003 edition of *American Idol*. Today, Moore continues to sing, but she devotes most of her time to raising public awareness of schizophrenia and the remarkable capacity for resilience that is displayed by many who are afflicted with the disease.

Symptoms of Schizophrenia

The *positive symptoms* of schizophrenia are the abnormal behaviors that are present in people with the disorder. (By the way, *positive* means "added" not "good.") One of the clearest positive symptoms of schizophrenia is the presence of hallucinations, or imaginary sensations. People with schizophrenia may see, hear, feel, taste, or smell strange things in the absence of any stimulus in the environment, but hearing voices is the most common type of hallucination. People with schizophrenia also may experience exceedingly frightening and painful bodily sensations and feel that they are being beaten, burned, or sexually violated.

Having delusions, or false beliefs not generally shared by others in the culture, is another positive symptom of schizophrenia. Those who have delusion of grandeur may believe they are a famous person (the president or Moses, for example) or a powerful or important person who possesses some great knowledge, ability, or authority. Those with delusion of persecution have the false notion that some person or agency is trying to harass, cheat, spy on, conspire against, injure, kill, or in some other way harm them.

Another positive symptom is the loosening of associations, or *derailment*, that is evident when a person with schizophrenia does not follow one line of thought to completion but, on the basis of vague connections, shifts from one subject to another in conversation or writing. *Grossly disorganized behavior*, another positive symptom, can include such things as childlike silliness, inappropriate sexual behavior (masturbating in public), disheveled appearance, and peculiar dress. There may also be unpredictable agitation, including shouting and swearing, and unusual or inappropriate motor behavior, including strange gestures, facial expressions, or postures. People with schizophrenia may also display *inappropriate affect*; that is, their facial expressions, tone of voice, and gestures may not reflect the emotion that would be expected under the circumstances.

A person might cry when watching a TV comedy and laugh when watching a news story about a fatal automobile accident.

A *negative symptom* of schizophrenia is a loss of or deficiency in thoughts and behaviors that are characteristic of normal functioning. Negative symptoms include social withdrawal, apathy, loss of motivation, lack of goal-directed activity, very limited speech, slowed movements, poor hygiene and grooming, poor problem-solving abilities, and a distorted sense of time (Davalos, Kisley, & Ross, 2002; Hatashita-Wong et al., 2002; Skrabalo, 2000). Many also have difficulty forming new memories (Matthews & Barch, 2004). Some with schizophrenia have another negative symptom called *flat affect,* showing practically no emotional response at all, even though they often report feeling the emotion. These patients may speak in a monotone, have blank and emotionless facial expressions, and act and move more like robots than humans.

◀ A person with catatonic schizophrenia may become frozen in an unusual position, like a statue, for hours at a time.

Not all people with schizophrenia have negative symptoms. Those who do seem to have the poorest outcomes (Fenton & McGlashan, 1994). Negative symptoms are predictors of impaired overall social and vocational functioning. People who have negative symptoms tend to withdraw from normal social contacts and retreat into their own world. They have difficulty relating to people, and often their functioning is too impaired for them to hold a job or even to care for themselves. ✳ Explore on **mypsychlab.com**

✳ Explore the **Concept** *Types and Symptoms of Schizophrenia* on **mypsychlab.com**

Types of Schizophrenia

12.12 What are the four types of schizophrenia?

Even though various symptoms are commonly shared by people with schizophrenia, certain features distinguish one type of schizophrenia from another. For example, people with paranoid schizophrenia usually have delusions of grandeur or persecution. They may be convinced that they have an identity other than their own—that they are the president, the Virgin Mary, or God—or that they possess great ability or talent. They may feel that they are in charge of the hospital or on a secret assignment for the government and often show exaggerated anger and suspiciousness. If they have delusions of persecution and feel that they are being harassed or threatened, they may become violent in an attempt to defend themselves against their imagined persecutors. Usually, the behavior of a person with paranoid schizophrenia is not so obviously disturbed as that of one with the catatonic or disorganized type, and the chance for recovery is better.

paranoid schizophrenia (PAIR-uh-noid) A type of schizophrenia characterized by delusions of grandeur or persecution.

Disorganized schizophrenia, the most serious type, tends to occur at an earlier age than the other types and is marked by extreme social withdrawal, hallucinations, delusions, silliness, inappropriate laughter, grimaces, grotesque mannerisms, and other bizarre behavior. These individuals show flat or inappropriate affect and are frequently incoherent. They often exhibit obscene behavior and may masturbate openly. Disorganized schizophrenia results in the most severe disintegration of the personality, and its victims have the poorest chance of recovery (Fenton & McGlashan, 1991).

Persons with catatonic schizophrenia may display complete stillness and stupor or great excitement and agitation. Frequently, they alternate rapidly between the two. They may become frozen in a strange posture or position and remain there for hours without moving. Undifferentiated schizophrenia is the general term used when schizophrenic symptoms either do not conform to the criteria of any one type of schizophrenia or conform to more than one type.

disorganized schizophrenia The most serious type of schizophrenia, marked by extreme social withdrawal, hallucinations, delusions, silliness, inappropriate laughter, grotesque mannerisms, and other bizarre behavior.

catatonic schizophrenia (KAT-uh-TAHN-ik) A type of schizophrenia characterized by complete stillness or stupor or great excitement and agitation; patients may assume an unusual posture and remain in it for long periods of time.

undifferentiated schizophrenia A catchall term used when schizophrenic symptoms either do not conform to the criteria of any one type of schizophrenia or conform to more than one type.

12.13 What factors increase the risk of developing schizophrenia?

Explaining Schizophrenia

Despite more than 100 years of research, the cause of schizophrenia remains a mystery. According to leading schizophrenia researcher Elaine Walker and her colleagues (2004), a key assumption underlying recent work on the puzzle of schizophrenia is that there is no single cause. Risk factors interact in complex ways such that an individual might have all of the relevant risk factors but never develop the disorder. Walker's model is shown in Figure 12.4 and includes several components. Walker and her team summarize these components as follows.

Constitutional Vulnerability. *Constitutional vulnerability* refers to the aspects of an individual's congenital (at birth) risk of developing schizophrenia that are attributable to factors within the person. One such factor is gender; that is, males are more likely to develop schizophrenia than females are. Moreover, scientists have known for some time that heredity contributes to schizophrenia (Cannon et al., 1998; Gottesman, 1991; Kendler & Diehl, 1993; Owen & O'Donovan, 2003). Figure 12.5 shows how the chance of developing schizophrenia varies with the degree of relationship to a person with schizophrenia. However, researchers do not yet know exactly what it is that vulnerable individuals inherit. It is possible that the genes that contribute to schizophrenia affect the structure of the developing fetal brain. On the other hand, they may shape later developmental processes or influence the actions of neurotransmitters such as dopamine in an individual's brain throughout life. Genes are also known to play a role in how well or how poorly individuals with schizophrenia respond to treatment with antipsychotic drugs (Yasui-Furukori et al., 2006).

Some aspects of constitutional vulnerability are acquired as a result of prenatal and/or postnatal experiences. These experiences include, for example, fetal exposure to maternal stress hormones and to substances such as alcohol and drugs that the mother ingests. They also include nutrients that the fetus receives from the mother as well as viruses and bacteria that cross the placenta. Postnatal stressors include birth trauma and other threats to the infant's health that occur during or immediately after birth.

Researchers have also examined the contribution of microorganisms to constitutional vulnerability. For example, schizophrenia is linked to the influenza virus (Perron et al., 2008). Recent studies suggest that the influenza virus activates a group of viruses called *HERV-W* that is dormant in all humans. The HERV-W viruses then trigger an inflammatory process in the brain that leads to schizophrenia. A number of investigations also suggest that the risk of schizophrenia is elevated in people with *cytomegalovirus*, a type of herpes virus, and *toxoplasmosis*, a condition caused by parasites in cat feces (Yolken & Torrey, 2008).

FIGURE 12.4 How Risk Factors Lead to Schizophrenia
This diagram shows how many researchers today view the risk factors for schizophrenia. The central concept is "constitutional vulnerability." Prenatal and postnatal factors derived from both heredity and environmental factors cause some people to be born with a greater sensitivity to stress than others. Stress and neuromaturational processes interact with constitutional vulnerability to produce the symptoms of schizophrenia.
Source: Walker et al. (2004).

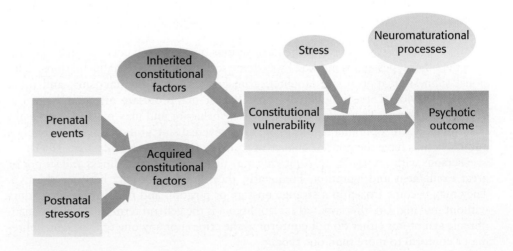

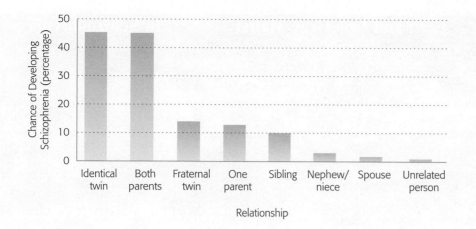

FIGURE 12.5 Genetic Similarity and Probability of Developing Schizophrenia Research strongly indicates a genetic factor associated with schizophrenia. Identical twins have identical genes, and if one twin develops schizophrenia, the other twin has a 46% chance of also developing it. In fraternal twins, the chance is only 14%. A person with one schizophrenic parent has a 13% chance of developing schizophrenia, but a 46% chance if both parents are schizophrenic. *Source:* Data from Nicol & Gottesman (1983).

Stress. Walker and her colleagues point out that there is no evidence suggesting that individuals who develop schizophrenia experience more stress than others. Instead, researchers believe that the constitutional factors described above cause some individuals to be more vulnerable to stress than others (Walker, Mittal, & Tessner, 2008). Thus, stress plays a role in the development of schizophrenia, but only among those who have the relevant constitutional vulnerability. Researchers hypothesize that the constitutional vulnerabilities of individuals who develop schizophrenia include some kind of neurological sensitivity to the biochemical changes that go along with being under stress. To use a crude analogy to illustrate this idea, stress hormones appear to flip switches in the brains of individuals who are constitutionally vulnerable to schizophrenia that they do not flip in the brains of others.

Neuromaturational Processes. Walker reports that many studies have shown that the brains of individuals with schizophrenia differ both structurally and functionally from those of people who do not have the disorder. For example, levels of neural activity in the frontal lobes tend to be lower in the brains of people with schizophrenia than they are in others (Glantz & Lewis, 2000; Kim et al., 2000). Many individuals with schizophrenia have defects in the neural circuitry of the cerebral cortex and the limbic system (Rasetti, et al., 2009). Further, on average, people with schizophrenia display slower than normal communication between the left and right hemispheres of the brain (Florio et al., 2002).

Because schizophrenia is most often diagnosed in the late teens and early twenties, the theoretical model in Figure 12.4 assumes that the neurological correlates of schizophrenia are somehow linked to the neuromaturational processes that normally occur during late adolescence. Once schizophrenia sets in, the progressive neurological deterioration that is part of the disorder itself also induces changes in the brain. These changes include decreases in gray matter (see Figure 12.6, p. 398) and in overall brain size, along with deterioration of the cerebral cortex and the hippocampus.

According to Walker and her colleagues (2004), studies of the brains of individuals with schizophrenia after death have shown that the disease is associated with damage to the neurons themselves. Most such damage is found in the parts of the neurons that make up the brain's neurotransmitter system that you learned about in Chapter 2. Some researchers suggest that this damage leads to impaired communication between the emotional and intellectual parts of the brain. Others contend that the damaged neurons ineffectively govern the overall coordination of the brain's various functional subsystems.

With regard to neurotransmitters themselves, Walker states that many studies suggest that dopamine plays an important role in schizophrenia, primarily because medications that are known to act on dopamine are usually helpful in the treatment of psychoses (Müller et al., 2006). However, the nature of the brain's neurotransmitter system is such that it is unlikely that deficiencies, excesses, or malfunctions that

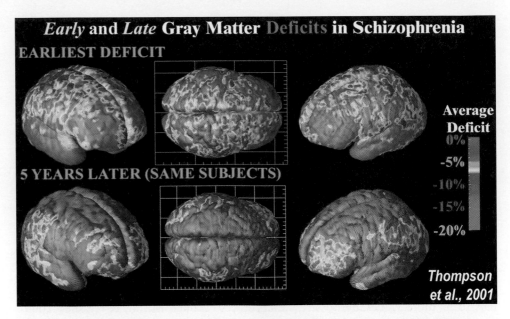

FIGURE 12.6 Destruction of Gray Matter in the Brains of Adolescents Diagnosed with Schizophrenia
This figure dramatically depicts the devastating effects of schizophrenia on gray matter in the brains of people with the disorder. The images on the first line of this figure show the average gray matter deficits in the brains of 15 adolescents who ranged from 12 to 15 years of age who had just been diagnosed with schizophrenia. Those on the second line represent the amount of gray matter they had lost to the disease five years later.
Source: Thompson et al. (2001).

involve a single neurotransmitter can fully account for the complex features of schizophrenia. It is more likely, says Walker, that many other neurotransmitters, notably glutamate and GABA, also participate in the neurological processes that underlie the symptoms of schizophrenia.

Other Psychological Disorders

In August 2005, a homeless man who could not remember who he was or how he had gotten to their city pleaded with Chicago police to help him determine his identity. He believed that his name was Jay Tower, but he knew nothing more about himself. The police helped the desperate man send his fingerprints to the FBI, but these efforts were to no avail. Months later, one of the residents who lived in the same homeless shelter as Tower recognized him in a picture that was shown on the television program *America's Most Wanted* during February 2006. The report claimed that the man in the picture was Ray Power, a New York attorney who had disappeared on August 1, 2005. Apparently, Power suffered from a form of amnesia known as *dissociative fugue,* one of several disorders you will read about in this section.

12.14 What are somatoform disorders?

Somatoform Disorders

Have you heard the word *psychosomatic* applied to a symptom or illness? Laypersons usually use this term to refer to physical disorders of psychological origin. The *DSM-IV-TR* uses the term *somatoform disorder* to refer to such conditions. The somatoform disorders involve physical symptoms that are due to psychological causes rather than any known medical condition. Although their symptoms are psychological in origin, patients are sincerely convinced that they spring from real physical disorders. People with somatoform disorders are not consciously faking illness to avoid work or other activities.

somatoform disorders (so-MAT-uh-form) Disorders in which physical symptoms are present that are due to psychological causes rather than any known medical condition.

People with hypochondriasis are overly concerned about their health and fear that their bodily symptoms are a sign of some serious disease. A person with this somatoform disorder "might notice a mole and think of skin cancer or read about Lyme disease and decide it might be the cause of that tired feeling" (Barsky, 1993, p. 8). Yet the symptoms are not usually consistent with known physical disorders, and even when a medical examination reveals no physical problem, people with hypochondriasis are not convinced. They may "doctor shop," going from one physician to another, seeking confirmation of their worst fears. Unfortunately, hypochondriasis is not easily treated, and there is usually a poor chance for recovery.

A person is diagnosed with a conversion disorder when there is a loss of motor or sensory functioning in some part of the body, which is not due to a physical cause but which solves a problem (Powsner & Dufel, 2009). For instance, debilitating headaches that are triggered by driving a car might provide a person who has a driving-related phobia with a socially acceptable reason for avoiding driving. A person may become blind, deaf, or unable to speak or may develop a paralysis in some part of the body. Many of Freud's patients suffered from conversion disorder, and he believed that they unconsciously developed a physical disability to help resolve an unconscious sexual or aggressive conflict.

Research suggests that hypochondriasis results from the same kinds of neurological deficits that give rise to obsessive-compulsive disorder (OCD) and depression (Xiong et al., 2009). Experts point out that it is often difficult to distinguish it from diagnoses such as generalized anxiety disorder. Moreover, drugs that are effective for OCD and depression are often effective for hypochondriasis as well, another finding that supports the hypothesis that these disorders share a common origin.

Similarly, there is some degree of overlap with conversion disorder and the anxiety disorders (Xiong et al., 2009). Psychologists think that a conversion disorder can act as an unconscious defense against any intolerable anxiety situation that the person cannot otherwise escape. For example, a soldier who desperately fears going into battle might escape the anxiety by developing a paralysis or some other physically disabling symptom. One reason for this hypothesis is that those with conversion disorder exhibit a calm and cool indifference to their symptoms, called "la belle indifference." Furthermore, many seem to enjoy the attention, sympathy, and concern their disability brings them.

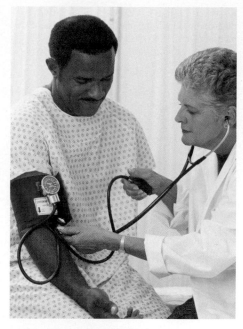

▲ A person who continually complains of various symptoms and seeks medical treatment for them, even though doctors can discover nothing wrong, may be suffering from a somatoform disorder.

Dissociative Disorders ▶

Imagine how disconcerting it would be if you were unable to recognize your own leg. In his book *A Leg to Stand On,* neurologist Oliver Sacks (1984) described the case of a hospitalized man who could not feel or even recognize his own leg. This patient insisted that the leg wasn't even connected to his body, and his attempts to throw the leg out of his bed resulted in numerous falls. This unfortunate man was suffering from a profound disintegration of his physical and psychological self. Mental health professionals refer to this process as *dissociation*—the loss of one's ability to integrate all the components of self into a coherent representation of one's identity. In this case, the patient's dissociation was the result of an underlying physical illness. In many other instances, dissociation has a psychological rather than a physical cause.

In response to unbearable stress, some people develop a dissociative disorder, in which they lose the ability to consciously integrate their identities. Their consciousness becomes dissociated from their identity or their memories of important personal events, or both. For example, dissociative amnesia is a complete or partial loss of the ability to recall personal information or identify past experiences that cannot be attributed to ordinary forgetfulness or substance use. It is often caused by a traumatic experience—a psychological blow, so to speak—or a situation that creates unbearable anxiety, causing the person to escape by "forgetting."

[**12.15** How do dissociative disorders affect behavior?

hypochondriasis (HI-poh-kahn-DRY-uh-sis) A somatoform disorder in which persons are preoccupied with their health and fear that their physical symptoms are a sign of some serious disease, despite reassurance from doctors to the contrary.

conversion disorder A somatoform disorder in which a person suffers a loss of motor or sensory functioning in some part of the body; the loss has no physical cause but solves some psychological problem.

dissociative disorders Disorders in which, under unbearable stress, consciousness becomes dissociated from a person's identity or her or his memories of important personal events, or both.

dissociative amnesia A dissociative disorder in which there is a complete or partial loss of the ability to recall personal information or identify past experiences.

dissociative fugue (FEWG) A dissociative disorder in which one has a complete loss of memory of one's entire identity, travels away from home, and may assume a new identity.

dissociative identity disorder (DID) A dissociative disorder in which two or more distinct, unique personalities occur in the same person, and there is severe memory disruption concerning personal information about the other personalities.

Even more puzzling than dissociative amnesia is dissociative fugue, in the disorder that afflicted Ray Power, whose story you read at the beginning of this section. In a fugue state, people not only forget their identity but, like Power, they also travel away from home. Some take on a new identity that is usually more outgoing and uninhibited than their former identity. The fugue state may last for hours, days, or even months. The fugue is usually a reaction to some severe psychological stress, such as a natural disaster, a serious family quarrel, a deep personal rejection, or military service in wartime. Fortunately for most people, recovery from dissociative fugue is rapid, although they may have no memory of the initial stressor that brought on the fugue state. When people recover from the fugue, they often have no memory of events that occurred during the episode.

In dissociative identity disorder (DID), two or more distinct, unique personalities exist in the same individual, and there is severe memory disruption concerning personal information about the other personalities. In 50% of the cases, there are more than 10 different personalities. The change from one personality to another often occurs suddenly and usually during stress. The personality in control of the body the largest percentage of time is known as the *host personality* (Kluft, 1984). The alternate personalities, or *alter personalities,* may differ radically in intelligence, speech, accent, vocabulary, posture, body language, hairstyle, taste in clothes, manners, and even handwriting and sexual orientation. In 80% of the cases of dissociative identity disorder, the host personality does not know of the alter personalities, but the alters have varying levels of awareness of each other (Putnam, 1989). The host and alter personalities commonly show amnesia for certain periods of time or for important life events, such as a graduation or wedding. A common complaint is of "lost time"—periods for which a given personality has no memory because he or she was not in control of the body.

Dissociative identity disorder usually begins in early childhood but is rarely diagnosed before adolescence (Vincent & Pickering, 1988). About 90% of the treated cases have been women (Ross, Norton, & Wozny, 1989), and more than 95% of the patients reveal early histories of severe physical and/or sexual abuse (Coons, 1994; Putnam, 1992). However, the connection between abuse and DID is not an absolute one (Brenner, 2009). That is, abuse does not lead to DID in every case, or even in most cases. Likewise, many cases of DID occur in individuals who do not have histories of abuse. Moreover dissociative identity disorder can be treated, often by psychotherapy, and some evidence indicates that DID patients respond well to treatment (Pais, 2009).

12.16 What are the characteristics of the various sexual disorders?

Sexual Disorders

sexual disorders Disorders with a sexual basis that are destructive, guilt- or anxiety-producing, compulsive, or a cause of discomfort or harm to one or both parties involved.

sexual dysfunctions Persistent, recurrent, and distressing problems involving sexual desire, arousal, or the pleasure associated with sex or orgasm.

Most psychologists define sexual disorders as behavior patterns that are related to sexuality or sexual functioning and are destructive, guilt- or anxiety-producing, compulsive, or a cause of discomfort or harm to one or both parties involved.

Perhaps the most common of all of the sexual disorders are the sexual dysfunctions—persistent, recurrent, and distressing problems involving sexual desire, sexual arousal, or the pleasure associated with sex or orgasm (see Chapter 9). Drug treatments for sexual dysfunctions have been successful for both men and women. For men, the drug *sildenafil citrate (Viagra)* has been proven effective in restoring erectile function. And orgasmic disorders and other sexual dysfunctions in women are increasingly being treated with hormones such as *dehydroepiandrosterone (DHEA)* (Munarriz et al., 2002). However, experts in sexual dysfunction point out that while biochemical treatments may restore or enhance physiological functions, other interventions, including individual and couples therapy, are required to improve the intimate relationships of people with sexual dysfunctions (Besharat, 2001; Heiman, 2002; Lieblum, 2002).

Another important aspect of treatment concerns the link between depression and sexual dysfunction in both men and women (Seidman, 2002). Depression is both a cause and an effect of sexual dysfunctions. Consequently, researchers advise health professionals to question people who complain of sexual difficulties about factors that may indicate the presence of depression. However, antidepressant drugs often increase the incidence of sexual difficulties (Coleman et al., 2001). Thus, experts advocate combined biochemical and psychological interventions that address both mood and sexual functioning for people with depression (Montejo et al., 2001).

Paraphilias are disorders in which a person experiences recurrent sexual urges, fantasies, or behaviors involving children, other nonconsenting persons, nonhuman objects, or the suffering or humiliation of the individual or his or her partner. To be diagnosed as having a paraphilia, the person must experience considerable psychological distress or an impairment in functioning in an important area of his or her life.

Gender identity disorder is characterized by a problem accepting one's identity as male or female. In childhood, people with gender identity disorder express a desire to be or insist that they are the other gender. They show a strong preference for the clothes, games, pastimes, and playmates of the opposite sex. In adulthood, an individual may feel so strongly that she or he is psychologically of the other gender that *sex-reassignment surgery* is undergone. Twin studies suggest that genes strongly influence the development of gender identity disorder (Coolidge, Thede, & Young, 2002).

Personality Disorders ▶

Do you know someone who is impossible to get along with and who always blames others for his or her problems? Such a person may have a personality disorder—a long-standing, inflexible, maladaptive pattern of behaving and relating to others, which usually begins early in childhood or adolescence. Personality disorders are among the most common of mental disorders; the *DSM-IV-TR* indicates that 10 to 15% of North Americans have one or more personality disorders. People who suffer from other disorders, especially mood disorders, are often diagnosed with personality disorders as well (Kopp et al., 2009; Valtonen et al., 2009). In most cases, the causes of personality disorders have yet to be identified.

People with personality disorders are extremely difficult to get along with and often blame others for their problems. As a result, most have unstable work and social histories. Because medications have not proved to be very useful in the treatment of personality disorders, treatment options are few. After all, to seek and benefit from therapy, a person must realize that he or she has a problem and be somewhat cooperative with the therapist.

Several types of personality disorders exist, and the criteria used to differentiate among them overlap considerably. For this reason, the *DSM-IV-TR* groups personality disorders into *clusters,* as shown in Table 12.3 (p. 402). The individual disorders within each cluster share certain similarities. For example, all of the disorders in Cluster A are characterized by odd behavior, such as extreme suspiciousness.

Cluster B disorders involve erratic, overly dramatic behavior. A person with a Cluster B disorder might complain loudly in a store when he feels slighted by a clerk. These disorders carry a higher risk of suicide than other personality disorders (Lambert, 2003). Individuals with borderline personality disorder are especially prone to suicidal thoughts and to self-mutilation (Joiner et al., 2009). Many have histories of childhood abuse and experience intense fears of abandonment in adult relationships (Allen, 2008).

Another Cluster B disorder, antisocial personality disorder, is believed to be present in 20% or more of the men and women who are serving prison sentences in the United States (American Psychiatric Association, 2000a). In most of these individuals, a pattern of behavior characterized by lying, cheating, and cruelty to others became established in childhood (Arehart-Treichel, 2002). People with Cluster B disorders typically lack empathy, and many experts believe that this feature of their thinking predisposes them to antisocial behavior (Habel et al., 2002).

Cluster C disorders are characterized by intense feelings of anxiety. Individuals with obsessive-compulsive disorder, for example, may become severely distressed if their normal routines are disrupted. The anxieties of those with either avoidant or dependent personality disorder center on social relationships.

Despite the apparently grim prognosis associated with personality disorders, research indicates that their features change over time. In one longitudinal study

paraphilias Sexual disorders in which recurrent sexual urges, fantasies, or behavior involve nonhuman objects, children, other nonconsenting persons, or the suffering or humiliation of the individual or his or her partner.

gender identity disorder Sexual disorder characterized by a problem accepting one's identity as male or female.

12.17 **What are the similarities and differences among the various personality disorders?**

personality disorder A long-standing, inflexible, maladaptive pattern of behaving and relating to others, which usually begins in early childhood or adolescence.

TABLE 12.3 Types of Personality Disorders

PERSONALITY DISORDER	SYMPTOMS
Cluster A: Odd behavior	
Paranoid	Individual is highly suspicious, untrusting, guarded, hypersensitive, easily slighted, lacking in emotion; holds grudges.
Schizoid	Individual isolates self from others; appears unable to form emotional attachments; behavior may resemble that of autistic children.
Schizotypal	Individual dresses in extremely unusual ways; lacks social skills; may have odd ideas resembling the delusions of schizophrenia.
Cluster B: Erratic, overly dramatic behavior	
Narcissistic	Individual has exaggerated sense of self-importance and entitlement; is self-centered, arrogant, demanding, exploitive, envious; craves admiration and attention; lacks empathy.
Histrionic	Individual seeks attention and approval; is overly dramatic, self-centered, shallow, demanding, manipulative, easily bored, suggestible; craves excitement; often, is attractive and sexually seductive.
Borderline	Individual is unstable in mood, behavior, self-image, and social relationships; has intense fear of abandonment; exhibits impulsive and reckless behavior and inappropriate anger; makes suicidal gestures and performs self-mutilating acts.
Antisocial	Individual disregards rights and feelings of others; is manipulative, impulsive, selfish, aggressive, irresponsible, reckless, and willing to break the law, lie, cheat, and exploit others for personal gain, without remorse; fails to hold jobs.
Cluster C: Anxious, fearful behavior	
Obsessive-compulsive	Individual is concerned with doing things the "right" way and is generally a perfectionist; relationships are emotionally shallow.
Avoidant	Individual fears criticism and rejection; avoids social situations in order to prevent being judged by others.
Dependent	Person overly dependent on others for advice and approval; may cling to lovers and friends, fearing abandonment.

involving individuals who were diagnosed with personality disorders in adolescence, researchers found that, on average, these diagnoses were fairly stable over a 10-year period (Durbin & Klein, 2006). However, many individuals in the study no longer met the diagnostic criteria for personality disorders at the 10-year follow-up. Of course, these individuals may have been incorrectly diagnosed in the first place. However, the study also identified declines in specific features of these disorders, such as the high prevalence of neuroticism among personality disorder sufferers. Such trends support the view that, in some individuals, the psychological and behavioral factors that lead to a personality disorder diagnosis may be resolved to some degree or become less severe over time.

Because the characteristics involved in personality disorders closely resemble normal variations in personality, it is especially important when thinking about them to remember the criteria for abnormality discussed at the beginning of this chapter. So, if a friend suspects a neighbor of poisoning his cat, and you think this is an unreasonable suspicion, don't jump to the conclusion that your friend has paranoid personality disorder. This tendency toward suspiciousness is likely to be simply a personality trait of your friend.

⟡ Looking Back

In this chapter, you may have found similarities between your own behavior and the patterns associated with one or more psychological disorders. This phenomenon, known as *intern's syndrome,* is common among students of introductory psychology. You need only look at the discussion of the criteria used by mental health professionals to define abnormality at the beginning of the chapter to determine that unless your behavior is interfering with some important domain of functioning—school, work, relationships, and so on—it is probably not indicative of a psychological disorder. If you or someone close to you does suffer from such a disorder, take heart from the many stories of resilience that we included and be aware that there are thousands more like these. There are many people who not only survive the experience of having a disorder or loving someone who does but also manage to grow stronger through the process.

CHAPTER 12 SUMMARY

DEFINING PSYCHOLOGICAL DISORDERS (pp. 380-384)

12.1 What criteria do psychologists use to classify behavior as abnormal? (pp. 380-381)

Behavior might be considered abnormal if it differs radically from what is considered normal in the person's own culture, if it leads to personal distress or impaired functioning, or if it results in the person's being a danger to self and/or others.

Key Term
psychological disorders, p. 380

12.2 How do clinicians use the *DSM-IV-TR*? (pp. 381-383)

Clinicians use the *DSM-IV-TR* to classify and keep track of psychological disorders. It includes diagnositic criteria for about 300 psychological disorders. They are organized into several major categories. Clinicians use its multiaxial system to describe individual cases. Tracking studies show that psychological disorders are more prevalent than physical diseases. Nearly half of people are diagnosed with some kind of psychological disorder during their lifetimes. The two most prevalent categories are anxiety and mood disorders.

Key Term
DSM-IV-TR, p. 381

12.3 What are the five perspectives that psychologists use to explain psychological disorders? (pp. 383-384)

Five theoretical perspectives on the causes of psychological disorders are the biological perspective, the biopsychosocial perspective, the psychodynamic perspective, the learning perspective, and the cognitive perspective. The biological perspective emphasizes genetics and other physiological factors. The biopsychosocial focuses on interactions among biological, psychological, and social factors. Learning theorists explain psychological disorders as the result of experiences, while the cognitive perspective focuses on faulty thinking. The psychodynamic perspective is based on Freud's psychoanalytic theory and emphasizes unconscious processes.

ANXIETY DISORDERS (pp. 384-389)

12.4 What are the characteristics of panic attacks, agoraphobia, and panic disorder? (pp. 385-386)

Poeple who have panic attacks respond to ordinary changes in the body as though they were life-threatening. The symptoms of panic attacks include intense fear, rapidly beating heart, and other signs of physiological distress. Repeated panic attacks can lead to agoraphobia, the fear of being in places from which escape is difficult. Panic disorder occurs when panic attacks are so frequent that they interfere with a person's social, occupational, and/or academic functioning.

Key Terms
anxiety disorders, p. 385
panic attack, p. 385
agoraphobia, p. 385
panic disorder, p. 385

12.5 How do generalized anxiety disorder, social phobia, and specific phobia differ? (pp. 386-388)

Generalized anxiety disorder (GAD) involves chronic, excessive worry. Social phobias arise out of the fear of embarrassment, whereas specific phobias represent irrational fear responses to objects or situations. The Big Five personality traits contribute to the development of GAD and phobias.

People who are high in the trait of neuroticism are more likely to develop them.

Key Terms
generalized anxiety disorder, p. 386
phobia, p. 386
social phobia, p. 386
specific phobia, p. 387

12.6 What are the symptoms of obsessive-compulsive disorder? (pp. 388-389)

Obsessive-compulsive disorder is characterized by recurrent obsessions (persistent, involuntary thoughts, images, or impulses that cause great distress) and/or compulsions (persistent, irresistible, irrational urges to perform an act or ritual repeatedly). Early infections and a tendency to exhibit exaggerated responses to stimuli that are universally undesirable contribute to the development of obsessive-compulsive disorder.

Key Terms
obsessive-compulsive disorder (OCD), p. 388
obsession, p. 388
compulsion, p. 388

MOOD DISORDERS (pp. 389-394)

12.7 What are the characteristics of major depressive disorder? (p. 390)

Major depressive disorder is characterized by feelings of great sadness, despair, and hopelessness, as well as a loss of the ability to feel pleasure. Other symptoms include psychomotor disturbance and, possibly, psychotic depression.

Key Terms
mood disorders, p. 389
major depressive disorder, p. 389

12.8 What kinds of mood changes do people with bipolar disorder experience? (p. 390)

Bipolar disorder is a mood disorder in which a person has manic episodes (periods of wild optimism, inflated self-esteem, excessive euphoria, and hyperactivity) that alternate with periods of major depression.

Key Terms
bipolar disorder, p. 390
manic episode, p. 390

12.9 What are some risk factors for mood disorders? (pp. 390-392)

Risk factors for mood disorders include (1) a genetic predisposition; (2) disturbances in the brain's serotonin levels; (3) abnormal patterns in the neurotransmitters dopamine, GABA, and norepinephrine; (4) the personality trait of neuroticism; and (5) major life stress.

12.10 What are some of the risk factors for suicide? (pp. 393-394)

Depression, mood disorders, schizophrenia, and substance abuse are major risk factors for suicide. Other risk factors include particularly troubling life stressors and a genetic tendency to suicidal behavior. Elderly, White males commit suicide more often than members of other race or age groups, perhaps because of poor health or loneliness. Research shows that women are more likely to attempt suicide, but men are more likely to be successful.

SCHIZOPHRENIA (pp. 394-398)

12.11 What are the positive and negative symptoms of schizophrenia? (pp. 394-395)

The positive symptoms of people with schizophrenia are abnormal behaviors and characteristics, including hallucinations, delusions, derailment, grossly disorganized behavior, and inappropriate affect. The negative symptoms of schizophrenia represent loss of or deficiencies in thoughts and behavior that are characteristic of normal functioning. They include social withdrawal, apathy, loss of motivation, lack of goal-directed activity, very limited speech, slowed movements, flat affect, poor problem-solving abilities, a distorted sense of time, and poor hygiene and grooming.

Key Terms
psychosis, p. 394   *delusion*, p. 394
schizophrenia, p. 394   *delusion of grandeur*, p. 394
hallucination, p. 394   *delusion of persecution*, p. 394

12.12 What are the four types of schizophrenia? (p. 395)

The four types of schizophrenia are paranoid, disorganized, catatonic, and undifferentiated schizophrenia. People with

paranoid schizophrenia have delusions of persecution and/or grandeur. Those with disorganized schizophrenia exhibit bizarre behavior and hallucinations. People with catatonic schizophrenia display complete stillness or agitation. Undifferentiated schizophrenia is the term for people with the disorder who do not fit into any of the categories.

Key Terms
paranoid schizophrenia, p. 395
disorganized schizophrenia, p. 395
catatonic schizophrenia, p. 395
undifferentiated schizophrenia, p. 395

12.13 What factors increase the risk of developing schizophrenia? (pp. 396-398)

Theorists propose that schizophrenia arises from an interaction of constitutional vulnerability and external factors. Constitutional vulnerability includes heredity and prenatal risks, such as exposure to teratogens. Stress is an important external factor. Neuromaturational development is also believed to contribute to the finding that schizophrenia usually appears in the late adolescent or early adult years.

OTHER PSYCHOLOGICAL DISORDERS (pp. 398-402)

12.14 What are somatoform disorders? (pp. 398-399)

Somatoform disorders involve physical symptoms that cannot be identified as any of the known medical conditions. Hypochondriasis involves a persistent fear that bodily symptoms are the sign of some serious disease, and conversion disorder involves a loss of motor or sensory functioning in some part of the body, which has no physical cause but does solve a psychological problem.

Key Terms

somatoform disorders, p. 398
hypochondriasis, p. 399
conversion disorder, p. 399

12.15 How do dissociative disorders affect behavior? (pp. 399-400)

Dissociative disorders cause people to lose the ability to consciously integrate their identities in some important way. People with dissociative amnesia have a complete or partial loss of the ability to recall personal information or identify past experiences. In dissociative fugue, people forget their entire identity, travel away from home, and may assume a new identity somewhere else. In dissociative identity disorder, two or more distinct, unique personalities exist in the same person, and there is severe memory disruption concerning personal information about the other personalities.

Key Terms

dissociative disorder, p. 399
dissociative amnesia, p. 399
dissociative fugue, p. 400
dissociative identity disorder (DID), p. 400

12.16 What are the characteristics of the various sexual disorders? (pp. 400-401)

Sexual disorders are destructive, guilt- or anxiety-producing, compulsive, or a cause of discomfort or harm to those who have them and/or others around them. A sexual dysfunction is a problem with sexual desire, sexual arousal, or the pleasure associated with sex or orgasm. Paraphilias are disorders in which people have recurrent sexual urges, fantasies, and behaviors that involve children, other nonconsenting persons, nonhuman objects, or the suffering and humiliation of the individual or his/her partner. People who feel that their psychological gender identity is different from that typically associated with their biological sex may suffer from gender identity disorder.

Key Terms

sexual disorders, p. 400
sexual dysfunctions, p. 400
paraphilias, p. 401
gender identity disorder, p. 401

12.17 What are the similarities and differences among the various personality disorders? (pp. 401-402)

People with personality disorders have long-standing, inflexible, maladaptive patterns of behavior that cause problems in their social relationships and at work. Cluster A disorders are characterized by unusual behavior. The disorders in Cluster B involve erratic, overly dramatic behavior. Cluster C includes disorders that are associated with fearful and anxious behaviors.

Key Term

personality disorder, p. 401

MAP IT

Log on to MyPsychLab and click on "Map It" to prepare a unique digital map of the chapter that you can save for later use, email to your instructor, or print out to use as a study tool. Or, create your own map by drawing one on paper. Use the starter map below as a model for your own map. Use the chapter summary as your guide for what to include. For each item in your map, be sure to include the page number.

Here's one way to *Map It*:

1. Draw a box at the top of the page for the section title.
2. Underneath the section title box, working horizontally across the page, draw a box for each learning question in the section. Write the learning questions in the boxes and draw a line from the section title to each questions box. After you read each subsection, jot an answer for the learning question in the subsection's box.
3. Below each learning question box, insert another box for all of the key terms that are related to the question, along with a very brief reminder of each term's definition. Draw a line from the question box to the key terms box.
4. Below each key terms box, create another box and list all of the helpful figures, tables, and other elements of the text, such as *Try It* and *Apply It* boxes. Draw a line from the key terms box to the helpful elements box.

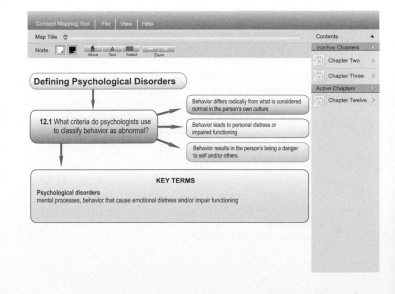

Chapter 12 Study Guide

Answers to all the Study Guide questions are provided at the end of the book.

SECTION ONE: Chapter Review

Defining Psychological Disorders (pp. 380–384)

1. It is relatively easy to differentiate normal behavior from abnormal behavior. (true/false)

2. The *DSM-IV-TR* is a manual that is published by the American Psychiatric Association and is used to
   a. diagnose psychological disorders.
   b. explain the causes of psychological disorders.
   c. outline the treatments for various psychological disorders.
   d. assess the effectiveness of treatment programs.

3. Match the perspective with its suggested cause of abnormal behavior.
   _____ (1) faulty learning
   _____ (2) unconscious, unresolved conflicts
   _____ (3) genetic inheritance or biochemical or structural abnormalities in the brain
   _____ (4) faulty thinking
   a. psychodynamic   c. learning
   b. biological   d. cognitive

Anxiety Disorders (pp. 384–389)

4. Anxiety disorders are the least common of all psychological disorders. (true/false)

5. Psychologists often use principles of learning to treat phobias. (true/false)

6. Obsessive-compulsive disorder appears to be caused primarily by psychological rather than biological factors. (true/false)

7. Match the anxiety disorder with the example.
   _____ (1) Lana refuses to eat in front of others for fear her hand will shake.
   _____ (2) Ronin is excessively anxious about his health and his job, even though there is no concrete reason to be.
   _____ (3) Kyla has been housebound for four years.
   _____ (4) Jackson gets hysterical when a dog approaches him.
   _____ (5) Lauren has incapacitating attacks of anxiety that come on her suddenly.
   _____ (6) Michael repeatedly checks his doors, windows, and appliances before he goes to bed.
   a. panic disorder
   b. agoraphobia
   c. specific phobia
   d. generalized anxiety disorder
   e. social phobia
   f. obsessive-compulsive disorder

Mood Disorders (pp. 389–394)

8. Monteil has periods in which he is so depressed that he becomes suicidal. At other times he is wildly euphoric. He would probably receive the diagnosis of
   a. antisocial personality disorder.
   b. dissociative fugue.
   c. bipolar disorder.
   d. major depressive disorder.

9. Match the type of factor with the proposed cause of depression.
   _____ (1) negative thoughts about oneself, the world, and one's future
   _____ (2) hereditary predisposition or biochemical imbalance
   _____ (3) negative life events
   a. stress
   b. cognitive factor
   c. biological factor

10. Drugs are seldom used in the treatment of mood disorders. (true/false)

11. The suicide rate is lower for
   a. males than for females.
   b. African American males than for White males.
   c. the elderly than for teenagers.
   d. people who have psychological disorders than for those who do not.

Schizophrenia (pp. 394–398)

12. Match the symptom of schizophrenia with the example.
   _____ (1) Brendon believes he is Moses.
   _____ (2) Dina thinks her family is spreading rumors about her.
   _____ (3) Avi hears voices cursing him.
   _____ (4) Dean laughs at tragedies and cries when he hears a joke.
   a. delusions of grandeur   c. inappropriate affect
   b. hallucinations   d. delusions of persecution

13. There is substantial research evidence that all of the following have roles as causes of schizophrenia *except*
   a. genetic factors.
   b. stress in people predisposed to the disorder.
   c. abnormal dopamine activity.
   d. unhealthy family interaction patterns.

14. Match the subtype of schizophrenia with the example.
   _____ (1) Amy stands for hours in the same strange position.
   _____ (2) Trevin believes the CIA is plotting to kill him.
   _____ (3) Matt makes silly faces, laughs a lot, and masturbates openly.
   _____ (4) Francesca has the symptoms of schizophrenia but does not fit any one type.
   a. paranoid schizophrenia
   b. disorganized schizophrenia
   c. catatonic schizophrenia
   d. undifferentiated schizophrenia

Other Psychological Disorders (pp. 398–402)

15. Somatoform disorders have physiological rather than psychological causes. (true/false)

16. Dissociative disorders are often associated with trauma. (true/false)

17. Match the psychological disorder with the example.
_____ **(1)** Jan is convinced he has some serious disease, although his doctors can find nothing physically wrong.
_____ **(2)** Lonnie is found far away from his home town, calling himself by another name and having no memory of his past.
_____ **(3)** Natalia suddenly loses her sight, but doctors can find no physical reason for the problem.
_____ **(4)** Colane has no memory of being in the boat with other family members the day her older brother drowned.
_____ **(5)** Cassandra has no memory for blocks of time in her life and often finds clothing in her closet that she cannot remember buying.

a. dissociative identity disorder
b. dissociative fugue
c. dissociative amnesia
d. hypochondriasis
e. conversion disorder

18. (Sexual dysfunctions, Paraphilias) are disorders in which sexual urges, fantasies, and behaviors involve children, other nonconsenting partners, or objects.

19. Which statement is true of personality disorders?
a. Personality disorders usually begin in adulthood.
b. Persons with these disorders usually realize that they have a problem.
c. Personality disorders typically cause problems in social relationships and at work.
d. Persons with these disorders typically seek professional help.

20. Bruce lies, cheats, and exploits others without feeling guilty. His behavior best fits the diagnosis of _____ personality disorder.
a. avoidant   **c.** antisocial
b. histrionic   **d.** narcissistic

SECTION TWO: Identifying the Disorder

Name the disorder characterized by each set of symptoms.

Symptoms

1. Markedly diminished interest or pleasure in all or most activities, combined with psychomotor disturbances, fatigue, insomnia, feelings of worthlessness, and recurrent thoughts of death

2. Grossly disorganized behavior combined with inappropriate affect, disturbed speech and loose associations, and delusions of grandeur—for example, a belief that one is working for a secret government agency and is being followed by foreign spies

3. Intense mood swings, ranging from euphoric and hyperactive highs marked by delusions of grandeur to extreme depression

4. Intense fear of being in a situation from which immediate escape is not possible or help is not available in the case of panic

5. Complete loss of the ability to recall personal information or past experiences, with no physical explanation for the problem

6. A pattern of unstable and intense interpersonal relationships combined with impulsivity, inappropriate and intense anger, a poor self-image, and recurrent thoughts of suicide

7. Problems involving sexual desire, sexual arousal, or the pleasure associated with sex or orgasm

8. Spending excessive amounts of time engaged in daily rituals such as counting and cleaning, accompanied by obsessions

Disorder

_____

_____

_____

_____

_____

_____

_____

_____

SECTION THREE: Fill in the Blank

1. The _____ perspective views abnormal behavior as a symptom of an underlying physical disorder.

2. Hallucinations, delusions, and disorganized speech are considered to be _____ symptoms of schizophrenia.

3. Ricardo believes that there are three men who follow him around and whisper messages in his ear, telling him to do bad things. Ricardo's false belief is called a _____.

4. Symptoms such as social withdrawal, apathy, slowed movements, and limited speech are examples of the _____ symptoms of schizophrenia.

5. Alice has been unable to make herself go to work for several weeks. She lies in bed for hours wishing for death. Alice may have _____ _____ _____.

6. Yolanda called her best friend one night at 2 a.m., extremely excited about her great idea: She was going to have U2 perform in her backyard for her birthday. She planned to call the band members as soon as she got off the phone with her friend. Yolanda was probably having a _____ episode.

7. Hypochondriasis is an example of a _____ disorder.

8. Taryn experiences sudden and unexplained waves of fear that seem to come out of nowhere. She is suffering from _____ disorder.

9. An obsession is characterized by _____ _____ _____; a compulsion involves a _____ _____ _____.

10. There seems to be no physical reason for Jason's paralysis. It is likely that he is suffering from _____ disorder.

11. The disorder in which an individual has two or more distinct personalities is called _____ _____ disorder.

12. Histrionic, borderline, antisocial, and narcissistic disorders are collectively known as _____ disorders.

13. Kim has never felt comfortable with her gender and believes she should have been a male. According to the *DSM-IV-TR* she has _____ _____ disorder.

14. _____ are sensory perceptions in the absence of any external stimulation—for example, seeing things that are not really there.

15. A _____ is a persistent, irrational fear of an object, situation, or activity that a person feels compelled to avoid.

16. The _____ personality disorder is marked by a lack of feeling for others, selfishness, aggressive and irresponsible behavior, and a willingness to break the law or exploit others for personal gain.

SECTION FOUR: Comprehensive Practice Test

1. Which perspective sees abnormal behavior as a symptom of an underlying physical disorder?
   a. cognitive
   b. psychodynamic
   c. biological
   d. behavioral

2. Which perspective sees abnormal behavior as the result of faulty and negative thinking?
   a. psychodynamic
   b. cognitive
   c. behavioral
   d. biological

3. Which perspective sees abnormal behavior as the result of early childhood experiences and unconscious sexual and aggressive conflicts?
   a. cognitive
   b. biological
   c. humanistic
   d. psychodynamic

4. Which perspective sees psychological disorders as resulting from both physical and psychological causes?
   a. cognitive
   b. biopsychosocial
   c. biological
   d. behavioral

5. Psychosis is a loss of contact with reality. (true/false)

6. Panic disorder, phobia, and obsessive-compulsive disorder are all examples of _____ disorders.
   a. neurotic
   b. anxiety
   c. personality
   d. somatoform

7. Dawn is convinced that she has a disease and goes from one doctor to another searching for a diagnosis; however, every doctor she consults says there is nothing physically wrong with her. Dawn is suffering from
   a. hypochondriasis.
   b. dissociative identity disorder.
   c. a conversion disorder.
   d. body dysmorphic disorder.

8. Dissociative amnesia, characterized by loss of memory of one's identity, is generally brought on by physical trauma. (true/false)

9. A common early experience of people with dissociative identity disorder is
   a. drug use by their mother while pregnant.
   b. measles or mumps when young.
   c. parental divorce.
   d. early physical and/or sexual abuse.

10. Hallucinations, delusions, and disorganized thinking and speech are _____ symptoms of schizophrenia.
    a. negative
    b. positive
    c. dissociative
    d. obsessive

11. Thao's belief that he is a secret agent for the devil is a good example of a delusion. (true/false)

12. A patient who sits completely still for hours as if he were in a stupor and sometimes experiences periods of great agitation and excitement is suffering from _____ schizophrenia.
    a. disorganized
    b. undifferentiated
    c. paranoid
    d. catatonic

13. Major depression and bipolar disorder are examples of _____ disorders.
    a. personality
    b. psychotic
    c. mood
    d. emotional

14. Depression is diagnosed more often in women than in men. (true/false)

15. _____ is characterized by periods of inflated self-esteem, wild optimism, and hyperactivity known as manic episodes.
    a. Schizophrenia
    b. Major depression
    c. Borderline personality disorder
    d. Bipolar disorder

16. The risk of suicide is especially high in patients who suffer from
    a. catatonic schizophrenia.
    b. paraphilias.
    c. depression.
    d. simple phobia.

17. Psychological disorders are more common than physical diseases. (true/false)

18. Depression seems to be the result of
    a. biological factors only.
    b. both biological and environmental factors.
    c. environmental factors only.
    d. poor parenting in early childhood.

SECTION FIVE: Critical Thinking

1. Formulate a specific plan that will help you recognize and avoid the five cognitive traps that contribute to unhealthy thinking. You might enlist the help of a friend to monitor your negative statements.

2. Some psychological disorders are more common in women (depression, agoraphobia, and simple phobia), and some are more common in men (antisocial personality disorder and substance abuse). Give some possible reasons for such gender differences in the prevalence of these disorders. Support your answer.

3. There is continuing controversy over whether specific psychological disorders are chiefly biological in origin (nature) or result primarily from learning and experience (nurture). Select any two disorders from this chapter, and prepare arguments for both the nature and nurture positions for both disorders.

Therapies

Think About It

Do you believe that you have to get good grades to be a "good person"? Or perhaps you believe that no matter what you do you are destined to get mediocre or even failing grades. Either way, unrealistic expectations for success or failure may be causing you some unpleasant feelings or perhaps even setting you up for a case of depression. A brief exercise can help you determine the extent to which such thinking may be compromising your mental health. First, identify an unrealistic expectation that you have for your own behavior or for some future outcome. Perhaps you think you can't be happy until you find "Mr. Right" or "Ms. Right." Or you may think it is impossible to achieve your ideal body image. Once you've identified the expectation, read and answer the following questions about it:

- Where does this belief come from? Can you identify the time in your life when it began?

- Why do you think this belief is true? What evidence can you think of that "proves" your belief?

- Can you think of any evidence to suggest that this belief is false? What evidence contradicts your belief? Do you know anyone who does not cling to this belief?

- How does holding this belief affect your life, both negatively and positively?

- How would your life be different if you stopped holding this belief? What would you do differently?

You have just completed an "assignment" that a *cognitive behavioral therapist* might give you to help you gain insight into and better control over thoughts that trigger feelings and behavior that you would like to change. But before we give you the details about cognitive behavior therapy, we will introduce you to a few other types of *psychotherapy*. The practice of psychotherapy has grown and changed enormously since its beginnings more than 100 years ago, when Freud and his colleagues began using it. Drug therapies and other physically based approaches to treatment are also far more important today than they were in Freud's time.

Insight Therapies

Do you recall a form of learning called *insight* that you read about in Chapter 5? Such learning is the foundation of several approaches to psychotherapy, treatments that use psychological rather than biological means to treat emotional and behavioral disorders. These approaches, fittingly enough, are collectively referred to as insight therapies because their assumption is that psychological well-being depends on self-understanding—the understanding of one's own thoughts, emotions, motives, behavior, and coping mechanisms.

psychotherapy Any type of approach that uses psychological rather than biological means to treat psychological disorders.

insight therapies Approaches to psychotherapy based on the notion that psychological well-being depends on self-understanding.

13.1 What are the basic techniques of psychodynamic therapies?

psychodynamic therapies Psychotherapies that attempt to uncover repressed childhood experiences that are thought to explain a patient's current difficulties.

psychoanalysis (SY-ko-uh-NAL-ul-sis) The first psychodynamic therapy, which was developed by Freud and uses free association, dream analysis, and transference.

free association A psychoanalytic technique used to explore the unconscious by having patients reveal whatever thoughts, feelings, or images come to mind.

transference An emotional reaction that occurs during psychoanalysis, in which the patient displays feelings and attitudes toward the analyst that were present in another significant relationship.

Psychodynamic Therapies

Psychodynamic therapies attempt to uncover repressed childhood experiences that are thought to explain a client's current difficulties. The techniques associated with the first such therapy—Freud's psychoanalysis—are still used by some psychodynamic therapists today (Epstein, Stern, & Silbersweig, 2001). One such technique is free association, in which the client is asked to reveal whatever thoughts, feelings, or images come to mind, no matter how trivial, embarrassing, or terrible they might seem. The analyst then pieces together the free-flowing associations, explains their meanings, and helps clients gain insight into the thoughts and behaviors that are troubling them. Some individuals may avoid revealing certain painful or embarrassing thoughts while engaging in free association, a phenomenon Freud called *resistance*. Resistance may take the form of halting speech during free association, "forgetting" appointments with the analyst, or arriving late.

Dream analysis is another technique used by psychoanalysts. Freud believed that areas of emotional concern repressed in waking life are sometimes expressed in symbolic form in dreams. He claimed that patient behavior may have a symbolic quality as well. At some point during psychoanalysis, Freud said, the patient reacts to the analyst with the same feelings that were present in another significant relationship—usually with the mother or father. This reaction of the patient is called transference. Freud believed that encouraging patients to achieve transference was an essential part of psychotherapy. He claimed that transference allows the patient to relive troubling experiences from the past with the analyst as a parent substitute, thereby resolving any hidden conflicts.

Object relations therapists represent a somewhat different take on classical psychoanalysis. From their perspective, the main goal of the personality is to forge functional links between the self (the subject) and others in the environment (the objects of the self's pursuit of relationships). The techniques that object relations therapists use are based on the notion that the emotional features of our early relationships become blueprints for future relationships. Thus, if our early relationships involve passive acceptance of another's abusive behavior, then we will follow that pattern in our adult relationships. When faced with clients who are involved in potentially damaging relationships, an object relations therapist would attempt to get them to identify the early relationships they are attempting to act out in the context of their current relationships. In addition, an object relations therapist would help the client change the maladaptive behavior patterns that arise when he or she uses current relationships to act out conflicts that originated in earlier relationships (Martinez, 2006).

Many therapists today practice brief psychodynamic therapy, in which the therapist and client decide on the issues to explore at the outset rather than waiting for them to emerge in the course of treatment. The therapist assumes a more active role and places more emphasis on the present than in traditional psychoanalysis. Brief psychodynamic therapy may require only one or two visits per week for as few as 12 to 20 weeks. In a meta-analysis of 11 well-controlled studies, Crits-Christoph (1992) found brief psychodynamic therapy to be as effective as other psychotherapies. More recent research has also shown brief psychodynamic therapy to be comparable to other forms of psychotherapy in terms of successful outcomes (Crits-Christoph et al., 2008). Brief psychodynamic psychotherapy appears to be most effective with clients who do not have multiple psychological disorders, who lack significant social relationship problems, and who believe that the therapy will be effective (Crits-Christoph et al., 2004).

▲ Freud's famous couch was used by his patients during psychoanalysis.

Interpersonal therapy (IPT) is a brief psychodynamic therapy that has been found to be very effective in the treatment of depression and bipolar disorder (Blatt et al., 2009; Swartz et al., 2009). It can be carried out with individual clients or with groups (Mufson et al., 2004). IPT is designed specifically to help clients understand and cope with four types of interpersonal problems commonly associated with major depression:

interpersonal therapy (IPT) A brief psychotherapy designed to help people with depression better understand and cope with problems relating to their interpersonal relationships.

1. *Unusual or severe responses to the death of a loved one.* The therapist and client discuss the client's relationship with the deceased person and feelings (such as guilt) that may be associated with the death.

2. *Interpersonal role disputes.* The therapist helps the client to understand others' points of view and to explore options for bringing about change.

3. *Difficulty in adjusting to role transitions, such as divorce, career change, and retirement.* Clients are helped to see the change not as a threat but as a challenge that they can master and an opportunity for growth.

4. *Deficits in interpersonal skills.* Through role-playing and analysis of the client's communication style, the therapist tries to help the client develop the interpersonal skills necessary to initiate and sustain relationships.

Interpersonal therapy is relatively brief, consisting of 12 to 16 weekly sessions. A large study conducted by the National Institute of Mental Health found IPT to be an effective treatment even for severe depression and to have a low dropout rate (Elkin et al., 1989, 1995). Research also indicates that clients who recover from major depression can enjoy a longer period without relapse when they continue with monthly sessions of IPT (Frank et al., 1991).

Humanistic Therapies ▶

13.2 What is the goal of the therapist in person-centered therapy?

Humanistic therapies assume that people have the ability and freedom to lead rational lives and make rational choices. One of the innovations that was introduced into the field by humanistic therapists was the use of the word *client* rather than the word *patient* to refer to individuals who are receiving psychotherapeutic services. Humanistic therapists believe that *patient* conjures up images of an individual with a disease

humanistic therapies Psychotherapies that assume that people have the ability and freedom to lead rational lives and make rational choices.

▲ Carl Rogers (at upper right) facilitates discussion in a therapy group.

person-centered therapy A nondirective, humanistic therapy developed by Carl Rogers, in which the therapist creates an accepting climate and shows empathy, freeing clients to be themselves and releasing their natural tendency toward self-actualization.

nondirective therapy Any type of psychotherapy in which the therapist allows the direction of the therapy sessions to be controlled by the client; an example is person-centered therapy.

13.3 What is the major emphasis of Gestalt therapy?

Gestalt therapy A therapy that was originated by Fritz Perls and that emphasizes the importance of clients' fully experiencing, in the present moment, their feelings, thoughts, and actions and then taking responsibility for them.

directive therapy Any type of psychotherapy in which the therapist takes an active role in determining the course of therapy sessions and provides answers and suggestions to the client; an example is Gestalt therapy.

relationship therapies Therapies that attempt to improve clients' interpersonal relationships or create new relationships to support clients' efforts to address psychological problems.

who needs to be healed by a professional who has skills that they lack. By contrast, the word *client* fits better with the humanistic notion that the goal of psychotherapy is to help individuals learn how to better facilitate their own personal growth.

One of the founders of the humanistic approach, Carl Rogers (1951), developed person-centered therapy, also called *client-centered therapy*. His approach is one of the most frequently used humanistic therapies. According to this view, people are innately good and, if allowed to develop naturally, will grow toward *self-actualization*—the realization of their inner potential. The humanistic perspective suggests that psychological disorders result when a person's natural tendency toward self-actualization is blocked either by oneself or by others. In the 1940s and 1950s, person-centered therapy enjoyed a strong following among psychologists.

The person-centered therapist attempts to create an accepting climate, based on *unconditional positive regard* (explained in Chapter 11) for the client. The therapist also empathizes with the client's concerns and emotions. To convey empathic understanding to the client, Rogers claimed that the therapist must adopt an attitude of *congruence* or *genuineness,* that is, a willingness to communicate with the client on a person-to-person basis rather than as an authority figure who will pass judgment on and give advice to the client. When the client speaks, the therapist responds by restating or reflecting back her or his ideas and feelings, a strategy known as *active listening*. Using these techniques, the therapist allows the client to control the direction of the therapy sessions. Rogers rejected all forms of therapy that cast the therapist in the role of expert and clients in the role of patients who expect the therapist to prescribe something that "cures" their problem. Thus, person-centered therapy is called a nondirective therapy.

Gestalt Therapy

Gestalt therapy, developed by Fritz Perls (1969), emphasizes the importance of clients' fully experiencing, in the present moment, their feelings, thoughts, and actions and then taking responsibility for them. The goal of Gestalt therapy is to help clients achieve a more integrated self and become more authentic and self-accepting. In addition, they learn to assume personal responsibility for their behavior rather than blaming society, past experiences, parents, or others.

Gestalt therapy is a directive therapy, one in which the therapist takes an active role in determining the course of therapy sessions and provides answers and suggestions to the client. The well-known phrase "getting in touch with your feelings" is a major objective of Gestalt therapy. Perls suggested that those of us who are in need of therapy carry around a heavy load of unfinished business, which may be in the form of resentment toward or conflicts with parents, siblings, lovers, employers, or others. If not resolved, these conflicts are carried forward into our present relationships. One method for dealing with unfinished business is the "empty chair" technique (Paivio & Greenberg, 1995). The client sits facing an empty chair and imagines, for example, that a wife, husband, father, or mother sits there. The client proceeds to tell the chair what he or she truly feels about that person. Then, the client moves to the empty chair and role-plays what the imagined person's response would be to what was said.

Relationship Therapies

Insight therapies focus on the self, which is not always the most appropriate approach to a psychological problem. Relationship therapies look not only at the individual's internal struggles but also at his or her interpersonal relationships. Some deliberately create new relationships for people that can support them in their efforts to address their problems.

Family Therapy and Couple Therapy ▶

Some therapists specialize in treating troubled families. In family therapy, parents and children enter therapy as a group. The therapist pays attention to the dynamics of the family unit—how family members communicate, how they act toward one another, and how they view one another (Dattilio, 2010). The goal of the therapist is to help family members reach agreement on certain changes that will help heal the wounds of the family unit, improve communication patterns, and create more understanding and harmony within the group (Doherty & McDaniel, 2010).

Couple therapy can take place at any phase of an intimate relationship and may focus either on behavior change or on partners' emotional responses to each other or on both aspects of an intimate relationship. For example, premarital sessions can help future spouses prepare for their life together. Couples who are considering divorce also often consult with a couple therapist for help in effecting a reconciliation or moderating the effects of a divorce on their children. Experimental studies indicate that couple therapy is effective at raising partners' levels of relationship satisfaction (Christensen et al., 2008; Snyder et al., 2006).

In addition to raising levels of satisfaction, couple therapy and family therapy appear to have positive effects in treating a number of disorders and clinical problems (Lebow & Gurman, 1995; Walitzer & Demen, 2004). Couple therapy can be helpful in the treatment of sexual dysfunctions (Gehring, 2003). And when it accompanies medication, family therapy can be beneficial in the treatment of schizophrenia and can reduce relapse rates (Snyder et al., 2006).

[**13.4** **What are the goals of family and couple therapy?**

family therapy Therapy involving an entire family, with the goal of helping family members reach agreement on changes that will help heal the family unit, improve communication problems, and create more understanding and harmony within the group.

▲ Therapists working with couples pay attention to the dynamics between the two people—how they communicate, act toward each other, and view each other.

Group Therapy ▶

Group therapy is a form of therapy in which several clients (usually 7 to 10) meet regularly with one or more therapists to resolve personal problems. Besides being less expensive than individual therapy, group therapy gives the individual a sense of belonging and opportunities to express feelings, to get feedback from other members, and to give and receive help and emotional support. Learning that others also share their problems helps people feel less alone and ashamed. A meta-analysis of studies comparing prisoners who participated in group therapy to those who did not found that group participation was helpful for a variety of problems, including anxiety, depression, and low self-esteem (Morgan & Flora, 2002).

A variant of group therapy is the *self-help group*. Approximately 12 million people in the United States participate in roughly 500,000 self-help groups, most of which focus on a single problem, such as substance abuse or depression. Self-help groups usually are not led by professional therapists. They are simply groups of people who share a common problem and meet to give and receive support.

One of the oldest and best-known self-help groups is Alcoholics Anonymous, which claims 1.5 million members worldwide. Other self-help groups patterned after Alcoholics Anonymous have been formed to help individuals overcome many other addictive behaviors, from overeating (Overeaters Anonymous) to gambling (Gamblers Anonymous). One study indicated that people suffering from anxiety-based problems were helped by participating in groups that used a multimedia self-help program called Attacking Anxiety. Of the 176 individuals who participated in the study, 62 were reported to have achieved significant improvement, and another 40 reported some improvement (Finch, Lambert, & Brown, 2000).

[**13.5** **What are some advantages of group therapy?**

couple therapy Therapy involving intimate partners in which behavior change or partners' emotional responses to each other or both are the focus of treatment.

group therapy A form of therapy in which several clients (usually 7 to 10) meet regularly with one or more therapists to resolve personal problems.

▲ Group therapy can give individuals a sense of belonging and an opportunity to give and receive emotional support.

Behavior Therapies

behavior therapy A treatment approach that is based on the idea that abnormal behavior is learned and that applies the principles of operant conditioning, classical conditioning, and/or observational learning to eliminate inappropriate or maladaptive behaviors and replace them with more adaptive responses.

behavior modification An approach to therapy that uses learning principles to eliminate inappropriate or maladaptive behaviors and replace them with more adaptive responses.

13.6 How do behavior therapists modify clients' problematic behavior?

▲ A time out is effective because it prevents a child from receiving reinforcers for undesirable behaviors. The child learns that once the behavior is under control, he or she will again have access to reinforcers. Similar behavioral techniques, such as token economies, are useful with adults in mental hospitals and other institutions.

token economy A behavior modification technique that rewards appropriate behavior with tokens that can be exchanged later for desired goods and/or privileges.

time out A behavior modification technique used to eliminate undesirable behavior, especially in children and adolescents, by withdrawing all reinforcers for a period of time.

Sometimes individuals seek help from a mental health professional because they want to rid themselves of a troublesome habit, or they want to develop a better way to respond to specific situations in their lives. In such cases, psychotherapists may employ a behavioral approach.

A behavior therapy is a treatment approach consistent with the learning perspective on psychological disorders—that abnormal behavior is learned. Instead of viewing maladaptive behavior as a symptom of some underlying disorder, the behavior therapist sees the behavior itself as the disorder. If a person comes to a behavior therapist with a fear of flying, that fear of flying is seen as the problem. Behavior therapies use learning principles to eliminate inappropriate or maladaptive behaviors and replace them with more adaptive responses—an approach referred to as behavior modification. The goal is to change the troublesome behavior, not to change the individual's personality structure or to search for the origin of the problem behavior.

Behavior Modification Techniques Based on Operant Conditioning

Behavior modification techniques based on operant conditioning seek to control the consequences of behavior. Extinction of an undesirable behavior is accomplished by terminating or withholding the reinforcement that is maintaining that behavior (Lerman & Iwata, 1996). Behavior therapists also seek to reinforce desirable behavior to increase its frequency. Institutional settings such as hospitals, prisons, and school classrooms are well suited to behavior modification techniques because they provide a restricted environment where the consequences of behavior can be strictly controlled.

Some institutions use a token economy that rewards appropriate behavior with tokens such as poker chips, play money, gold stars, or the like. These tokens can later be exchanged for desired goods (candy, gum, cigarettes) and/or privileges (weekend passes, free time, participation in desirable activities). Sometimes, individuals are fined a certain number of tokens for undesirable behavior. Mental hospitals have successfully used token economies with patients for decades to improve their self-care skills (Kopelowicz, Liberman, & Zarate, 2007). Similar interventions have been helpful in motivating clients at substance abuse clinics to remain abstinent (Petry et al., 2004).

Other behavior therapies based on operant conditioning have been effective in modifying some behaviors of seriously disturbed people. Although these techniques do not cure schizophrenia, autism, or mental retardation, they can increase the frequency of desirable behaviors and decrease the frequency of undesirable behaviors. For example, some children with autism display self-injurious behaviors, such as head-banging and skin-picking. Therapists use operant conditioning techniques to reduce the frequency of these behaviors (Luiselli, 2009). As a result, the family members of children with autism are better able to accept and care for them.

Another effective method used to eliminate undesirable behavior, especially in children and adolescents, is time out (Kazdin & Benjet, 2003). Children are told in advance that if they engage in certain undesirable behaviors, they will be removed from the situation and will have to pass a period of time (usually no more than 15 minutes) in a place containing no reinforcers (no television, books, toys, friends, and so on). Theoretically, the undesirable behavior will stop if it is no longer followed by attention or any other positive reinforcers.

Behavior modification techniques can also be used by people who want to break bad habits such as smoking and overeating or to develop good habits such as a regular exercise regime. If you want to modify any of your behaviors, devise a reward system for desirable behaviors, and remember the principles of shaping. Reward gradual changes in the direction of your ultimate goal. If you are trying to develop better eating habits, don't try to change a lifetime of bad habits all at once. Begin with a small step, such as substituting frozen yogurt for ice cream. Set realistic weekly goals that you are likely to be able to achieve.

Behavior Therapies Based on Other Learning Theories

► **13.7** What behavior therapies are based on classical conditioning and social-cognitive theory?

Behavior therapies based on classical conditioning can be used to rid people of fears and other undesirable behaviors. These therapies employ different means of exposing patients to feared objects or situations or to triggers that elicit undesirable behaviors such as substance abuse. Recent research also suggests that exposing individuals to such stimuli via *virtual reality* can be a useful addition to the standard ways in which such therapies are implemented (Mühlberger et al., 2006). Therapies of this type include systematic desensitization, flooding, exposure and response prevention, and aversion therapy.

One of the pioneers in the application of classical conditioning techniques to therapy, psychiatrist Joseph Wolpe (1958, 1973), reasoned that if he could get people to relax and stay relaxed while they thought about a feared object, person, place, or situation, they could conquer their fear. In Wolpe's therapy, known as systematic desensitization, clients are trained in deep muscle relaxation. Then, they confront a hierarchy of fears—a graduated series of anxiety-producing situations—either *in vivo* (in real life) or in their imagination, until they can remain relaxed even in the presence of the most feared situation. The technique can be used for everything from fear of animals to claustrophobia, social phobia, and other situational fears. Try creating such a hierarchy in the *Try It*.

systematic desensitization A behavior therapy that is based on classical conditioning and used to treat fears by training clients in deep muscle relaxation and then having them confront a graduated series of anxiety-producing situations (real or imagined) until they can remain relaxed while confronting even the most feared situation.

TRY IT ▷ A Possible Hierarchy of Fears

Use what you have learned about systematic desensitization to create a step-by-step approach to help someone overcome a fear of taking tests. The person's hierarchy of fears begins with reading in the syllabus that a test will be given and culminates in actually taking the test. Fill in successive steps, according to a possible hierarchy of fears, that will lead to the final step. One set of possible steps is given below.

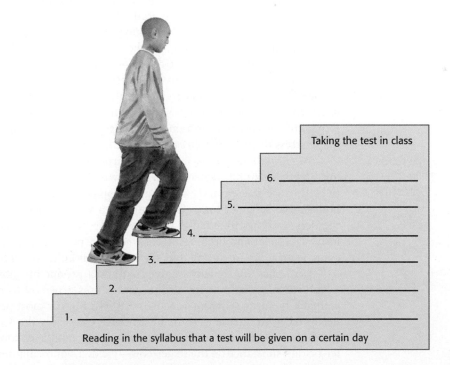

Taking the test in class

6. _____

5. _____

4. _____

3. _____

2. _____

1. _____

Reading in the syllabus that a test will be given on a certain day

SUGGESTED ANSWERS: (1) Preparing for each class session by reading the assigned material and/or completing any homework assignments. (2) Attending each class session and taking notes on the material the test will cover. (3) Reviewing the new notes after each class period. (4) Reviewing all class materials beginning one week before the test. (5) Reciting key information from memory the day before the test. (6) Arriving early to take the test, having gotten a good night's sleep.

▲ Flooding can be a useful treatment for phobias, such as fear of dogs.

flooding A behavior therapy based on classical conditioning and used to treat phobias by exposing clients to the feared object or event (or asking them to imagine it vividly) for an extended period, until their anxiety decreases.

exposure and response prevention A behavior therapy that exposes patients with obsessive-compulsive disorder to stimuli that trigger obsessions and compulsive rituals, while patients resist performing the compulsive rituals for progressively longer periods of time.

aversion therapy A behavior therapy in which an aversive stimulus is paired with a harmful or socially undesirable behavior until the behavior becomes associated with pain or discomfort.

participant modeling A behavior therapy in which an appropriate response to a feared stimulus is modeled in graduated steps and the client attempts to imitate the model step by step, encouraged and supported by the therapist.

Many experiments, demonstrations, and case reports confirm that systematic desensitization is a highly successful treatment for eliminating fears and phobias in a relatively short time (Kolivas, Riordan, & Gross, 2008; Zinbarg & Griffith, 2008). It has proved effective for specific problems, such as test anxiety, stage fright, and anxiety related to sexual disorders.

Flooding is a behavior therapy used in the treatment of phobias. It involves exposing clients to the feared object or event (or asking them to imagine it vividly) for an extended period, until their anxiety decreases. The person is exposed to the fear all at once, not gradually as in systematic desensitization. An individual with a fear of heights, for example, might have to go onto the roof of a tall building and remain there until the fear subsided.

Flooding sessions typically last from 30 minutes to 2 hours and should not be terminated until clients are markedly less afraid than they were at the beginning of the session. Additional sessions are required until the fear response is extinguished or reduced to an acceptable level. It is rare for a client to need more than six treatment sessions (Marshall & Segal, 1988). *In vivo* flooding, the real-life experience, works faster and is more effective than simply imagining the feared object (Chambless & Goldstein, 1979; Marks, 1972). Thus, a person who fears flying would benefit more from taking an actual plane trip than from just thinking about one.

Exposure and response prevention has been successful in treating obsessive-compulsive disorder (Baer, 1996; Foa, 1995; Rhéaume & Ladouceur, 2000). The first component of this technique involves *exposure*—exposing clients to objects or situations they have been avoiding because they trigger obsessions and compulsive rituals. The second component is *response prevention,* in which clients agree to resist performing their compulsive rituals for progressively longer periods of time.

Initially, the therapist identifies the thoughts, objects, or situations that trigger the compulsive ritual. For example, touching a doorknob, a piece of unwashed fruit, or a garbage bin might send people with a fear of contamination to the nearest bathroom to wash their hands. Clients are gradually exposed to stimuli that they find more and more distasteful and anxiety provoking. They must agree not to perform the normal ritual (hand washing, bathing, or the like) for a specified period of time after each exposure. A typical treatment course—about 10 sessions over a period of three to seven weeks—can bring about considerable improvement in 60 to 70% of patients (Jenike, 1990). And clients treated with exposure and response prevention are less likely to relapse after treatment than those treated with drugs alone (Greist, 1992). Exposure and response prevention has also proved useful in the treatment of posttraumatic stress disorder (Cloitre et al., 2002).

Aversion therapy is used to stop a harmful or socially undesirable behavior by pairing it with a painful, sickening, or otherwise aversive stimulus. Electric shock, emetics (which cause nausea and vomiting), or other unpleasant stimuli are paired with the undesirable behavior time after time until a strong negative association is formed and the person comes to avoid that behavior. Treatment continues until the bad behavior loses its appeal and becomes associated with pain or discomfort. Aversion therapy is controversial because it involves the intentional infliction of harm on a client.

Alcoholics are sometimes given a nausea-producing substance such as Antabuse, which reacts violently with alcohol and causes a person to retch and vomit until the stomach is empty (Grossman & Ruiz, 2004). But for most problems, aversion therapy need not be so intense as to make a person physically ill. A controlled comparison of treatments for chronic nail biting revealed that mild aversion therapy—painting a bitter-tasting substance on the fingernails—yielded significant improvement (Allen, 1996).

Therapies derived from Albert Bandura's work on observational learning are based on the belief that people can overcome fears and acquire social skills through modeling. The most effective type of therapy based on observational learning theory is called participant modeling (Bandura, 1977; Bandura, Adams, & Beyer, 1977; Bandura, Jeffery, & Gajdos, 1975). In this therapy, not only does the model demonstrate the appropriate response in graduated steps, but the client also attempts to imitate the model step by step while the therapist gives encouragement and support. Most specific phobias can be extinguished in only 3 or 4 hours of client participation in modeling therapy. For instance, participant modeling could be used to help someone overcome a fear of dogs. A session would begin with the client watching others petting and playing with a dog. As the client becomes more comfortable, he or she would be encouraged to join in. Alternatively, a client would be shown a video of people playing with a dog and then would be encouraged to play with a live dog.

Cognitive Behavior Therapies

In the *Think about It* activity at the beginning of the chapter, we introduced you to a type of psychotherapy that focuses on people's beliefs and ways of thinking about their problems. Cognitive behavior therapies (CBTs) assume that maladaptive behavior results from irrational thoughts, beliefs, and ideas, which the therapist tries to change (Dowd, Clen, & Arnold, 2010). This approach to therapy has been shown to be effective for treating a wide variety of problems, including anxiety disorders (Kellett et al., 2004), psychological drug dependence (Babor, 2004), and mood disorders (Totterdell & Kellett, 2008). The two best known types of CBT are Albert Ellis's *rational emotive behavior therapy (REBT)* and Aaron Beck's *cognitive therapy (CT)*.

cognitive behavior therapies (CBT) Therapies that assume maladaptive behavior can result from irrational thoughts, beliefs, and ideas.

Rational Emotive Behavior Therapy ▶

13.8 What is the aim of rational emotive behavior therapy?

The late clinical psychologist Albert Ellis (1913–2007) developed rational emotive behavior therapy (REBT) in the 1950s (Ellis, 1961, 1977, 1993). Ellis claimed to have developed the technique as a way of addressing his own problems with incapacitating anxiety (Ellis, 2004a). This type of therapy is based on Ellis's *ABC theory*. The *A* refers to the activating event, the *B* to the person's belief about the event, and the *C* to the emotional consequence that follows. Ellis claims that it is not the event itself that causes the emotional consequence but rather the person's belief about the event. In other words, *A* does not cause *C*; *B* causes *C*. If the belief is irrational, then the emotional consequence can be extreme distress, as illustrated in Figure 13.1 (p. 418).

rational emotive behavior therapy (REBT) A directive form of psychotherapy, developed by Albert Ellis and designed to challenge clients' irrational beliefs about themselves and others.

Rational emotive behavior therapy is a directive form of psychotherapy designed to challenge clients' irrational beliefs about themselves and others. Most clients in REBT see a therapist individually, once a week, for 5 to 50 sessions. In Ellis's view, clients do not benefit from warm, supportive therapeutic approaches that help them feel better but do not address the irrational thoughts that underlie their problems (Ellis, 2004b). Instead, he argues, as clients begin to replace irrational beliefs with rational ones, their emotional reactions become more appropriate, less distressing, and more likely to lead to constructive behavior. For example, a client might tell a therapist that he is feeling anxious and depressed because of his supervisor's unreasonable demands. Using Ellis's REBT model, the therapist would help the client distinguish between the supervisor's demands and the client's emotional reactions to them. The goal would be to help the client understand that his reactions to his supervisor's demands are the source of his anxiety and depression, not the demands themselves. Ultimately, the rational emotive behavior therapist would lead the client to the conclusion that while he may not be able to control his supervisor's demands, he is capable of controlling his emotional reactions to them. Once the client changes his thinking about the problem, the rational emotive behavior therapist helps him learn behavioral strategies, such as relaxation techniques, that can help him control his emotional reactions. Studies show that individuals receiving REBT do better than those receiving no treatment or a placebo (Browne, Dowd, & Freeman, 2010).

> How would you apply Ellis's model to a different kind of activating event such as failing an exam or failing to get a job you applied for?

Harry's View: Sally's refusal caused his upset. *A* caused *C*.

A (Activating Event)

Harry asked Sally to the concert and was turned down without a reason.

Harry believes Sally's refusal caused his upset.
A causes C

C (Consequence)

Harry was shocked, dejected, angry, and depressed.

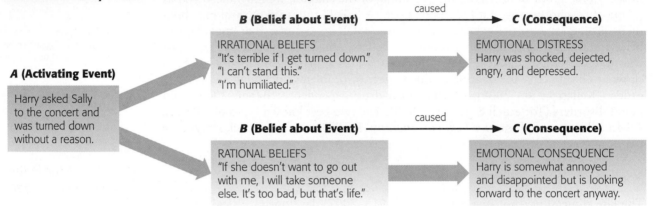

Ellis's View: Harry's belief about the event caused his upset. *B* caused *C*.

A (Activating Event)

Harry asked Sally to the concert and was turned down without a reason.

B (Belief about Event) — caused → **C (Consequence)**

IRRATIONAL BELIEFS
"It's terrible if I get turned down."
"I can't stand this."
"I'm humiliated."

EMOTIONAL DISTRESS
Harry was shocked, dejected, angry, and depressed.

B (Belief about Event) — caused → **C (Consequence)**

RATIONAL BELIEFS
"If she doesn't want to go out with me, I will take someone else. It's too bad, but that's life."

EMOTIONAL CONSEQUENCE
Harry is somewhat annoyed and disappointed but is looking forward to the concert anyway.

FIGURE 13.1 The ABCs of Rational Emotive Behavior Therapy (REBT)
Rational emotive behavior therapy teaches clients that it is not the activating event *(A)* that causes the upsetting consequences *(C)*. Rather, it is the client's beliefs *(B)* about the activating event. According to Albert Ellis, irrational beliefs cause emotional distress. Rational emotive behavior therapists help clients identify their irrational beliefs and replace them with rational ones.

13.9 How does Beck's cognitive therapy approach psychotherapy?

Beck's Cognitive Therapy

Psychiatrist Aaron T. Beck (1976) claims that much of the misery endured by a person with depression and anxiety can be traced to *automatic thoughts*—unreasonable but unquestioned ideas that rule the person's life ("To be happy, I must be liked by everyone"; "If people disagree with me, it means they don't like me"). Beck (1991) believes that persons with depression hold "a negative view of the present, past, and future experiences" (p. 369). These individuals notice only negative, unpleasant things and jump to upsetting conclusions.

The goal of Beck's cognitive therapy (CT) is to help clients overcome the impact of *cognitive errors* such as those listed in Table 13.1 on their emotions and behavior. This approach is designed to deal with such thoughts as they occur and replace them with more objective thoughts. After identifying and challenging the client's irrational thoughts, the therapist sets up a plan and guides the client so that her or his personal experience can provide actual evidence in the real world to refute the false beliefs. Clients are given homework assignments (see Figure 13.2), such as keeping track of automatic thoughts and the feelings evoked by them and then substituting more rational thoughts.

Cognitive therapy is brief, usually lasting only 10 to 20 sessions (Beck, 1976). This therapy has been researched extensively and is reported to be highly successful in the treatment of individuals with mild to moderate depression (Whisman 2008). There is some evidence that people who have received cognitive therapy are less likely to relapse than those who have been treated with antidepressant drugs (Hallon, Stewart, & Struck, 2006).

Beck's cognitive therapy (CT) A therapy designed by Aaron Beck to help clients stop their negative thoughts as they occur and replace them with more objective thoughts.

TABLE 13.1 Cognitive Errors

ERROR	DEFINITION	EXAMPLE
All-or-nothing thinking	Client sees only two options.	"If I don't get into Harvard, I might as well not go to college at all."
Catastrophizing (fortune-telling)	Client predicts negative future outcome.	"If I don't find a partner by the time I get out of college, I'll have to spend the rest of my life alone."
Discounting the positive	Client attributes positive outcome to forces outside his or her control.	"I only passed that exam because I got lucky."
Emotional reasoning	Client believes something because he or she feels it is true when evidence suggests it is not.	"Even though he hasn't called me, my heart tells me that we're meant to be together."
Labeling	Client attaches labels to self and others that block evidence that contradicts the label.	"She's too stuck-up to go out with a loser like me."
Magnification or minimization	Client exaggerates the negative or minimizes the positive.	"Since I missed class today, it won't matter that I have As on the exams. The professor will fail me because she can see how irresponsible I really am."
Mental filter	Client focuses on one small detail instead of the overall situation.	"I can't go on any interviews because I still haven't found the right shoes to go with my black suit."
Mind reading	Client thinks he or she knows what others are thinking.	"Since I said 'call me any time,' he probably thinks I'm desperate."
Overgeneralization	Client makes a general conclusion about himself or herself based on one situation or event.	"I didn't do well in that interview. I'm just not a 'people person' I guess."
Personalization	Client believes he or she is at fault for others' behavior.	"The professor seemed to be in a hurry to get out of the classroom. She must have thought my question was really dumb."
Inappropriate use of "should" and "must" statements	Client has rigid beliefs about how he or she and others should behave.	"A 'good' daughter should call her mother every day and report everything that she has done in the last 24 hours."
Tunnel vision	Client sees only negative aspects of a situation.	"This is my worst semester ever. I don't see how I'll survive it. I'll probably wreck my GPA."

Source: Beck (1995). Derived from pp. 118–120 in *Cognitive Therapies: Basics and Beyond* by J. Beck, Copyright © 1995 by The Gullford Press. Reprinted by permission of Gullford Publications, Inc.

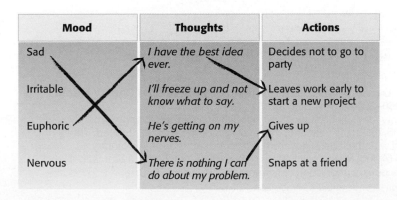

Mood	Thoughts	Actions
Sad	*I have the best idea ever.*	Decides not to go to party
Irritable	*I'll freeze up and not know what to say.*	Leaves work early to start a new project
Euphoric	*He's getting on my nerves.*	Gives up
Nervous	*There is nothing I can do about my problem.*	Snaps at a friend

FIGURE 13.2 Cognitive Therapy Homework
Cognitive therapists often assign "homework" exercises like this one that is designed to help clients with bipolar disorder gain control of their behavior. The therapist instructs the client to draw a line from each mood to the thought and action that it triggers during periods of depression and mania.
Source: Basco (2006).

Cognitive therapy has also been shown to be effective for treating panic disorder (Clark & Beck, 2010). By teaching clients to change the catastrophic interpretations of their symptoms, cognitive therapy helps prevent the symptoms from escalating into panic. Studies have shown that after 3 months of cognitive therapy, about 90% of individuals with panic disorder are panic free.

Biomedical Therapies

biomedical therapy A therapy (drug therapy, electroconvulsive therapy, or psychosurgery) that is based on the assumption that psychological disorders are symptoms of underlying physical problems.

Do you know someone who takes or has taken a drug prescribed by a physician or psychiatrist as a means of overcoming a psychological problem? Chances are good that you do because millions of people the world over are now taking various medications for just such reasons. Treatment with drugs is a cornerstone of the biological approach to therapy. Predictably, professionals who favor the biological perspective— the view that psychological disorders are symptoms of underlying physical problems— usually favor a biomedical therapy. The three main biological therapies are drug therapy, electroconvulsive therapy (ECT), and psychosurgery.

13.10 What are the advantages and disadvantages of using drugs to treat psychological disorders?

Drug Therapy

The most frequently used biological treatment is drug therapy. The drugs that mental health professionals prescribe for people with psychological disorders fit the definition of *psychoactive drugs* that you read about in Chapter 4. That is, they are drugs that alter moods, perceptions, and thoughts through their action on the brain's neurotransmitters. In fact, as we point out in the *Explain It*, some researchers believe that people with psychological disorders turn to *self-medication* when they find that a psychoactive substance such as nicotine relieves their symptoms. As a result, substance use and abuse often coexist with psychological disorders. ✳—Explore on **mypsychlab.com**

✳—Explore the Concept *Drugs Commonly Used to Treat Psychiatric Disorders* on **mypsychlab.com**

Breakthroughs in drug therapy, coupled with the federal government's effort to reduce involuntary hospitalization of people with psychological disorders, lowered the mental hospital patient population in the United States from about 560,000 in 1955, when the drugs were introduced, to about 100,000 by 1990 (see Figure 13.3); this figure continued to drop throughout the 1990s. Furthermore, the average stay of patients who do require hospitalization is now usually a matter of days.

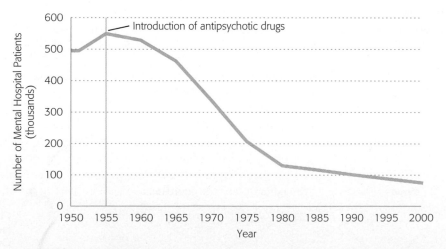

FIGURE 13.3 Decrease in Patient Populations in State and County Mental Hospitals (1950–2000)
State and county mental hospital patient populations peaked at approximately 560,000 in 1955, the same year that antipsychotic drugs were introduced. These drugs, coupled with the federal government's efforts to reduce involuntary hospitalization of people with psychological disorders, resulted in a dramatic decrease in the patient population to fewer than 100,000 in 2000.
Source: Data from Mandersheid & Henderson (2001).

EXPLAIN IT   **Why Are Smoking Rates So High among People with Schizophrenia?**

Studies show that 58–88% of individuals with schizophrenia smoke cigarettes (Moss et al., 2009). Is it possible then that, prior to being formally diagnosed, many individuals with schizophrenia accidentally happen on an effective biomedical treatment for their disorder when they take up the habit of smoking cigarettes? Among psychological researchers, this idea is known as the *self-medication hypothesis*. According to this view, the stimulant properties of nicotine help people with schizophrenia deal with the attention, thinking, and memory deficits that often go along with the disease. Studies show that nicotine increases activity in the parts of the brain that carry out these functions in people with schizophrenia (Moss et al., 2009; Yip et al., 2009). It may also protect individuals with schizophrenia from some of the more unpleasant side effects that are associated with antipsychotic drugs (George & Vessicchio, 2001). Advocates of the self-medication hypothesis also point out that, in general, smokers with schizophrenia smoke more heavily than smokers who do not have the disease, and smoking rates have remained constant among them while the rates of tobacco use in the general population have declined (Kelly & McCreadie, 2000).

Critics of the self-medication hypothesis argue that smoking rates are high among individuals with schizophrenia because smoking increases vulnerability to the disorder (Kelly & McCreadie, 2000). Recall from Chapter 12 that researchers believe that schizophrenia arises from a complex interaction of genetic, developmental, and environmental factors. Nicotine dependence, some researchers say, may be one of several factors that contribute to a series of biochemical changes that produce the symptoms of schizophrenia. Evidence in favor of this view comes from studies showing that most smokers with schizophrenia started smoking long before they had their first symptoms (Smith et al., 2009). As a result, they could not have initiated the habit as the result of a search for symptom relief.

The verdict on the self-medication hypothesis has yet to be decided. One thing is certain, though. As you would probably predict, cigarette smoking has a deleterious effect on the physical health of individuals with schizophrenia just as it does on the rest of us. Death rates from smoking-related diseases such as lung cancer and the prevalence of chronic conditions such as emphysema that are associated with smoking are far higher among individuals with schizophrenia than in the general population (Schizophrenia.com, 2006). Thus, whatever their differences with regard to the self-medication hypothesis, most researchers and clinicians agree that giving up smoking is just as important for them as for people who do not have a serious psychological disorder. Furthermore, smokers with schizophrenia are just as likely to want to quit smoking as smokers who do not have the disease.

Despite an equivalent desire to quit, individuals with schizophrenia have a more difficult time overcoming nicotine addiction than other people do. For one thing, antipsychotic drugs appear to intensify the unpleasant feelings that are associated with nicotine withdrawal. For another, nicotine moderates the effects of antipsychotic drugs such that an effort to quit smoking often leaves an individual with schizophrenia reeling from the effects of a dosage level of an antipsychotic drug that is too high (George & Vessicchio, 2001). Therefore, clinicians who have studied smoking cessation in individuals with schizophrenia strongly discourage them from quitting "cold turkey." Nicotine replacement, these experts say, is needed to ensure that an individual with schizophrenia remains stable throughout the withdrawal period as well as to increase the person's success. Above all, failing to urge individuals with schizophrenia to quit smoking because they may be getting symptom relief from nicotine is a subtle form of discrimination against them.

Antipsychotics. Antipsychotic drugs known as *neuroleptics* are prescribed primarily for schizophrenia. You may have heard of these drugs by their brand names—Thorazine, Stelazine, Compazine, and Mellaril. Their purpose is to control hallucinations, delusions, disorganized speech, and disorganized behavior (Andreasen et al., 1995). The neuroleptics work primarily by inhibiting the activity of the neurotransmitter dopamine. About 50% of patients have a good response to the standard antipsychotics (Bobes et al., 2003). But many patients, particularly those with an early onset of schizophrenia, are not helped by them (Meltzer et al., 1997), and others show only slight or modest improvement in symptoms. The long-term use of typical antipsychotic drugs carries a high risk of a severe side effect, *tardive dyskinesia*—almost continual twitching and jerking movements of the face and tongue, and squirming movements of the hands and trunk (Glazer, Morgenstern, & Doucette, 1993).

Newer antipsychotic drugs called *atypical neuroleptics* (clozapine, risperidone, olanzipine) can treat not only the positive symptoms of schizophrenia but also the negative symptoms, leading to marked improvement in patients' quality of life (Lauriello et al., 2005; Worrel et al., 2000). Atypical neuroleptics target both dopamine and serotonin receptors (Kawanishi, Tachikawa, & Suzuki, 2000). About 10% of patients who take clozapine find the results so dramatic that they almost feel as though they have been reborn. Clozapine produces fewer side effects than standard neuroleptics, and patients taking it are less likely to develop tardive dyskinesia (Soares-Weiser & Fernandez, 2007). It may also be more effective at suicide prevention than other antipsychotic

antipsychotic drugs Drugs used to control severe psychotic symptoms, such as delusions, hallucinations, disorganized speech, and disorganized behavior, by inhibiting dopamine activity; also known as neuroleptics.

drugs (Meltzer et al., 2003). However, the levels of various liver enzymes and other substances in patients who take the drug must be monitored regularly (Erdogan et al., 2004).

antidepressant drugs Drugs that act as mood elevators for people with severe depression and are also prescribed to treat some anxiety disorders.

Antidepressants. Antidepressant drugs act as mood elevators for people with severe depression and are also helpful in the treatment of certain anxiety disorders (Boren, Leventhal & Pigott, 2009). About 65 to 75% of people who take antidepressants find themselves significantly improved, and 40 to 50% of those are essentially completely recovered (Frazer, 1997). It is important to note, though, that most antidepressant research involves people with severe depression—those who are most likely to show a significant change after treatment (Zimmerman, Posternak, & Chelminski, 2002). Thus, these studies may not apply to individuals with milder cases of depression. Moreover, research has shown that participants respond almost as frequently to placebo treatments as to real drugs (Walsh et al., 2002). In fact, EEG studies of people who receive placebos have documented neurological changes that, while different from those in people receiving real drugs, are associated with improvements in mood (Leuchter et al., 2002). Recall from Chapter 1 that placebo effects are attributable to the belief that a given treatment will help. Consequently, many researchers think that some people's responses to antidepressant drugs result from a combination of the physiological effects of these medications on the brain and confidence in the effectiveness of drug treatment.

The first-generation antidepressants are known as the *tricyclics* (amitriptyline, imipramine) (Nutt, 2000). The tricyclics work against depression by blocking the reuptake of norepinephrine and serotonin into the axon terminals, thus enhancing the action of these neurotransmitters in the synapses. But tricyclics can have some unpleasant side effects, including sedation, dizziness, nervousness, fatigue, dry mouth, forgetfulness, and weight gain (Frazer, 1997). Progressive weight gain (an average of more than 20 pounds) is the main reason people stop taking tricyclics, in spite of the relief these drugs provide from distressing psychological symptoms.

The second-generation antidepressants, the *selective serotonin reuptake inhibitors (SSRIs),* block the reuptake of the neurotransmitter serotonin, increasing its availability at the synapses in the brain (Dayan & Huys, 2008). SSRIs (fluoxetine, clomipramine) have fewer side effects (Nelson, 1997) and are safer than tricyclics if an overdose occurs (Thase & Kupfer, 1996). SSRIs have been found to be promising in treating many disorders. Currently, the U.S. Food and Drug Administration (FDA) lists depression, obsessive-compulsive disorder, bulimia nervosa, and panic disorder as the conditions for which it approves the use of most SSRIs (FDA, 2006). It's also important to note that the FDA recommends that people younger than 18 be closely monitored during the first few weeks of SSRI treatment because of some studies showing that the drugs increase the risk of suicide among children and teens (FDA, 2004).

Reports indicating that SSRIs, especially fluoxetine (Prozac), increase the risk of suicide in adults have not been substantiated (Ham, 2003; Warshaw & Keller, 1996). However, SSRIs can cause sexual dysfunction, although normal sexual functioning returns when the drug is discontinued. Studies suggest that a newer group of antidepressants, the *serotonin-norepinephrine reuptake inhibitors (SNRIs)*, appears to be more effective than the SSRIs and to produce fewer side effects (Ravindran & Ravindran, 2009).

Another line of treatment for depression is the use of *monoamine oxidase (MAO) inhibitors* (sold under the names Marplan, Nardil, and Parnate). By blocking the action of an enzyme that breaks down norepinephrine and serotonin in the synapses, MAO inhibitors increase the availability of these neurotransmitters. MAO inhibitors are usually prescribed for people with depression who do not respond to other antidepressants (Tobin, 2007). They are also effective in treating panic disorder (Sheehan & Raj, 1988) and social phobia (Marshall et al., 1994). But MAO inhibitors have many of the same unpleasant side effects as tricyclic antidepressants, and people taking MAO inhibitors must avoid certain foods or run the risk of stroke.

Lithium and Anticonvulsant Drugs. Lithium, a naturally occurring salt, is considered a wonder drug for 40 to 50% of people who have bipolar disorder (Thase & Kupfer, 1996). It is said to begin to quiet the manic state within 5 to 10 days. This is an amazing accomplishment because the average episode, if untreated, lasts about 3 to 4 months. A proper maintenance dose of lithium reduces depressive episodes as well as manic ones. Studies show that the clinical effectiveness of lithium for treating depression and bipolar disorder is unmatched (Ross, Baldessarini, & Tondo, 2000). But 40 to 60% of those who take a maintenance dose will experience a recurrence (Thase & Kupfer, 1996). Also, monitoring the level of lithium in the patient's blood every 2 to 6 months is necessary to guard against lithium poisoning and permanent damage to the nervous system (Schou, 1997).

Recent research suggests that *anticonvulsant drugs,* such as Depakote (divalproex), may be just as effective for managing bipolar symptoms as lithium, with fewer side effects (Kowatch et al., 2000). Moreover, many people with bipolar disorder, especially those whose manic states include symptoms of psychosis, benefit from taking antipsychotic drugs along with the anticonvulsants (Bowden et al., 2004; Vieta, 2003).

lithium A drug used to treat bipolar disorder, which at proper maintenance dosage reduces both manic and depressive episodes.

Antianxiety Drugs. The family of minor tranquilizers called *benzodiazepines* includes, among others, the well-known drugs sold as Valium and Librium and the newer high-potency drug Xanax (pronounced "ZAN-ax"). Used primarily to treat anxiety, benzodiazepines are prescribed more often than any other class of psychoactive drugs (Cloos & Ferreira, 2009). They have been found to be effective in treating panic disorder (Davidson, 1997; Noyes et al., 1996) and generalized anxiety disorder (Lydiard, Brawman-Mintzer, & Ballenger, 1996).

Xanax, the largest-selling psychiatric drug (Famighetti, 1997), appears to be particularly effective in relieving anxiety and depression. When used to treat panic disorder (Noyes et al., 1996), Xanax works faster and has fewer side effects than antidepressants (Ballenger et al., 1993; Jonas & Cohon, 1993). However, if people discontinue treatment, relapse is likely (Rickels et al., 1993). There is a downside to Xanax. Many people, once they no longer experience panic attacks, find themselves unable to discontinue the drug because they experience moderate to intense withdrawal symptoms, including intense anxiety (Otto et al., 1993). Valium seems to be just as effective as Xanax for treating panic disorder, and withdrawal is easier. Although withdrawal is a problem with benzodiazepines, the abuse and addiction potential of these drugs is fairly low (Romach et al., 1995). The *Summarize It* lists the various drugs that are used to treat the symptoms of psychological disorders.

Drugs Used to Treat Psychological Disorders

TYPE OF DRUG	BRAND NAMES	SYMPTOMS TREATED
Neuroleptics	Compazine, Mellaril, Stelazine, Thorazine	Hallucinations, delusions
Atypical neuroleptics	Clozaril, Olanzapine, Risperdal	Hallucinations, delusions Negative symptoms of schizophrenia
Tricyclics	Elavil, Tofranil	Depressed mood/Anxiety
SSRIs	Celexa, Paxil, Prozac, Zoloft	Depressed mood/Anxiety
SNRIs	Effexor, Pristiq, Remeron	Depressed mood/Anxiety
MAOIs	Ensam, Nardil, Parnate, Marplan	Depressed mood/Anxiety
Lithium	Eskalith, Lithobid	Mania
Anticonvulsants	Depakote, Depacon, Depakene	Mania
Benzodiazepines	Librium, Valium, Xanax	Anxiety

SUMMARIZE IT

Disadvantages of Drug Therapy. Beyond the drugs' unpleasant or dangerous side effects, another disadvantage in using drug therapy is the difficulty in establishing the proper dosages. Also, it's important to note that drugs do not cure psychological disorders. Thus, people who take them usually experience a relapse if they stop taking the drugs when their symptoms lift. Maintenance doses of antidepressants following a major depressive episode reduce the probability of recurrence (Prien & Kocsis, 1995). Maintenance doses are usually required with anxiety disorders as well, or symptoms are likely to return (Hallon et al., 2006). Further, some studies suggest that the trend away from involuntary hospitalization brought about by the availability of antipsychotic and other psychiatric drugs has led to an increase in homelessness among people who have chronic mental illnesses such as schizophrenia (Carson et al., 2000). Unfortunately, after being discharged from mental hospitals because they have shown favorable responses to antipsychotic drugs, many people with schizophrenia do not get adequate follow-up care. As a result, some stop taking their medications, relapse into psychotic states, and are unable to support themselves. Finally and perhaps most importantly, critics of drug therapy point out that it often prevents people with psychological disorders from being advised of other forms of therapy that may reduce or eliminate the need for psychiatric drugs (Calton & Spandler, 2009).

13.11 What is electroconvulsive therapy (ECT) used for?

electroconvulsive therapy (ECT) A biological therapy in which an electric current is passed through the right hemisphere of the brain; usually reserved for patients with severe depression who are suicidal.

Electroconvulsive Therapy

Antidepressant drugs are relatively slow acting. A person with severe depression needs at least two to six weeks to obtain relief, and 30% of these patients don't respond at all. This situation can be too risky for people who are at risk for suicide (Keitner & Boschini, 2009). Electroconvulsive therapy (ECT), a biological therapy in which an electric current is passed through the right hemisphere of the brain, is sometimes used in such cases. ECT has a bad reputation because it was misused and overused in the 1940s and 1950s. Nevertheless, when used appropriately, ECT is a highly effective treatment for major depression (Scott & Fraser, 2008).

For many years, ECT was performed by passing an electric current through both cerebral hemispheres, a procedure known as *bilateral ECT.* Today, electric current is administered to the right hemisphere only, and the procedure is called *unilateral ECT.* Research suggests that unilateral ECT is as effective as the more intense bilateral form while producing milder cognitive effects (Sackeim et al., 2000). Also, a patient undergoing ECT today is given anesthesia, controlled oxygenation, and a muscle relaxant.

Experts think that ECT changes the biochemical balance in the brain, resulting in a lifting of depression. When ECT is effective, cerebral blood flow in the prefrontal cortex is reduced, and delta waves (usually associated with slow-wave sleep) appear (Sackeim et al., 1996). Some psychiatrists and neurologists have spoken out against the use of ECT, claiming that it causes pervasive brain damage and memory loss. But advocates of ECT say that claims of brain damage are based on animal studies in which dosages of ECT were much higher than those now used in human patients. No structural brain damage from ECT has been revealed by studies comparing MRI or CT scans before and after a series of treatments (Devanand et al., 1994).

Toward the end of the 20th century, a new brain-stimulation therapy known as *rapid transcranial magnetic stimulation (rTMS)* was developed. This magnetic therapy is not invasive in any way. Performed on people who are not sedated, it causes no seizures, leads to no memory loss, and has no known side effects. Its therapeutic value is similar to that of ECT, and it is much more acceptable to the public (Higgins & George, 2009).

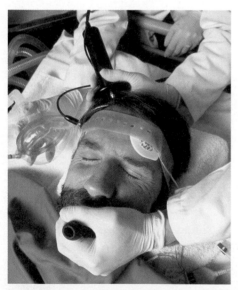

▲ In electroconvulsive therapy, a mild electric current is passed through the right hemisphere of the brain for 1 to 2 seconds, causing a brief seizure.

13.12 For what problems is psychosurgery used?

psychosurgery Brain surgery performed to alleviate serious psychological disorders or unbearable chronic pain.

Psychosurgery

An even more drastic procedure than ECT is psychosurgery—brain surgery performed to alleviate serious psychological disorders, such as severe depression, severe anxiety, or obsessions, or to provide relief from unbearable chronic pain. The first experimental brain surgery for human patients, the *lobotomy,* was developed by Portuguese neurologist Egas Moniz in 1935 to treat severe phobias, anxiety, and obsessions. Surgeons performing a lobotomy would sever the neural connections between the frontal lobes and the deeper brain centers involved in emotion. But no brain tissue was removed. At first, the procedure was considered a tremendous contribution, and Moniz won the Nobel Prize in medicine in 1949. Eventually, however, it became apparent that this treatment left patients in a severely deteriorated condition. You may recall, for example, the case of H. M. that we discussed in Chapter 6. As a result of an operation of this kind, H. M. lost the ability to form new memories. Devastating after-effects of the lobotomy and similar operations led to their discontinuation.

Modern psychosurgery procedures result in less intellectual impairment because, rather than using conventional surgery, surgeons deliver electric currents through electrodes to destroy a much smaller, more localized area of brain tissue. In one procedure, called a *cingulotomy*, electrodes are used to destroy the *cingulum*, a small bundle of nerves connecting the cortex to the emotional centers of the brain. Several procedures, including cingulotomy, have been helpful for some extreme cases of obsessive-compulsive disorder (Baer et al., 1995; Trivedi, 1996). But the results of psychosurgery are still not predictable, and the consequences—whether positive or negative—are irreversible. For these reasons, the treatment is considered experimental and absolutely a last resort (Clannon, 2006).

Practical Issues in Psychotherapy

If you decided that you were ready to enter into a long-term relationship with a romantic partner, would you open the telephone directory and select a name at random? Of course not. Admittedly, establishing a relationship with a therapist isn't quite as momentous as selecting a life partner. But, in both situations, it is wise to arm yourself with relevant information. Becoming familiar with the various professionals who offer therapeutic services is an important step toward that goal. Likewise, you should consider how comfortable you feel with a therapist whose gender or cultural background is different from your own. Finally, you would probably want to know which type of therapy is most effective.

Choosing a Therapist ▷

Perhaps you are one of the thousands of people who have considered turning to the Internet for therapy. If so, then you will find the tips in the *Apply It* to be very helpful. Regardless of the mode through which therapy occurs—online, by telephone, or in person—choosing a therapist with the type of training best suited to your problem can be crucial to how helpful the therapy turns out to be. Table 13.2 (p. 427) lists the various types of mental health professionals. One important difference among professionals, about which many people are confused, is that a psychologist has an advanced degree, usually at the doctoral level, in psychology, while a psychiatrist is a medical doctor. Historically, drug therapy has been available only from psychiatrists. At present, however, there is a movement that is gaining momentum in the United States to allow psychologists with special training in psychopharmacology to prescribe drugs. Only the U.S. military and a few states have authorized prescribing privileges for psychologists so far.

Regardless of their training or theoretical orientation, all therapists are bound by ethical standards established by professional organizations and, in most cases, codified in state laws. Each profession (e.g., psychologists, social workers) has its own ethical standards, but certain features are common to all of them and are exemplified by the ethics code of the American Psychological Association (2002). All of the ethical standards in the APA code are governed by the principle that therapists must take reasonable steps to ensure the well-being and rights of their client and to avoid causing them any kind of immediate or long-term harm. One important standard that serves these

13.13 What are the similarities and differences among the various types of therapists?

psychologist A mental health professional who possesses a doctoral degree in psychology.

psychiatrist A mental health professional who is a medical doctor.

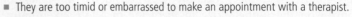

APPLY IT   Is E-therapy Right for You?

If you were trying to overcome a substance abuse problem or needed help getting through a period of bereavement, would you turn to an online support group? Some studies suggest that therapy delivered via the Internet can be highly effective (Kenwright & Marks, 2004). But people aren't waiting for scientific studies that demonstrate the effectiveness of these innovative treatments. Thousands have already turned to *e-therapy*—ongoing online interaction with a trained therapist (Warmerdam et al., 2010; Taylor & Luce, 2003). This form of therapy typically involves the exchange of e-mail messages over a period of hours or days but can also include video-conferencing and telephone sessions (Day & Schneider, 2002). In addition, therapists have begun experimenting with virtual environments that

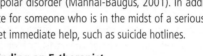

are similar to the popular online environment *Second Life*. In these virtual environments, therapists and clients manipulate *avatars* (graphic online identities) and settings to interact with each other and to create situations in which clients can practice the coping skills that they learn in either face-to-face or e-therapy (Cho et al., 2008; Gaggioli & Riva, 2007).

Advantages of E-therapy

E-therapy enables clients to be much less inhibited than they might be in a face-to-face situation. It is also less expensive than traditional therapy (Roan, 2000). Another advantage is that the therapist and the client do not have to be in the same place at the same time. The client can write to the therapist whenever he or she feels like it and can keep records of "sessions" (e-mail correspondence) to refer to later (Ainsworth, 2000; Stubbs, 2005). A therapist can also keep accurate records of communications with clients and can answer their questions at times of day when telephone calls are inconvenient, thus making his or her therapy practice more efficient (Andrews & Erskine, 2003). Ainsworth (2000) and Walker (2000) have found that e-therapy can be an especially helpful alternative to psychotherapy for people with any of several characteristics:

- They are often away from home or have full schedules.
- They cannot afford traditional therapy.
- They live in rural areas and do not have access to mental health care.
- They have disabilities.

- They are too timid or embarrassed to make an appointment with a therapist.
- They are good at expressing their thoughts and feelings in writing.

Disadvantages of E-therapy

Because of the anonymity of Internet interactions, it is easy for imposters to pose as therapists. So far, there is no system for regulating or licensing e-therapists. In addition, e-therapy poses some potential ethical problems, such as the possibility of breaches of confidentiality. But like all reputable therapists, the best e-therapists do everything they can to protect clients' privacy and confidentiality—except when it is necessary to protect them or someone else from immediate harm (Ainsworth, 2000). Perhaps the most serious drawback of e-therapy is the fact that the therapist cannot see the client and therefore cannot use visual and auditory cues to determine when the person is becoming anxious or upset. This reduces the effectiveness of treatment (Roan, 2000).

Another important limitation of e-therapy is that it is not appropriate for diagnosing and treating serious psychological disorders, such as schizophrenia or bipolar disorder (Manhal-Baugus, 2001). In addition, e-therapy is not appropriate for someone who is in the midst of a serious crisis. There are better ways to get immediate help, such as suicide hotlines.

Finding an E-therapist

If you wish to locate an e-therapist, the best place to start is *http://www.metanoia.org*. This site lists online therapists whose credentials have been checked by Mental Health Net. It provides information about the location of the therapist, the services offered, the payment method, and so forth (Roan, 2000).

When choosing a therapist, be sure to do the following (Ainsworth, 2000):

- Make sure the person's credentials have been verified by a third party.
- Get real-world contact information.
- Verify that you'll receive a personal reply to your messages.
- Find out in advance how much the therapist charges.

If you decide to contact an e-therapist, bear this in mind: While e-therapy may be a good way to get started, if you have persistent problems, it would be wise in the long run to obtain traditional psychotherapy (Roan, 2000).

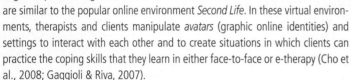

goals is *informed consent*. Therapists must inform clients of the cost and expected duration of therapy prior to beginning any intervention. Moreover, clients must be informed of the legal limits of confidentiality. For example, if a client reveals that she or he has committed a crime, in most cases the therapist is obligated to report the confession to the appropriate authorities. In addition, some insurance companies require that therapists' notes be available for review without regard to clients' confidentiality.

The nature of the therapeutic relationship is also governed by ethical standards. Therapists are forbidden to engage in any kind of intimate relationship with a client or with anyone close to the client. They are also prohibited from providing therapeutic services to former intimate partners. When ending a therapeutic relationship, a thera-

TABLE 13.2 Mental Health Professionals

PROFESSIONAL TITLE	TRAINING	SERVICES PROVIDED
Psychiatrist	Medical degree (M.D. or O.D.); residency in psychiatry	Psychotherapy; drug therapy; hospitalization for serious psychological disorders
Psychoanalyst	M.D., Ph.D., or Psy.D.; additional training in psychoanalysis	Psychodynamic therapy
Clinical psychologist	Ph.D. or Psy.D.; internship in clinical psychology	Diagnosis and treatment of psychological disorders; can prescribe drugs in some settings after additional training; psychological testing
Counseling psychologist	Ph.D. or Ed.D.; internship in counseling psychology	Assessment and therapy for normal problems of life (e.g., divorce); psychological testing
School psychologist	Ph.D., Ed.D., or master's degree; internship in school psychology	Assessment and treatment of school problems in children and adolescents; psychological testing
Clinical or psychiatric social worker (M.S.W.)	Master's degree; internship in psychiatric social work	Diagnosis and treatment of psychological disorders; identification of supportive community services
Licensed professional counselor (L.P.C.)	Master's degree; internship in counseling	Assessment and therapy for normal problems of life; some psychological testing
Licensed marriage and family therapist (L.M.F.T.)	Master's degree; internship in couple therapy and family therapy	Assessment and therapy for relationship problems
Licensed chemical dependency counselor (L.C.D.C.)	Educational requirements vary from one state to another	Treatment and education for substance abuse problems

pist must counsel a client about the reason for terminating therapy and provide him or her with alternatives.

With regard to testing, therapists are ethically obligated to use tests that are reliable and valid. Moreover, they must have appropriate training for administering, scoring, and evaluating each test they use. They are also required to explain the purpose of testing to clients and to provide them with test results in a timely and confidential manner.

Culturally Sensitive Therapy ▶

13.14 What are the characteristics of culturally sensitive therapy?

Among most psychotherapists, there is a growing awareness of the need to consider cultural variables in diagnosing and treating psychological disorders (Field, 2009). In fact, the American Psychological Association published guidelines to help psychologists be more sensitive to cultural issues (American Psychological Association, 2003b). According to Kleinman and Cohen (1997), people experience and suffer from psychological disorders within a cultural context that may dramatically affect the meaning of symptoms, outcomes, and responses to therapy. And cultural differences between therapist and client may undermine the *therapeutic alliance,* the bond between therapist and client that is known to be a factor in the effectiveness of psychotherapy (Blatt et al., 1996). Thus, many experts advocate an approach called culturally sensitive therapy in which knowledge of clients' cultural backgrounds guides the choice of therapeutic interventions (Kumpfer et al., 2002).

Culturally sensitive therapists recognize that language differences between therapists and clients can pose problems (Santiago-Rivera & Altarriba, 2002). For

culturally sensitive therapy An approach to therapy in which knowledge of clients' cultural backgrounds guides the choice of therapeutic interventions.

▲ When therapist and client have the same racial or ethnic background, they are more likely to share cultural values and communication styles, which can facilitate the therapeutic process.

example, a client who speaks both Spanish and English but is more fluent in Spanish may exhibit hesitations, backtracking, and delayed responses to questions when being interviewed in English. As a result, the therapist may erroneously conclude that this client is suffering from the kind of disordered thinking that is often displayed by people with schizophrenia (Martinez, 1986). Such language differences may also affect clients' results on standardized tests used by clinicians. In one frequently cited study, researchers found that when a group of Puerto Rican clients took the Thematic Apperception Test (TAT) in English, their pauses and their choices of words were incorrectly interpreted as indications of psychological problems (Suarez, 1983). Thus, culturally sensitive therapists become familiar with clients' general fluency in the language in which they will be assessed prior to interviewing and testing them.

When working with recent immigrants to the United States, culturally sensitive therapists take into account the impact of the immigration experience on clients' thoughts and emotions (Lijtmaer, 2001; Sluzki, 2004; Smolar, 1999; Ying, 2009). Some researchers who have studied the responses of recent Asian immigrants to psychotherapy recommend that, prior to initiating diagnosis and treatment, therapists encourage clients who are immigrants to talk about the feelings of sadness they have experienced as a result of leaving their native culture, as well as their anxieties about adapting to life in a new society. Using this strategy, therapists may be able to separate depression and anxiety related to the immigration experience from true psychopathology.

Some advocates of culturally sensitive therapy point out that cultural practices can be used as models for therapeutic interventions. Traditional Native American *healing circles,* for example, are being used by many mental health practitioners who serve Native Americans (Garrett, Garrett, & Brotherton, 2001). Members of a healing circle are committed to promoting the physical, mental, emotional, and spiritual well-being of one another. Healing circle participants typically engage in member-led activities such as discussion, meditation, and prayer. However, some more structured healing circles include a recognized Native American healer who leads the group in traditional healing ceremonies.

Culturally sensitive therapists also attempt to address group differences that can affect the results of therapy. For example, many studies have found that African Americans with mental disorders are less likely than white Americans with the same diagnoses to follow their doctor's or therapist's instruction about taking medications (Fleck et al., 2002; Hazlett-Stevens et al., 2002). A culturally sensitive approach to this problem might be based on a therapist's understanding of the importance of kinship networks and community relationships in African American culture. A therapist might increase an African American client's compliance level by having the client participate in a support group with other African Americans suffering from the same illness and taking the same medications (Muller, 2002). In addition, researchers and experienced therapists recommend that non–African American therapists and African American clients openly discuss their differing racial perspectives prior to beginning therapy (Bean, Perry, & Bedell, 2002).

13.15 Why is gender-sensitive therapy important?

Gender-Sensitive Therapy

Many psychotherapists also note the need for gender-sensitive therapy, a therapeutic approach that takes into the account the effects of gender on both the therapist's and the client's behavior (Gehart & Lyle, 2001). To implement gender-sensitive therapy, therapists must examine their own gender-based prejudices. They may assume men to be more analytical and women to be more emotional, for example. These stereotypical beliefs may be based on a therapist's socialization background or knowledge of research findings on gender differences.

gender-sensitive therapy An approach to therapy that takes into account the effects of gender on both the therapist's and the client's behavior.

Advocates of gender-sensitive therapy point out that knowledge of real differences between the sexes is important to the practice of gender-sensitive therapy. For instance, because of men's gender role socialization, interventions focused on emotional expression may be less effective for them than for women (Gillon, 2008). Moreover, men may view seeking therapy as a sign of weakness or as a threat to their sense of masculinity (Addis & Mahalik, 2003). As a result, researchers advise therapists to try to avoid creating defensiveness in their male clients (Greer, 2005). Nevertheless, therapists must guard against using research findings as a basis for stereotyping either male or female clients. They have to keep in mind that there is more variation within each gender than across genders, and thus each man or women must be considered as an individual.

Some therapists who are motivated by a sincere desire to be sensitive to gender issues may place too much emphasis on gender issues and misinterpret clients' problems (Addis & Mahalik, 2003). For example, in one study, researchers found that therapists expect people who are working in nontraditional fields—female engineers and male nurses, for instance—to have more psychological problems (Rubinstein, 2001). As a result, therapists may assume that such clients' difficulties arise from gender role conflicts, when, in reality, their problems have completely different origins.

Evaluating the Therapies ▶

If you look over the summaries of the various therapeutic approaches in the *Summarize It* (p. 430), you will notice that they share many similarities. For example, several therapies help clients reflect on their own thoughts and/or emotions. Analyses of therapy sessions representing different perspectives suggest that therapists use a core set of techniques no matter which perspective they adopt; at the same time, each therapeutic approach has elements that distinguish it from others (Crits-Cristoph et al., 2008; de Groot, Verheul, & Trijsburg, 2008). ✳—Explore on mypsychlab.com

But to what degree do the various therapies differ in effectiveness? In a classic study of therapeutic effectiveness, Smith and his colleagues (1980) analyzed the results of 475 studies, which involved 25,000 clients. Their findings revealed that psychotherapy was better than no treatment, but that no one type of psychotherapy was more effective than another. A subsequent reanalysis of the same data by Hans Eysenck (1994), however, showed a slight advantage for behavior therapies over other types. A study by Hollon and others (2002) found that cognitive and interpersonal therapies had an advantage over psychodynamic approaches for clients with depression. Moreover, socioeconomic status and other personal variables interact with clients' problems, and these interactions influence therapeutic outcomes (Falconnier, 2009). For example, a technique that has proven to be effective for people with adequate means may not be so for people who are struggling financially. Thus, the most important determinant of the effectiveness of any therapeutic technique is its appropriateness for a given client's problems and the circumstances of his or her life (Crits-Christoph et al., 2008).

But how do the clients themselves rate the therapies? To answer this question, *Consumer Reports* (1995) conducted the largest survey to date on client attitudes toward psychotherapy. Martin Seligman (1995, 1996), a consultant for the study, summarized its findings:

- Overall, clients believed that they benefited substantially from psychotherapy.
- Patients seemed equally satisfied with their therapy, whether it was provided by a psychologist, a psychiatrist, or a social worker.
- Clients who were in therapy for more than 6 months did considerably better than the rest; generally, the longer patients stayed in therapy, the more they improved.
- Patients who took a drug such as Prozac or Xanax believed it helped them, but overall, psychotherapy alone seemed to work about as well as psychotherapy plus drugs.

13.16 What does research suggest about the effectiveness of psychotherapy?

✳—Explore the **Concept** *Closer Look Simulation: Therapies* on **mypsychlab.com**

Summarize and Comparison of the Therapies

TYPE OF THERAPY	PERCEIVED CAUSE OF DISORDER	GOALS OF THERAPY	METHODS USED	PRIMARY DISORDERS OR SYMPTOMS TREATED
INSIGHT THERAPIES				
Psychoanalysis	Unconscious sexual and aggressive urges or conflicts; fixations; weak ego; object relations; life stress	Help patient bring disturbing, repressed material to consciousness and work through unconscious conflicts; strengthen ego functions	Psychoanalyst analyzes and interprets dreams, free associations, resistance, and transference, and past relationships.	General feelings of unhappiness; unresolved problems from childhood
Person-centered therapy	Blocking of normal tendency toward self-actualization; incongruence between real and desired self; overdependence on positive regard of others	Increase self-acceptance and self-understanding; help client become more inner-directed; increase congruence between real and desired self; enhance personal growth	Therapist shows empathy, unconditional positive regard, and genuineness, and reflects client's expressed feelings back to client.	General feelings of unhappiness; interpersonal problems
Gestalt therapy	Difficulties are caused by blaming society, past experiences, parents, or others	Help clients achieve a more integrated self and become more self-accepting	Directive therapy; the "empty chair" technique; role-play	Depression
RELATIONSHIP THERAPIES				
Family therapy and couples therapy	Problems caused by faulty communication patterns, unreasonable role expectations, drug and/or alcohol abuse, and so on	Create more understanding and harmony within the relationships; improve communication patterns; heal wounds of family unit	Therapist sees clients individually or several family members at a time and explores such things as communication patterns, power struggles, and unreasonable demands and expectations.	Family problems such as marriage or relationship problems, troubled or troublesome teenagers, abusive relationships, drug or alcohol problems, schizophrenia family member
Group therapy	None	Give clients sense of belonging, opportunity to express feelings, opportunity to give and receive feedback from others with similar problems	7 to 10 clients meet regularly with one or more therapists to resolve personal problems	Anxiety, depression, low self-esteem
BEHAVIOR THERAPIES				
Behavior therapy	Learning of maladaptive behaviors or failure to learn appropriate behaviors	Extinguish maladaptive behaviors and replace with more adaptive ones; help client acquire needed social skills	Therapist uses methods based on classical and operant conditioning and modeling, which include systematic desensitization, flooding, exposure and response prevention, and aversion therapy.	Fears, phobias, panic disorder, obsessive-compulsive disorder, bad habits
COGNITIVE THERAPIES				
Cognitive therapy	Irrational and negative assumptions and ideas about self and others	Change faulty, irrational, and/or negative thinking	Therapist helps client identify irrational and negative thinking and substitute rational thinking.	Depression, anxiety, panic disorder, general feelings of unhappiness
BIOMEDICAL THERAPIES				
Biomedical therapy	Underlying physical disorder caused by structural or biochemical abnormality in the brain; genetic inheritance	Eliminate or control biological cause of abnormal behavior; restore balance of neurotransmitters	Physician prescribes drugs such as antipsychotics, antidepressants, lithium, or tranquilizers; uses ECT or psychosurgery.	Schizophrenia, depression, bipolar disorder, anxiety disorders

⚙ Looking Back

Now that you have read about the various therapies and a few important aspects of the therapeutic relationship, what sort of therapist do you think you would look for if you needed one? Remember that a psychodynamic therapist will probably engage you in an exploration of past relationships, while a humanistic therapist will try to facilitate your search for self-actualization. A family or couple therapist might be the best professional to consult if you would like to change the interaction patterns that have developed between you and the significant people in your life. A behavior therapist can help you modify a troublesome behavior pattern, and a cognitive therapist will do the same for any maladaptive thought patterns that you have. Recall, too, that any of these techniques can be used by any of the professionals listed in Table 13.2. In fact, most therapists are skilled in the use of more than one approach, although most have preferences. Finally, before entering into a therapeutic relationship think about how cultural and gender issues may affect the course of your therapy. As you can see, the information you have acquired from studying this chapter has helped you become a savvier consumer of psychotherapeutic services should a need for such services ever arise in your life.

CHAPTER 13 SUMMARY

INSIGHT THERAPIES (pp. 410–412)

13.1 What are the basic techniques of psychodynamic therapies? (pp. 410-411)

The techniques associated with psychoanalysis are free association, dream analysis, object relations, and transference. They are used to uncover the repressed memories, impulses, and conflicts presumed to be the cause of the patient's problems. Interpersonal therapy (IPT) is designed to help people with depression cope with unusual or severe responses to the death of a loved one, interpersonal role disputes, difficulty in adjusting to role transitions, and deficits in interpersonal skills.

Key Terms
psychotherapy, p. 410
insight therapies, p. 410
psychodynamic therapies, p. 410
psychoanalysis, p. 410
free association, p. 410
transference, p. 410
interpersonal therapy (IPT), p. 411

13.2 What is the goal of the therapist in person-centered therapy? (pp. 411-412)

Person-centered therapy is a nondirective therapy in which the therapist provides empathy and a climate of unconditional positive regard. The goal is to allow the client to determine the direction of the therapy sessions and to move toward self-actualization.

Key Terms
humanistic therapies, p. 411
person-centered therapy, p. 411
nondirective therapy, p. 412

13.3 What is the major emphasis of Gestalt therapy? (p. 412)

Gestalt therapy emphasizes the importance of clients' fully experiencing, in the present moment, their feelings, thoughts, and actions and taking personal responsibility for their behavior.

Key Terms
Gestalt therapy, p. 412
directive therapy, p. 412

RELATIONSHIP THERAPIES (pp. 412–413)

13.4 What are the goals of family and couple therapy? (pp. 412-413)

In couple therapy, therapists help intimate partners change their behavior and their emotional responses to each other in order to improve their relationships. The goals of family therapy include helping family members improve communication patterns and create more interpersonal understanding and harmony.

Key Terms

relationship therapies, p. 412   *couple therapy*, p. 413
family therapy, p. 413

13.5 What are some advantages of group therapy? (p. 413)

Group therapy is less expensive than individual therapy, and it gives people opportunities to express their feelings, get feed-back from other group members, and give and receive help and emotional support.

Key Term

group therapy p. 413

BEHAVIOR THERAPIES (pp. 414–417)

13.6 How do behavior therapists modify clients' problematic behavior? (p. 414)

Behavior therapists use operant conditioning techniques such as the use of reinforcement to shape or increase the frequency of desirable behaviors (token economies) and the withholding of reinforcement to eliminate undesirable behaviors (time out).

Key Terms

behavior therapy, p. 414   *token economy*, p. 414
behavior modification, p. 414   *time out*, p. 414

13.7 What behavior therapies are based on classical conditioning and social-cognitive theory? (pp. 415-417)

Behavior therapies based on classical conditioning are systematic desensitization, flooding, exposure and response preven-tion, and aversion therapy. In participant modeling, an appro-priate response to a feared stimulus is modeled in graduated steps, and the client is asked to imitate each step with the encouragement and support of the therapist.

Key Terms

systematic desensitization, p. 415
flooding, p. 416
exposure and response prevention, p. 416
aversion therapy, p. 416
participant modeling, p. 416

COGNITIVE BEHAVIOR THERAPIES (pp. 417–420)

13.8 What is the aim of rational emotive behavior therapy? (pp. 417-418)

Rational emotive behavior therapy is a directive form of therapy designed to challenge and modify a client's irra-tional beliefs, which are believed to be the cause of personal distress.

Key Terms

cognitive behavior therapies, p. 417
rational emotive behavior therapy (REBT), p. 417

13.9 How does Beck's cognitive therapy approach psychotherapy (pp. 418-420)

Beck's cognitive therapy helps people overcome depression and panic disorder by pointing out the irrational thoughts causing them misery and by helping them learn other, more realistic ways of looking at themselves and their experiences.

Key Term

Beck's cognitive therapy (CT), p. 418

especially the simple act of smiling, influences our perceptions of their attractiveness (Reis et al., 1990). But physical appearance matters as well.

Symmetrical faces and bodies are seen as more attractive and sexually appealing (Green et al., 2008). In a review of 11 meta-analyses of cross-cultural studies of attractiveness, Langlois and others (2000) found that males and females across many cultures have similar ideas about the physical attractiveness of members of the opposite sex. When native Asian, Hispanic American, and White American male students rated photographs of Asian, Hispanic, African American, and White females on attractiveness, Cunningham and others (1995) reported a very high mean correlation (.93) among the groups in attractiveness ratings. When African American and White American men rated photos of African American women, their agreement on facial features was also very high—a correlation of .94. Evolutionary psychologists suggest that this cross-cultural similarity exists because of a tendency, shaped by natural selection, to look for indicators of health in potential mates (Fink & Penton-Voak, 2002).

Why does physical attractiveness matter? When people have one trait that we either admire or dislike very much, we often assume that they have other positive or negative traits—a phenomenon known as the halo effect (Nisbett & Wilson, 1977). Dion, Berscheid, and Walster (1972) found that people generally attribute additional favorable qualities to those who are attractive. Attractive people are seen as more exciting, personable, interesting, and socially desirable than unattractive people. As a result, job interviewers are more likely to recommend highly attractive people (Dipboye, Fromkin, & Wilback, 1975). Similarly, when asked to rate pictures of women with regard to the likelihood of career success, research participants give higher ratings to those who are thin than to those who are overweight or obese (Wade & DiMaria, 2003).

Does this mean that unattractive people don't have a chance? Fortunately not. Eagly and her colleagues (1991) suggest that the impact of physical attractiveness is strongest in the perception of strangers. But once we get to know people, other qualities assume more importance. In fact, as we come to like people, they begin to look more attractive to us, while people with undesirable personal qualities begin to look less attractive. ◉–Watch on mypsychlab.com

halo effect The tendency to assume that a person has generally positive or negative traits as a result of observing one major positive or negative trait.

◉–Watch the **Video** *Explore Attractiveness* on **mypsychlab.com**

Intimate Relationships ▷

14.4 What factors contribute to the formation and maintenance of intimate relationships?

Most of the factors that influence attraction in general, such as physical attractiveness, also influence romantic attraction. But what about love? As you will learn, the kind of love that intimate partners experience influences their relationship throughout its duration.

Romantic Attraction. You probably have heard that opposites attract, but is this really true? The matching hypothesis suggests that we are likely to end up with a partner similar to ourselves in physical attractiveness and other assets (Berscheid et al., 1971; Feingold, 1988; Walster & Walster, 1969). Furthermore, couples mismatched in attractiveness are more likely to end the relationship (Cash & Janda, 1984). It has been suggested that we estimate our social assets and realistically expect to attract someone with approximately equal assets. Fear of rejection prevents many people from pursuing those who are much more attractive than they are. Nevertheless, once a relationship is formed, both men and women develop the ability to screen out the attractiveness of alternative partners (Maner, Gailliot, & Miller, 2009). Thus, while continuing to be attentive to a partner's attractiveness is important to maintaining a romantic relationship, ignoring the attractiveness of other potential partners may be just as important to relationship stability and longevity.

Most research indicates that similarity in needs is mainly what attracts (Buss, 1984; Phillips et al., 1988). Similarities in personality, physical traits, intellectual

matching hypothesis The notion that people tend to have lovers or spouses who are similar to themselves in physical attractiveness and other assets.

▲ You are more likely to be attracted to someone who is similar to you than to someone who is your opposite.

triangular theory of love Sternberg's theory that three components—intimacy, passion, and commitment—singly and in various combinations, produce seven different kinds of love.

ability, education, religion, ethnicity, socioeconomic status, and attitudes are also related to partner choice (Luo & Klohnen, 2005; O'Leary & Smith, 1991). And similarities in needs and in personality appear to be related to marital success as well as to marital choice (O'Leary & Smith, 1991). Similarities wear well. If you were to select a life partner, what qualities would attract you? Complete the *Try It* to evaluate your own preferences.

Compare your rankings from the *Try It* to those of men and women from 33 countries and 5 major islands around the world. Generally, men and women across those cultures rate these four qualities as most important in life partner selection: (1) mutual attraction/love, (2) dependable character, (3) emotional stability and maturity, and (4) pleasing disposition (Buss et al., 1990). Aside from these first four choices, however, women and men differ somewhat in the attributes they prefer. According to the views of evolutionary psychologist David Buss (1994), "Men prefer to mate with beautiful young women, whereas women prefer to mate with men who have resources and social status" (p. 239). These preferences, he claims, have been adaptive in human evolutionary history. To a male, beauty and youth suggest health and fertility—the best opportunity to send his genes into the next generation. To a female, resources and social status provide security for her and her children (Buss & Shackelford, 2008). As was noted in Chapter 9, social role theorists maintain that gender differences in mate preferences are influenced by economic and social forces as well as evolutionary forces (Wood & Eagly, 2007).

Sternberg's Triangular Theory of Love. In Western culture, affection is an important part of most relationships, including friendships, and being "in love" is the most important factor in the formation of long-term romantic relationships. But what is love? Robert Sternberg (1986b, 1987), whose triarchic theory of intelligence was discussed in Chapter 7, has also proposed a triangular theory of love. Its three components are intimacy, passion, and commitment. Sternberg explains intimacy as "those feelings in a relationship that promote closeness, bondedness, and connectedness" (1987, p. 339). Passion refers to those drives in a loving relationship "that lead to romance, physical attraction, [and] sexual consummation" (1986b, p. 119). The commitment component consists of (1) a short-term aspect, the decision that one loves another person, and (2) a long-term aspect, a commitment to maintaining that love over time.

Sternberg proposes that these three components, singly and in various combinations, produce seven different kinds of love (see Figure 14.1).

TRY IT ▶ Choosing a Life Partner

In your choice of a life partner, which qualities are most and least important to you? Rank these 18 qualities of a potential life partner from most important (1) to least important (18) to you.

_____ Ambition and industriousness
_____ Chastity (no previous sexual intercourse)
_____ Desire for home and children
_____ Education and intelligence
_____ Emotional stability and maturity
_____ Favorable social status or rating
_____ Good cooking and housekeeping skills
_____ Similar political background
_____ Similar religious background
_____ Good health
_____ Good looks

_____ Similar education
_____ Pleasing disposition
_____ Refinement/neatness
_____ Sociability
_____ Good financial prospects
_____ Dependable character
_____ Mutual attraction/love

Alexander
Biology & Pre-Med

◉ Watch on mypsychlab.com

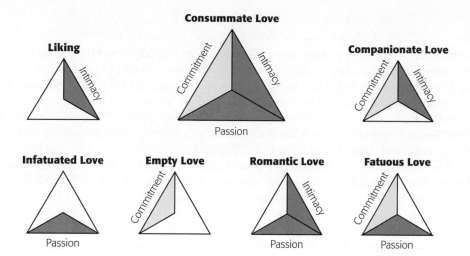

FIGURE 14.1 Sternberg's Triangular Theory of Love
Sternberg identifies three components of love—passion, intimacy, and commitment—and shows how the three, singly and in various combinations, produce seven different kinds of love. Consummate love, the most complete form of love, has all three components.
Source: Sternberg (1986b).

1. *Liking* includes only one of the love components—intimacy. In this case, liking is not used in a trivial sense. Sternberg says that this intimate liking characterizes true friendships, in which a person feels a bondedness, a warmth, and a closeness with another but not intense passion or long-term commitment.

2. *Infatuated love* consists solely of passion and is often what is felt as "love at first sight." But without the intimacy and the commitment components of love, infatuated love may disappear suddenly.

3. *Empty love* consists of the commitment component without intimacy or passion. Sometimes, a stronger love deteriorates into empty love, in which the commitment remains, but the intimacy and passion have died. In cultures in which arranged marriages are common, relationships often begin as empty love.

4. *Romantic love* is a combination of intimacy and passion. Romantic lovers are bonded emotionally (as in liking) and physically through passionate arousal.

5. *Fatuous love* has the passion and the commitment components but not the intimacy component. This type of love can be exemplified by a whirlwind courtship and marriage in which a commitment is motivated largely by passion, without the stabilizing influence of intimacy.

6. *Companionate love* consists of intimacy and commitment. This type of love is often found in marriages in which the passion has gone out of the relationship, but a deep affection and commitment remain.

7. *Consummate love* is the only type of love that includes all three components—intimacy, passion, and commitment. Consummate love is the most complete form of love, and it represents the ideal love relationship for which many people strive but which apparently few achieve. Sternberg cautions that maintaining a consummate love may be even harder than achieving it. He stresses the importance of translating the components of love into action. "Without expression," he warns, "even the greatest of loves can die" (1987, p. 341).

consummate love According to Sternberg's theory, the most complete form of love, consisting of all three components—intimacy, passion, and commitment.

Conformity, Obedience, and Compliance

Do you think of yourself as independently minded? Most people do. In Western cultures in particular, individuality and independent thinking are highly valued. But what happened to your independent-mindedness the last time that someone talked you into doing something that you really didn't want to do? As you have probably learned through experience, we are all subject to social influences in one way or another.

14.5 **What did Asch find in his classic experiment on conformity?**

conformity Changing or adopting a behavior or an attitude in an effort to be consistent with the social norms of a group or the expectations of other people.

social norms The attitudes and standards of behavior expected of members of a particular group.

Standard Line

1   2   3

FIGURE 14.2 Asch's Classic Study of Conformity
If you were one of eight participants in the Asch experiment who were asked to pick the line (1, 2, or 3) that matched the standard line shown above them, which line would you choose? If the other participants all chose line 3, would you conform and answer line 3?
Source: Based on Asch (1955).

Conformity

Conformity is changing or adopting a behavior or an attitude in an effort to be consistent with the social norms of a group or the expectations of other people. Social norms are the standards of behavior and the attitudes that are expected of members of a particular group. Some conformity is necessary if we are to have a society at all. We cannot drive on the other side of the road anytime we please. And we conform to other people's expectations to have their esteem or approval, their friendship or love, or even their company (Christensen et al., 2004).

The best-known experiment on conformity was conducted by Solomon Asch (1955), who designed the simple test shown in Figure 14.2. Eight male participants were seated around a large table and were asked, one by one, to tell the experimenter which of the three lines matched the standard line. But only one of the eight was an actual participant; the others were confederates assisting the experimenter. There were 18 trials—18 different lines to be matched. During 12 of these trials, the confederates all gave the same wrong answer, which of course puzzled the naive participant. Remarkably, Asch found that 5% of the subjects conformed to the incorrect, unanimous majority all of the time, 70% conformed some of the time, but 25% remained completely independent and were never swayed by the group.

Varying the experiment with groups of various sizes, Asch found that the tendency to go along with the majority opinion remained in full force even when there was a unanimous majority of only three confederates. Surprisingly, unanimous majorities of 15 confederates produced no higher conformity rate than did those of three. Asch also discovered that if just one other person voices a dissenting opinion, the tendency to conform is not as strong. When just one confederate in the group disagreed with the incorrect majority, the naive subjects' errors dropped drastically, from 32% to 10.4%.

Other research on conformity and the Big Five personality dimensions reveals that people who are low in neuroticism but high in agreeableness and conscientiousness are more likely to conform than those who score oppositely on those dimensions (DeYoung, Peterson, & Higgins, 2002). But, contrary to conventional wisdom, women are no more likely to conform than men (Eagly & Carli, 1981). And an individual's

▲ In this scene from Asch's experiment on conformity, all but one of the "subjects" were really confederates of the experimenter. They deliberately chose the wrong line to try to influence the naive subject (second from right) to go along with the majority.

conformity is greater if the sources of influence are perceived as belonging to that person's own group (Abrams et al., 1990). Even so, those who hold minority opinions on an issue have more influence in changing a majority view if they present a well-organized, clearly stated argument and if they are especially consistent in advocating their views (Wood et al., 1994).

Obedience ▶

[**14.6** What did Milgram's classic study reveal about obedience?

Can you imagine a world in which each person always did exactly what he or she wanted, without regard for rules or respect for authority? We would stop at red lights only when we felt like it or weren't in a hurry. Someone might decide that he liked your car better than his own and take it. Or worse, someone might kill you because of an interest in your intimate partner.

Clearly, obedience—behaving in accordance with the rules and commands of those in authority—helps to ensure that society survives and functions smoothly. However, unquestioned obedience can cause humans to commit unbelievably horrible acts. One of the darkest chapters in human history arose from the obedience of officials in Nazi Germany who carried out Adolf Hitler's orders to exterminate Jews and other "undesirables." ◉ Watch on mypsychlab.com

obedience Behaving in accordance with the rules and commands of those in authority.

◉ Watch the **Video** *Obedience* on **mypsychlab.com**

Intrigued by questions about what drove the guards in Nazi death camps to obey their superiors, social psychologist Stanley Milgram conducted one of the most startling experiments in the history of psychology in the early 1960s. He placed an advertisement in various newspapers in the New Haven, Connecticut, area that read: "Wanted: Volunteers to serve as subjects in a study of memory and learning at Yale University." Many people responded to the ad, and 40 male participants between the ages of 20 and 50 were selected. Yet, instead of a memory experiment, a staged drama was planned. The cast of characters was as follows:

- The Experimenter: A 31-year-old high school biology teacher, dressed in a gray laboratory coat, who assumed a stern and serious manner

- The Learner: A middle-aged man (an actor and accomplice of the experimenter)

- The Teacher: One of the volunteers

The experimenter led the teacher and the learner into one room, where the learner was strapped into an electric chair apparatus. The teacher was delivered a sample shock of 45 volts, supposedly for the purpose of testing the equipment and showing the teacher what the learner would feel. Next, the script called for the learner to complain of a heart condition and say that he hoped the electric shocks would not be too painful. The experimenter admitted that the stronger shocks would hurt but hastened to add, "Although the shocks can be extremely painful, they cause no permanent tissue damage" (Milgram, 1963, p. 373).

Then the experimenter took the teacher to an adjoining room and seated him in front of an instrument panel with 30 lever switches arranged horizontally across the front. The first switch on the left, he was told, delivered only 15 volts, but each successive switch was 15 volts stronger than the previous one, up to the last switch, which carried 450 volts. The switches on the instrument panel were labeled with designations ranging from "Slight Shock" to "Danger: Severe Shock" to "XXX." The experimenter instructed the teacher to read a list of word pairs to the learner and then test his memory. When the learner made the right choice, the teacher was supposed to go on to the next pair. If the learner missed a question, the teacher was told to flip a switch and shock him, moving one switch to the right—delivering 15 additional volts—each time the learner missed a question.

The learner performed well at first but then began missing about three out of every four questions. The teacher began flipping the switches. When he hesitated, the experimenter urged him to continue. If he still hesitated, the experimenter said, "The experiment requires that you continue," or more strongly, "You have no other choice, you must go on" (Milgram, 1963, p. 374). At the 20th switch, 300 volts, the script

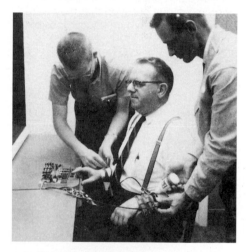

▲ In Stanley Milgram's experiments on obedience, "teachers" were led to believe that they could deliver electric shocks to "learners" who were hooked to devices such as the one shown here.
Courtesy of Alexandra Milgram. Copyright 1968 by Stanley Milgram. Copyright renewed 1993 by Alexandra Milgram. From the film OBEDIENCE, distributed by Penn State Media Sales.

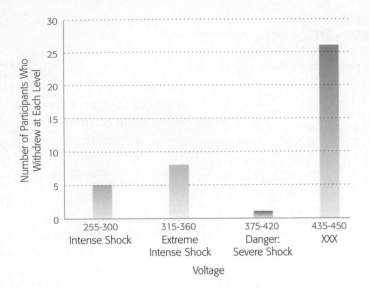

FIGURE 14.3 Milgram's Obedience Experiment
Sixty-five percent of the "teachers" in Milgram's study believed that they were delivering the maximum shock possible to the "learner."
Source: Milgram, 1963.

required the learner to pound on the wall and scream, "Let me out of here, let me out, my heart's bothering me, let me out!" (Meyer, 1972, p. 461). From this point on, the learner answered no more questions. If the teacher expressed concern or a desire to discontinue the experiment, the experimenter answered, "Whether the learner likes it or not, you must go on" (Milgram, 1963, p. 374). At the flip of the next switch—315 volts—the teacher heard only groans from the learner. Again, if the teacher expressed reluctance to go on, the experimenter said, "You have no other choice, you must go on" (Milgram, 1963, p. 374). If the teacher insisted on stopping at this point, the experimenter allowed him to do so.

How many of the 40 participants in the Milgram study do you think obeyed the experimenter to the end—450 volts? Surprisingly not a single participant stopped before the 20th switch, at supposedly 300 volts, when the learner began pounding the wall (see Figure 14.3). Amazingly, 26 participants—65% of the sample—obeyed the experimenter to the bitter end and only withdrew when they reached the maximum voltage level. But this experiment took a terrible toll on the participants. They "were observed to sweat, tremble, stutter, bite their lips, groan, and dig their fingernails into their flesh. These were characteristic rather than exceptional responses to the experiment" (Milgram, 1963, p. 375). Moreover, in an effort to avoid administering further shocks, some teachers begged the learners to respond correctly. Curiously, too, some participants began to laugh as the experiment progressed and the "learner" exhibited increasing degrees of distress. In a few, the laughter developed into seizures. Milgram suggested that participants' psychological distress resulted from a conflict between a desire to avoid harming others and a need to conform to the demands of those who hold legitimate authority.

A study like Milgram's could not be performed today because it would violate the American Psychological Association's code of ethics for researchers. Still, deception has traditionally been a part of social psychologists' research. To accomplish this deception, a researcher often must use one or more *confederates*—people who pose as participants in a psychology experiment but who are actually assisting the researcher, like the learner in the Milgram experiment. A *naive subject*—like the teacher in Milgram's study—is a person who has agreed to participate in an experiment but is not aware that deception is being used to conceal its real purpose.

Deception was a key element of follow-up studies that Milgram conducted in order to address questions about the limits of obedience. In one such study, Milgram (1965) varied the procedures of the original experiment: Each trial involved three teachers, two of whom were confederates and the other, a naive participant. One confederate was instructed to refuse to continue after 150 volts, and the other confederate after 210 volts. In this situation, 36 out of 40 naive participants (90%) defied the experimenter before the maximum shock could be given, compared with only 14 out of 40 participants in the original experiment (Milgram, 1965). In Milgram's experiment, as in Asch's conformity study, the presence of another person who refused to go along gave many of the participants the courage to defy authority.

14.7 What techniques do people use to gain compliance from others?

compliance Acting in accordance with the direct requests of other people.

foot-in-the-door technique A strategy designed to gain a favorable response to a small request at first, with the intent of making the person more likely to agree later to a larger request.

Compliance

How often do you do what others want you to do? There are many times when people act in accordance with the direct requests of others. This type of action is called compliance. One strategy people use to gain the compliance of others, the foot-in-the-door technique, is designed to gain a favorable response to a small request first. The intent is to make the person more likely to agree later to a larger request (the result desired from the beginning). For example, your roommate might ask you to throw a few extra items in the washer for her when you're doing a load of laundry in the hope that you will include her laundry with yours on a regular basis in the future.

In a classic study of the foot-in-the-door technique, a researcher claiming to represent a consumers' group called a number of homes and asked whether the people answering the phone would mind responding to a few questions about the soap products they used. Then, a few days later, the same person called those who had agreed to the first request and asked if he could send five or six of his assistants to conduct an inventory of the products in their home. The researcher told the people that the inventory would take about 2 hours and that the inventory team would have to search all drawers, cabinets, and closets in the house. Nearly 53% of those asked preliminary questions agreed to the larger request, compared to 22% of a control group who were contacted only once with the larger request (Freedman & Fraser, 1966).

How would you respond to a friend who asked to borrow 50 dollars? Suppose that you told your friend that you couldn't afford to loan him the money, and he reduced his request to 20 dollars. If you agree, your compliance was gained through a strategy called the door-in-the-face technique, a technique in which a large, unreasonable request is made first. The expectation is that the person will refuse but will then be more likely to respond favorably to a smaller request later (the result desired from the beginning). In a classic study of the door-in-the-face technique, college students were approached on campus. They were asked to agree to serve without pay as counselors to juvenile delinquents for 2 hours each week for a minimum of two years. As you would imagine, not a single person agreed (Cialdini et al., 1975). Then, the experimenters presented a much smaller request, asking if the students would agree to take a group of juveniles on a 2-hour trip to the zoo. Half the students agreed, a fairly high compliance rate. The researchers used another group of college students as controls, asking them to respond only to the smaller request, for the zoo trip. Only 17% agreed when the smaller request was presented alone.

door-in-the-face technique A strategy in which someone makes a large, unreasonable request with the expectation that the person will refuse but will then be more likely to respond favorably to a smaller request later.

Another method used to gain compliance is the low-ball technique. A very attractive initial offer is made to get people to commit themselves to an action, and then the terms are made less favorable. For example, suppose you receive a coupon for a free dinner at an expensive restaurant, and when you go the restaurant you learn that you have to listen to a one-hour sales pitch for a financial services company before you can order your dinner. You have just been subjected to the low-ball technique.

low-ball technique A strategy in which someone makes a very attractive initial offer to get a person to commit to an action and then makes the terms less favorable.

In a classic study of this technique, college students were asked to enroll in an experimental course for which they would receive credit. After the students had agreed to participate, they were informed that the class would meet at 7:00 a.m. Control group participants were told about the class meeting time when first asked to enroll. More than 50% of the low-balled group agreed to participate, but only 25% of control participants did so (Cialdini et al., 1978).

Group Influence

Have you ever seen a movie in which you really weren't interested or gone to the beach when you would have preferred to stay home? Being part of a group often means giving up a bit of individuality, but the reward is the support and camaraderie of the group. Clearly, we behave differently in a variety of ways when we are part of a group, small or large. What happens when the group of which we are a part is made up of strangers? Do such groups influence our behavior as well?

social facilitation Any positive or negative effect on performance that can be attributed to the presence of others, either as an audience or as coactors.

Social Facilitation and Social Loafing

14.8 How do social facilitation and social loafing affect performance?

In certain cases, individual performance can be either helped or hindered by the mere physical presence of others. The term social facilitation refers to any effect on performance, whether positive or negative, that can be attributed to the presence of others. Research on this phenomenon has focused on two types of effects: (1) audience effects, the impact of passive spectators on performance, and (2) coaction effects, the impact on performance caused by the presence of other people engaged in the same task.

audience effects The impact of passive spectators on performance.

coaction effects The impact on performance of the presence of other people engaged in the same task.

In one of the first studies in social psychology, Norman Triplett (1898) looked at coaction effects. He had observed in official records that bicycle racers pedaled faster

Presence of Others
(Audience effects, coaction effects)

Arousal is heightened, and dominant response is enhanced.

Performance is enhanced
on tasks at which we are skilled and on simple tasks.

Performance suffers
on tasks at which we are unskilled and on difficult tasks.

FIGURE 14.4 Social Facilitation: Performing in the Presence of Others
The presence of others (either as an audience or as coactors engaged in the same task) may have opposite effects, either helping or hindering an individual's performance. Why? First, the presence of others heightens arousal. Second, heightened arousal leads to better performance on tasks the individual is good at and worse performance on tasks that are difficult for him or her.
Source: Based on Zajonc & Sales (1966).

social loafing The tendency to put forth less effort when working with others on a common task than when working alone.

when they were pedaling against other racers than when they were racing against the clock. Was this pattern of performance peculiar to competitive bicycling? Or was it part of a more general phenomenon whereby people would work faster and harder in the presence of others than when performing alone? Triplett set up a study in which he told 40 children to wind fishing reels as quickly as possible under one of two conditions: (1) alone, or (2) in the presence of other children performing the same task. He found that children worked faster when other reel turners were present. But later studies on social facilitation found that in the presence of others people's performance improves on easy tasks but suffers on difficult tasks (Michaels et al., 1982). See Figure 14.4.

Have you ever been assigned by a teacher or professor to work in a group and, at the end of the project, felt that you had carried more than your fair share of the workload? Such feelings are not uncommon. Researcher Bibb Latané used the term social loafing to refer to people's tendency to put forth less effort when working with others on a common task than they do when they are working alone (Latané, Williams, & Harkins, 1979). Social loafing occurs in situations where no one person's contribution to the group can be identified and individuals are neither praised for a good performance nor blamed for a poor one (Williams, Harkins, & Latané, 1981). Social loafing is a problem in many workplaces, especially where employees have unlimited access to the Internet (Lim, 2002). However, individuals who display high levels of the Big Five trait conscientiousness are less likely to engage in social loafing than their peers (Tan & Tan, 2008).

Similarly, achievement motivation influences social loafing (Hart et al., 2004). Researchers tested participants with regard to their levels of achievement motivation and then assigned them to pairs. Each pair was asked to generate as many uses for a knife that they could think of. The amount of effort exhibited by participants who were low in achievement motivation depended on their partner's effort. When paired with partners who worked hard, individuals with low achievement motivation contributed little; that is, they engaged in social loafing. They did the opposite, however, when paired with others who didn't work. By contrast, participants who were high in achievement motivation worked hard at the task no matter what their partner's level of participation was.

Some 80 experimental studies have been conducted on social loafing in diverse cultures, including those of Taiwan, Japan, Thailand, India, China, and the United States. Social loafing on a variety of tasks was evident to some degree in all of the cultures studied. But it appears to be more common in individualistic Western cultures, such as the United States (Karau & Williams, 1993).

▲ Studying in a group could lead to social loafing through a diffusion of responsibility effect.

14.9 How do groups influence individual decision making?

Group Decision Making

It is commonly believed that groups tend to make more moderate decisions than individuals. However, research shows that group discussion often causes members of a group to shift to a more extreme position after participating in a discussion in which other group members strongly express agreement with them, a phenomenon known as group polarization (Kerr & Tindale, 2004). An example will help you see how this finding applies to everyday discussions of issues about which some people have very strong opinions. Suppose you haven't fully decided whether you support or oppose the death penalty but lean toward favoring it. Research on group polarization suggests that discussing the issue with people who strongly support the death penalty will make you more likely to end up supporting it yourself. By contrast, if you are undecided but lean toward opposing the death penalty, discussing it with people who strongly oppose it will make you more likely to make a firm commitment to opposing the death penalty yourself.

In classic research, Myers and Bishop (1970) found that, as a result of group polarization, group discussions of racial issues can either increase or decrease prejudice, depending on the average "leanings" of the group at the beginning of the discussion. However, studies also show that lower degrees of polarization are exhibited in groups in which two sides of an issue are presented in a balanced manner (Kuhn & Lao, 1996). Moreover, when a group includes two or more factions, or subgroups, that are strongly committed to opposing views, compromise rather than polarization is the most likely outcome.

Groupthink is the term that social psychologist Irving Janis (1982, 2007) applied to the kind of decision making that is sometimes seen in tightly knit groups. For instance, you may have heard news stories about college fraternity parties at which members and guests dress in costumes that are deeply offensive to some ethnic groups. Social psychologists would say that groupthink plays a role in the decision-making process that leads to such parties. That is, when members are planning such a party, most of them get caught up in the idea and think it will be great fun. Members who realize that the party is inappropriate and will offend others keep their doubts to themselves in order to maintain relationships with others in the group, that is, so that they won't be seen as spoiling others' fun.

Some social psychologists believe that the officers and soldiers who took part in the abuse of prisoners at Abu Ghraib during the first year of the Iraq War may have constituted such a group (Reicher & Haslam, 2004). When tightly knit groups of this kind are more concerned with preserving group solidarity and uniformity than with objectively evaluating all possible alternatives in decision making, individual members may hesitate to voice any dissent. Those individuals who turn against the group may face retaliation for their actions (see the *Explain It* feature on page 452.) The group may also discredit opposing views from outsiders and begin to believe it is incapable of making mistakes.

To guard against groupthink, Janis (1982) suggests that it is necessary to encourage open discussion of alternative views and the expression of any objections and doubts. He further recommends that outside experts sit in and challenge the views of the group. At least one group member should take the role of devil's advocate whenever a policy alternative is evaluated. To avoid groupthink in workplace situations, managers should withhold their own opinions when problem-solving and decision-making strategies are being considered (Bazan, 1998).

There are some situations in which group decision making appears to be better than that of individuals. In one study, college students' attitudes toward risky behaviors such as driving under the influence of alcohol were measured after the students participated in experimental conditions in which they (1) drank alcohol alone, (2) drank alcohol in a group, (3) drank a placebo they believed to be alcohol alone, or (4) drank a placebo they believed to be alcohol in a group (Abrams et al., 2006). Students who drank alcohol alone were more likely than either those who drank in groups (both alcohol and placebo) or those who drank a placebo alone to exhibit a willingness to engage in risky behaviors. The study's authors concluded that drinking in a small group may afford drinkers some protection against making poor decisions about risky behaviors.

group polarization A group member's adoption of a more extreme position about an issue than she or he originally held after participating in a discussion in which other group members strongly express agreement with her or him.

groupthink The tendency for members of a tightly knit group to be more concerned with preserving group solidarity and uniformity than with objectively evaluating all alternatives in decision making.

Why Doesn't Groupthink Occur in Every Tightly Knit Group?

Suppose that a group of girlfriends who are sophomores in high school promise each other that they will always be friends. To be sure that they stick together, the girls take a solemn oath that they will all attend the same college. Is this an example of groupthink? To determine whether these girls have succumbed to groupthink, predict what will happen if one member of the group changes her mind and goes to a different school. Do you think the other girls will retaliate against her?

You probably predicted that the other girls would be disappointed but would not retaliate in any serious way against the nonconforming member of their group. Groupthink typically occurs only in groups that are characterized by very high levels of interpersonal pressure, or even coercion, to conform to the group. Furthermore, groupthink is likely to be found in groups that have authoritarian leaders who remind members of the need for loyalty. Once groupthink is established, individuals are expected to give greater weight to group loyalty than to their own moral values or those of the larger society. Any member who fails to do so is likely to be punished by the group. Consequently, retaliation against members who turn against the group is another feature of groupthink. There are many real-world examples of individuals who have experienced groupthink-induced retaliation:

- *Joe Darby: reported abuse of inmates by his fellow guards at Abu Ghraib prison in Iraq*
- *Sherron Watkins: revealed fraudulent accounting practices that were used to hide financial losses of Enron*
- *Cathy Harris: reported racial profiling of African Americans at Hartsfield Airport in Atlanta*

- *Marc Hodler: exposed the role of bribery in the awarding of the 2002 Winter Games bid to Salt Lake City, Utah, by the International Olympic Committee*
- *Jeffrey Wigand: exposed the efforts of the tobacco company for which he worked to increase the addictive power of cigarettes and to hide research findings about smoking and lung disease*
- *Frank Serpico: exposed a number of his colleagues on the New York City Police force who were accepting bribes from criminals*
- *John Dean: member of President Nixon's staff who revealed the role that White House staffers and the president himself played in the complex scandal known as "Watergate"*

Researching a few of these cases will help you gain insight into how groupthink develops and how it affects group members. You will also learn a great deal about courage. Each of these individuals regretted hurting the friends he or she left behind and feared retaliation. Moreover, each has experienced varying degrees of retaliation. However, these individuals do not regret the actions they took because they know that doing the right thing is more important than group loyalty.

Jennifer
ARCHITECTURES

▶ Watch on mypsychlab.com

14.10 How do social roles influence individual behavior?

social roles Socially defined behaviors considered appropriate for individuals occupying certain positions within a given group.

deindividuation A social psychological process in which individuals lose their sense of personal identity as a result of identification with a group.

social identity A social psychological process in which individuals join with others to construct a group identity to insulate themselves from stressors.

Social Roles

Social roles are socially defined behaviors that are considered appropriate for individuals occupying certain positions within a given group. These roles can shape our behavior, sometimes quickly and dramatically. Consider a classic experiment (the Stanford Prison Experiment) in which psychologist Philip Zimbardo (1972) simulated a prison experience. College student volunteers were randomly assigned to be either guards or prisoners. The guards, wearing uniforms and carrying small clubs, strictly enforced harsh rules. The prisoners were stripped naked, searched, and deloused. Then, they were given prison uniforms, assigned numbers, and locked away in small, bare cells. The guards quickly adapted to their new role, some even to the point of becoming heartless and sadistic. One guard remembered forcing prisoners to clean toilets with their bare hands. And the prisoners began to act debased and subservient. The role playing became all too real—so much so that the experiment had to be ended in only 6 days.

Zimbardo invoked social psychologist Leon Festinger's concept of deindividuation to explain the study's outcome (Festinger, Pepitone, & Newcomb, 1952; Zimbardo, 1969). Deindividuation occurs when individuals lose their sense of personal identity as a result of identification with a group. Many social psychologists think that deindividuation explains phenomena such as looting, in which being part of a large group causes people to violate norms that they would obey if they were alone.

British psychologists Alexander Haslam and Stephen Reicher (2008) have challenged the deindividuation hypothesis, however. They argue that the outcome of the Stanford Prison Experiment was shaped by social identity, or the tendency to join with others to construct a group identity that insulates individual members against a stressor (Haslam et al., 2009). Thus, they say that the participants in the Stanford Prison Experiment were strongly influenced by the stressors that were associated with the instructions they were given by Zimbardo in his role as the "Superintendent" of the prison (Haslam & Reicher, 2006). Zimbardo instructed the guards to do whatever was necessary, including inflicting harm on them if needed, to convince the prisoners that they were powerless.

In their own similar experiment, the BBC Prison Study, Reicher and Haslam did not align themselves with either the guards or the prisoners. The guards were given control of the prisoners' physical environment, their schedule, and so on, but the researchers did not give either group instructions as to how to treat the other. Under these conditions, the guards did not behave abusively toward the prisoners. When asked to explain why they had treated the prisoners humanely, the guards explained that when they were faced with opportunities to treat prisoners abusively, imagining how authority figures in their own lives, such as their parents, would judge their actions motivated them to treat the prisoners well.

The prisoners in the BBC study also behaved differently than those in the Stanford study. Several days into the study, the researchers introduced a new prisoner into the group who had a background in union negotiations. As a result of ideas that were introduced to them by the new member of their group, the prisoners' beliefs about their status in relation to the guards changed. Moreover, the new prisoner taught them how to use collective bargaining strategies to persuade the guards to comply with their demands. As a result, the study's surprising result was that the guards felt themselves to be the more bullied of the two groups and reported experiencing more stress.

The findings of the BBC Prison Study call into question a role-based explanation for the results of the Stanford Prison Experiment. They also show that the degree to which deindividuation occurs when individuals take on social roles may depend on the kind of leadership that the group receives. Moreover, identification with a group may be adaptive in some situations, as it was when the prisoners learned to be good collective bargainers.

Another important point to be made about social roles is that they can have positive effects on behavior. In classic research examining adolescents with learning disabilities, Palinscar and Brown (1984) reported that students' learning behaviors were powerfully affected by their being assigned to play either the "teacher" or the "student" role in group study sessions. Participants summarized reading assignments more effectively, and as a result learned more from them, when functioning as a teacher than when functioning as a student. ◉⊣Watch on **mypsychlab.com**

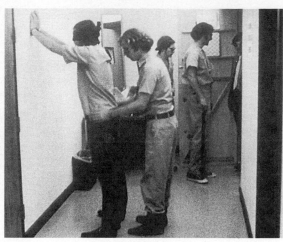

▲ Zimbardo's experiment simulated the prison environment by randomly assigning participants to the social roles of prison guards or inmates. The social roles influenced the participants' behavior: The prisoners began acting like real prisoners, and the prison guards like real prison guards.

◉⊣Watch the **Video** *Stanford Prison Experiment* on **mypsychlab.com**

Attitudes and Attitude Change

We use the word *attitude* frequently in everyday speech. We say that someone has a "bad attitude," for instance. But what is an attitude?

Attitudes ▶ ~~DON'T READ~~

[**14.11** What are the three components of an attitude?

Essentially, attitudes are relatively stable evaluations of persons, objects, situations, or issues, along a continuum ranging from positive to negative (Petty, Wegener, & Fabrigar, 1997). Most attitudes have three components: (1) a cognitive component, consisting of thoughts and beliefs about the attitudinal object; (2) an emotional component, made up of feelings toward the attitudinal object; and (3) a behavioral component, composed of predispositions concerning actions toward the object (Breckler, 1984). See Figure 14.5 (p. 454). Attitudes enable us to appraise people, objects, and situations, and provide structure and consistency in the social environment (Fazio, 1989). Attitudes also help us process social information (Pratkanis, 1989), guide our behavior (Sanbonmatsu & Fazio, 1990), and influence our social judgments and decisions (Jamieson & Zanna, 1989).

Some attitudes are acquired through firsthand experiences with people, objects, situations, and issues. Others are acquired when children hear parents, family, friends, and teachers express positive or negative attitudes toward certain issues or people. The mass media, including advertising, influence people's attitudes and reap billions of

attitude A relatively stable evaluation of a person, object, situation, or issue, along a continuum ranging from positive to negative.

FIGURE 14.5 The Three Components of an Attitude
An attitude is a relatively stable evaluation of a person, object, situation, or issue. Most of our attitudes have (1) a cognitive component, (2) an emotional component, and (3) a behavioral component.

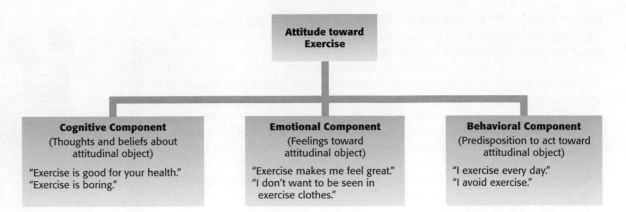

Attitude toward Exercise

Cognitive Component
(Thoughts and beliefs about attitudinal object)

"Exercise is good for your health."
"Exercise is boring."

Emotional Component
(Feelings toward attitudinal object)

"Exercise makes me feel great."
"I don't want to be seen in exercise clothes."

Behavioral Component
(Predisposition to act toward attitudinal object)

"I exercise every day."
"I avoid exercise."

dollars annually for their efforts. As you might expect, however, the attitudes that people form through their own direct experience are stronger than those they acquire vicariously and are also more resistant to change (Nieto-Hernandez et al., 2008). Once formed, however, attitudes tend to strengthen when we associate with others who share them (Visser & Mirabile, 2004).

Lively discussions of controversial topics, even when those discussions take place only with others who agree with us, may improve our ability to think analytically about our attitudes. Researchers Joseph Lao and Deanna Kuhn (2002) asked college students to engage in a series of six discussions of a controversial topic with another student. Participants were assigned to three experimental conditions. In one arm of the study, all of the discussions involved a partner who agreed with them. In another, all of the partners disagreed. In the third condition, three discussion partners agreed and three disagreed with the participant. Six weeks later, Lao and Kuhn found that participants who had discussed the topic either with those who agreed with them or with an equal number of agreers and disagreers showed the greatest improvement in critical thinking about the topic. They inferred from these findings that discussing a controversial issue with people who disagree with you is helpful only if it is balanced by discussions with others who share your views. Despite ageist stereotypes, many studies have found that older adults are more likely to change their attitudes than are middle-aged adults (Visser & Krosnick, 1998).

We often hear that attitude change is the key to behavior change. However, a number of studies in the mid-20th century showed that attitudes predict behavior only about 10% of the time (Wicker, 1969). People, for example, may express strong attitudes in favor of protecting the environment and conserving natural resources, yet not recycle or join a carpool (Knussen & Yule, 2008). However, attitudes are better predictors of behavior if they are strongly held, are readily accessible in memory (Bassili, 1995; Fazio & Williams, 1986; Kraus, 1995), and vitally affect the holder's interests (Sivacek & Crano, 1982).

14.12 What factors influence cognitive dissonance?

Cognitive Dissonance

What happens when attitudes contradict one another, or when attitudes and behaviors are inconsistent? According to psychologist Leon Festinger (1957), if people discover that some of their attitudes are in conflict or that their attitudes are not consistent with their behavior, they are likely to experience an unpleasant state called cognitive dissonance. Psychologists believe that cognitive dissonance results from a desire to maintain self-esteem (Stone, 2003). People usually try to reduce the dissonance by changing the behavior or the attitude or by somehow explaining away the inconsistency or minimizing its importance (Crano & Prislin, 2006; Matz & Wood, 2005). By changing the attitude, individuals retain their self-esteem and reduce the discomfort caused by dissonance (Elliot & Devine, 1994).

cognitive dissonance The unpleasant state that can occur when people become aware of inconsistencies between their attitudes or between their attitudes and their behavior.

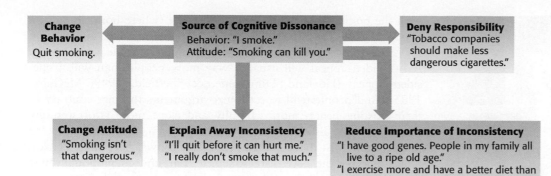

FIGURE 14.6 Methods of Reducing Cognitive Dissonance
Cognitive dissonance can occur when people become aware of inconsistencies in their attitudes or between their attitudes and their behavior. People try to reduce dissonance by (1) changing their behavior, (2) changing their attitude, (3) explaining away the inconsistency, or (4) reducing its importance. Here are examples of how a smoker might use these methods to reduce the cognitive dissonance created by his or her habit.

Smoking creates a perfect situation for cognitive dissonance. Faced with a mountain of evidence linking smoking to a number of diseases, what are smokers to do? The healthiest, but perhaps not the easiest, way to reduce cognitive dissonance is to change the behavior—quit smoking. Another way is to change the attitude, to convince oneself that smoking is not as dangerous as it is said to be. Smokers may also tell themselves that they will stop smoking long before any permanent damage is done, or that medical science is advancing so rapidly that a cure for cancer or emphysema is just around the corner. Figure 14.6 illustrates the methods a smoker may use to reduce cognitive dissonance.

In classic research, Festinger and Carlsmith (1959) placed research participants alone in a room to play a boring game. On completing the game, participants were instructed to tell the next participants that the game was fun. Participants were randomly assigned to two experimental groups. One group was paid $1 for following instructions, while the other was paid $20. Festinger and Carlsmith assumed that the conflict between participants' self-esteem and their lying behavior would cause cognitive dissonance. How could participants resolve this dissonance and get rid of the threat to self-esteem caused by lying? Just as Festinger and Carlsmith had hypothesized, participants who were paid $1 resolved the conflict by convincing themselves that the game really had been fun—a change in attitude. By contrast, participants who were paid $20 resolved the conflict by justifying their actions on the basis of having been paid a fairly large sum of money relative to the amount of effort it had required to lie to the next participant. Consequently, they did not view the lie as a threat to their self-esteem.

Persuasion ▶

14.13 What are the elements of persuasion?

Have you ever tried to convince another person to agree with your political opinions or to do something you wanted them to do? Persuasion is a deliberate attempt to influence the attitudes and/or the behavior of another person. Attempts at persuasion are pervasive parts of work experience, social experience, and even family life. Researchers have identified four elements of persuasion: (1) the source of the communication (who is doing the persuading), (2) the audience (who is being persuaded), (3) the message (what is being said), and (4) the medium (the means by which the message is transmitted).

persuasion A deliberate attempt to influence the attitudes and/or behavior of another person.

Some factors that make the source (the communicator) more persuasive are credibility, attractiveness, and likability (Klucharev, Smidts, & Fernandez, 2008). A credible communicator is one who has expertise (knowledge of the topic at hand) and trustworthiness (truthfulness and integrity). Other characteristics of the source—including physical attractiveness, celebrity status, and similarity to the audience—also contribute to our responses to the sources of persuasive messages.

Audience characteristics influence responses to persuasion as well. In general, people with low IQs are easier to persuade than those with high IQs (Rhodes & Wood, 1992). Evidence suggests that a one-sided message is usually most persuasive if the audience is not well informed on the issue, is not highly intelligent, or already agrees

▲ Marketers say that the campaign for the 2008 film *The Dark Knight* exemplified the power of viral strategies (Maymann, 2008). Through their innovative whysoserious.com website and a variety of other communication strategies—such as "I Believe in Harvey Dent" billboards, T-shirts, bumper stickers, and campaign vans that toured the country—the movie's marketing team attracted millions of participants the world over to virtual and real-world events, games, and scavenger-hunt activities that promoted the film.

with the point of view. A two-sided message (where both sides of an issue are mentioned) works best when the audience is well informed on the issue, is fairly intelligent, or is initially opposed to the point of view. A two-sided appeal will usually sway more people than will a one-sided appeal (Hovland, Lumsdaine, & Sheffield, 1949; McGuire, 1985). And people tend to scrutinize arguments that are contrary to their existing beliefs more carefully and exert more effort refuting them; they are also more likely to judge such arguments as being weaker than those that support their beliefs (Edwards & Smith, 1996).

A message can be well reasoned, logical, and unemotional ("just the facts"); it can be strictly emotional ("make their hair stand on end"); or it can be a combination of the two. Arousing fear seems to be an effective method for persuading people to quit smoking, get regular chest X-rays, wear seat belts, and get flu vaccine shots (Dillard & Anderson, 2004). Appeals based on fear are most effective when the presentation outlines definite actions the audience can take to avoid the feared outcomes (Buller et al., 2000; Stephenson & Witte, 1998). However, nutritional messages are more effective when framed in terms of the benefits of dietary change rather than the harmful effects of a poor diet (van Assema et al., 2002).

The role that the medium plays in persuasion has gained a larger share of researchers' attention in recent years as people have increasingly turned to the Internet for information rather than to television, radio, and print media. Surprisingly, though, experimental studies show that television continues to be the most effective medium through which to communicate a persuasive message (Dijkstra, Buijtels, & van Raaij, 2005). Furthermore, text-based messages on the Internet are no more effective than those that are presented in print media (Murphy et al., 2005). However, *viral marketing strategies* may soon change this. Such strategies employ Internet pop-up ads, text messages, instant messages, social networking sites, blogs, microblogs, podcasts, mass e-mails, and targeted e-mails that recipients are encouraged to forward to friends to publicize a message more quickly than traditional mass media such as television can disseminate it. Not surprisingly, research shows that product sales go up when marketers augment traditional approaches such as television advertising with viral strategies (Dhar & Chang, 2009).

Interestingly, the effectiveness of persuasive e-mail messages varies by gender (Guadagno & Cialdini, 2007). Men seem to be more open to such messages when they are delivered by e-mail, while women are more amenable to persuasive messages that are delivered in person. However, for both men and women, persuasive messages that are contained in personal e-mails are far more effective than those that are sent to impersonal mailing lists (Chesney, 2006).

Another important factor in persuasion is repetition. The more often a product or a point of view is presented, the more people will be persuaded to buy it or embrace it. Advertisers apparently believe in the mere-exposure effect because they repeat their messages over and over (Bornstein, 1989). But messages are likely to be less persuasive if they include vivid elements (colorful language, striking examples) that hinder the reception of the content (Frey & Eagly, 1993).

Prosocial Behavior

prosocial behavior Behavior that benefits others, such as helping, cooperation, and sympathy.

Psychologists define prosocial behavior as any behavior that benefits others, such as helping, cooperation, and sympathy. Examples of prosocial behavior abound in everyday life: A customer at a convenience store check-out counter turns up a few cents short, and the next person in line hands him the money. A parent pushing a stroller has difficulty negotiating her way through a heavy shopping mall door, and a customer on the way out of the mall holds the door open for her. And when large-scale tragedies strike, people demonstrate remarkable levels of generosity through donations of money, blood, and supplies. But what does it mean when people ignore others in need? In a now-famous case from 1964, New York City resident Kitty Genovese was murdered while her neighbors looked on, apparently indifferent to her plight. More recently, in early 2003, several people were caught on videotape doing nothing as a man who had just been shot lay dying in a gas station driveway (CNN.com, 2003). One person even stared at the victim for a few minutes and then calmly returned to the task of filling a can with kerosene. What causes such extreme variations in helping behavior?

Reasons for Helping ▶

There are many kinds of prosocial behavior and such impulses arise early in life. Researchers agree that young children respond sympathetically to companions in distress, usually before their second birthday (Hoffman, 2007). The term altruism is usually reserved for behavior that is aimed at helping others, requires some self-sacrifice, and is not performed for personal gain. Batson (2006) believes that we help out of *empathy*—the ability to take the perspective of others, to put ourselves in their place.

Commitment is another factor influencing altruism. We are more likely to behave in an altruistic fashion in the context of relationships to which we are deeply committed (Powell & Van Vugt, 2003). The influence of commitment is strongest when the cost of an altruistic act is high. For instance, you would probably be more likely to volunteer to donate a kidney, let's say, to a family member than to a stranger.

The degree to which society values altruism is another variable that can influence individual decisions about altruistic behavior. Cultures vary in their norms for helping others—that is, their *social responsibility norms*. According to Miller and others (1990), people in the United States tend to feel an obligation to help family members, friends, and even strangers in life-threatening circumstances, but only family members in moderately serious situations. In contrast, in India the social responsibility norm extends to strangers whose needs are only moderately serious or even minor.

Whatever the motive for altruism, people who regularly engage in behavior that helps others reap significant benefits (Poulin & Cohen Silver, 2008). One interesting benefit is that, the more people help, the more altruistic they become. In other words, behaving altruistically generates or enhances an individual's altruistic attitudes. Along with this attitude change comes an increased appreciation for life. Thus, the costs of altruistic behavior are balanced by its benefits, both for those who are helped and for the helpers themselves.

The Bystander Effect ▶

A variety of social circumstances contribute to the decision to help another person. One example is the bystander effect: As the number of bystanders at an emergency increases, the probability that the victim will receive help from them decreases, and the help, if given, is likely to be delayed. Psychologists have suggested that the bystander effect explains the failure of Kitty Genovese's neighbors to help her.

In now-classic research, Darley and Latané (1968a) placed a series of research participants alone in a small room and told them that they would be participating in a discussion group by means of an intercom system. Some participants were told that they would be communicating with only one other participant, some believed that two other participants would be involved, and some were told that five other people would participate. There really were no other participants in the study—only the prerecorded voices of confederates assisting the experimenter. Shortly after the discussion

[**14.14** What motivates people to help others?

altruism Behavior that is aimed at helping another, requires some self-sacrifice, and is not performed for personal gain.

▲ Altruistic acts, such as helping build houses for low-income families, may be motivated by social responsibility norms.

[**14.15** How do psychologists explain the bystander effect?

bystander effect A social factor that affects prosocial behavior: As the number of bystanders at an emergency increases, the probability that the victim will receive help decreases, and the help, if given, is likely to be delayed.

FIGURE 14.7 The Bystander Effect
In their intercom experiment, Darley and Latané showed that the more people a participant believed were present during an emergency, the longer it took the participant to respond and help a person in distress.
Source: Data from Darley & Latané (1968a).

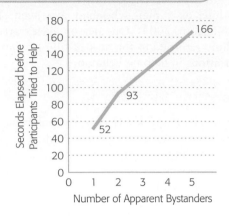

How do you think learning about the bystander effect in a psychology class might influence a person's behavior in a situation in which the effect is likely to occur?

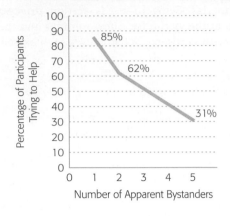

began, the voice of one confederate was heard over the intercom calling for help, indicating that he was having an epileptic seizure. Of the participants who believed that they alone were hearing the victim, 85% went for help before the end of the seizure. When participants believed that one other person heard the seizure, 62% sought help. But when they believed that four other people were aware of the emergency, only 31% tried to get help before the end of the seizure. Figure 14.7 shows how the number of bystanders affects both the number of people who try to help and the speed of response.

Darley and Latané (1968a) suggest that, when bystanders are present in an emergency, they generally feel that the responsibility for helping is shared by the group, a phenomenon known as diffusion of responsibility. Consequently, each person feels less compelled to act than if she or he were alone and felt the total responsibility; each bystander thinks, "Somebody else must be doing something." Another reason for the bystander effect is the influence of other bystanders who appear calm. When others seem calm, we may conclude that nothing is really wrong and that no intervention is necessary (Darley & Latané, 1968b).

Ironically, with regard to catastrophes, such as the terrorist attacks of September 11, 2001, the Indonesian tsunami that occurred in 2004, and the numerous powerful hurricanes that have hit the coastal communities of the United States over the past several years, the bystander effect is greatly reduced. In fact, people are likely to put forth extraordinary effort to help others in such situations. We noted how much money people donated to Hurricane Katrina victims within the first few days after the storm made landfall. But this phenomenon is also seen in the countless individual acts of altruism that occur in the context of such events. Often, too, people who can't help directly witness the events via the media and contribute money to the families of victims within hours of these tragedies. Research on public responses to large-scale disasters predicts such responses (Shepperd, 2001). ✳─|Explore on **mypsychlab.com**

▲ Why do people ignore someone who is unconscious on the sidewalk? Diffusion of responsibility is one possible explanation.

diffusion of responsibility The feeling among bystanders at an emergency that the responsibility for helping is shared by the group, making each person feel less compelled to act than if he or she alone bore the total responsibility.

✳─|Explore the **Concept** *Bystander Intervention* on **mypsychlab.com**

Aggression

One of the enduring themes of research in social psychology for many years has been the study of aggression. Aggression is the intentional infliction of physical or psychological harm on others. Aggression has many forms and takes place in a variety of locations—at home, at work, and even among drivers on the road. Being the target of an aggressive act is an all-too-common experience. Of course, domestic violence represents only one of many forms of aggression. But why does one person intentionally harm another?

aggression The intentional infliction of physical or psychological harm on others.

Biological Factors in Aggression ▶

[14.16 What biological factors influence aggression?

Sigmund Freud believed that humans have an aggressive instinct that can be turned inward as self-destruction or outward as aggression or violence toward others. While rejecting this view, many psychologists do concede that biological factors are involved. A meta-analysis of 24 twin and adoption studies of several personality measures of aggression revealed a heritability estimate of about .50 for aggression (Miles & Carey, 1997). Twin and adoption studies have also revealed a genetic link for criminal behavior (Baker et al., 2007). Cloninger and others (1982) found that adoptees with a criminal biological parent were four times as likely as members of the general population to commit crimes, while adoptees with a criminal adoptive parent were at twice the risk of committing a crime. But adoptees with both a criminal biological and a criminal adoptive parent were 14 times as likely to commit crimes, indicating the power of the combined influences of nature and nurture. Thus, many researchers believe that genes that predispose individuals to aggressive behavior may cause them to be more sensitive to models of aggressiveness in the environment (Rowe, 2003).

One biological factor that seems very closely related to aggression is a low arousal level of the autonomic nervous system (Caramaschi de Boer & Koolhaas, 2008). Low arousal level (low heart rate and lower reactivity) has been linked to antisocial and violent behavior (Herpetz, et al., 2007). People with a low arousal level tend to seek stimulation and excitement and often exhibit fearlessness, even in the face of danger.

Men are more physically aggressive than women (Hyde, 2005), and a correlation between high testosterone levels and aggressive behavior has been found in males (Archer, 1991; Dabbs & Morris, 1990). However, testosterone and aggression are most strongly correlated in individuals who display the types of low levels of arousal that we discussed earlier (Popma et al., 2007). Moreover, the connection between testosterone and aggression has a social component. Adolescent males with both high testosterone levels and a tendency to take risks that can lead to aggression, such as insulting someone without provocation, prefer to associate with peers who have similar hormonal and behavioral profiles (Vermeersch et al., 2008). Researchers speculate that a cycle of risky behavior and aggression maintains high levels of testosterone secretion among such males. Furthermore, violent behavior has been associated with low levels of the neurotransmitter serotonin (Gartner & Whitaker-Azimitia, 1996; Mitsis et al., 2000; Toot et al., 2004). Brain damage, brain tumors, and temporal lobe epilepsy are also related to aggressive and violent behavior (Mednick et al., 1988; van Elst et al., 2000).

Alcohol and aggression are frequent partners. A meta-analysis of 30 experimental studies indicated that alcohol is related to aggression (Foran & O'Leary, 2008). The use of alcohol and other drugs that affect the brain's frontal lobes may lead to aggressive behavior in humans and other animals by disrupting normal executive functions (Lyvers, 2000). Law enforcement officials estimate that perpetrators who are under the influence of alcohol or drugs commit about one-third of all violent crimes (Bureau of Justice Statistics, 2005).

The *Summarize It* (p. 460) summarizes the possible biological causes of aggression.

Other Influences on Aggression ▶

[14.17 What other factors contribute to aggression?

Beyond biological factors, what other variables contribute to aggression? The frustration-aggression hypothesis suggests that frustration produces aggression (Dollard et al., 1939; Miller, 1941). If a traffic jam caused you to be late for an appointment and you were frustrated, would you lean on your horn, shout obscenities out of your window, or just sit patiently and wait? Frustration doesn't always cause aggression, but it is especially likely to do so if it is intense and seems to be unjustified (Doob & Sears, 1939; Pastore, 1950). Berkowitz (1988) points out that even if frustration is justified and not aimed specifically at an individual, it can cause aggression if it arouses negative emotions.

frustration-aggression hypothesis The hypothesis that frustration produces aggression.

SUMMARIZE IT

Possible Biological Causes of Aggression

CAUSE	EVIDENCE
Heredity	If one identical twin is aggressive, there is a 50% chance that the other twin is aggressive as well. Adopted children's aggressive tendencies are more like those of their biological parents than their adopted parents.
Low arousal level	People with low levels of arousal seek stimulation and excitement to increase arousal.
High testosterone level	High levels of testosterone have been found to be correlated with some forms of aggression, such as intimate partner abuse, in both men and women.
Neurological disorders	Brain tumors and other neurological diseases have been linked to aggressive behavior.
Alcohol abuse	People who are intoxicated commit the majority of murders and most other violent crimes.

▲ Alcohol impairs the brain's ability to process information, a condition that often leads to poor decisions. For this reason, alcohol is frequently involved in acts of aggression.

scapegoating Displacing aggression onto members of minority groups or other innocent targets not responsible for the frustrating situation.

personal space An area surrounding each person, much like an invisible bubble, that the person considers part of himself or herself and uses to regulate the level of intimacy with others.

crowding The subjective judgment that there are too many people in a confined space.

Aggression in response to frustration is not always focused on the actual cause of the frustration. If the preferred target is too threatening or not available, the aggression may be displaced. For example, children who are angry with their parents may take out their frustration on a younger sibling. Sometimes, members of minority groups or other innocent targets who are not responsible for a frustrating situation become targets of displaced aggression, a practice known as scapegoating (Koltz, 1983).

People often become aggressive when they are in pain (Berkowitz, 1983) or are exposed to loud noise or foul odors (Rotton et al., 1979). Extreme heat has also been linked to aggression in several studies (Anderson & Anderson, 1996; Rotton & Cohn, 2000). These and other studies lend support to the *cognitive-neoassociationistic model* proposed by Berkowitz (1990). He has suggested that anger and aggression result from aversive events and from unpleasant emotional states, such as sadness, grief, and depression. The cognitive component of Berkowitz's model occurs when the angered person appraises the aversive situation and makes attributions about the motives of the people involved. As a result of the cognitive appraisal, the initial reaction of anger can be intensified, reduced, or suppressed. This process makes the person either more or less likely to act on his or her aggressive tendency.

Personal space is an area surrounding each individual, much like an invisible bubble, that the person considers part of himself or herself and uses to regulate the closeness of interactions with others. Personal space serves to protect privacy and to regulate the level of intimacy with others. The size of personal space varies according to the person or persons with whom an individual is interacting and the nature of the interaction. When personal space is reduced, aggression can result.

Crowding—the subjective judgment that there are too many people in a confined space—often leads to higher physiological arousal, and males typically experience its effects more negatively than females do. The effects of crowding also vary across cultures and situations. Researchers have studied its effects on such diverse populations as male heads of households in India and middle-class male and female college students in the United States (Evans & Lepore, 1993). In both of these studies, psychological distress was linked to household crowding. Furthermore, studies in prisons have shown that the more inmates per cell, the greater the number of violent incidents (Paulus, Cox, & McCain, 1988). However, keep in mind that a prison is an atypical environment with a population whose members have been confined precisely because they tend to be aggressive.

Finally, researchers Roy and Judy Eidelson have identified several beliefs that may lead members of a group of people to act aggressively toward outsiders (Eidelson & Eidelson, 2003). One such belief is a group's conviction that its members are superior to others, together with a sense of "chosenness" for a particular task. The view that one's own group has a legitimate grievance against outsiders can also spark aggression. Group members who believe themselves to be vulnerable may justify aggression as a form of defense. Similarly, those who are convinced that promises made by outsiders to respect the rights of group members cannot be trusted may act aggressively. Finally, group members who believe that aggression is the only strategy available to them for addressing grievances or protecting themselves may resort to violence. Group leaders play an important role in either encouraging or discouraging these beliefs among group members. For example, positive leadership may be able to prevent intergroup aggression.

The Social Learning Theory of Aggression

The *social learning theory of aggression* holds that people learn to behave aggressively by observing aggressive models and by having their aggressive responses reinforced (Bandura, 1973). It is well known that aggression levels are higher in groups and subcultures that condone violent behavior and accord high status to aggressive members. A leading advocate of the social learning theory of aggression, Albert Bandura (1976), claims that aggressive models in the subculture, the family, and the media all play a part in increasing the level of aggression in society.

There is some truth to this belief. Abused children certainly experience aggression and see it modeled day after day. Moreover, having been abused as a child clearly increases the risk that a person will grow up to abuse his or her own children (Burton, 2003). Nevertheless, on the basis of original research and an analysis of 60 other studies, Oliver (1993) concludes that only one-third of people who are abused go on to become abusers, one-third do not, and the final one-third may become abusers if their lives are highly stressful.

Although abused and neglected children are at higher risk of becoming delinquent, criminal, or violent, the majority do not become abusive themselves (DuMont et al., 2007). Several researchers suggest that the higher risk for aggression may not be due solely to an abusive family environment but may be partly influenced by the genes (DiLalla & Gottesman, 1991). Some abused children become withdrawn and isolated rather than aggressive and abusive (Dodge et al., 1990).

The research evidence overwhelmingly supports a relationship between TV violence and viewer aggression (Coyne et al., 2004; Eron, 1987; Huesmann et al., 2003). And the negative effects of TV violence are even worse for individuals who are, by nature, highly aggressive (Bushman, 1995). Researchers have also found a correlation between playing violent video games and aggression (Anderson & Dill, 2000; Carnagey & Anderson, 2004). Moreover, aggressiveness increases as more time is spent playing such games (Colwell & Payne, 2000). However, researchers in the Netherlands found that boys who choose aggressive video games tend to be more aggressive, less intelligent, and less prosocial in their behavior (Weigman & van Schie, 1998). So, the link between aggression and video games may be due to the tendency of aggressive individuals to prefer entertainment media that feature aggression.

14.18 How does social learning theory explain aggression?

Prejudice and Discrimination

Do you know the difference between *prejudice* and *discrimination*? Prejudice consists of attitudes (usually negative) toward others based on their gender, religion, race, or membership in a particular group. Prejudice involves beliefs and emotions (not actions) that can escalate into hatred. Discrimination consists of behavior—actions (usually negative) toward others based on their gender, religion, race, or membership in a particular group. Many Americans have experienced prejudice and discrimination—minority racial groups (racism), women (sexism), the elderly (ageism), people with disabilities, homosexuals, religious groups, and others. What are the roots of prejudice and discrimination?

prejudice Attitudes (usually negative) toward others based on their gender, religion, race, or membership in a particular group.

discrimination Behavior (usually negative) directed toward others based on their gender, religion, race, or membership in a particular group.

14.19 What factors contribute to the development of prejudice and discrimination?

The Roots of Prejudice and Discrimination

Social psychologists have proposed several theories to explain the psychological bases for prejudice and discrimination. Moreover, a number of studies have provided insight into their origins.

One of the oldest explanations as to how prejudice arose cites competition among various social groups that must struggle against each other for scarce resources—good jobs, homes, schools, and so on. Commonly called the realistic conflict theory, this view suggests that as competition increases, so do prejudice, discrimination, and hatred among the competing groups. Some historical evidence supports the realistic conflict theory. Prejudice and hatred were high between the American settlers and the Native Americans, who struggled over land during the westward expansion. The multitudes of Irish and German immigrants who came to the United States in the 1830s and 1840s felt the sting of prejudice and hatred from other Americans who were facing economic scarcity. But prejudice and discrimination are attitudes and actions too complex to be explained solely by economic conflict and competition.

Prejudice can also spring from the distinct social categories into which people divide the world, employing an "us-versus-them" mentality (Turner et al., 1987). An in-group is a social group with a strong sense of togetherness, from which others are excluded. Members of college fraternities and sororities often exhibit strong in-group feelings. The out-group consists of individuals specifically identified by the in-group as not belonging. Us-versus-them thinking can lead to excessive competition, hostility, prejudice, discrimination, and even war. Prejudiced individuals are reluctant to admit outsiders to their racial in-group if there is the slightest doubt about the outsiders' racial purity (Blascovich et al., 1997).

A famous study by Sherif and Sherif (1967) shows how in-group/out-group conflict can escalate into prejudice and hostility rather quickly, even between groups that are very much alike. The researchers set up their experiment at the Robber's Cave summer camp. Their subjects were 22 bright, well-adjusted, 11- and 12-year-old White middle-class boys from Oklahoma City. Divided into two groups and housed in separate cabins, the boys were kept apart for all their daily activities and games. During the first week, in-group solidarity, friendship, and cooperation developed within each of the groups. One group called itself the "Rattlers"; the other group took the name "Eagles."

During the second week of the study, competitive events were purposely scheduled so that the goals of one group could be achieved "only at the expense of the other group" (Sherif, 1958, p. 353). The groups were happy to battle each other, and intergroup conflict quickly emerged. Name-calling began, fights broke out, and accusations were hurled back and forth. During the third week of the experiment, the researchers tried to put an end to the hostility and to turn rivalry into cooperation. They simply brought the groups together for pleasant activities, such as eating meals and watching movies. "But far from reducing conflict, these situations only served as opportunities for the rival groups to berate and attack each other. ... They threw paper, food and vile names at each other at the tables" (Sherif, 1956, pp. 57–58).

Finally, experimenters manufactured a series of crises that could be resolved only if all the boys combined their efforts and resources and cooperated. The water supply, sabotaged by the experimenters, could be restored only if all the boys worked together. After a week of several activities requiring cooperation, cutthroat competition gave way to cooperative exchanges. Friendships developed between groups, and before the end of the experiment, peace was declared. Working together toward shared goals had turned hostility into friendship.

realistic conflict theory The view that as competition increases among social groups for scarce resources, so do prejudice, discrimination, and hatred.

in-group A social group with a strong sense of togetherness, from which others are excluded.

out-group A social group made up of individuals specifically identified by the in-group as not belonging.

▼ Can you perceive differences among the young girls shown here? Research shows that people typically perceive more variability among members of groups to which they belong and more similarity among members of groups with which they are unfamiliar.

According to *social-cognitive theory*, people learn attitudes of prejudice and hatred the same way they learn other attitudes. If children hear their parents, teachers, peers, and others openly express prejudices toward different racial, ethnic, or cultural groups, they may be quick to learn such attitudes. And if parents, peers, and others reward children with smiles and approval for parroting their own prejudices (operant conditioning), children may learn these prejudices even more quickly. Phillips and Ziller (1997) suggest that people learn to be nonprejudiced in the same way.

Earlier in the chapter we told you that *social cognition* refers to the ways in which people typically process social information. The very processes we use to simplify, categorize, and order the social world are the same processes that distort our views of it. So, prejudice may arise not only from heated negative emotions and hatred toward other social groups, but also from cooler cognitive processes that govern how we think and process social information (Kunda & Oleson, 1995).

One way people simplify, categorize, and order the world is by using stereotypes. Stereotypes are widely shared beliefs about the characteristic traits, attitudes, and behaviors of members of various social groups (racial, ethnic, or religious), including the assumption that "they" are usually all alike. Once a stereotype is in place, people tend to pay more attention to information that confirms their beliefs than to information that challenges them (Wigboldus, Dijksterhuis, & Van Knippenberg, 2003).

Stereotyping allows people to make quick, automatic (thoughtless) judgments about others and apply their mental resources to other activities (Sherman et al., 2009). However, individuals who are prejudiced do not necessarily apply stereotypes equally to all members of a given group. For one thing, people are less likely to apply stereotypes to others with whom they have personal relationships than they are to strangers (Turner et al., 2008). And even when stereotypes are applied to strangers, they can be moderated, or amplified, by other relevant information. For example, Cheryl Kaiser and Jennifer Pratt-Hyatt (2009) asked White college students to rate the "likeability" of several fictitious peers on the basis of personality test results. Along with the test results, the researchers provided participants with information about the fictitious peers' ethnicity and their responses to questions such as "The racial/ethnic group I belong to is an important reflection of who I am." Kaiser and Pratt-Hyatt found that participants were most likely to report having negative first impressions of fictitious African American and Latino peers if the peers attached high levels of importance to racial/ethnic identity.

Some research has revealed that people tend to perceive more diversity or more variability within the groups to which they belong (in-groups), but they see more similarity among members of other groups (out-groups) (Ostrom, Carpenter, & Sedikides, 1993). For example, White Americans see more diversity among themselves but more sameness within groups of African Americans or Asian Americans. This tendency in thinking can also be based on gender, age, or any other characteristic. One study showed that a group of 100 young college students believed there was much more variability or diversity in their group than in a group of 100 elderly Americans, whom the students perceived to be much the same (Linville, Fischer, & Salovey, 1989). And a study involving elderly adults showed that they perceived more variability within their own age group than among college students. Age stereotypes can be even more pronounced and negative than gender stereotypes (Kite, Deaux, & Miele, 1991).

The tendency to be less sensitive to variations among members of other groups may arise from a general tendency to look at people and situations from the perspective of one's own racial or cultural group. This tendency is often called ethnocentrism. In work settings, ethnocentrism may prevent us from realizing that co-workers from different backgrounds sometimes perceive the same incidents quite differently. For example, researchers have found that African Americans are more likely than Whites to perceive negative encounters between supervisors and subordinates of different races as being racial in nature (J. Johnson et al., 2003). To complicate matters further, members of each group believe that such opinions are either right or wrong. Because of ethnocentrism, Whites will insist that their view is the correct one; African Americans will take

stereotypes Widely shared beliefs about the characteristic traits, attitudes, and behaviors of members of various social groups (racial, ethnic, or religious), including the assumption that the members of such groups are usually all alike.

ethnocentrism The tendency to look at situations from one's own racial or cultural perspective.

the same position about their view. To address this problem, many organizations provide workers with training geared toward helping them understand that such differences do not involve one view that is right and another that is wrong. Instead, each perspective is deserving of respect by the other.

14.20 What evidence suggests that prejudice and discrimination are decreasing?

Is Prejudice Decreasing?

Few people will readily admit to being prejudiced. Gordon Allport (1954), a pioneer in research on prejudice, said, "Defeated intellectually, prejudice lingers emotionally" (p. 328). Even those who are sincerely intellectually opposed to prejudice may still harbor some prejudiced feelings (Devine, 1989). However, most people feel guilty when they catch themselves having prejudiced thoughts or engaging in discriminatory behavior (Amodio, Devine, & Harmon-Jones, 2007).

Is there any evidence that prejudice is decreasing in U.S. society? One positive indicator was the election of Barack Obama to the presidency in 2008. Not only was President Obama the first African American to be elected to the nation's highest office, but most people in the United States, especially African Americans, perceived his election to be an enormous step forward in race relations (Rasmusenreports.com, 2009). Moreover, Gallup polls have revealed that White Americans became more racially tolerant over the final decades of the 20th century (Gallup & Hugick, 1990). When White Americans were asked in 1990 whether they would move if African Americans were to move next door to them, 93% said no, compared with 65% in 1965. Moreover, both White and African Americans overwhelmingly agree that conditions have improved for minorities in the United States over the past several decades (Public Agenda Online, 2002). However, there are still marked differences of opinion among ethnic groups as to whether racism continues to be a problem in the United States. About 50% of African Americans and 40% of Hispanic

APPLY IT   **"Unlearning" Prejudice**

Today's college population is more diverse than ever before. In the United States, members of minority groups are attending college in higher numbers. And people from cultures all over the world come to the United States to further their educations. Consequently, for many young people, campus life represents a unique opportunity to interact with others of different racial, ethnic, or cultural groups. How can students make the most of this opportunity to "unlearn" the prejudices they may bring with them to college?

Intergroup Contact
As you learned from the Robber's Cave experiment (Sherif & Sherif, 1967), intergroup contact can sometimes lead to increased stereotyping. Under the right conditions, though, intergroup contact can reduce prejudice. College can provide a context in which students from diverse backgrounds study together, endure the same trials (midterms and finals), develop a shared sense of school spirit, join clubs in which members from different backgrounds share common goals, and so on. Thus, under the right conditions, intergroup contact can reduce prejudice (Page-Gould, Mendoza-Denton, & Tropp, 2008).

The Jigsaw Technique
Methods such as the *jigsaw technique,* a strategy that works well in college classrooms and as a game in less formal interactions, represent a more direct approach. Each participant in a jigsaw group is given a small amount of information and asked to teach it to other participants. The group must use all the individual pieces of information to solve a problem. This approach increases interaction among participants and helps them develop empathy for members of other ethnic and racial groups (Aronson, 1988; Aronson et al., 1978; Singh, 1991; Walker & Crogan, 1998). A side benefit is that it is an effective way of learning a new solution to a problem.

Diversity Education
Many colleges offer students and faculty opportunities to participate in seminars and workshops designed to combat racism. In such settings, participants learn about racial and cultural perspectives that may differ from their own. They also learn to identify behaviors that may be construed as racist by others, even when that may not be what they intend. Researchers have found that such programs help to reduce automatic stereotyping among participants (Hill & Augoustinos, 2001; Rudman, Ashmore, & Gary, 2001).

Open Discussions of Prejudice and Discrimination
Perhaps the greatest potential of the college campus for reducing prejudice and discrimination lies in the nature of its intellectual climate. Traditionally, college classes, as well as club meetings, gatherings at restaurants, all-night study sessions in coffee shops, and late-night debates in dorm rooms, often feature lively discussions of a variety of topics. And when we hear others speak passionately about racism, sexism, and other types of injustice, we are likely to adopt more tolerant attitudes ourselves.

So, the next time you hear someone make a statement you feel is racist or sexist or prejudiced in any way, speak up! You never know how influential your voice might be.

Americans believe racial discrimination is a significant factor in education, employment, and housing, while less than one-third of White Americans agree (Kaiser Family Foundation, 1999). Moreover, studies show that people continue to cite fear of rejection as the reason they don't engage in more social contact with others of different races (Shelton & Richeson, 2005).

Recall, too, that attitudes do not always predict behavior. In one study, researchers asked participants to judge whether a fictitious woman was qualified to be the president of a parent-teacher organization (Lott & Saxon, 2002). Participants were provided with information about the woman's occupation and education. In addition, they were told, based on random assignment, that the woman was Hispanic, Anglo-Saxon, or Jewish in ethnic origin. The experimenters found that participants who believed the woman to be Hispanic were more likely to say that she was not qualified for the position than those who thought her to be Anglo-Saxon or Jewish. Such studies suggest that racial stereotyping is still evident in the United States. But there are many things we can do to combat prejudice and discrimination as discussed in the *Apply It* on page 464.

⊙º Looking Back

At the beginning of the chapter, you learned that people sometimes do a poor job of forming judgments about others and themselves. Likewise, at the end of the chapter, you learned about the roots of racial prejudice and discrimination. Much of the work of social psychologists seeks to explain and find remedies for human failings such as these. For example, Milgram's brilliant experiment began as an effort to comprehend what appeared to be an incomprehensible event, the Holocaust. His work and that of other social psychologists demonstrate that psychology is a field with a great deal of relevance to the real world, whether that world consists of momentous historical events or the more ordinary happenings of everyday life.

CHAPTER 14 SUMMARY

SOCIAL COGNITION (pp. 439-442)

14.1 How do we form opinions of others and manage their opinions of us? (pp. 439-440)

First impressions shape our opinions of others because we attend more carefully to the first information we receive about another person; and, once formed, an impression acts as a framework through which later information is interpreted. Through impression management, we influence others' opinions of us when they have the ability to provide us with something we want or need and when we believe that their opinions of us are inaccurate.

Key Terms

social psychology, p. 439
social cognition, p. 439
impression formation, p. 439
primacy effect, p. 440
impression management, p. 440

14.2 How do we explain our own and others' behavior? (pp. 440-442)

An attribution is an opinion about another person that is based on an inference about the causes of their behavior. In making a situational attribution, people attribute the cause of the behavior to some factor operating within the situation. With a dispositional attribution, the inferred cause is internal, such as some personal trait, motive, or attitude. People tend to attribute their own shortcomings primarily to situational factors and those of others primarily to dispositional factors, a tendency known as the actor-observer effect.

Key Terms

attribution, p. 440   *self-serving bias*, p. 441
situational attribution, p. 440   *actor-observer effect*, p. 441
dispositional attribution,   *fundamental attribution*
   p. 441   *error*, p. 441

ATTRACTION (pp. 442-445)

14.3 What factors contribute to attraction? (pp. 442-443)

Proximity contributes to attraction because it is easier to develop relationships with people close at hand. Proximity also increases the likelihood that there will be repeated contacts, and there is a tendency to feel more positively toward a stimulus as a result of repeated exposure to it (the mere-exposure effect). Our moods and emotions influence how much we are attracted to those we meet. We also tend to like people who like us (reciprocity). Other factors that contribute to attraction are similarities in age, gender, race, and socioeconomic class and similar views and interests. Physical attractiveness is a major factor in attraction for people of all ages. People attribute positive qualities to those who are physically attractive, a phenomenon called the halo effect.

Key Terms

proximity, p. 442   *halo effect*, p. 443
mere-exposure effect, p. 442

14.4 What factors contribute to the formation and maintenance of intimate relationships? (pp. 443-445)

Psychologists have proposed the matching hypothesis to explain the finding that people are often select intimate partners who are similar to themselves. Others argue that individuals choose partners whose characteristics complement their own. Evolutionary psychologists argue that men and women are attracted to one another on the basis of what each can contribute to the creation and support of a family. Sternberg's triangular theory of love describes different types of intimate relationships, and the changes that happen in relationships over time, in terms of three interactive components: intimacy, passion, and commitment.

Key Terms

matching hypothesis, p. 443
triangular theory of love, p. 444
consummate love, p. 445

CONFORMITY, OBEDIENCE, AND COMPLIANCE (pp. 445-449)

14.5 What did Asch find in his classic experiment on conformity? (pp. 446-447)

In Asch's classic study on conformity, 5% of the participants went along with the incorrect, unanimous majority all the time; 70% went along some of the time; and 25% remained completely independent.

Key Terms

conformity, p. 446   *social norms*, p. 446

14.6 What did Milgram's classic study reveal about obedience? (pp. 447-448)

Participants were almost as likely to obey experimenters when the study was repeated at a shabby office building rather than at Yale University. However, when participants were paired with confederates who refused to obey the experimenter, they were less likely to obey.

Key Term

obedience, p. 447

14.7 What techniques do people use to gain compliance from others? (pp. 448-449)

One technique that can lead to compliance is the foot-in-the-door technique, in which a person gains compliance with a small request with the intent of making another agree to a larger request later. In the door-in-the-face technique, someone makes a large request with the expectation that another will refuse but be open to a smaller request later. A person who makes an attractive initial offer to gain compliance from another before making the offer less attractive is using the low-ball technique.

Key Terms

compliance, p. 448
foot-in-the-door technique, p. 448
door-in-the-face technique, p. 449
low-ball technique, p. 449

GROUP INFLUENCE (pp. 449-453)

14.8 How do social facilitation and social loafing affect performance? (pp. 449-450)

When others are present, either as an audience or as co-actors, people's performance on easy tasks is usually improved through social facilitation. However, performance on difficult tasks is usually impaired. Social loafing is people's tendency to put forth less effort when they are working with others on a common task than when working alone. It is less likely to occur when individual output can be monitored or when people have a personal stake in the outcome.

Key Terms

social facilitation, p. 449   *coaction effects*, p. 450
audience effects, p. 449   *social loafing*, p. 450

14.9 How do groups influence individual decision making? (pp. 450-452)

Group polarization occurs when, after a discussion, a group's decision shifts to a more extreme position in whatever direction the members were leaning initially. Groupthink happens when a group's desire to maintain solidarity outweighs other considerations, a process that often leads to poor decisions.

Key Terms
group polarization, p. 451   *groupthink,* p. 451

14.10 How do social roles influence individual behavior? (pp. 452-453)

Individual behavior can be guided by the expectations associated with certain social roles. The effects of such roles can be either negative or positive.

Key Terms
social roles, p. 452
deindividuation, p. 452
social identity, p. 452

ATTITUDES AND ATTITUDE CHANGE (pp. 453-456)

14.11 What are the three components of an attitude? (pp. 453-454)

An attitude usually has a cognitive, an emotional, and a behavioral component.

Key Term
attitude, p. 453

14.12 What factors influence cognitive dissonance? (pp. 454-455)

Cognitive dissonance is an unpleasant state that can occur when people become aware of inconsistencies among their attitudes or between their attitudes and their behavior. People can reduce cognitive dissonance by changing the behavior or the attitude, by denying responsibility, or by explaining away the inconsistency or minimizing its importance.

Key Term
cognitive dissonance, p. 454

14.13 What are the elements of persuasion? (pp. 455-456)

The four elements of persuasion are the source of the communication, the audience, the message, and the medium.

Key Term
persuasion, p. 455

PROSOCIAL BEHAVIOR (pp. 456-458)

14.14 What motivates people to help others? (p. 457)

Some prosocial behavior is motivated by altruism. In other cases, cultural norms influence helping behavior. We are more likely to help those in need if we are in a committed relationship with them or we perceive them to be similar to us.

Key Terms
prosocial behavior, p. 456
altruism, p. 457

14.15 How do psychologists explain the bystander effect? (pp. 457-458)

The bystander effect is a social factor that affects prosocial behavior: As the number of bystanders at an emergency increases, the probability that the victim will receive help decreases, and the help, if given, is likely to be delayed. The bystander effect may be due in part to diffusion of responsibility or the influence of other bystanders who seem calm.

Key Terms
bystander effect, p. 457   *diffusion of responsibility,* p. 457

AGGRESSION (pp. 458-461)

14.16 What biological factors influence aggression? (p. 459)

Biological factors thought to be related to aggression are a genetic link in criminal behavior, low arousal level, high testosterone level, low level of serotonin, brain damage or certain brain disorders, and alcohol abuse.

Key Term
aggression, p. 458

14.17 What other factors contribute to aggression? (pp. 459-461)

The frustration-aggression hypothesis holds that frustration produces aggression and that this aggression may be directed at the person, causing the frustration or displaced onto another target, as in scapegoating. Aggression has been associated with such aversive conditions as pain, heat, loud noise, and foul odors and with unpleasant emotional states, such as sadness, grief, and depression. Invasions of privacy and crowding may also contribute to aggression. Finally, belief in the superiority of one's own group may lead to aggression toward outsiders.

Key Terms

frustration-aggression hypothesis, p. 459
scapegoating, p. 460

personal space, p. 460
crowding, p. 460

14.18 How does social learning theory explain aggression? (p. 461)

According to social learning theory, people acquire aggressive responses by observing aggressive models in the family, the subculture, and the media, and by having aggressive responses reinforced.

PREJUDICE AND DISCRIMINATION (pp. 461-465)

14.19 What factors contribute to the development of prejudice and discrimination? (pp. 462-464)

Prejudice consists of attitudes (usually negative) toward others based on their gender, religion, race, or membership in a particular group. Discrimination consists of actions (usually negative) against others based on the same factors. Prejudice can arise out of competition for scarce resources or from people's tendency to divide the world into distinct social categories—in-groups and outgroups. According to social-cognitive theory, prejudice is learned in the same way that other attitudes are—through modeling and reinforcement.

Key Terms

prejudice, p. 461   *out-group*, p. 462
discrimination, p. 461   *stereotypes*, p. 463
realistic conflict theory, p. 462   *ethnocentrism*, p. 463
in-group, p. 462

14.20 What evidence suggests that prejudice and discrimination are decreasing? (pp. 464-465)

Many Americans believe that the election of the first African American president in 2008 was a sign that prejudice and discrimination have declined significantly. From the 1960s to the 1980s, White Americans became less likely to object to living in racially mixed neighborhoods. But ethnic groups still have varying views of the degree to which prejudice and discrimination continue to be problematic in the United States.

MAP IT

Log on to MyPsychLab and click on "Map It" to prepare a unique digital map of the chapter that you can save for later use, email to your instructor, or print out to use as a study tool. Or, create your own map by drawing one on paper. Use the starter map below as a model for your own map. Use the chapter summary as your guide for what to include. For each item in your map, be sure to include the page number.

Here's one way to *Map It*:

1. Draw a box at the top of the page for the section title.
2. Underneath the section title box, working horizontally across the page, draw a box for each learning question in the section. Write the learning questions in the boxes and draw a line from the section title to each questions box. After you read each subsection, jot an answer for the learning question in the subsection's box.
3. Below each learning question box, insert another box for all of the key terms that are related to the question, along with a very brief reminder of each term's definition. Draw a line from the question box to the key terms box.
4. Below each key terms box, create another box and list all of the helpful figures, tables, and other elements of the text, such as *Try It* and *Apply It* boxes. Draw a line from the key terms box to the helpful elements box.

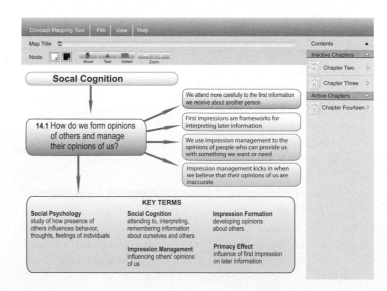

Map the Chapter on **mypsychlab.com**

Chapter 14 Study Guide

Answers to all the Study Guide questions are provided at the end of the book.

SECTION ONE: Chapter Review

Social Cognition (pp. 439–442)

1. Which of the following statements about first impressions is *false*?
   a. People usually pay closer attention to early information they receive about a person than to later information.
   b. Early information forms a framework through which later information is interpreted.
   c. First impressions often serve as self-fulfilling prophecies.
   d. The importance of first impressions is greatly overrated.

2. People tend to make _____ attributions to explain their own behavior and _____ attributions to explain the behavior of others.
   a. situational; situational
   b. situational; dispositional
   c. dispositional; situational
   d. dispositional; dispositional

3. Attributing Mike's poor grade to his lack of ability is a dispositional attribution. (true/false)

Attraction (pp. 442–445)

4. Match each term with a description.
   _____ (1) Brian sees Kelly at the library often and begins to like her.
   _____ (2) Lori assumes that because Michael is handsome, he must be popular and sociable.
   _____ (3) Kate and Kurt are dating and are both very attractive.
   a. matching hypothesis
   b. halo effect
   c. mere-exposure effect

5. Physical attractiveness is a very important factor in initial attraction. (true/false)

6. People are usually drawn to those who are more opposite than similar to themselves. (true/false)

7. Sternberg refers to commitment with passion but without intimacy as _____
   a. empty love
   b. liking
   c. fatuous love
   d. companionate love

Conformity, Obedience, and Compliance (pp. 445–449)

8. What percentage of subjects in the Asch study never conformed to the majority's unanimous incorrect response?
   a. 70%
   b. 33%
   c. 25%
   d. 5%

9. What percentage of the subjects in Milgram's original obedience experiment administered what they thought was the maximum 450-volt shock?
   a. 85%
   b. 65%
   c. 45%
   d. 25%

10. Match the technique for gaining compliance with the appropriate example.
    _____ (1) Meghan agrees to sign a letter supporting an increase in taxes for road construction. Later she agrees to make 100 phone calls urging people to vote for the measure.
    _____ (2) Jude refuses a phone request for a $24 donation to send four needy children to the circus but does agree to give $6.
    _____ (3) Lexie agrees to babysit for her next-door neighbors' two girls and then is informed that their three nephews will be there, too.
    a. door-in-the-face technique
    b. low-ball technique
    c. foot-in-the-door technique

Group Influence (pp. 449–453)

11. Which of the following statements regarding the effects of social facilitation (the presence of other people) is true?
    a. Performance improves on all tasks.
    b. Performance worsens on all tasks.
    c. Performance improves on easy tasks and worsens on difficult tasks.
    d. Performance improves on difficult tasks and worsens on easy tasks.

12. What occurs when members of a very cohesive group are more concerned with preserving group solidarity than with evaluating all possible alternatives in making a decision?
    a. groupthink
    b. group polarization
    c. social facilitation
    d. social loafing

13. Social roles cannot cause an individual to behave in ways that conflict with his/her own moral standards. (true/false)

Attitudes and Attitude Change (pp. 453–456)

14. Which of the following is *not* one of the three components of an attitude?
    a. cognitive component
    b. emotional component
    c. physiological component
    d. behavioral component

15. All of the following are ways to reduce cognitive dissonance *except*
    a. changing an attitude.
    b. changing a behavior.
    c. explaining away the inconsistency.
    d. strengthening the attitude and behavior.

16. People who have made a great sacrifice to join a group usually decrease their liking for the group. (true/false)

17. Credibility relates most directly to the communicator's
    a. attractiveness.
    b. expertise and trustworthiness.
    c. likability.
    d. personality.

18. With a well-informed audience, two-sided messages are more persuasive than one-sided messages. (true/false)

19. High-fear appeals are more effective than low-fear appeals if they provide definite actions that people can take to avoid dreaded outcomes. (true/false)

Prosocial Behavior (pp. 456–458)

20. The bystander effect is influenced by all of the following *except*
    a. the number of bystanders.
    b. the personalities of bystanders.
    c. whether the bystanders appear calm.
    d. whether the situation is ambiguous.

21. Altruism is one form of prosocial behavior. (true/false)

22. As the number of bystanders at an emergency increases, the probability that the victim will receive help decreases. (true/false)

23. In an ambiguous situation, a good way to determine if an emergency exists is to look at the reactions of other bystanders. (true/false)

Aggression (pp. 458–461)

24. Social psychologists generally believe that aggression stems from an aggressive instinct. (true/false)

25. Pain, extreme heat, loud noise, and foul odors have all been associated with an increase in aggressive responses. (true/false)

26. According to the frustration-aggression hypothesis, frustration _____ leads to aggression.
    a. always
    c. rarely
    b. often
    d. never

27. Which of the following statements is *not* true of personal space?
    a. It functions to protect privacy and regulate intimacy.
    b. How much personal space a person requires is affected by culture, race, gender, and personality.
    c. The size of a person's personal space is fixed.
    d. Invasions of personal space are usually perceived as unpleasant.

28. The social learning theory of aggression emphasizes all of the following *except* that
    a. aggressive responses are learned from the family, the subculture, and the media.
    b. aggressive acts are learned through modeling.
    c. most aggression results from frustration.
    d. when aggression responses are reinforced, they are more likely to continue.

29. Research tends to support the notion that a person can drain off aggressive energy by watching others behave aggressively in sports or on television. (true/false)

30. Research suggests that media violence is probably related to increased aggression. (true/false)

Prejudice and Discrimination (pp. 461–465)

31. Match the example with the term.
    _____ (1) Carlotta hired a woman to be her assistant because she doesn't like working with men.
    _____ (2) Darlene thinks that all Asian students are good at math.
    _____ (3) Bill canceled a blind date with Ellen when he heard that she was overweight.
    a. stereotypic thinking
    b. discrimination
    c. prejudice

32. Social learning theory asserts that prejudice develops and is maintained through
    a. competition.
    c. modeling and reinforcement.
    b. us-versus-them thinking.
    d. genetic inheritance.

33. African Americans no longer believe that racism is a major problem in U.S. society. (true/false)

34. Ethnocentrism is the tendency to look at others from the perspective of one's own racial or cultural group. (true/false)

SECTION TWO: Match Terms with Definitions

_____ (1) effect of one major positive or negative trait

_____ (2) as more viewers gather at the scene of an emergency, a victim's chances of help are reduced

_____ (3) geographic closeness

_____ (4) the blocking of an impulse

_____ (5) attitudes and standards of a group

_____ (6) relatively stable evaluation of a person, object, situation, or issue

_____ (7) impact of passive spectators on performance

_____ (8) the tendency of individuals to go along with the group even if they disagree

_____ (9) widely shared beliefs about traits of members of certain groups

_____ (10) the fact that one's overall impression is influenced by a first impression

_____ (11) displacing aggression onto innocent people

_____ (12) making a large request in the hope of gaining compliance with a subsequent small request

_____ (13) the intentional infliction of harm on another

a. frustration
b. proximity
c. aggression
d. scapegoating
e. bystander effect
f. halo effect
g. door-in-the-face technique
h. social norms
i. attitude
j. groupthink
k. stereotypes
l. audience effect
m. primacy effect

SECTION THREE: Fill in the Blank

1. A(n) _____ is a relatively stable evaluation of a person, object, situation, or issue.

2. Research reveals that our overall impression of another person is more influenced by the first information we have about the individual than by later information about the person. This tendency is called the

   _____ _____.

3. Jaime explained his poor grade on his math test by saying that he is a right-brained person and, therefore, more the artistic type than the analytical type. He is making a _____ attribution.

4. We tend to use _____ factors to explain our own behavior and _____ factors to explain the behavior of others.

5. Sal tends to attribute his successes to internal factors and his failure to situational factors. This tendency is known as the _____ _____.

6. People tend to infer generally positive or negative traits in a person as a result of observing one major positive or negative trait. This tendency is known as the _____ effect.

7. A classic study in social psychology is Milgram's research on _____. His experiment revealed that most participants were willing to follow orders and deliver the strongest possible shock to a confederate for giving wrong answers in a memory test.

8. Individual performance may be affected by the mere physical presence of others. This effect is known as _____ _____.

9. Group polarization refers to the tendency of group members, following a discussion, to take a more _____ position on the issue at hand.

10. A(n) _____ is a widely shared belief about the characteristics of members of various social groups and includes the assumption that all members of a social group are alike.

11. As the number of bystanders at an emergency increases, the probability that anyone will help a victim decreases. This phenomenon is known as the _____ effect.

12. Theo suffered serious injury while attempting to save a child from being run over by a car. Theo's action is an example of _____.

13. The _____ hypothesis suggests that frustration can result in aggression.

14. _____ occurs when a person is the undeserving victim of someone else's displaced aggression, which is due to that person's frustration.

15. A(n) _____ is an inference about the cause of our own or another's behavior.

16. _____ is changing or adopting an attitude or behavior to be consistent with the norms of a group or the expectations of others.

SECTION FOUR: Comprehensive Practice Test

1. Dispositional attribution is to _____ as situational attribution is to _____.
   a. external factors; internal factors
   b. others; self
   c. self; others
   d. internal factors; external factors

2. Crystal attributed Asher's poor oral presentation to his basic lack of motivation to be a good student and to be prepared for class. Assuming Crystal was wrong and Asher's poor performance was due to some other, external factor, Crystal was making an error called the self-serving bias. (true/false)

3. Crystal's own oral presentation was also poor. She explained that the students in the front row were goofing off and distracting her. Crystal was excusing her performance with the
   a. primary attribution error.
   b. fundamental self-bias error.
   c. self-serving bias.
   d. error of external factors.

4. The concept of proximity relates to
   a. attribution.
   b. attraction.
   c. aggression.
   d. prejudice.

5. In the past few decades people have become less influenced by physical attractiveness and more influenced by internal factors such as personality. (true/false)

6. Jesse's mother reminded him to check his tie and comb his hair prior to meeting the interviewer at his college admissions interview. Jesse's mother was probably concerned about the _____ effect.
   a. attenuation
   b. Soloman
   c. Harvard
   d. halo

7. The old adage "Birds of a feather flock together" summarizes the concept of _____, one of the factors that influence attraction.
   a. attribution
   b. social influence
   c. similarity
   d. proximity

8. Research reveals that low autonomic nervous system arousal levels seem to be related to aggressive behavior. (true/false)

9. Messsages about smoking are most effective if framed _____, while those about dietary change are best if framed _____.
   a. positively, negatively
   b. negatively, positively

10. The terms *stereotype* and *prejudice* are actually different words for the same thing. (true/false)

11. A negative attitude toward a person based on gender, religion, race, or membership in a certain group is known as
    a. discrimination.
    b. prejudice.
    c. a stereotype.
    d. social dissonance.

12. Strategies such as changing a behavior, changing an attitude, explaining away an inconsistency, or minimizing the importance of an inconsistency are all used to reduce
    a. cognitive distortion bias.
    b. relative attribution frustration.
    c. cognitive dissonance.
    d. inconsistency anxiety.

13. _____ are the attitudes and standards of behavior expected of members of a particular group.
    a. Values
    b. Social rules
    c. Social norms
    d. Social postures

14. Those who hold a minority opinion have more influence on a majority group if
    a. the opinion is stated vaguely so its departure from the majority opinion is disguised.
    b. the opinion is clearly stated and well organized.
    c. the opinion is stated as a question.
    d. the opinion is stated with qualifications that complement the majority opinion.

15. One strategy to induce compliance to a request is known as the _____ technique. In this strategy, the person making the request secures a favorable response to a small request with the aim of making the person more likely to agree to a larger request later.
    a. door-in-the-face
    b. low-ball
    c. foot-in-the-door
    d. risky shift

16. A good example of the door-in-the-face technique is to ask $10,000 for your used car, hoping that the buyer, who is likely to refuse to pay that much, will then be willing to agree to pay $8,000, the price you wanted in the first place. (true/false)

17. Social loafing refers to
    a. the tendency to avoid social contact and interpersonal relationships.
    b. the tendency to exert less effort when working with others on a common task.
    c. the tendency to be less productive when working alone than with others.
    d. the tendency to see others' work as more externally motivated than one's own.

18. A common finding on audience effects is that when we are being watched, we tend to do better on easy tasks and on more difficult tasks at which we are more proficient. (true/false)

19. Which of the following is *not* listed as a component of an attitude?
    a. social component
    b. behavioral component
    c. cognitive component
    d. emotional component

SECTION FIVE: Critical Thinking

1. Prepare a convincing argument supporting each of these positions:
   a. The Milgram study should have been conducted because it provided vitally important information about the troubling human tendency to inflict pain and suffering on others in obedience to authority figures.
   b. Despite the value of the knowledge the Milgram study provided, it should never have been conducted because it subjected research participants to tremendous stress.

2. Prepare a convincing argument supporting each of these positions:
   a. Aggression results largely from biological factors (nature).
   b. Aggression is primarily learned (nurture).

3. Review the factors influencing impression formation and attraction discussed in this chapter. Prepare a dual list of behaviors indicating what you should and should not do if you wish to make a better impression on other people and to increase their liking for you.

Appendix

Statistical Methods

If you want to know how tall a person is, all you have to do is get hold of a tape measure. But if you want to know whether someone is an extravert or how well he or she solves problems or how large his or her vocabulary is, you have to use a tool that is indispensable to psychological researchers, an operational definition. An operational definition is a way of assigning numerical values to a variable that cannot be observed directly. Tests are one type of operational definition, as are survey results. The bits of numerical information that researchers get from these operational definitions are known as data. The mathematical techniques that are used to analyze data are collectively called statistics. Psychologists and other scientists use statistics to organize, describe, and draw conclusions about the quantitative results of their studies. We will explore the two basic types of statistics that psychologists use—descriptive statistics and inferential statistics.

operational definition Way of assigning numerical values to a variable that cannot be observed directly, (e.g., test, survey).

data Bits of numerical information that are derived from operational definitions.

statistics Mathematical techniques that are used to analyze data.

Descriptive Statistics

Descriptive statistics are statistics used to organize, summarize, and describe data. Simply put, descriptive methods are sophisticated ways of counting things and describing the results of the counting process. For instance, you might count your money and describe it in terms of the total sum, the number of bills of various denominations, and the number of coins you have. You could even make a graph of the number of $1 bills, $5 bills, quarters, dimes, and so on that you have. You might count your money each day for a week and then say something like, "I had a daily average of $22.43 this week. On Monday I had nearly $50, but by Friday, I was down to just $5." All of these actions—counting your money, categorizing your bills and coins, and graphing the results, averaging your money for a week, and describing how your money varied from the beginning to the end of the week—yield descriptive statistics. Researchers use similar strategies to describe the data they gather in experiments and other kinds of studies. Typically, they display the data itself in tables and graphs. To gain more insight into the data, researchers also calculate descriptive statistics that include measures of central tendency, measures of variability, and correlation coefficients. Quite often psychologists and others apply these methods to the results of tests like those you learned about in Chapter 7 and Chapter 11 as well as to the kinds of tests that are used in classrooms. Descriptive statistics include measures of central tendency, variability, and relationship.

descriptive statistics Statistics used to organize, summarize, and describe data.

Describing Data with Tables and Graphs

Visual representations of data, such as graphs and tables, allow researchers to see data in an organized fashion. For example, a researcher tested 100 students for recall of 20 new vocabulary words 24 hours after they had memorized the list. The researcher organized the scores in a frequency distribution—an arrangement showing the number of times each score occurred. In other words, the frequency distribution shows how many students obtained each score. To organize the 100 test scores, the researcher decided to group the scores into 2-point intervals. Next, the researcher tallied the frequency (number of scores) within each 2-point interval. Table A.1 on the next page presents the resulting frequency distribution.

frequency distribution An arrangement showing the numbers of scores that fall within equal-sized intervals.

TABLE A.1 *Frequency Distribution of 100 Vocabulary Test Scores*

INTERVAL	TALLY OF SCORES IN EACH INTERVAL	NUMBER OF SCORES IN EACH INTERVAL (FREQUENCY)
1–2	|	1
3–4	||	2
5–6	⊬⊬ |	6
7–8	⊬⊬ ⊬⊬ ⊬⊬ |||	18
9–10	⊬⊬ ⊬⊬ ⊬⊬ ⊬⊬ |||	23
11–12	⊬⊬ ⊬⊬ ⊬⊬ ⊬⊬ |||	23
13–14	⊬⊬ ⊬⊬ ⊬⊬ ||	17
15–16	⊬⊬ |||	8
17–18	|	1
19–20	|	1

histogram A bar graph that depicts the number of scores within each class interval in a frequency distribution.

frequency polygon A line graph that depicts the frequency, or number, of scores within each class interval in a frequency distribution.

The researcher then made a histogram, a bar graph that depicts the number of scores within each interval in the frequency distribution. The intervals are plotted along the horizontal axis, and the frequency of scores in each interval is plotted along the vertical axis. Figure A.1 shows the histogram for the 100 test scores.

Another common method of representing frequency data is the frequency polygon. As in a histogram, the intervals are plotted along the horizontal axis, and the frequencies are plotted along the vertical axis. However, in a frequency polygon, each interval is represented by a graph point that is placed at the middle (midpoint) of the interval so that its vertical distance above the horizontal axis shows the frequency of that interval. Lines are drawn to connect the points, as shown in Figure A.2. The histogram and the frequency polygon are simply two different ways of presenting data.

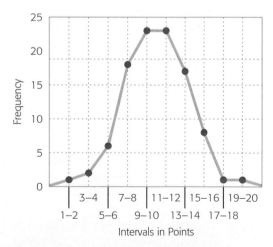

FIGURE A.2 A Frequency Polygon
Vocabulary test scores from the frequency distribution in Table A.1 are plotted here in the form of a frequency polygon. Intervals of 2 points each appear on the horizontal axis. Frequencies of the scores in each class interval are plotted on the vertical axis.

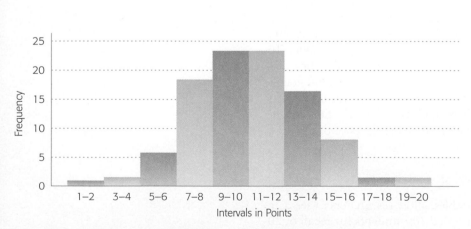

FIGURE A.1 A Frequency Histogram
Vocabulary test scores from the frequency distribution in Table A.1 are plotted here in the form of a histogram. Intervals of 2 points each appear on the horizontal axis. Frequencies of the scores in each interval are plotted on the vertical axis.

Measures of Central Tendency

A measure of central tendency is a measure or score that describes the center, or middle, of a distribution of scores. The most widely used and most familiar measure of central tendency is the mean, the arithmetic average of a group of scores. The mean is computed by adding all the single scores and dividing the sum by the number of scores.

For instance, consider the case of Carl. Carl sometimes studies and does well in his classes, but he occasionally procrastinates and fails a test. Table A.2 shows how Carl performed on the seven tests in his psychology class last semester. Carl computes his mean score by adding up all his test scores and dividing the sum by the number of tests. Carl's mean, or average, score is 80.

The mean is an important and widely used statistical measure of central tendency, but it can be misleading when a group of scores contains one or several extreme scores. Table A.3 lists the annual incomes of 10 people in rank order. When an income of $1 million is averaged with several more modest incomes, the mean does not provide a true picture of the group. Therefore, when one or a few individuals score far above or below the middle range of a group, a different measure of central tendency should be used. The median is the middle score or value when a group of scores are arranged from highest to lowest. When there is an odd number of scores, the score in the middle is the median. When there is an even number of scores, the median is the average of the two middle scores. For the 10 incomes arranged from highest to lowest in Table A.3, the median is $27,000, which is the average of the middle incomes, $28,000 and $26,000. The $27,000 median income is a truer reflection of the comparative income of the group than is the $124,700 mean.

Another measure of central tendency is the mode. The mode is easy to find because it is the score that occurs most frequently in a group of scores. The mode of the annual-income group in Table A.3 is $22,000.

measure of central tendency A measure or score that describes the center, or middle, of a distribution of scores (example: mean, median, or mode).

mean The arithmetic average of a group of scores; calculated by adding all the single scores and dividing the sum by the number of scores.

TABLE A.2 *Carl's Psychology Test Scores*

Test 1	98
Test 2	74
Test 3	86
Test 4	92
Test 5	56
Test 6	68
Test 7	86
Sum:	560

Mean: 560 ÷ 7 = 80

median The middle score or value when a group of scores are arranged from highest to lowest.

mode The score that occurs most frequently in a group of scores.

TABLE A.3 *Annual Income for Ten People*

SUBJECT	ANNUAL INCOME
1	$1,000,000
2	$50,000
3	$43,000
4	$30,000
5	$28,000
6	$26,000
7	$22,000
8	$22,000
9	$16,000
10	$10,000
Sum:	$1,247,000

$28,000 and $26,000 → $27,000 = Median

$22,000 and $22,000 → Mode

Mean: $1,247,000 ÷ 10 = $124,700

Median: $27,000

Mode: $22,000

Measures of Variability

variability How much the scores in a distribution spread out, away from the mean.

In addition to a measure of central tendency, researchers need a measure of the variability of a set of scores—how much the scores spread out, away from the mean. Both groups in Table A.4 have a mean and a median of 80. However, the scores in Group II cluster tightly around the mean, while the scores in Group I vary widely from the mean.

range The difference between the highest score and the lowest score in a distribution of scores.

The simplest measure of variability is the range—the difference between the highest and lowest scores in a distribution of scores. Table A.4 reveals that Group I has a range of 47, indicating high variability, while Group II has a range of only 7, showing low variability. Unfortunately, the range reveals only the difference between the lowest score and the highest score; it tells nothing about the scores in between.

standard deviation A descriptive statistic reflecting the average amount that scores in a distribution deviate, or vary, from their mean.

The standard deviation is a descriptive statistic reflecting the average amount that scores in a distribution deviate, or vary, from their mean. The larger the standard deviation, the greater the variability in a distribution of scores. Refer to Table A.4 and note the standard deviations for the two distributions of test scores. In Group I, the relatively large standard deviation of 18.1 reflects the wide variability in that distribution. By contrast, the small standard deviation of 2.14 in Group II indicates that the variability is low, and you can see that the scores cluster tightly around the mean.

TABLE A.4 *Comparison of Range and Standard Deviation for Two Small Groups of Scores Having Identical Means and Medians*

GROUP I		GROUP II	
TEST	**SCORE**	**TEST**	**SCORE**
1	99	1	83
2	99	2	82
3	98	3	81
4	80 Median	4	80 Median
5	72	5	79
6	60	6	79
7	52	7	76
Sum:	560	Sum:	560

Mean: 560 ÷ 7 = 80

Median: 80

Range: 99 − 52 = 47

Standard deviation: 18.1

Mean: 560 ÷ 7 = 80

Median: 80

Range: 83 − 76 = 7

Standard deviation: 2.14

The Normal Curve

normal curve A symmetrical, bell-shaped frequency distribution that represents how scores are normally distributed in a population; most scores fall near the mean, and fewer and fewer scores occur in the extremes either above or below the mean.

In Chapter 7 we introduced you to the normal curve, pictured in Figure A.3. Psychologists and other scientists often use descriptive statistics in connection with an important type of frequency distribution. If a large number of people are measured on any of a wide variety of traits (such as height or IQ score), the great majority of values will cluster in the middle, with fewer and fewer individuals measuring extremely low or high on these variables. Note that slightly more than 68% of the scores in a normal distribution fall within 1 standard deviation of the mean (34.13% within 1 standard deviation above the mean, and 34.13% within 1 standard deviation below the mean). Almost 95.5% of the scores in a normal distribution lie between 2 standard deviations above and below the mean. The vast majority of scores in a normal distribution—99.72%—fall between 3 standard deviations above and below the mean.

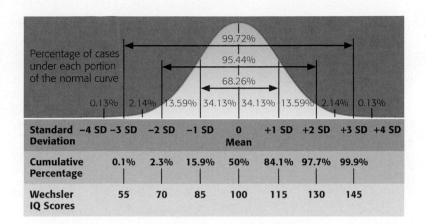

FIGURE A.3 The Normal Curve
The normal curve is a symmetrical, bell-shaped curve that represents how scores are normally distributed in a population. Slightly more than 68% of the scores in a normal distribution fall within 1 standard deviation above and below the mean. Almost 95.5% of the scores lie between 2 standard deviations above and below the mean, and about 99.75% fall between 3 standard deviations above and below the mean.

Using the properties of the normal curve and knowing the mean and the standard deviation of a normal distribution, we can find where any score stands (how high or low) in relation to all the other scores in the distribution. For example, on the Wechsler intelligence scales, the mean IQ is 100 and the standard deviation is 15. Thus, 99.72% of the population has an IQ score within 3 standard deviations above and below the mean, ranging from an IQ of 55 to an IQ of 145.

The Correlation Coefficient

As you learned in Chapter 1, a correlation coefficient is a number that indicates the degree and direction of relationship between two variables. Correlation coefficients can range from +1.00 (a perfect positive correlation) to .00 (no correlation) to −1.00 (a perfect negative correlation), as illustrated in Figure A.4. A positive correlation indicates that two variables vary in the same direction. An increase in one variable is associated with an increase in the other variable, or a decrease in one variable is associated with a decrease in the other. There is a positive correlation between the number of hours college students spend studying and their grades. The more hours they study, the higher their grades are likely to be. A negative correlation means that an increase in one variable is associated with a decrease in the other variable. There may be a negative correlation between the number of hours students spend watching television and studying. The more hours they spend watching TV, the fewer hours they may spend studying, and vice versa.

correlation coefficient A numerical value indicating the strength and direction of relationship between two variables, which ranges from +1.00 (a perfect positive correlation) to −1.00 (a perfect negative correlation).

positive correlation A relationship between two variables in which both vary in the same direction.

negative correlation A relationship between two variables in which an increase in one variable is associated with a decrease in the other variable.

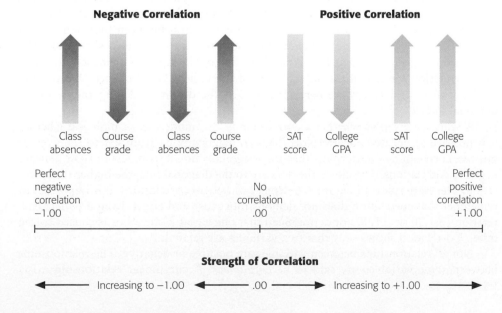

FIGURE A.4 Understanding Correlation Coefficients
Correlation coefficients can range from −1.00 (a perfect negative correlation) through .00 (no correlation) to +1.00 (a perfect positive correlation). As the arrows indicate, a negative correlation exists when an increase in one variable is associated with a decrease in the other variable, and vice versa. A positive correlation exists when both variables tend to either increase or decrease together.

TABLE A.5 *High School and College GPAs for 11 Students*

STUDENT	HIGH SCHOOL GPA (VARIABLE X)	COLLEGE GPA (VARIABLE Y)
1	2.0	1.8
2	2.2	2.5
3	2.3	2.5
4	2.5	3.1
5	2.8	3.2
6	3.0	2.2
7	3.0	2.8
8	3.2	3.3
9	3.3	2.9
10	3.5	3.2
11	3.8	3.5

The sign (+ or −) in a correlation coefficient merely tells whether the two variables vary in the same or opposite directions. (If no sign appears, the correlation is assumed to be positive.) The number in a correlation coefficient indicates the relative strength of the relationship between the two variables—the higher the number, the stronger the relationship. For example, a correlation of −.70 is higher than a correlation of +.56; a correlation of −.85 is just as strong as one of +.85. A correlation of .00 indicates that no relationship exists between the variables. IQ and shoe size are examples of two variables that are not correlated.

Table A.5 shows the measurements of two variables—high school GPA and college GPA for 11 college students. Looking at the data, we can see that 6 of the 11 students had a higher GPA in high school, while 5 of the students had a higher GPA in college. A clearer picture of the actual relationship is shown by the *scatterplot* in Figure A.5. High school GPA (variable X) is plotted on the horizontal axis, and college GPA (variable Y) is plotted on the vertical axis.

One dot is plotted for each of the 11 students at the point where high school GPA, variable X, and college GPA, variable Y, intersect. For example, the first student is represented by a dot at the point where her high school GPA of 2.0 on the horizontal (x) axis and college GPA of 1.8 on the vertical (y) axis intersect. The scatterplot in Figure A.5 reveals a relatively high correlation between high school and college GPAs because the dots cluster near the diagonal line. It also shows that the correlation is positive, because the dots run diagonally upward from left to right. The correlation coefficient for the high school and college GPAs of these 11 students is .71. If the correlation were perfect (1.00), all the dots would fall exactly on the diagonal line.

A scatterplot shows whether a correlation is low, moderate, or high and whether it is positive or negative. Scatterplots that run diagonally up from left to right reveal positive correlations. Scatterplots that run diagonally down from left to right indicate negative correlations. The closer the dots are to the diagonal line, the higher the correlation. The scatterplots in Figure A.6 depict a variety of correlations. It is important to remember that correlation does not demonstrate cause and effect. Even a perfect correlation (+1.00 or −1.00) does not mean that one variable causes or is caused by the other. Correlation shows only that two variables are related.

Not all relationships between variables are positive or negative. The relationships between some variables are said to be *curvilinear*. A curvilinear relationship exists

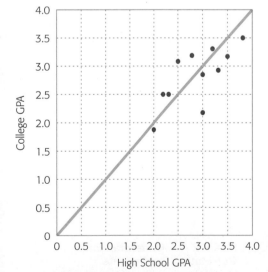

FIGURE A.5 A Scatterplot
A scatterplot reveals a relatively high positive correlation between the high school and college GPAs of the 11 students listed in Table A.5. One dot is plotted for each of the 11 students at the point where high school GPA (plotted on the horizontal axis) and college GPA (plotted on the vertical axis) intersect.

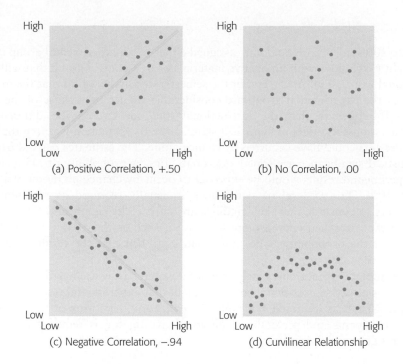

A scatterplot moving diagonally up from left to right, as in (a), indicates a positive correlation. A scatterplot moving diagonally down from left to right, as in (c), indicates a negative correlation. The more closely the dots cluster around a diagonal line, the higher the correlation. Scatterplot (b) indicates no correlation. Scatterplot (d) shows a curvilinear relationship that is positive up to a point and then becomes negative. Age and strength of handgrip have a curvilinear relationship: Handgrip increases in strength up to about age 40 and then decreases with continued aging.

when two variables correlate positively (or negatively) up to a certain point and then change direction. For example, there is a positive correlation between physical strength and age up to about 40 or 45 years of age. As age increases from childhood to middle age, so does the strength of handgrip pressure. But beyond middle adulthood, the relationship becomes negative, and increasing age is associated with decreasing handgrip strength. Figure A.6(d) shows a scatterplot of this curvilinear relationship.

Inferential Statistics

As you have learned, descriptive statistics are about counting, tabulating, and using numbers in other ways to communicate information about data. By contrast, inferential statistics is based on probabilities. For instance, you know that the probability of getting a "head" when you flip a coin is 1 in 2, or 50%. Knowing that, you *infer* that if you could flip a coin an infinite number of times, heads would turn up half the time. In so doing, you are practicing inferential statistics.

When researchers use inferential statistics, they do so in order to determine how well their findings represent the probabilities that exist outside the confines of the research setting. For example, if the participants in a study obtain a certain average on a test, the psychologist doing the research wants to know how well that average corresponds to the mean that would be obtained if she could test everyone in the group of interest. As such, inferential statistics allow researchers (1) to make inferences about the characteristics of the larger population from their observations and measurements of a sample and (2) to derive estimates of how much faith or confidence can be placed in those inferences. In statistical theory, a population is the entire group that is of interest to researchers—the group to which they wish to apply their findings. For example, a population could be all the registered voters in the United States. Usually, researchers cannot directly measure and study the entire population of interest. Consequently, they make inferences about a population from a relatively small sample selected from that population. For researchers to draw conclusions about the larger population, the sample must be representative—that is, its characteristics must mirror those of the larger population. (See Chapter 1 for more information about representative samples.)

inferential statistics Statistical procedures that allow researchers to make inferences about the characteristics of the larger population from observations and measurements of a sample and to derive estimates of how much confidence can be placed in those inferences.

population The entire group of interest to researchers and to which they wish to generalize their findings; the group from which a sample is selected.

sample The portion of any population that is selected for study and from which generalizations are made about the entire population.

Statistical Significance

Suppose 200 students are randomly assigned either to an experimental group that will be taught psychology with innovative materials or to a control group that will receive traditional instruction. At the end of the semester, researchers find that the mean test scores of the experimental group are considerably higher than those of the control group. To conclude that the instructional methods caused the difference, the researchers must use tests of statistical significance to estimate how often the experimental results could have occurred by chance alone. The estimates derived from tests of statistical significance are stated as probabilities. A probability of .05 means that the experimental results would be expected to occur by chance no more than 5 times out of 100. The .05 level of significance is usually required as a minimum for researchers to conclude that their findings are statistically significant. Often the level of significance reached is even more impressive, such as the .01 level. The .01 level means that the probability is no more than 1 in 100 that the results occurred by chance.

The inferences researchers make are not absolute. They are based on probability, and there is always a possibility, however small, that experimental results could occur by chance. Thus, as we noted in Chapter 1, replication, repetition of a study with different participants and preferably a different investigator, is required to determine whether a given result is reliable.

tests of statistical significance Statistical tests that estimate the probability that a particular research result could have occurred by chance.

replication the process of repeating a study with different participants and preferably a different investigator to verify research findings

Answers to Study Guide Questions

Chapter 1

Section One: Chapter Review 1. scientific method; 2. describe, explain, predict, influence; 3. true; 4. (1) b, (2) b, (3) b, (4) a, (5) a, (6) a, (7) a, b; 5. (1) c, (2) a, (3) d, (4) e, (5) b; 6. (1) d, (2) c, (3) b, (4) a, (5) c, (6) b; 7. (1) d, (2) a, (3) f, (4) e, (5) b, (6) c; 8. (1) b, (2) c, (3) a, (4) b, (5) a, (6) c; 9. (1) b, (2) c, (3) d, (4) a, (5) e, (6) g, (7) f; 10. (1) Yes, (2) No, (3) No, (4) Yes; 11. counseling; 12. d; 13. independent thinking, suspension of judgment, willingness to modify or abandon prior judgments; 14. b; 15. (1) d, (2) a, (3) b, (4) c; 16. case studies; 17. false; 18. false; 19. correlation coefficient; 20. b; 21. positive; 22. negative; 23. false; 24. true; 25. independent variable, dependent variable; 26. (1) d, (2) c, (3) a, (4) b; 27. c; 28. d; 29. b; 30. c; 31. true

Section Two: Who Said This? 1. Skinner; 2. Wundt; 3. James; 4. Watson; 5. Maslow; 6. Sumner; 7. Calkins; 8. Rogers; 9. Wertheimer

Section Three: Fill in the Blank 1. theory; 2. naturalistic observation; 3. population, representative sample; 4. hypothesis; 5. independent, dependent; 6. sociocultural; 7. predictions, cause, effect; 8. structuralism; 9. functionalism; 10. psychoanalysis; 11. cognitive; 12. psychoanalytic; 13. Developmental

Section Four: Comprehensive Practice Test 1. b; 2. b; 3. d; 4. c; 5. c; 6. b; 7. a; 8. d; 9. c; 10. a; 11. c; 12. false; 13. false; 14. true; 15. false; 16. true; 17. false; 18. false; 19. false; 20. false

Chapter 2

Section One: Chapter Review 1. (1) b, (2) c, (3) a; 2. b; 3. a; 4. a; 5. c; 6. a; 7. Glial cells; 8. c; 9. d; 10. action; 11. b; 12. d; 13. dopamine; 14. endorphins; 15. dopamine, glutamate; 16. b; 17. c; 18. (1) b, (2) a, (3) f, (4) c, (5) e, (6) d, (7) g; 19. b; 20. hippocampus; 21. amygdala, hippocampus; 22. b; 23. a; 24. (1) d, (2) c, (3) a, (4) b; 25. (1) d, (2) a, (3) e, (4) b, (5) c; 26. (1) a, (2) b, (3) a, (4) a, (5) b; 27. c; 28. c; 29. myelination; 30. white matter; 31. different; 32. decreases; 33. strokes; 34. (1) d, (2) a, (3) e, (4) c, (5) b, (6) f; 35. recessive; 36. d; 37. twin studies, adoption studies

Section Two: Label the Brain 1. frontal lobe; 2. motor cortex; 3. parietal lobe; 4. occipital lobe; 5. cerebellum; 6. pons; 7. medulla; 8. corpus callosum

Section Three: Fill in the Blank 1. dendrite; 2. neurotransmitters; 3. limbic; 4. primary visual cortex; 5. parietal; 6. frontal; 7. left;

8. axon; 9. brain, spinal cord; 10. sympathetic; 11. hypothalamus; 12. action potential; 13. Broca's; 14. hippocampus; 15. temporal; 16. cerebellum; 17. peripheral; 18. substantia nigra; 19. left hippocampus; 20. fragile-X syndrome; 21. language processing

Section Four: Comprehensive Practice Test 1. b; 2. c; 3. true; 4. d; 5. d; 6. a; 7. c; 8. b; 9. c; 10. b; 11. d; 12. b; 13. a; 14. c; 15. d; 16. true; 17. spatial perception; 18. right parietal cortex; right frontal cortex; 19. X chromosome

Chapter 3

Section One: Chapter Review 1. sensation; 2. absolute; 3. false; 4. c; 5. transduction; 6. b; 7. (1) d (2) c (3) b (4) e (5) a; 8. rods, cones; 9. c; 10. d; 11. hertz, decibels; 12. (1) b (2) a (3) c; 13. d; 14. c; 15. kinesthetic; 16. vestibular, inner ear; 17. olfaction; 18. c; 19. sweet, sour, salty, bitter, umami; 20. taste bud; 21. false; 22. inattentional blindness; 23. bottom-up processing; 24. cross-modal perception; 25. top-down; 26. c; 27. (1) c (2) a (3) b; 28. binocular; 29. (1) c (2) b (3) a (4) d; 30. false; 31. c; 32. false; 33. Ganzfeld procedure

Section Two: Multiple Choice 1. a; 2. d; 3. d; 4. c; 5. d; 6. d; 7. b; 8. c; 9. a; 10. c; 11. c; 12. a; 13. c; 14. a; 15. a; 16. a; 17. b; 18. b; 19. c; 20. d; 21. b; 22. b; 23. c; 24. c; 25. c

Section Three: Fill in the Blank 1. seeing, hearing, etc.; interpreting what is seen, heard, etc.; 2. difference; 3. sensory; 4. transduction; 5. sensory adaptation; 6. cornea; 7. opponent process; 8. frequency; 9. umami; 10. Gestalt; 11. figure–ground; 12. closure; 13. binocular disparity; 14. facial expressions; 15. subliminal perception

Section Four: Comprehensive Practice Test 1. c; 2. a; 3. d; 4. c; 5. b; 6. d; 7. a; 8. c; 9. a; 10. c; 11. c; 12. b; 13. d; 14. a; 15. d; 16. b; 17. true; 18. d; 19. true; 20. c; 21. false; 22. a; 23. c; 24. d; 25. c; 26. b; 27. a; 28. b; 29. d

Chapter 4

Section One: Chapter Review 1. a; 2. suprachiasmatic nucleus; 3. d; 4. false; 5. evolutionary, adaptive; 6. (1) a (2) b (3) a (4) a (5) a; 7. c; 8. false; 9. d; 10. b; 11. (1) c (2) b (3) a; 12. c; 13. false; 14. (1) d (2) a (3) c (4) b; 15. c; 16. false; 17. b; 18. false; 19. b; 20. true; 21. true; 22. c; 23. a; 24. sociocognitive, neodissociation, dissociated control; 25. nucleus accumbens; 26. d; 27. true; 28. true; 29. (1) b (2) a (3) d (4) c; 30. b; 31. b; 32. a; 33. c; 34. false; 35. c;

Section Two: Identify the Drug   (1) b (2) d (3) f (4) c (5) e (6) a (7) g

Section Three: Fill in the Blank   1. consciousness; 2. delta; 3. REM rebound; 4. REM; 5. parasomnias; 6. apnea; 7. narcolepsy; 8. mood, perception, thought; 9. Meditation; 10. dependence; 11. crash; 12. dopamine; 13. cocaine

Section Four: Comprehensive Practice Test   1. melatonin; 2. b; 3. a; 4. c; 5. c; 6. b; 7. false; 8. d; 9. c; 10. d; 11. true; 12. b; 13. b; 14. false; 15. false; 16. c; 17. c; 18. false

Chapter 5

Section One: Chapter Review   1. Pavlov; 2. conditioned; 3. extinction; 4. existing conditioned stimulus; 5. b; 6. conditioned, unconditioned; 7. a; 8. cognitive; 9. false; 10. true; 11. b; 12. c; 13. d; 14. negative; 15. continuous; 16. d; 17. a; 18. false; 19. false; 20. true; 21. learned helplessness; 22. biofeedback; 23. behavior modification; 24. insight; 25. d; 26. b; 27. b; 28. (1) c (2) a (3) d (4) b; 29. (1) c (2) a (3) b; 30. Bandura

Section Two: Identify the Concept   1. variable-ratio schedule of reinforcement; 2. classical conditioning of emotions; 3. positive reinforcement for Joey; negative reinforcement for his mother; 4. generalization; 5. positive reinforcement; 6. extinction; 7. fixed-interval reinforcement schedule; 8. positive punishment; 9. observational learning, modeling effect; 10. secondary reinforcer; 11. insight; 12. electronic multitasking environment

Section Three: Fill in the Blank   1. stimuli, behavior, consequences; 2. Learning; 3. the sound of the truck; 4. the food; 5. salivation; 6. neutral; 7. generalization; 8. discrimination; 9. higher-order; 10. conditioned, unconditioned; 11. effect, Thorndike; 12. successive approximations; 13. negative, positive; 14. discriminative; 15. primary, secondary; 16. continuous, partial; 17. aggressive; 18. television, the Internet

Section Four: Comprehensive Practice Test   1. a; 2. c; 3. c; 4. d; 5. b; 6. c; 7. b; 8. c; 9. b; 10. d; 11. b; 12. false; 13. b; 14. b; 15. d; 16. c; 17. a

Chapter 6

Section One: Chapter Review   1. d; 2. (1) b (2) c (3) a; 3. (1) b (2) c (3) a; 4. c; 5. c; 6. (1) a (2) c (3) b (4) a (5) c; 7. c; 8. true; 9. true; 10. b; 11. d; 12. source monitoring; 13. a; 14. b; 15. true; 16. positive; 17. d; 18. a; 19. (1) c (2) e (3) a (4) b (5) d; 20. d; 21. false; 22. true; 23. true; 24. episodic, semantic; 25. a; 26. true; 27. c; 28. a; 29. false

Section Two: Complete the Diagrams   1. large; 2. visual, fraction of a second; auditory, 2 seconds; 3. about 7 items; 4. less than 30 seconds; 5. unlimited; 6. from minutes to a lifetime; 7. declarative; 8. episodic; 9. motor; 10. classically

Section Three: Fill in the Blank   1. encoding; 2. rehearsal; 3. working; 4. chunking; 5. semantic; 6. recall; 7. middle;

8. state-dependent; 9. flashbulb; 10. proactive; 11. encoding; 12. hippocampal region; 13. potentiation; 14. anterograde amnesia; 15. retroactive, source monitoring; 16. repression

Section Four: Comprehensive Practice Test   1. c; 2. a; 3. c; 4. b; 5. nondeclarative; 6. a; 7. d; 8. b; 9. true; 10. false; 11. false; 12. d; 13. a; 14. c; 15. true; 16. a; 17. b; 18. true; 19. false; 20. d

Chapter 7

Section One: Chapter Review   1. c; 2. b; 3. d; 4. Framing; 5. a; 6. b; 7. c; 8. false; 9. false; 10. (1) c (2) d (3) b (4) e (5) a; 11. false; 12. true; 13. true; 14. (1) b (2) c (3) a; 15. a; 16. b; 17. a; 18. false; 19. true; 20. (1) b (2) a (3) a (4) b (5) a; 21. c; 22. false; 23. c

Section Two: Important Concepts and Psychologists   1. Simon; 2. Tversky; 3. Whorf; 4. Spearman; 5. Sternberg; 6. Terman; 7. Wechsler; 8. Galton; 9. Steele; 10. Gardner

Section Three: Fill in the Blank   1. cognition; 2. Imagery; 3. exemplars; 4. elimination by aspects; 5. psycholinguistics; 6. syntax; 7. linguistic relativity; 8. Gardner; 9. validity; 10. contextual; 11. reliability; 12. creativity

Section Four: Comprehensive Practice Test   1. c; 2. b; 3. prototype; 4. true; 5. a; 6. a; 7. d; 8. a; 9. false; 10. false; 11. false; 12. c; 13. a; 14. b; 15. true; 16. true; 17. true

Chapter 8

Section One: Chapter Review   1. b; 2. d; 3. (1) b (2) c (3) b; 4. true; 5. (1) c (2) a (3) b; 6. a; 7. b; 8. c; 9. true; 10. (1) c (2) b (3) a (4) e (5) d; 11. false; 12. (1) c (2) b (3) a; 13. false; 14. b; 15. false; 16. a; 17. true; 18. c; 19. Crystallized; 20. b; 21. a; 22. a; 23. d

Section Two: Important Concepts and Psychologists   1. cognitive development; 2. psychosocial development; 3. temperament; 4. attachment; 5. nativist view of language development; 6. moral reasoning; gender role development; 7. death and dying; 8. gender-schema theory

Section Three: Fill in the Blank   1. scheme; 2. personal fable; 3. conventional; 4. identity versus role confusion; 5. zygote; 6. teratogens; 7. maturation; 8. avoidant; 9. overextension; 10. overregularization; 11. Kohlberg; 12. Crystallized, fluid; 13. Bargaining

Section Four: Comprehensive Practice Test   1. b; 2. b; 3. d; 4. d; 5. b; 6. a; 7. b; 8. b; 9. true; 10. b; 11. d; 12. c; 13. c; 14. c; 15. true; 16. b; 17. c; 18. b; 19. true; 20. b

Chapter 9

Section One: Chapter Review   1. true; 2. extrinsic; 3. a; 4. d; 5. c; 6. true; 7. performance; 8. d; 9. expectancy; 10. feeding, satiety;

11. c; 12. c; 13. d; 14. maintain; 15. d; 16. biological; 17. c; 18. anorexia, bulimia; 19. a; 20. c; 21. true; 22. true; 23. b; 24. true; 25. b; 26. b; 27. c; 28. a; 29. b; 30. c; 31. d; 32. c; 33. a; 34. c

Section Two: Important Concepts and Psychologists   1. drive-reduction theory; 2. hierarchy of needs; 3. need for achievement; 4. event creates physical arousal which is identified as an emotion; 5. event creates physical arousal plus emotion; 6. cognitive appraisal of a stimulus results in emotion; 7. facial-feedback hypothesis

Section Three: Fill in the Blank   1. Motives; 2. intrinsic; 3. extrinsic; 4. arousal; 5. valence; 6. lateral, ventromedial; 7. exercise; 8. Anorexia, bulimia; 9. James–Lange; 10. Cannon–Bard; 11. Schachter–Singer; 12. basic; 13. excitement; 14. testosterone; 15. homeostasis; 16. heterosexual, homosexual

Section Four: Comprehensive Practice Test   1. a; 2. a; 3. c; 4. a; 5. c; 6. d; 7. true; 8. d; 9. c; 10. c; 11. true; 12. c; 13. true; 14. true; 15. false; 16. d; 17. b; 18. a

Chapter 10

Section One: Chapter Review   1. false; 2. false; 3. false; 4. true; 5. true; 6. c; 7. d; 8. d; 9. c; 10. c; 11. resistance; 12. exhaustion; 13. physiological, psychological; 14. a; 15. problem-focused, emotion-focused; 16. true; 17. true; 18. d; 19. false; 20. b; 21. a; 22. false; 23. b; 24. d; 25. a; 26. b; 27. Alcohol; 28. false; 29. c; 30. c; 31. c; 32. false

Section Two: The Biopsychosocial Model of Health and Illness   1. genetics, relaxation, healthy lifestyle; 2. lack of exercise, poor diet, disease and injury, toxic chemicals, pollution; 3. stress management skills, giving and receiving love, optimism; 4. depression, pessimism, worry, anxiety, poor coping skills, stress; 5. social responsibility, social policy, social groups; 6. loneliness, poverty, exploitation, violence

Section Three: Fill in the Blank   1. biomedical, biopsychosocial; 2. health psychology; 3. sympathetic nervous system; 4. alarm; 5. resistance; 6. cognitive; 7. proactive; 8. HIV/AIDS; 9. homosexual men; 10. hassles; 11. health psychology; 12. A; 13. cognition; 14. Primary; 15. high blood pressure; 16. stressor; 17. approach-avoidance; 18. life events

Section Four: Comprehensive Practice Test   1. true; 2. b; 3. a; 4. b; 5. a; 6. true; 7. true; 8. c; 9. racism; 10. true; 11. c; 12. false; 13. a; 14. true; 15. true

Chapter 11

Section One: Chapter Review   1. true; 2. unconscious; 3. a; 4. c; 5. b; 6. false; 7. true; 8. birth; 9. d; 10. b; 11. Oedipus complex; 12. c; 13. collective; 14. c; 15. c; 16. d; 17. c; 18. a; 19. true; 20. d; 21. true; 22. a; 23. b; 24. negligible; 25. false; 26. b; 27. c; 28. a; 29. d; 30. (1) a (2) c (3) d (4) b (5) e; 31. d; 32. c

Section Two: Complete the Table   1. Freud; behavior arises mostly from unconscious conflict between pleasure-seeking id and moral-perfectionistic superego, with ego as mediator; 2. Maslow, Rogers; behavior springs from the person's motivation to become self-actualized or fully functioning and reflects the person's unique perception of reality and conscious choices; 3. Allport, Cattell, Eysenck, McCrae, Costa; behavior springs from personality traits that are influenced by both heredity and environment.; 4. Mischel, Bandura, Rotter; behavior results from an interaction between internal cognitive factors and environmental factors

Section Three: Fill in the Blank   1. id; 2. ego; 3. preconscious; 4. oral, anal, phallic, latency, genital; 5. cardinal; 6. surface; 7. reciprocal determinism; 8. collective unconscious; 9. observation; 10. Jung's; 11. projective; 12. MMPI; 13. Self-efficacy; 14. source; 15. archetype; 16. collectivist, individualistic/collectivist; 17. self-esteem

Section Four: Comprehensive Practice Test   1. c; 2. c; 3. b; 4. true; 5. b; 6. c; 7. a; 8. a; 9. b; 10. d; 11. b; 12. c; 13. true; 14. false; 15. c; 16. d

Chapter 12

Section One: Chapter Review   1. false; 2. a; 3. (1) c (2) a (3) b (4) d; 4. false; 5. true; 6. false; 7. (1) e (2) d (3) b (4) c (5) a (6) f; 8. c; 9. (1) b (2) c (3) a; 10. false; 11. b; 12. (1) a (2) d (3) b (4) c; 13. d; 14. (1) c (2) a (3) b (4) d; 15. false; 16. true; 17. (1) d (2) b (3) e (4) c (5) a; 18. paraphilias; 19. c; 20. c

Section Two: Identifying the Disorder   1. major depressive disorder; 2. schizophrenia; 3. bipolar disorder; 4. social phobia; 5. dissociative amnesia; 6. borderline personality disorder; 7. sexual dysfunctions; 8. obsessive-compulsive disorder

Section Three: Fill in the Blank   1. biological; 2. positive; 3. delusion; 4. negative; 5. major depressive disorder; 6. manic; 7. somatoform; 8. panic; 9. persistent involuntary thoughts, persistent impulsive urge; 10. conversion; 11. dissociative identity; 12. personality; 13. gender identity; 14. Hallucinations; 15. phobia; 16. antisocial

Section Four: Comprehensive Practice Test   1. c; 2. b; 3. d; 4. b; 5. true; 6. b; 7. a; 8. false; 9. d; 10. b; 11. true; 12. d; 13. c; 14. true; 15. d; 16. c; 17. true; 18. b

Chapter 13

Section One: Chapter Review   1. d; 2. Gestalt; 3. Person-centered; 4. Psychodynamic; 5. c; 6. c; 7. false; 8. operant; 9. b; 10. d; 11. (1) c (2) b (3) a (4) d; 12. c; 13. false; 14. b; 15. d; 16. true; 17. (1) c (2) b (3) a (4) c (5) c; 18. b; 19. d; 20. a; 21. false; 22. false; 23. c; 24. are; 25. b; 26. (1) a (2) c (3) b (4) c

Section Two: Identify the Therapy   1. e; 2. a; 3. d; 4. f; 5. b; 6. g; 7. c

Section Three: Fill in the Blank   1. psychological, biological; 2. transference; 3. directive; 4. interpersonal; 5. family; 6. self-help group; 7. operant; 8. behavior modification; 9. cognitive behavior; 10. schizophrenia; 11. depression; 12. bipolar disorder; 13. suicidal depression; 14. clinical; 15. free association; 16. time out; 17. lobotomy; 18. gender-based prejudices

Section Four: Comprehensive Practice Test   1. c; 2. c; 3. c; 4. false; 5. d; 6. a; 7. b; 8. a; 9. a; 10. b; 11. b; 12. a; 13. c; 14. a; 15. b; 16. d; 17. c; 18. true; 19. false; 20. false

Chapter 14

Section One: Chapter Review   1. d; 2. b; 3. true; 4. (1) c (2) b (3) a; 5. true; 6. false; 7. c; 8. c; 9. b; 10. (1) c (2) a (3) b; 11. c;

12. a; 13. false; 14. c; 15. d; 16. true; 17. b; 18. true; 19. true; 20. b; 21. true; 22. true; 23. false; 24. false; 25. true; 26. b; 27. c; 28. c; 29. false; 30. true; 31. (1) b (2) a (3) c; 32. c; 33. false; 34. true

Section Two: Match Terms with Definitions   1. f; 2. e; 3. b; 4. a; 5. h; 6. i; 7. l; 8. j; 9. k; 10. m; 11. d; 12. g; 13. c

Section Three: Fill in the Blank   1. attitude; 2. primacy effect; 3. dispositional; 4. situational, dispositional; 5. self-serving bias; 6. halo; 7. obedience; 8. social facilitation; 9. extreme; 10. stereotype; 11. bystander; 12. altruism; 13. frustration-aggression; 14. Scapegoating; 15. attribution; 16. Conformity

Section Four: Comprehensive Practice Test   1. d; 2. false; 3. c; 4. b; 5. false; 6. d; 7. c; 8. true; 9. b; 10. false; 11. b; 12. c; 13. c; 14. b; 15. c; 16. true; 17. b; 18. true; 19. a

Glossary

absolute threshold The minimum amount of sensory stimulation that can be detected 50% of the time.

accommodation In vision, the flattening and bulging action of the lens as it focuses images of objects on the retina. In learning, the process by which existing schemes are modified and new schemes are created to incorporate new objects, events, experiences, or information.

acetylcholine (ah-SEET-ul-KOH-leen) A neurotransmitter that plays a role in learning new information, causes the skeletal muscle fibers to contract, and keeps the heart from beating too rapidly.

achievement motivation Factors that move people to seek success in academic settings.

acquired immune deficiency syndrome (AIDS) A devastating and incurable illness that is caused by infection with the human immun-odeficiency virus (HIV) and progressively weakens the body's immune system, leaving the person vulnerable to opportunistic infections that usually cause death.

action potential The sudden reversal of the resting potential, which initiates the firing of a neuron.

activation-synthesis hypothesis of dreaming The hypothesis that dreams are the brain's attempt to make sense of the random firing of brain cells during REM sleep.

actor-observer effect The tendency to attribute one's own behavior primarily to situational factors and the behavior of others primarily to dispositional factors.

adolescence The developmental stage that begins at puberty and encompasses the period from the end of childhood to the beginning of adulthood.

adrenal glands (ah-DREE-nal) A pair of endocrine glands that release hormones that prepare the body for emergencies and stressful situations and also release corticoids and small amounts of the sex hormones.

aerobic exercise Exercise that uses the large muscle groups in continuous, repetitive action and increases oxygen intake and breathing and heart rates.

affective neuroscience The study of the neurological foundations of emotion.

afterimage A visual sensation that remains after a stimulus is withdrawn.

aggression The intentional infliction of physical or psychological harm on others.

agoraphobia (AG-or-uh-FO-bee-ah) An intense fear of being in a situation from which escape is not possible or in which help would not be available if one experienced overwhelming anxiety or a panic attack.

alarm stage The first stage of the general adaptation syndrome, in which the person experiences a burst of energy that aids in dealing with the stressful situation.

algorithm A systematic, step-by-step procedure, such as a mathematical formula, that guarantees a solution to a problem of a certain type if applied appropriately and executed properly.

alpha wave The brain-wave pattern associated with deep relaxation.

altered state of consciousness Changes in awareness produced by sleep, meditation, hypnosis, and drugs.

alternative medicine Any treatment or therapy that has not been scientifically demonstrated to be effective.

altruism Behavior that is aimed at helping another, requires some self-sacrifice, and is not performed for personal gain.

Alzheimer's disease (ALZ-hye-mers) An incurable form of dementia characterized by progressive deterioration of intellect and personality, resulting from widespread degeneration of brain cells.

amnesia A partial or complete loss of memory due to loss of consciousness, brain damage, or some psychological cause.

amplitude The measure of the loudness of a sound; expressed in the unit called the decibel.

amygdala (ah-MIG-da-la) A structure in the limbic system that plays an important role in emotion, particularly in response to unpleasant or punishing stimuli.

analogy heuristic A rule of thumb that applies a solution that solved a problem in the past to a current problem that shares many features with the past problem.

anchoring Overestimation of the importance of a factor by focusing on it to the exclusion of other relevant factors.

anorexia nervosa An eating disorder characterized by an overwhelming, irrational fear of gaining weight or becoming fat, compulsive dieting to the point of self-starvation, and excessive weight loss.

anterograde amnesia The inability to form long-term memories of events occurring after a brain injury or brain surgery, although memories formed before the trauma are usually intact and short-term memory is unaffected.

antidepressant drugs Drugs that act as mood elevators for people with severe depression and are also prescribed to treat some anxiety disorders.

antipsychotic drugs Drugs used to control severe psychotic symptoms, such as delusions, hallucinations, disorganized speech, and disorganized behavior, by inhibiting dopamine activity; also known as neuroleptics.

anxiety disorders Psychological disorders characterized by frequent fearful thoughts about what might happen in the future.

aphasia (uh-FAY-zyah) A loss or impairment of the ability to use or understand language, resulting from damage to the brain.

applied research Research conducted specifically to solve practical problems and improve the quality of life.

approach-approach conflict A conflict arising from having to choose between equally desirable alternatives.

approach-avoidance conflict   A conflict arising when the same choice has both desirable and undesirable features.

aptitude test   A test designed to predict a person's achievement or performance at some future time.

archetype   (AR-ka-type) Existing in the collective unconscious, an inherited tendency to respond to universal human situations in particular ways.

arousal   A state of alertness and mental and physical activation.

arousal theory   A theory of motivation suggesting that people are motivated to maintain an optimal level of alertness and physical and mental activation.

artificial intelligence   The programming of computer systems to simulate human thinking in solving problems and in making judgments and decisions.

artificial neural networks (ANNs)   Computer systems that are intended to mimic human cognitive functioning.

assimilation   The process by which new objects, events, experiences, or information is incorporated into existing schemes.

association areas   Areas of the cerebral cortex that house memories and are involved in thought, perception, and language.

attachment   The strong affectionate bond a child forms with the mother or primary caregiver.

attention   The process of sorting through sensations and selecting some of them for further processing.

attitude   A relatively stable evaluation of a person, object, situation, or issue, along a continuum ranging from positive to negative.

attribution   An assignment of a cause to explain one's own or another's behavior.

audience effects   The impact of passive spectators on performance.

audition   The sensation and process of hearing.

authoritarian parents   Parents who make arbitrary rules, expect unquestioned obedience from their children, punish transgressions, and value obedience to authority.

authoritative parents   Parents who set high but realistic standards, reason with the child, enforce limits, and encourage open communication and independence.

autobiographical memories   Recollections that a person includes in an account of the events of his or her own life.

automacity   The ability to recall information from long-term memory without effort.

availability heuristic   A cognitive rule of thumb that says that the perceived probability of an event or the importance assigned to it is based on its availability in memory.

aversion therapy   A behavior therapy in which an aversive stimulus is paired with a harmful or socially undesirable behavior until the behavior becomes associated with pain or discomfort.

avoidance learning   Learning to avoid events or conditions associated with aversive consequences or phobias.

avoidance-avoidance conflict   A conflict arising from having to choose between undesirable alternatives.

axon   (AK-sahn) The slender, tail-like extension of the neuron that transmits signals to the dendrites or cell body of other neurons and to muscles, glands, and other parts of the body.

axon terminal   Bulbous end of the axon where signals move from one end of the axon of one neuron to the dendrites or cell body of another.

babbling   Vocalization of the basic speech sounds (phonemes), which begins between 4 and 6 months.

bacterial STDs   Sexually transmitted diseases that are caused by bacteria and can be treated with antibiotics.

basic emotions   Emotions that are unlearned and universal, that are reflected in the same facial expressions across cultures, and that emerge in children according to their biological timetable of development; fear, anger, disgust, surprise, happiness, and sadness are usually considered basic emotions.

basic research   Research conducted to seek new knowledge and to explore and advance general scientific understanding.

behavior modification   A method of changing behavior through a systematic program based on the learning principles of classical conditioning, operant conditioning, or observational learning. An approach to therapy that uses learning principles to eliminate inappropriate or maladaptive behaviors and replace them with more adaptive responses.

behavior therapy   A treatment approach that is based on the idea that abnormal behavior is learned and that applies the principles of operant conditioning, classical conditioning, and/or observational learning to eliminate inappropriate or maladaptive behaviors and replace them with more adaptive responses.

behavioral genetics   A field of research that uses twin studies and adoption studies to investigate the relative effects of heredity and environment on behavior.

behaviorism   The school of psychology that views observable, measurable behavior as the appropriate subject matter for psychology and emphasizes the key role of environment as a determinant of behavior.

beta wave   (BAY-tuh) The brain-wave pattern associated with mental or physical activity.

binocular depth cues   Depth cues that depend on both eyes working together.

biofeedback   The use of sensitive equipment to give people precise feedback about internal physiological processes so that they can learn, with practice, to exercise control over them.

biological psychology   The school of psychology that looks for links between specific behaviors and equally specific biological processes that often help explain individual differences.

biological therapy   A therapy (drug therapy, electroconvulsive therapy, or psychosurgery) that is based on the assumption that psychological disorders are symptoms of underlying physical problems.

biomedical model   A perspective that explains illness solely in terms of biological factors.

biopsychosocial model   A perspective that focuses on health as well as illness and holds that both are determined by a combination of biological, psychological, and social factors.

bipolar disorder   A mood disorder in which manic episodes alternate with periods of depression, usually with relatively normal periods in between.

blind spot   The point in each retina where there are no rods or cones because the cable of ganglion cells is extending through the retinal wall.

body mass index (BMI)   A measure of weight relative to height.

bottom-up processing   Information processing in which individual components or bits of data are combined until a complete perception is formed.

brainstem   The structure that begins at the point where the spinal cord enlarges as it enters the brain and handles functions critical to physical survival. It includes the medulla, the pons, and the reticular formation.

brightness   The intensity of light energy perceived as a color; based on amplitude of light wave.

Broca's aphasia   (BRO-kuz uh-FAY-zyah) An impairment in the physical ability to produce speech sounds or, in extreme cases, an inability to speak at all; caused by damage to Broca's area.

Broca's area   (BRO-kuz) The area in the frontal lobe, usually in the left hemisphere, that controls the production of speech sounds.

bulimia nervosa   An eating disorder characterized by repeated and uncontrolled (and often secretive) episodes of binge eating.

bystander effect   A social factor that affects prosocial behavior: As the number of bystanders at an emergency increases, the probability that the victim will receive help decreases, and the help, if given, is likely to be delayed.

California Personality Inventory (CPI)   A highly regarded personality test developed especially for typical individuals aged 13 and older.

Cannon-Bard theory   The theory that an emotion-provoking stimulus is transmitted simultaneously to the cerebral cortex, providing the conscious mental experience of the emotion, and to the sympathetic nervous system, causing the physiological arousal.

case study   A descriptive research method in which a single individual or a small number of persons are studied in great depth.

catatonic schizophrenia   (KAT-uh-TAHN-ik) A type of schizophrenia characterized by complete stillness or stupor or great excitement and agitation; patients may assume an unusual posture and remain in it for long periods of time.

causal hypothesis   A prediction about a cause–effect relationship between two or more variables.

cell body   The part of a neuron that contains the nucleus and carries out the metabolic functions of the neuron.

central nervous system (CNS)   The part of the nervous system comprising the brain and the spinal cord.

cerebellum   (sehr-uh-BELL-um) The brain structure that helps the body execute smooth, skilled movements and regulates muscle tone and posture.

cerebral cortex   (seh-REE-brul KOR-tex) The gray, convoluted covering of the cerebral hemispheres that is responsible for the higher mental processes of language, memory, and thinking.

cerebral hemispheres   (seh-REE-brul) The right and left halves of the cerebrum, covered by the cerebral cortex and connected by the corpus callosum; they control movement and feeling on the opposing sides of the body.

cerebrum   (seh-REE-brum) The largest structure of the human brain, consisting of the two cerebral hemispheres connected by the corpus callosum and covered by the cerebral cortex.

chromosomes   Rod-shaped structures in the nuclei of body cells, which contain all the genes and carry all the genetic information necessary to make a human being.

chunking   A memory strategy that involves grouping or organizing bits of information into larger units, which are easier to remember.

circadian rhythm   (sur-KAY-dee-un) Within each 24-hour period, the regular fluctuation from high to low points of certain bodily functions and behaviors.

circadian theory of sleep   The theory that sleep evolved to keep humans out of harm's way during the night; also known as the evolutionary or adaptive theory.

classical conditioning   A type of learning through which an organism learns to associate one stimulus with another.

co-action effects   The impact on performance of the presence of other people engaged in the same task.

cochlea   (KOK-lee-uh) The fluid-filled, snail-shaped, bony chamber in the inner ear that contains the basilar membrane and its hair cells (the sound receptors).

cognition   The mental processes that are involved in acquiring, storing, retrieving, and using information and that include sensation, perception, imagery, concept formation, reasoning, decision making, problem solving, and language.

cognitive dissonance   The unpleasant state that can occur when people become aware of inconsistencies between their attitudes or between their attitudes and their behavior.

cognitive map   A mental representation of a spatial arrangement such as a maze.

cognitive processes   (COG-nih-tiv) Mental processes such as thinking, knowing, problem solving, remembering, and forming mental representations.

cognitive psychology   The school of psychology that sees humans as active participants in their environment; studies mental processes such as memory, problem solving, reasoning, decision making, perception, language, and other forms of cognition.

cognitive therapies   Therapies that assume maladaptive behavior can result from irrational thoughts, beliefs, and ideas.

cognitive therapy   A therapy designed by Aaron Beck to help clients stop their negative thoughts as they occur and replace them with more objective thoughts.

collective unconscious   In Jung's theory, the most inaccessible layer of the unconscious, which contains the universal experiences of humankind.

color blindness   The inability to distinguish certain colors from one another.

compliance   Acting in accordance with the wishes, suggestions, or direct requests of other people.

compulsion   A persistent, irresistible, and irrational urge to perform an act or ritual repeatedly.

concept   A mental category used to represent a class or group of objects, people, organizations, events, situations, or relations that share common characteristics or attributes.

conditioned response (CR)   The learned response that comes to be elicited by a conditioned stimulus as a result of its repeated pairing with an unconditioned stimulus.

conditioned stimulus (CS)   A neutral stimulus that, after repeated pairing with an unconditioned stimulus, becomes associated with it and elicits a conditioned response.

conditions of worth   Conditions on which the positive regard of others rests.

cones The light-sensitive receptor cells in the retina that enable humans to see color and fine detail in adequate light but do not function in very dim light.

confederate A person who poses as a participant in an experiment but is actually assisting the experimenter.

conformity Changing or adopting a behavior or an attitude in an effort to be consistent with the social norms of a group or the expectations of other people.

confounding variables Factors other than the independent variable(s) that are unequal across groups.

conscious (KON-shus) The thoughts, feelings, sensations, or memories of which a person is aware at any given moment.

consciousness Everything of which we are aware at any given time—our thoughts, feelings, sensations, and external environment.

conservation The concept that a given quantity of matter remains the same despite being rearranged or changed in appearance, as long as nothing is added or taken away.

consolidation A physiological change in the brain that allows encoded information to be stored in memory.

consolidation failure Any disruption in the consolidation process that prevents a long-term memory from forming.

context effect The tendency to encode elements of the physical setting in which information is learned along with memory of the information itself.

control group In an experiment, a group similar to the experimental group that is exposed to the same experimental environment but is not given the treatment; used for purposes of comparison.

conventional level Kohlberg's second level of moral development, in which right and wrong are based on the internalized standards of others; "right" is whatever helps or is approved of by others, or whatever is consistent with the laws of society.

conversion disorder A somatoform disorder in which a person experiences a loss of motor or sensory functioning in some part of the body; the loss has no physical cause but solves some psychological problem.

coping Efforts through action and thought to deal with demands that are perceived as taxing or overwhelming.

cornea (KOR-nee-uh) The tough, transparent, protective layer that covers the front of the eye and bends light rays inward through the pupil.

corpus callosum (KOR-pus kah-LO-sum) The thick band of nerve fibers that connects the two cerebral hemispheres and makes possible the transfer of information and the synchronization of activity between the hemispheres.

correlation coefficient A numerical value that indicates the strength and direction of the relationship between two variables; ranges from +1.00 (a perfect positive correlation) to −1.00 (a perfect negative correlation).

correlational method A research method used to establish the degree of relationship (correlation) between two characteristics, events, or behaviors.

creativity The ability to produce original, appropriate, and valuable ideas and/or solutions to problems.

critical period A period so important to development that a harmful environmental influence at that time can keep a bodily structure from developing normally or can impair later intellectual or social development.

critical thinking The process of objectively evaluating claims, propositions, and conclusions to determine whether they follow logically from the evidence presented.

cross-modal perception A process whereby the brain integrates information from more than one sense.

crowding The subjective judgment that there are too many people in a confined space.

crystallized intelligence Aspects of intelligence involving verbal ability and accumulated knowledge which tend to increase over the lifespan.

CT scan (computerized axial tomography) A brain-scanning technique that uses a rotating, computerized X-ray tube to produce cross-sectional images of the structures of the brain.

culturally sensitive therapy An approach to therapy in which knowledge of clients' cultural backgrounds guides the choice of therapeutic interventions.

culture-fair intelligence test An intelligence test that uses questions that will not penalize those whose culture differs from the mainstream or dominant culture.

curve of forgetting The pattern of forgetting discovered by Ebbinghaus which shows that forgetting tapers off after a period of rapid information loss that immediately follows learning.

decay theory The oldest theory of forgetting, which holds that memories, if not used, fade with time and ultimately disappear altogether.

decibel (dB) (DES-ih-bel) A unit of measurement for the loudness of sounds.

decision making The process of considering alternatives and choosing among them.

declarative memory The subsystem within long-term memory that stores facts, information, and personal life events that can be brought to mind verbally or in the form of images and then declared or stated; also called explicit memory.

defense mechanism A means used by the ego to defend against anxiety and to maintain self-esteem.

delusion A false belief, not generally shared by others in the culture.

delusion of grandeur A false belief that one is a famous person or a powerful or important person who has some great knowledge, ability, or authority.

delusion of persecution A false belief that some person or agency is trying in some way to harm one.

dementia A state of mental deterioration characterized by impaired memory and intellect and by altered personality and behavior.

dendrites (DEN-drytes) In a neuron, the branchlike extensions of the cell body that receive signals from other neurons.

dependent variable The factor or condition that is mea-sured at the end of an experiment and is presumed to vary as a result of the manipulations of the independent variable(s).

depressants A category of drugs that decrease activity in the central nervous system, slow down bodily functions, and reduce sensitivity to outside stimulation; also called "downers."

depth perception The ability to perceive the visual world in three dimensions and to judge distances accurately.

descriptive research methods Research methods that yield descriptions of behavior.

developmental psychology The study of how humans grow, develop, and change throughout the lifespan.

difference threshold A measure of the smallest increase or decrease in a physical stimulus that is required to produce a difference in sensation that is noticeable 50% of the time.

diffusion of responsibility The feeling among bystanders at an emergency that the responsibility for helping is shared by the group, making each person feel less compelled to act than if he or she alone bore the total responsibility.

directive therapy Any type of psychotherapy in which the therapist takes an active role in determining the course of therapy sessions and provides answers and suggestions to the client; an example is Gestalt therapy.

discrimination Behavior (usually negative) directed toward others based on their gender, religion, race, or membership in a particular group. The learned ability to distinguish between similar stimuli so that the conditioned response occurs only to the original conditioned stimulus but not to similar stimuli.

discriminative stimulus A stimulus that signals whether a certain response or behavior is likely to be rewarded, ignored, or punished.

disinhibitory effect Displaying a previously suppressed behavior because a model does so without receiving punishment.

disorganized schizophrenia The most serious type of schizophrenia, marked by extreme social withdrawal, hallucinations, delusions, silliness, inappropriate laughter, grotesque mannerisms, and other bizarre behavior.

displacement The event that occurs when short-term memory is filled to capacity and each new, incoming item pushes out an existing item, which is then forgotten.

display rules Cultural rules that dictate how emotions should generally be expressed and when and where their expression is appropriate.

dispositional attribution Attributing a behavior to some internal cause, such as a personal trait, motive, or attitude; an internal attribution.

dissociative amnesia A dissociative disorder in which there is a complete or partial loss of the ability to recall personal information or identify past experiences.

dissociative disorders Disorders in which, under unbearable stress, consciousness becomes dissociated from a person's identity or her or his memories of important personal events, or both.

dissociative fugue (FEWG) A dissociative disorder in which one has a complete loss of memory of one's entire identity, travels away from home, and may assume a new identity.

dissociative identity disorder (DID) A dissociative disorder in which two or more distinct, unique personalities occur in the same person, and there is severe memory disruption concerning personal information about the other personalities.

divergent thinking The ability to produce multiple ideas, answers, or solutions to a problem for which there is no agreed-on solution.

dominant-recessive pattern A set of inheritance rules in which the presence of a single dominant gene causes a trait to be expressed but two genes must be present for the expression of a recessive trait.

door-in-the-face technique A strategy in which someone makes a large, unreasonable request with the expectation that the person will refuse but will then be more likely to respond favorably to a smaller request later.

dopamine (DOE-pah-meen) A neurotransmitter that plays a role in learning, attention, movement, and reinforcement.

double-blind technique A procedure in which neither the participants nor the experimenter knows who is in the experimental and control groups until after the data have been gathered; a control for experimenter bias.

drive An internal state of tension or arousal that is brought about by an underlying need and that an organism is motivated to reduce.

drive-reduction theory A theory of motivation suggesting that biological needs create internal states of tension or arousal—called drives—which organisms are motivated to reduce.

drug tolerance A condition in which the user becomes progressively less affected by the drug and must take increasingly larger doses to maintain the same effect or high.

DSM-IV *Diagnostic and Statistical Manual of Mental Disorders,* 4th edition, a manual published by the American Psychiatric Association, which describes the criteria used to classify and diagnose mental disorders.

ego (EE-go) In Freud's theory, the logical, rational, largely conscious system of personality, which operates according to the reality principle.

elaborative rehearsal A memory strategy that involves relating new information to something that is already known.

electroconvulsive therapy (ECT) A biological therapy in which an electric current is passed through the right hemisphere of the brain; usually reserved for patients with severe depression who are suicidal.

electroencephalogram (EEG) (ee-lek-tro-en-SEFF-uh-lo-gram) A record of brain-wave activity made by a machine called the electroencephalograph.

elicitation effect Exhibiting a behavior similar to that shown by a model in an unfamiliar situation.

elimination by aspects A decision-making approach in which alternatives are evaluated against criteria that have been ranked according to importance.

embryo The developing human organism during the period (week 3 through week 8) when the major systems, organs, and structures of the body develop.

emotion A state involving physiological arousal, a cognitive appraisal of the situation that produced the state, and an outward behavior expressing the state.

emotional intelligence The ability to apply knowledge about emotions to everyday life.

emotion-focused coping A response involving reappraisal of a stressor to reduce its emotional impact.

encoding The process of transforming information into a form that can be stored in memory.

encoding failure A cause of forgetting that occurs when information was never put into long-term memory.

endocrine system (EN-duh-krin) A system of ductless glands in various parts of the body that manufacture hormones and secrete them into the bloodstream, thus affecting cells in other parts of the body.

endorphins (en-DOR-fins) The body's own natural painkillers, which block pain and produce a feeling of well-being. Chemicals produced naturally by the brain that reduce pain and the stress of vigorous exercise and positively affect mood.

epinephrine (EP-ih-NEF-rin) A neurotransmitter that affects the metabolism of glucose and nutrient energy stored in muscles to be released during strenuous exercise.

episodic memory (ep-ih-SOD-ik) The type of declarative memory that records events as they have been subjectively experienced.

ethnocentrism The tendency to look at situations from one's own racial or cultural perspective.

evolutionary psychology The school of psychology that studies how humans have adapted the behaviors required for survival in the face of environmental pressures over the long course of evolution.

exemplars The individual instances, or examples, of a concept that are stored in memory from personal experience.

exhaustion stage The third stage of the general adaptation syndrome, which occurs if the organism fails in its efforts to resist the stressor.

expectancy theory An approach that explains work motivation in terms of workers' beliefs about the effectiveness and value of the effort they put forth on the job.

experimental group In an experiment, the group that is exposed to an independent variable.

experimental method The only research method that can be used to identify cause-effect relationships between two or more conditions or variables.

experimenter bias A phenomenon that occurs when a researcher's preconceived notions or expectations in some way influence participants' behavior and/or the researcher's interpretation of experimental results.

expert systems Computer programs designed to carry out highly specific functions within a limited domain.

expertise An extensive amount of background knowledge that is relevant to a reconstructive memory task.

exposure and response prevention A behavior therapy that exposes patients with obsessive-compulsive disorder to stimuli that trigger obsessions and compulsive rituals, while patients resist performing the compulsive rituals for progressively longer periods of time.

extinction In classical conditioning, the weakening and eventual disappearance of the conditioned response as a result of repeated presentation of the conditioned stimulus without the unconditioned stimulus. In operant conditioning, the weakening and eventual disappearance of the conditioned response as a result of the withholding of reinforcement.

extrasensory perception (ESP) Gaining information about objects, events, or another person's thoughts through some means other than the known sensory channels.

extrinsic motivation The desire to behave in a certain way to gain some external reward or to avoid some undesirable consequence.

facial-feedback hypothesis The idea that the muscular movements involved in certain facial expressions produce the corresponding emotions (for example, smiling makes one feel happy).

family therapy Therapy involving an entire family, with the goal of helping family members reach agreement on changes that will help heal the family unit, improve communication problems, and create more understanding and harmony within the group.

feature detectors Neurons in the brain that respond only to specific visual patterns (for example, to lines or angles).

fetal alcohol syndrome A condition, caused by maternal alcohol intake during pregnancy, in which the baby is born mentally retarded, with a small head and facial, organ, and behavioral abnormalities.

fetus The developing human organism during the period (week 9 until birth) when rapid growth and further development of the structures, organs, and systems of the body occur.

fight-or-flight response A response to stress in which the sympathetic nervous system and the endocrine glands prepare the body to fight or flee.

five-factor theory A mode that describes personality using five broad dimensions, each of which is composed of a constellation of personality traits.

fixation Arrested development at a psychosexual stage occurring because of excessive gratification or frustration at that stage.

fixed-interval schedule A schedule in which a reinforcer is given following the first correct response after a specific period of time has elapsed.

fixed-ratio schedule A schedule in which a reinforcer is given after a fixed number of correct, nonreinforced responses.

flashbulb memories Memories for shocking, emotion-provoking events that include information about the source from which the information was required.

flooding A behavior therapy based on classical conditioning and used to treat phobias by exposing clients to the feared object or event (or asking them to imagine it vividly) for an extended period, until their anxiety decreases.

fluid intelligence Aspects of intelligence involving abstract reasoning and mental flexibility, which peak in the early 20s and decline slowly as people age.

foot-in-the-door technique A strategy designed to gain a favorable response to a small request at first, with the intent of making the person more likely to agree later to a larger request.

forgetting The inability to bring to mind information that was previously remembered.

formal concept A concept that is clearly defined by a set of rules, a formal definition, or a classification system.

fovea (FO-vee-uh) A small area at the center of the retina that provides the clearest and sharpest vision because it has the largest concentration of cones.

framing The way information is presented so as to emphasize either a potential gain or a potential loss as the outcome.

free association A psychoanalytic technique used to explore the unconscious by having patients reveal whatever thoughts, feelings, or images come to mind.

frequency The number of cycles completed by a sound wave in one second, determining the pitch of the sound; expressed in the unit called the hertz.

frequency theory The theory of hearing that holds that hair cell receptors vibrate the same number of times per second as the sounds that reach them.

frontal lobes The largest of the brain's lobes, which contain the motor cortex, Broca's area, and the frontal association areas.

frustration-aggression hypothesis The hypothesis that frustration produces aggression.

functional fixedness The failure to use familiar objects in novel ways to solve problems because of a tendency to view objects only in terms of their customary functions.

functional MRI (fMRI) A brain-imaging technique that reveals both brain structure and brain activity more precisely and rapidly than PET.

functionalism An early school of psychology that was concerned with how humans and animals use mental processes in adapting to their environment.

fundamental attribution error The tendency to give more attention to dispositional factors than is appropriate for a situation.

***g* factor** Spearman's term for a general intellectual ability that underlies all mental operations to some degree.

GABA Primary inhibitory neurotransmitter in the brain.

gender identity disorder Sexual disorder characterized by a problem accepting one's identity as male or female.

gender roles Cultural expectations about the behavior appropriate for each gender.

gender-sensitive therapy An approach to therapy that takes into account the effects of gender on both the therapist's and the client's behavior.

general adaptation syndrome (GAS) The predictable sequence of reactions (alarm, resistance, and exhaustion stages) that organisms show in response to stressors.

generalization In classical conditioning, the tendency to make a conditioned response to a stimulus that is similar to the original conditioned stimulus. In operant conditioning, the tendency to make the learned response to a stimulus similar to that for which the response was originally reinforced.

generalized anxiety disorder An anxiety disorder in which people experience chronic, excessive worry for 6 months or more.

genes The segments of DNA that are located on the chromosomes and are the basic units for the transmission of all hereditary traits.

Gestalt (geh-SHTALT) A German word that roughly refers to the whole form, pattern, or configuration that a person perceives.

Gestalt psychology The school of psychology that emphasizes that individuals perceive objects and patterns as whole units and that the perceived whole is more than the sum of its parts.

Gestalt therapy A therapy that was originated by Fritz Perls and that emphasizes the importance of clients' fully experiencing, in the present moment, their feelings, thoughts, and actions and then taking responsibility for them.

glial cells (GLEE-ul) Specialized cells in the brain and spinal cord that support neurons, remove waste products such as dead neurons, and perform other manufacturing, nourishing, and cleanup tasks.

glutamate (GLOO-tah-mate) Primary excitatory neurotransmitter in the brain.

goal orientation theory The view that achievement motivation depends on which of four goal orientations (mastery/approach, mastery/avoidance, performance/approach, performance/avoidance) an individual adopts.

goal setting An approach to work motivation that involves establishing specific, difficult goals rather than simply telling people to do their best in the absence of assigned goals.

gonads The ovaries in females and the testes in males; endocrine glands that produce sex hormones.

group polarization A group member's adoption of a more extreme position about an issue than she originally held after participating in a discussion in which other group members strongly express agreement with her.

group therapy A form of therapy in which several clients (usually 7 to 10) meet regularly with one or more therapists to resolve personal problems.

groupthink The tendency for members of a tightly knit group to be more concerned with preserving group solidarity and uniformity than with objectively evaluating all alternatives in decision making.

gustation The sense of taste.

hair cells Sensory receptors for hearing that are attached to the basilar membrane in the cochlea.

hallucination An imaginary sensation.

hallucinogens (hal-LU-sin-o-jenz) A category of drugs that can alter and distort perceptions of time and space, alter mood, produce feelings of unreality, and cause hallucinations; also called *psychedelics.*

halo effect The tendency to assume that a person has generally positive or negative traits as a result of observing one major positive or negative trait.

hardiness A combination of three psychological qualities—commitment, control, and challenge—shared by people who can handle high levels of stress and remain healthy.

hassles Irritating demands that occur daily, and may cause more stress than major life changes do.

health psychology The subfield within psychology that is concerned with the psychological factors that contribute to health, illness, and recovery.

heritability An index of the degree to which a characteristic is estimated to be influenced by heredity.

heuristic (yur-RIS-tik) A rule of thumb that is derived from experience and used in decision making and problem solving, even though there is no guarantee of its accuracy or usefulness.

higher-order conditioning Conditioning that occurs when conditioned stimuli are linked together to form a series of signals.

hippocampal region A part of the limbic system, which includes the hippocampus itself and the underlying cortical areas, involved in the formation of semantic memories.

hippocampus (hip-po-CAM-pus) A structure in the limbic system that plays a central role in the storing of new memories, the response to new or unexpected stimuli, and navigational ability.

homeostasis The natural tendency of the body to maintain a balanced internal state in an effort to ensure physical survival.

homophobia An intense, irrational hostility toward or fear of homosexuals.

hormone A chemical substance that is manufactured and released in one part of the body and affects other parts of the body.

hue The dimension of light that refers to the specific color perceived.

human immunodeficiency virus (HIV) The virus that causes AIDS.

humanistic psychology   The school of psychology that focuses on the uniqueness of human beings and their capacity for choice, growth, and psychological health.

humanistic therapies   Psychotherapies that assume that people have the ability and freedom to lead rational lives and make rational choices.

hypnosis   A procedure through which one person, the hypnotist, uses the power of suggestion to induce changes in thoughts, feelings, sensations, perceptions, or behavior in another person, the subject.

hypochondriasis   (HI-poh-kahn-DRY-uh-sis) A somatoform disorder in which persons are preoccupied with their health and fear that their physical symptoms are a sign of some serious disease, despite reassurance from doctors to the contrary.

hypothalamus   (HY-po-THAL-uh-mus) A small but influential brain structure that regulates hunger, thirst, sexual behavior, internal body temperature, other body functions, and a wide variety of emotional behaviors.

hypothesis   A testable prediction about the conditions under which a particular behavior or mental process may occur.

hypothetico-deductive thinking   The ability to base logical reasoning on a hypothetical premise.

id   The unconscious system of the personality, which contains the life and death instincts and operates on the pleasure principle; source of the libido.

illusion   A false perception or a misperception of an actual stimulus in the environment.

imagery   The representation in the mind of a sensory experience—visual, auditory, gustatory, motor, olfactory, or tactile.

imaginary audience   A belief of adolescents that they are or will be the focus of attention in social situations and that others will be as critical or approving as they are of themselves.

impression formation   The mental process of developing opinions about other people.

impression management   The intentional steps we take to influence others' opinions of us.

inattentional blindness   The phenomenon in which we shift our focus from one object to another and, in the process, fail to notice changes in objects to which we are not directly paying attention.

incentive   An external stimulus that motivates behavior (for example, money or fame).

inclusion   Educating students with mental retardation by placing them in classes with nonhandicapped students for part or all of the day; also called *mainstreaming*.

independent variable   In an experiment, a factor or condition that is deliberately manipulated to determine whether it causes any change in another behavior or condition.

individualism/collectivism dimension   A measure of a culture's emphasis on either individual achievement or social relationships.

industrial/organizational (I/O) psychologists   Psychologists who apply their knowledge in the workplace and are especially interested in work motivation and job performance.

infantile amnesia   The relative inability of older children and adults to recall events from the first few years of life.

information-processing theory   An approach to the study of mental structures and processes that uses the computer as a model for human thinking.

in-group   A social group with a strong sense of togetherness, from which others are excluded.

inhibitory effect   Suppressing a behavior because a model is punished for displaying the behavior.

inner ear   The innermost portion of the ear, containing the cochlea, the vestibular sacs, and the semicircular canals.

insight   The sudden realization of the relationship between elements in a problem situation, which makes the solution apparent.

insight therapies   Approaches to psychotherapy based on the notion that psychological well-being depends on self-understanding.

insomnia   A sleep disorder characterized by difficulty falling or staying asleep, by waking too early, or by sleep that is light, restless, or of poor quality.

intelligence   An individual's ability to understand complex ideas, to adapt effectively to the environment, to learn from experience, to engage in various forms of reasoning, and to overcome obstacles through mental effort.

intelligence quotient (IQ)   An index of intelligence, originally derived by dividing mental age by chronological age and then multiplying by 100, but now derived by comparing an individual's score with the scores of others of the same age.

interference   A cause of forgetting that occurs because information or associations stored either before or after a given memory hinder the ability to remember it.

interpersonal therapy (IPT)   A brief psychotherapy designed to help people with depression better understand and cope with problems relating to their interpersonal relationships.

intrinsic motivation   The desire to behave in a certain way because it is enjoyable or satisfying in and of itself.

intuition   Rapidly formed judgments based on "gut feelings" or "instincts."

inventory   A paper-and-pencil test with questions about a person's thoughts, feelings, and behaviors, which measures several dimensions of personality and can be scored according to a standard procedure.

James-Lange theory   The theory that emotional feelings result when an individual becomes aware of a physiological response to an emotion-provoking stimulus (for example, feeling fear because of trembling).

just noticeable difference (JND)   The smallest change in sensation that a person is able to detect 50% of the time.

kinesthetic sense   The sense providing information about the position and movement of body parts.

laboratory observation   A descriptive research method in which behavior is studied in a laboratory setting.

language   A means of communicating thoughts and feelings, using a system of socially shared but arbitrary symbols (sounds, signs, or written symbols) arranged according to rules of grammar.

latent content   Freud's term for the underlying meaning of a dream.

latent learning   Learning that occurs without apparent reinforcement and is not demonstrated until the organism is motivated to do so.

lateral hypothalamus (LH) The part of the hypothalamus that acts as a feeding center to incite eating.

lateralization The specialization of one of the cerebral hemispheres to handle a particular function.

law of effect One of Thorndike's laws of learning, which states that the consequence, or effect, of a response will determine whether the tendency to respond in the same way in the future will be strengthened or weakened.

Lazarus theory The theory that a cognitive appraisal is the first step in an emotional response and all other aspects of an emotion, including physiological arousal, depend on it.

learned helplessness A passive resignation to aversive conditions that is learned through repeated exposure to inescapable or unavoidable aversive events.

learning A relatively permanent change in behavior, knowledge, capability, or attitude that is acquired through experience and cannot be attributed to illness, injury, or maturation.

left hemisphere The hemisphere that controls the right side of the body, coordinates complex movements, and, in most people, handles most of the language functions.

lens The transparent disk-shaped structure behind the iris and the pupil that changes shape as it focuses on objects at varying distances.

levels-of-processing model The memory model that describes maintenance rehersal as "shallow" processing and elaborative rehearsal as "deep" processing.

life events approach The view that a person's state of well-being can be threatened by major life changes.

limbic system A group of structures in the brain, including the amygdala and hippocampus, that are collectively involved in emotional expression, memory, and motivation.

linguistic relativity hypothesis The notion that the language a person speaks largely determines the nature of that person's thoughts.

lithium A drug used to treat bipolar disorder, which at proper maintenance dosage reduces both manic and depressive episodes.

locus of control Rotter's concept of a cognitive factor that explains how people account for what happens in their lives—either seeing themselves as primarily in control of their behavior and its consequences (internal locus of control) or perceiving what happens to them to be in the hands of fate, luck, or chance (external locus of control).

long-term memory (LTM) The memory system with a virtually unlimited capacity that contains vast stores of a person's permanent or relatively permanent memories.

long-term potentiation (LTP) An increase in the efficiency of neural transmission at the synapses that lasts for hours or longer.

low-ball technique A strategy in which someone makes a very attractive initial offer to get a person to commit to an action and then makes the terms less favorable.

low-birth-weight baby A baby weighing less than 5.5 pounds.

lucid dream A dream that an individual is aware of dreaming and whose content the individual is often able to influence while the dream is in progress.

lymphocytes The white blood cells—including B cells and T cells—that are the key components of the immune system.

maintenance rehearsal Repeating information over and over again until it is no longer needed; may eventually lead to storage of information in long-term memory.

major depressive disorder A mood disorder marked by feelings of great sadness, despair, and hopelessness as well as the loss of the ability to experience pleasure.

manic episode (MAN-ik) A period of excessive euphoria, inflated self-esteem, wild optimism, and hyperactivity, often accompanied by delusions of grandeur and by hostility if activity is blocked.

manifest content Freud's term for the content of a dream as recalled by the dreamer.

massed practice Learning in one long practice session without rest periods.

matching hypothesis The notion that people tend to have lovers or spouses who are similar to themselves in physical attractiveness and other assets.

maturation Changes that occur according to one's genetically determined biological timetable of development.

means-end analysis A heuristic strategy in which the current position is compared with the desired goal and a series of steps are formulated and taken to close the gap between them.

meditation A group of techniques that involve focusing attention on an object, a word, one's breathing, or one's body movements in an effort to block out all distractions, to enhance well-being, and to achieve an altered state of consciousness.

medulla (muh-DUL-uh) The part of the brainstem that controls heartbeat, blood pressure, breathing, coughing, and swallowing.

memory The process of encoding, storage, and retrieval of information.

menarche (men-AR-kee) The onset of menstruation.

menopause The cessation of menstruation, occurring between ages 45 and 55 and signifying the end of reproductive capacity.

mental set The tendency to apply a familiar strategy to the solution of a problem without carefully considering the special requirements of that problem.

mentally retarded Subnormal intelligence reflected by an IQ below 70 and by adaptive functioning severely deficient for one's age.

mere-exposure effect The tendency to feel more positively toward a stimulus as a result of repeated exposure to it.

metabolic rate (meh-tuh-BALL-ik) The rate at which the body burns calories to produce energy.

microelectrode A small wire used to monitor the electrical activity of or stimulate activity within a single neuron.

middle ear The portion of the ear containing the ossicles, which connect the eardrum to the oval window and amplify sound waves.

Minnesota Multiphasic Personality Inventory (MMPI) The most extensively researched and widely used personality test, which is used to screen for and diagnose psychiatric problems and disorders; revised as MMPI-2.

misinformation effect Erroneous recollections of witnessed events that result from information learned after the fact.

model The individual who demonstrates a behavior or whose behavior is imitated.

modeling Another name for observational learning.

modeling effect   Learning a new behavior from a model through the acquisition of new responses.

monocular depth cues   (mah-NOK-yu-ler) Depth cues that can be perceived by one eye alone.

mood disorders   Disorders characterized by extreme and unwarranted disturbances in emotion or mood.

morphemes   The smallest units of meaning in a language.

motivated forgetting   Forgetting through suppression or repression in an effort to protect oneself from material that is painful, frightening, or otherwise unpleasant.

motivation   All the processes that initiate, direct, and sustain behavior.

motives   Needs or desires that energize and direct behavior toward a goal.

motor cortex   The strip of tissue at the rear of the frontal lobes that controls voluntary body movement and participates in learning and cognitive events.

MRI (magnetic resonance imagery)   A diagnostic scanning technique that produces high-resolution images of the structures of the brain.

multifactorial inheritance   A pattern of inheritance in which a trait is influenced by both genes and environmental factors.

myelin sheath   (MY-uh-lin) The white, fatty coating wrapped around some axons that acts as insulation and enables impulses to travel much faster.

Myers-Briggs Type Indicator (MBTI)   A personality inventory useful for measuring individual differences; based on Jung's theory of personality.

naive idealism   A type of thought in which adolescents construct ideal solutions for problems.

naive subject   A person who has agreed to participate in an experiment but is not aware that deception is being used to conceal its real purpose.

narcolepsy   An incurable sleep disorder characterized by excessive daytime sleepiness and uncontrollable attacks of REM sleep.

narcotics   A class of depressant drugs derived from the opium poppy that produce both pain-relieving and calming effects.

natural concept   A concept acquired not from a definition but through everyday perceptions and experiences.

naturalistic observation   A descriptive research method in which researchers observe and record behavior in its natural setting, without attempting to influence or control it.

nature-nurture controversy   The debate over whether intelligence and other traits are primarily the result of heredity or environment.

need for achievement   (*n* Ach) The need to accomplish something difficult and to perform at a high standard of excellence.

negative reinforcement   The termination of an unpleasant condition after a response, which increases the probability that the response will be repeated.

neodissociation theory of hypnosis   A theory proposing that hypnosis induces a split, or dissociation, between two aspects of the control of consciousness: the planning function and the monitoring function.

neonate   A newborn infant up to 1 month old.

neuron   (NEW-ron) A specialized cell that conducts impulses through the nervous system.

neuroscience   An interdisciplinary field that combines the work of psychologists, biologists, biochemists, medical researchers, and others in the study of the structure and function of the nervous system.

neurotransmitters   Specialized chemicals that facilitate or inhibit the transmission of impulses from one neuron to the next.

nondeclarative memory   The subsystem within long-term memory that stores motor skills, habits, and simple classically conditioned responses; also called implicit memory.

nondirective therapy   Any type of psychotherapy in which the therapist allows the direction of the therapy sessions to be controlled by the client; an example is person-centered therapy.

norepinephrine   (nor-EP-ih-NEF-rin) A neurotransmitter affecting eating, alertness, and sleep.

norms   Aged-based averages.

NREM dream   A type of dream occurring during NREM sleep that is typically less frequent and memorable than REM dreams are.

NREM sleep   Non–rapid eye movement sleep, which consists of four sleep stages and is characterized by slow, regular respiration and heart rate, little body movement, an absence of rapid eye movements, and blood pressure and brain activity that are at their 24-hour low points.

obedience   Behaving in accordance with the rules and commands of those in authority.

obesity   BMI over 30.

object permanence   The realization that objects continue to exist, even when they can no longer be perceived.

observational learning   Learning by observing the behavior of others and the consequences of that behavior; learning by imitation.

obsession   A persistent, involuntary thought, image, or impulse that invades consciousness and causes great distress.

obsessive-compulsive disorder (OCD)   An anxiety disorder in which a person has recurrent obsessions and/or compulsions.

occipital lobes   (ahk-SIP-uh-tul) The lobes that are involved in the reception and interpretation of visual information; they contain the primary visual cortex.

Oedipus complex   (ED-uh-pus) Occurring in the phallic stage, a conflict in which the child is sexually attracted to the opposite-sex parent and feels hostility toward the same-sex parent.

olfaction   (ol-FAK-shun) The sense of smell.

olfactory bulbs   Two matchstick-sized structures above the nasal cavities, where smell sensations first register in the brain.

olfactory epithelium   Two 1-square-inch patches of tissue, one at the top of each nasal cavity, which together contain about 10 million olfactory neurons, the receptors for smell.

operant   A voluntary behavior that accidentally brings about a consequence.

operant conditioning   A type of learning in which the consequences of behavior are manipulated so as to increase or decrease the frequency of an existing response or to shape an entirely new response.

opponent-process theory   The theory of color vision suggesting that three kinds of cells respond by increasing or decreasing their rate of firing when different colors are present.

optic nerve   The nerve that carries visual information from each retina to both sides of the brain.

outer ear   The visible part of the ear, consisting of the pinna and the auditory canal.

out-group   A social group made up of individuals specifically identified by the in-group as not belonging.

overextension   The act of using a word, on the basis of some shared feature, to apply to a broader range of objects than is appropriate.

overlearning   Practicing or studying material beyond the point where it can be repeated once without error.

overregularization   The act of inappropriately applying the grammatical rules for forming plurals and past tenses to irregular nouns and verbs.

pancreas   The endocrine gland responsible for regulating the amount of sugar in the bloodstream.

panic attack   An episode of overwhelming anxiety, fear, or terror.

panic disorder   An anxiety disorder in which a person experiences recurring, unpredictable episodes of overwhelming anxiety, fear, or terror.

paranoid schizophrenia   (PAIR-uh-noid) A type of schizophrenia characterized by delusions of grandeur or persecution.

paraphilias   Sexual disorders in which recurrent sexual urges, fantasies, or behavior involve nonhuman objects, children, other nonconsenting persons, or the suffering or humiliation of the individual or his or her partner.

parasomnias   Sleep disturbances in which behaviors and physiological states that normally take place only in the waking state occur while a person is sleeping.

parasympathetic nervous system   The division of the autonomic nervous system that brings the heightened bodily responses back to normal following an emergency.

parathyroid glands   The endocrine glands that produce PTH, a hormone that helps the body absorb minerals from the diet.

parental investment   A term used by evolutionary psychologists to denote the amount of time and effort men or women must devote to parenthood.

parietal lobes   (puh-RY-uh-tul) The lobes that contain the somatosensory cortex (where touch, pressure, temperature, and pain register) and other areas that are responsible for body awareness and spatial orientation.

participant modeling   A behavior therapy in which an appropriate response to a feared stimulus is modeled in graduated steps and the client attempts to imitate the model step by step, encouraged and supported by the therapist.

participant-related bias   A type of bias in which a study's participants are not representative of the population to which results will be generalized.

perception   The process by which the brain actively organizes and interprets sensory information.

perceptual constancy   The phenomenon that allows us to perceive objects as maintaining stable properties, such as size, shape, and brightness, despite differences in distance, viewing angle, and lighting.

perceptual set   An expectation of what will be perceived, which can affect what actually is perceived.

peripheral nervous system (PNS)   (peh-RIF-er-ul) The nerves connecting the central nervous system to the rest of the body.

permeability   (perm-ee-uh-BIL-uh-tee) The capability of being penetrated or passed through.

permissive parents   Parents who make few rules or demands and allow children to make their own decisions and control their own behavior.

personal fable   An exaggerated sense of personal uniqueness and indestructibility, which may be the basis for adolescent risk taking.

personal space   An area surrounding each person, much like an invisible bubble, that the person considers part of himself or herself and uses to regulate the level of intimacy with others.

personal unconscious   In Jung's theory, the layer of the unconscious that contains all of the thoughts, perceptions, and experiences accessible to the conscious, as well as repressed memories, wishes, and impulses.

personality   A person's characteristic patterns of behaving, thinking, and feeling.

personality disorder   A long-standing, inflexible, maladaptive pattern of behaving and relating to others, which usually begins in early childhood or adolescence.

person-centered therapy   A nondirective, humanistic therapy developed by Carl Rogers, in which the therapist creates an accepting climate and shows empathy, freeing clients to be themselves and releasing their natural tendency toward self-actualization.

persuasion   A deliberate attempt to influence the attitudes and/or behavior of another person.

PET scan (positron-emission tomography)   A brain-imaging technique that reveals activity in various parts of the brain, based on patterns of blood flow, oxygen use, and glucose consumption.

phobia   (FO-bee-ah) A persistent, irrational fear of some specific object, situation, or activity that poses little or no real danger.

phonemes   The smallest units of sound in a spoken language.

physical drug dependence   A compulsive pattern of drug use in which the user develops a drug tolerance coupled with unpleasant withdrawal symptoms when the drug use is discontinued.

pineal gland   The endocrine gland that secretes the hormone that controls the sleep/wakefulness cycle.

pituitary gland   The endocrine gland located in the brain that releases hormones that activate other endocrine glands as well as growth hormone; often called the "master gland."

place theory   The theory of hearing that holds that each individual pitch a person hears is determined by the particular location along the basilar membrane of the cochlea that vibrates the most.

placebo   (pluh-SEE-bo) An inert or harmless substance given to the control group in an experiment as a control for the placebo effect.

placebo effect   The phenomenon that occurs in an experiment when a participant's response to a treatment is due to his or her expectations about the treatment rather than to the treatment itself.

plasticity   The capacity of the brain to adapt to changes such as brain damage.

polygenic inheritance   A pattern of inheritance in which many genes influence a trait.

population The entire group of interest to researchers, to which they wish to generalize their findings; the group from which a sample is selected.

positive bias The tendency for pleasant autobiographical memories to be more easily recalled than unpleasant ones and memories of unpleasant events to become more emotionally positive over time.

positive psychology The view that psychologists should study and promote the development of human strengths such as optimism.

positive reinforcement Any pleasant or desirable consequence that follows a response and increases the probability that the response will be repeated.

postconventional level Kohlberg's highest level of moral development, in which moral reasoning involves weighing moral alternatives; "right" is whatever furthers basic human rights.

posttraumatic stress disorder (PTSD) A prolonged and severe stress reaction to a catastrophic event or to severe, chronic stress.

pragmatics The patterns of intonation and social roles associated with a language.

preconscious The thoughts, feelings, and memories that a person is not consciously aware of at the moment but that may be easily brought to consciousness.

preconventional level Kohlberg's lowest level of moral development, in which moral reasoning is based on the physical consequences of an act; "right" is whatever avoids punishment or gains a reward.

prejudice Attitudes (usually negative) toward others based on their gender, religion, race, or membership in a particular group.

prenatal development Development from conception to birth.

presbyopia (prez-bee-O-pee-uh) A condition, occurring in the mid- to late 40s, in which the lenses of the eyes no longer accommodate adequately for near vision, and reading glasses or bifocals are required for reading.

preterm infant An infant born before the 37th week and weighing less than 5.5 pounds; a premature infant.

primacy effect The tendency for an overall impression of another to be influenced more by the first information that is received about that person than by information that comes later. The tendency to recall the first items in a sequence more readily than the middle items.

primary appraisal A cognitive evaluation of a potentially stressful event to determine whether its effect is positive, irrelevant, or negative.

primary auditory cortex The part of each temporal lobe where hearing registers in the cerebral cortex.

primary drives States of tension or arousal that arise from a biological need and are unlearned.

primary mental abilities According to Thurstone, seven relatively distinct capabilities that singly or in combination are involved in all intellectual activities.

primary reinforcer A reinforcer that fulfills a basic physical need for survival and does not depend on learning.

primary visual cortex The area at the rear of the occipital lobes where vision registers in the cerebral cortex. The part of the brain in which visual information is processed.

proactive coping Active measures taken in advance of a potentially stressful situation in order to prevent its occurrence or to minimize its consequences.

problem solving Thoughts and actions required to achieve a desired goal that is not readily attainable.

problem-focused coping A direct response aimed at reducing, modifying, or eliminating a source of stress.

projective test A personality test in which people respond to inkblots, drawings of ambiguous human situations, or incomplete sentences by projecting their inner thoughts, feelings, fears, or conflicts onto the test materials.

prosocial behavior Behavior that benefits others, such as helping, cooperation, and sympathy.

prospective forgetting Not remembering to carry out some intended action.

prototype An example that embodies the most common and typical features of a concept.

proximity Physical or geographic closeness; a major influence on attraction.

pruning The process through which the developing brain eliminates unnecessary or redundant synapses.

psychiatrist A mental health professional who is a medical doctor.

psychoactive drug Any substance that alters mood, perception, or thought; called a controlled substance if approved for medical use.

psychoanalysis (SY-ko-ah-NAL-ih-sis) The term Freud used for both his theory of personality and his therapy for the treatment of psychological disorders; the unconscious is the primary focus of psychoanalytic theory. The first psychodynamic therapy, which was developed by Freud and uses free association, dream analysis, and transference.

psychodynamic therapies Psychotherapies that attempt to uncover repressed childhood experiences that are thought to explain a patient's current difficulties.

psycholinguistics The study of how language is acquired, produced, and used and how the sounds and symbols of language are translated into meaning.

psychological disorders Mental processes and/or behavior patterns that cause emotional distress and/or substantial impairment in functioning.

psychological drug dependence A craving or irresistible urge for a drug's pleasurable effects.

psychological perspectives General points of view used for explaining people's behavior and thinking, whether normal or abnormal.

psychologist A mental health professional who possesses a doctoral degree in psychology.

psychology The scientific study of behavior and mental processes.

psychoneuroimmunology (sye-ko-NEW-ro-IM-you-NOLL-oh-gee) A field in which psychologists, biologists, and medical researchers combine their expertise to study the effects of psychological factors on the immune system.

psychosexual stages A series of stages through which the sexual instinct develops; each stage is defined by an erogenous zone around which conflict arises.

psychosis (sy-CO-sis) A condition characterized by loss of contact with reality.

psychosocial stages Erikson's eight developmental stages for the entire lifespan; each is defined by a conflict that must be resolved satisfactorily for healthy personality development to occur.

psychosurgery Brain surgery performed to alleviate serious psychological disorders or unbearable chronic pain.

psychotherapy Any type of approach that uses psychological rather than biological means to treat psychological disorders.

puberty A period of rapid physical growth and change that culminates in sexual maturity.

punishment The removal of a pleasant stimulus or the application of an unpleasant stimulus, thereby lowering the probability of a response.

random assignment The process of selecting participants for experimental and control groups by using a chance procedure to guarantee that each participant has an equal probability of being assigned to any of the groups; a control for selection bias.

rational emotive therapy A directive form of psychotherapy, developed by Albert Ellis and designed to challenge clients' irrational beliefs about themselves and others.

realistic conflict theory The view that as competition increases among social groups for scarce resources, so do prejudice, discrimination, and hatred.

recall A memory task in which a person must produce required information by searching memory.

recency effect The tendency to recall the last items in a sequence more readily than those in the middle.

receptors Protein molecules on the surfaces of dendrites and cell bodies that have distinctive shapes and will interact only with specific neurotransmitters.

reciprocal determinism Bandura's concept of a mutual influential relationship among behavior, cognitive factors, and environment.

recognition A memory task in which a person must simply identify material as familiar or as having been encountered before.

recognition heuristic A strategy in which decision making stops as soon as a factor that moves one toward a decision has been recognized.

reconstruction An account of an event that has been pieced together from a few highlights.

reflexes Built-in responses to certain stimuli that neonates need to ensure survival in their new world.

rehearsal The act of purposely repeating information to maintain it in short-term memory.

reinforcement Any event that follows a response and strengthens or increases the probability that the response will be repeated.

reinforcer Anything that follows a response and strengthens it or increases the probability that it will occur.

relationship therapies Therapies that attempt to improve clients' interpersonal relationships or create new relationships to support clients' efforts to address psychological problems.

relearning method A measure of memory in which retention is expressed as the percentage of time saved when material is relearned compared with the time required to learn the material originally.

reliability The ability of a test to yield nearly the same score when the same people are tested and then retested on the same test or an alternative form of the test.

REM dream A type of dream occurring almost continuously during each REM period and having a storylike quality; typically more vivid, visual, and emotional than NREM dreams.

REM rebound The increased amount of REM sleep that occurs after REM deprivation; often associated with unpleasant dreams or nightmares.

REM sleep A type of sleep characterized by rapid eye movements, paralysis of large muscles, fast and irregular heart and respiration rates, increased brain-wave activity, and vivid dreams.

replication The process of repeating a study with different participants and preferably a different investigator to verify research findings.

representative sample A sample that mirrors the population of interest; it includes important subgroups in the same proportions as they are found in that population.

representative heuristic A thinking strategy based on how closely a new object or situation is judged to resemble or match an existing prototype of that object or situation.

repression Completely removing unpleasant memories from one's consciousness, so that one is no longer aware that a painful event occurred.

resistance stage The second stage of the general adaptation syndrome, when there are intense physiological efforts to either resist or adapt to the stressor.

resting potential The slight negative electrical potential of the axon membrane of a neuron at rest, about −70 millivolts.

restorative theory of sleep The theory that the function of sleep is to restore body and mind.

reticular formation A structure in the brainstem that plays a crucial role in arousal and attention and that screens sensory messages entering the brain.

retina The layer of tissue that is located on the inner surface of the eyeball and contains the sensory receptors for vision.

retrieval The process of bringing to mind information that has been stored in memory.

retrieval cue Any stimulus or bit of information that aids in retrieving particular information from long-term memory.

retrieval failure Not remembering something one is certain of knowing.

retrograde amnesia (RET-ro-grade) A loss of memory for experiences that occurred shortly before a loss of consciousness.

reuptake The process by which neurotransmitters are taken from the synaptic cleft back into the axon terminal for later use, thus terminating their excitatory or inhibitory effect on the receiving neuron.

reversibility The realization that any change in the shape, position, or order of matter can be reversed mentally.

right hemisphere The hemisphere that controls the left side of the body and, in most people, is specialized for visual-spatial perception.

risk/resilience model A perspective that proposes that risk and protective factors interact to produce or protect us from illness.

rods   The light-sensitive receptor cells in the retina that look like slender cylinders and allow the eye to respond to as few as five photons of light.

Rorschach Inkblot Method   (ROR-shok) A projective test composed of 10 inkblots that the test taker is asked to describe; used to assess personality, make differential diagnoses, plan and evaluate treatment, and predict behavior.

sample   A part of a population that is studied to reach conclusions about the entire population.

saturation   The purity of a color, or the degree to which the light waves producing it are of the same wavelength.

scaffolding   A type of instruction in which an adult adjusts the amount of guidance provided to match a child's present level of ability.

scapegoating   Displacing aggression onto members of minority groups or other innocent targets not responsible for the frustrating situation.

Schachter-Singer theory   A two-factor theory stating that for an emotion to occur, there must be (1) physiological arousal and (2) a cognitive interpretation or explanation of the arousal, allowing it to be labeled as a specific emotion.

schedule of reinforcement   A systematic process for administering reinforcement.

schemas   Frameworks of knowledge and assumptions we have about people, objects, and events.

scheme   Plans of action, based on previous experiences, to be used in similar circumstances.

schizophrenia   (SKIT-soh-FREE-nee-ah) A severe psychological disorder characterized by loss of contact with reality, hallucinations, delusions, inappropriate or flat affect, some disturbance in thinking, social withdrawal, and/or other bizarre behavior.

scientific method   The orderly, systematic procedures that researchers follow as they identify a research problem, design a study to investigate the problem, collect and analyze data, draw conclusions, and communicate their findings.

secondary appraisal   A cognitive evaluation of available resources and options prior to deciding how to deal with a stressor.

secondary reinforcer   A reinforcer that is acquired or learned through association with other reinforcers.

secondary sex characteristics   Those physical characteristics that are not directly involved in reproduction but distinguish the mature male from the mature female.

selection bias   The assignment of participants to experimental or control groups in such a way that systematic differences among the groups are present at the beginning of the experiment.

self-actualization   Developing to one's fullest potential.

self-efficacy   The perception a person has of his or her ability to perform competently whatever is attempted.

self-esteem   A person's sense of self-worth.

self-serving bias   The tendency to attribute one's successes to dispositional causes and one's failures to situational causes.

semantic memory   The type of declarative memory that stores general knowledge, or objective facts and information.

semantics   The meaning or the study of meaning derived from morphemes, words, and sentences.

semicircular canals   Three fluid-filled tubular canals in the inner ear that sense the rotation of the head.

sensation   The process through which the senses pick up visual, auditory, and other sensory stimuli and transmit them to the brain.

sensory adaptation   The process in which sensory receptors grow accustomed to constant, unchanging levels of stimuli over time.

sensory memory   The memory system that holds information from the senses for a period of time ranging from only a fraction of a second to about 2 seconds.

sensory receptors   Highly specialized cells in the sense organs that detect and respond to one type of sensory stimulus light, sound, or odor, for example—and transduce (convert) the stimuli into neural impulses.

separation anxiety   The fear and distress shown by a toddler when the parent leaves, occurring from 8 to 24 months and reaching a peak between 12 and 18 months.

serial position effect   The finding that, for information learned in a sequence, recall is better for the beginning and ending items than for the middle items in the sequence.

serotonin   (ser-oh-TOE-nin) A neurotransmitter that plays an important role in regulating mood, sleep, impulsivity, aggression, and appetite.

set point   The weight the body normally maintains when one is trying neither to gain nor to lose weight.

sexual disorders   Disorders with a sexual basis that are destructive, guilt- or anxiety-producing, compulsive, or a cause of discomfort or harm to one or both parties involved.

sexual dysfunctions   Persistent, recurrent, and distressing problems involving sexual desire, arousal, or the pleasure associated with sex or orgasm.

sexual orientation   The direction of one's sexual preference—toward members of the opposite sex (heterosexuality), toward one's own sex (homosexuality), or toward both sexes (bisexuality).

sexual response cycle   The four phases—excitement, plateau, orgasm, and resolution—that make up the human sexual response in both males and females, according to Masters and Johnson.

sexually transmitted diseases   Infections that are spread primarily through intimate sexual contact.

shaping   An operant conditioning technique that consists of gradually molding a desired behavior (response) by reinforcing any movement in the direction of the desired response, thereby gradually guiding the responses toward the ultimate goal.

short-term memory (STM)   The memory system that codes information according to sound and holds about seven (from five to nine) items for less than 30 seconds without rehearsal; also called working memory.

situational attribution   Attributing a behavior to some external cause or factor operating within the situation; an external attribution.

Skinner box   A soundproof chamber with a device for delivering food to an animal subject; used in operant conditioning experiments.

sleep apnea   A sleep disorder characterized by periods during sleep when breathing stops and the individual must awaken briefly to breathe.

sleep cycle   A period of sleep lasting about 90 minutes and including one or more stages of NREM sleep, followed by REM sleep.

sleep spindles   Sleep Stage 2 brain waves that feature short periods of calm interrupted by brief flashes of intense activity.

slow-wave sleep   Deep sleep; associated with Stage 3 and Stage 4 sleep.

social cognition   The process of attending to, interpreting, and remembering information about ourselves and others.

social facilitation   Any positive or negative effect on performance that can be attributed to the presence of others, either as an audience or as co-actors.

social loafing   The tendency to put forth less effort when working with others on a common task than when working alone.

social motives   Motives (such as the needs for affiliation and achievement) that are acquired through experience and interaction with others.

social norms   The attitudes and standards of behavior expected of members of a particular group.

social phobia   An irrational fear and avoidance of any social or performance situation in which one might embarrass or humiliate oneself in front of others by appearing clumsy, foolish, or incompetent.

social psychology   The subfield that attempts to explain how the actual, imagined, or implied presence of others influences the thoughts, feelings, and behavior of individuals.

Social Readjustment Rating Scale (SRRS)   Holmes and Rahe's measure of stress, which ranks 43 life events from most to least stressful and assigns a point value to each.

social roles   Socially defined behaviors considered appropriate for individuals occupying certain positions within a given group.

social support   Tangible and/or emotional support provided in time of need by family members, friends, and others; the feeling of being loved, valued, and cared for by those toward whom we feel a similar obligation.

socialization   The process of learning socially acceptable behaviors, attitudes, and values.

sociocognitive theory of hypnosis   A theory suggesting that the behavior of a hypnotized person is a function of that person's expectations about how subjects behave under hypnosis.

sociocultural approach   The view that social and cultural factors may be just as powerful as evolutionary and physiological factors in affecting behavior and mental processing and that these factors must be understood when interpreting the behavior of others.

somatoform disorders   (so-MAT-uh-form) Disorders in which physical symptoms are present that are due to psychological causes rather than any known medical condition.

somatosensory cortex   (so-MAT-oh-SENS-or-ee) The strip of tissue at the front of the parietal lobes where touch, pressure, temperature, and pain register in the cerebral cortex.

source memory   A recollection of the circumstances in which you formed a memory.

source monitoring   Intentionally keeping track of the sources of incoming information.

spaced practice   Learning in short practice sessions with rest periods in between.

specific phobia   A marked fear of a specific object or situation; a general label for any phobia other than agoraphobia and social phobia.

spinal cord   An extension of the brain, from the base of the brain through the neck and spinal column, that transmits messages between the brain and the peripheral nervous system.

split-brain operation   A surgical procedure, performed to treat severe cases of epilepsy, in which the corpus callosum is cut, separating the cerebral hemispheres.

spontaneous recovery   The reappearance of an extinguished response (in a weaker form) when an organism is exposed to the original conditioned stimulus following a rest period.

SQ3R method   A study method involving the following five steps: (1) survey, (2) question, (3) read, (4) recite, and (5) review.

Stage 4 sleep   The deepest stage of NREM sleep, characterized by an EEG pattern of more than 50% delta waves.

standardization   Establishing norms for comparing the scores of people who will take a test in the future; administering tests using a prescribed procedure.

state-dependent memory effect   The tendency to recall information better if one is in the same pharmacological or psychological state as when the information was encoded.

stereotypes   Widely shared beliefs about the characteristic traits, attitudes, and behaviors of members of various social groups (racial, ethnic, or religious), including the assumption that the members of such groups are usually all alike.

stimulants   A category of drugs that speed up activity in the central nervous system, suppress appetite, and can cause a person to feel more awake, alert, and energetic; also called "uppers."

stimulus   (STIM-yu-lus) Any event or object in the environment to which an organism responds; plural is *stimuli*.

stimulus motives   Motives that cause humans and other animals to increase stimulation when the level of arousal is too low (examples are curiosity and the motive to explore).

storage   The process of keeping or maintaining information in memory.

stranger anxiety   A fear of strangers common in infants at about 6 months and increasing in intensity until about 12 months, and then declining in the second year.

stress   The physiological and psychological response to a condition that threatens or challenges a person and requires some form of adaptation or adjustment.

stressor   Any stimulus or event capable of producing physical or emotional stress.

stroke   An event in the cardiovascular system in which a blood clot or plug of fat blocks an artery and cuts off the blood supply to a particular area of the brain.

structuralism   The first formal school of thought in psychology, aimed at analyzing the basic elements, or structure, of conscious mental experience.

subjective night   The time during a 24-hour period when the biological clock is telling a person to go to sleep.

subliminal perception   The capacity to perceive and respond to stimuli that are presented below the threshold of awareness.

substance abuse   Continued use of a substance that affects an individual's work, education, and social relationships.

substantia nigra (sub-STAN-sha NI-gra) The structure in the mid-brain that controls unconscious motor movements.

successful aging Maintaining one's physical health, mental abilities, social competence, and overall satisfaction with life as one gets older.

successive approximations A series of gradual steps, each of which is more similar to the final desired response.

superego (sue-per-EE-go) The moral system of the personality, which consists of the conscience and the ego ideal.

suprachiasmatic nucleus (SCN) A pair of tiny structures in the brain's hypothalamus that control the timing of circadian rhythms; the biological clock.

survey A descriptive research method in which researchers use interviews and/or questionnaires to gather information about the attitudes, beliefs, experiences, or behaviors of a group of people.

symbolic function The understanding that one thing—an object, a word, a drawing—can stand for another.

sympathetic nervous system The division of the autonomic nervous system that mobilizes the body's resources during stress and emergencies, preparing the body for action.

synapse (SIN-aps) The junction where the axon terminal of a sending neuron communicates with a receiving neuron across the synaptic cleft.

synesthesia The capacity for experiencing unusual sensations along with ordinary ones.

syntax The aspect of grammar that specifies the rules for arranging and combining words to form phrases and sentences.

systematic desensitization A behavior therapy that is based on classical conditioning and used to treat fears by training clients in deep muscle relaxation and then having them confront a graduated series of anxiety-producing situations (real or imagined) until they can remain relaxed while confronting even the most feared situation.

tactile Pertaining to the sense of touch.

taste aversion The intense dislike and/or avoidance of a particular food that has been associated with nausea or discomfort.

taste buds Structures in many of the tongue's papillae that are composed of 60 to 100 receptor cells for taste.

telegraphic speech Short sentences that follow a strict word order and contain only essential content words.

temperament A person's behavioral style or characteristic way of responding to the environment.

temporal lobes The lobes that are involved in the reception and interpretation of auditory information; they contain the primary auditory cortex, Wernicke's area, and the temporal association areas.

teratogens Harmful agents in the prenatal environment, which can have a negative impact on prenatal development or even cause birth defects.

thalamus (THAL-uh-mus) The structure, located above the brainstem, that acts as a relay station for information flowing into or out of the forebrain.

Thematic Apperception Test (TAT) A projective test consisting of drawings of ambiguous human situations, which the test taker describes; thought to reveal inner feelings, conflicts, and motives, which are projected onto the test materials.

theory A general principle or set of principles proposed to explain how a number of separate facts are related.

theory of dissociated control The theory that hypnosis weakens the control that the executive function exerts over other subsystems of consciousness.

thymus gland The endocrine gland that produces hormones that are essential to immune system functioning.

thyroid gland The endocrine gland that produces thyroxine and regulates metabolism.

timbre (TAM-burr) The distinctive quality of a sound that distinguishes it from other sounds of the same pitch and loudness.

time out A behavior modification technique used to eliminate undesirable behavior, especially in children and adolescents, by withdrawing all reinforcers for a period of time.

token economy A behavior modification technique that motivates and rewards appropriate behavior with tokens that can be exchanged later for desired goods or privileges.

top-down processing Information processing in which previous experience and conceptual knowledge are applied to recognize the whole of a perception and thus easily identify the simpler elements of that whole.

trait A personal characteristic that is stable across situations and is used to describe or explain personality.

transduction The process through which sensory receptors convert the sensory stimulation into neural impulses.

transference An emotional reaction that occurs during psychoanalysis, in which the patient displays feelings and attitudes toward the analyst that were present in another significant relationship.

triarchic theory of intelligence Sternberg's theory that there are three types of intelligence: componential (analytical), experiential (creative), and contextual (practical).

trichromatic theory The theory of color vision suggesting that three types of cones in the retina each make a maximal chemical response to one of three colors—blue, green, or red.

Type A behavior pattern A behavior pattern marked by a sense of time urgency, impatience, excessive competitiveness, hostility, and anger; considered a risk factor in coronary heart disease.

Type B behavior pattern A behavior pattern marked by a relaxed, easygoing approach to life, without the time urgency, impatience, and hostility of the Type A pattern.

unconditional positive regard Unqualified caring and nonjudgmental acceptance of another.

unconditioned response (UR) A response that is elicited by an unconditioned stimulus without prior learning.

unconditioned stimulus (US) A stimulus that elicits a specific unconditioned response without prior learning.

unconscious (un-KON-shus) For Freud, the primary motivating force of human behavior, containing repressed memories as well as instincts, wishes, and desires that have never been conscious.

underextension Restricting the use of a word to only a few, rather than to all, members of a class of objects.

undifferentiated schizophrenia A catch-all term used when schizophrenic symptoms either do not conform to the criteria of any one type of schizophrenia or conform to more than one type.

uplifts The positive experiences in life, which may neutralize the effects of many hassles.

validity The ability of a test to measure what it is intended to measure.

variable Any condition or factor that can be manipulated, controlled, or measured.

variable-interval schedule A schedule in which a reinforcer is given after the first correct response that follows a varying time of nonreinforcement, based on an average time.

variable-ratio schedule A schedule in which a reinforcer is given after a varying number of nonreinforced responses, based on an average ratio.

ventromedial hypothalamus (VMH) The part of the hypothalamus that acts as a satiety (fullness) center to inhibit eating.

vestibular sense (ves-TIB-yu-ler) The sense that provides information about the body's orientation in space.

viral STDs Sexually transmitted diseases that are caused by viruses and are considered to be incurable.

visible spectrum The narrow band of electromagnetic waves that are visible to the human eye.

visual cliff An apparatus used to test depth perception in infants.

wavelength A measure of the distance from the peak of a light wave to the peak of the next.

Weber's law The law stating that the just noticeable difference (JND) for all the senses depends on a proportion or percentage of change in a stimulus rather than on a fixed amount of change.

Wernicke's aphasia (VUR-nih-keys) Aphasia that results from damage to Wernicke's area and in which the person's speech is fluent and clearly articulated but does not make sense to listeners.

Wernicke's area The language area in the left temporal lobe involved in comprehending the spoken word and in formulating coherent speech and written language.

withdrawal symptoms The physical and psychological symptoms that occur when a regularly used drug is discontinued and that terminate when the drug is taken again.

work motivation The conditions and processes responsible for the arousal, direction, magnitude, and maintenance of effort of workers on the job.

working backward A heuristic strategy in which a person discovers the steps needed to solve a problem by defining the desired goal and working backward to the current condition; also called *backward search*.

working memory The memory subsystem that we use when we try to understand information, remember it, or use it to solve a problem or communicate with someone.

Yerkes-Dodson law The principle that performance on tasks is best when the arousal level is appropriate to the difficulty of the task: higher arousal for simple tasks, moderate arousal for tasks of moderate difficulty, and lower arousal for complex tasks.

zone of proximal development A range of cognitive tasks that a child cannot yet do but can learn to do through the guidance of an older child or adult.

zygote Cell that results from the union of a sperm and an ovum.

Name Index

Subject Index

early and middle adulthood, 266–270. *See also under* Social development
  body and mind change in, 266–267
  menopause, 266
  physical and cognitive changes, 266–267
  presbyopia, 266
Emotion, 302–309
  and brain, 304–306
  attitude and, 453–454
  Cannon–Bard theory, 303
  emotion-focused stress coping, 329
  expression of, 307–309
   basic emotions, 307
   display rules, 308
   facial expressions, 307–309
  gender differences in, 306–307
  James–Lange theory of emotion, 303
  Lazarus theory, 304
  neuroimaging of, 305
  positive psychology, 309
  Schachter–Singer theory, 304
  theories of, 303–304
  two-factor theory, 303
Emotional conditioning, 140–141
  'Little Albert' experiment, 140–141
  John Watson and, 140–141
Emotional intelligence, 230–231
  components of, 230–231
  interpersonal aspects, 230
  personal aspects, 230
Emotional quotient (EQ), 230
Empathy, 230
'Empty chair' technique, 412
Empty love, 445
Empty nest syndrome, 270
Encoding, 168
  failure, 183
Endocrine system, 58–59
  adrenal glands, 59
  glands, functions of, 58–60
  parathyroid glands, 58–59
  pineal gland, 58–59
  pituitary gland, 58–59
  thymus gland, 59
  thyroid gland, 58–59
Endorphins, 87, 254
Environment effects on personality traits, 363–364
Episodic memory, 174–175
Escaliers, 172
Escape learning, 151–152
Esteem needs, 290
Estrogen, 59, 188, 299
Ethnic group differences
  in health, 335
  in IQ scores, 226–227
   dynamic assessment, 227
   stereotype threat, 227
Ethnocentrism, 463
Evaluating research, 15–16
Evaluating theories, 15
Everyday stressors, 320–321
Evolutionary perspective, 13
Evolutionary psychology, 10
Evolutionary theory of dreaming, 119

Excitement phase, 299
Exemplars, 203
Exercise and health, 342–343
  aerobic exercise, 343
Exhaustion stage, 327
Existential intelligence, 217
Expectancy theory, 287–288, 291
Experiential intelligence, 217
Experimental groups, 23
Experimental method, 21–25
  causal hypothesis, 21
  control group, 23
  experimental group, 23
  experiments and hypothesis testing, 21–23
  limitations of, 23–25
   confounding variables, 24
   double-blind technique, 24
   experimenter bias, 24
   placebo effect, 24
   random assignment, 24
   selection bias, 24
  variable, 21
Experimental psychologists, 14
Experimenter bias, 24
Expert systems, 209
Expertise influencing reconstructive memory, 180–181
Explicit memory. *See* Declarative memory
Exposure, 416
Expression of emotion, 307–309. *See also under* Emotion
External cues, hunger, 291–292
External locus of control, 367
Extinction, 139–140, 145
Extrasensory perception (ESP), 98
Extraversion, 361, 362
Extrinsic motivation, 284–285
Eye function in vision, 74–7. *See also under* Vision
Eyewitness testimony, 191–192
  misinformation effect, 191
  reliability of, 191

F
Facial expressions, 307–309
Facilitation effect, observational learning, 157
Family therapy, 413
Fantasies, sexual, 300
Farsightedness (*hyperopia*), 74
Fatuous love, 445
Feeding center, 291
Fetal alcohol syndrome, 253
Fetus, 252
Fight-or-flight response, 44, 188, 303
  affecting health, 325–328
Figure–ground, 92
Five-factor model, 361–363
  agreeableness, 362
  conscientiousness, 361–362
  extraversion, 362
  gender differences in, 362
  neuroticism, 362
  openness, 361
Fixation, 353
Fixed-interval (FI) schedule, 148

Fixed-ratio (FR) schedule, 147
Flashbacks, 128
Flashbulb memories, 179
Flat affect, 395
Flooding, 416
  In vivo flooding, 416
Fluid intelligence, 267
Fluoxetine, 422
Flynn effect, 225
Foot-in-the-door technique, 448
Forebrain, 45–46
  cerebral cortex, 46
  cerebrum, 46
  corpus callosum, 46
  hippocampus, 48
  hypothalamus, 46–47
  limbic system, 46–47
  thalamus, 46–47
Forensic psychologists, 14
Forgetting, 182–186
  curve of forgetting, 182–183
  Ebbinghaus discovery, 182–183
  mastery, 182
  reason for, 183
   consolidation failure, 185
   decay, 183
   encoding failure, 183
   interference, 184
   motivated forgetting, 185
   prospective forgetting, 185
   repression, 185
   retrieval failure, 185
   suppression, 185
Formal academic knowledge, 217
Formal concepts, 203
Formal education, 245
Formal operational thinking, 251
Formal operations development stage, 242, 245
Fovea, 74–75
Fragile-X syndrome, 61
Frames of mind, 216
  Gardner's eight frames of mind, 216
   bodily-kinesthetic intelligence, 216
   interpersonal intelligence, 216
   intrapersonal intelligence, 216
   linguistic intelligence, 216
   logical-mathematical intelligence, 216
   musical intelligence, 216
   naturalistic intelligence, 216
   spatial intelligence, 216
Framing, 206, 208
Free association, 410
Frequency, 79
  frequency theory, 82
Frontal lobe, 53–54
  aphasia, 53
  Broca's aphasia, 53
  Broca's area, 53–54
  motor cortex, 53
Frustration-aggression hypothesis, 459
Full-scale IQ score, 221
Fully functioning person, 358
Functional fixedness, 208
Functional MRI (fMRI), 37

References

Aaltola, E. (2005). The politics and ethics of animal experimentation. *International Journal of Biotechnology, 7,* 234–249.

Abboud, T., Sarkis, F., Hung, T., Khoo, S., Varakian, L., Henriksen, E., Houehihed, R., & Goebelsmann, U. (1983). Effects of epidural anesthesia during labor on maternal plasma beta-endorphin levels. *Anesthesiology, 59,* 1–5.

Abraham, H., & Duffy, F. (2001). EEG coherence in post-LSD visual hallucinations. *Psychiatry Research: Neuroimaging, 107,* 151–163.

Abramowitz, J. S. (1997). Effectiveness of psychological and pharmacological treatments for obsessive-compulsive disorder: A quantitative review. *Journal of Consulting and Clinical Psychology, 65,* 44–52.

Abrams, D., Crisp, R., Marques, S., Fagg, E., Bedford, L., & Provias, D. (2008). Threat inoculation: Experienced and imagined intergenerational contact prevents stereotype threat effects on older people's math performance. *Psychology and Aging, 23,* 934–939.

Abrams, D., Wetherell, M., Cochrane, S., Hogg, M. A., & Turner, J. C. (1990). Knowing what to think by knowing who you are: Self-categorization and the nature of norm formation, conformity and group polarization. *British Journal of Social Psychology, 29*(Pt. 2), 97–119.

Achtman, R., Green, C., & Bavelier, D. (2008). Video games as a tool to train visual skills. *Restorative Neurology and Neuroscience, 26,* 435–436.

Adam, M., & Reyna, V. (2005). Coherence and correspondence criteria for rationality: Experts' estimation of risks of sexually transmitted infections. *Journal of Behavioral Decision Making, 18,* 169–186.

Adams, J. H., Graham, D. I., & Jennett, B. (2000). The neuropathology of the vegetative state after an acute brain insult. *Brain, 123,* 1327–1338.

Adams, R., and Boscarino, J. (2006). Predictors of PTSD and delayed PTSD after disaster: The impact of exposure and psychosocial resources. *Journal of Nervous and Mental Disease, 194,* 485–493.

Addis, M., & Mahalik, J. (2003). Men, masculinity, and the contexts of help seeking. *American Psychologist, 58,* 5–14.

Addis, M., Hatgis, C., Krasnow, A., Jacob, K., Bourne, L., & Mansfield, A. (2004). Effectiveness of cognitive-behavioral treatment for panic disorder versus treatment as usual in a managed care setting. *Journal of Consulting & Clinical Psychology, 72,* 625–635.

Ader, R. (2000). On the development of psychoneuroimmunology. *European Journal of Pharmacology, 405,* 167–176.

Adesman, A. (1996). Fragile X syndrome. In A. Capute & P. Accardo (Eds.). *Developmental disabilities in infancy and childhood* (2nd ed., Vol. 2, pp. 255–269). Baltimore: Brookes.

Adler, A. (1927). *Understanding human nature.* New York: Greenberg.

Adler, A. (1956). In H. L. Ansbacher & R. R. Ansbacher (Eds.), *The individual psychology of Alfred Adler: A systematic presentation in selections from his writings.* New York: Harper & Row.

Adler, J. (1997, Spring/Summer). It's a wise father who knows. . . . *Newsweek* [Special Edition], 73.

Agras, W. S., Walsh, T., Fairburn, C. G., Wilson, T., & Kraemer, H. C. (2000). A multicenter comparison of cognitive-behavioral therapy and interpersonal psychotherapy for bulimia nervosa. *Archives of General Psychiatry, 57,* 459–466.

Ainsworth, M. (2000). ABCs of "internet therapy." *Metanoia* [Electronic version]. Retrieved 2000 from *www.metanoia.org*

Ainsworth, M. D. S. (1973). The development of infant-mother attachment. In B. Caldwell & H. Ricciuti (Eds.), *Review of child development research* (Vol. 3). Chicago: University of Chicago Press.

Ainsworth, M. D. S. (1979). Infant-mother attachment. *American Psychologist, 34,* 932–937.

Ainsworth, M. D. S., Blehar, M. C., Walters, E., & Wall, S. (1978). *Patterns of attachment.* Hillsdale, NJ: Erlbaum.

Ajdacic-Gross, V., Ring, M., Gadola, E., Lauber, C., Bopp, M., Gutzwiller, F., & Rossler, W. (2008). Suicide after bereavement: An overlooked problem. *Psychological Medicine, 38,* 673–676.

Å kerstedt, T. (1990). Psychological and psychophysiological effects of shift work. *Scandinavian Journal of Work and Environmental Health, 16,* 67–73.

Aksan, N., & Kochanska, G. (2005). Conscience in childhood: Old questions, new answers. *Developmental Psychology, 41,*506–516.

Al'absi, M., Hugdahl, K., & Lovallo, W. (2002). Adrenocortical stress responses and altered working memory performance. *Psychophysiology, 39,* 95–99.

Alberts, A., Elkind, D., & Ginsberg, S. (2007). The personal fable and risk-taking in early adolescence. *Journal of Youth and Adolescence, 36,* 71–76.

Albrecht, K. (1979). *Stress and the manager: Making it work for you.* Englewood Cliffs, NJ: Prentice-Hall.

Alexander, G. E., Furey, M. L., Grady, C. L., Pietrini, P., Brady, D. R., Mentis, M. J., et al. (1997). Association of premorbid intellectual function with cerebral metabolism in Alzheimer's disease: Implications for the cognitive reserve hypotheses. *American Journal of Psychiatry, 154,* 165–172.

Ali, M., Blades, M., Oates, C., & Blumberg, F. (2009). Young children's ability to recognize advertisements in web page designs. *British Journal of Developmental Psychology, 27,* 71–83.

Alleman, J. (2002). Online counseling: The Internet and mental health treatment. *Psychotherapy: Theory, Research, Practice, Training, 39,* 199–209.

Allen, B. (2008). An analysis of the impact of diverse forms of childhood psychological maltreatment on emotional adjustment in early adulthood. *Child Maltreatment, 13,* 307–312.

Allen, B. P. (1997). *Personality theories: Development, growth, and diversity* (2nd ed.). Boston: Allyn & Bacon.

Allen, G., Buxton, R. B., Wong, E. C., & Courchesne, E. (1997). Attentional activation of the cerebellum independent of motor involvement. *Science, 275,* 1940–1943.

Allen, K. W. (1996). Chronic nailbiting: A controlled comparison of competing response and mild aversion treatments. *Behaviour Research and Therapy, 34,* 269–272.

Allison, T., Puce, A., & McCarthy, G. (2000). Social perception from visual cues: Role of the STS region. *Trends in Cognitive Sciences, 4,* 267–278.

Allport, G. W. (1954). *The nature of prejudice.* Reading, MA: Addison-Wesley.

Allport, G. W. (1961). *Pattern and growth in personality.* New York: Holt, Rinehart & Winston.

Allport, G. W., & Odbert, J. S. (1936). Trait names: A psycholexical study. *Psychological Monographs, 47*(1, Whole No. 211), 1–171.

Almeida, D. (2005). Resilience and vulnerability to daily stressors assessed with diary methods. *Current Directions in Psychological Science, 14,* 62–68.

Alsaker, F. D. (1995). Timing of puberty and reactions to pubertal changes. In M. Rutter (Ed.), *Psychosocial disturbances in young people* (pp. 37–82). New York: Cambridge University Press.

Alter, A., Aronson, J., Darley, J., Rodriguez, C., & Ruble, D. (2010). Rising to the threat: Reducing stereotype threat by reframing the threat as a challenge. *Journal of Experimental Social Psychology, 46,* 166–171.

Altermatt, E., & Pomerantz, E. (2003). The development of competence-related and motivational beliefs: An investigation of similarity and influence among friends. *Journal of Educational Psychology, 95,* 111–123.

Aluja, A., & Blanch, A. (2004). Replicability of first-order 16PF-5 factors: An analysis of three parcelling methods. *Personality & Individual Differences, 37,* 667–677.

Amado, S., & Ulupinar, P. (2005). The effects of conversation on attention and peripheral detection: Is talking with a passenger and talking on the cell phone different? *Transportation Research, 8,* 383–395.

Amato, S. (1998). Human genetics and dysmorphy. In R. Behrman & R. Kliegman (Eds.), *Nelson essentials of pediatrics* (3rd ed., pp. 167–225). Philadelphia: W. B. Saunders.

American Association of Retired Persons. (2002). *Evaluating health information on the Internet: How good are your sources?* Retrieved November 1, 2002, from *http://www.aarp.org/confacts/health/wwwhealth.html.*

American Cancer Society. (2002). *Cancer facts & figures/2002.* Retrieved November 10, 2002, from *http://www.cancer.org/downloads/STT/CancerFacts&Figures2002TM*

American Cancer Society. (2009). *Cancer facts & figures.* Retrieved March 12, 2010 from *http://www.cancer.org/downloads/STT/500809web.pdf.*

American Cancer Society. (2009). *Cancer facts & figures.* Retrieved March 12, 2010 from *http://www.cancer.org/downloads/STT/500809web.pdf.*

American Medical Association. (1994). *Report of the Council on Scientific Affairs: Memories of childhood abuse.* CSA Report 5-A-94.

American Psychiatric Association. (1993a). *Statement approved by the Board of Trustees, December 12, 1993.* Washington, DC: Author.

American Psychiatric Association. (1994). *Diagnostic and statistical manual of mental disorders* (4th ed.). Washington DC: Author.

American Psychiatric Association. (1997). Practice guideline for the treatment of patients with Alzheimer's disease and other dementias of late life. *American Journal of Psychiatry, 154,* 1–39.

American Psychiatric Association. (2000a). *The Diagnostic and Statistical Manual of Mental Disorders* (4th ed., Text Revision). Washington, DC: Author.

American Psychiatric Association. (2000b). *Practice guidelines for eating disorders.* Retrieved January 31, 2005, from *http://www.psych.org.*

American Psychological Association (APA). (1994). *Interim report of the APA Working Group on Investigation of Memories of Childhood Abuse.* Washington, DC: Author.

American Psychological Association (APA). (1995). *Psychology: Scientific problem-solvers—Careers for the 21st century.* Retrieved March 7, 2002, from *http://www.apa.org/students/brochure/outlook.html#bachelors*

American Psychological Association (APA). (2000). *Psychologists in the red* [Online factsheet]. Retrieved March 7, 2002, from *http://www.apa.org/ppo/issues/ebsinthered.html*

American Psychological Association (APA). (2002). Ethical principles of psychologists and code of conduct. *American Psychologist, 57,* 1060–1073.

American Psychological Association (APA). (2003a). *Graduate study in psychology.* Washington, DC: APA.

American Psychological Association (APA). (2003b). Guidelines on multicultural education, training, research, practice, and organizational change for psychologists. *American Psychologist, 58,* 377–402.

American Psychological Association (APA). (2006a). *Practice guidelines for treatment of patients with eating disorders* (3rd edition). Retrieved October 12, 2006, from *http://psych.org/psych_pract/treatg/pg/EatingDisorders3ePG_04-28-06.pdf*

American Psychological Association. (2008). *2007 APA Early career psychologists survey.* Retrieved January 12, 2010 from *http://www.apa.org/careers/early-career/2007-survey.pdf.*

American Society of Bariatric Surgeons. (2005). *Rationale for the surgical treatment of morbid obesity.* Retrieved January 25, 2007, from *http://www.asbs.org/html/patients/rationale.html*

Amodio, D., Devine, P., & Harmon-Jones, E. (2007). A dynamic model of guilt: Implications for motivation and self-regulation in the context of prejudice. *Psychological Science, 18,* 524–530.

Amsterdam, B. (1972). Mirror self-image reactions before age two. *Developmental Psychobiology, 5,* 297–305.

Anand, B. K., & Brobeck, J. R. (1951). Hypothalamic control of food intake in rats and cats. *Yale Journal of Biological Medicine, 24,* 123–140.

Andersen, B. L., & Cyranowski, J. M. (1995). Women's sexuality: Behaviors, responses, and individual differences. *Journal of Consulting and Clinical Psychology, 63,* 891–906.

Anderson, C. A., & Anderson, K. B. (1996). Violent crime rate studies in philosophical context: A destructive testing approach to heat and southern culture of violence effects. *Journal of Personality and Social Psychology, 70,* 740–756.

Anderson, C. A., & Dill, K. E. (2000). Video games and aggressive thoughts, feelings, and behavior in the laboratory and in life. *Journal of Personality & Social Psychology, 78,* 772–790.

Anderson, C., & Bushman, B. (2001). Effects of violent video games on aggressive behavior, aggressive cognition, aggressive affect, physiological arousal, and prosocial behavior: A meta-analytic review of the scientific literature. *Psychological Science, 12,* 353–359.

Anderson, C., & Carnagey, N. (2009). Causal effects of violent sports video games on aggression: Is it competitiveness or violent content? *Journal of Experimental Social Psychology, 45,* 731–739.

Anderson, R. (2002). Deaths: Leading causes for 2000. *National Vital Statistics Reports, 50*(16), 1–86.

Anderson, S. M., Klatzky, R. L., & Murray, J. (1990). Traits and social stereotypes: Efficiency differences in social information processing. *Journal of Personality and Social Psychology, 59,* 192–201.

Anderson, S., & Patrick, A. (2006). *Doctor Dolittle's delusion: Animals and the uniqueness of human language.* New Haven, CT: Yale University Press.

Andreasen, N. C., & Black, D. W. (1991). *Introductory textbook of psychiatry.* Washington, DC: American Psychiatric Press.

Andreasen, N. C., Arndt, S., Alliger, R., Miller, D., & Flaum, M. (1995). Symptoms of schizophrenia: Methods, meanings, and mechanisms. *Archives of General Psychiatry, 52,* 341–351.

Andreasen, N. C., Flaum, M., Swayze, V., O'Leary, D. S., Alliger, R., Cohen, G., Ehrhardt, J., & Yuh, W. T. C. (1993). Intelligence and brain structure in normal individuals. *American Journal of Psychiatry, 150,* 130–134.

Andrews, G., & Erskine, A. (2003). Reducing the burden of anxiety and depressive disorders: The role of computerized clinician assistance. *Current Opinion in Psychiatry, 16,* 41–44.

Angeleri, F., Angeleri, V. A., Foschi, N., Giaquinto, S., Nolfe, G., Saginario, A., & Signorino, M. (1997). Depression after stroke: An investigation through catamnesis. *Journal of Clinical Psychiatry, 58,* 261–265.

Anglin, J. (1995, March). *Word learning and the growth of potentially knowable vocabulary.* Paper presented at the biennial meetings of the Society for Research in Child Development, Indianapolis, IN.

Anokhin, A., Vedeniapin, A., Sitevaag, E., Bauer, L., O'Connor, S., Kuperman, S., et al. (2000). The P300 brain potential is reduced in smokers. *Psychopharmacology, 149,* 409–413.

Apgar, V., & Beck, J. (1982). A perfect baby. In H. E. Fitzgerald & T. H. Carr (Eds.), *Human Development 82/83* (pp. 66–70). Guilford, CT: Dushkin.

Aram, D., & Levitt, I. (2002). Mother-child joint writing and storybook reading: Relations with literacy among low SES kindergarteners. *Merrill-Palmer Quarterly, 48,* 202–224.

Araujo, L. (2009). Stochastic parsing and evolutionary algorithms. *Applied Artificial Intelligence, 23,* 346–372.

Archer, J. (1991). The influence of testosterone on human aggression. *British Journal of Social Psychology, 82*(Pt. 1), 1–28.

Archer, J. (1996). Sex differences in social behavior: Are the social role and evolutionary explanations compatible? *American Psychologist, 51,* 909–917.

Arehart-Treichel, J. (2002). Researchers explore link between animal cruelty, personality disorders. *Psychiatric News, 37,* 22.

Arendt, J. (2009). Managing jet lag: Some of the problems and possible new solutions. *Sleep Medicine Reviews, 13,* 249–256.

Ariatti, A., Benuzzi, F., & Nichelli, P. (2008). Recognition of emotions from visual and prosodic cues in Parkinson's disease. *Neurological Sciences, 29,* 219–227.

Arim, R., & Shapka, J. (2008). The impact of pubertal timing and parental control on adolescent problem behaviors. *Journal of Youth and Adolescence, 37,* 445–455.

Ariznavarreta, C., Cardinali, D., Villanua, M., Granados, B., Martin, M., Chiesa, J., Golombek, D., & Tresguerres, J. (2002). Circadian rhythms in airline pilots submitted to long-haul transmeridian flights. *Aviation, Space, and Environmental Medicine, 73,* 445–455.

Armstrong, M., & Shikani, A. (1996). Nasal septal necrosis mimicking Wegener's granulomatosis in a cocaine abuser. *Ear Nose Throat Journal, 75,* 623–626.

Arnett, J. (2000). Emerging adulthood: A theory of development from the late teens through the twenties. *American Psychologist, 57,* 774–783.

Aronson, E. (1976). Dissonance theory: Progress and problems. In E. P. Hollander & R. C. Hunt (Eds.), *Current perspectives in social psychology* (4th ed., pp. 316–328). New York: Oxford University Press.

Aronson, E. (1988). *The social animal* (3rd ed.). San Francisco: W. H. Freeman.

Aronson, E., Stephan, W., Sikes, J., Blaney, N., & Snapp, M. (1978). *Cooperation in the classroom.* Beverly Hills, CA: Sage.

Arriaga, P., Esteves, F., Carneiro, P., & Monteiro, M. (2006). Violent computer games and their effects on state hostility and physiological arousal. *Aggressive Behavior, 32,* 146–158.

Arushanyan, E., & Shikina, I. (2004). Effect of caffeine on light and color sensitivity of the retina in healthy subjects depending on psychophysiological features and time of day. *Human Physiology, 30,* 56–61.

Asch, S. E. (1955). Opinions and social pressure. *Scientific American, 193,* 31–35.

Assadi, S., Noroozian, M., Pakravannejad, M., Yahyazadeh, O., Aghayan, S., Shariat, S., et al. (2006). Psychiatric morbidity among sentenced prisoners: Prevalence study in Iran. *British Journal of Psychiatry, 188,* 159–164.

Assefi, S., & Garry, M. (2003). Absolute memory distortions: Alcohol placebos influence the misinformation effect. *Psychological Science, 14,* 77–80.

Astin, S. (August, 2004). After the storm: My mother taught me to turn pain into strength. *Reader's Digest.* Retrieved February 12, 2007, from *http://www.rd.com/content/openContent.do?contentId=27665*

Athanasselis, T., Bakamadis, S., Dologlou, I., Cowie, R., Douglas-Cowie, E., & Cox, C. (2005). ASR for emotional speech: Clarifying the issues and enhancing performance. *Neural Networks, 18,* 437–444.

Atkinson, R. C., & Shiffrin, R. M. (1968). Human memory: A proposed system and its controlled processes. In K. W. Spence & J. T. Spence (Eds.), *The psychology of learning and motivation* (Vol. 2, pp. 89–195). New York: Academic.

Augestad, L. B. (2000). Prevalence and gender differences in eating attitudes and physical activity among Norwegians. *Eating and Weight Disorders: Studies on Anorexia, Bulimia, and Obesity, 5,* 62–72.

Austenfeld, J., & Stanton, A. (2004). Coping through emotional approach: A new look at emotion, coping, and health-related outcomes. *Journal of Personality, 72,* 1335–1363.

Avraham, K. (2001). Modifying with mitochondria. *Nature Genetics, 27,* 136–137.

Axel, R. (1995, October). The molecular logic of smell. *Scientific American, 273,* 154–159.

Ayllon, T., & Azrin, N. (1965). The measurement and reinforcement of behavior of psychotics. *Journal of the Experimental Analysis of Behavior, 8,* 357–383.

Ayllon, T., & Azrin, N. (1968). *The token economy: A motivational system for therapy and rehabilitation.* New York: Appleton-Century-Crofts.

Azar, B. (2000). A web of research. *Monitor on Psychology, 31* [Online version]. Retrieved March 13, 2002, from *http://www.apa.org/monitor/*

Azrin, N. H., & Holz, W. C. (1966). Punishment. In W. K. Honig (Ed.), *Operant behavior: Areas of research and application* (pp. 380–447). New York: Appleton-Century-Crofts.

Békésy, G. von. (1957). The ear. *Scientific American, 197,* 66–78.

Babor, T. (2004). Brief treatments for cannabis dependence: Findings from a randomized multisite trial. *Journal of Consulting & Clinical Psychology, 72,* 455–466.

Bach, P., & Hayes, S. (2002). The use of acceptance and commitment therapy to prevent the rehospitalization of psychotic patients: A randomized controlled trial. *Journal of Consulting and Clinical Psychology, 70,* 1129–1139.

Baddeley, A. (1998). *Human memory: Theory and practice.* Boston, MA: Allyn & Bacon.

Baddeley, A. (2009). Working memory. In A., Baddeley, M., Eysenck, & M. Anderson (Eds), *Memory* (pp. 41–68). New York: Psychology Press.

Baddeley, A. D. (1990). *Human memory.* Boston, MA: Allyn & Bacon.

Baddeley, A. D. (1992). Working memory. *Science, 255,* 556–559.

Baddeley, A. D. (1995) Working memory. In M. S. Gazzaniga (Ed.), *The cognitive neurosciences.* Cambridge, MA: MIT Press.

Baer, J. (1996). The effects of task-specific divergent-thinking training. *Journal of Creative Behavior, 30,* 183–187.

Baer, L., Rauch, S. L., Ballantine, T., Jr., Martuza, R., Cosgrove, R., Cassem, E., et al. (1995). Cingulotomy for intractable obsessive-compulsive disorder. *Archives of General Psychiatry, 52,* 384–392.

Bagley, C., & Tremblay, P. (1998). On the prevalence of homosexuality and bisexuality in a random community survey of 750 men aged 18 to 27. *Journal of Homosexuality, 36,* 1–18.

Bahrick, H. P., Bahrick, P. O., & Wittlinger, R. P. (1975). Fifty years of memory for names and faces: A cross-sectional approach. *Journal of Experimental Psychology: General, 104,* 54–75.

Bahrick, H. P., Hall, L. K., & Berger, S. A. (1996). Accuracy and distortion in memory for high school grades. *Psychological Science, 7,* 265–271.

Bailey, J. M., & Pillard, R. C. (1991). A genetic study of male sexual orientation. *Archives of General Psychiatry, 48,* 1089–1096.

Bailey, J. M., & Pillard, R. C. (1994). The innateness of homosexuality. *Harvard Mental Health Letter, 10*(7), 4–6.

Bailey, J. M., Pillard, R. C., Neale, M. C., & Agyei, Y. (1993). Heritable factors influence sexual orientation in women. *Archives of General Psychiatry, 50,* 217–223.

Baird, A. (2010). The terrible twelves. In P., Zalazo, M., Chandler, & E. Crone (Eds.), *Developmental social cognitive neuroscience,* The Jean Piaget symposium (pp. 191–207). New York: Psychology Press.

Bajic, D., & Rickard, T. (2009). The temporal dynamics of strategy execution in cognitive skill learning. *Journal of Experimental Psychology: Learning, Memory, and Cognition, 35,* 113–121.

Baker, M., & Bendabis, S. (2005). Narcolepsy. Retrieved December 16, 2006, from *http://www.emedicine.com/neuro/topic522.htm*

Baldwin, J. D., & Baldwin, J. I. (1997). Gender differences in sexual interest. *Archives of Sexual Behavior, 26,* 181–210.

Ball, S. G., Baer, L., & Otto, M. W. (1996). Symptom subtypes of obsessive-compulsive disorder in behavioral treatment studies: A quantitative review. *Behaviour Research and Therapy, 34,* 47–51.

Ballenger, J. C., Pecknold, J., Rickels, K., & Sellers, E. M. (1993). Medication discontinuation in panic disorder. *Journal of Clinical Psychiatry, 54*(10, Suppl.), 15–21.

Baltes, P. B., Reese, H. W., & Lipsitt, L. P. (1980). Life-span developmental psychology. *Annual Review of Psychology, 31,* 65–110.

Baltes, P., & Baltes, M. (1990). Psychological perspectives on successful aging: The model of selective optimization with compensation. In P. Baltes & M. Baltes (Eds.), *Successful aging* (pp. 1–34). Cambridge, U.K.: Cambridge University Press.

Baltimore, D. (2000). Our genome unveiled. *Nature, 409,* 814–816.

Bandura, A. (1969). *Principles of behavior modification.* New York: Holt, Rinehart & Winston.

Bandura, A. (1973). *Aggression: A social learning analysis.* Englewood Cliffs, NJ: Prentice-Hall.

Bandura, A. (1976). On social learning and aggression. In E. P. Hollander & R. C. Hunt (Eds.), *Current perspectives in social psychology* (4th ed., pp. 116–128). New York: Oxford University Press.

Bandura, A. (1977). *Social learning theory.* Englewood Cliffs, NJ: Prentice-Hall.

Bandura, A. (1986). *Social functions of thought and action: A social-cognitive theory.* Englewood Cliffs, NJ: Prentice-Hall.

Bandura, A. (1989). Social cognitive theory. *Annals of Child Development, 6,* 1–60.

Bandura, A. (1997a, March). Self-efficacy. *Harvard Mental Health Letter, 13*(9), 4–6.

Bandura, A. (1997b). *Self-efficacy: The exercise of control.* New York: Freeman.

Bandura, A., Adams, N. E., & Beyer, J. (1977). Cognitive processes mediating behavioral change. *Journal of Personality and Social Psychology, 35,* 125–139.

Bandura, A., Jeffery, R. W., & Gajdos, E. (1975). Generalizing change through participant modeling with self-directed mastery. *Behaviour Research and Therapy, 13,* 141–152.

Bandura, A., Ross, D., & Ross, S. A. (1961). Transmission of aggression through imitation of aggressive models. *Journal of Abnormal and Social Psychology, 63,* 575–582.

Bandura, A., Ross, D., & Ross, S. A. (1963). Imitation of film-mediated aggressive models. *Journal of Abnormal and Social Psychology, 66,* 3–11.

Barbarich, N., McConaha, C., Gaskill, J., La Via, M., Frank, G., Achenbach, S., Plotnicov, K., & Kaye, W. (2004). An open trial of olanzapine in anorexia nervosa. *Journal of Clinical Psychiatry, 65,* 1480–1482.

Bard, P. (1934). The neurohumoral basis of emotional reactions. In C. A. Murchison (Ed.), *Handbook of general experimental psychology* (pp. 264–311). Worcester, MA: Clark University Press.

Bargmann, C. (1996). From the nose to the brain. *Nature, 384,* 512–513.

Barker, L. (2006). Teaching evolutionary psychology: An interview with David M. Buss. *Teaching of Psychology, 33,* 69–76.

Barlow, D. H. (1997). Cognitive-behavioral therapy for panic disorder: Current status. *Journal of Clinical Psychiatry, 58*(6, Suppl.), 32–36.

Barnes, P., Bloom, B., & Nahin, R. (2008). Complementary and alternative medicine use among adults and children: United States, 2007. *National Health Statistics Reports, 12,* 1–24.

Barrett. D. (2007). An evolutionary theory of dreams and problem-solving. In D. Barrrett & P. McNamara, (Eds.), *The new science of dreaming, Volume 3: Cultural and theoretical perspectives* (pp. 133–153). Westport, CT: Praeger Publishers.

Barrick, M., Mount, M., & Judge, T. (2001). Personality and performance at the beginning of the new millennium: What do we know and where do we go next? *International Journal of Selection and Assessment, 9,* 9–30.

Barrick, M., Shaffer, J., & DeGrassi, S. (2009). What you see may not be what you get: Relationships among self-presentation tactics and ratings of interview and job performance. *Journal of Applied Psychology, 94,* 1394–1411.

Barsh, G. S., Farooqi, I. S., & O'Rahilly, S. (2000). Genetics of bodyweight regulation. *Nature, 404,* 644–651.

Barsky, A. J. (1993, August). How does hypochondriasis differ from normal concerns about health? *Harvard Mental Health Letter, 10*(3), 8.

Bartlett, A. (2002). Current perspectives on the goals of psychoanalysis. *Journal of the American Psychoanalytic Association, 50,* 629–638.

Bartlett, F. C. (1932). *Remembering: A study in experimental and social psychology.* London: Cambridge University Press.

Bartoshuk, L. M., & Beauchamp, G. K. (1994). Chemical senses. *Annual Review of Psychology, 45,* 419–449.

Bartzokis, G., Sultzer, D., Lu, P., Huechterlein, K., Mintz, J., & Cummings, J. (2004). Heterogeneous age-related breakdown of white matter structural integrity: Implications for cortical "disconnection" in aging and Alzheimer's disease. *Neurobiology of Aging, 25,* 843–851.

Basco, M. (2006). *The bipolar workbook.* New York: Guilford Press.

Bassili, J. N. (1995). Response latency and the accessibility of voting intentions: What contributes to accessibility and how it affects vote choice. *Personality and Social Psychology Bulletin, 21,* 686–695.

Bateson, G. (1982). Totemic knowledge in New Guinea. In U. Neisser (Ed.), *Memory observed: Remembering in natural contexts* (pp. 269–273). San Francisco: W. H. Freeman.

Batson, C. (2006). "Not all self-interest after all": Economics of empathy-induced altruism. In D., De Cremer, M., Zeelenberg, & J. Murnighan (Eds.), *Social psychology and economics* (pp. 281–299). Mahwah, NJ: Lawrence Erlbaum Associates.

Batson, C. D., Batson, J. G., Griffitt, C. A., Barrientos, S., Brandt, J. R., Sprengelmeyer, P., et al. (1989). Negative-state relief and the empathy-altruism hypothesis. *Journal of Personality and Social Psychology, 56,* 922–933.

Bauchowitz, A., Gonder-Frederick, L., Olbrisch, M., Azarbad, L., Ryee, M., Woodson, M., et al. (2005). Psychosocial evaluation of bariatric surgery candidates: A survey of present practices. *Psychosomatic Medicine, 67,* 825–832.

Baumgardner, A. H., Heppner, P. P., & Arkin, R. M. (1986). Role of causal attribution in personal problem solving. *Journal of Personality and Social Psychology, 50,* 636–643.

Baumrind, D. (1967). Child care practices anteceding three patterns of preschool behavior. *Genetic Psychology Monographs, 75,* 43–88.

Baumrind, D. (1971). Current patterns of parental authority. *Developmental Psychology Monographs, 4*(1, Pt. 2).

Baumrind, D. (1980). New directions in socialization research. *American Psychologist, 35,* 639–652.

Baumrind, D. (1991). The influence of parenting style on adolescent competence and substance use. *Journal of Early Adolescence, 11,* 56–95.

Bavelier, D., Tomann, A., Hutton, C., Mitchell, T., Corina, D., Liu, G., & Neville, H. (2000). Visual attention to the periphery is enhanced in congenitally deaf individuals. *Journal of Neuroscience, 20,* 1–6.

Bazan, S. (1998). Enhancing decision-making effectiveness in problem-solving teams. *Clinical Laboratory Management Review, 12,* 272–276.

BBC World Service. (2007). *Figure it out: Winning the lottery—probability and coincidence.* Retrieved January 27, 2007, from *http://www.bbc.co.uk/worldservice/sci_tech/features/figure_it_out/lottery.shtml*

Bean, P., Loomis, C., Timmel, P., Hallinan, P., Moore, S., Mammel, J., et al. (2004). Outcome variables for anorexic males and females one year after discharge from residential treatment. *Journal of Addictive Diseases, 23,* 83–94.

Bean, R., Perry, B., & Bedell, T. (2002). Developing culturally competent marriage and family therapists: Treatment guidelines for non-African American therapists working with African American families. *Journal of Marital & Family Therapy, 28,* 153–164.

Beare, P., Severson, S., & Brandt, P. (2004). The use of a positive procedure to increase engagement on-task and decrease challenging behavior. *Behavior Modification, 28,* 28–44.

Beck, A. T. (1976). *Cognitive therapy and the emotional disorders.* New York: New American Library.

Beck, A. T. (1991). Cognitive therapy: A 30-year retrospective. *American Psychologist, 46,* 368–375.

Beck, A. T. (1993). Cognitive therapy: Past, present, and future. *Journal of Consulting and Clinical Psychology, 61,* 194–198.

Beck, J. (1995). *Cognitive therapy: Basics and beyond.* New York: Guilford Press.

Becker, K., & Wallace, J. (2010). *Central sleep apnea.* Retrieved April 29, 2010 from *http://emedicine.medscape.com/article/304967-overview.*

Beede, K., & Kass, S. (2006). Engrossed in conversation: The impact of cell phones on simulated driving performance. *Accident Analysis & Prevention, 38,* 415–421.

Beirut, L., Dinwiddie, S., Begleiter, H., Crowe, R., Hesselbrock, V., Nurnberger, J., et al. (1998). Familial transmission of substance dependence: Alcohol, marijuana, cocaine, and habitual smoking: A report from the collaborative study on the genetics of alcoholism. *Archives of General Psychiatry, 55,* 982–988.

Bekinschtein, T., Cardozo, J., & Manes, F. (2008). Strategies of Buenos Aires waiters to enhance memory capacity in a real-life setting. *Behavioural Neurology, 20,* 65–70.

Belcourt-Dittloff, A., & Stewart, J. (2000). Historical racism: Implications for Native Americans. *American Psychologist, 55,* 1164–1165.

Bell, A. P., Weinberg, M. S., & Hammersmith, S. K. (1981). *Sexual preference: Its development in men and women.* Bloomington: Indiana University Press.

Belsky, J., & Fearon, R. (2002). Infant-mother attachment security, contextual risk, and early development: A moderational analysis. *Development & Psychopathology, 14,* 293–310.

Bem, D., & Honorton, C. (1994). Does psi exist? Replicable evidence for an anomalous process of information transfer. *Psychological Bulletin, 115,* 4–18.

Bem, S. L. (1981). Gender schema theory: A cognitive account of sex typing. *Psychological Review, 88,* 354–364.

Ben-Porath, Y. S., & Butcher, J. N. (1989). The comparability of MMPI and MMPI-2 scales and profiles. *Psychological Assessment: A Journal of Consulting and Clinical Psychology, 1,* 345–347.

Benarroch, E. (2008). Suprachiasmatic nucleus and melatonin: Reciprocal interactions and clinical correlations. *Neurology, 71,* 594–598.

Benes, F. M. (2000). Emerging principles of altered neural circuitry in schizophrenia. *Brain Research Reviews, 31,* 251–269.

Benjafield, J. G. (1996). *A history of psychology.* Boston: Allyn & Bacon.

Benjamin, L. T. (2000). The psychology laboratory at the turn of the 20th century. *American Psychologist, 55,* 318–321.

Benjamin, L., & Crouse, E. (2002). The American Psychological Association's response to Brown v. Board of Education: The case of Kenneth B. Clark. *American Psychologist, 57,* 38–50.

Bennett, S. K. (1994). The American Indian: A psychological overview. In W. J. Lonner & R. Malpass (Eds.), *Psychology and culture* (pp. 35–39). Boston: Allyn & Bacon.

Bennett, W. I. (1990, November). Boom and doom. *Harvard Health Letter, 16,* 1–4.

Bensafi, M., Zelano, C., Johnson, B., Mainland, J., Khan, R., & Sobel, N. (2004). Olfaction: From sniff to percept. In M. Gazzaniga (Ed.), *The cognitive neurosciences* (pp. 259–280). Cambridge, MA: MIT Press.

Beran, M. (2004). Long-term retention of the differential values of Arabic numerals by chimpanzees (Pan troglodytes). *Animal Cognition, 7,* 86–92.

Beran, M., & Rumbaugh, D. (2001). "Constructive" enumeration by chimpanzees (Pan troglodytes) on a computerized task. *Animal Cognition, 4,* 81–89.

Berckmoes, C., & Vingerhoets, G. (2004). Neural foundations of emotional speech processing. *Current Directions in Psychological Science, 13,* 182–185.

Berenbaum, S. A., & Snyder, E. (1995). Early hormonal influences on childhood sex-typed activity and playmate preferences: Implications for the development of sexual orientation. *Developmental Psychology, 31,* 31–42.

Berenbaum, S. A., Korman, K., & Leveroni, C. (1995). Early hormones and sex differences in cognitive abilities. *Learning and Individual Differences, 7,* 303–321.

Bergen, G., Chen, L., Warner, M., & Fingerhut, L. (2008). *Injury in the United States: 2007 chartbook.* Retrieved June 11, 2009 from *http://www.cdc.gov/nchs/data/misc/injury2007.pdf.*

Bergman, O., Hakansson, A., Westberg, l., Nordenstrom, K., Belin, A., Sydow, O., Olson, L., Holmberg, B., Eriksson, E., & Nissbrandt, H. (2010). PITX3 polymorphism is associated with early onset Parkinson's disease. *Neurobiology of Aging, 31,* 114–117.

Bergström, M., Kieler, H., & Waldenström, U. (2009). Effects of a natural childbirth preparation versus standard antenatal education on epidural rates, experience of childbirth and parental stress in mothers and fathers: A randomised controlled multicentre trial. *British Journal of Obstetrics and Gynaecology, 116,* 1167–1176.

Berkowitz, L. (1983). Aversively stimulated aggression: Some parallels and differences in research with animals and humans. *American Psychologist, 38,* 1135–1144.

Berkowitz, L. (1988). Frustrations, appraisals, and aversively stimulated aggression. *Aggressive Behavior, 14,* 3–11.

Berkowitz, L. (1990). On the formation and regulation of anger and aggression: A cognitive-neoassociationistic analysis. *American Psychologist, 45,* 494–503.

Bernal, M. E., & Castro, F. G. (1994). Are clinical psychologists prepared for service and research with ethnic minorities? Report of a decade of progress. *American Psychologist, 49,* 797–805.

Bernardi, L., Sleight, P., Bandinelli, G., Cencetti, S., Fattorini, L., Wdowczyc-Szulc, J., & Lagi, A. (2001). Effect of rosary prayer and yoga mantras on autonomic cardiovascular rhythms: Comparative study. *BMJ: British Medical Journal, 323,* 1446–1449.

Bernat, E., Shevrin, H., & Snodgrass, M. (2001). Subliminal visual oddball stimuli evoke P300 component. *Clinical Neurophysiology, 112,* 159–171.

Berndt, E. R., Koran, L. M., Finkelstein, S. N., Gelenberg, A. J., Kornstein, S. G., Miller, I. M., et al. (2000). Lost human capital from early-onset chronic depression. *American Journal of Psychiatry, 157,* 940–947.

Berndt, T. J. (1992). Friendship and friends' influence in adolescence. *Current Directions in Psychological Science, 1,* 156–159.

Bernstein, I. L. (1985). Learned food aversions in the progression of cancer and its treatment. *Annals of the New York Academy of Sciences, 443,* 365–380.

Bernstein, I. L., Webster, M. M., & Bernstein, I. D. (1982). Food aversions in children receiving chemotherapy for cancer. *Cancer, 50,* 2961–2963.

Berridge, (2009). "Liking" and "wanting" food rewards: Brain substrates and roles in eating disorders. *Physiology & Behavior, 97,* 537–550.

Berry, J. W. (2003). Conceptual approaches to understanding acculturation. In K. M. Chun, P. B. Organista, & G. Marín (Eds.), *Acculturation: Advances in theory, measurement, and applied research* (pp. 17–38). Washington, DC: American Psychological Association.

Berry, J. W., Kim, U., Minde, T., & Mok, D. (1987). Comparative studies of acculturative stress. *International Migration Review, 21,* 491–511.

Berscheid, E., Dion, K., Walster, E., & Walster, G. W. (1971). Physical attractiveness and dating choice: A test of the matching hypothesis. *Journal of Experimental Social Psychology, 7,* 173–189.

Besharat, M. (2001). Management strategies of sexual dysfunctions. *Journal of Contemporary Psychotherapy, 31,* 161–180.

Beyenburg, S., Watzka, M., Clusmann, H., Blümcke, I., Bidlingmaier, F., Stoffel-Wagner, et al. (2000). Androgen receptor mRNA expression in the human hippocampus. *Neuroscience Letters, 294,* 25–28.

Bhalla, R., Moraille-Bhalla, P., & Aronson, S. (2010). *Depression.* Retrieved March 15, 2010 from *http://emedicine.medscape.com/article/286759-overview.*

Bhugra, D. (2005). The global prevalence of schizophrenia. *Public Library of Science, 5.* [Online only, no pages.] Retrieved July 18, 2006, from *http://medicine.plosjournals.org/perlserv?request=getdocument&doi=10.1371/journal.pmed.0020151.*

Bialystok, E., Shenfield, T., & Codd, J. (2000). Languages, scripts, and the environment: Factors in developing concepts of print. *Developmental Psychology, 36,* 66–76.

Bienenfeld, D. (2008). *Personality disorders.* Retrieved March 15, 2010 from *http://emedicine.medscape.com/article/294307-overview.*

Bierman, A., Fazio, & Milkie, M. (2006). A multifaceted approach to the mental health advantage of the married: Assessing how explanations vary by outcome measure and unmarried group. *Journal of Family Issues, 27,* 554–582.

Billiard, M., Pasquiré-Magnetto, V., Heckman, M., Carlander, B., Besset, A., Zachariev, Z., et al. (1994). Family studies in narcolepsy. *Sleep, 17,* S54–S59.

Biondi, M., & Picardi, A. (2003). Increased probability of remaining in remission from panic disorder with agoraphobia after drug treatment in patients who received concurrent cognitive-behavioural therapy: A follow-up study. *Psychotherapy & Psychosomatics, 72,* 34–42.

Bird, T. (2001). *Alzheimer overview* [Online brochure]. Retrieved March 25, 2002, from *http://www.geneclincis.org.*

Birren, J. E., & Fisher, L. M. (1995). Aging and speed of behavior: Possible consequences for psychological functioning. *Annual Review of Psychology, 46,* 329–353.

Bishop, J., & Lane, R. C. (2000). Father absence and the attitude of entitlement. *Journal of Contemporary Psychotherapy, 30,* 105–117.

Bishop, R. (2005). Cognitive psychology: Hidden assumptions. In B. Slife, J. Reber, & F. Richardson (Eds.), *Critical thinking about psychology: Hidden assumptions and plausible alternatives* (151–170). Washington, DC: American Psychological Association.

Bisiach, E. (1996). Unilateral neglect and the structure of space representation. *Current Directions in Psychological Science, 5,* 62–65.

Bjorklund, D. F., Cassel, W. S., Bjorklund, B. R., Brown, R. D., Park, C. L., Ernst, K., et al. (2000). Social demand characteristics in children's and adults' memory and suggestibility: The effect of different interviewers on free recall and recognition. *Applied Cognitive Psychology, 14,* 421–433.

Blagrove, M., & Hartnell, S. (2000). Lucid dreaming: Associations with internal locus of control, need for cognition and creativity. *Personality & Individual Differences, 28,* 41–47.

Blascovich, J., Wyer, N. A., Swart, L. A., & Kibler, J. L. (1997). Racism and racial categorization. *Journal of Personality and Social Psychology, 72,* 1364–1372.

Blatt, S. J., Sanislow, C. A., III, Zuroff, D. C., & Pilkonis, P. A. (1996). Characteristics of effective therapists: Further analyses of data from the National Institute of Mental Health Treatment of Depression Collaborative Research Program. *Journal of Consulting and Clinical Psychology, 64,* 1276–1284.

Blatt, S., Zuroff, D., & Hawley, L. (2009). Factors contributing to sustained therapeutic gain in outpatient treatments of depression. In R., Levy, & J. Ablon, (Eds.), *Handbook of evidence-based psychodynamic psychotherapy: Bridging the gap between science and practice* (pp. 279–301). Totowa, NJ: Humana Press.

Bliese, P. D., & Castro, C. A. (2000). Role clarity, work overload and organizational support: Multilevel evidence of the importance of support. *Work & Stress, 14,* 65–73.

Blinn-Pike, L., Berger, T., Hewett, J., & Oleson, J. (2004). Sexually abstinent adolescents: An 18-month follow-up. *Journal of Adolescent Research, 19,* 495–511.

Bliss, T. V., & Lomo, T. (2000). Plasticity in a monosynaptic cortical pathway. *Journal of Physiology, 207,* 61.

Bloom, B. S. (Ed.). (1985). *Developing talent in young people.* New York: Ballantine.

Bloomer, C. M. (1976). *Principles of visual perception.* New York: Van Nostrand Reinhold.

Blyth, D. A., Simmons, R. G., Bulcroft, R., Felt, D., VanCleave, E. F., & Bush, D. M. (1981). The effects of physical development on self-image and satisfaction with body-image for early adolescent males. In R. G. Simmons (Ed.), *Research in community and mental health* (Vol. 2 pp. 43–73). Greenwich, CT: JAI.

Bogen, J. E., & Vogel, P. J. (1963). Treatment of generalized seizures by cerebral commissurotomy. *Surgical Forum, 14,* 431.

Bohannon, J. N., III. (1988). Flashbulb memories for the Space Shuttle disaster: A tale of two theories. *Cognition, 29,* 179–196.

Bohannon, R., Larkin, P., Cook, A., Gear, J., & Singer, J. (1984). Decrease in timed balance test scores with aging. *Physical Therapy, 64,* 1067–1070.

Boivin, D. B., Czeisler, C. A., Dijk, D-J., Duffy, J. F., Folkard, S., Minors, D. S., et al. (1997). Complex interaction of the sleep-wake cycle and circadian phase modulates mood in healthy subjects. *Archives of General Psychiatry, 54,* 145–152.

Bompas, A., & O'Regan, J. (2006). Evidence for a role of action in colour perception. *Perception, 35,* 65–78.

Bonanno, G. A., Keltner, D., Holen, A., & Horowitz, M. J. (1995). When avoiding unpleasant emotions might not be such a bad thing: Verbal-autonomic response dissociation and midlife conjugal bereavement. *Journal of Personality and Social Psychology, 69,* 975–989.

Bonnefond, A., Härmä, M., Hakola, T., Sallinen, M., Kandolin, I., & Virkkala, J. (2006). Interaction of age with shift-related sleep-wakefulness, sleepiness, performance, and social life. *Experimental Aging Research, 32,* 185–208.

Bonson, K., Grant, S., Contoreggi, C., Links, J., Metcalfe, J., Weyl, H., et al. (2002). Neural systems and cue-induced cocaine craving. *Neuropsychopharmacology, 26,* 376–386.

Borbely, A. A., Achermann, P., Trachsel, L., & Tobler, I. (1989). Sleep initiation and initial sleep intensity: Interactions of homeostatic and circadian mechanisms. *Journal of Biological Rhythms, 4,* 149–160.

Borden, W. (2009). *Contemporary psychodynamic theory and practice.* Chicago: Lyceum Books.

Boren, J., Leventhal, A., & Pigott, H. (2009). Just how effective are antidepressant medications? Results of a major new study. *Journal of Contemporary Psychotherapy, 139,* 93–100.

Borge, C. (2007, January 3). *Basic instincts: The science of evil.* Retrieved March 24, 2010 from *http://abcnews.go.com/Primetime/story?id=2765416&page=1.*

Bornstein, R. F. (1989). Exposure and affect: Overview and meta-analysis of research, 1968–1987. *Psychological Bulletin, 106,* 265–289.

Borzekowski, D., Fobil, J., & Asante, K. (2006). Online access by adolescents in Accra: Ghanaian teens' use of the Internet for health information. *Developmental Psychology, 42,* 450–458.

Bosse, R., Aldwin, C. M., Levenson, M. R., & Workman-Daniels, K. (1991). How stressful is retirement? *Journal of Gerontology, 46,* 9–14.

Bouchard, T. (2004). Genetic influence on human psychological traits: A survey: *Current Directions in Psychological Science, 13,* 148–151.

Bouchard, T. J., Jr. (1994). Genes, environment, and personality. *Science, 264,* 1700–1701.

Bouchard, T. J., Jr. (1997, September/October). Whenever the twain shall meet. *The Sciences, 37,* 52–57.

Bouchard, T. J., Jr., & McGue, M. (1981). Familial studies of intelligence: A review. *Science, 212,* 1055–1058.

Bouchard, T. J., Jr., Lykken, D. T., McGue, M., Segal, N. L., & Tellegen, A. (1990). Sources of human psychological differences: The Minnesota study of twins reared apart. *Science, 250,* 223–228.

Boul, L. (2003). Men's health and middle age. *Sexualities, Evolution, & Gender, 5,* 5–22.

Bourassa, M., & Vaugeois, P. (2001). Effects of marijuana use on divergent thinking. *Creativity Research Journal, 13,* 411–416.

Bowden, C., Lecrubier, Y., Bauer, M., Goodwin, G., Greil, W., Sachs, G., et al. (2000). Maintenance therapies for classic and other forms of bipolar disorder. *Journal of Affective Disorders, 59*(1), S57–S67.

Bowden, C., Myers, J., Grossman, F., & Xie, Y. (2004). Risperidone in combination with mood stabilizers: A 10-week continuation phase study in bipolar I disorder. *Journal of Clinical Psychiatry, 65,* 707–714.

Bowen-Reid, T., & Harrell, J. (2002). Racist experiences and health outcomes: An examination of spirituality as a buffer. *Journal of Black Psychology, 28,* 18–36.

Bower, G. H. (1973, October). How to . . . uh . . . remember! *Psychology Today*, 63–70.

Bower, G. H., Thompson-Schill, S., & Tulving, E. (1994). Reducing retroactive interference: An interference analysis. *Journal of Experimental Psychology: Learning, Memory, and Cognition, 20*, 51–66.

Bowers, K. S. (1992). Imagination and dissociative control in hypnotic responding. *International Journal of Clinical and Experimental Hypnosis, 40*, 253–275.

Bowers, K. S., & Farvolden, P. (1996). Revisiting a century-old Freudian slip—from suggestion disavowed to the truth repressed. *Psychological Bulletin, 119*, 355–380.

Bowers, K. S., & Woody, E. Z. (1996). Hypnotic amnesia and the paradox of intentional forgetting. *Journal of Abnormal Psychology, 105*, 381–390.

Boyce, J., & Shone, G. (2006). Effects of aging on smell and taste. *Postgraduate Medical Journal, 82*, 239–241.

Bozorg, A., & Benbadis, S. (2009). *Narcolepsy*. Retrieved February 5, 2010 from *http://emedicine.medscape.com/article/1188433-overview*.

Brönte-Tinkew, J., Moore, K. A., & Carrano, J. (2006). The father-child relationship, parenting styles, and adolescent risk behaviors in intact families. *Journal of Family Issues, 27*, 850–881.

Brackbill, R., Hadler, J., DiGrande, L., Ekenga, C., Farfel, M., Friedman, S., Perlman, S., Stellman, S., Walker, D., Wu, D., Yu, S., & Thorpe, L. (2009). Asthma and posttraumatic stress symptoms 5 to 6 years following exposure to the World Trade Center terrorist attack. *JAMA: Journal of the American Medical Association, 302*, 502–516.

Brady, S., & Matthews, K. (2006). Effects of media violence on health-related outcomes among young men. *Archives of Pediatric Adolescent Medicine, 160*, 341–347.

Brain imaging and psychiatry—Part I. (1997, January). *Harvard Mental Health Letter, 13*(7), 1–4.

Brannon, L., & Feist, J. (2010). *Health psychology: An introduction to behavior and health* (7th ed.). Wadsworth Publishing.

Braun, A., Balkin, T., Wesensten, N., Gwadry, F., Carson, R., Varga, M., et al. (1998). Dissociated pattern of activity in visual cortices and their projections during human rapid eye movement sleep. *Science, 279*, 91–95.

Braun, S. (1996). New experiments underscore warnings on maternal drinking. *Science, 273*, 738–739.

Brawman-Mintzer, O., & Lydiard, R. B. (1996). Generalized anxiety disorder: Issues in epidemiology. *Journal of Clinical Psychiatry, 57*(7, Suppl.), 3–8.

Brawman-Mintzer, O., & Lydiard, R. B. (1997). Biological basis of generalized anxiety disorder. *Journal of Clinical Psychiatry, 58*(3, Suppl.), 16–25.

Bray, G. A., & Tartaglia, L. A. (2000). Medicinal strategies in the treatment of obesity. *Nature, 404*, 672–677.

Brecht, M., Greenwell, L., & Anglin, M. (2007). Substance use pathways to methamphetamine use among treated users. *Addictive Behaviors, 32*, 24–38.

Breckler, S. J. (1984). Empirical validation of affect, behavior, and cognition as distinct attitude components. *Journal of Personality and Social Psychology, 47*, 1191–1205.

Brennan, P. A., Raine, A., Schulsinger, F., Kirkegaard-Sorensen, L., Knop, J., Hutchings, B., et al. (1997). Psychophysiological protective factors for male subjects at high risk for criminal behavior. *American Journal of Psychiatry, 154*, 853–855.

Brenner, I. (2009). A new view from the Acropolis: Dissociative identity disorder. *Psychoanalytic Quarterly, 78*, 57–105.

Brent, D. A., Bridge, J., Johnson, B. A., & Connolly, J. (1996). Suicidal behavior runs in families: A controlled family study of adolescent suicide victims. *Archives of General Psychiatry, 53*, 1145–1152.

Brent, D., Oquendo, M., Birmaher, B., Greenhill, L., Kolko, D., Stanley, B., et al. (2002). Familial pathways to early-onset suicide attempt. *Archives of General Psychiatry, 59*, 801.

Breslau, N., Davis, G. C., Peterson, E. L., & Schultz, L. (1997). Psychiatric sequelae of posttraumatic stress disorder in women. *Archives of General Psychiatry, 54*, 81–87.

Bressan, P., & Pizzighello, S. (2008). The attentional cost of inattentional blindness. *Cognition, 106*, 379–383.

Brewer, W. F. (1992). The theoretical and empirical status of the flashbulb memory hypothesis. In E. Winograd, & U. Neisser, (Eds.), *Affect and accuracy in recall* (pp. 274–305). Cambridge, UK: Cambridge University Press.

Brickman, P., & Campbell, D. (1971). Hedonic relativism and planning the good society. In N. H. Appley (Ed.), *Adaptation level theory: A symposium* (pp. 287–302). New York: Academic Press.

Brieger, P., Ehrt, U., & Marneros, A. (2003). Frequency of comorbid personality disorders in bipolar and unipolar affective disorders. *Comprehensive Psychiatry, 44*, 28–34.

Brigham, J., Bennett, L., Meissner, C., & Mitchell, T. (2007). The influence of race on eyewitness memory. In R., Lindsay, D., Ross, J., Read, & M. Toglia (Eds.), *Handbook of Eyewitness Psychology: Memory for People* (pp. 257–281). Mahwah, NJ: Lawrence Erlbaum & Associates.

Britt, R. (2006). *Sound science: Pete Townshend blames headphones for hearing loss.* Retrieved December 13, 2006, from *http://www.foxnews.com/story/0,2933.180844,00.html*

Broadbent, D. E. (1958). *Perception and communication.* New York: Pergamon Press

Brody, A., Saxena, S., Fairbanks, L., Alborzian, S., Demaree, H., Maidment, K., & Baxter, L. (2000). Personality changes in adult subjects with major depressive disorder or obsessive-compulsive disorder treated with paroxetine. *Journal of Clinical Psychiatry, 61*, 349–355.

Brody, L. R. (1985). Gender differences in emotional development: A review of theories and research. *Journal of Personality, 53*, 102–149.

Brooks-Gunn, J. (2003). Do you believe in magic? What we can expect from early childhood intervention programs. *Social Policy Report, 17*, 3–14.

Brooks-Gunn, J., & Furstenberg, F. F. (1989). Adolescent sexual behavior. *American Psychologist, 44*, 249–257.

Brotman, A. W. (1994). What works in the treatment of anorexia nervosa? *Harvard Mental Health Letter, 10*(7), 8.

Broughton, W. A., & Broughton, R. J. (1994). Psychosocial impact of narcolepsy. *Sleep, 17*, S45–S49.

Brown, A. (1996, Winter). Mood disorders in children and adolescents. *NARSAD Research Newsletter*, 11–14.

Brown, A. (2004). The déjà vu illusion. *Current Directions in Psychological Science, 13*, 256–259.

Brown, G. W., Harris, T. O., & Hepworth, C. (1994). Life events and endogenous depression: A puzzle reexamined. *Archives of General Psychiatry, 51*, 525–534.

Brown, J. D., & Rogers, R. J. (1991). Self-serving attributions: The role of physiological arousal. *Personality and Social Psychology Bulletin, 17*, 501–506.

Brown, R. (1973). *A first language: The early stages.* Cambridge, MA: Harvard University Press.

Brown, R., & Kulik, J. (1977). Flashbulb memories. *Cognition, 5*, 73–99.

Brown, R., & McNeil, D. (1966). The "tip of the tongue" phenomenon. *Journal of Verbal Learning and Verbal Behavior, 5*, 325–337.

Brown, R., Cazden, C., & Bellugi, U. (1968). The child's grammar from I to III. In J. P. Hill (Ed.), *Minnesota symposium on child psychology* (Vol. 2, pp. 28–73). Minneapolis: University of Minnesota Press.

Brown, W. A. (1998, January). The placebo effect. *Scientific American, 278*, 90–95.

Browne, C., Dowd, E., & Freeman, A. (2010). Rational and irrational beliefs and psychopathology. In D., David, S., Lynn, & A. Ellis (Eds.), *Rational and irrational beliefs: Research, theory, and clinical practice.* (pp. 149–171). New York: Oxford University Press.

Bruch, M., Fallon, M., & Heimberg, R. (2003). Social phobia and difficulties in occupational adjustment. *Journal of Counseling Psychology, 50,* 109–117.

Brummett, B., Babyak, M., Williams, R., Barefoot, J., Costa, P., & Siegler, I. (2006). NEO personality domains and gender predict levels and trends in body mass index over 14 years during midlife. *Journal of Research in Personality, 40,* 222–236.

Brundage, S. (2002). *Preconception health care.* Retrieved November 30, 2006, from *http://www.aafp.org/afp/20020615/2507.html*

Brunetti, A., Carta, P., Cossu, G., Ganadu, M., Golosio, B., Mura, G., et al. (2002). A real-time classification system of thalassemic pathologies based on artificial neural networks. *Medical Decision Making, 22,* 18–26.

Brunila, T., Lincoln, N., Lindell, A., Tenovuo, O., & Haemelaeinen, H. (2002). Experiences of combined visual training and arm activation in the rehabilitation of unilateral visual neglect: A clinical study. *Neuropsychological Rehabilitation, 12,* 27–40.

Bruno-Petrina, A. (2009). *Motor recovery in stroke.* Retrieved January 15, 2010 from *http://emedicine.medscape.com/article/324386-overview.*

Brydon, L., Magid, K., & Steptoe, A. (2006). Platelets, coronary heart disease, and stress. *Brain, Behavior, and Immunity, 20,* 113–119.

Buchanan, N., & Fitzgerald, L. (2008). Effects of racial and sexual harassment on work and the psychological well-being of African American women. *Journal of Occupational Health Psychology, 13,* 137–151.

Buchert, R., Thomasius, R., Wilke, F., Petersen, K., Nebeling, B., Obrocki, J., Schulze, O., Schmidt, U., & Clausen, M. (2004). A voxel-based PET investigation of the long-term effects of "ecstasy" consumption on brain serotonin transporters. *American Journal of Psychiatry, 161,* 1181–1189.

Buchert, S., Laws, E., Apperson, J., & Bregman, N. (2008). First impressions and professor reputation: Influence on student evaluations of instruction. *Social Psychology of Education, 11,* 397–408.

Buck, L. B. (1996). Information coding in the vertebrate olfactory system. *Annual Review of Neuroscience, 19,* 517–544.

Buckingham, H. W., Jr., & Kertesz, A. (1974). A linguistic analysis of fluent aphasics. *Brain and Language, 1,* 29–42.

Buhusi, C., & Meck, W. (2002). Differential effects of methamphetamine and haloperidol on the control of an internal clock. *Behavioral Neuroscience, 116,* 291–297.

Buller, D. B., Burgoon, M., Hall, J. R., Levine, N., Taylor, A. M., Beach, B. H., et al. (2000). Using language intensity to increase the success of a family intervention to protect children from ultraviolet radiation: Predictions from language expectancy theory. *Preventive Medicine, 30,* 103–113.

Burchinal, M., Campbell, F., Bryant, D., Wasik, B., & Ramey, C. (1997). Early intervention and mediating processes in cognitive performance of children of low-income African American families. *Child Development, 68,* 935–954.

Bureau of Justice Statistics. (2005). *Criminal victimization in the United States: Statistics tables.* Retrieved February 14, 2009 from *http://www.ojp.gov/bjs/abstract/cvusst.htm.*

Burke, A., Heuer, F., & Reisberg, D. (1992). Remembering emotional events. *Memory and Cognition, 20,* 277–290.

Burt, D. B., Zembar, M. J., & Niederehe, G. (1995). Depression and memory impairment: A meta-analysis of the association, its pattern, and specificity. *Psychological Bulletin, 117,* 285–305.

Burton, D. (2003). Male adolescents: Sexual victimization and subsequent sexual abuse. *Child & Adolescent Social Work Journal, 20,* 277–296.

Busch, C. M., Zonderman, A. B., & Costa, P. T. (1994). Menopausal transition and psychological distress in a nationally representative sample: Is menopause associated with psychological distress? *Journal of Aging and Health, 6,* 209–228.

Bushman, B. (2002). Does venting anger feed or extinguish the flame? Catharsis rumination, distraction, anger and aggressive responding. *Personality & Social Psychology Bulletin, 28,* 724–731.

Bushman, B. J. (1995). Moderating role of trait aggressiveness in the effects of violent media on aggression. *Journal of Personality and Social Psychology, 69,* 950–960.

Bushman, B. J., & Cooper, H. M. (1990). Effects of alcohol on human aggression: An integrative research review. *Psychological Bulletin, 107,* 341–354.

Bushman, B., & Huesmann, R. (2006). Short-term and long-term effects of violent media on aggression in children and adults. *Archives of Pediatric Adolescent Medicine, 160,* 348–352.

Busnel, M. C., Granier-Deferre, C., & Lecanuet, J. P. (1992). Fetal audition. *Annals of the New York Academy of Sciences, 662,* 118–134.

Buss, D. M. (1984). Marital assortment for personality dispositions: Assessment with three different data sources. *Behavioral Genetics, 14,* 111–123.

Buss, D. M. (1994). The strategies of human mating. *American Scientist, 82,* 238–249.

Buss, D. M. (1999). *Evolutionary psychology: The new science of the mind.* Boston: Allyn & Bacon.

Buss, D. M. (2000a). *The dangerous passion: Why jealousy is as necessary as sex and love.* New York: Free Press.

Buss, D. M. (2000b). Desires in human mating. *Annals of the New York Academy of Sciences, 907,* 39–49.

Buss, D. M., Abbott, M., Angleitner, A., Asherian, A., Biaggio, A., Blanco-Villasenor, A., et al. (1990). International preferences in selecting mates: A study of 37 cultures. *Journal of Cross-Cultural Psychology, 21,* 5–47.

Buss, D. M., Shackelford, T., Kirkpatrick, L., & Larsen, R. (2001). A half century of mate preferences: The cultural evolution of values. *Journal of Marriage and the Family, 63,* 491–503.

Buss, D., & Shackelford, T. (2008). Attractive women want it all: Good genes, economic investment, parenting proclivities, and emotional commitment. *Evolutionary Psychology, 6,* 134–146.

Buss, D., & Shackelford, T. (2008). Attractive women want it all: Good genes, economic investment, parenting proclivities, and emotional commitment. *Evolutionary Psychology, 6,* 134–146.

Bussey, K., & Bandura, A. (1999). Social cognitive theory of gender development and differentiation. *Psychological Review, 106,* 676–713.

Butcher, J. N., & Graham, J. R. (1989). *Topics in MMPI–2 interpretation.* Minneapolis: Department of Psychology, University of Minnesota.

Butcher, J. N., & Rouse, S. V. (1996). Personality: Individual differences and clinical assessment. *Annual Review of Psychology, 47,* 89–111.

Butcher, J. N., Dahlstrom, W. G., Graham, J. R., Tellegen, A., & Kaemmer, B. (1989). *Manual for the restandardized Minnesota Multiphasic Personality Inventory: MMPI–2. An administrative and interpretive guide.* Minneapolis: University of Minnesota Press.

Butler, L., Waelde, L., Hastings, T., Chen, X., Symons, B., Marshall, J., Kaufman, A., & Nagy, T. (2008). Meditation with yoga, group therapy with hypnosis, and psychoeducation for long-term depressed mood: A randomized pilot trial. *Journal of Clinical Psychology, 64,* 806–820.

Butler, R., & Lewis, M. (1982). *Aging and mental health* (3rd ed.). St. Louis: Mosby.

Byne, W. (1993). *Sexual orientation and brain structure: Adding up the evidence.* Paper presented at the annual meeting of the International Academy of Sex Research. Pacific Grove, CA.

Caby'oglu, M., Ergene, N., & Tan, U. (2006). The mechanism of acupuncture and clinical applications. *International Journal of Neuroscience, 116,* 115–125.

Cahill, L., & McGaugh, J. (1995). A novel demonstration of enhanced memory associated with emotional arousal. *Consciousness & Cognition, 4,* 410–421.

Cahn, B., & Polich, J. (2006). Meditation states and traits: EEG, ERP, and neuroimaging studies. *Psychological Bulletin, 132,* 180–211.

Cain, C., & LeDoux, J. (2008). Emotional processing and motivation: In search of brain mechanisms. In A. Eliot (Ed.), *Handbook of approach and avoidance motivation* (pp. 17–34). New York: Psychology Press.

Calton, T., & Spandler, H. (2009). Minimal-medication approaches to treating schizophrenia. *Advances in Psychiatric Treatment, 15,* 209–217.

Camerer, C. (2005). Three cheers—psychological, theoretical, empirical—for loss aversion. *Journal of Marketing Research, 42,* 129–133.

Camp, D. S., Raymond, G. A., & Church, R. M. (1967). Temporal relationship between response and punishment. *Journal of Experimental Psychology, 74,* 114–123.

Campbell, F., & Ramey, C. (1994). Effects of early intervention on intellectual and academic achievement: A follow-up study of children from low-income families. *Child Development, 65,* 684–698.

Campbell, F., Pungello, E., Miller-Johnson, S., Burchinal, M., & Ramey, C. (2001). The development of cognitive and academic abilities: Growth curves from an early childhood educational experiment. *Developmental Psychology, 37,* 231–242.

Campbell, F., Wasik, B., Pungello, E., Burchinal, M., Barbarin, O., Kainz, K., Sparling, J., & Ramey, C. (2008). Young adult outcomes of the Abecedarian and CARE early childhood educational interventions. *Early Childhood Research Quarterly, 23,* 452–466.

Campbell, P., & Dhand, R. (2000). Obesity. *Nature, 404,* 631.

Cannon, T. D., Kaprio, J., Lönnqvist, J., Huttunen, M., & Koskenvuo, M. (1998). The genetic epidemiology of schizophrenia in a Finnish twin cohort: A population-based modeling study. *Archives of General Psychiatry, 55,* 67–74.

Cannon, W. B. (1927). The James-Lange theory of emotions: A critical examination as an alternative theory. *American Journal of Psychology, 39,* 106–112.

Cannon, W. B. (1929). *Bodily changes in pain, hunger, fear and rage* (2nd ed.). New York: Appleton.

Cannon, W. B. (1935). Stresses and strains of homeostasis. *American Journal of Public Health, 189,* 1–14.

Capel, B. (2000). The battle of the sexes. *Mechanisms of Development, 92,* 89–103.

Caramaschi, D., de Boer, S., & Koolhaas, J. (2008). Is hyper-aggressiveness associated with physiological hypoarousal? A comparative study on mouse lines selected for high and low aggressiveness. *Physiology & Behavior, 95,* 591–598.

Cardoso, S. H., de Mello, L. C., & Sabbatini, R. M. E. (2000). How nerve cells work. Retrieved June 10, 2007 from *http://www.cerebromente.org.br/n10/fundamentos/pot2_i.htm.org.br/cm/n09/fundamentos/transmissao/voo_i.htm*

Carlat, D. J., Camargo, C. A., Jr., & Herzog, D. B. (1997). Eating disorders in males: A report on 135 patients. *American Journal of Psychiatry, 154,* 1127–1132.

Carlson, N. R. (1998). *Foundations of physiological psychology* (4th ed.). Boston: Allyn & Bacon.

Carlsson, I., Wendt, P. E., & Risberg, J. (2000). On the neurobiology of creativity. Differences in frontal activity between high and low creative subjects. *Neuropsychologia, 38,* 873–885.

Carnagey, N., & Anderson, C. (2004). Violent video game exposure and aggression: A literature review. *Minerva Psichiatrica, 45,* 1–18.

Carnagey, N., & Anderson, C. (2005). The effects of reward and punishment in violent video games on aggressive affect, cognition, and behavior. *Psychological Science, 16,* 882–889.

Carnagey, N., Anderson, C., & Bushman, B. (2007). The effect of video game violence on physiological desensitization to real-life violence. *Journal of Experimental Social Psychology, 43,* 489–496.

Carpenter, S. (2001). Sights unseen. *Monitor on Psychology, 32* [Electronic version]. Retrieved May 13, 2003, from *http://www.apa.org/monitor/apr01/blindness.html*

Carpenter, S. (2001, March). Everyday fantasia: The world of synesthesia. *APA Monitor on Psychology* [Online version], *32.*

Carpenter, W. T., Jr. (1996). Maintenance therapy of persons with schizophrenia. *Journal of Clinical Psychiatry, 57*(9, Suppl.), 10–18.

Carrier, J. (1980). Homosexual behavior in cross-cultural perspective. In J. Marmor (Ed.), *Homosexual behavior* (pp. 100–122). New York: Basic Books.

Carroll, K. M., Rounsaville, B. J., Nich, C., Gordon, L. T., Wirtz, P. W., & Gawin, F. (1994). One-year follow-up of psychotherapy and pharmacotherapy for cocaine dependence: Delayed emergence of psychotherapy effects. *Archives of General Psychiatry, 51,* 989–997.

Carroll, M., & Perfect, T. (2002). Students' experiences of unconscious plagiarism: Did I beget or forget? In T., Perfect, & B. Schwartz (Eds.), *Applied metacognition* (pp. 146–166). New York: Cambridge University press.

Carskadon, M. A., & Dement, W. C. (1989). Normal human sleep: An overview. In M. H. Kryger, T. Roth, & W. C. Dement (Eds.), *Principles and practice of sleep medicine* (pp. 3–13). Philadelphia: W. B. Saunders.

Carskadon, M. A., & Rechtschaffen, A. (1989). Monitoring and staging human sleep. In M. H. Kryger, T. Roth, & W. C. Dement (Eds.), *Principles and practice of sleep medicine* (pp. 665–683). Philadelphia: W. B. Saunders.

Carson, R. C. (1989). Personality. *Annual Review of Psychology, 40,* 227–248.

Carson, R., Butcher, J., & Mineka, S. (2000). *Abnormal psychology and modern life* (11th ed.). Boston: Allyn & Bacon.

Carver, C. S., Pozo, C., Harris, S. D., Noriega, V., Scheier, M. F., Robinson, D. S., et al. (1993). How coping mediates the effect of optimism on distress: A study of women with early stage breast cancer. *Journal of Personality and Social Psychology, 65,* 375–390.

Case, A., & Paxson, C. (2004). Sex differences in morbidity and mortality. *National Bureau of Economic Research Working Paper No. 10653.* Retrieved July 7, 2006, from *http://www.nber.org/papers/W10653*

Case, R. (Ed.). (1992). *The mind's staircase: Exploring the conceptual underpinnings of children's thought and knowledge.* Hillsdale, NJ: Erlbaum.

Casey, D. E. (1996). Side effect profiles of new antipsychotic agents. *Journal of Clinical Psychiatry, 57*(11, Suppl.), 40–45.

Cash, T. F., & Janda, L. H. (1984, December). The eye of the beholder. *Psychology Today,* 46–52.

Caspi, A. (2000). The child is father of the man: Personality continuities from childhood to adulthood. *Journal of Personality & Social Psychology, 78,* 158–172.

Caspi, A., Lynam, D., Moffitt, T. E., & Silva, P. A. (1993). Unraveling girls' delinquency: Biological, dispositional, and contextual contributions to adolescent misbehavior. *Developmental Psychology, 29,* 19–30.

Cassell, M., Halperin, D., Shelton, J., & Stanton, D. (2006). Risk compensation: The Achilles' heel of innovations in HIV protection? *British Medical Journal, 332,* 605–607.

Cattapan-Ludewig, K., Ludewig, S., Jaquenoud, S., Etzensberger, M., & Hasler, F. (2005). Why do schizophrenic patients smoke? *Nervenarzt, 76,* 287–294.

Cattell, R. B. (1950). *Personality: A systematic, theoretical, and factual study.* New York: McGraw-Hill.

Cattell, R., & Schuerger, J. (2003). *Essentials of 16PF assessment.* New York: John Wiley & Sons.

Cavanaugh, S. (2004). The sexual debut of girls in early adolescence: The intersection of race, pubertal timing, and friendship group. *Journal of Research on Adolescence, 14,* 285–312.

CBS News. (July 31, 2002). *Fear of public speaking.* Retrieved February 14, 2003, from *http://www.cbsnews.com/stories/2002/07/30*

Centers for Disease Control (CDC). (2008). *About the childhood lead poisoning prevention program.* Retrieved May 8, 2009 from *http://www.cdc.gov/nceh/lead/about/program.htm.*

Centers for Disease Control (CDC). (2008). *Youth risk behavior surveillance: United States, 2007.* Retrieved February 27, 2010 from *http://www.cdc.gov/mmwr/PDF/ss/ss5704.pdf.*

Centers for Disease Control (CDC). (2009a). *Sexually transmitted diseases surveillance: National Profile.* Retrieved March 12, 2010 from *http://www.cdc.gov/std/stats08/surv2008-NationalProfile.pdf.*

Centers for Disease Control and Prevention (CDC). (1999). *Physical activity and health.* Retrieved January 29, 2003, from *http://www.cdc.gov/needphp/sgr/ataglan.htm.*

Centers for Disease Control and Prevention (CDC). (2000). Youth risk behavior surveillance—United States, 1999. *Morbidity and Mortality Weekly Report, 49,* 1–96.

Centers for Disease Control and Prevention (CDC). (2002). Nonfatal self-inflicted injuries treated in hospital emergency departments—United States, 2000. *Morbidity & Mortality Weekly Report, 51,* 436–438.

Centers for Disease Control and Prevention (CDC). (2003a). *About minority health.* Retrieved August 8, 2003, from *http://www.cdc.gov/omh/AMH/AMH.htm.*

Centers for Disease Control and Prevention (CDC). (2003b). Sexually transmitted disease surveillance, 2002. Retrieved August 18, 2004, from *http://www.cdc.gov/std/stats/natoverview.htm.*

Centers for Disease Control and Prevention (CDC). (2004a). Surveillance summaries. *Morbidity & Mortality Weekly Report, 53,* 1–100.

Centers for Disease Control and Prevention (CDC). (2004b). *Syphilis and men who have sex with men.* Retrieved July 3, 2006, from *http://www.cdc.gov/std/syphilis/STDFact-MSM&Syphilis.htm.*

Centers for Disease Control and Prevention (CDC). (2005a). *About minority health.* Retrieved February 2, 2005, from *http://www.cdc.gov/omh/AMH/AMH.htm.*

Centers for Disease Control and Prevention (CDC). (2005b). *Trends in reportable sexually transmitted diseases in the United States, 2004.* Retrieved July 3, 2006, from *http://www.cdc.gov/std/stats/04pdf/trends2004.pdf.*

Centers for Disease Control and Prevention (CDC). (2006a). *HPV Vaccine questions and answers.* Retrieved June 29, 2006, from *http://www.cdc.gov/std/hpv/STDFact-HPV-vaccine.htm#vaccine.*

Centers for Disease Control and Prevention (CDC). (2006b). Growing stronger: Strength training for older adults. Retrieved July 7, 2006 from *http://www.cdc.gov/nccdphp/dnpa/physical/growing_stronger/index.htm.*

Centers for Disease Control and Prevention (CDC). (2006c). National youth risk behavior survey 1991–2005. Retrieved June 13, 2006 from *http://www.cdc.gov/healthyyouth/yrbs/pdf/trends/2005_YRBS_Sexual_Behaviors.pdf.*

Centers for Disease Control and Prevention (CDC). (2006d). *Nutrition topics.* Retrieved July 7, 2006, from *http://www.cdc.gov/nccdphp/dnpa/nutrition/index.htm.*

Centers for Disease Control and Prevention (CDC). (2006e). Quick stats: General information on alcohol use and health. Retrieved July 7, 2006 from *http://www.cdc.gov/alcohol/quickstats/general_info.htm.*

Centers for Disease Prevention and Control (CDC). (2009b). *HIV/AIDS surveillance report.* Retrieved March 12, 2010 from *http://www.cdc.gov/hiv/topics/surveillance/resources/reports/2007report/pdf/2007SurveillanceReport.pdf.*

Chaitow, L., & DeLany, J. (2002). *Clinical application of neuromuscular techniques.* London: Elsevier Science Limited.

Chambless, D. L., & Goldstein, A. J. (1979). Behavioral psychotherapy. In R. J. Corsini (Ed.), *Current psychotherapies* (2nd ed., pp. 230–272). Itasca, IL: F. E. Peacock.

Chamorro-Premuzic, T., & Furnham, A. (2003). Personality predicts academic performance: Evidence from two longitudinal university samples. *Journal of Research in Personality, 37,* 319–338.

Chan, J., Thomas, A., & Bulevich, J. (2009). Recalling a witnessed event increases eyewitness suggestibility: The reversed testing effect. *Psychological Science, 20,* 66–73.

Chang, E., & Merzenich, M. (2003). Environmental noise retards auditory cortical development. *Science, 300,* 498–502.

Chao, R. (2001). Extending research on the consequences of parenting style for Chinese Americans and European Americans. *Child Development, 72,* 1832–1843.

Chao, R., & Aque, C. (2009). Interpretations of parental control by Asian immigrant and European American youth. *Journal of Family Psychology, 23,* 342–354.

Chaplin, W. F., Philips, J. B., Brown, J. D., Clanton, N. R., & Stein, J. L. (2000). Handshaking, gender, personality, and first impressions. *Journal of Personality and Social Psychology, 19,* 110–117.

Charles, S., Mather, M., & Carstensen, L. (2003). Aging and emotional memory: The forgettable nature of negative images for older adults. *Journal of Experimental Psychology, 132,* 310–324.

Charness, N. (1989). Age and expertise: Responding to Talland's challenge. In L. W. Poon, D. C. Rubin, & B. A. Wilson (Eds.), *Everyday cognition in adulthood and old age* (pp. 437–456). New York: Cambridge University Press.

Chart, H., Grigorenko, E., & Sternberg, R. (2008). Identification: The Aurora battery. In J., Plucker & C. Callahan (Eds.), *Critical issues and practices in gifted education: What the research says* (pp. 281–301). Waco, TX: Prufrock Press.

Chase, M. H., & Morales, F. R. (1990). The atonia and myoclonia of active (REM) sleep. *Annual Review of Psychology, 41,* 557–584.

Chase, W. G., & Simon, H. A. (1973). Perception in chess. *Cognitive Psychology, 4,* 55–81.

Chassin, L., Presson, C., Sherman, S., & Kim, K. (2003). Historical changes in cigarette smoking and smoking-related beliefs after 2 decades in a midwestern community. *Health Psychology, 22,* 347–353.

Chen-Sea, M.-J. (2000). Validating the Draw-A-Man Test as a personal neglect test. *American Journal of Occupational Therapy, 54,* 391–397.

Cherry, E. (1953). Some experiments on the recognition of speech with one and two ears. *Journal of the Acoustical Society of America, 25,* 975–979.

Chesney, T. (2006). The effect of communication medium on research participation decisions. *Journal of Computer-Mediated Communication, 11,* 877–883.

Chi, S., Park, C., Lim, S., Park, E., Lee, Y., Lee, K., et al. (2005). EEG and personality dimensions: A consideration based on the rain oscillatory systems. *Personality and Individual Differences, 39,* 669–681.

"Children spend more time playing video games than watching TV, MSU survey shows." (2004, April 4). Retrieved July 23, 2005, from *http://www.newsroom.msu.edu/site/indexer/1943/content.htm*

Chilosi, A., Cipriani, P., Bertuccelli, B., Pfanner, L., & Cioni, G. (2001). Early cognitive and communication development in children with focal brain lesions. *Journal of Child Neurology, 16,* 309–316.

Cho, K. (2001). Chronic "jet lag" produces temporal lobe atrophy and spatial cognitive deficits. *Nature Neuroscience, 4,* 567–568.

Cho, K., Ennaceur, A., Cole, J., & Kook Suh, C. (2000). Chronic jet lag produces cognitive deficits. *Journal of Neuroscience, 20,* RC66.

Cho, S., Ku, J., Park, J., Han, K., Lee, H., Choi, Y., Jung, Y., Namkoong, K., Kim, J., Kim, I., Kim, S., & Shen, D. (2008). Development and verification of an alcohol craving-induction tool using virtual reality: Craving characteristics in social pressure situations. *CyberPsychology & Behavior, 11,* 302–309.

Choi, H., & Smith, S. (2005). Incubatin and the resolution of tip-of-the-tongue states. *Journal of General Psychology, 132,* 365–376.

Choi, I., Dalal, R., Kim-Prieto, C., & Park, H. (2003). Culture and judgment of causal relevance. *Journal of Personality & Social Psychology, 84,* 46–59.

Choi, J., & Silverman, I. (2002). The relationship between testosterone and route-learning strategies in humans. *Brain & Cognition, 50,* 116–120.

Chollar, S. (1989). Conversation with the dolphins. *Psychology Today, 23,* 52–57.

Chomsky, N. (1957). *Syntactic structures.* The Hague: Mouton.

Chomsky, N. (1968). *Language and mind.* New York: Harcourt, Brace & World.

Chowdhury, R., Ferrier, I., & Thompson, J. (2003). Cognitive dysfunction in bipolar disorder. *Current Opinion in Psychiatry, 16,* 7–12.

Christakis, D., Zimmerman, F., DiGiuseppe, D., & McCarty, C. (2004). Early television exposure and subsequent attentional problems in children. *Pediatrics, 113,* 708–713.

Christensen, A., Atkins, D., Berns, S., Wheeler, J., Baucom, D., & Simpson, L. (2004). Traditional versus integrative behavioral couple therapy for significantly and chronically distressed married couples. *Journal of Consulting and Clinical Psychology, 72,* 176–191.

Christensen, A., Wheeler, J., & Jacobson, N. (2008). In D. Barlow (Ed.), *Clinical handbook of psychological disorders: A step-by-step treatment manual* (4th ed.) (pp. 662–689). New York: Guilford Press.

Christianson, S-Å. (1992). Emotional stress and eyewitness memory: A critical review. *Psychological Bulletin, 112,* 284–309.

Church, M., Elliot, A., & Gable, S. (2001). Perceptions of classroom enviornment, achievement goals, and achievement outcomes. *Journal of Educational Psychology, 93,* 43–54.

Church, R. M. (1963). The varied effects of punishment on behavior. *Psychological Review, 70,* 369–402.

Cialdini, R. B., Cacioppo, J. T., Basset, R., & Miller, J. A. (1978). Lowball procedure for producing compliance: Commitment then cost. *Journal of Personality and Social Psychology, 36,* 463–476.

Cialdini, R. B., Vincent, J. E., Lewis, S. K., Catalan, J., Wheeler, D., & Darby, B. L. (1975). Reciprocal concessions procedure for inducing compliance: The door-in-the-face technique. *Journal of Personality and Social Psychology, 31,* 206–215.

Clément, K., Vaisse, C., Lahlou, N., Cabrol, S., Pelloux, V., Cassuto, D., et al. (1998). A mutation in the human leptin receptor gene causes obesity and pituitary dysfunction. *Nature, 392,* 398–401.

Clark, D. M., & Teasdale, J. D. (1982). Diurnal variation in clinical depression and accessibility of memories of positive and negative experiences. *Journal of Abnormal Psychology, 91,* 87–95.

Clark, D., & Beck, A. (2010). *Cognitive therapy of anxiety disorders: Science and practice.* New York: Guilford Press.

Clark, L., Bechara, A., Damasio, H., Atiken, M., Sahakian, B., & Robbins, T. (2008). Differential effects of insular and ventromedial prefrontal cortex lesions on risky decision-making. *Brain: A Journal of Neurology, 131,* 1311–1322.

Clark, L., Watson, D., & Reynolds, S. (1995). Ciagnosis and classification of psychopathology: Challenges to the current system and future directions. *Annual Review of Psychology, 46,* 121–153.

Clark, M. (2009). Suppose Freud had chosen Orestes instead. *Journal of Analytical Psychology, 54,* 233–252.

Clark, M. L., & Ayers, M. (1992). Friendship similarity during early adolescence: Gender and racial patterns. *Journal of Psychology, 126,* 393–405.

Classen, J., Liepert, J., Wise, S., Hallett, M., & Cohen, L. (1998). Rapid plasticity of human cortical movement representation induced by practice. *Journal of Neurophysiology, 79,* 1117–1123.

Clay, R. (2003). Researchers replace midlife myths with facts. *APA Monitor on Psychology, 34,* 36.

Clayton, V. (2004, September 8). *What's to blame for the rise in ADHD?* Retrieved November 22, 2004, from *http://www.msnbc.msn.com/id/5933775/*

Clifford, E. (2000). Neural plasticity: Merzenich, Taub, and Greenough. *Harvard Brain [Special Issue], 6,* 16–20.

Cloitre, M., Koenen, K., Cohen, L., & Han, H. (2002). Skills training in affective and interpersonal regulation followed by exposure: A phase-based treatment for PTSD related to childhood abuse. *Journal of Consulting and Clinical Psychology, 70,* 1067–1074.

Cloninger, C. R., Sigvardsson, S., Bohman, M., & von Knorring, A. L. (1982). Predispositions to petty criminality in Swedish adoptees, II. Cross-fostering analysis of gene-environment interaction. *Archives of General Psychiatry, 39,* 1242–1249.

Cloos, J., & Ferreira, V. (2009). Current use of benzodiazepines in anxiety disorders. *Current Opinion in Psychiatry, 22,* 90–95.

CNN.com. (February 16, 2003). *Fatal shooting caught on tape.* Retrieved February 17, 2003, from *http://www.cnn.com/2003/US/South/02/16/gas.shooting.ap/index.html.*

Cohen, L. L., & Shotland, R. L. (1996). Timing of first sexual intercourse in a relationship: Expectations, experiences, and perceptions of others. *Journal of Sex Research, 33,* 291–299.

Cohen, R., & Stussman, B. (2010). *Health information technology use among men and women aged 18–64: Early release of estimates from the National Health Interview Survey, January–June 2009.* Retrieved March 12, 2010 from *http://www.cdc.gov/nchs/data/hestat/healthinfo2009/healthinfo2009.htm.*

Cohen, S., & Herbert, T. B. (1996). Health psychology: Psychological factors and physical disease from the perspective of human psychoneuroimmunology. *Annual Review of Psychology, 47,* 113–142.

Cohen, S., & Williamson, G. M. (1991). Stress and infectious disease in humans. *Psychological Bulletin, 109,* 5–54.

Cohen, S., Doyle, W. J., Skoner, D. P., Rabin, B. S., & Gwaltney, J. M., Jr. (1997). Social ties and susceptibility to the common cold. *Journal of the American Medical Association, 277,* 1940–1944.

Cohen, S., Doyle, W., & Baum, A. (2006). Socioeconomic status is associated with stress hormones. *Psychosomatic Medicine, 68,* 414–420.

Cohn, M., Brown, S., Fredrickson, B., & Mikels, J. (2009). Happiness unpacked: Positive emotions increase life satisfaction by building resilience. *Emotion, 9,* 361–368.

Colby, A., Kohlberg, L., Gibbs, J., & Lieberman, M. (1983). A longitudinal study of moral judgment. *Monographs of the Society for Research in Child Development, 48*(1–2, Serial No. 200).

Cole, R., Smith, J., Alcala, Y., Elliott, J., & Kripke, D. (2002). Bright-light mask treatment of delayed sleep phase syndrome. *Journal of Biological Rhythms, 17,* 89–101.

Coleman, C., King, B., Bolden-Watson, C., Book, M., Segraves, R., Richard, N., et al. (2001). A placebo-controlled comparison of the effects on sexual functioning of bupropion sustained release and fluoxetine. *Clinical Therapeutics: The International Peer-Reviewed Journal of Drug Therapy, 23,* 1040–1058.

Collaer, M. L., & Hines, M. (1995). Human behavioral sex differences: A role for gonadal hormones during early development. *Psychological Bulletin, 118,* 55–107.

Colwell, J., & Payne, J. (2000). Negative correlates of computer game play in adolescents. *British Journal of Psychology, 91*(Pt. 3), 295–310.

Conca, A., Swoboda, E., König, P., Koppi, S., Beraus, W., Künz, A., et al. (2000). Clinical impacts of single transcranial magnetic stimulation (sTMS) as an add-on therapy in severely depressed patients under SSRI treatment. *Human Psychopharmacology: Clinical and Experimental, 15,* 429–438.

Condon, W. S., & Sander, L. W. (1974). Neonatal movement is synchronized with adult speech: Interactional participation and language acquisition. *Science, 183,* 99–101.

Coney, J., & Fitzgerald, J. (2000). Gender differences in the recognition of laterally presented affective nouns. Cognition and Emotion, 14, 325–339.

Conrad, P., & Leiter, V. (2004). Medicalization, markets, and consumers. *Journal of Health and Social Behavior, 45* (Supplement), 158–176.

Conroy, D., Poczwardowski, A., & Henschen, K. (2001). Evaluative criteria and consequences associated with failure and success for elite athletes and performing artists. *Journal of Applied Sport Psychology, 13,* 300–322.

Consumer *Reports.* (1995, November) Mental health: Does therapy help?, 734–739.

Coolidge, F., Thede, L., & Young, S. (2002). The heritability of gender identity disorder in a child and adolescent twin sample. *Behavior Genetics, 32,* 251–257.

Coons, P. M. (1994). Confirmation of childhood abuse in child and adolescent cases of multiple personality disorder and dissociative disorder not otherwise specified. *Journal of Nervous and Mental Disease, 182,* 461–464.

Cooper, R. (1994). Normal sleep. In R. Cooper (Ed.), *Sleep.* New York: Chapman & Hall.

Coplan, J. D., Papp, L. A., Pine, D., Marinez, J., Cooper, T., Rosenblum, L. A., et al. (1997). Clinical improvement with fluoxetine therapy and noradrenergic function in patients with panic disorder. *Archives of General Psychiatry, 54,* 643–648.

Corballis, M. C. (1989). Laterality and human evolution. *Psychological Review, 96,* 492–509.

Coren, S. (1996a). Accidental death and the shift to daylight savings time. *Perceptual and Motor Skills, 83,* 921–922.

Coren, S. (1996b). Daylight savings time and traffic accidents. *New England Journal of Medicine, 334*, 924.

Corenblum, B., & Meissner, C. (2006). Recognition of faces of ingroup and outgroup children and adults. *Journal of Experimental Child Psychology, 93*, 187–206.

Cornelius, M. D., Leech, S. L., Goldschmidt, L., & Day, N. L. (2000). Prenatal tobacco exposure: Is it a risk factor for early tobacco experimentation? *Nicotine & Tobacco Research, 2*, 45–52.

Cortina, L., & Magley, V. (2003). Raising voice, risking retaliation: Events following interpersonal mistreatment in the workplace. *Journal of Occupational Health Psychology, 8*, 247–265.

Cosmides, L., & Tooby, J. (2000). Evolutionary psychology and the emotions. In M. Lewis, Jr., & J. M. Haviland-Jones (Eds.), *Handbook of emotions* (2nd ed.) (pp. 91–115). New York: Guilford.

Costa E Silva, J. A., Chase, M., Sartorius, N., & Roth, T. (1996). Special report from a symposium held by the World Health Organization and the World Federation of Sleep Research Societies: An overview of insomnias and related disorders—recognition, epidemiology, and rational management. *Sleep, 19*, 412–416.

Costa, P. T., Jr., & McCrae, R. R. (1985). *The NEO Personality Inventory*. Odessa, FL: Psychological Assessment Resources.

Costa, P., & McCrae, R. (2009). The five-factor model and the NEO Inventories. In J. Butcher, (Ed.), *Oxford handbook of personality assessment*, Oxford Library of Psychology (pp. 299–322). New York: Oxford University Press.

Courage, M. L., & Adams, R. J. (1990). Visual acuity assessment from birth to three years using the acuity card procedures: Cross-sectional and longitudinal samples. *Optometry and Vision Science, 67*, 713–718.

Covey, S. (1989). *The 7 habits of highly effective people*. New York: Simon & Shuster.

Cowan, N. (1988). Evolving conceptions of memory storage, selective attention, and their mutual constraints within the human information-processing system. *Psychological Bulletin, 104*, 163–191.

Cowley, E. (2005). Views from consumers next in line: The fundamental attribution error in a service setting. *Journal of the Academy of Marketing Science, 33*, 139–152.

Coyle, J., & Draper, E. S. (1996). What is the significance of glutamate for mental health? *Harvard Mental Health Letter, 13*(6), 8.

Coyne, S. (2004). Indirect aggression on screen: A hidden problem? *The Psychologist, 17*, 688–690.

Coyne, S., Archer, J., & Eslea, M. (2004). Cruel intentions on television and in real life: Can viewing indirect aggression increase viewers' subsequent indirect aggression? *Journal of Experimental Child Psychology, 88*, 234–253.

Craig, I., & Plomin, R. (2006). Quantitative trait loci for IQ and other complex traits: Single-nucleotide polymorphism genotyping using pooled DNA and microarrays. *Genes, Brain & Behavior, 5*, 32–37.

Craik, F., & Bialystok, E. (2010). Bilingualism and aging: Costs and benefits. In L., Bäckman & L. Nyberg, (Eds.), *Memory, aging and the brain: A Festschrift in honour of Lars-Göran Nilsson* (pp. 115–131). New York: Psychology Press.

Craik, F. I. M., & Lockhart, R. S. (1972). Levels of processing: A framework for memory research. *Journal of Verbal Learning and Verbal Behavior, 11*, 671–684.

Craik, F. I. M., & Tulving, E. (1975). Depth of processing and the retention of words in episodic memory. *Journal of Experimental Psychology: General, 104*, 268–294.

Crandall, C., & Reser, A. (2005). Attributions and weight-based prejudice. In K. Brownell, R., Puhl, M., Schwartz, & L. Rudd (Eds.), *Weight bias: Nature, consequences, and remedies*. New York: Guilford Press.

Criglington, A. (1998). Do professionals get jet lag? A commentary on jet lag. *Aviation, Space, & Environmental Medicine, 69*, 810.

Crits-Christoph, P. (1992). The efficacy of brief dynamic psychotherapy: A meta-analysis. *American Journal of Psychiatry, 149*, 151–158.

Crits-Christoph, P., Gibbons, M., Losardo, D., Narducci, J., Schamberger, M., & Gallop, R. (2004). Who benefits from brief psychodynamic therapy for generalized anxiety disorder? *Canadian Journal of Psychoanalysis, 12*, 301–324.

Crits-Christoph, P., Gibbons, M., Ring-Kurtz, S., Gallop, R., Stirman, S., Present, J., Temes, C., & Goldstein, L. (2008). Changes in positive quality of life over the course of psychotherapy. *Psychotherapy, Theory, Research, Practice, Training, 45*, 419–430.

Crockenberg, S., & Leerkes, E. (2005). Infant temperament moderates associations between childcare type and quantity and externalizing and internalizing behaviors at 2 1/2 years. *Infant Behavior & Development, 28*, 20–35.

Crombag, H., & Robinson, T. (2004). Drugs, environment, brain, and behavior. *Current Directions in Psychological Science, 13*, 107–111.

Crone, E., Wendelken, C., Donohue, S., van Leijenhorst, L., & Bunge, S. (2006). Neurocognitive development of the ability to manipulate information in working memory. *Proceedings for the National Academy of Sciences, 103*, 9315–9320.

Crowder, R. G. (1992) Sensory memory. In L. R. Squire (Ed.), *Encyclopedia of learning and memory*. New York: Macmillan.

Crowe, L. C., & George, W. H. (1989). Alcohol and human sexuality: Review and integration. *Psychological Bulletin, 105*, 374–386.

Crowley, B., Hayslip, B., & Hobdy, J. (2003). Psychological hardiness and adjustment to life events in adulthood. *Journal of Adult Development, 10*, 237–248.

Crowther, J., Kichler, J., Shewood, N., & Kuhnert, M. (2002). The role of familial factors in bulimia nervosa. *Eating Disorders: The Journal of Treatment & Prevention, 10*, 141–151.

Cruess, D., Localio, A., Platt, A., Brensinger, C., Christie, J., Gross, R., Parker, C., Price, M., Metlay, J., Cohen, A., Newcomb, C., Strom, B., & Kimmel, S. (2010). Patient attitudinal and behavioral factors associated with warfarin non-adherence at outpatient anticoagulation clinics. *International Journal of Behavioral Medicine, 17*, 33–42.

Csikszentmihalyi, M. (1996, July/August). The creative personality. *Psychology Today, 29*, 36–40.

Cui, X-J., & Vaillant, G. E. (1996). Antecedents and consequences of negative life events in adulthood: A longitudinal study. *American Journal of Psychiatry, 153*, 21–26.

Culbertson, F. M. (1997). Depression and gender: An international review. *American Psychologist, 52*, 25–31.

Cullen, M., Hardison, C., & Sackett, P. (2004). Using SAT-grade and ability-job performance relationships to test predictions derived from stereotype threat theory. *Journal of Applied Psychology, 89*, 220–230.

Cunningham, M. R., Roberts, A. R., Barbee, A. P., Druen, P. B., & Wu, C-H. (1995). "Their ideas of beauty are, on the whole, the same as ours": Consistency and variability in the cross-cultural perception of female physical attractiveness. *Journal of Personality and Social Psychology, 68*, 261–279.

Cupach, W. R., & Canary, D. J. (1995). Managing conflict and anger: Investigating the sex stereotype hypothesis. In P. J. Kalbfleisch & M. J. Cody (Eds.), *Gender, power, and communication in human relationships* (pp. 233–252). Hillsdale, NJ: Erlbaum.

Curci, A. (2009). Measurement issues in the study of flashbulb memory. In O., Luminet & A. Curci (Eds.), *Flashbulb memories: New issues and perspectives* (pp. 13–32). New York: Psychology Press.

Curci, A., Luminet, O., Finkenauer, C., & Gisler, L. (2001). Flashbulb memories in social groups: A comparative test-retest study of the memory of French president Mitterrand's death in a French and a Belgian group. *Memory, 9*, 81–101.

Curran, P. J., Stice, E., & Chassin, L. (1997). The relation between adolescent alcohol use and peer alcohol use: A longitudinal random coefficients model. *Journal of Consulting and Clinical Psychology, 65*, 130–140.

Cyranowski, J. M., Frand, E., Young, E., & Shear, M. K. (2000). Adolescent onset of the gender difference in lifetime rates of major depression. *Archives of General Psychiatry, 57*, 21–27.

Cytowic, R. (1993). *The man who tasted shapes*. Cambridge, MA: MIT Press.

Cytowic, R. (2002). *Synesthesia: A union of the senses* (2nd ed.). Cambridge, MA: MIT Press

D'Azevedo, W. A. (1982). Tribal history in Liberia. In U. Neisser (Ed.), *Memory observed: Remembering in natural contexts* (258-268). San Francisco: W. H. Freeman.

Dabbs, J. M., Jr., & Morris, R. (1990). Testosterone, social class, and antisocial behavior in a sample of 4,462 men. *Psychological Science, 1,* 209–211.

Dadds., M., Fraser, J., Frost, A., & Hawes, D. (2005). Disentangling the underlying dimensions of psychopathy and conduct problems in childhood: A community study. *Journal of Consulting and Clinical Psychology, 73,* 400–410.

Dahloef, P., Norlin-Bagge, E., Hedner, J., Ejnell, H., Hetta, J., & Haellstroem, T. (2002). Improvement in neuropsychological performance following surgical treatment for obstructive sleep apnea syndrome. *Acta Oto-Laryngologica, 122,* 86–91.

Dale, N., & Kandel, E. R. (1990). Facilitatory and inhibitory transmitters modulate spontaneous transmitter release at cultured *Aplysia* sensorimotor synapses. *Journal of Physiology, 421,* 203–222.

Daley, T., Whaley, S,. Sigman, M., Espinosa, M., & Neumann, C. (2003). IQ on the rise: The Flynn Effect in rural Kenyan children. *Psychological Science, 14,* 215–219.

Dalgleish, T. (2004). The emotional brain. *Nature Neuroscience Reviews, 5,* 582–589.

Dallard, I., Cathebras, P., & Sauron, C. (2001). Is cocoa a psychotropic drug? Psychopathological study of self-labeled "chocolate addicts." *Encephale, 27,* 181–186.

Damasio, A. (1995). On some functions of the human prefrontal cortex. *Annals of the National Academy of Sciences, 769,* 241–251.

Damasio, A. R. (1994). *Descartes' error: Emotion, reason, and the human brain.* New York: Lyons Press.

Damasio, A. R. (1999). *The feeling of what happens: Body and emotion in the making of consciousness.* New York: Harcourt.

Dandy, J., & Nettelbeck, T. (2002). The relationship between IQ, homework, aspirations and academic achievement for Chinese, Vietnamese and Anglo-Celtic Australian school children. *Educational Psychology, 22,* 267–276.

Dang-Vu, T., Schabus, M., Desseilles, M., Schwartz, S., & Maquet, P. (2007). Neuroimaging of REM sleep and dreaming. In D. Barrett & P. McNamara (Eds.), *The new science of dreaming: Volume 1. Biological aspects* (pp. 95–113). Westport, CT: Praeger Publishers.

Danielides, V., Katotomichelakis, M., Balatsouras, D., Riga, M., Tripsianis, G., Simopoulou, M., & Nikolettos, N. (2009). Improvement of olfaction after endoscopic sinus surgery in smokers and nonsmokers. *Annals of Otology, Rhinology, & Laryngology, 118,* 13–20.

Danielsson, N., Jansson-Fröjmark, M., Linton, S., Jutengren, G., & Stattin, H. (2010). Neuroticism and sleep-onset: What is the long-term connection? *Personality and Individual Differences, 48,* 463–468.

Dantzker, M., & Eisenman, R. (2003). Sexual attitudes among Hispanic college students: Differences between males and females. *International Journal of Adolescence & Youth, 11,* 79–89.

Darley, J. M., & Latané, B. (1968a). Bystander intervention in emergencies: Diffusion of responsibility. *Journal of Personality and Social Psychology, 8,* 377–383.

Darley, J. M., & Latané, B. (1968b, December). When will people help in a crisis? *Psychology Today, 54–57,* 70–71.

Darwin, C. (1872/1965). *The expression of emotion in man and animals.* Chicago: University of Chicago Press. (Original work published 1872).

Dasen, P. R. (1994). Culture and cognitive development from a Piagetian perspective. In W. J. Lonner & R. Malpass (Eds.), *Psychology and culture* (pp. 145–149). Boston: Allyn & Bacon.

Dattilio, F. (2010). *Cognitive-behavioral therapy with couples and families: A comprehensive guide for clinicians.* New York: Guilford Press.

Dauringnac, E., Toga, A., Jones, D., Aronen, H., Hommer, D., Jernigan, T., Krystal, J., & Mathalon, D. (2005). Applications of morphometric and diffusion tensor magnetic resonance imaging to the study of brain abnormalities in the alcoholism spectrum. *Alcoholism: Clinical and Experimental Research, 29,* 159–166.

Davalos, D., Kisley, M., & Ross, R. (2002). Deficits in auditory and visual temporal perception in schizophrenia. *Cognitive Neuropsychiatry, 7,* 273–282.

Davidson, A., Castanon-Cervantes, O., Leise, T., Molyneux, P., & Harrington, M. (2009). Visualizing jet lag in the mouse suprachiasmatic nucleus and peripheral circadian timing system. *European Journal of Neuroscience, 29,* 171–180.

Davidson, J. R. T. (1997). Use of benzodiazepines in panic disorder. *Journal of Clinical Psychiatry, 58*(2, Suppl.), 26–28.

Davies, L. (2003). Singlehood: Transitions within a gendered world. *Canadian Journal on Aging, 22,* 343–352.

Davis, S., Butcher, S. P., & Morris, R. G. M. (1992). The NMDA receptor antagonist D-2-amino-5-phosphonopentanoate (D-AP5) impairs spatial learning and LTP in vivo at intracerebral concentrations comparable to those that block LTP in vitro. *Journal of Neuroscience, 12,* 21–34.

Day, S., & Schneider, P. (2002). Psychotherapy using distance technology: A comparison of face-to-face, video, and audio treatment. *Journal of Counseling Psychology, 49,* 499–503.

Dayan, P., & Huys, Q. Serotonin, inhibition, and negative mood. *Public Library of Science: Computational Biology.* Retrieved July 26, 2009 from *http://www.ploscompbiol.org/article/info:doi/10.1371/journal.pcbi.0040004.*

De Brito, S., Mechelli, A., Wilke, M., Laurens, K., Jones, A., Barker, G., Hodgins, S., & Viding, E. (2009). Size matters: Increased grey matter in boys with conduct problems and callous-unemotional traits. *Brain: A Journal of Neurology, 132,* 843–852.

de Groot, E., Verheul, R., & Trijsburg, R. (2008). An integrative perspective on psychotherapeutic treatments for borderline personality disorder. *Journal of Personality Disorders, 22,* 332–352.

de Jong, P., & vander Leij, A. (2002). Effects of phonological abilities and linguistic comprehension on the development of reading. *Scientific Studies of Reading, 6,* 51–77.

de Lacoste, M., Horvath, D., & Woodward, J. (1991). Possible sex differences in the developing human fetal brain. *Journal of Clinical and Experimental Neuropsychology, 13,* 831.

De Martino, B., Kumaran, O., Seymour, B., & Dolan, R. (2006). Frames, biases, and rational decision-making in the human brain. *Science, 313,* 684–687.

de Mello, M., Esteves, M., Pires, D., Santos, L., Bittencourt, R., & Tufik, S. (2008). Relationship between Brazilian airline pilot errors and time of day. *Brazilian Journal of Medical and Biological Research, 41,* 1129–1131.

De Raad, B., & Kokkonen, M. (2000). Traits and emotions: A review of their structure and management. *European Journal of Personality, 14,* 477–496.

De Roo, M., Klauser, P., Muller, D., & Sheng, M. (2008). LTP promotes a selective long-term stabilization and clustering of dendritic spines. *Public Library of Science: Biology, 6,* e219.

De Vos, S. (1990). Extended family living among older people in six Latin American countries. *Journal of Gerontology: Social Sciences, 45,* S87–S94.

Deacon, B., & Olatunji, B. (2007). Specificity of disgust sensitivity in the prediction of behavioral avoidance in contamination fear. *Behaviour Research and Therapy, 45,* 2110–2120.

DeCasper, A. J., & Spence, M. J. (1986). Prenatal maternal speech influences newborns' perception of speech sounds. *Infant Behavior and Development, 9,* 133–150.

Dedert, E., Studts, J., Weissbecker, I., Salmon, P., Banis, P., & Sephton, S. (2004). Religiosity may help preserve the cortisol rhythm in women with stress-related illness. *International Journal of Psychiatry in Medicine, 34,* 61–77.

Deinzer, R., Kleineidam, C., Stiller-Winkler, R., Idel, H., & Bach, D. (2000). Prolonged reduction of salivary immunoglobulin (sIgA) after a major academic exam. *International Journal of Psychophysiology, 37,* 219–232.

Delgado, J. M. R., & Anand, B. K. (1953). Increased food intake induced by electrical stimulation of the lateral hypothalamus. *American Journal of Physiology, 172,* 162–168.

DeLongis, A., Folkman, S., & Lazarus, R. S. (1988). The impact of daily stress on health and mood: Psychological and social resources as mediators. *Journal of Personality and Social Psychology, 54,* 486–495.

Dement, W., & Kleitman, N. (1957). The relation of eye movements during sleep to dream activity: An objective method for the study of dreaming. *Journal of Experimental Psychology, 53,* 339–346.

Denny, C., Tsai, J., Floyd, R., & Green, P. (2009). Alcohol use among pregnant and nonpregnant women of childbearing age: United States, 1991–2005. *Morbidity & Mortality Weekly Report, 58,* 529–532.

Denollet, J. (1997). Personality, emotional distress and coronary heart disease. *European Journal of Personality, 11,* 343–357.

Deovell, L. Y., Bentin, S., & Soroker, N. (2000). Electrophysiological evidence for an early (pre-attentive) information processing deficit in patients with right hemisphere damage and unilateral neglect. *Brain, 123,* 353–365.

DePrince, A., & Freyd, J. (2004). Forgetting trauma stimuli. *Psychological Science, 15,* 488–492.

DeSpelder, L., & Strickland, A. (1983). *The last dance: Encountering death and dying.* Palo Alto, CA: Mayfield.

Devanand, D. P., Dwork, A. J., Hutchinson, M. S. E., Bolwig, T. G., & Sackeim, H. A. (1994). Does ECT alter brain structure? *American Journal of Psychiatry, 151,* 957–970.

Devine, P. G. (1989). Stereotypes and prejudice: Their automatic and controlled components. *Journal of Personality and Social Psychology, 56,* 5–18.

Dewsbury, D. A. (2000). Introduction: Snapshots of psychology circa 1900. *American Psychologist, 55,* 255–259.

DeYoung, C., Peterson, J., & Higgins, D. (2002). Higher-order factors of the Big Five predict conformity: Are there neuroses of health? *Personality & Individual Differences, 33,* 533–552.

Dhar, V., & Chang, E. (2009). Does chatter matter: The impact of user-generated content on music sales. *Journal of Interactive Marketing, 23,* 300–307.

Di Fabio, A., & Palazzeschi, L. (2009). An in-depth look at scholastic success: Fluid intelligence, personality traits or emotional intelligence? *Personality and Individual Differences, 46,* 581–585.

Diaper, A., & Hindmarch, I. (2005). Sleep disturbance and its management in older patients. In S. Curran & R. Bullock (Eds.), *Practical old age psychopharmacology* (pp. 177–194). Oxon, Oxford, United Kingdom: Radcliffe Publishing.

Dickens, W., & Flynn, R. (2001). Heritability estimates versus large environmental effects: The IQ paradox resolved. *Psychological Review, 108,* 346–369.

Dickey, M. (2005). Engaging by design: How engagement strategies in popular computer and video games can inform instructional design. *Educational Technology Research and Development, 53,* 67–83.

Diefendorff, J., & Richard, E. (2003). Antecedents and consequences of emotional display rule perceptions. *Journal of Applied Psychology, 88,* 284–294.

Diener, E., Lucas, R., & Scollon, C. (2006). Beyond the hedonic treadmill: Revising the adaptation theory of well-being. *American Psychologist, 61,* 305–314.

Dijkstra, M., Buijtels, H., & van Raaij, W. (2005). Separate and joint effects of medium type on consumer response: A comparison of television, print, and the Internet. *Journal of Business Research, 58,* 2005.

DiLalla, L. F., & Gottesman, I. I. (1991). Biological and genetic contributors to violence—Widom's untold tale. *Psychological Bulletin, 109,* 125–129.

Dillard, J., & Anderson, J. (2004). The role of fear in persuasion. *Psychology & Marketing, 21,* 909–926.

Dilorio, C., McCarty, F., DePadilla, L., Resnicow, K., Holstad, M., Yeager, k., Sharma, S., Morisky, D., & Lundberg, B. (2009). Adherence to antiretroviral medication regimens: A test of a psychosocial model. *AIDS and Behavior, 13,* 10–22.

Din-Dzietham, R., Nembhard, W., Collins, R., & Davis, S. (2004). Perceived stress following race-based discrimination at work is associated with hypertension in African-Americans. *Social Science & Medicine, 58,* 449–461.

Dion, K., Berscheid, E., & Walster, E. (1972). What is beautiful is good. *Journal of Personality and Social Psychology, 24,* 285–290.

Dipboye, R. L., Fromkin, H. L., & Wilback, K. (1975). Relative importance of applicant sex, attractiveness, and scholastic standing in evaluation of job applicant resumes. *Journal of Applied Psychology, 60,* 39–43.

Dixon, K., Keefe, F., Scipio, C., Perri, L., & Abernethy, A. (2007). Psychologica interventions for arthritis pain management in adults: A meta-analysis. *Health Psychology, 26,* 241–250.

Dobson, R., & Baird, T. (2006, May 28). "Women learn to play it like a man." *Timesonline.co.uk* Retrieved March 2, 2010 from *http://www.timesonline.co.uk/article/0,,2089-2200093.html*

Dodge, K. A., Bates, J. E., & Pettit, G. S. (1990). Mechanisms in the cycle of violence. *Science, 250,* 1678–1683.

Dodson, C. S., Koutstaal, W., & Schacter, D. L. (2000). Escape from illusion: Reducing false memories. *Trends in Cognitive Sciences, 4,* 391–397.

Doghramji, K., Brainard, G., & Balaicuis, J. (2010). Sleep and sleep disorders. In D. Monti & B. Beitman, (Eds.), *Integrative psychiatry.* Weil integrative medicine library. (pp. 195–239). New York: Oxford University Press.

Dohanich, G. (2003). Ovarian steroids and cognitive function. *Current Directions in Psychological Science, 12,* 57–61.

Doherty, W., & McDaniel, S. (2010). History. In W., Doherty, & S. McDaniel (Eds.), *Family therapy: Theories of psychotherapy* (pp. 5–27). Washington, DC: American Psychological Association.

Dohrenwend, B. (2006). Inventorying stressful life events as risk factors for psychopathology: Toward resolution of the problem of intracategory variability. *Psychological Bulletin, 132,* 477–495.

Dollard, J., Doob, L. W., Miller, N., Mowrer, O. H., & Sears, R. R. (1939). *Frustration and aggression.* New Haven: Yale University Press.

Domino, G. (1984). California Psychological Inventory. In D. J. Keyser & R. C. Sweetland (Eds.), *Test Critiques* (Vol. 1, pp. 146–157). Kansas City, MO: Test Corporation of America.

Domjan, M. (2005). Pavlovian conditioning: A functional perspective. *Annual Review of Psychology, 56,* 179–206.

Domjan, M., Cusato, B., & Krause, M. (2004). Learning with arbitrary versus ecological conditioned stimuli: Evidence from sexual conditioning. *Psychonomic Bulletin & Review, 11,* 232–246. [5]

Doob, L. W., & Sears, R. R. (1939). Factors determining substitute behavior and the overt expression of aggression. *Journal of Abnormal and Social Psychology, 34,* 293–313.

Dorz, S., Lazzarini, L., Cattelan, A., Meneghetti, F., Novara, C., Concia, E., et al. (2003). Evaluation of adherence to antiretroviral therapy in Italian HIV patients. *AIDS Patient Care & STDs, 17,* 33–41.

Dowd, E., Clen, S., & Arnold, K. (2010). The specialty practice of cognitive and behavioral psychology. *Professional Psychology: Research and Practice, 41,* 89–95.

Downing, P., Jiang, Y., Shuman, M., & Kanwisher, N. (2001). A cortical area selective for visual processing of the human body. *Science, 293,* 2470–2473.

Doyle, J. A., & Paludi, M. A. (1995). *Sex and gender* (3rd ed.). Madison, WI: Brown & Benchmark.

Dreikurs, R. (1953). *Fundamentals of Adlerian psychology.* Chicago: Alfred Adler Institute.

Drevets, W. C., Price, J. L., Simpson, J. R., Jr., Todd, R. D., Reich, T., Vannier, M., et al. (1997). Subgenual prefrontal cortex abnormalities in mood disorders. *Nature, 386,* 824–827.

Drevets, W., Neugebauer, V., Li, W., Bird, G., & Han, J. (2004). The amygdala and persistent pain. *Neuroscientist, 10,* 221–234.

Drevets, W., Price, J., & Furey, M. (2008). Brain structural and functional abnormalities in mood disorders: Implications for neurocircuitry models of depression. *Brain Structure and Function, 213,* 93–118.

Druckman, D., & Bjork, R. A. (Eds.) (1994). *Learning, remembering, believing: Enhancing human performance.* Washington, DC: National Academy Press.

Drug Enforcement Administration. National Drug Intelligence Center. (2003). *National Drug Threat Assessment/2003.* Retrieved October 22, 2003, from *http://www.usdoj.gov/ndic/pubs3/3300/pharm.htm*

Drug Free Workplace. (2002, September). *Designer Drugs. National Medical Report* [Electronic version]. Retrieved May 25, 2003, from *http://www.drugfreeworkplace.com/drugsofabuse/designer.htm*

Drummond, S. P. A., Brown, G. G., Gillin, J. C., Stricker, J. L., Wong, E. C., & Buxton, R. B. (2000). Altered brain response to verbal learning following sleep deprivation. *Nature, 403,* 655–657.

Drummond, S., Brown, G., Salamat, J., & Gillin, J. (2004). Increasing task difficulty facilitates the cerebral compensatory response to total sleep deprivation. *Sleep: Journal of Sleep & Sleep Disorders Research, 27,* 445–451.

Duck, S. (1983). *Friends for life: The psychology of close relationships.* New York: St. Martin's Press.

Duckworth, A., & Seligman, M. (2006). Self-discipline gives girls the edge: Gender in self-discipline, grades, and achievement test scores. *Journal of Educational Psychology, 98,* 198–208.

Duke, P., & Hochman, G. (1992). *A brilliant madness: Living with manic-depressive illness.* New York: Bantam Books.

Duke, P., & Turan, K. (1987). *Call me Anna.* New York: Bantam Books.

DuMont, K., Widom, C., & Czaja, S. (2007). Predictors of resilience in abused and neglected children grown-up: The role of individual and neighborhood characteristics. *Child Abuse and Neglect, 31,* 255–274.

Dunkel-Schetter, C., Feinstein, L. G., Taylor, S. E., & Falke, R. L. (1992). Patterns of coping with cancer. *Health Psychology, 11,* 79–87.

Dunn, J., Cutting, A., & Fisher, N. (2002). Old friends, new friends: Predictors of children's perspective on their friends at school. *Child Development, 73,* 621–635.

Durbin, C., & Klein, D. (2006). Ten-year stability of personality disorders among outpatients with mood disorders. *Journal of Abnormal Psychology, 115,* 75–84.

Durex. (2005). *Durex Global Sex Survey 2005.* Retrieved July 3, 2006, from *http://www.durex.com/cm/gss2005results.asp*

Dutton, M., Lee, E., & Zukowska, Z. (2006). NPY and extreme stress: Lessons learned from posttraumatic stress disorder. In Z., Zukowska, & G. Feuerstei, (Eds.), *NPY family of peptides in neurobiology, cardiovascular and metabolic disorders: From genes to therapeutics* (pp. 213–222). Basel, Switzerland: Birkhauser Publishing.

Duyme, M. (1988). School success and social class: An adoption study. *Developmental Psychology, 24,* 203–209.

Dy-Liacco, G., Piedmont, R., Murray, P., Swank, N., Rodgerson, T., & Sherman, M. (2009). Spirituality and religiosity as cross-cultural aspects of human experience. *Psychology of Religion and Spirituality, 1,* 35–52.

Dye, M., Hauser, P., & Bavelier, D. (2008). Visual skills and cross-modal plasticity in deaf readers: Possible implications for acquiring meaning from print. *Annals of the New York Academy of Science, 1145,* 71–82.

Dyl, J., Kittler, J., Phillips, K., & Hunt, J. (2006). Body dysmorphic disorder and other clinically significant body image concerns in adolescent psychiatric inpatients: Prevalence and clinical characteristics. *Child Psychiatry and Human Development, 36,* 369–382.

Dywan, J., & Bowers, K. (1983). The use of hypnosis to enhance recall. *Science, 222,* 184–185.

Eagly, A. H., & Carli, L. (1981). Sex of researchers and sex-typed communications as determinants of sex differences in influence-ability: A meta-analysis of social influence studies. *Psychological Bulletin, 90,* 1–20.

Eagly, A. H., & Wood, W. (1999). The origins of sex differences in human behavior: Evolved dispositions versus social roles. *American Psychologist, 54,* 408–423.

Eagly, A. H., Ashmore, R. D., Makhijani, M. G., & Longo, L. C. (1991). What is beautiful is good . . . : A meta-analytic review of research on the physical attractiveness stereotype. *Psychological Bulletin, 110,* 109–128.

Earlandsson, L., & Eklund, M. (2003). The relationships among hassles and uplifts to experience of health in working women. *Women & Health, 38,* 19–37.

Ebbinghaus, H. (1913). *Memory* (H. A. Ruger & C. E. Bussenius, Trans.). New York: Teacher's College Press. (Original work published 1885)

Ebbinghaus, H. E. (1885/1964). *Memory: A contribution to experimental psychology* (H. A. Ruger & C. E. Bussenius, Trans.). New York: Dover. (Original work published 1885).

Ebersbach, M. (2009). Achieving a new dimension: Children integrate three stimulus dimensions in volume estimations. *Developmental Psychology, 45,* 877–883.

Edwards, B., Atkinson, G., Waterhouse, J., Reilly, T., Godfrey, R., & Budgett, R. (2000). Use of melatonin in recovery from jet-lag following an eastward flight across 10 time-zones. *Ergonomics, 43,* 1501–1513.

Edwards, K., & Smith, E. E. (1996). A disconfirmation bias in the evaluation of arguments. *Journal of Personality and Social Psychology, 71,* 5–24.

Egeth, H. E. (1993). What do we not know about eyewitness identification? *American Psychologist, 48,* 577–580.

Ehlers, C., Gizer, I., Vieten, C., Gilder, D., Stouffer, G., Lau, P., & Wilhelmsen, K. (2010). Cannabis dependence in the San Francisco family study: Age of onset of use, DSM-IV symptoms, withdrawal, and heritability. *Addictive Behaviors, 35,* 102–110.

Eichenbaum, H. (1997). Declarative memory: Insights from cognitive neurobiology. *Annual Review of Psychology, 48,* 547–572.

Eichenbaum, H., & Fortin, N. (2003). Episodic memory and the hippocampus: It's about time. *Current Directions in Psychological Science, 12,* 53–57.

Eichenbaum, H., & Otto, T. (1993). LTP and memory: Can we enhance the connection? *Trends in Neurosciences, 16,* 163.

Eidelson, R., & Eidelson, J. (2003). Dangerous ideas. *American Psychologist, 58,* 182–192.

Eisold, B. (2005). Notes on lifelong resilience: Perceptual and personality factors implicit in the creation of a particular adaptive style. *Psychoanalytic Psychology, 22,* 411–425.

Ekman, P. (1972). Universals and cultural differences in facial expression of emotion. In J. Cole (Ed.), *Nebraska symposium on motivation* (Vol. 19). Lincoln: University of Nebraska Press.

Ekman, P. (1993). Facial expression and emotion. *American Psychologist, 48,* 384–392.

Ekman, P., & Friesen, W. V. (1975). *Unmasking the face: A guide to recognizing emotions from facial clues.* Englewood Cliffs, NJ: Prentice-Hall.

Ekman, P., Levenson, R. W., & Friesen, W. V. (1983). Autonomic nervous system activity distinguishes among emotions. *Science, 221,* 1208–1210.

Elal, G., Altug, A., Slade, P., & Tekcan, A. (2000). Factor structure of the Eating Attitudes Test (EAT) in a Turkish university sample. *Eating and Weight Disorders: Studies on Anorexia, Bulimia, and Obesity, 5,* 46–50.

Elkin, I., Gibbons, R. D., Shea, M. T., Sotsky, S. M., Watkins, J. T., Pikonis, P. A., & Hedeker, D. (1995). Initial severity and differential treatment outcome in the National Institute of Mental Health Treatment of Depression Collaborative Research Program. *Journal of Consulting and Clinical Psychology, 63,* 841–847.

Elkin, I., Shea, M. T., Watkins, J. T., et al. (1989). National Institute of Mental Health Treatment of Depression Collaborative Research Program: General effectiveness of treatments. *Archives of General Psychology, 46,* 971–982.

Elkind, D. (1967). Egocentrism in adolescence. *Child Development, 38,* 1025–1034.

Elkind, D. (1974). *Children and adolescents: Interpretive essays on Jean Piaget* (2nd ed.). New York: Oxford University Press.

Ellason, J. W., & Ross, C. A. (1997). Two-year follow-up of inpatients with dissociative identity disorder. *American Journal of Psychiatry, 154*, 832–839.

Elliot, A. J., & Devine, P. G. (1994). On the motivational nature of cognitive dissonance: Dissonance as psychological discomfort. *Journal of Personality and Social Psychology, 67*, 382–394.

Ellis, A. (1961). *A guide to rational living.* Englewood Cliffs, NJ: Prentice-Hall.

Ellis, A. (1977). The basic clinical theory of rational-emotive therapy. In A. Ellis & R. Grieger (Eds.), *Handbook of rational-emotive therapy* (pp. 3–33). New York: Springer.

Ellis, A. (1993). Reflections on rational-emotive therapy. *Journal of Consulting and Clinical Psychology, 61*, 199–201.

Ellis, A. (2004a). Why I (really) became a therapist. *Journal of Rational-Emotive & Cognitive Behavior Therapy, 22*, 73–77.

Ellis, A. (2004b). Why rational-emotive behavior therapy is the most comprehensive and effective form of behavior therapy. *Journal of Rational-Emotive & Cognitive Behavior Therapy, 22*, 85–92.

Ellison, P., & Nelson, A. (2009). Brain development: Evidence of gender differences. In E., Fletcher-Janzen (Ed.), *The neuropsychology of women: Issues of diversity in clinical neuropsychology* (pp. 11–30). New York: Springer Science and Business Media.

Else-Quest, N., Hyde, J., Goldsmith, H., & Van Hulle, C. (2006). Gender differences in temperament: A meta-analysis. *Psychological Bulletin, 132*, 33–72.

Engel, G. L. (1977). The need for a new medical model: A challenge for biomedicine. *Science, 196*, 126–129.

Engel, G. L. (1980). The clinical application of the biopsychosocial model. *American Journal of Psychiatry, 137*, 535–544.

Engels, G. I., Garnefski, N., & Diekstra, R. F. W. (1993). Efficacy of rational-emotive therapy: A quantitative analysis. *Journal of Consulting and Clinical Psychology, 61*, 1083–1090.

Engen, T. (1982). *The perception of odors.* New York: Academic Press.

Epstein, D., Willner-Reid, J., & Preston, K. (2010). Addiction and emotion: Theories, assessment techniques, and treatment implications. In J. Kassel, (Ed.), *Substance abuse and emotion* (pp. 259–260). Washington, DC: American Psychological Association.

Epstein, J. (1983). Examining theories of adolescent friendships. In J. Epstein & N. Karweit (Eds.), *Friends in school* (pp. 39–61). New York: Academic Press.

Epstein, J., Stern, E., & Silbersweig, D. (2001). Neuropsychiatry at the millennium: The potential for mind/brain integration through emerging interdisciplinary research strategies. *Clinical Neuroscience Research, 1*, 10–18.

Equifax. (2006). *How lenders see you.* Retrieved November 29, 2006, from *https://www.econsumer.equifax.com/consumer/sitepage.ehtml?forward=cps_hlsysample*

Erdogan, A., Kocabasoglu, N., Yalug, I., Ozbay, G., & Senturk, H. (2004). Management of marked liver enzyme increase during clozapine treatment: A case report and review of the literature. *International Journal of Psychiatry in Medicine, 34*, 83–89.

Erikson, E. (1968). *Identity, youth, and crisis.* (New York: W. W. Norton & Company.

Erikson, E. H. (1980). *Identity and the life cycle.* New York: Norton.

Erikson, E., & Erikson, K. (1957). The confirmation of the delinquent. *Chicago Review, 10*, 15–23.

Erlacher, D., & Schredl, M. (2008). Cardiovascular responses to dreamed physical exercise during REM lucid dreaming. *Dreaming, 18*, 112–121.

Erlenmeyer-Kimling, L., & Jarvik, L. F. (1963). Genetics and intelligence: A review. *Science, 142*, 1477–1479.

Eron, L. D. (1987). The development of aggressive behavior from the perspective of a developing behaviorism. *American Psychologist, 42*, 435–442.

Eronen, M., Hakola, P., & Tiihonen, J. (1996). Mental disorders and homicidal behavior in Finland. *Journal of Personality and Social Psychology, 53*, 497–501.

Espeland, M., Tindle, H., Bushnell, C., Jaramillo, S., Kuller, L., Margolis, K., Mysiw, W., Maldjian, J., Melhem, E., & Resnick, S., for the Women's Health Initiative Memory Study. (2009). Brain volumes, cognitive impairment, and conjugated equine estrogens. *Journals of Gerontology Series A: Biological Sciences and Medical Sciences, 64A*, 1243–1250.

Estes, W. K. (1994). *Classification and cognition.* New York: Oxford University Press.

Etcoff, N., Ekman, P., Magee, J., & Frank, M. (2000). Lie detection and language comprehension. *Nature, 405*, 139.

Evans, D., & Zarate, O. (2000). *Introducing evolutionary psychology.* New York: Totem Books.

Evans, G. W., & Lepore, S. J. (1993). Household crowding and social support: A quasiexperimental analysis. *Journal of Personality and Social Psychology, 65*, 308–316.

Evans, S., Huxley, P., Gately, C., Webber, M., Mears, A., Pajak, S., Medina, J., Kendall, T., & Katona, C. (2006). Mental health, burnout and job satisfaction among mental health social workers in England and Wales. *British Journal of Psychiatry, 188*, 75–80.

Everson, S. A., Goldberg, D. E., Kaplan, G. A., Cohen, R. D., Pukkala, E., Tuomilehto, J., et al. (1996). Hopelessness and risk of mortality and incidence of myocardial infarction and cancer. *Psychosomatic Medicine, 58*, 113–121.

Exner, J. E. (1993). *The Rorschach: A comprehensive system: Vol. 1. Basic foundations* (3rd ed.). New York: Wiley.

Eysenbach, G., Powell, J., Kuss, O., & Sa, E. (2002). Empirical studies of health information for consumers on the World Wide Web: A systematic review. *JAMA: Journal of the American Medical Association, 287*, 2691–2700.

Eysenck, H. J. (1990). Genetic and environmental contributions to individual differences: The three major dimensions of personality. *Journal of Personality, 58*, 245–261.

Eysenck, H. J. (1994). The outcome problem in psychotherapy: What have we learned? *Behaviour Research and Therapy, 32*, 477–495.

Eysenck, M., & Keane, M. (2010). *Cognitive psychology.* 6th ed. New York: Taylor & Francis.

Fackelmann, K. (1997). Marijuana on trial: Is marijuana a dangerous drug or a valuable medicine? *Science News, 151*, 178–179, 183.

Fagot, B. (1995). Observations of parent reactions to sex-stereotyped behavior: Age and sex effects. *Child Development, 62*, 617–628.

Faisal-Cury, A., Tedesco, J., Kahhale, S., Menezes, P., & Zugaib, M. (2004). Postpartum depression: In relation to life events and patterns of coping. *Archives of Women's Mental Health, 7*, 123–131.

Falconnier, L. (2009). Socioeconomic status in the treatment of depression. *American Journal of Orthopsychiatry, 79*, 148–158.

Fallon, J., Irvine, D., & Shepherd, R. (2008). Cochlear implants and brain plasticity. *Hearing Research, 238*, 110–117.

Famighetti, R. (Ed.). (1997). *The world almanac and book of facts 1998.* Mahwah, NJ: World Almanac Books.

Fan, J., Wong, C., Carroll, S., & Lopez, F. (2008). An empirical investigation of the influence of social desirability on the factor structure of the Chinese 16PF. *Personality and Individual Differences, 45*, 790–795.

Fang, C., & Myers, H. (2001). The effects of racial stressors and hostility on cardiovascular reactivity in African American and Caucasian men. *Health Psychology, 20*, 64–70.

Fanous, A., Gardner, C., Prescott, C., Cancro, R., & Kendler, K. (2002). Neuroticism, major depression and gender: A population-based twin study. *Psychological Medicine, 32*, 719–728.

Fantz, R. L. (1961). The origin of form perception. *Scientific American, 204*, 66–72.

Farber, B., Khurgin-Bott, R., & Feldman, S. (2009). The benefits and risks of patient self-disclosure in the psychotherapy of women with a history of childhood sexual abuse. *Psychotherapy: Theory, Research, Practice, Training, 46*, 52–67.

Farde, L. (1996). The advantage of using positron emission tomography in drug research. *Trends in Neurosciences, 19,* 211–214.

Farrer, L. A., & Cupples, A. (1994). Estimating the probability for major gene Alzheimer disease. *American Journal of Human Genetics, 54,* 374–383.

Fasano, S., D'Antoni, A., Orban, P., Valjent, E., Putigano, E., Vara, H., Pizzorusso, T., Giusetto, M., Yoon, B., Soloway, P., Maldonado, R., Caboche, J., & Brambilla, R. (2009). Ras-guanine nucleotide-releasing factor 1 (Ras-GRF1) controls activation of extracellular signal-regulated kinase (ERK) signaling in the striatum and long-term behavioral responses to cocaine. *Biological Psychiatry, 66,* 758–768.

Fasotti, L. (2003). Executive function retraining. In J. Grafman, & I. Robertson, (Eds.), *Handbook of Neuropsychology: Volume 9: Plasticity and Rehabilitation* (pp. 67–78). Amsterdam, The Netherlands: Elsevier Science.

Fauerbach, J., Lawrence, J., Haythornthwaite, J., & Richter, L. (2002). Coping with the stress of a painful medical procedure. *Behaviour Research & Therapy, 40,* 1003–1015.

Faunce, G. (2002). Eating disorders and attentional bias: A review. *Eating Disorders: The Journal of Treatment & Prevention, 10,* 125–139.

Fazio, R. H. (1989). On the power and functionality of attitudes: The role of attitude accessibility. In A. R. Pratkanis, S. J. Breckler, & A. G. Greenwald (Eds.), *Attitude structure and function* (pp. 153–179). Hillsdale, NJ: Erlbaum.

Fazio, R. H., & Williams, C. J. (1986). Attitude accessibility as a moderator of the attitude perception and attitude-behavior relations: An investigation of the 1984 presidential election. *Journal of Personality and Social Psychology, 51,* 505–514.

Federal Interagency Forum on Aging—Related Statistics (FIFARS). (2000). *Older Americans 2000: Key indicators of well-being.* Retrieved July 30, 2003, from *http://www.agingstats.gov*

Federal Interagency Forum on Aging—Related Statistics (FIFARS). (2004). *Older Americans 2004: Key indicators of well-being.* Retrieved January 27, 2005, from *http://www.agingstats.gov/ chartbook2004/default.htm.*

Federal Interagency Forum on Aging-Related Statistics (FIFARS). (2008). *Older Americans 2008: Key indicators of well-being.* Retrieved February 27, 2010 from *http://www.agingstats.gov/ agingstatsdotnet/main_site/default.aspx.*

Feeney, K. (2007). The legal bases for religious peyote use. In M. Winkelman, & T. Roberts, (Eds.), *Psychedelic medicine: New evidence for hallucinogenic substances as treatments (Vol. 1)* (pp. 233–250). Westport, CT: Praeger Publishers.

Feingold, A. (1988). Matching for attractiveness in romantic partners and same-sex friends: A meta-analysis and theoretical critique. *Psychological Bulletin, 104,* 226–235.

Fenn, K., Nusbaum, H., & Margoliash, D. (2003). Consolidation during sleep of perceptual learning of spoken language. *Nature, 425,* 614–616.

Fenton, W. S., & McGlashan, T. H. (1991). Natural history of schizophrenia subtypes: I. Longitudinal study of paranoid, hebephrenic, and undifferentiated schizophrenia. *Archives of General Psychiatry, 48,* 969–977.

Fenton, W. S., & McGlashan, T. H. (1994). Antecedents, symptom progression, and long-term outcome of the deficit syndrome in schizophrenia. *American Journal of Psychiatry, 151,* 351–356.

Fernald, A. (1993). Approval and disapproval: Infant responsiveness to vocal affect in familiar and unfamiliar languages. *Child Development, 64,* 637–656.

Ferreira, S., de Mello, M., Pompeia, S., & de Souza-Formigoni, M. (2006). Effects of energy drink ingestion on alcohol intoxication. *Alcoholism: Clinical and Experimental Research, 30,* 598.

Festinger, L. (1957). *A theory of cognitive dissonance.* Evanston, IL: Row, Peterson.

Festinger, L., & Carlsmith, J. M. (1959). Cognitive consequences of forced compliance. *Journal of Abnormal and Social Psychology, 58,* 203–210.

Festinger, L., Pepitone, A., & Newcomb, T. (1952). Some consequences of de-individuation in a group. *Journal of Abnormal and Social Psychology, 47,* 382–389.

Fiatarone, M. A., Morley, J. E., Bloom, E. T., Benton, D., Makinodan, T., & Solomon, G. F. (1988). Endogenous opioids and the exercise-induced augmentation of natural killer cell activity. *Journal of Laboratory and Clinical Medicine, 112,* 544–552.

Fiatarone, M. A., O'Neill, E. F., Ryan, N. D., Clements, K. M., Solares, G. R., Nelson, M. E., et al. (1994). Exercise training and nutritional supplementation for physical frailty in very elderly people. *New England Journal of Medicine, 330,* 1769–1775.

Field, M., & Duka, T. (2002). Cues paired with a low dose of alcohol acquire conditioned incentive properties in social drinkers. *Psychopharmacology, 159,* 325–334.

Field, T. (2002). Infants' need for touch. *Human Development, 45,* 100–103.

Field, T. (2009). Biofeedback. In T. Field, (Ed.), *Complementary and alternative therapies research* (pp. 119–126). Washington, DC: American Psychological Association.

Field, T. (2009). Origins of complementary and alternative therapies. In T. Field (Ed.), *Complementary and alternative therapies research* (pp. 13–21). Washington, DC: American Psychological Association.

Field, T. M., Cohen, D., Garcia, R., & Greenberg, R. (1984). Mother–stranger face discrimination by the newborn. *Infant Behavior and Development, 7,* 19–25.

Field, T., Schanberg, S. M., Scfidi, F., Bauer, C. R., Vega-Lahr, N., Garcia, R., et al. (1986, May). Tactile/kinesthetic stimulation effects on preterm neonates. *Pediatrics, 77,* 654–658.

Fields, J., Walton, K., & Schneider, R. (2002). Effect of a multimodality natural medicine program on carotid atherosclerosis in older subjects: A pilot trial of Maharishi Verdic Medicine. *American Journal of Cardiology, 89,* 952–958.

Finch, A. E., Lambert, M. J., & Brown, G. (2000). Attacking anxiety: A naturalistic study of a multimedia self-help program. *Journal of Clinical Psychology, 56,* 11–21.

Fink, B., & Penton-Voak, I. (2002). Evolutionary psychology of facial attractiveness. *Current Directions in Psychological Science, 11,* 154–158.

Fischbach, G. D. (1992). Mind and brain. *Scientific American, 267,* 48–56.

Fischer, K., & Rose, S. (1994). Dynamic development of coordination of components in brain and behavior: A framework for theory and research. In K. Fischer & G. Dawson (Eds.), *Human Behavior and the Developing Brain* (pp. 3–66). New York: Guilford Press.

Fivush, R., & Nelson, K. (2004). Culture and language in the emergence of autobiographical memory. *Psychological Science, 15,* 573–577.

Fixx, J. F. (1978). *Solve It! A perplexing profusion of puzzles.* New York: Doubleday.

Flavell, J. H. (1985). *Cognitive development.* Englewood, NJ: Prentice-Hall.

Flavell, J. H. (1992). Cognitive development: Past, present, and future. *Developmental Psychology, 28,* 998–1005.

Flavell, J. H. (1996). Piaget's legacy. *Psychological Science, 7,* 200–203.

Fleck, D., Hendricks, W., DelBellow, M., & Strakowski, S. (2002). Differential prescription of maintenance antipsychotics to African American and White patients with new-onset bipolar disorder. *Journal of Clinical Psychiatry, 63,* 658–664.

Fleming, J. D. (1974, July). Field report: The state of the apes. *Psychology Today,* pp. 31–46.

Fleshner, M., & Laudenslager, M. (2004). Psychoneuroimmunology: Then and now. *Behavioral & Cognitive Neuroscience Reviews, 3,* 114–130.

Fletcher, J. M., Page, B., Francis, D. J., Copeland, K., Naus, M. J., Davis, C. M., Morris, R., Krauskopf, D., & Satz, P. (1996). Cognitive correlates of long-term cannabis use in Costa Rican men. *Archives of General Psychiatry, 53,* 1051–1057.

Flynn, J. (1999). Searching for justice: The discovery of IQ gains over time. *American Psychologist, 54,* 5–20.

Flynn, J. R. (1987). Race and IQ: Jensen's case refuted. In S. Modgil, & C. Modgil (Eds.), *Arthur Jensen: Consensus and controversy* (221–232). New York: Palmer Press.

Foa, E. B. (1995). How do treatments for obsessive-compulsive disorder compare? *Harvard Mental Health Letter, 12*(1), 8.

Fogel, S., Smith, C., & Beninger, R. (2010). Increased GABAergic activity in the region of the pedunculopontine and deep mesencephalic reticular nuclei reduces REM sleep and impairs learning in rats. *Behavioral Neuroscience, 124,* 79–86.

Foley, D. J., Monjan, A. A., Brown, S. L., Simonsick, E. M., Wallace, R. B., & Blazer, D. G. (1995). Sleep complaints among elderly persons: An epidemiologic study of three communities. *Sleep, 18,* 425–432.

Folkman, S. (1984). Personal control and stress and coping processes: A theoretical analysis. *Journal of Personality and Social Psychology, 46,* 839–852.

Folkman, S., & Lazarus, R. S. (1980). An analysis of coping in a middle-aged community sample. *Journal of Health and Social Behavior, 21,* 219–239.

Folkman, S., Chesney, M., Collette, L., Boccellari, A., & Cooke, M. (1996). Postbereavement depressive mood and its prebereavement predictors in HIV+ and HIV– gay men. *Journal of Personality and Social Psychology, 70,* 336–348.

Foran, H., & O'Leary, K. (2008). Alcohol and intimate partner violence: A meta-analytic review. *Clinical Psychology Review, 28,* 1222–1234.

Ford, C. S., & Beach, F. A. (1951). *Patterns of sexual behavior.* New York: Harper & Row.

Foster, R., Hankins, M., & Peirson, S. (2007). Light, photoreceptors, and circadian clocks. In E. Rosato, (Ed.), *Circadian rhythms: Methods and protocols* (pp. 3–28). Totowa, NJ: Humana Press.

Foulkes, D. (1996). Sleep and dreams: Dream research: 1953–1993. *Sleep, 19,* 609–624.

Fourkas, A., Bonavolonta, V., Avenanti, A., & Aglioti, S. (2008). Kinesthetic imagery and tool-specific modulation of corticospinal representations in expert tennis players. *Cerebral Cortex, 18,* 2382–2390.

Fourkas, A., Ionta, S., & Aglioti, S. (2006). Influence of imagined posture and imagery modality on corticospinal excitability. *Behavioural Brain Research, 168,* 190–196.

Fox, N. A., & Bell, M. A. (1990). Electrophysiological indices of frontal lobe development: Relations to cognitive and affective behavior in human infants over the first year of life. *Annals of the New York Academy of Sciences, 608,* 677–698.

Francis-Smythe, J., & Smith, P. (1997). The psychological impact of assessment in a development center. *Human Relations, 50,* 149–167.

Francks, C., DeLisi, L., Fisher, S., Laval, S., Rue, J., Stein, J., et al. (2003). Confirmatory evidence for linkage of relative hand skill to 2p12-q11. *American Journal of Human Genetics, 72,* 499–502.

Francks, C., Maegawa, S., Lauren, J., Abrahams, B., Velayos-Baeza, A., Medland, S., Colella, S., Groszer, M., McAuley, E., Caffrey, T., Timmusk, T., Pruunsild, P., Koppel, I., Lind, P., Natsummoto-Itaba, N., Nicok, J., Xiong, L., Joober, R., Enard, W., Krinsky, B., Nanba, E., Richardson, A., Riley, B., Martin, N., Strittmatter, S., Miller, H., Rejuescu, D., St. Clair, D., Muglia, P., Roos, J., Fisher, S., Wade-Martins, R., Rouleau, G., Stain, J., Karayiorgou, M., Geschwind, D., Ragoussis, J., Kendler, K., Airaksinen, M., Oshimura, M., DeLisi, L., & Monaco, A. (2007). LRRTM1 on chromosome 2p12 is a maternally suppressed gene that is associated paternally with handedness and schizophrenia. *Molecular Psychiatry, 12,* 1129–1139.

Frank, E., Anderson, B., Reynolds, C. F., III, Ritenour, A., & Kupfer, D. J. (1994). Life events and the research diagnostic criteria endogenous subtype. *Archives of General Psychiatry, 51,* 519–524.

Frank, E., Kupfer, D. J., Wagner, E. F., McEachran, A. B., & Cornes, C. (1991). Efficacy of interpersonal psychotherapy as a maintenance treatment of recurrent depression: Contributing factors. *Archives of General Psychiatry, 48,* 1053–1059.

Franklin, A., Pilling, M., & Davies, I. (2005). The nature of infant colour categorization: Evidence from eye-movements on a target detection task. *Journal of Experimental Child Psychology, 91,* 227–248.

Franks, P., Gold, M., & Fiscella, K. (2003). Sociodemographics, self-rated health, and mortality in the U. S. *Social Science & Medicine, 56,* 2505–2514.

Frantz, K., Hansson, K., Stouffer, D., & Parsons, L. (2002). 5-HT-sub-6 receptor antagonism potentiates the behavioral and neurochemical effects of amphetamine but not cocaine. *Neuropharmacology, 42,* 170–180.

Fratiglioni, L., & Wang, H. (2007). Brain reserve hypothesis in dementia. *Journal of Alzheimers Disease, 12,* 11–22.

Frazer, A. (1997). Antidepressants. *Journal of Clinical Psychiatry, 58*(6, Suppl.), 9–25.

Frazer, N., Larkin, K., & Goodie, J. (2002). Do behavioral responses mediate or moderate the relation between cardiovascular reactivity to stress and parental history of hypertension? *Health Psychology, 21,* 244–253.

Fredricks, J., & Eccles, J. (2002). Children's competence and value beliefs from childhood through adolescence growth trajectories in two male-sex-typed domains. *Developmental Psychology, 38,* 519–533.

Fredrickson, B. (2001). The role of positive emotions in positive psychology. *American Psychologist, 56,* 218–226.

Fredrickson, B. (2009). *Positivity: Groundbreaking research reveals how to embrace the hidden strength of positive emotions, overcome negativity, and thrive.* New York: Crown Publishers/Random House.

Fredrikson, M., Annas, P., Fischer, H., & Wik, G. (1996). Gender and age differences in the prevalence of specific fears and phobias. *Behaviour Research and Therapy, 34,* 33–39.

Freedman, J. L., & Fraser, S. C. (1966). Compliance without pressure: The foot-in-the-door technique. *Journal of Personality and Social Psychology, 4,* 195–202.

Freeman, C. (2004). Trends in educational equity of girls & women. Retrieved July 3, 2006 from *http://nces.ed.gov/pubs2005/2005016.pdf*

Freeman, E., Colpe, L., Strine, T., Dhingra, S., McGuire, L., Elam-Evans, L., & Perry, G. (2010). Public health surveillance for mental health. *Preventing Chronic Disease: Public Health Research, Practice, and Policy, 7,* 1–7.

Freeman, W. J. (1991). The physiology of perception. *Scientific American, 264,* 78–85.

Freud, S. (1900/1953a). The interpretation of dreams. In J. Strachey (Ed. and trans.), *The standard edition of the complete psychological works of Sigmund Freud* (Vols. 4 and 5). London: Hogarth Press. (Original work published 1900).

Freud, S. (1905/1953b). Three essays on the theory of sexuality. In J. Strachey (Ed. and Trans.), *The standard edition of the complete psychological works of Sigmund Freud* (Vol. 7). London: Hogarth Press. (Original work published 1905).

Freud, S. (1920/1963b). *A general introduction to psycho-analysis* (J. Riviere, Trans.). New York: Simon & Schuster. (Original work published 1920).

Freud, S. (1922). *Beyond the pleasure principle.* London: International Psychoanalytic Press.

Freud, S. (1925/1963a). *An autobiographical study* (J. Strachey, Trans.). New York: W.W. Norton. (Original work published 1925).

Freud, S. (1930/1962). *Civilization and its discontents* (J. Strachey, Trans.). New York: W. W. Norton. (Original work published 1930).

Freud, S. (1933/1965). *New introductory lectures on psychoanalysis* (J. Strachey, Trans.). New York: W. W. Norton. (Original work published 1933).

Freudenberger, H., & Richelson, G. (1981). *Burnout.* New York: Bantam Books.

Frey, K. P., & Eagly, A. H. (1993). Vividness can undermine the persuasiveness of messages. *Journal of Personality and Social Psychology, 65,* 32–44.

Frey, M., & Detterman, D. (2004). Scholastic assessment or *g*? The relationship between the scholastic assessment test and general cognitive ability. *Psychological Science, 15,* 373–378.

Frick, P., Cornell, A., Bodin, S., Dane, H., Barry, C., & Loney, B. (2003). Callous-unemotional traits and developmental pathways to severe conduct problems. *Developmental Psychology, 39,* 246–260.

Friedland, N., Keinan, G., & Regev, Y. (1992). Controlling the uncontrollable: Effects of stress on illusory perceptions of controllability. *Journal of Personality and Social Psychology, 63,* 923–931.

Friedman, J. M. (1997). The alphabet of weight control. *Nature, 385,* 119–120.

Friedman, J. M. (2000). Obesity in the new millennium. *Nature, 404,* 632–634.

Friedman, M. I., Tordoff, M. G., & Ramirez, I. (1986). Integrated metabolic control of food intake. *Brain Research Bulletin, 17,* 855–859.

Friedman, M., & Rosenman, R. H. (1974). *Type A behavior and your heart.* New York: Fawcett.

Fujita, F., Diener, E., & Sandvik, E. (1991). Gender differences in negative affect and well-being: The case for emotional intensity. *Journal of Personality and Social Psychology, 61,* 427–434.

Fuzhong, L., Harmer, P., Fisher, K., & McAuley, E. (2004). Tai Chi: Improving balance and predicting subsequent falls in older persons. *Medicine & Science in Sports & Exercise, 36,* 2046–2052.

Gackenbach, J., Kuruvilla, B., & Dopko, R. (2009). Video game play and dream bizarreness. *Dreaming, 19,* 218–231.

Gadea, M., Martinez-Bisbal, M., Marti-Bonmati, Espert, R., Casanova, B., Coret, F., & Celda, B. (2004). Spectroscopic axonal damage of the right locus coeruleus relates to selective attention impairment in early stage relapsing-remitting multiple sclerosis. *Brain, 127,* 89–98.

Gaertner, I., Sedikides, C., & Chang, K. (2008). On pancultural self-enhancement: Well-adjusted Taiwanese self-enhance on personally valued traits. *Journal of Cross-Cultural Psychology, 39,* 463–477.

Gaggioli, A., & Riva, G. (2007). A second life for telehealth? *Annual Review of CyberTherapy and Telemedicine, 5,* 29–36.

Galambos, N., Turner, P., & Tilton-Weaver, L. (2005). Chronological and subjective age in emerging adulthood: The crossover effect. *Journal of Adolescent Research, 20,* 538–556.

Gallagher, M., & Rapp, P. R. (1997). The use of animal models to study the effects of aging on cognition. *Annual Review of Psychology, 48,* 339–370.

Gallo, L., Troxel, W., Matthews, K., Jansen-McWilliams, L., Kuller, L., & Suton-Tyrrell, K. (2003). Occupation and subclinical carotid artery disease: Are clerical workers at greater risk? *Health Psychology, 22,* 19–29.

Gallup, G. (1970). Chimpanzees: Self-recognition. *Science, 167,* 86–87.

Gallup, G., Anderson, J., & Shillito, D. (2002). The mirror test. In M. Bekoff, C. Allen, & G. Burghardt (Eds.), *The cognitive animal: Empirical and theoretical perspectives on animal cognition* (pp. 325–334). Cambridge, MA: MIT Press.

Gallup, G., Jr., & Hugick, L. (1990). Racial tolerance grows, progress on racial equality less evident. *Gallup Poll Monthly, 297,* 23–32.

Ganellen, R. J. (1996). Comparing the diagnostic efficiency of the MMPI, MCMI-II, and Rorschach: A review. *Journal of Personality Assessment, 67,* 219–243.

Gao, J-H., Parsons, L. M., Bower, J. M., Xiong, J., Li, J., & Fox, P. T. (1996). Cerebellum implicated in sensory acquisition and discrimination rather than motor control. *Science, 272,* 545–547.

Garavan, H., Morgan, R. E., Levitsky, D. A., Hermer-Vasquez, L., & Strupp, B. J. (2000). Enduring effects of early lead exposure: Evidence for a specific deficit in associative ability. *Neurotoxicology and Teratology, 22,* 151–164.

Garcia, J., & Koelling, A. (1966). Relation of cue to consequence in avoidance learning. *Psychonomic Science, 4,* 123–124.

Gardner, H. (1983). *Frames of mind: The theory of multiple intelligences.* New York: Basic Books.

Gardner, H., & Hatch, T. (1989). Multiple intelligences go to school: Educational implication of the theory of multiple intelligences. *Educational Researcher, 18*(8), 6.

Gardner, R. A., & Gardner, B. T. (1969). Teaching sign language to a chimpanzee. *Science, 165,* 664–672.

Garfield, C. (1986). *Peak performers: The new heroes of American business.* New York: Morrow.

Garma, L., & Marchand, F. (1994). Non-pharmacological approaches to the treatment of narcolepsy. *Sleep, 17,* S97–S102.

Garmon, L. C., Basinger, K. S., Gregg, V. R., & Gibbs, J. C. (1996). Gender differences in stage and expression of moral judgment. *Merrill-Palmer Quarterly, 42,* 418–437.

Garrett, M., Garrett, J., & Brotherton, D. (2001). Inner circle/outer circle: A group technique based on Native American healing circles. *Journal for Specialists in Group Work, 26,* 17–30.

Garry, M., & Loftus, E. F. (1994). Pseudomemories without hypnosis. *International Journal of Clinical and Experimental Hypnosis, 42,* 363–373.

Garssen, B. (2004). Psychological factors and cancer development: Evidence after 30 years of research. *Clinical Psychology Review, 24,* 315–338.

Gartner, J., & Whitaker-Azimitia, P. M. (1996). Developmental factors influencing aggression: Animal models and clinical correlates. *Annals of the New York Academy of Sciences, 794,* 113–120.

Gavin, J., Scott, A., & Duffield, J. (2006). *Passion, intimacy and commitment in online dating: Time versus channel effects.* Paper presented at the International Association for Relationship Research Conference. July, 2006, University of Crete, Greece.

Gawin, F. H. (1991). Cocaine addiction: Psychology and neurophysiology. *Science, 251,* 1580–1586.

Gawronski, B., Alshut, E., Grafe, J., Nespethal, J., Ruhmland, A., & Schulz, L. (2002). Processes of judging known and unknown persons. *Zeitschrift fuer Sozialpsychologie, 33,* 25–34.

Gazzaniga, M. (1970). *The bisected brain.* New York: Appleton-Century-Crofts.

Gazzaniga, M. (1989). Organization of the human brain. *Science, 245,* 947–952.

Gazzola, N., & Stalikas, A. (2004). Therapist interpretations and client processes in three therapeutic modalities: Implications for psychotherapy integration. *Journal of Psychotherapy Integration, 14,* 397–418.

Ge, X., Brody, G., Conger, R., Simons, R., & Murry, V. (2002). Contextual amplification of pubertal transition effects on deviant peer affiliation and externalizing behavior among African American children. *Developmental Psychology, 38,* 42–54.

Geary, D. C. (1996). Sexual selection and sex differences in mathematical abilities. *Behavioral and Brain Sciences, 19,* 229–284.

Geary, N. (2004). Endocrine controls of eating: CCK, leptin, and ghrelin. *Physiology & Behavior, 81,* 719–733.

Geen, R. G. (1984). Human motivation: New perspectives on old problems. In A. M. Rogers & C. J. Scheier (Eds.), *The G. Stanley Hall lecture series* (Vol. 4, pp. 9–57). Washington, DC: American Psychological Association.

Gehart, D., & Lyle, R. (2001). Client experience of gender in therapeutic relationships: An interpretive ethnography. *Family Process, 40,* 443–458.

Gehring, D. (2003). Couple therapy for low sexual desire: A systematic approach. *Journal of Sex & Marital Therapy, 29,* 25–38.

Geiselman, R. E., Schroppel, T., Tubridy, A., Konishi, T., & Rodriguez, V. (2000). Objectivity bias in eye witness performance. *Applied Cognitive Psychology, 14,* 323–332.

Gentile, D., Anderson, C., Yukawa, S., Ihori, N., Saleem, M., Ming, L., Shibuya, A., Liau, A., Khoo, A., Bushman, B., Heusmann, L., & Sakamoto, A. (2009). The effects of prosocial video games on prosocial behaviors: International evidence from correlational, longitudinal, and experimental studies. *Personality and Social Psychology Bulletin, 36,* 752–763.

George, M. S., Ketter, T. A., & Post, R. M. (1993). SPECT and PET imaging in mood disorders. *Journal of Clinical Psychiatry, 54*(11, Suppl.), 6–13.

George, T., & Vessicchio, J. (2001). Nicotine addiction and schizophrenia. *Psychiatric Times*. Retrieved February 12, 2007, from *http://www.psychiatrictimes.com/p010239.html*

German, T., & Barrett, H. (2005). Functional fixedness in a technologically sparse culture. *Psychological Science, 16,* 1–5.

Gerrits, M., Petromilli, P., Westenberg, H., Di Chiara, G., & van Ree, J. (2002). Decrease in basal dopamine levels in the nucleus accumbens shell during daily drug-seeking behavior in rats. *Brain Research, 924,* 141–150.

Gevins, A., Leong, H., Smith, M. E., Le, J., & Du, R. (1995). Mapping cognitive brain function with modern high-resolution electroencephalography. *Trends in Neurosciences, 18,* 429–436.

Gibbons, A. (1991). Déjà vu all over again: Chimp-language wars. *Science, 251,* 1561–1562.

Gibbs, J., Basinger, K., Grime, R., & Snarey, J. (2007). Moral judgment development across cultures: Revisiting Kohlberg's universality claims. *Developmental Review, 27,* 443–500.

Gibson, E., & Walk, R. D. (1960). The "visual cliff." *Scientific American, 202,* 64–71.

Gibson, J. (1994). The visual perception of objective motion and subjective motion. *Psychological Review, 101,* 318–323.

Giedd, J. N., Rapoport, J. L., Garvey, M. A., Perlmutter, S., & Swedo, S. E. (2000). MRI assessment of children with obsessive-compulsive disorder or tics associated with streptococcal infection. *American Journal of Psychiatry, 157,* 2281–2283.

Gigerenzer, G. (2004). Dread risk, September 11, and fatal traffic accidents. *Psychological Science, 15,* 286–287.

Gilbert, D. (2006). *Stumbling on happiness.* New York: Alfred A. Knopf.

Gilbert, D. T., & Malone, P. S. (1995). The correspondence bias. *Psychological Bulletin, 117,* 21–38.

Gilligan, C. (1982). *In a different voice: Psychological theory and women's development.* Cambridge, MA: Harvard University Press.

Gillon, E. (2008). Men, masculinity, and person-centered therapy. *Person-Centered and Experiential Psychotherapies, 7,* 120–134.

Gingell, C., Nicolosi, A., Buvat, J., Glasser, D., Simsek, F., Hartmann, U., et al. (2003). *Sexual activity and dysfunction among men and women aged 40 to 80 years.* Poster presented at the XVIIIth Congress of the European Association of Urology. Madrid, March, 2003.

Ginty, D. D., Kornhauser, J. M., Thompson, M. A., Bading, H., Mayo, K. E., Takahashi, J. S., et al. (1993). Regulation of CREB phosphorylation in the suprachiasmatic nucleus by light and a circadian clock. *Science, 260,* 238–241.

Ginzburg, K., Solomon, Z., & Bleich, A. (2002). Repressive coping style, acute stress disorder, and post-traumatic stress disorder after myocardial infarction. *Journal of the American Psychosomatic Society, 64,* 748–757.

Giraud, A., Price, C., Graham, J., & Frackowisk, R. (2001). Functional plasticity of language-related brain areas after cochlear implantation. *Neuropsychopharmacology, 124,* 1307–1316.

Girolamo, G., & Bassi, M. (2003). Community surveys of mental disorders: Recent achievements and works in progress. *Current Opinion in Psychiatry, 16,* 403–411.

Glannon, W. (2006). Neuroethics. *Bioethics, 20,* 37–52.

Glantz, L. A., & Lewis, D. A. (2000). Decreased dendritic spine density on prefrontal cortical pyramidal neurons in schizophrenia. *Archives of General Psychiatry, 57,* 65–73.

Glass, D. C., & Singer, J. E. (1972). *Urban stress: Experiments in noise and social stressors.* New York: Academic Press.

Glazer, W. M., Morgenstern, H., & Doucette, J. T. (1993). Predicting the long-term risk of tardive dyskinesia in outpatients maintained on neuroleptic medications. *Journal of Clinical Psychiatry, 54,* 133–139.

Gleaves, D. J. (1996). The sociocognitive model of dissociative identity disorder: A reexamination of the evidence. *Psychological Bulletin, 120,* 42–59.

Global Fund to Fight AIDS, Tuberculosis, and Malaria, (2005). *Global Fund ARV factsheet.* Retrieved July 3, 2006, from *http://www.theglobalfund.org/en/files/publications/factsheets/aids/ARV_Factsheet_2006.pdf*

Glover, J. A., & Corkill, A. J. (1987). Influence of paraphrased repetitions on the spacing effect. *Journal of Educational Psychology, 79,* 198–199.

Gluck, M. A., & Myers, C. E. (1997). Psychobiological models of hippocampal function in learning and memory. *Annual Review of Psychology, 48,* 481–514.

Glucksman, M., & Kramer, M. (2004). Using dreams to assess clinical change during treatment. *Journal of the American Academy of Psychoanalysis and Dynamic Psychiatry, 32,* 345–358.

Gökcebay, N., Cooper, R., Williams, R. L., Hirshkowitz, M., & Moore, C. A. (1994). Function of sleep. In R. Cooper (Ed.), *Sleep* (pp. 47–59). New York: Chapman & Hall.

Godden, D. R., & Baddeley, A. D. (1975). Context-dependent memory in two natural environments: On land and underwater. *British Journal of Psychology, 66,* 325–331.

Goeders, N. (2004). Stress, motivation, and drug addiction. *Current Directions in Psychological Science, 13,* 33–35.

Goffman, E. (1959). *The presentation of self in everyday life.* Garden City, NY: Doubleday-Anchor.

Gogtay, N., Giedd, J., Lusk, L., Hayashi, K., Greenstein, D., Vaituzis, A., et al. (2004). Dynamic mapping of human cortical development during childhood through early adulthood. *Proceedings of the National Academy of Science, 101,* 8174–8179.

Goldberg, L. (1993). The structure of phenotypic personality traits. *American Psychologist, 48,* 26–34.

Goldstein, D. & Gigerenzer, G. (2002). Models of ecological rationality: The recognition heuristic. *Psychological Review, 109,* 75–90.

Goleman, D., Kaufman, P., & Ray, M. (1992). *The creative spirit.* New York: Dutton.

Gollan, T., & Brown, A. (2006). From tip-of-the-tongue (TOT) data to theoretical implications in two steps: When more TOTs means better retrieval. *Journal of Experimental Psychology: General, 135,* 462–483.

Gollan, T., & Silverberg, N. (2001). Tip-of-the-tongue states in Hebrew-English bilinguals. *Bilingualism: Language and Cognition, 4,* 63–83.

Golz, A., Netzer, A., Westerman, S., Westerman, L., Gilbert, D., Joachims, H., & Goldenberg, D. (2005). Reading performance in children with otitis media. *Otolaryngology: Head and Neck Surgery, 132,* 495-499.

Gonsalves, B., Reber, P., Gitelman, D., Parrish, T., Mesulam, M., & Paller, K. (2004). Neural evidence that vivid imagining can lead to false remembering. *Psychological Science, 15,* 655–660.

Gonzalez, R., Ellsworth, P. C., & Pembroke, M. (1993). Response biases in lineups and showups. *Journal of Personality and Social Psychology, 64,* 525–537.

Good, C., Aronson, J., & Inzlicht, M. (2003). Improving adolescents' standardized test performance: An intervention to reduce the effects of stereotype threat. *Applied Developmental Psychology, 24,* 645–662.

Goodglass, H. (1993). *Understanding aphasia.* San Diego, CA: Academic Press.

Goodman, E., McEwen, B., Huang, B., Dolan, L., & Adler, N. (2005). Social inequalities in biomarkers of cardiovascular risk in adolescence. *Psychosomatic Medicine, 67,* 9–15.

Goodman, G., Quas, J., & Ogle, C. (2010). Child maltreatment and memory. *Annual Review of Psychology, 61,* 325–351.

Goodwin, G. M. (1996). How do antidepressants affect serotonin receptors? The role of serotonin receptors in the therapeutic and side effect profile of the SSRIs. *Journal of Clinical Psychiatry, 57*(4, Suppl.), 9–13.

Goodwin, R., & Fitzgibbon, M. (2002). Social anxiety as a barrier to treatment for eating disorders. *International Journal of Eating Disorders, 32,* 103–106.

Goodwin, R., & Gotlib, I. (2004). Gender differences in depression: The role of personality factors. *Psychiatry Research, 126,* 135–142.

Gordon, H. (2002). Early environmental stress and biological vulnerability to drug abuse. *Psychoneuroendocrinology, 27,* 115–126.

Gorman, C. (1996, Fall). Damage control. *Time* [Special Issue], 31–35.

Gorman, J. (2007). *The essential guide to psychiatric drugs* (4th ed.). New York: St. Martin's Press.

Gottesman, I. I. (1991). *Schizophrenia genesis: The origins of madness.* New York: W. H. Freeman.

Gottesmann, C. (2000). Hypothesis for the neurophysiology of dreaming. *Sleep Research Online, 3,* 1–4.

Gottfried, J. (2010). Olfaction and its pleasures: Human neuroimaging perspectives. In Kringelbach, M., & Berridge, K. (Eds.). *Pleasures of the brain.* (pp. 125–145). New York: Oxford University Press.

Gough, H. (1987). *California Psychological Inventory: Administrator's Guide.* Palo Alto: Consulting Psychologists Press.

Gould, E. R., Reeves, A. J., Graziano, M. S. A., & Gross, C. (1999). Neurogenesis in the neocortex of adult primates. *Science, 286,* 548.

Gow, A., Whiteman, M., Pattie, A., & Deary, I. (2005). Goldberg's IPIP Big-Five factor markers: Internal consistency and concurrent validation in Scotland. *Personality and Individual Differences, 39,* 317–329.

Grünbaum, A. (2006). Is Sigmund Freud's psychoanalytic edifice relevant to the 21st century? *Psychoanalytic Psychology, 23,* 257–284.

Granic, I., & Patterson, G. (2006). Toward a comprehensive model of antisocial development: A dynamic systems approach. *Psychological Review, 113,* 101–131.

Grant, D., & Harari, E. (2005). Psychoanalysis, science and the seductive theory of Karl Popper. *Australian and New Zealand Journal of Psychiatry, 39,* 446–452.

Greden, J. F. (1994). Introduction Part III. New agents for the treatment of depression. *Journal of Clinical Psychiatry, 55*(2, Suppl.), 32–33.

Green, B. L., Lindy, J. D., & Grace, M. C. (1985). Post-traumatic stress disorder: Toward DSM-IV. *Journal of Nervous and Mental Disorders, 173,* 406–411.

Green, J. P., & Lynn, S. J. (2000). Hypnosis and suggestion-based approaches to smoking cessation: An examination of the evidence. *International Journal of Clinical Experimental Hypnosis, 48,* 195–224.

Green, J., & Shellenberger, R. (1990). *The dynamics of health and wellness: A biopsychosocial approach.* Fort Worth: Holt, Rinehart & Winston.

Green, L. R., Richardson, D. R., & Lago, T. (1996). How do friendship, indirect, and direct aggression relate? *Aggressive Behavior, 22,* 81–86.

Green, R., MacDorman, K., Ho, C., & Vasudevan, S. (2008). Sensitivity to the proportions of faces that vary in human likeness. *Computers in Human Behavior, 24,* 2456–2474.

Greenberg, W. (2009). *Obsessive-compulsive disorder.* Retrieved March 15, 2010 from *http://emedicine.medscape.com/article/287681-overview.*

Greenfield, S., & Hennessy, G. (2008). Assessment of the patient. In M. Galanter & H. Kleber (Eds.), *The American Psychiatric Publishing textbook of substance abuse* (4th ed., pp. 55–78). Arlington, VA: American Psychiatric Publishing.

Greenglass, E., & Fiksenbaum, L. (2009). Proactive coping, positive affect, and well-being: Testing for mediation using path analysis. *European Psychologist, 14,* 29–39.

Greenwald, A. (1992). New look 3: Unconscious cognition reclaimed. *American Psychologist, 47,* 766–779.

Greenwald, A., Spangenberg, E., Pratkanis, A., & Eskenazi, J. (1991). Double-blind tests of subliminal self-help audiotapes. *Psychological Science, 2,* 119–122.

Greer, M. (2005). Keeping them hooked in. *APA Monitor on Psychology, 36,* 60.

Gregory, R. J. (1996). *Psychological testing: History, principles, and applications* (2nd ed.). Boston: Allyn & Bacon.

Greist, J. H. (1992). An integrated approach to treatment of obsessive compulsive disorder. *Journal of Clinical Psychiatry, 53*(4, Suppl.), 38–41.

Greist, J. H. (1995). The diagnosis of social phobia. *Journal of Clinical Psychiatry, 56*(5, Suppl.), 5–12.

Greitmeyer, T., & Osswald, S. (2010). Effects of prosocial video games on prosocial behavior. *Journal of Personality and Social Psychology, 98,* 211–221.

Grey, N., Salkovskis, P., Quigley, A., Clark, D., & Ehlers, A. (2008). Dissemination of cognitive therapy for panic disorder in primary care. *Behavioural and Cognitive Psychotherapy, 36,* 509–520.

Griffiths, M. (2003). Communicating risk: Journalists have responsibility to report risks in context. *British Medical Journal, 327,* 1404.

Grigorenko, E. (2003). Epistasis and the genetics of complex traits. In R. Plomin, J. DeFries, I. Craig, & P. McGuffin (Eds.), *Behavioral genetics in the postgenomic era* (pp. 247–266). Washington, DC: American Psychological Association.

Grigorenko, E., Jarvin, L., & Sternberg, R. (2002). School-based tests of the triarchic theory of intelligence: Three settings, three samples, three syllabi. *Contemporary Educational Psychology, 27,* 167–208.

Grigorenko, E., Meier, E., Lipka, J., Mohatt, G., Yanez, E., & Sternberg, R. (2004). Academic and practical intelligence: A case study of the Yup'ik in Alaska. *Learning & Individual Differences, 14,* 183–207.

Grinker, J. A. (1982). Physiological and behavioral basis for human obesity. In D. W. Pfaff (Ed.), The physiological mechanisms of motivation. New York: Springer-Verlag.

Grochowicz, P., Schedlowski, M., Husband, A., King, M., Hibberd, A., & Bowen, K. (1991). Behavioral conditioning prolongs heart allograft survival in rats. *Brain, Behavior, and Immunity, 5,* 349–356.

Gron, G., Wunderlich, A. P., Spitzer, M., Tomczrak, R., & Riepe, M. W. (2000). Brain activation during human navigation: Gender-different neural networks as substrate of performance. *Nature Neuroscience, 3,* 404–408.

Gross, J. (2002). Emotion regulation: Affective, cognitive, and social consequences. *Psychophysiology, 39,* 281–291.

Grossenbacher, P., & Lovelace, C. (2001). Mechanisms of synesthesia: Cognitive and physiological constraints. *Trends in Cognitive Sciences, 5,* 36–41.

Grossman, H. J. (Ed.). (1983). *Manual on terminology and classification in mental retardation.* Washington, DC: American Association on Mental Deficiency.

Grossman, J., & Ruiz, P. (2004). Shall we make a leap-of-faith to disulfiram (Antabuse)? *Addictive Disorders & Their Treatment, 3,* 129–132.

Grossman, M., & Wood, W. (1993). Sex differences in intensity of emotional experience: A social role interpretation. *Journal of Personality and Social Psychology, 65,* 1010–1022.

Guadagno, R., & Cialdini, R. (2007). Persuade him by email, but see her in person: Online persuasion revisited. *Computers in Human Behavior, 23,* 99–1015.

Guenole, N., & Chernyshenko, O. (2005). The suitability of Goldberg's Big Five IPIP personality markers in New Zealand: A dimensionality, bias, and criterion validity evaluation. *New Zealand Journal of Psychology, 34,* 86–96.

Guenther, K. (2002). Memory. In D. Levitin, (Ed.), *Foundations of cognitive psychology.* Cambridge, MA: MIT Press.

Guilford, J. P. (1967). *The nature of human intelligence.* New York: McGraw-Hill.

Guilleminault, C. (1993). Amphetamines and narcolepsy: Use of the Stanford database. *Sleep, 16,* 199–201.

Gulick, D., & Gould, T. (2009). Effects of ethanol and caffeine on behavior in C57BL/6 mice in the plus-maze discriminative avoidance task. *Behavioral Neuroscience, 123,* 1271–1278.

Gur, R. C., Turetsky, B., Mastsui, M., Yan, M. Bilker, W., Hughett, P., & Gur, R. E. (1999). Sex differences in brain gray and white matter in healthy young adults: correlations with cognitive performance. *Journal of Neuroscience, 19,* 4067–4072.

Gur, R., Gunning-Dixon, F., Bilker, W., & Gur, R. (2002). Sex differences in temporolimbic and frontal brain volumes of healthy adults. *Cerebral Cortex, 12,* 998–1003.

Gurin, J. (1989, June). Leaner, not lighter. *Psychology Today,* 32–36.

Guthrie, R. (2004). *Even the rat was white* (classic ed.). Boston, MA: Allyn & Bacon.

Häkkänen, H., & Summala, H. (1999). Sleepiness at work among commercial truck drivers. *Sleep, 23,* 49–57.

Hänggi, J., Buchmann, A., Mondadori, C., Henke, K., Jäncke, L., & Hock, C. (2010). Sexual dipmorphism in the parietal substrate associated with visuospatial cognition independent of general intelligence. *Journal of Cognitive Neuroscience, 22,* 139–155.

Hébert, S., Béland, R., Dionne-Fournelle, O., Crête, M., & Lupien, S. (2005). Physiological stress response to video-game playing: The contribution of built-in music. *Life Sciences, 76,* 2371–2380.

Haag, L., & Stern, E. (2003). In search of the benefits of learning Latin. *Journal of Educational Psychology, 95,* 174–178.

Haaken, J., & Reavey, P. (2010). Memory matters: Contexts for understanding sexual abuse recollections (pp. 1–13). New York: Routledge/Taylor & Francis Group.

Habel, U., Kuehn, E., Salloum, J., Devos, H., & Schneider, F. (2002). Emotional processing in psychopathic personality. *Aggressive Behavior, 28,* 394–400.

Haber, R. N. (1980). How we perceive depth from flat pictures. *American Scientist, 68,* 370–380.

Haberlandt, D. (1997). *Cognitive psychology* (2nd ed.). Boston: Allyn & Bacon.

Hackel, L. S., & Ruble, D. N. (1992). Changes in the marital relationship after the first baby is born: Predicting the impact of expectancy disconfirmation. *Journal of Personality and Social Psychology, 62,* 944–957.

Hada, M., Porjesz, B., Begleiter, H., & Polich, J. (2000). Auditory P3a assessment of male alcoholics. *Biological Psychiatry, 48,* 276–286.

Hada, M., Porjesz, B., Chorlian, D., Begleiter, H., & Polich, J. (2001). Auditory P3a deficits in male subjects at high risk for alcoholism. *Biological Psychiatry, 49,* 726–738.

Hahn, I., & Yew, D. (2009). *Toxicity, MDMA.* Retrieved February 8, 2010 from *http://emedicine.medscape.com/article/821572-overview.*

Hakuta, K., Bialystok, E., & Wiley, E. (2003). Critical evidence: A test of the critical-period hypothesis for second-language acquisition. *Psychological Science, 14,* 31–38.

Halaas, J. L., Gajiwala, K. S., Maffei, M., Cohen, S. L., Chait, B. T., Rabinowitz, D., et al. (1995). Weight-reducing effects of the plasma protein encoded by the obese gene. *Science, 269,* 543–546.

Halama, P., & Strízenec, M. (2004). Spiritual, existential or both? Theoretical considerations on the nature of "higher" intelligences. *Studia Psychologica, 46,* 239–253.

Halaris, A. (2003). Neurochemical aspects of the sexual response cycle. *CNS Spectrums, 8,* 211–216.

Hald, A., Nedergaard, S., Hansen, R., Ding, M., & Heegaard, A. (2009). Differential activation of spinal cord glial cells in murine models of neuropathic and cancer pain. *European Journal of Pain, 13,* 138–145.

Halford, G. S. (1989). Reflections on 25 years of Piagetian cognitive developmental psychology, 1963–1988. *Human Development, 32,* 325–327.

Halligan, P. W., & Marshall, J. C. (1994). Toward a principled explanation of unilateral neglect. *Cognitive Neuropsychology, 11,* 167–206.

Hallon, S., Stewart, M., & Strunk, D. (2006). Enduring effects for cognitive therapy in the treatment of depression and anxiety. *Annual Review of Psychology, 57,* 285–316.

Hallschmid, M., Benedict, C., Born, J., Fehm, H., & Kern, W. (2004). Manipulating central nervous mechanisms of food intake and body weight regulation by intranasal administration of neuropeptides in man. *Physiology & Behavior, 83,* 55–64.

Halmi, K. A. (1996). Eating disorder research in the past decade. *Annals of the New York Academy of Sciences, 789,* 67–77.

Ham, P. (2003). Suicide risk not increased with SSRI and antidepressants. *Journal of Family Practice, 52,* 587–589.

Hamilton, C. S., & Swedo, S. E. (2001). Autoimmune-mediated, childhood onset obsessive-compulsive disorder and tics: A review. *Clinical Neuroscience Research, 1,* 61–68.

Hampson, S., Goldberg, L., Vogt, T., & Dubanoski, J. (2006). Forty years on: Teachers' assessments of children's personality traits predict self-reported health behaviors and outcomes at midlife. *Health Psychology, 25,* 57–64.

Hancock, P., & Ganey, H. (2003). From the inverted-u to the extended-u: The evolution of a law of psychology. *Journal of Human Performance in Extreme Environments, 7,* 5–14.

Hanley, S., & Abell, S. (2002). Maslow and relatedness: Creating an interpersonal model of self-actualization. *Journal of Humanistic Psychology, 42,* 37–56.

Hannover, B., & Kuehnen, U. (2002). "The clothing makes the self" via knowledge activation. *Journal of Applied Social Psychology, 32,* 2513–2525.

Hanoch, Y., & Vitouch, O. (2004). When less is more: Information, emotional arousal and the ecological reframing of the Yerkes-Dodson law. *Theory & Psychology, 14,* 427–452.

Harackiewicz, A., Barron, A., Pintrich, A., Elliot, A., & Thrash, A. (2002). Revision of achievement goal theory: Necessary and illuminating. *Journal of Educational Psychology, 94,* 638–645.

Hare, R. (1998). The Hare PCL-R: Some issues concerning its use and misuse. *Legal and Criminological Psychology, 3,* 99–119.

Hargadon, R., Bowers, K. S., & Woody, E. Z. (1995). Does counterpain imagery mediate hypnotic analgesia? *Journal of Abnormal Psychology, 104,* 508–516.

Harlow, H. F., & Harlow, M. K. (1962). Social deprivation in monkeys. *Scientific American, 207,* 137–146.

Harlow, J. M. (1848). Passage of an iron rod through the head. *Boston Medical and Surgical Journal, 39,* 389–393.

Harms, P., Roberts, B., & Winter, D. (2006). Becoming the Harvard Man: Person–environment fit, personality development, and academic success. *Personality and Social Psychology Bulletin, 32,* 851–865.

Harp, S., & Mayer, R. (1998). How seductive details do their damage: A theory of cognitive interest in science learning. *Journal of Educational Psychology, 90,* 414–434.

Harris, J. A., Rushton, J. P., Hampson, E., & Jackson, D. N. (1996). Salivary testosterone and self-report aggressive and pro-social personality characteristics in men and women. *Aggressive Behavior, 22,* 321–331.

Harris, R. A., Brodie, M. S., & Dunwiddie, T. V. (1992). Possible substrates of ethanol reinforcement: GABA and dopamine. *Annals of the New York Academy of Sciences, 654,* 61–69.

Harrison, Y., & Horne, J. A. (2000). Sleep loss and temporal memory. *Journal of Experimental Psychology, 53,* 271–279.

Harrold, L., Ware, C., Mason, J., McGuire, E., Lewis, D., Pagano, L., & Alley, W. (2009). *The distracted teenage driver.* Paper presented at the annual meeting of the Pediatric Academic Society. Baltimore, MD.

Hart, J., Karau, S., Stasson, M., & Kerr, N. (2004). Achievement motivation, expected coworker performance, and collective task motivation: Working hard or hardly working? *Journal of Applied Social Psychology, 34,* 984–1000.

Hart, S., Petrill, S., Thompson, L., & Plomin, R. (2009). The ABCs of math: A genetic analysis of mathematics and its links with reading ability and general cognitive ability. *Journal of Educational Psychology, 101,* 388–402.

Haslam, S. A., & Reicher, S. (2006). Stressing the group: Social identity and the unfolding dynamics of responses to stress. *Journal of Applied Psychology, 91,* 1037–1052.

Haslam, S., Jetten, J., Postmes, T., & Haslam, C. (2009). Social identity, health and well-being: An emerging agenda for applied psychology. *An International Review, 58,* 1–23.

Haslam, S., & Reicher, S. (2008). Questioning the banality of evil. *The Psychologist, 21,* 16–19.

Hatashita-Wong, M., Smith, T., Silverstein, S., Hull, J., & Willson, D. (2002). Cognitive functioning and social problem-solving skills in schizophrenia. *Cognitive Neuropsychiatry, 7,* 81–95.

Hauser, M. D. (1993). Right hemisphere dominance for the production of facial expression in monkeys. *Science, 261,* 475–477.

Hauser, M., Li, Y., Xu, H., Noureddine, M., Shao, Y., Gullans, S., et al. (2005). Expression profiling of substantia nigra in Parkinson disease, progressive supranuclear palsy, and frontotemporal dementia with Parkinsonism. *Archives of Neurology, 62,* 917–921.

Hawley, K., & Weisz, J. (2003). Child, parent and therapist (dis)agreement on target problems in outpatient therapy: The therapist's dilemma and its implications. *Journal of Consulting & Clinical Psychology, 71,* 62–70.

Haxby, J., Gobbini, M., Furey, M., Ishai, A., Schouten, J., & Pietrini, P. (2001). Distributed and overlapping representations of faces and objects in ventral temporal cortex. *Science, 293,* 2425–2430.

Hay, D. F. (1994). Prosocial development. *Journal of Child Psychology and Psychiatry, 35,* 29–71.

Haywood, H., & Lidz, C. (2007). *Dynamic assessment in practice: Clinical and educational applications.* New York: Cambridge University Press.

Hazlett-Stevens, H., Craske, M., Roy-Byrne, P., Sherbourne, C., Stein, M., & Bystritsky, A. (2002). Predictors of willingness to consider medication and psychosocial treatment for panic disorder in primary care patients. *General Hospital Psychology, 24,* 316–321.

HCF Nutrition Foundation. (2003). *The benefits of fiber.* Retrieved January 29, 2003, from *http://www.hcf-nutrition.org/fiber/fiber-ben_article.html*

He, Y., Colantonio, A., & Marshall, V. (2003). Later-life career disruption and self-rated health: An analysis of General Social Survey data. *Canadian Journal on Aging, 22,* 45–57.

Heap, M. (2000). The alleged dangers of stage hypnosis. *Contemporary Hypnosis, 17,* 117–126.

Heatherton, T., Macrae, N., & Kelley, W. (2004). What the social brain sciences can tell us about the self. *Current Directions in Psychological Science, 13,* 190–193.

Hebb, D. O. (1949). *The organization of behavior.* New York: John Wiley & Sons.

Hecht, S., Shlaer, S., & Pirenne, M. H. (1942). Energy, quanta, and vision. *Journal of General Physiology, 25,* 819.

Heckhausen, J., & Brian, O. (1997). Perceived problems for self and others: Self-protection by social downgrading throughout adulthood. *Psychology & Aging, 12,* 610–619.

Hedges, L. B., & Nowell, A. (1995). Sex differences in mental test scores, variability, and numbers of high-scoring individuals. *Science, 269,* 41–45.

Heider, F. (1958). *The psychology of interpersonal relations.* Mahwah, NJ: Lawrence Erlbaum Associates.

Heil, M., Rolke, B., & Pecchinenda, A. (2004). Automatic semantic activation is no myth. *Psychological Science, 15,* 852–857.

Heiman, J. (2002). Psychologic treatments for female sexual dysfunction: Are they effective and do we need them? *Archives of Sexual Behavior, 31,* 445–450.

Heitjtz, R., Kolb, B., & Forssberg, H. (2003). Can a therapeutic dose of amphetamine during pre-adolescence modify the pattern of synaptic organization in the brain? *European Journal of Neuroscience, 18,* 3394–3399.

Held, R. (1993). What can rates of development tell us about underlying mechanisms? In C. E. Granrud (Ed.), *Visual perception and cognition in infancy* (pp. 75–89). Hillsdale, NJ: Erlbaum.

Hellige, J. B. (1990). Hemispheric asymmetry. *Annual Review of Psychology, 41,* 55–80.

Hellstrom, Y., & Hallberg, I. (2004). Determinants and characteristics of help provision for eldery people living at home and in relation to quality of life. *Scandinavian Journal of Caring Sciences, 18,* 387–395.

Hendin, H., & Haas, A. P. (1991). Suicide and guilt as manifestations of PTSD in Vietnam combat veterans. *American Journal of Psychiatry, 148,* 586–591.

Henkel, L. A., Franklin, N., & Johnson, M. K. (2000). Cross-modal source monitoring confusions between perceived and imagined events. *Journal of Experimental Psychology: Learning, Memory, and Cognition, 26,* 321–335.

Herbert, T. B., & Cohen, S. (1993). Depression and immunity: A meta-analytic review. *Psychological Bulletin, 113,* 472–486.

Herek, G. (2002). Gender gaps in public opinion about lesbians and gay men. *Public Opinion Quarterly, 66,* 40–66.

Herkenham, M. (1992). Cannabinoid receptor localization in brain: Relationship to motor and reward systems. *Annals of the New York Academy of Sciences, 654,* 19–32.

Herman, L. (1981). Cognitive characteristics of dolphins. In L. Herman (Ed.), *Cetacean behavior* (pp. 363–430). New York: Wiley.

Hernandez, L., & Hoebel, B. G. (1989). Food intake and lateral hypothalamic self-stimulation covary after medial hypothalamic lesions or ventral midbrain 6-hydroxydopamine injections that cause obesity. *Behavioral Neuroscience, 103,* 412–422.

Herness, S. (2000). Coding in taste receptor cells: The early years of intracellular recordings. *Physiology and Behavior, 69,* 17–27.

Herpertz., S., Kielmann, R., Wolf, A., Hebebrand, J., & Senf, W. (2004). Do psychosocial variables predict weight loss or mental health after obesity surgery? A systematic review. *Obesity Research, 12,* 1554–1569.

Hershberger, S., & Segal, N. (2004). The cognitive, behavioral, and personality profiles of a male monozygotic triplet set discordant for sexual orientation. *Archives of Sexual Behavior, 33,* 497–514.

Hertzog, C. (1991). Aging, information processing speed, and intelligence. In K. W. Schaie & M. P. Lawton (Eds.), *Annual Review of Gerontology and Geriatrics* (Vol. 11, pp. 55–79). New York: Springer Publishing Company.

Hespos, S., & Baillargeon, R. (2006). Décalage in infants' knowledge about occlusion and containment events: Converging evidence from action tasks. *Cognition, 99,* B31–B41.

Hctherington, A. W., & Ranson, S. W. (1940). Hypothalamic lesions and adiposity in the rat. *Anatomical Record, 78,* 149–172.

Heyman, G., Gee, C., & Giles, J. (2003). Preschool children's reasoning about ability. *Child Development, 74,* 516–534.

Hickman, J., & Geller, E. (2003). A safety self-management intervention for mining operations. *U.S. Journal of Safety Research, 34,* 299–308.

Higbee, K. L. (1977). *Your memory: How it works and how to improve it.* Englewood Cliffs, NJ: Prentice-Hall.

Higgins, A. (1995). Educating for justice and community: Lawrence Kohlberg's vision of moral education. In W. M. Kurtines & J. L. Gerwirtz (Eds.), *Moral development: An introduction* (pp. 49–81). Boston: Allyn & Bacon.

Higgins, E., & George, M. (2009). *Brain stimulation therapies for clinicians.* Arlington, VA: American Psychiatric Publishing.

Hilgard, E. R. (1975). Hypnosis. *Annual Review of Psychology, 26,* 19–44.

Hilgard, E. R. (1986). *Divided consciousness: Multiple controls in human thought and action.* New York: Wiley.

Hilgard, E. R. (1992). Dissociation and theories of hypnosis. In E. Fromm & M. R. Nash (Eds.), *Contemporary hypnosis research* (pp. 69–101). New York: Guilford.

Hill, M., & Augoustinos, M. (2001). Stereotype change and prejudice reduction: Short- and long-term evaluation of a cross-cultural awareness programme. *Journal of Community & Applied Social Psychology, 11,* 243–262.

Hillebrand, J. (2000). New perspectives on the manipulation of opiate urges and the assessment of cognitive effort associated with opiate urges. *Addictive Behaviors, 25,* 139–143.

Hirst, W., Phelps, E., Buckner, R., Budson, A., Cuc, A., Gabrieli, J., Johnson, M., Lustig, C., Lyle, K., Mather, M., Meksin, R., Mitchell, K., Ochsner, K., Schacter, D., Simons, J., & Vaidya, C. (2009). Long-term memory for the terrorist attack of September 11: Flashbulb memories, event memories, and the factors that influence their retention. *Journal of Experimental Psychology: General, 138,* 161–176.

Hobson, C., & Delunas, L., (2001). National norms and life-event frequencies for the revised Social Readjustment Rating Scale. *International Journal of Stress Management, 8,* 299–314.

Hobson, J. A. (1988). *The dreaming brain*. New York: Basic Books.

Hobson, J. A. (1989). *Sleep*. New York: Scientific American Library.

Hobson, J. A., & McCarley, R. W. (1977). The brain as a dream state generator: An activation-synthesis hypothesis of the dream process. *American Journal of Psychiatry, 134*, 1335–1348.

Hockett, C. (1959). Animal "language" and human language. *Human Biology, 31*, 32–39.

Hodgins, S., Mednick, S. A., Brennan, P. A., Schulsinger, F., & Engberg, M. (1996). Mental disorder and crime: Evidence from a Danish birth cohort. *Journal of Personality and Social Psychology, 53*, 489–496.

Hoenig, K., & Scheef, L. (2005). Mediotemporal contributions to semantic processing: fMRI evidence from ambiguity processing during semantic context verification. *Hippocampus, 15*, 597–609.

Hofer, H., Carroll, J., Neitz, J., Neitz, M., & Williams, D. (2005). Organization of the human trichromatic cone mosaic. *Journal of Neuroscience, 25*, 9669–9679.

Hoffman, M. (2007). The origins of empathic morality in toddlerhood. In C., Brownell, & C. Kopp (Eds.), *Socioemotional development in the toddler years: Transitions and transformations* (pp. 132–145). New York: Guilford Press.

Hofstede, G. (1980). *Culture's consequences: International differences in work-related values*. Beverly Hills, CA: Sage.

Hofstede, G. (1983). Dimensions of national cultures in fifty countries and three regions. In J. Deregowski, S. Dziurawiec, and R. Annis (Eds.), *Explications in cross-cultural psychology* (pp. 335–355). Lisse, The Netherlands: Swets and Zeitlinger.

Hogan, E., & McReynolds, C. (2004). An overview of anorexia nervosa, bulimia nervosa, and binge eating disorders: Implications for rehabilitation professionals. *Journal of Applied Rehabilitation Counseling, 35*, 26–34.

Holden, C. (1996). Sex and olfaction. *Science, 273*, 313.

Holland, J. L. (1973). *Making vocational choices: A theory of careers*. Englewood Cliffs, NJ: Prentice Hall.

Holland, J. L. (1992). *Making vocational choices: A theory of vocational personalities and work environments* (2nd ed.). Odessa, FL: Psychological Assessment Resources.

Hollon, S., Thase, M., & Markowitz, J. (2002). Treatment and prevention of depression. *Psychological Science in the Public Interest, 3*, 39–77.

Holmes, T. H., & Masuda, M. (1974). Life change and illness susceptibility. In B. S. Dohrenwend & B. P. Dohrenwend (Eds.), *Stressful life events: Their nature and effects* (pp. 45–72). New York: Wiley.

Holmes, T. H., & Rahe, R. H. (1967). The social readjustment rating scale. *Journal of Psychosomatic Research, 11*, 213–218.

Holt-Lunstad, J., Uchino, B., Smith, T., Olson-Cerny, C., & Nealey-Moore, J. (2003). Social relationships and ambulatory blood pressure: Structural and qualitative predictors of cardiovascular function during everyday social interactions. *Health Psychology, 22*, 388–397.

Home, S., & Biss, W. (2005). Sexual satisfaction as more than a gendered concept: The roles of psychological well-being and sexual orientation. *Journal of Constructivist Psychology, 18*, 25–38.

Hooten, W., Wolter, T., Ames, S., Hurt, R., Viciers, K., Offord, K., & Hays, J. (2005). Personality correlates related to tobacco abstinence following treatment. *International Journal of Psychiatry in Medicine, 35*, 59–74.

Hopkins, W., & Cantalupo, C. (2004, in press). Handedness in chimpanzees (*Pan troglodytes*) is associated with asymmetries of the primary motor cortex but not with homologous language areas. *Behavioral Neuroscience, 118*, 1176–1183.

Horberry, T., Anderson, J., Regan, M., Triggs, T., & Brown, J. (2006). Driver distraction: The effects of concurrent in-vehicle tasks, road environment complexity and age on driving performance. *Accident Analysis & Prevention, 38*, 185–191.

Horn, J. L. (1982). The theory of fluid and crystallized intelligence in relation to concepts of cognitive psychology and aging in adulthood. In F. I. M. Craik & S. Trehub (Eds.), *Aging and cognitive processes* (pp. 201–238). New York: Plenum Press.

Horn, L. J., & Zahn, L. (2001). *From bachelor's degree to work: Major field of study and employment outcomes of 1992–93 bachelor's degree recipients who did not enroll in graduate education by 1997* (NCES 2001–165). Retrieved March 7, 2002, from *http://nces.ed.gov/pubs2001/quarterly/spring/q5_2.html*

Horney, K. (1937). *The neurotic personality of our time*. New York: W. W. Norton.

Horney, K. (1939). *New ways in psychoanalysis*. New York: W. W. Norton.

Horney, K. (1945). *Our inner conflicts*. New York: W. W. Norton.

Horney, K. (1950). *Neurosis and human growth*. New York: W. W. Norton.

Horney, K. (1967). *Feminine psychology*. New York: W. W. Norton.

Hoshi, R., Pratt, H., Mehta, S., Bond, A., & Curran, H. (2006). An investigation into the sub-acute effects of ecstasy on aggressive interpretive bias and aggressive mood—Are there gender differences? *Journal of Psychopharmacology, 20*, 291–301.

Houzel, D. (2004). The psychoanalysis of infantile autism. *Journal of Child Psychotherapy, 30*, 225–237.

Hovland, C. I., Lumsdaine, A. A., & Sheffield, F. D. (1949). *Experiments on mass communication*. Princeton, NJ: Princeton University Press.

Howard, A. D., Feighner, S. D., Cully, D. F., Arena, J. P., Liberator, P. A., Rosenblum, C. I., et al. (1996). A receptor in pituitary and hypothalamus that functions in growth hormone release. *Science, 273*, 974–977.

Hrushesky, W. J. M. (1994, July/August). Timing is everything. *The Sciences,* pp. 32–37.

Hubel, D. H. (1963). The visual cortex of the brain. *Scientific American, 209*, 54–62.

Hubel, D. H. (1995). *Eye, brain, and vision*. New York: Scientific American Library.

Hubel, D. H., & Wiesel, T. N. (1959). Receptive fields of single neurons in the cat's striate cortex. *Journal of Physiology, 148*, 547–591.

Hubel, D. H., & Wiesel, T. N. (1979). Brain mechanisms of vision. *Scientific American, 241*, 130–144.

Hudson, J. I., Carter, W. P., & Pope, H. G., Jr. (1996). Antidepressant treatment of binge-eating disorder: Research findings and clinical guidelines. *Journal of Clinical Psychiatry, 57*(8, Suppl.), 73–79.

Huesmann, L., Dubow, E., & Boxer, P. (2009). Continuity of aggression from childhood to early adulthood as a predictor of life outcomes: Implications for the adolescent-limited and life-course-persistent models. *Aggressive Behavior, 35*, 136–149.

Huesman, L., Moise-Titus, J., Podolski, C., & Eron, L. (2003). Longitudinal relations between children's exposure to television violence and their aggressive and violent behavior in young adulthood. *Developmental Psychology, 39*, 201–221.

Huesmann, L., & Podolski, C. (2003). Punishment: A psychological perspective. In S. McConville, (Ed.), *The use of punishment* (pp. 55–88). Portland, OR: Willan Publishing.

Huesmann, L. R., & Moise, J. (1996, June). Media violence: A demonstrated public health threat to children. *Harvard Mental Health Letter, 12*(12), 5–7.

Hughes, S., Harrison, M., & Gallup, G. (2004). Sex differences in mating strategies: Mate guarding, infidelity and multiple concurrent sex partners. *Evolution & Gender, 6*, 3–13.

Hughes, S., Levinson, G., Rosen, M., & Shnider, S. (2002). *Shnider and Levinson's anesthesia for obstetrics*. Chicago, IL: Wolters Kluwer Health.

Hull, C. L. (1943). *Principles of behavior*. New York: Appleton-Century-Crofts.

Hultsch, D. F., & Dixon, R. A. (1990). Learning and memory in aging. In J. E. Birren & K. W. Schaie (Eds.), *Handbook of the psychology of aging* (3rd ed., pp. 359–374). San Diego: Academic Press.

Hunter, C., & Lewis, M. (2010). Coping with racism: A spirit-based psychological perspective. In J. Chin, (Ed.), *The psychology of prejudice and discrimination: A revised and condensed edition* (pp. 209–222). Santa Barbara, CA: Praeger/ABC-CLIO.

Hunton, J., & Rose, J. (2005). Cellular telephones and driving performance: The effects of attentional demands on motor vehicle crash risk. *Risk Analysis, 25,* 855–866.

Hur, Y. (2009). Genetic and environmental covariations among obsessive-compulsive, symptoms, neuroticism, and extraversion in South Korean adolescent and young adult twins. *Twin Research and Human Genetics, 12,* 142–149.

Huttenlocher, P. (1994). Synaptogenesis, synapse elimination, and neural plasticity in human cerebral cortex. In C. Nelson (Ed.), *The Minnesota symposia on child psychology* (Vol. 27, pp. 35–54). Hillsdale, NJ: Erlbaum.

Hyde, J. (2005). The gender similarities hypothesis. *American Psychologist, 60,* 581–592.

Hyman, I. E., Jr., & Pentland, J. (1996). The role of mental imagery in the creation of false childhood memories. *Journal of Memory and Language, 35,* 101–117.

Hyman, I. E., Jr., Husband, T. H., & Billings, E. J. (1995). False memories of childhood. *Applied Cognitive Psychology, 9,* 181–197.

Insel, T. R. (1990). Phenomenology of obsessive compulsive disorder. *Journal of Clinical Psychiatry, 51*(2, Suppl.), 4–8.

Intons-Peterson, M. J., & Fournier, J. (1986). External and internal memory aids: When and how often do we use them? *Journal of Experimental Psychology: General, 115,* 267–280.

Isaksson, K., Johansson, G., Bellaagh, K., & Sjöberg, A. (2004). Work values among the unemployed: Changes over time and some gender differences. *Scandinavian Journal of Psychology, 45,* 207–214.

Ishii, K., Reyes, J., & Kitayama, S. (2003). Spontaneous attention to word content versus emotional tone: Differences among three cultures. *Psychological Science, 14,* 39–46.

Ito, T. A., Miller, N., & Pollock, V. E. (1996). Alcohol and aggression: A meta-analysis on the moderating effects of inhibitory cues, triggering events, and self-focused attention. *Psychological Bulletin, 120,* 60–82.

Izard, C. E. (1971). *The face of emotion.* New York: Appleton-Century-Crofts.

Izard, C. E. (1977). *Human emotions.* New York: Plenum Press.

Izard, C. E. (1990). Facial expressions and the regulation of emotions. *Journal of Personality and Social Psychology, 58,* 487–498.

Izard, C. E. (1992). Basic emotions, relations among emotions, and emotion-cognition relations. *Psychological Review, 99,* 561–565.

Izard, C. E. (1993). Four systems for emotion activation: Cognitive and noncognitive processes. *Psychological Review, 100,* 68–90.

Jacklin, C. N. (1989). Female and male: Issues of gender. *American Psychologist, 44,* 127–133.

Jackson, J., Bogg, T., Walton, K., Wood, D., Harms, P., Lodi-Smith, J., Edmonds, G., & Roberts, B. (2009). Not all conscientiousness scales change alike: A multimethod, multisample study of age differences in the facets of conscientiousness. *Journal of Personality and Social Psychology, 96,* 446–459.

Jackson, S. (2002). A study of teachers' perceptions of youth problems. *Journal of Youth Studies, 5,* 313–322.

Jacobson, C. (2009). The nightmares of Puerto Ricans: An embodied 'altered states of consciousness' perspective. *Culture, Medicine, and Psychiatry, 33,* 323–331.

James, W. (1884). What is an emotion? *Mind, 9,* 188–205.

Jamieson, D. W., & Zanna, M. P. (1989). Need for structure in attitude formation and expression. In A. R. Pratkanis, S. J. Breckler, & A. G. Greenwald (Eds.), *Attitude structure and function* (pp. 383–406). Hillsdale, NJ: Erlbaum.

Janis, I. (2007). Groupthink. In R. Vecchio (Ed.), *Leadership: Understanding the dynamics of power and influence in organizations* (2nd ed.) (pp. 157–169). Notre Dame, IN: University of Notre Dame Press.

Janis, I. L. (1982). *Groupthink: Psychological studies of policy decisions and fiascoes* (2nd ed.). Boston: Houghton Mifflin.

Janssen, T., & Carton, J. (1999). The effects of locus of control and task difficulty on procrastination. *Journal of Genetic Psychology, 160,* 436–442.

Jansz, J. (2005). The emotional appeal of violent video games for adolescent males. *Communication Theory, 15,* 219–241.

Jansz, J., & Martens, L. (2005). Gaming at a LAN event: The social context of playing video games. *New Media & Society, 7,* 333–355.

Jarvin, L., Newman, T., Randi, J., Sternberg, R., & Grigorenko, E. (2008). Matching instruction and assessment. In J., Plucker, & C. Callahan, (Eds.), *Critical issues and practices in gifted education: What the research says* (pp. 345–365). Waco, TX: Prufrock Press.

Jefferson, J. W. (1995). Social phobia: A pharmacologic treatment overview. *Journal of Clinical Psychiatry, 56*(5, Suppl.), 18–24.

Jefferson, J. W. (1997). Antidepressants in panic disorder. *Journal of Clinical Psychiatry, 58*(2, Suppl.), 20–24.

Jeffrey, S. (2009, April 3). Wyeth, Elan amend phase 3 procols for bapineuzumab in Alzheimer's. Retrieved May 29, 2009 from *http://www.medscape.com/viewarticle/590592.*

Jelicic, M., & Bonke, B. (2001). Memory impairments following chronic stress? A critical review. *European Journal of Psychiatry, 15,* 225–232.

Jellinek, E. M. (1960). *The disease concept of alcoholism.* New Brunswick, NJ: Hillhouse Press.

Jeltova, I., Birney, D., Fredine, N., Jarvin, L., Sternberg, R., & Grigorenko, E. (2007). Dynamic assessment as a process-oriented assessment in educational settings. *Advances in Speech Language Pathology, 9,* 273–285.

Jenike, M. A. (1990, April). Obsessive-compulsive disorder. *Harvard Medical School Health Letter, 15,* 4–8.

Jenkins, J. J., Jimenez-Pabon, E., Shaw, R. E., & Sefer, J. W. (1975). *Schuell's aphasia in adults: Diagnosis, prognosis, and treatment* (2nd ed.). Hagerstown, MD: Harper & Row.

Jewell, J. (2009). *Fragile X syndrome.* Retrieved January 15, 2010 from *http://emedicine.medscape.com/article/943776-overview.*

Jimerson, D. C., Wolfe, B. E., Metzger, E. D., Finkelstein, D. M., Cooper, T. B., & Levine, J. M. (1997). Decreased serotonin function in bulimia nervosa. *Archives of General Psychiatry, 54,* 529–534.

Jing, L., (2004). Neural correlates of insight. *Acta Psychologica Sinica, 36,* 219–234.

John, L. (2004). Subjective well-being in a multicultural urban population: Structural and multivariate analyses of the Ontario Health Survey well-being scale. *Social Indicators Research, 68,* 107–126.

Johnson, J., Simmons, C., Trawalter, S., Ferguson, T., & Reed, W. (2003). Variation in Black anti-White bias and target distancing cues: Factors that influence perceptions of "ambiguously racist" behavior. *Personality & Social Psychology Bulletin, 29,* 609–622.

Johnson, M., Hashtroudi, S., & Lindsay, S. (1993). Source monitoring. *Psychological Bulletin, 114,* 3–28.

Johnson, M. P., Duffy, J. F., Dijk, D-J., Ronda, J. M., Dyal, C. M., & Czeisler, C. A. (1992). Short-term memory, alertness and performance: A reappraisal of their relationship to body temperature. *Journal of Sleep Research, 1,* 24–29.

Johnson, W. G., Tsoh, J. Y., & Varnado, P. J. (1996). Eating disorders: Efficacy of pharmacological and psychological interventions. *Clinical Psychology Review, 16,* 457–478.

Johnson, W., Bouchard, T., McGue, M., Segal, N., Tellegen, A., Keyes, M., & Gottesman, I. (2007). Genetic and environmental influences on the verbal-perceptual-image rotation (VPR) model of the structure of mental abilities in the Minnesota study of twins reared apart. *Intelligence, 35,* 542–562.

Johnson, W., Turkheimer, E., Gottesman, I., & Bouchard, T. (2009). Beyond heritability: Twin studies in behavioral research. *Current Directions in Psychological Science, 18,* 207–220.

Johnston, D. (2000). A series of cases of dementia presenting with PTSD symptoms in World War II combat veterans. *Journal of the American Geriatrics Society, 48,* 70–72.

Johnston, L. D., O'Malley, P. M., Bachman, J. G., & Schulenberg, J. E. (2010). *Monitoring the future national results on adolescent drug use: Overview of key findings, 2009* (NIH Publication No. [yet to be assigned]). Bethesda, MD: National Institute on Drug Abuse.

Johnston, L. E., O'Malley, P. M., & Bachman, J. G. (2001). *Monitoring the future national results on adolescent drug use: Overview of key findings, 2000* (NIH Publication No. 01-4923). Rockville MD: National Institute on Drug Abuse.

Joiner, T., Van Orden, K., Witte, T., & Rudd, M. (2009). Diagnoses associated with suicide. In T., Joiner, K., Van Orden, T., Witte, & M. Rudd (Eds.), *The interpersonal theory of suicide: Guidance for working with suicidal clients* (pp. 21–51). Washington, DC: American Psychological Association.

Jolicoeur, D., Richter, K., Ahgluwalia, J., Mosier, M., & Resnicow, K. (2003). Smoking cessation, smoking reduction, and delayed quitting among smokers given nicotine patches and a self-help pamphlet. *Substance Abuse, 24,* 101–106.

Jonas, J. M., & Cohon, M. S. (1993). A comparison of the safety and efficacy of alprazolam versus other agents in the treatment of anxiety, panic, and depression: A review of the literature. *Journal of Clinical Psychiatry, 54*(10, Suppl.), 25–45.

Jones, E. E. (1976). How do people perceive the causes of behavior? *American Scientist, 64,* 300–305.

Jones, E. E. (1990). *Interpersonal perception.* New York: Freeman.

Jones, E. E., & Nisbett, R. E. (1971). *The actor and the observer: Divergent perceptions of the causes of behavior.* New York: General Learning.

Jones, H. E., Herning, R. I., Cadet, J. L., & Griffiths, R. R. (2000). Caffeine withdrawal increases cerebral blood flow velocity and alters quantitative electroencephalography (EEG) activity. *Psychopharmacology, 147,* 371–377.

Jones, M. C. (1924). A laboratory study of fear: The case of Peter. *Pedagogical Seminary, 31,* 308–315.

Jones, P. (2005). The American Indian Church and its sacramental use of peyote: A review for professionals in the mental-health arena. *Mental Health, Religion, & Culture, 8,* 227–290.

Jones, R. (2003). Listen and learn. *Nature Reviews Neuroscience, 4,* 699.

Jones, S. (2003). *Let the games begin: Gaming technology and entertainment among college students.* Washington, DC: Pew Internet and American Life Project. Retrieved May 17, 2006, from *http://www.pewinternet.org/PPF/r/93/report_display.asp*

Jorgensen, G. (2006). Kohlberg and Gilligan: Duet or duel? *Journal of Moral Education, 35,* 179–196.

Jorgensen, M., & Keiding, N. (1991). Estimation of spermarche from longitudinal spermaturia data. *Biometrics, 47,* 177–193.

Josephs, R., Newman, M., Brown, R., & Beer, J. (2003). Status, testosterone, and human intellectual performance. *Psychological Science, 14,* 158–163.

Joyce, P., Mulder, R., Luty, S., McKenzie, J., Sullivan, P., & Cloninger, R. (2003). Borderline personality disorder in major depression: Symptomatology, temperament, character, differential drug response, and 6-month outcome. *Comprehensive Psychiatry, 44,* 35–43.

Joynt, R. (2000). Chapter 42: Aging and the nervous system. In T. Beers (Ed.) *Merck Manual of Geriatrics* (3rd Ed.). [Online edition] Retrieved October 12, 2006, from *http://www.merck.com/mrkshared/mmg/sec6/ch42/ch42a.jsp*

Judd, L. L., Akiskal, H. S., Zeller, P. J., Paulus, M., Leon, A. C., Maser, J. D., et al. (2000). Psychosocial disability during the long-term course of unipolar major depressive disorder. *Archives of General Psychiatry, 57,* 375–380.

Juengling, F., Schmahl, C., Heblinger, B., Ebert, D., Bremner, J., Gostomzyk, J., et al. (2003). Positron emission tomography in female patients with borderline personality disorder. *Journal of Psychiatric Research, 37,* 109–115.

Juliano, S. L. (1998). Mapping the sensory mosaic. *Science, 279,* 1653–1654.

Julien, R. M. (1995). *A primer of drug action* (7th ed.). New York: W.H. Freeman.

Jung, C. G. (1933). *Modern man in search of a soul.* New York: Harcourt Brace Jovanovich.

Köhler, W. (1925). *The mentality of apes* (E. Winter, Trans.). New York: Harcourt Brace Jovanovich.

Kübler-Ross, E. (1969). *On death and dying.* New York: Macmillan.

Kagan, J. (2003). Foreword: A behavioral science perspective. In R. Plomin, J. DeFries, I. Craig, & P. McGuffin (Eds.), *Behavioral genetics in the postgenomic era* (pp. xvii–xxiii). Washington, DC: American Psychological Association.

Kahneman, D., Krueger, A., Schkade, D., Schwarz, N., & Stone, A. (2006). Would you be happier if you were richer? A focusing illusion. *Science, 312,* 1908–1910.

Kahneman, D., & Tversky, A. (1984). Choices, values, and frames. *American Psychologist, 39,* 341–350.

Kail, R. (2000). Speed of information processing: Developmental change and links to intelligence. *Journal of School Psychology, 38,* 51–61.

Kaiser, C., & Pratt-Hyatt, J. (2009). Distributing prejudice unequally: Do whites direct their prejudice toward strongly identified minorities? *Journal of Personality and Social Psychology, 96,* 432–445.

Kaiser Family Foundation. (2010). *The global HIV/AIDS timeline.* Retrieved March 12, 2010 from *http://www.kff.org/hivaids/timeline/hivtimeline.cfm*

Kakkar, R. (2008). *Central sleep apnea.* Retrieved February 7, 2009 from *http://emedicine.medscape.com/article/914360-overview.*

Kalidindi, S., & McGuffin, P. (2003). The genetics of affective disorders: Present and future. In R. Plomin, J. Defries, I. Craig, & P. McGuffin (Eds.), *Behavioral genetics in the postgenomic era* (pp. 481–502). Washington, DC: American Psychological Association.

Kalish, H. I. (1981). *From behavioral science to behavior modification.* New York: McGraw-Hill.

Kallio, S., & Revonsuo, A. (2003). Hypnotic phenomena and altered states of consciousness: A multilevel framework of description and explanation. *Contemporary Hypnosis, 20,* 111–164.

Kaltiala-Heino, R., Rimpelae, M., Rissanen, A., & Rantanen, P. (2001). Early puberty and early sexual activity are associated with bulimic-type eating pathology in middle adolescence. *Journal of Adolescent Health, 28,* 346–352.

Kamarajan, C., Porjesz, B., Jones, K., Chorlian, D., Padmanabhapillai, A., Rangaswamy, M., et al. (2006). Event-related oscillations in offspring of alcoholics: Neurocognitive disinhibition as a risk for alcoholism. *Biological Psychiatry, 59,* 625–634.

Kampman, M., Keijsers, G., Hoogduin, C., & Hendriks, G. (2002). A randomized, double-blind, placebo-controlled study of the effects of adjunctive paroxetine in panic disorder patients unsuccessfully treated with cognitive-behavioral therapy alone. *Journal of Clinical Psychiatry, 63,* 772–777.

Kane, J. M. (1996). Treatment-resistant schizophrenic patients. *Journal of Clinical Psychiatry, 57*(9, Suppl.), 35–40.

Kanner, A. D., Coyne, J. C., Schaefer, C., & Lazarus, R. S. (1981). Comparison of two modes of stress measurement: Daily hassles and uplifts versus major life events. *Journal of Behavioral Medicine, 4,* 1–39.

Kaplowitz, P. (2009). *Precocious puberty.* Retrieved February 27, 2010 from *http://emedicine.medscape.com/article/924002-overview.*

Karau, S. J., & Williams, K. D. (1993). Social loafing; a meta-analytic review and theoretical integration. *Journal of Personality and Social Psychology, 65,* 681–706.

Karlson, B., Eek, F., Ørbæk, P., & Österberg, K. (2009). Effects on sleep-related problems and self-reported health after a change of shift schedule. *Journal of Occupational Health Psychology, 14,* 97–109.

Karni, A., Tanne, D., Rubenstein, B. S., Askenasy, J. J. M., & Sagi, D. (1994). Dependence on REM sleep of overnight improvement of a perceptual skill. *Science, 265,* 679–682.

Karpicke, J., Butler, A., & Roediger, H. (2009). Metacognitive strategies in student learning: Do students practise retrieval when they study on their own? *Memory, 17,* 471–479.

Kastenbaum, R. (1992). *The psychology of death.* New York: Springer-Verlag.

Katerndahl, D., Burge, S., & Kellogg, N. (2005). Predictors of development of adult psychopathology in female victims of childhood sexual abuse. *Journal of Nervous and Mental Disease, 193,* 258–264.

Katz-Wise, S., Priess, H., & Hyde, J. (2010). Gender-role attitudes and behavior across the transition to parenthood. *Developmental Psychology, 46,* 18–28.

Katzell, R. A., & Thompson, D. E. (1990). Work motivation: Theory and practice. *American Psychologist, 45,* 144–153.

Kawanishi, Y., Tachikawa, H., & Suzuki, T. (2000). Pharmacogenomics and schizophrenia. *European Journal of Pharmacology, 410,* 227–241.

Kazdin, A. (2000). Token economy. In A. Kazdin, (Ed.), *Encyclopedia of psychology,* Volume 8 (pp. 90–92). Washington, DC: American Psychological Association.

Kazdin, A., & Benjet, C. (2003). Spanking children: Evidence and issues. *Current Directions in Psychological Science, 12,* 99–103.

Keating, C. R. (1994). World without words: Messages from face and body. In W. J. Lonner & R. Malpass (Eds.), *Psychology and culture* (pp. 175–182). Boston: Allyn & Bacon.

Keenan, J., Gallup, G., & Falk, D. (2003). *The face in the mirror: The search for the origins of consciousness.* New York: HarperCollins.

Keenan, J., Wheeler, M., Gallup, G., & Pascual-Leone, A. (2000). Self-recognition and the right prefrontal cortex. *Trends in Cognitive Sciences, 4,* 338–344.

Keitner, G. I., Ryan, C. E., Miller, I. W., & Norman, W. H. (1992). Recovery and major depression: Factors associated with twelve-month outcome. *American Journal of Psychiatry, 149,* 93–99.

Keitner, N., & Boschini, D. (2009). Electroconvulsive therapy. *Perspectives in Psychiatric Care, 45,* 66–70.

Kellett, S., Newman, D., Matthews, L., & Swift, A. (2004). Increasing the effectiveness of large group format CBT via the application of practice-based evidence. *Behavioural & Cognitive Psychotherapy, 32,* 231–234.

Kelly, C., & McCreadie, R. (2000). Cigarette smoking and schizophrenia. *Advances in Psychiatric Treatment, 6,* 327–331.

Kelly, D., Wehring, H., Linthicum, J., Feldman, S., McMahon, R., Love, R., Wagner, T., Shim, J., & Fowler, D. (2009). Cardiac-related findings at autopsy in people with severe mental illness treated with clozapine or risperidone. *Schizophrenia Research, 107,* 134–138.

Kelner, K. L. (1997). Seeing the synapse. *Science, 276,* 547.

Kendler, K. S., & Diehl, S. R. (1993). The genetics of schizophrenia: A current genetic-epidemiologic perspective. *Schizophrenia Bulletin, 19,* 261–285.

Kendler, K. S., MacLean, C., Neale, M., Kessler, R., Heath, A., & Eaves, L. (1991). The genetic epidemiology of bulimia nervosa. *American Journal of Psychiatry, 148,* 1627–1637.

Kendler, K. S., Neale, M. C., Kessler, R. C., Heath, A. C., & Eaves, L. J. (1992). The genetic epidemiology of phobias in women. *Archives of General Psychiatry, 49,* 273–281.

Kendler, K. S., Neale, M. C., Kessler, R. C., Heath, A. C., & Eaves, L. J. (1993). The lifetime history of major depression in women: Reliability of diagnosis and heritability. *Archives of General Psychiatry, 50,* 863–870.

Kennedy, Q., Mather, M., & Carstensen, L. (2004). The role of motivation in the age-related positivity effect in autobiographical memory. *Psychological Science, 15,* 208–214.

Kenney-Benson, G., Pomerantz, E., Ryan, A., & Patrick, H. (2006). Sex differences in math performance: The role of children's approach to schoolwork. *Developmental Psychology, 42,* 11–26.

Kenwright, M., & Marks, I. (2004). Computer-aided self-help for phobia/panic via Internet at home: A pilot study. *British Journal of Psychiatry, 184,* 448–449.

Kerr, N., & Tindale, S. (2004). Group performance and decision making. *Annual Review of Psychology, 55,* 623–655.

Kesner, R. (2009). Tapestry of memory. *Behavioral Neuroscience, 123,* 1–13.

Kessler, R. C., Stein, M. B., & Berglund, P. (1998). Social phobia subtypes in the National Comorbidity Survey. *American Journal of Psychiatry, 155,* 613–619.

Kessler, R., Berglund, P., Demler, O., Jin, R., & Walters, E. (2005a). Lifetime prevalence and age-of-onset distributions of DSM-IV disorders in the National Comorbidity Survey Replication. *Archives of General Psychiatry, 62,* 593–602.

Kessler, R., Chiu, W., Demler, O., & Walters, E. (2005b). Prevalence, severity, and comorbidity of 12-month DSM-IV disorders in the National Comorbidity Survey replication. *Archives of General Psychiatry, 62,* 617–627.

Khaleefa, O., Abdelwahid, S., Abdulradi, F., & Lynn, R. (2008). The increase of intelligence in Sudan 1964–2006. *Personality and Individual Differences, 45,* 412–413.

Kiecolt-Glaser, J. (2000). *Friends, lovers, relaxation, and immunity: How behavior modifies health. Cortisol and the language of love: Text analysis of newlyweds' relationship stories.* Paper presented at the annual meeting of the American Psychological Association, Washington, DC.

Kiecolt-Glaser, J. K., Fisher, L. D., Ogrocki, P., Stout, J., Speicher, C. E., & Glaser, R. (1987). Marital quality, marital disruption, and immune function. *Psychosomatic Medicine, 49,* 13–34.

Kiecolt-Glaser, J. K., Glaser, R., Gravenstein, S., Malarkey, W. B., & Sheridan, J. (1996). Chronic stress alters the immune response to influenza virus vaccine in older adults. *Proceedings of the National Academy of Science, 93,* 3043–3047.

Kiecolt-Glaser, J., Gouin, J., & Hantsoo, L. (2010, in press). Close relationships, inflammation, and health. *Neuroscience and Biobehavioral Reviews.*

Kihlstrom, J. (2007). Consciousness in hypnosis. In P. Zelazo, M. Moscovitch, & E. Thompson (Eds.), *The Cambridge handbook of consciousness* (pp. 445–479). New York: Cambridge University Press.

Kihlstrom, J. F. (1985). Hypnosis. *Annual Review of Psychology, 26,* 557–591.

Kihlstrom, J. F. (1986). Strong inferences about hypnosis. *Behavioral and Brain Sciences, 9,* 474–475.

Kihlstrom, J. F., & Barnhardt, T. M. (1993). The self-regulation of memory: For better and for worse, with and without hypnosis. In D. M. Wegner & J. W. Pennebaker (Eds.), *Handbook of mental control.* Englewood Cliffs, NJ: Prentice Hall.

Kilbride, J. E., & Kilbride, P. L. (1975). Sitting and smiling behavior of Baganda infants. *Journal of Cross-Cultural Psychology, 6,* 88–107.

Kilpatrick, D., Ruggiero, K., Acierno, R., Saunders, B., Resnick, H., & Best, C. (2003). Violence and risk of PTSD, major depression, substance abuse/dependence, and comorbidity: Results from the National Survey of Adolescents. *Journal of Consulting and Clinical Psychology, 71,* 692–700.

Kim, H., & Chung, R. (2003). Relationship of recalled parenting style to self-perception in Korean American college students. *Journal of Genetic Psychology, 164,* 481–492.

Kim, J. J., Mohamed, S., Andreasen, N. C., O'Leary, D. S., Watkins, L., Ponto, L. L. B., et al. (2000). Regional neural dysfunctions in chronic schizophrenia studied with positron emission tomography. *American Journal of Psychiatry, 157,* 542–548.

Kim, K. H. S., Relkin, N. R., Lee, K-M., & Hirsch, J. (1997). Distinct cortical areas associated with native and second languages. *Nature, 388,* 171–174.

Kim, L., & Makdissi, A. (2009). *Hyperparathyroidism.* Retrieved January 20, 2010 from *http://emedicine.medscape.com/article/127351-overview.*

Kimber, L., McNabb, M., McCourt, C., Haines, A., & Brocklehurst, P. (2008). Massage or music for pain relief in labour: A pilot randomised placebo controlled trial. *European Journal of Pain, 12,* 961–969.

Kimura, D. (1992). Sex differences in the brain. *Scientific American, 267,* 118–125.

Kimura, D. (2000). *Sex and cognition.* Cambridge, MA: MIT Press.

King, B. (2006). The rise, fall, and resurrection of the ventromedial hypothalamus in the regulation of feeding behavior and body weight. *Physiology & Behavior, 87,* 221–244.

Kinnunen, T., Zamansky, H. S., & Block, M. L. (1994). Is the hypnotized subject lying? *Journal of Abnormal Psychology, 103,* 184–191.

Kinomura, S., Larsson, J., Gulyás, B., & Roland, P. E. (1996). Activation by attention of the human reticular formation and thalamic intralaminar nuclei. *Science, 271,* 512–515.

Kinsey, A. C., Pomeroy, W. B., & Martin, C. E. (1948). *Sexual behavior in the human male.* Philadelphia: W. B. Saunders.

Kinsey, A. C., Pomeroy, W. B., Martin, C. E., & Gebhard, P. H. (1953). *Sexual behavior in the human female.* Philadelphia: W. B. Saunders.

Kirchner, T., & Sayette, M. (2003). Effects of alcohol on controlled and automatic memory processes. *Experimental & Clinical Psychopharmacology, 11,* 167–175.

Kirkcaldy, B., Shephard, R., & Furnham, A. (2002). The influence of Type A behavior and locus of control upon job satisfaction and occupational health. *Personality & Individual Differences, 33,* 1361–1371.

Kirsch, I., & Lynn, S. J. (1995). The altered state of hypnosis: Changes in the theoretical landscape. *American Psychologist, 50,* 846–858.

Kirshner, H., & Jacobs, D. (2008). *Aphasia.* Retrieved February 3, 2009 from *http://emedicine.medscape.com/article/1135944-overview.*

Kirvan, C., Swedo, S., Snider, L., & Cunningham, M. (2006). Antibody-mediated neuronal cell signaling in behavior and movement disorders. *Journal of Neuroimmunology, 179,* 173–179.

Kisilevsky, B., Hains, S., Lee, K., Xie, X., Huang, H., Ye, H., et al. (2003). Effects of experience on fetal voice recognition. *Psychological Science, 14,* 220–224.

Kitayama, S., & Markus, H. R. (2000). The pursuit of happiness and the realization of sympathy: Cultural patterns of self, social relations, and well-being. In E. Diener & E. M. Suh (Eds.), *Subjective well-being across cultures* (pp. 113–164). Cambridge, MA: MIT Press.

Kite, M. E., Deaux, K., & Miele, M. (1991). Stereotypes of young and old: Does age outweigh gender? *Psychology and Aging, 6,* 19–27.

Kittler, J., Menard, W., & Phillips, K. (2007). Weight concerns in individuals with body dysmorphic disorder. *Eating Behavior, 8,* 115–120.

Kiyatkin, E., & Wise, R. (2002). Brain and body hyperthermia associated with heroin self-administration in rats. *Journal of Neuroscience, 22,* 1072–1080

Klaczynski, P., Fauth, J, & Swanger, A. (1998). Adolescent identity: Rational vs. experiential processing, formal operations, and critical thinking beliefs. *Journal of Youth & Adolescence, 17,* 185–207.

Klar, A. (2003). Human handedness and scalp hair-whorl direction develop from a common genetic mechanism. *Genetics, 165,* 269–276.

Klatzky, R. L. (1980). *Human memory: Structures and processes* (2nd ed.). New York: W. H. Freeman.

Klatzky, R. L. (1984). *Memory and awareness: An information-processing perspective.* New York: W. H. Freeman.

Kleinman, A., & Cohen, A. (1997, March). Psychiatry's global challenge. *Scientific American, 276,* 86–89.

Klerman, E., & Dijk, D. (2008). Age-related reduction in the maximal capacity for sleep: Implications for insomnia. *Current Biology, 18,* 1118–1123.

Klerman, G. L., Weissman, M. N., Rounsaville, B. J., & Chevron, E. S. (1984). *Interpersonal therapy of depression.* New York: Academic Press.

Kliegman, R. (1998). Fetal and neonatal medicine. In R. Behrman & R. Kliegman (Eds.), *Nelson essentials of pediatrics* (3rd ed., pp. 167–225). Philadelphia: W. B. Saunders.

Kline, G., Stanley, S., Markan, H., Olmos-Gallo, P., St. Peters, M., Whitton, S., et al. (2004). Timing is everything: Pre-engagement cohabitation and increased risk for poor marital outcomes. *Journal of Family Psychology, 18,* 311–318.

Klucharev, V., Smidts, A., & Fernandez, G. (2008). Brain mechanisms of persuasion: How "expert power" modulates memory and attitudes. *Social Cognitive and Affective Neuroscience, 3,* 353–366.

Kluft, R. P. (1984). An introduction to multiple personality disorder. *Psychiatric Annals, 14,* 19–24.

Kluwer, E., & Johnson, M. (2007). Conflict frequency and relationship quality across the transition to parenthood. *Journal of Marriage and Family, 69,* 1089–1106.

Kmietowicz, Z. (2002). US and UK are top in teenage pregnancy rates. *British Medical Journal, 324,* 1354.

Knafo, D. (2009). Freud's memory erased. *Psychoanalytic Psychology, 26,* 171–190.

Knapp, C., Ciraulo, D., & Kranzler, H. (2008). Neurobiology of alcohol. In M. Galanter & H. Kleber (Eds.), *The American Psychiatric Publishing textbook of substance abuse* (4th ed., pp. 111–128). Arlington, VA: American Psychiatric Publishing.

Knipe, J. (2010). Dysfunctional positive affect: Procrastination. In M. Luber, (Ed.). *Eye movement desensitization and reprocessing (EMDR) scripted protocols: Special populations* (pp. 453–458). New York: Springer Publishing Company.

Knussen, C., & Yule, F. (2008). "I'm not in the habit of recycling": The role of habitual behavior in the disposal of household waste. *Environment and Behavior, 40,* 683–702.

Knyazev, G. (2009). Is cortical distribution of spectral power a stable individual characteristic? *International Journal of Psychophysiology, 72,* 123–133.

Kobasa, S. (1979). Stressful life events, personality, and health: An inquiry into hardiness. *Journal of Personality and Social Psychology, 37,* 1–11.

Kobasa, S. C., Maddi, S. R., & Kahn, S. (1982). Hardiness and health: A prospective study. *Journal of Personality and Social Psychology, 42,* 168–177.

Kochanska, G. (1993). Toward a synthesis of parental socialization and child temperament in early development of conscience. *Child Development, 64,* 325–347.

Kochavi, D., Davis, J., & Smith, G. (2001). Corticotropin-releasing factor decreases meal size by decreasing cluster number in Koletsky (LA/N) rats with and without a null mutation of the leptin receptor. *Physiology & Behavior, 74,* 645–651.

Koehler, T., Tiede, G., & Thoens, M. (2002). Long and short-term forgetting of word associations: An experimental study of the Freudian concepts of resistance and repression. *Zeitschrift fuer Klinische Psychologie, Psychiatrie und Psychotherapie, 50,* 328–333.

Koenig, L., & Vaillant, G. (2009). A prospective study of church attendance and health over the lifespan. *Health Psychology, 28,* 117–124.

Koerner, B. (2002, July/August). Disorders made to order. *Mother Jones.* [Online, no pages specified.] Retrieved July 25, 2006, from *http://www.motherjones.com/news/feature/2002/07/disorders.html*

Kohlberg, L. (1966). A cognitive-developmental analysis of children's sex-role concepts and attitudes. In E. E. Maccoby (Ed.), *The development of sex differences* (pp. 82–173). Palo Alto, CA: Stanford University Press.

Kohlberg, L. (1968, September). The child as a moral philosopher. *Psychology Today,* 24–30.

Kohlberg, L. (1969). *Stages in the development of moral thought and action.* New York: Holt, Rinehart & Winston.

Kohlberg, L., & Ullian, D. Z. (1974). In R. C. Friedman, R. M. Richart, & R. L. Vande Wiele (Eds.), *Sex differences in behavior* (pp. 209–222). New York: Wiley.

Kolivas, E., Riordan, P., & Gross, A. (2008). Overview of behavioral treatment with children and adolescents. In M., Hersen, & D. Reitman, (Eds.), *Handbook of psychological assessment, case conceptualization, and treatment, Vol. 2: Children and adolescents.* Hoboken, NJ: John Wiley & Sons.

Koltz, C. (1983, December). Scapegoating. *Psychology Today,* 68–69.

Kon, M. A., & Plaskota, L. (2000). Information complexity of neural networks. *Neural Networks, 13,* 365–375.

Konishi, M. (1993). Listening with two ears. *Scientific American, 268,* 66–73.

Koob, G. (2008). Neurobiology of addiction. In M. Galanter & H. Kleber (Eds.), *The American Psychiatric Publishing textbook of substance abuse* (4th ed., pp. 3–16). Arlington, VA: American Psychiatric Publishing.

Koob, G., & Le Moal, M. (2008). Addiction and the brain antireward system. *Annual Review of Psychology, 59,* 29–53.

Kopelowicz, A., Liberman, R., & Zarate, R. (2007). In P. Nathan, & J. Gorman, (Eds.), *A guide to treatments that work* (3rd ed.). New York: Oxford University Press.

Kopinska, A., & Harris, L. (2003). Spatial representation in body coordinates: Evidence from errors in remembering positions of visual and auditory targets after active eye, head, and body movements. *Canadian Journal of Experimental Psychology, 57,* 23–37.

Kopp, C. P., & Kaler, S. R. (1989). Risk in infancy: Origins and implications. *American Psychologist, 44,* 224–230.

Kopp, D., Spitzer, C., Kuwert, P., Barnow, S., Orlob, S., Lüth, H., Freyberger, H., & Dudeck, M. (2009). Psychiatric disorders and childhood trauma in prisoners with antisocial personality disorder. *Fortschiritte der Neurologie, Psychiatrie, 77,* 152–159.

Korobov, N., & Thorne, A. (2006). Intimacy and distancing: Young men's conversations about romantic relationships. *Journal of Adolescent Research, 21,* 27–55.

Kosslyn, S. M. (1988). Aspects of a cognitive neuroscience of mental imagery. *Science, 240,* 1621–1626.

Kouider, S., deGardelle, V., Dehaene, S., Dupoux, E., & Pallier, C. (2009). Cerebral bases of subliminal speech priming. *Neuroimage, 49,* 922–929.

Kounios, J., Fleck, J., Green, D., Payne, L., Stevenson, J., Bowden, E., & Jung-Beeman, M. (2008). The origins of insight in resting-state brain activity. *Neuropsychologia, 46,* 281–291.

Kovacs, D., Mahon, J., & Palmer, R. (2002). Chewing and spitting out food among eating-disordered patients. *International Journal of Eating Disorders, 32,* 112–115.

Kovas, Y., Haworth, C., Dale, P., & Plomin, R. (2007). The genetic and environmental origins of learning abilities and disabilities in the early school years. *Monographs of the Society for Research in Child Development, 72,* 1–144.

Kowatch, R., Suppes, T., Carmody, T., Bucci, J., Hume, J., Kromelis, M., et al. (2000). Effect size of lithium, divalproex sodium, and carbamazepine in children and adolescents with bipolar disorder. *Journal of the American Academy of Child & Adolescent Psychiatry, 39,* 713–720.

Kozak, M. J., Foa, E. B., & McCarthy, P. R. (1988). Obsessive-compulsive disorder. In C. G. Last & M. Herson (Eds.), *Handbook of anxiety disorders* (pp. 87–108). New York: Pergamon Press.

Kozel, F., Padgett, T., & George, M. (2004). A replication study of the neural correlates of deception. *Behavioral Neuroscience, 118,* 852–856.

Krantz, D. S., Grunberg, N. E., & Baum, A. (1985). Health psychology. *Annual Review of Psychology, 36,* 349–383.

Kranzler, H. R. (1996). Evaluation and treatment of anxiety symptoms and disorders in alcoholics. *Journal of Clinical Psychiatry, 57*(6, Suppl.).

Kraus, S. J. (1995). Attitudes and the prediction of behavior: A meta-analysis of the empirical literature. *Personality and Social Psychology Bulletin, 21,* 58–75.

Krcmar, M., & Cooke, M. (2001). Children's moral reasoning and their perceptions of television violence. *Journal of Communication, 51,* 300–316.

Krebs, D., & Denton, K. (2005). Toward a more pragmatic approach to morality: A critical evaluation of Kohlberg's model. *Psychological Review, 112,* 629–649.

Kripke, D., Garfinkel, L., Wingard, D., Klauber, M., & Marler, M. (2002). Mortality associated with sleep duration. *Archives of General Psychiatry, 59,* 131–136.

Kripke, D., Youngstedt, S., Elliott, J., Tuunainen, A., Rex, K., Hauger, R., et al. (2005). Circadian phase in adults of contrasting ages. *Chronobiology International, 22,* 695–709.

Kroll, N. E. A., Ogawa, K. H., & Nieters, J. E. (1988). Eyewitness memory and the importance of sequential information. *Bulletin of the Psychonomic Society, 26,* 395–398.

Krueger, J. M., & Takahashi, S. (1997). Thermoregulation and sleep: Closely linked but separable. *Annals of the New York Academy of Sciences, 813,* 281–286.

Krueger, R., & Johnson, W. (2004). Genetic and environmental structure of adjectives describing the domains of the Big Five model of personality: A nationwide U.S. twin study. *Journal of Research in Personality, 38,* 448–472.

Krueger, W. C. F. (1929). The effect of overlearning on retention. *Journal of Experimental Psychology, 12,* 71–81.

Kruk, M., Meelis, W., Halasz, J., & Haller, J. (2004). Fast positive feedback between the adrenocortical stress response and a brain mechanism involved in aggressive behavior. *Behavioral Neuroscience, 118,* 1062–1070

Kubzansky, L., Cole, S., Kawachi, I., Vokonas, P., & Sparrow, D. (2006). Shared and unique contributions of anger, anxiety, and depression to coronary heart disease: A prospective study in the normative aging study. *Annals of Behavioral Medicine, 31,* 21–29.

Kucharska-Pietura, K., & Klimkowski, M. (2002). Perception of facial affect in chronic schizophrenia and right brain damage. *Acta Neurobiologiae Experimentalis, 62,* 33–43.

Kuhn, D. (1984). *Cognitive development.* In M. H. Bernstein & M. E. Lamb (Eds.), *Developmental psychology.* Hillsdale, NJ: Erlbaum.

Kuhn, D. (2008). Formal operations from a twenty-first century perspective. *Human Development, 51,* 48–55.

Kuhn, D., & Lao, J. (1996). Effects of evidence on attitudes: Is polarization the norm? *Psychological Science, 7,* 115–120.

Kumar, R., O'Malley, P., Johnston, L., Schulenberg, J., & Bachman, J. (2002). Effects of school-level norms on student substance abuse. *Prevention Science, 3,* 105–124.

Kumpfer, K., Alvarado, R., Smith, P., & Ballamy, N. (2002). Cultural sensitivity and adaptation in family-based prevention interventions. *Prevention Science, 3,* 241–246.

Kunda, Z., & Oleson, K. C. (1995). Maintaining stereotypes in the face of disconfirmation: Construction grounds for subtyping deviants. *Journal of Personality and Social Psychology, 68,* 565–579.

Kunz, D., & Herrmann, W. M. (2000). Sleep-wake cycle, sleep-related disturbances, and sleep disorders: A chronobiological approach. *Comparative Psychology, 41*(2, Suppl. 1), 104–105.

Kuo, C., & Tsaur, C. (2004). Locus of control, supervisory support and unsafe behavior: The case of the construction industry in Taiwan. *Chinese Journal of Psychology, 46,* 392–405.

Kuo, L., Abe, K., & Zukowska, Z. (2007). Stress, NPY and vascular remodeling: Implications for stress-related diseases. *Peptides, 28,* 435–440.

Kuo, W., Sjorstrom, T., Chen, Y, Wang, Y, & Huang, C. (2009). Intuition and deliberation: Two systems for strategizing in the brain. *Science, 324,* 519–522.

Kurdek, L. (2009). Assessing the health of a dyadic relationship in heterosexual and same-sex partners. *Personal Relationships, 16,* 117–127.

Kuroda, K. (2002). An image retrieval system by impression words and specific object names-IRIS. *Neurocomputing: An International Journal, 43,* 259–276.

Kurup, R., & Kurup, P. (2002). Detection of endogenous lithium in neuropsychiatric disorders. *Human Psychopharmacology: Clinical & Experimental, 17,* 29–33.

Lafferty, K. (2008). *Toxicity, barbiturate.* Retrieved February 8, 2010 from *http://emedicine.medscape.com/article/813155-overview.*

Laitinen, H. (2005). Factors affecting the use of hearing protectors among classical music players. *Noise & Health, 7,* 21–29.

Lal, S. (2002). Giving children security: Mamie Phipps Clark and the racialization of child psychology. *American Psychologist, 57,* 20–28.

Lam, L., & Kirby, S. (2002). Is emotional intelligence an advantage? An exploration of the impact of emotional and general intelligence on individual performance. *Journal of Social Psychology, 142,* 133–143.

Lambe, E. K., Katzman, D. K., Mikulis, D. J., Kennedy, S. H., & Zipursky, R. B. (1997). Cerebral gray matter volume deficits after weight recovery from anorexia nervosa. *Archives of General Psychiatry, 54,* 537–542.

Lamberg, L. (1996). Narcolepsy researchers barking up the right tree. *Journal of the American Medical Association, 276,* 265–266.

Lambert, M. (2003). Suicide risk assessment and management: Focus on personality disorders. *Current Opinion in Psychiatry, 16,* 71–76.

Lamborn, S. D., Mounts, N. S., Steinberg, L., & Dornbusch, S. M. (1991). Patterns of competence and adjustment among adolescents from authoritative, authoritarian, indulgent, and neglectful families. *Child Development, 62,* 1049–1065.

Lambright, L. (2004). *Lessons from Vietnam.* Paper presented at International Intercultural Education Conference, St Louis, MO, April, 2004.

Lamplugh, C., Berle, D., Millicevic, D., & Starcevic, V. (2008). Pilot study of cognitive behaviour therapy for panic disorder augmented by panic surfing. *Clinical Psychology & Psychotherapy, 15,* 440–445.

Landers, D. (2007). The arousal-performance relationship revisited. In D., Smith & M. Bar-Eli (Eds.), *Essential readings in sport and exercise psychology* (pp. 211–218). Champaign, IL: Human Kinetics.

Landry, D. W. (1997, February). Immunotherapy for cocaine addiction. *Scientific American, 276,* 42–45.

Laney, C., & Loftus, E. (2009). Eyewitness memory. In R. Koscis, (Ed.), *Applied criminal psychology: A guide to forensic behavioral sciences* (pp. 121–145). Springfield, IL: Charles C. Thomas Publisher.

Lang, A. R., Goeckner, D. J., Adesso, V. J., & Marlatt, G. A. (1975). Effects of alcohol on aggression in male social drinkers. *Journal of Abnormal Psychology, 84,* 508–518.

Lang, A., Craske, M., Brown, M., & Ghaneian, A. (2001). Fear-related state dependent memory. *Cognition & Emotion, 15,* 695–703.

Lange, C. G., & James, W. (1922). *The emotions* (I. A. Haupt, Trans.). Baltimore: Williams and Wilkins.

Langer, E. J., & Rodin, J. (1976). The effects of choice and enhanced personal responsibility for the aged: A field experiment in an institutional setting. *Journal of Personality and Social Psychology, 34,* 191–198.

Langer, P., Holzner, B., Magnet, W., & Kopp, M. (2005). Hands-free mobile phone conversation impairs the peripheral visual system to an extent comparable to an alcohol level of 4–5g/100 ml. *Human Psychopharmacology: Clinical and Experimental, 20,* 65–66.

Langevin, B., Sukkar, F., Léger, P., Guez, A., & Robert, D. (1992). Sleep apnea syndromes (SAS) of specific etiology: Review and incidence from a sleep laboratory. *Sleep, 15,* S25–S32.

Langlois, J. H., Kalakanis, L., Rubenstein, A. J., Larson, A., Hallam, M., & Smoot, M. (2000). Maxims or myths of beauty? A meta-analytic and theoretical review. *Psychological Bulletin, 126,* 390–423.

Lao, J., & Kuhn, D. (2002). Cognitive engagement and attitude development. *Cognitive Development, 17,* 1203–1217.

Larson, M. (2003). Gender, race, and aggression in television commercials that feature children. *Sex Roles, 48,* 67–75.

Larsson, H., Andershed, H., & Lichtenstein, P. (2006). A genetic factor explains most of the variation in the psychopathic personality. *Journal of Abnormal Psychology, 115,* 221–230.

Latané, B., Williams, K., & Harkins, S. (1979). Many hands make light the work: The causes and consequences of social loafing. *Journal of Personality and Social Psychology, 37,* 822–832.

Latham, G., & Pinder, C. (2005). Work motivation theory and research at the dawn of the twenty-first century. *Annual Review of Psychology, 56,* 485–516.

Latner, J., & Wilson, T. (2004). Binge eating and satiety in bulimia nervosa and binge eating disorder: Effects of macronutrient intake. *International Journal of Eating Disorders, 36,* 402–415.

Laumann, E. O., Gagnon, J. H., Michael, R. T., & Michaels, S. (1994). *The social organization of sexuality.* Chicago: University of Chicago Press.

Laurent, J., Swerdik, M., & Ryburn, M. (1992). Review of validity research on the Stanford-Binet Intelligence Scale: Fourth Edition. *Psychological Assessment, 4,* 102–112.

Lauriello, J., McEvoy, J., Rodriguez, S., Bossie, C., & Lasser, R. (2005). Long-acting risperidone vs. placebo in the treatment of hospital inpatients with schizophrenia. *Schizophrenia Research, 72,* 249–258.

Lavie, P., Herer, P., Peled, R., Berger, I., Yoffe, N., Zomer, J., et al. (1995). Mortality in sleep apnea patients: A multivariate analysis of risk factors. *Sleep, 18,* 149–157.

Lawton, B. (2001). *Damage to human hearing by airborne sound of very high frequency or ultrasonic frequency.* Contract Research Report No. 343/2001. Highfield, Southampton, U.K.: Institution of Sound and Vibration Research, University of Southampton/Highfield. Retrieved December 13, 2006, from *http://www.compoundsecurity.co.uk/download/HSE.pdf*

Layton, L., Deeny, K., Tall, G., & Upton, G. (1996). Researching and promoting phonological awareness in the nursery class. *Journal of Research in Reading, 19,* 1–13.

Lazarus, R. S. (1966). *Psychological stress and the coping process.* New York: McGraw-Hill.

Lazarus, R. S. (1984). On the primacy of cognition. *American Psychologist, 39,* 124–129.

Lazarus, R. S. (1991a). Cognition and motivation in emotion. *American Psychologist, 46,* 352–367.

Lazarus, R. S. (1991b). Progress on a cognitive-motivational-relational theory of emotion. *American Psychologist, 46,* 819–834.

Lazarus, R. S. (1995). Vexing research problems inherent in cognitive-mediational theories of emotion—and some solutions. *Psychological Inquiry, 6,* 183–187.

Lazarus, R. S., & DeLongis, A. (1983). Psychological stress and coping in aging. *American Psychologist, 38,* 245–253.

Lazarus, R. S., & Folkman, S. (1984). *Stress, appraisal, and coping.* New York: Springer.

Lebow, J. L., & Gurman, A. S. (1995). Research assessing couple and family therapy. *Annual Review of Psychology, 46,* 27–57.

Lecomte, T., & Lecomte, C. (2002). Toward uncovering robust principles of change inherent to cognitive-behavioral therapy for psychosis. *American Journal of Orthopsychiatry, 72,* 50–57.

LeDoux, J. E. (1994). Emotion, memory, and the brain. *Scientific American, 270,* 50–57.

LeDoux, J. E. (1995). Emotion: clues from the brain. *Annual Review of Psychology, 46,* 209–235.

LeDoux, J. E. (1996). *The emotional brain: The mysterious underpinnings of emotional life.* New York: Simon & Schuster.

LeDoux, J. E. (2000). Emotion circuits in the brain. *Annual Review of Neuroscience, 23,* 155–184.

Lee, I., & Kesner, R. (2002). Differential contribution of NMDA receptors in hippocampal subregions to spatial working memory. *Nature Neuroscience, 5,* 162–168.

Lee, J., Kelly, K., & Edwards, J. (2006). A closer look at the relationships among trait procrastination, neuroticism, and conscientiousness. *Personality and Individual Differences, 40,* 27–37.

Lefebvre, P., & Merrigan, P. (1998). *Family background, family income, maternal work and child development.* Human Resources Development Canada Report #[[commat]]-98-12E. Retrieved November 28, 2006 from *http://www.hrsdc.gc.ca/en/cs/sp/sdc/pkrf/publications/research/1998-002345/page01.shtml*

Leichtman, M. D., & Ceci, S. J. (1995). The effects of stereotypes and suggestions on preschoolers' reports. *Developmental Psychology, 31,* 568–578.

Leitenberg, H., & Henning, K. (1995). Sexual fantasy. *Psychological Bulletin, 117,* 469–496.

Lenhart, A., Jones, S., & Macgill, A. (2008). *Video games: Adults are players too.* Pew Internet & American Life Project. Retrieved February 11, 2010 from *http://pewresearch.org/pubs/1048/video-games-adults-are-players-too.*

Lenneberg, E. (1967). *Biological foundations of language.* New York: Wiley.

Leon, M. (1992). The neurobiology of filial learning. *Annual Review of Psychology, 43,* 337–398.

Leonardo, E., & Hen, R. (2006). Genetics of affective and anxiety disorders. *Annual Review of Psychology, 57,* 117–137.

Lerman, D. C., & Iwata, B. A. (1996). Developing a technology for the use of operant extinction in clinical settings: An examination of basic and applied research. *Journal of Applied Behavior Analysis, 29,* 345–382.

Lesch, K. (2003). Neuroticism and serotonin: A developmental genetic perspective. In R. Plomin, J. DeFries, I. Craig, & P. McGuffin (Eds.), *Behavioral genetics in the postgenomic era* (pp. 389–423). Washington, DC: American Psychological Association.

Lester, B., Hoffman, J., & Brazelton, T. (1985). The rhythmic structure of mother-infant interaction in term and preterm infants. *Child Development, 56,* 15–27.

Leuchter, A., Cook, I., Witte, E., Morgan, M., & Abrams, M. (2002). Changes in brain function of depressed subjects during treatment with placebo. *American Journal of Psychiatry, 159,* 122–129.

LeVay, S. (1991). A difference in hypothalamic structure between heterosexual and homosexual men. *Science, 253,* 1034–1037.

Levenson, R. W., Ekman, P., & Friesen, W. (1990). Voluntary facial action generates emotion-specific autonomic nervous system activity. *Psychophysiology, 27,* 363–385.

Levy, J. (1985, May). Right brain, left brain: Fact and fiction. *Psychology Today,* pp. 38–44.

Levy-Shiff, R., Lerman, M., Har-Even, D., & Hod, M. (2002). Maternal adjustment and infant outcome in medically defined high-risk pregnancy. *Developmental Psychology, 38,* 93–103.

Lewald, J. (2004). Gender-specific hemispheric asymmetry in auditory space perception. *Cognitive Brain Research, 19,* 92–99.

Lewinsohn, P. M., & Rosenbaum, M. (1987). Recall of parental behavior by acute depressives, remitted depressives, and nondepressives. *Journal of Personality and Social Psychology, 52,* 611–619.

Lewis, D. O., Pincus, J. H., Feldman, M., Jackson, L., & Bard, B. (1986). Psychiatric, neurological, and psychoeducational characteristics of 15 death row inmates in the United States. *American Journal of Psychiatry, 143,* 838–845.

Leyens, J-P., Yzerbyt, V., & Olivier, C. (1996). The role of applicability in the emergence of the overattribution bias. *Journal of Personality and Social Psychology, 70,* 219–229.

Li, J. (2003). U.S. and Chinese cultural beliefs about learning. *Journal of Educational Psychology, 95,* 258–267.

Li, L., Lee, E., Ji, H., & Zukowska, Z. (2003). Neuropeptide Y-induced acceleration of postangioplasty occlusion of rat carotid artery. *Arteriosclerosis, Thrombosis, and Vascular Biology, 23,* 1204–1210.

Lidz, C., & Macrine, S. (2001). An alternative approach to the identification of gifted culturally and linguistically diverse learners: The contribution of dynamic assessment. *School Psychology International, 22,* 74–96.

Lieblum, S. (2002). After sildenafil: Bridging the gap between pharmacologic treatment and satisfying sexual relationships. *Journal of Clinical Psychiatry, 63,* 17–22.

Liepert, J., Terborg, C., & Weiller, C. (1999). Motor plasticity induced by synchronized thumb and foot movements. *Experimental Brain Research, 125,* 435–439.

Lievens, F., Coetsier, P., De Fruyt, F., & De Maeseneer, J. (2002). Medical students' personality characteristics and academic performance: A five-factor model perspective. *Medical Education, 36,* 1050–1056.

Lijtmaer, R. (2001). Splitting and nostalgia in recent immigrants: Psychodynamic considerations. *Journal of the American Academy of Psychoanalysis, 29,* 427–438.

Lilienfeld, S., Lynn, S., Namy, L., & Woolf, N. (2009). *Psychology: From inquiry to understanding.* Boston: Allyn & Bacon.

Lim, V. (2002). The IT way of loafing on the job: Cyberloafing, neutralizing and organizational justice. *Journal of Organizational Behavior, 23,* 675–694.

Lin, H., Mao, S., Chen, P., & Gean, P. (2008). Chronic cannabinoid administration in vivo compromises extinction of fear memory. *Learning & Memory, 15,* 876–884.

Lindenberger, U., Mayr, U., & Kliegl, R. (1993). Speed and intelligence in old age. *Psychology and Aging, 8,* 207–220.

Linder, J., & Gentile, D. (2009). Is the television rating system valid? Indirect, verbal, and physical aggression in programs viewed by fifth grade girls and associations with behavior. *Journal of Applied Developmental Psychology 30,* 286–297.

Lindsay, D., Hagen, L., Read, J., Wade, K., & Garry, M. (2004). True photographs and false memories. *Psychological Science, 15,* 149–154.

Linville, P. W., Fischer, G. W., & Salovey, P. (1989). Perceived distributions of the characteristics of in-group and out-group members: Empirical evidence and a computer simulation. *Journal of Personality and Social Psychology, 57,* 165–188.

Liossi, C. (2006). Hypnosis in cancer care. *Contemporary Hypnosis, 23,* 47–57.

Lishman, W. A. (1990). Alcohol and the brain. *British Journal of Psychiatry, 156,* 635–644.

Little, J., McFarlane, J., & Ducharme, H. (2002). ECT use delayed in the presence of comorbid mental retardation: A review of clinical and ethical issues. *Journal of ECT, 18,* 218–222.

Little, R. E., Anderson, K. W., Ervin, C. H., Worthington-Roberts, B., & Clarren, S. K. (1989). Maternal alcohol use during breast-feeding and infant mental and motor development at one year. *New England Journal of Medicine, 321,* 425–430.

Liu, B., & Lee, Y. (2006). In-vehicle workload assessment: Effects of traffic situations and cellular telephone use. *Journal of Safety Research, 37,* 99–105.

Liu, O., & Wilson, M. (2009). Gender differences and similarities in PISA 2003 mathematics: A comparison between the United States and Hong Kong. *International Journal of Testing, 9,* 20–40.

Liu, S., Liao, H., & Pratt, J. (2009). The impact of media richness and flow on e-learning technology acceptance. *Computers & Education, 52,* 599–607.

Livingston, E., Huerta, S., Arthur, D., Lee, S., De Shields, S., & Heber, D. (2002). Male gender is a predictor of morbidity and age a predictor of mortality for patients undergoing gastric bypass surgery. *Annals of Surgery, 236,* 576–582.

Lock, C. (2004). Deception detection: Psychologists try to learn how to spot a liar. *Science News, 166,* 72.

Loeber, R., & Hay, D. (1997). Key issues in the development of aggression and violence from childhood to early adulthood. *Annual Review of Psychology, 48,* 371–410.

Loehlin, J. (2009). History of behavior genetics. In Kim, Y. (Ed.), *Handbook of behavior genetics* (pp. 3–14). New York: Spring Science + Business Media, LLC.

Loehlin, J. C. (1992). *The limits of family influence: Genes, experience, and behavior.* New York: Guilford.

Loehlin, J. C., Horn, J. M., & Willerman, L. (1990). Heredity, environment, and personality change: Evidence from the Texas Adoption Project. *Journal of Personality, 58,* 221–243.

Loehlin, J. C., Lindzey, G., & Spuhler, J. N. (1975). *Race differences in intelligence.* San Francisco: Freeman.

Loehlin, J. C., Willerman, L., & Horn, J. M. (1987). Personality resemblance in adoptive families: A 10-year follow-up. *Journal of Personality and Social Psychology, 53,* 961–969.

Loehlin, J. C., Willerman, L., & Horn, J. M. (1988). Human behavior genetics. *Annual Review of Psychology, 39,* 101–133.

Loewenstein, G., Rick, S., & Cohen, J. (2008). Neuroeconomics. *Annual Review of Psychology, 59,* 647–672.

Loftus, E. (2003). Our changeable memories: Legal and practical impli-cations. *Nature Reviews: Neuroscience, 4,* 231–234.

Loftus, E. (2004). Memories of things unseen. *Current Directions in Psychological Science, 13,* 145–147.

Loftus, E. F. (1979). *Eyewitness testimony.* Cambridge, MA: Harvard University Press.

Loftus, E. F. (1993). Psychologists in the eyewitness world. *American Psychologist, 48,* 550–552.

Loftus, E. F. (1997). Creating false memories. *Scientific American, 277,* 71–75.

Loftus, E. F., & Hoffman, H. G. (1989). Misinformation and memory: The creation of new memories. *Journal of Experimental Psychology: General, 118,* 100–104.

Loftus, E. F., & Loftus, G. R. (1980). On the permanence of stored information in the human brain. *American Psychologist, 35,* 409–420.

Loftus, E. F., & Pickrell, J. (1995). The formation of false memories. *Psychiatric Annals, 25,* 720–725.

Loftus, E., & Bernstein, D. (2005). Rich false memories: The royal road to success. In A. Healy (Ed.), *Experimental cognitive psychology and its applications* (pp. 101–113). Washington, DC: American Psychological Association.

Logothetis, N. (2008). What we can do and what we cannot do with fMRI. *Nature, 453,* 869–878.

Lohr, J., Olatunji, B., Baumeister, R., & Bushman, B. (2007). The psy-chology of anger venting and empirically supported alternatives that do no harm. *The Scientific Review of Mental Health Practice, 5,* 53–64.

London, E. D., Ernst, M., Grant, S., Bonson, K., & Weinstein, A. (2000). Orbitofrontal cortex and human drug abuse: Functional imaging. *Cerebral Cortex, 10,* 334–342.

Long, D., & Baynes, K. (2002). Discourse representation in the two cerebral hemispheres. *Journal of Cognitive Neuroscience, 14,* 228–242.

Long, G. M., & Crambert, R. F. (1990). The nature and basis of age-related changes in dynamic visual acuity. *Psychology and Aging, 5,* 138–143.

Lonsdorf, T., Weike, A., Nikamo, P., Schalling, M., Hamm, A., & Ohman, A. (2009). Genetic gating of human fear learning and extinction: Possible implications for gene-environment interaction in anxiety disorder. *Psychological Science, 20,* 198–206.

Lott, B., & Saxon, S. (2002). The influence of ethnicity, social class and context on judgments about U.S. women. *Journal of Social Psychology, 142,* 481–499.

Lotze, M., Montoya, P., Erb, M., Hulsmann, E., Flor, H., Klose, U., Birbaumer, N., & Grodd, W. (1999). Activation of cortical and cerebellar motor areas during executed and imagined hand move-ments: An fMRI study. *Journal of Cognitive Neuroscience, 11,* 491–501.

Lubart, T. (2003). In search of creative intelligence. In R. Sternberg, J. Lautrey, & T. Lubart (Eds.), *Models of intelligence: International perspective* (pp. 279–292). Washington, DC: American Psychological Association.

Lubit, R., Bonds, C., & Lucia, M. (2009). *Sleep disorders.* Retrieved February 5, 2010 from *http://emedicine.medscape.com/article/287104-overview.*

Luchins, A. S. (1957). Experimental attempts to minimize the impact of first impressions. In C. I. Hovland (Ed.), *Yale studies in attitude and communication: Vol. 1. The order of presentation in persua-sion* (pp. 62–75). New Haven, CT: Yale University Press.

Luiselli, J. (2009). Nonsuicidal self-injury among people with develop-mental disabilities. In M. Nock, (Ed.), *Understanding nonsuicidal self-injury: Origins, assessment, and treatment* (pp. 157–179). Washington, DC: American Psychological Association.

Luo, L., Luk, G., & Bialystok, E. (2010). Effect of language proficiency and executive control on verbal fluency performance bilinguals. *Cognition, 114,* 29–41.

Luo, S., & Klohnen, E. (2005). Assortative mating and marital quality in newlyweds: A couple-centered approach. *Journal of Personality & Social Psychology, 88,* 304–326.

Lustig, C., & Hasher, L. (2002). Working memory span: The effect of prior learning. *American Journal of Psychology, 115,* 89–101.

Lustig, C., Konkel, A., & Jacoby, L. (2004). Which route to recovery? Controlled retrieval and accessibility bias in retroactive interfer-ence. *Psychological Science, 15,* 729–735.

Lutchmaya, S., Baron-Cohen, S., & Raggatt, P. (2002). Foetal testos-terone and vocabulary size in 18- and 24-month-old infants. *Infant Behavior & Development, 24,* 418–424.

Lutz, A., Brefczynski-Lewis, J., Johnstone, T., & Davidson, R. (2008). Regulation of the neural circuitry of emotion by compassion medi-tation: Effects of meditative expertise. *Public Library of Science One, 3,* e1897.

Lutz, A., Greischar, L., Rawlings, N., Ricard, M., & Davidson, R. (2004). Long-term meditators self-induce high-amplitude gamma synchrony during mental practice. *Proceedings of the National Academy of Sciences, 101,* 16369–16373.

Lydiard, R. B., Brawman-Mintzer, O., & Ballenger, J. C. (1996). Recent developments in the psychopharmacology of anxiety disorders. *Journal of Consulting and Clinical Psychology, 64,* 660–668.

Lynn, R. (2006). *Race differences in intelligence: An evolutionary analy-sis.* Atlanta, GA: Washington Summit Books.

Lynn, S. J., & Nash, M. R. (1994). Truth in memory: Ramifications for psychotherapy and hypnotherapy. *American Journal of Clinical Hypnosis, 36,* 194–208.

Lynn, S. J., Kirsch, I., Barabasz, A., Cardena, E., & Patterson, D. (2000). Hypnosis as an empirically supported clinical intervention: The state of the evidence and a look to the future. *International Journal of Clinical Experimental Hypnosis, 48,* 239–259.

Lyvers, M. (2000). "Loss of control" in alcoholism and drug addiction: A neuroscientific interpretation. *Experimental and Clinical Psychopharmacology, 8,* 225–245.

Mühlberger, A., Weik, A., Pauli, P., & Wiedemann, G. (2006). One-ses-sion virtual reality exposure treatment for fear of flying: 1-year fol-low-up and graduation flight accompaniment effects. *Psychotherapy Research, 16,* 26–40.

Müller, M., Regenbogen, B., Sachse, J., Eich, F., Härtter, S., & Hiemke, C. (2006). Gender aspects in the clinical treatment of schizophrenic inpatients with amisulpride: A therapeutic drug monitoring study. *Pharmacopsychiatry, 39,* 41–46.

Maccoby, E. E. (1992). The role of parents in the socialization of children: An historical overview. *Developmental Psychology, 28,* 1006–1017.

Maccoby, E. E., & Martin, J. A. (1983). Socialization in the context of the family: Parent-child interaction. In P. H. Mussen (Ed.), *Handbook of child psychology* (4th ed., Vol. 4. pp. 1–101). New York: John Wiley.

MacDonald, A., Pogue-Geile, M., Johnson, M., & Carter, C. (2003). A spe-cific deficit in context processing in the unaffected siblings of patients with schizophrenia. *Archives of General Psychiatry, 60,* 57–65.

Macey, P., Henderson, L., Macey, K., Alger, J., Frysinger, R., Woo, M., et al. (2002). Brain morphology associated with obstructive sleep apnea. *American Journal of Respiratory and Critical Care Medicine, 166,* 1382–1387.

Macht, M., & Mueller, J. (2007). Immediate effects of chocolate on experimentally induced mood states. *Appetite, 49,* 667–674.

Mack, A. (2003). Inattentional blindness: Looking without seeing. *Current Directions in Psychological Science, 12,* 180–184.

Mack, A., & Rock, I. (1998). *Inattentional blindness.* Cambridge, MA: MIT Press.

MacWhinney, B. (2005). Language development. In M. Bornstein & M. Lamb, (Eds.), *Developmental science: An advanced textbook* (5th ed., pp. 359–387). Hillsdale, NJ: Lawrence Erlbaum Associates.

Madden, M., & Lenhart, A. (2006). *Pew Internet and American life project: Online dating.* Retrieved July 3, 2006 from *http://www.pewinternet.org/pdfs/PIP_Online_Dating.pdf*

Maguire, E. A., Gadian, D. G., Johnsrude, I. S., Good, C. D., Ashburner, J., Frackowiak, R. S. J., & Frith, C. D. (2000). Navigation-related structural change in the hippocampi of taxi drivers. *Proceedings of the National Academy of Science, 97,* 4398–4403.

Maguire, E., Nannery, R., & Spiers, H. (2006). Navigation around London by a taxi driver with bilateral hippocampal lesions. *Brain, 129,* 2894–2907.

Maguire, E., Spiers, H., Good, C., Hartley, T., Frackowiak, R., & Burgess, N. (2003). Navigation expertise and the human hippocampus: A structural brain imaging analysis. *Hippocampus, 13,* 208–217.

Mahler, H., Kulik, J., Gibbons, F., Gerrard, M., & Harrell, J. (2003). Effects of appearance-based intervention on sun protection intentions and self-reported behaviors. *Health Psychology, 22,* 199–209.

Maiden, R., Peterson, S., Caya, M., & Hayslip, B. (2003). Personality changes in the old-old: A longitudinal study. *Journal of Adult Development, 10,* 31–39.

Maier, S. F., & Laudenslager, M. (1985, August). Stress and health: Exploring the links. *Psychology Today,* 44–49.

Main, M., & Solomon, J. (1990). Procedures for identifying infants as disorganized/disoriented during the Ainsworth Strange Situation. In M. Greenberg, D. Cicchetti, & M. Cummings (Eds.), *Attachment in the preschool years: Theory, research, and intervention* (pp. 121–160). Chicago: University of Chicago Press.

Maj, M. (1990). Psychiatric aspects of HIV–1 infection and AIDS. *Psychological Medicine, 20,* 547–563.

Malik, A., & D'Souza, D. (2006). Gone to pot: The association between cannabis and psychosis. *Psychiatric Times, 23.* Retrieved May 15, 2006 from *http://www.psychiatrictimes.com/article/showArticle .jhtml?articleId=185303874.*

Malkoff, S. B., Muldoon, M. F., Zeigler, Z. R., & Manuck, S. B. (1993). Blood platelet responsivity to acute mental stress. *Psychosomatic Medicine, 55,* 477–482.

Malle, B. (2006). The actor-observer asymmetry in attribution: A (surprising) meta-analysis. *Psychological Bulletin, 132,* 895–919.

Maltz, W. (1991). *The sexual healing journey: A guide for survivors of sexual abuse.* New York: HarperCollins.

Mancini, J., Lethel, V., Hugonenq, C., & Chabrol, B. (2001). Brain injuries in early foetal life: Consequences for brain development. *Developmental Medicine & Child Neurology, 43,* 52–60.

Manderscheid, R., & Henderson, M. (2001). *Mental health, United States, 2000.* Rockville, MD: Center for Mental Health Services. Retrieved January 14, 2003, from *http://www.mentalhealth.org/publications/allpubs/SMA01-3537/*

Mandler, J. M. (1990). A new perspective on cognitive development in infancy. *American Scientist, 78*(3), 236–243.

Maner, J., Gailliot, M., & Miller, S. (2009). The implicit cognition of relationship maintenance: Inattention to attractives. *Journal of Experimental Social Psychology, 45,* 174–179.

Mangen, A. (2008). Hypertext fiction reading: Haptics and immersion. *Journal of Research in Reading, 31,* 404–419.

Manhal-Baugus, M. (2001). E-therapy: Practical, ethical, and legal issues. *CyberPsychology and Behavior, 4,* 551–563.

Manton, K. G., Siegler, I. C., & Woodbury, M. A. (1986). Patterns of intellectual development in later life. *Journal of Gerontology, 41,* 486–499.

Mantooth, R. (2010). *Toxicity, benzodiazepine.* Retrieved February 8, 2010 from *http://emedicine.medscape.com/article/813255-overview.*

Manzardo, A., Stein, L., & Belluzi, J. (2002). Rats prefer cocaine over nicotine in a two-level self-administration choice test. *Brain Research, 924,* 10–19.

Maratsos, M., & Matheny, L. (1994). Language specificity and elasticity: Brain and clinical syndrome studies. *Annual Review of Psychology, 45,* 487–516.

Marcia, J. (2002). Identity and psychosocial development in adulthood. *Identity, 2,* 7–28.

Marcus, G. F. (1996). Why do children say "breaked"? *Current Directions in Psychological Science, 5,* 81–85.

Marder, S. R. (1996). Clinical experience with risperidone. *Journal of Clinical Psychiatry, 57*(9, Suppl.), 57–61.

Mares, M., & Woodard, E. (2005). Positive effects of television on children's social interactions: A meta-analysis. *Media Psychology, 7,* 301–322.

Markowitsch, H., Welzer, H., & Emmans, D. (2010). *The development of autobiographical memory.* New York: Psychology Press.

Marks, I. (1987). The development of normal fear: A review. *Journal of Child Psychology and Psychiatry, 28,* 667–697.

Marks, I. M. (1972). Flooding (implosion) and allied treatments. In W. S. Agras (Ed.), *Behavior modification* (pp. 151–211). New York: Little, Brown.

Marriott, L., & Wenk, G. (2004). Neurobiological consequences of long-term estrogen therapy. *Current Directions in Psychological Science, 13,* 173–176.

Marsh, A., Elfenbein, H., & Ambady, N. (2003). Nonverbal "accents": Cultural differences in facial expressions of emotion. *Psychological Science, 14,* 373–376.

Marsh, A., Elfenbein, H., & Ambady, N. (2007). Separated by a common language: Nonverbal accents and cultural stereotypes about Americans and Australians. *Journal of Cross-Cultural Psychology, 38,* 284–301.

Marshall, R. D., Schneier, F. R., Fallon, B. A., Feerick, J., & Liebowitz, M. R. (1994). Medication therapy for social phobia. *Journal of Clinical Psychiatry, 56*(6, Suppl.), 33–37.

Marshall, W. L., & Segal, Z. (1988). Behavior therapy. In C. G. Last & M. Hersen (Eds.), *Handbook of anxiety disorders* (pp. 338–361). New York: Pergamon.

Marshall, W., Marshall, L., & Serran, G. (2009). Empathy and offending behavior. In M., McMurran, & R. Howard (Eds.), *Personality, personality disorder and violence: An evidence based approach* (pp. 229–244). New York: Wiley-Blackwell.

Martikainen, P., & Valkonen, R. (1996). Mortality after the death of a spouse: Rates and causes of death in a large Finnish cohort. *American Journal of Public Health, 86,* 1087–1093.

Martin, C. L., & Little, J. K. (1990). The relation of gender understanding to children's sex-typed preferences and gender stereotypes. *Child Development, 61,* 1427–1439.

Martin, C., & Ruble, D. (2002). Cognitive theories of early gender development. *Psychological Bulletin, 128,* 903–933.

Martin, J., Hamilton, B., Sutton, P., Ventura, S., Menacker, F., & Munson, M. (2003). Births: Final data for 2002. *National Vital Statistics Reports, 52,* 1–50.

Martinez, C. (1986). Hispanics: Psychiatric issues. In C. B. Wilkinson (Ed.), *Ethnic psychiatry* (pp. 61–88). New York: Plenum.

Martinez, C. (2006). Abusive family experiences and object relation disturbances: A case study. *Clinical Case Studies, 5,* 209–219.

Martinez, I. (2002). The elder in the Cuban American family: Making sense of the real and ideal. *Journal of Comparative Family Studies, 33,* 359–375.

Martinez, J. L., Jr., & Derrick, B. E. (1996). Long-term potentiation and learning. *Annual Review of Psychology, 47,* 173–203.

Martinez, M., & Belloch, A. (2004). The effects of a cognitive-behavioural treatment for hypochondriasis on attentional bias. *International Journal of Clinical & Health Psychology, 4,* 299–311.

Maruna, S., & Mann, R. (2006). A fundamental attribution error? Rethinking cognitive distortions. *Legal and Criminological Psychology, 11,* 155–177.

Masataka, N. (1996). Perception of motherese in a signed language by 6-month-old deaf infants. *Developmental Psychology, 32,* 874–879.

Masland, R. H. (1996). Unscrambling color vision. *Science, 271,* 616–617.

Mason, B., Goodman, A., Chabac, S., & Lehert, P. (2006). Effect of oral acamprosate on abstinence in patients with alcohol dependence in a double-blind, placebo-controlled trial: The role of patient motivation. *Journal of Psychiatric Research, 40,* 383–393.

Mason, R., & Just, M. (2004). How the brain processes causal inferences in text: A theoretical account of generation and integration component processes utilizing both cerebral hemispheres. *Psychological Science, 15,* 1–7.

Massey Cancer Center. (2006). *Familial cancer: Genetic counseling and consultation services.* Retrieved November 30, 2006, from *http://www.massey.vcu.edu/discover/?pid=1888*

Masters, W. H., & Johnson, V. E. (1966). *Human sexual response.* Boston: Little, Brown.

Mata, I., Perez-Iglesias, R., Roiz-Santianez, R., Tordesillas-Gutierez, D., Pazos, A., Gutierrez, A., Vazquez-Barquero, J., & Crespo-Facorro, B. (2010, in press). Gyrification brain abnormalities associated with adolescence and early-adulthood cannabis use. *Brain Research,* [pages not available].

Mathew, R. J., & Wilson, W. H. (1991). Substance abuse and cerebral blood flow. *American Journal of Psychiatry, 148,* 292–305.

Mathy, R. (2002). Suicidality and sexual orientation in five continents: Asia, Australia, Europe, North America, and South America. *International Journal of Sexuality & Gender Studies, 7,* 215–225.

Matlin, M. W. (1989). *Cognition* (2nd ed.). New York: Holt, Rinehart & Winston.

Matlin, M. W., & Foley, H. J. (1997). *Sensation and perception* (4th ed.). Boston: Allyn & Bacon.

Matsuda, L., Lolait, S. J., Brownstein, M. J., Young, A. C., & Bonner, T. I. (1990). Structure of a cannabinoid receptor and functional expression of the cloned CDNA. *Nature, 346,* 561–564.

Matsunami, H., Montmayeur, J-P., & Buck, L. B. (2000). A family of candidate taste receptors in human and mouse. *Nature, 404,* 601–604.

Matta, D., & Knudson-Martin, C. (2006). Father responsivity: Couple processes and the coconstruction of fatherhood. *Family Process, 45,* 19–37.

Matthews, K. A. (1992). Myths and realities of the menopause. *Psychosomatic Medicine, 54,* 1–9.

Matthews, K. A., Shumaker, S. A., Bowen, D. J., Langer, R. D., Hunt, J. R., Kaplan, R. M., et al. (1997). Women's health initiative: Why now? What is it? What's new? *American Psychologist, 52,* 101–116.

Matthiesen, S., & Einarsen, S. (2004). Psychiatric distress and symptoms of PTSD among victims of bullying at work. *British Journal of Guidance and Counseling, 32,* 335–356.

Matz, D., & Wood, W. (2005). Cognitive dissonance in groups: The consequences of disagreement. *Journal of Personality & Social Psychology, 88,* 22–37.

Mayer, R. (2010). Fostering scientific reasoning with multimedia instruction. In H. Waters & W. Schneider, (Eds.), *Metacognition, strategy use, and instruction* (pp. 160–175). New York: Guilford Press.

Mayer, R., Heiser, J., & Lonn, S. (2001). Cognitive constraints on multimedia learning: When presenting more material results in less understanding. *Journal of Educational Psychology, 93,* 187–198.

Maymann, J. (2008). *The Dark Knight Batman movie and attention planning for viral campaigns.* Retrieved March 26, 2010 from *http://www.goviral.com/articles/GOV-WARC-DarkKnight-161008.pdf.*

Mayo Clinic. (2005). *Weight loss: 6 strategies for success.* Retrieved June 16, 2006, from *https://www.mayoclinic.com/health/weight-loss/HQ01625*

Mayo Clinic. (2006a). *Hearing loss: MP3 players can pose risk.* Retrieved December 13, 2006, from *http://mayoclinic.com/health/hearing-loss/GA00046*

Mayo Clinic. (2006b). *Sleep tips for the perpetually awake.* Retrieved December 16, 2006, from *http://mayoclinic.com/health/sleep/HQ01387*

Mayo Clinic. (2009). *Exercise: 7 benefits of regular physical activity.* Retrieved March 12, 2010 from *http://www.mayoclinic.com/health/exercise/HQ01676.*

Mayo Clinic. (2009). *Hypnosis.* Retrieved February 8, 2010 from *http://www.mayoclinic.com/health/hypnosis/SA00084*

Mayo Clinic. (2009). *Ten tips for better sleep.* Retrieved February 5, 2010 from *http://www.mayoclinic.com/health/sleep/hq01387.*

Mazur, E., & Kozarian, L. (2010). Self-presentation and interaction in blogs of adolescents and young emerging adults. *Journal of Adolescent Research, 25,* 124–144.

Mazzoni, G., & Memon, A. (2003). Imagination can create false autobiographical memories. *Psychological Science, 14,* 186–188.

McAdams, D. P. (1992). The five-factor model in personality: A critical appraisal. *Journal of Personality, 60,* 329–361.

McCabe, R., & Gifford, S. (2009). Psychological treatment of panic disorder and agoraphobia. In M., Antony, & M. Stein, (Eds.), *Oxford handbook of anxiety and related disorders* (pp. 308–320). New York: Oxford University Press.

McCall, W., Dunn, A., & Rosenquist, P. (2004). Quality of life and function after electroconvulsive therapy. *British Journal of Psychiatry, 185,* 405–409.

McClearn, G. E., Johansson, B., Berg, S., Pedersen, N. L., Ahern, F., Petrill, S. A., et ak. (1997). Substantial genetic influence on cognitive abilities in twins 80 or more years old. *Science, 276,* 1560–1563.

McClelland, D. C. (1961). *The achieving society.* Princeton, NJ: Van Nostrand.

McClelland, D. C. (1985). *Human motivation.* New York: Cambridge University Press.

McClelland, D. C., Atkinson, J. W., Clark, R. W., & Lowell, E. L. (1953). *The achievement motive.* New York: Appleton-Century-Crofts.

McClelland, J. L., McNaughton, B. L., & O'Reilly, R. C. (1995). Why there are complementary learning systems in the hippocampus and neocortex: Insights from the successes and failures of connectionist models of learning and memory. *Psychological Bulletin, 102,* 419–457.

McCormick, C. B., & Kennedy, J. H. (2000). Father–child separation, retrospective and current views of attachment relationship with father and self-esteem in late adolescence. *Psychological Reports, 86,* 827–834.

McCrae, R. (1984). Situational determinants of coping responses: Loss, threat, and challenge. *Journal of Personality and Social Psychology, 46,* 919–928.

McCrae, R. (2002). The maturation of personality psychology: Adult personality development and psychological well-being. *Journal of Research in Personality, 36,* 307–317.

McCrae, R. R. (1993). Moderated analyses of longitudinal personality stability. *Journal of Personality and Social Psychology, 65,* 577–583.

McCrae, R. R., & Costa, P. T., Jr. (1990). *Personality in adulthood.* New York: Guilford.

McCrae, R. R., Costa, P. T., Jr., Ostendorf, F., Angleitner, A., Hrebickova, M., Avia, S. J., et al. (2000). Nature over nurture: Temperament, personality, and life span development. *Journal of Personality & Social Psychology, 78,* 173–186.

McCrae, R., & Costa, P. (2003). *Personality in adulthood: A five-factor theory perspective* (2nd ed.). New York: Guilford Press.

McCue, J. M., Link, K. L., Eaton, S. S., & Freed, B. M. (2000). Exposure to cigarette tar inhibits ribonucleotide reductase and blocks lymphocyte proliferation. *Journal of Immunology, 165,* 6771–6775.

McCullough, M. E., Hoyt, W. T., Larson, D. B., Koenig, H. G., & Thoresen, C. (2000). Religious involvement and mortality: A meta-analytic review. *Health Psychology, 19,* 211–222.

McDonald, A. D., Armstrong, B. G., & Sloan, M. (1992). Cigarette, alcohol, and coffee consumption and prematurity. *American Journal of Public Health, 82,* 87–90.

McDonald, J. L. (1997). Language acquisition: The acquisition of linguistic structure in normal and special populations. *Annual Review of Psychology, 48,* 215–241.

McDowell, C., & Acklin, M. W. (1996). Standardizing procedures for calculating Rorschach interrater reliability: Conceptual and empirical foundations. *Journal of Personality Assessment, 66,* 308–320.

McElree, B., Jia, G., & Litvak, A. (2000). The time course of conceptual processing in three bilingual populations. *Journal of Memory & Language, 42*, 229–254.

McElwain, N., & Volling, B. (2004). Attachment security and parental sensitivity during infancy: Associations with friendship quality and false-belief understanding at age 4. *Journal of Social & Personal Relationships, 21*, 639–667.

McGaugh, J., & Cahill, L. (2009). Emotion and memory: Central and peripheral contributions. In R., Davidson, K., Scherer, & H. Goldsmith, (Eds.), *Handbook of affective sciences*. Series in affective science. (pp. 93–116). New York: Oxford University Press.

McGlashan, T. H., & Hoffman, R. E. (2000). Schizophrenia as a disorder of developmentally reduced synaptic connectivity. *Archives of General Psychiatry, 57*, 637–648.

McGuire, W. J. (1985). Attitudes and attitude change. In G. Lindzey & E. Aronson (Ed.), *Handbook of social psychology* (Vol. 2, 3rd ed.). New York: Random House.

McKelvie, S. (1984). Relationship between set and functional fixedness: A replication. *Perceptual and Motor Skills, 58*, 996–998.

McMahon, F., Akula, N., Schulze, T., Pierandrea, M., Tozzi, F., Detera-Wadleigh, S., Steele, C., Breuer, R., Strohmaier, J., Wendland, J., Mattheisen, M., Muhleisen, T., Maier, W., Nothen, M., Cichon, S., Farmer, A., Vincent, J., Holsboer, F., Preisig, M., & Reitschel, M. (2010). Meta-analysis of genome-wide association data identifies a risk locus for major mood disorders on 3p21.1. *Nature, 42*, pp. 128–131.

McNally, R. (2003). The demise of pseudoscience. *The Scientific Review of Mental Health Practice, 2*, 97–101.

McNally, R., Lasko, N., Clancy, S., Macklin, M., Pitman, R., & Orr, S. (2004). Psychophysiological responding during script-driven imagery in people reporting abduction by space aliens. *Psychological Science, 15*, 493–497.

McNamara, P., McLaren, D., & Durso, K. (2007). Representation of the self in REM and NREM dreams. *Dreaming, 17*, 113–126.

Medina, J. H., Paladini, A. C., & Izquierdo, I. (1993). Naturally occurring benzodiazepines and benzodiazepine-like molecules in brain. *Behavioural Brain Research, 58*, 1–8.

Mednick, S. A., & Mednick, M. T. (1967). *Examiner's manual, Remote Associates Test.* Boston: Houghton-Mifflin.

Mednick, S. A., Brennan, P., & Kandel, E. (1988). Predisposition to violence. *Aggressive Behavior, 14*, 25–33.

Meehan, W., & Adelman, S. (2010). *Opioid use*. Retrieved February 8, 2010 from *http://emedicine.medscape.com/article/287790-overview*.

Meltzer, H. Y., Rabinowitz, J., Lee, M. A., Cola, P. A., Ranjan, R., Findling, R. L., et al. (1997). Age at onset and gender of schizophrenic patients in relation to neuroleptic resistance. *American Journal of Psychiatry, 154*, 475–482.

Meltzer, H., Alphs, L., Green, A., Altamura, A., Anand, R., Bertoldi, A., et al. (2003). Clozapine treatment for suicidality in schizophrenia: International suicide prevention trial. *Archives of General Psychiatry, 60*, 82–91.

Melzack, R., & Wall, P. D. (1965). Pain mechanisms: A new theory. *Science, 150*, 971–979.

Melzack, R., & Wall, P. D. (1983). *The challenge of pain.* New York: Basic Books.

Memmert, D., Simons, D., & Grimme, T. (2009). The relationship between visual attention and expertise in sports. *Psychology of Sport and Exercise, 10*, 146–151.

Merck Manual of Diagnosis and Therapy. (2005). *Anxiolitics and sedatives.* Retrieved December 16, 2006, from *http://www.merck.com/mmpe/sec15/ch198/ch198e.html*

Meschyan, G., & Hernandez, A. (2002). Is native-language decoding skill related to second-language learning? *Journal of Educational Psychology, 94*, 14–22.

Meyer, A. (1997, March/April). Patching up testosterone. *Psychology Today, 30*, 54–57, 66–70.

Meyer, C., Hagmann-von Arx, P., Lemola, S., & Grob, A. (2010). Correspondence between the general ability to discriminate sensory stimuli and general intelligence. *Journal of Individual Differences, 31*, 46–56.

Meyer, P. (1972). If Hitler asked you to electrocute a stranger, would you? In R. Greenbaum & H. A. Tilker (Eds.), *The challenge of psychology* (pp. 456–465). Englewood Cliffs, NJ: Prentice-Hall.

Meyers, L. (2006). Still wearing the "kick me" sign. *APA Monitor on Psychology, 37*, 68–69.

Mezulis, A., Abramson, L., Hyde, J., & Hankin, B. (2004). Is there a universal positivity bias in attributions? A meta-analytic review of individual, developmental, and cultural differences in the self-serving attributional bias. *Psychological Bulletin, 130*, 711–747.

Michaels, J. W., Bloomel, J. M., Brocato, R. M., Linkous, R. A., & Rowe, J. S. (1982). Social facilitation and inhibition in a natural setting. *Replications in Social Psychology, 2*, 21–24.

Middlebrooks, J. C., & Green, D. M. (1991). Sound localization by human listeners. *Annual Review of Psychology, 42*, 135–159.

Miles, D. R., & Carey, G. (1997). Genetic and environmental architecture of human aggression. *Journal of Personality and Social Psychology, 72*, 207–217.

Miles, J., & Hempel, S. (2004). The Eysenck Personality Scales: The Eysenck Personality Questionnaire-Revised (EPQ-R) and the Eysenck Personality Profiler (EPP). In M. Hilsenroth & D. Segal (Eds.), *Comprehensive handbook of psychological assessment, personality assessment* (Vol. 2, pp. 99–107). New York: John Wiley & Sons.

Miles, R. (1999). A homeostatic switch. *Nature, 397*, 215–216.

Milgram, S. (1963). Behavioral study of obedience. *Journal of Abnormal and Social Psychology, 67*, 371–378.

Milgram, S. (1965). Liberating effects of group pressure. *Journal of Personality and Social Psychology, 1*, 127–134.

Miller, B., Norton, M., Curtis, T., Hill, E., Schvaneveldt, P., & Young, M. (1998). The timing of sexual intercourse among adolescents: Family, peer, and other antecedents: Erratum. *Youth & Society, 29*, 390.

Miller, G. A. (1956). The magical number seven, plus or minus two: Some limits on our capacity for processing information. *Psychological Review, 63*, 81–97.

Miller, G., Cohen, S., & Ritchey, A. (2002). Chronic psychological stress and the regulation of pro-inflammatory cytokines: A glucocorticoid-resistance model. *Health Psychology, 21*, 531–541.

Miller, J. G., Bersoff, D. M., & Harwood, R. L. (1990). Perceptions of social responsibilities in India and in the United States: Moral imperatives or personal decisions? *Journal of Personality and Social Psychology, 58*, 33–47.

Miller, J., Lynam, D., Zimmerman, R., Logan, T., Leukefeld, C., & Clayton, R. (2004). The utility of the Five Factor Model in understanding risky sexual behavior. *Personality and Individual Differences, 36*, 1611–1626.

Miller, L. (1989, November). What biofeedback does (and doesn't) do. *Psychology Today*, pp. 22–23.

Miller, N. E. (1941). The frustration-aggression hypothesis. *Psychological Review, 48*, 337–342.

Miller, N. E. (1985, February). Rx: Biofeedback. *Psychology Today*, pp. 54–59.

Miller, N. S., & Gold, M. S. (1994). LSD and Ecstasy: Pharmacology, phenomenology, and treatment. *Psychiatric Annals, 24*, 131–133.

Miller, T. Q., Smith, T. W., Turner, C. W., Guijarro, M. L., & Hallet, A. J. (1996). A meta-analytic review of research on hostility and physical health. *Psychological Bulletin, 119*, 322–348.

Miller, W., & Thoresen, C. (2003). Spirituality, religion, and health: An emerging research field. *American Psychologist, 58*, 24–35.

Milling, L., Coursen, E., Shores, J., & Waszkiewica, J. (2010). The predictive utility of hypnotizability: The change in suggestibility produced by hypnosis. *Journal of Consulting and Clinical Psychology, 78*, 126–130.

Millman, R. (2005). Excessive sleepiness in adolescents and young adults: Causes, consequences, and treatment strategies. *Pediatrics, 115*, 1774–1786.

Milner, B. (1966). Amnesia following operation on the temporal lobes. In C. W. M. Whitty & O. L. Zangwill (Eds.), *Amnesia* (pp. 109–133). London: Butterworth.

Milner, B., Corkin, S., & Teuber, H. L. (1968). Further analysis of the hippocampal amnesic syndrome: 14-year follow-up study of H. M. *Neuropsychologia, 6*, 215–234.

Milos, G., Spindler, A., & Schnyder, U. (2004). Psychiatric comorbidity and Eating Disorder Inventory (EDI) profiles in eating disorder patients. *Canadian Journal of Psychiatry, 49*, 179–184.

Milos, G., Spindler, A., Ruggiero, G., Klaghofer, R., & Schnyder, U. (2002). Comorbidity of obsessive-compulsive disorders and duration of eating disorders. *International Journal of Eating Disorders, 31*, 284–289.

Milton, J., & Wiseman, R. (2001). Does psi exist? Reply to Storm and Ertel (2001). *Psychological Bulletin, 127*, 434–438.

Mineka, S., & Oehlberg, K. (2008). The relevance of recent developments in classical conditioning to understanding the etiology and maintenance of anxiety disorder. *Acta Psychologica, 127*, 567–580.

Mischel, W. (1966). A social-learning view of sex differences in behavior. In E. E. Maccoby (Ed.), *The development of sex differences* (pp. 56–81). Palo Alto, CA: Stanford University Press.

Mischel, W. (1968). *Personality and assessment.* New York: Wiley.

Mischel, W. (1973). Toward a cognitive social learning reconceptualization of personality. *Psychological Review, 80*, 252–283.

Mischel, W. (1977). The interaction of person and situation. In D. Magnusson & N. S. Endler (Eds.), *Personality at the crossroads: Current issues in interactional psychology* (pp. 333–352). Hillsdale, NJ: Lawrence Erlbaum.

Mischel, W. (2004). Toward an integrative science of the person. *Annual Review of Psychology, 55*, 1–22.

Mishra, R. (1997). Cognition and cognitive development. In J. Berry, P. Dasen, & T. Saraswathi (Eds.), *Handbook of cross-cultural psychology* (Vol. 2). Boston, MA: Allyn & Bacon.

Mishra, R., & Singh, T. (1992). Memories of Asur children for locations and pairs of pictures. *Psychological Studies, 37*, 38–46.

Mistry, J., & Rogoff, B. (1994). Remembering in cultural context. In W. J. Lonner & R. Malpass (Eds.), *Psychology and culture* (pp. 139–144). Boston: Allyn & Bacon.

Mitler, M. M., Aldrich, M. S., Koob, G. F., & Zarcone, V. P. (1994). Narcolepsy and its treatment with stimulants. *Sleep, 17*, 352–371.

Mitsis, E. M., Halperin, J. M., & Newcorn, J. H. (2000). Serotonin and aggression in children. *Current Psychiatry Reports, 2*, 95–101.

Mogg, K., Baldwin, D., Brodrick, P., & Bradley, B. (2004). Effect of short-term SSRI treatment on cognitive bias in generalised anxiety disorder. *Psychopharmacology, 176*, 466–470.

Mohan, J. (2006). Cardiac psychology. *Journal of the Indian Academy of Applied Psychology, 32*, 214–220.

Mohanty, A., & Perregaux, C. (1997). Language acquisition and bilingualism. In J. Berry, P. Dasen, & T. Saraswathi (Eds.), *Handbook of cross-cultural psychology* (pp. 217–254). Boston: Allyn & Bacon.

Mohr, D., Goodkin, D., Nelson, S., Cox, D., & Weiner, M. (2002). Moderating effects of coping on the relationship between stress and the development of new brain lesions in multiple sclerosis. *Psychosomatic Medicine, 64*, 803–809.

Molloy, G., Perkins-Porras, L., Strike, P., & Steptoe, A. (2008). Type-D personality and cortisol in survivors of acute coronary syndrome. *Psychosomatic Medicine, 70*, 863–868.

Molnar, M., Potkin, S., Bunney, W., & Jones, E. (2003). MRNA expression patterns and distribution of white matter neurons in dorsolateral prefrontal cortex of depressed patients differ from those in schizophrenia patients. *Biological Psychiatry, 53*, 39–47.

Mombereau, C., Kaupmann, K., Froestl, W., Sansig, G., van der Putten, H., & Cryan, J. (2004). Genetic and pharmaceutical evidence of a role for GABA-sub(b) receptors in the modulation of anxiety- and antidepressant-like behavior. *Neuropsychopharmacology, 29*, 1050–1062.

Mondloch, C., & Maurer, D. (2004). Do small white balls squeak? Pitch-object correspondences in young children. *Cognitive, Affective, & Behavioral Neuroscience, 4*, 133–136.

Monk, T. H. (1989). Circadian rhythms in subjective activation, mood, and performance efficiency. In M. H. Kryger, T. Roth, & W. C. Dement (Eds.), *Principles and practice of sleep medicine* (pp. 163–172). Philadelphia: W. B. Saunders.

Montejo, A., Llorca, G., Izquierdo, J., & Rico-Villademoros, F. (2001). Incidence of sexual dysfunction associated with antidepressant agents: A prospective multicenter study of 1022 outpatients. *Journal of Clinical Psychiatry, 62*, 10–21.

Montgomery, G. (2003). Color blindness: More prevalent among males. *Seeing, Hearing, and Smelling the World.* Retrieved May 13, 2003, from *http://www.hhmi.org/senses/b130.html*

Montgomery, G. H., DuHamel, K. N., & Redd, W. H. (2000). A meta-analysis of hypnotically induced analgesia: How effective is hypnosis? *International Journal of Clinical Experimental Hypnosis, 48*, 138–153.

Montgomery, G., Weltz, C., Seltz, M., & Bovbjerg, D. (2002). Brief presurgery hypnosis reduces distress and pain in excisional breast biopsy patients. *International Journal of Clinical & Experimental Hypnosis, 50*, 17–32.

Montoya, M. (2008). I'm hot, so I'd say you're not: The influence of objective physical attractiveness on mate selection. *Personality and Social Psychology Bulletin, 34*, 1315–1331.

Moran, M. G., & Stoudemire, A. (1992). Sleep disorders in the medically ill patient. *Journal of Clinical Psychiatry, 53*(6, Suppl.), 29–36.

Moreno, R., Mayer, R. E., Spires, H., & Lester, J. (2001). The case for social agency in computer-based teaching: Do students learn more deeply when they interact with animated pedagogical agents? *Cognition and Instruction, 19*, 177–213.

Morewedge, C., & Norton, M. (2009). When dreaming is believing: The (motivated) interpretation of dreams. *Journal of Personality and Social Psychology, 96*, 249–264.

Morgan, C. D., & Murray, H. A. (1935). A method for investigating fantasies: The Thematic Apperception Test. *Archives of Neurology and Psychiatry, 34*, 289–306.

Morgan, C. D., & Murray, H. A. (1962). Thematic Apperception Test. In H. A. Murray et al. (Eds.), *Explorations in personality: A clinical and experimental study of fifty men of college age* (pp. 530–545). New York: Science Editions.

Morgan, C. L. (1996). Odors as cues for the recall of words unrelated to odor. *Perceptual and Motor Skills, 83*, 1227–1234.

Morgan, R. E., Levitsky, D. A., & Strupp, B. J. (2000). Effects of chronic lead exposure on learning and reaction time in a visual discrimination task. *Neurotoxicology and Teratology, 22*, 337–345.

Morgan, R., & Flora, D. (2002). Group psychotherapy with incarcerated offenders: A research synthesis. *Group Dynamics: Theory, Research, and Practice, 6*, 203–218.

Morgenthaler, T., Lee-Chiong, T., Alessi, C., Friedman, L., Aurora, R., Boehlecke, B., Brown, T., Chesson, A., Kapur, V., Maganti, R., Owens, J., Pancer, J., Swick, T., & Zak, R. (2007). Practice parameters for the clinical evaluation and treatment of circadian rhythm sleep disorders: An American Academy of Sleep Medicine report. *Sleep: Journal of Sleep and Sleep Disorders Research, 30*, 1445–1459.

Morofushi, M., Shinohara, K., Funabashi, T., & Kimura, F. (2000). Positive relationship between menstrual synchrony and ability to smell 5alpha-androst-16-en-3alpha-ol. *Chemical Senses, 25*, 407–411.

Morra, S., Gobbo, C., Marini, Z., & Sheese, R. (2008). *Cognitive development: Neo-Piagetian perspectives.* New York: Taylor & Francis Group/Lawrence Erlbaum Associates.

Morris, J. S., Frith, C. D., Perrett, D. I., Rowland, D., Young, A. W., Calder, A. J., & Dolan, R. J. (1996). A differential neural response in the human amygdala to fearful and happy facial expressions. *Nature, 383*, 812–815.

Morsella, E., Krieger, S., & Bargh, J. (2010). Minimal neuroanatomy for a conscious brain: Homing in on the networks constituting consciousness. *Neural Networks, 23*, 14–15.

Mos'cicki, E. K. (1995). Epidemiology of suicidal behavior. *Suicide and Life-Threatening Behavior, 25*, 22–31.

Moser, G., & Robin, M. (2006). Environmental annoyances: An urban-specific threat to quality of life? *European Review of Applied Psychology, 56*, 35–41.

Mosher, W., Chandra, A., & Jones, J. (2005). Sexual behavior and selected health measures: Men and women 15–44 years of age, United States, 2002. *Advance Data from Vital and Health Statistics, 362*, 1–56.

Moss, T., Sacco, K., Allen, T., Weinberger, A., Vessicchio, J., & George, T. (2009). Prefrontal cognitive dysfunction is associated with tobacco dependence treatment failure in smokers with schizophrenia. *Drug and Alcohol Dependence, 104*, 94–99.

Most, S., Simons, D., Scholl, B., Jimenez, R., Clifford, E., & Chabris, C. (2001). How not to be seen: The contribution of similarity and selective ignoring to sustained inattentional blindness. *Psychological Science, 12*, 9–17.

Mourtazaev, M. S., Kemp, B., Zwinderman, A. H., & Kamphuisen, H. A. C. (1995). Age and gender affect different characteristics of slow waves in the sleep EEG. *Sleep, 18*, 557–564.

Moynihan, J., Larson, M., Treanor, J., Dubersetein, P., Power, A., Shre, B., et al. (2004). Psychosocial factors and the response to influenza vaccination in older adults. *Psychosomatic Medicine, 66*, 950–953.

Moynihan, R., & Cassels, A. (2005). *Selling sickness: How the world's biggest pharmaceutical companies are turning us all into patients.* New York: Nation Books.

Mufson, L., Gallagher, T., Dorta, K., & Young, J. (2004). A group adaptation of interpersonal psychotherapy for depressed adolescents. *American Journal of Psychotherapy, 58*, 220–237.

Mukerjee, M. (1997). Trends in animal research. *Scientific American, 276*, 86–93.

Mukherjee, R., & Turk, J. (2004). Fetal alcohol syndrome. *Lancet, 363*, 1556.

Muller, L. (2002). Group counseling for African American males: When all you have are European American counselors. *Journal for Specialists in Group Work, 27*, 299–313.

Mumtaz, S., & Humphreys, G. (2002). The effect of Urdu vocabulary size on the acquisition of single word reading in English. *Educational Psychology, 22*, 165–190.

Munarriz, R., Talakoub, L., Flaherty, E., Gioia, M., Hoag, L., Kim, N., et al. (2002). Androgen replacement therapy with dehydroepiandrosterone for androgen insufficiency and female sexual dysfunction: Androgen and questionnaire results. *Journal of Sex & Marital Therapy, 28*, 165–173.

Munroe, R. H., Shimmin, H. S., & Munroe, R. L. (1984). Gender role understanding and sex role preference in four cultures. *Developmental Psychology, 20*, 673–682.

Munzar, P., Li, H., Nicholson, K., Wiley, J., & Balster, R. (2002). Enhancement of the discriminative stimulus effects of phencyclidine by the tetracycline antibiotics doxycycline and minocycline in rats. *Psychopharmacology, 160*, 331–336.

Murphy, E. (2003). Being born female is dangerous to your health. *American Psychologist, 58*, 205–210.

Murray, B. (2002). Finding the peace within us. *APA Monitor on Psychology, 33*, 56–57.

Murray, D. (2009). Infectious diseases. In C., Rudolph, A., Rudolph, M., Hostetter, G., Lister, & N. Siegel (Eds.), *Rudolph's pediatrics* (22nd ed.) (pp. 867–1174). New York: McGraw-Hill.

Murray, H. (1938). *Explorations in personality.* New York: Oxford University Press.

Murray, J., Liotti, M., Ingmundson, P., Mayburg, H., Pu, Y., Zamarripa, F., et al. (2006). Children's brain activations while viewing televised violence revealed by fMRI. *Media Psychology, 8*, 24–37.

Must, O., te Njienhuis, J., Must, A., & van Vianen, A. (2009). Comparablity of IQ scores over time. *Intelligence, 37*, 25–33.

Mustanski, B., Chivers, M., & Bailey, J. (2002). A critical review of recent biological research on human sexual orientation. *Annual Review of Sex Research, 13*, 89–140.

Myers, D. G., & Bishop, G. D. (1970). Discussion effects on racial attitudes. *Science, 169*, 778–779.

Nader, K. 2003. Re-recording human memories. *Nature, 425*, 571–572.

Nadon, R., Hoyt, I. P., Register, P. A., & Kilstrom, J. F. (1991). Absorption and hypnotizability: Context effects reexamined. *Journal of Personality and Social Psychology, 60*, 144–153.

Namie, G., & Namie, R. (2000). Naperville, IL: Sourcebooks.

Narita, M., Kaneko, C., Miyoshi, K., Nagumo, Y., Kuzumaki, N., Nakajima, M., et al. (2006). Chronic pain induces anxiety with concomitant changes in opioidergic function in the amygdala. *Neuropsychopharmacology, 31*, 739–750.

Narr, K., Woods, R., Thompson, P., Szeszko, P., Robinson, D., Dimtcheva, T., Gurbani, M., Toga, A., & Bilder, R. (2007). Relationships between IQ and regional cortical gray matter thickness in healthy adults. *Cerebral Cortex, 17*, 2163–2171.

Narvaez, D. (2002). Does reading moral stories build character? *Educational Psychology Review, 14*, 155–171.

Nash, M. (1987). What, if anything, is regressed about hypnotic age regression? A review of the empirical literature. *Psychological Bulletin, 102*, 42–52.

Nash, M. R. (1991). Hypnosis as a special case of psychological regression. In S. J. Lynn & J. W. Rhue (Eds.), *Theories of hypnosis: Current models and perspectives* (pp. 171–194). New York: Guilford.

Nash, M., & Baker, E. (1984, February). Trance encounters: Susceptibility to hypnosis. *Psychology Today*, pp. 18, 72–73.

National Alliance for Mental Illness (NAMI). (2003). *Panic disorder.* Retrieved July 19, 2006, from *http://www.nami.org/Template.cfm? Section=By_Illness&Template=/TaggedPage/TaggedPageDisplay.cfm& TPLID=54&ContentID=23050*

National Cancer Institute. (2000). *Questions and answers about smoking cessation.* Retrieved January 29, 2003, from *http://cis.nci.nih .gov/fact/8_13.htm*

National Center for Chronic Disease Prevention and Health Promotion. (2006). *The health consequences of involuntary exposure to tobacco smoke: A report of the surgeon general.* Retrieved July 7, 2006, from *http://www.cdc.gov/TOBACCO/sgr/sgr_2006/ index.htm*

National Center for Health Statistics (NCHS). (2000). *Health, United States, 2000 with adolescent health chartbook.* Retrieved June 10, 2007 from *http://www.cdc.gov/nchs/data/hus/hus00.pdf*

National Center for Health Statistics (NCHS). (2002). *Fast stats A to Z: Mental health.* [Online fact sheet]. Retrieved November 9, 2002, from *http://www.cdc.gov/nchs/fastats/mental.htm*

National Center for Health Statistics (NCHS). (2004a). *Health in the U.S. 2004.* Retrieved February 1, 2005, from *http://www.cdc.gov/nchs/hus.htm*

National Center for Health Statistics (NCHS). (2004b). *Prevalence of overweight and obesity among adults: United States, 1999–2002.* Retrieved February 1, 2005, from *http://www.cdc.gov/nchs/ products/pubs/pubd/hestats/obese/obse99.htm*

National Center for Health Statistics (NCHS). (2005). *Health, United States, 2005.* Retrieved July 5, 2006, from *http://www.cdc.gov/ nchs/data/hus/hus05.pdf#053*

National Center for Education Statistics (NCES). (2006). *Digest of Education Statistics, 2005.* Retrieved January 31, 2009 from *http://nces.ed.gov/programs/digest/d06/index.asp.*

National Center for Education Statistics (NCES). (2006). *Digest of Education Statistics, 2005.* Retrieved November 28, 2006 from *http://nces.ed.gov/fastfacts/display.asp?id=98*National Center for Health Statistics (NCHS). (2006a). *Health, United States, 2006.* Retrieved February 12, 2007, from *http://www.cdc .gov/nchs/data/hus/hus06.pdf#046*

National Center for Health Statistics (NCHS). (2006b). *Teen births.* Retrieved January 28, 2007, from *http://www.cdc.gov/nchs/fastats/ teenbrth.htm*

National Center for Education Statistics (NCES). (2008). *Digest of Education Statistics, 2007.* Retrieved January 31, 2009 from *http://nces.ed.gov/programs/digest/d07/index.asp.*

National Center for Health Statistics (NCHS). (2008). *Prevalence of overweight, obesity and extreme obesity among adults: United States, trends 1976–1980 through 2005–2006.* Retrieved June 1, 2009 from *http://www.cdc.gov/nchs/products/pubs/pubd/hestats/overweight/overweight_adult.pdf.*

National Center for Health Statistics (NCHS). (2010). *Health, United States, 2009.* Retrieved March 12, 2010 from *http://www.cdc.gov/nchs/data/hus/hus09.pdf#062*

National Health and Nutrition Examination Survey (NHANES). (2002). *NHANES 2001-2002.* Retrieved March 24, 2010 *http://www.cdc.gov/nchs/nhanes/nhanes01-02.htm*

National Highway and Traffic Safety Administration (NHTSA). (2007). *Alcohol poisoning.* Retrieved February 7, 2007, from *http://www.nhtsa.dot.gov/PEOPLE/outreach/safesobr/15qp/web/idalc.html*

National Institute of Mental Health. (1999b). *The invisible disease—depression.* Retrieved June 10, 2007 from *http://www.nimh.nih.gov/publicat/invisible.cfm*

National Institute of Mental Health (NIMH). (2001). *The numbers count: Mental disorders in America (NIMH Report No. 01–4584).* Washington, DC: Author.

National Institute of Mental Health (NIMH). (2009). *Suicide in the U.S.: Statistics and prevention.* Retrieved June 11, 2009 from *http://www.nimh.nih.gov/health/publications/suicide-in-the-us-statistics-and-prevention/index.shtml*

National Institute of Neurological Disorders and Stroke rt-PA Stroke Study Group. (1995). Tissue plasminogen activator for acute ischemic stroke. *New England Journal of Medicine, 333,* 1581–1587.

National Institute on Aging. (2001). Progress report on Alzheimer's Disease: Taking the next steps. Silver Spring, MD: Alzheimer's Disease Education and Referral Center (ADEAR) of the National Institute on Aging.

National Institute on Drug Abuse (NIDA). (2001). *Ecstasy: What we know and don't know about MDMA: A scientific review.* Retrieved October 17, 2003, from *http://www.nida.nih.gov/Meetings/MDMA/MDMAExSummary.html*

National Science Foundation (NSF). (2000a). *Characteristics of scientists and engineers in the United States: 1999.* Washington, DC: Author. Retrieved April 25, 2006, from *http://srsstats.sbe.nsf.gov/preformatted-tables/1999/DST1999.html*

National Science Foundation (NSF). (2002). *Science and engineering: Indicators 2002.* Retrieved January 29, 2003, from *http://www.nsf.gov/sbc/srs/seind02/toc.htm*

Nawrot, M., Nordenstrom, B., & Olson, A. (2004). Disruption of eye movements by ethanol intoxication affects perception of depth from motion parallax. *Psychological Science, 15,* 858–865.

Needleman, H. L., Riess, J. A., Tobin, M. J., Biesecker, G. E., & Greenhouse, J. B. (1996). Bone lead levels and delinquent behavior. *Journal of the American Medical Association, 275,* 363–369.

Neimark, E. D. (1981). Confounding with cognitive style factors: An artifact explanation for the apparent nonuniversal incidence of formal operations. In I. Sigel, D. Brodzinsky, & R. Golinkoff (Eds.), *New directions in Piagetian research and theory.* Hillsdale, NJ: Erlbaum.

Neisser, U., & Harsch, N. (1992). Phantom flashbulbs: False recollections of hearing the news about *Challenger.* In E. Winograd & U. Neisser (Eds.), *Affect and accuracy in recall: Studies of "flashbulb" memories* (pp. 9–31). New York: Cambridge University Press.

Neisser, U., Boodoo, G., Bouchard, T. J., Jr., Boykin, A. W., Brody, N., Ceci, S. J., et al. (1996). Intelligence: Knowns and unknowns. *American Psychologist, 51,* 77–101.

Neitz, J., Neitz, M., & Kainz, M. (1996). Visual pigment gene structure and the severity of color vision defects. *Science, 274,* 801–804.

Neitz, M., & Neitz, J. (1995). Numbers and ratios of visual pigment genes for normal red-green color vision. *Science, 267,* 1013–1016.

Nelson, J. C. (1997). Safety and tolerability of the new antidepressants. *Journal of Clinical Psychiatry, 58*(6, Suppl.), 26–31.

Nelson, T. (1996). Consciousness and metacognition. *American Psychologist, 51,* 102–116.

Nestadt, G., Samuels, J., Riddle, M., Bienvenu, J., Liang, K., LaBuda, M., Walkup, J., Grados, M., & Hoehn-Saric, R. (2000). A family study of obsessive-compulsive disorder. *Archives of General Psychiatry, 57,* 358–363.

Nestor, P., Graham, K., Bozeat, S., Simons, J., & Hodges, J. (2002). Memory consolidation and the hippocampus: Further evidence from studies of autobiographical memory in semantic dementia and frontal variant frontotemporal dementia. *Neuropsychologia, 40,* 633–654.

Neumann, I. (2008). Brain oxytocin: A key regulator of emotional and social behaviours in both females and males. *Journal of Neuroendocrinology, 20,* 858–865.

Newberg, A. (2010). The neurobiology of meditation. In D. Monti, & B. Beitman, (Eds.), *Integrative psychiatry: Well integrative medicine library;* (pp. 339–358). New York: Oxford University Press.

Newberg, A., Alavi, A. Baime, M., Pourdehnad, M., Santanna, J. d'Aquili. E. (2001). The measurement of cerebral blood flow during the complex cognitive task of meditation: A preliminary SPECT study. *Psychiatry Research: Neuroimaging, 106,* 113–122.

Newell, B., Lagnado, D., & Shanks, D. (2007). *Straight choices: The psychology of decision making.* New York: Psychology Press.

Newell, B., & Shanks, D. (2003). Take the best or look at the rest? Factors influencing "one-reason" decision making. *Journal of Experimental Psychology: Learning, Memory, and Cognition, 29,* 53–65.

Newell, B., & Shanks, D. (2004). On the role of recognition in decision making. *Journal of Experimental Psychology: Learning, Memory and Cognition, 30,* 923–935.

Newell, P., & Cartwright, R. (2000). Affect and cognition in dreams: A critique of the cognitive role in adaptive dream functioning and support for associative models. *Psychiatry: Interpersonal & Biological Processes, 63,* 34–44.

Nguyen, P. V., Abel, T., & Kandel, E. R. (1994). Requirement of a critical period of transcription for induction of a late phase of LTP. *Science, 265,* 1104–1107.

Nickerson, R. S., & Adams, M. J. (1979). Long-term memory for a common object. *Cognitive Psychology, 11,* 287–307.

Nicol, S. E., & Gottesman, I. I. (1983). Clues to the genetics and neurobiology of schizophrenia. *American Scientist, 71,* 398–404.

Nieto-Hernandez, R., Rubin, G., Cleare, A., Weinman, J., & Wessely, S. (2008). Can evidence change belief? Reported mobile phone sensitivity following individual feedback of an inability to discriminate active from sham signals. *Journal of Psychosomatic Research, 65,* 453–460.

Nigg, J., & Breslau, N. (2007). Prenatal smoking exposure, low birth weight, and disruptive behavior disorders. *Child & Adolescent Psychiatry, 46,* 362–369.

Nisbett, R. E., & Wilson, T. D. (1977). The halo effect: Evidence for unconscious alteration of judgments. *Journal of Personality and Social Psychology, 35,* 250–256.

Nishida, M., Pearsall, J., Buckner, R., & Walker, M. (2008). REM sleep, prefrontal theta, and the consolidation of human emotional memory. *Cerebral Cortex, 19,* 1158–1166.

Niyuhire, F., Varvel, S., Martin, B., & Lichtman, A. (2007). Exposure to marijuana smoke impairs memory retrieval in mice. *Journal of Pharmacology and Experimental Therapeutics, 322,* 1067–1075.

Nogrady, H., McConkey, K. M., & Perry, C. (1985). Enhancing visual memory: Trying hypnosis, trying imagination, and trying again. *Journal of Abnormal Psychology, 94,* 195–204.

Noise Pollution Council. (2003). *Comparing standards for safe noise exposure.* Retrieved May 16, 2003, from *http://www.nonoise.org/hearing/exposure/standardschart.htm*

Nordentoft, M., Lou, H. C., Hansen, D., Nim, J., Pryds, O., Rubin, P., et al. (1996). Intrauterine growth retardation and premature delivery: The influence of maternal smoking and psychosocial factors. *American Journal of Public Health, 86,* 347–354.

Noriko, S. (2004). Identity development pre- and post-empty nest women. *Japanese Journal of Developmental Psychology, 15,* 52–64.

Norman, S., Norman, G., Rossi, J., & Prochaska, J. (2006). Identifying high- and low-success smoking cessation subgroups using signal detection analysis. *Addictive Behaviors, 31,* 31–41.

Norman, W. (1963). Toward an adequate taxonomy of personality attributes: Replicated factor structure in peer nomination personality ratings. *Journal of Abnormal & Social Psychology, 66,* 574–583.

Norris, J. E., & Tindale, J. A. (1994). *Among generations: The cycle of adult relationships.* New York: Freeman.

Norton, M., Moniu, B., Cooper, J., & Hogg, M. (2003). Vicarious dissonance: Attitude change from the inconsistency of others. *Journal of Personality & Social Psychology, 85,* 47–62.

Noyes, R., Jr., Burrows, G. D., Reich, J. H., Judd, F. K., Garvey, M. J., Norman, T. R., et al. (1996). Diazepam versus alprazolam for the treatment of panic disorder. *Journal of Clinical Psychiatry, 57,* 344–355.

Nunn, J., Gregory, L., Brammer, M., Williams, S., Parslow, D., Morgan, M., Morris, R., Bullmore, E., Baron-Cohen, S., & Gray, J. (2002). Functional magnetic resonance imaging of synesthesia: Activation of V4/V8 by spoken words. *Nature Neuroscience, 5,* 371–375.

Nutt, D. (2000). Treatment of depression and concomitant anxiety. *European Neuropsychopharmacology, 10* (Suppl. 4), S433–S437.

Nyberg, L., Eriksson, J., Larsson, A., & Marklund, P. (2006). Learning by doing versus learning by thinking. An fMRI study of motor and mental training. *Neuropsychologia, 44,* 711–717.

O'Brien, C. P. (1996). Recent developments in the pharmacotherapy of substance abuse. *Journal of Consulting and Clinical Psychology, 64,* 677–686.

O'Kane, G., Kensinger, E., & Corkin, S. (2004). Evidence for semantic learning in profound amnesia: An investigation with patient H. M. *Hippocampus, 14,* 417–425.

O'Leary, K. D., & Smith, D. A. (1991). Marital interactions. *Annual Review of Psychology, 42,* 191–212.

Ogawa, A., Mizuta, I., Fukunaga, T., Takeuchi, N., Honaga, E., Sugita, Y., Mikami, A., Inoue, Y., & Takeda, M. (2004). Electrogastrography abnormality in eating disorders. *Psychiatry & Clinical Neurosciences, 58,* 300–310.

Ohman, A., & Mineka, S. (2003). The malicious serpent: Snakes as a prototypical stimulus for an evolved module of fear. *Current Directions in Psychological Science, 12,* 5–8.

Okura, Y., Akira, M., Kuniko, K., Park, I., Matthias, S., & Matsumoto, Y. (2006). Nonviral amyloid-beta DNA vaccine therapy against Alzheimer's disease: Long-term effects and safety. *Proceedings of the National Academy of Sciences, 103,* 9619–9624.

Olatunji, B., Lohr, J, Sawchuk, C., & Tolin, D. (2007). Multimodal assessment of disgust in contamination-related obsessive-compulsive disorder. *Behaviour Research and Therapy, 45,* 263–276.

Oliver, J. E. (1993). Intergenerational transmission of child abuse: Rates, research, and clinical implications. *American Journal of Psychiatry, 150,* 1315–1324.

Olson, M., Krantz, D., Kelsey, S., Pepine, C., Sopko, G., Handberg, E., Rogers, W., Gierach, G., McClure, C., & Merz, C. (2005). Hostility scores are associated with increased risk of cardiovascular events in women undergoing coronary angiography: A report from the NHLBI-sponsored WISE study. *Psychosomatic Medicine, 67,* 546–552.

Ono, H. (2003). Women's economic standing, marriage timing and cross-national contexts of gender. *Journal of Marriage & Family, 65,* 275–286.

Ophir, E., Nass, C., & Wagner, A. (2009). Cognitive control in media multitaskers. *PNAS Proceedings of the National Academy of Sciences of the United States of America, 106,* 15583–15587.

Oquendo, M., Placidi, G., Malone, K., Campbell, C., Kelp, J., Brodsky, B., et al. (2003). Positron emission tomography of regional brain metabolic responses to a serotonergic challenge and lethality of suicide attempts in major depression. *Archives of General Psychiatry, 60,* 14–22.

Orban, P., Peigneux, P., Lungu, O., Albouy, G., Breton, E., Laberenne, F., Benali, H., Maquet, P., & Doyon, J. (2009). The multifaceted nature of the relationship between performance and brain activity in motor sequence learning. *Neuroimage, 49,* 694–702.

Orman, M. (1996). *How to conquer public speaking fear.* Retrieved February 15, 2003, from *http://www.stresscure.com/jobstress/speak.html*

Ortega-Alvaro, A., Gilbert-Rahola, J., & Micó, J. (2006). Influence of chronic treatment with olanzapine, clozapine, and scopolamine on performance of a learned 8-arm radial maze task in rats. *Progress in Neuro-Psychopharmacology & Biological Psychiatry, 30,* 104–111.

Osborn, D., Fletcher, A., Smeeth, L., Sitrling, S., Bulpitt, C., Breeze, E., et al. (2003). Factors associated with depression in a representative sample of 14,217 people aged 75 and over in the United Kingdom: Results from the MRC trial of assessment and management of older people in the community. *International Journal of Geriatric Psychiatry, 18,* 623–630.

Öst, L-G., & Westling, B. E. (1995). Applied relaxation vs. cognitive behavior therapy in the treatment of panic disorder. *Behavior Research and Therapy, 33,* 145–158.

Ostrom, T. M., Carpenter, S. L., Sedikides, C., & Li, F. (1993). Differential processing of in-group and out-group information. *Journal of Personality and Social Psychology, 64,* 21–34.

Otto, M. W., Pollack, M. H., Sachs, G. S., Reiter, S. R., Meltzer-Brody, S., & Rosenbaum, J. F. (1993). Discontinuation of benzodiazepine treatment: Efficacy of cognitive-behavioral therapy for patients with panic disorder. *American Journal of Psychiatry, 150,* 1485–1490.

Overby, K. (2002). Pediatric health supervision. In A. Rudolph, R. Kamei, & K. Overby (Eds.), *Rudolph's fundamentals of pediatrics* (3rd ed., pp. 1–69). New York: McGraw-Hill.

Overmeier, J. B., & Seligman, M. E. P. (1967). Effects of inescapable shock upon subsequent escape and avoidance responding. *Journal of Comparative and Physiological Psychology, 67,* 28–33.

Owen, M., & O'Donovan, M. (2003). Schizophrenia and genetics. In R. Plomin, J. Defries, I. Craig, & P. McGuffin (Eds.), *Behavioral genetics in the postgenomic era* (pp. 463–480). Washington, DC: American Psychological Association.

Ozcan, L., Ergin, A., Lu, A., Chung, J., Sarkar, S., Nie, D., Myers, M., & Ozcan, U. (2009). Endoplasmic reculum stress plays a central role in development of leptin resistance. *Cell Metabolism, 9,* 35–51.

Pöysti, L., Rajalin, S., & Summala, H. (2005). Factors influencing the use of cellular (mobile) phone during driving and hazards while using it. *Accident Analysis & Prevention, 37,* 47–51.

Packard, M. (2009). Anxiety, cognition, and habit: A multiple memory systems perspective. *Brain Research, 1293,* 121–128.

Page-Gould, E., Mendoza-Denton, R., & Tropp, L. (2008). With a little help from my cross-group friend: Reducing anxiety in intergroup contexts through cross-group friendshps. *Journal of Personality and Social Psychology, 95,* 1080–1094.

Pais, S. (2009). A systemic approach to the treatment of dissociative identity disorder. *Journal of Family Psychotherapy, 20,* 72–88.

Paivio, S. C., & Greenberg, L. S. (1995). Resolving "unfinished business": Efficacy of experiential therapy using empty-chair dialogue. *Journal of Consulting and Clinical Psychology, 63,* 419–425.

Pal, S. (2005). Prevalence of chronic pain and migraine. *U.S. Pharmacist, 3,* 12–15.

Palinscar, A. S., & Brown, A. L. (1984). Reciprocal teaching of comprehension-fostering and comprehension-monitoring activities. *Cognition and Instruction, 1,* 117–175.

Panksepp, J. (2010). Evolutionary substrates of addiction: The neurochemistries of pleasure seeking and social bonding in the mammalian brain. In J. Kassel, (Ed.), *Substance abuse and emotion* (pp. 137–167). Washington, DC: American Psychological Association.

Pansu, P., & Gilibert, D. (2002). Effect of causal explanations on work-related judgments. *Applied Psychology: An International Review, 51,* 505–526.

Papousek, I., & Schulter, G. (2002). Covariations of EEG asymmetries and emotional states indicate that activity at frontopolar locations is particularly affected by state factors. *Psychophysiology, 39,* 350–360.

Paquette, D. (2004). Dichotomizing paternal and maternal functions as a means to better understand their primary contributions. *Human Development, 47,* 237–238.

Paraherakis, A., Charney, D., & Gill, K. (2001). Neuropsychological functioning in substance-dependent patients. *Substance Use & Misuse, 36,* 257–271.

Parke, R. D. (1977). Some effects of punishment on children's behavior—revisited. In E. M. Hetherington, E. M. Ross, & R. D. Parke (Eds.), *Contemporary readings in child psychology.* New York: McGraw-Hill.

Parker, K. (2009). *The harried life of the working mother.* Retrieved February 27, 2010 from *http://pewsocialtrends.org/pubs/745/the-harried-life-of-the-working-mother.*

Parkinson, W. L., & Weingarten, H. P. (1990). Dissociative analysis of ventromedial hypothalamic obesity syndrome. *American Journal of Physiology, 259,* 829–835.

Parry, R. (2010, March 16). *Contestants turn torturers in French TV experiment.* Retrieved March 24, 2010 from *http://news.yahoo.com/s/afp/20100316/ts_afp/francetelevisionpsychologyentertainment.*

Partinen, M., Hublin, C., Kaprio, J., Koskenvuo, M., & Guilleminault, C. (1994). Twin studies in narcolepsy. *Sleep, 17,* S13–S16.

Parvizi, J., & Damasio, A. (2001). Consciousness and the brainstem. *Cognition, 79,* 135–159.

Pascual-Leone, A., Dhuna, A., Altafullah, I., & Anderson, D. C. (1990). Cocaine-induced seizures. *Neurology, 40,* 404–407.

Passaro, E. (2009). *Insomnia.* Retrieved February 5, 2010 from *http://emedicine.medscape.com/article/1187829-overview.*

Pastore, N. (1950). The role of arbitrariness in the frustration-aggression hypothesis. *Journal of Abnormal and Social Psychology, 47,* 728–731.

Patterson, C. J. (1995). Sexual orientation and human development: An overview. *Developmental Psychology, 31,* 3–11.

Patterson, D. (2004). Treating pain with hypnosis. *Current Directions in Psychological Science, 13,* 252–255.

Paul, T., Schroeter, K., Dahme, B., & Nutzinger, D. (2002). Self-injurious behavior in women with eating disorders. *American Journal of Psychiatry, 159,* 408–411.

Paul, W. E. (1993). Infectious diseases and the immune system. *Scientific American, 269,* 90–99.

Paulhus, D., Harms, P., Bruce, M., & Lysy, D. (2003). The over-claiming technique: Measuring self-enhancement independent of ability. *Journal of Personality & Social Psychology, 84,* 890–904.

Paulus, P. B., Cox, V. C., & McCain, G. (1988). *Prison crowding: A psychological perspective.* New York: Springer-Verlag.

Paunonen, S. V., Keinonen, M., Trzebinski, J., Forsterling, F., Grishenko-Roze, N., Kouznetsova, L., et al. (1996). The structure of personality in six cultures. *Journal of Cross-Cultural Psychology, 27,* 339–353.

Pause, B. (2004). Are androgen steroids acting as pheromones in humans? *Physiology & Behavior, 83,* 21–29.

Pavlov, I. P. (1927/1960). *Conditioned reflexes: An investigation of the physiological activity of the cerebral cortex* (G. V. Anrep, Trans.). New York: Dover. (Original translation published 1927).

Payami, H., Montee, K., & Kaye, J. (1994). Evidence for familial factors that protect against dementia and outweigh the effect of increasing age. *American Journal of Human Genetics, 54,* 650–657.

Pedersen, A., Zachariae, R., Jensen, A., Bovbjerg, D., Andersen, O., & von der Masse, H. (2009). Psychological stres predicts the risk of febrile episodes in cancer patients during chemotherapy. *Psychotherapy and Psychosomatics, 78,* 258–260.

Pedersen, D. M., & Wheeler, J. (1983). The Müller-Lyer illusion among Navajos. *Journal of Social Psychology, 121,* 3–6.

Pedersen, S., & Denollet, J. (2003). Type D personality, cardiac events, and impaired quality of life: A review. *European Journal of Cardiovascular Prevention and Rehabilitation, 10,* 241–248.

Pederson, S., Van Domburg, R., & Theuns, D. (2004). Type D personality is associated with increased anxiety and depressive symptoms in patients with an implantable cardioverter defibrillator and their partners. *Psychosomatic Medicine, 66,* 714–719.

Peeters, M., & Oerlemans, W. (2009). The relationship between acculturation orientations and work-related well-being: Differences between ethnic minority and majority employees. *International Journal of Stress Management, 16,* 1–24.

Penfield, W. (1969). Consciousness, memory, and man's conditioned reflexes. In K. Pribram (Ed.), *On the biology of learning* (pp. 129–168). New York: Harcourt Brace Jovanovich.

Pennebaker, J., & Seagal, J. (1999). Forming a story: The health benefits of narrative. *Journal of Clinical Psychology, 55,* 1243–1254.

Pennisi, E. (1997). Tracing molecules that make the brain–body connection. *Science, 275,* 930–931.

Peplau, L. (2003). Human sexuality: How do men and women differ? *Current Directions in Psychological Science, 12,* 37–40.

Pepperberg, I. (2006). Grey parrot *(Psittacus erithacus)* numerical abilities: Addition and further experiments on a zero-like concept. *Journal of Comparative Psychology, 120,* 1–11.

Pepperberg, I. M. (1991, Spring). Referential communication with an African grey parrot. *Harvard Graduate Society Newsletter,* 1–4.

Pepperberg, I. M. (1994a). Numerical competence in an African grey parrot (Psittacus erithacus). *Journal of Comparative Psychology, 108,* 36–44.

Pepperberg, I. M. (1994b). Vocal learning in grey parrots (Psittacus erithacus): Effects of social interaction, reference, and context. *The Auk, 111,* 300–314 .

Perez-Navarro, J., Lawrence, T., & Hume, I. (2009). Personality, mental state and procedure in the experimental replication of ESP: A preliminary study of new variables. *Journal of the Society for Psychical Research, 73,* 17–32.

Perls, F. S. (1969). *Gestalt therapy verbatim.* Lafayette, CA: Real People Press.

Perron, H., Mekaoui, L., Bernard, C., Veas, F., Stefas, I., & Leboyer, M. (2008). Endogenous retrovirus type W GAG and envelope protein antigenemia in serium of schizophrenic patients. *Biological Psychiatry, 64,* 1019–1023.

Perry, S., Wallace, N., & Wilhelm, I. (2005). Donations for victims of Katrina reach $404 million. *Chronicle of Philanthropy.* [Online edition] Retrieved October 29, 2006, from *http://philanthropy.com/free/update/2005/09/2005090201.htm.*

Pesonen, A., Raeikkoenen, K., Keskivaara, P., & Keltikangas-Jaervinen, L. (2003). Difficult temperament in childhood and adulthood: Continuity from maternal perceptions to self-ratings over 17 years. *Personality & Individual Differences, 34,* 19–31.

Peters, A., Leahu, D., Moss, M. B., & McNally, J. (1994). The effects of aging on area 46 of the frontal cortex of the rhesus monkey. *Cerebral Cortex, 6,* 621–635.

Peterson, A. C. (1987, September). Those gangly years. *Psychology Today,* 28–34.

Peterson, L. R., & Peterson, M. J. (1959). Short-term retention of individual verbal items. *Journal of Experimental Psychology, 58,* 193–198.

Petry, N. (2002). Psychosocial treatments for pathological gambling: Current status and future directions. *Psychiatric Annals, 32,* 192–196.

Petry, N., Tedford, J., Austin, M., Nich, C., Carroll, K., & Rounsaville, B. (2004). Prize reinforcement contingency management for treating cocaine users: How low can we go, and with whom? *Addiction, 99,* 349–360.

Pettus, A. (2006). Psychiatry by prescription. *Harvard Magazine, 108,* 38–44, 90–91. Retrieved July 8, 2006, from *http://www.harvardmagazine.com/on-line/070646.html*

Petty, R. E., Wegener, D. T., & Fabrigar, L. R. (1997). Attitudes and attitude change. *Annual Review of Psychology, 48,* 609–647.

Pew Research Center. (2006). *Global gender gaps.* Retrieved June 29, 2006, from *http://pewglobal.org/commentary/display.php?AnalysisID=90*

Phillips, K., Fulker, D. W., Carey, G., & Nagoshi, C. T. (1988). Direct marital assortment for cognitive and personality variables. *Behavioral Genetics, 18,* 347–356.

Phillips, S. T., & Ziller, R. C. (1997). Toward a theory and measure of the nature of nonprejudice. *Journal of Personality and Social Psychology, 72,* 420–434.

Piaget, J. (1927/1965). *The moral judgment of the child.* New York: Free Press.

Piaget, J. (1963). *Psychology of intelligence.* Patterson, NJ: Littlefield, Adams.

Piaget, J. (1964). *Judgment and reasoning in the child.* Patterson, NJ: Littlefield, Adams.

Piaget, J., & Inhelder, B. (1969). *The psychology of the child.* New York: Basic Books.

Piazza, M., & Dehaene, S. (2004). From number neurons to mental arithmetic: The cognitive neuroscience of number sense. In M. Gazzaniga (Ed.), *The cognitive neurosciences* (pp. 865–876). Cambridge, MA: MIT Press.

Pich, E. M., Pagliusi, S. R., Tessari, M., Talabot-Ayer, D., van Huijsduijnen, R. H., & Chiamulera, C. (1997). Common neural substrates for the addictive properties of nicotine and cocaine. *Science, 275,* 83–86.

Pieringer, W., Fazekas, C., & Pieringer, C. (2005). Schizophrenia: An existential disease. *Fortschritte der Neurologie, Psychiatrie, 73,* S25–S31.

Pigott, T. A. (1996). OCD: Where the serotonin selectivity story begins. *Journal of Clinical Psychiatry, 57*(6, Suppl.), 11–20.

Pihl, R. O., Lau, M. L., & Assaad, J-M. (1997). Aggressive disposition, alcohol, and aggression. *Aggressive Behavior, 23,* 11–18.

Pilcher, J. J., Lambert, B. J., & Huffcutt, A. I. (2000). Differential effects of permanent and rotating shifts on self-report sleep length: A meta-analytic review. *Sleep, 23,* 155–163.

Pillemer, D. B. (1990). Clarifying the flashbulb memory concept: Comment on McCloskey, Wible, and Cohen (1988). *Journal of Experimental Psychology: General, 119,* 92–96.

Pillow, D. R., Zautra, A. J., & Sandler, I. (1996). Major life events and minor stressors: Identifying mediational links in the stress process. *Journal of Personality and Social Psychology, 70,* 381–394.

Pillsworth, E., Haselton, M., & Buss, D. (2004). Ovulatory shifts in female sexual desire. *Journal of Sex Research, 41,* 55–65.

Pinel, J. (2007). *Basics of Biopsychology.* Boston: Allyn & Bacon.

Pinel, J. P. L. (2000). *Biopsychology* (4th ed.). Boston: Allyn & Bacon.

Pinikahana, J., Happell, B., & Keks, N. (2003). Suicide and schizophrenia: A review of literature for the decade (1990–1999) and implications for mental health nursing. *Issues in Mental Health Nursing, 24,* 27–43.

Pinker, S. (1994). *The language instinct: How the mind creates language.* New York: Morrow.

Pinker, S. (2007). *The stuff of thought: Language as a window into human nature.* New York: Viking.

Pinquart, M., & Sörensen, S. (2000). Influences of socioeconomic status, social network, and competence on subjective well-being in later life: A meta-analysis. *Psychology and Aging, 15,* 187–224.

Pittenger, D. J. (1993). The utility of the Myers-Briggs Type Indicator. *Review of Educational Research, 63,* 467–488.

Plaks, J., Grant, H., & Dweck, C. (2005). Violations of implicit theories and the sense of prediction and control: Implications for motivated person perception. *Journal of Personality & Social Psychology, 88,* 245–262.

Platek, S., Loughead, J., Gur, R., Busch, S., Ruparel, K., Phend, N., et al. (2006). Neural substrates for functionally discriminating self-face from personally familiar faces. *Human Brain Mapping, 27,* 91–98.

Platek, S., Thomson, J., & Gallup, G. (2004). Cross-modal self-recognition: The role of visual, auditory, and olfactory primes. *Consciousness and Cognition: An International Journal, 13,* 197–210.

Pleis, J., Lucas, J., & Ward, B. (2009). Summary health statistics for U.S. adults: National Health Interview Survey, 2008. *Vital and Health Statistics, 10,* 1–167.

Plomin, R., DeFries, J. C., & Fulker, D. W. (1988). *Nature and nurture during infancy and early childhood.* New York: Cambridge University Press.

Plomin, R., DeFries, J. C., McClearn, G. E., & Rutter, M. (1997). *Behavioral genetics* (3rd ed.). New York: Freeman.

Plomin, R., Defries, J., Craig, I., & McGuffin, P. (2003). *Behavioral genetics in the postgenomic era.* Washington, DC: American Psychological Association.

Plomin, R., Owen, M. J., & McGuffin, P. (1994). The genetic basis of complex human behaviors. *Science, 264,* 1733–1739.

Plotnik, J., de Waal, F., & Reiss, D. (2006). Self-recognition in an Asian elephant. *Proceedings of the National Academy of Science, 103,* 17053–17057.

Plumer, B. (2005, July). Licensed to ill. *Mother Jones.* [Online. No pages specified.] Retrieved July 25, 2006, from *http://www.motherjones.com/commentary/columns/2005/07/selling_sickness.html*

Poldrack, R., & Wagner, A. (2004). What can neuroimaging tell us about the mind? Insights from prefrontal cortex. *Current Directions in Psychological Science, 13,* 177–181.

Pontieri, F. C., Tanda, G., Orzi, F., & Di Chiara, G. (1996). Effects of nicotine on the nucleus accumbens and similarity to those of addictive drugs. *Nature, 382,* 255–257.

Popma, A., Vermeiren, R., Geluk, C., Rinne, T., van den Brink, W., Knol, D., Jansen, L., van Engeland, H., & Doreleijers, T. (2007). Cortisol moderates the relationship between testosterone and aggression in delinquent male adolescents. *Biological Psychiatry, 61,* 405–411.

Poponoe, D., & Whitehead, B. D. (2000). Sex without strings, relationships without rings: Today's young singles talk about mating and dating. In *National Marriage Project, The State of Our Unions, 2000.* Retrieved June 10, 2007 from *http://marriage.rutgers.edu/Publications/SOOU/NMPAR2000.pdf.*

Popper, K. (1972). *Objective knowledge: An evolutionary approach.* New York: Oxford University Press.

Porjesz, B., Begleiter, H., Reich, T., Van Eerdewegh, P., Edenberg, H., Foroud, T., et al. (1998). Amplitude of visual P3 event-related potential as a phenotypic marker for a predisposition to alcoholism: Preliminary results from the COGA project. *Alcoholism: Clinical & Experimental Research, 22,* 1317–1323.

Porrino, L. J., & Lyons, D. (2000). Orbital and medial prefrontal cortex and psychostimulant abuse: Studies in animal models. *Cerebral Cortex, 10,* 326–333.

Porte, H. S., & Hobson, J. A. (1996). Physical motion in dreams: One measure of three theories. *Sleep, 105,* 3329–3335.

Porter, F. L., Porges, S. W., & Marshall, R. E. (1988). Newborn pain cries and vagal tone: Parallel changes in response to circumcision. *Child Development, 59,* 495–505.

Porter, S., Bellhouse, S., McGougall, A., ten Brinke, L., & Wilson, K. (2010). A prospective investigation of the vulnerability of memory for positive and negative emotional scenes to the misinformation effect. *Canadian Journal of Behavioural Science, 42,* 55–61.

Posada, G., Jacobs, A., Richmond, M., Carbonell, O., Alzate, G., Bustamante, M., et al. (2002). Maternal caregiving and infant security in two cultures. *Developmental Psychology, 38,* 67–78.

Posner, M. I. (1996, September). Attention and psychopathology. *Harvard Mental Health Letter, 13*(3), 5–6.

Postman, L., & Phillips, L. W. (1965). Short-term temporal changes in free recall. *Quarterly Journal of Experimental Psychology, 17,* 132–138.

Potts, N. L. S., Davidson, J. R. T., & Krishman, K. R. R. (1993). The role of nuclear magnetic resonance imaging in psychiatric research. *Journal of Clinical Psychiatry, 54*(12, Suppl.), 13–18.

Poulin, M., & Cohen Silver, R. (2008). World benevolence beliefs and well-being across the life span. *Psychology and Aging, 23,* 13–23.

Powell, C., & Van Vugt, M. (2003). Genuine giving or selfish sacrifice? The role of commitment and cost level upon willingness to sacrifice. *European Journal of Social Psychology, 33,* 403–412.

Powell, L., Shahabi, L., & Thoresen, C. (2003). Religion and spirituality: Linkages to physical health. *American Psychologist, 58,* 36–52.

Power, F. C., Higgins, A., & Kohlberg, L. (1989). *Lawrence Kohlberg's approach to moral education.* New York: Columbia University Press.

Power, K. G., Sharp, D. M., Swanson, V., & Simpson, R. J. (2000). Therapist contact in cognitive behaviour therapy for panic disorder and agoraphobia in primary care. *Clinical Psychology & Psychotherapy, 7,* 37–46.

Powlishta, K. K. (1995). Intergroup processes in childhood: Social categorization and sex role development. *Developmental Psychology, 31,* 781–788.

Powsner, S., & Dufel, S. (2009). *Conversion disorder.* Retrieved March 17, 2010 from *http://emedicine.medscape.com/article/805361-overview.*

Poznanski, M., & Thagard, P. (2005). Changing personalities: Towards realistic virtual characters. *Journal of Experimental & Theoretical Artificial Intelligence, 17,* 221–241.

Prabhu, V., Porjesz, B., Chorlian, D., Wang, K., Stimus, A., & Begleiter, H. (2001). Visual P3 in female alcoholics. *Alcoholism: Clinical & Experimental Research, 25,* 531–539.

Prati, G., & Pietrantoni, L. (2009). Optimism, social support, and coping strategies as factors contributing to posttraumatic growth: A meta-analysis. *Journal of Loss and Trauma, 14,* 364–388.

Pratkanis, A. R. (1989). The cognitive representation of attitudes. In A. R. Pratkanis, S. J. Breckler, & A. G. Greenwald (Eds.), *Attitude structure and function* (pp. 71–93). Hillsdale, NJ: Erlbaum.

Preda, A., & Albucher, R. (2008). *Phobic disorders.* Retrieved March 15, 2010 from *http://emedicine.medscape.com/article/288016-overview.*

Premack, D. (1971). Language in chimpanzees. *Science, 172,* 808–822.

Premack, D., & Premack, A. J. (1983). *The mind of an ape.* New York: Norton.

Price, D., Finniss, D., & Benedetti, F. (2008). A comprehensive review of the placebo effect: Recent advances and current thought. *Annual Review of Psychology, 59,* 565–590.

Prien, R. F., & Kocsis, J. H. (1995). Long-term treatment of mood disorders. In F. E. Bloom & D. J. Kupfer (Eds.), *Psychopharmacology: The fourth generation of progress* (pp. 1067–1079). New York: Raven.

Prigerson, H. G., Bierhals, A. J., Kasl, S. V., Reynolds, C. F., III, Shear, M. K., Day, N., et al. (1997). Traumatic grief as a risk factor for mental and physical mortality. *American Journal of Psychiatry, 154,* 616–623.

Prinz, P. N., Vitiello, M. V., Raskind, M. A., & Thorpy, M. J. (1990). Geriatrics: Sleep disorders and aging. *New England Journal of Medicine, 323,* 520–526.

Pryke, S., Lindsay, R. C. L., & Pozzulo, J. D. (2000). Sorting mug shots: Methodological issues. *Applied Cognitive Psychology, 14,* 81–96.

Public Agenda Online. (2002). *The issues: Race.* Retrieved November 13, 2002, from *http://www.publicagenda.com/issues/overview.dfm?issue_type=race*

Public Health Agency of Canada. (2006). *Hearing loss info-sheet for seniors.* Retrieved December 13, 2006, from *http://www.phac-aspc.gc.ca/seniors-aines/pubs/info_sheets/hearing_loss/index.htm*

Putnam, F. W. (1989). *Diagnosis and treatment of multiple personality disorder.* New York: Guilford Press.

Putnam, F. W. (1992). Altered states: Peeling away the layers of a multiple personality. *The Sciences, 32,* 30–36.

Quaid, K., Aschen, S., Smiley, C., Nurnberger, J. (2001). Perceived genetic risks for bipolar disorder in patient population: An exploratory study. *Journal of Genetic Counseling, 10,* 41–51.

Querido, J., Warner, T., & Eyberg, S. (2002). Parenting styles and child behavior in African American families of preschool children. *Journal of Clinical Child & Adolescent Psychology, 31,* 272–277.

Quesnel, C., Savard, J., Simard, S., Ivers, H., & Morin, C. (2003). Efficacy of cognitive-behavioral therapy for insomnia in women treated for nonmetastatic breast cancer. *Journal of Consulting & Clinical Psychology, 71,* 189–200.

Quick, N., & Janik, V. (2008). Whistle rates of wild bottlenose dolphins (Tursiops truncatus): Influences of group size and behavior. *Journal of Comparative Psychology, 122,* 305–311.

Quill, T. (2007). Legal regulation of physician-assisted death: The latest report cards. *New England Journal of Medicine, 356,* 1911–1913.

Quiroga, T., Lemos-Britton, Z., Mostafapour, E., Abbott, R., & Berninger, V. (2002). Phonological awareness and beginning reading in Spanish-speaking ESL first graders: Research into practice. *Journal of School Psychology, 40,* 85–111.

Rönnqvist, L., & Domellöf, E. (2006). Quantitative assessment of right and left reaching movements in infants: A longitudinal study from 6 to 36 months. *Developmental Psychobiology, 48,* 444–459.

Rabinowitz, P. (2000). Noise-induced hearing loss. *American Family Physician, 61,* 1053.

Rachman, S. J., & Wilson, G. T. (1980). *The effects of psychological therapy* (2nd ed.). New York: Pergamon.

Raeikkoenen, K., Matthews, K., & Salomon, K. (2003). Hostility predicts metabolic syndrome risk factors in children and adolescents. *Health Psychology, 22,* 279–286.

Rahe, R. J., Meyer, M., Smith, M., Kjaer, G., & Holmes, T. H. (1964). Social stress and illness onset. *Journal of Psychosomatic Research, 8,* 35–44.

Rahman, Q. (2005). Fluctuating asymmetry, second to fourth finger length ratios and human sexual orientation. *Psychoneuroendocrinology, 30,* 382–391.

Rahman, Q., & Wilson, G. (2003). Born gay? The psychobiology of human sexual orientation. *Personality and Individual Differences, 34,* 1337–1382.

Raine, A. (1996). Autonomic nervous system factors underlying disinhibited, antisocial, and violent behavior: Biosocial perspectives and treatment implications. *Annals of the New York Academy of Sciences, 794,* 46–59.

Ralph, M. R. (1989, November/December). The rhythm maker: Pinpointing the master clock in mammals. *The Sciences, 29,* 40–45.

Ramey, C. (1993). A rejoinder to Spitz's critique of the Abecedarian experiment. *Intelligence, 17,* 25–30.

Ramey, C., & Campbell, F. (1987). The Carolina Abecedarian project. An educational experiment concerning human malleability. In J. J. Gallagher & C. T. Ramey (Eds.), *The malleability of children* (pp. 127–140). Baltimore: Brookes.

Ramey, C., & Ramey, S. (2004). Early learning and school readiness: Can early intervention make a difference? 471–491.

Ramey, S., Ramey, C., & Lanzi, R. (2007). In J., Jacobson, J., Mulick, & J. Rojahn (Eds.), *Handbook of intellectual and developmental disabilities: Issues in clinical child psychology* (pp. 445–463). New York: Springer Publishing Co.

Ramsay, D. S., & Woods, S. C. (1997). Biological consequences of drug administration: Implications for acute and chronic tolerance. *Psychological Review, 104,* 170–193.

Ramsey, J., Langlois, J., Hoss, R., Rubenstein, A., & Griffin, A. (2004). Origins of a stereotype: Categorization of facial attractiveness by 6-month-old infants. *Developmental Science, 7,* 201–211.

Rangaswamy, M., Jones, K., Porjesz, B., Chorlian, D., Padmanabhapillai, A., Karajan, C., Kuperman, S., Rohrbaugh, J., O'Connor, S., Bauer, L., Schuckit, M., & Begleiter, H. (2007). Delta and theta oscillations as risk markers in adolescent offspring of alcoholics. *International Journal of Psychophysiology, 63,* 3–15.

Ranjan, A., & Gentili, A. (2005). Primary insomnia. Retrieved December 16, 2006, from *http://www.emedicine.com/med/topic3128.htm*

Rantanen, J., Pulkkinen, L., & Kinnunen, U. (2005). The Big Five personality dimensions, work-family conflict, and psychological distress: A longitudinal view. *Journal of Individual Differences, 26,* 155–166.

Rapp, S., Espeland, M., Shumaker, S., Henderson, V., Brunner, R., Manson, J., et al. (2003). Effect of estrogen plus progestin on global cognitive function in postmenopausal women: The Women's Health Initiative Memory Study: A randomized controlled trial. *Journal of the American Medical Association (JAMA), 289,* 2663–2672.

Rasetti, R., Mattay, V., Wiedholz, L., Kolachana, B., Hariri, A., Callicott, J., Meyer-Lindenberg, A., & Weinberger, D. (2009). Evidence that altered amygdala activity in schizophrenia is related to clinical state and not genetic risk. *American Journal of Psychiatry, 166,* 216–225.

Rasmussen, S. A., & Eisen, J. L. (1990). Epidemiology of obsessive compulsive disorder. *Journal of Clinical Psychiatry, 51*(2, Suppl.), 10–13.

Ratty, H., Vaenskae, J., Kasanen, K., & Kaerkkaeinen, R. (2002). Parents' explanations of their child's performance in mathematics and reading: A replication and extension of Yee and Eccles. *Sex Roles, 46,* 121–128.

Ravindran, A., & Ravindran, L. (2009). Depression and comorbid anxiety: An overview of pharmacological options. *Psychiatric Times, 26.* Retrieved June 18, 2009 from *http://www.psychiatrictimes.com/cme/display/article/10168/1421225?pageNumber=2.*

Ravindran, A., da Silva, T., Ravindran, L., Richter, M., & Rector, N. (2009). Obsessive-compulsive spectrum disorders: A review of the evidence-based treatments. *Canadian Journal of Psychiatry, 54,* 331–343.

Ray, S., & Bates, M. (2006). Acute alcohol effects on repetition priming and word recognition memory with equivalent memory cues. *Brain and Cognition, 60,* 118–127.

Raz, A., Deouell, L., & Bentin, S. (2001). Is pre-attentive processing compromised by prolonged wakefulness? Effects of total sleep deprivation on the mismatch negativity. *Psychophysiology, 38,* 787–795.

Raz, N., Lindenberger, U., Rodrigue, K., Kennedy, K., Head, D., Williamson, A., Dahle, C., Gerstorf, D., & Acker, J. (2006). Regional brain changes in aging healthy adults: General trends, individual differences and modifiers. *Cerebral Cortex, 15,* 1679–1689.

Razoumnikova, O. M. (2000). Functional organization of different brain areas during convergent and divergent thinking: An EEG investigation. *Cognitive Brain Research, 10,* 11–18.

Reading, R. (2009). "Reducing immunization discomfort in r- to y-year-old children." A randomized clinical trial. *Child Care, Health & Development, 35,* p. 890.

Rebs, S., & Park, S. (2001). Gender differences in high-achieving students in math and science. *Journal for the Education of the Gifted, 25,* 52–73.

Reicher, S., & Haslam, A. (2004). The banality of evil: Thoughts on the psychology of atrocity. *Anthropology News, 45,* 14–15.

Reichle, B., & Gefke, M. (1998). Justice of conjugal divisions of labor—you can't always get what you want. *Social Justice Research, 11,* 271–287.

Reinhardt, J., Boerner, K., Horowitz, A., & Lloyd, S. (2006). Good to have but not to use: Differential impact of perceived and received support on well-being. *Journal of Social and Personal Relationships, 23,* 117–129.

Reis, H. T., Wilson, I. M., Monestere, C., Bernstein, S., Clark, K., Seidl, E., et al. (1990). What is smiling is beautiful and good. *European Journal of Social Psychology, 20,* 259–267.

Reiss, D., & Marino, L. (2001). Mirror self-recognition in the bottlenose dolphin: A case of cognitive convergence. *Proceedings of the National Academy of Science, 98,* 5937–5942.

Reite, M., Buysse, D., Reynolds, C., & Mendelson, W. (1995). The use of polysomnography in the evaluation of insomnia. *Sleep, 18,* 58–70.

Reitman, D., Murphy, M., Hupp, S., & O'Callaghan, P. (2004). Behavior change and perceptions of change: Evaluating the effectiveness of a token economy. *Child & Family Behavior Therapy, 26,* 17–36.

Reneman, L., Booij, J., Schmand, B., van den Brink, W., & Gunning, B. (2000). Memory disturbances in "Ecstasy" users are correlated with an altered brain serotonin neurotransmission. *Psychopharmacology, 148,* 322–324.

Rentfrow, P., & Gosling, S. (2003). The do re mi's of everyday life: The structure and personality correlates of music preferences. *Journal of Personality & Social Psychology, 84,* 1236–1256.

Rescorla, R. (2008). Conditioning of stimuli with nonzero initial value. *Journal of Experimental Psychology: Animal Behavior Processes, 34,* 315–323.

Rescorla, R. A. (1967). Pavlovian conditioning and its proper control procedures. *Psychological Review, 74,* 71–80.

Rescorla, R. A. (1968). Probability of shock in the presence and absence of CS in fear conditioning. *Journal of Comparative and Physiological Psychology, 66,* 1–5.

Rescorla, R. A. (1988). Pavlovian conditioning: It's not what you think it is. *American Psychologist, 43,* 151–160.

Rescorla, R. A., & Wagner, A. R. (1972). A theory of Pavlovian conditioning: Variations in the effectiveness of reinforcement and nonreinforcement. In A. Black & W. F. Prokasy (Eds.), *Classical conditioning: II. Current research and theory* (pp. 64–99). New York: Appleton.

Restak, R. (1988). *The mind.* Toronto: Bantam.

Restak, R. (1993, September/October). Brain by design. *The Sciences,* pp. 27–33.

Reuters News Service. (2006, June 30). *Japan elderly population ratio now world's highest.* Retrieved July 3, 2006, from *http://today.reuters.co.uk/news/newsArticle.aspx?type=worldNews&storyID=2006-06-30T084625Z_01_T83766_RTRUKOC_0_UKJAPANPOPULATION.xml&archived=False*

Revensuo, A. (2000). The reinterpretation of dreams: An evolutionary hypothesis of the function of dreaming. *Behavioral & Brain Science, 23.*

Reyna, V. (2004). How people make decisions that involve risk: A dual-processes approach. *Current Directions in Psychological Science, 13,* 60–66.

Reyna, V., & Adam, M. (2003). Fuzzy-trace theory, risk communication, and product labeling in sexually transmitted diseases. *Risk Analysis, 23,* 325–342.

Reyner, A., & Horne, J. A. (1995). Gender- and age-related differences in sleep determined by home-recorded sleep logs and actimetry from 400 adults. *Sleep, 18,* 127–134.

Reynolds, A., & Temple, J. (2008). Cost-effective early childhood development programs from preschool to third grade. *Annual Review of Clinical Psychology, 4,* 109–139.

Rhéaume, J., & Ladouceur, R. (2000). Cognitive and behavioural treatments of checking behaviours: An examination of individual cognitive change. *Clinical Psychology & Psychotherapy, 7,* 118–127.

Rhodes, N., & Wood, W. (1992). Self-esteem and intelligence affect influenceability: The medicating role of message reception. *Psychological Bulletin, 111,* 156–171.

Rich, L. (2004). Along with increased surgery, a growing need for support. *APA Monitor on Psychology, 35,* 54.

Richter, W., Somorjai, R., Summers, R., Jarmasz, M., Ravi, S., Menon, J. S., et al. (2000). Motor area activity during mental rotation studied by time-resolved single-trial fMRI. *Journal of Cognitive Neuroscience, 12,* 310–320.

Rickels, K., Schweizer, E., Weiss, S., & Zavodnick, S. (1993). Maintenance drug treatment for panic disorder II. Short- and long-term outcome after drug taper. *Archives of General Psychiatry, 50,* 61–68.

Ricks, T., & Wiley, J. (2009). The influence of domain knowledge on the functional capacity of working memory. *Journal of Memory and Language, 61,* 519–537.

Riedel, G. (1996). Function of metabotropic glutamate receptors in learning and memory. *Trends in Neurosciences, 19,* 219–224.

Riegle, R. (2005). Viewpoint: Online courses as video games. *Campus Technology*, June 15, 2005. Retrieved May 5, 2006, from *http://www.campus-technology.com*

Rieker, P., & Bird, C. (2005). Rethinking gender differences in health: Why we need to integrate social and biological perspectives. *The Journals of Gerontology Series B: Psychological Sciences and Social Sciences, 60*, S40–S47.

Rini, C., Manne, S., DuHamel, K., Austin, J., Ostroff, J., Boulad, F., et al. (2004). Mothers' perceptions of benefit following pediatric stem cell transplantation: A longitudinal investigation of the roles of optimism, medical risk, and sociodemographic resources. *Annals of Behavioral Medicine, 28*, 132–141.

Ritz, S. (2006). The bariatric psychological evaluation: A heuristic for determining the suitability of the morbidly obese patient for weight loss surgery. *Bariatric Nursing and Surgical Patient Care, 1*, 97–105.

Roan, S. (2000, March 6). *Cyberanalysis*. Retrieved June 10, 2007 from *http://www.doctorchase.com/html/cyberanalysis.html*.

Roberts, B. W., & DelVecchio, W. F. (2000). The rank-order consistency of personality traits from childhood to old age: A quantitative review of longitudinal studies. *Psychological Bulletin, 126*, 3–25.

Roberts, B., Chernyshenko, O., Stark, S., & Goldberg, L. (2005). The structure of conscientiousness: An empirical investigation based on seven major personality questionnaires. *Personnel Psychology, 58*, 103–139.

Roberts, G., Treasure, D., & Conroy, D. (2007). Understanding the dynamics of motivation in sport and physical activity: An achievement goal interpretation. In G., Tenenbaum, & R. Eklund (Eds.), *Handbook of sport psychology* (3rd ed.) (pp. 3–30). Hoboken, NJ: John Wiley & Sons.

Roberts, J., & Bell, M. (2000). Sex differences on a mental rotation task: Variations in electroencephalogram hemispheric activation between children and college students. *Developmental Neuropsychology, 17*, 199–223.

Roberts, P., & Moseley, B. (1996, May/June). Fathers' time. *Psychology Today, 29*, 48–55, 81.

Robins, C. J., & Hayes, A. M. (1993). An appraisal of cognitive therapy. *Journal of Consulting and Clinical Psychology, 61*, 205–214.

Robins, R. W., Gosling, S. D., & Craik, K. H. (1999). An empirical analysis of trends in psychology. *American Psychologist, 54*, 117–128.

Robinson, D., Phillips, P. Budygin, E., Trafton, B., Garris, P., & Wightman, R. (2001). Sub-second changes in accumbal dopamine during sexual behavior in male rats. *Neuroreport: For Rapid Communication of Neuroscience Research, 12*, 2549–2552.

Robinson, F. (1970). *Effective study* (4th ed.). New York: Harper & Row.

Robinson, M., & Tamir, M. (2005). Neuroticism as mental noise: A relation between neuroticism and reaction time standard deviations. *Journal of Personality and Social Psychology, 89*, 107–114.

Robles, T., Glaser, R., & Kiecolt-Glaser, J. (2005). Out of balance: A new look at chronic stress, depression, and immunity. *Current Directions in Psychological Science, 14*, 111–115.

Rock, I., & Palmer, S. (1990). The legacy of Gestalt psychology. *Scientific American, 263*, 84–90.

Rodin, J., & Salovey, P. (1989). Health psychology. *Annual Review of Psychology, 40*, 533–579.

Rodin, J., Wack, J., Ferrannini, E., & DeFronzo, R. A. (1985). Effect of insulin and glucose on feeding behavior. *Metabolism, 34*, 826–831.

Rodríguez, C., & Church, A. (2003). The structure and personality correlates of affect in Mexico: Evidence of cross-cultural comparability using the Spanish language. *Journal of Cross-Cultural Psychology, 34*, 211–223.

Roediger, H. (1980). Memory metaphors in cognitive psychology. *Memory & Cognition, 8*, 231–246.

Roediger, H. L., III. (1980). The effectiveness of four mnemonics in ordering recall. *Journal of Experimental Psychology: Human Learning and Memory, 6*, 558–567.

Roehrich, L., & Kinder, B. N. (1991). Alcohol expectancies and male sexuality: Review and implications for sex therapy. *Journal of Sex and Marital Therapy, 17*, 45–54.

Roesch, S. C., & Amirkhan, J. H. (1997). Boundary condition for self-serving attributions: Another look at the sports pages. *Journal of Applied Social Psychology, 27*, 245–261.

Rogers, C. R. (1951). *Client-centered therapy: Its current practice, implications, and theory*. Boston: Houghton Mifflin.

Rogers, M., Blumberg, N., Heal, J., & Hicks, G. (2007). Increased risk of infection and mortality in women after cardiac surgery related to allogeneic blood transfusion. *Journal of Women's Health, 16*, 1412–1420.

Rogers, M., Langa, K., Kim, C., Nallamothu, B., McMahon, L., Malani, P., Fries, B., Kaufman, S., & Saint, S. (2006). Contribution of infection to increased mortality in women after cardiac surgery. *Archives of Internal Medicine, 166*, 437–443.

Rogge, R., Bradbury, T., Hahlweg, K., Engl, J., & Thurmaier, F. (2006). Predicting marital distress and dissolution: Refining the two-factor hypothesis. *Journal of Family Psychology, 20*, 156–159.

Rogoff, B. (1990). *Apprenticeship in thinking: Cognitive development in social context*. New York: Oxford University Press.

Roisman, G., Masten, A., Coatsworth, J., & Tellegen, A. (2004). Salient and emerging developmental tasks in the transition to adulthood. *Child Development, 75*, 123–133.

Romach, M., Busto, U., Somer, G., Kaplan, A., et al. (1995). Clinical aspects of chronic use of alprazolam and lorazepam. *American Journal of Psychiatry, 152*, 1161–1167.

Roorda, A., & Williams, D. R. (1999). The arrangement of the three cone classes in the living human eye. *Nature, 397*, 520–521.

Roozendaal, B., Catello, N., Vedana, G., Barsegyan, A., & McGaugh, J. (2008). Noradrenergic activation of the basolateral amygdala modulates consolidation of object recognition memory. *Neurobiology of Learning and Memory, 90*, 576–579.

Rosch, E. & Lloyd, B. (1978). *Cognition and categorization*. Hillsdale, NJ: Erlbaum.

Rosch, E. H. (1973). Natural categories. *Cognitive Psychology, 4*, 328–350.

Rosch, E. H. (1987). Linguistic relativity. *Et Cetera, 44*, 254–279.

Rose, J., (2006). Nicotine and nonnicotine factors in cigarette addiction. *Psychopharmacology, 184*, 274–285.

Rose, R. J., Koskenvuo, M., Kaprio, J., Sarna, S., & Langinvainio, H. (1988). Shared genes, shared experiences, and similarity of personality: Data from 14,288 adult Finnish co-twins. *Journal of Personality and Social Psychology, 54*, 161–171.

Rosekind, M. R. (1992). The epidemiology and occurrence of insomnia. *Journal of Clinical Psychiatry, 53*(6, Suppl.), 4–6.

Roselli, C., Larkin, K., Schrunk, J., & Stormshak, F. (2004). Sexual partner preference, hypothalamic morphology and aromatase in rams. *Physiology & Behavior, 83*, 233–245.

Rosenblatt, M. (2008). *Fetal alcohol syndrome*. Retrieved February 26, 2010 from *http://www.acog.org/acog_districts/dist_notice.cfm?recno=1&bulletin=2646*.

Rosenbloom, T. (2006). Sensation seeking and pedestrian crossing compliance. *Social Behavior and Personality, 34*, 113–122.

Rosenbluth, R., Grossman, E. S., & Kaitz, M. (2000). Performance of early-blind and sighted children on olfactory tasks. *Perception, 29*, 101–110.

Rosengren, A., Tibblin, G., & Wilhelmsen, L. (1991). Self-perceived psychological stress and incidence of coronary artery disease in middle-aged men. *American Journal of Cardiology, 68*, 1171–1175.

Rosenhan, D. L. (1973). On being sane in insane places. *Science, 179*, 250–258.

Rosenvinge, J. H., Matinussen, M., & Ostensen, E. (2000). The comorbidity of eating disorders and personality disorders: A meta-analytic review of studies published between 1983 and 1998. *Eating and Weight Disorders: Studies on Anorexia, Bulimia, and Obesity, 5*, 52–61.

Rosenzweig, M. R. (1961). Auditory localization. *Scientific American, 205,* 132–142.

Rosenzweig, S., Greeson, J., Reibel, D., Green, J., Jasser, S., & Beasley, D. (2010). Mindfulness-based stress reduction for chronic pain conditions: Variation in treatment outcomes and role of home meditation practice. *Journal of Psychosomatic Research, 68,* 29–36.

Ross, C. A., Norton, G. R., & Wozney, K. (1989). Multiple personality disorder: An analysis of 236 cases. *Canadian Journal of Psychiatry, 34,* 413–418.

Ross, J., Baldessarini, R. J., & Tondo, L. (2000). Does lithium treatment still work? Evidence of stable responses over three decades. *Archives of General Psychiatry, 57,* 187–190.

Ross, L. (1977). The intuitive psychologist and his shortcomings: Distortions in the attribution process. In L. Berkowitz (Ed.), *Advances in experimental social psychology* (pp. 173–220). New York: Academic Press.

Rossow, I., & Amundsen, A. (1997). Alcohol abuse and mortality: A 40-year prospective study of Norwegian conscripts. *Social Science & Medicine, 44,* 261–267.

Roth, T. (1996). Social and economic consequences of sleep disorders. *Sleep, 19,* S46–S47.

Rotter, J. B. (1966). Generalized expectancies for internal versus external control of reinforcement. *Psychological Monographs, 80*(1, Whole No. 609).

Rotter, J. B. (1971, June). External control and internal control. *Psychology Today,* 37–42, 58–59.

Rotter, J. B. (1990). Internal versus external control of reinforcement: A case history of a variable. *American Psychologist, 45,* 489–493.

Rotton, J., & Cohn, E. G. (2000). Violence is a curvilinear function of temperature in Dallas: A replication. *Journal of Personality & Social Psychology, 78,* 1074–1082.

Rotton, J., Frey, J., Barry, T., Milligan, M., & Fitzpatrick, M. (1979). The air pollution experience and physical aggression. *Journal of Applied Social Psychology, 9,* 397–412.

Rouch, I., Wild, P., Ansiau, D., & Marquie, J. (2005). Shiftwork experience, age and cognitive performance. *Ergonomics, 48,* 1282–1293.

Rowe, D. (2003). Assessing genotype-environment interactions and correlations in the postgenomic era. In R. Plomin, J. DeFries, I. Craig, & P. McGuffin (Eds.), *Behavioral genetics in the postgenomic era* (pp. 71–86). Washington, DC: American Psychological Association.

Rowe, D. C. (1987). Resolving the person-situation debate: Invitation to an interdisciplinary dialogue. *American Psychologist, 42,* 218–227.

Rowe, J., & Kahn, R. (1998). *Successful aging.* New York: Pantheon.

Rozell, E., Pettijohn, C., & Parker, R. (2002). An empirical evaluation of emotional intelligence: The impact on management development. *Journal of Management Development, 21,* 272–289.

Rubin, D., Boals, A., & Klein, K. (2010). Autobiographical memories for very negative events: The effects of thinking about and rating memories. *Cognitive Therapy and Research, 34,* 35–48.

Rubino, T., Realini, N., Braida, Da., Guidi, S., Capurro, V., Vigano, D., Guidali, C., Pinter, M., Sala, M., Bartesaghi, R., & Parolaro, D. (2009). Changes in hippocampal morphology and neuroplasticity induced by adolescent THC treatment are associated with cognitive impairment in adulthood. *Hippocampus, 19,* 763–772.

Rubinstein, G. (2001). Sex-role reversal and clinical judgment of mental health. *Journal of Sex & Marital Therapy, 27,* 9–19.

Ruble, D., Taylor, L., Cyphers, L., Greulich, F., Lurye, L., & Shrout, P. (2007). The role of gender constancy in early gender development. *Child Development, 78,* 1121–1136.

Ruby, N., Dark, J., Burns, D., Heller, H., & Zucker, I. (2002). The suprachiasmatic nucleus is essential for circadian body temperature rhythms in hibernating ground squirrels. *Journal of Neuroscience, 22,* 357–364.

Rudebeck, P., Walton, M., Millette, B., Shirley, E., Rushworth, M., & Bannerman, D. (2007). *European Journal of Neuroscience, 26,* 2315–2326.

Rudman, L., Ashmore, R., & Gary, M. (2001). "Unlearning" automatic biases: The malleability of implicit prejudice and stereotypes. *Journal of Personality & Social Psychology, 81,* 856–868.

Ruggero, M. A. (1992). Responses to sound of the basilar membrane of the mammalian cochlea. *Current Opinion in Neurobiology, 2,* 449–456.

Rumbaugh, D. (1977). *Language learning by a chimpanzee: the Lana project.* New York: Academic Press.

Ruscio, J. (2001). Administering quizzes at random to increase students' reading. *Teaching of Psycholog, 28,* 204–206.

Rushton, J. P., Fulker, D. W., Neale, M. C., Nias, D. K. B., & Eysenck, H. J. (1986). Altruism and aggression: The heritability of individual differences. *Journal of Personality and Social Psychology, 50,* 1192–1198.

Rushton, J., & Jensen, A. (2003). African–White IQ differences from Zimbabwe on the Wechsler Intelligence Scale for Children-Revised are mainly on the g factor. *Personality & Individual Differences, 34,* 177–183.

Rushton, P., & Jensen, A. (2005). Thirty years of research on race differences in cognitive ability. *Psychology, Public Policy, and Law, 11,* 235–294.

Russell, T., Rowe, W., & Smouse, A. (1991). Subliminal self-help tapes and academic achievement: An evaluation. *Journal of Counseling and Development, 69,* 359–362.

Ryan, R., Kim, Y., & Kaplan, U. (2003). Differentiating autonomy from individualism and independence: A self-determination theory perspective on internalization of cultural orientations and well-being. *Journal of Personality and Social Psychology, 84,* 97–110.

Sachs, G., Grossman, F., Ghaemi, S., Okamoto, A., & Bosden, C. (2002). Combination of a mood stabilizer with risperidone or haloperidol for treatment of acute mania: A double-blind, placebo-controlled comparison of efficacy and safety. *American Journal of Psychiatry, 159,* 1146–1154.

Sack, R., Auckley, D., Auger, R., Carskadon, M., Wright, K., Vitiello, M., & Zhdanova, I. (2007a). Circadian rhythm sleep disorders: Part I, Basic principles, shift work and jet lag disorders. An American Academy of Sleep Medicine review. *Sleep, 30,* 1460–1483.

Sackeim, H. A., Luber, B., Katzman, G. P., Moeller, J. R., Prudic, J., Devanand, D. P., et al. (1996). The effects of electroconvulsive therapy on quantitative electroencephalograms. *Archives of General Psychiatry, 53,* 814–824.

Sackeim, H. A., Prudic, J., Devanand, D. P., Nobler, M. S., Lisanby, S. H., Peyser, S., et al. (2000). A prospective, randomized, double-blind comparison of bilateral and right unilateral electroconvulsive therapy at different stimulus intensities. *Archives of General Psychiatry, 57,* 425–434.

Sackett, P., Hardison, C., & Cullen, M. (2004). On interpreting stereotype threat as accounting for African American-White differences on cognitive tests. *American Psychologist, 59,* 7–13.

Sacks, O. (1984). *A leg to stand on.* New York: Harper & Row.

Sacks, O. (1995). An anthropologist on Mars. New York: Macmillan.

Saczynski, J., Willis, S., & Schaie, K. W. (2002). Strategy use in reasoning training with older adults. *Aging, Neuropsychology, & Cognition, 9,* 48–60.

Sadeh, A., Gruber, R., & Raviv, A. (2003). The effect of sleep restriction and extension on school-age children: What a difference an hour makes. *Child Development, 74,* 444–455.

Saevarsson, S., Kristiansson, A., & Hjaltason, H. (2009). Unilateral neglect: A review of causes, anatomical localization, theories and interventions. *Laeknabladid, 95,* 27–33.

Safdar, S., Friedmeier, W., Matsumoto, D., Yoo, S., Kwantes, C., Kakai, H., & Shigemasu, E. (2009). Variations of emotional display rules within and across cultures: A comparison between Canada, USA, and Japan. *Canadian Journal of Behavioural Science, 41,* 1–10.

Sahoo, F., Sahoo, K., & Harichandan, S. (2005). Big Five factors of personality and human happiness. *Social Science International, 21,* 20–28.

Sajdyk, T., Johnson, P., Leitermann, R., Fitz, S., Dietrich, A., Morin, M., Gehlert, D., Urban, J., & Shekhar, A. (2008). Neuropeptide Y in the amygdala induces long-term resilience to stress-induced reductions in social responses but not hypothalamic-adrenal-pituitary axis activity or hyperthermia. *Journal of Neuroscience, 28,* 893–903.

Salat, D., van der Kouwe, A., Tuch, D., Quinn, B., Fischl, A., & Corkin, S. (2006). Neuroimaging H. M.: A 10-year follow-up examination. *Hippocampus, 16,* 936–945.

Salisch, M. (2001). Children's emotional development: Challenges in their relationships to parents, peers, and friends. *International Journal of Behavioural Development, 25,* 310–319.

Salmon, D., & Bondi, M. (2009). The neuropsychology of Alzheimer's disease. *Neurology, 72,* 521–527.

Salmon, J., Owen, N., Crawford, D., Bauman, A., & Sallis, J. (2003). Physical activity and sedentary behavior: A population-based study of barriers, enjoyment, and preference. *Health Psychology, 22,* 178–188.

Salovey, P., & Pizarro, D. (2003). The value of emotional intelligence. In R. Sternberg, J. Lautrey, & T. Lubart (Eds.), *Models of intelligence: International perspective* (pp. 263–278). Washington, DC: American Psychological Association.

Salthouse, T. (2004). What and when of cognitive aging. *Current Directions in Psychological Science, 13,* 140–144.

Salthouse, T. (2009). When does age-related cognitive decline begin? *Neurobiology of Aging, 30,* 507–514.

Salthouse, T. A. (1996). The processing-speed theory of adult age differences in cognition. *Psychological Review, 103,* 403–428.

Sample, J. (2004). The Myers-Briggs type indicator and OD: Implications for practice from research. *Organization Development Journal, 22,* 67–75.

Sanbonmatsu, D. M., & Fazio, R. H. (1990). The role of attitudes in memory-based decision making. *Journal of Personality and Social Psychology, 59,* 614–622.

Sanes, J. N., & Donoghue, J. P. (2000). Plasticity and primary motor cortex. *Annual Review of Neuroscience, 23,* 393–415.

Sanes, J. N., Donoghue, J. P., Thangaraj, V., Edelman, R. R., & Warach, S. (1995). Shared neural substrates controlling hand movements in human motor cortex. *Science, 268,* 1775.

Santiago-Rivera, A., & Altarriba, J. (2002). The role of language in therapy with the Spanish-English bilingual client. *Professional Psychology: Research & Practice, 33,* 30–38.

Saper, C., Scammell, T., & Lu, J. (2005). Hypothalamic regulation of sleep and circadian rhythms. *Nature, 437,* 1257–1263.

Sarrio, M., Barbera, E., Ramos, A., & Candela, C. (2002). The glass ceiling in the professional promotion of women. *Revista de Psicologia Social, 17,* 167–182.

Sastry, R., Lee, D., & Har-El, G. (1997). Palate perforation from cocaine abuse. *Otolaryngol Head Neck Surgery, 116,* 565–566.

Sateia, M. J., Doghramji, K., Hauri, P. J., & Morin, C. M. (2000). Evaluation of chronic insomnia. An American Academy of Sleep Medicine review. *Sleep, 23,* 243–308.

Sattler, J. (2008). *Assessment of children: Cognitive foundations* (5th ed.). San Diego, CA: Jerome M. Sattler, Publisher.

Sattler, J., & Dumont, R. (2004). *Assessment of children: WISC-IV and WPPSI-III supplement.* San Diego, CA: Jerome M. Sattler, Publisher.

Saudino, K. (2005). Special article: Behavioral genetics and child temperament. *Journal of Developmental & Behavioral Pediatrics, 26,* 214–223.

Savage, M., & Holcomb, D. (1999). Adolescent female athletes' sexual risk-taking behaviors. *Journal of Youth and Adolescence, 28,* 583–594.

Savage-Rumbaugh, E. S. (1986). *Ape language.* New York: Columbia University Press.

Savage-Rumbaugh, E. S. (1990). Language acquisition in a nonhuman species: Implications for the innateness debate. *Developmental Psychology, 26,* 599–620.

Savage-Rumbaugh, E. S. (1993). Language learnability in man, ape, and dolphin. In H. L. Roitblat, L. M. Herman, & P. E. Nachtigall (Eds.), *Language and communication: Comparative perspectives. Comparative cognition and neuroscience* (pp. 457–484). Hillsdale, NJ: Erlbaum.

Savage-Rumbaugh, E. S., Sevcik, R. A., Brakke, K. E., & Rumbaugh, D. M. (1992). Symbols: Their communicative use, communication, and combination by bonobos (Pan paniscus). In L. P. Lipsitt & C. Rovee-Collier (Eds.). *Advances in infancy research* (Vol. 7, pp. 221–278). Norwood, NJ: Ablex.

Scarr, S., & Weinberg, R. (1976). The influence of "family background" on intellectual attainment. *American Sociological Review, 43,* 674–692.

Schachter, S., & Singer, J. E. (1962). Cognitive, social, and physiological determinants of emotional state. *Psychological Review, 69,* 379–399.

Schaie, K. (2005). *Developmental influences on adult intelligence: The Seattle longitudinal study.* New York: Oxford University Press.

Schaie, K. (2008). Historical processes and patterns of cognitive aging. In S., Hofer, & D. Alwin (Eds.), *Handbook of cognitive aging: Interdisciplinary perspectives.* (pp. 368–383). Thousand Oaks, CA: Sage Publications.

Schauer, P., Ikramuddin, S., Gourash, W., Ramanathan, R., & Luketich, J. (2000). Outcomes after laparoscopic roux-en-Y gastric bypass for morbid obesity. *Annals of Surgery, 232,* 515–529.

Schellenberg, E. (2004). Music lessons enhance IQ. *Psychological Science, 15,* 511–514.

Schenck, C. H., & Mahowald, M. W. (2000). Parasomnias. Managing bizarre sleep-related behavior disorders. *Postgraduate Medicine, 107,* 145–156.

Scherer, K. R., & Wallbott, H. G. (1994). Evidence for universality and cultural variation of differential emotion response patterning. *Journal of Personality and Social Psychology, 66,* 310–328.

Schieber, M. H., & Hibbard, L. S. (1993). How somatotopic is the motor cortex hand area? *Science, 261,* 489–492.

Schiff, M., & Lewontin, R. (1986). *Education and class: The irrelevance of IQ genetic studies.* Oxford, England: Clarendon.

Schizophrenia.com. (2006). *Brain disorders, smoking and nicotine addiction: A special report.* Retrieved February 12, 2007, from *http://www.schizophrenia.com/smokerreport.htm*

Schlosberg, S. (2004). *The curse of the singles table: A true tale of 1001 nights without sex.* New York: Warner Books.

Schmidt, P., Murphy, J., Haq, N., Rubinow, D., & Danaceau, M. (2004). Stressful life events, personal losses, and perimenopause-related depression. *Archives of Women's Mental Health, 7,* 19–26.

Schmitt, N., Fuchs, A., & Kirch, W. (2008). Mental health disorders and work-life balance. In A. Linos & W. Kirch (Eds.), *Promoting health for working women.* (pp. 117–136). New York: Springer.

Schmitt, N., Keeney, J., Oswald, F., Pleskac, T., Billington, A., Sinha, R., & Zorzie, M. (2009). Prediction of 4-year college student performance using cognitive and noncognitive predictors and the impact on demographic status of admitted students. *Journal of Applied Psychology, 94,* 1479–1497.

Schneider, E., Lang, A., Shin, M., & Bradley, S. (2004). Death with a story: How story impacts emotional, motivational, and physiological responses to first-person shooter video games. *Human Communication Research, 30,* 361–375.

Schofield, J. W., & Francis, W. D. (1982). An observational study of peer interaction in racially mixed "accelerated" classrooms. *Journal of Educational Psychology, 74,* 722–732.

Scholz, U., Dona, B., Sud, S., & Schwarzer, R. (2002). Is general self-efficacy a universal construct? Psychometric findings from 25 countries. *European Journal of Psychological Assessment, 18,* 242–251.

Schou, M. (1997). Forty years of lithium treatment. *Archives of General Psychiatry, 54,* 9–13.

Schuckit, M., Edenberg, H., Kalmijn, J., Flury, L., Smith, T., Reich, T., Beirut, L., Goate, A., & Foroud, T. (2001). A genome-wide search for gens that relate to a low level of response to alcohol. *Alcoholism: Clinical & Experimental Research, 25,* 323–329.

Schultz, W. (2006). Behavioral theories and the neurophysiology of reward. In S. Fiske, A. Kazdin, & D. Schacter (Eds.). *Annual Review of Psychology* (Vol. 57, pp. 87–116). Palo Alto, CA: Annual Reviews.

Schulz, T., Whitehead, H., Gero, S., & Rendell, L. (2008). Overlapping and matching of codas in vocal interactions between sperm whales: Insights into communication function. *Animal Behavior, 76,* 1977–1988.

Schwabe, L., & Wolf, O. (2009). The context counts: Congruent learning and testing environments prevent memory retrieval impairment following stress. *Cognitive, Affective & Behavioral Neuroscience, 9,* 229–236.

Schwartz, G. E. (1982). Testing the biopsychosocial model: The ultimate challenge facing behavioral medicine? *Journal of Consulting and Clinical Psychology, 50,* 1040–1052.

Schwartz, S., & Maquet, P. (2002). Sleep imaging and the neuro-psychological assessment of dreams. *Trends in Cognitive Sciences, 6,* 23–30.

Schwartz, S., & Zamboanga, B. (2008). Testing Berry's model of acculturation: A confirmatory latent class approach. *Cultural Diversity and Ethnic Minority Psychology, 14,* 275–285.

Scott, A., & Fraser, T. (2008). Decreased usage of electroconvulsive therapy: Implications. *British Journal of Psychiatry, 192,* 476.

Scott, S. K., Young, A. W., Calder, A. J., Hellawell, D. J., Aggleton, J. P., & Johnson, M. (1997). Impaired auditory recognition of fear and anger following bilateral amygdala lesions. *Nature, 385,* 254–257.

Scully, J., Tosi, H., & Banning, K. (2000). Life event checklists: Revisiting the Social Readjustment Rating Scale after 30 years. *Educational & Psychological Measurement, 60,* 864–876.

Sedikides, C., Gaertner, L., & Toguchi, Y. (2003). Pancultural self-enhancement. *Journal of Personality & Social Psychology, 84,* 60–79.

Seegert, C. (2004). Token economies and incentive programs: Behavioral improvement in mental health inmates housed in state prisons. *Behavior Therapist, 26,* 210–211.

Seeman, T., Dubin, L., & Seeman, M. (2003). Religiosity/spirituality and health. *American Psychologist, 58,* 53–63.

Seenoo, K., & Takagi, O. (2003). The effect of helping behaviors on helper: A case study of volunteer work for local resident welfare. *Japanese Journal of Social Psychology, 18,* 106–118.

Segal, Z., Williams, M., & Teasdale, J. (2001). *Mindfulness-based cognitive therapy for depression.* New York: Guilford Press.

Segall, M. H. (1994). A cross-cultural research contribution to unraveling the nativist/empiricist controversy. In J. Lonner & R. Malpass (Eds.), *Psychology and culture* (pp. 135–138). Boston: Allyn & Bacon.

Segall, M. H., Campbell, D. T., & Herskovitz, M. J. (1966). *The influence of culture on visual perception.* Indianapolis: Bobbs-Merrill.

Seger, C. A., Desmond, J. E., Glover, G. H., & Gabrieli, J. D. E. (2000). Functional magnetic resonance imaging evidence for right-hemisphere involvement in processing unusual semantic relationships. *Neuropsychology, 14,* 361–369.

Seidman, S. (2002). Exploring the relationship between depression and erectile dysfunction in aging men. *Journal of Clinical Psychiatry, 63,* 5–12.

Self, M., & Zeki, S. (2005). The integration of colour and motion by the human visual brain. *Cerebral Cortex, 15,* 1270–1279.

Seligman, M. E. P. (1970). On the generality of the laws of learning. *Psychological Review, 77,* 406–418.

Seligman, M. E. P. (1972). Phobias and preparedness. In M. E. P. Seligman & J. L. Hager (Eds.), *Biological boundaries of learning* (pp. 307–320). Englewood Cliffs, NJ: Prentice Hall.

Seligman, M. E. P. (1975). *Helplessness: On depression, development and death.* San Francisco: Freeman.

Seligman, M. E. P. (1990). *Learned optimism: How to change your mind and your life.* New York: Simon & Schuster.

Seligman, M. E. P. (1991). *Learned optimism.* New York: Knopf.

Seligman, M. E. P. (1995). The effectiveness of psychotherapy: The *Consumer Reports* Study. *American Psychologist, 50,* 965–974.

Seligman, M. E. P. (1996). Science as an ally of practice. *American Psychologist, 51,* 1072–1079.

Seligman, M., & Csikszentmihalyi, M. (2000). Positive psychology: An introduction. *American Psychologist, 55,* 5–14.

Seligman, M., Steen, T., Park, N., & Peterson, C. (2005). Positive psychology progress: Empirical validation of interventions. *American Psychologist, 60,* 410–421.

Seligman, M., Steen, T., Park, N., & Peterson, C. (2005). Positive psychology progress: Empirical validation of interventions. *American Psychologist, 60,* 410–421.

Selye, H. (1956). *The stress of life.* New York: McGraw-Hill.

Sensky, T., Turkington, D., Kingdon, D., Scott, J. L., Scott, J., Siddle, R., O'Carroll, M., & Barnes, T. R. E. (2000). A randomized controlled trial of cognitive-behavioral therapy for persistent symptoms in schizophrenia resistant to medication. *Archives of General Psychiatry, 57,* 165–172.

Sentenac, J. (2007). *Anger erupts over insurance company's IQ test for weight-loss surgery.* Retrieved January 25, 2007, from *http://www.foxnews.com/story/0,2933,246519,00.html*

Serido, J., Almeida, D., & Wethington, E. (2004). Chronic stressors and daily hassles: Unique and interactive relationships with psychological distress. *Journal of Health and Social Behavior, 45,* 17–33.

Serpell R., & Hatano, G. (1997). Education, schooling, and literacy. In J. Berry, P. Dasen, & T. Sarswthi (Eds.), *Handbook of cross-cultural psychology* (Vol. 2, pp. 339–376). Boston: Allyn & Bacon.

Shackelford, T., Schmitt, T., & Buss, D. (2005). Universal dimensions of human mate preferences. *Personality and Individual Differences, 39,* 447–458.

Shackelford, T., Voracek, M., Schmitt, D., Buss, D., Weekes-Shackelford, V., & Michalski, R. (2004). Romantic jealousy in early adulthood and in later life. *Human Nature, 15,* 283–300.

Shaffer, D., Gould, M. S., Fisher, P., Trautman, P., Moreau, D., Kleinman, M., et al. (1996). Psychiatric diagnosis in child and adolescent suicide. *Archives of General Psychiatry, 53,* 339–348.

Sharma, S. (2006). Parasomnias. Retrieved December 16, 2006, from *http://www.emedicine.com/med/topic3131.html*

Sharp, D., Cole, M., & Lave, C. (1979). Education and cognitive development: The evidence from experimental research. *Monographs of the Society for Research in Child Development, 44*(1–2, Serial No. 178).

Shaunessy, E., Karnes, F., & Cobb, Y. (2004). Assessing potentially gifted students from lower socioeconomic status with nonverbal measures of intelligence. *Perceptual & Motor Skills, 98,* 1129–1138.

Shaw, J. I., & Steers, W. N. (2001). Gathering information to form an impression: Attribute categories and information valence. *Current Research in Social Psychology, 6,* 1–21.

Shaw, J. S., III. (1996). Increases in eyewitness confidence resulting from postevent questioning. *Journal of Experimental Psychology: Applied, 2,* 126–146.

Shaw, V. N., Hser, Y.-I., Anglin, M. D., & Boyle, K. (1999). Sequences of powder cocaine and crack use among arrestees in Los Angeles County. *American Journal of Drug and Alcohol Abuse, 25,* 47–66.

Shears, J., Robinson, J., & Emde, R. (2002). Fathering relationships and their associations with juvenile delinquency. *Infant Mental Health Journal, 23,* 79–87.

Sheehan, D. V., & Raj, A. B. (1988). Monoamine oxidase inhibitors. In C. G. Last & M. Hersen (Eds.), *Handbook of anxiety disorders* (pp. 478–506). New York: Pergamon.

Sheets, R., & Mohr, J. (2009). Perceived social support from friends and family and psychosocial functioning in bisexual young adult college students. *Journal of Counseling Psychology, 56,* 152–163.

Shelton, J., & Richeson, J. (2005). Intergroup contact and pluralistic ignorance. *Journal of Personalty & Social Psychology, 88,* 91–107.

Shepperd, J. (2001). The desire to help and behavior in social dilemmas: Exploring responses to catastrophes. *Group Dynamics, 5,* 304–314.

Sher, A. E., Schechtman, K. B., & Piccirillo, J. F. (1996). The efficacy of surgical modifications of the upper airway in adults with obstructive sleep apnea syndrome. *Sleep, 19,* 156–177.

Sher, L. (2004a). Hypothalamic-pituitary-adrenal function and preventing major depressive episodes. *Canadian Journal of Psychiatry, 49,* 574–575.

Sher, L. (2004b). Type D personality, cortisol and cardiac disease. *Australian and New Zealand Journal of Psychiatry, 38,* 652–653.

Sherif, M. (1956). Experiments in group conflict. *Scientific American, 195,* 53–58.

Sherif, M. (1958). Superordinate goals in the reduction of intergroup conflict. *American Journal of Sociology, 63,* 349–358.

Sherif, M., & Sherif, C. W. (1967). The Robbers' Cave study. In J. F. Perez, R. C. Sprinthall, G. S. Grosser, & P. J. Anastasiou, *General psychology: Selected readings* (pp. 411–421). Princeton, NJ: D. Van Nostrand.

Sherman, J., Kruschke, J., Sherman, S., Percy, E., Petrocelli, J., & Conrey, F. (2009). Attentional processes in stereotype formation: A common model for category accentuation and illusory correlation. *Journal of Personality and Social Psychology, 96,* 305–323.

Shimamura, A. P., Berry, J. M., Mangela, J. A., Rusting, C. L., & Jurica, P. J. (1995). Memory and cognitive abilities in university professors: Evidence for successful aging. *Psychological Science, 6,* 271–277.

Shinar, D., Tractinsky, N., & Compton, R. (2005). Effects of practice, age, and task demands, on interference from a phone task while driving. *Accident Analysis & Prevention, 37,* 315–326.

Shiner, R. (2000). Linking childhood personality with adaptation: Evidence for continuity and change across time into late adolescence. *Journal of Personality and Social Psychology, 78,* 310–325.

Shneidman, E. (1989). The Indian summer of life: A preliminary study of septuagenarians. *American Psychologist, 44,* 684–694.

Shneidman, E. S. (1994). Clues to suicide, reconsidered. *Suicide and Life-Threatening Behavior, 24,* 395–397.

Shumaker, S., Legault, C., Rapp, S., Thal, L., Wallace, R., Ockene, J., et al. (2003). Estrogen plus progestin and the incidence of dementia and mild cognitive impairment in postmenopausal women: The Women's Health Initiative Memory Study: A randomized controlled trial. *Journal of the American Medical Association (JAMA), 289,* 2651–2662.

Siahpush, M., Yong, H., Borland, R., Reid, J., & Hammond, D. (2009). Smokers with financial stress are more likely to want to quit but less likely to try or succeed: Findings from the International Tobacco Control (ITC) Four Country Survey. *Addiction, 104,* 1382–1890.

Siegel, J. (2009). Sleep viewed as a state of adaptive inactivity. *Nature Reviews Neuroscience, 10,* 747–753.

Siegel, R. (2005). *Intoxication: The universal drive for mind-altering substances.* Rochester, VT: Park Street Press.

Siegfried, N., Muller, M., Deeks, J., & Volmink, J. (2009). Male circumcision for prevention of heterosexual acquisition of HIV in men. *Cochrane Database of Systematic Reviews, 2,* Online article No. CD003362.

Siegler, R. S. (1991). *Children's thinking* (2nd ed.). Englewood Cliffs, NJ: Prentice-Hall.

Siegrist, J., Peter, R., Junge, A., Cremer, P., & Seidel, D. (1990). Low status control, high effort at work and ischemic heart disease: Prospective evidence from blue-collar men. *Social Science and Medicine, 31,* 1127–1134.

Silva, C. E., & Kirsch, I. (1992). Interpretive sets, expectancy, fantasy proneness, and dissociation as predictors of hypnotic response. *Journal of Personality and Social Psychology, 63,* 847–856.

Simon, G., Cherkin, D., Sherman, K., Eisenberg, D., Deyo, R., & Davis, R. (2004). Mental health visits to complementary and alternative medicine providers. *General Hospital Psychiatry, 26,* 171–177.

Simon, H. (1956). Rational choice and the structure of the environment. *Psychological Review, 63,* 129–138.

Simon, H. B. (1988, June). Running and rheumatism. *Harvard Medical School Health Letter, 13,* 2–4.

Simons, D. & Chabris, C. (1999). Gorillas in our midst: Sustained inattentional blindness for dynamic events. *Perception, 28,* 1059–1074.

Simons, D., & Rensink, R. (2005). Change blindness: Past, present, and future. *Trends in Cognitive Sciences, 9,* 16–20.

Simons, J., & Carey, K. (2002). Risk and vulnerability for marijuana use problems. *Psychology of Addictive Behaviors, 16,* 72–75.

Simpson, P., & Stroh, L. (2004). Gender differences: Emotional expression and feelings of personal inauthenticity. *Journal of Applied Psychology, 89,* 715–721.

Simunovic, M. (2010, in press). Colour vision deficiency. *Eye, 24,* [pages not available].

Singer, M. I., Miller, D. B., Guo, S., Flannery, D. J., Frierson, T., & Slovak, K. (1999). Contributors to violent behavior among elementary and middle school children. *Pediatrics, 104*(Pt. 1), 878–884.

Singh, B. (1991). Teaching methods for reducing prejudice and enhancing academic achievement for all children. *Educational Studies, 17,* 157–171.

Singh, I. (2004). Doing their jobs: Mothering with Ritalin in a culture of mother-blame. *Social Science & Medicine, 59,* 1193–1205.

Singh, S., & Darroch, J. (2000). Adolescent pregnancy and childbearing: Levels and trends in industrialized countries. *Family Planning Perspectives, 32,* 14–23.

Sivacek, J., & Crano, W. D. (1982). Vested interest as a moderator of attitude-behavior consistency. *Journal of Personality and Social Psychology, 43,* 210–221.

Skinner, B. F. (1953). *Science and human behavior.* New York: Macmillan.

Skinner, B. F. (1957). *Verbal behavior.* New York: Appleton Century.

Skrabalo, A. (2000). Negative symptoms in schizophrenia(s): The conceptual basis. *Harvard Brain, 7,* 7–10.

Slawinski, E. B., Hartel, D. M., & Kline, D. W. (1993). Self-reported hearing problems in daily life throughout adulthood. *Psychology and Aging, 8,* 552–561.

Slobin, D. (1972, July). Children and language: They learn the same all around the world. *Psychology Today,* 71–74, 82.

Sluzki, C. (2004). House taken over by ghosts: Culture, migration, and the developmental cycle of a Moroccan family invaded by hallucination. *Families, Systems, & Health, 22,* 321–337.

Small, G. (2005). *Effects of a 14-day healthy aging lifestyle program on brain function.* Paper presented at the 44th Annual Meeting of the American College of Neuropsychopharmacology. December 11–15, 2005. Waikoloa, Hawaii.

Smith, G., Wong, H., MacEwan, G., Kopala, L., Ehmann, T., Thornton, A., Lang, D., Barr, A., Procyshyn, R., Austin, J., Flynn, S., & Honer, W. (2009). *Schizophrenia Research, 108,* 258–264.

Smith, J., & Brennan, B. (2009). *Management of the third stage of labor.* Retrieved February 27, 2010 from *http://emedicine. medscape.com/article/275304-overview.*

Smith, M. L., Glass, G. V., & Miller, T. I. (1980). *The benefits of psychotherapy.* Baltimore, MD: Johns Hopkins University Press.

Smith, N., Young, A., & Lee, C. (2004). Optimism, health-related hardiness and well-being among older Australian women. *Journal of Health Psychology, 9,* 741–752.

Smith, S. M., Glenberg, A., & Bjork, R. A. (1978). Environmental context and human memory. *Memory & Cognition, 6,* 342–353.

Smith, T., & Ruiz, J. (2002). Psychosocial influences on the development and course of coronary heart disease: Current status and implications for research and practice. *Journal of Consulting and Clinical Psychology, 70,* 548–568.

Smith, Y., Stohler, C., Nichols, T., Bueller, J., Koeppe, R., & Zubieta, J. (2006). Pronociceptive and antinociceptive effects of estradiol through endogenous opioid neurotransmission in women. *The Journal of Neuroscience, 26,* 5777–5785.

Smolar, A. (1999). Bridging the gap: Technical aspects of the analysis of an Asian immigrant. *Journal of Clinical Psychoanalysis, 8,* 567–594.

Smolensky, M., & Lamberg, L. (2000). *The body clock guide to better health.* New York: Macmillan/Henry Holt.

Snarey, J. R. (1985). Cross-cultural universality of social-moral development: A critical review of Kohlbergian research. *Psychological Bulletin, 97*, 202–232.

Snarey, J. R. (1995). In communitarian voice: The sociological expansion of Kohlbergian theory, research, and practice. In W. M. Kurtines & J. L. Gerwirtz (Eds.), *Moral development: An introduction* (pp. 109–134). Boston: Allyn & Bacon.

Snow, C. E. (1993). Bilingualism and second language acquisition. In J. B. Gleason & N. B. Ratner (Eds.), *Psycholinguistics* (pp. 391–416). Fort Worth, TX: Harcourt.

Snyder, D., Castellani, A., & Whisman, M. (2006). Current status and future directions in couple therapy. *Annual Review of Psychology, 57*, 317–344.

Soares-Weiser, K., & Fernandez, H. (2007). Tardive dyskinesia. *Seminars in Neurology, 27*, 159–69.

Sobin, C., & Sackeim, H. A. (1997). Psychomotor symptoms of depression. *American Journal of Psychiatry, 154*, 4–17.

Soei, E., Koch, B., Schwarz, M., & Daum, I. (2008). Involvement of the human thalamus in relational and non-relational memory. *European Journal of Neuroscience, 28*, 2533–2541.

Sokolov, E. N. (2000). Perception and the conditioning reflex: Vector encoding. *International Journal of Psychophysiology, 35,* 197–217.

Solano, L., Donati, V., Pecci, F., Perischetti, S., & Colaci, A. (2003). Postoperative course after papilloma resection: Effects of written disclosure of the experience in subjects with different alexithymia levels. *Psychosomatic Medicine, 65*, 477–484.

Solomon, S., Rothblum, E, & Balsam, K. (2004). Pioneers in partnership: Lesbian and gay male couples in civil unions compared with those not in civil unions and married heterosexual siblings. *Journal of Family Psychology, 18*, 275–286.

Solso, R., MacLin, O., & MacLin, M. (2008). *Cognitive psychology* (8th ed.). Upper Saddle River, NJ: Pearson Prentice-Hall.

Somers, V., White, D., Amin, R., Abraham, W., Costa, F., Culebras, A., Daniels, S., Floras, J., Hunt, C., Olson, L., Pickering, T., Russell, R., Woo, M., & Young, T. (2008). Expert consensus document: Sleep apnea and cardiovascular disease. *Journal of the American College of Cardiology, 52*, 686–717.

Sonnentag, S. (2003). Recovery, work engagement, and proactive behaviour: A new look at the interface between work and non-work. *Journal of Applied Psychology, 88*, 518–528.

Soreff, S., & McInnes, L. (2008). *Bipolar affective disorder.* Retrieved June 11, 2009 from *http://emedicine.medscape.com/article/286342-overview.*

Sotres-Bayon, F., Bush, D., & LeDoux, J. (2004). Emotional perseveration: An update on prefrontal–amygdala interactions in fear extinction. *Learning & Memory, 11*, 525–535.

Soussignan, R. (2002). Duchenne smile, emotional experience, and autonomic reactivity: A test of the facial feedback hypothesis. *Emotion, 2*, 52–74.

Spangler, D. L., Simons, A. D., Monroe, S. M., & Thase, M. E. (1996). Gender differences in cognitive diathesis-stress domain match: Implications for differential pathways to depression. *Journal of Abnormal Psychology, 105*, 653–657.

Spanos, N. P. (1986). Hypnotic behavior: A social-psychological interpretation of amnesia, analgesia, and "trance logic." *Behavioral and Brain Sciences, 9*, 499–502.

Spanos, N. P. (1991). A sociocognitive approach to hypnosis. In S. J. Lynn & J. W. Rhue (Eds.), *Theories of hypnosis: Current models and perspectives* (pp. 324–361). New York: Guilford.

Spanos, N. P. (1994). Multiple identity enactments and multiple personality disorder: A sociocognitive perspective. *Psychological Bulletin, 116*, 143–165.

Spataro, L., Sloane, E., Milligan, E., Wieseler-Frank, J., Schoeniger, D., Jakich, B., et al. (2004). Spinal gap junctions: Potential involvement in pain facilitation. *Journal of Pain, 5*, 392–405.

Spearman, C. (1927). *The abilities of man.* New York: Macmillan.

Spector, F., & Maurer, D. (2009). Synesthesia: A new approach to understanding the development of perception. *Developmental Psychology, 45*, 175–189.

Spencer, R., Zelaznik, H., Diedrichsen, J., & Ivry, R. (2003). Disrupted timing of discontinuous but not continuous movements by cerebellar lesions. *Science, 300*, 1437–1439.

Sperling, G. (1960). The information available in brief visual presentations. *Psychological Monographs: General and Applied 74* (Whole No. 498), 1–29.

Sperry, R. W. (1964). The great cerebral commissure. *Scientific American, 210*, 42–52.

Sperry, R. W. (1968). Hemisphere deconnection and unity in conscious experience. *American Psychologist, 23*, 723–733.

Spiers, H., Maguire, E., & Burgess, N. (2001). Hippocampal amnesia. *Neurocase, 7*, 357–382.

Spitzer, M. W., & Semple, M. N. (1991). Interaural phase coding in auditory midbrain: Influence of dynamic stimulus features. *Science, 254*, 721–724.

Sporer, S. L., Penrod, S., Read, D., & Cutler, B. (1995). Choosing, confidence, and accuracy: A meta-analysis of the confidence-accuracy relation in eyewitness identification studies. *Psychological Bulletin, 118*, 315–327.

Spreen, O., Risser, A., & Edgell, D. (1995). *Developmental neuropsychology.* New York: Oxford University Press.

Squire, L. R., Knowlton, B., & Musen, G. (1993). The structure and organization of memory. *Annual Review of Psychology, 44*, 453–495.

Srivastava, S., John, O., Gosling, S., & Potter, J. (2003). Development of personality in early and middle adulthood: Set like plaster or persistent change? *Journal of Personality & Social Psychology, 84*, 1041–1053.

Stabell, B., & Stabell, U. (2009). *Duplicity theory of vision: From Newton to the present.* New York: Cambridge University Press.

Stea, R. A., & Apkarian, A. V. (1992). Pain and somatosensory activation. *Trends in Neurosciences, 15*, 250–251.

Steblay, N. M. (1992). A meta-analytic review of the weapon focus effect. *Law and Human Behavior, 16*, 413–424.

Steele, C., & Aronson, J. (1995). Stereotype threat and the intellectual test performance of African Americans. *Journal of Personality & Social Psychology, 69*, 797–811.

Steele, J., & Mayes, S. (1995). Handedness and directional asymmetry in the long bones of the human upper limb. *International Journal of Osteoarchaeology, 5*, 39–49.

Steeves, R. (2002). The rhythms of bereavement. *Family & Community Health, 25*, 1–10.

Steffens, A. B., Scheurink, A. J., & Luiten, P. G. (1988). Hypothalamic food intake regulating areas are involved in the homeostasis of blood glucose and plasma FFA levels. *Physiology and Behavior, 44*, 581–589.

Steffensen, M., & Calker, L. (1982). Intercultural misunderstandings about health care: Recall of descriptions of illness and treatments. *Social Science and Medicine, 16*, 1949–1954.

Stein, J., Milburn, N., Zane, J., & Rotheram-Borus, M. (2009). Paternal and maternal influences on problem behaviors among homeless and runaway youth. *American Journal of Orthopsychiatry, 79*, 39–50.

Stein, M. B., & Kean, Y. M. (2000). Disability and quality of life in social phobia: Epidemiologic findings. *American Journal of Psychiatry, 157*, 1606–1613.

Stein-Behrens, B., Mattson, M. P., Chang, I., Yeh, M., & Sapolsky, R. (1994). Stress exacerbates neuron loss and cytoskeletal pathology in the hippocampus. *Journal of Neuroscience, 14*, 5373–5380.

Steinberg, L. (1990). Autonomy, conflict, and harmony in the family relationship. In S. S. Feldman & R. E. Glen (Eds.). *At the threshold: The developing adolescent* (pp. 255–276). Cambridge, MA: Harvard University Press.

Steinberg, L., & Dornbusch, S. (1991). Negative correlates of part-time employment during adolescence: Replication and elaboration. *Developmental Psychology, 27*, 304–313.

Steinberg, L., Blatt-Eisengart, I., & Cauffman, E. (2006). Patterns of competence and adjustment among adolescents from authoritative, authoritarian, indulgent, and neglectful homes: A replication in a sample of serious juvenile offenders. *Journal of Research on Adolescence, 16*, 47–58.

Steinberg, L., Elman, J. D., & Mounts, N. S. (1989). Authoritative parenting, psychosocial maturity, and academic success among adolescents. *Child Development, 60*, 1424–1436.

Steinberg, L., Lamborn, S. D., Darling, N., Mounts, N. S., & Dornbusch, S. M. (1994). Over-time changes in adjustment and competence among adolescents from authoritative, authoritarian, indulgent, and neglectful families. *Child Development, 65*, 754–770.

Steinman, L. (1993). Autoimmune disease. *Scientific American, 269*, 106–114.

Stelmachowicz, P., Beauchaine, K., Kalberer, A., & Jesteadt, W. (1989). Normative thresholds in the 8- to 20-kHz range as a function of age. *Journal of the Acoustical Society of America, 86*, 1384–1391.

Stephan, K. M., Fink, G. R., Passingham, R. E., Silbersweig, D., Ceballos-Baumann, A. O., Frith, C. D., et al. (1995). Functional anatomy of the mental representation of upper extremity movements in healthy subjects. *Journal of Neurophysiology, 73*, 373–386.

Stephenson, M. T., & Witte, K. (1998). Fear, threat, and perceptions of efficiency from frightening skin cancer messages. *Public Health Review, 26*, 147–174.

Steptoe, A. (2000). Stress, social support and cardiovascular activity over the working day. *International Journal of Psychophysiology, 37*, 299–308.

Steriade, M. (1996). Arousal: Revisiting the reticular activating system. *Science, 272*, 225–226.

Sternberg, R. (2003a). Issues in the theory and measurement of successful intelligence: A reply to Brody. *Intelligence, 31*, 331–337.

Sternberg, R. (2003b). Our research program validating the triarchic theory of successful intelligence: Reply to Gottfredson. *Intelligence, 31*, 399–413.

Sternberg, R. J. (1985). *Beyond IQ: A triarchic theory of human intelligence.* New York: Cambridge University Press.

Sternberg, R. J. (1986a). *Intelligence applied: Understanding and increasing your intellectual skills.* San Diego: Harcourt Brace Jovanovich.

Sternberg, R. J. (1986b). A triangular theory of love. *Psychological Review, 93*, 119–135.

Sternberg, R. J. (1987). Liking versus loving: A comparative evaluation of theories. *Psychological Bulletin, 102*, 331–345.

Sternberg, R. J. (2000). The holey grail of general intelligence. *Science, 289*, 399–401.

Sternberg, R. J., Wagner, R. K., Williams, W. M., & Horvath, J. A. (1995). Testing common sense. *American Psychologist, 50*, 912–927.

Sternberg, R., Castejon, J., Prieto, M., Hautamacki, J., & Grigorenko, E. (2001). Confirmatory factor analysis of the Sternberg Triarchic Abilities Test in three international samples: An empirical test of the triarchic theory of intelligence. *European Journal of Psychological Assessment, 17*, 1–16.

Stevenson, H. W. (1992). Learning from Asian schools. *Scientific American, 267*, 70–76.

Stewart, G., Fulmer, I., & Barrick, M. (2005). An exploration of member roles as a multilevel linking mechanism for individual traits and team outcomes. *Personnel Psychology, 58*, 343–365.

Stewart, N. (2009). The cost of anchoring on credit-card minimum repayments. *Psychological Science, 20*, 39–41.

Stigler, J., & Stevenson, H. (1991). How Asian teachers polish each lesson to perfection. *American Educator*, 12–20, 43–47.

Still, C. (2001). *Health benefits of modest weight loss.* Retrieved January 29, 2003, from *http://abcnews.go.com/sections/living/Healthology/weightloss_benefits011221.html*

Stilwell, N., Wallick, M., Thal, S., & Burleson, J. (2000). Myers-Briggs type and medical specialty choice: A new look at an old question. *Teaching & Learning in Medicine, 12*, 14–20.

Stockhorst, U., Gritzmann, E., Klopp, K., Schottenfeld-Naor, Y., Hübinger, A., Berresheim, H., Stingrüber, H., & Gries, F. (1999). Classical conditioning of insulin effects in healthy humans. *Psychosomatic Medicine, 61*, 424–435.

Stockhorst, U., Mayl, N., Krueger, M., Huenig, A., Schottenfeld-Naor, Y., Huebinger, A., Berreshaim, H., Steingrueber, H., & Scherbaum, W. (2004). Classical conditioning and conditionability of insulin and glucose effects in healthy humans. *Physiology & Behavior, 81*, 375–388.

Stokes, D. (1986). Chance can play key role in life, psychologist says. *Stanford Campus Report*, June 10, 1986, 1–4.

Stone, J. (2003). Self-consistency for low self-esteem in dissonance processes: The role of self-standards. *Personality & Social Psychology Bulletin, 29*, 846–858.

Stone, K., Karem, K., Sternberg, M., McQuillan, G., Poon, A., Unger, E., & Reeves, W. (2002). Seroprevalence of human papillomavirus type 16 infection in the United States. *Journal of Infectious Diseases, 186*, 1396–1402.

Strack, F., Martin, L. L., & Stepper, S. (1988). Inhibiting and facilitating conditions of facial expressions: A nonobtrusive test of the facial feedback hypothesis. *Journal of Personality and Social Psychology, 54*, 768–777.

Strange, B., Hurlemann, R., & Dolan, R. (2003). An emotion-induced retrograde amnesia in humans is amygdala- and b-adrenergic-dependent. *Proceedings of the National Academy of Science, 100*, 13626–13631.

Strayer, D., & Drews, F. (2004). Profiles in driver distraction: Effects of cell phone conversations on younger and older drivers. *Human Factors, 46*, 640–649.

Strickland, B. R. (1995). Research on sexual orientation and human development: A commentary. *Developmental Psychology, 31*, 137–140.

Stroebe, M., & Schut, H. (1999). The dual process model of coping with bereavement: Rationale and description. *Death Studies, 23*, 197–224.

Strohmetz, D., Rind, B., Fisher, R., & Lynn, M. (2002). Sweetening the till: The use of candy to increase restaurant tipping. *Journal of Applied Social Psychology, 32*, 300–309.

Stromeyer, C. F., III. (1970, November). Eidetikers. *Psychology Today*, pp. 76–80.

Stubbs, P. (2005). *A consumer's guide to online mental health care.* Retrieved June 10, 2007 from *http://www.m-a-h.net/hip/index.html.*

Stuss, D. T., Gow, C. A., & Hetherington, C. R. (1992). "No longer Gage": Frontal lobe dysfunction and emotional changes. *Journal of Consulting and Clinical Psychology, 60*, 349–359

Suarez, M. G. (1983). *Implications of Spanish-English bilingualism in the TAT stories.* Unpublished doctoral dissertation, University of Connecticut.

Sugita, M., & Shiba, Y. (2005). Genetic tracing shows segregation of taste neuronal circuitries for bitter and sweet. *Science, 309*, 781–785.

Sullivan, A. D., Hedberg, K., & Fleming, D. W. (2000). Legalized physician-assisted suicide in Oregon—The second year. *New England Journal of Medicine, 342*, 598–604.

Sullivan, A., Maerz, J., & Madison, D. (2002). Anti-predator response of red-backed salamanders (Plethodon cinereus) to chemical cues from garter snakes (Thamnophis sirtalis): Laboratory and field experiments. *Behavioral Ecology & Sociobiology, 51*, 227–233.

Sullivan, M. J. L., Bishop, S. R., & Pivik, J. (1995). The pain catastrophizing scale: Development and validation. *Psychological Assessment, 7*, 524–532.

Summerfeldt, L., Kloosterman, P., Antony, M., & Parker, J. (2006). Emotional intelligence, and interpersonal adjustment. *Journal of Psychopathology and Behavioral Assessment, 28*, 57–68.

Sun, W., & Rebec, G. (2005). The role of prefrontal cortex D1-like and D2-like receptors in cocaine-seeking behavior in rats. *Psychopharmacology, 177*, 315–323.

Sung, K. (2008). Serial and parallel attentive visual searches: Evidence from cumulative distribution functions of response times. *Journal of Experimental Psychology: Human Perception and Performance, 34*, 1372–1388.

Sung, K-T. (1992). Motivations for parent care: The case of filial children in Korea. *International Journal of Aging and Human Development, 34*, 109–124.

Super, C. W. (1981). Behavioral development in infancy. In R. H. Munroe, R. L. Munroe, & B. B. Whiting (Eds.), *Handbook of cross-cultural human development* (pp. 181–269). Chicago: Garland.

Super, D. (1971). A theory of vocational development. In N. H. J. Peters & J. C. Hansen (Eds.), *Vocational guidance and career development* (pp. 111–122). New York: MacMillan.

Super, D. (1986). Life career roles: Self-realization in work and leisure. In D. T. H. & Associates (Eds.), *Career development in organizations* (pp. 95–119). San Francisco: Jossey-Bass.

"Survey: Four in 10 American adults play video games." (2006, May 9). Retrieved May 12, 2006, from *http://www.foxnews.com*

Susman, E., & Dorn, L. (2009). Puberty: Its role in development. In R., Lerner & L. Steinberg (Eds.), *Handbook of adolescent psychology*. Volume I: Individual bases of adolescent development (3rd ed.) (pp. 116–151). Hoboken, NJ: John Wiley & Sons.

Sussman, S., & Dent, C. W. (2000). One-year prospective prediction of drug use from stress-related variables. *Substance Use & Misuse, 35*, 717–735.

Swann, W., & Bosson, J. (2008). Identity negotiation: A theory of self and social interaction. In O., John, R., Robins, & L. Pervin (Eds.), *Handbook of personality psychology: Theory and research* (3rd ed.) (pp. 448–471). New York: Guilford Press.

Swann, W., Rentfrow, P., & Guinn, J. (2003). Self-verification: The search for coherence. In M. Leary, and J. Tangney, J. (Eds.), *Handbook of Self and Identity* (pp. 367–383). New York: Guilford Publications.

Swanson, L. W. (1995). Mapping the human brain: past, present, and future. *Trends in Neurosciences, 18*, 471–474.

Swanson, N. G. (2000). Working women and stress. *Journal of the American Medical Women's Association, 55*, 276–279.

Swartz, H., Frank, E., Frankel, D., Novick, P., & Houck, P. (2009). Psychotherapy as monotherapy for the treatment of bipolar II depression: A proof of concept study. *Bipolar Disorders, 11*, 89–94.

Sweatt, J. D., & Kandel, E. R. (1989). Persistent and transcriptionally dependent increase in protein phosphorylation in long-term facilitation of *Aplysia* sensory neurons. *Nature, 339*, 51–54.

Swedo, S., & Grant, P. (2004). PANDAS: A model for autoimmune neuropsychiatric disorders. *Primary Psychiatry, 11*, 28–33.

Sweller, J., & Levine, M. (1982). Effects of goal specificity on means-end analysis and learning. *Journal of Experimental Psychology: Learning, Memory, and Cognition, 8*, 463–474.

Symister, P., & Friend, R. (2003). The influence of social support and problematic support on optimism and depression in chronic illness: A prospective study evaluating self-esteem as a mediator. *Health Psychology, 22*, 123–129.

Talarico, J., & Rubin, D. (2009). Flashbulb memories result from ordinary memory processes and extraordinary event characteristics. In O., Luminet, & A. Curci, (Eds.), *Flashbulb memories: New issues and perspectives* (pp. 13–32). New York: Psychology Press.

Tamminga, C. A. (1996, Winter). The new generation of antipsychotic drugs. *NARSAD Research Newsletter*, 4–6.

Tamminga, C. A., & Conley, R. R. (1997). The application of neuroimaging techniques to drug development. *Journal of Clinical Psychiatry, 58*(10, Suppl.), 3–6.

Tamminga, C., & Vogel, M. (2005). Images in neuroscience: The cerebellum. *American Journal of Psychiatry, 162*, 1253.

Tan, H., & Tan, M. (2008). Organizational citizenship behavior and social loafing: The role of personality, motives, and contextual factors. *Journal of Psychology: Interdisciplinary and Applied, 142*, 89–108.

Tanda, G., Pontieri, F. E., & Di Chiara, G. (1997). Cannabinoid and heroin activation of mesolimbic dopamine transmission by a common μ1 opioid receptor mechanism. *Science, 276*, 2048–2050.

Tanner, J. M. (1990). *Fetus into man* (2nd ed.). Cambridge MA: Harvard University Press.

Tate, D., Paul, R., Flanigan, T., Tashima, K., Nash, J., Adair, C., et al. (2003). The impact of apathy and depression on quality of life in patients infected with HIV. *AIDS Patient Care & STDs, 17*, 117–120.

Taub, G., Hayes, B., Cunningham, W., & Sivo, S. (2001). Relative roles of cognitive ability and practical intelligence in the prediction of success. *Psychological Reports, 88*, 931–942.

Tay, C., Ang, S., & Dyne, L. (2006). Personality, biographical characteristics, and job interview success: A longitudinal study of the mediating effects of interviewing self-efficacy and the moderating effects of internal locus of causality. *Journal of Applied Psychology, 91*, 446–454.

Taylor, C., & Luce, K. (2003). Computer- and Internet-based psychotherapy interventions. *Current Directions in Psychological Science, 12*, 18–22.

Taylor, S. E. (1991). *Health psychology* (2nd ed.). New York: McGraw-Hill.

Taylor, S. E., & Repetti, R. L. (1997). Health psychology: What is an unhealthy environment and how does it get under the skin? *Annual Review of Psychology, 48*, 411–447.

Tchanturia, K., Serpell, L., Troop, N., & Treasure, J. (2001). Perceptual illusions in eating disorders: Rigid and fluctuating styles. *Journal of Behavior Therapy & Experimental Psychiatry, 32*, 107–115.

Teachman, B., Marker, C., & Smith-Janik, S. (2008). Automatic associations and panic disorder; Trajectories of change over the course of treatment. *Journal of Consulting and Clinical Psychology, 76*, 988–1002.

Teachman, J. (2003). Premarital sex, premarital cohabitation and the risk of subsequent marital dissolution among women. *Journal of Marriage and Family, 65*, 444-455.

Teitelbaum, P. (1957). Random and food-directed activity in hyperphagic and normal rats. *Journal of Comparative and Physiological Psychology, 50*, 486–490.

Tellegen, A., Lykken, D. T., Bouchard, T. J., Jr., Wilcox, K. J., Segal, N. L., & Rich, S. (1988). Personality similarity in twins reared apart and together. *Journal of Personality and Social Psychology, 54*, 1031–1039.

Tennant, C. (2002). Life events, stress and depression: A review of the findings. *Australian & New Zealand Journal of Psychiatry, 36*, 173–182.

Tepper, B. (2008). Nutritional implications of genetic taste variation: The role of PROP sensitivity and other taste phenotypes. *Annual Review of Nutrition, 28*, 367–388.

Tepper, B., & Ullrich, N. (2002). Influence of genetic taste sensitivity to 6-n-propylthiouracil (PROP), dietary restraint and disinhibition on body mass index in middle-aged women. *Physiology & Behavior, 75*, 305–312.

Tercyak, K., Johnson, S., Roberts, S., & Cruz, A. (2001). Psychological response to prenatal genetic counseling and amniocentesis. *Patient Education & Counseling, 43*, 73–84.

Terlecki, M., & Newcombe, N. (2005). How important is the digital divide? The relation of computer and videogame usage to gender differences in mental rotation ability. *Sex Roles, 53*, 433–441.

Terman, L. M. (1925). *Genetic studies of genius, Vol. 1: Mental and physical traits of a thousand gifted children*. Palo Alto, CA: Stanford University Press.

Terman, L. M., & Oden, M. H. (1947). *Genetic studies of genius, Vol. 4: The gifted child grows up*. Palo Alto, CA: Stanford University Press.

Terman, L. M., & Oden, M. H. (1959). *Genetic studies of genius, Vol. 5: The gifted group at mid-life*. Palo Alto, CA: Stanford University Press.

Terrace, H. (1979, November). How Nim Chimpski changed my mind. *Psychology Today*, 65–76.

Terrace, H. S. (1981). A report to an academy. *Annals of the New York Academy of Sciences, 364*, 115–129.

Terrace, H. S. (1985). In the beginning was the "name." *American Psychologist, 40*, 1011–1028.

Terrace, H. S. (1986). *Nim: A chimpanzee who learned sign language.* New York: Columbia University Press.

Tew, J. D., Mulsant, B. H., Haskett, R. F., Prudic, J., Thase, M. E., Crowe, R. R., et al. (1999). Acute efficacy of ECT in the treatment of major depression in the old-old. *American Journal of Psychiatry, 156,* 1865–1870.

Thaakur, S., & Himabindhu, G. (2009). Effect of alpha lipoic acid on the tardive dyskinesia and oxidative stress induced by haloperidol in rats. *Journal of Neural Transmission, 116,* 807–814.

Tham, K., Borell, L., & Gustavsson, A. (2000). The discovery of disability: A phenomenological study of unilateral neglect. *American Journal of Occupational Therapy, 54,* 398–406.

Thase, M. E., & Kupfer, D. J. (1996). Recent developments in the pharmacotherapy of mood disorders. *Journal of Consulting and Clinical Psychology, 64,* 646–659.

Thase, M. E., Frank, E., Mallinger, A. G., Hammer, T., & Kupfer, D. J. (1992). Treatment of imipramine-resistant recurrent depression, III: Efficacy of monoamine oxidise inhibitors. *Journal of Clinical Psychiatry, 53*(1, Suppl.), 5–11.

Thirthalli, J., & Benegal, V. (2006). Psychosis among substance users. *Current Opinion in Psychiatry, 19,* 239–245.

Thomas, A., Chess, S., & Birch, H. G. (1970). The origin of personality. *Scientific American, 223,* 102–109.

Thomas, S., & Jordan, T. (2004). Contributions of oral and extraoral facial movement to visual and audiovisual speech perception. *Journal of Experimental Psychology: Human Perception & Performance, 30,* 873–888.

Thompson, P., Dutton, R., Hayashi, K., Toga, A., Lopez, O., Aizenstein, H., & Becker, J. (2005). Thinning of the cerebral cortex visualized in HIV/AIDS reflects CD4+ T lymphocyte decline. *Proceedings of the National Academies of Science, 102,* 15642–15647.

Thompson, P., Vidal, C., Giedd, J., Gochman, P., Blumenthal, J., Nicolson, R., et al. (2001). Mapping adolescent brain change reveals dynamic wave of accelerated gray matter loss in very early-onset schizophrenia. *Proceedings of the National Academy of Sciences, 98,* 11650–11655.

Thompson, R., Emmorey, K., & Gollan, T. (2005). "Tip of the fingers" experiences by deaf signers. *Psychological Science, 16,* 856–860.

Thompson, S. C., Sobolew-Shubin, A., Galbraith, M. E., Schwankovsky, L., & Cruzen, D. (1993). Maintaining perceptions of control: Finding perceived control in low-control circumstances. *Journal of Personality and Social Psychology, 64,* 293–304.

Thorndike, E. (1898). Some experiments on animal intelligence. *Science, 7*(181), 818–824.

Thorndike, E. L. (1911/1970). *Animal intelligence: Experimental studies.* New York: Macmillan. (Original work published 1911).

Thorne, B. (2000). Extra credit exercise: A painless pop quiz. *Teaching of Psychology, 27,* 204–205.

Thorsteinsson, E., & Brown, R. (2009). Mediators and moderators of the stressor-fatigue relationship in nonclinical samples. *Journal of Psychosomatic Research, 66,* 21–29.

Thurstone, L. L. (1938). *Primary mental abilities.* Chicago: University of Chicago Press.

Tidey, J., O'Neill, S., & Higgins, S. (2002). Contingent monetary reinforcement of smoking reductions, with and without transferal nicotine, in outpatients with schizophrenia. *Experimental and Clinical Psychopharmacology, 10,* 241–247.

Tiedemann, J. (2000). Parents' gender stereotypes and teachers' beliefs as predictors of children's concept of their mathematical ability in elementary school. *Journal of Educational Psychology, 92,* 144–151.

Tiihonen, J., Isohanni, M., Räsänen, P., Koiranen, M., & Moring, J. (1997). Specific major mental disorders and criminality: A 26-year prospective study of the 1966 northern Finland birth cohort. *American Journal of Psychiatry, 154,* 840–845.

Toastmasters International. (2003). *Ten tips for successful public speaking.* Retrieved November 25, 2003, from *http://www.toastmasters.org/pdfs/top10.pdf*

Tobin, M. (2007). Psychopharmacology column: Why choose selegiline transderman system for refractory depression. *Issues in Mental Health Nursing, 28,* 223–228.

Todorov, A., & Bargh, J. (2002). Automatic sources of aggression. *Aggression & Violent Behavior, 7,* 53–68.

Tohidian, I. (2009). Examining linguistic relativity hypothesis as one of the main views on the relationship between language and thought. *Journal of Psycholinguistic Research, 38,* 65–74.

Tolman, E. C. (1932). *Purposive behavior in animals and men.* New York: Appleton-Century-Crofts.

Tolman, E. C., & Honzik, C. H. (1930). Introduction and removal of reward, and maze performance in rats. *University of California Publications in Psychology, 4,* 257–275.

Tooby, J., & Cosmides, L. (2005). Conceptual foundations of evolutionary psychology. In Buss, D. (Ed.). *Handbook of evolutionary psychology* (pp. 5–67). Hoboken, NJ: Wiley.

Toot, J., Dunphy, G., Turner, M., & Ely, D. (2004). The SHR Y-chromosome increases testosterone and aggression, but decreases serotonin as compared to the SKY Y-chromosome in the rat model. *Behavior Genetics, 34,* 515–524.

Topolinski, S., & Strack, F. (2009). The architecture of intuition: Fluency and affect determine intuitive judgments of semantic and visual coherence and judgments of grammaticality in artificial grammar learning. *Journal of Experimental Psychology: General, 138,* 39–63.

Tori, C., & Bilmes, M. (2002). Multiculturalism and psychoanalytic psychology: The validation of a defense mechanism's measure in an Asian population. *Psychoanalytic Psychology, 19,* 701–721.

Torrey, E. (1992). *Freudian fraud: The malignant effect of Freud's theory on American thought and culture.* New York: Harper Collins.

Totterdell, P., & Kellett, S. (2008). Restructuring mood in cyclothymia using cognitive behavior therapy: An intensive time-sampling study. *Journal of Clinical Psychology, 64,* 501–518.

Tourangeau, R., Smith, T. W., & Rasinski, K. A. (1997). Motivation to report sensitive behaviors on surveys: Evidence from a bogus pipeline experiment. *Journal of Applied Social Psychology, 27,* 209–222.

Traverso, A., Ravera, G., Lagattolla, V., Testa, S., & Adami, G. F. (2000). Weight loss after dieting with behavioral modification for obesity: The predicting efficiency of some psychometric data. *Eating and Weight Disorders: Studies on Anorexia, Bulimia, and Obesity, 5,* 102–107.

Triandis, H. C. (1994). *Culture and social behavior.* New York: McGraw-Hill.

Trijsburg, R., Perry, J., & Semeniuk, T. (2004). An empirical study of the differences in interventions between psychodynamic therapy and cognitive-behavioural therapy for recurrent major depression. *Canadian Journal of Psychoanalysis, 12,* 325–345.

Triplett, N. (1898). The dynamogenic factors in pacemaking and competition. *American Journal of Psychology, 9,* 507–533.

Trivedi, M. J. (1996). Functional neuroanatomy of obsessive-compulsive disorder. *Journal of Clinical Psychiatry, 57*(8, Suppl.), 26–36.

Troglauer, T., Hels, T., & Christens, P. (2006). Extent and variations in mobile phone use among drivers of heavy vehicles in Denmark. *Accident Analysis & Prevention, 38,* 105–111.

Troxel, W., Matthews, K., Bromberger, J., & Sutton-Tyrrell, K. (2003). Chronic stress burden, discrimination, and subclinical carotid artery disease in African American and Caucasian women. *Health Psychology, 22,* 300–309.

Trull, T., Stepp, S., & Durrett, C. (2003). Research on borderline personality disorder: An update. *Current Opinion in Psychiatry, 16,* 77–82.

Tsai, J., Knutson, B., & Fung, H. (2006). Cultural variation in affect valuation. *Journal of Personality and Social Psychology, 90,* 288–307.

Tsai, S., Kuo, C., Chen, C., & Lee, H. (2002). Risk factors for completed suicide in bipolar disorder. *Journal of Clinical Psychiatry, 63,* 469–476.

Tulving, E. (1995). Organization of memory: Quo vadis? In M. S. Gazzaniga (Ed.), *The cognitive neurosciences* (pp. 839–847). Cambridge, MA: MIT Press.

Tulving, E. (2002). Episodic memory: From mind to brain. *Annual Review of Psychology, 53,* 1–25.

Tulving, E., & Thompson, D. M. (1973). Encoding specificity and retrieval processes in episodic memory. *Psychological Review, 80,* 352–373.

Turner, J. C., Hogg, M. A., Oakes, P. J., Reicher, S. D., & Wetherell, M. S. (1987). *Rediscovering the social group: A self-categorization theory.* Oxford, England: Blackwell.

Turner, R., Hewstone, M., Voci, A., & Vonofakou, C. (2008). A test of extended intergroup contact hypothesis: The mediating role of intergroup anxiety, perceived ingroup and outgroup norms, and inclusion of the outgroup in the self. *Journal of Personality and Social Psychology, 95,* 843–860.

Tversky, A. (1972). Elimination by aspects: A theory of choice. *Psychological Review, 79,* 281–299.

Tversky, A., & Kahneman, D. (1974). Judgment under uncertainty: Heuristics and biases. *Science, 185,* 1124–1130.

Tweed, R., & Lehman, D. (2002). Learning considered within a cultural context: Confucian and Socratic approaches. *American Psychologist, 57,* 89–99.

Tye, K., Stuber, G., Ridder, B., Bonci, A., & Janak, P. (2008). Rapid strengthing of thalamo-amygdala synapses mediates cue-reward learning. *Nature, 453,* 1253–1257.

U. S. Census Bureau. (2006). *2005 American community survey.* Retrieved November 19, 2006, from *http://www.census.gov/acs/www/index.html*

U.S. Census Bureau. (2001). *Statistical abstract of the United States.* Washington, DC: U.S. Government Printing Office.

U.S. Census Bureau. (2004). Income 2003: Press release. Retrieved July 5, 2006, from *http://www.census.gov/Press-elease/www/releases/archives/income_wealth/002484.html*

U.S. Census Bureau. (2010). *2006–2008 American Community Survey 3-Year Estimates.* Retrieved March 12, 2010 from *http://factfinder.census.gov/servlet/STTable?_bm=y&-geo_id=01000US&-qr_name=ACS_2008_3YR_G00_S1702&-ds_name=ACS_2008_3YR_G00.*

U.S. Census Bureau. (2010). *Estimated median age at first marriage, by sex: 1890 to the present.* Historical Time Series. Retrieved February 27, 2010 from *http://www.census.gov/population/www/socdemo/hh-fam.html#ht.*

U.S. Department of Energy. (2003). *International consortium completes Human Genome Project.* Retrieved January 16, 2005, from *http://www.ornl.gov/sci/techresources/Human_Genome/*

U.S. Department of Energy. (2009). *Human genome project information.* Retrieved January 17, 2010 from *http://www.ornl.gov/sci/techresources/Human_Genome/home.shtml.*

U.S. Department of Health and Human Services. (2000). *Reducing tobacco use: A report of the Surgeon General—executive summary.* Atlanta: Department of Health and Human Services, Centers for Disease Control and Prevention, National Center for Chronic Disease Prevention and Health Promotion, Office on Smoking and Health.

U.S. Department of Health and Human Services. (2001). *Ecstasy: Teens speak out* [Online factsheet]. Retrieved October 22, 2003, from *http://www.health.org/govpubs/prevalert/v4/8.aspx*

U.S. Department of Justice. (1999). *Eyewitness evidence: A guide for law enforcement.* Retrieved February 22, 2010 from *http://www.ncjrs.gov/pdffiles1/nij/178240.pdf.*

U.S. Food and Drug Administration (FDA). (2004, October 15). *Suicidality in children and adolescents being treated with antidepressant medication.* Retrieved May 12, 2005, from *http://www.fda.gov/cder/drug/antidepressants/SSRIPHA200410.htm.*

U.S. Food and Drug Administration (FDA). (2006a, April 20). Interagency advisory regarding claims that smoked marijuana is a medicine. Retrieved May 15, 2006, from *http://www.fda.gov/bbs/topics/NEWS/2006/NEW01362.html*

U.S. Food and Drug Administration (FDA). (2006b). *Prozac patient information sheet.* Retrieved July 26, 2006, from *http://www.fda.gov/cder/drug/InfoSheets/patient/fluoxetinePIS.htm*

Uchida, Y., Norasakkunkit, V., & Kitayama, S. (2004). Cultural constructions of happiness: Theory and empirical evidence. *Journal of Happiness Studies, 5,* 223–239.

Uchino, B. N., Cacioppo, J. T., & Kiecolt-Glaser, J. K. (1996). The relationship between social support and physiological processes: A review with emphasis on underlying mechanisms and implications for health. *Psychological Bulletin, 119,* 488–531.

Uman, L., Chambers, C., McGrath, P., & Kisely, S. (2008). A systematic review of randomized controlled trials examining psychological interventions for needle-related procedural pain and distress in children and adolescents: An abbreviated Cochrone review. *Journal of Pediatric Psychology, 33,* 842–854.

Umberson, D., Williams, K., Powers, D., Liu, H., & Needham, B. (2006). You make me sick: Marital quality and health over the life course. *Journal of Health and Social Behavior, 47,* 1–16.

Underwood, B. J. (1957). Interference and forgetting. *Psychological Review, 64,* 49–60.

Underwood, B. J. (1964). Forgetting. *Scientific American, 210,* 91–99.

United Nations. (2008). *Millennium development goals report.* Retrieved March 12, 2010 from *http://www.un.org/millenniumgoals/2008highlevel/pdf/newsroom/mdg%20reports/MDG_Report_2008_ENGLISH.pdf.*

University of Michigan Transportation Research Institute (UMTRI). (2003). Ready for the road: Software helps teens drive safely. *UMTRI Research Review, 34,* 1–2.

Urry, H., Nitschke, J., Dolski, I., Jackson, D., Dalton, K., Mueller, C., Rosenkranz, M., Ryff, C., Singer, B., & Davidson, R. (2004). Making a life worth living: Neural correlates of well-being. *Psychological Science, 15,* 367–372.

Ushikubo, M. (1998). A study of factors facilitating and inhibiting the willingness of the institutionalized disabled elderly for rehabilitation: A United States–Japanese comparison. *Journal of Cross-Cultural Gerontology, 13,* 127–157.

Utsey, S., Chae, M., Brown, C., & Kelly, D. (2002). Effect of ethnic group membership on ethnic identity, race-related stress and quality of life. *Cultural Diversity & Ethnic Minority Psychology, 8,* 367–378.

Vaccarino, V., Abramson, J., Veledar, E., & Weintraub, W. (2002). Sex differences in hospital mortality after coronary artery bypass surgery: Evidence for a higher mortality in younger women. *Circulation, 105,* 1176.

Valeo, T. (2008). Role of sleep in memory and learning elucidated in new studies. *Neurology Today, 8,* 16.

Valipour, A., Lothaller, H., Rauscher, H., Zwick, H., Burghuber, O., & Lavie, P. (2007). Gender-related differences in symptoms of patients with suspected breathing disorders in sleep: A clinical population study using the Sleep Disorders Questionnaire. *Sleep: Journal of Sleep and Sleep Disorders Research, 30,* 312–319.

Valtonen, H., Suominen, K., Haukka, J., Mantere, O., Arvilommi, P., Leppämäki, S., & Isometsä, E. (2009). Hopelessness across phases of bipolar I or II disorder: A prospective study. *Journal of Affective Disorders, 115,* 11–17.

Van Assema, P., Martens, M., Ruiter, A., & Brug, J. (2002). Framing of nutrition education messages in persuading consumers of the advantages of a healthy diet. *Journal of Human Nutrition & Dietetics, 14,* 435–442.

Van Boven, L., White, K., Kamada, A., & Gilovich, T. (2003). Intuitions about situational correction in self and others. *Journal of Personality & Social Psychology, 85,* 249–258.

Van Cauter, E. (2000). Slow-wave sleep and release of growth hormone. *Journal of the American Medical Association, 284,* 2717–2718.

Van der Elst, W., Van Boxtel, M., Van Breukelen, G., & Jolles, J. (2006). The Stroop color-word test: Influence of age, sex, and education;

and normative data for a large sample across the adult age range. *Assessment, 13,* 62–79.

Van der Zee, K., Thijs, M., & Schakel, L. (2002). The relationship of emotional intelligence with academic intelligence and the Big Five. *European Journal of Personality, 16,* 103–125.

van Elst, L. T., Woermann, F. G., Lemieux, L., Thompson, P. J., & Trimble, M. R. (2000). Affective aggression in patients with temporal lobe epilepsy. *Brain, 123,* 234–243.

Van Groen, T., Kadish, I., & Wyss, J. (2002). The role of the laterodoral nucleus of the thalamus in spatial learning and memory in the rat. *Behavior and Brain Research, 136,* 329–337.

Van Lancker, D. (1987, November). Old familiar voices. *Psychology Today,* pp. 12–13.

Van Lommel, S., Laenen, A., & d'Ydewalle, G. (2006). Foreign-grammar acquisition while watching subtitled television programmes. *British Journal of Educational Psychology, 76,* 243–258.

van Schoor, G., Bott, S., & Engels, R. (2008). Alcohol drinking in young adults: The predictive value of personality when peers come around. *European Addiction Research, 14,* 125–133.

van Vianen, A., & Fischer, A. (2002). Illuminating the glass ceiling: The role of organizational culture preferences. *Journal of Occupational & Organizational Psychology, 75,* 315–337.

Vargha-Khadem, F., Gadian, D. G., Watkins, D. E., Connelly, A., Van Paesschen, W., & Mishkin, M. (1997). Differential effects of early hippocampal pathology on episodic and semantic memory. *Science, 277,* 376–380.

Varley, A., & Blasco, M. (2003). Older women's living arrangements and family relationships in urban Mexico. *Women's Studies International Forum, 26,* 525–539.

Vasterling, J., Duke, L., Brailey, K., Constans, J., Allain, A., & Sutker, P. (2002). Attention, learning, and memory performances and intellectual resources in Vietnam veterans: PTSD and no disorder comparisons. *Neuropsychology, 16,* 5–14.

Vawter, L., & Fisher, C. (2007). *Cannabis compound abuse.* Retrieved February 8, 2010 from *http://emedicine.medscape.com/ article/286661-overview.*

Verdejo-García, A., López-Torrecillas, F., Aguilar de Arcos, F., & Pérez-García, M. (2005). Differential effects of MDMA, cocaine, and cannabis use severity on distinctive components of the executive functions in polysubstance users: A multiple regression analysis. *Addictive Behaviors, 30,* 89–101.

Verhaeghen, P., Marcoen, A., & Goossens, L. (1993). Facts and fiction about memory aging. A quantitative integration of research findings. *Journal of Gerontology, 48,* 157–171.

Vermeersch, H., T'Sjoen, G., Kaufman, J., & Vincke, J. (2008). The role of testosterone in aggressive and non-aggressive risk-taking in adolescent boys. *Hormones and Behavior, 53,* 463–471.

Vetulani, J., & Nalepa, I. (2000). Antidepressants: Past, present and future. *European Journal of Pharmacology, 405,* 351–363.

Viding, E., Blair, R., Moffitt, T., & Plomin, R. (2005). Evidence of substantial genetic risk for psychopathy in 7-year-olds. *Journal of Child Psychology and Psychiatry, 46,* 592–597.

Viemerö, V. (1996). Factors in childhood that predict later criminal behavior. *Aggressive Behavior, 22,* 87–97.

Vieta, E. (2003). Atypical antipsychotics in the treatment of mood disorders. *Current Opinion in Psychiatry, 16,* 23–27.

Villegas, A., Sharps, M., Satterthwaite, B., & Chisholm, S. (2005). Eyewitness memory for vehicles. *Forensic Examiner, 14,* 24–28.

Vincent, M., & Pickering, M. R. (1988). Multiple personality disorder in childhood. *Canadian Journal of Psychiatry, 33,* 524–529.

Violari, A., Cotton, M., Gibb, D., Babiker, A., Steyn, J., Madhi, S., Jean-Philippe, P., & McIntyre, J. (2008). Early antiretroviral therapy and mortality among HIV-infected infants. *New England Journal of Medicine, 359,* 2233–2244.

Visser, P. S., & Krosnick, J. A. (1998). Development of attitude strength over the life cycle: Surge and decline. *Journal of Personality & Social Psychology, 75,* 1389–1410.

Visser, P., & Mirabile, R. (2004). Attitudes in the social context: The impact of social network composition on individual-level attitude strength. *Journal of Personality & Social Psychology, 87,* 779–795.

Vitello, P. (2006, June 12). A ring tone meant to fall on deaf ears. *New York Times* [Online]. Retrieved December 13, 2006, from *http://www.nytimes.com/06/12/technology/12ring.html?ex_130776 4899&en_2a80*

Vitousek, K., & Manke, F. (1994). Personality variables and disorders in anorexia nervosa and bulimia nervosa. *Journal of Abnormal Psychology, 103,* 137–147.

Volis, C., Ashburn-Nardo, L., & Monteith, M. (2002). Evidence of prejudice-related conflict and associated affect beyond the college setting. *Group Processes & Intergroup Relations, 5,* 19–33.

Volkow, N. D., & Fowler, J. S. (2000). Addiction, a disease of compulsion and drive: Involvement of the orbitofrontal cortex. *Cerebral Cortex, 10,* 318–325.

Volkow, N., Wang, G., Kollins, S., Wigal, T., Newcorn, J., Telang, F., Fowler, J., Zhu, W., Logan, J., Ma, Y., Pradhan, K., Wong, C., & Swanson, J. (2009). Evaluating dopamine reward pathway in ADHD: Clinical implications. *JAMA: Journal of the American Medical Association, 302,* 1084–1091.

Von Dras, D. D., & Siegler, I. C. (1997). Stability in extraversion and aspects of social support at midlife. *Journal of Personality and Social Psychology, 72,* 233–241.

Votruba, S., Horvitz, M., & Schoeller, D. (2000). The role of exercise in the treatment of obesity. *Nutrition, 16,* 179–188.

Voyer, D., & Rodgers, M. (2002). Reliability of laterality effects in a dichotic listening task with nonverbal material. *Brain & Cognition, 48,* 602–606.

Vygotsky, L. (1926/1992). *Educational psychology.* Boca Raton, FL: St. Lucie Press.

Vygotsky, L. S. (1936/1986). *Thought and language* (A. Kozulin, Trans.). Cambridge, MA: MIT Press. (Original work published 1936).

Wacker, J., Chavanon, M., & Stemmler, G. (2006). Investigating the dopaminergic basis of extraversion in humans: A multilevel approach. *Journal of Personality and Social Psychology, 91,* 171–187.

Wade, T., & DiMaria, C. (2003). Weight halo effects: Individual differences in personality evaluations as a function of weight. *Sex Roles, 48,* 461–465.

Wagner, D., Wenzlaff, R., & Kozak, M. (2004). Dream rebound: The return of suppressed thoughts in dreams. *Psychological Science, 15,* 232–236.

Wald, G. (1964). The receptors of human color vision. *Science, 145,* 1007–1017.

Wald, G., Brown, P. K., & Smith, P. H. (1954). Iodopsin. *Journal of General Physiology, 38,* 623–681.

Waldron, S., & Helm, F. (2004). Psychodynamic features of two cognitive-behavioural and one psychodynamic treatment compared using the analytic process scales. *Canadian Journal of Psychoanalysis, 12,* 346–368,

Walitzer, K., & Demen, K. (2004). Alcohol-focused spouse involvement and behavioral couples therapy: Evaluation of enhancements to drinking reduction treatment for male problem drinkers. *Journal of Consulting & Clinical Psychology, 72,* 944–955.

Walker, E., Kestler, L., Bollini, A., & Hochman, K. (2004). Schizophrenia: Etiology and course. *Annual Review of Psychology, 55,* 401–430.

Walker, E., Mittal, V., & Tessner, K. (2008). Stress and the hypothalamic pituitary adrenal axis in the developmental course of schizophrenia. *Annual Review of Clinical Psychology, 4,* 189–216.

Walker, I., & Crogan, M. (1998). Academic performance, prejudice and the jigsaw classroom: New pieces to the puzzle. *Journal of Community & Applied Social Psychology, 8,* 381–393.

Walker, L. (1989). A longitudinal study of moral reasoning. *Child Development, 60,* 157–166.

Walker, M., & Stickgold, R. (2006). Sleep, memory, and plasticity. *Annual Review of Psychology: 57*, 139–166.

Walker, M., Brakefield, T., Hobson, J., & Stickgold, R. (2003). Dissociable stages of human memory consolidation and reconsolidation. *Nature, 425,* 616–620.

Wallentin, M. (2009). Putative sex differences in verbal abilities and language cortex: A critical review. *Brain and Language, 108,* 175–183.

Walsh, B., Seidman, S., Sysko, R., & Gould, M. (2002). Placebo response in studies of major depression: Variable, substantial, and growing. *JAMA: Journal of the American Medical Association, 287,* 1840–1847.

Walsh, D., Gentile, D., VanOverbeke, M., & Chasco, E. (2002). *MediaWise video game report card.* National Institute on Media and the Family. Retrieved May 18, 2006, from *http://www.mediafamily.org/research/report_vgrc_2002-2.shtml*

Walster, E., & Walster, G. W. (1969). The matching hypothesis. *Journal of Personality and Social Psychology, 6,* 248–253.

Walters, C. C., & Grusec, J. E. (1977). *Punishment.* San Francisco: Freeman.

Wang, J., Keown, L., Patten, S., Williams, J., Currie, S., Beck, C., Maxwell, C., & El-Guebaly, N. (2009). A population-based study on ways of dealing with daily stress: Comparisons among individuals with mental disorders, with long-term general medical conditions and healthy people. *Social Psychiatry and Psychiatric Epidemiology, 44,* 666–674.

Wang, P., & Li, J. (2003). An experimental study on the belief bias effect in syllogistic reasoning. *Psychological Science (China), 26,* 1020–1024.

Wang, X., & Perry, A. (2006). Metabolic and physiologic responses to video game play in 7- to 10-year-old boys. *Archives of Pediatric Adolescent Medicine, 160,* 411–415.

Wang, Z., & Chen, M. (2002). Managerial competency modeling: A structural equation testing. *Psychological Science (China), 25,* 513–516.

Warburton, J., McLaughlin, D., & Pinsker, D. (2006). Generative acts: Family and community involvement of older Australians. *International Journal of Aging & Human Development, 63,* 115–137.

Ward, C. (1994). Culture and altered states of consciousness. In W. J. Lonner & R. Malpass (Eds.), *Psychology and culture* (pp. 59–64). Boston: Allyn & Bacon.

Wark, G. R., & Krebs, D. L. (1996). Gender and dilemma differences in real-life moral judgment. *Developmental Psychology, 32,* 220–230.

Warmerdam, L., van Straten, A., Jongsma, J., Twisk, J., & Cuijpers, P. (2010). Online cognitive behavioral therapy and problem-solving therapy for depressive symptoms: Exploring mechanisms of change. *Journal of Behavior Therapy and Experimental psychiatry, 41,* 64–70.

Warshaw, M. G., & Keller, M. B. (1996). The relationship between fluoxetine use and suicidal behavior in 654 subjects with anxiety disorders. *Journal of Clinical Psychiatry, 57,* 158–166.

Washington University School of Medicine. (2003). *Epilepsy surgery* [Online factsheet]. Retrieved September 29, 2003, from *http://neurosurgery.wustl.edu/clinprog/epilepsysurg.htm*

Waterman, A. (1985). Identity in the context of adolescent psychology. *Child Development, 30,* 5–24.

Watson, D. (2002). Predicting psychiatric symptomatology with the Defense Style Questionnaire-40. *International Journal of Stress Management, 9,* 275–287.

Watson, J. B., & Rayner, R. (1920). Conditioned emotional reactions. *Journal of Experimental Psychology, 3,* 1–14.

Weaver, M., & Schnoll, S. (2008). Hallucinogens and club drugs. In M. Galanter & H. Kleber (Eds.), *The American Psychiatric Publishing Textbook of Substance Abuse* (4th ed., pp. 191–200). Arlington, VA: American Psychiatric Publishing, Inc.

Webb, R., Lubinski, D., & Benbow, C. (2002). Mathematically facile adolescents with math-science aspirations: New perspectives on their educational and vocational development. *Journal of Educational Psychology, 94,* 785–794.

Webb, W. (1995). The cost of sleep-related accidents: A reanalysis. *Sleep, 18,* 276–280.

Webb, W. B. (1975). *Sleep: The gentle tyrant.* Englewood Cliffs, NJ: Prentice-Hall.

Weber, R., Ritterfeld, U., & Mathiak, K. (2006). Does playing violent video games induce aggression? Empirical evidence of a functional magnetic resonance imaging study. *Media Psychology, 8,* 39–60.

Wechsler, D. (1939). *The measurement of adult intelligence.* Baltimore: Williams & Wilkins.

Weekes, J. R., Lynn, S. J., Green, J. P., & Brentar, J. T. (1992). Pseudomemory in hypnotized and task-motivated subjects. *Journal of Abnormal Psychology, 101,* 356–360.

Weeks, D. L., & Anderson, L. P. (2000). The interaction of observational learning with overt practice: Effects on motor skill learning. *Acta Psychologia, 104,* 259–271.

Weigman, O., & van Schie, E. G. (1998). Video game playing and its relations with aggressive and prosocial behaviour. *British Journal of Social Psychology, 37*(Pt. 3), 367–378.

Weinbrenner, A., Peus, V., Inta, D., English, S., & Zink, M. (2009). Risperidone-associated increase in triglyceride levels. *American Journal of Psychiatry, 166,* 113–114.

Weiner, I. (2004). Monitoring psychotherapy with performance-based measures of personality functioning. *Journal of Personality Assessment, 83,* 323–331.

Weiner, I. B. (1996). Some observations on the validity of the Rorschach Inkblot Method. *Psychological Assessment, 8,* 206–213.

Weiner, I. B. (1997). Current status of the Rorschach Inkblot Method. *Journal of Personality Assessment, 68,* 5–19.

Weinstock, M., Assor, A., & Broide, G. (2009). Schools as promoters of moral judgment: The essential role of teachers' encouragement of critical thinking. *Social Psychology of Education, 12,* 137–151.

Weisberg, M. (2008). 50 years of hypnosis in medicine and clinical health psychology: A synthesis of cultural crosscurrents. *American Journal of Clinical Hypnosis, 51,* 13–27.

Weissman, M. M., Bland, R. C., Canino, G. J., Faravelli, C., Greenwald, S., Hwu, H-G., et al. (1996). Cross-national epidemiology of major depression and bipolar disorder. *Journal of the American Medical Association, 276,* 293–299.

Wells, B., & Twenge, J. (2006). Changes in young people's sexual behavior and attitudes, 1943–1999: A cross-temporal meta-analysis. *Review of General Psychology, 9,* 249–261.

Wells, D. L., & Hepper, P. G. (2000). The discrimination of dog odours by humans. *Perception, 29,* 111–115.

Wells, G. L. (1993). What do we know about eyewitness identification? *American Psychologist, 48,* 553–571.

Wells, G. L., Malpass, R. S., Lindsay, R. C., Fisher, R. P., Turtle, J. W., & Fulero, S. M. (2000). From the lab to the police station. A successful application of eyewitness research. *American Psychologist, 55,* 6581–6598.

Welsh, D. (2009). Predictors of depressive symptoms in female medical-surgical hospital nurses. *Issues in Mental Health Nursing, 30,* 320–326.

Wertheimer, M. (1912). Experimental studies of the perception of movement. *Zeitschrift fuer Psychologie, 61,* 161–265.

Wesensten, N., Balenky, G., Kautz, M., Thorne, D., Reichardt, R., & Balkin, T. (2002). Maintaining alertness and performance during sleep deprivation: Modafinil versus caffeine. *Psychopharmacology, 159,* 238–247.

Westerhof, G., Katzko, M., Dittmann-Kohli, F., & Hayslip, B. (2001). Life contexts and health-related selves in old age: Perspectives from the United States, India and Congo-Zaire. *Journal of Aging Studies, 15,* 105–126.

Westling, E., Andrews, J., Hampson, S., & Peterson, M. (2008). Pubertal timing and substance use: The effects of gender, parental monitoring, and deviant peers. *Journal of Adolescent Health, 42,* 555–563.

Wetherell, J., Gatz, M., & Craske, M. (2003). Treatment of generalized anxiety disorder in older adults. *Journal of Consulting & Clinical Psychology, 71,* 31–40.

Wheeler, M., & McMillan, C. (2001). Focal retrograde amnesia and the episodic-semantic distinction. *Cognitive, Affective & Behavioral Neuroscience, 1,* 22–36.

Whisenhunt, B. L., Williamson, D. A., Netemeyer, R. G., & Womble, L. G. (2000). Reliability and validity of the Psychosocial Risk Factors Questionnaire (PRFQ). *Eating and Weight Disorders: Studies on Anorexia, Bulimia, and Obesity, 5,* 1–6.

Whisman, M. (2008). *Adapting cognitive therapy for depression: Managing complexity and comorbidity.* New York: Guilford Press.

Whitam, F. L., Diamond, M., & Martin, J. (1993). Homosexual orientation in twins: A report on 61 pairs and three triplet sets. *Archives of Sexual Behavior, 22,* 187–296.

White, D. P. (1989). Central sleep apnea. In M. H. Kryger, T. Roth, & W. C. Dement (Eds.), *Principles and practice of sleep medicine* (pp. 513–524). Philadelphia: W. B. Saunders.

White, S. D., & DeBlassie, R. R. (1992). Adolescent sexual behavior. *Adolescence, 27,* 183–191.

Whitehead, B., & Popenoe, D. (2005). *The state of our unions: The social health of marriage in America: 2005: What does the Scandinavian experience tell us?* Retrieved June 15, 2006, from *http://marriage.rutgers.edu/Publications/SOOU/TEXTSOOU2005.htm*

Whitehurst, G. J., Fischel, J. E., Caulfield, M. B., DeBaryshe, B. D., & Valdez-Menchaca, M. C. (1989). Assessment and treatment of early expressive language delay. In P. R. Zelazo & R. Barr (Eds.), *Challenges to developmental paradigms: Implications for assessment and treatment* (pp. 113–135). Hillsdale, NJ: Erlbaum.

Whorf, B. L. (1956). Science and linguistics. In J. B. Carroll (Ed.), *Language, thought, and reality: Selected writings of Benjamin Lee Whorf* (pp. 207–219). Cambridge, MA: MIT Press.

Wickelgren, I. (1996). For the cortex, neuron loss may be less than thought. *Science, 273,* 48–50.

Wicker, A. W. (1969). Attitudes versus action: The relationship of verbal and overt behavioral responses to attitude objects. *Journal of Social Issues, 25,* 41–78.

Widom, C. S. (1989). Does violence beget violence? A critical examination of the literature. *Psychological Bulletin, 106,* 3–28.

Widom, C. S., & Maxfield, M. G. (1996). A prospective examination of risk for violence among abused and neglected children. *Annals of the New York Academy of Sciences, 794,* 224–237.

Widom, C. S., & Morris, S. (1997). Accuracy of adult recollections of childhood victimization: Part 2. Childhood sexual abuse. *Psychological Bulletin, 9,* 34–46.

Wiederhold, B., & Wiederhold, M. (2008). Virtual reality with fMRI: A breakthrough cognitive treatment tool. *Virtual Reality, 12,* 259–267.

Wigboldus, D., Dijksterhuis, A., & Van Knippenberg, A. (2003). When stereotypes get in the way: Stereotypes obstruct stereotype-inconsistent trait inferences. *Journal of Personality & Social Psychology, 84,* 470–484.

Wilcox, D., & Hager, R. (1980). Toward realistic expectation for orgasmic response in women. *Journal of Sex Research, 16,* 162–179.

Wilhelm, K., Kovess, V., Rios-Seidel, C., & Finch, A. (2004). Work and mental health. *Social Psychiatry & Psychiatric Epidemiology, 39,* 866–873.

Wilken, J. A., Smith, B. D., Tola, K., & Mann, M. (2000). Trait anxiety and prior exposure to non-stressful stimuli: Effects on psychophysiological arousal and anxiety. *International Journal of Psychophysiology, 37,* 233–242.

Wilkinson, R. (2004). The role of parental and peer attachment in the psychological health and self-esteem of adolescents. *Journal of Youth & Adolescence, 33,* 479–493.

Williams, J. (2003). Dementia and genetics. In R. Plomin, J. de Fries, I. Craig, & P. McGuffin (Eds.), *Behavioral genetics in the postgenomic era* (pp. 503–528). Washington, DC: APA.

Williams, K., Harkins, S. G., & Latané, B. (1981). Identifiability as a deterrent to social loafing: Two cheering experiments. *Journal of Personality and Social Psychology, 40,* 303–311.

Williams, L. M. (1994). Recall of childhood trauma: A prospective study of women's memories of child sexual abuse. *Journal of Consulting and Clinical Psychology, 62,* 1167–1176.

Willoughby, T., Anderson, S., Wood, E., Mueller, J., & Ross, C. (2009). Fast searching for information on the Internet to use in a learning context: The impact of domain knowledge. *Computers & Education, 52,* 640–648.

Wilson, F. R. (1998). *The hand: How its use shapes the brain, language, and human culture.* New York: Pantheon.

Wilson, G., & Sysko, R. (2006). Cognitive-behavioral therapy for adolescents with bulimia nervosa. *European Eating Disorders Review, 14,* 8–16.

Wilson, M. A., & McNaughton, B. L. (1993). Dynamics of the hippocampal ensemble code for space. *Science, 261,* 1055–1058.

Wilson, W., Mathew, R., Turkington, T., Hawk, T., Coleman, R. E., & Provenzale, J. (2000). Brain morphological changes and early marijuana use: A magnetic resonance and positron emission tomography study. *Journal of Addictive Diseases, 19,* 1–22.

Winerman, L. (2006). Reaching out to Muslim and Arab Americans. *APA Monitor on Psychology, 37,* 54–55.

Winograd, E. (1988). Some observations on prospective remembering. In M. M. Gruneberg, P. E. Morris, & R. N. Sykes (Eds.), *Practical aspects of memory: Current research and issues: Vol. 1* (pp. 348–353). Chichester, England: John Wiley & Sons.

Winokur, G., Coryell, W., Keller, M., Endicott, J., & Akiskal, H. S. (1993). A prospective follow-up of patients with bipolar and primary unipolar affective disorder. *Archives of General Psychiatry, 50,* 457–465.

Wirth, S., Yanike, M., Frank, L., Smith, A., Brown, E., & Suzuki, W. (2003). Single neurons in the monkey hippocampus and learning of new associations. *Science, 300,* 1578–1581.

Wirz-Justice, A. (2009). From the basic neuroscience of circadian clock function to light therapy for depression: On the emergence of chronotherapeutics. *Journal of Affective Disorders, 116,* 159–160.

Witt, L., Burke, L., Barrick, M., & Mount, M. (2002). The interactive effects of conscientiousness and agreeableness on job performance. *Journal of Applied Psychology, 87,* 164–169.

Wittenberg, M., Bremmer, F., & Wachtler, T. (2008). Perceptual evidence for saccadic updating of color stimuli. *Journal of Vision, 8,* 1–9.

Wolf, O. (2009). Stress and memory in humans: Twelve years of progress? *Brain Research, 1293,* 142–154.

Wolford, G., Miller, M. B., & Gazzaniga, M. (2000). The left hemisphere's role in hypothesis formation. *Journal of Neuroscience, 20,* 1–4.

Wolpe, J. (1958). *Psychotherapy by reciprocal inhibition.* Palo Alto, CA: Stanford University Press.

Wolpe, J. (1973). *The practice of behavior therapy* (2nd ed.). New York: Pergamon.

Wolsko, P., Eisenberg, D., Davis, R., & Phillips, R. (2004). Use of mind-body medical therapies: Results of a national survey. *Journal of General Internal Medicine, 19,* 43–50.

Wolters, C. (2003). Understanding procrastination from a self-regulated learning perspective. *Journal of Educational Psychology, 95,* 179–187.

Wolters, C. (2004). Advancing achievement goal theory using goal structures and goal orientations to predict students' motivation, cognition, and achievement. *Journal of Educational Psychology, 96,* 136–250.

Wood, J. M., Nezworski, M. T., & Stejskal, W. J. (1996). The Comprehensive System for the Rorschach: A critical examination. *Psychological Science, 7,* 3–10.

Wood, J., Cowan, P., & Baker, B. (2002). Behavior problems and peer rejection in preschool boys and girls. *Journal of Genetic Psychology, 163,* 72–88.

Wood, W., & Conway, M. (2006). Subjective impact, meaning making, and current and recalled emotions for self-defining memories. *Journal of Personality, 75,* 811–846.

Wood, W., & Eagly, A. (2007). Social structure origins of sex differences in human mating. In S. Gangestad, & J. Simpson (Eds.), *The evolution of mind: Fundamental questions and controversies* (pp. 383–390). New York: Guilford Press.

Wood, W., Lundgren, S., Ovellette, J. A., Busceme, S., & Blackstone, T. (1994). Minority influence: A meta-analytic review of social influence processes. *Psychological Bulletin, 115,* 323–345.

Wood, W., Wong, F. Y., & Chachere, J. G. (1991). Effects of media violence on viewers' aggression in unconstrained social interaction. *Psychological Bulletin, 109,* 371–383.

Woodman, G., & Luck, S. (2003). Serial deployment of attention during visual search. *Journal of Experimental Psychology: Human Perception and Performance, 29,* 121–138.

Woodward, A. L., Markman, E. M., & Fitzsimmons, C. M. (1994). Rapid word learning in 13- and 18-month-olds. *Developmental Psychology, 30,* 553–566.

Woody, E. Z., & Bowers, K. S. (1994). A frontal assault on dissociated control. In S. J. Lynn & J. W. Rhue (Eds.), *Dissociation: Clinical, theoretical and research perspectives* (pp. 52–79). New York: Guilford.

Woolley, J., & Boerger, E. (2002). Development of beliefs about the origins and controllability of dreams. *Developmental Psychology, 38,* 24–41.

World Health Organization (WHO). (2000b). *Violence against women.* [Online report] Retrieved September 1, 2000, from *http://www.who.int*

World Health Organization. (2010). *Gender and women's mental health.* Retrieved March 18, 2010 from *http://www.who.int/ mental_health/prevention/genderwomen/en/.*

Worrel, J. A., Marken, P. A., Beckman, S. E., & Ruehter, V. L. (2000). Atypical antipsychotic agents: A critical review. *American Journal of Health System Pharmacology, 57,* 238–255.

Worthen, J., & Wood, V. (2001). Memory discrimination for self-performed and imagined acts: Bizarreness effects in false recognition. *Quarterly Journal of Experimental Psychology, 54A,* 49–67.

Wright, J. C., & Mischel, W. (1987). A conditional approach to dispositional constructs: The local predictability of social behavior. *Journal of Personality and Social Psychology, 53,* 1159–1177.

Wright, K. (2002, September). Times of our lives. *Scientific American,* 58–65.

Wu, C., & Shaffer, D. R. (1987). Susceptibility to persuasive appeals as a function of source credibility and prior experience with the attitude object. *Journal of Personality and Social Psychology, 52,* 677–688.

Wyrobek, A., Eskenazi, B., Young, S., Arnheim, N., Tiemann-Boege, I., Jahs, E., et al. (2006). Advancing age has differential effects on DNA damage, chromatin integrity, gene mutations, and aneuploidies. *Proceedings of the National Academies of Sciences, 103,* 9601–9606.

Xiong, G., Bourgeois, J., Marks, S., Liu, D., Chang, C., Yellowlees, P., & Hilty, D. (2009). *Hypochondriasis.* Retrieved March 15, 2010 from *http://emedicine.medscape.com/article/290955-overview.*

Xu, J., Kochanek, K., & Tejada-Vera, B. (2009). Deaths: Preliminary data for 2007. *National Vital Statistics Reports, 58,* 1–51.

Yackinous, C., & Guinard, J. (2002). Relation between PROP (6-n-propylthiouracil) taster status, taste anatomy and dietary intake measures for young men and women. *Appetite, 38,* 201–209.

Yale-New Haven Hospital. (2003). *Making the right choice: Speak up about complementary and alternative therapies.* Retrieved August 6, 2003, from *http://www.ynhh.org/choice/cam.html*

Yanagita, T. (1973). An experimental framework for evaluation of dependence liability in various types of drugs in monkeys. *Bulletin of Narcotics, 25,* 57–64.

Yang, C., & Spielman, A. (2001). The effect of a delayed weekend sleep pattern on sleep and morning functioning. *Psychology & Health, 16,* 715–725.

Yapko, M. D. (1994). Suggestibility and repressed memories of abuse: A survey of psychotherapists' beliefs. *American Journal of Clinical Hypnosis, 36,* 163–171.

Yasui-Furukori, N., Saito, M., Nakagami, T., Kaneda, A., Tateishi, T., & Kaneko, S. (2006). Association between multidrug resistance 1 (MDR1) gene polymorphisms and therapeutic response to bromperidol in schizophrenic patients: A preliminary study. *Progress in Neuro-Psychopharmacology & Biological Psychiatry, 30,* 286–291.

Yates, W. (2009). *Anxiety disorders.* Retrieved March 15, 2010 from *http://emedicine.medscape.com/article/286227-overview.*

Yeh, S., & Lo, S. (2004). Living alone, social support, and feeling lonely among the elderly. *Social Behavior & Personality, 32,* 129–138.

Ying, Y. (2009). Strengthening intergenerational/intercultural ties in immigrant families (SITIF): A parenting intervention to bridge the Chinese American intergenerational acculturation gap. In N., Trinh, Y., Rho, F., Lu, & K. Sanders (Eds.), *Handbook of mental health and acculturation in Asian American families: Current clinical psychiatry* (pp. 45–64). Totowa, NJ: Humana Press.

Yip, S., Sacco, K., George, T., & Potenza, M. (2009). Risk/reward decision-making in schizophrenia: A preliminary examination of the influence of tobacco smoking and relationship to Wisconsin Card Sorting Task performance. *Schizophrenia Research, 110,* 156–164.

Yolken, R., & Torrey, E. (2008). Are some cases of psychosis caused by microbial agents? A review of the evidence. *Molecular Psychiatry, 13,* 470–479.

Young, G. (2009). Coma. In Schiff, N., & Laureys, S. (Eds.), *Disorders of consciousness. Annals of the New York Academy of Sciences* (pp. 32–47). New York: Wiley-Blackwell.

Yovell, Y., Bannett, Y., & Shalev, A. (2003). Amnesia for traumatic events among recent survivors: A pilot study. *CNS Spectrums, 8,* 676–685.

Zajonc, R. B. (1980). Feeling and thinking: Preferences need no inferences. *American Psychologist, 35,* 151–175.

Zajonc, R. B. (1984). On the primacy of affect. *American Psychologist, 39,* 117–123.

Zajonc, R. B., & Sales, S. M. (1966). Social facilitation of dominant and subordinate responses. *Journal of Experimental Social Psychology, 2,* 160–168.

Zaragoza, M. S., & Mitchell, K. J. (1996). Repeated exposure to suggestion and the creation of false memories. *Psychological Science, 7,* 294–300.

Zatorre, R., Belin, P., & Penhune, V. (2002). Structure and function of the auditory cortex: Music and speech. *Trends in Cognitive Sciences, 6,* 37–46.

Zhang, D., Li, Z., Chen, X., Wang, Z., Zhang, X., Meng, X., et al. (2003). Functional comparison of primacy, middle and recency retrieval in human auditory short-term memory: An event-related fMRI study. *Cognitive Brain Research, 16,* 91–98.

Zhang, L. (2002). Thinking styles and the Big Five personality traits. *Educational Psychology, 22,* 17–31.

Zhang, X., Cohen, H., Porjesz, B., & Begleiter, H. (2001). Mismatch negativity in subjects at high risk for alcoholism. *Alcoholism: Clinical & Experimental Research, 25,* 330–337.

Zimbardo, P. (1969). The human choice: Individuation, reason, and order versus deindividuation, impulse, and chaos. *Nebraska Symposium on Motivation, 17,* 237–307.

Zimbardo, P. G. (1972). Pathology of imprisonment. *Society, 9,* 4–8.

Zimmerman, M., Posternak, K., & Chelminski, I. (2002). Symptom severity and exclusion from antidepressant efficacy trials. *Journal of Clinical Psychopharmacology, 22,* 610–614.

Zinbarg, R., & Griffith, J. (2008). Behavior therapy. In J. Lebow, (Ed.), *Twenty-first century psychotherapies: Contemporary approaches to theory and practice* (pp. 8–42). Hoboken, NJ: John Wiley & Sons.

Zinkernagel, C., Naef, M., Bucher, H., Ladewig, D., Gyr, N., & Battegay, M. (2001). Onset and pattern of substance use in intravenous drug users of an opiate maintenance program. *Drug & Alcohol Dependence, 64,* 105–109.

Zisapel, N. (2001). Circadian rhythm sleep disorders: Pathophysiology and potential approaches to management. *CNS Drugs, 15,* 311–328.

Zubieta, J., Bueller, J., Jackson, L., Scott, D., Xu, Y., Koeppe, R., Nichols, T., & Stohler, C. (2005). Placebo effects mediated by endogenous opioid activity on μ-opioid receptors. *Journal of Neuroscience, 25,* 7754–7762.

Zucker, A., Ostrove, J., & Stewart A. (2002). College-educated women's personality development in adulthood: Perceptions and age differences. *Psychology & Aging, 17,* 236–244.

"48% say Obama's inauguration signals new era of race relations." (January 20, 2009). Retrieved February 14, 2009 from *http://www.rasmussenreports.com/public_content/politics/obama_administration/january_2009/48_say_obama_s_inauguration_signals_new_era_of_race_relations.*

Credits

Photos

355 middle: Purestock/Alamy Images; 355 bottom middle: Somos Images/Alamy Images; 355 bottom: Frederic Cirou/PhotoAlto, inc. 355 top middle: Sean Boggs/iStockphoto.com; 357: © Bettmann/ CORBIS All Rights Reserved; 365: Chris Arend/Stone/Getty Images; 366: © Ariel Skelley/CORBIS All Rights Reserved; 367: dpa/Landov Media; 372: Getty Images, Inc - Purestock Royalty Free.

Chapter 12: p. 379: Rosanne Olson/Getty Images—Digital Vision; 381 left: Robert Harbison/Robert Harbison; 381 right: © Dean Conger/ COR-BIS All Rights Reserved; 384: Richard Drew/AP Wide World Photos; 389: Bubbles Photolibrary/Alamy Images; 393: AP Wide World Photos; 394: Frazer Harrison/Getty Images, Inc. 395: William Hart/Will Hart; 399: Arthur Tilley/Taxi/Getty Images.

Chapter 13: p. 409: Zigy Kaluzny/Getty Images Inc.—Stone Allstock; 411: AP Wide World Photos; 412: Michaek Rougier/Getty Images/Time Life Pictures; 413 top: Corbis RF; 413 bottom: Bruce Ayers/Stone/Getty Images; 414: David Young-Wolff/PhotoEdit Inc. 416: Geri Enberg Photography/The Image Works; 424: W & D McIntyre/Photo Researchers, Inc. 426: © David and Les Jacobs/Blend Images/CORBIS All Rights Reserved; 428: Michael Newman/PhotoEdit Inc.

Chapter 14: p. 438: Chrissie Cowan/The Image Works; 439: Charles Gatewood/The Image Works; 441: Jonathan Kirn/Stock Connection; 442: Aijaz Rahi/AP Wide World Photos; 444: Tony Freeman/PhotoEdit Inc. 446: William Vandevert/Scientific American Magazine; 447: Mark Richards/Alexandra Milgram Courtesy of Alexandra Milgram/From the film, Obedience ©1965 by Stanley Milgram and distributed by Penn State Media sales. 450: Mark Richards/PhotoEdit Inc. 453: Philip G. Zimbardo, Inc., Department of Psychology, Stanford University; 456: zumaredwestphotos/Newscom; 457: David Young-Wolff/PhotoEdit Inc. 458: Robert Brenner/PhotoEdit Inc. 460: Getty Images; 462: Gary Conner/PhotoEdit Inc.

Text and Art

Figure 1.5, p. 22: Lang et. al.

Figure 2.2, p. 40: Lilienfeld, et. al., Prentice-Hall, Inc. (electronic rights).

Figure 2.5, p. 44: Lilienfeld, et. al., Prentice-Hall, Inc. (electronic rights).

Figure 2.6, p. 45: Lilienfeld, et. al., Prentice-Hall, Inc. (electronic rights).

Figure 2.10, p. 51: Gazzaniga.

Figure 2.11, p. 52: Gazzaniga.

Figure 3.5, p. 79: NYT Graphics, The New York Times (Figures/Images).

Figure 3.7, p. 82: House Ear Institute.

Figure 3.11, p. 91: Highlights for Children.

Figure 3.16, p. 96: E. G. Boring.

Table 4.1, p. 121: Nash and Benham, Scientific American.

Figure 5.3, p. 140 top: Pavlov.

Figure 5.4, p. 140 bottom: Pavlov.

Figure 5.7, p. 156: Tolman & Honzik.

Figure 5.8, p. 160: Lenhart, Jones, & Macgill, Pew Internet & American Life Project.

Figure 6.2, p. 169: Atkinson and Shiffrin.

Figure 6.8, p. 187: Maguire et al., Proceedings of the National Academy of Sciences.

Try It, p. 183: Nickerson & Adam, Rightslink.

Figure 6.5, p. 183: From p. 297 in "Long-Term Memory for a Common Object" by R. S. Nickerson & M. J. Adams, (1979), Cognitive Psychology, 11, pp. 287–307. Copyright © 1979. Reprinted by permission of Elsevier, Inc.

Figure 6.8, p. 187: From E. A. Maguire, D. G. Gadian, I. S. Johnsrude, C. D. Good, J. Ashburner, R. S. J. Frackowiak, and C. D. Frick, "Navigation-Related Structural Change in the Hippocamp of Taxi Drivers", (2000), Proceedings of the National Academy of Sciences of the United States of America, 97, pp. 4398–4403. Copyright © 2000 by National Academy of Sciences. Reprinted by permission.

Figure 7.1, p. 212: David Premack, Rightslink.

Figure 7.2, p. 215: Hakuta et al., Rightslink.

Figure 7.8, p. 225: Frances Campbell; Craig Ramey, Rightslink.

Figure 7.9, p. 228: Kimura, Jared Schneidman Design.

Figure 7.10, p. 232: Carlsson et al., Rightslink.

Figure 8.1, p. 244: Bee & Boyd.

Figure 8.2, p. 249: Colby et al., Wiley-Blackwell Publishing Ltd.

Figure 8.4, p. 256: Frankenburg et al., Denver Developmental Materials.

Figure 9.3, p. 290: American Psychological Association (APA).

Table 9.4, p. 294: Mayo Clinic.

Figure 9.6, p. 305: Figure 3, p. 1051 from "Subcortical and Cortical Brain Activity during the Feeling of Self-Generated Emotions" by A. R. Damasio, T. J. Grabowski, A. Bechara, H. Damasio, L. L. B. Ponto, J. Parvizi, and R. D. Hichwa, (October 2000), Nature Neuroscience, 3 (10), pp. 1049–1056. Copyright © 2000. Reprinted by permission of Copyright Clearance Center on behalf of the publisher.

Think About It, p. 318: Kanner et al., Springer Science+Business Media.

Try It, p. 319: Holmes, Matsuda, John Wiley & Sons, Inc.

Figure 10.1, p. 322: Albrecht.

Figure 10.2, p. 325: Green & Shellenberger, Cengage Learning/Global Rights and Permissions Administration.

Figure 10.3, p. 327: Selye.

Figure 10.7, p. 343: Barnes et al.

Figure 11.3, p. 360: Cattell, Cattell, & Cattell, John Wiley & Sons, Inc.

Figure 11.4, p. 363: Bouchard.

Table 12.1, p. 382: Based on DSM-IV-TR, American Psychiatric Association.

Table 12.2, p. 383: American Psychiatric Association.

Figure 12.4, p. 396: Walker et al., Copyright Clearance Center.

Figure 12.6, p. 398: Thompson et al., Proceedings of the National Academy of Sciences.

Table 13.1, p. 419: Judith Beck, Guilford Press.

Figure 13.2, p. 419: Monica Ramirez Basco, Guilford Press.

Figure 14.1, p. 445: Sternberg, American Psychological Association (APA).

Figure 14.2, p. 446: Based on Asch, Scientific American.

Figure 14.3, p. 448: Milgram.

Figure 14.4, p. 450: Zajonc & Sales.

Practice Tests

Answers can be found in the *Student Solutions Manual*.

CHAPTER 1: Introduction to Psychology

Multiple Choice

1. Psychology is defined as
   a. a survey of the mind's abilities.
   b. an informal study of human behavior and learning processes.
   c. the scientific study of behavior and mental processes.
   d. nothing more than common sense.

2. A counseling psychologist is working with a married couple to promote better communication in their relationship. Which goal of psychology is the psychologist trying to accomplish?
   a. description
   b. explanation
   c. prediction
   d. influence

3. Which of the following is true regarding basic and applied research?
   a. Applied research would seek to find out why memory abilities sometimes change over time.
   b. Basic research would allow us to help the quality of life for those who have Alzheimer's type dementia.
   c. Neither basic nor applied research allows us to determine cause and effect.
   d. Basic research would allow us to learn about memory changes, and applied research allows us to help those with memory problems cope with everyday life.

4. One of the first psychological laboratories was established by _____ where he used _____ as the primary method of research.
   a. Ernst Weber; introspection
   b. Gustav Fechner; metromes
   c. Wilhelm Wundt; introspection
   d. Sigmund Freud; behavioral modification

5. The early psychological school of thought devoted to studying the basic elements of conscious mental experiences was _____, developed by _____.
   a. functionalism; Freud
   b. structuralism; Titchener
   c. behaviorism; Skinner
   d. humanism; Watson

6. _____ is the school of thought that focuses on unconscious wishes, desires, and impulses.
   a. Humanistic psychology
   b. Behaviorism
   c. Functionalism
   d. Psychoanalytic psychology

7. _____ is associated with _____, the school of thought that studies only observable, measurable behavior.
   a. John B. Watson; behaviorism
   b. Sigmund Freud; psychoanalytic psychology
   c. Abraham Maslow; humanistic psychology
   d. Max Wertheimer; structuralism

8. Dr. Smith believes that depression is a consequence of faulty thinking, decision making, and problem solving. With which theoretical perspective would Dr. Smith most agree?
   a. biological
   b. humanistic
   c. psychoanalytic
   d. cognitive

9. Dr. Jarrod, a psychologist, is part of an interdisciplinary team that includes biologists, biochemists, and medical researchers, who study the nervous system. To which field does Dr. Jarrod likely belong?
   a. evolutionary psychology
   b. biocultural psychology
   c. chemical psychology
   d. neuroscience

10. Dr. Benson studies the factors that promote productivity in an office environment for a large company. Which type of psychologist is Dr. Benson likely to be?
    a. social psychologist
    b. industrial-organizational psychologist
    c. educational psychologist
    d. counseling psychologist

11. Which type of psychologist is most likely to study how human behavior is affected by the presence of other people?
    a. social psychologist
    b. developmental psychologist
    c. educational psychologist
    d. clinical psychologist

12. Which of the following is *not* a characteristic exhibited when one engages in critical thinking?
    a. independent thinking
    b. suspension of judgment
    c. open-minded acceptance
    d. willingness to modify prior judgments

13. A researcher is studying patterns of social play in 8-year-olds by watching children on a playground and documenting their behaviors. Which research method is she using?
    a. survey
    b. laboratory observation
    c. case study
    d. naturalistic observation

14. A survey taker makes sure that the people surveyed closely mirror the population of interest. He is ensuring that he has a
    a. representative sample.
    b. representative population.
    c. biased sample.
    d. random population.

15. A professor asks her class to record how often they study. Her students may tend to report studying more than they really do, thereby giving a
    a. candid response.
    b. social desirability response.
    c. representative response.
    d. random response.

16. The variable that is presumed to vary as a result of the manipulation of another variable is called a(n)
    a. confounding variable.
    b. dependent variable.
    c. independent variable.
    d. mitigating factor.

17. Dr. Needles is testing the effects of a new drug. One group receives the drug, while a comparison group receives an injection of a harmless solution. The group that receives the drug is called the
    a. experimental group.
    b. control group.
    c. prediction group.
    d. placebo group.

18. In Dr. Needles's experiment, neither he nor the participants know who gets the drug and who gets the harmless solution. This method is called
    a. the single-blind method.
    b. the double-blind technique.
    c. the hidden-purpose method.
    d. deception.

19. Which of the following correlation coefficients indicates the strongest relationship between two variables?
    a. .67
    b. −.43
    c. −.85
    d. 1.25

20. Research participants must be told the purpose of the study in which they are participating and its potential for harming them. This is the ethical consideration known as
    a. prior approval.
    b. applicable disclosure.
    c. appropriate disclosure.
    d. informed consent.

True/False

21. Replication is used to verify a study's findings with a different group of participants.

22. Wilhelm Wundt and John Watson belonged to the same early school of psychology.

23. Humanistic psychology focuses on the uniqueness of human beings and their capacity for growth.

24. Information-processing theory compares the human brain's workings to those of a computer.

25. The view that human behavior is shaped by physiological factors is called the sociocultural approach.

26. Descriptive research methods, such as surveys and observation, accomplish all four goals of psychology equally well.

27. The experimental method allows for the greatest experimenter control as well as permitting cause and effect conclusions to be drawn.

28. A perfect positive correlation is indicated by the coefficient 1.00.

29. If stress and illness are positively correlated, it means that stress causes illness.

30. The APA permits the use of animals in research.

Essay

31. Explain what separates the science of psychology from common sense. Include in your response reasons that a theory cannot rely on anecdotal evidence.

32. Name and describe at least four current, major schools of thought in psychology. According to each school selected, what is the primary reason for an individual's behavior?

33. Suppose you wanted to test whether a new drug helped improve scores on a memory test for college students. Design an experiment to do so. Include how you would select your sample and label the independent and dependent variables, as well as the experimental and control groups. Also, describe one confounding variable you would avoid.

CHAPTER 2: Biology and Behavior

Multiple Choice

1. During an exam, which brain-wave pattern are you most likely to exhibit?
   a. alpha wave
   b. beta wave
   c. delta wave
   d. slow wave

2. Kevin is undergoing some tests to look for signs of physical damage to his brain. He also needs to be sure that certain parts of his brain are working properly. Which type of diagnostic technique would reveal both structures and activity?
   a. fMRI
   b. MRI
   c. CT scan
   d. PET scan

3. The neurons that relay messages from the sense organs to the central nervous system are
   a. afferent (sensory) neurons.
   b. efferent (motor) neurons.
   c. interneurons.
   d. operant neurons.

4. Which part of the neuron receives messages from other cells?
   a. dendrite
   b. myelin sheath
   c. axon
   d. synapse

5. When a neuron's axon carries a positive electrical potential of about 50 millivolts for a brief moment, it is said to be firing. This is called the
   a. resting potential.
   b. synaptic charge.
   c. action potential.
   d. ionic storm.

6. Sarah seems to be depressed, isn't sleeping well, and has little appetite. Which neurotransmitter is most likely to be involved in the problem?
   a. serotonin
   b. dopamine
   c. epinephrine
   d. acetylcholine

7. Which part of the nervous system is primarily responsible for regulating the body's involuntary, internal environment?
   a. autonomic nervous system
   b. somatic nervous system
   c. central nervous system
   d. synaptic nervous system

8. Marisa is riding a roller coaster. As it surges over the high point to plunge downward, her heart races, her breathing quickens, and blood flow to her skeletal muscles increases. Which division of the peripheral nervous system is most active?

   a. somatic
   b. central
   c. sympathetic
   d. parasympathetic

9. Jesse is wiring together his home theater system, and he accidentally touches a live wire. He gets a painful shock and quickly jerks his hand away. The reflex of pulling his hand back is dictated by the
   a. hypothalamus.
   b. spinal cord.
   c. hippocampus.
   d. medulla.

10. A severe injury to the medulla would likely result in
    a. coma.
    b. paralysis.
    c. memory loss.
    d. death.

11. Which area of the brain regulates several body functions, including hunger, thirst, sexual behavior, and internal body temperature?
    a. thalamus
    b. hypothalamus
    c. amygdala
    d. substantia nigra

12. Danielle is left-handed. When she is taking notes in class, which part of her brain is directing the movements of her hand?
    a. left frontal lobe
    b. right frontal lobe
    c. left temporal lobe
    d. right temporal lobe

13. The visual cortex is located in the
    a. frontal lobe.
    b. parietal lobe.
    c. temporal lobe.
    d. occipital lobe.

14. Coral has epilepsy. Her seizures begin on the left side of her brain and then travel to the right side; this occurs repeatedly. Her doctor wants to perform an operation that he believes will improve the quality of Coral's life. Because medications are not controlling her seizures, which of the following is Coral's doctor likely considering?
    a. He plans to perform a prefrontal lobotomy.
    b. He plans to remove her amygdala.
    c. He plans to sever her corpus callosum.
    d. He plans to scrape the Broca's area.

15. Which individual is most likely to recover or at least partially recover a lost brain function following a head injury?
    a. 15-year-old boy
    b. 25-year-old man
    c. 45-year-old woman
    d. 7-year-old girl

16. Which of the following statements about gender differences in the adult brain is true?

    a. Men have less white matter in the brain than do women.

    b. Women have more white matter in the left brain than do men.

    c. Women have more gray matter in the area of the brain that controls emotions than do men.

    d. There is no evidence of gender differences in the adult brain.

17. _____ are to the central nervous system as _____ are to the endocrine system.

    a. Neurons; electrons

    b. Electrons; neurons

    c. Hormones; neurotransmitters

    d. Neurotransmitters; hormones

18. Which organ is responsible for regulating blood sugar by releasing insulin and glucagon into the bloodstream?

    a. pancreas

    b. pituitary

    c. spleen

    d. thyroid

19. In a dominant-recessive pattern set of inheritance rules, which pair of genes would result in the expression of a recessive trait?

    a. two dominant genes

    b. one dominant gene and one recessive gene

    c. two recessive genes

    d. none of the above

20. Which of the following is *true* regarding the field of behavioral genetics?

    a. The researchers are trying to understand how heredity affects behavior.

    b. Twin studies are used in the field of behavioral genetics.

    c. Adoption studies are used in the field of behavioral genetics.

    d. All of the above are true.

True/False

21. An MRI is a more powerful way to view the brain's structures than an EEG.

22. The myelin sheath allows neural impulses to travel faster.

23. Any neurotransmitter can fit into any receptor.

24. The somatic nervous system can be divided into the sympathetic and parasympathetic nervous systems.

25. The limbic system is a series of brain structures involved in emotion.

26. Wernicke's aphasia involves difficulty with comprehension of speech.

27. The right hemisphere of the brain is responsible for most language functions.

28. Pain perception occurs in the somatosensory area of the cerebrum.

29. The gonads are primarily responsible for the production of sex hormones.

30. There are 22 pairs of chromosomes in the human body.

Essay

31. Describe the process of neural transmission across the synapse.

32. Name and describe the effects of five neurotransmitters.

33. Name and describe the components that make up the peripheral nervous system.

CHAPTER 3: Sensation and Perception

Multiple Choice

1. Jenna accidentally steps on a pin. The stimulation of her skin and transmission of the information regarding this touch to the central nervous system is the process of
   a. penetration.
   b. sensation.
   c. perception.
   d. registration.

2. To sense a change in weights being carried, the additional weight added must be 2% higher than what you carried before. This difference threshold is calculated using
   a. Weber's law.
   b. an absolute threshold.
   c. Planck's law.
   d. Gestalt laws.

3. The process of converting sensory information into neural impulses is called
   a. sensory conduction.
   b. transformation.
   c. sensory adaptation.
   d. transduction.

4. Jake and Abby walked into their local Starbucks to get some coffee. Jake immediately noticed the smell of freshly ground coffee beans. Abby couldn't smell them until she walked closer to the counter where the beans were being ground. Jake and Abby likely have different
   a. sensory adaptation abilities.
   b. olfactory accommodations.
   c. absolute thresholds.
   d. saturation levels.

5. The outer part of the eye that serves to protect the eye, and on which you would place your contact lenses, is called the
   a. lens.
   b. cornea.
   c. pupil.
   d. iris.

6. The _____ is the structure responsible for transduction for vision.
   a. retina
   b. optic nerve
   c. fovea
   d. iris

7. Which theory best explains visual phenomena such as afterimages?
   a. trichromatic theory
   b. opponent-process theory
   c. Weber's law
   d. signal detection theory

8. The loudness of a sound corresponds to which physical characteristic of a sound wave?
   a. amplitude
   b. frequency
   c. wavelength
   d. timbre

9. Which of the following best describes where transduction for hearing takes place?
   a. eardrum
   b. pinna
   c. ossicles
   d. hair cells in the cochlea

10. Which theory of hearing best explains how sensory receptors in our ear encode sound wave frequencies over 1,000 Hz?
    a. frequency theory
    b. place theory
    c. both frequency theory and place theory
    d. neither frequency theory nor place theory

11. Glenda purchases some new perfume to attract her boyfriend's attention. The perfume is meant to stimulate which sensory system?
    a. olfactory
    b. gustatory
    c. tactile
    d. auditory

12. Linda's friends all drink coffee, but Linda finds the taste of coffee very bitter, more so than do her friends. Which is one explanation for Linda's dislike of coffee?
    a. She is has an aversion to caffeine.
    b. She is a "nontaster."
    c. She is a "supertaster."
    d. She has damaged taste buds.

13. Monique experiences a leg cramp in her calf. She massages the muscle while gritting her teeth and finds she feels less pain. Which theory explains this decrease in pain?
    a. place theory
    b. frequency theory
    c. opponent-process theory
    d. gate-control theory

14. A toddler plays with blocks by sorting them into piles by color, so that the red blocks make up one pile, the blue blocks make up a second pile, and the green blocks make up a third pile. He is using which Gestalt principle of perceptual organization?
    a. proximity
    b. similarity
    c. continuity
    d. closure

15. Gary sees a friend standing near a fence. The fence partially blocks his view of his friend, so Gary realizes the fence is closer to him than is his friend. Which monocular depth cue is Gary using?
    a. linear perspective
    b. relative size
    c. interposition
    d. texture gradient

16. The "old woman/young woman" image is an example of
    a. the phi phenomenon.
    b. an impossible figure.
    c. an ambiguous figure.
    d. an autokinetic illusion.

17. Which of the following involves an illusion using two equal lines with diagonals extending outward from one line, making it appear longer than the line with diagonals extending inward?
    a. Müller-Lyer illusion
    b. moon illusion
    c. Ponzo illusion
    d. linear perspective illusion

18. Brandi is learning to read by sounding out a word one letter at a time. Which type of processing is she using?
    a. bottom-up processing
    b. top-down processing
    c. perceptual set
    d. Gestalt principle of closure

19. Leroy is studying and trying to ignore his roommate's phone conversation in the other room. He is engrossed in his psychology textbook until he hears his name mentioned, when he suddenly becomes aware of what his roommate is saying on the phone. Which perceptual concept does this example demonstrate?
    a. phi phenomenon
    b. cross-modal perception
    c. just noticeable difference
    d. cocktail party phenomenon

20. Which type of extrasensory perception might be claimed by individuals who try to predict the outcome of a football game?
    a. clairvoyance
    b. synesthesia
    c. precognition
    d. telepathy

True/False

21. The lens in the eye is a muscle that dilates or constricts depending on the amount of light in the environment.

22. A blind spot exists in our vision due to an area on the retina that lacks rods and cones.

23. Someone with color blindness cannot perceive any colors at all.

24. The same note played on different musical instruments sounds different because of a change in timbre.

25. Receptors in our muscles, joints, and ligaments allow us to obtain information as to where our body is in space.

26. The sensory receptors for the olfactory system are located in the olfactory bulbs.

27. Specific areas of the tongue specialize in processing different taste sensations.

28. The body has the ability to produce natural painkillers called endorphins in times of need.

29. Illusions fool our perceptual system only when our attention decreases.

30. Subliminal perception can influence behavior to some degree.

Essay

31. Explain the progression of a sound wave from its arrival at the pinna to its arrival in the brain.

32. Describe how the gate-control theory explains our perception of pain. How do psychological factors affect this perception?

33. Name and describe five Gestalt principles of perceptual organization.

CHAPTER 4: States of Consciousness

Multiple Choice

1. A mental state other than wakefulness, such as sleep or meditation, is called
   a. consciousness.
   b. meta-consciousness.
   c. an altered state of consciousness.
   d. conscientiousness.

2. Circadian rhythms exist for
   a. appetite.
   b. learning efficiency.
   c. energy level.
   d. all of the above.

3. Which hormone is most related to the sleep/wake cycle?
   a. adrenaline
   b. serotonin
   c. melatonin
   d. glucagons

4. _____ occurs in four stages.
   a. Biorhythm
   b. Consciousness
   c. REM sleep
   d. NREM sleep

5. Which EEG pattern is typical of someone who is relaxed and drowsy but not yet asleep?
   a. alpha waves
   b. beta waves
   c. delta waves
   d. sleep spindles

6. Jonas stayed up all night at a party. The next night, he had nightmares when he slept. This was probably because of
   a. somnambulism.
   b. REM rebound effect.
   c. NREM sleep disturbance.
   d. more time spent in stage 3 sleep.

7. Which theory explains the function of sleep in humans?
   a. restorative theory of sleep
   b. circadian theory of sleep
   c. a combination of both the restorative and circadian theories of sleep
   d. neither the restorative nor the circadian theory of sleep

8. Laura describes a dream she had to her friend, Jessica. Jessica explains her view of what the dream means. According to Freud, Jessica is offering her opinion of which aspect of Laura's dream?
   a. manifest content
   b. latent content
   c. lucid content
   d. symbiotic content

9. Which of the following best describes the activation-synthesis hypothesis of dreaming?
   a. Dreams are symbolic of unconscious conflicts.
   b. Dreams offer a symbolic opportunity to rehearse solutions to real-world problems.
   c. Dreams are the brain's way of consolidating memories.
   d. Dreams are the brain's attempt to make sense of the random firing of brain cells during REM sleep.

10. The technical term for talking in one's sleep is
    a. somniloquy.
    b. somnambulism.
    c. parasomnia.
    d. hypersomnia.

11. Which of the following major sleep disorders may be treated through surgery?
    a. insomnia
    b. sleep apnea
    c. narcolepsy
    d. somniloquy

12. Nightmares and sleep terrors
    a. occur during different stages of sleep.
    b. are both seen during REM sleep.
    c. are the same thing.
    d. predict mental illness.

13. Terrell spends time every morning sitting alone, quietly concentrating on the sound of his own breathing. He says that the 20 minutes of quiet time clear his mind and cause him to feel rested and alert. Terrell is experiencing the benefits of
    a. hypnosis.
    b. somniloquy.
    c. dyssomnia.
    d. meditation.

14. Which of the following statements about hypnosis is true?
    a. Memory is more accurate under hypnosis.
    b. People can perform superhuman acts while under hypnosis.
    c. People are more suggestible while hypnotized.
    d. Hypnosis can be used to regress adults back to their childhood.

15. Which theory of hypnosis states that the behavior of a hypnotized person is a function of his or her own expectations about how people behave while hypnotized?
    a. sociocognitive theory of hypnosis
    b. theory of dissociated control
    c. cognitive dissonance theory
    d. neodissociated theory of hypnosis

16. Which of the following is not a psychoactive drug?
    a. marijuana
    b. nicotine
    c. caffeine
    d. All of the above are psychoactive drugs.

17. Alcohol is classified as a
a. stimulant.
b. depressant.
c. hallucinogen.
d. narcotic.

18. Blake uses cocaine. He finds he needs more cocaine now to receive the same effect he once received from smaller amounts of the drug. This symptom of cocaine dependence is called
a. withdrawal.
b. drug escalation.
c. drug tolerance.
d. psychological drug dependence.

19. According to psychologists, at what point does casual use of a psychoactive drug become abuse?
a. when the use of the substance occurs regularly
b. when the individual feels a craving for the drug
c. when use of the drug has begun to negatively affect important aspects of the person's life and functioning
d. when the individual realizes that he or she wants to stop using the substance

20. The neurotransmitter associated with the feelings of reward or pleasure produced by many psychoactive substances is
a. serotonin.
b. dopamine.
c. acetylcholine.
d. diazepam.

True/False

21. Chronic jet lag can result in permanent memory deficits.

22. Exposure to bright sunlight during early morning hours and avoidance of bright light in the evening may help restore circadian rhythms for those experiencing jet lag.

23. Sleep deprivation may negatively affect mood but has little effect on cognitive performance.

24. Dreams occur only during REM sleep.

25. Chronic insomnia can last for years.

26. Meditation can help some people with depression.

27. Hypnosis has been effective in helping people control pain.

28. Substance abuse is a more severe problem than substance dependence.

29. An individual who is addicted to cocaine and tries to quit using will often feel irritable and may have trouble sleeping.

30. Marijuana has been associated with lung diseases.

Essay

31. Describe the NREM and REM progression of the sleep cycle. Include the EEG pattern typical of each stage.

32. Distinguish between the dream theories espoused by Freud and Hobson.

33. Distinguish between the general effects of stimulants, depressants, and hallucinogens, including the typical pattern of withdrawal symptoms for each.

CHAPTER 5: Learning

Multiple Choice

1. The individual most directly responsible for the process of classical conditioning is
   a. B. F. Skinner.
   b. Ivan Pavlov.
   c. John B. Watson.
   d. Edward Thorndike.

2. Vinny's professor always says, "Here we go!!" before administering an exam. For some reason now, Vinny becomes nervous every time he hears someone say, "Here we go!!" In this example of classical conditioning, which is the conditioned stimulus?
   a. the exam
   b. becoming nervous
   c. hearing the phrase, "Here we go!!"
   d. Vinny's professor

3. Twenty-two year old Sofia drank too much vodka and cranberry juice one evening and became very ill. Now, anytime Sofia tastes cranberry juice, she feels very ill. Based on classical conditioning, _____ is the unconditioned stimulus whereas _____ is the conditioned stimulus.
   a. too much vodka; cranberry juice
   b. feeling very ill; too much vodka
   c. cranberry juice; feeling very ill
   d. cranberry juice; vodka

4. The weakening and eventual disappearance of a conditioned response that is caused by repeated presentation of the conditioned stimulus without the presence of the unconditioned stimulus is called
   a. discrimination.
   b. generalization.
   c. spontaneous recovery.
   d. extinction.

5. Jerry bought a dog specifically to serve as a watch dog. He teaches his dog to bark whenever the doorbell rings. However, the dog also barks at the telephone or a doorbell rung on television. Which process explains these additional responses?
   a. spontaneous recovery
   b. higher-order conditioning
   c. generalization
   d. discrimination

6. John B. Watson's work with Little Albert was significant because it demonstrated
   a. a conditioned fear response.
   b. the limitations of classical conditioning.
   c. discrimination procedures.
   d. conditioning the behavior of a rat.

7. Janie once ate fish at a restaurant and later felt ill. Now the very smell of cooked fish makes her nauseous. What has Janie experienced?
   a. a conditioned fear response
   b. a taste aversion
   c. a taste generalization
   d. an unconditioned aversion response

8. Bill completes his drug rehabilitation program. His counselor strongly urges him to avoid going to places where he used to use drugs. His counselor, knowledgeable about classical conditioning, says this so that
   a. Bill doesn't experience peer pressure to use drugs.
   b. Bill can start fresh in more areas of his life.
   c. Bill doesn't get rewarded for drug use.
   d. Bill doesn't come into contact with stimuli previously associated with drug use.

9. Thorndike's experiments using the cat that had to learn to escape the puzzle box for food illustrated which behavioral law?
   a. law of rewards
   b. law of consequence
   c. law of effect
   d. law of gravity

10. _____ are the major concepts of operant conditioning, a type of learning devised by _____.
    a. Positive and negative reinforcement; Pavlov
    b. Stimulus and reinforcement; Skinner
    c. The law of effect and classical conditioning; Thorndike
    d. Reinforcement and punishment; Skinner

11. The process of shaping a response involves reinforcing each of a series of steps that become increasingly more similar to the desired response. This is called
    a. successive approximations.
    b. gradual discovery.
    c. the "eureka" phenomenon.
    d. planning with foresight.

12. What causes extinction in operant conditioning?
    a. withholding punishment
    b. withholding reinforcement
    c. shaping
    d. reinforcing successive approximations

13. Cindy cries for candy when in the store with her mother. Her mother, wanting Cindy to be quiet, gives in and gets her some candy, at which point Cindy becomes silent. The next time they go to the store, the process repeats itself. Which of the following best describes what has happened?
    a. Cindy's behavior is positively reinforced, and her mother's behavior is positively reinforced.
    b. Cindy's behavior is positively reinforced, and her mother's behavior is negatively reinforced.
    c. Cindy's behavior is negatively reinforced, and her mother's behavior is positively reinforced.
    d. Cindy's behavior is negatively reinforced, and her mother's behavior is negatively reinforced.

14. Positive reinforcement _____ the likelihood of a behavior happening again; negative reinforcement _____ the likelihood of a behavior happening again.
    a. decreases; increases
    b. increases; decreases
    c. decreases; decreases
    d. increases; increases

15. Which of the following is the best example of a primary reinforcer?
    a. money
    b. a diploma
    c. water
    d. a greeting card

16. A professor gives his class a quiz each Monday. Consequently, students do not study much during the week, but "cram" throughout the weekend to earn a good grade. Their behavior best corresponds to which schedule of reinforcement?
    a. fixed ratio
    b. variable ratio
    c. fixed interval
    d. variable interval

17. When Billy misbehaves, his parents make sure to apply punishment immediately and consistently and to use the harshest possible punishment so that Billy will "get the message." According to the research in your text, which of the following is a recommendation you might make to help their use of punishment be more effective?
    a. make punishment less severe
    b. make punishment more severe
    c. punish him less consistently
    d. wait a bit after his misbehavior before punishing him

18. Seligman's experiments with dogs that did not escape the shock administered, even when they could have, demonstrates which principle?
    a. avoidance learning
    b. learned helplessness
    c. escape learning
    d. positive reinforcement

19. Carrie is trying to complete a jigsaw puzzle. She struggles with it for some time until she suddenly sees how the pieces fit together. Which type of learning is Carrie exhibiting?
    a. insight learning
    b. latent learning
    c. shaping
    d. observational learning

20. Carl learned how to change a flat tire by watching his mother do so. She would change a tire and then have him show her each step as well. Which type of learning does this demonstrate?
    a. insight learning
    b. latent learning
    c. classical conditioning
    d. observational learning

True/False

21. Memorizing a phone number long enough to dial it, and then forgetting it, fits the text definition of learning.

22. Classical conditioning takes place most readily when the unconditioned stimulus occurs just before the conditioned stimulus.

23. John B. Watson was one of the researchers who demonstrated that fear could be conditioned in humans.

24. Rescorla's cognitive view of classical conditioning suggests that the repeated pairing of the conditioned stimulus and the unconditioned stimulus is the critical element for conditioning to occur.

25. The "operant" in operant conditioning refers to a voluntary behavior.

26. Negative reinforcement is designed to have the same outcome as punishment.

27. According to Skinner, punishment can suppress behavior but not extinguish it.

28. Biofeedback can be used to train individuals to control internal responses such as heart rate and anxiety-tension states.

29. Behavior modification programs require a therapist to administer them.

30. The process of latent learning depends on reinforcement taking place.

Essay

31. Distinguish between the process of extinction in classical conditioning and the process of extinction in operant conditioning.

32. Design a reinforcement plan to teach your dog to roll over. Include the type of reinforcement used, the schedule of reinforcement, and the reason why you made those particular choices.

33. Describe Bandura's "Bobo doll" study and its implications for television violence.

CHAPTER 6: Memory

Multiple Choice

1. Any steps you take to try to commit something to memory are part of the _____ process.
   a. consolidation
   b. encoding
   c. retrieval
   d. placement

2. When you call information for a phone number, but you don't have a pen to write down the number, which part of your memory must attempt to maintain the number while you run around looking for a pen?
   a. implicit memory
   b. long-term memory
   c. short-term memory
   d. nondeclarative memory

3. The strategy of grouping bits of information into larger units that are easier to remember is called
   a. displacement.
   b. rehearsal.
   c. assimilation.
   d. chunking.

4. For information stored in long-term memory to be used, it must first be
   a. grouped.
   b. moved into sensory memory.
   c. retrieved.
   d. chunked.

5. Memories of a vacation spent with your family would be considered
   a. implicit memories
   b. episodic memories
   c. procedural memories
   d. nondeclarative memories

6. Which of the following is not one of the three types of nondeclarative memories?
   a. information learned in class
   b. motor skills
   c. simple classically conditioned responses
   d. habits

7. A memory researcher asks subjects to memorize a list of words and finds it takes them 30 minutes to do so. Two weeks later, he asks the same subjects to memorize the list of words again, and they do so in 15 minutes. The percentage of time saved, 50%, is known as the
   a. savings score.
   b. relearning score.
   c. rote score.
   d. recognition score.

8. Which of the following techniques is used to measure memory?
   a. the relearning method
   b. tests of recall
   c. tests of recognition
   d. all of the above

9. According to the serial position effect, which items on a list are least likely to be recalled?
   a. the first few
   b. the middle few
   c. the last few
   d. All items are equally likely to be remembered or forgotten.

10. Vern had a bit too much to drink at a party one night. The next day he got a phone call from a woman he met at the party, but he cannot remember her name. According to the state-dependent memory effect, under which condition will Vern most likely remember her name?
    a. when he is sober
    b. when he hears her voice
    c. when he sees her face
    d. when he has a bit too much to drink

11. An integrated framework about people, objects, and events that is stored in long-term memory is called a
    a. memory.
    b. schema.
    c. reconstruction.
    d. retrieval cue.

12. There is a good chance that you remember exactly where you were and what you were doing when you first heard about the attacks on September 11, 2001. Such a vivid memory is called a(n) _____ memory.
    a. flashbulb
    b. snapshot
    c. autobiographical
    d. first-order

13. Jacquez believes that as you get older, memories that haven't been used will just fade away and disappear. His position is most consistent with which cause of forgetting?
    a. decay theory
    b. encoding failure
    c. consolidation failure
    d. proactive interference

14. David studied French in high school but switched to learning Italian in college. Whenever he tries to speak French, he catches himself instead translating his English phrases into Italian. Why is David forgetting his French?
    a. encoding failure
    b. proactive interference
    c. retroactive interference
    d. decay theory

15. Which of the following is not a form of motivated forgetting according to your text?
    a. anterograde amnesia
    b. progressive forgetting
    c. suppression
    d. retrograde amnesia

16. Cassie is playing Trivial Pursuit with friends. She is asked a question and knows she knows the answer. However, she becomes frustrated because although she knows the answer, she cannot seem to retrieve it. What is Cassie likely experiencing?
    a. state-dependent memory
    b. the tip-of-the-tongue phenomenon
    c. retrograde amnesia
    d. repression

17. Which of the following hormones has *not* been related to memory processes, according to your text?
    a. cortisol
    b. estrogen
    c. testosterone
    d. noradrenalin (epinephrine)

18. Which type of memory is reconstructive?
    a. autobiographical
    b. flashbulb
    c. source
    d. all of the above

19. While passing on an interesting bit of gossip to a friend, the friend asks where you heard the information. Try as you might, you can't recall. You have experienced a failure of _____ memory.
    a. semantic
    b. short-term
    c. source
    d. flashbulb

20. Henry, a college student, has difficulty remembering events from the first few years of his life. This is likely due to
    a. repression of early traumas.
    b. a negative bias.
    c. infantile amnesia.
    d. the fact that he has yet to experience recovered memories.

True/False

21. Elaborative rehearsal is the best method for remembering complex information like material for this class.

22. Recall tasks are typically considered to be easier than recognition tasks.

23. A reconstruction of an event may sometimes be based on inaccurate information.

24. Hermann Ebbinghaus conducted the first experimental studies on learning and memory.

25. The tip-of-the-tongue phenomenon is an example of retrieval failure.

26. The brain structure associated with transfer of information from short- to long-term memory is the amygdala.

27. If a person's hippocampus is damaged, she may be unable to store new information in long-term memory.

28. Your strongest, most long-lasting memories are usually those fueled by your emotions.

29. Research suggests that eyewitness testimony is too unreliable to be considered as evidence in criminal court cases.

30. Repressed memories are controversial in that the event never really occurred.

Essay

31. Describe the "reconstructive" nature of memory, including the impact of schemas and cognitive bias.

32. What is long-term potentiation, and how is it related to learning?

33. Describe a plan for studying that incorporates at least two recommendations from your text to improve your memory.

CHAPTER 7: Cognition, Language, and Intelligence

Multiple Choice

1. Acquiring, storing, retrieving, and using information, based on sensation, perception, problem solving, and conceptualizing, is called
   a. a formal concept.
   b. memorizing.
   c. cognition.
   d. recognition.

2. Which of the following would not be considered a concept?
   a. animals
   b. your cat Spike
   c. mammals
   d. dogs

3. Individual instances of a concept that are stored in memory based on personal experience are called
   a. prototypes.
   b. specifics.
   c. phonemes.
   d. exemplars.

4. Which of the following is the most likely prototype of a bird?
   a. sparrow
   b. penguin
   c. ostrich
   d. turkey

5. You are trying to decide what kind of breakfast cereal to buy. You notice a new cereal that you recall seeing advertised on television and choose to buy it. This kind of decision making fits best with the concept of the
   a. elimination by aspects strategy.
   b. recognition heuristic.
   c. algorithm.
   d. representativeness heuristic.

6. The _____ is a sort of mental short cut that helps us make decisions based on what is easiest to call to mind.
   a. probability heuristic
   b. representative heuristic
   c. recognition heuristic
   d. availability heuristic

7. Kayla is playing blackjack and has a hand totaling 17. She knows that she will likely lose if she gets another card but she does so anyway because she has a "gut feeling" she will get a lucky card. On what is Kayla's decision making based?
   a. probability heuristic
   b. elimination by aspects
   c. intuition
   d. analogy heuristic

8. When you use a specific procedure for solving a math problem that will always lead you to the correct answer, providing you correctly follow the steps, you are using a(n)

   a. analogy.
   b. availability heuristic.
   c. algorithm.
   d. means-end analysis.

9. Juanita visits her advisor at college and afterward figures out when she will graduate by counting how many classes she has left and determining how many terms it will take to complete them. She is using
   a. the recognition heuristic.
   b. means-end analysis.
   c. pragmatics.
   d. an algorithm.

10. _____ refers to word arrangement, whereas _____ refers to the meaning of words.
    a. Syntax; semantics
    b. Semantics; phonemes
    c. Morphemes; pragmatics
    d. Semantics; syntax

11. How many phonemes are in the word *psychology*?
    a. 4
    b. 6
    c. 8
    d. 10

12. Intonation and social rules are part of which component of language?
    a. phonics
    b. pragmatics
    c. syntax
    d. semantics

13. The language in which you think largely determines the nature of your thoughts. This is called the
    a. bilingual theory.
    b. relative cognition model.
    c. meta-cognitive strategy.
    d. linguistic relativity hypothesis.

14. Thurston believed that seven distinct capabilities are involved in all intellectual activities, which he referred to as
    a. primary mental abilities.
    b. the *g* factor.
    c. IQ.
    d. the triarchic theory.

15. Wes is a con artist who flunked out of school, though he always got along with teachers and students. He is currently unemployed but runs "scams" to earn his living. He has played a bum, a cop, a priest, and a businessman as part of his efforts to cheat people, and he has never been caught. Wes would likely have a high degree of Gardner's _____ intelligence.
    a. interpersonal
    b. musical
    c. componential intelligence
    d. existential

16. Phillip is an 8-year-old with a mental age of 6. According to Terman's formula, what is his IQ?
    a. 60
    b. 75
    c. 100
    d. 133

17. When you take a psychology test and afterward believe it did not accurately measure your knowledge of the psychology, you are questioning the test's
    a. validity.
    b. cultural fairness.
    c. reliability.
    d. standardization.

18. When administered properly, the results of a standardized intelligence test
    a. can be used to determine which individuals will enjoy a successful life.
    b. should not be considered at all because IQ tests are culturally unfair.
    c. can help explain why a child may be struggling in school.
    d. are completely useless.

19. Early interventions designed to enrich the environment of poor children
    a. rarely have an effect.
    b. have demonstrated that such efforts can have lasting effects.
    c. support the heritability of intelligence.
    d. demonstrate that nature cannot be altered by nurturing.

20. When you figure out a solution to your problem and you put it into action, you are engaging in the process of
    a. preparation.
    b. incubation.
    c. illumination.
    d. translation.

True/False

21. A rose would be a likely prototype for the concept of flowers.

22. Framing, or presenting information a certain way to emphasize an outcome or gain, has a limited effect on decision making.

23. Anything the human brain can do, an artificial intelligence program can do just as well or better.

24. Morphemes, the smallest units of meaning in the English language, are always words.

25. Bilingualism during childhood is associated with an improved ability to think about language.

26. The SAT is an aptitude test designed to predict college performance.

27. Mental retardation is based solely on one's IQ score.

28. Lewis Terman's study found that mentally gifted individuals had more mental health/psychological problems than the general population.

29. Research shows that racial differences in IQ are largely due to genetic factors.

30. Women tend to do better than men on mathematical calculation tests.

Essay

31. Discuss the advantages and disadvantages of relying on heuristics in making decisions.

32. What have attempts to teach language to nonhuman primates demonstrated?

33. Distinguish between Spearman's *g* factor approach to intelligence and Gardner's theory of multiple intelligences.

CHAPTER 8: Human Development

Multiple Choice

1. The idea that development occurs in distinctive phases that are easily distinguishable from each other is the central premise of
   a. continuous development.
   b. stage theories.
   c. environmental theory.
   d. nature versus nurture.

2. Wendy is 18 months old and just learning to speak. She meows whenever she sees a cat. One day, while she is watching television, a rabbit appears, and Wendy points and meows. What process has Wendy attempted regarding her existing scheme of cats?
   a. assimilation
   b. conservation
   c. accommodation
   d. hypothetico-deductive thinking

3. Sanford enjoys playing hide-and-seek with his mother. Sanford can play this game only because he has achieved what Piaget would call
   a. conservation.
   b. reversibility.
   c. hypothetico-deductive thinking.
   d. object permanence.

4. Piaget's cognitive stages in chronological order are
   a. sensorimotor, concrete operations, preoperations, formal operations.
   b. preoperations, concrete operations, formal operations, sensorimotor.
   c. preoperations, formal operations, concrete operations, sensorimotor.
   d. sensorimotor, preoperations, concrete operations, formal operations.

5. During which of Piaget's stages are children able to understand abstract concepts such as "freedom"?
   a. formal operations
   b. preoperations
   c. concrete operations
   d. sensorimotor

6. Luis behaves well at school because he wants to please his teacher. Which of Kohlberg's levels of moral development best fits Luis?
   a. sensorimotor
   b. preconventional
   c. conventional
   d. postconventional

7. According the Erikson, adolescence is known as the period of
   a. industry versus inferiority.
   b. autonomy versus shame and doubt.
   c. identity versus role confusion.
   d. trust versus mistrust.

8. Ginny is 82 years old. She often looks back on her life with satisfaction, believing that she accomplished a lot, had a loving family, and contributed to the world. Which of Erikson's stages best fits Ginny?
   a. industry versus inferiority
   b. ego integrity versus despair
   c. generativity versus stagnation
   d. autonomy versus shame and doubt

9. The developing human organism as it develops from the ninth week until birth is called a(n)
   a. embryo.
   b. zygote.
   c. gamete.
   d. fetus.

10. Because of the risk of fetal alcohol syndrome, pregnant women are advised to
    a. drink no more than one glass of wine per day.
    b. limit their drinking during the first trimester of pregnancy.
    c. completely abstain from alcohol during pregnancy.
    d. abstain from all hard liquor and limit consumption of other alcoholic beverages.

11. Harmful agents in the environment that can have a negative effect on prenatal development are called
    a. critical periods.
    b. teratogens.
    c. prenatal poisons.
    d. antagonists.

12. Brandi is 2 months old. She is generally happy most of the time, enjoys meeting new people, and has a regular routine to her day. Which temperament best describes her?
    a. slow-to-warm-up
    b. inconsistent
    c. easy
    d. difficult

13. Shawn is 18 months old. Lately, whenever his mother leaves him with his grandmother, he cries as if he is afraid. Their pediatrician said not to worry because _____ is common among children his age.
    a. stranger anxiety
    b. separation anxiety
    c. attachment disorder
    d. avoidance anxiety

14. "Want cookie!" could be an example of
    a. babbling.
    b. underextension.
    c. overextension.
    d. telegraphic speech.

15. Barry tells his father that he and his mother "goed to the store." This error is an example of
    a. overextension.
    b. overregularization.
    c. underextension.
    d. underregularization.

16. Which parenting style generally appears to be the most effective in the United States?
    a. authoritative
    b. authoritarian
    c. permissive
    d. indulgent

17. Cassandra is a teenager who hates school. She has developed a plan to have a perfect life that involves quitting school with her boyfriend and getting rich and famous by being on *American Idol*. Cassandra's plan would best be described by which term?
    a. a personal fable
    b. naive idealism
    c. imaginary audience
    d. hypothetico-deductive thinking

18. The most common symptom of menopause is
    a. menarche.
    b. hot flashes.
    c. dizziness.
    d. high blood pressure.

19. The only intellectual ability to show a continuous decline from about the mid-twenties to 80 is
    a. spatial ability.
    b. perceptual speed.
    c. creativity.
    d. general mathematic ability.

20. John has just learned that he has a terminal illness. According to Kübler-Ross, which reaction is he likely to experience first?
    a. acceptance
    b. anger
    c. a fighting spirit
    d. denial

True/False

21. Developmental psychology as it is studied today focuses on childhood and adolescence as times of change and adulthood as a time of stagnation.

22. According to Piaget, a 3-year-old child would assume that you can see what she sees.

23. Vygotsky's sociocultural approach to cognitive development puts more emphasis on the impact of language development than does Piaget's theory.

24. Newborns can recognize some stimuli to which they were exposed prior to birth.

25. One conclusion drawn from the visual cliff experiment was that babies have no perception of depth until they learn to walk.

26. Securely attached infants tend to develop more advanced social skills when they are preschoolers than their peers who were not securely attached.

27. The nativist position suggests that language development occurs primarily through operant conditioning.

28. Gender roles occur through the sole influence of biological factors.

29. Fluid intelligence peaks in one's twenties, but crystallized intelligence increases throughout the lifespan.

30. Kübler-Ross's stages of death and dying appear to be universal.

Essay

31. Name and describe the stages of prenatal development.

32. Distinguish between how learning theorists, nativists, and interactionists explain language development.

33. Describe how social learning, cognitive developmental, and gender-schema theorists explain gender role development.

CHAPTER 9: Motivation and Emotion

Multiple Choice

1. Keisha wants to make good grades because her parents promised her a new car if she makes the honor roll. Keisha's motivation is
   a. intrinsic.
   b. extrinsic.
   c. social.
   d. homeostatic.

2. Which of the following statements is true according to the Yerkes-Dodson law?
   a. Performance on simple tasks is best when the arousal level is low.
   b. Performance on both simple and difficult tasks is best when the arousal level is high.
   c. Performance on moderately difficult tasks is best when the arousal level is low.
   d. Performance on difficult tasks is better when arousal is low.

3. Which needs did Maslow believe must be satisfied first?
   a. need to feel competent
   b. need for shelter
   c. need for self-actualization
   d. need for affiliation

4. Inez devotes all of her energy to school. She sets high standards of performance for herself in an effort to accomplish all she can. According to research on motivation, Inez could be said to have a high need for
   a. success.
   b. recognition.
   c. achievement.
   d. glory.

5. Yvonne insists she must get the highest grade on every test so that she can exceed her peers and enhance her own self-worth. According to goal orientation theory, which goal orientation best fits Yvonne?
   a. mastery approach orientation
   b. mastery avoidance orientation
   c. performance approach orientation
   d. performance avoidance orientation

6. Which of the following factors *inhibits* eating?
   a. low blood levels of glucose
   b. stomach contractions
   c. increased levels of cholecystokinin (CCK)
   d. increased levels of insulin

7. All of the following are true *except*
   a. a taste aversion may inhibit eating.
   b. foods high in fat and sugar may stimulate eating.
   c. raised blood glucose levels stimulate eating.
   d. a full (or distended) stomach may inhibit eating.

8. You conduct a hunger experiment with rats. In one rat, you damage the ventromedial hypothalamus. In the second rat, you stimulate the lateral hypothalamus. Then you offer food to each of the rats. What will happen?
   a. The first rat will eat; the second rat will not eat.
   b. The first rat will not eat; the second rat will eat.
   c. Both rats will eat.
   d. Neither rat will eat.

9. Cherelle has weighed approximately 120 pounds for most of her adult life. She doesn't work hard to lose weight, nor does she try to gain weight. You conclude that 120 pounds represents Cherelle's
   a. set point.
   b. metabolic rate.
   c. body mass index.
   d. homeostatic score.

10. The hormone, produced in the body's fat tissues, that affects the hypothalamus and plays a primary role in weight regulation is
    a. adrenalin.
    b. leptin.
    c. serotonin.
    d. insulin.

11. Based on the research with males, which factor seems most highly correlated with bulimia?
    a. age
    b. education
    c. sexual orientation
    d. intelligence

12. What is the shortest of the four phases in the sexual response cycle?
    a. plateau
    b. resolution
    c. excitement
    d. orgasm

13. The area of the hypothalamus that governs sexual behavior is twice as large in heterosexual men than it is in homosexual men, according to research done by LeVay. What is the *main* criticism of LeVay's research?
    a. He did not use universal precautions.
    b. He did not account for AIDS as a variable.
    c. LeVay used only CT scans of the subjects' brains.
    d. His research was never replicated.

14. On realizing that the shadow behind you is a man with a gun, your heart begins to race *just as* you feel afraid. With which of the following theories of emotion is this scenario most consistent?
    a. Cannon-Bard theory
    b. Lazarus theory
    c. James-Lange theory
    d. Schachter-Singer theory

15. Which two-factor theory of emotion says that physiological arousal is followed by a cognitive interpretation of the situation?

    a. James-Lange theory

    b. Cannon-Bard theory

    c. Schachter-Singer theory

    d. Lazarus theory

16. Which of the following would not be considered a basic emotion?

    a. embarrassment

    b. fear

    c. anger

    d. joy/happiness

17. Many members of traditional British culture consider Americans to be vulgar because of Americans' tendency to spontaneously demonstrate whatever emotion they feel. The conflict between cultures is caused by differing

    a. impressions.

    b. display rules.

    c. emotional ranges.

    d. basic emotions.

18. The facial feedback hypothesis states that

    a. we recognize the emotions of others in their facial expression and change our own emotions to match.

    b. our emotions directly affect our facial muscles so that we produce an expression to match the emotion.

    c. muscular movements involved in certain facial expressions produce the corresponding emotion.

    d. seeing an individual's emotional response innately triggers a corresponding emotion.

19. Mary Ann is at a restaurant when she sees someone she thinks she knows. He turns around, and she realizes it is her ex-boyfriend. She decides that this is not a good situation. She becomes nervous, and sweaty palms and an increased heart rates follow. Which theory of motivation best describes this scenario?

    a. Lazarus theory

    b. Cannon-Bard theory

    c. James-Lange theory

    d. Schachter-Singer theory

20. The _____ is the part of the brain that is involved in the suppression of emotional impulses.

    a. hypothalamus

    b. anterior cingulate cortex

    c. corpus calossum

    d. hippocampus

True/False

21. According to psychologists, motivation is thought to have three basic components: activation, persistence, and intensity.

22. Extrinsic motivation is consistent with Skinner's concept of reinforcement.

23. Drive-reduction theory is largely based on the concepts of tension and homeostasis.

24. With regard to bulimia, bingeing is characterized by eating an extraordinary amount of food coupled with the feeling of loss of control over one's eating.

25. Women appear to have the strongest desire for sex around the time of ovulation when they are most likely to conceive a child, as evolutionary theory would predict.

26. Androgens are present only in men; estrogen and progesterone are present only in women.

27. Based on the Global Sex Survey, individuals in Japan reported the highest frequency of intercourse and the highest satisfaction regarding their sex lives.

28. The amygdala is activated by fear before any direct involvement of the cerebral cortex occurs.

29. Facial expressions for the basic emotions are very similar across cultures.

30. Some studies show that women are more attuned to verbal and nonverbal expressions of emotions than are men.

Essay

31. Describe environmental cues for hunger.

32. Define anorexia nervosa and bulimia nervosa and describe the negative effects of each disorder.

33. Discuss the role of cognition in each of the four theories of emotion discussed in this chapter.

CHAPTER 10: Health and Stress

Multiple Choice

1. Based on the Social Readjustment Rating Scale (SRRS), which of the following have the largest life-changing unit value?
   a. change in school
   b. jail term
   c. getting fired at work
   d. death of a spouse

2. A prolonged stress reaction following a catastrophic experience is called
   a. acute stress disorder.
   b. posttraumatic stress disorder.
   c. general adaptation syndrome.
   d. reactive attachment disorder.

3. According to Lazarus, which types of stressors seem to cause more stress?
   a. hassles
   b. uplifts
   c. annoyances
   d. catastrophes

4. Hank has a stressful job, but he always looks forward to coming home to his wife, who never fails to bring a smile to his face and relieve some of his stress. According to Richard Lazarus, Hank's time with his wife would be described as
   a. a hassle.
   b. an approach-approach situation.
   c. a counter-stressor.
   d. an uplift.

5. Would you rather have a terrible toothache or the undesirable experience of having the tooth drilled and the cavity filled? This choice represents which type of conflict?
   a. approach-avoidance
   b. approach-approach
   c. avoidance-avoidance
   d. avoidance-approach

6. According to Albrecht (1979), which of the following factors is *not* related to job satisfaction and effective functioning at work?
   a. the clarity of the job description and evaluation criteria
   b. having a variety of tasks to accomplish
   c. being one's own boss
   d. having some amount of accountability on the job

7. According to Utsey (2002), _____ has been found to moderate the levels of racial stress in African Americans.
   a. a strong sense of ethnic identity
   b. a high degree of hostility
   c. historical racism
   d. being one of only a few African Americans in a given setting, such as a classroom or workplace

8. The key components of the immune system are the white blood cells known as
   a. antigens.
   b. antibodies.
   c. lymphocytes.
   d. leukocytes.

9. Which of the following infectious diseases has *not* been correlated with periods of high stress?
   a. rubella
   b. mononucleosis
   c. flu
   d. genital herpes

10. According to Seyle's General Adaptation Syndrome theory, what happens when an organism fails in its efforts to resist or adapt to a stressor?
    a. resistance failure
    b. exhaustion
    c. fight-or-flight syndrome
    d. alarm

11. According to Richard Lazarus, an event appraised as stressful could involve
    a. harm or loss.
    b. threat.
    c. challenge.
    d. all of the above

12. Which of the following statements reflects a secondary appraisal?
    a. "I refuse to accept that I have cancer."
    b. "It's good to know my sister can watch my kids while I have chemotherapy. At least I don't have to worry about that."
    c. "It is not fair that I have been diagnosed with cancer at such a young age!"
    d. "Why is this happening to *me?*"

13. Mrs. Genova has been told that she has terminal cancer and only a few months left to live. After a brief time, she set out to tie up the loose ends of her life, updating her will, giving away special possessions, and saying her goodbyes. Mrs. Genova is employing which approach to coping with her illness?
    a. variate-focused
    b. problem-focused
    c. emotion-focused
    d. solution-focused

14. All of the following are qualities of the hardiness trait *except*
    a. control.
    b. commitment.
    c. caring.
    d. challenge.

15. Which element of the Type A behavior pattern is most strongly related to coronary heart disease?
    a. time urgency
    b. hostility
    c. competitiveness
    d. impatience

16. Which of the following is a risk factor for cancer, according to health psychologists?
    a. smoking
    b. promiscuous sexual behavior
    c. excessive alcohol consumption
    d. all of the above

17. What percentage of the adult population in the United States still smokes, according to your text?
    a. 65%
    b. less than 25%
    c. 35%
    d. 50%

18. Blake has been at his friend's party for about two hours now. He has consumed a large amount of alcohol (about five drinks) in those few hours. He gets a call from his girlfriend who tells him to sober up and come to the party she is attending. Based on the research in your text, which of the following is the best advice Blake gets from his friends?
    a. "Blake, wait another hour, and you should be sober enough to drive."
    b. "Blake, just go crash on my bed for one or two hours . . . you can sleep it off and then leave."
    c. "Blake, buddy, there is no way to sober up in time for you to get to that party. Looks like you are staying here tonight."
    d. "Blake, drink two cans of Red Bull and then take a walk outside. The fresh air and caffeine will help you sober up before you leave."

19. Which of the following STDs can successfully be treated with antibiotics?
    a. genital warts
    b. HPV
    c. syphilis
    d. genital herpes

20. Though research shows exercise is the simplest and most effective way to enhance one's health, what proportion of Americans still don't exercise at all?
    a. one-third
    b. one-half
    c. three-quarters
    d. two-thirds

True/False

21. Survivor guilt may be a symptom experienced by individuals who live through a catastrophic event.

22. The hassle most commonly cited by college students is not getting enough sleep.

23. The parasympathetic nervous system initiates the fight-or-flight response.

24. According to Selye, prolonged stress can lead to permanent increases in blood pressure, suppression of the immune system, and weakening of muscles.

25. Engaging in problem-focused coping helps manage stress by reducing, modifying, or eliminating the stressor.

26. A sedentary lifestyle is the primary modifiable risk factor contributing to death from coronary heart disease.

27. The Type D behavior pattern appears to buffer the negative effects of stress.

28. Women are more likely than men to seek medical care.

29. Being exposed to secondhand smoke doubles one's risk of having a heart attack when compared to those who are not exposed to it.

30. The most common infectious disease in the United States is AIDS.

Essay

31. Describe the biopsychosocial model of health and illness.

32. Describe the Type A, Type B, and Type D behavior patterns.

33. Describe four factors that reduce the impact of stress and illness.

CHAPTER 11: Personality Theory and Assessment

Multiple Choice

1. You don't usually think about your phone number, but if someone asked you for it, you could easily recall it and make yourself aware of it. According to Freud's levels of consciousness, your phone number is likely stored in your
   a. unconscious.
   b. conscious.
   c. preconscious.
   d. subconscious.

2. George wants a new stereo badly. He decides he will buy a new one by putting it on his credit card, without worrying too much about the debt he is accruing. George is acting based on the wishes of his
   a. id.
   b. ego.
   c. superego.
   d. unconscious mind.

3. Alice feels good about how neat and organized she keeps her room. This pride represents her
   a. ego.
   b. conscience.
   c. id.
   d. ego ideal.

4. Lysette cannot believe it when her friends tell her that her boyfriend is cheating on her. She insists they must be mistaken. Which Freudian defense mechanism might Lysette be exhibiting?
   a. repression
   b. projection
   c. displacement
   d. denial

5. Tabitha has always been a flirtatious and promiscuous woman. She is very vain, and she tends to seek attention from anyone around her. Freud might suggest that she had problems at which psychosexual stage of development?
   a. anal
   b. phallic
   c. oral
   d. latency

6. Which theorist suggested that we share the universal experiences of humankind throughout evolution?
   a. Carl Jung
   b. Sigmund Freud
   c. Karen Horney
   d. Alfred Adler

7. Which theorist suggested that behavior, cognitive factors, and the environment have a mutually influential relationship?
   a. Abraham Maslow
   b. Julian Rotter
   c. Albert Bandura
   d. Karen Horney

8. Which of the following statements about the differences between people with high self-efficacy and low self-efficacy is *false*?
   a. People with high self-efficacy show greater persistence than those with low self-efficacy.
   b. People with high self-efficacy set lower goals that are more realistic than those with low self-efficacy.
   c. People with high self-efficacy have more confidence than those with low self-efficacy.
   d. People with low self-efficacy appear to have higher rate of depression than those with high self-efficacy.

9. Someone with an internal locus of control is most likely to explain a high test grade as due to
   a. luck.
   b. an easy exam.
   c. hard work.
   d. prayer.

10. Which group of theories is most likely to suggest that individuals can reach their full potential for growth?
    a. psychoanalytic
    b. trait
    c. learning
    d. humanistic

11. Ben goes along with what his friends want to do even though he would prefer to do something else. He does so because he wants to be accepted. Carl Rogers would explain Ben's behavior by saying that he has been exposed to conditions of
    a. worth.
    b. self-actualization.
    c. unconditional positive regard.
    d. friendship.

12. You are trying to set up two of your friends for a date. One asks you to describe the other's personality, which you do using the four characteristics the person is known for. According to Allport, what kind of traits have you listed?
    a. cardinal traits
    b. surface traits
    c. central traits
    d. source traits

13. Zach is an emotional, nervous, and moody person, but he is always good-natured, warm, and cooperative. On which two Big Five traits would Zach likely be rated highly?
    a. extroversion and neuroticism
    b. openness to experience and agreeableness
    c. conscientiousness and extroversion
    d. agreeableness and neuroticism

14. According to the Minnesota twin study, which of the following statements concerning twins and personality is true?
    a. Identical twins are similar on several personality factors, whether reared together or apart.
    b. Identical twins are similar on several personality factors, but only if they were reared together.

c. Identical twins are similar on several personality factors, but only if they were reared apart.

d. Identical twins are not similar on any personality factors.

15. Genes exert more influence on which Big Five traits?

a. extroversion and neuroticism

b. openness to experience and agreeableness

c. conscientiousness and extroversion

d. agreeableness and neuroticism

16. Nicole responds to some questionnaires that ask her questions about her behaviors and personality characteristics. What kind of personality assessment has she undergone?

a. behavioral assessment

b. personality inventory

c. projective test

d. structured interview

17. Which of the following provides a standardized format for the data from observations or interviews?

a. personality inventory

b. rating scale

c. projective test

d. the TAT

18. Which of the following is often used by career counselors?

a. Minnesota Multiphasic Personality Inventory (MMPI)

b. Myers-Briggs Type Indicator (MBTI)

c. Thematic Apperception Test (TAT)

d. California Personality Inventory (CPI)

19. Which of the following is a projective test?

a. Minnesota Multiphasic Personality Inventory (MMPI)

b. Myers-Briggs Type Indicator (MBTI)

c. Thematic Apperception Test (TAT)

d. California Personality Inventory (CPI)

20. Which of the following is considered by the examiner in evaluating responses to the Rorschach Inkblot method?

a. the content of the response

b. whether shape or color influenced the response

c. whether the whole blot or only part of it is used in the response

d. all of the above

True/False

21. The ego operates according to a principle that demands immediate gratification.

22. Freud's theories, when tested, show no scientific evidence supporting them.

23. Low self-efficacy is correlated with an increased risk for depression.

24. People with an internal locus of control are more likely to procrastinate than people with an external locus of control.

25. According to Maslow, self-actualized individuals are autonomous and thus do not pursue personal relationships.

26. According to Raymond Cattell, observable qualities of personality are referred to as source traits.

27. The Big Five traits have been found in cross-cultural studies in Canada, Poland, Germany, Hong Kong, and Russia.

28. The trait of aggressiveness is solely influenced by parental upbringing.

29. The MMPI contains validity scales to detect faking or lying.

30. The Rorschach Inkblot method continues to have poor interrater agreement due to the lack of a scoring system.

Essay

31. What are the primary distinctions between the theories of the neo-Freudians and Freud's theory?

32. Describe the situation versus trait debate.

33. How does personality differ based on the individualism/collectivism dimension of a culture?

CHAPTER 12: Psychological Disorders

Multiple Choice

1. Gretchen likes to keep everything. She has things stacked in corners, and every closet is filled to the top. Lots of people save things, but Gretchen's "saving" has reached the point that every surface in her home is covered. She is embarrassed to have company, to the point that she refuses to allow anyone in her house. However, she continues to save things. What is it about Gretchen's behavior that makes it considered abnormal?
   a. It is illegal.
   b. It is maladaptive.
   c. It is dangerous.
   d. It is culturally influenced.

2. Which perspective contends that early childhood experiences are behind the manifestation of psychological disorders?
   a. psychosocial
   b. psychodynamic
   c. cognitive
   d. biopsychosocial

3. Which of the following is considered an anxiety disorder?
   a. schizophrenia
   b. bipolar disorder
   c. substance abuse/dependence
   d. panic disorder

4. Eric does not like to be in public places—especially where there are a lot of people, and escape would be difficult. He fears he will have a panic attack and will not be able to get away or obtain help. Eric could probably be diagnosed with
   a. agoraphobia.
   b. obsessive-compulsive disorder.
   c. bipolar disorder.
   d. generalized anxiety disorder.

5. Which of the following would be considered a social phobia?
   a. fear of enclosed places
   b. fear of injections
   c. fear of public speaking
   d. fear of flying

6. Mark spends hours upon hours mopping, dusting, and in general sanitizing his house. This cleaning behavior is Mark's way to mute the frightening visual images that frequently pop into his mind. Mark's cleaning behaviors might be described as a(n)
   a. phobia.
   b. obsession.
   c. delusion.
   d. compulsion.

7. Which individual is *most* at risk for a recurrent episode of depression?
   a. John, who first became depressed at age 24
   b. Mary, who first became depressed at age 50
   c. Carol, who first became depressed at age 14
   d. Henry, who first became depressed at age 40

8. The rate of depression among women is generally _____ that of men.
   a. about half
   b. twice
   c. about four times
   d. one-fourth

9. How does the prevalence of bipolar disorder compare to the prevalence of major depressive disorder?
   a. Bipolar disorder is much less common.
   b. Major depressive disorder is much less common.
   c. Bipolar disorder is three times more common.
   d. Their prevalence rates are strikingly similar.

10. In the field of psychology, the word *psychosis* refers to
    a. dangerousness.
    b. nervousness.
    c. a loss of contact with reality.
    d. social isolation.

11. Marianne truly believes that she is a world-famous movie star. Her neighbors see her occasionally in her front yard, waving to them as if they were her adoring crowd. Marianne likely has
    a. delusions of grandeur.
    b. delusions of persecution.
    c. an anxiety disorder.
    d. dissociative identity disorder.

12. Which of the following neurotransmitters has been associated with schizophrenia?
    a. serotonin
    b. norepinephrine
    c. acetylcholine
    d. dopamine

13. Individuals with which type of schizophrenia have periods where they display little or no body movement, often remaining in bizarre positions for hours?
    a. undifferentiated
    b. disorganized
    c. paranoid
    d. catatonic

14. Which of the following disorders is diagnosed more often in men than in women?
    a. major depression
    b. generalized anxiety disorder
    c. schizophrenia
    d. phobia

15. On waking one morning, Michael could not see. However, doctors could find no medical cause for his blindness. They should consider a diagnosis of
    a. conversion disorder.
    b. dissociative disorder.
    c. reaction formation.
    d. hypochondriasis.

16. The disorder that involves an individual having more than one personality, generally one host and at least one alter, is called
    a. dissociative identity disorder.
    b. dissociative fugue.
    c. dissociative amnesia.
    d. conversion disorder.

17. Sarah is a female, although she believes she was born into the wrong body. Since she was a very young child, she has proclaimed that she is a boy. Sarah might be considered to have
    a. gender identity disorder.
    b. conversion disorder.
    c. sexual dysfunction.
    d. personality disorder.

18. James finds it arousing when his girlfriend wears a sexy negligee. James would be diagnosed with
    a. a paraphilia.
    b. gender identity disorder.
    c. a sexual dysfunction.
    d. no disorder at all.

19. Which cluster of personality disorders includes disorders that are most likely to be confused with schizophrenia, especially paranoid schizophrenia?
    a. cluster A
    b. cluster B
    c. cluster C
    d. cluster D

20. Tina is one of those people you can never predict. One minute she's your best friend; the next, she hates you and considers you to be her worst enemy. She has fits of inappropriate anger, recklessness, and occasional suicidal gestures. Tina may be an example of a(n)
    a. histrionic personality.
    b. dependent personality.
    c. borderline personality.
    d. antisocial personality.

True/False

21. *Insanity* is a term used by mental health professionals to describe those with psychological disorders.

22. Just under half of people in the United States develop a psychological disorder at some time during their lives.

23. Antidepressant drugs are effective in the treatment of obsessive-compulsive disorder (OCD) for some individuals.

24. Research indicates that one year after their initial diagnosis of major depressive disorder, more than 90% of individuals still show symptoms.

25. About 90% of individuals who commit suicide leave clues.

26. Schizophrenia involves the possession of multiple personalities within the same body.

27. Smelling something that is not there is an example of a hallucination.

28. An individual with hypochondriasis is someone who fakes an illness to get attention.

29. Dissociative amnesia is typically caused by a traumatic head injury that impairs the functioning of the hippocampus.

30. Twin studies show that genes strongly influence the development of gender identity disorder.

Essay

31. Review the questions that may be asked to determine whether someone's behavior is abnormal.

32. Describe the risk factors for suicide, including gender, age, and ethnic differences in suicide rates.

33. Distinguish between the positive and the negative symptoms of schizophrenia.

CHAPTER 13: Therapies

Multiple Choice

1. Which group of psychotherapy approaches is based on the notion is that psychological well-being depends on self-understanding?
   a. behavior therapies
   b. relationship therapies
   c. insight therapies
   d. All forms of psychotherapy are based on that notion.

2. Which approach attempts to uncover repressed childhood experiences in an effort to explain a person's current difficulties?
   a. psychodynamic therapy
   b. interpersonal therapy
   c. person-centered therapy
   d. cognitive therapy

3. Valora became angry with her therapist and shouted at him, "You are just like my father!" Freud would consider her outburst to be an example of
   a. dissociation.
   b. empathy.
   c. transference.
   d. genuineness.

4. What is the goal of person-centered therapy?
   a. to uncover unconscious conflicts and resolve them
   b. to assist clients' growth toward self-actualization
   c. to replace maladaptive behaviors with more adaptive responses
   d. to challenge clients' irrational beliefs about themselves and others

5. The individual most closely associated with Gestalt therapy is
   a. Fritz Perls.
   b. Sigmund Freud.
   c. Carl Rogers.
   d. Aaron Beck.

6. Interpersonal therapy (IPT) is especially helpful in treating
   a. alcoholism.
   b. narcissism.
   c. specific phobias.
   d. depression.

7. Which type of problem is interpersonal therapy (IPT) not specifically designed to address?
   a. severe problems in coping with the death of a loved one
   b. deficits in interpersonal skills
   c. the highs and lows of bipolar disorder
   d. difficulties in adjusting to life after a divorce

8. Which of the following is true regarding behavior therapy?
   a. It is based on the idea that inappropriate thoughts are the basis for abnormal behavior.
   b. It is based on the notion that abnormal behavior is learned.
   c. It is a type of therapy that uses medication to control behaviors.
   d. It assumes that abnormal behavior is primarily caused by aggressive forces within the unconscious.

9. Juan's school uses a reward system to encourage students to do their homework and have good behavior. Children earn gold stars for completing assignments and paying attention to the teacher and later can exchange stars for snacks or even a day without homework. Which behavior modification technique is Juan's school using?
   a. time out
   b. systematic desensitization
   c. flooding
   d. token economy

10. Which technique is designed to treat phobias by exposing the client to extended periods of contact with the feared object or event until the anxiety decreases?
    a. aversion therapy
    b. flooding
    c. systematic desensitization
    d. free association

11. Exposure and response prevention is an approach that has proved successful in treating
    a. personality disorders.
    b. narcissism.
    c. depression.
    d. obsessive-compulsive disorder.

12. In Ellis's ABC model, the A represents the
    a. action taken.
    b. actual problem.
    c. activity of the client.
    d. activating event.

13. Joan's therapist encourages her to look for unrealistic thoughts that may be "automatic." Joan's therapist is likely providing therapy based on the theory proposed by
    a. Sigmund Freud
    b. Fritz Perls
    c. Carl Rogers
    d. Aaron Beck

14. *Neuroleptics* is another term for
    a. antipsychotics.
    b. benzodiazepines.
    c. mood stabilizers.
    d. antidepressants.

15. Which of the following drugs is most likely to be prescribed for bipolar disorder?
    a. Xanax
    b. Clozapine
    c. Lithium
    d. Prozac (fluoxetine)

16. Cynthia wants to be a psychiatrist. What degree will she need after college?
    a. Ph.D.
    b. M.D.
    c. Psy.D.
    d. Ed.D.

17. The bond between therapist and client that is thought to be a factor in the effectiveness of psychotherapy is called
    a. attachment.
    b. counselor–client bonding.
    c. the psychosocial relationship.
    d. the therapeutic alliance.

18. All of the following behaviors would be considered ethical for a therapist *except*
    a. informing clients about the cost and expected duration of a therapy.
    b. alerting the authorities if a client confesses to a crime.
    c. treating an ex-girlfriend in therapy.
    d. explaining the purpose of tests given to clients as part of therapy.

19. Culturally sensitive therapy is important because
    a. it ensures that proper medication will be prescribed.
    b. cultural factors need to be considered when choosing a therapeutic intervention.
    c. the development of a therapeutic alliance is not possible if the client and therapist have different backgrounds.
    d. cultural insensitivity is the underlying cause of most mood disorders.

20. What does research suggest about the success of psychotherapy?
    a. It is most successful with single adults.
    b. The longer someone is in therapy, the more improvement he or she seems to make.
    c. Psychotherapy is not nearly as effective as treatment involving medication.
    d. People in therapy do better with psychologists than with psychiatrists.

True/False

21. A psychodynamic therapist would interpret a client's being late to a session as a form of resistance.

22. Person-centered therapy is an example of a directive therapy.

23. A Gestalt therapist might help a client with unfinished business using the empty chair technique.

24. Family therapy, in addition to medication, tends to be effective as a treatment option for schizophrenia.

25. Alcoholics Anonymous (AA) is a form of self-help group.

26. Aversion therapy is no longer used due to ethical concerns about it.

27. Tardive dyskinesia is a movement disorder brought on by long-term use of antidepressants.

28. Tricyclics, SSRIs, and MAO inhibitors are forms of antipsychotic medications.

29. Rapid transcranial magnetic stimulation (rTMS) appears to have the same benefits as electroconvulsive therapy (ECT) with significantly fewer risks.

30. Acknowledging that there are, in fact, differences between males and females is an important facet of gender-sensitive therapy.

Essay

31. Compare and contrast Ellis's rational emotive behavior therapy and Beck's cognitive therapy.

32. What are the three types of antidepressant drugs, and how do they work?

33. Explain the similarities and differences between psychologists and psychiatrists.

CHAPTER 14: Social Psychology

Multiple Choice

1. Your grandmother always told you that first impressions create lasting impressions. She is essentially describing
   a. the actor-observer effect.
   b. the recency effect.
   c. the primacy effect.
   d. a situational attribution.

2. Creighton's boss is particularly grumpy today. He knows that she's been under a lot of stress at home and figures that is the reason for her grumpiness. Creighton is making a
   a. self-serving bias.
   b. random attribution.
   c. dispositional attribution.
   d. situational attribution.

3. Shea failed her law school entrance exams. She said it was because there was too much noise in the room and the questions were ridiculous. When she passed on taking it a second time, she concluded she was intellectually gifted. Shea demonstrated
   a. a false attribution.
   b. the primacy effect.
   c. the actor-observer effect.
   d. the self-serving bias.

4. Heather never gave Bobby much thought until she found out that he likes her. Lately she's been thinking that she likes him, too. Her attraction is largely based on
   a. the mere-exposure effect.
   b. proximity.
   c. reciprocity.
   d. a situational attribution.

5. All of the following factors influence attraction *except*
   a. physical attractiveness.
   b. the mere-exposure effect.
   c. proximity.
   d. deindividuation.

6. The matching hypothesis is similar to the idea that
   a. birds of a feather flock together.
   b. opposites attract.
   c. a bird in the hand is worth two in the bush.
   d. familiarity breeds contempt.

7. Changing or adopting an attitude or behavior to be consistent with the social norms of a group or their expectation is called
   a. obedience.
   b. conformity.
   c. familiarity.
   d. triangulation.

8. All of the following are true regarding Asch's study of conformity *except*
   a. 70% of the true subjects conformed at least some of the time.
   b. 5% of the true subjects conformed all of the time.

c. 25% of the true subjects did not conform.
   d. the majority of participants refused to conform.

9. In Stanley Milgram's obedience study, the "learner" was a(n)
   a. confederate.
   b. naive subject.
   c. unwilling participant.
   d. victim.

10. Phillip was offered a job that provided the majority of the weekends off. Once he said yes and gave notice at his old job, the new employer told him he would have to work every Saturday until noon. Phillip's new boss used the
    a. mere-exposure effect.
    b. door-in-the-face technique.
    c. foot-in-the-door technique.
    d. low-ball technique.

11. Two teams were playing a game of tug-of-war. Gerald was tired, so he just pretended to be pulling, knowing that no one could tell the difference. Gerald's approach to the game is an example of
    a. socialization.
    b. social facilitation.
    c. social loafing.
    d. the triangular effect.

12. If you work better in front of other people, the effect of those other people is called a(n)
    a. audience effect in social facilitation.
    b. coaction effect in social facilitation.
    c. audience effect in social loafing.
    d. coaction effect in social loafing.

13. Investigations following the latest NASA shuttle disaster suggested that many of the engineers and other workers saw problems but failed to speak up because no one else did. They all work well together and were accustomed to everything going right. In their zeal to launch the shuttle and continue to work effectively and cohesively, they failed to investigate problems that were quite evident. Some suggested that the NASA scientists were victims of:
    a. groupthink.
    b. social facilitation.
    c. obedience.
    d. compliance.

14. Zimbardo's prison study showed that
    a. social roles influence behavior.
    b. behavior is beyond the influence of social bias.
    c. prisons are inherently corrupt.
    d. social loafing is culturally bound.

15. Which of the following is a deliberate attempt to change the attitude or behavior of another person?
    a. stereotyping
    b. persuasion
    c. extortion
    d. cognitive dissonance

16. Frank is overweight and seems unable to stick to any diet. Although his diet efforts suggest that he wants to lose weight, he denies it and says that he is happy with his body the way it is. Frank is trying to reduce his feelings of

   a. cognitive dissonance.

   b. negative persuasion.

   c. self-esteem.

   d. attributional asymmetry.

17. According to your text, which of the following is *not* one of the identified elements of persuasion?

   a. the source of the communication

   b. the message

   c. the decision-making process

   d. the audience

18. When Kitty Genovese was stabbed to death near her apartment, later investigations found that nearly 40 people witnessed the attack—yet no one called for help. Some would say that this case is an example of

   a. altruism.

   b. prejudice.

   c. the bystander effect.

   d. antisocial behavior.

19. Which of the following has been shown to help people unlearn prejudice?

   a. an open discussion on prejudice and discrimination

   b. the jigsaw technique

   c. intergroup contact

   d. all of the above

20. Kathy's sorority has a rule against dating boys from certain fraternities. Kathy may date only boys who belong to two specific fraternities. Her sorority considers any other boys to be "undesirables." According to the definitions in your chapter, Kathy's sorority is an example of _____ whereas the "undesirables" are an example of _____.

   a. an in-group; an in-group

   b. an out-group; an in-group

   c. an out-group; an out-group

   d. an in-group; an out-group

True/False

21. Research has indicated that culture contributes to attributional biases.

22. There are significant cultural differences in attractiveness ratings of the opposite sex.

23. In Asch's conformity experiments, 75% of the participants conformed to the incorrect response of the majority at least once.

24. The degree to which a person who is low in achievement motivation exhibits social loafing depends on the behavior of others in his or her group.

25. Social loafing is more common in collectivistic cultures such as China than in the United States.

26. Zimbardo's Stanford prison experiment had to be ended in six days because the behavior of the participants began to get out of hand.

27. Generally speaking, people with low IQs are easier to persuade than people with high IQs.

28. Altruistic acts are usually performed for some gain.

29. Individuals who were abused as children are more likely to be aggressive than adults who were not abused in childhood.

30. According to some research, people perceive more diversity among members of their own ethnic group and more similarity among members of other groups.

Essay

31. What do men and women rate as the most important qualities in a mate? Review both the similarities and the differences in what men and women seek.

32. Describe Stanley Milgram's obedience study. What conclusions could be drawn from it? Could the same study be conducted today?

33. Describe the social learning theory of aggression. What does the research say about a relationship between TV violence and viewer aggression?